A Handbook of Modern Arabic Historical Scholarship on the Ancient and Medieval Periods

A Handbook of Modern Arabic Historical Scholarship on the Ancient and Medieval Periods

Edited by

Amar S. Baadj

BRILL

LEIDEN | BOSTON

Originally published in hardback in 2021 as Volume 155 in the series *Handbook of Oriental Studies, Section 1: The Near and Middle East*.

Cover illustration: Scholars in an ʿAbbāsid period library with shelves full of books in the background, *Maqāmāt al-Ḥarīrī*, Bibliothèque nationale de France, MS Arabe 5847, fol. 5v, copied and illustrated in 634/1236–37 by Yaḥyā b. Maḥmūd al-Wāsiṭī.

Library of Congress Cataloging-in-Publication Data

Names: Baadj, Amar Salem, editor.
Title: A handbook of modern Arabic historical scholarship on the ancient and medieval periods / edited by Amar S. Baadj.
Description: Leiden ; Boston : Brill, [2021] | Series: Handbook of Oriental studies. section 1 the Near and Middle East, 0169-9423 ; vol.155 | Includes index. | Preface in English and Arabic; articles in English, German, and French.
Identifiers: LCCN 2021018995 (print) | LCCN 2021018996 (ebook) | ISBN 9789004460072 (hardback) | ISBN 9789004460089 (ebook)
Subjects: LCSH: Islamic Empire—History. | Islamic Empire—Historiography. | Arab countries—History. | Middle Ages—Historiography.
Classification: LCC DS38.14 .H36 2021 (print) | LCC DS38.14 (ebook) | DDC 909/.097492701—DC23
LC record available at https://lccn.loc.gov/2021018995
LC ebook record available at https://lccn.loc.gov/2021018996

Typeface for the Latin, Greek, and Cyrillic scripts: "Brill". See and download: brill.com/brill-typeface.

ISSN 0169-9423
ISBN 978-90-04-69596-2 (paperback, 2024)
ISBN 978-90-04-46007-2 (hardback)
ISBN 978-90-04-46008-9 (e-book)

Contents

English Preface

1   **Why Modern Arabic Historiography?**

The present volume brings together sixteen studies concerning modern Arabic academic scholarship on the ancient and medieval worlds. Most of the chapters are concerned with specific disciplines or sub-disciplines (such as Egyptology, Byzantine Studies, Mamluk Studies, etc.) while others focus on what can be characterized as "schools" or movements of historiography. Some of the studies focus on a single country in the Arab world while others look at developments across several countries. The arrangement of the chapters is broadly chronological, beginning with those disciplines that study the earliest civilizations in North Africa and the Middle East, and concluding with the disciplines and historiographical schools that are concerned with the study of what, for lack of a better commonly accepted term, we may refer to as the "late medieval" history of the region, prior to the period of Ottoman domination. Though the great bulk of the scholarly work under consideration in this volume is – as one would expect – in Arabic, some of the chapters also discuss works written by Arab historians in European languages such as English and French.

Many, though not all, of the chapters developed out of papers presented at an international conference held in Trier, Germany between October 21 and October 23, 2017, entitled "Modern Arabic Historical Scholarship on the Ancient and Medieval Periods". This conference, sponsored by Trier University and the Thyssen Foundation, was the first of its kind. It brought together specialists in various fields from the Arab world, Europe, and North America who discussed the development and current state of the pre-modern historical disciplines in the Arab countries, and the problem of the lack of visibility of this scholarship in Western academic circles.

The editor is painfully aware that some very important topics are missing from this volume such as chapters on the fields of Abbasid, Fatimid, and Crusade studies in the Arab world as well as studies on the rise and development of modern historical scholarship in Bilād al-Shām, the Arabian Peninsula, Sudan, and Libya. These unfortunate gaps are due, in large part, to circumstances that were beyond the editor's control, such as unexpected and late withdrawals of contributions for various reasons. It is hoped that these omissions can be redressed in a second volume. At a later stage perhaps modern Arabic historiography of the Ottoman, Colonial, and Post-Independence periods can receive similar treatment. It should be pointed out that there is also a need for reference works of this nature on modern academic Persian and Turkish historical scholarship.

This volume has a number of aims. It was conceived within the wider framework of a collaborative research project on "The Contemporary History of Historiography," led by Professor Lutz Raphael at Trier University and funded by the German Research Foundation (DFG), which seeks to view the contemporary history of this discipline from a truly international perspective, taking into account developments not only in Europe and North America but also in the less studied non-Western regions. Therefore, one of the goals of this volume is to contribute to increasing our knowledge about the rise, development, and present state of the modern academic field of historical studies in the Arab countries. To date only a small handful of studies have been written on this subject in English and other European languages. Even these works are overwhelmingly concerned with Arabic scholarship on the Early Modern (Ottoman) and Modern periods. The histories of entire fields (such as Assyriology, Byzantine Studies, Mamluk Studies, etc.) and important historiographical schools and trends in the Arab world have yet to be written in Western languages and sometimes even in Arabic itself. As a result, most of the studies presented in this volume are the very first of their kind and will no doubt be of value for those who seek a global perspective on modern historiography and its various sub-disciplines.

The second goal of this book is to meet the needs of specialists in the various disciplines of ancient and medieval studies who are based outside of the Arab countries and who wish to be better acquainted with the state of their field in the Arab world and with the work done by their Arab colleagues. This is obviously a pressing need in the case of fields whose geographical areas of focus wholly (as in the case of Egyptology) or partially (as in the case of Greco-Roman studies) overlap with a portion of the Arab world and which at the same time do not employ Arabic as a language of research at an international level. For example, the vast majority of Assyriologists outside of the Arab countries do not read Arabic, therefore, they have limited knowledge of and access to a fairly large body of Assyriological scholarship (including publications of cuneiform tablets) that has been produced by Iraqi scholars over the last 70 years. Information about the history and current state of the Assyriological discipline in Iraq, and the Arabic publications in this field, is thus of great practical value to the international community of Assyriology and can facilitate cooperation between Iraqi scholars and their colleagues abroad.

Surprisingly, the same problem also exists in the field of Arabic and Islamic studies. It is still the case that many monographs and dissertations on Islamic history written in the West make no reference at all to secondary literature in written in Arabic and other "oriental" languages such as Persian or Turkish.

With a few exceptions, Arabic studies are seldom reviewed in Western journals and they are often missing from bibliographies. The standard bibliographical resource for the field of Islamic Studies, the renowned *Index Islamicus*, is, according to its website, limited to "… material published by Western scholars in the fields of Humanities and Social Sciences, specialist area- and subject-based areas, and by Muslims writing in European languages."[1] In order to remedy this gap, the editor and many of the contributors to the present volume hope to eventually create an open-access database of discipline-specific bibliographies of Arabic secondary works on pre-modern history for the benefit of international researchers.

In the European languages there is also a serious lack of basic summaries or introductions to modern Arabic scholarship on the various sub-fields of Islamic history that identify important scholars, historical "schools", publications, and intellectual trends. There has been little interest in the history and development of professional historical studies in the modern Arab world in comparison to the rich body of literature on the history of the various European schools of oriental studies.[2] Due to the lack of such studies as well as of bibliographical aids and reviews it is difficult for specialists in medieval Islamic history who are based in the West to gain an accurate picture of the state of their field in the Arab world and identify Arabic works which might be helpful in their research.

Non-Arab scholars specializing in the history of the Islamic period should be familiar with contemporary Arabic historical scholarship, not only in order to better "know their field" by mastering a comprehensive bibliography of the discipline which is not limited to Western studies, but also because their own work will be enriched and enhanced by utilizing and engaging with Arabic scholarship.

To illustrate the importance of contemporary Arabic historical scholarship we can look briefly at the field of medieval Maghribī history, the branch of Islamic history with which the editor of this volume is most familiar. Until the 1970s this field was clearly dominated at an international level by French scholarship, though it is important to note that, by the 1950s, an Arab school of Andalusī and Maghribī studies already existed in Egypt, which included some pioneering historians such as Ḥusayn Muʾnis, Muḥammad ʿAbdallāh ʿInān, and Ḥasan Aḥmad Maḥmūd. From the 1980s onward many new universities (with

---

1 "Index Islamicus," accessed October 11, 2019, https://bibliographies.brillonline.com/browse/index-islamicus.

2 A notable exception, which includes coverage of contemporary Arabic scholarship on the pre-modern periods, is Choueiri's survey. See Youssef M. Choueiri, "Arab Historical Writing," in *The Oxford History of Historical Writing*, vol. 5, *Historical Writing Since 1945*, ed. A. Schneider and D. Woolf (Oxford, Oxford University Press, 2011) 496–514.

new History departments) were established in the countries of the Maghrib and as a result the number of Moroccan, Algerian, and Tunisian medievalists has increased dramatically along with an accompanying surge in the volume of publications (journals, theses, monographs, and editions of texts). At the same time every respectable history department in the eastern Arab world has at least one professor of medieval Maghribī and Andalusī history. Due to these factors, today the overwhelming majority of academic studies on the medieval Maghrib (and a very considerable portion of the studies on al-Andalus as well) are in Arabic and they cover a great variety of topics, many of which have been only lightly treated in Western scholarship.

A notable feature of Arabic scholarship on the medieval Maghrib and al-Andalus since at least the 1980s is the great attention that has been given to economic and social history. A considerable number of pioneering, sophisticated studies have been produced in this area, and they deserve greater recognition from specialists outside of the Arab world. A few randomly selected examples of outstanding and thought-provoking works of this nature (some with very different methodological approaches) include the magisterial studies of Muḥammad Ḥasan and Ṣāliḥ Baʿayzīq on the society and economy of Ḥafsid Ifrīqīya and Bijāya respectively, ʿUmar Binmīra's study on society in the Moroccan countryside under the Merinids, the works of Brahim Kadiri Boutchich (Ibrāhīm al-Qādirī Būtashīsh) on Almoravid society and on the feudal question in Umayyad al-Andalus, Maḥmūd Ismāʿīl ʿAbd al-Rāziq's (often referred to as Maḥmūd Ismāʿīl) class-based, Marxian analysis of medieval Islamic history, ʿIzz al-Dīn Mūsā's foundational work on the economic history of the Islamic West under the Almoravids and Almohads, and Saʿīd Binḥamāda's remarkable study on water in al-Andalus.[3] Suffice it to say that

---

3 Maḥmūd Ismāʿīl ʿAbd al-Rāziq, *Sūsiyūlūjiyyā al-Fikr al-Islāmī*, vols. 1–7 (Cairo: Sīnāʾ li al-Nashr; Beirut: Al-Intishār al-ʿArabī, 2000), vols. 8–10 (Cairo: Miṣr al-Maḥrūsa, 2005); Ṣāliḥ Baʿayzīq, *Bijāya fī al-ʿAhd al-Ḥafṣī: Dirāsa Iqtiṣādiyya wa Ijtimāʿiyya*, (Tunis: Manshūrāt Jāmiʿat Tūnis, 2006); Saʿīd Binḥamāda, *Al-Māʾ wa al-Insān fī al-Andalus khilāl al-Qarnayn 7–8 h./13–14 m.*, (Beirut: Dār al-Ṭalīʿa, 2007); ʿUmar Binmīra, *Al-Nawāzil wa al-Mujtamaʿ: Musāhama fī Dirāsat Tārīkh al-Bādiya fī al-Maghrib al-Wasīṭ*, (Rabat: Manshūrāt Kulliyyat al-Adāb wa al-ʿUlūm al-Insāniyya, 2012); Ibrāhīm al-Qādirī Būtashīsh [Brahim Kadiri Boutchich], *Athar al-Iqṭāʿ fī Tārīkh al-Andalus al-Sīyāsī min Muntaṣaf al-Qarn al-Thālith al-Hijrī ḥattā Ẓuhūr al-Khilāfa (250h.–316h.)*, (Rabat: Manshūrāt ʿUkāẓ, 1992); Idem, *Mabāḥith fī al-Tārīkh al-Ijtimāʿī li al-Maghrib wa al-Andalus khilāl ʿAṣr al-Murābiṭīn*, (Beirut: Dār al-Ṭalīʿa, 1997?); Idem, *Al-Maghrib wa al-Andalus fī ʿAṣr al-Murābiṭīn: Al-Mujtamaʿ, al-Dhihnīyāt, al-Awliyyāʾ*, (Beirut: Dār al-Ṭalīʿa, 1993); Muḥammad Ḥasan, *Al-Madīna wa al-Bādiya bi Ifrīqiyya fī al-ʿAṣr al-Ḥafṣī*, 2 vols, (Tunis: University of Tunis 1, 1999); ʿIzz al-Dīn Aḥmad Mūsā, *Al-Nashāṭ al-Iqtiṣādī fī al-Maghrib al-Islāmī khilāl al-Qarn al-Sādis al-Hijrī*, (Beirut: Dār al-Shurūq, 1983). See also Chapter 11 and Chapter 15 in this volume and Amar S. Baadj, "Maḥmūd Ismāʿīl and his Historical-Materialist Approach to the History of the Medieval Islamic World," in *What's Left of Marxism: Historiography and the Possibilities of Thinking with Marxian Themes and*

at present any scholar wishing to specialize in the history and civilization of the medieval Islamic West must be familiar not only with secondary literature produced in the traditional European research languages of the field (mainly French, Spanish, and English) but also with the substantial body of contemporary Arabic studies.

2   A Summary of the Contents

Chapter 1 is possibly the first overview of the Iraqi school of Assyriology from its foundation in the 1940s by the great philologist and archaeologist Ṭāhā Bāqir down to the present. We see that, despite extremely difficult circumstances, the discipline continues to grow as new departments are founded, more scholars than ever before enter the field, and an impressive body of dissertations and published works covering all the major branches of the field are produced.

Chapter 2 discusses the development of the field of Egyptology in Egypt. We learn, contrary to what some in the West may imagine, that already in the second half of the nineteenth century Egyptian scholars such as Aḥmad Kamāl had begun serious study of the archaeology, history, and languages of ancient Egypt and that colonial officials during the period of British domination did everything in their power to hamper these efforts, including preventing the publication of the first ancient Egyptian-Arabic dictionary and removing native Egyptians from positions in the antiquities service in order to preserve it as a monopoly for Europeans. Nonetheless, Egyptian Egyptology survived these setbacks and it has grown and flourished since the end of colonial rule in 1952.

In recent decades tens of thousands of inscriptions in various ancient North and South Arabian dialects have been discovered throughout the Arabian Peninsula as well as in neighboring lands such as Jordan and Syria. Scholarship is still in the early stages of understanding and exploiting these valuable sources, which have the potential to shed a great deal of new light on what we know about the history of the Near East, the development of the Semitic languages (especially Arabic), and the cultural and historical milieu out of which Islam arose. Chapter 3 focuses on the contributions made by researchers from throughout the Arab world to the study of the epigraphy and archaeology of ancient Yemen.

Chapters 4 and 5 are concerned with the study of Antiquity in Morocco and Algeria, respectively. Major themes in the development of the disciplines of

---

Concepts, ed. Benjamin Zachariah, Lutz Raphael and Brigitta Bernet (Berlin: De Gruyter, 2020) 147–170.

archaeology and ancient history in the post-independence Maghrib are the process of decolonization of these fields, the quest to establish a uniquely North African perspective on the region's ancient past, and the replacement of French by Arabic as the principal language of instruction and publication in the universities. The last four decades have seen a great increase in the number of archaeology and history departments in the region and a considerable body of MA and PhD theses concerned with the pre-Islamic period has been produced. One of the weaknesses confronting the field of ancient studies in Morocco and Algeria is that the study of primary source languages (Latin, Greek, Phoenician, and Lybic, as well as of Afro-Asiatic linguistics, which is essential for understanding the context of the latter two languages) is largely absent from the university curricula.

Chapter 6 explores Classical Studies in the Arab world. Egypt has a rich tradition of Greek and Latin studies extending back to the 1940s thanks in part to the pioneering efforts of Tāhā Ḥusayn, one of the greatest Arab intellectuals and authors of the twentieth century. Since that time thousands of studies have been produced in Arabic covering all facets of Greco-Roman Civilization. The author emphasizes that Classics in the Arab world holds a particular interest as an example of Classics in a non-Western context in a region which was once part of the Classical world and whose culture has been profoundly influenced by Greek thought as a result of the Greco-Arabic translation movement of the ʿAbbāsid period.

Chapter 7 is the first account of Byzantine Studies in an Arab context. The focus again is on Egypt, for though there are individual Byzantinists in some of the other Arab countries, only in Egypt does there exist what we may call, for lack of a better term, a "school" of Byzantine Studies that has developed continuously from the middle of the twentieth century down to the present. In this chapter we learn about the changing concerns and preoccupations of Egyptian Byzantinists. The author explains how this field has evolved from a focus in its early years on Byzantine history seen from the perspective of Arab-Islamic civilization (Muslim-Byzantine relations) to an increased concern in recent years with what he calls "pure Byzantine studies", including such topics as the internal history of the Byzantine Empire, its society, culture, and economy, and its relations with non-Muslim powers. He also provides us with valuable information about how the study of the medieval period in general (Byzantine, Islamic, and Western European) has been approached in the major Egyptian universities.

The Tunisian scholar Hichem Djaït (Hishām Jaʿayṭ) is one of the most famous living Arab historians and he is also well known in Western specialist circles for his important studies on early Islamic history, some of which were published in French and translated into English. In his works he has explored topics such as the life of the Prophet Muḥammad, the Great Fitna (Civil War), the early Islamic city, and early Islamic provincial administration in North Africa, taking a standpoint that is critical both of traditional historical scholarship in the Arab world and of orientalist scholarship. Chapter 8 discusses the groundbreaking work of Djaït as well as the historiographical "school" which he has established in Tunisia, where a number of distinguished historians who were trained by him have produced a body of important and innovative work on the formative period of Islamic history.

Chapter 9 presents an overview of modern Arabic historical scholarship on the Umayyad period. Different trends in historical writing are analyzed, including the Arab nationalist, sectarian Sunni, and sectarian Shīʿī trends as well as the works of "modernist" historians, particularly from North Africa, who have brought a more critical approach to the field. This chapter also discusses important new research in Arabic epigraphy, particularly in the Arabian Peninsula, which has resulted in the discovery of many new inscriptions from the early Islamic period (including Umayyad inscriptions) which provide a valuable supplement to the manuscript tradition.

Iraq boasts one of the oldest national schools of historiography in the Arab world (along with Egypt and Syria) and many distinguished historians such as ʿAbd al-ʿAzīz al-Dūrī, Jawād ʿAlī, and Ṣāliḥ Aḥmad al-ʿAlī, to name only a few. Chapter 10 traces the development of the Iraqi historiographical school from its origins in the early twentieth century until the present through a series of vignettes of prominent historians who are representative of some of the dominant trends in Iraqi history-writing. Close attention is also paid to the influence of political events on the historians and their work. Thus, we see how the anticolonialist, Arab nationalist, Baathist, Marxist and, more recently, following the American invasion of 2003, sectarian religious trends have impacted historical scholarship in Iraq.

Chapter 11 looks at the remarkable scholarship that has been done by a group of Moroccan scholars on the economic and social history of the Maghrib and al-Andalus during the medieval period. The origins of this historiographical movement extend back to the 1970s and 1980s when the Egyptian historian Maḥmūd Ismāʿīl ʿAbd al-Rāziq was a visiting professor at the University of Fez. Several of his Moroccan students themselves became prominent historians of the medieval Islamic West, and they in turn have trained a third generation of historians who are concerned with socio-economic history. These scholars have produced important studies on such topics as economic history, class relations, the effects of natural disasters and war on society, marginalized groups, and mentalities in medieval North Africa and al-Andalus.

Chapter 12 concerns the study of medieval history in the Algerian universities since independence in 1962. The Algerian historiographical school is one of the younger national schools in the Arab world and it has grown enormously since independence. At the time of independence there was only one university in the country, the University of Algiers, and the only language of education was French. Today there are over 100 institutions of higher education in Algeria and the humanities and social sciences have been fully Arabized. The author of the chapter discusses the processes of decolonization and Arabization and also undertakes an analysis of the large corpus of MA and PhD dissertations in medieval Islamic history that has been produced by the Algerian universities in recent decades. This analysis reveals the topics and fields of research that have received the most attention from contemporary Algerian medievalists as well as those that have been relatively neglected.

The Mamluks and the Mamluk period (1250–1517) have received a great deal of attention in Western Islamicist scholarship in recent years, perhaps more so than any other medieval Islamic dynasty. Surprisingly, until now no attempt has been made to present an overview of the vast and diverse body of Arabic scholarship on the Mamluk period. Chapter 13 gives a comprehensive survey of the Mamluks in modern Arabic historiography from the late nineteenth century to the present. A wide range of studies are considered, not only from Egypt and Bilād al-Shām, but also from the Gulf states, Iraq, and the Maghrib. These works span the fields of political, economic, social, and cultural history. Attention is also given to the place of Mamluk history within Egyptian history departments and how the Mamluk period is viewed in relation to the preceding dynasties. There is no question that this chapter fills a major gap in our understanding of the development and present state of the field of Mamluk studies.

Chapter 14 complements the preceding chapter by focusing on the study of the art and architecture of the Mamluk period in Egypt. The history and development of this field of study is surveyed from its origins to the present, followed by a detailed discussion of how Islamic art and architecture are taught in Egyptian universities and careful analysis of the research produced (especially theses). The author provides us with a good picture of the state of the field in Egypt today, along with its strengths, weaknesses and future prospects.

In general, Western orientalists have tended to be more interested in relations between Europe and North Africa in the medieval period rather than relations between the Maghrib and the Mashriq.[4] In the Arab countries, by

---

4 Although this trend is fortunately changing. See for example the forthcoming volume *The Maghrib in the Mashriq: Knowledge, Travel and Identity*, ed. Maribel Fierro and Mayte Penelas (Berlin: De Gruyter, 2021 [expected]).

contrast, the topic of Maghribī–Mashriqī relations has been a major theme for medievalists since the 1940s, for obvious historical and cultural reasons, and a great deal of work has been and continues to be published on this subject. Chapter 15 presents a thorough survey of the literature on this topic from across the Arab world, covering all aspects of Maghribī–Mashriqī contacts such as diplomatic relations, intellectual and cultural relations, trade, travel, and migrations of tribes.

The final chapter in this volume, Chapter 16, is about the study of Medieval (non-Byzantine) Europe in the Arab world. Academics specializing in Medieval Europe can be found in most of the Arab countries today, particularly in Egypt, where there is a tradition of Latin studies in the larger universities (both in the classics and history departments) and as a consequence, nearly all students of medieval European history there have had some formal instruction in the language and a few have become quite proficient in it and have done extensive research in the Latin primary sources. The present condition and state of the discipline are discussed, and the author analyzes the output of Arab researchers in this field (including theses, monographs, articles, translation of primary and secondary sources, etc.) in order to draw some conclusions about their major interests and preoccupations.

3   Concluding Remarks

It would be very unfortunate if, rather than existing in one large global community, each of the various disciplines discussed in this book is allowed to bifurcate into largely separate communities of Western and non-Western scholars with limited contact between the two. Such a situation leads to inefficiency (for example there is the problem on both sides of scholars "reinventing the wheel" due to being unaware of research published in another language) and hampers dialogue and exchange of ideas, essential conditions for the growth and development of any field of scholarship. The present volume is a modest attempt to create a bridge between the Arab and Western communities of pre-modern historians and it is the sincere hope of the editor and all of the contributors that their work will encourage others on both sides to take the initiative in opening new avenues for collaboration, dialogue, and exchange of ideas and research.

المقدمة

1   ما الهدف من دراسة علم التأريخ العربي الحديث؟

يضم هذا المجلد الحالي ستة عشر بحثا تتناول الدراسات الأكاديمية العربية الحديثة المتعلّقة بالعالم القديم والعصور الوسطى. وتتعلق معظم الفصول بتخصصات معينة أو بتخصصات فرعية (مثل علم المصريات والدراسات البيزنطية والدراسات المملوكية، إلخ)، بينما يركّز البعض الآخر منها على ما يمكن وصفه بـ"المدارس" أو تيّارات علم التاريخ. وتركّز بعض الدراسات على دولة محددة في العالم العربي بينما تتعلق دراسات أخرى بالتطورات التاريخية في العديد من تلك البلدان. تمّ ترتيب الفصول على أساس زمني، وتبدأ بتلك التخصصات التي تدرس الحضارات الأولى في شمال إفريقيا والشرق الأوسط، وتنتهي بالتخصصات والمدارس التاريخية التي تهتم بدراسة ما يمكن أن نسميه "بالعصور الوسطى المتأخرة"، هذه التسمية جاءت بسبب عدم توفر مصطلح شائع ومقبول عند الباحثين للإشارة إلى تاريخ المنطقة في فترة ما قبل السيطرة العثمانية. وعلى الرغم من أن الجزء الأكبر من العمل الأكاديمي قيد الدراسة في هذا المجلد خاص بالدراسات المنشورة باللغة العربية كما يتوقع المرء، فإن بعض الفصول تناقش أيضًا الأعمال التي كتبها مؤرخون عرب باللغات الأوروبية مثل الإنجليزية والفرنسية.

هذا المجلد متعدد الأهداف. تم تصميمه ضمن الإطار الأوسع لمشروع بحثي مشترك حول "دراسة علم التأريخ المعاصر" تحت إشراف البروفسور لوتز رافائيل من جامعة ترير وبتمويل من مؤسسة البحوث الألمانية (DFG)، ويسعى هذا المشروع إلى دراسة علم التأريخ المعاصر من منظور عالمي حقيقي، مع مراعاة التطورات الحديثة، ليس في أوروبا وأمريكا الشمالية فقط بل أيضا في المناطق غير الغربية والأقل دراسة. فلذلك فإن أحد أهداف هذا المجلد هو المساهمة في زيادة معرفتنا بنهضة وحالة التطورات الحديثة في المجال الأكاديمي للدراسات التاريخية في البلدان العربية في الوقت الحاضر. وهناك عدد قليل من الدراسات حول هذا الموضوع باللغة الإنجليزية واللغات الأوروبية الأخرى. حتى هذه الأعمال تهتم بشكل كبير بأعمال الأكاديمية العربية في العصور الحديثة المبكرة (العثمانية) والعصور الحديثة. وهناك حقول تاريخية عربية يجب أن تكتب الآن باللغات الغربية والعربية (مثل علم الآشوريات، والدراسات البيزنطية، والدراسات المملوكية، إلخ) وكذلك المدارس والتيارات التأريخية الهامة في العالم العربي. لذلك نجد أنّ معظم الدراسات المقدمة في هذا المجلد هي فريدة من نوعها وستكون بلا شك ذات قيمة لأولئك الذين يبحثون عن منظور عالمي في كتابة التاريخ الحديث وتخصصاته الفرعية المختلفة.

الهدف الثاني من هذا الكتاب هو تلبية احتياجات المتخصصين في مختلف تخصصات الدراسات القديمة والعصور الوسيطة والمتواجدين خارج البلاد العربية، والذين يرغبون في التعرف بشكل أفضل على أوضاع اهتماماتهم العلمية في البلدان العربية وكذلك التعرف على أعمال زملائهم العرب الآخرين. من الواضح أن هناك حاجة ملحّة فيما يخصّ التخصصات التي تتداخل فيها مناطق جغرافية مختلفة إمّا كلياً (كما هو الحال في علم المصريات) أو جزئياً (كما هو الحال في الدراسات اليونانية والرومانية) والتي تغطّي بعض البلدان العربية. وهذه التخصصات بشكل عام لا تستخدم اللغة العربية كلغة بحث على المستوى الدولي. فعلى سبيل المثال، فإن الغالبية العظمى من علماء الدراسات المسمارية خارج البلدان العربية لا يعرفون اللغة العربية، وبالتالي فإن لديهم معرفة محدودة بالإنتاج الأكاديمي العربي، وليس لديهم إمكانية الوصول إلى مجموعة كبيرة من الدراسات العربية الخاصة بالمسمارية (بما في ذلك المنشورات التي تتعلق بالألواح المسمارية) التي أنتجها العلماء العراقيون منذ أكثر من 70 سنة مضت. إن المعلومات حول تاريخ وحالة الدراسات المسمارية في العراق، والمنشورات العربية في هذا المجال لها قيمة علمية كبيرة لجماعة الدراسات المسمارية الدولية، ويمكن أن تسهّل التعاون ما بين العلماء العراقيين وزملائهم في الخارج.

والمثير للدهشة أن نفس مشكلة الدراسات المسمارية موجودة أيضًا في مجال الدراسات العربية والإسلامية في الغرب، فلا يزال الحال كذلك بالنسبة للعديد من الدراسات والأطروحات الأكاديمية حول التاريخ الإسلامي والمكتوبة في الغرب والتي عادة لا تشير على الإطلاق إلى المراجع الثانوية والمكتوبة باللغة العربية واللغات الشرقية الأخرى مثل الفارسية أو التركية، طبعا مع استثناءات قليلة. ونادرًا ما تتم مُراجعة الدراسات العربية في المجلات الغربية، وغالبًا لا تجدها في المصادر والمراجع الخاصة بالدراسات البيليوغرافية. فثلا، المصدر البيليوغرافي الأساسي في مجال الدراسات الإسلامية هو الفهرس الإسلامي الشهير، ووفقًا لموقعه على الإنترنت، يذكر بأن البيليوغرافيا فيه تقتصر فقط على "... المواد المنشورة من قبل العلماء الغربيين في مجالات العلوم الإنسانية والاجتماعية، والمجالات المتخصصة والموضوعات المتفرقة، والمواد المنشورة من قبل مسلمين يكتبون باللغات الأوروبية".

ومن أجل إغلاق هذه الثغرة، يأمل المحرر والعديد من المساهمين في المجلد الحالي في إنشاء قاعدة بيانات مفتوحة وتتيح الوصول إلى البيليوغرافيات العربية والخاصة بالمراجع العربية في مرحلة ما قبل الحداثة بما يخدم الباحثين على المستوى الدولي. سيكون من المؤسف حقًّا، بدلاً من العمل العلمي ضمن مجتمع عالمي واحد وكبير، بأن يتم تقسيم الدراسات المختلفة التي نوقشت في هذا الكتاب إلى مجموعات منفصلة عن بعضها البعض، العلماء الغربيون وغير الغربيين، ومع تواصل محدود بينهما. سيؤدي مثل هذا الموقف إلى نقص كبير في المهنية العلمية (خاصةً عندما

لا يكون العلماء على معرفة بالأبحاث المنشورة بلغة أخرى) وسيعيق هذا الحوار وتبادل الأفكار، وهذه مقومات أساسية للتطوير العلمي في أي مجال من مجالات البحث. يمكن اعتبار هذا المجلد الحالي محاولة متواضعة لتدشين جسر من التعاون ما بين جماعة المؤرخين العرب والمؤرخين الغربيين ومؤرخي ما قبل الحداثة، ويأمل المحرر وجميع المساهمين أن يخدم عملهم هذا المؤرخين من كلا الطرفين، وأن يكون خطوة إلى الأمام لأخذ زمام المبادرة لفتح آفاق جديدة للتعاون والحوار وتبادل الأفكار والبحوث المشتركة.

2 ملخص المحتويات

يلقي الفصل الأول نظرة عامة على المدرسة العراقية التي تُعنى بالدراسات المسمارية منذ تأسيسها في الأربعينيات من قبل عالم اللغة وعالم الآثار الكبير طه باقر وحتى الوقت الحاضر. وبالرغم من الظروف الصعبة للغاية، فإن هذا الحقل العلمي استمر في النمو وتمّ إنشاء أقسام جديدة، ورافق ذلك دخول المزيد من العلماء أكثر من أي وقت مضى إلى هذا الحقل، وتمّ انجاز مجموعة رائعة من الأطروحات والمنشورات العلمية التي تغطي جميع الفروع الرئيسية لهذا المجال.

يناقش الفصل الثاني تطور علم الدراسات المصرية القديمة في مصر. ونرى، وعلى عكس ما قد يتصوره البعض في الغرب، فقد تمّ في النصف الثاني من القرن التاسع عشر تأسيس علم الدراسات المصرية القديمة، حيث بدأ العلماء المصريون مثل أحمد كمال بدراسات جادة لآثار وتاريخ ولغات مصر القديمة، ورغم محاولة المسؤولين الاستعماريين خلال فترة الاستعمار البريطانية والذين حاولوا بكل ما في وسعهم عرقلة هذه الجهود بما في ذلك منع نشر أول قاموس مصري قديم-عربي وكذلك قاموا بطرد المواطنين المصريين من وظائف دائرة الآثار المصرية من أجل الحفاظ عليها باعتبارها حكرا على الأوروبيين. ومع كل ذلك، فقد استمر علم الدراسات المصريات كعلم مصري أصيل رغم هذه المعوقات وتطوّر وازدهر منذ نهاية الحكم الاستعماري عام 1952.

في العقود الأخيرة، تم اكتشاف عشرات الآلاف من النقوش في جميع أنحاء شبه الجزيرة العربية وكذلك في البلدان المجاورة مثل الأردن وسوريا، وهي مكتوبة باللغة العربية الشمالية بلهجاتها المختلفة وكذلك باللغة الجنوبية القديمة بلهجاتها المختلفة خاصة السبئية. ولا تزال الدراسات العربية الخاصة بلغات العرب قبل الإسلام في مراحلها الأولى، وهناك محاولات جادّة لفهم المادة اللغوية والتاريخية لهذه النقوش من قبل الباحثين العرب وذلك من أجل توظيف قيمتها اللغوية والتاريخية في كتابة التاريخ العربي والتاريخ اللغة العربية والاعتماد عليها كمصدر أساسي. وتشكّل هذه النقوش، وخاصة النقوش العربية الجنوبية المادة الأساسية لكتابة التاريخ، ليس فقط

تاريخ اليمن القديم بل تاريخ الجزيرة بشكل عام. يقدّم الفصل الثالث بعض مساهمات الباحثين العربِ من جميع أنحاء العالم العربي لدراسة النقوش والآثار في اليمن القديم.

يعنى الفصلان الرابع والخامس بدراسة الآثار والتاريخ القديم في المغرب والجزائر. وتتعلق الموضوعات الرئيسية هنا بعملية تطوير تخصصات علم الآثار والتاريخ القديم في المغرب والجزائر بعد الاستقلال وتشمل عملية إنهاء التأثيرات الاستعمارية في هذه التخصصات والسعي لتأسيس منظور منهجي فريد من نوعه لدراسة شمال إفريقيا في العصور القديمة، واستبدال الفرنسية بالعربية كلغة رئيسية للتعليم والنشر في الجامعات. شهدت العقود الأربعة الماضية زيادة كبيرة في عدد أقسام علم الآثار والتاريخ في المنطقة، وتم انجاز مجموعة كبيرة من رسائل الماجستير والدكتوراه التي تعالج فترة ما قبل الإسلام. ومن نقاط الضعف التي تواجه تخصصات الدراسات القديمة في المغرب والجزائر هو عدم توفّر أقسام لدراسة اللغات القديمة (اللاتينية واليونانية والفينيقية والليبية القديمة وكذلك اللغويات الأفرو-آسيوية التي تعتبر ضرورية) والتي تشكّل مصدرا أساسيا لهذه الدراسات، وهي للأسف غائبة إلى حد كبير عن المناهج الجامعية.

يعطينا الفصل السادس صورة استكشافية عن الدراسات الكلاسيكية في العالم العربي، حيث تتمتع مصر بتقاليد غنية في الدراسات اليونانية واللاتينية وتعود إلى أربعينيات القرن الماضي، ويرجع الفضل في ذلك جزئيًا إلى الجهود الرائدة التي بذلها طه حسين، أحد أعظم المفكرين والكتّاب العرب في القرن العشرين. منذ ذلك الوقت تم إتتاج آلاف الدراسات باللغة العربية والتي تغطي جميع جوانب الحضارة اليونانية والرومانية. ويؤكّد الباحث بأن الدراسات الكلاسيكية في العالم العربي تحظى باهتمام خاص، وتقدّم مثالا جيدا للدراسات الكلاسيكية في سياق غير غربي في منطقة كانت ذات يوم تُشكّل جزءًا من العالم اليوناني-الروماني، وتأثرت ثقافتها بعمق بالفكر اليوناني نتيجة لذلك، هذا التأثير الذي نجده في حركة الترجمة من اليونانية الى العربية في العصر العباسي.

الفصل السابع يعرض الرواية الأولى للدراسات البيزنطية في سياق عربي. ويقوم بالتركيز هنا مرة أخرى على مصر، وعلى الرغم من وجود باحثين في الدراسات البيزنطية كأفراد في بعض البلدان العربية، إلاّ الأمر مختلف في مصر والتي ظهر فيها ما يمكن أن نسميه تجاوزا "مدرسة" للدراسات البيزنطية، وكانت قد تطوّرت باستمرار من منتصف القرن العشرين وحتى الوقت الحاضر. وفي هذا الفصل محاولة للتعرف على اهتمامات وانشغالات الباحثين المصريين في الدراسات البيزنطية. ويقدّم الباحث شرحا لتطور الدراسات البيزنطية في مصر مع التركيز على السنوات الأولى من التاريخ البيزنطي من منظور الحضارة العربية الإسلامية (العلاقات الإسلامية البيزنطية) والتي زاد الاهتمام فيها في الأعوام الأخيرة تحت ما يسمى "الدراسات البيزنطية الخالصة" والتي ترتكّز على التاريخ الحضاري للإمبراطورية البيزنطية، ومجتمعها، وثقافتها،

واقتصادها، وعلاقاتها مع القوى غير المسلمة. ويزوّدنا هذا البحث بمعلومات قيّمة تتعلق بكيفية التعامل مع دراسة العصور الوسطى بشكل عام (البيزنطية، والإسلامية، وأوروبا الغربية) في الجامعات المصرية الكبرى.

يناقش الفصل الثامن العمل الرائد الذي قام به المؤرخ هشام جعيط، وكذلك "مدرسة" الدراسات التاريخية التي أنشأها في تونس، حيث قام عدد من المؤرخين المتميزين الذين تدربوا على يديه بإنتاج مجموعة من الأعمال الهامة والمبتكرة عن فترة التكوين التاريخ الإسلامي. ويعتبر العالم التونسي جعيط من أشهر المؤرخين العرب الأحياء، وهو معروف أيضًا في الأوساط الأكاديمية الغربية بدراساته المهمة عن التاريخ الإسلامي المبكر، والتي نُشرت بالفرنسية وترجمت إلى العربية وأحيانًا إلى الإنجليزية. وكان جعيط قد تناول في أعماله دراسة موضوعات مختلفة مثل سيرة النبي محمد، والفتنة الكبرى، والمدينة الإسلامية المبكرة، وإدارة الأمصار الإسلامية المبكرة في شمال إفريقيا، متخذًا وجهة نظر نقدية من الدراسات التاريخية التقليدية في العالم العربي والدراسات الاستشراقية.

يقدّم الفصل التاسع لمحة عامة عن الدراسات التاريخية العربية الحديثة المتعلّقة بالعصر الأموي. وهنا يتمّ تحليل اتجاهات مختلفة من الكتابة التاريخية بما في ذلك الاتجاهات القومية العربية والطائفية السنية والطائفية الشيعية وكذلك أعمال المؤرخين "الحداثيين"، وخاصة من شمال إفريقيا والذين قدموا نهجًا أكثر نقدية في هذا الإطار. يناقش هذا الفصل أيضًا مدخلا جديدًا ومهمًا في البحث العلمي وهو اعتماد النقوش العربية كمصدر تاريخي، ولا سيما الاكتشافات الأثرية في شبه الجزيرة العربية، حيث تمّ الكشف عن العديد من النقوش الجديدة من العصر الإسلامي المبكر (بما في ذلك نقوش من العصر الأموي) والتي تقدّم تكملة قيّمة لمادة المخطوطات في كتابة التاريخ الأموي.

يعالج الفصل العاشر تطور المدرسة التاريخية العراقية منذ نشأتها في أوائل القرن العشرين وحتى الوقت الحاضر من خلال سلسلة من المقالات القصيرة للمؤرخين البارزين الذين يمثلون بعض الاتجاهات السائدة في كتابة التاريخ العراقي. ويفتخر العراق بواحدة من أقدم المدارس الوطنية للتاريخ في العالم العربي (إلى جانب مصر وسوريا) وهناك العديد من المؤرخين المتميزين مثل عبد العزيز الدوري، وجواد علي، وصالح أحمد العلي، على سبيل المثال لا الحصر. وسيتناول هذا البحث تأثير الأحداث السياسية على المؤرخين وعملهم، ونلمس هذا التأثير عند المؤرخين المناهضين للاستعمار وهناك أيضا التيار القومي العربي والبعثي والماركسي، ومؤخرا، وعقب الغزو الأمريكي عام 2003، فقد أثرت الاتجاهات الدينية الطائفية على الدراسات التاريخية في العراق.

يتناول الفصل الحادي عشر الدراسات الأكاديمية الرائعة التي قامت بها مجموعة من العلماء المغاربة حول التاريخ الاقتصادي والاجتماعي للمغرب والأندلس خلال فترة العصور الوسطى.

وتعود أصول هذه الحركة التاريخية إلى السبعينيات والثمانينيات عندما كان المؤرخ المصري محمود إسماعيل عبد الرازق أستاذًا زائرًا في جامعة فاس، وكان العديد من طلابه المغاربة أنفسهم قد أصبحوا مؤرخين بارزين في مجال دراسة بلاد الغرب الإسلامي في العصور الوسطى، وكانوا قد قاموا بدورهم بتدريب جيل ثالث من المؤرخين المهتمين بالتاريخ الاجتماعي والاقتصادي. وقدّم هؤلاء العلماء دراسات مهمة حول مواضيع مختلفة مثل التاريخ الاقتصادي والعلاقات الطبقية وتأثيرات الكوارث الطبيعية والحرب على المجتمع ودراسات أخرى عن الفئات المهمشة ودراسات عن تاريخ العقليات في شمال أفريقيا والأندلس في العصور الوسطى.

يتعلق الفصل الثاني عشر بدراسة تاريخ العصور الوسطى في الجامعات الجزائرية منذ الاستقلال عام 1962. والمدرسة التاريخية الجزائرية هي إحدى المدارس الوطنية الأصغر سنًا في العالم العربي وقد تطوّرت بشكل كبير منذ الاستقلال. وكانت جامعة الجزائر في وقت الاستقلال هي الجامعة الوحيدة في البلاد، وكانت اللغة الفرنسية هي اللغة الوحيدة للتعليم. وأمّا اليوم فيوجد أكثر من 100 مؤسسة للتعليم العالي في الجزائر، وقد تم تعريب العلوم الإنسانية والاجتماعية بشكل كامل. ويناقش مؤلف هذا الفصل عمليات إنهاء الاستعمار والتعريب، كما يقوم بتحليل مجموعة كبيرة من رسائل الماجستير والدكتوراه في التاريخ الإسلامي في العصور الوسطى التي أنجزتها الجامعات الجزائرية في العقود الأخيرة. وتعرض هذه الدراسة تحليلات عن مواضيع ومجالات البحث العلمي في القرون الوسطى والتي حظيت بأكبر قدر من الاهتمام من قبل الباحثين الجزائريين المعاصرين وكذلك المواضيع تم إهمالهم نسبياً.

حظي المماليك والعصر المملوكي (1250–1517) باهتمام كبير في الدراسات الإسلامية الغربية في السنوات الأخيرة، ربما أكثر من أي دولة إسلامية أخرى في العصور الوسطى. والمثير للدهشة أنه حتى الآن ليس هناك أي محاولة لتقديم لمحة عامة عن الكم الهائل والمتنوع من الدراسات الأكاديمية العربية عن العصر المملوكي. يقدم الفصل الثالث عشر مسحاً شاملاً للدراسات العربية الحديثة حول المماليك من أواخر القرن التاسع عشر حتى الوقت الحاضر. وقد تمّ الأخذ بعين الاعتبار مجموعة كبيرة من الدراسات، ليس فقط من مصر وبلاد الشام، ولكن أيضًا من دول الخليج والعراق والمغرب العربي. وتعالج هذه الأعمال مجالات التاريخ السياسي والاقتصادي والاجتماعي والثقافي. وكما تمّ الاهتمام بمكانة التاريخ المملوكي في أقسام التاريخ المصرية، وكذلك مسألة النظر إلى الفترة المملوكية بالمقارنة بالدول السابقة. ومما لا شك فيه أن هذا الفصل يسد ثغوة كبيرة في فهمنا لتطور حقل الدراسات المملوكية ووضعها الحالي.

يُعدّ الفصل الرابع عشر استكمالا للفصل السابق ويقوم بالتركيز على دراسة الفن والعمارة في الفترة المملوكية في مصر. ويقوم بمسح تاريخ وتطور هذا الحقل العلمي من الدراسة منذ بداياته حتى الوقت الحاضر، ويلي ذلك مناقشة مفصلة لكيفية تدريس الفن والهندسة المعمارية

الإسلامية في الجامعات المصرية وتحليل دقيق للبحوث التي تمّ انجازها (خاصة الرسائل الجامعية). ويقدم لنا المؤلف صورة جيدة عن حالة هذا التخصص في مصر اليوم، إلى جانب مسائل القوة والضعف في هذا المجال وآفاق المستقبل.

كان المستشرقون الغربيون يميلون بشكل عام إلى الاهتمام بالعلاقات بين أوروبا وشمال إفريقيا في فترة العصور الوسطى أكثر من اهتمامهم بالعلاقات بين المغرب والمشرق. وعلى النقيض من ذلك فإن الاهتمام في البلدان العربية بموضوع العلاقات المغاربية-المشرقية كان دائمًا موضوعًا رئيسيًا لعالمي القرون الوسطى منذ الأربعينيات وذلك لأسباب تاريخية وثقافية واضحة. وقد نُشر الكثير من الانتاج العلمي ولا يزال يُنشر حول هذا الموضوع. يقدم الفصل الخامس عشر مسحًا شاملاً للأدبيات حول هذا الموضوع من جميع أنحاء العالم العربي والتي تغطي جميع جوانب العلاقات المغاربية والمشرقية مثل العلاقات الدبلوماسية والعلاقات الفكرية والثقافية وكذلك التجارة والسفر وهجرات القبائل.

والفصل الأخير في هذا المجلد هو الفصل السادس عشر ويدور حول دراسة أوروبا في العصور الوسطى (غير البيزنطية) في العالم العربي. وهناك اليوم مجموعة من الأكاديميين العرب المتخصصين في تاريخ أوروبا في العصور الوسطى في معظم الدول العربية ولا سيما في مصر حيث يوجد تقاليد للدراسات اللاتينية في الجامعات الكبيرة (في كل من أقسام التاريخ والدراسات الكلاسيكية)، ونتيجة لذلك، فإن كافة طلاب العصور الوسطى والمتخصصين في التاريخ الأوروبي يستفيدون من دراسة اللغة اللاتينية، واستطاعت مجموعة منهم أن تقوم بأبحاث بارعة بالاعتماد على المصادر الأولية أي اللاتينية. ويناقش هذا البحث الوضع الحالي لهذا التخصص، وكذلك يقوم بتحليل مخرجات الباحثين العرب في هذا المجال (بما في ذلك الأطروحات والدراسات والمقالات وترجمة المصادر الأولية والثانوية إلخ) من أجل استخلاص بعض الاستنتاجات حول تخصصهم، وكذلك اهتماماتهم وانشغالاتهم العلمية.

Acknowledgements

It goes without saying that an edited volume of this nature requires the assistance of many people and institutions around the world. First and foremost I would like to thank Professor Lutz Raphael of Trier University. He is the director of the DFG-Leibniz Research Group "The Contemporary History of Historiography", of which I am honored to be a member, and it is safe to say that without his enthusiastic support this volume would not have been realized. I am also very grateful for the support and camaraderie of my fellow group members Dr. Benjamin Zachariah, Dr. Brigitta Bernet, and Mr. Debojit Thakur from whom I have learned a great deal. During the period of preparing this book I held positions first at Trier University, then at Bonn University and now once again at Trier University, and I am grateful to both of these institutions, as well as to the DFG (German Research Foundation) which has funded the research project of which this book is the result.

Many of the studies in this volume developed out of presentations given at a conference in Trier, Germany between October 21 and October 23, 2017, entitled "Modern Arabic Historical Scholarship on the Ancient and Medieval Periods". I would like to thank Trier University, the Thyssen Foundation, and the DFG for their support of the conference and the Hotel Deutscher Hof Trier for providing a pleasant venue. I am also deeply grateful to all of the individuals who were in any way involved in the conference whether as presenters, panel chairs, panel discussants, or as providers of administrative assistance and logistical support.

I would like to extend my sincere thanks to all of the members of the editorial committee for the series *Handbook of Oriental Studies*, in which this volume appears, to the two anonymous reviewers for their helpful comments, and to the staff of Brill Publishers. Of the latter, I would like to mention in particular Ms. Kathy van Vliet who was my main contact at Brill during the early stages of planning this volume, Dr. Abdurraouf Oueslati who oversaw the critical stage in this volume's life from acceptance to publication and who was ever helpful and generous with his time, and Dr. Carina van den Hoven who oversaw technical production of the book.

I am also very thankful to have had help from the following individuals in editing parts of this volume: Ms. Ouennassa Khiari (Montreal) and Professor Ismet Touati (Tlemcen) who edited the French chapters for language and style, Professor Lutz Raphael (Trier) who edited the German chapter for language and style, and Professor Allaoua Amara (Constantine) who helped to correct the French transliteration of Arabic words in some of the chapters.

Dr. Mohammed Maraqten (Heidelberg) kindly assisted with preparing an Arabic preface for the volume. Ms. Sarah Jane Campbell did a meticulous job of copy-editing the final draft for which I am most grateful. I would also like to thank Ms. Pierke Bosschieter for preparing the index. Last, but certainly not least, I would like to express my gratitude to all of the authors who participated in this volume for their hard work and for their patience.

Amar S. Baadj

Notes on Contributors

Emad Abou-Ghazi
(PhD Cairo University, 1995) is an Egyptian historian and archivist and Professor Emeritus of Medieval Arabic Documents in the faculty of Arts, Cairo University. He has worked in the fields of history, archives, diplomatics, and cultural policies since 1976. He has written more than 60 articles and seven books in Arabic including: *Ṭūmān Bāy al-Sulṭān al-Shahīd* (1999); *Taṭawwur al-Ḥiyāza al-Zirāʿiyya fī Miṣr Zaman al-Mamālīk al-Jarākisa* (2000); *Ḥikāyat Thawrat 1919* (2009); *1517 Al-Iḥtilāl al-ʿUthmānī li Miṣr wa Suqūṭ Dawlat al-Mamālīk* (2019).

Al-Amin Abouseada
(PhD Birmingham University, 2000) is professor of Medieval History at Tanta University, Egypt, and currently visiting professor of Medieval History at King Faisal University, Saudi Arabia. His research interests include: Byzantine history, Byzantine-Muslim relations, relics, Medieval Poland and Christian-Muslim polemics. He has several publications on these topics.

Youcef Aibeche
(Doctorat d'état, Mentouri University, Constantine, Algeria, 2007) is professor of ancient history at the University of Sétif 2 where he is also vice-rector of postgraduate studies and research. He is a specialist on Late Antiquity whose research focuses on the transition from the ancient to the Islamic period in North Africa. He is responsible for the archaeological mapping project of the Sétifienne region, co-director of the archaeological research project of Lambaesis (with the Algerian Ministry of Culture CNRS-ENS) since 2014, and he directs projects at other sites such as Cuicul, Milev and the prehistoric site of Ain el-Hennech near Sétif.

Sidi Mohammed Alaioud
(PhD Moulay Ismail University, Meknes, 2005) is professor at the École Normale Supérieure (ENS) at Mohammed V University in Rabat. His research focuses on urbanization and architectural development in the cities of pre-Islamic Morocco. His publications include *Mudun wa Marākiz al-Maghrib al-Qadīm* (2015); *Al-Taṭawwur al-Ḥaḍārī li Walīlī min al-Fatra al-Mūriyya ilā al-Fatra al-Islāmiyya: Musāhama fī Dirāsat Mudun al-Maghrib* (2015); *Min Salā ilā Shāla: Dhākirat Madīna* (2nd ed. 2020).

Abdulhadi Alajmi

(PhD Durham University, 2004) is professor of history at Kuwait University, where he was also chair of the history department and assistant dean of academic affairs. He specializes in early Islamic history and historiography, and the Umayyad period in particular. In 2020 he received the prestigious pan-Arab award for historical studies *Shawāmikh al-Muʾarrikhīn al-ʿArab* from the Union of Arab Historians (*Ittiḥād al-Muʾarrikhīn al-ʿArab*) in Cairo. He has published more than 30 studies in English and Arabic including *Political Legitimacy in Early Islam: Al-Awzāʿī's Interactions with the Umayyad and ʿAbbasid States* (2009); "ʿUlama and caliphs new understanding of the "God's Caliph" term" in *Journal of Islamic Law and Culture* (2011); *Al-Brājmātiyyūn fī al-Qarn al-Hijrī al-Awwal* (Cairo, 2019).

Allaoua Amara

(PhD University of Paris 1 Panthéon Sorbonne, 2002) is a historian of the medieval Islamic Maghrib. He teaches in the History Department of Emir Abdelkader University in Constantine. He is an associate researcher at the National Center for Prehistoric, Anthropological and Historical Research (CNRPAH, Algiers) and the National Center for Scientific Research (CNRS, Paris). He is the author of a number of books, including *Dirāsāt fī Tārīkh al-Jazāʾir wa al-Gharb al-Islāmī* (2nd ed., 2016); *L'histoire de l'Algérie dans la recherche historique en France* (2010), *Madīnat Qusanṭīna* (2016), and numerous articles.

Lotfi Ben Miled

(PhD University of Tunis, 2009) is assistant professor of medieval history at the University of Tunis (Manouba). He is particularly interested in relations between the Maghrib and the Mashriq in the period from 1030 to 1530 CE. His publications include *Ifrīqīya wa al-Mashriq al-Mutawassiṭī min Awāsiṭ al-Qarn 5 h./11 m. ilā Maṭlaʿ al-Qarn 10 h./16m.* (Tunis, 2011); "Tracking down the Hafsid Diplomats all the way to the Turco-Mamluk Border 1487–1491" in *Mamluk Cairo, a Crossroads for Embassies* (Leiden, 2019).

Brahim El Kadiri Boutchich

(PhD Moulay Ismail University, Meknes, 1991) is professor of history at the University of Meknes. He specializes in the history of the Maghrib and al-Andalus in the Islamic period. He has previously taught in Oman and he has been a visiting professor in several other Arab countries. He has published dozens of studies on social history and the history of mentalities in the medieval Islamic West including *Al-Muhammashūn fī Tārīkh al-Gharb al-Islāmī: Qirāʾat al-Tārīkh min al-Asfal* (2014).

Usama Gad

(PhD Heidelberg University, 2016) is assistant professor of papyrology and Classics at ʿAyn Shams University in Cairo. His interests include Greek and Latin language pedagogy, papyrology, Greco-Roman Egypt, the medieval Greek-Arabic and Arabic-Latin translation movements, modern Arabic translations of the Classics, the history of Classical Studies in Egypt, Digital Classics, Orientalism, and Classics and Colonialism. His publications include "Who Was Who in the Aristocracy of Byzantine Oxyrhynchus" in *Proceedings of the 27th International Congress of Papyrology, Warsaw, 29 July–3 August 2013* (Warsaw 2016); "Sale on Delivery for Reeds," in *Archiv für Papyrusforschung und verwandte Gebiete* (2014).

Azeddine Guessous

(PhD El Jadida, Morocco, 2002) is currently professor of history and civilization at Chouaib Doukkali University in El Jadida. He specializes in the history of the Maghrib and al-Andalus during the Islamic period. His publications include: *Mawqif al-Raʿiyya min al-Sulṭa al-Siyāsiyya fī al-Maghrib wa al-Andalus ʿalā ʿAhd al-Murābiṭīn: Dirāsa fī ʿIlm al-Ijtimāʿ al-Siyāsī* (2014); *Al-Sulṭa al-Murābiṭiyya: al-Ramzī wa al-Mutakhayyal* (2019).

Fayza Haikal

(PhD Oxford, 1965) is currently professor emerita of Egyptology at the American University in Cairo, where she continues her research on many aspects of Ancient Egyptian culture and their transmission to the modern world. She previously taught in the Faculty of Archaeology of Cairo University and was visiting professor at the University of Paris IV- La Sorbonne, at Charles University in Prague, and at the University of Rome "La Sapienza". She was the first Egyptian woman to work in Nubia during the international campaign for the salvage of its monuments in the 1960s, and in the 1990s she directed the international campaign for the salvage of archeological sites in North Sinai during the digging of the Peace Canal. Her recent publications include "De la natte au Tapis Rouge. Symbolisme de la natte hier et aujourd'hui", in *Du Sinai au Soudan: itinéraire d'une égyptologue. Mélanges offerts au Professeur Dominique Valbelle,* (2017); (with Amr Omar) "Egyptology in Egypt: the founding institutions," in Navratilova, H., Th. L. Gertzen, A. Dodson, A. Bednarsk (eds.) *Towards a History of Egyptology: Proceedings of the Egyptological Section of the 8th ESHS Conference in London* (2018).

Hani Hamza

(PhD Cairo University, 2004) is an independent scholar who lives in Cairo, where he researches, writes, and lectures on the history of Mamluk architecture and other Mamluk-related topics. His academic articles in English have been published in the journal *Mamluk Studies Review* (MSR) in Chicago, by the AUC Press in Cairo, and by Brill in Leiden. He has also published a monograph in English on the Northern Cemetery of Cairo and three Arabic books on the general history of the Mamluk sultanate.

Laith M. Hussein

(PhD Philipps-University Marburg, Altorientalistik, Center for Near and Middle Eastern Studies, 2006) specializes in Cuneiform Studies. He is currently Director General of the State Board of Antiquities and Heritage of Iraq. He previously taught in and chaired the department of archaeology in the College of Arts at the University of Baghdad where he was also Head of the Consulting Office and Vice-Dean for Scientific Affairs and Graduate Studies. He has participated in many international conferences, seminars and workshops and published numerous articles in the areas of Assyriology and Mesopotamian archaeology.

Nasir al-Kaabi

(PhD University of Kufa and University of Tehran, 2008) is professor of history at the University of Kufa, Iraq. He was a post-doctoral research fellow at the University of Toronto (2014–2016). He specializes in the history of the Sasanian Empire. His publications include: *Musammā al-ʿIrāq wa Tukhūmuhu fī al-Mudawwanāt al-Bahlawiyya al-Sāsāniyya: Dirāsa fī al-Tārīkh al-Thaqāfī wa al-Īdiyūlūjī li al-Mafhūm* (2018); *A Short Chronicle on the End of the Sasanian Empire and Early Islam: 590–660* (2016); *Jadaliyyat al-Dawla wa al-Dīn fī al-ʿAṣr al-Sāsānī* (2010); *Al-Dawla al-Sāsāniyya fī al-Maṣādir al-ʿArabiyya: Dirāsa fī al-Tārīkh al-Siyāsī* (2008).

Khaled Kchir

(PhD University of Tunis, 1994) is professor of medieval history at the University of Tunis, where he has also directed the *Laboratoire du Monde arabo-islamique médiéval* since 2013 and served as vice-president of the university from 2017 to 2020. His research interests include the transmission of knowledge in the later medieval period, medieval Arabic biographical dictionaries, Ibn Khaldūn, Arabic codicology and diplomatics. His latest works concern the Berbers and Persians viewed by Ibn Khaldūn.

Mohammed Maraqten
(PhD Philipps-University Marburg, Semitic and Ancient Near Eastern Studies, 1987), born in Palestine and based in Germany, is a specialist of Ancient Near Eastern languages and cultures. He is now affiliated with the University of Heidelberg, Germany, and he also works for the Berlin-Brandenburg Academy of Sciences and Humanities. He has conducted archaeological excavations and surveys in Jordan, Bahrain, Yemen, Oman, Morocco, Algeria and Tunisia, and published intensively on the cultures and epigraphy of Ancient Arabia and especially on ancient South Arabian inscriptions. His recent work includes *Altsüdarabische Texte auf Holzstäbchen: Epigraphische und kulturhistorische Untersuchungen* (Beiruter Texte und Studien Nr. 103), Orient-Institut/Beirut; Würzburg: Ergon (2014).

Amr Omar
(PhD Cairo University, 2020) is curator of the Egyptology and Coptology collection at the Rare Books and Special Collections Library of the American University in Cairo. He has participated in many archaeological projects such as Eternal Egypt, Archaeological Map of Egypt, Mediterranean Defense Architecture Preservation Project, Theban Mapping Project, and currently the Egyptian Archaeological Database Project. His publications include "Battle of Qadesh in Ramesses II's Memory: A Brief Note," in *Abgadiyat* (2014); "Note on Beth Shan Stela of Ramesses II," *Annales du Service des Antiquités de l'Égypte* (2019); (with Salima Ikram) "Egypt" in Bednarski, A., A. Dodson & S. Ikram (eds.) *A History of World Egyptology* (2020).

Abdelaziz Ramadan
(PhD ʿAyn Shams University, 2003) is a historian of early Byzantium and its relations with the Arabs. He taught at ʿAyn Shams University from 2003 to 2018 and is now Professor of medieval history in King Khalid University, Saudi Arabia. He has conducted research abroad at the University of Rome "La Sapienza" (2002–2003) and at the Freie Universität Berlin (2013). He is the author of a number of Arabic books including *Al-Marʾa wa al-Mujtamaʿ fī al-Imbrāṭūriyyat al-Bīzanṭiyya* (2005); *Al-Ṭarīq ilā Bīzanṭa: Dirāsāt ḥawl al-Fikr wa al-Dīn wa al-Siyāsa fī Sharq al-Imbrāṭūriyya al-Rūmāniyya al-Mutaʾakhkhira* (2017); and articles in English including "Treatment of Arab Prisoners of War in Byzantium", in *Annales Islamologiques* (2009); "Arab Apostates in Byzantium", in *Byzantina Symmeikta* (2019).

PART 1

The Study of the Ancient World

1

Assyriologie im Irak: Ein kurzer Überblick

Laith M. Hussein

Das Department of Archaeology ist die älteste wissenschaftliche Abteilung am College of Arts der Universität Bagdad, verantwortlich für alle Themen, die mit den alten Kulturen Mesopotamiens und Umgebung verbunden sind. Gründer des Department of Archaeology waren Taha Baqir, Zaki Hassan und Fuad Safar.[1] Der ursprüngliche Name der Abteilung war „Department of Archaeology and Civilization" und das Studium begann im Gründungsjahr der Abteilung 1949–1950 mit einer Klasse. Der Lehrplan bestand damals aus einer Mischung von Themen zur antiken und islamischen Archäologie, für dessen Bewältigung das Dekanat des Colleges of Arts bestrebt war, genügend Professoren anzustellen. Im akademischen Jahr 1964–1965 war das Studium in zwei Abschnitte unterteilt: Archäologie und Geschichte der antiken Gesellschaft sowie arabisch-islamische Archäologie und Geschichte der islamischen Gesellschaft. Die Keilschriftforschung wurde im Jahr 1988–1989 als eigenständiges Fach unter der Bezeichnung „Keilschriftstudien" hinzugefügt. In dieser letzten Form wird die Lehre in den drei Fächern bis heute fortgesetzt. In der Regel erreichen Studierende nach vier Jahren den Abschluss als Bachelor of Arts (B.A.). Auf den Bachelor of Arts aufbauend kann ein Master Studium folgen, das nach zwei Jahren abgeschlossen wird. Wer promovieren und einen Doktortitel erwerben möchte, muss einen guten wissenschaftlichen Hochschulabschluss (Magister of Arts) vorweisen. Der Promotionsstudiengang dauert normalerweise drei Jahre.

Die Abteilung für Archäologie legt seit ihrer Gründung Wert darauf, dass das akademische Studium eine starke praktische Komponente (Feldforschung, Arbeit an Originalen) aufweist. Deshalb wurde die archäologische Untersuchung von Sippar (modern: Tell Abū Ḥabbah) als Ausgrabungsprojekt des Departments ausgewählt. Das *State Board of Antiquities and Heritage of Iraq* (SBAH) erteilte im Jahr 1978 die Genehmigung für die Ausgrabung an diesem Ort, die in 24 Kampagnen bis 2002 fortgesetzt wurde.

---

1 Ich bedanke mich bei Margarete van Ess für ihre Vorschläge. Ein Großteil der Informationen basiert auf internen Dokumenten des Department of Archaeology. Khaled Nashef hat in *American Journal of Archaeology* zwei Artikel zu „Archaeology in Iraq" publiziert, s. *AJA* Vol. 94, No. 2 (Apr. 1990), 259–289; Vol. 96, Nr. 2 (Apr. 1992), 301–323.

Die Leiter das Department of Archaeology / College of Arts / University of Baghdad seit der Gründung waren:

Dr. Zaki Mohammad Hassan (aus Ägypten)	1950–1958
Prof. Dr. Taqi al-Dabbagh	1958–1969
Prof. Dr. Fadhil Abdulwahed Ali	1969–1979
Prof. Dr. Taqi al-Dabbagh	1979–1981
Prof. Dr. Ghazi Rajab Muhammed	1982–1984
Prof. Dr. Salah Hussein al-ʿUbaydi	1984–1986
Prof. Dr. Tahir Muzaffar al-ʿAmid	1986–1990
Prof. Dr. Farouk Nasir al-Rawi	1990–1993
Prof. Dr. Talʿat Rashad al-Yawir	1993–1999
Prof. Dr. Abdulillah Fadhil Muhammed	1999–2003
Prof. Dr. Ghazi Rajab Muhammed	2003–2007
Ass. Prof. Dr. Sabah Jasim al-Shukri	2007–2009
Prof. Dr. Nusaybah al-Hashimi	2009–2012
Ass. Prof. Dr. Munther Ali Abdulmalik	2012–2014
Prof. Dr. Rafah Jasim al-Samarraʾi	2014–2016
Prof. Dr. Nawala A. al-Mutawalli	2016–2018
Ass. Prof. Dr. Laith M. Hussein	2018–2020

Die größte Anzahl von Abschlüssen im Magister- und Promotionsprogramm in der Vorderasiatischen Altertumskunde (Studium der Zivilisationen des antiken Mesopotamien) verlieh das Department of Archaeology im Laufe der letzten 20 Jahre.

Der Masterstudien- und der Promotionsstudiengang im Fach Altorientalistik umfasst folgende Themen:
- Geschichte des antiken Mesopotamien (prähistorische und historische Perioden)
- Keilschriftstudien: die zwei Grundsprachen Mesopotamiens, Sumerisch und Akkadisch
- Alt-Ägypten und Alter Orient (Anatolien, Iran und die Levante)
- Arabisch-islamische Zivilisation, islamische Kunst und Architektur
- Griechische und römische Geschichte
- Archäologie des Golfs und der Arabischen Halbinsel sowie Geologie

Gründer der Altorientalischen Forschungen und des Studiums der antiken Zivilisationen im Irak war Taha Baqir[2] (1912–1984). Er hatte Archäologie,

---

2　Fawzi Rashid legte die Biografie Baqirs monographisch vor, s. Taha Baqir – Ḥayātuhu wa Āṯāruh (Taha Baqir – His life and effects) 1987.

Anthropologie, Ausgrabungsmethoden, Alte Geschichte sowie Alte Sprachen wie Akkadisch, Sumerisch und Hebräisch am Oriental Institute in Chicago studiert. Im November 1938 wurde er in die Antikenverwaltung in Bagdad berufen. Dieses Datum ist der Beginn einer langen und bedeutsamen Karriere, in der er nicht nur im Irak, sondern auch in der arabischen Welt archäologische Studien initiierte und entwickelte. Seit 1951 lehrte Baqir im Department of Archaeology, er war ein sehr vielseitiger Gelehrter, der mehrere wichtige Studien verfasste. Nicht nur in seinem Heimatland, sondern in der gesamten arabischen Welt wurde er durch sein zweibändiges Hauptwerk, „Einführung in die Geschichte der alten Zivilisationen" (Baqir 1973) bekannt, das lange Zeit als Standardwerk galt.

In Bibliographien zu Studien des antiken Irak und zur arabischen Welt war in dieser Zeit der Verweis auf Baqir, dem der Ehrentitel „Lehrer für Kultur und Zivilisation" verliehen wurde, fast obligatorisch. Seine Beiträge zu Ausgrabungen, zur Restaurierung und zur archäologischen Feldforschung legten den Grundstein für die irakische Archäologie, der er über vierzig Jahre lang diente.

1   Staatliche Behörde des Irak für Antiken und Kulturerbe

Das *State Board of Antiquities and Heritage of Iraq* (SBAH) verwaltet das nationale Kulturerbe und die Nationalmuseen des Irak und gilt als eine der herausragenden Institutionen für Archäologie und Kulturerbe im Nahen Osten. Die Geschichte der Staatlichen Behörde reicht bis in das Jahr 1922 zurück, als die englische Reisende und Archäologieliebhaberin Gertrude Bell (1868–1926) Direktorin des archäologischen Departments des Königreichs Irak wurde. Sie wurde auch als die Frau, die den Irak erfand, bezeichnet. Ihr ist zu verdanken der Aufbau des ersten archäologischen Museums von Bagdad sowie das wegweisende Antikengesetz zum Umgang mit Grabungsstätten und -funden.[3] Das State Board arbeitet seit vielen Jahrzehnten mit internationalen Institutionen und großen nationalen Projekten zusammen.

Das Programm des Department of Archaeology / University of Baghdad im Fach Assyriologie z.B. ist eng mit dem Irak Museum, das die größte Sammlung von Tontafeln und anderen mesopotamischen Artefakten im Irak beherbergt, verbunden. Studenten haben dort die Möglichkeit, im Rahmen ihres B.A. Studiums sowie insbesondere für eigenständige wissenschaftliche Arbeiten (Magister und Doktorarbeiten) originale Keilschrifttexte zu entziffern,

---

3   http://www.orient-gesellschaft.de/forschungen/projekt.php?a=54.

zu interpretieren und zu veröffentlichen. Da der größte Teil der Sammlung noch veröffentlicht werden muss, werden qualifizierte Forscher angeregt, ihre Arbeiten auf Sammlungsbestände zu stützen. Das (SBAH) enthält auch eine fast vollständige Bibliothek auf den Gebieten der Altorientalistik. Häufige Besuche von Wissenschaftlern und Studierenden, regelmäßige Kolloquien und tägliche Erfahrungen mit einer der weltweit wichtigsten Sammlungen mesopotamischer Materialien bereichern das Studium der Assyriologie im Irak.

2   Einige im Irak durchgeführte Projekte

2.1   *Iraq Cultural Heritage Conservation Initiative* (2004–2011)

Diese Initiative,[4] eine Partnerschaft zwischen dem GCI, dem World Monuments Fund, dem irakischen Kulturministerium und dem irakischen Staatliche Behörde des Irak für Antiken und Kulturerbe (SBAH), zielte darauf ab, Bedrohungen für das irakische Kulturerbe zu mindern, Schäden zu reparieren und das Land wieder aufzubauen sowie professionelle Kapazitäten zur Erhaltung und Verwaltung des kulturellen Erbes bereitzustellen.

2.2   *Iraq Cultural Heritage Project* (ICHP)

Im Jahr 2008 vergab das Außenministerium der USA über die amerikanische Botschaft in Bagdad einen Zuschuss in Höhe von 13 Millionen US-Dollar an die International Relief und Development (IRD)-Organisation, eine gemeinnützige Nichtregierungsorganisation, die Hilfe in verschiedenen „Regionen der Welt" koordiniert.[5]

2.3   *Creation of Master's Programmes and Development of a Professional Sector for the Conservation of Archaeological and Heritage Monuments and Sites in Iraq* (2019–2023)

Dieses internationale Kooperationsprojekt,[6] das seit Dezember 2016 gemeinsam mit irakischen und internationalen Partnern gestartet wurde, soll die Entwicklung eines professionellen Sektors für den Erhalt von archäologischen Denkmälern und Stätten im Irak unterstützen. Ein solcher Sektor ist derzeit trotz der gewaltigen Herausforderungen, denen das kulturelle Erbe des Landes seit Jahrzehnten gegenübersteht, unterentwickelt. Die Aussicht auf groß angelegte Restaurierungs- und Rekonstruktionsmaßnahmen an historischen Stätten, Denkmälern und städtischen Gebieten, die in den letzten Jahren in

---

4   https://www.getty.edu/conservation/our_projects/field_projects/iraq/index.html.
5   https://eca.state.gov/highlight/iraq-cultural-heritage-project.
6   https://www.tandfonline.com/doi/full/10.1080/13527258.2019.1608585.

und um Mosul beschädigt oder zerstört wurden, macht die Behebung des Mangels an qualifizierten irakischen Kulturwissenschaftlern umso dringlicher.

2.4   *Irakisch-Deutsches Zentrum für Archäologie und Assyriologie*

Am 20. Juni 2017 wurde in Bagdad das Irakisch-Deutschen Zentrum für Archäologie und Assyriologie gegründet.[7] Während der Eröffnungszeremonie am College of Arts der Universität Bagdad wurde die Gründungserklärung durch Prof. Dr. Alaa Abdul Hussain Abdul Rasoul, Präsident der Universität von Bagdad, und Dr. Dr. h.c. Margarete van Ess, wissenschaftliche Direktorin der Orient-Abteilung des Deutschen Archäologischen Instituts in Berlin, unterzeichnet. Zu den eingeladenen Gästen zählten Dr. Qais Hussein Rashid, Staatssekretär des Ministeriums für Kultur sowie der deutsche Botschafter in Irak, Herr Franz Josef Kremp.

Die wissenschaftliche Zusammenarbeit zwischen der Universität Bagdad und deutschen Institutionen, insbesondere dem Deutschen Archäologischen Institut, verspricht eine Verbesserung der Forschungsförderung, eine verstärkte Zusammenarbeit zwischen Einzelwissenschaftlern sowie auf institutioneller Ebene zwischen den Fakultäten im College of Arts und internationalen Wissenschafts- und Forschungseinrichtungen.

2.5   *WALADU Projekt*

Das Waladu Projekt[8] war ein dreijähriges internationales Projekt (2017–2019), das von der Europäischen Union finanziert wurde. Sechs Universitäten, die Universitäten München, Bologna, Koç sowie im Irak die Universitäten Bagdad, Al-Kufa und Al-Qadisiyah waren beteiligt. Ziel war es, einen Beitrag zur Verbesserung der Ausbildung in der Archäologie, Assyriologie und der alten Geschichte zu leisten sowie zur Verbesserung der Möglichkeiten für Graduierte auf dem Arbeitsmarkt im Irak.

2.6   *EDUU Projekt*

EDUU (Education and Cultural Heritage Enhancement for Social Cohesion in Iraq)[9] war ein 30-monatiges internationales Projekt (2017–2019), das von der Europäischen Union finanziert wurde. Die Bezeichnung EDUU ist abgeleitet vom Verb „Wissen" in akkadischer Sprache, die von den Einwohnern des antiken Mesopotamien vom 3. bis zum 1. Jahrtausend v. Chr. gesprochen wurde. Das Projekt versuchte, eine Partnerschaft zwischen der EU und dem Irak im

---

7   https://www.archernet.org/2017/07/22/irakisch-deutsches-zentrum-fuer-archaeologie-und-assyriologie-eroeffnet/.

8   https://site.unibo.it/waladu/en.

9   https://site.unibo.it/eduu/en/project.

Bereich von Bildung und Kulturerbe zu schaffen und somit Universitäten, weiterführende Schulen und Museen zu verbinden. Die Partnerschaft hatte zum Ziel, den Pluralismus und das Bewusstsein für die vielfältige und multikulturelle Vergangenheit des Irak in der irakischen Zivilgesellschaft zu stärken.

2.7   *Das Nahrein-Netzwerk*

Das Nahrein-Netzwerk[10] hat das Ziel, die Entwicklung der Altertumswissenschaften, des Kulturerbes und der Geisteswissenschaften in Irak nachhaltig zu fördern. Das Projekt unterstützt interdisziplinäre Forschung, um Universitäten, Museen und Gemeindegruppen die Möglichkeit zu geben, den Bedürfnissen der lokalen Bevölkerung besser gerecht zu werden. Das Netzwerk ist am University College London, an der University of Kurdistan Hewlêr und am Ashmolean Museum in Oxford angesiedelt und hat viele internationale Partner. Das Netzwerk wird vom britischen Arts and Humanities Research Council und dem Global Challenges Research Fund Network Plus-Programm für vier Jahre (2017–2021) unterstützt.

2.8   *BANUU-Projekt*

BANUU (Designing new pathways for employability and entrepreneurship of Iraqi students in Archaeology and Cultural Heritage)[11] ist ein dreijähriges Projekt (von 01/01/2020 bis 31/12/2022), das von Universitäten, Ministerien und privaten Unternehmen aus Italien, der Türkei und Irak getragen wird.

Das BANUU-Projekt stützt sich auf die Erfahrungen und Ergebnisse der EU-finanzierten WALADU- und EDUU-Projekte, die auf verschiedenen Ebenen im Bereich der Archäologie und des kulturellen Erbes im Irak gute Auswirkungen hatten. Ziel des Projekts ist, die Beschäftigungsfähigkeit der Studierenden im Bereich der Geisteswissenschaften in Irak zu verbessern.

2.9   *Die Neugründung anderer Fakultäten und Departments*

Mehrere irakische Universitäten evaluierten einen zunehmenden Bedarf an Ausbildungsmöglichkeiten in den Altertumswissenschaften und etablierten daher mit dem vorhandenen, wissenschaftlich gut ausgebildeten Personal auf dem Gebiet der Archäologie eigene Fakultäten und Abteilungen für Archäologie. Der Bedarf an Nachwuchs führte auch zur Notwendigkeit der Einrichtung eines archäologischen und kulturellen Forschungszentrums. Die bisher gegründeten Fakultäten und Departments für Archäologie sind:

---

10   https://www.ucl.ac.uk/nahrein/.
11   https://site.unibo.it/banuu/en.

1. Bereits im Jahr 1970 wurde an der Universität Mosul das Archäologische Department / College of Arts etabliert, das im Jahr 2008 in eine Fakultät für Archäologie umgewandelt wurde, um spezialisiertes Personal auf dem Gebiet der archäologischen Forschung in allen Bereichen – antike und islamische Archäologie, alte Sprachen und Zivilisationen sowie archäologische Ausgrabungen – auszubilden.

2. Das College of Arts / Archäologische Department der Universität Babylon in al-Ḥillah wurde 2004 gegründet.

3. Das College of Arts / Department of Archaeology der Al-Muthanna Universität in Samawa wurde 2007 gegründet.

4. Die Fakultät für Archäologie / Kufa Universität of wurde im Jahr 2011 etabliert.

5. An der Universität von Samarra wurde die Abteilung für Archäologie zusammen mit der Fakultät für Archäologie zu Beginn des akademischen Jahrs 2011–2012 gegründet.

6. Die Fakultät für Archäologie / University of Al-Qadisiyah / Abteilung für Keilschriftstudien in Diwaniyah wurde mit der Einrichtung des Colleges im akademischen Jahr 2014–2015 gegründet.

7. Die Fakultät für Archäologie / Dhi-Qar Universität in der Provinz Dhi-Qar wurde zu Beginn des neuen akademischen Jahres 2015–16 am neuen Hauptsitz in Suq al-Shuyukh gegründet.

3   **Wissenschaftliche Zeitschriften, universitäre Abschlussarbeiten sowie universitäre Lehrpläne im Irak**

Im Folgenden gebe ich einen Überblick über einschlägige wissenschaftliche Zeitschriften im Irak, über Abschlussarbeiten, die von irakischen Wissenschaftlern im Ausland und im Irak verfasst wurden, sowie am Schluss einen Überblick über die Lehrpläne in den Fächern Archäologie / Altorientalistik an ausgewählten Universitäten.

Zu den irakischen wissenschaftlichen Fachzeitschriften, die sich mit Archäologie, Philologie und Kulturerbe des Irak beschäftigen, zählen:

1. *Sumer* (Zeitschrift für Archäologie und Geschichte im Irak), Staatliche Behörde des Irak für Antiken und Kulturerbe, Bagdad.

2. *Majallat Dirāsāt fi al-Tārīḫ wa al-Āṯār* (Zeitschrift für historische und archäologische Studien), College of Arts – Universität Bagdad.

3. *Majallat Kullīyat al-Ādāb* (Bulletin des College of Arts), herausgeben vom College of Arts – Universität Bagdad.

4. *Ādāb al-Rāfidayn* (Universität Mosul – College für Archäologie).

5. *Al-Turāṯ wa-al-Ḥaḍāra* (Zeitschrift des regionalen Zentrums für Konservierung und Kulturgut in den arabischen Ländern – Bagdad).
6. *Āṯār al-Rāfidayn* (Universität Mosul – College für Archäologie).
7. *Bayn al-Nahrayn* (Kulturzeitschrift, vierteljährlich, herausgegeben von der chaldäischen Kirche in Mosul).
8. *Historical Bulletin* (Irakische Gesellschaft für Geschichte und Archäologie), Bagdad.
9. *Al-Malwīya li-l Dirāsāt al-Āṯārīya wa-l Tārīḫīya* (Al Malweah Zeitschrift für archäologische und historische Studien), Samarra Universität.

Irakische und arabische Gelehrte haben die Wichtigkeit erkannt, Bücher über Archäologie, Keilschriftforschung und über die Geschichte des älteren Orients zu übersetzen und selbst zu schreiben, um insbesondere den arabischen Lesern die Bedeutung ihres kulturellen Erbes näher zu bringen. Die folgenden, ausgewählten Fachbücher sind in arabischer Sprache verfasst oder ins Arabische übersetzt worden:

3.1 *Monographien für Akkadische und Sumerische Texte*

'Abd, Bāsīma J. & al-Ḏāhāb, Amīra E.
2015 Nuṣūṣ mismārīya ġayr manšūra fi al-Matḥaf al-'Iraqi – al-silsila al-Akkadīya / I (Unpublished cuneiform texts in the Iraqi Museum – Akkadian Series/I), Bagdad.

'Abd, Bāsīma J.
2016 Nuṣūṣ mismārīya ġayr manšūra fi al-Matḥaf al-'Iraqi – al-silsila al-Akkadīya / II (Unpublished cuneiform texts in the Iraqi Museum – Akkadian Series / II), Bagdad.

'Abd, Bāsīma J.
2017 Nuṣūṣ mismārīya ġayr manšūra min 'aṣr sulālat Ūr al-ṯāliṯa min madīnat Irisagrig/Al-Šarraki (Unpublished cuneiform texts from the Ur III Dynasty from the city Iri-sag-rig$_7$/Al-Šarraki), Bagdad.

'Abd, Bāsīma J.
2018 Al-aršīf al-malakī lil-malik Ilūni min madīnat Bāsī (The royal archive of the king Iluni from Basi city), Bagdad.

'Abd, Bāsīma J.
2020 Aršīf Šamaš-zēr-ibnī min madīnat Šāṭir (The archive of Šamaš-zer-ibni from the city of Šaṭir), Bagdad.

al-Fuʾādi, ʿAbdu l-Hādī (al-Fouadi, Abdul-Hadi)
1979   Nuṣūṣ fi al-Matḥaf al-ʿIrāqī, al-Nuṣūṣ al-madrasīya al-Qurṣīyat al-šakil
        (Texts in the Iraq Museum: Lenticular exercise school texts), Band 10/1,
        Bagdad.

Rašīd, Fāuzi (Rashid, Fawzi)
1971   Nuṣūṣ fi al-mathaf al-ʿIrāqī – Nuṣūṣ mismārīya – Nuṣūṣ idārīya min
        sulālat Ūr al-tālita (Texts in the Iraq Museum – cuneiform texts,
        administrative texts from the Ur III Dynasty), Vol. VI, Bagdad.

Rašīd, Fāuzi (Rashid, Fawzi)
1981   Aqdam al-kitābāt al-mismārīya al-muktašafa fi ḥauḍ sadd Ḥimrīn (The
        ancient inscriptions in Himrin area: Results of the salvage excavations
        at Himrin Reservoir), Himrin 4. Bagdad.

3.2   *Monographien für Akkadische und Sumerische Grammatik*
Caplice, Richard
1995   Introduction to Akkadian (Muqaddima tamhīdīya lil-luġa al-Akkadīya)
        Übersetzer: Abdul Rahman Darkazalli, Aleppo Universität.

Ḥānnūn, Nāʾil (Hannon, Naʾil)
2011   Dirāsāt fi ʿilm al-āṯār wa al-luġat al-qadīma (Studies in archeology and
        ancient languages) (zwei Bände), Damaskus.

Ḥānnūn, Nāʾil (Hannon, Naʾil)
2015   Nuṣuṣ mismārīya tārīḫīya wa adabīya (Historische und literarische
        Keilschrifttexte), Kufa Universität.

Ḥānnūn, Nāʾil (Hannon, Naʾil)
2016   Al-luġatān al-Sūmarīya wa al-Akkadīya- Qawāʿid – Nuṣuṣ – Mufradāt
        (Die sumerische und akkadische Sprache. Grammatik- Texte-
        Wortschätze), Beirut.

Rašīd, Fauzī (Rashid, Fawzi)
1971   Qawāʿid al-luġa al-Sūmarīya (Grammatik der sumerischen Sprache),
        Bagdad.

Rašīd, Fauzī (Rashid, Fawzi)
2009   Qawāʿid al-luġa al-Akkadīya (Grammatik der akkadischen Sprache),
        Damaskus.

Sulaimān, ʿĀmir (Sulaiman, Amer)
1991   al-luġa al-Akkadīya (Die akkadische Sprache), Mosul Universität.

3.3   *Werke zur Mythologie des Alten Orients*
Al-Aḥmad, Sāmī Saʿīd (al-Ahmad, Sami Said)
1984   Malḥamat Ǧilǧāmiš (Gilgamesch-Epos), Bagdad.

ʿAlī, Fāḍil ʿAbdul Wāḥid (Ali, Fadhil Abdul-Wahed)
1986   ʿIštār wa-ma'sāt Tammūz (Ištar and the tragedy of Dumuzi), Bagdad.

Bāqir, Ṭāhā (Baqir, Taha)
1962   Malḥamat Ǧilǧāmiš (Gilgamesch-Epos), Bagdad.

Ismāʿīl, Fārūq (Ismail, Faruk)
1998   Erra wa Malik kull al-Diyār (Erra und der König aller Wohnstädte),
         Aleppo.

Kramer, Samuel N.
1971   Sumerian Mythology (al-Aṣāṭīr al-Sūmarīya), Übersetzer: Yūsuf Dāwūd
         ʿAbd al-qādir.

3.4   *Monographien zur Geschichte, Literatur und Archäologie des*
            Alten Orients
ʿAlī, Fāḍil ʿAbdul Wāḥid & Sulaimān, ʿĀmir
1979   ʿĀdāt wa-taqalīd al-šuʿūb al-qadīma (Bräuche und Traditionen der
         alten Völker), Bagdad.

ʿAlī, Fāḍil ʿAbdul Wāḥid
1989   Von den Sumer Tontafeln bis zur Bibel (min 'Alwaḥ Sūmer 'ila al-
         Tawrat) Bagdad.

al-Badrī, ʿAbd al-Laṭīf (al-Badri, Abd-allatief)
1976   min al-Ṭibb al-Āššūrī (Aus der assyrischen Medizin), Bagdad.

Bāqir, Ṭāhā
1959   Bābil wa Būrsibbā (Babylon und Borsippa), Bagdad.

Bāqir, Ṭāhā
1973   Muqaddima fī Tārīḫ al-Ḥaḍārāt al-qadīma (Einführung in die Geschichte
         der alten Zivilisationen).

Bāqir, Ṭāhā
1976   Muqaddima fī Ādāb al-ʿIraq al-qadīm (Eine Einführung in die Literatur des alten Irak) Bagdad.

Bottéro, Jean
1952   La religion babylonienne (al-Diyāna ʿind al-Babilīyyn), Übersetzer: Walīd al-Ġādir, Bagdad.

Bottéro, Jean
1990   Mesopotamie: l'écriture, la ration et les dieux (Bilād al-Rāfidayn: al-kitāba al-ʿaql al-ʾaliha), Übersetzer: Albert Abūna, Bagdad.

Cancik-Kirschbaum, Eva
2008   Die Assyrer – Geschichte, Gesellschaft, Kultur (Tārīḫ al-Āššūrīyīn al-qadīm), Übersetzer: Fārūq Ismāʿīl, Damaskus.

Chamard, Georges Boyer
1981   Responsabilité pénale dans les littératures Babylonienne et Assyrienne (al-masʾūlīya al-Ġazāʾīya fī al-ādāb al-Āššūrīya wa al-Bābilīya), Übersetzer: Sālim al-Sūways, Bagdad.

Contenau, Georges
1979   Everyday life in Babylon and Assyria (al-Ḥayāt al-yawmīya fī Bilād Bābil wa Āššūr), Übersetzer: Salīm Ṭāhā al-Tikrītī & Burhān ʿAbd al-Tikrītī.

Frankfort, Henri
1965   The birth of civilization in the Near East (Faǧr al-Ḥaḍāra fī al-Šarq al-adnā), Übersetzer: Mīḫaīl Ḫūri.

Ḥānnūn, Nāʾil
2003   Šarīʿat Ḥamūrābī: tarǧamat al-Naṣṣ al-mismārī maʿa al-šurūḥāt al-luġawīya (Kodex Hammurabi: Übersetzung des Keilschrifttextes mit sprachlichen Erklärungen), Bagdad.

Ḥānnūn, Nāʾil
2007   Ḥaqīqat al-Sūmarīyīn wa Dirāsāt uḫrā fī ʿilm al-āṯār wa al-Nuṣūṣ al-mismārīya (Die Realitäten der Sumerer und andere Studien in Archäologie und Keilschrifttexten), Damaskus.

al-Hāšimī, Riḍā, (al-Hashimi, Ridha)
1971   Niẓam al-ʿAʾila fī al-ʿahd al-Bābilī al-qadīm (Familiensystem in der alt-
        babylonischen Zeit), Bagdad.

Klengel, Horst
1990   Hammurapi von Babylon und seine Zeit (Ḥammurabi al-Bābilī wa
        ʿAṣrūhū), Übersetzer: Muḥammad Waḥīd Ḥayyāṭa, Syrien.

Koldewey, Robert
1985   The temples of Babylon and Borsippa (Maʿābid Bābil wa-Burssība)
        Übersetzer: Nawāl Ḥuršīd Saʿīd, Bagdad.

Kramer, Samuel N.
1975   From the tablets of Sumer (min Alwāḥ Sūmar). Übersetzer: Ṭāhā Bāqir,
        Bagdad.

Kramer, Samuel N.
2012   The Sumerians: Their history, culture and character (al-sūmarīyyīn:
        Tārīḫuhum, Ḥaḍāratuhum wa Ḥaṣåiṣuhum), Übersetzer: Faiṣal al-
        Wāilī, Bagdad.

Krischen, Fritz
1976   Weltwunder der Baukunst in Babylonien und Ionien (ʿAǧåib al-Dunyā
        fiʾImārat Bābil), Übersetzer: Ṣubḥī Anwar Rašīd, Bagdad.

Lloyd, Seton
1980   The archaeology of Mesopotamia: From the Old Stone Age to the
        Persian conquest (Āṯār bilād al-Rāfidayn min al-ʿaṣr al-ḥaǧǧarī al-
        qadīm ḥattā al-iḥtilāl al-Fārisi), Übersetzer: Sāmī Saʿīd Al-Aḥmad,
        Bagdad.

Moortgat, Anton
1975   Art of ancient Mesopotamia (al-Fann fī al-ʿIrāq al-qadīm) Übersetzer:
        ʿĪsā Salmān & Salīm Ṭāhā al-Tikrītī, Bagdad.

al-Naǧafi, Ḥasan (al-Najafi, Hassan)
1982   al-tiǧara wa al-Qānūn badaʾa fī Sūmer (Handel und Recht begannen in
        Sumer), Bagdad.

al-Nāṣirī, Ṭāriq (al-Nasiry, Tariq)
1983   al-Riyāḍa fī Bilād mā Bayna al-Nahrayn al-qadīma (Sport im alten
        Mesopotamien), Bagdad.

Oates, David and Joan
1988   The rise of civilization (Nušūʾ al-Ḥaḍāra), Übersetzer: Luṭfi al-Ḫūrī,
        Bagdad.

Oates, Joan
1990   Babylon (Bābil), Übersetzer: Samīr ʿAbd ar-Raḥīm al-Ǧalabī, Bagdad.

Oppenheim, Leo
1981   Ancient Mesopotamia (Bilād mā Bayna al-Nahrayn), Übersetzer: Saʿdī
        Fāyḍī ʿAbd ar-Razzāq, Bagdad.

Parrot, André
1977   Sumer: The dawn of art (Sūmir: funūnuhā wa-ḥaḍāratuhā), Übersetzer:
        ʿĪsā Salmān & Salīm Ṭāhā al-Tikrītī.

Parrot, André
1980   The tower of Babylon (Burǧ Bābil), Übersetzer: Ǧabra Ibrāhīm Ǧabra,
        Bagdad.

Parrot, André
1980   Assyria – Nineveh and Babylon (Bilād Āššūr- Nīnawā wa-Bābil),
        Übersetzer: ʿĪsā Salmān and Salīm Ṭāhā al-Tikrītī.

Qāšā, Suhāil (Qāshā, Suhail)
2010   Tārīḫ al-fikr fī al-ʿIrāq al-qadīm (Geschichte des Denkens im alten
        Irak), Beirut.

Rašīd, Fauzī
1979   al-Šarāʾiʿ al-ʿIrāqīya al-qadīma (Die alten irakischen Gesetze), Bagdad.

Rašīd, Fauzī
2010   Ḍawāhir ḥaḍārīya wa Ǧamālīya min al-tārīḫ al-qadīm (Kulturelle und
        ästhetische Phänomene aus der alten Geschichte).

Reuter, Oscar
1985   Bābil al-madīna al-dāḫilīya „al-markaz" (Die Innenstadt von Babylon
        „Merkes"), Übersetzer: Nawāl Ḫuršīd Saʿīd and ʿAlī Yaḥyā Manṣūr,
        Deutschland.

Roux, Georges
1984   Ancient Iraq (al-ʿIrāq al-qadīm), Übersetzer: Ḥusain ʿAlwan Ḥusain,
        Bagdad.

Rutten, Marguerite
1980   La science des chaldéens (ʿUlūm al-Bābīlien) Übersetzer: Yūsuf Ḥabbī,
        Bagdad.

Saggs, H.W.F.
1979   The greatness that was Babylon (ʿAẓamat Bābil), Übersetzer: ʿĀmir
        Sulaimān.

Saggs, H.W.F.
2010   Everyday life in Babylonia and Assyria (al-Ḥayāt al-yawmīya fi al-ʿIrāq
        al-qadīm (Bilād Bābil wa-Aššūr)). Übersetzer: Kaẓem Saʿad al-Dīn.

Šḫālat, ʿAlī; al-Ḥamadānī, ʿAbd al-ʿAzīz Ilyās (Shuhaylat, Ali; al-Hamadani, Abd
al-Aziz Ilyas)
2012   Muḫtaṣar Tārīḫ al-ʿIrāq: Tārīḫ al-ʿIrāq al-qadīm (Eine kurze Geschichte
        des Irak: Geschichte des alten Irak), Beirut.

al-Sīwāni, Šāh Muḥammad ʿAlī (al-Siwani, Shah Muhammad Ali)
1976   Ūr, Bagdad.

von Soden, Wolfram
2003   Einführung in die Altorientalistk (Madḫal ilā Ḥaḍārāt al-Šarq al-
        qadīm), Übersetzer: Fārūq Ismāʿīl, Damaskus.

al-Ṭaʿān, ʿAbd al-Riḍā (al-Ta'an, Abd al-Ridha)
1981   Al-fikr al-Siyāsī fī al-ʿIrāq al-qadīm (Das politische Denken im alten
        Irak), Bagdad.

Wolfensohn, Israel
1980   Tārīḫ al-luġāt al-Sāmīya (Geschichte der semitischen Sprachen), Kairo.

Woolley, Leonard
1947   Mesopotamia: Cradle of civilization (Wādi al-Rāfidayn: Mahd al-
         Ḥaḍāra), Übersetzer: Aḥmad ʿAbd al-Bāqi, Bagdad.

Woolley, Leonard
1982   Digging up the past (Nabš al-Māḍī), Übersetzer: ʿAzīz al-ʿAlī al-ʿIzzī,
         Bagdad.

al-ʿAzāwī, ʿUmar Jassām (al-Azzawi, Omar Jassam)
2019   Aqsām ʿIlm al-āṯār fī al-Jāmiʿāt al-ʿIrāqīya wa-subul Taṭwīr al-Dirāsāt
         al-Akādīmīya fīhā (Departments of archeology in Iraqi universities
         and methods of development of academic studies).

3.5   *Wörterbücher*

Baqir, Ṭāhā
1980   Min turāṯinā al-luġawī al-qadīm – mā yusamma fī al-ʿarabīya bi-al-
         Daḫīl (Von unserem alten sprachlichen Kulturerbe – Die sogenannten
         Lehnwörter).

Bīṭār, Ilyās (Bitar, Ilyas)
2011   al-Nabātāt as-sūmarīya wa-al-Āššūrīya – al-Bābilīya: muʿğam wa-
         dirāsa muqārana fī ḍawʾ al-ʿArabīya (Sumerische und assyrische
         babylonische Pflanzen: Wörterbuch und Vergleichsstudie im Lichte
         des Arabischen), Beirut.

Ḥānnūn, Nāʾil
2001   al-muʿğam al-mismārī – muʿğam al-luġat al-akkadīya wa as-sūmarīya
         wa al-ʿarabīya (Keilschriftwörterbuch – Wörterbuch der akkadischen,
         sumerischen und arabischen Sprache), (Band 1), Bagdad.

al-Ǧubūrī, ʿAlī Yāsīn (al-Jubouri, Ali Yasin)
2010   Qāmūs al-luġat al-akkadīya – al-ʿarabīya (Das Akkadisch-Arabische
         Sprachwörterbuch), Abu Dhabi.

al-Ǧubūrī, ʿAlī Yāsīn (al-Jubouri, Ali Yasin)
2018   Muʿğam al-kalimāt as-sūmarīya fī al-luġatain al-akkadīya wa-al-
         ʿarabīya wa-uḫra akkadīya fī al-ʿarabīya (Dictionary of Sumerian words
         in Akkadian and Arabic languages and other Akkadians in Arabic),
         Bibliothek von Alexandria.

Ḫāšīm, ʿAlī Fāhmī (Khashim, Ali Fahmi)
2005   al-Akkadīya al-ʿArabīya: muʿǧam muqāran wa-muqaddima (Akka-
        disches Arabisch: Vergleichendes Wörterbuch und Einleitung), Kairo.

Labat, René
1995   Manuel d'épigraphie akkadienne (Qāmūs al-ʿalamat al-mismaria),
        Übersetzer: Walid al-Jadir, Albēr Abona, Khalid Salim Ismail.

Nūmān, Faḍīlah Ṣabīḥ
2017   Alfāẓ al-ṭabīʿa al-muštarakā bayna al-ʿarabīya wa-al-akkadīya –
        dirāsa luġawīya (Gemeinsame Naturwörter zwischen Arabisch und
        Akkadisch – Sprachliche Studie), Damaskus.

al-Rāwi, Fārūq Nāṣir (al-Rawi, Farouk Nasir)
        Qāmūs al-mufīd li-ṭālib al-luġa as-sūmarīya (Nützliches Wörterbuch
        für den Student des Sumerischen).

Sallūm, Muḥammad Dāwūd (Sallum, Muhammad Dawud)
2003   Muʿǧam al-kalimāt al-akkadīya: fi al-luġāt al-šarraqīya al-qadīma wa-
        al-iġrīqīya wa-al-lātīnīya (Wörterbuch der Akkadischen Wörter in den
        altorientalischen, der altgriechischen und lateinischen Sprachen),
        Beirut.

Sulaimān, ʿĀmir
1999   al-muʿǧam al-akkadī: muʿǧam al-luġāt al-akkadīya, al-Bābilīya – al-
        āššūrīya, bi-al-luġāt al-ʿarabīya wa-al-ḥarf al-ʿarabī (Akkadisches Sprach-
        wörterbuch: Wörterbuch der Akkadischen, Babylonisch-Assyrischen
        Sprache, übersetzt ins Arabische und in arabischer Schrift), Bagdad.

3.6   *Verzeichnis der Abschlussarbeiten irakischer Altorientalisten (Assyriologen) an ausländischen Universitäten (nach Jahren geordnet)*

ʿAlī, Fāḍil ʿAbd al-Wāḥid (Ali, Fadhil Abdulwahid)
1964   Sumerian letters: Two collections from the Old Babylonian schools,
        Philadelphia.

al-Zībārī, Akrām (Al-Zeebari, Akram)
1964   Altbabylonische Briefe des Iraq-Museums, Münster.

Rašīd, Fauzī (Rashid, Fawzi)
1965   Archiv des Nūršamaš und andere Darlehungsurkunden aus der alt-
          babylonischen Zeit, Heidelberg.

Sulaimān, ʿĀmir (Suleiman, Amir)
1966   A study of land tenure in the Old Babylonian Period with special
          reference to the Diyala region, based on published and unpublished
          texts, London.

Ismāʿīl-Ṣābir, Bāhīǧa Ḥalīl (Ismail-Sabir, Bahija Khalil)
1967   Mittelassyrische Keilschrifttexte aus Assur, Berlin.

al-Fuʾādi, ʿAbd al-Hādī (Al-Fouadi, Abdul-Hadi)
1969   Enki's journey to Nippur: The journeys of the gods, Philadelphia.

al-Āʿdamī, Ḥālid Aḥmad (Al-Aʿdami, Khalid Ahmed)
1971   Some Old Babylonian letters in the Iraq Museum, Birmingham.

al-Rāwī, Fārūq Nāṣir (Al-Rawi, Farouk Nasir)
1977   Studies in the commercial life of an administrative area of Eastern
          Assyria in the fifteenth century BC, based on published and unpublished
          cuneiform texts, Cardiff.

Fāḍil, ʿAbdu l-Ilāh (Fadhil, Abdulillah)
1978   Studien zur Topographie und Prosopographie der Provinzstädte des
          Königreiches Arrapḫe, Heidelberg.

ʿAbd al-Qādir ʿAbd al-Ǧabbār Muṣṭafā, Abdul-Kader Abdul-Jabbar
1983   The Old Babylonian tablets from Me-Turan (Tell Al-Sib and Tell
          Haddad), Glasgow.

al-Ǧubūrī, ʿAlī Yāsīn (Al-Juboori, Ali Yasin)
1984   Some Neo-Assyrian provincial administrators, London.

Ḥānnūn, Nāʾil (Hannoon, Naʾil)
1986   Studies in the historical geography of Northern Iraq during the Middle
          and Neo-Assyrian periods, Toronto.

Ḥusain, Layṯ Maǧīd (Hussein, Laith Majeed)
2006   Tell Ḥarmal: Die Texte aus dem Hauptverwaltungsgebäude „Serai",
          Marburg.

Fāḍil, Anmār ʿAbdu l-Ilāh (Fadhil, Anmar Abdulillah)
2012   Eine kleine Tontafelbibliothek aus Assur (Ass. 15426), Heidelberg.

Aḥmad, Kūzād Muḥammad (Ahmed, Kozad Mohamed)
2012   The beginnings of ancient Kurdistan (c. 2500–1500 BC): A historical
        and cultural synthesis, Leiden.

al-Maʿmūri, Ḥaidar ʿAbd al-Wāḥid (al-Mamori, Haider Abdollwahed)
2013   Umm al-Aqarib: An architectural and textual study of a Sumerian city,
        Kokushikan.

Kāmil, Arrī (Kamil, Ari)
2015   L'archive d'Esidum, un entrepreneur du temps du rois d'Ur (XXI av.
        J.-C.). D'après les textes cunéiformes inédits conserves au musée de
        Suleymaniyeh (Kurdistan Irakien), Université de Sorbonne, Paris 1,
        Paris.

Mūrād, ʿAlī, (Murad, Ali)
2017   Textes cunéiformes de Larsa de l'époque paléo-babylonienne
        (Isin-Larsa), Paris.

Ẓāhir, ʿIštār S. (Dhahir, Ishtar S.)
2018   Das Archiv der Šāt-Eštar Keilschrifturkunden aus der Zeit der Dritten
        Dynastie von Ur, Berlin.

**3.7   *Verzeichnis der M.A.-Arbeiten an der University of Baghdad College
        of Arts / Department of Archaeology (nach Jahren geordnet)***

Vgl. Fadhil, Abdulillah, Qualifikationsarbeiten zum Magister oder Doktor Phil.
des Department of Archaeology der Universität Baghdad, Teil 1: BaM 32 (2001),
289–321; Teil 2: BaM 33 (2002), 331–354; Teil 3: BaM 34 (2003), 267–285; Teil 4:
BaM 35 (2005), 173–219; Teil 5: ZOrA 2 (2009), 88–104.

Al-Hāšimī, Riḍā (Al-Hashimi, Ridha)
1964   Some Old Babylonian purchase contracts in the Iraq Museum from
        Harmal and Dhibaʾi (Betreuer: Lubor Matuš).[12]

---

12   Lubor Matouš war ein aus Tschechien stammender Altorientalist (Assyriologe und
      Sumerologe), der bei Benno Landsberger an der Universität Leipzig studiert hatte.

'Abd Allāh, 'Abd al-Karīm (Abdullah, Abdul-Karim)
1964   Old Babylonian loan contracts in the Iraq Museum from Tell al-Dhiba'i
        and Tell Harmal (Betreuer: Lubor Matuš).

'āl-'Ubaid, Īmān J. (Al-Ubaid, Iman J.)
1983   Nuṣūṣ mismārīya ġayr manšūra min al-'aṣr al-Bābilī al-qadīm / manṭiqat
        Diyālā (Unpublished cuneiform texts from the Old Babylonian period,
        Diyala Region, Tell Muhammad).

Muḥammad, Aḥmad K. (Mohammed, Ahmed K.)
1985   Dirāsāt fi Nuṣūṣ mismārīya ġayr manšūra min manṭiqat Diyālā / ḥauḍ
        Ḥimrīn / Tall Ḥaddād (Studies in unpublished cuneiform texts from
        the Diyala Region – Himrin Basin, Tell Haddad).

al-Mutawallī, Nawāla A. (Al-Mutawali, Nawala A.)
1986   Dirāsāt fi Nuṣūṣ mismārīya ġayr manšūra min sulalat Ūr al-ṯāliṯa (Tall
        Mazyad) Ḥafriyāt al-mausim al-ṯānī 1980 (Studies in unpublished
        cuneiform texts from the Ur III Dynasty, Tell Mazyad, excavation of
        the second season – 1980).

Ḥamīd, Aḥmad M. (Hamid, Ahmed M.)
1990   Dirāsāt fi Nuṣūṣ ġayr manšūra min fatrat al-'ahd al-Bābilī al-qadīm /
        manṭiqat Diyālā / Tall Ḥarmal (Studies of unpublished Old Babylonian
        cuneiform texts from the Diyala Region, Tell Harmal).

Ismā'īl, Ḥālid S. (Ismaeel, Khalid S.)
1990   Nuṣūṣ mismārīya ġayr manšūra min al-'aṣr al-Bābilī al-qadīm /
        manṭiqat Diyālā / Tulūl Ḥaṭṭāb (Unpublished cuneiform texts from the
        Old Babylonian period/ Diyala Region – Tulul Khatab).

al-Qaradāġī, Rāfida A.A. (Al-Qaradagi, Rafida A.A.)
1990   Nuṣūṣ ġayr manšūra min Sippar (Unpublished texts from Sippar).

Ḥusain, Layṯ M. (Hussein, Laith Mohammed)
1991   al-Kāhin fi al-'aṣr al-Bābilī al-qadīm (The priest in the Old Babylonian
        period).

Aḥmad, Kwzād M. (Ahmed, Kozad M.)
1993   Tukulti-Ninurta – Munġazātuhu fi ḍaw' al-kitābāt al- mismārīya al-
        manšūra wa ġayr al-manšūra (Tukulti-Ninurta – His achievements in
        the light of the published and unpublished cuneiform inscriptions).

Fahd, Saʿd S. (Fahad, Saad S.)

1996   Nuṣūṣ mismārīya min al-ʿahd al-Bābilī al-qadīm (manṭiqat Diyālā / Tall Ḥarmal (cuneiform texts from the Old Babylonian period (Diyala Region / Tell Harmal)).

Minšid, Minšid (Menshed, Menshed M.)

1997   Nuṣūṣ mismārīya ġayr manšūra min al-ʿaṣr al-Bābilī al-qadīm / manṭiqat Diyālā / Tall Ḥarmal (Unpublished cuneiform texts from the Old Babylonian period (Diyala Region – Tell Harmal)).

ʿAbd al-Laṭīf, Saǧa M. (Abdullateef, Saja M.)

1997   al-Ḥaywān fi adab al-ʿIrāq al-qadīm (Animal in ancient Iraqi literature).

ʿAbd, Bāsīma J. (Abed, Basima J.)

1998   Nuṣūṣ mismārīya ġayr manšūra min al-ʿahd al-Bābilī al-qadīm fi al-Matḥaf al-ʿIrāqī (Unpublished cuneiform texts from the Old Babylonian period in the Iraq Museum).

Macelaru, Adrian

1999   Madḫal ʾilā al-luġatayn al-akkadīya wa al-ʿarabīya – Dirāsā Muʿǧamīya (Introduction to Akkadian and Arabic – A lexical study).

al-Ḏahab, Amīra E. (Al-Dahab, Amira E.)

1999   al-Kāhinat fi al-ʿaṣr al-Bābilī al-qadīm (The priestesses in the Old Babylonian period).

ʿAbd al-Mālik, Munḏir A. (Abdul-Malik, Munther A.)

1999   Nuṣūṣ ʾIdāriya wa qaḍāʾīya min Tall al-faḫḫār (madīnat Kurruḫānni) (Nuṣūṣ ġayr manšūra) (Administrative and legal texts from Tell Al-Fahhar (the city Kurukhani) (Unpublished texts)).

ʾāl -Affandī, Mahā S.S., (Al-Afandi, Maha S.S.)

2000   Nuṣūṣ mismārīya ġayr manšūra min al-ʿaṣr al-Āšūrī al-wasīṭ min Tall al-faḫḫār (Kurruḫānni) (Unpublished cuneiform texts from the Middle Assyrian period from Tell Al-Fahhar (Kurukhani)).

al-Zūbādī, Maha H.R. (Al-Zubadi, Maha H.R.)

2003   Nuṣūṣ mismārīya ġayr manšūra min al-ʿaṣr al-Bābilī al-wasīṭ (al-fatra al-Kāššīya) ʿAqārqūf (Dūr- Kūrīgālzu) (Unpublished cuneiform texts from the Middle Babylonian period (Kassite Period) Aqar Quf (Dur- Kurigalzu)).

al-Sāmarrā'ī, Aḥmad N.S. (Al-Samraee, Ahmed N.S.)
2006 Nuṣūṣ mismārīya ġayr manšūra min al-'aṣr al-Bābilī al-qadīm fi al-Matḥaf al-'Irāqī – Sippar (Tall Abū Ḥabbā). (Unpublished cuneiform texts from the Old Babylonian period – Sippar (Tell Abu Habbah)).

al-Ǧannābī, Samrā' H.N. (Al-Janabe, Samraa H.N.)
2006 Nuṣūṣ mismārīya ġayr manšūra min al-'aṣr al-Bābilī al-qadīm – Sippar (Unpublished cuneiform texts from the Old Babylonian period – Sippar).

al-Ḥālidī, Šaymā' N.H. (Al-Khalidy, Shaimaa N.H.)
2006 Nuṣūṣ mismārīya ġayr manšūra min 'ahd al-Malik Ammi-Ṣāduqa (Unpublished cuneiform texts from the reign of the king Ammi-Saduqa).

Ẓāhir, 'Ištār S. (Dahir, Ishtar S.)
2007 Dirāsah Nuṣūṣ mismārīya ġayr manšūra min 'aṣr Ur al-ṯāliṯa (2112–2004 BC) (A study of unpublished cuneiform texts from the Ur III period (2112–2004 BC)).

Murād, Nādiā A. (Muwrad, Nadia A.)
2007 Dirāsah Nuṣūṣ mismārīya ġayr manšūra min 'aṣr Ur al-ṯāliṯa min madīnat Ur (A study of unpublished cuneiform texts from the Ur III period from the city of Ur).

Ḥalīl, Yāsir J. (Khalil, Yassir J.)
2007 Nuṣūṣ mismārīya ġayr manšūra min al-'aṣr al-Bābilī al-muta'aḫḫir – Sippar (Unpublished cuneiform texts from the late Old Babylonian period from Sippar).

al-Māʿmūri, Fāṭima A.S. (Al-Ma'muri, Fattima A.S.)
2008 Nuṣūṣ mismārīya ġayr madrūsa min 'aṣr sulalat Ūr al-ṯāliṯa fi Silsilat al-Matḥaf al-'Irāqī (TIM/6) (Unpublished cuneiform texts from the Ur III Dynasty (TIM/6)).

Muʿaḍḍad, 'Alī H. (Meadhed, Ali H.)
2009 Nuṣūṣ iqtiṣādīyah ġayr maqrū'a min al-Matḥaf al-'Irāqī (Unread cuneiform texts from the Iraqi Museum).

Saʿdūn, Abā Ḏarr R. (Sadoon, Abather R.)
2010   Nuṣūṣ mismārīya ġayr manšūra fi al-Matḥaf al-ʿIrāqī min ʿaṣr sulalat
         Ūr al-ṭāliṯa (2114–2004 BC) (Unpublished cuneiform texts in the Iraq
         Museum from the Ur III Dynasty (2114–2004 BC)).

al-Mayālī, Walīd S.M. (Al-Mayali, Waleed S.M.)
2010   Nuṣūṣ mismārīya ġayr manšūra min al-ʿaṣr al-Bābilī al-qadīm
         (muṣādara) (Unpublished cuneiform texts from the Old Babylonian
         period (Confiscation)).

Ǧawād, Aḥmad A. (Jawad, Ahmed A.)
2011   Nuṣūṣ mismārīya ġayr manšūra min al-ʿaṣr al-Bābilī al-qadīm min
         Sippar (Unpublished cuneiform texts from the Old Babylonian period
         from Sippar).

ʿUmrān, Naš’at A. (Omran, Nashat A.)
2011   Tall Abū ʿantīk (Pikasi) min al-ʿaṣr al-Bābilī al-qadīm fi ḍaw’ al-tanqībāt
         al-āṯārīya lil-mawsim (1999–2002) (Dirāsa taḥlīlīya) (Tell Abu-Inteek
         (Pikasi) at the Old Babylonian period according to archaeological
         excavations seasons "1999–2002" (an analysis study)).

al-Lāmī, Ṣabrīn Q.R. (Al-Lami, Sabreen Q.R.)
2012   Nuṣūṣ iqtiṣādīyah ġayr manšūra min zaman al-Malikīn Šu-Sin wa
         Ibbi-Sin (2038–2004 BC) (Unpublished economic texts from the reign
         of the two kings (Šu-Sin and Ibbi-Sin) (2038–2004 BC)).

ʿAṭṭa, Saḥar D. (Atta, Sahar D.)
2012   Nuṣūṣ mismārīya min al-ʿaṣr al-sūmarī al-qadīm (min al-Matḥaf al-
         ʿIrāqī) (A study of unpublished cuneiform texts from the Old Sumerian
         period (from the Iraqi Museum)).

al-Baldawī, Šaymā’ I.A. (Al-Baldawi, Shaimaa I.A.)
2012   Nuṣūṣ mismārīya ġayr manšūra min al-ʿaṣr al-Bābilī al-qadīm min
         al-Matḥaf al-ʿIrāqī min zaman ḥukm al-Malik Rīm-Sin al-’awal
         (1822–1763 BC) (Unpublished cuneiform texts from the Old Babylonian
         period from the Iraqi Museum from the time of the reign the king
         Rim-Sin I (1822–1763 BC)).

Zwaīd, Wafā’ H. (Zwaid, Wafaa H.)
2012   Nuṣūṣ al-nafaqāt min al-ʿaṣr al-sūmarī al-ḥadīṯ (Expenses texts from
         the Neo-Sumerian period (2112–2004 BC)).

al-Nidawī, Hūda H.A. (Al-Nidawi, Huda H.A.)
2013   Nuṣūṣ iqtiṣādīyah ġayr manšūra min al-ʿaṣr al-akkadī al-qadīm (Unpublished economic tablets from the Old Akkadian period).

al-Fanharawī, Walāʾ S.A. (Al-Fanharawi, Walaa S.A.)
2013   Nuṣūṣ mismārīya ġayr manšūra min al-ʿaṣr al-Bābilī al-qadīm min al-Matḥaf al-ʿIrāqī (Tall Abū ʿantīk) (The unpublished cuneiform texts from the Old Babylonian period in the Iraq Museum (Tell Abu Anteek)).

Ṣālih, Isrāʾ S. (Salih, Israa S.)
2014   Nuṣūṣ iqtiṣādīyah ġayr manšūra min ʿaṣr faġr al-sulalat (The unpublished economic texts from the Early Dynastic period).

Ǧawdat, Yaʿqūb A.H. (Jawdat, Jacob A.H.)
2014   Rasāʾil ġayr manšūra min al-ʿaṣr al-Bābilī al-qadīm fi al-Matḥaf al-ʿIrāqī (Unpublished Old Babylonian letters in the Iraqi Museum).

Ǧāsim, Qāsim ʿAbd al-Ḥamīd (Jasim, Qasim Abdul-Hamed)
2014   al-ṣiyāġa al-Balāġīya fi Nuṣūṣ Māri al-Malakīya fi ḍawʾ al-Nuṣūṣ al-manšūra – Dirāsa muqārana maʿa al-luġa al-ʿarabīya (The rhetoric arts of Mari royal texts on the light of published ones – A comparative study with the Arabic language).

ʿAbd al-Raḥman, Šaymāʾ W. (Abdul-Rahman, Shaymaʿa W.)
2014   Nuṣūṣ (sa$_2$-du$_{11}$) fi ḍawʾ Nuṣūṣ manšūra wa ġayr manšūra min sulālat Ūr al-t̲ālit̲a (2112–2004 BC) ((sa$_2$-du$_{11}$) (Texts in the light of published and unpublished economic cuneiform texts from the Ur III Dynasty (2112–2004 BC)).

ʿAbd, Ḥaidar A. (Abed, Haider A.)
2014   Nuṣūṣ mismārīya ġayr manšūra min ʿahd al-Malik Ibbī-Suʾen (2028–2004 BC) (Unpublished economic texts from the reign of the king ^{d}Ibbi-^{d}Suʾen (2028–2004 BC)).

al-Ǧannābī, Ǧāsim ʿAbd al-Amīr J. (Al-Janabi, Jasim Abdul-Amir J.)
2014   Nuṣūṣ mismārīya ġayr manšūra min ʾaršīf Turām-īlī (2046–2004 BC) (Unpublished cuneiform texts from the archive of Turam-ili (2046–2004 BC)).

al-ʿIsāwī, Ḥanān A.B. (Al-Essawy, Hanan A.B.)
2014   al-Ḥayawānāt al-mudaǧana wa-dauruha fi iqtiṣād al-ʿaṣr al-akkadī al-qadīm fi ḍawʾ al-Nuṣūṣ al-mismārīya al-manšūra wa ġayr al-manšūra (The domesticated animals and their rule in the economics of the Old Akkadian period on the light of the published and unpublished cuneiform texts).

al-ʿUbaydī, Hind S.A. (Al-Obaidi, Hind S.A.)
2015   Nuṣūṣ mismārīya ġayr manšūra min al-ʿaṣr al-Bābilī al-qadīm (Unpublished cuneiform texts from the Old Babylonian period).

al-Māʿmūri, Lwʾāi K.S. (Al-Maʾmuri, Luay K.S.)
2015   Nuṣūṣ mismārīya iqtiṣādīya ġayr manšūra min al-ʿaṣr al-Akkadī (Unpublished economic texts from the Akkadian period).

Aḥmad, Afrāḥ J. (Ahmed, Afrah J.)
2015   Nuṣūṣ iqtiṣādīya ġayr manšūra min nihāyat al-ʾalf al-ṯaliṯ Qabl al-Mīlad (Unpublished economic cuneiform texts from the end of the third millennium BC).

al-Ḥamīdawi, Wiǧdān N.H. (Al-Hamidawi, Wejdan N.H.)
2015   Nuṣūṣ iqtiṣādīya wa idārīya ġayr manšūra min ʿaṣr sulalat Ūr aṯ-ṯālita (2112–2004 BC) (Unpublished economic and administrative texts from the time of the Third Dynasty of Ur (2112–2004 BC)).

Aḥmad, ʿAlī A. (Ahmed, Ali A.)
2015   al-fʿāl wa mukawinatah fi al-luǧa al-sūmarīya fi ḍawʾ Nuṣūṣ iqtiṣādīyah manšūra wa ġayr manšūra min sulalat Ūr al-ṯālita (The verb and its components in the Sumerian language in light of the published and unpublished economic texts from the Third Dynasty of Ur).

al-Naʿīmī, Ṣafāʾ ʿAbd al-Karīm H. (Al-Naimi, Safa Abdul-Kareem H.)
2015   Dirāsā Nuṣūṣ iqtiṣādīya ġayr manšūra min fatrat Ūr aṯ-ṯālita (2112–2004 BC) (Study of unpublished economic texts from the Third Period of Ur (2112–2004 BC)).

al-Ǧubūrī, Raǧad J.M.G. (Al-Jubouri, Raghad J.M.G.)
2015   Nuṣūṣ mismārīya ġayr manšūra min al-ʿaṣr al-Bābilī al-qadīm min mauqiʿ Tall Ibzyḫ (Unpublished cuneiform texts from the Old Babylonian Era from Tell Ibzikh).

Hāl, Taḥrīr D. (Hel, Tahreer D.)
2016   Nuṣūṣ iqtiṣādīya muṣādara min al-Matḥaf al-ʿIrāqī min al-ʿaṣr al-Bābilī al-qadīm (Confiscation economic texts from the Iraqi Museum from the Old Babylonian period).

al-ʿIbādī, ʿAlī H. Ḥuḍayr (Al-Abady, Ali H. Khudair)
2016   Nuṣūṣ iqtiṣādīya ġayr manšūra min Tall Abū Ḥabba (Sippar Yaḫrurum) nihāya al-ʿaṣr al-Bābilī al-qadīm (Unpublished economic texts from Tell Abu Habbah (Sippar Yaḫrurum), end of the Old Babylonian period).

al-Ḥimyarī, Ḥusain M.R. (Al-Hummeri, Hussein M.R.)
2016   Nuṣūṣ mismārīya ġayr manšūra min al-ʿaṣr al-Bābilī al-qadīm – Sippar (Mawsim tanqībāt 24) (Unpublished cuneiform texts from the Old Babylonian period – Sippar (excavation season 24)).

al-ʿUkaylī, Saǧǧād ʿAbd al- Ḥasan M. (Al-Egaily, Sajjad Abd al-Hassan M.)
2017   Nuṣūṣ iqtiṣādīya ġayr manšūra min al-ʿaṣr al-sūmarī al-ḥadīt̠ (2112–2004 BC) (Unpublished economic texts of the Neo-Sumerian period (2112–2004 BC)).

al-Kurwī, ʾaswār T. ʿAlī (Al-Kurwi, Aswaar T. Ali)
2017   Nuṣūṣ iqtiṣādīya ġayr manšūra min al-ʿaṣr al-Bābilī al-qadīm min al-Matḥaf al-ʿIrāqī (Tall Abū ʿantīk) (Unpublished economic texts from the Old Babylonian period in the Iraqi Museum (Tal Abu Anteeq)).

ʿAbd al-Razzāq, Nūra Q. (Abdul-Razzaq, Noora Q.)
2017   Al-ʿImmāʿ fi al-ʿIrāq al-qadīm fi ḍawʾ Nuṣūṣ mismārīya manšūra wa ġayr manšūra (Female slaves in ancient Iraq in the light of published and unpublished cuneiform texts).

ʿAṭīya, Nūra R. (Ataiya, Nora R.)
2017   Nuṣūṣ iqtiṣādīyah ġayr manšūra min ʿaṣr faǧr al-sulālāt (Unpublished economic texts from the Early Dynastic period).

al-Ṭāʾī, ʿAmmār M.A.D. (Al-Taee, Ammar M.A.D.)
2018   Nuṣūṣ mismārīya ġayr manšūra min ʿaṣr Ūr al-t̠ālita (2112–2004 BC) (Unpublished cuneiform texts from the age of Ur III (2112–2004 BC)).

al-Dulaimī, Anǧām S.M. (Al-Dulaymi, Angham S.M.)
2018   Nuṣūṣ mismārīya ġayr manšūra min al-ʿaṣr al-sūmarī al-ḥadīṯ (2112–
        2004 BC) (Unpublished cuneiform texts from the Neo-Sumerian age
        (2112–2004 BC)).

al-Ḥasnawī, ʿAlī H.M. (Al-Hasnawi, Ali H.M.)
2018   Nuṣūṣ mismārīya min al-ʿaṣr al-Sūmarī al-Ḥadīṯ (cuneiform texts from
        the Neo-Sumerian period).

al-Qaṭṭān, Šuʿayb F.I. (Al-Qattan, Shuaib F.I.)
2018   Masāʾil Riyāḍiya fi ḍawʾ Nuṣūṣ mismārīya manšūra wa ġayr manšūra
        (Mathematical issues in the light of published and unpublished
        cuneiform texts).

Al-Tamīmī, Šaymāʾ A. Ḥ (Al-Tamimi, Shaymaa A.H.)
2018   Nuṣūṣ mismārīya ġayr manšūra min al-ʿaṣr al-Bābilī al-qadīm –
        madīnat Pikasi (Tall Abū ʿantīk) (Unpublished cuneiform texts from
        the Old Babylonian period – Pikasi city – Tell Abu Anteek).

al-Rubayʿī, ʿAmmār Y.M. (Al-Rubayee, Ammar Y.M.)
2018   Nuṣūṣ mismārīya ġayr manšūra fi al-Matḥaf al-ʿIrāqī min al-ʿaṣr al-
        Akkadī (Unpublished cuneiform texts in the Iraqi Museum).

al-Ḥafaǧī, Nūr Ḥ.Ḥ. (Al-Khafaji, Noor H.H.)
2018   Nuṣūṣ iqtiṣādīya min sulālat Ūr al-ṯāliṯa (muṣādara) (Economic texts
        from the Ur III Dynasty (Confiscated)).

al-Šiblāwī, Muḥammad R.S. (Al-Shiblawi, Mohammed R.S.)
2019   Nuṣūṣ mismārīya muṣādarah ġayr manšūra min al-ʿaṣr al-Sūmerī
        al-ḥadīṯ (Unpublished expropriated cuneiform texts from the Neo-
        Sumerian period, 2112–2004 BC).

al-Rikābī, Nāʾil H.O. (Al-Rikabi, Nael H.O.)
2019   al-murāqib fi Nuṣūṣ mismārīya al-manšūra wa ġayr al-manšūra min ʿaṣr
        Ūr al-ṯālita (The observer in the published and unpublished cuneiform
        texts from the Ur III period).

3.8   *Verzeichnis der irakischen Promovierten an der University of*
       Baghdad College of Arts / Department of Archaeology

S. Al-Mutawalli, N. A; Al-Wash, H.H.; Muhammed, N.M., A guide of a
achievement thesis and dissertations in the Department of Archaeology,
College of Arts – University of Baghdad 1964–2014, 2018, Baghdad.

al-Mutawallī, Nawāla A. (Al-Mutawali, Nawala A.)

1994   Madḫal fi Dirāsāt al-Ḥayāt al-Iqtiṣādīya li-dawlat Ūr al-ṯāliṯa fi ḍaw'
        al-Waṯā'iq al- mismārīya (al-manšūra wa ġayr al-manšūra) (An
        introduction study to the state economy of the Ur III Dynasty in the
        light of some published and unpublished cuneiform documents).

Muḥammad, Aḥmad K. (Muhammed, Ahmed K.)

1996   Rasā'il ġayr manšūra min al-'ahd al-Bābilī al-qadīm fi al-Matḥaf al-
        'Irāqī (Unpublished letters from the Old Babylonian period in the Iraq
        Museum).

Ḥamīd, Aḥmad M. (Hameed, Ahmed M.)

2002   Nuṣūṣ mismārīya min al-'aṣr al-Bābilī al-qadīm fi al-Matḥaf al-
        'Irāqī (Tall as-Sīb: ḥauḍ sadd Ḥimrīn) (cuneiform texts from the Old
        Babylonian period in Iraqi Museum (Tell Al-Seeb: Hemrin Basin)).

'Abd, Bāsīma J. (Abed, Basima J.)

2003   Nuṣūṣ mismārīya ġayr manšūra min al-'ahd al-Bābilī al-qadīm
        (Unpublished cuneiform texts from the Old Babylonian period).

al-Ḏahab, Amīra E. (Al-Dahab, Amira E.)

2004   Dirāsā Nuṣūṣ mismārīya ġayr manšūra min al-'aṣr al-akkadī al-qadīm
        (min al-Matḥaf al-'Irāqī) (Study of unpublished cuneiform texts from
        the Old Akkadian period (from Iraq Museum)).

'Abd al-Mālik, Munḏir A. (Abdul Malik, Munther A.)

2004   Nuṣūṣ mismārīya ġayr manšūra min al-'aṣr al-Āšūrī al-ḥadīṯ (min al-
        Matḥaf al-'Irāqī) (Unpublished cuneiform texts from the Neo-Assyrian
        period in the Iraq Museum).

'Abd al-Laṭīf, Saǧa M. (Abdullateef, Saja M.)

2004   Qawā'id al-luġa as-sūmarīya fi ḍaw' Nuṣūṣ sulālat Lagaš al-Ulā
        (Sumerian language grammar in the light of the texts of the First
        Dynasty of Lagash).

Fahd, Saʿd S. (Fahad, Saad S.)

2010   Nuṣūṣ mismārīya ġayr manšūra min al-ʿaṣr al-Bābilī al-qadīm min Tall
        Ibzyḫ (Zabalam) wa Tall Abū ʿantīk (Pikasi) (Unpublished cuneiform
        texts from the Old Babylonian period from Tell Ibzikh (Zabalam) and
        Tell Abu Intewek (Pikasi)).

al-Quṭbī, Muhannad A. (Al-Qutbee, Muhanad A.)

2011   Nuṣūṣ iqtiṣādīya ġayr manšūra min al-ʿaṣr al-Sūmerī al-ḥadīṯ min al-
        Matḥaf al-ʿIrāqī (Unpublished economic texts from the Neo-Sumerian
        period in the Iraq Museum).

Al-Māʿmūrī, Fāṭima A.S. (Al-Maamory, Fatimah A.S.)

2013   Nuṣūṣ al-madḫūlāt (mu-du) fi ḍawʾ al-Nuṣūṣ al- mismārīya al-manšūra
        wa ġayr al-manšūra (2112–2004 BC) (The delivery texts (mu-du) in the
        light of published and unpublished cuneiform texts (2112–2004 BC)).

Murād, Nādiā A. (Murad, Nadia A.)

2014   Nuṣūṣ Ǧirāyāt ġayr manšūra min ʿaṣr Ūr al-ṯāliṯa (2112–2004 BC)
        (Unpublished ration texts of the Third Dynasty of Urs (2112–2004 BC)).

al-Qāysī, Ibrāhīm H.H. (Al-Qaisy, Ibrahim H.H.)

2014   al-waṣf al-muštaqq ġayr al-ʿāmil fi al-luġa al-akkadīya – Dirāsa
        muqārana maʿa al-luġa al-ʿArabīya (The inactive denominatives in the
        Akkadian language. A comparative study with the Arabic language).

al-Ǧubūrī, Muṣṭafā M. (Al-Gubury, Mustafa M.)

2014   al-awṣāf al-muštaqqa al-ʿāmila fi al-luġa al-akkadīya – Dirāsa muqārana
        maʿa al-luġa al-ʿibrīya (The active denominative in the Akkadian
        language. A comparative study with the Hebrew language).

al-Tamīm, ʿAbdallāh ʿAlī M. (Al-Tameem, Abdullah Ali M.)

2015   aṣ-ṣīġa as-sabbabīya fi al-luġa al-akkadīya – Dirāsa muqārana maʿa
        al-luġa al-ʿArabīya (The causative stem in the Akkadian language. A
        comparative study with the Arabic language).

al-Ǧannābī, Samrāʾ H.N. (Al-Janaby, Samraa H.N.)

2015   al-milkīya fi al-ʿaṣr al-Bābilī al-qadīm fi ḍawʾ al-Nuṣūṣ al-mismārīya
        ġayr al-manšūra (Property in the Old Babylonian period in the light of
        the unpublished cuneiform texts).

'Umrān, Naš'at A. (Omran, Nashat A.)
2016   Nuṣūṣ mismārīya ġayr manšūra min al-'aṣr al-akkadī (Unpublished
        cuneiform texts from the Akkadian period).

Sa'dūn, Abā Ḍarr R. (Saadoon, Abather R.)
2016   al-'arāḍī al-zira'iya fi Nuṣūṣ mismārīya ġayr manšūra min al-'aṣr al-
        akkadī – Tall al-Wilāyah -tanqibat al-mawsim al-rābi' 2002 (Agricultural
        lands in unpublished cuneiform texts from the Akkadian period – Tell
        Al-Wilayah, fourth season of excavations, 2002).

al-Sāmarrā'ī, Aḥmad N.S. (Al-Samarra'e, Ahmed N.S.)
2016   Nuṣūṣ mismārīya ġayr manšūra min al-'aṣr al-Bābilī al-qadīm Īsin-
        Larsa (2004–1595 BC) (Unpublished cuneiform texts from the Old
        Babylonian period, Isin-Larsa (2004–1595 BC)).

Al-Bayāti, Āmina Fāḍil J. (Al-Bayati, Aminah Fadhil J.)
2016   Nuṣūṣ mismārīya ġayr manšūra min al-'aṣr al-Bābilī al-muta'aḫḫir
        (Unpublished cuneiform texts from the Late Babylonian period).

al-Na'īmī, Haifā' A.A.M. (Al-Ny'amy, Haifaa A.A.M.)
2018   aḍ-ḍarā'ib fi Bilād al-rāfidain fi ḍaw' al-maṣādir al-mismārīya (Taxation
        in Mesopotamia in light of cuneiform sources).

al-Ǧannābī, Ǧāsim 'Abd al-Amīr J. (Al-Janabi, Jasim Abdul Amir J.)
2018   Nuṣūṣ idārīya ġayr manšūra min (2112–2004 BC) (Unpublished
        administrative texts from (2112–2004 BC)).

al-Ḫālidī, Šaymā' N.H. (Al-Khalidy, Shaimaa N.H.A.)
2018   Ṣīyaġ al-'af'āl fi al-Nuṣūṣ al-mismārīya al-manšūra wa ġayr al-manšūra
        min madīnat Sippar (2004–1595 BC) Dirāsa muqārana ma'a al-luġa al-
        'Arabīya (Verb aspects in published and unpublished cuneiform texts
        from Sippar city (2004–1595 BC): A contrastive study with Arabic).

Zwaīd, Waffā' H. (Zwaid, Wafaa H.)
2018   Nuṣūṣ mismārīya ġayr manšūra min 'aṣr sulālat Ūr al-ṯāliṯa Ummā –
        Dryhm (muṣādara) (Unpublished cuneiform texts of the Third Dynasty
        of Ur from Umma-Drehem – (Confiscated)).

al-Fanharawī, Walā' S.A. (Al-Fanharawi, Walaa S.A.)
2018   Rasā'il ġayr manšūra min al-'aṣr al-Bābilī al-qadīm fi al-Matḥaf al-'Irāqī
        (Tall Abū 'antīk) (Unpublished letters from the Old Babylonian period
        in the Iraqi Museum (Tel Abu Antik)).

al-Šammarī, Muhannad J. (Al-Shamari, Mohanad J.)
2018   Nuṣūṣ mismārīya ġayr manšūra min al-ʿaṣr al-Bābilī al-Ḥadīṯ (Unpublished cuneiform texts from the Neo-Babylonian period).

al-ʿIsāwī, Ḥanān A.B. (Al-Esawee, Hanan A.B.)
2018   Nuṣūṣ iqtiṣādīya ġayr manšūra min al-ʿaṣr al-Akkadī al-qadīm (fī al-Matḥaf al-ʿIrāqī) (Unpublished economic texts from the Old Akkadian period (in the Iraqi Museum)).

al-Mafraġī, Isrāʾ S.S. (Al-Mifraji, Israa S.S.)
2019   Nuṣūṣ mismārīya ġayr manšūra min ʿaṣr faġr al-sulālāt (Unpublished cuneiform texts from the Early Dynastic period).

al-Ǧubūrī, Riyāḍ I.M.A. (Al-Juboury, Reyadh I.M.A.)
2019   Nuṣūṣ mismārīya ġayr manšūra lil-ʿaṣr al-Bābilī al-qadīm – Tall as-sīb (Unpublished cuneiform texts from the Old Babylonian period – Tell Al-Seeb).

Al-Māʿmūrī, Lwʾāi K.S. (Al-Maʾmuri, Luay K.S.)
2019   Nuṣūṣ Akkadīya iqtiṣādīya ġayr manšūra fī al-Matḥaf al-ʿIrāqī (Unpublished economic Akkadian texts in the Iraqi Museum).

al-ʿUbaidī, Hind S.A. (Al-Obaidi, Hind S.A.)
2019   Tall Abū ʿantīk fī ḍawʾ al-Nuṣūṣ al-mismārīya al-manšūra wa ġayr al-manšūra (Tell-Abu antique in the light of the published and unpublished cuneiform texts).

3.9   *Verzeichnis der irakischen M.A.-Arbeiten an anderen Universitäten, Colleges oder Departments of Archaeology*

al-Dulaimī, Muʾayad M.S. (Dulaimy, Muʾayad M.S.)
2001   al-Awzān fī al-ʿIrāq al-qadīm fī ḍawʾ al-Kitābāt al-mismārīya al-manšūra wa ġayr al-manšūra (Weights in ancient Mesopotamia in the light of published and unpublished cuneiform texts), Mosul Universität.

al-Ǧubūrī, Riyāḍ I. (Al-Juboury, Reyadh I.)
2004   Nuṣūṣ mismārīya ġayr manšūra min al-ʿaṣr al-Āššūrī al-Ḥadīṯ – madīnat Aššur (Unpublished cuneiform texts from the Neo-Assyrian period, Assur city), Mosul Universität.

Al-Mi'māri, Maḥmūd H.A. (Al-Me'mari, Mahmood H.A.)
2007   Nuṣūṣ Āšūrīya ḥadīṯa ġayr manšūra min madīnat Aššur (Unpublished
        Neo-Assyrian texts from the town of Ashur), Mosul Universität.

Fāḍil, Aḥmad M. (Fadhil, Ahmad M.)
2007   Nuṣūṣ mismārīya ġayr manšūra min al-'aṣr al-Bābilī al-qadīm – Larsa
        (Unpublished cuneiform texts from the Old Babylonian period –
        Larsa), Mosul Universität.

Ṭāhir, Srrūd T.M. (Tahir, Srood T.M.)
2009   Dirāsā fī Nuṣūṣ mismārīya ġayr manšūra min fatrat Ūr aṯ-ṯāliṯa
        (2112–2004 BC) fi Matḥaf as-Sulaimānīya (A study of unpublished
        cuneiform texts from the Ur III Period (2112–2004 BC) in Sulaymaniyah
        Museum), Salahaddin Universität / Erbil.

Bahnām, Sarġun N. (Behnam, Sargon N.)
2010   Nuṣūṣ mismārīya ġayr manšūra min sulālat Ūr aṯ-ṯāliṯa (Unpublished
        cuneiform texts from the Ur III Dynasty), Mosul Universität.

'Abd ar-Raḥmān, Šayma' W. (Abdul-Rahman, Shayma'a W.)
2010   Nuṣūṣ mismārīya ġayr manšūra min al-Matḥaf al-'Irāqī – fatrat Ūr
        aṯ-ṯāliṯa (Unpublished cuneiform texts from Iraqi Museum – Ur III
        Period), Mosul Universität.

Dāwūd, Suzānnā A. (Daood, Suzanne A.)
2010   Nuṣūṣ mismārīya iqtiṣādīya min al-'aṣr al-Āšūrī al-ḥadīṯ (Economic
        cuneiform texts from the Neo-Assyrian period), Mosul Universität.

Ibrāhīm, Yāsir J.K. (Ibrahim, Yassir J.K.)
2012   'uqūd Bābilī qadīm ġayr manšūra min Tall Abū 'antīk (Unpublished
        Old Babylonian contracts from Tell Abu-Anteek), Mosul Universität.

al-Ṭā'ī, Ranā W.F. (Al-Taye, Rana W.F.)
2013   Nuṣūṣ iqtiṣādīya ġayr manšūra min al-'aṣr al-Akkadī al-qadīm
        (Unpublished economic texts from the Old Akkadian period), Mosul
        Universität.

al-Šammarī, Muhannad J. (Al-Shamary, Mohannad J.)
2013   Nuṣūṣ mismārīya ġayr manšūra min al-'aṣr al-Bābilī al-qadīm – Īsin
        (Unpublished cuneiform texts from the Old Babylonian period – Isin),
        Mosul Universität.

al-ʿIzzī, ʿAbd-Al-Mukarim M. (Al-Ezzy, Abd-Almukarim M.)

2014   Nuṣūṣ iqtiṣādīya ġayr manšūra min al-ʿaṣr al-Akkadī al-qadīm (Unpublished economic texts from the Old Akkadian period), Mosul Universität.

3.10   BA *Studiengang im Department of Archaeology / College of Arts / Bagdad Universität*

Erstes Jahr	
Einheitsname	**Einheiten**
Einführung in die alten Sprachen	2
Kunst und Architektur des alten Irak	2
Geschichte des antiken Irak	2
Einführung in die Archäologie und Museologie	2
Arabisch-islamische Architektur im Irak	2
IT	2
Menschenrechte	2
Englische Sprache	2
Arabische Sprache	2

Zweites Jahr	
Einheitsname	**Einheiten**
Kunst und Architektur des alten Irak	3
Archäologische Texte (auf Englisch)	2
Arabisch-islamische Architektur im Irak	2
Islamische Geschichte	2
Dekorative Kunst	2
Zivilisation des alten Irak	2
Einführung in die Geologie	2
Alte Sprachen	3

Drittes Jahr/ Antikenabteilung	
Einheitsname	Einheiten
Methodik der wissenschaftlichen Forschung	2
Archäologische Texte (auf Englisch)	2
Konservierung und Restaurierung	2
Prähistorische Geschichte	2
Vermessung und geometrisches Zeichnen	2
Geschichte, Kunst und Architektur des Irak während der Zeit der Achämeniden, Alexander des Großen, Seleukiden, Parther und Sassaniden	3
Archäologie des Alten Vorderen Orients	2
Alte Sprachen	3

Drittes Jahr / Islamische Abteilung	
Einheitsname	Einheiten
Archäologie des Irak und der arabischen Halbinsel	3
Archäologische Texte (auf Englisch)	2
Orient / islamische Architektur	2
Vermessung und geometrisches Zeichnen	2
Dekorative Kunst	3
Kalligraphie und Numismatik	2
Konservierung und Restaurierung	2
Methodik der wissenschaftlichen Forschung	2

Drittes Jahr / Keilschriftabteilung	
Einheitsname	**Einheiten**
Grammatik der akkadischen Sprache	2
Sumerische Sprache	3
Akkadische Texte	2
Geschichte und Kultur des Alten Irak	3
Einführung in die semitischen Sprachen	3
Methodik der wissenschaftlichen Forschung	2
Vermessung und geometrisches Zeichnen	2
Archäologische Texte (auf Englisch)	2

Viertes Jahr / Keilschriftabteilung	
Einheitsname	**Einheiten**
Grammatik der akkadischen Sprache	2
Sumerische Sprache	3
Akkadische Texte	2
Keilschrift: Paläographie und Kopieren	2
Abschluss: Forschungsbericht	2
Geschichte des alten Vorderen Orients	3
Ausgrabungsmethoden	2
Archäologische Texte (auf Englisch)	2

Viertes Jahr / Antikenabteilung	
Einheitsname	**Einheiten**
Abschluss: Forschungsbericht	2
Archäologische Texte (auf Englisch)	2
Archäologie der Golfregion und der Arabischen Halbinsel	2
Alte Keramik	2
Archäologie der griechischen und römischen Kulturen	2
Ausgrabungsmethoden	3
Archäologie des Alten Vorderen Orients (Ägypten und Syrien)	3
Alte Sprachen	3

Viertes Jahr / Islamische Abteilung	
Einheitsname	**Einheiten**
Archäologie von Marokko und Andalusien	2
Archäologische Texte (auf Englisch)	2
Stadtplanung	3
Ausgrabungsmethoden	3
Dekorative Kunst	2
Abschluss Forschungsbericht	2
Ägyptische Architektur	3
Keramik	2

3.11   M.A. *Studiengang in Department of Iraqi Ancient Languages /
College of Archaeology / Mosul Universität*

Siehe: http://archeology.uomosul.edu.iq/page.php?details=46. Zum Curriculum
für das Bachelorstudium des Departments für Archäologie an der Universität
Mosul – College für Archäologie, siehe: http://archeology.uomosul.edu.iq/files/
pages/page_6992450.pdf. Zum Curriculum des Departments für alte irakische
Sprachen siehe: http://archeology.uomosul.edu.iq/files/pages/page_1862690.pdf.

Material (Erste Semester)	
Einheitsname	**Einheiten**
Sumerische Grammatik	3
Akkadische Grammatik	3
Wissenschaftliche Forschungsmethodik	2
Englische Texte	2
Kopieren von Keilschrifttexten (Fakultative Materialien)	2
Geschichte der alten Sprachen (Fakultative Materialien)	2
Assyrische Königsinschriften (Fakultative Materialien)	2

Material (Zweites Semester)	
Einheitsname	**Einheiten**
Sumerische Grammatik	3
Akkadische Grammatik	3
Lesen und Analysieren von Keilschrifttexten	2
IT	2
Englische Texte	2
Monumentale Inschriften (Fakultative Materialien)	2
Altbabylonische Texte (Fakultative Materialien)	2
Assyrische Texte (Fakultative Materialien)	2

3.12   *M.A. Studiengang im Department of Archaeology College of Arts / Bagdad Universität*

Material (Erste Semester) Antikenabteilung	
Einheitsname	**Einheiten**
Sumerische Grammatik	2
Akkadische Grammatik	3
Seminar	2
Politische Geschichte	2
Englische Texte	1
Alte Kunst	2

Material (Zweites Semester) Antikenabteilung	
Einheitsname	**Einheiten**
Sumerische Grammatik	3
Akkadische Grammatik	2
Seminar	2
Politische Geschichte	2
Englische Texte	1
Alte Architektur	2

Material (Erste Semester) Islamische Abteilung	
Einheitsname	**Einheiten**
Islamische Architektur	2
Stadtplanung	3
Islamische Kunst	2
Seminar	2
Englische Texte	1
Arabische Kalligraphie	2

Material (Zweites Semester) Islamische Abteilung	
Einheitsname	**Einheiten**
Islamische Architektur	3
Stadtplanung	2
Islamische Kunst	2
Seminar	2
Englische Texte	1
Numismatik	2

3.13 *PhD Studiengang im Department of Archaeology College of Arts / Bagdad Universität*

Material (Erste Semester) Antikenabteilung	
Einheitsname	**Einheiten**
Sumerische Grammatik	2
Akkadische Grammatik	3
Alte Kunst und Architektur	2
Seminar	2
Englische Texte	1
Zivilisation des Irak	2

Material (Zweites Semester) Antikenabteilung	
Einheitsname	**Einheiten**
Sumerische Grammatik	2
Akkadische Grammatik	3
Alte Kunst und Architektur	2
Seminar	2
Englische Texte	1
Zivilisation des Irak	2

Material (Erste Semester) / Islamische Abteilung	
Einheitsname	Einheiten
Islamische Architektur	2
Islamische Kunst	2
Stadtplanung	3
Seminar	2
Arabische Kalligraphie	2
Englische Texte	1

Material (Zweites Semester) / Islamische Abteilung	
Einheitsname	Einheiten
Islamische Architektur	3
Islamische Kunst	2
Stadtplanung	2
Seminar	2
Numismatik	2
Englische Texte	1

2

Egyptian Egyptology, from Its Birth in the Late Nineteenth Century until the Early 2000s: The Founding Generations

Fayza Haikal and Amr Omar

This chapter will present an account of Egyptian Egyptology, from its beginning in the late nineteenth century, with the Egyptian people's struggle to re-appropriate their national heritage under very difficult socio-political and economic circumstances, until the beginning of the twenty-first century, a full century after the inception of this discipline. This paper will focus in particular on a selection of Egyptian Egyptologists who had the most impact on their discipline, whether they wrote in Arabic or in a European language, in an attempt to be better understood by their international colleagues and to convey to them that there can be another way of approaching ancient Egyptian culture and of understanding it better via what is known today as ethno-archeology. This approach also underscores the symbiotic relationship between ancient Egypt and Egyptians, even if most of them do not realize it yet fully, with the hope that they will be more aware of their cultural heritage and the urgency of its preservation, particularly because, in its own country, Egyptology is far from being simply a science. For Egyptian Egyptologists, it is a revelation, a kind of mirror in which they recognize themselves. It is a mood, a sense of belonging and a very long cultural memory: a memory stimulated by landscapes, specific words or expressions, particular artifacts, and so many traditions and superstitions.

Because of space limitation, the authors decided to limit their presentation to graduates of archeological departments in the faculties of arts of the oldest national universities, those who replaced foreigners and who carried the responsibility to teach further generations in Egypt. In their turn, these would later transmit this knowledge in all the younger universities created in the country and would also develop the *Service des Antiquités Égyptiennes* into what is today the Ministry of Antiquities. The main references used by the authors to present them are the latest edition of *Who was who in Egyptology*, D. Reid's *Contesting antiquity in Egypt: archaeologies, museums & the struggle for identities from World War I to Nasser*, and tributes to colleagues who have passed away. One of the authors, being from the last generation of pioneers, also added her own memories of her own professors and of many of her former students, hoping to flesh out and give more life to these people and to the Egyptological landscape in Egypt. Last but not least, the authors also apologize for leaving out some names that also contributed to Egyptian Egyptology in many ways.

1   Before Aḥmad Bāshā Kamāl

Although ancient Egypt was never totally forgotten in the course of history, whether in Egypt itself during the famous "Missing Millennium",[1] or in the West through the many accounts of travelers to the country, and through the many publications known today as Egyptomania, it is clear that, in Egypt, a noticeable increase in the political 're-appropriation of ancient Egypt' is particularly well documented since the French invasion of Egypt in 1798, and more precisely, since Muḥammad ʿAlī Bāshā came to power as wālī or viceroy in 1805, barely four years after the British occupation of the country. Muḥammad ʿAlī Bāshā is hailed as the man who modernized Egypt and shifted its orientation from the Ottoman Islamic world to Europe and the modern western world. Under his rule a number of young Egyptians were sent to study in Europe, particularly in Paris, chaperoned between 1826 and 1831 by Rifāʿa al-Ṭahṭāwī, one of Muḥammad ʿAlī 's most eminent and best remembered education ministers. He himself studied translation with a special focus on historical research while he was with them in France, and he later used these skills to translate into Arabic what he deemed most important in Egyptological publications on the history of ancient Egypt at the time. He and his students all returned to Egypt imbued with western culture and, most importantly for this chapter, quite taken by the love and admiration the western world had for ancient Egypt. Indeed, a new wave of Egyptomania raged in the West with Napoleon's scholars' publication of the *Description de l'Égypte* between 1809–1828, and particularly after Champollion announced his decipherment of Egyptian hieroglyphs in 1822, thanks to the Rosetta Stone with its bilingual inscriptions written in Greek and Egyptian which the French army unearthed in the fort of a city named Rosetta on the Mediterranean, not far from Alexandria. When these Egyptian students returned home, they relayed this western fascination in their own country and thus triggered national Egyptomania intensified by the 1922 British declaration of Egypt's partial independence and by the discovery of the tomb of Tutankhamun in that same year. Indeed, ancient Egypt

1   El-Dali, *Egyptology*.

provided the best emblematic representations of the country for all Egyptians, whether Jews, Christians or Muslims, to remind them of their glorious past and to encourage them to stand strong and united in front of the western colonial powers, particularly France and Great Britain with whom they were fighting or negotiating their independence.

Among the first visual manifestations of this political acknowledgement of the past, and official desire to link with it in Egypt, are stamps issued in 1867, under the Khédive Ismāʿīl,[2] showing the Great Pyramid and the Sphinx. From then on, ancient Egyptian monuments and other artifacts continued to appear on Egyptian stamps, while other manifestations of national Egyptomania began to surface in literature and in the visual arts. Indeed, many great Egyptian artists, writers, politicians and intellectuals contributed to Egyptomania in Egypt at the beginning of their careers, and their works certainly played a part in creating awareness of ancient Egypt among the Egyptian elite and the ruling class. They may even have helped Egyptology itself to develop in the country.

With the publication of the *Description de l'Égypte* between 1809 and 1828, and Champollion's decipherment of hieroglyphs in 1822, as mentioned above, Egyptology became a real science first in Europe (France, England, Germany and Italy) and, soon after, in the United States of America as well. It took only a few years before this science took off in Egypt. But archeology in general, and more specifically Egyptology, was one of the most important battlefields on which France and England competed in order to dominate the culture and treasures of ancient Egypt, at a time when museum building and collection gathering were very much in the forefront of the international cultural scene. The only thing these colonizing rival powers seemed to agree on in this domain was their dislike and distrust of Egyptians who wanted to study Egyptology and take part in the administration, study and preservation of their own national heritage. Aḥmad Kamāl, the "father of Egyptian Egyptology" lived in this period.

2 Aḥmad Kamāl (1851–1923) and the Birth of Egyptian Egyptology

The date and place of Kamāl's birth and his very name are a bit of a mystery: different accounts give his year of birth as 1849, 1850 or 1851, the last being the most likely as it is the one that corresponds best to the recorded Islamic year of his birth, the Islamic calendar being the one most used in those days. He could have been born in Crete, where his parents originally came from, or in Egypt after their arrival and settlement in Cairo. Many people consider that

---

2 Reid, *Whose pharaohs?*, 119, fig 22.

his passion for ancient Egypt and the difficulty he faced in his career would fit within the context of the negative attitude of colonialist powers towards Egyptians rather than towards foreigners. However, this argument is not totally convincing as Cretans were, like Egyptians in those days, under Ottoman control and therefore they all were considered to be Ottoman citizens. As for his name, it is difficult to relate it to that of his father Ḥassān ʿAbdallāh from Heraklion, and we do not know exactly where his last name "Kamāl" comes from.[3] He named his eldest son Ḥassān, probably after his father, as is the tradition in Egypt, up to the present day.

Aḥmad Kamāl lived in the time of the Khédive Ismāʿīl, a man who admired the Western world and who believed that education was the best path to modernization. To achieve this target, he multiplied the number of schools at all levels. Kamāl started his education at the *Mubtadiyan* elementary school of al-ʿAbbāsiyya at the age of 13, possibly after spending his earlier years in a traditional school or *kuttāb*, learning the Qurʾān and classical Arabic, as was common then. After completing four years in elementary school, he went to a secondary school for two years before joining, in 1869, the language school established by ʿAlī Bāshā Mubārak, and directed by H. Brugsch, where the ancient Egyptian language and some general Egyptology were taught to Egyptian students for the first time. Needless to say, this school had an immense impact on Kamāl's future.

Even before Kamāl was born, many things had happened in Egypt in this field. At the instigation of Champollion himself, who was distressed at the fast deterioration of the monuments and at the way they were looted, by foreign as well as Egyptian adventurers, Muḥammad ʿAlī Bāshā created in 1835 a *Service des Antiquités Égyptiennes* to be supervised by al-Ṭahṭāwī, where all ancient archeological finds would be gathered. This new institution was housed at the al-Azbakiyya gardens, in downtown Cairo, and entrusted to a certain Yūsuf Ḍiyāʾ, known as Ḍiyāʾ Afandī, who did his best to enlarge and curate the collection. However, it soon became a sort of depository for presents to be offered by the Egyptian rulers to distinguished foreign guests when they visited Egypt. The depleted collection was moved to a warehouse at the Citadel and soon after it was offered to the Archduke Maximillian of Austria as a souvenir of his visit to Egypt. A few years later, August Mariette, a French Egyptologist working for the Louvre, was sent to Cairo in search of Coptic manuscripts. Instead Mariette excavated in Saqqara and discovered its famous Serapeum. This fabulous discovery attracted international attention, and since at the time France was the rival of the British, who were colonizing Egypt, and because France had a great

---

3 Said, *Kamāl wa-Yūsuf*, 32.

deal of influence in the country, particularly in cultural matters, Mariette was appointed Director of Egyptian Antiquities in 1858. With him, the old museum and the *Service des Antiquités* were resurrected. In addition to excavating and establishing laws for regulating foreign excavations in Egypt, Mariette created a new museum in Būlāq where he could curate newly discovered or collected objects. It is in this newly created museum that Brugsch wanted his young Egyptian graduates to work. However, Mariette, probably because of colonial prejudice or fearing German influence in the museum, refused to hire them. And that was the first blow in "the struggle to develop Egyptian Egyptology and to integrate Egyptians as colleagues and scholars in this discipline totally appropriated by western colonizers" as so clearly expressed by D. Reid. As a result, the school closed in 1874.[4]

Thus, Kamāl had to work in many different jobs, such as French translator or German teacher in various schools or government institutions until 1881, when Prime Minister Riad Pasha forced Mariette to appoint him at the Būlāq Museum, where he was hired as a secretary translator. Mariette died in the same year and was replaced by Gaston Maspero, newly arrived in Cairo to head the French Institute of Archeology. Maspero, far more open-minded than Mariette, supported the school of Egyptology that Kamāl had created in the museum, and even hired its graduates. However, once again the school was closed in 1886 under the pretext of lack of funds. When Maspero had to leave for France, his interim successor Eugene Grébaut promoted Kamāl to the post of assistant curator. Maspero returned as museum director in 1899 and entrusted Kamāl with archeological and publication work, but he did not promote him –, in spite of his many contributions inside the museum and outside, on excavation sites – so he remained in this position of assistant curator in the museum until he retired in 1914, aged 65.

Among the most famous of these contributions while working for the museum, was his key role in transferring the royal and noble mummies and other artefacts found in the Deir el Bahri cachette, kept secret and long exploited by the 'Abd al-Rasūl family, to the Cairo Museum, amidst the complaints of the people of western Thebes and their animosity. The event is splendidly related by director Shādī 'Abd al-Salām in his film "The Night of Counting the Years" better known as "The Mummy". Kamāl also contributed more than 60 articles, in French and in English, to the *Annales du Service des Antiquités Égyptiennes*, along with reports of excavations he participated in

---

4 Reid, *Contesting antiquity in Egypt*, 30.

all over Egypt. He published another few articles in different scientific bulletins issued in Egypt[5] and authored books, each one in two volumes of the then recently created *Catalogue Général du Musée du Caire*.[6] He published an equivalent number of books and articles in Arabic and translated some others that he thought would be of interest to Arabic readers, thereby being the first Egyptian to publish scientific Egyptological research covering all aspects of ancient Egyptian life, in order to invite his compatriots to better appreciate their cultural heritage and take pride in it. He even wrote a textbook for students to learn ancient Egyptian, with exercises to practice and a small dictionary, predating Gardiner's famous Middle Egyptian Grammar which appeared after Kamāl's death and on which generations of Egyptologists were raised![7] His foremost work was his 23-volume Dictionary of Ancient Egyptian with the words translated into Arabic and French, accompanied by Coptic and Hebrew equivalents, demonstrating the Semitic nature of the ancient Egyptian language.[8] Kamāl's dictionary was already finished before the *Great Berlin Dictionary* began to be issued (1926–31). Nonetheless, when Kamāl's dictionary was presented for publication, Pierre Lacau, the then director of Antiquities, refused to have it published. This book had to wait until 2002 to see the light of day, when it was published by the Supreme Council of Antiquities press for the commemoration of the centennial of the Egyptian Museum in Cairo's Tahrir Square.

From 1906–1909 Kamāl also lectured intensively at the "Higher Schools Club" and in 1908–9 he gave a course at the private Egyptian University, as the National University had not opened yet, blocked as it was by Lord Cromer and the colonizers' attitude towards the country. Ṭāhā Ḥusayn, the great blind Egyptian writer, also attended these lectures, and later wrote a number of books inspired by ancient Egypt's history and culture.[9] Kamāl was also committed to creating provincial museums all over Egypt and his compelling writings in the daily newspaper *Al Ahram* must have greatly contributed to the creation of museums in Asyūṭ, Minyā and Ṭanṭa, followed later by others all over the country. In addition to his regular work at the *Service des Antiquités* and the Museum, Kamāl created another school of Egyptology at the 'High School of Instructors' known as *al-Khidiwiyya School*, to compensate for the one that was closed at the Cairo Museum in 1886. Among his students who graduated in 1912

---

5 Attiatallah, Die Rolle der einheimischen Ägyptologen in der Entwicklung der Ägyptologie als Wissenschaft, 75–77.

6 Kamal, *Stèles ptolémaiques et romaines*; and *Tables d'offrandes*.

7 Gardiner, *Egyptian grammar*.

8 Kamal, *Makhṭūṭ muʿjam al-Lughat al-Miṣriyya al-qadīma*.

9 Ḥusayn, *The days*.

were the great Egyptologist Salīm Ḥasan, and Maḥmūd Ḥamza, the future first Egyptian director of the Cairo Museum.

That same class of 1912 also counted among its graduates a number of students who played a role in the socio-political life of the country although not necessarily in Egyptology as they failed to penetrate this field, still dominated by foreigners in Egypt.[10] Sāmī Jabra, Bāhūr Labīb, ʿAbbās Bayyūmī, Salīm Ḥasan and Maḥmūd Ḥamza form the second generation of Egyptian Egyptologists. They helped, like their teacher Kamāl, to foster a greater awareness of ancient Egypt among their compatriots. As for the other Egyptians who studied with Kamāl and Brugsch in the very first school of Egyptology in Egypt, they were mostly overshadowed by Kamāl. Among them is Aḥmad Najīb Bey, who translated Brugsch's book on ancient Egyptian scripts into Arabic in 1872. In 1893 he also published in Arabic a history of ancient Egypt in the form of a guidebook of Egypt in which he reports Sir E.A. Wallis Budge's bitter criticism of the "Saidis" (people of Upper Egypt) for their lack of education, corruption and ignorance, addressing them as people who have no problem selling their antiquities to foreigners, thus killing the goose that lays golden eggs, or as he says: "You are like the one who cuts down the tree to pluck its fruits".[11] The book also included a list of the most recent Egyptian excavations in Egypt undertaken by the *Service des Antiquités*, whether by foreign scholars or by the author himself. This guidebook became the first textbook on ancient Egypt written in Arabic by an Egyptian Egyptologist for secondary and specialized schools. Of the same generation was Muḥammad Shaʿbān who also worked for a while at the Egyptian Museum, and conducted some excavation reports which were published in the early issues of the *Annales du Service des Antiquités Égyptiennes*.

When Kamāl died in 1923, a whole century had passed with Egyptology still totally controlled by foreigners fighting among themselves to dominate the scene in Egypt, but all agreeing in their reluctance to have "natives" as their colleagues. The discovery of Tutankhamun's tomb in 1922 provoked a new wave of enthusiasm for ancient Egypt all over the world and intellectuals in Egypt thought of exploiting this enthusiasm for political ends. The government even considered reopening the Secondary School of Archeology that Kamāl had started in the *al-Khidiwiyya* School. Instead, when the first Egyptian University (after the medieval religious university of al-Azhar) opened its door

---

10   For example, Aḥmad Pasha ʿAbd al-Wahhāb, who reoriented himself and later became Minister of Finances, Aḥmad al- Badrī, a future school director, Muḥammad Fahīm Bey, a vice minister at the Ministry of Social Affairs, Muḥammad Junaydī Malṭī, a director of an important secondary school, and Ramsīs Shāfiʿī who worked for the Arab League in Paris.

11   Najīb, *Kitāb al-athar*.

in Giza in 1925, the Faculty of Arts included, among the disciplines it taught, a department for Archeology, with two sub-sections, one for Egyptology and the other for Islamic Civilization, Art, and Architecture, replacing the old High School of Archeology. This department, like the *Service des Antiquités* and its Museums – the Islamic Arts Museum (1880) and the Coptic Museum (1908) in Cairo, and The Greco-Roman Museum in Alexandria (1892) – was first headed by foreign scholars. But with the increasing number of Egyptians having studied Egyptology abroad, sometimes as their own students in France, England or Germany and a little later in the United States, some of these foreign scholars began to be less prejudiced and even helped their Egyptian colleagues who had finally been commissioned with field missions, or with academic positions in the newly opened universities in Cairo or in Alexandria. This complex relationship between Egyptian and foreign scholars was characterized by a mixture of disapproval and need for cooperation from both sides, but slowly generated sympathies and friendly collaborations that increased after the 1952 revolution that finally liberated Egypt from the British "protectorate", and turned the page on both the colonizers and the royal regime.

Gradually more universities in which students could specialize in Egyptology, or related studies if they so wished, were established all over Egypt so that the number of Egyptian Egyptologists now increases by the thousands every year. A large number work for the government, as curators in museums, or inspectors on archeological sites. They all try to help keep the "administrative machine" going. However, their huge number sometimes blocks or hinders its progress. With the increase of the excavation missions, the new sites brought to light, the newly discovered artifacts filling the museums, and the site storage spaces, the *Service des Antiquités* gradually developed until it became the Ministry of Antiquities. The Ministry today has thirty-five thousand employees from various disciplines and oversees complex administration of all Egypt's cultural heritage older than 100 years, in a country whose past began so many millennia ago. All these institutions have to be acknowledged when speaking about Egyptology in Egypt. Let us now return to the earliest Egyptian Egyptologists and particularly to those who clearly contributed to their discipline.

3   **After Aḥmad Kamāl: The Second Generation**

3.1   *Salīm Bey Ḥasan: 1886–1961*

Salīm Ḥasan remains undoubtedly one of the most prolific scholars of his time, and a towering figure among his generation. Originally from the Delta (Mit Nagi in Daqahliya Governorate), he studied at *al-Khidiwiyya* School for

Languages in the morning and, in the evening, he followed the courses of the school of Egyptology that Aḥmad Bāshā Kamāl had managed to open in the *al-Khidiwiyya* school in 1910. When he graduated in 1912 Kamāl tried to have Ḥasan and his classmates hired by the Cairo Museum, but without success, leading Ḥasan to teach English and history in different schools before coming back to Egyptology in 1921 when he and Maḥmūd Ḥamza were hired by Pierre Lacau to work in the Egyptian Museum.

Salīm Ḥasan was not very happy in the museum as he was not allowed to take part in any museum work, so he left to study in Paris at the *École Pratique des Hautes Études* (EPHE) from 1923 to 1927. Back in Egypt he was offered a position of Associate Professor at Cairo University in 1928 and thus became the first Egyptian Egyptology professor there. He was also given an honorary position in the museum. In addition to teaching, Ḥasan was soon entrusted with the excavation of the university at the Pyramids' field in Giza. He received his PhD from the University of Vienna in 1935 on his research written in French on solar hymns in the Middle Kingdom.[12] This study remained for a long time the only reference on the subject. Ḥasan became Deputy Director of the *Service des Antiquités Égyptiennes* in 1936, the first Egyptian to hold such a high position in the field of Egyptology. In 1939–40 however, his interaction with his colleagues, the foreign ones in particular, began to deteriorate, and he had to quit the Antiquities Service and practically avoid public life for a while. He returned to teach at ʿAyn Shams University when it was created in 1950 (under the name of Ibrāhīm Pasha University) and presided in 1955 over the Egyptian mission to Nubia that was to investigate the possibilities for the salvage of the monuments that would be affected by the construction of the High Dam in Aswan. He then focused on his excavations in Nubia until 1958, when he returned to Cairo to lead a team in charge of the revision of the inventory of the Egyptian Museum in 1959.

During all this time Ḥasan never stopped his research and publications in Arabic, French and English. In fact, Ḥasan's publications enriched the discipline of Egyptology very much as he regularly published the results of his excavations at Giza, Saqqara or elsewhere in articles and in multi-volume books published in English or French, mainly by the government press.[13] He also wrote many books in Arabic on the history and culture of ancient Egypt that were a must-read for any Egyptian at this early stage of Egyptian Egyptology. In fact, it is a great shame that they were not read by foreigners as well as they

---

12   Hassan, *Hymnes religieux du moyen empire*.

13   Hassan, *Excavations at Gîza: 1929–1930, Excavations at Gîza I; Excavations at Gîza: 1930–1931, Excavations at Gîza* [2].

presented interesting new ideas that were later presented by western scholars and unjustly attributed to them in western literature simply because Arabic Egyptological literature was and still is not known in the western Egyptological community. Among the many examples of research by Egyptian Egyptologists whose results preceded those of their western counterparts yet went unacknowledged is Ḥasan's beautiful analysis and interpretation of Ramses II's account of the battle of Qadesh as a poem, to be recited or performed during the king's celebrations of victories.[14] Around 70 years later, in an excellent article on literature and audience in ancient Egypt[15] this very same idea was mentioned by Ch. Eyre, without any reference to Ḥasan's remarks in Arabic. This of course is just one example of many such instances.

In addition to his writing many books and articles in all fields of Egyptology known in his time, Ḥasan also translated foreign studies that he considered important to the Egyptian readers. Indeed, both national and international Egyptology are greatly indebted to him.

3.2   *Maḥmūd Ḥamza: 1890–1978*

Maḥmūd Ḥamza received his Diploma in Egyptology from Kamāl's Higher Teachers' College Egyptology program in the same year as Salīm Ḥasan. His career in Egyptology seems to have been a quieter one, perhaps due to the different temperaments of the two scholars. Ḥamza married Kamāl's daughter in 1919 and started working at the Museum in 1921. Then he was sent to Europe together with Sāmī Jabra to study in Liverpool under Garstand, Blackman and Peet. Ḥamza's doctoral thesis concerned the "Relations of Nubia and Egypt in the light of Recent Discoveries", emphasizing salvaged monuments during the 1907–11 heightening of the Aswan Dam. In 1925 Ḥamza and Jabra went to Paris where they joined Ḥasan at the EPHE and studied with Maspero and other professors there. They finished their European tour with the traditional stop in Berlin.

Ḥamza is best remembered as an Egyptologist for his excavations at Qantir in the Eastern Delta, as he rightly proved it to be the site of the famous Piramesse, the Ramesside Egyptian capital mentioned in the Bible,[16] thus contradicting the general western consensus of the time. He ended his career as Director of the Cairo Museum from 1941–50, then he retired.

---

14   Hassan, *Le poème dit de Pentaour et le rapport officiel sur la bataille de Qadesh; Al-Adab al-Misri al-Qadim, aw, adab al-Farāʿina.*

15   Eyre, Ch., The practice of literature, 103.

16   Hamza, The identification of "Khent-nefer" with "Qantîr", 647–655.

3.3   *Sāmī Jabra: 1892–1979*

Sāmī Jabra came from a different background. He was a native of Abnub, near Asyūṭ in Upper Egypt. Born to a wealthy family, he was sent as a child to a private school run by an American mission, and his family spoke French at home, French being the cultural language of the westernized upper class of these days. He then received a French Doctorate in Law from Bordeaux before turning his attention to Egyptology, which he had loved since he was a child. We do not know exactly where he studied it before he joined the *Service des Antiquités* and was sent to study in England, where he wrote his doctoral thesis on "Justice under the Old and New Kingdom", and later to France and Germany, as mentioned. Jabra is best known for his work at Tuna al-Jabal, a Late Period necropolis in Upper Egypt not far from Minyā. In 1939, Jabra became the first Egyptian head of the Archeology Department at Cairo University.

Together with the first and second generations of Egyptology, we have to mention the geographer and pre-historian Muṣṭafā ʿĀmir (1896–1973) who received both his BA and MA from Liverpool. He had a long career in academia culminating in the post of Rector of the University of Alexandria in 1950. He later held the position of Director General of the *Service des Antiquités Égyptiennes* from 1953–56, making him the first Egyptian to hold this post. He was also the first Director of the Documentation Centre created in 1955 to document the monuments of Nubia threatened by the building of the High Dam.

He excavated extensively (with O. Menghin) in the Maadi area south of Cairo, (1930–35), and in Wadi Degla (1950–53) discovering important early cemeteries belonging to people with close links to the city of Memphis. Muṣṭafā ʿĀmir is an example of people who were not from the "mainstream" of Egyptology but who served the discipline both academically and administratively, forming a bridge between the second generation of Egyptologists and their immediate successors.

Another example of these scholars who served Egyptology is al-Ḥājj Aḥmad Yūsuf (as he was best known, 1912–1999) who graduated from Cairo University in 1925. He is representative of the restoration specialists. Like Kamāl he was among the first Egyptians whose genius impressed Reisner, the famous American Egyptologist, and he was considered to be the best restorer of his time. Yūsuf was an expert restorer of all sorts of materials, from clay pots to metal tools. He treated and preserved artifacts from all over Egypt but he will always be remembered for his amazing work on the funerary equipment of Queen Hetepheres, the mother of King Khufu, which no foreign restorer had the courage to touch, and for his magnificent masterpiece, the study and restoration of the funerary boat of that same king, discovered by Kamāl Mallākh in 1954, to which he dedicated 27 years of his life.[17]

3.4   *ʿAbbās Bayyūmi: 1904–1983*

Bayyūmi was born in Asyūṭ in Upper Egypt. After he finished school his family sent him to Paris where he studied Egyptology at the EPHE like his Egyptian predecessors, from 1924–31, but due to his age he was closer to the third generation of Egyptologists. He returned from France in 1931 with a Doctorate on the Elysean fields in ancient Egyptian afterlife,[18] and started a career at the *Service des Antiquités Égyptiennes*, where he was chief inspector of Upper Egypt, before he joined the Cairo Museum as curator, then as Director after Maḥmūd Ḥamza (1950–56). He succeeded Muṣṭafā ʿĀmir as Director-General for Antiquities for a brief period before resigning in 1957.

4   The Third Generation and After

After Ḥasan, Ḥamza and Jabra and their colleagues, Egyptian Egyptology became more institutionalized as Egyptians began to graduate from Egyptian universities, an Egyptology department having been created at Cairo University Faculty of Arts at its opening in 1925. The first graduates of Cairo University were still taught mainly by foreigners. They worked for the *Service des Antiquités Égyptiennes*, Cairo University or the Alexandria and ʿAyn Shams Universities which were created in the following decades. They mostly taught the next generation of Egyptologists who graduated from these universities. The best known among them are discussed below.

4.1   *Labīb Ḥabashī: 1906–1984*

Ḥabashī was born in Salamun near Manṣūra in the Delta. He graduated from the newly opened department of the Faculty of Arts at Cairo University in 1928. Here, students were essentially instructed by foreigners: W. Golenischeff, who headed the department that he founded, and Ch. Kuentz, V. Vikentiev, and E. Peet for archeology, for example. Ḥabashī also attended classes by Salīm Ḥasan, Sāmī Jabra and Ṭāhā Ḥusayn. His curriculum included French and English along with some Latin and Greek. He also studied Coptic with Jūrjī Ṣubḥī and Aḥmad Labīb. These scholars, along with Aḥmad Fakhrī and Jirjis

---

17   Abu Bakr, The funerary boat of Khufu, 1–16.
18   Bayoumi, *Autour du champ des souchets et du champ des offrandes*.

Mattā, formed the vanguard of the class of 1928, the first class of graduates from Fuʾād (later Cairo) University.

Ḥabashī joined the *Service des Antiquités Égyptiennes* in 1930 where he was first appointed as an inspector and where he remained until the end of his career. He was the leading Egyptian archeologist of his generation and he conducted excavations all over Egypt which he published in more than 150 papers and books. Among these are his study of the famous Heka-ib complex in Aswan on the island of Elephantine that he excavated and proved to be a center of pilgrimage for this deified personality until at least the end of the XIIIth dynasty.[19] In Karnak he discovered and published the famous Kamose stela that recounts the wars against the Hyksos and their expulsion from Egypt.[20] He also published tombs that he excavated in the west of Thebes[21] and he was among the first to draw attention to the features of deification of Ramses II,[22] a topic that was picked up again later by other scholars and applied to other pharaohs as well. He also contributed to the research on Nubia and its monuments during the salvage campaign before, during, and after the construction of the High Dam in the late 1950s and early 1960s.[23] In the Delta he is best known for his work at Bubastis and at Tell el Dabʾa/Avaris that he was the first to identify as the capital of the Hyksos dynasty during the Second Intermediate Period.[24] Ḥabashī also lectured extensively abroad. Because of his immense scholarship and humility Ḥabashī was appreciated and honored by all. He received many international recognitions in the form of honorary membership of different institutions, honorary doctorates, orders of merit and the presidencies of different institutions.[25]

4.2 *Aḥmad Fakhrī: 1905–1973*

Aḥmad Fakhrī was born in the Fayum Oasis, from Bedouin ancestry, a fact that explains his taste for the desert and his work on the oases of the western desert

---

19   Ḥabachi, *The sanctuary of Heqaib.*

20   Ḥabachi, *The second stela of Kamose and his struggle against the Hyksos ruler and his capital.*

21   Habachi, Clearance of the area to the east of Luxor temple and discovery of some objects; Clearance of the tomb of Kheruef at Thebes (1957–1958).

22   Ḥabachi, *Features of the deification of Ramesses II*; Rosenvasser, The stela Aksha 505 and the cult of Ramesses II as a god in the army; and Eaton-Krauss, Ramesses: Re who creates the gods.

23   Habachi, (ed), *Actes du IIe Symposium International sur la Nubie, Février 1–3*; and Collaboration of Egyptian Egyptologists with foreign expeditions in facing problems threatening the pharaonic monuments.

24   Ḥabachi, Khatâ'na-Qantîr: importance; *Tell el-Dab'a I.*

25   Kamil, *Labib Habachi.*

later in his life. Like Ḥabashī, Fakhrī received his BA in Egyptology from the Fuʾād I (later Cairo) University in 1928. Like his colleagues before him, he was sent to Europe from 1929 to 1932 where he studied with Jean Capart in Brussels, Eric Peet in Liverpool, F.L. Griffith in Oxford and Kurt Sethe in Berlin. Back in Cairo, he joined the *Service des Antiquités Égyptiennes* where he first worked under Salīm Ḥasan at Giza and was then sent to Luxor for a first stay.[26] His short stays there, as in Giza and other sites, always resulted in immediate publications of his work.[27] He returned to Luxor as Chief Inspector of Upper Egypt between 1942 and 1944, after having been Chief Inspector for Middle Egypt and the Oases from 1936 and Chief Inspector for the Delta from 1938, having thus served all over Egypt. His interest in the oases resulted in a number of extremely interesting publications, tackling archeology and anthropology. Most notable was his book on the Siwa oasis for which he received his doctorate in 1944.[28] This oasis seems to have fascinated him more than any other part of Egypt. From 1944 to 1950, Fakhrī served as Director of Desert Researches and during this period, he discovered and first published the archeological site of Wādī al-Hūdī.[29] He then visited Yemen in 1947 where he made a survey resulting in a book that introduced the country to the archeological world.[30] From 1950 to 1955 he was Director of Pyramids Research and worked mainly in Dahshur where he discovered the "valley temple" of Snefru's Bent Pyramid.[31] Fakhrī also served briefly as curator in the Cairo Museum and from 1952 to 1965 as professor of Egyptian and Middle Eastern history at Cairo University. He retired in 1965 and started lecturing intensively abroad, particularly in the USA, where he had already been a visiting professor at Brown University in 1953–54. In 1966 he went to Pennsylvania. After that he went to Amman in Jordan, and then to California in 1969. He also lectured in Beijing in 1956 and his lectures published in Chinese are probably the first Egyptological material published in that language. Fakhrī gave lecture tours in north and central America as well as in the Middle and Far East and in Europe. He died in Paris in 1973, collapsing during a lecture he was giving there. Fakhrī received many honors from many different countries and many different scientific organizations, the latest

---

26   Fakhry, Tomb of Paser (no. 367 at Thebes).

27   Fakhri, *Sept tombeaux à l'est de la grande pyramide de Guizeh*.

28   Fakhri, *Siwa Oasis: its history and antiquities*.

29   Fakhri, *The Egyptian deserts*.

30   Fakhri, *An archaeological journey to Yemen (March–May, 1947)*; *An archaeological journey to Yemen (March–May, 1947)*; *al-Yaman, māḍīhā wa-ḥāḍiruhā: muḥāḍarāt alqāhā Aḥmad Fakhrī ʿalā ṭalabat qism al-dirāsāt al-tārīkhiyya wa-al-jughrāfiyya*.

31   Fakhri, *The Bent Pyramid of Dahshur*.

being his election as member of the famous and prestigious *Institut d'Égypte* in January 1973, a few months before his death.

4.3   *Jirjis Mattā: 1905–1967*

Mattā was also a graduate of the famous class of 1928, the first to graduate from Fu'ād I (later Cairo) University. He then went to Europe as was the practice at this time, first to study at the *Institut Catholique* in Paris, where he received a Diploma in 1930, then to Oxford in England where he studied with Francis Llewellyn Griffith until 1937. After he received his DPhil, he returned to Egypt to teach at the University in Cairo. Mattā is the first Egyptian to have specialized in demotic. He is best remembered for his *Demotic legal code of Hermopolis*.[32]

4.4   *'Abd al-Mun'im Abū Bakr: 1907–1976*

Abū Bakr was born in Cairo where he went to *al-Ḥilmiyya* School before attending Fu'ād I University, where he studied under Wladimir Golenischeff and Charles Kuentz, who taught in Arabic. He continued his studies in Germany, first at the university of Berlin and then at Heidelberg, where he received his PhD in 1937 for his dissertation on ancient Egyptian crowns.[33] Back in Egypt he made a career mainly in teaching, first at the recently opened Fārūq I University of Alexandria (later Alexandria University), then at Cairo University where he was professor and head of the Antiquities Department of the Faculty of Arts, later becoming Dean of the Faculty. He headed excavations at Giza and at Hermopolis in 1949–50 and later at Aniba in Nubia (1959–64), when he was the Egyptian representative on the UNESCO campaign for the salvage of the monuments of Nubia threatened by the erection of the High Dam in Aswan. His excavations at Giza as well as various other excavation reports were partially published during his lifetime.[34] His unpublished manuscripts on the Giza Western Cemetery have been used by the late Professor Tuḥfa Ḥandūsa (of Cairo University) and Professor Ed Brovarski (Brown University) and their team to resume research in this site.[35]

4.5   *Zakī Yūsuf Sa'd: 1901–1982*

Born in the Daqahliya province in the Delta, Sa'd studied there before joining Cairo University. He is particularly remembered for his work with Emery on archaic royal tombs at Saqqara, and for his own excavations there as Director of

---

32   Matta, *The demotic legal code of Hermopolis West*.
33   Abu Bakr, *Untersuchungen über die ägyptischen Kronen*.
34   Abu Bakr, *Excavations at Giza 1949–1950*.
35   Handoussa and Brovarski, *The Abu Bakr cemetery at Giza*.

Works and then Chief Inspector between 1939 and 1942. He also worked extensively in Ḥilwān (1942–54) where he mainly discovered Old Kingdom tombs.[36]
Among his publications are his work with Emery in Saqqara on the tomb of
Hemaka and the tomb of Hor-Aha, in addition to other work in Ḥilwān. He
died in North Carolina in the United States.

4.6   *Aḥmad Badawī: 1905–1980*

Born in Abu Girg, a village in Middle Egypt near Banī Mazar and Minyā, Badawī
first studied at the Muslim Benevolent Society school at Minyā before he moved
to the Fu'ād I school in Cairo and then to Cairo University where he received
his BA in 1930. He started his career at the *Service des Antiquités* and was sent a
year later to the University of Berlin where he studied with H. Grapow and K.
Sethe for five years ending with a PhD on the god Khnum.[37] He then went to
study with Herman Kees in Heidelberg and was granted a habilitation degree
in 1938 on Memphis as Second Capital of Egypt in the New Kingdom.[38] Back in
Egypt he began a brilliant career as lecturer (1938–47), then associate professor
at Cairo University (1947–1950). He later became a full professor and moved to
'Ayn Shams university. He was rector of 'Ayn Shams University from 1956 until
1962 and director of the newly created Documentation Centre of Egyptian
Antiquities established initially to house the documentation on the monuments of Nubia during the salvage campaign. In 1962, Badawī returned to Cairo
University as its rector and as head of the council of Egyptian Universities. He
occupied this position until he retired.

Despite his numerous teaching and administrative obligations, Badawī
lectured frequently in various institutions in Egypt after he returned from
Germany. He was also an honorary curator at the Cairo Museum and was
entrusted for a number of years with the supervision of excavations in Saqqara
and Mit Rahina. Among his discoveries at Mit Rahina were the tomb of the
prince Sheshonq – now reconstructed in the garden of the Cairo Museum –
a beautiful Apis mummification table, and a stela of Amenhotep II. Badawī
will be remembered for his two-volume book in Arabic on the history and culture of ancient Egypt[39] as well as for his translation into Arabic of the most
commonly used entries of the great Berlin Dictionary, which he presented,

---

36   Saad, *Royal excavations at Saqqara and Helwan (1941–1945)*.
37   Badawi, *Der Gott Chnum.*
38   Badawi, *Memphis als zweite Landeshauptstadt im Neuen Reich.*
39   Badawi, *Fī mawkib al-Shams.*

along with his Professor H. Kees, as the first concise dictionary of the ancient Egyptian language to be published in Arabic.[40]

Badawī was an extremely cultured man who enjoyed the company of historians as well as philosophers and writers. Because of his deep knowledge of and eloquence in classical Arabic, perhaps due to his early education in an Islamic institution and his rural roots, Badawī was elected to the Arabic Language Academy ('Academy of the Immortals'/Majma' al-Khālidīn) in 1960. In the same year he also became a member of the Egyptian Scientific Institute. He was a member of a number of other academic institutions as well and he presided over the Historical Institute for a number of years. He died in Riyadh, Saudi Arabia, in 1980.

4.7   *'Abd al-Muhsin Bakīr: 1908–1992*

Bakīr was born and partly raised in Alexandria. He joined the then Institute of Egyptology at Cairo University to study under V. Vikentiev, Salīm Ḥasan, and Hermann Junker who gave him his first taste of the ancient Egyptian language. After graduating in 1935 he studied in Berlin under Herman Grapow and then in Oxford under Battiscombe Gunn and specialized in grammar and in the hieratic script. He received his DPhil in 1946 on slavery in ancient Egypt[41] after having done an MA on Egyptian epistolography.[42] Back in Egypt, he first worked briefly at the Cairo Egyptian Museum before moving back to his native city, where he became lecturer in 1949, then associate professor in 1952 at Alexandria University, and afterwards professor of Egyptian philology at Cairo University from 1954 to 1968. He later held research and teaching posts at the universities of Gottingen, Oxford and Cambridge.

In addition to his various articles, Bakīr was the second person, after Aḥmad Kamāl (whose works were unpublished or outdated by this time), to have written a grammar of Egyptian in Arabic[43] and others in English[44] in which he stressed the Semitic aspects of the ancient Egyptian language, thus impressing upon his students the need to approach ancient Egyptian culture from a new angle.

---

40   Badawi and Kees, *Handwörterbuch der ägyptischen Sprache.*
41   Bakir, *Slavery in pharaonic Egypt.*
42   Bakir, *Egyptian epistolography.*
43   Bakir, *Qawā'id al-lughat al-Miṣriyya fī 'aṣrihā al-dhahabī.*
44   Bakir, *An introduction to the study of the Egyptian language; Notes on Late Egyptian grammar; Notes on Middle Egyptian grammar.*

4.8   *Muṣṭafā al-Amīr: 1914–1974*

Born and raised in Upper Egypt (first Idfū then Asyūṭ) al-Amīr joined Cairo University in 1933. He received his BA in 1937 and then joined the Institute of Archeology, receiving his diploma in 1940. Afterwards he started his career at the *Service des Antiquités Égyptiennes* as inspector in Saqqara until 1943. He was transferred to Thebes, where he stayed until 1945. He then worked briefly at the Cairo Egyptian Museum until he was sent to England for graduate studies, first at UCL in London and then in Cambridge where he studied under S.R.K. Glanville. He specialized in demotic and received his DPhil in 1950. He returned to Egypt to start an academic career first at the University of Alexandria in 1952, then at the University of Khartoum from 1961–65 and finally at Cairo University from 1965 until his death in 1974. Al-Amīr was also visiting professor at Mainz and Peking Universities. His main work was the publication of the demotic texts of *A family archive from Thebes*.[45]

4.9   *Alexander Badawī: 1913–1986*

Alexander Badawī was born in Cairo. He first studied architecture at Cairo University, graduating in 1936. He then received his first Diploma from the Institute of Archeology in 1939, followed by a PhD in 1942. He then took part in a number of excavations in Egypt and taught at the universities of Cairo and Alexandria between 1941 and 1955 until he left for the United States where he was hired consecutively as Professor of Architecture, Art Design and Art History at the University of Kansas 1957–61, at UCLA 1961–81, and then again at the University of Chicago as Fulbright Professor. During this period, he also conducted excavations in Egypt at Askut/Nubia during the salvage campaign from 1962 to 1964,[46] as well as in Giza[47] and Saqqara in 1973–74.[48] Alexander Badawī published the tombs which he excavated in Giza and Saqqara, but he will be particularly remembered for his pioneering research on architecture and architectural design in ancient Egypt.[49] He died in Egypt in 1986.

4.10   *Muḥammad Jamāl al-Dīn Mukhtār: 1918–1998*

Jamāl Mukhtār, as he was best known, was at the heart of the Egyptian archeological scene from the 1960s until his death in 1998. Born in Alexandria, Jamāl Mukhtār graduated from Cairo University with a BA in geography in 1939.

---

45   Al-Amīr, *A family archive from Thebes*.
46   Badawy, Excavation under the threat of the High Dam.
47   Badawy, *The tombs of Iteti, Sekhem'ankh-Ptah, and Kaemnofert at Giza*.
48   Badawy, *The tomb of Nyhetep-Ptah at Giza and the tomb of 'Ankhm'ahor at Saqqara*.
49   Badawy, *Ancient Egyptian architectural design*.

In 1940 he earned a Diploma in Pedagogy from the High Institute of Pedagogy, then he returned to Cairo University to study Egyptology and received his MA in 1943. He then returned to Alexandria as an assistant at the High Institute of Pedagogy in 1946–47. He left for the USA to obtain a further Diploma in Education from the Iowa State Teachers College. In 1957 he received his PhD in Egyptology from the University of ʿAyn Shams[50] under the mentorship of Aḥmad Badawī and Herman Kees. He then started his career at the *Service des Antiquités Égyptiennes* as head of the scientific department of the Center of Documentation on Ancient Egypt created in 1955 for the documentation of Nubian monuments endangered by the building of the high dam of Aswan. Despite his heavy administrative work as scientific director of the Center, he managed to work with Aḥmad Badawī and Herman Kees on an abridged Arabic translation of the *Wörterbuch der ägyptischen Sprache* in order to present the Egyptian public with a reliable 'Concise Dictionary of Ancient Egyptian' in Arabic. He also wrote, in Arabic, a series of little books on the monuments of Nubia and on ancient Egyptian culture in general. With the beginning of the work on the Nubian Salvage Project, he became an expert for UNESCO, a position that required him to travel and allowed him to meet a very large number of international colleagues whose appreciation, friendship and respect he won very quickly, as can be seen from the number of contributors (at least 73) to the two volume *Mélanges Gamal Mokhtar* published by the IFAO in 1985 on the occasion of his 65th birthday.

While working with UNESCO, Mukhtār established a permanent collaboration agreement between the CEDEG and the CEDAE and directed the second volume of UNESCO's *General History of Africa*. In 1967 Mukhtār became professor of ancient history at Cairo University, in succession to Aḥmad Fakhrī, as well as director of *the Service des Antiquités Égyptiennes*, and later President of the Egyptian Antiquities Organization, a new name for the *Service des Antiquités* that he conducted, thus giving the Institution a higher and more independent status. He remained in this position until the end of the Nubian Salvage campaign, which he directed with so much diplomacy and perseverance.

In 1977, Mukhtār left Egypt for a few years to work for the University of Riyadh in Saudi Arabia, where, in addition to his teaching, he conducted one of the earliest excavations in that country.

During his long career Mukhtār received many honors from all over the world. Back in Egypt in 1982, he was offered an Emeritus Professorship at the University of Alexandria and from 1995 onwards he taught mostly at the Ḥilwān Faculty of Tourism in Cairo. He continued supervising graduate research at

---

50   Mokhtar, *Ihnâsya El-Medina (Herakleopolis Magna)*.

national universities and served on the jury of many MA and PhD dissertations. Among the honors he received from abroad were an Honorary PhD from the University of Montpellier (1972) and the French *Légion d'Honneur*.

4.11 *'Abd al-'Azīz Ṣāliḥ: 1921–2001*

Ṣāliḥ was born and raised in Cairo. He received his BA in History from Cairo University and pursued graduate studies at the Institute of Archeology, receiving his Diploma in 1951 and his PhD in 1956. Ṣāliḥ worked for most of his career at Cairo University, where he started as assistant lecturer in 1953. In 1970 he was offered the Chair of Ancient History of Egypt and the Near East and in 1977 he became the Dean of the Faculty of Archeology at Cairo University. Ṣāliḥ also taught at the University of Riyadh in Saudi Arabia from 1965–68, and again at King Abdulaziz University in Jeddah in 1973. In addition to teaching, Ṣāliḥ contributed to Cairo University excavation missions at Tuna al-Jabal in Middle Egypt in 1954–55 when the mission discovered eight important legal papyri, and at Aniba in Nubia in 1963. From 1970–74 he directed important excavations at Giza around the Pyramid complex of Menkaure, bringing to light an entire workers' village dating to the Old Kingdom, including what seemed to be a papyrus workshop in addition to a few tombs of the same period. Later, in 1976 he excavated at Tell al-Hisn/Matareya, and uncovered a huge settlement dating to the Ramesside Period and the beginning of the Third Intermediate Period.

Ṣāliḥ wrote many important articles and books on the culture and history of ancient Egypt and the Near East. His studies are extremely thorough, allowing the reader to understand the culture of Egypt from within, always underscoring the importance of ethno-Egyptology to a real understanding of ancient Egypt and the continuity of its culture. Ṣāliḥ expressed many opinions before they appeared in western Egyptology, among which is his analysis of the double nature of the pharaoh, who was considered to be divine in official texts and human in literary texts[51] as was demonstrated later by G. Posener.[52] Unfortunately, because he wrote most of his books in Arabic, he was not well-known in the West. One can only lament here again the lack of interest that the Western Egyptological community has shown towards research published in Arabic. Among his most celebrated books in Arabic were his studies of ancient Egyptian and ancient Arabian society and religion.[53] He also wrote important books on the history of the ancient world, and a few articles on the relation of

---

51   Saleh, Qissat al-dīn fī Misr Misr al-qadīmah Mantiq al- ta'līh.
52   Posener, *De la divinité du pharaon.*
53   Saleh, *Tārīkh Shibh al-Jazīra al-'Arabiyya fī 'usūrihā al-qadīma*, Cairo 1988.

ancient Egyptian to the Semitic languages.[54] His English publications include the results of his excavations[55] and many articles, on a variety of topics, which appeared in international journals and conference proceedings. He had a great impact on his students and his field.

Ṣāliḥ was also a member of many scientific societies and sat on many councils, but he was first and foremost a remarkable professor and scholar and he was duly presented with the highest government awards for his scientific contributions. He was also a member of the *Institut d'Égypte* and of the most important scientific and cultural institutions in Egypt. He even chaired some of them like the Egyptian Antiquities Committee in the Supreme Council of Arts Sciences and Literature and the Society of Archeological and Historical studies of the University of Riyadh while he was teaching there. Ṣāliḥ died in 2001.

4.12 *Ḍiyāʾ Abū Ghāzī: 1924–2001*

Abū Ghāzī was born and raised in Cairo. She received her first degree from Cairo University in 1949 and began a doctoral dissertation under Jabra which she did not complete until 1966. Abū Ghāzī worked for her entire career at the Cairo Egyptian Museum, starting as a Librarian in 1950 and ending her career as Director-General of the Museum service. During Abū Ghāzī's tenure, the Museum library was greatly expanded. She also revised and wrote catalogues for the museum but her main contribution lies in the number of articles she wrote on the excavation sites and the people who excavated them regardless of whether they were Egyptians or foreigners, directors or workers, giving each person his or her due and thereby presenting a much more lively and realistic scene of an archeological site.[56]

4.13 *ʿAbd al-Munʿim ʿAbd al-Ḥalīm Sayyid: 1925–2011*

Born in Cairo in the *al-Ḥilmiyya* district, he studied at *al-Ḥusayniyya* School and continued with a diploma in Egyptology in 1950, followed by another one in Education and Psychology in 1954. A.A. Sayyid is considered the pioneer of Red Sea archeological studies. In fact, Sayyid started his relationship with the Red Sea when he was sent to Somalia in 1957 by the Egyptian ministry of education to teach social studies in the schools of Mogadishu. While there he wrote a book in Arabic, published in 1960, on Somalia's environment, economy, society, culture and its relations with Egypt throughout history. In 1959 he was sent to Yemen, where he studied the ancient South Arabian inscriptions. Back

---

54   Saleh, Notes on the phonetic values of some Egyptian letters.
55   Saleh, Excavations around Mycerinus pyramid complex; *Excavations at Heliopolis*.
56   Abou-Ghazi, Discoveries of Selim Hassan at Saqqarah.

in Cairo, he started specializing in ancient Egypt and the Red Sea, and earned his MA degree in history from the University of Alexandria in 1969, working on ancient Egypt and its relationship with the land of Punt and its activities in the Red Sea.[57] In 1973 he received his PhD on further studies on ancient Egypt and its relations with other Red Sea civilizations. In 1974 he became a lecturer in the Department of History in the Faculty of Arts of Alexandria University. As was to be expected, Sayyid returned to the Red Sea to excavate on the Egyptian coast in 1976–77 and made his most groundbreaking discovery of a XIIth dynasty port at Wadi Gawasis[58] with remains of dismantled boats and all the necessary artifacts for navigation and inscriptions mentioning expeditions departing to Punt, among other things. This first discovery of an ancient Egyptian port on the Red Sea revolutionized Egyptologists' conceptions of ancient seafaring and opened the way to more, similar discoveries on the coast further north, the latest being the famous Wadi Jarf port with the wonderful finds of Pierre Tallet of the Sorbonne.[59]

In addition to a series of articles on the Wadi Gawasis finds in Arabic and English and on Egypt's relations with its Asian and African neighbors, Sayyid also provided Egyptological literature with the impressions these Red Sea cultures had of Egypt, thus opening a whole new chapter in the study of international relations in Antiquity.[60]

From 1979–1981 Sayed went back to the Red Sea shores to teach at King Abdulaziz University at Jeddah as Associate Professor and later as Professor. He then returned to the University of Alexandria where he taught as Professor Emeritus until he died in 2011. Sayed left behind many important Arabic and English publications and he shall always be remembered as the pioneer of Red Sea archeology.[61]

4.14   *Aḥmad Muḥammad Ḥilmī Qadrī: 1931–1990*

Born at Zaqāzīq in the Eastern Delta, Aḥmad Qadrī pursued a military career and received a BSc in Air Force Sciences in 1956 from the Air Force Academy and another in Law from Cairo University in 1964 before he was attracted to antiquities. He joined the Egyptian Antiquities Organization in 1965 as head of the Department for the Salvage of Nubian Monuments after having worked as head of Public Relations in the Ministry of Culture from 1957 to 1965. While

---

57   Sayed, Muḥāwala li-taḥdīd mawqiʿ Būnt; and On the geographical location of the Land of Punt.

58   Sayed, Discovery of the site of the 12th dynasty port at Wadi Gawasis on the Red Sea shore.

59   Tallet, *Les papyrus de la mer Rouge I*.

60   Sayed, *Al-Baḥr al-Aḥmar wa-ẓahīruhu fī al-ʿuṣūr al-qadīma*.

61   El-Saeed, Mahfouz, and Megahed (eds), *The Festschrift volume*.

at the Egyptian Antiquities Organization, Qadrī pursued a diploma in Islamic Antiquities which he received in 1976 and wrote a PhD dissertation at the University of Budapest under the supervision of L. Kakosy.[62] He made use of his own professional military experience in this study. He also wrote two works in Arabic, one on "The Military Institution in the Era of the Empire" and another on "Our national Heritage between Challenge and Response". From 1981 to 1987 Qadrī was a very dynamic president of the Egyptian Antiquities Organization. His administration conducted intense restoration work all over the country. Qadrī was the first to hire students during their summer vacations to take part in restoration and field work, thus pioneering in a way the current theories in Cultural Heritage Management programs stressing the importance of involving a population in the management of its own heritage. Qadrī died in Pittsburg, USA, in October 1990.

4.15   *Sayyid Tawfīq: 1936–1990*

Born and raised in Cairo, Tawfīq received his BA in Egyptology from The Faculty of Arts, Cairo University in 1959. He then went to Göttingen in Germany to study under Schott from 1961–66 and returned with a PhD to Cairo where he obtained a teaching post in Cairo University. His association with the Akhenaten temple project at the time prompted him to focus his research on the Amarna Period and resulted in a series of interesting articles on the royal succession at the end of the XVIIIth Dynasty.[63] Tawfīq served as head of the Egyptology Department in the Faculty of Archeology 1987–89 and then Vice Dean and Dean of the Faculty in 1980–83. During this period, he was in charge of the Cairo Faculty of Archeology excavations in Saqqara and discovered a series of New Kingdom Tombs,[64] but he did not have time to fully publish them as he was appointed president of the Egyptian Antiquities Organization in 1988 to replace A. Qadrī. He died two years later in December of 1990.

4.16   *Jāballāh ʿAlī Jāballāh: 1939–2012*

Born in Minūfiyya in the Egyptian Delta in 1939, Jāballāh came to Cairo in 1957 to join the Faculty of Arts of Cairo University from where he received his BA in Egyptology with honors in 1961. His first job was at the Documentation Centre of the *Service des Antiquités*, where he served for a year. He then moved for a couple of years to the position of assistant at Cairo University between 1962 and 1963 and then returned to the *Service des Antiquités* which offered him a

---

62   Kadry, *Officers and officials in the New Kingdom*.
63   Tewfik, Aton studies, *Mitteilungen des Deutschen Archäologischen Instituts*.
64   Tewfik, Recently excavated Ramesside tombs at Saqqara. 1.

scholarship to Liverpool in England to pursue graduate research with Professor Fairman. There he finished in 1967 his PhD on "Narrative in art in ancient Egypt", a very new topic at the time. Back in Egypt, Jāballāh returned to the *Service des Antiquités* to resume his activities as a curator of the Cairo museum and was assigned, in addition, the editorial responsibility of the *Annales du Service des Antiquités Égyptiennes*. In 1969 he was offered the position of lecturer at the Faculty of Arts of Cairo University, thus starting his teaching career. In 1974 he became an associate professor at the Institute of Archeology – which had developed out of the old Archeology Department of the Faculty of Arts – then professor in 1979, and head of department in 1994 in the Faculty of Archeology (which replaced the Institute of Archeology) and its Dean in 1996. However, he did not remain long as a dean, because the Ministry of Culture requested him in 1997 to become Secretary-General of the Supreme Council of Antiquities as the Egyptian Antiquities Organization was called in those days, having merged with the Ministry of Culture a few years before. He kept his position until 2002, then returned as professor emeritus to Cairo University where he stayed until he died in 2012.

During his long academic and administrative careers, Jāballāh taught students and supervised research in Egypt and elsewhere as he spent a year as visiting professor at the Muḥammad v University in Rabat, Morocco, where he established a department of archeology, another year at the University of Central Florida in the US and many years in the University of Kuwait. He conducted excavations in Memphis[65] and contributed to the Cairo University excavations on the Giza Plateau. During his years as Secretary-General of the Supreme council of Antiquities he was invited to be a member of the International Committee for the Development of the Turin Egyptian Museum. He also lectured abroad extensively and headed many international conferences and national committees. Among these was the Specialized National Committee for Archeology at the Ministry of Culture that he headed for many years, encouraging the translation of important books in History or Archeology into Arabic, as well as the creation of seminars and round tables around important cultural and scientific issues of the time. He was a member of many scientific organizations and honored by many countries (France, Germany, Austria and Italy) for his contributions to their work in Egypt and by Egypt itself for his scientific publications. Indeed, Jāballāh was a prolific author and he contributed greatly to Egyptology through his administration, his teaching and his publications, both in English and in Arabic. His publications include several studies on ancient Egyptian officials along with their monuments and titles in

---

65   Gaballa, Latest excavations in Memphis.

order to better understand the functioning of ancient Egyptian society and its administration,[66] essays on the religion of ancient Egypt[67] as well as his seminal thesis on narrative in art.[68] In Arabic he wrote several articles on different facets of social and religious life in ancient Egypt,[69] and he translated and revised a number of translations into Arabic of books on Egypt and the Near East.[70] His loss was deeply felt in the Egyptological scene in Egypt.

4.17   *Ḥasan al-ʿAshirī: 1928–1994*

Born in Cairo in 1928, al-ʿAshirī first studied architecture at the Faculty of Engineering at Cairo University, graduating in 1951. His interest in ancient Egypt led him to pursue graduate studies at the then Institute of Archeology of Cairo University which granted him a Diploma in ancient Egyptian architecture in 1955. He joined the Centre of Documentation and Studies on Ancient Egypt at the Antiquities Service in 1957, a crucial time in Egypt when scholars were engaged in the salvage of the Nubian monuments threatened by the building of the High Dam in Aswan. Al-ʿAshirī served there until 1979, as an architect and eventually as Director of the Department/Sector of Technical Affairs, always setting the highest standards of precision in his and his teams' work. His architectural surveys covered all Nubian monuments (1957–64), and a large number of temples in Aswan and the Theban area (1964–79). Results of his invaluable work have been published mainly in the *Collection Scientifique* of the CDEAE.[71]

Al-ʿAshirī's impact on the study of ancient architecture was also important in Saudi Arabia where he was the documentation expert for the preservation of the historic city of Der'eyya, capital of the Wahhabis. In addition to his skills as an architect/Egyptologist, al-ʿAshirī was a particularly cultured man, a music lover and a piano player. Those who knew him will remember him for a very long time.

4.18   *ʿAbd al-ʿAzīz Fahmī Ṣādiq: 1933–1995*

Ṣādiq was born in Cairo and was introduced to Egyptology as a child by Aḥmad Fakhrī who was his father's friend. After he graduated from the Department

---

66   Gaballa, The chief of records of the royal harbour Aniy (Amenemone); False-door stelae of some Memphite personnel; Harnakht, chief builder of Mi; Siese, naval standard-bearer of Amenophis III; and Three funerary stelae from the New Kingdom.

67   Gaballa and Kitchen, The festival of Sokar; and New light on the cult of Sokar.

68   Gaballa, *Narrative in Egyptian art*, Mainz am Rhein 1976.

69   Gaballa, *Tārīkh Miṣr al-qadīm*.

70   Fakhri, *al-Ṣaḥrāwāt al-Miṣriyya*.

71   Al-ʿAshirī, *Le temple d'Amada*.

of Egyptology of the Faculty of Arts at Cairo University, in 1958, Ṣādiq joined the *Service des Antiquités Égyptiennes* and after a very brief mission at Tura el Asmant he was transferred to the Documentation Center on Ancient Egypt, where he worked for his entire career, occupying posts from assistant Egyptologist in 1959 to Director of the Centre from 1989–93.

Ṣādiq contributed consistently to the epigraphic work of the Center, first in Nubia where he copied a vast number of texts in its temples during the salvation of its monuments, and then in Thebes, working on the Theban Mountain Graffiti on which he was trained by Prof. J. Černý (until 1970) and later with other members of the Documentation Center. This work resulted first in a series of small monographs of these temples published by the Documentation Center, in addition to an MA thesis on Ramses II's temples in Nubia and a series of volumes on the Theban graffiti also published by this Center[72].

In 1962 Ṣādiq went to Prague for a year to train at the Czechoslovak Academy of Sciences to better his archeological and philological knowledge. A decade later he went to Lyon in France to prepare a PhD on the *Amduat* Papyri in the Cairo Museum.[73] Ṣādiq was also interested in many other aspects of Egyptian culture. His publications include studies on astronomy and on a number of Theban tombs.[74] His love of modern technology also led him to advise and help in the first attempts at the computerization of museum objects and in the creation of a Multilingual Egyptological Thesaurus to fine-tune descriptions of site and museum artifacts. Ṣādiq has also served on many administrative committees in Egypt and was a member of the Royal Astronomical Society of Canada in addition to other International Archeological and Egyptological Societies.

4.19   *Aḥmad Maḥmūd Mūsā: 1934–1998*

Born in Damietta, Mūsā studied Egyptology at the Department of Archeology in the Faculty of Arts of Cairo University and graduated in 1959. Soon after, he joined the Antiquities Service where he worked for his entire career holding all positions from inspector to general director of Giza and Saqqara, as well as director of the Permanent Committee of Egyptology in charge of regulating all archeological missions doing field work in Egypt. Although he excavated in many sites under his jurisdiction, and brought to light a number of important artifacts, such as the Taharqa stela from Dahshour,[75] he is best known for his

---

72   Sadek and Černý, *Graffiti de la montagne thébaine III–IV.*

73   Sadek, *Contribution à l'étude de l'Amdouat.*

74   Sadek, Le plafond astronomique du Ramesseum.

75   Moussa, A stela of Taharqa from the desert road at Dahshur.

work at Saqqara where he discovered the tomb of Nefer[76] and that of the Two Brothers[77] while supervising the restauration of Unas' causeway.[78] In addition to his many articles, Mūsā published several tombs from Saqqara either alone or in collaboration with foreign scholars, in particular with H. Altenmuller. In 1995, a few years before his death, he obtained his PhD degree from the Eotvos Laurand University in Budapest.

4.20　　*Mayy Ṭarrād: 1929(?)–2016*

Mayy Ṭarrād, as she was best known in the Egyptological world, was an Egyptian Egyptologist of Lebanese origin called Hind Ṭarrād, Mayy being the nickname her family gave her in homage to the great Lebanese poet Mayy Ziyāda. She grew up in Cairo at a period when well-to-do families would send their children to schools supervised by nuns and, accordingly, she was schooled at the famous Sacré-Coeur, where schooling was done in French. Moreover, they did not necessarily want their daughters to go to university, so Ṭarrād came to study Egyptology at Cairo University at an unusually late age for Egyptian students. Her passion for this discipline and her comparatively large knowledge of the subject, in addition to her fluency in French and English, which allowed her to easily read foreign studies, put her immediately at the top of her class. After graduating in 1968, Ṭarrād worked for a number of years as librarian at the Chicago House in Luxor and later at the American Research Centre in Cairo, both institutions putting the most recent research at her disposal and allowing her to meet and discuss with the best international scholars who came to Egypt, so that Ṭarrād became well known on the international scene even before she came to work at the Cairo Museum in the 1980s. Ṭarrād immediately understood the most pressing needs of the museum: fixing the *Journal d'Entrée* of artefacts at the museum and helping its curators whenever their lack of training or ignorance of foreign languages impeded the fulfilment of their jobs.[79] Thus, Ṭarrād trained curators and assisted them with the correction and digitalization of the old, worn-out and dilapidated journals. Ṭarrād also found the time to write a number of short articles, often to honor her friends in dedicatory volumes offered to them or in catalogues of exhibitions they organized.[80] She died in December 2016.

76　　Moussa, *The tomb of Nefer and Ka-hay*.

77　　Moussa and Altenmüller, *Das Grab des Nianchchnum und Chnumhotep*.

78　　Moussa, Excavations in the valley temple of King Unas at Saqqara.

79　　Trad, Varia Musée du Caire, 1.

80　　Trad, The false-door stele of Ḥesi; "Given life again"; The sequence of the artist's strokes on a sherd from Hierakonpolis, in Friedman, R., and B. Adams (eds), *The followers of Horus: studies dedicated to Michael Allen Hoffman*, Oxford 1992, 65–68.

4.21   *Muḥammad ʿAbd al-Ḥalīm Nūr al-Dīn: 1943–2017*

Nūr al-Dīn was born near Banhā in the Qalyūbiyya province in the central
Delta of Egypt. He received his BA in Egyptology from the Cairo University
Faculty of Arts' Department of Archeology in 1963 and was immediately hired
as assistant there. Already at this early stage of his career his charisma, spon-
taneous leadership and sense of responsibility were evident so that students
flocked around him and he never failed to help them as much as he could. He
received his MA in 1966 from Cairo University on women in ancient Egypt[81]
and his PhD from Leiden on demotic ostraca at the Leiden Museum in 1974
under the supervision of the late Prof. P.W. Pestman.[82] He then returned to his
home university where he occupied a position of Lecturer/Assistant Professor.
In 1977 he became an honorary conservator of the papyri department of the
Cairo Museum. In 1979 however, he returned to Leiden as a visiting Professor at
the Institute of Papyrology for a year and in 1980 he received a fellowship from
Christ's College, Cambridge, for another year, a time he used to teach less and
concentrate more on his research. Although his degrees and career so far were
clearly related to ancient Egyptian language and scripts, Nūr al-Dīn accepted,
in 1982, an offer to teach at the University of Sanaa in Yemen. He stayed there
for four years, during which his creativity, leadership and academic curios-
ity were unleashed, as he founded there a department of archeology and a
museum to house the artefacts of the excavations which he started at Shebam
al Ghoras, southeast of Sanaa. In 1983 he discovered the first Yemeni mummies
in old tombs of this city. From 1983–86 he was director of topographical survey
and research in all the archeological sites of Yemen and he contributed also to
the development of its museums. Nūr al-Dīn wrote several books and articles
on Yemen and, like Aḥmad Fakhrī, he contributed greatly to Yemeni archeology and ancient history.[83] In 1986 he returned to his home university and
became full professor of Egyptology. In 1988 he was seconded to the Egyptian
Antiquities Organization as head of the museums sector and acting director
of this organization for a year. Back again at his university he served as Vice
Dean and as head of the Egyptology Department in addition to his teaching
obligations. His administrative skills were also remarkable, and he showed
them clearly when he was in charge of the EAO/SCA between 1993 and 1996,
and later when he created and headed the Archeology department of Fayoum
University, from 2000–2005, and the Faculty of Archaeology and Tourism at
Misr University for Sciences and Technology from 2010–17.

---

81   Nur el Din, *Dawr al-marʾa fī al-mujtamaʿ al-Miṣrī al-qadīm.*
82   Nur el Din, *The demotic ostraca in the National Museum of Antiquities at Leiden.*
83   Nur el Din, *Muqaddima fī al-Āthār al-Yamaniyya.*

Nūr al-Dīn lectured all over the world. In Egypt he taught at all national universities and his students are widespread. He had a particularly close relationship with the faculties of tourism as he considered guides to be ambassadors of Egyptian culture and he wanted them to be well prepared to transmit their love of Egypt to the tourists they guided.

Nūr al-Dīn was also a very prolific writer and he published in both English and Arabic. Most of his publications on demotic are in English.[84] He also published essential books on what he deemed lacking in Arabic Egyptological literature, such as a book on Egyptian archeological sites,[85] with specific references to their various names across history, their precise locations, archeological monuments, and their role in the history of the country in addition to many other books and articles on different topics in ancient Egyptian culture and history.[86]

4.22   *ʿAlī Radwān: 1941–2020*

Radwān was born in Ismailia in 1941, he graduated from the department of archeology in the Faculty of Arts at Cairo University in 1962 and received his PhD from the University of Munich in Germany in 1968.[87] He then returned to Egypt and dedicated his whole career to Cairo University where he was first appointed as lecturer/Assistant Professor. Although he was an excellent teacher in all different fields of ancient Egyptian culture, Radwān's lectures on art were particularly brilliant, so that he was often solicited to lecture at the different faculties of Fine Art as well.

In addition to his teaching and mentoring activities, Radwān occupied a number of administrative positions as well in the Faculty of Archeology: head of the Egyptology Department from 1980–87 and Dean of the Faculty, from 1987–93. During his administration as Dean, Radwān established a branch of the Faculty of Archeology in the Fayoum area, this branch later developed into a full-fledged faculty which continues to grow, and which collaborates intensively with international universities. Radwān excavated at Abusir for a number of years and duly published a series of articles on his finds there, mainly dating to the early periods of Egyptian History.[88]

---

84   Nur el Din, Report on new demotic texts from Tuna-el-Gebel, in Johnson.

85   Nur el Din, *al-Lughah al-Miṣriyya al-qadīma; Mawāqiʿ wa-matāḥif al-āthār al-Miṣriyya; and Matāḥif al-āthār fī Miṣr wa-al-waṭan al-ʿArabī.*

86   Nur el Din, *Tārīkh wa-ḥaḍārat Miṣr al-qadīma.*

87   Radwan, *Die Darstellungen des regierenden Königs.*

88   Radwan, Mastaba XVII at Abusir (First Dynasty); Small mastabas and subsidiary graves from the archaic cemetery at Abusir; Ein Jenseitsboot der 1. Dynastie aus Abusir – Teil I.

Among Radwān's important contributions to Egyptology was his role as consultant to the head of the Secretary General of the Supreme Council of Antiquities during which he represented Egypt at UNESCO. During the sessions on heritage there, his profound knowledge of archeological sites in Egypt and the Arab world and the eloquence and arguments with which he presented them as important sites of Human Heritage won the appreciation of the audiences, so that many archeological sites owe Radwān for being on the lists of the UNESCO. Inside Egypt he showed the same concern and enthusiasm for ancient heritage sites and artefacts and he constantly shared in protecting them and in enhancing museums' roles in society. Indeed, among his list of publications is one on "Museology, Egyptology and Marketing Interests: A Contradiction?"[89] Because of his concern for all Arab as well as Egyptian heritage, Radwān started the Arab Archeologists Association in Cairo to create a forum for Arabs concerned with heritage of all periods to meet annually and interact, share and publish their research.

4.23   *Zāhī Ḥawwās: 1947*

Zāhī Ḥawwās is today the most renowned Egyptologist in the world. Because of his energy, frequent public appearances and charisma, Ḥawwās has conveyed his love for Egyptology to thousands of people, including women and children everywhere. He had an impressive career, beginning as an assistant inspector and eventually becoming a secretary-general of the Supreme Council of Antiquities, and finally the first Minister of State for Egyptian Antiquities in 2011. He continues to be active on the Egyptological scene even after his official retirement.

Born near the port of Damietta on the Mediterranean, Ḥawwās received his BA from Alexandria University in Greek and Roman archaeology in 1967. Because he worked on Pharaonic sites all over Egypt as an inspector at the Egyptian Antiquities Organization, he decided to become more familiar with the topic and enrolled for a diploma in Egyptology, which he received in 1979, at Cairo University. Awarded a Fulbright fellowship, he left for the United States for further studies and was granted both his MA and PhD by the University of Pennsylvania in 1984 and 1987 respectively. Additionally, Ḥawwās would later receive five honorary doctorates from various foreign universities in the course of his career. Back in Cairo, he was appointed to work at the Giza Plateau where he brought to light among other things, the tombs of the Great Pyramid's builders.[90] At Bahariya Oasis he discovered the famous Valley of the Golden

---

89   Radwan, Response to R. Schulz.
90   Hawass, Tombs of the pyramid builders.

mummies dating to the Hellenistic period which he had first studied as an undergraduate.[91] In the Valley of the Kings in Western Thebes (Luxor), he and his team rediscovered a 'lost tomb' KV 53,[92] and he conducted the cleaning of the famous tunnel in Sethi I's tomb.[93] He also excavated near Amenhotep III's mortuary temple and uncovered the northern entrance to the temple and a series of statues and other artifacts.[94] Ḥawwās is also very much interested in modern technologies that can help us better understand ancient Egyptian monuments and other artifacts as can be shown by his directing a scientific team using a robot inside the "ventilation" tunnels of the Great Pyramid, in the hope of better understanding their architecturally enigmatic roles.[95] His most important endeavor in science and technology however, is probably the Egyptian Mummies Project which uses modern forensic techniques including CT scans and DNA analysis to investigate human remains and better understand royal genealogies, and more importantly their health conditions and other problems these analyses can reveal.[96]

While director general of the Giza Plateau in the 90s he supervised the latest restoration of the Great Sphinx.[97] Later, as secretary general of the Supreme Council of Antiquities he conducted an extensive restoration and site management program for Coptic and Islamic archeological sites. He also created children's programs in all the great museums of the country and encouraged sending exhibitions of Egyptian artefacts all over the world to enhance the image of Egypt abroad. Ḥawwās also worked hard to raise the academic standard of his employees by sending the better ones to pursue graduate studies abroad or by sending others for shorter periods to interact with international colleagues through museum visits or training in different fields of Egyptology and to be exposed to new ideas and new cultures. Through his vast international network, the process for repatriation of stolen artefacts has been largely reactivated. Ḥawwās also took part in the completion, enlargement or creation of a number of museums all over Egypt.

In addition to his very frequent appearances in national and international media, Ḥawwās is also a prolific writer both in English and in Arabic who published a great many books and articles on Egyptology-related topics for

---

<ol start="91">
<li>Hawass, Valley of the golden mummies, Cairo, 2000.</li>
<li>Hawass and el-Laithy, The Egyptian expedition in the Valley of the Kings.</li>
<li>Hawass and el Awady, The tunnel inside the tomb of Seti I (KV 17).</li>
<li>Hawass and Wagdy, Excavations northwest of Amenhotep III's temple at Kom el-Hetan.</li>
<li>Hawass, The so-called secret doors inside Khufu's pyramid.</li>
<li>Hawass and Saleem, Scanning the pharaohs.</li>
<li>Hawass, History of the Sphinx conservation.</li>
</ol>

specialists and laymen and he has been highly decorated with awards and honors for his scientific work both in Egypt and abroad.

4.24   *Muḥammad Ṣāliḥ: 1939–*

Muḥammad Ṣāliḥ was born in Cairo in the Citadel district. After graduating in 1960 from the department of Archeology at Cairo University's faculty of Arts and finishing his military service, Ṣāliḥ was hired in 1962 by the *Service des Antiquités* and sent to Upper Egypt as an assistant inspector, first to Aswan, where he supervised the reconstruction of Ramses II's Nubian temple of Beit el Wali, and soon after to Thebes, where he first worked with the Polish mission at Deir el Bahri followed by the German mission in the Assasif. In 1964 Ṣāliḥ became Inspector of Antiquities at Thebes and started his own excavations, resulting in the first discovery of Old Kingdom tombs in western Thebes, which he published later in a monograph entitled *Three Old Kingdom Tombs at Thebes*.[98] He also discovered several New Kingdom tombs, among them that of Qen-Amun at Khokha, TT 412. He presented the preliminary findings in different articles.[99] He was then offered a scholarship to study in Germany and went to Heidelberg where he wrote his PhD dissertation on The Book of the Dead texts and vignettes on the walls of Theban tombs under the supervision of E. Otto and J. Assmann.[100] Back in Cairo in 1975, Ṣāliḥ was appointed curator at the Cairo Egyptian Museum, then deputy director and then director until he retired in 1999. As director of the Museum and its exhibits in Egypt as well as its touring exhibitions abroad, Ṣāliḥ traveled and lectured all over the world. While director, Muḥammad Ṣāliḥ updated and modernized the museum and supervised a committee of Egyptologists from among his Egyptian colleagues who could best establish the concordance between Arabic and foreign terminology in the description of museum contents. This important tool of research was published by CultNat in 2010.

Ṣāliḥ was the first to encourage school students to visit the museum under the guidance of volunteer students from the national Faculties of Egyptology and Tourism, so that these future guides and Egyptologists would become more familiar with the museum and its masterpieces.

Ṣāliḥ co-authored two guide books of the museum to facilitate visits, as well as writing important articles in several catalogues for international exhibitions and many articles on different topics in Egyptology, in English as well as in Arabic.

---

98   Saleh, *Three Old Kingdom tombs at Thebes.*
99   Saleh, The tomb of the royal scribe Qen-Amun at Khokha, 15–28.
100   Saleh, *Das Totenbuch in den thebanischen Beamtengräbern des Neuen Reiches.*

After retiring from the Cairo Egyptian Museum, Ṣāliḥ continued to contribute his vast museum experience as member of the administrative board of the Grand Egyptian Museum at Giza and consultant for the selection of objects to be exhibited there. He has also been working as a consultant for CultNat, the institution in charge of the digital documentation of ancient Egyptian cultural and natural heritage in which he was in charge of editing all scientific work on ancient Egypt and for which he translated many ancient Egyptian texts and wrote scripts for a number of digital programs which "reproduce" ancient rituals like the chanting of the *Book of the Dead* for example. He also continues his activities as guest professor at several national universities. Ṣāliḥ was also a visiting professor at The American University in Cairo (1991) and at the University of Heidelberg (2004). Since 2008 he has been a visiting Professor of ancient history and civilization at 'Ayn Shams University's Women's Faculty. Ṣāliḥ is currently finishing a four-volume book on ancient Egyptian civilization in Arabic, and working on the long *Book of the Dead* papyrus of Her-si-ese from the Late Ptolemaic period in the Egyptian Museum.

4.25   *Fayza Haikal [Fā'iza Haykal]: 1938–*

Born in Cairo, Haykal was schooled at the *Lycée Français du Caire* before she joined the Department of Archeology of the Faculty of Arts at Cairo University. She received her BA in 1960 and worked for a year (1960–61) at the documentation center of the *Services des Antiquités Égyptiennes* created for the documentation and study of the monuments of Nubia. There she was officially responsible for revising all the scientific material before its publication, and also for subsequent press coverage. Although Egyptian traditions did not allow young women to work in Nubia, she broke this tradition and went to work on missions there, doing epigraphic work in the temple of Abu-Simbel, and an archeological description of the tomb of Pennut at Aniba,[101] thus opening the way for other women to fulfil their dreams after her.

She then left for England (1961–65) on a Cairo University scholarship to pursue graduate studies, as she had by then been appointed as an assistant at the Faculty of Arts. In England she spent a year (1961–62) at UCL where she was tutored by R.O. Faulker in ancient Egyptian and by M. Drower in the history of ancient civilization. At the end of her first year there however, she transferred to Oxford and matriculated at St Anne's college where she started to work on her thesis about Religious Papyri from the British Museum under J. Černý, receiving her DPhil in 1965.[102] Back in Cairo she returned to her university as a lecturer and stayed there until 1984 when she became a full professor. While

---

101   Haikal and Abu Bakr, *Tombeau de Pennout.*
102   Haikal, *Two hieratic funerary papyri of Nesmin.*

at Cairo University, Haykal's contacts with Egyptian students from all over Egypt and her discussions with them about ancient Egyptian language and cultural traditions confirmed her ideas on transmission of culture in Egypt, ideas that had been evoked by a number of scholars in the past, but which had never actually been fully investigated. She systematically drew attention to the phenomenon of cultural transmission every time vocabulary, expressions or traditions that have survived in later periods appeared in the texts she was teaching to her students and as a result a large number of her students wrote their dissertations or subsequent articles on analogies and transmission of culture between ancient and modern Egypt so that ethno-Egyptology has almost become the norm for many Egyptian researchers. In 1984 the American University in Cairo hired her to create a program for a BA in Egyptology which was accredited by the Egyptian Board of Universities. She is still teaching at the American University where she has promoted her ideas on transmission of culture and on the importance of ethno-Egyptology to understanding ancient Egypt.

Haykal has also participated in MA, PhD and habilitation committees at foreign universities, particularly in France where she was a visiting Professor at Paris-Sorbonne in 1994 (February–June) and again for a year from November 2006 to October 2007. She also taught at Roma-La Sapienza from 1978–79 and in 1994 for a short period, and at Charles University in Prague for several short periods. From 1991–98 she was Vice President of the International Association of Egyptologists and from 1998–2000 she was President of that same association.

As Vice President of the International Association of Egyptologists, in 1992 she initiated the North Sinai Archeological Salvage Project to investigate and protect archeological sites threatened by the digging of the Peace Canal that was to bring fresh water to the region. She directed the project from 1992–96, gathering and coordinating international help. Her field experience also includes her previous work in Nubia in 1961 and several seasons of epigraphical work in TT 23 in Thebes for the Egyptian Antiquities Organization from 1983–86.

Her academic publications, which concentrated essentially on ancient Egyptian hieratic literary or religious papyri in the first part of her career, have gradually come to focus more and more on the study of ancient traditions, expressions, metaphors, beliefs and national Egyptomania.[103] Haykal believes that whenever Egyptian Egyptologists recognize these cultural analogies

---

103   Haikal, The roots of modern Egypt; Of cats and twins in Egyptian folklore; Echoes from ancient Egypt; Spiritualité égyptienne; Performativité du nom divin en Égypte; A definition of identity; and Egypt's past regenerated by its own people.

and transmissions in today's language and folklore, it is their duty to make them known to their foreign colleagues as well as to Egyptians interested in their roots. Haikal received many homages and awards from Egypt and abroad and is currently a Professor Emerita at the American University in Cairo.

4.26   *'Ulā Al-Ajuizi: 1948–*

Born in Cairo, Al-Ajuizi was instructed at the francophone *Lycée al-Horreya* of Maadi before she joined the Department of Egyptology of the Faculty of Arts at Cairo University from which she graduated in 1970, making her one of the last graduates of this faculty, before the department was severed from it to be transformed briefly into an institute prior to becoming the Faculty of Archeology of Cairo University. She was recruited as an assistant at the Faculty of Arts in that same year and later worked at the Faculty of Archeology. She received her MA in 1977 for her research on dwarfs and pygmies in ancient Egyptian daily life[104] under the supervision of 'Abd al-'Azīz Ṣāliḥ and her PhD in 1985 on her 'Paleography of demotic texts until the end of the Ptolemaic Period' under 'Abd al-Ḥalīm Nūr al-Dīn.[105] This work, later published by the IFAO, became an essential tool for all students of demotic texts of that period. In 1998 Al-Ajuizi became a Professor and as such began to assume more administrative duties in her faculty alongside her teaching.

In 2002 she became head of the Egyptology Department for an academic year (2002–2003) and then Dean of the Faculty (2004–2006). Her tenure as Dean was extremely active, as in addition to her considerable administrative load, Al-Ajuizi took it upon herself to reopen the Cairo University excavation site in Saqqara that had remained closed for a number of years. Al-Ajuizi is still working on this site where she was initiated into archeology and which became her passion. Her excavations there brought to light several important Ramesside tombs of exceptional beauty.[106]

As Dean, Al-Ajuizi renovated the Faculty and recuperated its lost or forgotten assets and landed property in Upper Egypt and elsewhere and established agreements for academic collaboration with universities all over the world including in Africa and Asia. She also reinforced and activated the links between the Faculty of Archeology and the Supreme Council of Antiquities to collaborate more closely and to allow her young students to train in field schools organized by the Council. Under her leadership the faculty also contributed to the reorganization and documentation of important historical archives at the university's central library.

---

104   Al-Aguizy, Dwarfs and pygmies in ancient Egypt.
105   Al-Aguizy, *A palaeographical study of demotic papyri in the Cairo Museum.*
106   Al-Aguizy, Une nouvelle "tombe-sarcophage à puits" à Saqqâra.

As a professor, Al-Ajuizi taught and supervised graduate students in Egyptian national universities. She lectured in many foreign institutions and contributed to a large number of congresses, attending most of the international congresses on demotic that took place in the last three decades in addition to the more general ones organized by the IAE (International Association of Egyptologists). Al-Ajuizi is on the editing board of several Egyptological journals, including that of the Faculty of Archeology and that of *Abgadeyat* at the Bibliotheca Alexandrina, the ASAE, the *Bulletin of the Egyptian Museum* and the *Göttinger Miszellen*. She currently heads a committee at the Ministry of Culture for enhancing awareness and research on historical and archeological matters.

In addition to her main work at the Faculty of Archeology, Al-Ajuizi was an affiliate researcher at the IFAO from 1998–2011. As such she worked with the Franco-Italian mission at Tebtynis in the Fayyūm for a number of years on demotic ostraca found during the excavations there. The result of her work is to be published by the IFAO. In 2015 she was offered the *Mélanges offerts à Ula el Agulzy* as a tribute from her colleagues.[107] She is currently an Emerita Professor at Cairo University and devotes most of her time to her excavations in Saqqara.

5   After the Pioneers

After ʿUlā Al-Ajuizi's class, the Faculty of Archeology graduated hundreds of students every year and many other public universities have been created in addition to the older Cairo, ʿAyn Shams and Alexandria Universities so that it becomes more difficult to classify students as belonging to specific generations or to follow their careers, except maybe for the most brilliant among them who clearly contributed to Egyptology, either academically or in its administration or both. Among these younger generations are a few that cannot be omitted in this chapter, and they will also serve as examples for many others who cannot be mentioned for lack of space. Foremost among these is Muḥammad ʿAbd al-Maqṣūd.

5.1   *Muḥammad ʿAbd al-Maqṣūd ʿAbd al-Raḥīm: 1953–*
ʿAbd al-Maqṣūd, as he is known, was born in Ismailia in 1953. He received his BA in Egyptology from the recently renamed Faculty of Archeology at Cairo University in 1977 and after working for a few years in many different places in

---

107   Haikal, *Mélanges offerts à Ola el-Aguizy.*

Egypt for the then Egyptian Antiquities Organization and with different foreign archeological missions, he went to Lille in France to pursue graduate studies under Prof. Dominique Valbelle. There he first received a DEA in 1986 on a Memoire he wrote on Sinai archeological sites, an MA in 1987 on Roman baths in Northern Sinai, and finally a PhD in 1992 on the old fortresses of North Sinai, on the route to Palestine.[108]

His first mission when he came back to Egypt was to be the field director of the North Sinai Archeological Salvage Project created to protect and document archeological sites threatened by the digging of the Peace Canal in north Sinai. He fulfilled his job perfectly, caring for the sites as well as for his colleagues who, at the beginning of the project lived under very difficult conditions. He did his best to find better accommodations for them and ultimately built for them, near Tell Abu Seifi not far from el Qantarah East, what is known today as the Sinai Research Center with living spaces for the members of the team, laboratories and storing facilities for objects discovered during the work, along with all the necessary facilities to have training sessions for students in the Center. 'Abd al-Maqṣūd was also well aware of all the potential financial problems resulting from obstructing the progress of the digging of the canal or of diverting its course in order to save a specific site, however, he never hesitated to ask the authorities to do so whenever the need arose. After a few years of this intensive work, the mission was accomplished and the topography of the place and views on its history completely changed. In the meantime, 'Abd al-Maqṣūd was also commissioned with the difficult task of bringing back to Egypt all the artefacts that were found in Sinai and transferred to Israel during its occupation of the Sinai.

From 1997–2000 'Abd al-Maqṣūd was Director of Antiquities for the Eastern Delta and Sinai. As such he carried out site management activities in Tanis[109] and excavated at Tell Basta, where he discovered the magnificent colossus of Merytamon, Ramses II's daughter, after which he created a very interesting archeological park for the city.[110]

In 2005 he became responsible for the whole Delta. He cleaned and protected the site of Tell el Dekka in Alexandria, one of the most important sites of the city, as well as the site of Marina el Alamein on the Mediterranean coast, and opened it for tourists. He also created in Alexandria an open-air museum for statues and other artifacts salvaged through marine archeology.

---

108   Abd al Maqsud, *Tell Heboua (1981–1991)*.
109   Valbelle, Abd el-Maksoud and Carrez-Maratray, Ce nome qu'on dit "tanite".
110   Tietze and Abd El Maksoud, *Tell Basta*.

In 2011 he became secretary general of the Supreme Council of Antiquities. This position was followed by a series of other important posts, when in the turmoil of the post 2011 revolution period, the need was felt for a strong personality in one place or the other. In 2015, after his retirement, he was entrusted with the direction of new excavations at Tell Daphne near the Suez Canal. Since 2017 he has been a consultant for the 'Ayn Shams University excavations on the site of old Heliopolis/*Iwnw* in Matareya.

In addition to his important field work in many parts of Egypt, and the related publications, 'Abd al-Maqṣūd attended and spoke at many international congresses and co-supervised several MA and PhD theses related to Sinai and carried out in various Egyptian universities.

He has been a member of many important committees of the Ministry of Antiquities, through its different name changes, and has earned a reputation for taking courageous decisions to support or oppose proposals based on his moral conviction. 'Abd al-Maqsūd also played an important role in UNESCO where he pleaded for adding St. Catherine to the list of human heritage to be protected and vetoed Israel's claim over Jerusalem's archeological sites. 'Abd al-Maqṣūd is still present wherever needed as counselor on a number of archeological sites. He is particularly present now in Mattareya on the site of Old Heliopolis *Iwnw* at Kom el Hisn.

5.2   *Mamdūḥ al-Damātī: 1961–*

Born and raised in Cairo, al-Damātī joined the Faculty of Archaeology of Cairo University and received his BA in 1983. His first full-time job was as an Assistant Curator at the Egyptian Museum, from 1985–87, then he moved to Cairo University as a Curator of the Faculty of Archaeology Museum from 1988. During these years, he pursued his postgraduate studies at Cairo University and received his MA in 1989, under the supervision of 'Abd al-Ḥalīm Nūr al-Dīn and 'Ulā Al-Ajuizi on "The *St-Meskhnet* Hall of the Dendera Temple." He studied German at Cologne University and enrolled in the PhD program at Trier, where he studied under Erich Winter and defended his dissertation on the "Sokar-Osiris-Kapelle im Tempel von Dendera"[111] in 1995, after which he returned to Egypt, and resumed his work at Cairo University as Curator of its Archaeological Museum until 1996, when he was appointed as a lecturer at Cairo University's Faculty of Tourism and Hotels in the Fayyūm branch in 1996. In 1998 al-Damātī joined the newly founded Archaeology Department of the Faculty of Arts at 'Ayn Shams University. In 2001, he became Associate Professor of Egyptology and was appointed as director of the Egyptian Museum until

---

111   El Damaty, *Sokar-Osiris-Kapelle im Tempel von Dendera.*

2004. Then he returned to his university as full professor in 2006, and chaired the Archaeology Department until 2009, when he was elected dean of the Faculty of Arts, a post he occupied until 2011. He was then appointed as Egypt's cultural counsellor and director of its educational bureau in Berlin, where he was also in charge of the Egyptian educational missions in the Netherlands, Poland, Denmark, Finland and Sweden, from 2011–2014. Al-Damātī was called back to Egypt to become its Minister of Antiquities from 2014–16, then he returned to ʿAyn Shams University, where he is still teaching.

During these years, al-Damātī has been teaching and supervising research, excavations and restoration projects in Egypt, such as Historic Cairo (2014–16); Scan-Pyramids (2015–); Tomb of Tutankhamun (2015–) and the ʿAyn Shams excavation at Arab al-Hisn, ancient Heliopolis (2017–). In addition, he served as visiting professor at several universities around the world and he has received international awards for his Egyptological work. He published numerous books and articles in Arabic, English and German, covering different aspects of ancient Egyptian history, art and archaeology, especially during the Late and Greco-Roman Periods[112].

5.3   *Ḥasan Al-Saʿdī: 1957–*

Born and raised in Ṭanṭa, Gharbiya Governorate, Al-Saʿdī graduated from the History Department at the University of Ṭanṭa in 1979. He then joined the History Department at the Faculty of Arts, Alexandria University, where he pursued his postgraduate studies and started his academic career. First appointed as an assistant in 1980, he was promoted to assistant lecturer in 1984 after receiving his MA, under the supervision of Bayyūmi Mahrān on "Nomarchs until the End of the Middle Kingdom, Egypt," which was published in 1991 and again in 2002.[113] This study still is the main Arabic reference on this subject to date. In 1988, he went for two years to Liverpool, where he studied under Kenneth Kitchen and conducted his PhD research on the "Monuments of Seti I," which was later published in 2005.[114] Back in Egypt, he pursued his academic career and became full professor in 1999. He has chaired the History, Egyptian and Islamic Archaeology Department since 2011, and is also executive director of Alexandria University's International Program. Al-Saʿdī taught at several other Egyptian Universities as well and spent many years teaching in various universities of Saudi Arabia (King Abdulaziz University in Jeddah from

---

112   El Damaty, *Horus als Ka des Königs*; *The Third Intermediate Period and the Late Period*; and *Die leeren Kartuschen von Echnaton*.

113   Saady, *Ḥukkām al-aqālīm fī Miṣr al-Firʿawniyya*.

114   Saady, *Āthār Sītī al-Awwal*.

1991–2001, and King Saud University in Riyadh in 2006) and is currently teaching ancient history at Tiba University in the same country. He significantly contributed to Egyptology in Arabic and English, and his research interests and publications primarily concentrate on the culture and history of ancient Egypt and the ancient Near East.

5.4 *Ḥasan Aḥmad Ḥasan Salīm: 1960–*

Salīm graduated from Cairo University in 1979 and is now a professor in the Department of Archeology at ʿAyn Shams University after having taught at the Asyūṭ/South Valley University and trained in Museum Studies in Europe, mainly at the British Museum, the Berlin Museum and the Louvre. Today he is considered to be one of the best specialists on ancient Egyptian art in Egypt and is a counselor on most museum committees in the country. His publications, in English, German and Arabic, mostly focus on museum artifacts forgotten in the dark corners or storerooms of museums. They reveal his profound knowledge and understanding of his subject.[115]

5.5 *Muḥammad Sharīf ʿAlī: 1960–*

He received his BA in Egyptology from the Faculty of Archaeology of Cairo University in 1982 and his PhD from Gottingen in Germany in 1996.[116] After pursuing his academic career at Cairo University and teaching in various universities in Egypt for a number of years he is now teaching at the University of Bonn in Germany, where he continues his research and publications of hieratic inscriptions.

5.6 *Laylā Maḥmūd ʿAzzām: 1963–*

She joined the Faculty of Archaeology at Cairo University, and graduated with a BA in Egyptology in 1984. Currently she is as professor of Egyptology at the Faculty of Arts at Ḥilwān University. While researching for her PhD on magical spells to cure illnesses,[117] which she received from Helwan University in 2001, she spent a year in Leiden studying with Prof. Borghouts. She has published a number of articles on demons and on various topics related to life in ancient Egypt for which she received in 2010 the Helwan University prize for the best scientific research.

---

115 Selim, Two royal statue bases from Karnak in the basement of the Egyptian Museum in Cairo; and Three unpublished naophorous statues from Cairo Museum.

116 Ali, *Hieratische Ritzinschriften aus Theben.*

117 Azzam, Magical spells used in the treatment of diseases in ancient Egypt.

5.7   *Ashraf Muḥammad Fatḥī: 1958–*

Fatḥī graduated from the Faculty of Archeology of Cairo University in 1980 and pursued his graduate studies at the Archaeology Department of the Faculty of Arts of Minyā University, under the supervision of the late Prof. Ramaḍān ʿAbduh who introduced Egyptology there. In 2001, Fatḥī joined the Department of Archeology of the Faculty of Arts at ʿAyn Shams University, where he is continuing his academic career. Since 1999 his research interests have been in the area of the lexicography of ancient Egyptian, highlighting the abundance of Arabic words derived from, or sharing the same roots as their Egyptian equivalents, thus he can be seen as contributing to the Egyptian trend of ethno-Egyptology.[118]

5.8   *Zaynab Maḥrūs: 1957–*

Maḥrūs studied at the Faculty of Archeology of Cairo University with a two-year interim in Paris to follow Prof. Vernus' classes and collect material for her PhD dissertation (1994) on phonetics and metathesis in the language of ancient Egypt and the indication of potential dialects, and their comparison with other Semitic languages. She was employed in the Faculty of Archeology and is now a Professor Emerita after having been head of the Egyptology Department for a number of years. Her publications, all in philology, include a number of articles on comparison of hieroglyphic and Coptic grammatical elements with their Arabic counterparts.

5.9   *Hiba Muṣṭafā Nūḥ: 1960–*

Nūḥ graduated from the Faculty of Archeology and completed her entire academic career there. Her excellent PhD (1996) on auxiliary verbs in Egyptian and Arabic was only the start of her further research in grammatical analogies between Egyptian and Arabic. She also occupied a number of administrative positions and is currently dean of the Faculty of Archeology.

5.10   *Hishām al-Laythī: 1971–*

Al-Laythī graduated from the Faculty of Archaeology, Cairo University, in 1993. After his graduation, he joined the Supreme Council of Antiquities (now Ministry of Antiquities), first as a member of the Secretary-General's Technical Office, where he was responsible for, and supervised many of the Supreme Council's ongoing projects in addition to being a member of different committees of the Ministry of Antiquities. He then became Director of Scientific Publications (2011–15) and Director-General of the Documentation Center (2015 onwards), to which was recently added the responsibility over all the

---

118   Fathy, Identical familial terms in Egyptian and Arabic.

Greco-Roman monuments of the Delta. In spite of this heavy administrative load al-Laythī managed to pursue graduate studies in the faculty and received his MA on "Letters to the dead in ancient and modern Egypt" in 2001 and his PhD on "Theban wooden funerary stelae from the 21st–26th dynasties" in 2012. Al-Laythī lectured extensively and participated in many international conferences in Europe, the USA, and India. His main research interest focuses on Late Period stelae, produced mainly in Thebes and on their religious significance.

In addition to the abovementioned, it might be fair to remember here Egyptian Egyptologists who for personal reasons remained abroad and contribute to Egyptology from the different countries they are living in, like Shafīq ʿAllām, Emeritus Professor at Tübingen University, who, with his prolific writing greatly contributed to the understanding of life in ancient Egypt and whose research on commerce and law in ancient Egypt in particular will remain an essential reference in this domain.[119] Fikrī Ḥasan worked on the birth of Egyptian civilization and many other topics first from Washington State University, then from UCL where he was the Petrie Professor of Archeology for many years before returning to Egypt to concentrate on the management of cultural heritage. He created an MA degree for this discipline at the French University of Egypt in collaboration with other European Universities. Also deserving of mention are: Ṣāfīnāz-Āmāl Najīb, professor at the University of Oslo and her many contributions to ethno-Egyptology; Nādiya al-Shuhūmi for her excellent book on funerary traditions, archeology and beliefs in ancient Egypt and their analogies with Modern Egypt; ʿUkāsha al-Dālī and his groundbreaking books on *The missing millennium* and *Egypt in the eyes of Arab writers*; Hānī Rashwān and his excellent research on *Rhetoric in ancient Egyptian and its analogies with Arabic*, underlining the importance of the Semitic character of the Egyptian language; Ramaḍān Badrī who is excavating Saite tombs in Saqqara on behalf of the university of Tübingen and has excellent knowledge of their religious texts; Muḥammad Mujāhid who excavated at Abusir on behalf of Charles University in Prague; and ʿAmr Hawwārī and his research on ancient Egyptian knowledge and religion in Bonn. We also have to mention here Fathī Ṣāliḥ who created CultNat, one of the scientific institutes of the Bibliotheca Alexandrina, to digitize the documentation of Cultural and Natural Heritage in Egypt, the many faculties of tourism, and a growing number of NGOs concerned with Egyptian Archeological Heritage in general. All these contribute, in one way

---

119　Allam, Lieux de juridiction; Islamic foundations (*waqf*) in Egypt; Regarding the eisagogeus (εἰσαγωγεύς) at Ptolemaic law courts; Foundations in pharaonic Egypt; Religiöse Bindungen im Recht und Rechtswirksamkeit in Altägypten; Juristes inconnus dans l'Égypte pharaonique.

or another, in serving Egyptology and diffusing awareness of Egyptology in its own country and in the world.

6   Conclusion

After this survey of Egyptian scholars who most impacted the Egyptological scene so far, it may be useful to remind the readers of the main changes that developed slowly but surely in the discipline. It is clear that now Egyptians have recuperated their national heritage, politically as well as administratively. Because of the annual proliferation of Egyptology graduates and the authorities' increased awareness of the importance of this unique cultural heritage in the world and of its marketing value, efforts are seriously made to diffuse and enhance the population's pride in, and knowledge of their past while trying to improve the presentation and management of the sites.

On the academic side, serious Egyptian Egyptologists are now integrated in the international academic community and it is up to them to overcome whatever resistance or reluctance still exists. However, in order to be recognized internationally and read by their colleagues abroad, they are expected to publish in a European language, preferably English. As a result, Arabic is still not properly acknowledged as a language of research in the field and there even seems to be a decline in good academic publications in this language. Many good MA or PhD theses written in Arabic remain unpublished even when their publication is officially recommended, and this is a loss to Egyptology that needs to be rectified. Last but not least, although similarities and transmission of culture seem evident to most Egyptians Egyptologists, international scholars who have no time to study Arabic and/or Egyptian culture to fully understand and appreciate ethno-archeology seem reluctant to accept it. The Semitic approach to the ancient Egyptian language and the culture is not sufficiently widespread as yet and this field of research that attracts many Egyptians still needs more attention and more diffusion on an international level.

Select Bibliography

Abd al Maqsud, ['Abd al-Maqṣūd, M.], *Tell Heboua (1981–1991): enquête archéologique sur la Deuxième Période Intermédiaire et le Nouvel Empire à l'extrémité orientale du Delta*, Paris, 1998.

Abu Bakr, A. [Abū Bakr, A.], *Untersuchungen über die ägyptischen Kronen*, Glückstadt, Hamburg, New York, 1937.

Abu Bakr, A. [Abū Bakr, A.], *Al-Mujmal fī al-Tārīkh al-Miṣriyy*, Cairo, 1942.

Abu Bakr, A. [Abū Bakr, A.], Al-Nashāṭ al-ʿIlmiyy al-athariyy fī Miṣr 1945–1947, *Majallat al-jamʿiyya al-Miṣriyya li-al-Dirāsāt al-Tārīkhiyya* 1 (1948), 179–192.

Abu Bakr, A. [Abū Bakr, A.], *Asātīr Miṣriyya*, Cairo, 1954.

Abu Bakr, A. [Abū Bakr, A.], *Kifāḥunā Ḍidd al-Ghuzāt*, Cairo, 1957.

Abu Bakr, A. [Abū Bakr, A.], *Ḥaḍārat al-ʿIrāq al-Qadīm*, Cairo, 1957.

Abu Bakr, A. [Abū Bakr, A.], Al-Kushūf al-Athariyya wa Atharuha fī Kitābat al-Tārīkh al-qadīm, *Majallat al-jamʿiyya al-Miṣriyya li-al-Dirasāt al-Tārīkhiyya* 5 (1956), 3–46.

Abu Bakr, A. [Abū Bakr, A.], Qiṣṣat al-Matḥaf al-Miṣriyy, *al-Majalla* 24 (1958), 21–27.

Abu Bakr, A. [Abū Bakr, A.], *Ikhnātūn*, Cairo, 1961.

Abu Bakr, A. [Abū Bakr, A.], *Excavations at Giza 1949–1950*, Cairo, 1953.

Abu Bakr, A. [Abū Bakr, A.], Les nouvelles découvertes de la nécropole de Guizeh. Les grandes découvertes archéologiques de 1954, *La Revue du Caire* 33, no. 175 (1955), 32–36.

Abu Bakr, A. [Abū Bakr, A.], Découvertes récentes au cimetière occidental de la nécropole de Guizeh. Les grandes découvertes archéologiques de 1954, *La Revue du Caire* 33, no. 175 (1955), 46–49.

Abu Bakr, A. [Abū Bakr, A.], Qiṣṣat al-Ḥaḍāra al-Miṣriyya wa Nash'atuha, *al-Majalla* 123 (1967), 34–41.

Abu Bakr, A. [Abū Bakr, A.], *Bilād al-Nūba*, Cairo, 1962.

Abu Bakr, A. [Abū Bakr, A.], Lawḥāt al-Fayyūm, *al-Majalla* 86 (1964), 76–80.

Abu Bakr, A. [Abū Bakr, A.], and A. Youssef [Yūsuf, A.], The funerary boat of Khufu, in *Aufsätze zum 70. Geburtstag von Herbert Ricke*, edited by G. Haeny. Beiträge zur ägyptischen Bauforschung und Altertumskunde 12, Wiesbaden, 1971, 1–16.

Abou-Ghazi, D., Discoveries of Selim Hassan at Saqqarah, *Annales du Service des Antiquités de l'Égypte* 63 (1979), 1–4.

Al-Aguizy, O. [Al-Ajuizi, ʿU.], Dwarfs and pygmies in ancient Egypt, *Annales du Service des Antiquités de l'Égypte* 71 (1987), 53–60.

Al-Aguizy, O. [Al-Ajuizi, ʿU.], *A palaeographical study of demotic Papyri in the Cairo Museum from the reign of King Taharka to the end of the Ptolemic period, 684–30 B.C.*, Cairo, 1998.

Al-Aguizy, O. [Al-Ajuizi, ʿU.], Une nouvelle "tombe-sarcophage à puits" à Saqqâra, *Bulletin de l'Institut Français d'Archéologie Orientale* 110 (2010), 13–34.

Allam, Sch. [ʿAllam, Sch.], Lieux de juridiction, in Zivie-Coche, Ch., and Ivan Guermeur (eds.), *"Parcourir l'éternité": hommages à Jean Yoyotte* 1, Turnhout, 2012, 1–13. Allam, Sch. [ʿAllam, Sch.], Islamic foundations (*waqf*) in Egypt (back into pharaonic times) *Journal of the American Research Center in Egypt* 44 (2008), 105–112.

Allam, Sch. [ʿAllam, Sch.], Regarding the eisagogeus (εἰσαγωγεύς) at Ptolemaic law courts, *Journal of Egyptian History* 1 (2008), 3–19.

Allam, Sch. ['Allam, Sch.], Foundations in pharaonic Egypt: the oldest known private endowments in history, *Die Welt des Orients* 37 (2007), 8–30.

Allam, Sch. ['Allam, Sch.], Religiöse Bindungen im Recht und Rechtswirksamkeit in Altägypten, in Barta, H., R. Rollinger, and M. Lang (eds.), *Recht und Religion: menschliche und göttliche Gerechtigkeitsvorstellungen in den antiken Welten*, Wiesbaden, 2008, 109–134.

Allam, Sch. ['Allam, Sch.], Juristes inconnus dans l'Égypte pharaonique, *Boletín de la Asociación Española de Egiptología* 16 (2006), 7–18.

Ali, M. ['Alī, M.], *Hieratische Ritzinschriften aus Theben: Paläographie der Graffiti und Steinbruchinschriften*. Göttinger Orientforschungen 4, Reihe: Ägypten 34, Wiesbaden, 2002.

Al-Amir, M. [Al-Amīr, M.], *A family archive from Thebes: Demotic papyri in the Philadelphia and Cairo Museums from the Ptolemaic period*, Cairo, 1959.

Al-'Ashirī, H. [Achiery, H.], *Le temple d'Amada*, 5 vols., Cairo, 1967.

Attiatallah, H. ['Aṭiyyatallāh, H.], Die Rolle der einheimischen Ägyptologen in der Entwicklung der Ägyptologie als Wissenschaft, *Göttinger Miszellen* 75 (1984), 59–71.

Attiatallah, H. ['Aṭiyyatallāh, H.], Die Rolle der einheimischen Ägyptologen in der Entwicklung der Ägyptologie als Wissenschaft (Teil 2), *Göttinger Miszellen* 76 (1984), 73–94.

Atallah, M. ['Aṭiyyatallāh, M.], Some aspects of relations between the ancient Egyptian language and Arabic, *Annales du Service des Antiquités de l' Égypte* 76 (2001), 114–124.

Azzam, L. ['Azzām, L.], Magical spells used in the treatment of diseases in ancient Egypt, in El-Aguizy, O. [Al-Ajuizi, 'U] and Ali, M. ['Alī, M.], (eds), *Echoes of eternity: studies presented to Gaballa Aly Gaballa*, Wiesbaden, 2010, 183–193.

Badawi, A.M. [Badawī, A.], *Der Gott Chnum*, Glückstadt, Hamburg, New York, 1937.

Badawi, A.M. [Badawī, A.], *Memphis als zweite Landeshauptstadt im Neuen Reich*, Cairo, 1948.

Badawi, A.M. [Badawī, A.], *Fi mawkib al-Shams: Fī tārīkh Miṣr al-Fir'awniyyah min fajrihi al-ṣādiq ilā ākhir al-ḍuḥā. Vol. 2: Fī tārīkh Miṣr al-Fir'awniyya min ākhir al-ḍuḥā ilā awwal al-aṣīl*, Cairo, 1950–1955.

Badawi, A.M. [Badawī, A.], *al-Āthār al-Miṣriyya fī al-Adab al-'Arabiyy*, al-Maktaba al-Thaqāfiyya, Cairo, 1965.

Badawi, A.M. [Badawī, A.], *al-Azyā' fī Miṣr al-qadīma* [*Dress in ancient Egypt. Costume dans l'Égypte ancienne*], Cairo, 1981.

Badawi, A.M. [Badawī, A.], and H. Kees, *Handwörterbuch der ägyptischen Sprache*, Cairo, 1958.

Badawi, A., Excavation under the threat of the High Dam: the ancient Egyptian island fortress of Askut in the Sudan, *Illustrated London News* 242 (1963), 964–966.

Badawi, A., *A history of Egyptian architecture: The empire (the New Kingdom): from the Eighteenth Dynasty to the end of the Twentieth Dynasty, 1580–1085 B.C.*, Berkeley, 1968.

Badawi, A., *A history of Egyptian architecture: The First Intermediate Period, the Middle Kingdom, and the Second Intermediate Period*, Berkeley, 1966.

Badawi, A., *Ancient Egyptian architectural design: a study of the harmonic system.* University of California Publications: Near Eastern Studies 4, Berkeley, Los Angeles, 1965.

Badawi, A., *The tombs of Iteti, Sekhem'ankh-Ptah, and Kaemnofert at Giza.* University of California Publications: Occasional Papers 9, Los Angeles, 1976.

Badawi, A., *The tomb of Nyhetep-Ptah at Giza and the tomb of 'Ankhm'ahor at Saqqara.* University of California Publications: Occasional Papers 11, Los Angeles, 1978.

Bakir, A. [Bakīr, A.], *Slavery in Pharaonic Egypt*, Cairo, 1952.

Bakir, A. [Bakīr, A.], *The Cairo Calendar no. 86637*, Cairo, 1966.

Bakir, A. [Bakīr, A.], *Egyptian epistolography: from the Eighteenth to the Twenty-First dynasty*, Cairo, 1970.

Bakir, A. [Bakīr, A.], *Qawā'id al-lughat al-Miṣriyya fī 'aṣrihā al-dhahabī*, Cairo, 1977.

Bakir, A. [Bakīr, A.], *An introduction to the study of the Egyptian language: a Semitic approach*, Cairo, 1978.

Bakir, A. [Bakīr, A.], *Notes on Late Egyptian grammar: a Semitic approach*, Warminster, 1983.

Bakir, A. [Bakīr, A.], *Notes on Middle Egyptian grammar*, Warminster, 1984.

Bayoumi, A. [Bayyūmi, A.], *Autour du champ des souchets et du champ des offrandes*, Service des Antiquités de l'Égypte, Cairo, 1940.

Bayoumi, A. [Bayyūmi, A.], Survivances égyptiennes, *Bulletin de la Société Royale de Géographie d'Égypte* (1937), 279–287.

Bayoumi, A. [Bayyūmi, A.], Survivances égyptiennes, in *Revue de l'Égypte ancienne* 3 (1930), 110–116.

Bierbrier, M. *Who was Who in Egyptology*, 5th revised ed., London, 2019.

Butros, N.K., Coptic music and its relation to Pharaonic music, *Enchoria. Zeitschrift für Demotistik und Koptologie* 8 (1978), 67*–69* (113–115).

El-Dali, O., *Egyptology: The missing millennium, ancient Egypt in medieval Arabic writings*, London, 2003.

El Damaty, M. [Al-Damātī, M.], *Sokar-Osiris-Kapelle im Tempel von Dendera*, Hamburg, 1995.

El Damaty, M. [Al-Damātī, M.], Horus als Ka des Königs, *Göttinger Miszellen* 169 (1999), 31–45.

El Damaty, M. [Al-Damātī, M.], The Third Intermediate Period and the Late Period, in Radwan, A. (ed.), *Ancient Egypt at the Cairo Museum*, Cairo, 2009.

El Damaty, M. [Al-Damātī, M.], Die leeren Kartuschen von Echnaton, in D'Auria, S.H. (ed.), *Offerings of the Discerning Eye, an Egyptological medley in honour of Jack Josephson*, Leiden, 2010, 79–81.

Eaton-Krauss, M., Ramesses: Re who creates the gods, in Bleiberg, E., and R. Freed (eds), *Fragments of a shattered visage: the proceedings of the international symposium of Ramesses the Great*, Memphis, TN, 1991, 15–23.

Eyre, Ch., The practice of literature: the relationship between content, form, audience and performance, in Enmarch, R, and V. Lepper (eds), *Ancient Egyptian literature: theory and practice*. Proceedings of the British Academy 188, Oxford, 2013, 103.

Fakhri, A. [Fakhrī, A.], *Sept tombeaux à l'est de la grande pyramide de Guizeh*, Service des Antiquités de l'Égypte, Cairo, 1935.

Fakhri, A. [Fakhrī, A.], Tomb of Paser (no. 367 at Thebes), *Annales du Service des Antiquités de l'Égypte* 43 (1943), 389–414.

Fakhri, A. [Fakhrī, A.], *Siwa Oasis: its history and antiquities*, Cairo, 1944.

Fakhri, A. [Fakhrī, A.], *The Oasis of Siwa: its customs, history and monuments*, Cairo, 1950.

Fakhri, A. [Fakhrī, A.], al-Wāḥāt al-Miṣriyya fī al-tārīkh, *al-Majalla al-tārīkhiyya al-Miṣriya* 4 (1951), 177–196.

Fakhri, A. [Fakhrī, A.], *An archaeological journey to Yemen (March–May, 1947), part III: Plates*, Cairo, 1951.

Fakhri, A. [Fakhrī, A.], *An archaeological journey to Yemen (March–May, 1947), part II: Epigraphical texts*, Cairo, 1952.

Fakhri, A. [Fakhrī, A.], *The Egyptian deserts: the inscriptions of the amethyst quarries at Wadi el-Hudi*, Cairo, 1952.

Fakhri, A. [Fakhrī, A.], *The Bent Pyramid of Dahshur*, Cairo, 1954.

Fakhri, A. [Fakhrī, A.], *Miṣr al-Firʿawniyya*, Cairo, 1956.

Fakhri, A. [Fakhrī, A.], *al-Yaman, māḍīhā wa-ḥāḍiruhā: muḥāḍarāt alqāhū Aḥmad Fakhrī ʿalā ṭalabat qism al-dirāsāt al-tārīkhiyya wa-al-jughrāfiyya*, Cairo, 1957.

Fakhri, A. [Fakhrī, A.], *Dirāsāt fī tārīkh al-Sharq al-qadīm, Miṣr wa-al-ʿIrāq – Sūriyā – al-Yaman – Īrān*, [Cairo], 1958.

Fakhri, A. [Fakhrī, A.], *Miṣr al-firʿawniyya*, Cairo, 1960.

Fakhri, A. [Fakhrī, A.], *The monuments of Sneferu at Dahshur*, 3 vols., Cairo, 1959–61.

Fakhri, A. [Fakhrī, A.], *The Pyramids*, Chicago, 1961.

Fakhri, A. [Fakhrī, A.], *al-Ahrāmāt al-Miṣriyya*, Cairo, 1963.

Fakhri, A. [Fakhrī, A.], *The oases of Egypt*, Cairo, 1973.

Fathy, A. [Fatḥī, A.], Identical familial terms in Egyptian and Arabic: a sociolinguistic approach, in Hawass, Z., and P.B. Lyla (eds.), *Egyptology at the dawn of the twenty-first century: proceedings of the Eighth International Congress of Egyptologists, Cairo, 2000*, vol. 3, Cairo, New York, 2003, 183–190.

Gaballa, G.A. [Jāballāh, J.A.], *Narrative in Egyptian art*, Mainz am Rhein, 1976.

Gaballa, G.A. [Jāballāh, J.A.], *The Memphite tomb-chapel of Mose*, Warminster, 1977.

Gaballa, G.A. [Jāballāh, J.A.], The chief of records of the royal harbour Aniy (Amenemone), *Orientalia* 44 (1975), 388–394.

Gaballa, G.A. [Jāballāh, J.A.], The chief worker in fine gold, Ptahmay – an inquest, *Göttinger Miszellen* 26 (1977), 13–15.

Gaballa, G.A. [Jāballāh, J.A.], False-door stelae of some Memphite personnel, *Studien zur Altägyptischen Kultur* 7 (1979), 41–52.

Gaballa, G.A. [Jāballāh, J.A.], Harnakht, chief builder of Mi, *Annales du Service des Antiquités de l'Égypte* 64 (1981), 7–14.

Gaballa, G.A. [Jāballāh, J.A.], Siese, naval standard-bearer of Amenophis III, *Annales du Service des Antiquités de l'Égypte* 71 (1987), 87–9.

Gaballa, G.A. [Jāballāh, J.A.], Three funerary stelae from the New Kingdom, *Mitteilungen des Deutschen Archäologischen Instituts, Abteilung Kairo* 35 (1979), 75–85.

Gaballa, G.A. [Jāballāh, J.A.], Latest excavations in Memphis: progress report, in Bleiberg, E., and R. Freed (eds), *Fragments of a shattered visage: the proceedings of the international symposium of Ramesses the Great*. Monographs of the Institute of Egyptian Art and Archaeology 1, Memphis, TN, 1991, 25–27.

Gaballa, G.A. [Jāballāh, J.A.], Al-Ruwwād al-Miṣriyyūn li Kitābat al- Tārīkh al-Miṣriyy al-Qadīm, *al-Majalla al-Tārīkhiyya al-Miṣriyya* 39 (1996), 259–272.

Gaballa, G.A. [Jāballāh, J.A.], Fakhri, A. [Fakhrī, A.] *al-Ṣaḥrāwāt al-Miṣriyya. al-mujallad al-thānī, wāḥāt al-Baḥriyya wa-al-Farāfrah*, trans Jāballāh ʿAlī Jāballāh, Cairo, 1999.

Gaballa, G.A. [Jāballāh, J.A.], *Tārīkh Miṣr al-qadīm: min al-usrat al-ḥādiyya wa-al-ʿashrīn ḥattā al-usra al-ḥādiyya wa-al-thalāthīn*, Cairo, 2015.

Gaballa, G.A. [Jāballāh, J.A.], and K.A. Kitchen, The festival of Sokar, *Orientalia* 38 (1969), 1–76.

Gaballa, G.A. [Jāballāh, J.A.], and K.A. Kitchen, New light on the cult of Sokar, *Orientalia* 41 (1972), 178–179.

Gabra, S. [Jabrah, S.], Fouilles du Service des Antiquités à Deir Tassa, *Annales du Service des Antiquités de l'Égypte* 30 (1930), 147–15.

Gabra, S. [Jabrah, S.], Rapport préliminaire sur les fouilles de l'Université Égyptienne à Touna (Hermopolis Ouest), *Annales du Service des Antiquités de l'Égypte* 32 (1932), 56–77.

Gabra, S. [Jabrah, S.], Fouilles de l'Université "Fouad el Awal" à Touna el-Gebel (Hermopolis Ouest). *Annales du Service des Antiquités de l'Égypte* 39 (1939), 483–496.

Galal, A. [Jalāl, A.], Notes on the descriptive forms of Egyptian words, *History & the Future: Academic Bulletin* 3 (1993), 67–74.

Galal, A. [Jalāl, A.], Readings in the rhetorical language of some Middle Egyptian tales, *The Egyptian Historian* 10 (1993), 1–17.

Gardiner, A., *Egyptian Grammar*, Oxford, 1927.

Ḥabachi, L. [Ḥabashī, L.], Clearance of the area to the east of Luxor temple and discovery of some objects, *Annales du Service des Antiquités de l'Égypte* 51 (1951), 447–468.

Ḥabachi, L. [Ḥabashī, L.], Khatâ'na-Qantîr: importance, *Annales du Service des Antiquités de l'Égypte* 52 (1954), 443–562.

Ḥabachi, L. [Ḥabashī, L.], *Tell Basta*, Cairo, 1957.

Ḥabachi, L. [Ḥabashī, L.], Clearance of the tomb of Kheruef at Thebes (1957–1958), *Annales du Service des Antiquités de l'Égypte* 55 (1958), 325–350.

Ḥabachi, L. [Ḥabashī, L.], *Features of the deification of Ramesses II*, Gluckstadt, 1969.

Ḥabachi, L. [Ḥabashī, L.], *The second stela of Kamose and his struggle against the Hyksos ruler and his capital*, Gluckstadt, 1972.

Ḥabachi, L. [Ḥabashī, L.], *The obelisks of Egypt: skyscrapers of the past*, New York, 1977.

Ḥabachi, L. [Ḥabashī, L.], *Sixteen studies on Lower Nubia*, Cairo, 1981.

Ḥabachi, L. [Ḥabashī, L.], (ed.) *Actes du IIe Symposium International sur la Nubie, Février 1–3, 1971*. Supplément aux Annales du Service des Antiquités de l'Égypte 24, Cairo, 1981.

Ḥabachi, L. [Ḥabashī, L.], Collaboration of Egyptian Egyptologists with foreign expeditions in facing problems threatening the pharaonic monuments, in Grimal, N.-Ch. (ed.), *Prospection et sauvegarde des antiquités de l'Égypte: actes de la table ronde organisée à l'occasion du centenaire de l'IFAO, 8–12 janvier 1981*. Bibliothèque d'Étude 88, Cairo, 1981, 87–90.

Ḥabachi, L. [Ḥabashī, L.], *The sanctuary of Heqaib*, 2 vols., Mainz am Rhein, 1984.

Ḥabachi, L. [Ḥabashī, L.], *Tell el-Dab'a I: Tell el-Dab'a and Qantir: The site and its connection with Avaris and Piramesse*, Edited by Engel, E.-M., P. Jánosi, and Ch. Mlinar. Untersuchungen der Zweigstelle Kairo des Österreichischen Archäologischen Institutes 2, Vienna, 2001.

Haikal, F. [Haykal, F.], *Two hieratic funerary papyri of Nesmin. Part One: Introduction, transcriptions and plates*, Brussels, 1970.

Haikal, F. [Haykal, F.], *Two hieratic funerary papyri of Nesmin. Part Two: Translation*, Brussels, 1972.

Haikal, F. [Haykal, F.], L'eau dans les métaphores de l'Égypte ancienne, in *Les problèmes institutionnels de l'eau en Égypte ancienne et dans l'Antiquité méditerranéenne*, Edited by Menu, B. Bibliothèque d'Étude, 110, Cairo, 1994, 205–211.

Haikal, F. [Haykal, F.], The roots of modern Egypt: a proposal for a periodical on ancient Egyptian survivals, *Annales du Service des Antiquites Égyptiennes* 74 (1999), 163–169.

Haikal, F. [Haykal, F.], Continuity and cultural identity: an introduction, in Wendrich, W., and G. van der Kooij (eds.), *Moving matters: ethnoarchaeology in the Near East. Proceedings of the international seminar held at Cairo, 7–10 December 1998*, Leiden, 2002, 173–180.

Haikal, F. [Haykal, F.], Egypt's past regenerated by its own people, in MacDonald, S., and M. Rice (eds.), *Consuming Ancient Egypt*, London, 2003, 123–138.

Haikal, F. [Haykal, F.], A definition of identity: Neo-Pharaonic architecture in the XXth century, *The Bulletin of the American Research Center in Egypt* 185 (Summer 2004), 1–14.

Haikal, F. [Haykal, F.], Spiritualité égyptienne: transmission et évolution, in *Bulletin de la Société Française d'Égyptologie* 168 (2007), 12–48.

Haikal, F. [Haykal, F.], Cultural similarities, kinship terminology and ethno-Egyptology, in Thompson, S.E. and P. der Manuelian (eds.), *Egypt and beyond: essays presented to Leonard H. Lesko upon his retirement from the Wilbour chair of Egyptology at Brown University June 2005*, Providence, 2008, 145–148.

Haikal, F. [Haykal, F.], Performativité du nom divin en Égypte de l'antiquité à nos jours, in Piacentini, P., and Ch. Orsenigo (eds.), *Egyptian archives: proceedings of the first session of the International Congress Egyptian Archives* / Egyptological Archives, Milan, September 9–10, 2008, Milan, 2009, 197–217.

Haikal, F. [Haykal, F.], Of cats and twins in Egyptian folklore, in Hawass, Z., P. der Manuelian and R.B. Hussein (eds.), *Perspectives on ancient Egypt: studies in honor of Edward Brovarski*, Cairo, 2010, 131–135.

Haikal, F. [Haykal, F.], The mother's heart, the hidden name, and true identity: paternal/maternal descent and gender dichotomy, in El-Aguizy, O. and M. Sh. Ali (eds.), *Echoes of eternity: studies presented to Gaballa Ali Gaballa*, Wiesbaden, 2010, 195–198.

Haikal, F. [Haykal, F.], Echoes from ancient Egypt, in *The Scribe of Justice, Egyptological studies in honour of Schafik Allam*, Cairo, 2011, 179–191.

Haikal, F. [Haykal, F.], Tradition and religion: transmission of culture versus similarity of beliefs, in Vymazalová, H., M. Megahed and F. Ondráš (eds.), *Ancient echoes in the culture of modern Egypt*, Prague, 2011, 9–27.

Haikal, F. [Haykal, F.], The impact of religious initiation and restricted knowledge on daily life in ancient Egypt: an ethno-Egyptological perspective, in Frood, E., and A. McDonald (eds.), *Decorum and experience: essays in ancient culture for John Baines*, Oxford, 2013, 135–140.

Haikal, F. [Haykal, F.], (ed.), *Mélanges offerts à Ola el-Aguizy*. Bibliothèque d'Étude 164, Cairo, 2015.

Haikal, F. [Haykal, F.], De la natte au tapis rouge: symbolisme de la natte hier et aujourd'hui, in Favry, N., Ch. Ragazzoli and P. Tallet (eds.), *Du Sinaï au Soudan: itinéraires d'une Égyptologue. Mélanges offerts au Professeur Dominique Valbelle*, Paris, 2017, 131–138.

Haikal, F. [Haykal, F.], and Abu Bakr, A. [Abū Bakr, A.], *Tombeau de Pennout à Aniba: description archéologique*. Collection scientifique 75, Cairo, 1963.

Hamza, M. [Ḥamza, M.], Excavations of the Department of Antiquities at Qantîr (Faqûs district): (season, May 21st–July 7th, 1928), *Annales du Service des Antiquités de l'Égypte* 30 (1930), 31–68.

Hamza, M. [Ḥamza, M.], The identification of "Khent-nefer" with "Qantîr", in *Mélanges Maspero I: Orient Ancien vol. 2*, Cairo, 1935, 647–655.

Handoussa, T., and E. Brovarski, *The Abu Bakr cemetery at Giza.* Wilbour Studies in Egyptology and Assyriology 5, Atlanta, Georgia, Lockwood Press, 2021.

Hassan, S. [Ḥasan, S.], *Hymnes religieux du moyen empire*, Cairo, 1928.

Hassan, S. [Ḥasan, S.], *Le poème dit de Pentaour et le rapport officiel sur la bataille de Qadesh*, Cairo, 1929.

Hassan, S. [Ḥasan, S.], Remains of religious customs of ancient Egypt in modern Egypt, in *Actes du Ve Congrès International d'Histoire des Religions à Lund, 27–29 août 1929*, Lund, 1930, 162–166.

Hassan, S. [Ḥasan, S.], *Excavations at Gîza: 1929–1930, Excavations at Gîza I*, Oxford, 1930.

Hassan, S. [Ḥasan, S.], In the vicinity of the Sphinx: the excavations of the Egyptian University in the zone of the pyramid, 1934–1935, in *Atti del XIX Congresso Internazionale degli Orientalisti, Roma, 23–29 Settembre 1935*, Roma, 1938, 151–154.

Hassan, S. [Ḥasan, S.], *Excavations at Gîza: 1930–1931, Excavations at Gîza [2]*, Cairo, 1936.

Hassan, S. [Ḥasan, S.], Excavations at Saqqara 1937–1938, *Annales du Service des Antiquités de l'Égypte* 38 (1938), 503–521.

Hassan, S. [Ḥasan, S.], *Excavations at Gîza: 1931–1932, Excavations at Gîza 3*, Cairo, 1941.

Hassan, S. [Ḥasan, S.], *Excavations at Gîza: 1932–1933, Excavations of the Faculty of Arts, Fouad I University, Excavations at Gîza 4*, Cairo, 1943.

Hassan, S. [Ḥasan, S.], *Excavations at Gîza: 1933–1934, with special chapters on methods of excavation, the false-door, and other archaeological and religious subjects, Excavations of the Faculty of Arts, Fouad I University, Excavations at Gîza 5*, Cairo, 1944.

Hassan, S. [Ḥasan, S.], *Excavations at Gîza: 1934–1935, The solar-boats of Khafra, their origin and development, together with the mythology of the universe which they are supposed to traverse, Excavations of the Faculty of Arts, Fouad I University, Excavations at Gîza 6 (1)*, Cairo, 1946.

Hassan, S. [Ḥasan, S.], *Excavations at Gîza: 1934–1935, The offering-list in the Old Kingdom, Excavations of the Faculty of Arts, Fouad I University, Excavations at Gîza 6 (2)*, Cairo, 1948.

Hassan, S. [Ḥasan, S.], *Excavations at Gîza: 1934–1935, The mastabas of the sixth season and their description, Excavations of the Faculty of Arts, Fouad I University, Excavations at Gîza 6 (3)*, Cairo, 1950.

Hassan, S. [Ḥasan, S.], *Miṣr al-qadīma*, 16 vols., Cairo, 1940–1950.

Hassan, S. [Ḥasan, S.], *Excavations at Gîza: 1935–1936, The mastabas of the seventh season and their description, Excavations of the Faculty of Arts, Cairo University, Excavations at Gîza 7*, Cairo, 1953.

Hassan, S. [Ḥasan, S.], *The Great Sphinx and its secrets: historical studies in the light of recent excavations [Excavations at Gîza, 1936–1937], Excavations at Gîza 8*, Cairo, 1953.

Hassan, S. [Ḥasan, S.], *The mastabas of the eighth season and their description: excavations at Gîza 1936–37–38, Excavations at Gîza 9*, Cairo, 1960.

Hassan, S. [Ḥasan, S.], *The Great Pyramid of Khufu and its mortuary chapel: excavations at Gîza, season 1938–39, with names and titles of vols. i–x of the Excavations at Gîza, Excavations at Gîza 10*, Cairo, 1960.

Hassan, S. [Ḥasan, S.], *Al-Adab al-Miṣrī al-Qadīm, aw, adab al-Farāʿinah*, 2 vols., Cairo, 1945.

Hassan, S. [Ḥasan, S.], *The mastaba of Neb-Kaw-Ḥer*, edited by Iskander, Z., Excavations at Saqqara 1937–1938 (1), Cairo, 1975.

Hassan, S. [Ḥasan, S.], *Mastabas of Ny-ʿankh-Pepy and others*, edited by Iskander, Z., Excavations at Saqqara 1937–1938 (2), Cairo, 1975.

Hassan, S. [Ḥasan, S.], *Mastabas of Princess Ḥemet-Rʾ and others*, edited by Iskander, Z., Excavations at Saqqara 1937–1938 (3), Cairo, 1975.

Hawass, Z. [Ḥawāss, Z.], History of the Sphinx conservation, in Esmael, F.A. (ed.), *The First International Symposium on the Great Sphinx: book of proceedings*, [Cairo], 1992, 165–214.

Hawass, Z. [Ḥawāss, Z.], Tombs of the pyramid builders, *Archaeology* 50 (1999), 39–43.

Hawass, Z. [Ḥawāss, Z.], *Valley of the golden mummies*, Cairo, 2000.

Hawass, Z. [Ḥawāss, Z.], *Hidden treasures of the Egyptian museum: one hundred masterpieces from the Centennial Exhibit*, Cairo, 2002.

Hawass, Z. [Ḥawāss, Z.], *The Golden Age of Tutankhamun: divine might and splendor in the New Kingdom*, New York, Cairo, 2004.

Hawass, Z. [Ḥawāss, Z.], *Hidden treasures of ancient Egypt: unearthing the masterpieces of Egyptian history*, Washington, 2004.

Hawass, Z. [Ḥawāss, Z.], *The golden king: the world of Tutankhamun*, New York, Cairo, 2006.

Hawass, Z. [Ḥawāss, Z.], *Al-Matḥaf al-Qibṭī: marāyā al-tārīkh: ʿabaq al-ʿarāqah*, Cairo, 2006.

Hawass, Z. [Ḥawāss, Z.], *Life in paradise: the noble tombs of Thebes*, Cairo, 2009.

Hawass, Z. [Ḥawāss, Z.], *The secrets of the Sphinx*, Cairo, 2010.

Hawass, Z. [Ḥawāss, Z.], *Highlights of the Egyptian museum*, Cairo, 2010.

Hawass, Z. [Ḥawāss, Z.], *Discovering Tutankhamun: from Howard Carter to DNA*, Cairo, 2013.

Hawass, Z. [Ḥawāss, Z.], The so-called secret doors inside Khufu's pyramid, in Kondo, J. (ed.), *Quest for the dream of the pharaohs: studies in honour of Sakuji Yoshimura*. Supplément aux Annales du Service des Antiquités de l'Égypte 43, Cairo, 2014, 51–68.

Hawass, Z. [Ḥawāss, Z.], *Magic of the pyramids: my adventures in archaeology*, Milan, 2015.

Hawass, Z. [Ḥawāss, Z.], and A. el-Laithy, The Egyptian expedition in the Valley of the Kings: the rediscovery of KV 53, *Mitteilungen des Deutschen Archäologischen Instituts, Abteilung Kairo* 69 (2013), 91–101.

Hawass, Z. [Ḥawāss, Z.], and T. el Awady, The tunnel inside the tomb of Seti I (KV 17): the work of the Egyptian mission, 2007–2010, in Elleithy, H. (ed.), *Valley of the Kings since Howard Carter: proceedings of the Luxor Symposium November 4, 2009*. Supplément aux Annales du Service des Antiquités de l'Égypte 44, Cairo, 2016, 59–93.

Hawass, Z. [Ḥawāss, Z.], and A. Wagdy, Excavations northwest of Amenhotep III's temple at Kom el-Hetan: season 2010–2011, *Mitteilungen des Deutschen Archäologischen Instituts, Abteilung Kairo* 70–71 (2014–2015), 193–225.

Hawass, Z. [Ḥawāss, Z.], and S.N. Saleem, *Scanning the pharaohs: CT imaging of the New Kingdom royal mummies*, Cairo, New York, 2016.

Ḥusayn, T., *The days*, translated by Paxton, E.H., H. Wayment, and K. Cragg, Cairo, 1997.

Ishaq, E.M. *The phonetics and phonology of the Bohairic dialect of Coptic, and the survival of Coptic words in the colloquial and classical Arabic of Egypt, and of Coptic grammatical constructions in colloquial Egyptian Arabic*, D.Phil. thesis submitted to the University of Oxford, 4 vols., Oxford, 1975.

Kadry, A. [Qadrī, A.], *Officers and officials in the New Kingdom*. Studia Aegyptiaca 8, Budapest, 1982.

Kadry, A. [Qadrī, A.], *al-Muʾassasa al-ʿaskariyya al-Miṣriyya fī ʿaṣr al-imbirāṭūriyya: 1570 Q.M.–1087*, Cairo, 1988.

Kamal, A. [Kamāl, A.], *Al-ʿIqd al-thamīn fī maḥāsin akhbār wa-badāʾiʿ āthār al-aqdamīn min al-Miṣriyyīn*, Būlāq, 1882.

Kamal, A. [Kamāl, A.], *Bughyat al-ṭālibīn fī ʿulūm wa-ʿawāʾid wa-ṣanāʾiʿ wa-aḥwāl qudamāʾ al-Miṣriyyīn*, Būlāq, 1891.

Kamal, A. [Kamāl, A.], *Tarwīh al-nafs fī madīnat al-shams, al-maʿrūfa al-Ān bi ʿAyn Shams*, Būlāq, 1902.

Kamal, A. [Kamāl, A.], *Stèles ptolémaïques et romaines. Catalogue général des antiquités égyptiennes du Musée du Caire, nos. 22001–22208*, Cairo, 1904.

Kamal, A. [Kamāl, A.], *Tables d'offrandes. Catalogue général des antiquités égyptiennes du Musée du Caire, nos. 23001–23256*, Cairo, 1906.

Kamal, A. [Kamāl, A.], *Kitāb al-Durr al-Maknūz wa-al-Sirr al-Maʿzūz fī al-Dalāʾil wa-al-Khabāyā wa-al-Dafāʾin wa-al-Kanūz Naql ʿan al-Naskh Numarah 4609, 3826, 1300 al-Mahfūẓa fī Maktabat al-Mathaf al-Miṣrī*, Cairo, 1907.

Kamal, A. [Kamāl, A.], *Makhṭūṭ muʿjam al-Lughat al-Miṣriyya al-qadīma*, 22 vols., Cairo, 2002.

Kamil, J., *Labib Habachi: the life and legacy of an Egyptologist*, Cairo, 2007.

Al-Kholi, M.S. [al-Khūlī, M.S.], Taḥqīq Asmāʾ Mulūk Miṣr al-Qadīma fī Kitābāt al-Muʾarrikhīn al-ʿArab, *Majallat Kulliyyat al-Ādāb, Jāmiʿat Janūb al-Wādī* 5 (1995), 355–384.

Al-Kholi, M.S. [al-Khūlī, M.S.], Das Herz in der Bedeutung ‚Verstand‘ und ‚Gefühl‘, in: Grimal, N., A. Kamel, and C. May-Sheikholeslami (eds), *Hommages à Fayza Haikal*, (Biblithèque d'étude, 138), Cairo, 2003, 165–175.

Al-Leithy, H. [al-Laythī, H.], Letters to the dead in ancient and modern Egypt, in: Hawass, Z., and P.B. Lyla (eds.), *Egyptology at the dawn of the twenty-first century: proceedings of the Eighth International Congress of Egyptologists, Cairo, 2000, vol. 1, Archaeology*, Cairo, 2003, 304–313.

Al-Mahdi, I. [Mahdī, I.], Al-khubz fi Miṣr al-qadīma, *Majallat Al-Funūn al-Shaʿbiyyah* 34 (1991), 93–99.

Matta, G., *Demotic ostraca from the collections at Oxford, Paris, Berlin, Vienna and Cairo: introduction, texts and indexes*, Cairo, 1945.

Matta, G., *The demotic legal code of Hermopolis West*, 2 vols. Bibliothèque d'Étude 45, Cairo, 1975.

Mokhtar, G. [Mukhtār, J.], al-Tasjīl al-ḥadīth lil Āthār al-*Miṣriyya* al-qadīma, *Majallat al-jamʿiyya al-Miṣriyya li-al-Dirasāt al-Tārīkhiyya* 6 (1957), 195–200.

Mokhtar, G. [Mukhtār, J.], Aḥmad Kamāl al-ʿĀlim al-Athariyy al-Awwal fī Miṣr, *al-Majalla al-Tārīkhiyya al-Miṣriyya* 12 (1964–65), 43–57.

Mokhtar, G. [Mukhtār, J.], Salīm Ḥasan ka-munaqqib wa ʿĀlim Āthār, *al-Majalla al-Tārīkhiyya al-Miṣriyya* 19 (1972), 1–12.

Mokhtar, G. [Mukhtār, J.], *General history of Africa II: ancient civilizations of Africa*. London, 1981.

Mokhtar, G. [Mukhtār, J.], *Ihnâsya El-Medina (Herakleopolis Magna): its importance and its role in Pharaonic history*, Cairo, 1983.

Moussa, A. [Mūsā, A.] *The tomb of Nefer and Ka-hay: Old Kingdom tombs at the causeway of king Unas at Saqqara*. AV 5, Mainz, 1971.

Moussa, A. [Mūsā, A.] Excavations in the valley temple of king Unas at Saqqara, *Annales du Service des Antiquités de l'Égypte* 64 (1981), 75–77.

Moussa, A. [Mūsā, A.] A stela of Taharqa from the desert road at Dahshur, *Mitteilungen des Deutschen Archäologischen Instituts, Abteilung Kairo* 37 (1981), 331–337.

Moussa, A. [Mūsā, A.] and H. Altenmüller, *Das Grab des Nianchchnum und Chnumhotep: Old Kingdom tombs at the causeway of king Unas at Saqqara*. AV 21, Mainz, 1977.

Naguib, S.-A., *Miroirs du passé*. Cahiers de la Société d'Égyptologie 2, Geneva, 1993.

Najīb, A., *Kitāb al-athar al-jalīl li-qudamāʾ Wādī al-Nīl*, Būlāq, 1893.

Nur el-Din, A. [Nūr al-Dīn, A.], *The demotic ostraca in the National Museum of Antiquities at Leiden*. Collections of the National Museum of Antiquities at Leiden 1, Leiden, 1974.

Nur el-Din, A. [Nūr al-Dīn, A.], *Muqaddima fī al-Āthār al-Yamaniyya*, Ṣanaa, 1988.

Nur el-Din, A. [Nūr al-Dīn, A.], Report on new demotic texts from Tuna el-Gebel, in Johnson, J.H. (ed.), *Life in a multi-cultural society: Egypt from Cambyses to Constantine and beyond*. Studies in Ancient Oriental Civilization 51, Chicago, 1992, 253–254.

Nur el-Din, A. [Nūr al-Dīn, A.], *Tārīkh wa-ḥaḍārat Miṣr al-qadīma*, Cairo, 1997.

Nur el-Din, A. [Nūr al-Dīn, A.], *Dawr al-marʾah fī al-mujtamaʿ al-Miṣrī al-qadīm*, Cairo, 1995.

Nur el-Din, A. [Nūr al-Dīn, A.], *Al-Lugha al-Miṣriyya al-qadīma*, 2nd ed., Cairo, 1998.

Nur el-Din, A. [Nūr al-Dīn, A.], *Mawāqiʿ wa-matāhif al-āthār al-Miṣriyya*, Cairo, 2007.

Nur el-Din, A. [Nūr al-Dīn, A.], *Al-Lugha al-Miṣriyya al-qadīma: al-khaṭṭ al-Hīrāṭīqī*, Cairo, 2010.

Nur el-Din, A. [Nūr al-Dīn, A.], *Matāhif al-āthār fī Miṣr wa-al-waṭan al-ʿArabī: dirāsa fī ʿilm al-matāḥif*, Cairo, 2010.

Posener, G., *De la divinité du pharaon*. Cahiers de la Société Asiatique 15, Paris, 1960.

Radwan, A. [Raḍwān, ʿA.], *Die Darstellungen des regierenden Königs und seiner Familien-angehörigen in den Privatgräbern der 18. Dynastie*. Münchner Ägyptologische Studien 21, Berlin, 1968.

Radwan, A. [Raḍwān, ʿA.], *Die Kupfer- und Bronzegefässe Ägyptens, von den Anfängen bis zum Beginn der Spätzeit*. Prähistorische Bronzefunde, Abteilung II.2, Munich, 1983.

Radwan, A. [Raḍwān, ʿA.], Mastaba XVII at Abusir (First Dynasty): preliminary results and general remarks, in Bárta, M., and J. Krejčí (eds), *Abusir and Saqqara in the year 2000*. Archív orientální, Supplementa 9, Prague, 2000, 509–514.

Radwan, A. [Raḍwān, ʿA.], Response to R. Schulz, in Hawass, Z., and L.P. Brock (eds), *Egyptology at the dawn of the twenty-first century: proceedings of the Eighth International Congress of Egyptologists, Cairo, 2000, vol. 3*, Cairo, 2003, 102–104.

Radwan, A. [Raḍwān, ʿA.], Small mastabas and subsidiary graves from the archaic cemetery at Abusir, in Goyon, J.-C., and Ch. Cardin (eds), *Proceedings of the Ninth International Congress of Egyptologists: Grenoble, 6–12 September 2004, vol. 2*. Orientalia Lovaniensia Analecta 150, Leuven, 2007, 1559–1566.

Radwan, A. [Raḍwān, ʿA.], Ein Jenseitsboot der 1. Dynastie aus Abusir – Teil I, in Engel, E.-M., V. Müller, and U. Hartung (eds), *Zeichen aus dem Sand: Streiflichter aus Ägyptens Geschichte zu Ehren von Günter Dreyer*. Menes 5, Wiesbaden, 2008, 559–571.

Reid, D., *Whose pharaohs? Archaeology, museums, and Egyptian national identity from Napoleon to World War I*, Cairo, 2002.

Reid, D., *Contesting antiquity in Egypt: archaeologies, museums & the struggle for identities from World War I to Nasser*, Cairo, 2015.

Rizkana, I. [Rizqanah, I.], *al-Ḥaḍārāt al-Miṣriyya fī fajr al-tārīkh*, Cairo, 1948.

Rizkana, I. [Rizqanah, I.], *Ḥaḍārat Miṣr wa-al-sharq al-qadīm*, Cairo, 1954.

Rosenvasser, A., The stela Aksha 505 and the cult of Ramesses II as a god in the army, *Revista del Instituto de Historia Antigua Oriental* 1 (1972), 99–114.

Saad, Z. [Saʿd, Z.], Khazza Lawizza, *Annales du Service des Antiquités de l'Égypte* 37 (1937), 212–218.

Saad, Z. [Saʿd, Z.], *Royal excavations at Saqqara and Helwan (1941–1945)*, Cairo, 1947.

Saad, Z. [Saʿd, Z.], *Royal excavations at Helwan (1945–1947)*, Cairo, 1951.

Saady, H. [Saʿdī, H.], *Ḥukkām al-aqālīm fī Miṣr al-Firʿawniyya: dirāsa fī tārīkh al-aqālīm ḥattā nihāyat al-dawlat al-wusṭā*, Alexandria, 1991.

Saady, H. [Saʿdī, H.], Āthār Sītī al-Awwal = The monuments of Sety *I*, Alexandria, 2005.

Sadek, A.F. [Ṣādiq, A.], *Contribution à l'étude de l'Amdouat: les variantes tardives du Livre de l'Amdouat dans les papyrus du Musée du Caire*. Orbis Biblicus et Orientalis 65, Freiburg, Göttingen, 1985.

Sadek, A.F. [Ṣādiq, A.], Le plafond astronomique du Ramesseum, *Memnonia* 1 (1990–1991), 135–141.

Sadek, A.F. [Ṣādiq, A.], and J. Černý, *Graffiti de la montagne thébaine III–IV*. Collection scientifique 15, 17, 20, 21, Cairo, 1970–79.

El-Saeed, E., E. Mahfouz, and A. Megahed (eds), *The Festschrift volume: a collection of studies presented to Professor Abdel Monem Abdel Haleem Sayed, Emeritus Prof. of Ancient History and Archaeology, Faculty of Arts – University of Alexandria (Egyptian pioneer of the archaeological studies of the Red Sea) by his European and American colleagues and friends on the occasion of his 80th birthday*, Alexandria, 2006.

Said, L. [Saʿīd, L.], *Kamal wa-Yūsuf: athariyan min al-zaman al-jamīl*, Cairo, 2002.

Saleh, A. [Ṣāliḥ, A.], *Dirāsāt fī al-tārīkh al-ḥaḍārī li-Miṣr al-qadīma*, Cairo, 1958.

Saleh, A. [Ṣāliḥ, A.], Qiṣṣat al-dīn fī Miṣr Miṣr al-qadīmah Manṭiq al-taʾlīh, *al-Majjalla* 23 (1958), 36–56.

Saleh, A. [Ṣāliḥ, A.], *Ḥaḍārat Miṣr al-qadīma wa-āthāruhā*, Cairo, 1962.

Saleh, A. [Ṣāliḥ, A.], *al-Tarbiya wa al-taʿlīm fī Miṣr al-qadīma*, Cairo, 1966.

Saleh, A. [Ṣāliḥ, A.], Excavations around Mycerinus pyramid complex, *Mitteilungen des Deutschen Archäologischen Instituts, Abteilung Kairo* 30 (1974), 131–154.

Saleh, A. [Ṣāliḥ, A.], *al-Sharq al-Adnā al-qadīm*, Part I, *Miṣr wa al-ʿIrāq*, Cairo, 1976.

Saleh, A. [Ṣāliḥ, A.], Notes on the phonetic values of some Egyptian letters, in Reineke, W.F. (ed.), *Acts: First International Congress of Egyptology, Cairo October 2–10, 1976*. Schriften zur Geschichte and Kultur des Alten Orients 14, Berlin, 1979, 557–564.

Saleh, A. [Ṣāliḥ, A.], *Excavations at Heliopolis: ancient Egyptian Ounu*, 2 vols., Cairo, 1980.

Saleh, A. [Ṣāliḥ, A.], Between teachers and pupils in Pharaonic Egypt, *Bulletin de l'Institut d'Égypte* 60 (1987), 207–241.

Saleh, A. [Ṣāliḥ, A.], *Al-Usra al-Miṣriyya fī ʿuṣūrihā al-qadīma*, Cairo, 1988.

Saleh, M. [Ṣāliḥ, M.], *Three Old Kingdom tombs at Thebes. I, The tomb of Unas-Ankh no. 413. II, The tomb of Khenty no. 405. III, The tomb of Ihy no. 186*, Mainz, 1974.

Saleh, M. [Ṣāliḥ, M.], The tomb of the royal scribe Qen-Amun at Khokha (Theban necropolis no. 412), *Annales du Service des Antiquités de l'Égypte* 69 (1983), 15–28.

Saleh, M. [Ṣāliḥ, M.], *Das Totenbuch in den thebanischen Beamtengräbern des Neuen Reiches: Texte und Vignetten*, Mainz, 1988.

Sayed, A. [Sayyid, A.], Discovery of the site of the 12th dynasty port at Wadi Gawasis on the Red Sea shore, *Revue d'Égyptologie* 29 (1977), 140–178.

Sayed, A. [Sayyid, A.], *Al-Baḥr al-Aḥmar wa-ẓahīruhu fī al-ʿusūr al-qadīma: majmūʿat buḥūth nushirat fī al-dawriyyāt al-ʿArabiyya wa-al-Urubiyya*, Alexandria, 1993.

Sayed, A. [Sayyid, A.], Muḥāwala li-taḥdīd mawqiʿ Būnt, *Archaeological and historical studies, Alexandria* 5 (1974), 5–34.

Sayed, A. [Sayyid, A.], On the geographical location of the Land of Punt, in Győry, H. (ed.), *Aegyptus et Pannonia II: Acta symposii anno 2002*, Budapest, 2005, 203–237.

Sayed, T. [Sayyid, T.], Aton studies, *Mitteilungen des Deutschen Archäologischen Instituts, Abteilung Kairo* 29 (1973), 77–86.

Sayed, T. [Sayyid, T.], *Maʿālim tārīkh wa-ḥaḍārat Miṣr min aqdam al-ʿuṣūr ḥattā al-fatḥ al-ʿArabī*, Cairo, 1980.

Sayed, T. [Sayyid, T.], *Maʿālim tārīkh wa-ḥaḍārat Miṣr al-firʿawniyya*, Cairo, 1984.

Sayed, T. [Sayyid, T.], *Tārīkh al-fann fī al-Sharq al-Adnā al-qadīm, Miṣr wa-al-ʿIrāq*, Cairo, 1987.

Sayed, T. [Sayyid, T.], Tārīkh al-ʿimāra fī Miṣr al-qadīma (al-Uqṣur), Cairo, 1990.

Sayed, T. [Sayyid, T.], Recently excavated Ramesside tombs at Saqqara. I: Architecture, *Mitteilungen des Deutschen Archäologischen Instituts, Abteilung Kairo* 47 (1990), 403–409.

Selim, H. [Salīm, H.], Two royal statue bases from Karnak in the basement of the Egyptian Museum in Cairo, *Bulletin de l'Institut Français d'Archéologie Orientale* 111 (2011), 324–334.

Selim, H. [Salīm, H.], Three unpublished naophorous statues from Cairo Museum, *Mitteilungen des Deutschen Archäologischen Instituts, Abteilung Kairo* 60 (2004), 159–170.

Shehab al-Din, T., Ancient Egyptian proverbs, *Annales du Service des Antiquités de l'Égypte* 76 (2001), 157–171.

Shehab al-Din, T., The terms 'village' and 'town' in ancient Egypt and its conformity with the modern Egyptian concept, *Annales du Service des Antiquités de l'Égypte* 76 (2001), 173–178.

Al-Shohoumi, N., Burying the dead – vivifying the past: reflections on ancient Egyptian funerary rites and their parallels in modern Egypt, in Wendrich, W. and G. van der Kooij (eds.) *Moving matters, ethnoarchaeology in the Near East: proceedings of the International Seminar held at Cairo, 7–10 December 1988*, Leiden, 2002, 179–213.

Al-Shohoumi, N., *Der Tod im Leben: Eine vergleichende Analyse altägyptischer und rezenter ägyptischer Totenbräuche*, Vienna, 2004.

Tallet, P. *Les papyrus de la mer Rouge I: Le "journal de Merer" (Papyrus Jarf A et B)*. Mémoires publiés par les membres de l'Institut français d'archéologie orientale 136, Cairo, 2017.

Trad, M. [Ṭarrād, M.], Varia Musée du Caire, I: Journal d'Entrée et Catalogue Général, *Annales du Service des Antiquités de l'Égypte* 70 (1984–85), 352–357.

Trad, M. [Ṭarrād, M.], The sequence of the artist's strokes on a sherd from Hierakonpolis, in Friedman, R., and B. Adams (eds), *The followers of Horus: studies dedicated to Michael Allen Hoffman*, Oxford, 1992, 65–68.

Trad, M. [Ṭarrād, M.], "Given life again", in Eldamaty, M., and M. Trad (eds), *Egyptian museum collections around the world, vol. 2*, Cairo, 2002, 1167–1171.

Trad, M. [Ṭarrād, M.], The false-door stele of Ḥesi, in Grimal, N., A. Kamel, and C. May-Sheikholeslami (eds), *Hommages à Fayza Haikal*. Bibliothèque d'Étude 138, Cairo, 2003, 285–288.

Trad, M. [Ṭarrād, M.], M. el Halwagy, La tumba "Galarza", in Die, P., M. Carmen and W. al-Sadiik (eds), *120 años de arqueología española en Egipto*, [Madrid], 2009, 34–35 and 302.

3

Historiography of Pre-Islamic Arabia: Arab Scholars and Their Contributions to the Writing of the History of Ancient Yemen

Mohammed Maraqten

1 Introduction

Our knowledge of pre-Islamic Arabia, and in particular Yemen, has been completely transformed in the last four decades. The primary sources for writing the history of pre-Islamic Arabia, and in particular Yemen, are the pre-Islamic ancient North Arabian (Safaitic, Thamudic, Dadanic-Lihyanite, etc.),[1] and South Arabian (Sabaic, Qatabanic, Minaic, etc.) inscriptions as well as the archaeological discoveries.[2] Tens of thousands of these inscriptions have been discovered all over Arabia. More than 15,000 ancient South Arabian inscriptions have been discovered, primarily in Yemen,[3] among them the newly discovered minuscule texts (*zabūr*) written on palm leaf stalks.[4] These are the *Werkzeug* of the historian of ancient Yemen.

This chapter aims to introduce the works of the Arab scholars who have made distinguished contributions to the historiography of pre-Islamic South Arabia using the archaeological and epigraphic sources.[5] It draws attention to the significance of the Arabic language studies on the epigraphy and archaeology of ancient South Arabia. Further, this study will attempt to relate key elements of the history of pre-Islamic Arabia to the epigraphic sources of Southern Arabia and evaluate how modern Arab historians are dealing with these issues.

An assessment of the modern Arabic scholarship on ancient Yemen must include a critical evaluation of the contributions. A focus on some significant

---

1   Online Corpus of the Inscriptions of Ancient North Arabia: http://krc.orient.ox.ac.uk/ociana/index.php.

2   Simpson, *Queen of Sheba*.

3   Corpus of South Arabian Inscriptions: http://csai.humnet.unipi.it.

4   Maraqten, *Altsüdarabische Texte auf Holzstäbchen*.

5   Note that the Arabic transliteration system used for this chapter is that of the *Deutsche Morgenländische Gesellschaft* (DMG) as this is the standard transliteration system used by all scholars of South Arabian epigraphy including those in the English-speaking countries.

contributions will be offered. Furthermore, this paper will review the results of more than four decades of archaeological research in Arabia that have greatly changed our historical and linguistic knowledge of the region. The topics to be covered are as follows:

- Ancient Civilizations in Yemen: An Outline
- Archaeological Discoveries: The Contribution of Arab Scholarship
- Editing Ancient South Arabian Inscriptions
- Epigraphy and Writing the History of Ancient Yemen
- The Methodologies of Modern Arab Historians and an Assessment of their Contributions on Ancient Yemen

2   Ancient Civilizations in Yemen: An Outline

The contribution of the Arabian Peninsula, and in particular ancient Yemen, to World History cannot be overlooked.[6] Evidence from archaeological discoveries proves the major significance of ancient Yemen as a high culture in the ancient Near East. Ancient Yemen played an important role not only in creating cultural notions which partly impacted the emergence of Islam, but also as a mediator of merchandise and cultural trends between India and the Mediterranean World.[7] Events in Arabia in Late Antiquity and during the emergence of Islam, which developed in Arabia proper within the context of Late Antiquity, changed the face of the Ancient World.[8]

In ancient South Arabia (corresponding to modern-day Yemen) four major kingdoms existed during the period from at least the beginning of the first millennium BCE to the eve of Islam in the seventh century CE. These are Saba', Ma'īn, Qataban and Hadramawt.[9] Our knowledge of these cultures can only be obtained from the epigraphic evidence since no literary records in book form from ancient Yemen have survived. Ancient South Arabian (ASA) is a general term applied to four different languages, namely Sabaic, Qatabanic, Minaic and Hadramitic. Minaic is also designated by some scholars as Madhābic, from Wadi Madhāb in the Yemeni Jawf. There are also other languages, such as Awsanite, spoken in the kingdom of Awsān in Wadi Markha.[10]

---

6   There are several general works on the ancient civilizations in Yemen, see instance Simpson, *Queen of Sheba* and *al-Mawsū'a al-Yamanīya*.

7   Fisher, *Arabs and Empires before Islam*.

8   Al-Azmeh, *The Emergence of Islam in Late Antiquity*.

9   Simpson, *Queen of Sheba*.

10   Robin, Before Himyar: Epigraphic Evidence for the Kingdoms of South Arabia, 90–126.

The major ancient South Arabian languages or dialects are designated on the basis of a list of the four most important peoples (*ethnē*) of ancient South Arabia, namely, the Sabaeans, the Qatabanians, the Minaeans and the Hadramites, by the Greek geographer Eratosthenes (third century BCE). These languages are related to the major South Arabian kingdoms, namely Saba', Maʿīn, Qataban and Hadramawt. Some scholars refer to these languages as Epigraphic South Arabian, others as Old South Arabian, or sometimes as Ṣayhadic in reference to the Ṣayhad desert around the Empty Quarter, as it has been called by the classical Arabic authors.[11] Yemeni scholars called the ancient South Arabian language group the "ancient Yemeni language" and the texts "Yemeni inscriptions".[12]

Sabaic is the major language and the most well-attested in inscriptions. Three main phases of the languages of ancient South Arabian linguistic history are recognized. These are: Early Sabaic (tenth century to second century BCE), Middle Sabaic (first century BCE to the middle of the fourth century CE) and Late Sabaic (middle of the fourth century CE to the eve of Islam).[13] Two scripts have been used for writing the languages of ancient Yemen, namely *musnad* and *zabūr*. The linguistic phases correspond to the phases of the monumental *musnad* and the minuscule *zabūr* scripts.[14] These two scripts have been the standard scripts for writing thousands of ASA inscriptions which transmitted South Arabian cultural content all over ancient South Arabia throughout its ancient history.[15]

3   Archaeological Discoveries: The Contribution of Arab Scholarship

3.1   *Notes on the History of Research: Travelers and International Missions*

Evidence from archaeological discoveries proves the great importance of ancient Yemen as a high culture in the ancient Near East and our knowledge of pre-Islamic Arabia has been changed drastically in the last four decades through these discoveries.[16] Yemen is one of the most difficult countries for archaeological work and Yemeni studies have been largely neglected by many orientalists. Several western travelers and researchers carried out journeys to

---

11   Nebes and Stein, Ancient South Arabian, 145–178.

12   Bāfaqīh et al., *Muḫtārāt min an-nuqūš an-yamanīya al-qadīma.*

13   Robin, Before Himyar: Epigraphic Evidence for the Kingdoms of South Arabia, 90–126.

14   Maraqten, *Altsüdarabische Texte auf Holzstäbchen*, 41–56.

15   CSAI – Database: *Corpus of South Arabian Inscriptions*: http://csai.humnet.unipi.it.

16   Simpson, *Queen of Sheba.*

Yemen in the nineteenth century. Some of those travelers disappeared or were killed in Yemen.[17] However, today western researchers are much respected among Yemenis.

Since the time of Carsten Niebuhr (1733–1815) who directed the Danish expedition to Arabia (1761–1767),[18] numerous European travelers undertook expeditions to Yemen, among them the German Ulrich Jasper Seetzen (1767–1811) who traveled in several Arab countries, including Yemen, and was the first person to bring some of the South Arabian inscriptions to Europe. Seetzen disappeared in the area of Taʿizz.[19]

With the decipherment of the ancient South Arabian script by Wilhelm Gesenius (1786–1842) and Emil Rödiger (1801–1874), the discipline of ancient South Arabian studies began in Europe.[20] The Austrian traveler and scholar Edward Glaser (1855–1908) was one of the esteemed travelers who collected inscriptions in original form and squeezes and sent them to the European museums.[21] More than two thousand inscriptions bear the siglum of his name.[22]

Little has been written by modern Arab scholars on the history of research in Yemen. An exception is Bāfaqīh's study on the Swedish scholar Landberg and his scientific activities in Yemen.[23]

Archaeological research in Yemen has been organized and carried out by several Western archaeological institutions and missions since the 1970s. Archaeological investigations have been primarily carried out by the German Archaeological Institute (DAI), the French Archaeological Mission in the Republic of Yemen, and the Italian Archaeological Mission in the Republic of Yemen, as well as the American Foundation for the Study of Man (AFSM). DAI (Deutsches Archäologisches Institut – Section Ṣanʿāʾ) concentrated on the oasis of Maʾrib. Significant discoveries have been published by the DAI in several monographs (Archäologische Berichte aus dem Yemen vols. I–XIV).[24] The

---

17 Von Wissman, *Arabien. Dokumente zur Entdeckungsgeschichte.*

18 Niebuhr, *Reisebeschreibung nach Arabien und anderen umliegenden Ländern.*

19 Nebes, Ulrich Jasper Seetzen im Jemen, 39–52.

20 Gesenius, Himjaritische Sprache und Schrift, 369–399.

21 See the digitalized squeezes of the Glaser Collection: http://glaser.acdh.oeaw.ac.at/#/.

22 Dostal, *Eduard Glaser: Forschungen im Yemen*; Müller, Der böhmische Südarabienreisende Eduard Glaser, 195–220.

23 Bafaqīh, *Al-Mustašriqūn wa-āṯār al-Yaman.*

24 On the archaeological and epigraphic discoveries in Yemen, see Müller, *Südarabien im Altertum.* This volume contains a select bibliography of the international contributions on the ancient civilizations of South Arabia from 1973 to 2011. Some Arabic contributions are mentioned in this bibliography. For earlier studies see the general bibliography of Chr. Robin, *Bibliographie générale systématique,* which contains the bibliographic data relating to ancient Yemen until the middle of the 1970s.

AFSM carried out excavations in Wadī Bayḥān and at Awām temple/Maḥram Bilqīs (1950–52), in the 1980s at Wadī al-Jūba, south of Maʾrib, and again at the Awām temple/Maḥram Bilqīs (1998–2006).[25]

3.2   *Arab Scholars and Their Contributions to the Field*

3.2.1   Arab Scientific Expeditions to Yemen

After the journey of the Austrian E. Glaser to Maʾrib in 1888, no other European travelers were able to visit Maʾrib for a long time.[26] However, the Syrian traveler Nazīh Muʾayyad al-ʿAẓm (1890–1977) who had visited Yemen already in 1927, was able to visit Maʾrib in 1936. This was the first scientific visit to Maʾrib after Glaser. Al-ʿAẓm's visit was in arrangement with Imām Yaḥyā (1869–1948) and he was accompanied by the Imam's soldiers. Al-ʿAẓm visited the remains of the old of city of Maʾrib, the Great Dam, and the Awām temple/Maḥram Bilqīs and took the first photographs of them. He made also some sketches of the Great Dam and copied some inscriptions engraved around the exterior wall of the Awām temple/Maḥram Bilqīs, among them parts of the inscription Ja 555. Further, he copied two inscriptions from Wadi Dhana published by G. Ryckmans (RES 5099+RES 5098 = Ry 350+Ry 351).[27]

The first Arab archaeological activity in Arabia was the scientific expedition of Cairo University to Yemen in 1936 under the direction of the Egyptian scholars Sulaymān Aḥmad Ḥuzayyin (1909–99), Ḫalil Yaḥyā Nāmī, Naṣr Šukrī and Muḥammad Tawfīq al-Dasūqī.[28] Meanwhile, the first Arabic language contribution to the publication of ancient South Arabian inscriptions was carried out by the Egyptian scholar Ḫalīl Yaḥyā Nāmī, who had joined the Egyptian archaeological expedition that was sent to Yemen by the University of Cairo in 1936 and directed by Ḥuzzayin. Nāmī recorded during this expedition 64 inscriptions from the Taʿizz area and 79 inscriptions primarily from Naʿiṭ, north of Ṣanʿāʾ. Nāmī selected a good collection of inscriptions that he discovered and submitted them as a PhD thesis that was published in 1943.[29]

In 1943 Muḥammad Tawfīq al-Dasūqī was invited by the Yemeni government to prevent locust attacks in the country. During his work in the Yemeni Jawf (1943–45), he visited the archaeological sites there and made the first accurate

---

25   Maraqten, Sacred spaces in ancient Yemen – The Awām Temple, Maʾrib, 109–135.

26   Müller, Der böhmische Südarabienreisende Eduard Glaser, 195–220.

27   Al-ʿAẓm, *Rila fī bilād al-ʿArabīya as-Saʿīda*; Glanzman, Clarifying the Record: the Bayt ʾAwwam Revisited, 73–88.

28   Ḥuzayyin, *Baʿtat al-ǧāmiʿa al-miṣrīya ilā l-Yaman wa-Ḥaḍramawt*.

29   Namī, *Našr nuqūš sāmīya qadīma min ǧanūb Ǧazīrat al-ʿArab*.

scientific documentation of the archaeology of the Jawf.[30] The Minaic inscriptions that he documented were published by Nāmī in a separate volume.[31]

In December 1951 the Egyptian Ministry of Education organized an expedition which was sent to Ṣanʿāʾ to document and gather Arabic manuscripts. This Egyptian delegation was led by Fuʾād Sayyid ʿImāra, the head of the Arabic manuscripts division in the Egyptian National Library. The Egyptians arrived at ʿAdan on their way to Ṣanʿāʾ to microfilm Yemeni manuscripts. They were received in Taʿizz by Imam Aḥmad and the Foreign Minister Qadi al-ʿAmrī and then flew to Ṣanʿāʾ, where they had access to the Western Library of the Great Mosque. They were able to microfilm about 300 manuscripts, including some of the collections of the former Imam Yaḥyā and other private collections. The expedition published an important bibliographic volume.[32]

The Egyptian archaeologist Aḥmed Fakhry (1905–73) undertook a scientific journey to Yemen and carried out research visits to Ṣirwāḥ, Maʾrib and the Jawf in 1947 with further journeys in 1948 and 1959.[33] He made an archaeological description of the sites and copied 136 inscriptions, of which 120 were previously unknown.[34]

The inscriptions copied by A. Fakhry have been published by G. Ryckmans.[35] Fakhry visited Maʾrib in 1947 and was aware of the previous work at the Awām temple/Maḥram Bilqī, especially that of E. Glaser. He made a description of the Maḥram Bilqīs and a plan sketch and copied more inscriptions, among them CIH 375 (= Ja 555), and made a sketch of the temple as well. Fakhry took additional photographs of the demolition of various archaeological structures in the Maʾrib oasis and especially at the Awām temple/Maḥram Bilqīs. This demolition was carried out by the governor of Maʾrib for construction of the new government building in the Old City of Maʾrib.[36] Fakhry summarized his archaeological journey in several articles, book chapters and two books, one in English (three vols.) and the other in Arabic.[37] Of importance is his article about his discovery of a hitherto unknown major Sabaean temple al-Masāǧid (ancient Ḏū-Maʿarabum) in Wadī al-Jūba south of Maʾrib.[38]

---

30   Tawfīq, *Āṯār Maʿīn fī Ǧawf al-Yaman.*

31   Nāmī, *Nuqūš ḥirbat Maʿīn.*

32   Nāmī. *Al-Baʿṯa al-miṣrīya.*

33   On the archaeological journeys of Ahmad Fakhry to Yemen see al-Ḫaṭīb, *Nuṣūṣ al-ḫaṭṭ al-musnad min al-Yaman,* 12–202.

34   Fakhry, *An Archaeological Journey to Yemen* (March–May, 1947).

35   Ryckmans, G. Epigraphical Texts, in Fakhry, *An Archaeological Journey to Yemen.*

36   Fakhry, *An Archaeological Journey to Yemen* (March–May, 1947).

37   Faḫrī, *Al-Yaman: Māḍīhā wa-ḥāḍrihā.*

38   Faḫrī, A. Aḥdaṯ al-iktišāfāt al-aṯarīya fī l-Yaman.

3.2.2   The Contributions of Arab Archaeologists to Ancient Yemeni
         Studies: Archaeological Surveys and Excavations

Archaeological excavations have been carried out in Yemen primarily by international missions and a few small excavations have been accomplished by Yemeni archaeologists.[39] The GOAM (the General Organization of Antiquities and Museums in Yemen) has conducted many regional archaeological surveys throughout the country although most of the reports are not published. However, some of the results have been published in short studies. It is worth noting that several Yemeni MA and PhD theses using have been based on the results of archaeological surveys which the students carried out from their own funds.

There are some solid MA theses that have been written at Ṣanʿāʾ University, especially those which depended on fieldwork in specific areas or archaeological sites where archaeological and epigraphic discoveries were studied. Among them is the thesis of M.A. Bāsalāma on Shibām al-Ġirās to the northeast of Ṣanʿāʾ.[40] Several studies were written on specific regions such as the archaeology of al-Yamānīyatayn south of Ṣanʿāʾ.[41] There are also an archaeological study based on the results of a survey in the area of al-Kasr in Wādī Hadramawt,[42] a study about the antiquities of Wādī Ġirdān,[43] another on archaeological investigations in the area of Al-ʿAwāliq,[44] an archaeological study dealing with Wādī Ḍahr, near Ṣanʿāʾ,[45] and a very good archaeological and epigraphic study based on a survey in the region of Hamdan, specifically in the area of the local kingdom of Suʿay.[46] Archaeological surveys have been carried out in the area of al-Maʿāfir, south of Taʿizz.[47] Another archaeological survey concentrated on the ancient port of al-Sawā located in the district of Sharʿab, in the governorate of Taʿizz.[48]

A study has been carried out on the ancient port of Qanā (today Bīr ʿAlī) which is located on the Indian Ocean coast, east of ʿAdan. It was the main port for the incense route which started in Qanā and ended in Gaza.[49] This

---

39   See *Ḥawlīyat al-āṯār al-yamanīya*, vol. 1, 2008 and vol. 2, 2009.

40   Bāsalāmah, *Šibām al-Ġirās*.

41   Rawḍān, *Al-Yamānīyatain*.

42   Rubāʿ, Manṭiqat al-kasr fī Wādī Ḥaḍramawt.

43   As-Sadla, *Wādī Ġirdān*.

44   Al-Baʿsī, *Mustawṭanāt awdiyat kūr al-ʿAwāliq*.

45   Al-Bakīr, *Āṯār wādī ḍahr at-tārīḫīya*.

46   Aḥsan, *Ittiḥād sumʿay: aṯ-ṯulṯ ḥumlān*.

47   Al-Ġawrī, *Al-Maʿāfir al-ġarbīya*; Ḥamīd, *Dirāsa lil-mawāqiʿ al-qadīma fī manṭiqatay qadas-sāmiʿ*.

48   Al-Šarʿabī, *Al-Sawā*.

49   Aš-Šarʿabī, *Mīnāʾ Qanā ʿalā al-baḥr al-ʿarabī*.

route passed through many caravan trade stations such as the Hadrami capital Shabwa, the Qatabanian capital Timna', the Sabaean metropolis Ma'rib, the Minaean cities of Yaṯul (Baraqish), Qarnāw (modern Kharibat Ma'īn), and Najran, several other caravan stations in Central and Northern Arabia, followed by Petra before terminating in Gaza.[50]

Only a small amount of work has been done by Arab scholars on the study of burial customs in Yemen. A royal tomb was excavated by GOAM near the Himyarite capital of Ẓafār and published.[51] The results of a GOAM excavation at the site al-Ḥiṣma in the district of Abyan, east of 'Adan, were the subject of an MA thesis at Ṣan'ā' University which was published.[52] Al-Ḥusaynī has written a solid dissertation on landscape archaeology.[53]

Of special importance is the site of Qaryat Dhāt Kāhilum (*qryt ḏt khlm*), today Qaryat al-Faw, which was the royal headquarters of the kingdom of Kindah and which is located in Wādī ad-Dawāsir (today in Saudi Arabia). This site was excavated by King Saud University, Riyadh, under the direction of A. Al-Ansārī beginning in the early 1970s.[54]

4 Editing Ancient South Arabian Inscriptions

4.1 *Ancient South Arabian Languages* (ASA)

Egyptian, Syrian, Palestinian, Jordanian, Iraqi, Saudi and Yemeni scholars have all contributed to the field of South Arabian epigraphy. There is still no comprehensive grammar of ancient South Arabic written in Arabic for Arabic-speaking learners. However, there is an Arabic translation of A.F.L. Beeston's *Sabaic Grammar*, which is widely used,[55] while the chrestomathy written by Bāfaqīh and others serves as a useful guide for students and specialists.[56] Another essential tool for the field is the English–French–Arabic *Sabaic Dictionary*.[57]

---

50   Several Arabic studies were achieved on incense trade and the incense trade route, see Abd al-Mawlā, *Tiǧārat al-baḫḫūr fī ǧanūb šibh al-Ǧazīra al-'Arabīya*.

51   See Al-'Ansī, *al-Qabr al-malakī*.

52   Al-Ḥusaynī, *Ṭuruq ad-dafn wal-aṯāṯ al-ǧanā'izī fī l-Yaman*.

53   Al-Ḥusaynī, *Al-Ḥawāǧiz al-ǧidārīya fī l-manāṭiq al-maftūḥa fī l-Yaman al-qadīm*.

54   Final results of the excavations are not yet published, see the general book on this site of al-Anṣārī, *Qaryat al-Fau*.

55   Beeston, *Sabaic Grammar*; two translations of this book have been made, see Bīston, *Al-Qawā'id as-saba'īya* and Bīston, *Qawā'id al-luġa al-'arabīya al-ǧanūbīya*.

56   Bāfaqīh et al., *Muḫtārāt min an-nuqūš al-yamanīya al-qadīma*; Isma'īl, *Al-Luġa al-yamanīya al-qadīma*. This book is based primarily on the Bāfaqīh et al., *Muḫtārāt* and not on the corpus of the texts.

57   Beeston et al., *Sabaic Dictionary*.

A pioneering work for studying the relation between Classical Arabic and the language of the ancient South Arabian inscriptions has been written by M. Ghul.[58] Further studies were carried out by I. Al-Selwi,[59] 'A. Miḫlāfī[60] and H.A.M. al-Hilālī.[61]

There are also some important studies on the Yemeni Arabic dialects, which are very important for understanding specific architectural and agricultural terms such as the vocabulary related to irrigation,[62] in addition to the agricultural seasons.[63] The main Arabic dictionary on this topic was written by M. al-ʾIryānī.[64] General and introductory studies on Yemeni dialects have been written by several scholars including M. Kāmil,[65] and A. Sharafaddīn.[66]

4.2 *Studying Ancient South Arabian Inscriptions*

ASA texts are primarily composed in four languages commonly called Sabaic, Minaic, Qatabanic, and Hadramitic. Thousands of ASA inscriptions have been discovered. This amount varies depending on whether one includes all categories of inscriptions and whether or not inscribed small objects such as seals and graffiti are considered. The inscriptions serving as sources for the study of the ASA language-family cover a period of about sixteen centuries from the beginning of the first millennium BCE until the sixth century CE.[67]

The editing of ancient South Arabian inscriptions started in the second half of the nineteenth century.[68] Around 10,000 inscriptions have now been published.[69] At present, the *Corpus of South Arabian Inscriptions* (CSAI) comprises approximately 7,500 texts digitized by the team of the University of Pisa guided by A. Avanzini. These inscriptions are now available online.[70]

Two types of ASA script are known, the so-called *musnad* or monumental script and the so-called *zabūr* or minuscule script. Both scripts seem to have been used for all ASA languages. The ASA alphabet has 29 graphemes, in contrast

---

58   Ghul, *Early Southern Arabian Languages and Classical Arabic Sources*.

59   Al-Selwi, *Jemenitische Wörter in den Werken von al-Hamdānī und Našwān*.

60   Al-Miḫlāfī, *al-Mansūb ilā lahaǧāt al-Yaman fī kutub at-turāṯ*.

61   Al-Hilālī, *Dalālat al-alfāẓ al-yamanīya fī baʿḍ al-muʿǧamāt al-ʿarabīya*.

62   Dādiyyah, *Alfāẓ al-zirāʿah war-ray*; Aš-Šamārī, *Lahǧat Ḥubān*.

63   Al-ʿAnsī, *Al-Maʿālim al-zirāʿiyya fī l-Yaman*.

64   Al-Iryānī, *Al-Muʿǧam al-yamanī fī l-luǧa wat-turāṯ*.

65   Kāmil. *Al-Lahaǧāt al-ʿArabiyya al-ḥadīṯa fī l-Yaman*.

66   Šarafaddīn, *Lahaǧāt al-Yaman qadīman wa-ḥadīthan*.

67   http://dasi.humnet.unipi.it/index.php?id=42&prjId=1&corId=0&colId=0&navId=0.

68   On the history of research of the ancient South Arabian inscriptions see Leslau, Ethiopic and South *Arabian*, 467–527.

69   See Robin, *Bibliographie générale systématique* and Müller, *Südarabien im Altertum*.

70   http://dasi.humnet.unipi.it/index.php?id=42&prjId=1&corId=0&colId=0&navId=0.

with the limited repertoire of 22 letters found in the Northwest Semitic group of alphabets such Phoenician, Hebrew and Aramaic.[71] No Arabic contributions about the South Arabian script system or palaeography are available. However, a study on the South Arabian monograms, which are engraved in association with the inscriptions, was written in Arabic.[72] The first Arabic publication of ancient South Arabian inscriptions was the dissertation of Ḥ.Y. Nāmī submitted to the Egyptian University (Cairo) and published in 1943.[73]

The Awām temple (modern folkloric name Māḥram Bilqīs) is one of the most important archaeological sites in Yemen. This extramuros temple was the national and the central Sabaean temple and is located about 3.5 km south of the ancient Sabaean capital at Ma'rib. It was excavated at the beginning of the 1950s by the AFSM. Excavations were resumed there by the AFSM in 1998. More than 800 Sabaean inscriptions were discovered at this site by the AFSM in 1950s,[74] and additional inscriptions were discovered by the AFSM during the most recent excavations inside this temple.

The temple was built by the Sabaeans at the edge of what is now Ramlat as-Sab'atayn desert, known as Ṣayhad in the Islamic sources. It was built around the time of the emergence of Sabaean culture around the beginning of the first millennium BCE. The temple, which was called by the Sabaeans ʾwm/Awām, was in use until the end of the fourth century CE. It was the main centre of worship for the Sabaean national deity, Almaqah, and hence doubtless the key focus of the concepts of sacred space and sacred time in ancient Yemen. This temple was not only the main pilgrimage place for the Sabaeans, similar to Mecca on the eve of Islam, but also the socioeconomic centre of the Sabaean kingdom.[75]

M. al-Iryāni published in 1973 (reprinted 1990) 34 inscriptions without photographs from Awām temple/Maḥram Bilqīs.[76] In the second edition of his book, the number of inscriptions was increased. Furthermore, al-Iryāni published several other inscriptions in separate articles.[77] The Yemeni scholar Z. ʿInān (1908–1992) was the representative for the Yemeni government during

---

71   Maraqten, *Altsüdarabische Texte auf Holzstäbchen*, 41–56.

72   Aš-Šarʿī, *Aṭ-Ṭaġrāʾ fī l-Yaman al-Qadīm*.

73   Nāmī, *Našr nuqūš sāmīya qadīma min ǧanūb Ǧazīrat al-ʿArab*.

74   Jamme, *Sabaean Inscriptions from Mahram Bilqīs*. Some of the archaeological and epigraphic results which the author as an epigrapher of the AFSM has documented at the Awām temple, Mahram Bilqīs, Yemen in 9 seasons (1998–2006) are summarized in Maraqten, Sacred spaces in ancient Yemen – The Awām Temple, Ma'rib, 109–135.

75   The majority of the Sabaic inscriptions discovered by the AFSM were published in Jamme, *Sabaean Inscriptions from Mahram Bilqīs*.

76   Al-Iryānī, *Fī tārīḫ al-Yaman. Nuqūš musnadīya wa-taʿlīqāt*.

77   Müller, *Südarabien im Altertum*.

the AFSM excavations at the Awām temple/ Maḥram Bilqīs from 1951 until 1952. ʿInān claims to have been personally responsible for the excavation.[78] He gathered some of the latex squeezes of the AFSM expedition and sent them to the Yemeni government. Some of these were kept in Taʿizz and others at the National Museum in Ṣanʿāʾ.[79] ʿInān copied about 200 inscriptions and published 80 in his work *Tārīḫ ḥaḍārat al-Yaman al-qadīm* (published 1976). Most of them had already been published by A. Jamme.[80]

The Yemeni government sent Ḥ.Y. Nāmī, who was a member of the Egyptian expedition for collecting Arabic manuscripts in Yemen (1951), to Maʾrib in March 1952 to check the work of the AFSM at Awām temple/Maḥram Bilqīs.[81] This was shortly after the AFSM left (February 1952) and it was possible for him to copy and photograph a few inscriptions that were still visible in the northeast side of the Peristyle Hall. Ḥ.Y. Nāmī published several inscriptions in a series of articles in *Maǧallat kulliyat al-ādāb* (Ǧamiʿat al-Qāhira).[82]

Aḥmad Šarafaddīn was the first Yemeni scholar who published ancient South Arabian inscriptions. He published a booklet in 1961[83] and a major work in 1966.[84] Sharafaddīn was a traditional historian and was not trained in epigraphy. However, he visited the Awām temple/Maḥram Bilqīs after the AFSM left the site and copied and photographed some inscriptions, which he published in his two books. It is not clear if he copied the inscriptions himself during a visit to the site or just used the copies of ʿInān, who mentions clearly that he gave the copies to Sharafaddīn.[85]

The recent archaeological activities of the AFSM served as a continuation of the efforts of the earlier Wendell Phillips expedition (1951–52). The nine seasons of excavations (1998–2006) carried out by the American Foundation for the Study of Man (AFSM) in the Awām complex, revealed more than 500 inscriptions that have shed new light on religious practices in the temple and surrounding area as well as on the cultural history of Yemen. This corpus now forms the largest and most important archive of ancient Yemen.[86]

---

78   ʿInān, *Tārīḫ ḥaḍārat al-Yaman al-qadīm*, 139f.

79   ʿInān, *Tārīḫ ḥaḍārat al-Yaman al-qadīm*, 140.

80   Jamme, *Sabaean Inscriptions from Mahram Bilqīs*.

81   Nāmī, *Al-Biʿta al-miṣrīya*.

82   See the inscriptions under the sigla Nāmī in Kitchen, *Documentation for Ancient Arabia*.

83   Sharafaddīn, *Yemen. Arabia Felix*.

84   *Taʾrīḫ al-Yaman al-ṯaqāfī*.

85   *Taʾrīḫ al-Yaman al-ṯaqāfī*.

86   Some of the archaeological and epigraphic results which the author as an epigrapher of the AFSM has documented at the Awām temple, Maḥram Bilqīs, Yemen in 9 seasons (1998–2006) are summarized in Maraqten, Sacred spaces in ancient Yemen – The Awām Temple, Maʾrib, 109–135.

One of the most significant recent findings in Yemen is the discovery of thousands of ancient South Arabian minuscule texts incised on wood, primarily palm-leaf stalks (ʿasīb, plural ʿusub) and ʿarʿar (juniper). Their provenance is the Yemeni Jawf, in particular the town of Al-Sawdāʾ, known in ancient times as Naššān. The inscriptions contain essential information about everyday life and the socioeconomic structure of ancient Yemen. They include documents related to daily life such as letters, contracts and transactions dating from the beginning of the first millennium BCE to the eve of Islam. The first discovery was at the beginning of the 1970s. The Palestinian scholar Maḥmūd ʿAlī Ghul was the first person to succeed in deciphering the minuscule script of these documents which is known in the Arabic tradition as the zabūr script.[87] The whole corpus of minuscule inscriptions contains about five thousand texts.

The Yemeni scholar Y.M. ʿAbdallāh was the first person to publish a document in miniscule script.[88] More than three thousand minuscule documents are stored in the National Museum of Ṣanʿāʾ. About one hundred minuscule texts from this collection have been published by the author of this study,[89] including some texts of this collection which were submitted as an MA dissertation to the University of Ṣanʿāʾ by the Yemeni student A. Faqʿaṣ.[90] It is urgent to continue the publication of this collection.

Among the best studies and editions by modern Arab scholars of the ancient South Arabian inscriptions are those written by Yūsuf Muḥammad ʿAbdallāh (University of Ṣanʿāʾ).[91] In addition to his popular book on the ancient history of Yemen,[92] he published several studies including an edition of an inscription of a solar hymn discovered in Wādī Qāniya, east of Ṣanʿāʾ, which is similar to the pre-Islamic Arabic poems.[93] There are some dissertations of Yemeni students which focus on the publication of recently discovered inscriptions. For instance a group of Sabaic texts from Khawlān were published by M. al-Salāmī in his dissertation[94] and another group of Sabaic texts were the topic of a PhD submitted to the University of Pisa.[95] Recently a collection of inscriptions from Khawlān has been published.[96] Furthermore, some studies were dedicated to

---

87   See Beeston. Mahmoud ʿAli Ghul and the Sabaean Cursive Script, 15–19.

88   See ʿAbdallāh, Ḥaṭṭ al-musnad wan-nuqūš al-yamaniyya al-qadīmah; Risāla min imraʾa bi-ḫaṭṭ az-zabūr.

89   Maraqten. Altsüdarabische Texte auf Holzstäbchen.

90   Faqʿas, Nuqūš ḫašabiyya bi-ḫaṭṭ az-zabūr.

91   Müller, Südarabien im Altertum.

92   ʿAbdallāh, Awrāq fī tārīḫ al-Yaman.

93   ʿAbdallāh, Naqš al-qaṣīda al-ḥimyariyya.

94   Al-Salami, Sabäische Inschriften aus dem Ḥawlān.

95   Noman, A Study of south Arabian Inscriptions from the region of Dhamār (Yemen).

96   Al-Hayyāl, Min nuqūš al-musnad fī Ḥawlān.

specific groups of inscriptions such as the inscriptions of the Yemen exhibit in Paris in 1997.[97]

Some work has also been done on architectural terminology in ancient Yemen. A dissertation from the University of Ṣanʿāʾ deals with architectural terms,[98] and another thesis has been written on the royal palaces.[99] There is also a general study on the architectural characteristics of the town in ancient Yemen.[100] Domestic architecture has received little attention so far.

Recently discovered Sabaic and Minaic inscriptions in the Yemeni Jawf have been published. These inscriptions are stored in the Yemen National Museum of Ṣanʿāʾ.[101] M. Bāfaqīh has made important contributions to the study of the Hadramitic and Qatabanic inscriptions.[102] An important edition of Qatabanic inscriptions has been published by a team of Yemeni scholars including M. Al-Ḥāǧǧ.[103]

Another important topic related to the field of ancient South Arabian inscriptions is the linguistic study of proper names. This sub-discipline deals with the ancient South Arabian onomastica and proper names of families, clans and tribes. Ancient South Arabian personal names were studied primarily by Arab students in Germany and in France. Y.M. Abdallāh published a comparative study of the personal and tribal names mentioned in the pre-Islamic inscriptions and in the works of the medieval Yemeni scholar al-Hamdānī.[104] Proper names have been studied and analyzed in a number of doctoral dissertations. For instance, early Sabaic personal names were studied by S. Tairan,[105] Minaic by names S. Al-Said,[106] Qatabanic names by H. Hayajneh[107] and ancient South Arabian women's names by A. Sholan.[108] A specific study of the onomastica of the CIH (The South Arabian portion of the *Corpus Inscriptionum Semiticarum*)

97   Bākarmum, *Nuqūš ʿarabiyya ǧanūbiyya qadīma min al-Yaman.*

98   Al-Aġbarī, *Muʿǧam al-alfāẓ al-miʿmāriyya.*

99   Al-Ḥāyir, *Al-Qaṣr fī l-Yaman al-qadīm.*

100   Ḥanšūr, *Al-Ḥaṣāʾiṣ al-miʿmāriyya lil-madīna al-yamaniyya al-qadīma.*

101   Arbach and Schiettecatte, *Catalogue des pièces archéologiques et épigraphiques du Jawf*; Arbach and Audouin, *Collection of epigraphic and archaeological artifacts*; Arbach, Schiettecatte and al-Hādī, *Collection of Funerary Stelae from the Jawf Valley*. These three volumes are written in English and Arabic.

102   See Bāfaqīh, *Āṯār wa-nuqūš al-ʿUqla.*

103   Al-Ḥāǧǧ, *Nuqūš qatabāniyya min madīnat maryama.*

104   ʿAbdallāh, *Die Personennamen in al-Hamdānī's Iklīl.*

105   Tairan, *Die Personennamen in den altsabäischen Inschriften.*

106   Al-Said, *Die Personennamen in den minäischen Inschriften.*

107   Hayajneh, *Die Personennamen in den qatabānischen Inschriften.*

108   Sholan, *Frauennamen in den Altsüdarabischen Inschriften.*

was made by M. Arbach.[109] These researchers also wrote a few studies on this topic in Arabic.

5   Epigraphy and the Historiography of Ancient Yemen

5.1   *Natural Resources*
Little research has been done on the topic of natural resources in ancient Yemen. An MA thesis collected some data about this topic, which depending more or less on the work of A. Sima.[110] Natural catastrophes such as volcanic activities and floods which are recorded in inscriptions have received some attention from scholars.[111]

5.2   *Historical Geography: Toponomies and Tribes*
The study of the historical geography of Arabia in general, and specifically Yemen, still depends on the works of the medieval Yemeni scholars (tenth century CE) Abū Muḥammad al-Ḥasan al-Hamdānī[112] and Našwān al-Ḥimyarī.[113] The basic references for studying the tribal names and toponomies of Yemen are the works of M.A. al-Ḥaǧrī (1889–1960),[114] I.ʿA. al-Maqḥafī[115] and Ḥ.ʿA. Luqmān.[116]

No comprehensive studies on the tribes in the pre-Islamic period have yet been carried out, though some individual studies have been published.[117] There are studies on specific tribes such as Khawlān[118] and Ǧurat.[119] Another study has been written on the tribes of the Tihāma, which was known in the Sabaic inscriptions as Sahratān.[120] ʿA. Aš-Šayba wrote a dissertation on place names in the ancient South Arabian inscriptions. However, his work deals only

---

109   Arbach, *Les noms propres du corpus; Corpus Inscriptionum Semiticarum. Pars quarta: inscriptiones ḥimyariticas et sabœas continens.*

110   Al-Ǧāwīš, *Al-Mawārid aṭ-ṭabīʿya fī l-Yaman al-qadīm;* See also Sima, *Tiere, Pflanzen, Steine und Metalle in den altsüdarabischen Inschriften.*

111   Al-ʿAwīl, *Al-Aḫtār wal-kawārit fī l-Yaman al-qadīm.*

112   al-Hamdānī, *Ṣifat ǧazīrat al-ʿarab; Kitāb al-Iklīl* I, II, VIII, X.

113   Al-Ḥimyarī, *Šams al-ʿulūm wa-dawāʾ al-ʿarab.*

114   al-Ḥaǧrī, *Maǧmūʿ buldān al-Yaman wa-qabāʾilihā.*

115   Maqḥafī, *Muʿǧam al-buldān wal-qabāʾil al-yamanīya.*

116   Luqmān, *Tārīḫ al-Qabāʾil al-yamanīya.*

117   Mikyāš, *Asmāʾ al-qabāʾil fī an-nuqūš al-ʿarabīya al-ǧanūbīya;* Alsekaf, *La geographie tribale du Yemen antique.*

118   As-Salāmī, *Ḥawlān al-arḍ wal-qabīla fī l-maṣādir at-tārīḫiyya.*

119   An-Nāširī, *Ḏī Ǧurat wa-dawruhum fī ḥukm dawlat Sabaʾ.*

120   Wušāḥ, *Qabāʾil as-sahra.*

with the attestations and identification of the place names in the inscriptions and is not concerned with the etymological analysis of the names.[121]

Several studies have focused on specific cities such as the capitals of the ancient kingdoms of Yemen. Maraqten has written a case study on the capital of the Sabaean kingdom, Ma'rib. This study deals with the history of Ma'rib and includes an analysis of its administrative and social history in the light of the Sabaean inscriptions.[122] Another study is dedicated to the history of the city of Ṣanʿāʾ.[123] There are also studies on Ẓafār,[124] capital of the Himyarite kingdom, the Qatabanian capital of Timnaʿ,[125] and other ancient urban centers such as Baynūn[126] and Yaklāʾ (modern Naḥlat al-Ḥamrāʾ).[127]

5.3   *General History*

There are a few studies that deal with the general history of ancient Yemen.[128] Apart from Ǧ. ʿAlī's encyclopedic history of the Arabs before Islam, *al-Mufaṣṣal*, the first general history of ancient Yemen written by an Arab author in Arabic was by *Tārīḫ al-Yaman al-qadīm* by the Yemeni scholar Zayd ʿInān in 1949. This was followed by another important survey also entitled *Tārīḫ al-Yaman al-qadīm* by the Yemeni scholar M. Bāfaqīh.[129] A large number of MA and PhD theses written by Yemeni students deal with the general history of pre-Islamic Yemen, while others focus on particular historical issues or specific phases in the ancient history of Yemen. Unfortunately, several of these theses are meagre and depend exclusively on secondary literature rather than the primary sources. Some of the theses contain copies of inscriptions and inaccurate translations. Numerous studies have been written about the Kingdom of Sabaʾ. Several studies have been written about specific Sabaean dynasties such as the Hamdanite dynasty.[130] Some studies are concerned with specific periods such as the reigns of the kings of Sabaʾ and Ḏū-Raydān or the Himayarite epoch.[131]

---

121   Al-Sheiba, Die Ortsnamen in den altsüdarabischen Inschriften, 1–61.

122   Maraqṭan, *Al-ʿĀṣima as-sabaʾīya Maʾrib*.

123   Al-ʿArašī, *Ṣanʿāʾ al-qadīma*.

124   Al-Ḥakīm, *Madīnat Ẓafār*.

125   ʿAbdallāh, *Timnaʿ: Haǧar Kuḥlān*.

126   Ġānim, *Madīnat Baynūn*.

127   Al-Ḥayānī, *Madīnat Yaklāʾ "an-Naḥla al-ḥamrāʾ"*.

128   Abdallāh, *Awrāq fī tārīḫ al-Yaman*; Bafaqīh, *Tawḥīd al-Yaman al-qadīm*.

129   Bāfaqīh, *Fī l-ʿArabīya as-Saʿīda*; cf. also Abdallāh, *Awrāq fī tārīḫ al-Yaman* and Al-Anṣārī, *Al-Kitāb al-marǧiʿ fī tārīḫ al-umma al-ʿarabīya*.

130   Al-Qaylī, *Mamlakat Sabaʾ fī ʿahd al-usra al-hamdānīya*.

131   As-Saqqāf, *Mulūk Sabaʾ wa-ḏū-raydān wa-Ḥaḍramawt wa-yamanat*; as-Saqqāf, *Aḍwāʾ ǧadīda ʿalā t-tārīḫ. Tabābiʿat wa-mulūk al-Yaman*; Nāširī, ʿA. *Al-Yaman fī ʿaṣr mulūk Sabaʾ wa-ḏī raydān*.

The period of the Himyaritic kingdom has also attracted the attention of Arab researchers.[132] Only a few studies treat the Kingdom of Qataban.[133] There also studies that focus on specific social groups.[134]

Studies have also treated the political history of ancient Yemen covering topics such as the origin and the formation of the state[135] and the ancient political institutions.[136] The ancient Yemeni chiefdoms have received the attention of researchers.[137] An example is Nāṣir's study on the titles *Aḏwāʾ* and *Aqyāl* and the political powers associated with them.[138] There is also a dissertation that deals with the conflicts and rivalries between the different kingdoms of Southern Arabia.[139] Another historical study concerns the Tihāma during the rule of the kings of Sabaʾ and Ḏī-Raydān.[140]

5.4 *Social and Economic History*

There are several studies on the social and economic structures in ancient Yemen.[141] Al-ʿAzʿazī has written about the political structure of the Kingdom of Sabaʾ.[142] Two studies have been written about nomadism in ancient South Arabia based on the epigraphic evidence. The first of these is an MA thesis submitted to Ṣanʿāʾ University[143] and the other is a PhD thesis that was submitted to Ṭanta University (Egypt).[144] There are several studies on the structure of the tribes in modern Yemen which take into account their historical backgrounds.[145] ʿA. ʿAqīl has written about alliances in ancient Yemen.[146] The land-tenure system and private property in ancient Yemen was the topic of a thesis by Damāǧ.[147]

132　On the Himyarite kingdom, see the comprehensive study with a good bibliography of I. Gajda, *Le royaume de Himyar à l'époque monothéiste* and the PhD of al-Qaylī, *Al-Yaman fī ʿaṣr mulūk Sabaʾ wa-ḏī-raydān wa-Ḥaḍramawt wa-yamanat.*

133　See the genera study of Al-Ḍafīf. *Mamalakat Qatabān.*

134　Ḥabtūr, *Al-yazanīyūn.*

135　Maraqṭan, *Handasat ar-ray wa-dawruhā fī naśʾat ad-dawla.*

136　Baḥrī, *Taṭawwur nuẓum al-ḥukm fī l-Ǧazīra al-ʿArabīya.*

137　As-Sarīḥī, *Maqwalat Radmān wa-Ḥawlān.*

138　Nāṣir, *Al-Aḏwāʾ wal-aqyāl.*

139　ʿAṭbūš, *Aṣ-Ṣirāʿ bayna l-mamālik al-yamanīya al-qadīma.*

140　Wanas, *Tihāma wa-ʿalāqātuha bi-mamlakat Sabaʾ wa-Ḏī-Raydān.*

141　Al-Ḥamad, *Al-Aḥwāl al-iǧtimāʿīya wal-iqtiṣādīya fī l-Yaman;* ʿAbd al-Ġanī, *al-Ḥayāh al-iǧtimāʿīya fī l-Yaman al-qadīm.*

142　Al-ʿAzʿazī, *Dawlat sabaʾ wa-taṭawwurātihā as-siyāsīya.*

143　Al-Ašbaṭ, *Al-Aʿrāb fī tārīḫ al-Yaman al-qadīm.*

144　Rubāʿ, *Al-Aʿrāb fī an-nuqūš al-ʿarabīya al-ǧanūbīya.*

145　See for instance Abū Ġanim, *Al-Bunya l-qabalīya fī l-Yaman.*

146　ʿAqīl, *Al-Aḥlāf fī l-Yaman.*

147　Damāǧ, *Al-Milkīya fī l-Yaman al-qadīm.*

5.5 *Ancient Yemen and Her Neighbours*

Several studies have been written on the relations between the South Arabian kingdoms and neighboring lands. There are studies on relations between South and North Arabia,[148] between ancient Yemen and Bilād aš-Šām (Syria–Palestine),[149] as well as on the relations between Yemen and Abyssinia,[150] and Yemen's relations with the Greco-Roman World.[151] There is a good deal of information about the relations between the Arabian Peninsula and ancient Egypt.[152] One study has focused on the relations between ancient Arabia and Egypt in light of the ancient South Arabian inscriptions.[153] The kingdom of Maʿīn in the Yemeni Jawf has been the topic of several studies.[154]

5.6 *Daily Life*

The most important data about daily life in ancient Yemen, such as correspondence, contracts, and economic interactions is contained in the documents in minuscule script.[155] Theses have been written which deal with the subjects of clothing[156] and jewelry.[157]

5.7 *Legal Documents and Law*

More than four hundred legal documents recorded in monumental and minuscule scripts are known. Thus far, we lack a comprehensive study of the legal system in ancient South Arabia. A PhD dissertation on legal documents was submitted by N. Al-Naʿīm to King Saud University.[158] Al-Naʿīm collected most of the legal texts that were known before the year 2000. However, there are few translations and little analysis of the texts in this thesis. A comparative

---

148   Abū l-Ġayt, *Al-ʿAlāqāt as-siyāsiya.*

149   Maraqtan, Ḥawla al-ʿalāqāt mā bayna Bilād aš-Šām wal-Yaman fī ʿuṣūr mā qabla l-islām.

150   Al-Ašbaṭ, *Al-Aḥbāš fī tārīḫ al-Yaman al-qadīm.*

151   Al-Šuʿaybī, *Aṣ-Ṣilāt al-yūnānīya ar-rūmānīya bil-Yaman qabla l-islām*; Al-Ḥakīmī, *Malāmiḥ min al-ḥaḍāra al-klāsīkīya fī ḥaḍarat al-Yaman al-qadīm.*

152   Al-Sayyid, *Al-Baḥr al-Aḥmar wa-ẓahīruhu fī l-ʿuṣūr al-qadīma.*

153   Al-Sayyid, *Al-ʿAlāqāt al-ḥaḍārīya bayna l-Ǧazīra al-ʿArabīya wa-miṣr.*

154   ʿAbdallāh, *Mamlakat Maʿīn*; Aṯ-Ṭalāyā, *Mamlakat Maʿīn. Tārīḫ wa-ḥaḍara.*

155   ʿAbdallāh, Ḫaṭṭ al-musnad wan-nuqūš al-yamanīya al-qadīmah and Risāla min imraʾa bi-ḫaṭṭ az-zabūr; Maraqten, *Altsüdarabische Texte auf Holzstäbchen*; Faqʿas, *Nuqūš ḥašabīyah bi-ḫaṭṭ az-zabūr.*

156   Bāʿlaïyān, *Al-Malābis fī l-Yaman al-qadīm.*

157   Ṭayyib, *Al-Ḥulīy fī l-Yaman al-qadīm.*

158   An-Naʿīm, *At-Tašrīʿāt fī ǧanūb ġarb al-Ǧazīra al-ʿarabīya.* This work is a good collection of the legal texts until the year 1999 in ancient Yemen. However, dozens of texts have been published since that time in particular minuscule legal text, see for instance Maraqten, *Altsüdarabische Texte auf Holzstäbchen*, 121–132. Many of the translations of the text, which an-Naʿīm has suggested are not acceptable.

study between the Qatabanian legal system and the Aramaic legal documents of Hatra (in Iraq) has been written.[159]

5.8   *Agriculture and Irrigation Systems*

A PhD on the topic of agriculture in South Arabia has been furnished by F. al-Bārid.[160] Agricultural production has been treated in some university theses.[161] Several studies have been dedicated to irrigation systems and irrigated fields.[162] A solid study of irrigation depending on an archaeological survey has been carried out for the oasis of Ṣirwāḥ.[163]

Also of importance are some Yemeni studies on traditional agriculture and irrigation, such as the studies of Y. al-ʿAnsī which show that some agricultural terms known from the Sabaic inscriptions have survived into modern times.[164] Attention should be drawn to some significant early Islamic Yemeni texts on agriculture[165] and in particular the information from medieval Yemeni historical works such as those of Al-Hamdānī.[166] A modern study has been written on the Ghayls (water systems) of Ṣanʿāʾ.[167]

Of great importance are agricultural terms and the terms relating to irrigation in Yemeni dialects and oral traditions. Several studies have been written on this topic.[168] The main work on traditional water rights in Yemen is the study of Al-Maqṭarī.[169] A good MA thesis was written by Y.ʿA.Y. Dādiyya at ʿAdan University on the agricultural terms in the area of Ḍamār, south of Ṣanʿāʾ.[170]

5.9   *Trade and the Incense Road*

With the domestication of the camel in the second half of the second millennium BCE, international trade was established. The international incense route was active from at least the beginning of the first millennium BCE.[171]

---

159   Al-ʿAzʿazī, *At-Tašrīʿāt al-qatabāniyya al-ḥaḍāriyya.*

160   Al-Bārid, *Az-Zirāʿa fī ǧanūb ǧarb al-Ǧazīra al-ʿArabiyya.*

161   Damāǧ, *Al-Maḥāṣīl az-zirāʿiyya fī l-Yaman al-qadīm.*

162   Al-Bārid, *An-Nuqūš al-musnadiyya al-mutaʿalliqa bi-ʾalmāʾ*; Bāfaqīh, *Taqniyyāt anẓimat ar-ray fī mamlakatay Qatabān wa-Ḥaḍramawt.*

163   Ṭuʿaimān, *Anẓimat ar-ray fī wāḥat Ṣirwāḥ al-qadīma.*

164   Al-ʿAnsī, *Al-Maʿālim az-zirāʿiyya fī l-Yaman.*

165   *Milḥ al-malāḥa fī maʿrifat al-filāḥa.*

166   Al-Hamdānī, *Ṣifat ǧazīrat al-ʿarab; Kitāb al-Iklīl* I, II, VIII, X.

167   ʿAslān, *Ġuyūl Ṣanʿāʾ.*

168   Al-Ḥusaynī, *Muʿǧam al-muṣṭalaḥāt az-zirāʿiyya fī ʾalfāẓ al-lahǧa al-lahǧiyya.*

169   Maktari, *Water Rights and Irrigation Practices in Lahj.*

170   Dādīya, *Alfāẓ al-zirāʿah war-ray.*

171   Several studies have been achieved on the South Arabian trade, see Al-Malāʿiba, *Dawr mamālik šibh al-Ǧazīra al-ʿArabiyya fī at-tiǧāra ad-dawlīya.*

Several surveys of economic life in pre-Islamic Arabia have been written.[172] There are a number of studies focusing on the incense trade in particular.[173] One study is dedicated to the incense trade of the Kingdom of Hadramawt.[174] Important information has been published regarding South Arabian trade and diplomatic relations with Bilād aš-Šām.[175] There are also studies on the animals used for caravan trade such as camels.[176] Sea trade and the Yemeni seaports have also attracted the attention of scholars.[177]

Other specific topics such as the impact of the irrigation systems on the development and transformation of society and the emergence and formation of the state have been the subjects of studies.[178] Two studies have been written on the role of trade in the formation of the South Arabian kingdoms.[179]

5.10   *Arts, Crafts and Professions*

Arab scholars of ancient South Arabian studies have written relatively little on the topic of art in ancient Yemen. However, there are a few important studies on this topic that have been conducted in Arabic.[180] Among these are a study of bronze sculptures,[181] another on representations of animals in reliefs[182] and a study on birds in ancient South Arabian art.[183] An important collection of metal sculptures primary made of bronze discovered in Qaryat al-Faw has also been studied.[184] Only a few studies have been written on the topic of rock art in South Arabia, among these is a useful survey of rock art.[185]

Though the South Arabian inscriptions yield important information relating to crafts and professions, this topic has so far been little investigated. A general study on this topic has been written, however, it depends primarily on the *Sabaic Dictionary* and does not really deal with analysis of the inscriptions.[186]

---

172   An-Naʿīm, Al-Waḍāʿ *al-iqtiṣādī fī šibh al-Ğazīra al-ʿArabīya.*

173   Abd al-Mawlā, *Tiğārat al-baḥḥūr fī ğanūb šibh al-Ğazīra al-ʿArabīya;* Nāšir, *At-Tiğara bayna al-Ğazīra al-ʿArabīya wa-Sūrīya.*

174   Bāʿabbād, *Tiğārat al-baḥḥūr fī mamlakat Ḥaḍramaut al-qadīma.*

175   Maraqtan, Ḥawla al-ʿalāqāt mā bayna Bilād aš-Šām wal-Yaman.

176   Bāʿlaīyān, *Ḥayawānāt an-naql wal-ḥarb fī l-Yaman al-qadīm.*

177   Al-Muṭahhar, *Al-Mawānīʾ al-yamanīya al-qadīma: Dirāsa tārīḫīya.*

178   Maraqtan, Handasat ar-ray wa-dawruhā fī naš'at ad-dawla.

179   Nāšir, *At-Tiğāra wa-aṭaruhā fī taṭawwur mamālik al-Yaman al-qadīma;* Al-Wayyis, *Al-ʾImlāt al-yamanīya;* An-Nuqūd fī l-Yaman ʿabr al-ʿuṣūr.

180   Dāwūd, *Fann an-naḥt fī l-Ğazīra al-ʿArabīya.*

181   ʿAqīl, *Al-Burunz fī l-Yaman al-qadīm.*

182   Al-ʿUmaysī, *At-Tağsīdāt al-ḥayawānīya ʿala l-āṯār.*

183   Nağīm, *Aškāl aṭ-ṭuyūr fī l-fann al-yamanī al-qadīm.*

184   Al-Sinān, *Al-Funūn al-maʿdanīya min qaryat al-Fāw.*

185   Al-ʿAydarūs, *Ar-Rusūm al-ādamīya aṣ-ṣaḥrīya.*

186   Al-Brīhī, *Al-Ḥiraf waṣ-ṣināʿāt fī ḍawʾ nuqūš al-musnad al-ğanūbī.*

There is also a general survey of the crafts in pre-Islamic Arabia, which depends mainly on the medieval Arabic sources.[187] Unfortunately, very few studies have been done on the pottery in Yemen.[188]

5.11 *Hunting in Ancient Yemen*
We have good epigraphic data about hunting in pre-Islamic South Arabia from the early Sabaean period until the eve of Islam. Hunting scenes are also to be found in the rock art and the Sabaean reliefs.[189] An archaeological study on hunting in ancient Yemen has been published.[190]

5.12 *Warfare*
The written records yield plentiful information about warfare between the various tribes and the different kingdoms in ancient Yemen.[191] They also recount military campaigns in Central Arabia and inform us about the wars of the South Arabian kingdoms such as Saba' and Ḥimyar against the Abyssinians. Several modern studies have been written on this topic.[192] Of particular interest is Al-Waǧīh's study on weapons in ancient Yemen.[193]

5.13 *Women's Studies*
Although the primary sources provide a good deal of information on women in pre-Islamic South Arabia,[194] little has been written in Arabic on this topic.[195] Women are mentioned many times in the ancient South Arabian inscriptions and a specific category of these texts were written by women or authorized by women, making them of great importance.

---

187 ʿĀmir, *Al-Ḥiraf waṣ-ṣināʿāt al-yadawīya fī l-Ǧazīra al-ʿArabīya.*

188 See the study of Al-Qāḍī, *Dirāsa taḥlīlīya lil-fuḫḫār al-yamanī al-qadīm.* On the restoration of artifacts, see As-Sanabānī, I. *Dirāsa ʿilmīya wa-taṭbīqīya fī tarmīm wa-ṣiyānat al-luqā.*

189 On hunting in pre-Islamic Arabia in the light of rock art and the epigraphic evidence including Yemen see Maraqten, Hunting in pre-Islamic Arabia.

190 Ṭuʿaimān, *Maṣāʾid al-wuʿūl fī madīnat Ṣirwāḥ al-qadīma.*

191 ʿAṭbūš, *Aṣ-Ṣirāʿ bayna l-mamālik al-yamanīya al-qadīma.*

192 Al-ʿUtaybī, *At-Tanẓīmāt wal-maʿārik al-ḥarbīya fī Sabaʾ;* As-Surūrī, *Al-Ḥayāh al-ʿaskarīya fī Sabaʾ;* Ar-Raṣīn, *Alfāẓ al-ḥarb fī n-nuqūš al-yamanīya al-qadīma.* These studies are depending on Beeston, *Warfare in Ancient South Arabia.*

193 Al-Waǧīh, *Al-Asliḥa fī l-Yaman al-qadīm.*

194 Maraqten, Women's inscriptions, 231–250.

195 Ṣāliḥ, *Al-Marʾa fī n-nuṣūṣ wal-āṯār al-ʿarabīya al-qadīma;* Al-Ḥaddād, *Al-Marʾa fī l-Yaman al-qadīm.*

5.14   *Religions and Temples in Ancient Yemen*

Several MA and PhD theses have been written at ʿAdan and Ṣanʿāʾ universities on the topic of religion and temples.[196] Specific studies were dedicated to the national god of Hadramawt, the national god of Qataban, and to other Qatabanian deities.[197] A solid MA thesis was written by Ḥ. Al-Zubayrī on the supreme god in ancient South Arabia.[198]

A number of studies have also been written about temples in ancient Yemen.[199] Some research has been done on offerings and sacrifices as well.[200] An example is al-Ṣilwī's study on children who were dedicated to the service of the deities in their temples.[201] Research has also been published on monotheism, Christianity, and Judaism in pre-Islamic Yemen.[202]

5.15   *Chronology and Dating Systems*

Several methods have been used for dating inscriptions from ancient Yemen. In addition to the study of palaeography and attempts to synchronize the chronology of ancient Yemen with that of other parts of the ancient Near East, the indigenous dating systems used by the ancient South Arabian kingdoms such as Sabaʾ are very valuable. In Sabaʾ an eponymous dating system was used,[203] while the Himyarites used a dating system according to eras.[204] The contributions of M. Bāfaqīh to the study of the chronology of ancient Yemen are very significant.[205] In addition, two dissertations were written on this topic in Arabic.[206]

---

196 Al-Qaḥṭānī, *Ālihat al-Yaman al-qadīm*; al-ʿArīqī, *Al-Fann al-miʿmārī wal-fikr ad-dīnī fī l-Yaman al-qadīm*; Aš-Šihāb, *Al-Maʿābid wa-waẓīfatuhā ad-dīnīnīya fī Sabaʾ*.

197 al-Ḥasanī, *Al-Ilāh Sīn fī diyanat Ḥaḍramawt al-qadīma*; Al-Ḥasanī, *Al-Ilāh ʿAmm wa-ālihat Qatabān*.

198 Az-Zubayrī, *al-ʾIlāh ʿAṯtar fī diyānat Sabaʾ*.

199 Aš-Šihāb, *Al-Maʿābid wa-waẓīfatuhā ad-dīnīnīya fī Sabaʾ*.

200 Al-Ḥammādī, *Al-Qarābīn wan-nuḏūr*.

201 See Al-Ṣilwī, *Nuqūš al-ihdāʾāt fī l-Yaman al-qadīm*.

202 Mirʿī, *At-Taḥawwulāt ad-dīnīya*.

203 This dating system was a calendar system used primarily in the Kingdom of Sabaʾ, for a period of hundreds of years. Every year was related to the individual, an eponym, the person holding office. The office was fixed for several years for that specific person. It was in the hands of particular families, see Maraqten, *Altsüdarabische Texte auf Holzstäbchen*, 57–63.

204 Müller, *Sabäische Inschriften nach Ären datiert*.

205 Bafaqīh, *L'Unification du Yemen Antique*.

206 Al-Ḥammādī, *Anẓimat at-taʾrīḫ fī n-nuqūš as-sabaʾīya*; ʿAsīrī, *At-Taqwīm fī šibh al-Ǧazīra al-ʿArabīya*.

6 Methodologies of Arab Historians and an Assessment of Their Contributions to the Study of Ancient Yemen

Many Arab scholars have contributed to the study of the history, archaeology and epigraphy of pre-Islamic Yemen. The point of view of these scholars is that they are studying their own history, since Yemen played an in important role in the formation of pre-Islamic Arabian history.

This chapter has presented an overview of the contributions of modern Arab scholars to the writing of the history of ancient Yemen and some critical assessment of their work has been made. It should be stressed that this chapter does not present an exhaustive survey of all modern Arabic scholarship on Yemen. It has concentrated primarily on PhD and MA theses written by the current generation of Arab students dealing with the archaeology and epigraphy of ancient Yemen. Only a small number of articles in Arabic have been mentioned.

A review of the Arabic dissertations in this field reveals that there has been widespread interest in ancient Yemeni studies at universities across the Arab World including in Egypt (Cairo University, Az-Zaqāziq University, Asyūṭ University), Tunisia (Tunis University), Algeria (University of Algiers), Morocco (Hassan II University), Lebanon (American University of Beirut), Syria (Damascus University), Jordan (Yarmouk University), Iraq (University of Baghdad) and Saudi Arabia (King Saud University, Riyadh). At the same time, it should be stressed that the majority of the scholars who produced these theses are Yemeni.

Most of these studies focus on historical topics, a smaller number on the archaeology of ancient Yemen, and a very small number deal with epigraphy. Most of these dissertations are not published, though some of them can be accessed online. Unfortunately, some of the dissertations are not of high quality since the students could not use the epigraphic sources properly. Some of the students had no solid understanding of the epigraphic texts because they lacked a thorough training in ancient South Arabian epigraphy at the universities where they submitted their theses.[207] However, it should be emphasized that within this body of dissertations there are also some important, high-quality studies on the archeology and epigraphy of ancient Yemen which should be published and made widely available for scholarship.

---

207   Al-Qaylī, *Al-Yaman fī ʿaṣr mulūk Sabaʾ wa-ḏī-raydān wa-Ḥaḍramawt wa-yamanat.*

6.1   *The Traditional Historians*

Many traditional Arab scholars still seem to be arguing within the canons of established orthodox Islamic tradition and its mixture of historical, scholarly and legendary elements. These scholars still dominate the historiography of pre-Islamic Arabia.[208] Much of their writing is non-scholarly. It relies heavily on Classical Arabic sources and collective memories and less on critical study of the inscriptions and remains from the pre-Islamic era. They deal with pre-Islamic Arabia as the age of *al-jāhilīyya*, or ignorance.

6.2   *Public Historians: Non-Academic Historians*

This term is used in contrast to professional, academic historians. Arab public historians have flourished in recent years. These historians are mostly amateurs and the writing they produce consists heavily of non-scholarly work as well as ideological dogmas and therefore it is of little value.[209]

6.3   *Professional Academic Historians*

The study of the ancient civilizations in the Arab countries started in the nineteenth century, during the colonial period. The colonial method for dealing with writing ancient history was fixed according to the practices of colonial archaeology and influenced by Orientalism. This method continued, more or less, until the emergence of the post-colonial Arab states, and influenced to some extent the modern Arab academic historians.[210]

Fortunately, contemporary Western specialists in ancient Yemeni studies do not apply postcolonial historical approaches in studying pre-Islamic Yemen. The approaches of Biblical Archaeology have been applied to the Yemeni region only in a few very limited cases.

The Arab academic historians make use of the primary sources for the history of pre-Islamic Arabia, such as inscriptions. Yemen has a special status in the formation of Arab history and that is why several academic historians from other Arab countries contributed to the study of the ancient history of Yemen. In additions, dozens of Arabic MA and PhD dissertations on pre-Islamic Yemen have been written, primarily at Ṣanʿāʾ and ʿAdan universities.

---

208   Al-Akwaʿ, *Al-Yaman al-ḥaḍrāʾ*; Tarsīsī, *Bilād sabaʾ wa-ḥaḍārāt al-ʿarab al-ūlā*, ʿInān, *Tārīḫ al-Yaman al-qadīm*.

209   Among these public authors is the Iraqi F. Ar-Rubayʿī, who wrote several unscientific books such as *Ḥaqīqat as-saybī al-bābilī*.

210   Maraqten, Al-Ḥaḍārāt al-qadīma fī l-bilād al-ʿarabīya wa-masʾalat al-huwīya.

There are several general presentations in Arabic on the history and civilizations of ancient Yemen. The first is Ǧawād ʿAlīs *al-Mufaṣṣal fī tārīḫ al-ʿArab qabla l-islām* (10 vols).[211] This work is still considered to be a standard reference on Arabia before Islam, and to date no other general work has replaced it. In addition to his *Al-Mufaṣṣal*, Ǧawād ʿAlī wrote many shorter studies and articles on pre-Islamic Arab history.[212] Also of interest is the *Handbook on the History and Archaeology of the Arab world (Al-Kitāb al-marǧiʿ fī tārīḫ al-umma al-ʿarabīya)*, which includes several chapters on pre-Islamic Arabia. However, most of the chapters, including the ones on Yemen, are meagre and do not make use of the most up-to-date sources. The authors did not take into consideration the archaeological discoveries of the last four decades.[213]

Professional Yemeni historians such as Muḥammad Bāfaqīh and Yūsuf ʿAbdallāh have contributed extensively to the study of the ancient history of Yemen. A general presentation of the ancient civilizations of Yemen by Yūsuf ʿAbdallāh entitled *Pages from the History of Yemen (Awrāq fī tārīḫ al-Yaman)* is still widely used. The Arabic translation of the catalogue of the Yemen Exhibit in Paris is also very popular among students and scholars. This catalogue is the most solid introduction to studying ancient Yemen in Arabic. The historical studies on ancient Yemen by M. Bāfaqīh are widely respected.[214] Furthermore, Ḥ.Y. Nāmī wrote an outline of the history of the Arabs before Islam and their languages.[215]

7 Conclusion

This outline of Arab contributions to the study of the archaeology and history of pre-Islamic Yemen demonstrates that there are some very important studies composed in Arabic. Although some studies show academic weakness, there

---

211   There is no doubt that this work of Ǧawād ʿAlī is very solid. However, ʿAlī is more a collector of historical data than an analyzer. At the same time the data for Yemen is not up-to-date since it ended in his *al-Mufaṣṣal* around the beginning of the 1960s. Further, the chronology used in *al-Mufaṣṣal* on the kingdoms of ancient Yemen is currently unacceptable since our knowledge has been changed totally by recent archaeological and epigraphic discoveries.

212   The academic essays of Ǧawād ʿAlī were collected and published by two different people, each one published the articles in two volumes, see Abd ar-Raḥīm, *Al-Āṯār al-ʿarabīya* and Al-Kaʿbī, *Abḥāṯ fī tārīḫ al-ʿarab qabla l-islām.*

213   Al-Anṣārī, *Al-Kitāb al-marǧiʿ fī tārīḫ al-umma al-ʿarabīya.*

214   Bāfaqīh, *Tārīḫ al-Yaman al-qadīm, Fī l-ʿArabīya as-Saʿīda.*

215   Nāmī, *Al-ʿArab qabla l-islām.*

are also high-quality studies and it is not possible to deal with several topics relating to the ancient history of Yemen without taking into account modern Arabic scholarship. One problem facing the field is that Western epigraphers are generally only interested in the publications of inscriptions by Arab scholars and not with the Arabic translations of these inscriptions or the meanings of the technical terms found in them. Likewise, Arab scholars generally are only concerned with the editions of inscriptions by Western epigraphers and not the translations of the inscriptions into European languages. Another difficulty facing scholars on both sides is the lack of ability to read modern studies in all relevant languages, especially works in German, Italian, Russian or French. In addition, the majority of western archaeologists do not take into consideration Yemeni surveys and excavations. However, among the Arabic dissertations on South Arabian archaeology and epigraphy there are some works of great significance that could even be described as pioneering works, particularly those which are based on fieldwork and depend on the results of surveys or excavations.

References

Journals

Ancient South Arabian inscriptions and archaeological studies are published in Arabic primarily in the following journals:

Abjadiyyāt, Calligraphy Center, Bibliotheca Alexandrina.

Adūmatu: Semi-Annual Archaeological Journal, Abdulrahman Al-Sudairy Foundation Kingdom of Saudi Arabia. http://www.alsudairy.org.sa/en/publishing-programme/journals/adumatu/.

Ḥawlīyat al-āṯār al-yamanīya, al-Hay'a al-'āmma lil-āṯar, Ṣan'ā', vol. 1, 2008.

Ḥawlīyat al-āṯār al-yamanīya, al-Hay'a al-'āmma lil-āṯar, Ṣan'ā', vol. 2, 2009.

Dirāsāt Yamanīya, Ṣan'ā', Markaz ad-dirāsāt wal-buḥut al-yamanīya.

Al-Iklīl, Ṣan'ā', Yemen.

Maǧallat Kullïyyat al-Ādāb, Cairo University.

Maǧallat Kullïyyat al-Ādāb, Ṣan'ā' University.

Al-Musnad: Ḥawlīya tu'nā bi-šu'un al-āṯar wat-tārīḫ wat-turāṯ (only two issues).

Raydān: Journal of ancient Yemeni antiquities and epigraphy, 'Adan/Ṣan'ā' (only 8 volumes have been published).

Al-Yaman al-Ǧadīd, Ṣan'ā', Yemen.

Al-Yaman. Maǧalla muḥakkama tu'nā biš-šu'ūn al-Yaman, Markaz ad-dirāsāt wal-buḥūṯ al-yamanīya, University of Aden.

Bibliography (Cited in This Study)

ʿAbdallāh, A., *Mamlakat Maʿīn: Dirāsa fī n-našʾa wat-taṭawwur min ḫilāl al-āṯār wan-nuqūš*, PhD dissertation, Asyūṭ University, 2011.

ʿAbdallāh, A., Timnaʿ: Haǧar Kuḥlān, a historical and archaeological study, MA thesis, University of Aden, 2006.

ʿAbdallāh, Y., *Die Personennamen in al-Hamdānīʾs Iklīl und ihre Parallelen in den altsüdarabischen Inschriften: Ein Beitrag zur jemenitischen Namengebung*, PhD thesis, Tübingen, 1975.

ʿAbdallāh, Y., *Awrāq fī tārīḫ al-Yaman. Buḥūṯ wa-maqālāt*, Beirut, Dār al-Fikr al-muʿāṣir, 1990.

ʿAbdallāh, Y., Naqš al-qaṣīda al-ḥimyarīya aw tarnīmat al-šams (Ṣūra min al-adab ad-dīnī fī l-Yaman al-qadīm), *Raydān* 5 (1988), 81–100.

ʿAbdallāh, Y., Ḥaṭṭ al-musnad wan-nuqūš al-yamanīya al-qadīma: Dirasa li-kitāba yamanīya qadīma manqūša ʿala l-ḫašab, al-ḥalaqa aṯ-ṯāniya, *al-Yaman al-ǧadīd* 15/6 (1986), 10–28.

ʿAbdallāh, Y., Risāla min imraʾa bi-ḫaṭṭ az-zabūr, *New Arabian Studies* 3 (1996), 18–28 (Arabic pagination).

Abū Ġānim, F., *Al-Bunya l-qabalīya fī l-Yaman bayna l-istimrār wat-taġayyur*, Ṣanʿāʾ, Dār al-Ḥikma, 1991.

Abū l-Ġayṯ, ʿA., *Al-ʿAlāqāt as-siyāsīya bayna ǧanūb al-Ǧazīra al-ʿArabīya wa-šamālihā min al-qarn aṯ-ṯāliṯ ḥattā l-qarn as-sādis lil-mīlād*. Ṣanʿāʾ, Iṣdārāt wizārat aṯ-ṯaqāfa was-siyāḥa, 2004.

ʿAbd al-Ġanī, N., *Al-Ḥayāh al-iǧtimāʿīya fī l-Yaman al-qadīm min al-qarn al-awwal al-mīlādī ilā l-qarn as-sādis al-mīlādī*, PhD thesis, University of Aden, 2012.

ʿAbd al-Mawlā, U., Tiǧārat al-baḫḫūr fī ǧanūb šibh al-Ǧazīra al-ʿArabīya fī l-fatra min al-qarn ʿāšir ḥattā nihāyat al-qarn al-awwal qabla l-mīlād, MA thesis, Zaqāzīq University (Egypt), 2013.

ʿAbd ar-Raḥīm, A. (ed.), *Al-Āṯār al-ʿarabīya. Muntaḫabāt min Abḥāṯ al-muʾarriḫ ad-duktōr Ǧawād ʿAlī*, 2 vols., Alexandria, Maktabat Al-Iskandarīya, 2015.

Aḥsan, ʿA., Ittiḥād sumʿay: aṯ-ṯulṯ ḥumlān: Dirāsa min ḫilāl al-maṣadir al-aṯarīya wat-tārīḫiya, MA thesis, University of Ṣanʿāʾ, 2017.

Al-Aġbarī, F., *Muʿǧam al-alfāẓ al-miʿmārīya fī nuqūš al-musnad*, Ṣanʿāʾ, Iṣdārāt wizārat aṯ-ṯaqāfa was-siyāḥa, 2010.

Al-Akwaʿ, M., *Al-Yaman al-ḫaḍrāʾ*, 2nd edition, Ṣanʿāʾ, Dār al-ǧīl al-ǧadīd, 1982.

ʿAlī, Ǧ., *Al-Mufaṣṣal fī tārīḫ al-ʿarab qabla l-islām*, 2nd edition, 10 vols, Baghdad, Baghdad University, 1993.

ʿĀmir, Ǧ., Al-Ḥiraf waṣ-ṣināʿāt al-yadawīya fī l-Ǧazīra al-ʿArabīya, MA thesis, Zaqāzīq University, 2005.

Al-Anṣārī, 'A., *Qaryat al-Fau: A Portrait of Pre-Islamic Civilisation in Saudi Arabia*, London, Croom Helm, 1982.

Al-Anṣārī, 'A., (ed.), *Al-Kitāb al-marǧiʿ fī tārīḫ al-umma al-ʿarabīya. Al-Ǧuḏūr wal-bidāyāt*, vol. 1, Tunis, al-Munaẓẓama al-ʿarabīya lit-tarbīa waṯ-ṯaqāfa wal-ʿulūm, 2005.

Al-ʿAnsī, Ḥ., *Al-Qabr al-malakī: Dirāsa aṯarīya lil-qabr al-malakī fī l-ʿaṣībīya*, Ṣanʿāʾ, al-ʿālamīya Liṭ-ṭibāʿah wan-našr, 2012.

Al-ʿAnsī, Y.Y., *al-Maʿālim al-zirāʿiyya fī l-Yaman*, Ṣanʿāʾ, EFAS/AIYS, 1998.

'Aqīl, 'A., Al-Aḥlāf fī l-Yaman fī l-ʿaṣr as-sabaʾī wal-ḥimyarī, MA thesis, Zaqāzīq University (n.d.).

'Aqīl, Bin Yaḥyā, 'A., *Al-Burunz fī l-Yaman al-qadīm. Al-ǧuzʾ al-awwal: at-taqnīya, at-tamāṯīl, az-zīna al-miʿmārīya*. Ṣanʿāʾ, Aṣ-Ṣandūq al-ištimāʿī lit-tanmīya, 2010.

Al-ʿArašī, N., Ṣanʿāʾ al-qadīma min al-qarn al-awwal al-mīlādī ilā l-qarn as-sādis al-mīlādī: Dirāsa aṯarīya tārīḫīya, MA thesis, University of Ṣanʿāʾ, 2009.

Arbach, M., *Les noms propres du corpus inscriptionum semiticarum pars IV: inscriptions ḥimyariticas et sabœas continens*, (IDIS 7), Paris/Rome, Académie des inscriptions et Belles-Lettres/Istituto italiano per l'Africa et l'Oriente.

Arbach, M. and Schiettecatte, J., *Catalogue des pièces archéologiques et épigraphiques du Jawf au musée national de San'â'* (French-Arabic), UNESCO-CFAS, 2006.

Arbach, M. and Audouin, R., *Collection of epigraphic and archaeological artifacts from al-Jawf Sites. Ṣanʿâʾ National Museum*, Part II, (English-Arabic), Ṣanʿâʾ, UNESCO-SFD, 2007.

Arbach, M., Schiettecatte, J. and al-Hādī, I., *Collection of Funerary Stelae from the Jawf Valley*, Ṣanʿâʾ National Museum, Part III, (English-Arabic), Ṣanʿâʾ, UNESCO-SFD, 2008.

Al-ʿArīqī, M., *Al-Fann al-miʿmārī wal-fikr ad-dīnī fī l-Yaman al-qadīm*, Cairo, Madbūlī, 2004.

'Asīrī, W., At-Taqwīm fī šibh al-Ǧazīra al-ʿArabīya mina l-qarn al-ʿāšir qabla l-mīlād ḥattā l-qarn as-sādis al-mīlādī, MA thesis, Jedda, King ʿAbd al-ʿAzīz University, 2009.

'Aslān, A.M., Ġuyūl Ṣanʿāʾ, Dirāsa tārīḫīya ʾaṯarīya waṯāʾiqīya, Beirut, Dār al-Fikr al-Muʿāṣir, 2000.

Al-Ašbaṭ, 'A., *Al-Aʿrāb fī tārīḫ al-Yaman al-qadīm. Dirāsa min ḫilāl an-nuqūš min al-qarn al-awwal qabla l-mīlād wa-ḥatta l-qarn as-sādis mīlādī*, Ṣanʿāʾ, Iṣdārāt wizārat aṯ-ṯaqāfa was-siyāḥa, 2004.

Al-Ašbaṭ, 'A., Al-Aḥbāš fī tārīḫ al-Yaman al-qadīm min al-qarn al-awwal ḥattā al-qarn as-sādīs al-mīlādī, PhD thesis, University of Ṣanʿāʾ, Iṣdārāt Ǧāmiʿat Ṣanʿāʾ, 2010.

'Aṭbūš, 'A., Aṣ-Ṣirāʿ bayna al-mamālik al-yamanīya al-qadīma: asbābuhu wa-natāʾiǧuhu (al-qarn 7–2 qabla l-mīlād), PhD thesis, Damascus University, 2008.

Al-ʿUmaysī, F., At-Taġsīdāt al-ḥayawānīya ʿala l-āṯār fī ǧanūb ġarb al-ǧazīra al-ʿArabīya (al-Yaman) fatrat mā qabla t-tārīḫ: Dirāsa aṯarīya, PhD thesis, Hasan II University, 2013.

Al-'Utaybī, M., At-Tanẓīmāt wal-ma'ārik al-ḥarbīya fī Saba' min ḫilāl an-nuṣūṣ minḏu l-qarn as-sādis qabla l-mīlād ḥattā l-qarn as-sādis al-mīlādī, PhD thesis, Riyadh, Wakalat al-āṯār wal-matāḥif, 2007.

Al-'Awīl, A., Al-Aḫṭār wal-kawārit fī l-Yaman al-qadīm fī l-fatra min al-Qarn al-'āšir qabla l-mīlād ilā al-qarn as-sādis al-mīlādī, MA thesis, Zaqāzīq University, 2014.

Al-'Aydarūs, Ḥ., Ar-Rusūm al-ādamīya aṣ-ṣaḫrīya wa-dalālātuhā fī l-Yaman qabla l-islām: Dirāsa aṯarīya muqārana taḥlīlīya, PhD thesis, University of Ṣan'ā, 2017.

Al-'Az'azī, N., At-Tašrī'āt al-qatabānīya al-ḥaḍarīya: Dirāsa tārīḫīya muqārana, MA thesis, University of Baghdad, 2001.

Al-'Az'azī, N., Dawlat saba' wa-taṭwurātiha as-siyāsīya min al-qarn aṯ-ṯāmin qabla l-mīlād īlā al-qarn as-sādis al-mīlādī, PhD thesis, Damascus University, 2006.

Al-'Aẓm, N., *Riḥla fī bilād al-al-'Arabīya as-Sa'īda min Miṣr ilā Ṣan'ā'*, 2nd edition, Beirut, Manšūrāt al-madīna, 1986.

Al-Azmeh, A., *The Emergence of Islam in Late Antiquity: Allāh and His People*, Cambridge and New York, Cambridge University Press, 2014.

Bā'abbād, F., Tiǧārat al-baḫḫ fī mamlakat Ḥaḍramaut al-qadīma wa-dauruhā fī t-tawāṣul al-ḥaḍārī, MA thesis, University of Aden, 2014.

Bā'laīyān, M., Al-Malābis fī l-Yaman al-qadīm. Dirāsa min ḫilāl at-tamāṯīl wal-āṯār, MA thesis, University of Aden, 2007.

Bā'laīyān, M., Ḥayawānāt an-naql wal-ḥarb fī l-Yaman al-qadīm, PhD thesis, University of Aden, 2012.

Al-Ba'sī, F., Mustawṭanāt awdiyat kūr al-'Awāliq, al-ǧumhūrīya al-yamanīya, Šabwah. Dirāsa tārīḫīya āṯārīya, MA thesis, Algiers University, 2009.

Baḥrī, M., *Taṭawwur nuẓum al-ḥukm fī l-Ǧazīra al-'Arabīya munḏu bidāyat al-'uṣūr at-tārīḫya ḥatta al-qarn aṯ-ṯaliṯ qabla l-mīlād*, Abu Dhabi, Al-Maǧma' aṯ-ṯaqāfī, 2007.

Bāfaqīh, H., Taqnīyat anẓimat ar-ray fī mamalakatay Qatabān wa-Ḥaḍramawt fī ǧanūb al-ǧazīra al-'Arabīya ḫilāl al-alf al-awwal qabla l-mīlād. Dirāsa muqārana, PhD thesis, University of Tunis, 2008.

Bāfaqīh, M.A., Āṯār wa-nuqūš al-'Uqla, Cairo, Laǧna at-ta'līf wat-tarǧama wan-našr, 1967.

Bāfaqīh, M.A., *Tārīḫ al-Yaman al-qadīm*, Beirut, 1973.

Bāfaqīh, M.A., *L'Unification du Yemen Antique*, Paris, Geuthner, 1990.

Bāfaqīh, M.A., *Tawḥīd al-Yaman al-qadīm: aṣ-Ṣirā' bayna saba' wa-ḥimyar wa-ḥaḍramawt mā-bayn al-awwal waṯ-ṯāliṯ al-mīlādī*, trans. 'A.M. Zayd, Ṣan'ā', al-Ma'had al-faransī lil-āṯār wal-'ulūm al-'ǧtimā'īya bi-Ṣan'ā', 2007.

Bāfaqīh, M.A., *Fī l-'Arabīya as-Sa'īda: Dirāsāt tārīḫīya qaṣīra*, Ṣan'ā', 1993.

Bāfaqīh, M.A., *Al-Mustašriqūn wa-āṯār al-Yaman. Qiṣṣat al-mustašriq al-suwaydī al-kūnt Karlū dī Landberg min ḫilāl murāsalati-hi ma'a al-yamanīyīn, 1895–1911*, 2 vols, Ṣan'ā', Markaz al-Dirāsāt wa-l-Buḥūth al-Yamanī, 1988.

Bāfaqīh, M., Beeston, A.F.L., Robin, Chr. and Ghul, M., *Muḫtārāt min an-nuqūš al-yamanīya al-qadīma*, Tunis, al-Munaẓẓama al-'arabīya lit-tarbīa waṯ-ṯaqāfa wa al-'ulūm, 1985.

Bākarmum, R., Nuqūš ʿarabīya ǧanūbīya qadīma min al-Yaman: iʿtimādanʿalā manšūrāt maʿraḍ "al-Yaman fī bilād Saba'", MA thesis, Yarmuk University, 2014.

Al-Bakīr, M., Āṯār wādī ḍahr at-tārīḫīya (fatrat mā qabla l-islām): Dirāsa tawṯīqīyah waṣfīya, MA thesis, University of Ṣanʿāʾ, 2014.

Al-Bārid, F., An-Nuqūš al-musnadīyah al-mutaʿalliqah bi-ʾalmāʾ Wa-r-ray fī l-Yaman, MA thesis, Hassan II University, 2010.

Al-Bārid, F., Az-Zirāʿa fī ǧanūb ġarb al-Ǧazīra al-ʿArabīya (al-Yaman) qabla l-Islām: Dirāsa aṯarīya, PhD thesis, Hassan II University, 2014.

Bāsalāma, M., Šibām al-Ġirās. Dirāsa taʾrīḫīya aṯarīya, Beirut, Dār al-Fikr al-Muʿāṣir, 1990.

Beeston, A.F.L., *Warfare in Ancient South Arabia* (2nd-3rd centuries AD). Qahtan: Studies in Old South Arabian Epigraphy 3, London, Luzac, 1976 [reprinted Oxford, 2005].

Beeston, A.F.L., Mahmoud ʿAli Ghul and the Sabaean Cursive Script, in M. Ibrahim, (ed.), *Arabian Studies in Honour of Mahmoud Ghul: Symposium at Yarmouk University*, December 8–11, 1984, Wiesbaden, Harrassowitz, 1989, 15–19.

Beeston, A.F.L., Ghul, M.A., Müller, W.W., and Ryckmans, J., *Sabaic Dictionary*, Louvain-la-Neuve, Peters/Beirut, Librairie du Liban, 1982 (Arabic-English-French).

Bīston, A.F.L., Al-Qawāʿid as-sabaʾīya, trans., N. Abdulfattāḥ et al., *Maǧallat markaz ad-dirāsāt al-bardīya wan-nuqūš*, (ʿAyn Šams University), 19 (2002), 111–210.

Bīston, A.F.L., *Qawāʿid an-nuqūš al-ʿarabīya al-ǧunūbīya (Nuqūš al-musnad)*, Irbid, Muʾassasat Ḥamāda lil-ḫadamāt al-ǧāmiʿīya, 1995.

Al-Brīhī, I., *Al-Ḥiraf waṣ-ṣināʿāt fī ḍawʾ nuqūš al-musnad al-ǧanūbī*, Riyadh, Wakālat al-āṯār wal-matāḥif, 2000.

Corpus Inscriptionum Semiticarum. Pars quarta: inscriptiones ḥimyariticas et sabœas continens [CIH], Paris, E Reipublicae Typ., 1889.

Dādīya, Y., Alfāz al-zirāʿah war-ray fī lahǧat manṭiqat ʿAtma fī muḥāfazat Ḏamār, MA thesis, University of Aden, 2009.

Al-Ḍafīf, ʿA., Mamalakat Qatabān min al-qarn al-sābiʿ ḥattā nihayat al-ṯānī qabla l-mīlād. Dirāsah tārīḫīya min ḫilāl an-nuqūš, MA thesis, University of Ṣanʿāʾ, 2007.

Damāǧ, L., Al-Maḥāṣil az-zirāʿīya fī l-Yaman al-qadīm: Dirāsa tārīḫīa, MA thesis, University of Ṣanʿāʾ, 2009.

Damāǧ, L., Al-Milkīya fī l-Yaman al-qadīm: Dirāsa taṭbīqīya ʿalā dawlat Sabaʾ, PhD thesis, University of Ṣanʿāʾ, 2017.

Dāwūd, H., Fann an-naḥt fī l-Ǧazīra al-ʿArabīya minḏu mā qabla t-tārīḫ ilā l-qarn aṯ-ṯāliṯ qabla l-mīlād, PhD thesis, Helwan University, 2009.

Dostal, W., *Eduard Glaser – Forschungen im Yemen. Eine quellenkritische Untersuchung aus ethnologischer Sicht*. SAWW 545, Vienna, VÖAW, 1990.

Fakhry, A., *An Archaeological Journey to Yemen* (March–May, 1947), Part III. Plates, Cairo, Service des Antiquités de l'Égypte, 1951.

Fakhry, A., *An Archaeological Journey to Yemen (March–May, 1947)*, Part I, Cairo, Service des Antiquités de l'Égypte, 1952.

Epigraphical Texts, in: A. Fakhry, *An Archaeological Journey to Yemen (March–May 1947)*, Part II, Cairo, Service des Antiquités de l'Égypte, 1952.

Faḫrī, A., Aḥdat al-iktišāfāt al-atarīya fī l-Yaman: Maʿbad al-masāǧid fī bilād murād in *Kitāb al-muʾtamr aṭ-ṭāliṭ li-āṯar fī l-bilād al-ʿarabīya*, Fez, 1959 / Cairo, 1961.

Faḫrī, A., *Al-Yaman: Māḍīhā wa-ḥāḍrihā*, Ṣanʿāʾ, al-Maktaba al-yamanīya h lin-našr wat-tawzīʿ, 1988.

Faqʿas, A., Nuqūš ḫašabīyah bi-ḫaṭṭ az-zabūr min maǧmūʿat al-matḥaf al-waṭanī bi-Ṣanʿāʾ (taḥqīq wa-dirāsa), MA thesis, Ṣanʿāʾ, University of Sanʿāʾ, 2013.

Fisher, G. (ed.), *Arabs and Empires before Islam*, Oxford, Oxford University Press, 2015.

Gajda, I., *Le royaume de Himyar à l'époque monothéiste: L'histoire de l'Arabie du sud ancienne de la fin du IVe siècle de l'ère chrétienne jusqu'à l'avènement de l'Islam*. Mémoires de l'Académie des Inscriptions et Belles-Lettres, tome 40, Paris, De Boccard, 2009.

Ġānim, Z., Madīnat Baynūn: Dirāsa tārīḫīya atarīya, MA thesis, University of Aden, 2007.

Al-Ġāwīš, ʿA., Al-Mawārid aṭ-ṭabīʿīya fī l-Yaman al-qadīm, ḥaḍarat Sabaʾ unmūḏaǧan: Dirāsa min ḫilāl an-nuqūš al-yamaīya al-qadīma, MA thesis, University of Ṣanʿāʾ, 2012.

Al-Ġawrī, ʿA., Al-Maʿāfir al-ġarbīya (aš-Šamāytayn): Dirāsa atarīya itnūgrafīya, MA thesis, University of Ṣanʿāʾ, 2013.

Gesenius, W., Himjaritische Sprache und Schrift, und Entzifferung der letzteren, *Allgemeine Literatur-Zeitung* 123–126 (July 1841), 369–399.

Ghul, M.A., *Early Southern Arabian Languages and Classical Arabic Sources. A critical Examination of Literary and Lexicographical Sources by Comparison with the Inscriptions*, PhD thesis, London, 1963, ed. O. Al-Ghul, Irbid, Yarmuk University, 1993.

Glanzman, W., Clarifying the Record: the Bayt ʾAwwam Revisited, *Proceedings of the Seminar for Arabian Studies* 29 (1999), 73–88.

Al-Ḥāǧǧ, M., Nuqūš qatabānīya min madīnat maryama (haǧar al-ʿādī) bi-wādī ḥarīb. Dirāsa taḥlīlīya muqārana, PhD thesis, King Saʿūd University, 2017.

Ḥabtūr, N., *Al-Yazanīyūn: Mawṭinuhum wa-dawruhum fī tārīḫ al-Yaman al-qadīm*, Aden, University of ʿAdan, 2002.

Al-Ḥaddād, ʿA., Al-Marʾa fī l-Yaman al-qadīm, *Maǧallat markaz ad-dirāsāt al-bardīya wan-nuqūš*, ʿAyn Šams University, 2003, 427–461.

Al-Ḥaǧrī, M.A., *Maǧmūʿ buldān al-Yaman wa-qabāʾilihā*, 2nd Edition, 2 vols., Ṣanʿāʾ, Dār al-Ḥikma, 1996.

Al-Ḥakīm, A., Madīnat Ẓafār: Dirāsa tārīḫīya atarīya, MA thesis, University of Ṣanʿāʾ, 2014.

Al-Ḥakīmī, Š., Malāmiḥ min al-ḥaḍāra al-klāsīkīya fī ḥaḍarat al-Yaman al-Qadī, MA thesis, University of Ṣanʿāʾ, 2010.

Al-Ḥamad, *Al-Aḥwāl al-iǧtimāʿīya wal-iqtiṣādīya fī l-Yaman ḫilāl al-alf al-awwal qabla l-mīlād ḥattā ʿašīyat al-ġazū al-ḥabašī 525 mīlādī*, Aden, University of Aden; Sharjah, Dār aṯ-ṯaqāfa al-ʿarabīya, 2002.

Ḥamīd, B., Dirāsa lil-mawāqiʿ al-qadīma fī manṭiqatay qadas-sāmiʿ min al-maʿāfir, MA thesis, University of Ṣanʿāʾ, 2010.

Al-Hamdānī, Abū Muḥammad al-Ḥasan b. Aḥmad b. Yaʿqūb, *Ṣifat ǧazīrat al-ʿarab*, ed. by Muḥammad b. ʿAlī ʾl-Akwaʿ al-Ḥiwālī. Ṣanʿāʾ, Iṣdārāt wizārat aṯ-ṯaqāfa was-siyāḥa, 1990.

Al-Hamdānī, Abū Muḥammad al-Ḥasan b. Aḥmad b. Yaʿqūb, *Kitāb al-Iklīl* I, ed. by Muḥammad b. ʿAlī ʾl-Akwaʿ al-Ḥiwālī, Ṣanʿāʾ, Iṣdārāt Wizārat aṯ-ṯaqāfa was-siyāḥa, 2004.

Al-Hamdānī, Abū Muḥammad al-Ḥasan b. Aḥmad b. Yaʿqūb, *Kitāb al-Iklīl* II, ed. by Muḥammad b. ʿAlī ʾl-Akwaʿ al-Ḥiwālī, Ṣanʿāʾ, Iṣdārāt wizārat aṯ-ṯaqāfa was-siyāḥa, 2004.

Al-Hamdānī, Abū Muḥammad al-Ḥasan b. Aḥmad b. Yaʿqūb, *Kitāb al-Iklīl* VIII, ed. by Muḥammad b. ʿAlī ʾl-Akwaʿ al-Ḥiwālī, Ṣanʿāʾ, Wizārat aṯ-ṯaqāfa was-siyāḥa, 2004.

Al-Hamdānī, Abū Muḥammad al-Ḥasan b. Aḥmad b. Yaʿqūb, *Kitāb al-Iklīl* X, ed. by Muḥammad b. ʿAlī ʾl-Akwaʿ al-Ḥiwālī, Ṣanʿāʾ, Wizārat aṯ ṯaqāfa was-siyāḥa, 2004.

Al-Ḥammādī, H., Anẓimat at-taʾrīḫ fī n-nuqūš as-sabaʾīya, MA thesis, Yarmuk University, 1997.

Al-Ḥammādī, H., Al-Qarābīn wan-nuḏūr fī d-diyāna al-yamanīya al-Qadīma, PhD thesis, Cairo University, 2006.

Ḥanšūr, A., Al-Ḥaṣāʾiṣ al-miʿmārīya lil-madīna al-yamanīya al-qadīma: dirāsa taḥlīlīya muqārana, PhD thesis, University of Aden, 2007.

Al-Ḥasanī, Ǧ., Al-Ilāh sīn fī diyanat Ḥaḍramawt al-qadīma. Dirāsa min ḫilāl an-nuqūš wal-āṯār, MA thesis, University of Aden, 2006.

Al-Ḥasanī, Ǧ., Al-Ilāh ʿAmm wa-ālihat Qatabān (700 qabla l-mīlād-170 mīlādī), PhD thesis, Ṭanṭā University, 2012.

Al-Ḫaṭīb, F., Nuṣūṣ al-ḫaṭ al-musnad min al-Yaman: Dirāsa tārīḫīya ḥaḍārīya li-natāʾiǧ ar-riḥlat al-ʿilmīya li-ʿālim al-āṯar Aḥmad Faḫrī ilā l-Yaman, MA thesis, ʿAyn Šams University, 2018.

Hayajneh, H., *Die Personennamen in den qatabānischen Inschriften.* TSO 10, Hildesheim [u.a.], Olms Verlag, 1998.

Al-Ḥayānī, F., Madīnat Yaklāʾ, an-Naḫla al-ḥamrāʾ: Dirāsa aṯarīya tārīḫīya, MA thesis, University of Ṣanʿāʾ, 2014.

Al-Ḫāyir, A., Al-Qaṣr fī l-Yaman al-qadīm bayna al-ḫabar wal-aṯar, MA thesis, University of Ṣanʿāʾ, 2014.

Al-Hayyāl, ʿA., *Min nuqūš al-musnad fī Ḫawlān. Naqš wādī ramak*, Ṣanʿāʾ, Dār an-naẓarīya, 2016.

Al-Hilālī, H., *Dalālat al-alfāẓ al-yamānīya fī baʿḍ al-muʿǧamāt al-ʿarabīya*, Ṣanʿāʾ, Markaz ad-Dirāsāt wal-Buḥūṯ al-Yamanī, 1988.

Al-Ḥimyarī, Našwān b. Saʿīd, Šams al-ʿulūm wa-dawāʾ al-ʿarab min al-kulūm, eds. al-ʿAmrī, Ḥ.ʿA., M.ʿA. al-Iryānī and Y.M. ʿAbdallāh, 12 vols., Beirut, Dār al-Fikr al-Muʿāṣir/ Damascus, Dār al-Fikr, 1999.

Al-Ḥusaynī, ʿA. Muʿǧam al-muṣṭalaḥāt az-zirāʿīya fī ʾalfāẓ al-lahǧa al-lahǧīya, Aden, University of Aden, 2003.

Al-Ḥusaynī, Ṣ., Ṭuruq ad-dafn wal-atāt al-ǧanāʾizī fī l-Yaman qabla l-islām (mawqiʿ al-ḥiṣma-šaqra): Dirāsa taṭbīqīya, MA thesis, University of Aden, 2008.

Al-Ḥusaynī, Ṣ., Al-Ḥawāǧiz al-ǧidārīya fī l-manāṭiq al-maftūḥa fī l-Yaman al-qadīm, PhD thesis, Hassan II University, 2016.

Ḥuzayyin, S., Baʿtat al-ǧāmiʿa al-miṣrīya ilā l-Yaman wa-Ḥaḍramawt(1936): Taqrīr ʿan dirāsa maydānīya rāʾida, Maǧallat kullīyat al-ādāb, 1939.

ʿInān, Z., Tārīḫ al-Yaman al-qadīm, Cairo, al-Maṭbaʿa as-Salafīya, 1949.

ʿInān, Z., Tārīḫ ḥaḍārat al-Yaman al-qadīm, Cairo, al-Maṭbaʿa as-Salafīya, 1976 [reprint, Cairo, Dār al-Āfāq al-ʿArabīya, 2003].

Al-Iryānī M., Fī tārīḫ al-Yaman. Nuqūš musnadīya wa-taʿlīqāt, 2nd edition, Ṣanʿāʾ, Markaz ad-Dirāsāt wal-Buḥūt al-Yamanī, 1990.

Al-Iryānī M., Al-Muʿǧam al-Yamanī fī l-luǧa wat-turāt. Hawala mufradāt ḫāṣṣa min al-lahaǧāt al-yamanīya, Damascus, Dār al-Fikr, 1st edition, 1994.

Ismāʿīl, F., Al-Luǧa al-yamanīya al-qadīma, Taʿizz, Dār al-kutub al-ʿilmīya, 2000.

Jamme, A., Sabaean Inscriptions from Mahram Bilqis (Marib). Publications for the American Foundation for the Study of Man III, Baltimore, The Johns Hopkins Press, 1962.

Al-Kaʿbī, N. [Al-Kaabi, N.], Abḥāt fī tārīḫ al-ʿarab qabla l-islām, 2 vols., Beirut, Al-Markaz al-akādīmī al-arabī, 2011.

Kāmil, M., Al-Lahaǧāt al-ʿarabīya al-ḥadīta fī l-Yaman. Cairo, Maʿhad al-Buḥūth wa-al-dirāsāt al-ʿarabīyah, 1968.

Kitchen, K.A., Documentation for Ancient Arabia. Part II, Chronological Framework & Historical Sources. The World of Ancient Arabia Series, Liverpool, Liverpool University Press, 2000.

Leslau, W., Ethiopic and South Arabian, in T.A. Sebeok (ed.), Current Trends in Linguistics. Vol. 6: Linguistics in South West Asia and North Africa. The Hague/Paris, Mouton, 1970, 467–527.

Luqmān, ʿA., Tārīḫ al-Qabāʾil al-Yamanīya: Qabāʾil Ǧanūb al-Yaman wa-Ḥaḍramawt, Ṣanʿāʾ, Dar al-Kalima, 1985.

Maktari, A.M.A., Water Rights and Irrigation Practices in Lahj. University of Cambridge Oriental Publications 21, Cambridge, Cambridge University Press, 1971.

Al-Malāʿiba, N., Dawr mamālik šibh al-Ǧazīra al-ʿArabīya fī at-tiǧāra ad-dawlīya (al-qarn al-awwal qabla l-mīlād – al-qarn at-tālit al-mīlādī), MA thesis, The Jordanian University, 1995.

Maqḥafī, I.A., Muʿǧam al-buldān wal-qabāʾil al-yamanīya, 2 vols., Ṣanʿāʾ, Dār al-Kalima/ Beirut, al-Muʾassasa al-ǧāmiʿīya lid-dirāsāt wan-našr wat-tawzīʿ, 2002.

Maraqten, M., Women's inscriptions recently discovered by the AFSM at the Awām Temple/Mahram Bilqis in Marib, Yemen, *Proceedings of the Seminar for Arabian Studies* 38 (2008), 231–250.

Maraqten, M., Sacred spaces in ancient Yemen – The Awām Temple, Ma'rib: A case study in M. Arbach & J. Schiettecatte, eds., *Proceedings of the 17e Rencontres Sabéennes: Pre-Islamic South Arabia and its Neighbours: New Developments of Research*. British Foundation for the Study of Arabia Monographs, no. 16, BAR International Series 2740, Oxford, Archaeopress, 2015, 109–135.

Maraqtan, M., Al-ʿĀṣima as-sabaʾīya Maʾrib. Tārīḫuhā wu-bunyatuhā al-idārīya wal-iǧtimāʿīya fī ḍauʾ an-nuqūš as-sabaʾīya in: A.R. Al-Ansary, K.I. Muaikel, A.M. Alsharekh (eds.), *Proceedings of the first Adumatu Journal Symposium. The City in the Arab World in light of archaeological discoveries: Evolution and development (5–7 December 2005, Skaka, Saudi Arabia)*, Riyadh, Adumatu, 2010, 107–144.

Maraqtan, M., Handasat ar-ray wa-dawruhā fī našʾat ad-dawla fī ǧanūb ġarb al-ǧazīra al-ʿarabīya wa-taṭawurruhā in A. Al-Nasary et al., (eds.). *Proceedings of the Second Adumatu Journal Symposium. Man and Environment in the Arab World in the Light of Archaeological Discoveries (May 4–6, 2010, Skaka, Saudi Arabia)*, Riyadh, Adumatu, 2013, 199–242.

Maraqtan, M., Ḥawla al-ʿalāqāt mā bayna Bilād aš-Šām wal-Yaman fī ʿuṣūr mā qabla l-islām in M. Maraqten and Z. Kafāfī (eds). *A pioneer of Arabia. Studies in the Archaeology and Epigraphy of the Levant and the Arabian Peninsula in Honor of Moawiyah Ibrahim*. Studies on the Archaeology of Palestine & Transjordan 10, Rome « La Sapienza ». Rome, La Sapienza, 2014, 97–114.

Maraqtan, M., Al-Ḥaḍārāt al-qadīma fī l-bilād al-ʿarabīya wa-masaʾlat al-huwīya li-ummat al-ʿArab, in *At-Taʾrīḫ al-ʿarabī wa-tārīḫ al-ʿarab. Kayfa kutiba wa-kayfa yuktab? Al-iǧābāt al-mumkina*. Al-Muʾtamar as-sanawī aṯ-ṯāliṯ lid-dirāsāt at-tārīḫīya, Beirut, 22–24 April 2016. Beirut, Al-Markaz al-ʿarabī lil-abḥāṯ wa-dirāsat as-siyāsāt, 147–193.

Al-Mawsūʿa al-Yamanīya, 2. Edition, 4 vols., Ṣanʿāʾ, Muʾassasat al-ʿAfīf, 2003.

al-Miḫlāfī, ʿA., *al-Mansūb ilā lahaǧāt al-Yaman fī kutub at-turāṯ. Dirāsa luġawīya taḥlīlīya*, Ṣanāʾ, Iṣdārāt wizārat aṯ-ṯaqāfa was-siyāḥa, 2004.

Mikyāš, ʿA. *Asmāʾ al-qabāʾil fī an-nuqūš al-ʿarabīya al-ǧanūbīya*, MA thesis, Yarmūk University, 1993.

Milḥ al-malāḥa fī maʿrifat al-filāḥa. Ǧamʿ al-imām al-muʿaẓẓam al-malik al-Ašraf ʿUmar bin Yūsuf b. ʿUmar b. Rasūl (696 AH/1296 CE), ed. M. Ǧāzim, M., in al-Iklīl 3 (1985), 165–207; ed. ʿA.M.ʿA. al-Muǧāhid, Damascus, Dār al-Fikr, 1987.

Mirʿī, ʿA., At-Taḥawwulāt ad-dīnīya wan-ʿikāsātuhā ʿalā al-awḍāʿ al-iqtiṣādīya was-sīyāsīya fī l-Yaman al-qadīm min an-niṣf aṯ-ṯānī lil-qarn ar-rābiʿ al-mīlādī ilā ẓuhūr al-islām, MA thesis, University of Aden, 2014.

Müller, W.W., Der böhmische Südarabienreisende Eduard Glaser (1855–1908) und seine Bedeutung für die Erforschung des antiken Jemen, in *Forschungsbeiträge der Geisteswissenschaftlichen Klasse*. Ed. by Eduard Hlawitschka. Schriften der Sudetendeutschen Akademie der Wissenschaften und Künste, Band 23, Munich, Verlagshaus Sudetenland, 2002, 195–220.

Müller, W.W., *Südarabien im Altertum: kommentierte Bibliographie der Jahre 1997 bis 2011*. Epigraphische Forschungen auf der Arabischen Halbinsel, vol 6, Tübingen, Wasmuth, 2014.

Müller, W.W., *Sabäische Inschriften nach Ären datiert: Bibliographie, Texte und Glossar*. Veröffentlichungen der Orientalischen Kommission / Akademie der Wissenschaften und der Literatur 53, Wiesbaden, Harrassowitz, 2010.

Al-Muṭahhar, Ḏ., Al-Mawānī' al-yamanīya al-qadīma: Dirāsa tārīḫīya, PhD thesis, University of Aden, 2008.

An-Naʿīm, N., *Al-Waḍaʿ al-iqtiṣādī fī šibh al-Ǧazīra al-ʿArabīya qabla l-Islām*, Riyadh, Dār aš-šawwāf liṭ-ṭibaʿa wan-našr, 1993.

An-Naʿīm, N., *At-Tašrīʿāt fī ǧanūb ǧarb al-Ǧazīra al-ʿArabīya ḥattā nihāyat dawlat Ḥimyar*, Riyadh, Maktabat al-Malik Fahd, 2000.

Naǧīm, A., Aškāl aṭ-ṭuyūr fī l-fann al-yamanī al-qadīm: dirāsa fannīya muqārana, MA thesis, University of Ṣanʿāʾ, 2012.

Nāmī, Ḥ.Y., *Našr nuqūš sāmīya qadīma min ǧanūb Ǧazīrat al-ʿArab*. Cairo, Institut français d'archéologie orientale du Caire, 1943.

Nāmī, Ḥ.Y., *Al-Baʿta al-miṣrīya li-taṣwīr al-maḫṭūṭāt al-ʿarabīya fī bilād al-Yaman*, Cairo, Wizārat al-maʿārif al-ʿumūmīya, 1952.

Nāmī, Ḥ.Y., *Nuqūš ḫirbat Maʿīn: maǧmūʿat Muḥammad Tawfīq, Dirāsāt ʿan ǧanūbī Ǧazīrat al-ʿArab, 2*, Cairo, Publications de l'Institut français d'archéologie orientale, 1952.

Nāmī, Ḥ.Y., *Al-ʿArab qabla l-islām. Tārīḫuhum, luġātuhum, ālihatuhum*, Cairo, Dār al-Maʿārif, 1985.

Nāṣir, A.K., *Al-Aḍwāʾ wal-aqyāl: Dirāsa fī at-tārīḫ al-yamanī al-qadīm*, MA thesis, Baṣra University, 2014.

Nāšir, H., At-Tiǧāra bayna al-Ǧazīra al-ʿArabīya wa-Sūrīya fī l-alf al-awwal qabla l-mīlad, MA thesis, University of Aden, 2003.

Nāšir, H., At-Tiǧāra wa-aṯaruhā fī taṭawwur mamālik al-Yaman al-qadīma, PhD thesis, University of Aden, 2009.

An-Nāširī, ʿA., *Ḏī Ǧurat wa dawruhum fī ḥukm dawlat Sabaʾ wa-Ḏī-Raydān: Dirāsa fī at-tārīḫ as-siyāsī lil-Yaman al-qadīm*, Ṣanʿāʾ, Iṣdārāt wizārat aṯ-ṯaqāfa was-siyāḥa, 2004.

An-Nāširī, ʿA., Al-Yaman fī ʿaṣr mulūk Sabaʾ wa-ḏī raydān mina l-qarn al-awwal ilā muntaṣaf al-qarn aṯ-ṯānī al-mīlādī: Dirāsa tārīḫīya min ḫilāl an-nuqūš, PhD thesis, University of Ṣanʿāʾ, 2007.

Nebes, N., Ulrich Jasper Seetzen im Jemen, in: *Ulrich Jasper Seetzen (1767–1811). Leben und Werk. Die arabischen Länder und die Nahostforschung im napoleonischen Zeitalter, Vorträge des Kolloquiums vom 23. und 24. September 1994 in der Forschungs- und Landesbibliothek Gotha, Schloß Friedenstein, Gotha.* Veröffentlichungen der Forschungs- und Landesbibliothek Gotha, Heft 33, 1995, 39–52.

Nebes, N. and Stein, P., Ancient South Arabian, in R.D. Woodard ed., *The ancient languages of Syria-Palestine and Arabia*, Cambridge, Cambridge University Press, 2008, 145–178.

Niebuhr, C. *Reisebeschreibung nach Arabien und andern umliegenden Ländern*, Zürich, Stuttgart, Manesse Verlag, 1992.

Noman, Kh., A Study of south Arabian Inscriptions from the region of Dhamār (Yemen), PhD thesis, University of Pisa, 2012.

An-Nuqūd fī l-Yaman ʿabr al-ʿuṣūr, Ṣanʿāʾ, Al-bank al-markazī al-yamanī, 2005.

Al-Qaḥṭānī, M., Ālihat al-Yaman al-qadīm ar-raʾīsīya wa-rumūzā: Dirāsa āṯārīya tārīḫīya, PhD thesis, University of Ṣanʿāʾ, 1997.

Al-Qāḍi, M., Dirāsa taḥlīlīya lil-fuḫḫār al-yamanī al-qadīm wa-ṭuruq al-ʿilāǧ waṣ-ṣiyāna taṭbīqan ʿalā baʿḍ an-namāḏiǧ al-muḫtāra min mawāqiʿ muḫtalifa bil-Yaman, MA thesis, Cairo University, 2014.

Al-Qaylī, M., Mamlakat Sabaʾ fī ʿahd al-usra al-hamdānīya, MA thesis, University of Ṣanʿāʾ, 2003.

Al-Qaylī, M., Al-Yaman fī ʿaṣr mulūk Sabaʾ wa-ḏī-raydān wa-Ḥaḍramawt wa-yamanat, PhD thesis, University of Ṣanʿāʾ, 2009.

Ar-Raṣīn, R., Alfāẓ al-ḥarb fī n-nuqūš al-yamanīya al-qadīma, MA thesis, Baghdad University, 2002.

Rawḍān, M., Al-Yamānīyatain: Dirāsa aṯarīya, MA thesis, University of Ṣanʿāʾ, 2014.

Robin, Chr., "Before Himyar: Epigraphic Evidence for the Kingdoms of South Arabia," in G. Fisher, *Arabs and Empires before Islam*, Oxford, Oxford University Press, 2015, 90–126.

Robin, Chr., *Bibliographie générale systématique.* Corpus des inscriptions et antiquités sud-arabes, Académie des Inscriptions et Belles-Lettres, Louvain, Peeters, 1977.

Rubāʿ, M., Manṭiqat al-kasr fī Wādī Ḥaḍramawt: Dirāsa tārīḫīya āṯārīya, MA thesis, University of Aden, 2006.

Rubāʿ, M., Al-Aʿrāb fī an-nuqūš al-ʿarabīya al-ǧanūbīya, PhD thesis, Ṭanṭā University, 2017.

Ar-Rubayʿī, F., *Ḥaqīqat as-saybī al-bābilī. Al-Ḥamlāt al-āšūrīya ʿala al-Ǧazīra al-ʿArabīya wal-Yaman*, Beirut, Ǧadāwil, 2013.

Ṣāliḥ, ʿA., *Al-Marʾa fī n-nuṣūṣ wal-āṯar al-ʿarabīya al-qadīma. Maǧallat dirāsāt al-Ḫalīǧ wal-ǧazīra al-ʿarabīya*, Kuwait, Kuwait University, 1985.

As-Sadla, M., Wādī Ǧirdān: Dirāsa tārīḫīya li-aḥad al-marākiz al-ḥaḍārīya fī l-Yaman al-qadīm min al-qarn as-sābiʿ qabla l-mīlād ḥattā as-sādis al-mīlādī, MA thesis, University of Aden, 2014.

Al-Said, S., *Die Personennamen in den minäischen Inschriften: Eine etymologische und lexikalische Studie im Bereich der semitischen Sprachen.* VOK 41, Wiesbaden, Harrassowitz, 1995.

As-Saʿīd, S., *Al-ʿAlāqāt al-ḥaḍārīya bayna l-Ǧazīra al-ʿArabīya wa-miṣr fī ḍawʾ an-nuqūš al-ʿarabīya al-qadīma*, Riyadh, Maktabat al-Fahd, 2003.

As-Salāmī, M., Ḥawlān, Al-arḍ wal-qabīla fī l-maṣādir at-tārīḫīya: Dirāsa taḥlīlīya, MA thesis, University of Ṣanʿāʾ, 2002.

Al-Salami, M., *Sabäische Inschriften aus dem Ḥawlān.* Jenaer Beiträge zum Vorderen Orient 7, Wiesbaden, Harrassowitz Verlag, 2011.

Aš-Šamārī, M., *Lahǧat Ḥubān. Dirāsa liǧawīya*, Ṣanʿāʾ, Iṣdārāt wizārat aṯ-ṯaqāfa was-siyāḥa, 2004.

As-Sanabānī, I., *Dirāsa ʿilmīya wa-taṭbīqīya fī tarmīm wa-ṣiyānat al-luqā l-mustaḫraǧa min ḥafāʾir maqawala-sanḥān*, MA thesis, University of Ṣanʿāʾ, 2007.

As-Saqqāf, Ḥ., *Mulūk Sabaʾ wa-ḏū-raydān wa-Ḥaḍramawt wa-yamanat. Tārīḫ al-Yaman min šammar yuharʿiš ilā malkīkarib ḥawālī 270–378 mīlādī*, Ṣanʿāʾ, Markaz ʿabādī lid-dirāsāt wan-našr, 2004.

As-Saqqāf, Ḥ., *Aḍwāʾ ǧadīda ʿalā t-tārīḫ. Tahābiʿat wa-mulūk al-Yaman. Mulūk Sabaʾ wa-ḏī-raydān wa-aʿrābuhim fī ṭ-tawd/naǧd wa-tihāma. Tārīḫ al-Yaman min asʿad al-kāmil ḥattā abraha l-ašram (378–571 mīlādī)*, Ṣanʿāʾ, Markaz ʿabādī lid-dirāsāt wan-našr, 2004.

Aš-Šarʿabī, ʿA. *As-Sawā: Dirāsa tārīḫīya aṯarīya*, Ṣanʿāʾ, Iṣdārāt wizārat aṯ-ṯaqāfa was-siyāḥa, 2004.

Aš-Šarʿabī, M., *Mīnāʾ Qanā ʿalā al-baḥr al-ʿarabī*, MA thesis, University of Ṣanʿāʾ, 2014.

Aš-Šarʿī, M., Aṭ-Ṯaǧrāʾ fī l-Yaman al-Qadīm: Dirāsa fī aškālihā al-kitābīya wa-dalālat maḍāmīniha, MA thesis, University of Ṣanʿāʾ, 2014.

As-Sarīḫī, Maqwalat Radmān wa-Ḥawlān: Al-Ittiḥad wat-taḥālufāt, MA thesis, University of Aden, 2005.

Sharafaddīn, A., *Yemen: Arabia Felix,* Taʿizz, 1961.

Sharafaddīn, A., *Tārīḫ al-Yaman aṯ-ṯaqāfī*, Cairo, Maṭbaʿat al-kīlānī aṣ-ṣaġīr, 1967 [reprint, Ṣanʿāʾ, University of Ṣanʿāʾ, 2004].

Sharafaddīn, A., *Lahaǧāt al-Yaman qadīman wa-ḥadīthan* Cairo, 1970 [reprint, Cairo, Maktabat al-Anglu miṣrīya, 1998].

As-Sayyid, ʿA., *Al-Baḥr al-ḥmar wa-ẓahīruhu fī l-ʿuṣūr al-qadīma*, Alexandria, Dār al-maʿrifa al-ǧāmiʿīya, 1992.

Alsekaf, A.A., La géographie tribale du Yemen antique, PhD thesis, Paris III, 1985.

Al-Selwi, I., *Jemenitische Wörter in den Werken von al-Hamdānī und Naśwān und ihre Parallelen in den semitischen Sprachen.* Marburger Studien zur Afrika – und Asienkunde, Serie B, Bd. 10, Berlin, Reimer, 1987.

Al-Scheiba, A., Die Ortsnamen in den altsüdarabischen Inschriften (mit dem Versuch ihrer Identifizierung und Lokalisierung), PhD thesis, Marburg University, 1982. Republished in *Archäologische Berichte aus dem Yemen* 4 (1988), 1–62.

Aš-Šihāb, S., Al-Maʿābid wa-waẓīfatuhā ad-dīnīnīya fī Saba': al-Maʿābid (Awām, Barʾān, Awʿāl Ṣirwāḥ numūḏaǧan): Dirāsa fī ḍaw' al-iktišāfāt al-aṯarīya al-aḫīra, PhD thesis, University of Ṣanʿāʾ, 2016.

Sholan, A., *Frauennamen in den Altsüdarabischen Inschriften*, (TSO 11), Hildesheim, [etc.], Olms Verlag, 1999.

Al-Ṣilwī, H., Nuqūš al-ihdāʾāt fī l-Yaman al-qadīm: Al-Ihdāʾāt al-bašarīya numūḏaǧan. Dirāsa istiqrāʾīya taḥlīlīya, MA thesis, University of Ṣanʿāʾ, 2013.

Sima, A., *Tiere, Pflanzen, Steine und Metalle in den altsüdarabischen Inschriften: Eine lexikalische und realienkundliche Untersuchung*. Veröffentlichungen der Orientalischen Kommission der Akademie der Wissenschaften und Literatur Mainz 46, Wiesbaden, Harrassowitz, 2000.

Simpson, St. J., (ed.), *Queen of Sheba. Treasures from Ancient Yemen*. London, The British Museum Press, 2002.

Al-Sinān, M., Al-Funūn al-maʿdanīya min qaryat al-Fāw, Dirāsa fannīya muqārana, PhD thesis, King Saʿūd University, 2009.

Al-Šuʿaybī, Ḥ., Aṣ-Ṣilāt al-yūnānīya ar-rūmānīya bil-Yaman qabla l-islām. Dirāsa min ḫilāl al-maṣādir al-klāsīkīya waš-Šawāhid al-aṯarīya, MA thesis, University of Aden, 2004.

As-Surūrī, N., *Al-Ḥayāh al-ʿaskarīya fī Saba'. Dirāsa min ḫilāl nuqūš Maḥram Bilqīs*, Ṣanʿāʾ, University of Ṣanʿāʾ, 2004.

Tairan, S.A., *Die Personennamen in den altsabäischen Inschriften*. TSO 8, Hildesheim [etc.], Olms Verlag, 1992.

Aṯ-Ṭalāyā, A., *Mamlakat Maʿīn. Tārīḫ wa-ḥaḍara, Dirāsa ḥafrīya fī t-tārīḫ*, Damascus: Dār nūr ḥawrān/Dār al-ʿarrāb, 2018.

Tarsīsī, ʿA., *Bilād saba' wa-ḥaḍārāt alʿarab al-ūlā. Al-Yaman (Al-ʿArabīya as-saʿīda)*, Damascus, Dār al-fikr/Beirut: Dār al-fikr al-muʿāṣir, 2nd edition, 1990.

Tawfīq, M., *Aṯār Maʿīn fī Ǧawf al-Yaman (Les monuments de Maʿīn)*. Publications de l'Institut français d'archéologie orientale du Caire, Études sud-arabiques 1, Cairo, ʾal-Maʿhad ʾal-ʿIlmī ʾal-Faransī lil-Āṯār ʾal-Sharqīyah, 1951.

Ṭayyib, M., Al-Ḥulīy fī l-Yaman al-qadīm: Dirāsa min ḫilāl al-manḥūtāt, MA thesis, University of Aden, 2017.

Ṭuʿaimān, ʿA., Maṣāʾid al-wuʿūl fī madīnat Ṣirwāḥ al-qadīma wa-mā ḥawlahā: Dirāsa aṯarīya miʿmārīya, MA thesis, King Saʿūd University, 2014.

Ṭuʿaimān, ʿA., Anẓimat ar-ray fī wāḥat Ṣirwāḥ al-qadīma wa-mā ḥawlahā munḏu al-alf al-awwal qabla l-mīlad ḥattā al-qarn as-sādis al-mīlādī, PhD thesis, King Saʿūd University, 2018.

Al-Waǧīh, ʿA., Al-Asliḥa fī l-Yaman al-qadīm. Dirāsa aṯarīya min maǧmūʿāt al-qiṭaʿ al-aṯarīya fī l-matāḥif al-yamanīya, MA thesis, University of Ṣanʿāʾ.

Wanas, A., Tihāma wa-ʿalāqātuha bi-mamlakat Sabaʾ wa-Ḏī-Raydān min al-qarn aṯ-ṯāliṯ ilā s-sādis al-mīlādī: Dirāsa tārīḫīya min ḫilāl an-nuqūš al-yamanīya al-qadīma, PhD thesis, University of Damascus, 2014.

Al-Wayyis, N., Al-ʿUmlāt al-yamanīya: Dirāsa taḥlīlīya lil-ʿalāqāt al-ḫāriǧīya qadīman, MA thesis, University of Algiers, 2010.

Von Wissmann, H., *Arabien. Dokumente zur Entdeckungsgeschichte*, Stuttgart, Goverts, 1965.

Wušāḥ, M., Qabāʾil aṣ-ṣaḥrāʾ bayna l-qarnayn aṯ-ṯāliṯ was-sādis al-mīlādiyīn, MA thesis, University of Aden, 2001.

Az-Zubayrī, Kh., Al-ʾIlāh ʿAṭtar fī diyānat Sabaʾ, MA thesis, University of Aden, 2000.

Online Pages

CSAI – *Database (Corpus of South Arabian Inscriptions)*: http://csai.humnet.unipi.it

OCIANA – *Database (Online Corpus of the Inscriptions of Ancient North Arabia)*: http://krc.orient.ox.ac.uk/ociana/index.php

Sabäisches Wörterbuch: http://sabaweb.uni-jena.de/

The Glaser Collection: http://glaser.acdh.oeaw.ac.at/#/

Some of the cited Arabic references, such as the university dissertations that are mentioned in this study, can be found at the following Internet pages:

Dār al-Manẓūma: http://mandumah.com/

Network system for scientific research, Yemen: http://www.srs-mohe.gov.ye/Network ingsystem/index.php

4

Contributions des chercheurs marocains dans l'enseignement de l'histoire ancienne

Sidi Mohammed Alaioud

Dans cet article, nous aborderons l'évolution de la recherche scientifique dans les universités marocaines. C'est par ce biais que nous examinerons l'apport de l'histoire antique et sa position dans les programmes des universités. Nous traiterons également un échantillon à travers lequel nous présenterons le résumé de certaines thèses traitant de l'histoire ancienne, ayant été soutenues soit au Maroc, soit à l'étranger. Pour ce qui est des travaux réalisés par les chercheurs marocains, seuls ou en collaboration, nous en donnerons un petit aperçu car nous envisageons, dans l'avenir, de dresser un bilan des recherches afin d'en déterminer les axes les plus importants.

1 Recherches et contributions des chercheurs marocains

1.1 *Étapes de recherche scientifique au Maroc*

Les premières étapes de la recherche scientifique au Maroc débutent avec la création de l'Université Al-Qarawīyyin au IXᵉ siècle. Mais c'est sous le protectorat français que le Maroc a mis en place les premières institutions d'enseignement supérieur, comme l'Institut supérieur des langues arabes et berbères fondé en 1914 et l'Institut supérieur d'études supérieures juridiques, fondé en 1940. Les premières statistiques ont montré qu'en 1954, les étudiants dans l'enseignement supérieur étaient au nombre de 2443, dont 500 marocains[1]. Soulignons que dans ces centres, que ce soit pour l'enseignement ou pour la recherche, la principale source de contribution était étrangère. Le même constat s'applique à la zone sous protectorat espagnol où la plupart des ouvrages publiés étaient destinés aux chercheurs espagnols. Ainsi, l'enseignement supérieur au Maroc à l'indépendance du pays comptait un peu plus de 200 étudiants musulmans. En revanche, le nombre d'étudiants marocains

---

1 « Répertoire des thèses Universitaires enregistrées dans les Facultés des Lettres du Maroc 1961-1994 », https://majles.alukah.net/t74832/, consulté le 10 novembre 2020.

poursuivant leurs études supérieures à l'étranger était bien plus important à cette époque[2].

La période comprise entre l'instauration du protectorat français au Maroc et l'indépendance a connu l'apparition de plusieurs études sur l'histoire ancienne du Maroc : entre autres, *Souvenirs du Maroc* de H. De Lamartiniere, *Le Maroc antique* par J. Carcopino, et *Marruecos punico* de M. Tarradell, ainsi que des articles apparus dans des revues spécialisées[3].

Après l'indépendance, on peut citer l'ouvrage de Abdallah Laraoui, *L'histoire du Maghreb : un essai de synthèse*, dans lequel l'auteur rappelle les grandes lignes de l'histoire du Maroc mais surtout, critique l'idéologie coloniale présente dans ces ouvrages sur l'histoire du Maroc[4]. L'utilisation de la langue arabe dans l'enseignement supérieur, en particulier dans les sciences humaines, est le résultat direct de la politique étatique après l'indépendance, visant l'arabisation de l'enseignement en général et du secteur de la vie publique, faisant ainsi du français une langue secondaire. Cependant, cette politique d'arabisation n'a touché, au niveau des universités, que les sciences humaines, notamment l'histoire avec ses différentes options, tandis que l'enseignement des matières scientifiques a continué de se faire en français. Il convient de signaler que l'enseignement de l'histoire, notamment l'histoire ancienne, en langue arabe, n'a pas empêché la publication de plusieurs recherches et études en langue française qui ont largement devancé les publications en arabe, comme le confirment les travaux d'indexation des recherches publiés soit dans des actes de colloques, soit dans des revues nationales et internationales.

En parallèle de la production et de la lecture historique, des travaux de recherches archéologiques ont commencé dès 1915 sur plusieurs sites du Maroc, sous la direction de Louis Chatelain, d'après des directives du résident général au Maroc, le général Lyautey. Il en est de même dans la zone du protectorat espagnol où plusieurs fouilles ont été menées par César Luis De Montalban et Q. Atauri, permettant la découverte de plusieurs sites.

Les travaux de fouilles menés à l'époque du protectorat avaient généralement pour objectifs de dégager les monuments de l'époque romaine et de mettre en valeur l'importance de la civilisation romaine dans cette partie de l'Afrique du Nord. C'était une manière indirecte de justifier la colonisation du Maroc. Nous soulignons qu'en raison de l'idéologie coloniale, l'occupation

---

2 Mekki Zouaoui, « L'enseignement supérieur depuis l'Indépendance. La dégradation de la qualité était-elle inéluctable ? », dans *Rapport du développement humain 2005*, 162.

3 H. De Lamartinier, *Souvenirs du Maroc*, Paris, 1912 ; J. Carcopino, *Le Maroc antique*, 1943 ; M. Taradell, *Marruecos punico*, Tetuan, 1960.

4 Abdallah Laraoui, *L'histoire du Maghreb : un essai de synthèse*, 2 volumes, Paris, Maspero, 1970.

française et espagnole ont mis l'accent sur tout ce qui était en relation avec la civilisation romaine au Maroc. Cela était clair et déterminait la nature des sujets et les périodes étudiés. Mais malgré cet aspect colonial, ces travaux ont permis la découverte de nombreux sites archéologiques.

Après l'indépendance, la recherche archéologique au Maroc a continué à être dirigée par des chercheurs étrangers ayant intégré dans leurs équipes des cadres marocains spécialisés dans ce domaine. On assiste plus tard à l'apparition d'une nouvelle génération de chercheurs marocains formés en France, et qui commencent à créer des équipes avec de nouvelles orientations dans la recherche archéologique.

Après la création de l'Institut National des Sciences de l'Archéologie et du Patrimoine (I.N.S.A.P.), une nouvelle génération de jeunes chercheurs va enrichir la recherche en archéologie, toutes époques confondues ; on assiste surtout à un regain d'intérêt pour des époques autrefois marginalisées, comme la période maurétanienne et les niveaux post romains et islamiques. Cette nouvelle situation a donné lieu à plusieurs nouveaux programmes de fouilles sur divers sites et permis l'enrichissement de la bibliographie marocaine dans la recherche archéologique, ainsi que la découverte de nouvelles collection archéologique inédites datées des époques maures, romaine, islamiques, et qui font actuellement la fierté du Maroc. À l'exception de l'Université Al-Qarawīyyin, fondée en 889, toutes les universités furent construites après l'indépendance. L'université Mohammed V de Rabat, fut la première université publique. Conçue sur le modèle français, cet établissement est l'une des universités les plus anciennes au Maroc. Elle est caractérisée par un nombre significatif de départements ayant un fort potentiel de recherche et une réputation nationale. En outre, avant la création de nouvelles universités (Fès, Casablanca, Tétouan, Meknès, El Jadida, Agadir, Kenitra, Oujda ...), l'université de Rabat était la seule capable d'accueillir les effectifs croissants d'étudiants.

En plus des établissements cités plus haut, et pour développer la recherche scientifique, on assiste à la création d'un certain nombre d'instituts dont l'activité se limite uniquement à la recherche sans enseignement, tels que l'Institut universitaire de recherche scientifique, à Rabat en 1961 et l'Institut d'études africaines, à Rabat en 1987. Entre 1973 et 2003, le nombre total d'étudiants inscrits dans les établissements de l'enseignement supérieur est passé de 22 000 à 299 000, soit une progression moyenne de 9% par an[5]. Les premiers diplômes d'études supérieures en histoire ont été délivrés en 1963 à la faculté de lettres de Rabat et en 1982 à celle de Fès. Pour ce qui est des thèses d'état, cinq ont été soutenues vers 1980.

---

5   Zouaoui, « L'enseignement supérieur », 172.

La réforme pédagogique de 1997 introduit un nouveau modèle, très différent du système des filières et des modules mis en application dans les F.S.T. Il s'agit d'une politique de proximité, visant à rapprocher les institutions des populations, afin de soulager les Facultés submergées et de réduire les problèmes sociaux des étudiants (suite au changement gouvernemental en 1995)[6]. Cette réforme va contribuer à la multiplication des doctorats dans les universités. On assiste à la fin d'un cycle classique de réforme, amorcé en 1992. Une accélération induite par la Charte Nationale de l'Éducation et la Loi 01.00 en 1999-2000, atteint sa vitesse de croisière en 2003. La période de 1997 à 2003 est cruciale dans la réforme universitaire. Les premiers éléments de la réforme de 2003 ont été mis en application dès la rentrée universitaire 2003-2004. Elle est perçue comme un moyen d'améliorer le fonctionnement des établissements universitaires publics. En 2006/2007, le taux d'accès à l'université est de 10% de la population âgée de 18 à 24 ans, ce qui correspond à 300 000 étudiants. Cependant, un tel développement illustre les difficultés d'un rattrapage quantitatif, sans préjuger de la qualité de l'enseignement dispensé[7]. Dans ce volet de réforme, mentionnons le problème qu'a connu l'enseignement de l'histoire antique : les exemples concernent la civilisation gréco-romaine dans l'université marocaine ainsi que l'histoire de l'Afrique du Nord. Il faut attendre la fin des années 1970 pour voir les nouveaux programmes des cours d'histoire grecque et romaine introduits en premier cycle de licence. Mais la nouvelle réforme de 2002 a encore réduit la place de l'histoire gréco-romaine et l'histoire de l'Afrique du Nord antique dans les programmes, en faisant d'elle un simple module optionnel.

Ainsi, durant son parcours de quatre ans, l'étudiant se concentre sur l'histoire ancienne durant les trois premières, soit l'histoire de l'ancien Orient, de l'Égypte, de la Grèce, des Romains et de l'ancienne Afrique du Nord. Pour cette dernière, l'enseignement ne présente que le tiers du temps. Ajoutez à cela que la part réservée à la civilisation de l'Afrique du Nord était trop insuffisante dans les publications, qu'il s'agisse des livres ou des manuels scolaires. Citons comme exemple le livre de Charles André Julien, L'histoire de l'Afrique du Nord, dont 260 pages étaient réservées à l'histoire ancienne[8]. Avec le nouveau

---

6 Laḥcen Nabil, « La réforme de l'université au Maroc, de l'enseignement à l'entreprenariat-management (1ère partie) », Revue AFN Maroc, N° : 17-18 Décembre 2015, 44.

7 Florian Kohstall, « Les réformes de l'Université à l'heure de « l'internationalisation » Regards croisés sur l'Égypte et le Maroc », dans *L'enseignement supérieur dans la mondialisation libérale*, dir. Sylvie Mazzella, Tunis, 2007, 39-50.

8 Rafaḥ Zineb Aouad, « L'histoire de l'Afrique du Nord antique entre passé et présent » ; dans *Tadrīs Tarīkh Šimāl Ifrīqīya wa al-Mamālik al-Amāzīġiyya*, manšūrāt al-maʿhad al-malakī li-al-ṯaqāfa al-Amāzīġiyya, Rabat, 2010, 7-15.

programme LMD, la licence comprend six semestres et s'étale sur trois ans au lieu de quatre. A côté du nombre d'heures limité pour l'histoire antique, ajoutons l'absence de la période préhistorique.

1.2 *L'histoire antique dans les universités*

L'enseignement de l'histoire antique s'est heurté à une problématique de réécriture. En effet, les ouvrages qui s'intéressent à l'histoire du Maroc dans sa totalité ne cessent de recommander voire de réclamer cette dernière. Portée par la croissance du nombre de chercheurs universitaires, cette demande est apparue à partir des années 1980 dans des colloques concernant le Maroc antique. D'autant que cette période a connu l'insertion de la matière « l'Afrique du Nord antique » dans les programmes universitaires et la création de l'Institut des Sciences d'Archéologie et du Patrimoine en 1985.

Dans son étude et durant la période répertoriée, M. ʿUmar ʿAfāʾ déduit que cette spécialité ne dépasse pas 4% de l'ensemble des spécialités enseignées[9]. Cette pénurie touche l'ensemble des universités marocaines du fait d'un manque d'encadrants. Dans ce travail, nous n'avons pas inclus de références relatives à la période préhistorique, pour la simple raison que cette spécialisation n'est actuellement pas étudiée dans les universités marocaines et ne fait pas partie des décisions universitaires. Quant à l'enseignement de la préhistoire au Maroc, je parle uniquement des universités dans lesquelles la préhistoire n'est pas un domaine dans le cursus universitaire, même si dans certains modules quelques notions sur les différentes époques préhistoriques sont mentionnées par les professeurs.

En revanche, à l'Institut National des Sciences de l'Archéologie et du Patrimoine il existe une spécialité à part entière dans les formations dispensées par cette institution. Le département d'histoire assure des cours théoriques et pratiques dans différents domaines et les travaux de recherches et de fouilles, menés dans les différents sites préhistoriques du Maroc par les professeurs et étudiants, confirment l'évolution et la diversité des champs d'études en préhistoire (Sidi Abderrahmane à Casablanca, Tafoghalt près de Berkane, Jbel Iroud près de Youssoufia, etc.).

Signalons aussi que l'enseignement des langues anciennes (libyque, phénicien, néopunique, grec, latin, etc.) est quasiment absent, non seulement à cause de la rareté des spécialistes, mais aussi du fait que les modules choisis dans les formations fondamentales en histoire antique ne prennent pas en

---

9 ʿUmar ʿAfāʾ, *Dalīl al-aṭārīḥ wa-l-rasāʾil al-jāmiʿiyya al-musajjala bi-kullīyāt al-ādāb bi-al-Maġrib*, Rabat, 1997.

considération l'enseignement de ces langues anciennes. Toutefois, il convient de signaler que certains enseignants-chercheurs, en nombre très limité, ayant fait leurs doctorats en France sur des thématiques faisant surtout appel au latin, enseignent des notions d'épigraphie latine dans deux universités uniquement. Aucun cours magistral sur les langues et la grammaire latine n'est offert dans les universités du Maroc.

Une expérience à signaler dans l'enseignement du latin est celle de l'Institut National des Sciences de l'Archéologie et du Patrimoine, qui a assuré pendant quelques années l'apprentissage du latin et l'étude des inscriptions latines pour les options de l'archéologie classique. Toutefois, cette expérience n'a pas duré très longtemps : d'une part la formation en archéologie classique n'a pas été très régulière, et d'autre part les professeurs spécialisés dans le latin manquaient. Cet institut (I.N.S.A.P.) a souvent fait appel à des professeurs étrangers. Ce manque de formation en langues anciennes, en particulier en latin, se traduit dans le nombre de travaux académiques (mémoires et thèses) marocains ayant pour objet les inscriptions latines.

Autre point lié à notre thème : l'archéologie. Cette science est devenue une unité de module dans les programmes universitaires. Le nouveau système, adopté en 2003, n'en a fait qu'une des composantes de l'unité « Outils de recherche en histoire » dans le module « Histoire et civilisations ».

Parmi les problèmes soulevés dans les travaux de ceux qui se sont intéressés à cette histoire antique du Maroc, nous trouvons des difficultés d'accompagnement de la recherche dans ce domaine. Cela se reflète dans la bibliographie utilisée par ces chercheurs dans leurs ouvrages. Elle est vieille de deux décennies, si ce n'est plus.

En regardant de plus près les contributions dans ce domaine, on remarque un surplus de la production étrangère et une rareté de la contribution marocaine. Pour combler cette lacune, nous nous référerons aux travaux de chercheurs marocains au cours des dernières décennies dans des colloques internationaux, à l'étranger, avec des sujets sur le Maroc antique.

Dans ce contexte, la nouvelle génération de jeunes chercheurs issus des universités marocaines et étrangères ainsi que les missions mixtes, ont enrichi la connaissance sur cette période, à travers notamment les mémoires de thèses.

Quant aux travaux de coopération, nous pouvons citer le chantier de fouilles de Dchar Jdid qui a débuté en 1977 et dont la publication finale n'a jamais vu le jour. Mais quelques résultats ont été publiés par M. et Mme Lenoir ou encore par Depeyrot et Ali sur le numéraire de ce site. Citons aussi le programme de recherches archéologiques maroco-espagnol qui a débuté en 1991 à Lixus. En 1996, une équipe marocaine dirigée par Mohamed Habibi a entamé une première campagne de fouilles sur le versant sud de la colline, au sud-ouest de l'enceinte tardive, ce qui a permis de cerner les phases d'occupation finales dans le secteur.

La mission maroco-italienne (mission Rif) a démarré en 2000 et avait pour but la production d'une carte archéologique de la côte septentrionale du Maroc à travers des travaux de prospection sur le territoire. La mission franco-marocaine (mission des temples) dirigée par Véronique Brouquié-Réddé avait pour objectif de revoir des problèmes de stratigraphie et de datation des fouilles anciennes et de procéder à des sondages dans les temples de Lixus, Volubilis, Banasa. Même chose pour la mission franco-marocaine du site de Kouass. Pour la mission franco-marocaine de Rhira (site dans la plaine du Gharb), les premiers résultats ont été publiés dans quatre tomes par la Casa Velazquez[10].

2 Contribution des marocains dans l'écriture de l'histoire antique de leur pays

Pour examiner ce point, nous focaliserons notre analyse sur un échantillon d'articles afin de déterminer les axes de recherches traitées par les chercheurs marocains à travers des thèses soutenues dans des universités marocaines qui traitaient le sujet du Maroc antique.

Nous traiterons ce sujet en mettant l'accent sur trois époques de l'histoire du Maroc.

2.1 *L'époque Maure*

Cette époque s'étale du VIIIe siècle av. J.-C. jusqu'à l'an 40 ap. J.-C. Comme Kably l'écrit, cité dans le livre *Histoire du Maroc. Réactualisation et synthèse* dans la partie réservée à l'histoire antique : « Les données dont on dispose sur le Maroc antique s'avèrent sommaires, imprécises et parfois subjectives ». Elles sont issues des textes rédigés par des auteurs étrangers, grecs et latins, qui avaient pour objectif de relater l'histoire de la Grèce et de Rome et n'abordaient qu'indirectement les autres contrées méditerranéennes.

Cette étape pose des problèmes de périodisation et de terminologie. On a affaire à deux termes distincts : celui de "libyque" désignant la période allant du VIIIe au IIIe s. av. J.-C. et celui de "maurétanien" appliqué aux trois derniers siècles av. J.-C., concernés par le règne de la dynastie maure. Cette période, qui

---

10   Laurent Callegarin, Muḥammad Kbiri Alaoui, Abdelfattah Ichkhakh, Jean-Claude Roux, *Rirha : site antique et médiévale du Maroc*, tomes I, II, III, IV, Casa de Velázquez, Madrid, 2016.

s'étalant du VIIIe siècle av. J.-C. jusqu'au Ier siècle ap. J.-C., elle est divisée en quatre étapes qui restent à revoir suivant les découvertes[11].

L'époque maure a connu dans ces dernières décennies, un développement remarquable par le biais d'une génération de chercheurs marocains s'étant intéressés à cette période, tant pour le Maroc que pour le reste de l'Afrique du Nord, notamment à travers des thèses soutenues dans des universités marocaines ou étrangères, et qui traitaient de sujets aussi variés que les sites, la céramique, le monnayage, ou tout simplement de sujets d'ordre général.

Concernant les travaux sur les sites antiques, donnons comme exemple la ville antique de Tamuda, sur la rive droite de l'oued Martil, aux abords de la ville actuelle de Tétouan. Les fouilles qu'a connu ce site ont mis à jour, des structures d'habitat appartenant à une agglomération maurétanienne, détruite vers 40 ap. J.-C. Les sondages ont permis de dater les étapes successives de son occupation. Les recherches sur le site de Lixus sont présentées dans deux thèses sur l'histoire et les recherches chronologiques. Ce site est lié à l'expansion phénicienne en Afrique du Nord en général et à la présence phénicienne au Maroc en particulier.

Des études sur la Maurétanie, nous citerons les exemples de *La Maurétanie et ses relations avec Rome jusqu'à 33 av. J.-C.*, et *Études sur la vie économique de Maurétanie au Ier siècle av. J.-C.*, par Muḥammad Majdūb. Le premier travail a traité les conditions politiques et économiques au cours de la période comprise entre le troisième siècle avant J.-C. et le premier siècle avant J.-C. Le second concernait la vie économique au cours du premier siècle avant J.-C. Dans le même contexte, nous nous référons à un travail de Rachid Arharbi sur la carte archéologique du Maroc antique, intitulé : *Contribution à l'établissement de la carte archéologique de la Maurétanie occidentale à l'époque maurétanienne*. L'auteur de ce travail a dressé un catalogue réalisé à partir d'un dépouillement bibliographique de la documentation relative à l'époque préromaine. Il a appuyé sa contribution par une enquête dans les réserves de quelques musées.

Pour d'autres thèmes d'ordre général, nous nous référons à un sujet sur la contribution à la connaissance de la région du détroit de Gibraltar pendant l'Antiquité, intitulé : *De la légende à l'intervention romaine*. Cette thèse a traité la géographie de la région et l'apport des éléments étrangers depuis l'arrivée des phéniciens jusqu'à l'avènement de l'empire romain. L'Afrique du Nord est présentée par un sujet sur les relations entre l'Espagne et l'Afrique du Nord dans l'antiquité du VIIIe siècle av. J.-C. au IIe siècle ap. J.-C. d'après les sources littéraires. Autre exemple de thèse : *Carthage et l'Afrique du Nord au cours du*

---

11   Mohamed Kably, *Histoire du Maroc, Réactualisation et synthèse*, édition de l'Institut Royal pour la Recherche sur l'Histoire du Maroc, Rabat, 2011.

cinquième siècle avant l'ère chrétienne. Ce travail évoque que les anciens habitants de l'Afrique du Nord ont connu une civilisation rurale basée sur l'agriculture et l'élevage bien avant l'expansion carthaginoise en Afrique du Nord, et que l'influence de cette puissance s'opérait sur les plans culturel, industriel, politique, et surtout agricole et commercial.

Une autre thèse de Abdelmohcin Cheddad sur le détroit de Gibraltar était centrée sur deux grandes parties : la géographie de la région et les relations depuis l'arrivée des phéniciens jusqu'à l'avènement de l'empire romain. À partir de l'étude des textes anciens et l'examen des données archéologiques, l'auteur a signalé deux récits : l'un légendaire et l'autre historique. L'analyse de l'impact phénicien, grec et carthaginois a permis de mettre en évidence les particularités de la région et la nature de ses rapports avec le monde extérieur.

2.2 *L'époque romaine*

Cette époque s'étale sur la période allant du premier siècle ap. J.-C. jusqu'à la fin du troisième siècle. En raison du grand intérêt que les autorités coloniales ont porté à la période romaine, pour des raisons idéologiques, cette période est abondamment étudiée.

Tout d'abord, il faut préciser que contrairement à la zone sous occupation française où les fouilles ont débuté de façon régulière au début du XXe siècle (1915), en particulier à Volubilis sous instruction de la résidence générale, la région Nord sous contrôle espagnol n'a vu les débuts des fouilles qu'en 1923, menées par De Montalban. Soulignons qu'il existait une certaine concurrence entre les deux pays colonisateurs du Maroc. Cela s'est manifesté à travers la création du Musée archéologique de Tétouan en 1939, après celui de Rabat en 1933.

Ainsi, la plupart des études et des fouilles archéologiques qui ont été pratiquées durant la période coloniale ont apparu clairement dans les thèses soutenues.

Vu le très grand nombre de thèses soutenues, nous citerons des exemples sur des sites comme Lixus : *Recherches chronologiques sur le site de Lixus* de Mohamed Habibi ; sur Volubilis : *At-Taṭawwur al-ḥaḍāri li-Walīlī min-al-fatrat al-Muriyya ilā al-fatrat al-Islāmiyya* de Sidi Mohammed Alaioud [Sīdī Muḥammad Al-ʿAyyūd] ; *Étude de l'architecture du quartier sud de Volubilis*, d'Abdelouahed Oumlil ; *Le quartier de l'arc de triomphe : La rive nord du Decumanus Maximus* d'Abdelfattah Ichkhakh ; et *Le versant est de Volubilis*, de Mohamed Behel. Sur Sala : Sala (Chellah) : *Le quartier à vocation artisanale et commerciale de "Sala" dans l'Antiquité*, par Meriam Hansali – cette étude avait pour but de retracer son histoire à travers une série de sondages pour avoir afin d'avoir une vision claire du site de Sala (Chellah) durant l'Antiquité – ainsi que l'étude sur *Les monuments des eaux à Sala dans l'Antiquité* d'Ammar Hakim. Cette recherche s'inscrit dans la continuité des travaux conduits sur l'hydraulique en Maurétanie Tingitane. Elle a permis de parvenir à des résultats importants. Les résultats, sur l'aqueduc, le nymphée, le château d'eau et les fontaines, étaient importants.

Pour ce qui est de la vie religieuse dans des villes comme Volubilis, *Approche religieuse d'une cité de Maurétanie Tingitane (milieu Ier–fin IIIe siècles ap. J.-C.)*, de l'annexion de la cité à l'empire romain, au milieu du Ier siècle ap. J.-C., jusqu'à 285, de Najat Brahmi, l'objectif était de chercher à connaître le passé religieux de cette ville ; il s'agit donc d'une enquête sur la religion dans cette cité. Parmi les points soulevés dans ce travail, notons la question des bouleversements, nés de l'intégration à l'empire romain, du panthéon et de l'organisation cultuelle de la ville. Ces mutations incitent à poser des questions sur les conditions du développement de la romanisation dans ce pays.

Dans le domaine artisanal, parmi les exemples choisis, on évoque une thèse sur la céramique : Contribution à l'étude des sigillées d'importation en Maurétanie tingitane aux Ier et IIe siècles après J.-C. L'auteur avance que les terres sigillées d'importation en Maurétanie tingitane ont été traitées partiellement dans quelques articles réservés aux marques de potiers. Cette étude analyse la totalité du matériel. Les documents présents proviennent principalement de trois sites : Lixus, Banasa et Tamuda, dont une grande partie est inédite. Les sigillées d'importation les mieux représentées quantitativement sont : la sigillée italique, la céramique dite « julio-claudienne », la sigillée du sud de la Gaule, la sigillée hispanique et le type A de la sigillée claire africaine. Avec ces importations trois périodes sont définies : la période Auguste-Tibère, la période flavienne et la période des antonins[12]. Mentionnons d'autres thèses sur les motifs de décorations, comme celle sur Les chapiteaux de Banasa, dans laquelle l'auteur signale que les groupements typologiques les plus cohérents sont déterminés par la forme du chapiteau, et par les détails du décor sculpté. La typologie basée sur la structure décorative permet d'approcher les problèmes de datation et ceux de la diffusion des différents types[13]. Une autre thèse sur les 500 chapiteaux de Volubilis concerne cette fois-ci l'originalité profonde de cet art provincial, qui au lieu de se conformer aux canons de l'art romain, a su exploiter à sa manière les modèles proposés en les adaptant à

---

12   Hassan Limane, *Contribution à l'étude des sigillées d'importation en Maurétanie Tingitane aux 1°-2° siècles après J. C. : Étude du matériel de Lixus, Banasa et Tamuda*, thèse de doctorat, Aix Marseille, 1988.

13   'Abdellatif Ḥarbach, *Les chapiteaux de Banasa*, thèse de doctorat, Paris I, 1991.

un goût et à des savoir-faire locaux[14]. Une autre thèse intitulée, L'onomastique de la Maurétanie tingitane à partir du corpus des inscriptions latines du Maroc avait pour objectif de fournir une meilleure compréhension du paysage épigraphique de la Maurétanie tingitane[15].

Parmi les travaux qui ont traité le mouvement des tribus dans le Maroc antique, évoquons, par exemple, Recherches sur l'évolution des structures tribales en Maurétanie Tingitane de la fin du royaume au IIIe siècle. Ce travail s'articule autour de l'évolution interne des tribus maures de la Tingitanie de l'âge des rois maures à l'apparition de l'Islam. Il traite de l'évolution des tribus dans leurs spécificités sociales, leurs mouvements naturels, ainsi que leurs rapports avec Rome entre 40 av. J.C. et 285 ap. J.C.[16]. Un dernier exemple est celui intitulé, Maurisia, recherches sur la géographie historique du Maroc antique, d'Elmostafa Moulay Rachid. Cette étude évoque une unité ethnique et linguistique que constitue l'ensemble maghrébin[17].

2.3 L'époque post-romaine

Cette période est présentée par un sujet sur le Maroc du sud du Dioclétien aux Idrīsides, d'Aomar Akerraz. L'auteur a énuméré les vestiges post-romains de la partie orientale de la ville de Volubilis, il a essayé de retracer la grande ligne de l'évolution de la ville de la fin du IIIe siècle à l'arrivée d'Idrīs. Parmi les problèmes majeurs de cette période dans cette ville se trouve l'absence de documents graphiques ou photographiques des vestiges sur les premières fouilles : « C'est grâce à l'étude de J. Carcopino que les archéologues ont pris conscience de l'intérêt que représentent ces vestiges »[18]. C'est à partir de cette époque qu'ont été mentionnées dans les journaux de fouilles les constructions tardives. En ce qui concerne le passage de la ville antique à la ville médiévale, nous présentons l'exemple d'une étude sur l'urbanisme et l'architecture de Sanaa Ḥassab. Cette étude porte sur la ville de l'Antiquité tardive à travers l'étude d'un ensemble de villes au nord de l'oued Loukkos. L'auteur a essayé d'établir le bilan des connaissances actuelles sur la ville en antiquité tardive en l'étudiant dans une

---

14 Brahim Faddadi, *Chapiteaux de Volubilis : étude du décor architectural*, thèse de doctorat, Aix Marseille 1991.

15 Mustafa Elrhaiti, *Recherches sur l'onomastique de la Maurétanie tingitane*, thèse de doctorat, Strasbourg 2, 1997.

16 Haddou Bouaghaz, *Recherches sur l'évolution des structures tribales en Maurétanie tingitane de la fin du royaume au IIIe siècle*, thèse de doctorat, Paris I, 1994.

17 Elmostafa Moulay Rachid, *Maurisia : recherches sur la géographie historique du Maroc antique*, Doctorat d'État, Université de Besançon, 1987.

18 Aomar Akarraz, *Le Maroc du sud de Dioclétien aux Idrissides*, thèse de troisième cycle, Paris, 1985.

dialectique de rupture et de continuité par rapport à la ville antérieure et à la ville postérieure[19]. Tous ces travaux que l'on vient de citer sur l'époque tardive ont jeté la lumière sur l'histoire du Maroc antique avant l'arrivée des Vandales et le début d'une nouvelle ère de l'histoire du pays. Quant à la période chrétienne, plusieurs thèses portent sur ce sujet. Ceux qui ont traité le christianisme et la romanisation, de Dioclétien à l'invasion vandale, et la religion en Afrique du nord, nous citons les exemples suivants : *Al-Masīḥiyya wa al-tarawmun fī Šimāl Ifrīqīya min ʿahd Dīyūklītyānus ilā al-ġazw al-wandalī 284-429* (*Christianisme et Romanisation en Afrique du Nord depuis l'époque de Dioclétien jusqu'à l'invasion vandale*) de Muḥammad al-Mubakkir et *Al-Dīn wa al-Mujtamaʿ bi Šimāl Ifrīqīya min 180 ilā 430, namūḏaj al-Masīḥiyya* (*Religion et société en Afrique du Nord de 180 à 430, l'exemple du christianisme*) de Fawzīya Kūrtī.

Terminons ces phases historiques par la thèse soutenue sur l'Afrique du Nord antique à partir des textes arabes du Moyen Âge, histoire et géographie historique. Un exemple : Le Maroc septentrional, d'Ahmed Siraje. Ce travail est un essai d'amélioration de nos connaissances sur l'antiquité par l'exploitation des éléments conservés dans des sources. Parmi les conclusions de ce travail se trouve l'idée selon laquelle l'apport des textes arabes à l'étude de l'évolution des cités romaines, à leur localisation et à leur identification, a été démontré de façon incontestable[20].

On ajoute dans ce contexte les travaux sur les prospections archéologiques ; nous en citons comme exemple le travail intitulé *Le piémont rifain entre le Loukkos et le Sebou de la préhistoire à la période contemporaine étude historique et prospection archéologique*. Il s'agit d'une étude historique et archéologique de la région du piémont rifain, entre le Loukkos et le Sebou, dans laquelle l'auteur propose un inventaire de tous les sites depuis la préhistoire jusqu'a la période Idrīside[21].

19   Sanaa Hassab, *L'évolution du fait urbain au Maroc du Nord : de la ville maurétano-romaine à la ville amazigho-islamique*, thèse de doctorat, Paris I, 2009.

20   Ahmed Siraje, « L'image de la Tingitane historiographie arabe médiévale et antiquité maghrébine », *Les Cahiers du Centre de Recherches Historiques* [en ligne], 13, 1994, mis en ligne le 27 février 2009, consulté le 17 août 2018.

21   Nouzha Boudouhou, *Le piémont rifain entre le Loukkos et le Sebou de la préhistoire à la période contemporaine étude historique et prospection archéologique*, thèse de doctorat en Art et archéologie, Paris I, 1999.

3   **Exemples de thèses issues de l'histoire ancienne et l'archéologie préislamique soutenues par des marocains**

On classe ces travaux universitaires dans deux rubriques : les thèses soutenues au Maroc et celles soutenues dans des universités étrangères, notamment françaises. Pour les exemples de travaux soutenus dans les universités marocaines, nous nous nous sommes référés à un échantillon.

Du recensement des thèses, dont la plupart étaient en arabe, à l'exception des thèses soutenues à l'Institut National d'Archéologie et du Patrimoine (I.N.S.A.P.), qui étaient en langue française, il résulte que les sites arrivent en tête. Nous citerons les exemples des villes comme Volubilis, Banasa, ou Lixus. Pour ce qui a trait à l'évolution urbaine, nous donnons l'exemple du site de Volubilis : Sīdī Muḥammad Al-ʿAyyūd [Sidi Mohammed Alaioud], *Al-taṭawwur al-ḥaḍāri li-Walīlī min-al-fātrat al-Mūriyyā ilā al-fatrat al-Islāmiyya*, Meknes, 2005 ; Rachid Arharbi, *La Maurétanie occidentale à l'époque préromaine contribution à la carte archéologique du Maroc*, thèse pour l'obtention du diplôme de troisième cycle en archéologie préislamique, I.N.S.A.P., Rabat, 2002-2003 ; Rachid Bouzidi, *Recherches archéologiques sur le quartier du tumulus (Volubilis)*, thèse pour l'obtention du diplôme de troisième cycle des Sciences de l'archéologie et du patrimoine, option Archéologie préislamique, soutenue à l'I.N.S.A.P., 2000-2001 ; Abdelfattah Ichkhakh, *Le quartier de l'arc de triomphe, la rive nord du Decumanus Maximus*, thèse pour l'obtention du diplôme de troisième cycle des sciences de l'archéologie et du patrimoine, I.N.S.A.P., année 2000-2001.

L'activité artisanale est présentée par divers travaux comme, la thèse de Hicham Hassini, *Éléments d'histoire économique du Maroc antique : étude des amphores des sites du littoral atlantique*, thèse pour l'obtention du diplôme de troisième cycle des Sciences de l'Archéologie et du Patrimoine (I.N.S.A.P.), Rabat, 1999-2000. Cette étude sur les amphores des sites antiques du Maroc, Tanger et sa région, Cotta, Kouass, Lixus, Banasa, Thamusida, Sala et Mogador, revêt une grande importance pour la connaissance de l'histoire économique du pays.

Pour toute la Maurétanie, le travail de Rachid Arharbi sur *La Maurétanie occidentale à l'époque préromaine : Contribution à la carte archéologique du Maroc*, thèse pour l'obtention du diplôme de troisième cycle en archéologie préislamique, I.N.S.A.P., Rabat, 2002-2003, est une contribution à l'établissement d'une carte archéologique du Maroc, réalisée à partir d'un dépouillement bibliographique de la documentation relative à l'époque préromaine. Les constatations formulées à partir de l'inventaire des sites préromains de Maurétanie occidentale ouvrent de nouvelles perspectives de recherche.

Sur la vie politique en Maurétanie tingitane et les conséquences de l'annexion du pays à Rome, le travail de Muḥammad Maqdūm, *Tāwrãt Aydīmoun 40-44*, thèse de troisième cycle, Fès, 1982, jette la lumière sur une phase décisive dans l'histoire du Maroc antique. Nous ajoutons à ces travaux, ceux sur l'Afrique du Nord. Les exemples sont : Al-Bayḍāwiya Bilkāmil, *Maẓāhir Iqtisādiyya mīn khīlal fusayfisāʾ al-šimāl al-ifrīqī*, Rabat, 2000 ; Muḥammad al-Mubakkir, *Al-Masīḥiyya wa-l-t-tarawmun fī Šimāl Ifrīqīya, min ʿahd Dīyūklītyānus ilā al-ġazw al-wandalī 284-429*, Fès, 1999 ; ʿAbd al-ʿAzīz Bilfāʾida, *Al-ʿIbādāt fī Ifrīqīya al- Bruqūnsulīya bayn Iᵉ et le IVᵉ s. ap. J.-C. Šahādāt Ibiġrāfīya*, Fès, 2002.

Pour ce qui est des thèses soutenues à l'étranger, nous nous baserons sur l'étude parue dans Hésperis, par Abderrahim Benhadda et Mohammed Lmoubakir. Elle avait pour base le catalogue des microfiches des thèses françaises, bibliothèque inter-universitaire de Lyon, comprenant les références de 274 thèses au 13/01/93. Les conclusions tirées sont « qu'en dépit de l'essor non négligeable qu'ont connu les recherches historiques sur le Maroc dans les universités anglo-saxonnes et en particulier américaines, l'université française reste le lieu privilégié de la recherche universitaire sur ce pays à l'étranger ». L'usage de la langue française explique la proximité des deux pays.

A l'issue de cette recherche, nous pouvons établir une liste de 232 thèses, dont 28 sur l'histoire antique, soit 12% de l'ensemble des thèses recensées. La majorité (19 thèses) porte sur l'histoire et les relations du Maroc avec l'empire romain, trois autres sur les rapports avec Byzance et deux autres sur les Phéniciens et leurs comptoirs commerciaux en Afrique du Nord. Les quatre autres thèses s'intéressent au culte de la déesse africaine Caelestis, l'image du Maroc dans la géographie de Ptolémée, la représentation des Imazighen antiques dans l'historiographie contemporaine et l'activité des Méditerranéens aux confins de l'Afrique du VIᵉ siècle avant J.-C. au IVᵉ siècle après J.-C.

Les exemples sont les suivants : Abdelaziz Belfaida [ʿAbd al-ʿAzīz Bilfāʾida], *Le culte des divinités des eaux en Afrique du Nord à l'époque romaine*, doctorat de troisième cycle, Université Montpellier III, 1987 ; Ḥassan Limane, *Contribution à l'étude des sigillées d'importation en Maurétanie Tingitane aux Iᵉʳ-IIᵉ siècles après J.-C. : Étude du matériel de Lixus, Banasa et Tamuda*, sous la direction de Paul-Albert Février – Aix-Marseille I, 1988 ; Mustapha Elrhaiti, *Recherches sur l'onomastique de la Maurétanie tingitane*, sous la direction de Jean-Michel David, Strasbourg 2, 1997 ; Fatima-Zohra El-Harrif , *La circulation monétaire dans le Maroc septentrional : les monnaies de fouilles de Valentia Banasa (IIIᵉ s. avant J.-C.–début du IVᵉ s. après J.-C.)* thèse de doctorat, nouveau régime, sous la direction de René Rebuffat, Paris IV, 1992 ; Mohamed Habibi, *Recherches chronologiques sur le site de Lixus*, thèse de doctorat, Université, Paris IV,

1994 ; Nouzha Boudouḥou, *Le piémont rifain entre le Loukkos et le Sebou de la préhistoire a la période contemporaine étude historique et prospection archéologique*, thèse de doctorat en Art et archéologie, Paris I, 1999 ; Abdelouahed Oumlil, *Étude de l'architecture du quartier sud de Volubilis*, thèse pour l'obtention du grade de PhD, Québec, 1989 ; Ḥaddou Boughaz, *Recherches sur l'évolution des structures tribales en Maurétanie tingitane de la fin du royaume au IIIᵉ siècle*, thèse de doctorat nouveau régime université Paris I 1993-1994 ; et Aomar Akerraz, *Le Maroc du sud de Dioclétien aux Idrissides*, thèse de troisième cycle, Paris 1985 . Parmi ces chercheurs, il y a des étrangers ayant travaillé sur le Maroc antique ou l'Afrique du Nord. Leurs thèses constituent une référence pour la recherche en histoire ancienne. C'est aussi le cas de chercheurs marocains ayant publié leurs thèses, permettant ainsi de les mettre à la disposition du public.

4   Bilan des recherches historiques et archéologiques

Dans une communication présentée lors du premier colloque sur le patrimoine maure, intitulée « Recherches archéologiques et Historiques de l'époque Maure au Maroc antique »[22], nous avons dressé un bilan de recherches sur cette époque dans l'histoire du Maroc, afin de déterminer les axes traités. Nous nous sommes basés, dans ce dépouillement systématique des publications, sur les ouvrages, les thèses et articles publiés dans des revues spécialisées, colloques, séminaires et collectifs ayant un rapport avec l'histoire et l'archéologie maure.

Ce travail consiste à présenter ces recherches sur une période s'étalant sur douze siècles, à partir du VIIIᵉ siècle av. J.-C. Il vise à connaître les thèmes les plus souvent abordés et à avoir une idée sur les phases et les espaces qui n'ont pas eu la chance d'être étudiés à cette époque. Le classement des sujets est basé essentiellement sur ce que révèlent les titres de publication, avec les auteurs classés par ordre alphabétique. Cette tentative a été suivie d'une autre, sur les recherches historiques et archéologiques de l'époque Maure dans le Maghreb antique[23].

---

22   Sīdī Muḥammad Al-ʿAyyūd [Sidi Mohammed Alaioud] et ʿAbd al-ʿAzīz Bilfāʾida [Abdelaziz Belfaida], «Ḥaṣīlat Al-abḥāṯ al-Tārīkhiyya wa al-Aṯāriyya al-Lībiyya wa al-Mūrītāniyya : Dirāsa Bibliyūġrāfiyya », *Actes du premier colloque sur le patrimoine Maure (Amazigh) du Maroc antique, Fès 29-31 mars 2013*, Fès, 2014, 5-32.

23   Sidi Mohammed Alaioud et Abdelaziz Belfaida, « Bilan des recherches historiques et archéologique sur l'époque libyco-mauretanienne en Afrique du Nord : étude bibliographique », dans Colloque international, *Le patrimoine antique du Maghreb : des origines à la fin des royaumes africains, Fès, 7-8-9 mai 2015* (à paraître).

Il résulte du premier recensement que la langue française était la plus utilisée, considérant les liens historiques entre les deux pays, la proximité géographique, et le lien linguistique vient ensuite la langue espagnole[24].

La langue arabe est largement utilisée après les années 1980, en lien avec la croissance du nombre de chercheurs universitaires. On constate aussi, d'après ce travail, que les sites archéologiques arrivent en tête des publications, suivis de l'architecture, l'artisanat et l'épigraphie, le monnayage, et les recherches historiques. Nous considérons que ce travail est l'ébauche d'un inventaire d'articles publiés par des chercheurs marocains, ainsi qu'en collaboration avec d'autres chercheurs étrangers, que nous pourrions développer dans l'avenir.

5   Conclusion

Au terme de cet exposé, nous pouvons constater que la recherche scientifique a connu au fil des années une évolution assistée par la création d'un certain nombre d'instituts. L'enseignement de l'histoire antique dans les universités marocaines à connu un progrès, même s'il est relativement minime par rapports au reste des recherches dans ce domaine, où nous assistons à un accroissement de ces études dans les dernières décennies, du fait de la croissance du nombre de chercheurs universitaires.

Bibliographie

'Afā', 'Umar, *Dalīl al-uṭruḥāt wa-al-rasā'il al-jāmi'iyya al-musajjala bi-kullīyāt al-ādāb bi-al-Maghrib*, Collaborateur, Rabat, 1997.

Aġmir, 'Abd al-Wāḥid, « Tāṭawwur al-bāḥt al-'ilmī fī al-Maghrib mīn khīlal ar-rasā'il al-jāmī'iyya : al-'ulūm al-insāniyya namūḏajan » https://www.fikrwanakd.aljabri abed.net/n28_15akmir.%282%29.htm#_edn1.

Akerraz, Aomar, *Le Maroc du sud de Dioclétien aux Idrissides*, thèse de troisième cycle, Paris, 1985.

Alaioud, Sidi Mohammed [Al-'Ayyūd, Sīdī Muḥammad] et 'Abd al-'Azīz Bilfā'ida [Belfaida, Abdelaziz], « Haṣīlat Al-Abḥāt al-Tārīkhiyya wa al-Aṯāriyya al-Lībiyya wa al- Mūrītāniyya, Dirāsa Bibliyūġrāfiyya », *Actes du premier colloque sur le patrimoine Maure (Amazigh) du Maroc antique, Fès, 29-31 mars 2013*, Fès, 2014, 5.

---

24   Nous sommes conscients que d'autres publications nous ont échappé vu la période et l'espace traités.

Alaioud, Sidi Mohammed et Abdelaziz Belfaida, « Bilan des recherches historiques et archéologique sur l'époque libyco-mauretanienne en Afrique du Nord : étude bibliographique », dans *Colloque international, Le patrimoine antique du Maghreb : des origines à la fin des royaumes africains, Fès, 7-8-9 mai 2015* (à paraître).

Aouad, Rafaḥ Zineb, « l'Histoire de l'Afrique du Nord antique entre passé et présent » ; dans *Tadrīs Tārīkh Šimāl Ifrīqīya wa al-Mamālik al-Amāzīġiyya*, Rabat, Manšūrāt al-ma'had al-malakī li-al-ṯaqāfa al- Amāziġiyya, 2010, 7-15.

Arharbi, Rachid, *Contribution à la carte archéologique du Maroc*, thèse pour l'obtention du diplôme de troisième cycle en archéologie préislamique, I.N.S.A.P., Rabat, 2002-2003.

Araichi, Ḥamid, « Le Maroc antique dans l'historiographie contemporaine : continuité, rupture ou mutation ? », *Atti del xx Convegno Internazionale di Alghero – Porto Conte Ricerche, 26-29 settembre 2013*, Rome, 2015, 897-1007.

Belfaida, Abdelaziz [Bilfā'ida, ʿAbd al-ʿAzīz], *Le culte des divinités des eaux en Afrique du Nord à l'époque romaine*, thèse doctorat de troisième cycle, Université Montpellier III, 1987.

Belfaida, Abdelaziz [Bilfā'ida, ʿAbd al-ʿAzīz], *Al-ʿIbādāt fī Ifrīqīya al- Bruqūnsulīya bayn Iᵉ et le IVᵉ s. ap. J.-C. Šahādāt Ibiġrāfīya*, Fès, 2002.

Benhadda, Abderrahim et Mohammed Lmoubakir, « Vingt ans de recherches historiques et archéologiques sur le Maroc dans l'université française (1972-1992) », *Hespéris-Tamuda* 32 (1994), 163-186.

Bilkāmil, al-Bayḍāwiya, *Maẓāhir Iqtisādīya mīn khīlal fusayfisā' al-šimāl al-ifrīqī*, Rabat, 2000.

Bouaghaz, Haddou, *Recherches sur l'évolution des structures tribales en Maurétanie tingitane de la fin du royaume au IIIᵉ siècle*, thèse de doctorat, Paris I, 1994.

Boudouhou, Nouzha, *Le piémont rifain entre le Loukkos et le Sebou de la préhistoire a la période contemporaine étude historique et prospection archéologique*, thèse de doctorat en art et archéologie, Paris I, 1999.

Boudribila, Mohammed, *Carthage et l'Afrique du Nord au cours du cinquième siècle avant l'ère chrétienne*, thèse de doctorat, Besançon, 1992.

Callegarin, Laurent, Muḥammad KbiriAlaoui, Abdelfattah Ichkhakh, Jean-Claude Roux, *Rirha : site antique et médiévale du Maroc*, tomes I, II, III, IV, Madrid, Casa de Velazquez, 2016.

Cheddad, Abdelmohcin, *La contribution à la connaissance de la région du détroit de Gibraltar pendant l'Antiquité intitulé : De la légende à l'intervention romaine*, thèse de doctorat, Bordeaux 3, 1995.

Depeyrot, Georges, Zilil, I. *Colonia Iulia Constantia Zilil, Étude du numéraire*, Rome, 1999.

El-Harrif, Fatima-Zohra, *La circulation monétaire dans le Maroc septentrional : les monnaies de fouilles de Valentia Banasa (IIIᵉ s. avant J.-C.–début du IVᵉ s. après J.-C.)*, thèse de doctorat, Paris IV, 1992.

Elkhayari, Abdelaziz, *Tamuda : recherches archeologiques et historiques*, thèse de doctorat, Paris I, 1996.

Elrhaiti, Mustapha, *Recherches sur l'onomastique de la Maurétanie tingitane*, thèse de doctorat, Stasbourg 2, 1997.

Faddadi, Brahim, *Chapiteaux de Volubilis : étude du décor architectural*, thèse de doctorat, Aix Marseille, 1991.

Gougou, Mohammed, *La réforme de l'université au Maroc vue par les acteurs universitaires : Une étude de cas de l'Université Mohammed V, Rabat-Salé*, thèse présentée à la Faculté des études supérieures en vue de l'obtention du grade de Philosophiae Doctor (Ph.D.) en sciences de l'éducation, option en administration de l'éducation, Université de Montréal, 2011.

Habibi, Mohamed, *Recherches chronologiques sur le site de Lixus*, thèse de doctorat, Université Paris IV, 1994.

Hassab, Sanaa, *L'évolution du fait urbain au Maroc du Nord : de la ville maurétano-romaine à la ville amazigho-islamique*, thèse de doctorat, Paris I, 2009.

Hassini, Hicham, *Éléments d'histoire économique du Maroc antique : étude des amphores des sitcs du littoral atlantique*, thèse pour l'obtention du diplôme de troisième cycle des Sciences de l'Archéologie et du Patrimoine (I.N.S.A.P.), Rabat, 1999-2000.

Kably, Mohamed, *Histoire du Maroc, Réactualisation et synthèse*, éditions de l'Institut Royal pour la Recherche sur l'Histoire du Maroc, Rabat, 2011.

Kharbach, Abdellatif, *Les chapiteaux de Banasa*, thèse de doctorat, Paris, 1991.

Kohstall, Florian, « Les réformes de l'Université à l'heure de « l'internationalisation ». Regards croisés sur l'Égypte et le Maroc », *L'enseignement supérieur dans la mondialisation libérale*, dir. Sylvie Mazzella, Tunis, 2007, 39-50.

Kūrtī, Fawzīya, *Al-Dīn wa al-Mujtamaʿ bi Šimāl Ifrīqīya min 180 ilā 430, namūḏaj al-Masīḥiyya*, thèse de troisième cycle, Rabat, 1998.

Laraoui, Abdallah, *L'histoire du Maghreb : un essai de synthèse*, 2 volumes, Paris, Maspero, 1970.

Limane, Ḥassan, *Contribution à l'étude des sigillées d'importation en Maurétanie Tingitane aux Iᵉʳ-IIᵉ siècles après J.-C. : étude du matériel de Lixus, Banasa et Tamuda*, thèse de doctorat, Aix Marseille 1988.

Majdūb, Muḥammad, *Mamlakat al- Mūriyyin wa ʿalāqātihā bi rūma li- ǧāyat 33 q.m.*, thèse de troisième cycle, Fès, 1989-1990.

Majdūb, Muḥammad, *Dirāsāt ʿan al-ḥayāt al- Iqtiṣādīya bi Mūrītāniyya fī al-qarn al-akhīr qabla al-mīlād*, thèse de doctorat, Al-Muḥammadiyya, 1997-1998.

Maqdūm, Muḥammad, *Tāwrāt Aydīmoun 40-44*, thèse de troisième cycle, Fès, 1982.

Mansour, Mohamed, « Thèses de Doctorat soutenues aux universités américaines concernant les pays du Maghreb (Maroc, Algérie, Tunisie, Libye), 1952-1982 », dans *Revue de la Faculté des Lettres de Rabat*, WU, 1985, 251-274.

Moulay Rachid, Elmostafa, *Maurisia : recherches sur la géographie historique du Maroc antique*, doctorat d'État, Université de Besançon, 1987.

Al-Mubakkir, Muḥammad, *Al-Masīḥiyya wa al-tarawmun fī Šimāl Ifrīqīya min ʿahd Dīyūklītyānus ilā al-ġazw al-wandalī 284-429*, Fès, 1999.

Nabil, Lahcen, « La réforme de l'université au Maroc de l'enseignement à l'entreprenariat-management », *Revue AFN Maroc* N° 17-18 décembre 2015, 41-81.

Oumlil, Abdelouahed, *Étude de l'architecture du quartier sud de Volubilis*, thèse pour l'obtention du grade de Ph.D., Québec, 1989.

« Répertoire des thèses universitaires enregistrées dans les Facultés des Lettres du Maroc 1961-1994 », https://majles.alukah.net/t74832/, consulté le 10 novembre 2020.

Sebti, Abdelahad, Bibliographie *Hesperis*, Vol. 35, Fascicule 2, 1997, 153-155.

Siraje, Ahmed, *L'Afrique du Nord antique à partir des textes arabes du Moyen-âge. Histoire et géographie historique. Un exemple : le Maroc septentrional*, thèse de doctorat, Paris I, 1993.

Siraje, Ahmed, « L'image de la Tingitane : historiographie arabe médiévale et antiquité maghrébine », *Les Cahiers du Centre de Recherches Historiques* [en ligne], 13, 1994, mis en ligne le 27 février 2009, consulté le 17 août 2018, http://journals.openedition.org/ccrh/2698 ; DOI : 10.4000/ccrh.2698.

Zouaoui, Mekki, « L'enseignement supérieur depuis l'Indépendance. La dégradation de la qualité était-elle inéluctable ? », dans *Rapport du développement humain 2005*, 159-194, (http://www.abhatoo.net.ma).

5

Les sciences de l'antiquité en l'Algérie : bilan et perspectives

Youcef Aibeche

L'effet médiatique de la publication des résultats des recherches menées sur le site préhistorique d'Ain Bouchérit dans la prestigieuse revue « Science » a ouvert à nouveau le débat sur les enjeux de la recherche historique et archéologique en Algérie[1]. En effet en dépit de la richesse de ce patrimoine, les recherches liées aux sciences de l'antiquité en Algérie ont évolué différement des autres disciplines, en raison d'une nouvelle perception de l'antiquité conditionnée par le discours politique post indépendant.

Nous avons effectué un dépouillement d'environ 500 thèses de magister et de doctorat en histoire antique, en archéologie classique et en préhistoire, soutenues dans les universités algériennes[2], en vue d'esquisser un tableau le plus exhaustif possible des sujets de recherche en sciences de l'Antiquité depuis l'indépendance jusqu'à nos jours. Il s'agit de présenter les grandes lignes de cette production et d'examiner son évolution, tout en soulevant les questions liées à la conception de cette antiquité et de son appropriation. Il s'agit aussi, de comprendre en premier lieu comment les universités algériennes ont appréhendé les questions majeures liées à cette période. Nous nous intérrogerons sur la nature même de leur production scientifique et de quelle manière elle s'inscrit dans le débat national et international[3].

L'examen de cette documentation facile en apparence, grâce aux opportunités qu'offrent les nouvelles technologies de communication, se heurte d'emblée à plusieurs difficultés, à commencer par l'absence de bilans périodiques regroupant les axes de recherches. Effectivement la plupart des thèses ne sont pas publiées, elles demeurent en grande partie à l'état de manuscrit et le plus souvent indisponibles d'accès. Par ailleurs le positionnement par rapport aux concepts historiques initiés et instrumentalisés par l'idéologie coloniale se

---

1 https://science.sciencemag.org/content/362/6420/1297.
2 J'ai intégré dans ma démarche les thèses soutenues aux universités étrangères afin de constituer un corpus qui permet d'établir les tendances thématiques et le profil de chaque chercheur.
3 Je remercie Amar S. Baadj de m'avoir impliqué dans ce projet et de sa patience et soutien.

© KONINKLIJKE BRILL NV, LEIDEN, 2021 | DOI:10.1163/9789004460089_006

révèle très complexe, dans la mesure où ils persistent encore dans la documentation universitaire post-indépendante.

Après l'indépendance, les universités algériennes ont fait soutenir plus de 500 thèses[4], contre seulement une trentaine au cours de la période coloniale. Étrangement ce chiffre parait insignifiant, en raison de la timidité de cette production, aussi bien en matière de concepts historiques qu'en données et découvertes archéologiques. Depuis l'indépendance, le métier de l'antiquisant n'est plus considéré comme une priorité, le parcours pédagogique universitaire n'arrive plus à prendre en charge les exigences du patrimoine ; la formation en matière d'archéologie devenue très lacunaire, et surtout à la merci du hasard de quelques initiatives individuelles. Abandonnant l'apprentissage du latin et la maitrise du terrain archéologique, elle s'est restreinte aux concepts théoriques. Par ailleurs sans prétendre porter un jugement de valeur, contrairement aux autres pays du Maghreb, la politique de l'arabisation a réellement impacté le processus de la recherche historique qui s'est trouvé très éloigné du débat international. Effectivement force est de constater qu'a défaut de traductions, la diffusion de la production historique s'est réellement restreinte. Plutôt elle est condamnée à l'invisibilité dans la bibliographie thématique internationale.

Le paradoxe selon l'expression de H. Remaoun[5], réside « dans le fait que le ministère de l'enseignement supérieur n'a sous sa tutelle aucun centre spécifiquement orienté vers la recherche historiographique ». L'appropriation de ce domaine par le ministère de la culture, notamment à travers les interventions d'urgence, a favorisé un climat de tension entre la réflexion académique et le geste archéologique. Ce constat nous invite à réexaminer la nature du montage institutionnel et à tenter d'évaluer le processus de la production du discours sur les sciences de l'antiquité.

1   L'antiquité dans le discours colonial

L'usage de l'histoire antique par la colonisation française n'est abordé ici que dans une perspective comparative[6], il serait difficile de mener une analyse

---

4   Il s'agit principalement de thèses d'histoire d'archéologie classique et de préhistoire soutenus en Algérie.

5   H. Remaoun, « L'intervention institutionnelle et son impact sur la pratique historiographique en Algérie : la politique d'écriture et de réécriture de l'histoire, tendances et contre-tendances », *Insaniyat*, CRASC, Oran. 19-20, 2003, 7-40.

6   Cette question a été traitée par plusieurs auteurs : J.C. Vatin, *L'Algérie politique. Histoire et société*, Paris, Presse de la Fondation Nationale des Sciences Politiques, 1974 ; Ph. Lucas, *L'Algérie des anthropologues*, Paris, Maspéro, 1975 ; J.F. Leimdorfer, *Discours académique et*

approfondie en peu de pages. Il est question seulement de rappeller combien l'école coloniale s'est attelée à magnifier l'Afrique romaine en faisant un argument justifiant le fait colonial. En effet, la prétention d'être les descendants directs des Romains ainsi que l'attachement à ressusciter l'Afrique du Nord latine et chrétienne à partir des ruines antiques ont rapidement pris l'ampleur d'un programme idéologique[7]. L'Armée française a été particulièrement active dans l'exploration archéologique, en partie par les brigades topographiques, confortées par les efforts individuels de nombreux soldats et officiers. L'exemple du colonel Carbuccia est représentatif[8]. En réalité cette implication des armées d'occupation dans l'exploration archéologique n'a fait que répondre à leurs préocupations d'ordre militaire, orientant l'interprétation des sites ruraux selon des critères d'ordre défensif qui a donné lieu au rejet de la part de la population locale de la civilisation romaine[9]. La création de la commission de l'*Exploration scientifique de l'Algérie*[10] puis l'émergence des sociétés archéologiques régionales constituées en grande partie par des administrateurs et d'anciens militaires a renforcé la prédominance de cette hystérie[11]. Ce raisonnement idéologique, n'accordant aucune importance au rôle de la population locale, a produit un stéréotype des populations berbères incapables de vivre en paix ou de s'organiser politiquement. Celles-ci étaient en éternel soulèvement contre la succession des puissances colonisatrices : carthaginoise, romaine, vandale, byzantine, arabe, ottomane[12].

Il est vrai que le regard porté sur l'Algérie a évolué en fonction du projet colonial français. D'ailleurs l'université d'Alger a largement repris ces concepts en les vulgarisant dans un discours argumenté. Y. Moderan a bien illustré le processus de l'adoption de la théorie des migrations orientales développée

---

colonisation. Thèmes de recherche sur l'Algérie pendant la période coloniale, Paris, Publisud, 1992 ; F. Soufi, « Histoire et mémoire : l'historiographie coloniale », dans *Insaniyat*, CRASC, Oran, n. 3, 1997, 53-97.

7   N. Oulebsir, *Les usages du patrimoine. Monuments, musées et politique coloniale en Algérie 1830-1930*, Paris, Éditions de la Maison des sciences de l'homme, 2004, 284.

8   Commandant français à Batna, épigraphiste amateur, il avait restauré avec ses soldats le mausolée d'un préfet de la Legio III Augusta près de Lambèse en ajoutant une nouvelle dédicace en 1849 avec une nouvelle inscription rendant hommage à l'officier romain au nom de la légion étrangère française. Cf. M. Dondin-Payre, « L'*exercitus Africae* inspiratrice de l'armée française d'Afrique : *Ense et aratro* », dans *Ant. Afric.*, vol. 27, 1991, 148-149.

9   D. Mattingly, *Imperialism, power, and identity : experiencing the Roman Empire*, Princeton : Princeton University Press, 2013, 49.

10   M. Dondin-Payre, L'*exercitus Africae* ... op. cit. 143.

11   J. Malarkey, *The colonial encounter in French Algeria : a study of the development of power asymmetry and symbolic violence in the city of Constantine 1830-1970*, thèse d'anthropologie, Austin, Texas, 1980.

12   D. Mattingly, op. cit., 51.

par H. Tauxier, souvent occulté par l'historiographie académique[13]. De son
côté Dondin-Payre a expliqué comment l'épigraphie a servi comme un outil
clé dans la pratique historiographique des études romano-africaines. D'après
elle, si l'étude de l'Afrique du Nord s'est révélée très importante dans le développement de l'épigraphie latine en tant que discipline « elle n'a pas échappé
à sa mobilisation pour affirmer une lointaine communauté de destin entre
la France et l'Algérie »[14]. La structuration des villes aux normes coloniales,
notamment par l'introduction de nouveaux espaces publics et de la multiplication des musées lapidaires, a fortement contribué à renforcer ce sentiment
d'héritage[15]. La prospérité agricole du Maghreb antique n'a pas échappé à cet
enjeu histriographique, sa mise en avant positionnait la colonisation française
comme une continuité toute naturelle de l'époque romaine[16]. Le centenaire de
l'occupation de l'Algérie fut conçu comme une grande manifestation d'unani-
misme colonial destinée à vanter les louanges de l'œuvre civilisatrice de l'occupation française. Les universitaires eurent largement droit aux honneurs[17]. Ce
qui nous incombe également c'est de constater un certain parallélisme entre
le bilan économique romain et celui de l'occupation française[18]. Par ailleurs
au moment même de cette effervescence historiographique, l'idée de la chute
du Maghreb romain suscitait un réel souci historique, pour cette référence au
modèle Romain[19]. L'analyse des causes de cette chute orientait le regard vers
le Berbère remis en cause par sa composante ethnologique, ses origines orientales et son incapacité à se constituer et à s'unir[20].

13

H. Tauxier, « Études sur les migrations des tribus berbères avant l'islamisme », dans *Rev.
Af.* T. 6, 1862, 353-363.

13   H. Tauxier, « Études sur les migrations des tribus berbères avant l'islamisme », dans *Rev.
      Af.* T. 6, 1862, 353-363.

14   M. Dondin-Payre, *Un siècle d'épigraphie classique. Aspects de l'œuvre des savants français
      dans les pays du bassin méditerranéen*, Paris, 1988, 33.

15   J.C. Jansen, *Une « statuomanie » à l'algérienne. Histoire de l'Algérie à la période coloniale,
      1880-1914*, Paris, La Découverte, 2014.

16   Muḥammad al-Bašīr Šnītī, *Aḍwā' 'alā tārīḫ al-Maġrib al-qadīm, buḥūṯ wa dirāsāt*, Dār
      al-Haqq, al-Ǧazā'ir, 2003.

17   J. Cantier, « L'Algérie au regard de l'histoire : un exemple d'évolution de l'historiographie
      coloniale », *Les Cahiers d'Histoire Immédiate*, Groupe de recherche en histoire immédiate,
      1994, 29-55 ; J. Cl. Vatin, « Science historique et conscience historiographique de l'Algérie
      coloniale, I. 1840-1962 », *Annuaire de l'Afrique du Nord*, 1979, vol. 18, 1.

18   P.-A. Février, *Approches du Maghreb romain*, vol. 1, Aix-en Provence, 1989, 74.

19   E. Albertini, *L'Afrique romaine*, Alger, 1922 réimp. 1955, 123 ; E. Mercier, « La population
      indigène de l'Afrique sous la domination romaine vandale et byzantine », *R.S.A.C.*, t. 30,
      1895-96, 194.

20   Ch. Diehl, *L'Afrique byzantine. Histoire de la domination byzantine en Afrique 533-709*, Paris,
      1896, 64-314 ; C. Courtois, *Les Vandales et l'Afrique*, 1955, 6 et 359 ; J. Carcopino, « La fin
      du Maroc romain », Ext. des *Mélanges d'archéologie et d'histoire de l'École française de
      Rome*, 1940, 349-448 ; G. Camps, *Aux origines de la Berbérie : Massinissa ou les débuts de*

2   La décolonisation de l'histoire

Plusieurs chercheurs s'accordent à considérer que l'euphorie des festivités du centenaire a constitué une étape importante dans le développement des bases d'une anti-histoire coloniale[21]. Cette réaction historiographique nationaliste rédigée en arabe ou en français représentait un des aspects de l'émancipation intellectuelle et politique de l'Algérie. Dès l'entre-deux guerres le mouvement des oulémas réformistes dirigé par le Cheik Ben Badis œuvrait à la renaissance des principes fondateurs de l'Algérie arabo-musulmane. L'ouvrage fondateur de Mubārak al-Mīllī est considéré comme la première histoire nationale de l'Algérie en langue arabe : *Histoire de l'Algérie de l'Antiquité à nos jours*[22]. Tūfīq al-Madanī publia en 1932 un *Livre de l'Algérie* « œuvre d'histoire patriotique qui devint l'Encyclopédie du nationalisme algérien »[23]. Ces deux premiers ouvrages en langue arabe avaient pour objectif de réfuter les thèses colonialistes et d'affirmer l'idée fondamentale de l'existence de la nation algérienne[24]. Plusieurs autres intellectuels algériens en langue française se sont mis à diffuser les arguments historiques de l'existence de la nation algérienne[25]. Ce même phénomène s'est manifesté parallèlement dans le discours du mouvement national qui a bien pris conscience de l'importance de l'histoire dans le processus de défense de ses idées nationalistes[26]. Mais le concept de la décolonisation de l'histoire n'est apparu qu'en 1962 avec la parution de l'ouvrage

---

l'histoire, Alger, Imprimerie officielle, 1961 ; M. Dondin-Payre, *L'exercitus Africae*, op. cit., p. 149 ; P.A. Février, « Le monde rural du Maghreb antique. Approches de l'historiographie du XIXᵉ siècle », *Histoire et archéologie de l'Afrique du Nord*, 3e Colloque International Montpellier, 111e Congrès national des Sociétés savants, Paris, 1986, 102 ; Y. Modéran, « Mythe et histoire aux derniers temps de l'Afrique antique : à propos d'un texte d'Ibn Khaldûn », *Revue historique*, n. 618, 2001, 315-341 ; P. Salama, « Vues nouvelles sur l'insurrection Maurétanienne dite 'de 253' : le dossier numismatique », *L'armée et des affaires militaires*, 113e Congrès national des Sociétés savants, Paris, 1991, 455-70.

21   J.-C. Vatin, *Science historique et conscience historiographique de l'Algérie coloniale*, op. cit., 1106 ; « Les désillusions de l'après Centenaire de 1930 marquèrent le déclin de cette histoire a sens unique et la lente réhabilitation des Algériens musulmans comme sujets historiques. »

22   Mubārak Al-Mīllī, *Tārīḫ al-Ǧazāir fī-l-qadīm wa-l-ḥadīth*, al-Maṭbaʿa al-islāmiyya al-Ǧazāiriyya, 1928-1932, 2 vol.

23   Aḥmad Tawfīq Al-Madanī, *Tārīḫ al-Ǧazāir*, Ghardaïa, al-Maṭbaʿa al-ʿarabiyya, 1931 ; nouvelle édition al-Gazāir : al-Muʾassassah al-Waṭanīya lil-Kitāb, 1984.

24   M. Djender, *Introduction à l'histoire de l'Algérie. Systèmes historiques, conception générale de l'histoire nationale*, Alger, SNED, 1968, 119-127.

25   Cf. l'exemple de J. Amrouche dans son essai « L'éternel Jugurtha » publié en 1946.

26   Cf. le discours de M. Lamine Debaghine devant le parlement français ; M.S. Boukechour, « L'écriture de l'histoire de l'Algérie, période coloniale 1830-1962 : sources et perspectives », *Revue des études humaines et sociales*, Université de Chlef, n. 16, juin 2016, 5.

de Mohamed Cherif Sahli[27], et celui de Mostafa Lacheraf en 1965 corroborant la même vision de ce dernier, en proposant une réelle mise au point de la vérité historique[28].

3   Vers une histoire nationale

L'indépendance de l'Algérie a suscité l'émancipation progressive du discours historique. En ce sens les nouveaux défis identitaires, depuis le congrès de Tripoli, imposaient une nouvelle démarche constructive, sans que l'Antiquité garde le même engouement qu'a connu la période coloniale. Le discours officiel s'est concentré en priorité sur les figures de la résistance tel que l'Amir Abd el Kader ou les grandes personnalités de la révolution. L'initiative de création d'un Centre National des Etudes Historiques (C.N.E.H.) au niveau de la Présidence s'inscrivait dans cette démarche[29]. Mieux encore, il y'a eu la création d'une direction des études historiques et de la mise en valeur du patrimoine qui avait pour mission la préparation des conditions de l'émergence « d'une École nationale de l'histoire »[30].

Néanmoins en matière d'archéologie la direction des affaires culturelles, installée au niveau du ministère de l'éducation nationale[31], devait maintenir la continuité du même programme archéologique entamé depuis les années cinquante. Elle a eu pour mission la gestion des musées, des sites et des fouilles archéologiques, tout en conservant l'encadrement scientifique français. Cette nouvelle structuration, renforcée par le soutien du CNRS (Centre

---

27   M. Ch. Sahli, *Décoloniser l'histoire. Introduction à l'histoire du Maghreb*, Éditions Maspero, Paris, 1965.

28   M. Lacheraf, *L'Algérie : nation et société*, Éditions Maspero, Paris, 1965.

29   Le centre a publié entre 1974 et 1992, 25 numéros de la revue *Majallat al-Târîkh*, cf. « Intervention institutionnelle et son impact sur la pratique historiographique en Algérie : la politique d'écriture et de réécriture de l'histoire, tendances et contre-tendances », *Insaniyat*, n. 9-20, 2003, 7-40.

30   F. Soufi, « En Algérie : l'histoire et sa pratique », dans *Savoirs historiques au Maghreb*, Oran, CRASC, 2006, 123-145.

31   M. Bouchenaki, *Recherches*, op. cit., 9, note 3, « Après l'indépendance la Direction des Beaux-Arts qui relevait du Ministère de l'Intérieur a été transférée au Ministère de l'Éducation Nationale jusqu'en 1970. À partir de 1971 la Sous-Direction des Beaux-Arts dépendant de la Direction des Affaires culturelles est passée au sein de la Direction de la Culture au Ministère de l'Information et de la Culture. En 1975 un nouvel organisme élevait cette Sous-Direction au rang de Direction des Beaux-Arts Monuments et Sites avec deux Sous-Directions, l'une consacrée aux Beaux-Arts et Antiquités, l'autre aux Monuments Historiques et Sites. »

national de la recherche scientifique)[32], a permis de publier le *Bulletin d'Archéologie Algérienne* qui prend la relève du *Libyca*[33], ainsi qu'une série de brochures consacrée à Timgad[34], à Djemila[35], à Hippone[36] et à Tiddis[37]. Le passage symbolique de la section « archéologie et épigraphie » de la revue *Libyca* en *Bulletin d'Archéologie Algérienne* (B.A.A.) a noté dès la première édition, la priorité accordée à la période musulmane[38]. Néanmoins une poignée de chercheurs algériens comme A. Baghli[39], M. Bouchenaki[40], F. Kadra[41] ou

---

32   Il y a eu même la création à Alger d'une antenne du Centre de Recherches sur l'Afrique Méditerranéenne attaché au CNRS.

33   T. I 1962-1965 ; T. II 1966-1967 ; T. III 1968 ; T. IV 1970 ; T. V 1971-1974 ; T. VI 1975-1976 ; T. VII 1977-1979 avec deux suppléments.

34   J. Lassus, *Visite à Timgad*, Alger, Ministère de l'Éducation nationale, Direction des affaires culturelles, 1969, 146.

35   P.A. Février, *Djemila*, Alger, 1968.

36   S. Dahmani, *Hippo Regius. Hipponc à travers les siècles. Ministère de l'Information et de la Culture de la R.A.D.P.*, Alger, 1973.

37   A. Berthier, *Tiddis antique. Castellum Tidditanorum guide*, 1972, Sous-direction des Arts, Musées, Monuments historiques, Antiquités, Réédition, Alger, 1991.

38   N. Benseddik, « L'archéologie antique en Algérie hier et aujourd'hui », dans N. Benghabrit et M. Heddab, Dir., *L'Algérie 50 ans après. État des savoirs en sciences sociales et humaines 1954-2004*, Oran, CRASC, 2008, 193-203 ; F.X. Fauvelle et alii, « Les savoirs archéologiques au Maghreb », *Perspective* 2, 2017. Mis en ligne le 30 juin 2018, URL : http://journals.open edition.org/perspective/7422.

39   S.-A. Baghli, « Bilan des activités archéologiques dans la wilaya de Constantine », R.S.A.C. (Recueil de la société archéologique de Constantine), vol. 71, 1969-1971, 13-17 ; Avec P.-A. Février, « Recherches et travaux, 1962-1965 », B.A.A., vol. 1, 1962-1965, 3-6 ; « Recherches et travaux, 1966-1967 », B.A.A., vol. 2, 1966-1967, 1-10 ; « Recherches et travaux, 1967 », B.A.A., vol. 3, 1968, 1-34 ; « Recherches et travaux, 1968-1969 », B.A.A., vol. 4, 1970, 9-40 ; « Recherches et travaux, 1970-1971 », B.A.A., vol. 5, 1971-1974, 9-24 ; Avec M. Bouchenaki, « Recherches et travaux en 1975-1976 », B.A.A., vol. 6, 1975-1976, 7-14.

40   M. Bouchenaki, *Les magistrats de la Confédération Cirtéenne Alger*, DEA, Université d'Alger, 1967 ; Idem, *Le mausolée royal de Maurétanie*, Alger, SNED, 1970 ; Idem, *Cités antiques d'Algérie*, Alger, Ministère de la Culture, 1975 ; Idem, *Tipasa, site du patrimoine mondial*, Alger, ENAG, 1989 ; *Fouilles de la nécropole occidentale de Tipasa Matarès 1968-1972*, Alger, 1975, 194 ; « Récentes recherches et étude de l'antiquité en Algérie », *Ant. Afr.*, vol. 15, 1980, 9-28 ; Idem, « Contribution à la connaissance de la Numidie avant la conquête romaine », dans *Atti del I Congresso internazionale di studi fenici e punici Roma 5-10 novembre 1979*, Roma, 1983, 527-541.

41   F. Kadra, R. Lequement, « Découverte d'une nécropole de basse époque à El Hadjar », B.A.A., vol. 3, 1968, 259-270 ; F. Kadra, « Recherches et travaux, 1977-1979 », B.A.A. vol. 7, 1, 1977-1979, 9-28 ; Idem, « Note complémentaire sur les Djedars de la région de Frenda », B.A.A., vol. 7, 1, 1977-1979, 227-232 ; Idem, *Les Djedars, monuments funéraires berbères de la région de Frenda Wilaya de Tiaret*, Alger, 1983.

N. Benseddik[42], ont émergé dans le domaine de la gestion des fouilles et leurs publications. Leur intégration à la dynamique scientifique française ou étrangère, bien qu'elle ait permis d'exécuter quelques projets, n'a pas réussi à fédérer une réelle pratique archéologique algérienne[43]. Le souci de gestion et de préservation des sites et des monuments archéologiques est rapidement devenu prioritaire au détriment de la recherche scientifique qui atteint un niveau de la stagnation à partir des années quatre-vingts[44].

Par ailleurs, le Centre Algérien de Recherches Anthropologiques Préhistoriques et Ethnographiques (CARAPE) qui a fonctionné dans le cadre des accords d'Évian jusqu'a 1969 sous la direction des chercheurs français : G. Camps, G. Aumassip et C. Roubet, a été affecté au ministère de l'Enseignement Supérieur et de la Recherche Scientifique[45]. En 1984 il est rattaché au CNEH avant de devenir en 1993 un Centre National de Recherches Préhistoriques Anthropologiques et Historiques (CNRPAH). Il a assuré la publication de la revue *Libyca* jusqu'a 1989[46]. Il est important de noter que malgré les réticences constatées, concernant l'orientation ethnologique et anthropologique, l'évolution de cette institution a maintenu le développement des études préhistoriques sous la tutelle du Ministère de la Culture. La création en 1987 de

---

42   N. Benseddik, Ph. Leveau, et F. Romane, « Les nouvelles inscriptions de Cherchel », *B.A.A.*, vol. 5, 1971-1974, 195-206 ; N. Benseddik, « Nouvelles inscriptions de Sétif », *B.A.A.*, vol. 7, 1, 1977-1979, 1985, 33-52 ; Idem, *Les troupes auxiliaires de l'armée romaine en Maurétanie Césarienne sous le Haut-Empire*, Alger, 1982 ; N. Benseddik, T.W. Potter, *La fouille du forum de Cherchell 1977-1981*, Alger, 1993 ; N. Benseddik, *Thagaste, Souk Ahras, patrie de Saint Augustin*, Alger, INAS, 2005 ; Idem, « Esculape et Hygie en Afrique. Recherches sur les cultes guérisseurs », *Mémoires de l'AIBL*, vol. 44, I et II, Paris, 2010 ; Idem, *Cirta-Constantina et son territoire*, Errance-Actes Sud, Arles, 2012.

43   Il ne s'agit pas de porter un jugement de valeur. Souvent ces acteurs ont énuméré les causes de cette situation. Cf. N. Benseddik, « L'archéologie antique en Algérie hier et aujourd'hui », op. cit., 198.

44   M. Bouchenaki, « La recherche archéologique en Algérie », *Die Numider*, Bonn, Rheinisches Landes Museum, 1979, 2-3 ; Idem, « Récentes recherches et étude de l'antiquité en Algérie », 1979, 11.

45   K. Chachoua, « 2ᵉ festival culturel panafricain d'Alger 1-4 juillet 2009, Colloque international sur l'anthropologie africaine, Pour une Anthropologie Sud/Sud », *Journal des anthropologues*, n. 118-119, 2009, 375-380 ; « Deux organismes ont concrétisé cette transition : le C.A.R.A.P.E. dont la création remonte à l'année 1956. En 1964 est dénommé « CRAPE » sans la mention de l'adjectif « Algérien ». En 1971 on le rattacha au laboratoire de l'Office National de la Recherche Scientifique sous la tutelle du Ministère de l'Enseignement Supérieur et de la Recherche Scientifique. Ensuite en 1974 la mention d'ethnographie a été retirée. Il devient en 1993 le Centre National de Recherches Préhistoriques Anthropologiques et Historiques C.N.R.P.A.H. »

46   http://www.cnrpah.org/index.php/features/revue.

Office du Parc National de l'Ahaggar[47] et de l'Agence Nationale d'Archéologie et de Protection des Sites et Monuments Historiques (ANAPSMH)[48], puis sa restructuration en 2005 en un Centre National de Recherche Archéologique (CNRA)[49], explique le processus de concentration de l'action archéologique au niveau du ministère de la Culture et le conditionnement de la recherche aux mêmes dispositifs de la gestion et de la sauvegarde du patrimoine[50], au point de la déconnecter de l'enseignement supérieur et de la recherche académique[51].

3.1   *L'histoire antique*

Jusqu'aux années soixante-dix, l'Université d'Alger qui assurait l'enseignement de l'histoire en langue française a maintenu la même dynamique historiographique issue de l'école coloniale, notamment à travers la coopération française. Deux grands chercheurs furent parmi les principaux acteurs de l'Antiquité ; il s'agit d'A. Mandouze et de P.A. Février, connus pour leur détermination à l'algérianisation de l'archéologie et à leur engagement progressiste. L'Antiquité a rapidement cédé la place aux périodes contemporaines et médiévales, en la reléguant au second plan. La mise en place de la politique d'arabisation du secteur de l'enseignement a favorisé l'ouverture sur les universités du Proche-Orient[52], notamment dans le domaine des sciences sociales et humaines et l'instauration de la référence arabo-musulmane dans le nouveau discours. Ainsi, s'est établie une méfiance vis-à-vis de l'héritage de l'antiquité, en occurrence l'antiquité romaine, favorisant les questions des royaumes numides, les concepts de la résistance ou celles de l'origine orientale de la population maghrébine. On doit noter aussi, que devant le besoin grandissant de l'encadrement pédagogique, il a fallu sacrifier les prérequis nécessaires

---

47   Décret n. 87-231 du 3 Novembre 1987 portant création d'un office du Parc National de l'Ahaggar.

48   *Décret n. 87-10 du 6 Janvier 1987, portant création de l'Agence Nationale d'Archéologie et de Protection des Sites et Monuments Historiques.*

49   *Décret n. 05-491 du 22 Décembre 2005 portant création du Centre National de Recherches Archéologiques.*

50   F. Soufi, « En Algérie : l'histoire et sa pratique », dans *Savoirs historiques au Maghreb*, Oran, CRASC, 132.

51   F. Soufi, « En Algérie : l'histoire et sa pratique», ibid, 130 ; N. Benseddik, *L'archéologie antique en Algérie hier et aujourd'hui*, op. cit., 196 ; « Les services archéologiques furent partagés à partir de 1969 entre deux ministères, Préhistoire à l'Éducation, Antiquité et Moyen Âge à l'Information ce qui eut pour première conséquence grave une rupture entre l'enseignement supérieur et la recherche archéologique ».

52   Le processus d'arabisation des facultés d'histoire et des départements de sciences humaines a commencé en 1973, ce qui a encouragé la coopération avec le Proche Orient, et le recours aux enseignants égyptiens, irakiens ou syriens, ainsi que l'acquisition des ouvrages rédigés ou traduits en arabe.

en matière de compétences pour faciliter le recrutement de nouveaux enseignants dans cette spécialité (Fig. 5.2).

C'est seulement à partir des années quatre-vingt que la production historique de l'université algérienne a commencé à voir le jour. Il suffit de suivre
le parcours des premiers enseignants algériens pour saisir les fondements de
cette tendance. Muḥammad al-Bašīr Šnītī[53] a entamé sa carrière, à partir d'un
DEA sur la politique de la romanisation au Maghreb antique ; il s'est orienté
vers l'histoire économique sociale[54] et enfin, vers l'Antiquité tardive[55]. Sa
direction d'un nombre important de thèses d'histoire et d'archéologie, dans
les différentes universités algériennes lui confère le statut de doyen de cette
discipline. Par ailleurs, Muḥammad al-Ṣaġīr Ġanim s'est investi dans l'histoire
Libyco-Punique[56]. Il enseigna à l'université de Constantine produisant plusieurs ouvrages et encadrant plusieurs thèses dans cette spécialité[57]. Ces deux
chercheurs ont suivi le même parcours de formation en histoire à l'université
d'Alger encadrés par El Ūlfi[58] puis par M.H. Fantar[59]. Ils ont influencé l'histoire de l'Algérie post-indépendante par leurs publications, mais aussi par le
nombre élevé de thèses et mémoires encadrés. Dans cette même mouvance
Muḥammad al-Ṭāhar ʿAdwānī décédé prématurément a soutenu aussi une
thèse sur la période punique au Maghreb[60], ainsi que Muḥammad al-Hādī
Ḥāriš qui a soutenu, à son tour, une thèse de magister sur l'évolution politique
et économique de la Numidie[61].

---

53 Muḥammad al-Bašīr Šnītī, *Siyāsat al-rawmana fī bilād al-Maġrib min suqūṭ al-dawla
    al-Qarṭāġiyya li-suqūṭ Mūrīṭaniyya 140q.m-40m*, DEA, Université d'Alger, 1975.

54 Idem, *al-Awḍāʿ al-iqtiṣādiyya wa al-iġtimāʿiyya fī al-Maġrib al-rūmānī wa dawruhā fī aḥdāṯ
    al-qarn al-rābiʿ al-mīlādī*, thèse de doctorat, Université d'Alger, 1981.

55 Idem, *Murīṭāniyyā al-Qayṣariyya : Dirāsa ḥawla al-līmas wa muqāwamat al-Mūr*, thèse de
    doctorat, Université d'Alger, 1992.

56 Muḥammad al-Ṣaġīr Ġanim, *al-Tawassuʿ al-finīqī fī ġarb al-baḥr al-mutawassiṭ*, diplôme
    d'étude superieur, Université d'Alger, 1974.

57 Idem, *al-Tawāġud al-finīqī- al-būnī fī al-Ǧazāʾir*, doctorat troisième cycle, Université
    d'Alger, 1981 ; *al-Musāhama al-ḥaḍāriyya al-būniyya fī al-mamlaka al-nūmīdiyya*, thèse de
    doctorat d'État, Université de Constantine, 1996.

58 Professeur égyptien à l'Université d'Alger, en coopération depuis la fin des années
    soixante-dix.

59 Professeur tunisien, spécialiste d'histoire et d'archéologie punique.

60 Muḥammad al-Ṭāhar ʿAdwānī, *Dirāsa li-l-ḥaḍāra fī ʿuṣūr mā qabla al-tārīḫ bi-al-Ṣaḥrāʾ
    al-Ǧazāʾiriyya wa ḫāṣṣatan aṯnāʾ al-ʿaṣr al-ḥaǧarī al-ḥadīṯ*, mémoire de magister, Université
    d'Alexandrie, 1983.

61 Muḥammad al-Hādī Ḥāriš, *al-Taṭawwur al-siyāsī wa al-iqtiṣādī fī Nūmīdiyā munḏu iʿtilāʾ
    Māsīnīsā al-ʿarš ilā wafāt Yūbā al-awwal 203-46 qabla al-mīlād*, mémoire de magister,
    Université d'Alger*, 1985.

Il est important de souligner que cette production rédigée exclusivement en arabe a eu recours à la documentation coloniale ; elle a adopté la même périodisation historique tout en accordant une importance particulière à la période préromaine. L'histoire de Carthage s'est jumelée à l'histoire des royaumes numides afin d'argumenter une continuité historique remontant aux périodes les plus anciennes. Le territoire de la Numidie est considéré comme l'espace historique algérien[62], notamment à travers des personnalités clés tel que Massinissa ou Jugurtha. Par ailleurs si la dimension préhistorique a ouvert de nouvelles perspectives au concept identitaire, la reconquête historique algérienne s'est focalisée principalement sur les périodes contemporaine et islamique au dépend de l'Antiquité, montrant ainsi des limites de cette production.

Plusieurs étudiants ont poursuivi leurs études au Proche Orient, notamment en Égypte. Ils ont soutenu des mémoires de magister traitant en grande partie les questions des relations entre l'Égypte et le Maghreb préromain. Il s'agit d'étudiants de l'Université d'Alger ou de l'Université de Constantine qui ont fait des choix de sujets en fonction de leur nouvel environnement. Effectivement les projets de Šāfiya Šāran[63], Fatīḥa Farḥātī[64], Umm al-Ḥayr Al-ʿAqqūn[65] ou de Slīman Ban al-Saʿdī[66] ont introduit la documentation égyptienne dans la recherche sur l'Antiquité. Ces chercheurs ont même poursuivi cette démarche dans leurs projets de thèses et d'encadrement, sans pouvoir renouveler l'état de la recherche ni d'apporter de réelles réponses aux questionnements en lien avec l'Égypte pharaonique. Ainsi en dépit de l'importance des sources hiéroglyphes, l'apport de la documentation soutenue s'est limité à des généralités.

---

62   F. Soufi, « En Algérie : l'histoire et sa pratique », op. cit., 123-145.

63   Šāfiya Šāran, *Awḍāʿ al-Nūmīdiyyīn fī ẓill al-ḥukm al-rūmānī wa mawqifuhum minhu*, mémoire de magister, Université du Caire, 1983 ; Idem, *al-Našaṭ al-tiǧārī fī Nūmīdiyā wa Mūrṭīaniyā al-Qayṣariyya aṯnāʾ al-iḥtilāl al-rūmānī : al-ʿahd al-imbrāṭūrī al-awwal*, thèse de doctorat, Université d'Alger, 2001.

64   Fatīḥa Farḥātī, *Nūmīdiyā min ḥukm Ġāyā ilā bidāyat al-iḥtilāl al-rūmānī, al-ḥayāt al-siyāsiyya wa al-ḥaḍāriyya 213-46.m*, Université du Caire, 2003. Nous n'avons pu consulter que la publication de ce mémoire.

65   Umm al-Ḥayr Al-ʿAqqūn, *al-ʿAlāqāt al-ḥaḍāriyya wa al-siyāsiyya bayna Miṣr wa šamāl ǧarb Ifrīqiya munḏu aqdam al-ʿuṣūr ḥattā nihāyat al-alf al-ṯāniya qabla al-mīlād*, mémoire de magister, Université d'Alexandrie, 1988 ; Idem, *Al-Lībiyyūn wa taʾsīsihim li-l-dawla fī Miṣr al-firʿawniyya*, thèse de doctorat d'État, Université Oran, 1996.

66   Slīman Ban al-Saʿdī, *Šuʿūb al-baḥr wa ʿalāqatuhum bi-Miṣr 1300-1150 q.m : dirāsa tārīḫiyya*, mémoire de magister, Université d'Alexandrie, 1992 ; Idem, *ʿalāqat Miṣr bi-l-Maǧrib al-qadīm munḏu faǧr al-tārīḫ ḥattā al-qarn 7q. m.*, thèse de doctorat d'État, Université de Constantine, 2009.

Par ailleurs, le nombre de thèses d'histoire antique, soutenues en France, reste très modeste par rapport aux autres spécialités d'histoire. À Paris 1, M. Zidane a fait un état de la recherche comparée de Cuicul et de Sitifis[67]. À Lyon 3, O.A. Amara a étudié la question de la guerre chez les Numides et les Maures[68]. Enfin, à Aix, B. Mokrenta a réalisé une compilation importante des sources arabes servant à l'étude des cités à la fin de l'Antiquité[69].

Il est clair que la production scientifique préparée et soutenue dans les universités étrangères a véhiculé de nouvelles approches méthodologiques ; elle répondait en grande partie à l'état de la recherche de ces institutions d'accueil. Contrairement à la Tunisie ou au Maroc, l'Antiquité algérienne n'a entretenu qu'une discrète implication dans les milieux de publications et de recherches internationales, à une exception prés de quelques préhistoriens qui ont maintenu une certaine rigueur méthodologique. Cependant le contexte politique de l'algérianisation de l'université a favorisé, dés le début des années quatre vingt dix, l'émergence d'une nouvelle génération, formée exclusivement en Algérie et l'introduction de nouvelles pratiques et préoccupations.

En effet, les conditions politiques des années soixante-dix ont facilité la création de deux nouveaux départements d'histoire à Oran et à Constantine. Cependant, il a fallu attendre les années quatre-vingt dix pour constater l'émergence de quelques projets de thèses sur l'antiquité. Cette phase est caractérisée par l'ouverture de quelques dossiers de l'histoire du Maghreb antique tels que les réformes sévériennes traitées par Tasaʿdīt Ramaḍān[70] le donatisme étudié par Ḥadīǧa Manṣūrī[71], les Maures et les Byzantins par Yūsuf ʿAybaš[72], ou la période romaine étudiée par Ismāʿīl Ḥamīsī[73], et B'šārī Muḥammad

---

67   M. Zidane, *Djemila et Sétif : l'urbanisme comparé de deux villes romaines d'Afrique du nord*, thèse de doctorat, Paris-Sorbonne, Dir. M. Christol, 2002.

68   Wīza Āyt Aʿmāra, *Dawr al-safīna fī-l-tiǧāra wa al-tawassuʿ al-istiṭānī fī al-baḥr al-mutawassiṭ al-qadīm*, mémoire de magister, Université d'Alger, 1996 ; Idem, *Recherche sur les Numides et les maures face à la guerre depuis les guerres puniques jusqu'à l'époque de Juba 1er*, thèse de doctorat, Université Jean Moulin Lyon 3, Dir. Y. Le Bohec, 2007.

69   B. Mokrenta, *L'Algérie antique (Maurétanie, Césarienne, Sitifienne et Numidie) à travers les sources arabes du Moyen-Âge, thèse de doctorat*, Aix-Marseille 1, 2005.

70   Tasaʿdīt Ramaḍān, *al-Iṣlāḥāt al-Sīfīriyya fī bilād al-Maġrib al-qadīm 193-235 mīlādī*, mémoire de magister, Université d'Alger, 1990.

71   Ḥadīǧa Manṣūrī, *al-Dūnātiyya wa ṯawrāt al-qarn al-rābiʿ fī šamāl Ifrīqiyya*, mémoire de magister, Université d'Oran, 1987 ; Idem, *al-Taṭawwurāt al-iqtṣādiyya li-Mūrīṭāniyya al-Qayṣariyya aṯnāʾal-iḥtilāl al-rūmānī*, thèse de doctorat, Université d'Oran, 1996.

72   Yūsuf ʿAybaš, *al-Mūr wa al-bizanṭiyīn ḫilāl al-qarn 6 mīlādī*, mémoire de magister, Université de Constantine, 1996 ; Idem, *al-Awḍāʿ al-iǧtimāʿiyya wa al-iqtiṣādiyya fī bilad al-Maġrib aṯnāʾ al-iḥtilāl al-bizanṭī*, thèse de doctorat, Université de Constantine, 2007.

73   Ismāʿīl Ḥamīsī, *Taṭawwur al-muǧtamaʿ al-lātīnī min ḫilāl al-tašrīʿāt*, Université d'Alger, 1996.

al-Ḥabīb[74]. Il est clair que cette génération a appréhendé l'antiquité à travers le regard magrébin tout en empruntant une démarche méthodologique actualisée. Par ailleurs, l'intérêt pour l'Antiquité orientale s'est multiplié grâce à l'influence des enseignants coopérants venus du Proche Orient, il s'est traduit par l'inscription de plusieurs projets de recherche sur la Mésopotamie, dont celle de ʿAbd al-ʿAzīz Ban Laḥraš[75], de Āsiyā Masʿūdī[76], Ibrāhīm al-ʿĪd Bašī[77], ou de Ḥūriyya ʿAbd Allāh[78]. Balqāsam Raḥmānī s'est intéressé davantage à l'histoire de l'Arabie Sud[79], tandis que T. Drāʿ à étudié celle des religions préislamiques[80]. Ce choix, favorisé par les coopérants du Proche Orient, a trouvé son appui dans le besoin d'encadrement pédagogique et de la disponibilité de la documentation en langue arabe. Ainsi, à défaut de maitriser les outils de recherche dans cette discipline, l'orientation vers les sciences de l'Antiquité orientale ne pouvait se développer que d'une manière timide.

Ainsi, en matière d'histroire il est à noter que l'absence de fouilles archéologiques n'a pas empêché les universités d'engager des travaux de synthèse. Il était prévisible que cette tâche, centrée exclusivement sur la documentation de seconde main ne pouvait que reproduire les acquis scientifiques déjà

74　Muḥamad al-Ḥabīb B'šārī, *Dirāsa Tārīḫiyya li-Muqāṭaʿat Mūrīṭāniyyā al-Saṭāyfiyya*, *mémoire de magister, Université d'Alger*, 2000 ; Idem, *Dawr al-muqāṭʿāt al-ifrīqiyya fī iqtiṣād Rūmā bayna 146 qabla al-mīlād wa 285 li-l-mīlād*, thèse de doctorat d'État, Université d'Alger, 2007.

75　ʿAbd al-ʿAzīz Ban Laḥraš, *Niẓām al-ḥukm fī ǧanūb bilād al-Rāfidayn al-qadīm min 3500 qabla al-mīlād. ilā 2350 mīlādī, mémoire de magister*, Université de Constantine, 1987.

76　Āsiyā Masʿūdī, *al-Tabādul al-tiǧārī bayna al-Maǧrib al-qadīm wa Īṭāliyā ḫilāla al-ʿahd al-imbrāṭūrī al-awwal qarn 1-3 lil-mīlād, mémoire de magister, Université d'Alger*, 1988.

77　Ibrāhīm al-ʿĪd, Bašī, *al-Tawassuʿ al-ʿaskarī al-maqdūnī min ḫilal ḥamlāt al-Iskandar al-Akbar 336-323 qabla al-mīlād, mémoire de magister, Université d'Alger*, 1992 ; Idem, *al-Būnya al-ǧuǧrāfiyya wa al-ḥaḍāriyya fī al-ǧanūb al-šarqī al-ǧazāʾirī Tāsīlī – Nāǧar namūḏaǧan, dirāsa waṣfiyya li-l-minṭaqa fī al-marḥala al-qadīma*, thèse de doctorat d'État, Université d'Alger, 2005.

78　Ḥūriyya ʿAbd Allāh, *al-Tawassuʿ al-Āšūrī fī bilād al-Šām 911-612 qabla al-mīlād*, mémoire de magister, Université d'Alger, 1992 ; Idem, *al-Ḥayāt al-ṯaqāfiyya wa-al-fikriyya fī bilād al-Rāfidayn : dirāsa taḥlīliyya al-usṭūrāt wa al-malḥamāt namawḏaǧan, nihāyat al-qarn 25 qabla al-mīlād – nihāyat al-qarn 17 qabla al-mīlād*, thèse de doctorat, Université d'Alger, 2015.

79　Balqāsam Raḥmānī, *ʿAlāqāt ǧanūb šibh al-Ǧazīra al-ʿarabiyya bi-šarq Ifrīqiyyā munḏu qiyām al-duwaylāt al-ʿarabiyya al-ǧanūbiyya ḥattā al-fatḥ al-islāmī*, mémoire de magister, Université d'Alger, 1993 ; Idem, *al-Āṯār al-ḥaḍāriyya li-ʿalāqat al-Yaman bi-šamāl al-Ǧazīrat al-ʿArabiyya wa -Ifrīqiyyā qabla al-islām*, thèse de doctorat d'État, Université d'Alger, 2003.

80　Al-Ṭāhar Drāʿ, *al-Diyānāt al-qadīma fī al-Ḥiǧāz qabla al-Islām min ḫilāl al-maṣādir al-ʿarabiyya wa al-kutub al-samāwiyya, Mmmoire de magister*, Université de Constantine, 1991 ; Idem, *al-Muǧtamaʿ al-ʿarabī al-qadīm min ḫilāl kitābāt aṣḥāb al-siyar wa-al-kutāb al-qudamāʾ*, thèse de doctorat d'État, Université de Constantine, 2003.

connus. Néanmoins ces travaux de recherche ont commencé à diversifier les approches et les problématiques. Leur multiplication, à partir des années quatre-vingt-dix, est suivie d'une vertigineuse croissance, dès le debut des années deux milles. Ce qui nous a amené à les présenter selon leurs contextes thématiques, sans prendre en compte leur ordre chronologique.

3.1.1   Une approche historique de la préhistoire

La thématique de la préhistoire en Algérie a fait l'objet de plusieurs approches historiques. Une attention particulière est portée vers le Tassili, à travers la synthèse présentée par Ibrāhīm Bašī sur le Tassili[81], celle de Yuġūrṭa Ḥadadū sur la dualité des représentations animalières des gravures rupestres et de la vie humaine[82], ou d'Amḥammad Wā'il qui a analysé l'impact du climat sur la culture des sociétés sahariennes[83] et enfin celle de Laḥḍar Ban Būzīd qui a effectué une étude sur l'aspect religieux et l'activité pastorale qui se dégagent des gravures du Tassili[84]. Badr al-Dīn Slāḥǧa a réalisé une monographie sur les monuments funéraires dans la région du Zab à Biskra[85]. Nous signalons d'autres approches beaucoup plus générales, tels que l'étude de Mūḥammad Rušdī Ǧrāya sur les faciès de la préhistoire maghrébine[86], ou celle de ʿAbd al-ʿAzīz Ban Laḥraš[87].

---

81   Ibrāhīm Bašī, *al-Būnya al-ǧuġrāfiyya wa al-ḥaḍāriyya fī al-ǧanūb al-šarqī al-ǧazāʾirī Tāsīlī – Nāǧar namūḏaǧan, dirāsa waṣfiyya li-l-minṭaqa fī al-marḥala al-qadīma*, thèse de doctorat d'État, Université d'Alger, 2005.

82   Yuġūrṭa Ḥadadū, *Ahamm mašāhid al-ḥayawanāt al-ṭabīʿiyya al-kabīra fī maḥaṭṭat al-nuqūš al-ṣaḥriyya li-l-Aṭlas al-ṣaḥrāwī wa ʿalāqatuhā bi-l-insān min al-nāḥiyya al-iǧtimāʿiyya wa al-ʿaqadiyya*, mémoire de magister, Université d'Alger, 2006.

83   Amḥammad Wā'il, *Inʿikās marḥalat al-munāḥ al-amṭal ʿalā ṯaqāfat al-muǧtamʿāt fī al-Ṣaḥrāʾ al-wusṭā 7000 qabla al-mīlād ilā ġāyat 2500 qabla al-mīlād*, mémoire de magister, Université d'Oran 1, 2014.

84   Laḥḍar Ban Būzīd, *al-Aṯar al-dīnī fī mašāhid al-rusūm al-ṣaḥriyya li-minṭaqat al-Ṭāsīlī-Nāǧar ḥilal marḥalat al-ruʾūs al-mustadīra : 8000 q m-2500 q m*, mémoire de magister, Université d'Alger, 2010 ; Idem, *Ḥaḍārat al-ruʿāt fī al-niyūlītī bi-l-Ṭāsīlī-Nāǧar wa al-Hūǧar min ḥilāl al-fan al-ṣaḥrī : 6000 q.m. 1000 q.m.* , thèse de doctorat, Université d'Alger, 2016.

85   Badr al-Dīn Slāḥǧa, *al-Maʿālim al-ǧanāʾiziyya li-fatrat faǧr al-tārīḥ b-manṭiqat Biskra "Ǧabal al-Zāb" : dirāsa aṯariyya wa miʿmāriyya*, mémoire de magister, Université d'Alger, 2012.

86   Mūḥammad Rušdī Ǧrāya, *al-Ṣaḥrāʾ al-Ǧazāʾiriyya ḥilāl al-ʿaṣr al-ḥaǧarī al-ḥadīṯ 6100 qabla al-mīlād 1000 qabla al-mīlād*, mémoire de magister, Université de Constantine, 2007 ; Idem, *Malāmiḥ al-ʿaṣr al-ḥaǧarī al-qadīm fī bilād al-Maġrib : dirāsa ḥaḍāriyya aṯariyya*, thèse de doctorat, Université d'Alger, 2012.

87   ʿAbd al-ʿAzīz Ban Laḥraš, *Bašariyyāt mā qabla al-insān*, thèse de doctorat d'État, Université de Constantine, 2003.

En ce qui concerne l'histoire punique, le thème traditionnel de la vie religieuse à Carthage a été réouvert par Ǧamāl Maḥbūs[88], et Zīnab Balʿabad, qui a traité les stèles du temple punique d'el Hofra[89], ou Ṣabāḥ ʿAla[90]. Le thème des industries de Carthage a été traité par Fahīma Ḥamdāš[91], Wīza Āyt Aʿmāra, pour sa part a étudié le rôle des navires dans le commerce et la colonisation[92], suivi de ʿAbd al-Mālik Slāṭniyya, qui a étudié les comptoirs puniques à l'Ouest de la méditerranée[93], et de al-Saʿīd Qaʿr al-Maṭrad qui a étudié l'agriculture avant la chute de Carthage[94]. Le dossier des guerres carthaginoises a été réouvert par Murād Rīǧī[95], par Ḥalīma Larābī[96]et par Ḥasān Balʿīd qui a consacré son travaille à Hannibal[97]. Dans la même perspective Rīma Malīzīqui a mis en exergue la politique maritime de Carthage[98]. ʿAmr Ban Drīs a réalisé une thèse sur le conflit Cartago- grec[99], Karīma Nūr al-Dīn sur la politique des

88   Ǧamāl Maḥbūs, *al-Ḥayāt al-dīniyya fī Qarṭāǧanna*, Université d'Oran, 2011.

89   Zīnab Balʿabad, *al-Muqaddas wa-l-ramz min ḫilāl nuṣub maʿbad al-Ḥufra bi-Qasanṭīna al-qarnayn al-ṯāliṯ wu-l-ṯānī q.m.*, mémoire de magister, Université de Constantine, 2005 ; Idem, *al-Malāmiḥ al-ǧanaʾiziyya wa al-naḏriyya li-l-būniyyīn wa-l-nūmīdiyyīn fī al-mamlaka al-Nūmīdiyya : dirāsa taḥlīliyya min ḫilāl al-mʿālim al-aṯariyya*, thèse de doctorat, Université de Constantine, 2016.

90   Ṣabāḥ ʿAla, *al-Muʿtaqadāt al-dīniyya al-qarṭāǧiyya 814 q m-264 q m*, mémoire de magister, Université d'Alger, 2011 ; Idem, *Muʿtaqadāt bilād al-Maġrib wa ʿalāqatuhā bi-muʿtaqadāt al-Šarq al-Adnāal-qadīm. al-Maġrib wa Miṣr namūḏaǧan*, thèse de doctorat, Université d'Alger, 2017.

91   Fahīma Ḥamdāš, *al-Ṣināʿāt al-ḥirafiyya fī Qarṭāǧa al-būnīqiyya*, mémoire de magister, Université d'Alger, 2009 ; Idem, *al-Ḥayāt al-iqtiṣādiyya fī Ifrīqiyya al-Brūqunṣuliyya : min iṣlāḥāt aūǧusṭus ilā iṣlāḥāt Daqlidiyyānūs*, thèse de doctorat, Université d'Alger, 2018.

92   Āyt Aʿmāra, *Dawr al-Safīna*.

93   ʿAbd al-Mālik Slāṭniyya, *Al-Mustawṭanāt al-finīqiyya – al-būniyya fī al-Ḥawḍ al-Ġarbī li-l-baḥr al-mutawassiṭ*, thèse de doctorat, Université de Constantine, 2010.

94   al-Saʿīd Qaʿr al-Maṭrad, *al-Zirāʿa fī bilād al-Maġrib al-qadīm : malāmiḥ al-našʾa wa-al-taṭawur ḥattā tadmīr Qarṭāǧa -146 qabla al-mīlād*, mémoire de magister, Université de Constantine, 2008.

95   Murād Rīǧī, *Ḥurūb Ṣiqiliyya bayna al-Qarṭāǧiyyīn wa al-Iġrīq fī al-fatra bayn 580-265 q.m.*, mémoire de magister, Université d'Alger, 2011 ; Idem, *al-Tārīḫ al-ʿaskarī li-Qarṭāǧa bi-Ṣiqiliyya bayna al-qarnayn al-sādis wa al-ṯālit q.m.*, thèse de doctorat, Université d'Alger, 2017.

96   Ḥalīma Larābī, *al-ʿAlāqā bayna Qarṭāǧa wa Rūmā min ḫilāl al-muʿāhadāt – 509-146 qabla al-mīlād*, mémoire de magister, Université d'Alger, 2016.

97   Ḥasān Balʿīd, *Hannibaʿl wa al-ḥarb al-būniyya al-ṯāniyya 218-202 qabla al-mīlād*, mémoire de magister, Université d'Alger, 2014.

98   Rīma Malīzī, *Qarṭāǧa wa al-baḥr 814-146 q m.*, mémoire de magister, Université d'Alger, 2011.

99   ʿAmr Ban Drīs, *al-Ṣirāʿ al-qarṭāǧī al-iġrīqī fī ġarb al-mūtawassiṭ : mā bayna al-qarnayn al-sādis wa al-rābiʿ q.m.*, DEA, Université d'Alger, 1982.

Barcéens[100] et enfin, Nağla Saqwān sur la culture Carthaginoise[101]. Le sujet des guerres civiles romaines et leurs impacts sur le Maghreb a été étudié par Ḥasīna Zaġbīb[102].

Les études libyques ont fait l'objet de plusieurs mémoires. L'hypothèse d'éventuelles relations libyco-égyptiennes, à travers la documentation égyptienne a permis d'orienter le regard au-delà des sources carthaginoises, il s'agit des mémoires de Umm al-Ḥayr Al-ʿAqqūn[103], de Saʿīda Ūyaḥyā[104] et de al-Madanī Ṣawšat[105]. Néanmoins, l'ancienne problématique des relations avec l'empire de Carthage a été présentée à nouveau par Aḥmad Al-Sulīmānī[106], par Samīr Hamādī[107] et bien après par Nawāl Maġārī[108]. Signalons plusieurs études sur la langue et les inscriptions libyques par Farīda Būğamʿa[109], Mahā ʿAysawī[110] et Rūqiyya Bāmbārk[111]. Les thèmes liés à la société maghrébine ont été aussi traités par Nağat Sarḥān[112] et Ḥasība Bāḥmān[113]. Par ailleurs, l'emploi des sources égyptiennes à permis d'apporter quelques éléments de réflexions, sans pouvoir répondre aux grandes questions de l'émergence et de l'évolution de la population maghrébine.

100   Karīma Nūr al-Dīn, *Siyāsat Āl Barqa fī al-Ḥawḍ al-ġarbī li-l-mutawssiṭ : munḏu nihāyat al-ḥarb al-Būnīqiyya al-ūlā ilā wafāt Ḥannibaʿl 241-138 q.m.*, mémoire de magister, Université d'Alger, 2011.

101   Nağla Saqwān, *al-Taqāfa al-qarṭağiyya fī bilād al-Maġrib al-qadīm 814 q m-146 q m.*, mémoire de magister, Université d'Adrar, 2015.

102   Ḥasīna Zaġbīb, *al-Ḥurūb al-ahliyya fī Rūmā wa aṯaruhā ʿalā bilād al-Maġrib : 88-31 qabla al-mīlād*, mémoire de magister, Université d'Alger, 2012.

103   Umm al-Ḥayr Al-ʿAqqūn, *al-ʿAlāqāt al-ḥaḍāriyya*.

104   Saʿīda Ūyaḥyā, *Ṣilāt al-lībiyyīn bi-Miṣr munḏu fatrāt mā qabla al-ūsrāt li-nihāyat al-ḥukm al-lībī fī Miṣr*, mémoire de magister, Université d'Alger, 2003.

105   ʿAlī al-Madanī Ṣawšat, *al-ʿAlāqāt al-lībiyya al-miṣriyya fī ẓill al-ṣirāʿ al-fārīsī al-iġrīqī*, mémoire de magister, Université d'Oran, 2017.

106   Aḥmad Al-Sulīmānī, *al-Ṣilāt al-qarṭāğiyya al-lūbiyya min al-nawāḥī al-siyāsiyya wa al-iğtimāʿiyya wa al-ḥaḍāriyya wa dalālāti al-nuqūš al-maktūba ; al-qarn 5 wabla al-mīlād 146 qabla al-mīlād*, Université d'Alger, 2011.

107   Samīr Hamādī, *Maẓāhir al-taʾṯīr al-ḥaḍārī al-fīnīqī fī al-ḍiffa al-šamāliyya al-ġarbiyya li-ḥawḍ al-baḥr al-abyaḍ al-mutawissaṭ : ğuzur Ṣīqiliyya, Sardīniyya wa al-Balyar namū-dağan 1200-550 q.m.*, mémoire de magister, Université d'Alger, 2012.

108   Nawāl Maġārī, *Qarṭāğa wa al-lībyyūn : Dirāsa fī al-alāqa al-ḥaḍariyya 480-146 q.m.*, mémoire de magister, Université d'Alger, 2014.

109   Farīda Būğamʿa, *al-Kitāba al-Lībiyya*, mémoire de magister, Université d'Alger, 2012.

110   Mahā ʿAysawī, *al-Nuqūš al-lūbiyya fī Šamāl Ifrīqiyya : dirāsa tārīḫiyya – luġawiyya*, mémoire de magister, Université de Constantine, 2002.

111   Rūqiyya Bāmbārk, *al-Lūġa al-lūbiyya al-qadīma min ḫilāl al-maṣādir al-madiyya wa-l-kitābiyya*, mémoire de magister, Université d'Adrar, 2016.

112   Nağat Sarḥān, *Baʿḍ min malāmiḥ al-ḥayāt al-yawmiyya fī al-muğtamaʿ al-lībī al-qadīm*, mémoire de magister, Université de Constantine, 2005.

113   Ḥasība Bāḥmān, *Sukkān bilād al-Maġrib al-qadīm fī al-ʿahd al-qarṭāğī 814 qabla al-mīlād-146 qabla al-mīlād*, mémoire de magister, Université d'Adrar, 2015.

Outre les travaux de la première génération d'historiens algériens[114], l'histoire des Royaumes Numides se poursuit par de jeunes chercheurs. Mais au-delà de leurs intitulés, cette reprise des problématiques traditionnelles peine à renouveler la documentation essentielle, ne fait que reproduire le même discours littéraire. Il s'agit des mémoires de Maḍwī Ḫāldiyya sur les rois du Maghreb préromain[115] et d' ʿĪsā Ban Maqallātī sur le royaume de Maurétanie[116]. En ce qui concerne la religion, Nādiya Yafṣaḥ a étudié les divinités numido- puniques[117], ʿAbd al-Raḥmān Ḫalfa la religion païenne[118], al-Bašīr Kīḥal a travaillé sur l'influence relgieuse punique[119], Līnda ʿUṯman sur les pratiques religieuses et les rites funéraires[120]. L'influence carthaginoise a été étudiée par Aḥmad Būmaʿqal Mūlāy al-Ḥāǧǧ[121] et les relations de ces royaumes avec le monde méditerranéen, traités dans le même contexte par ʿAlī Aḥmad Šaʿbān[122], Dahbiyya Sī al-Hādī[123], Wafāʾ Būġrāra[124] et Tāwrīrt Muṣṭafā[125].

---

114 Cf. Fatīḥa Farḥātī, *Nūmīdiyā min ḥukm Ġāyā* ; Yammūna Baġdādī, *Dirāsa ḥawla Mūrīṭaniyya qabla al-iḥtilāl al-rūmanī*, mémoire de magister, Université d'Alger, 1994.

115 Maḍwī Ḫāldiyya, *Mulūk bilād al-Maġrib al-qadīm qabla al-iḥtilāl al-rūmānī*, mémoire de magister, Université d'Oran, 2009 ; Bulaḫluḫ, Muḥammad, *al-Tanẓīm al-ʿaskarī li-mamlkat Nūmīdiyā min sanat 220 ilā 46 q.m.*, mémoire de magister, Université d'Alger, 2016.

116 ʿĪsā Ban Maqallātī, *Mamlakat Murīṭāniyyā bayna al-tabaʿiyya li-Rūma wa al-istiqlāliyya : min 25 qabla al-mīlād ilā 40 li-l-mīlād, mémoire de magister, Université d'Alger*, 2015.

117 Nādiya Yafṣaḥ, *Ālihat al-ḥiṣb al-būniyya al-nūmīdiyya fī Šamāl Afrīqiyyā*, mémoire de magister, Université d'Alger, 2004.

118 ʿAbd al-Raḥmān Ḫalfa, *al-Diyānāt al-waṭaniyya al-maġrībiyya al-qadīma munḏu al-našʾa ilā suqūṭ Qarṭāǧa, 146 qabla al-mīlād, mémoire de magister*, Université de Constantine, 2008.

119 al-Bašīr Kīḥal, *al-Ḥuḍūr al-dīnī al-būnī fī Nūmīdiyā -814 qabla al-mīlād -146 qabla al-mīlād, mémoire de magister, Université d'Alger*, 2012.

120 Līnda ʿUṯmān, *al-ʿĀdāt al-dīniyya wa al-ṭuqūṣ wa al-šaʿāʾir al-ǧanāʾiziyya fī bilād al-Maġrib al-qadīm fī-l-fatra al-lībiyya al-būniyya*, mémoire de magister, Université d'Alger 2, 2014.

121 Aḥmad Būmaʿqal Mūlāy al-Ḥāǧǧ, *Maẓāhir min al-taʾṯīr al-qarṭāǧī fī Nūmīdiyā : al-zirāʿa, al-diyāna wa al-luġa, min al-Qarn al-ṯāliṯ ilā 146 qabla al-mīlād, mémoire de magister, Université d'Alger*, 2009 ; Idem, *al-Aǧānib fī madīnat Qarṭāǧa, min al-qarn al-rābiʿ ilā 146 qabla al-mīlād ; al-miṣriyyūn wa al-Iġrīqiyyūn namūḏaǧan*, thèse de doctorat, Université d'Alger, 2015.

122 ʿAlī, Aḥmad Šaʿbān, *al-Siyāsa al-ḫāriǧiyya li-mamlakatay Nūmīdiyā wa Murīṭāniyā fī ʿahd al-mamālik : min al-qarn al-ṯāliṯ qabla al-mīlād ilā 40 li-l-mīlād, mémoire de magister, Université d'Alger*, 2010.

123 Dahbiyya Sī al-Hādī, *al-Mamālīk al-nūmīdiyya bayna Qarṭāǧa wa Rūmā min nihāyat al-qarn al-ṯālit q.m li-l-qarn al-awwal q.m : dirāsa siyāsiyya waʿaskariyya*, mémoire de magister, Université d'Alger, 2014.

124 Wafāʾ Būġrāra, *al-Ḥayāt al-ṯaqāfiyya fī al-Maġrib al-qadīm bayna al-aṣāla wa taʾṯīr al-ṯaqāfa al-wāfida*, mémoire de magister, Université d'Adrar, 2014 ; Idem, *al-ʿAlāqa al-iǧtīmāʿiyya wa al-taqāfiyya bayna al-Maġrib al-qadīm wa šuʿūb al-baḥr al-abyaḍ al-mutawassaṭ*, thèse de doctorat, Université d'Adrar, 2018.

125 Tāwrīrt Muṣṭafā, *Al-ʿAlaqāt al-nūmīdiyya al-rūmāniyya bayna al-siyāda wa al-tabaʿiyya, 203 q, m-46 q, m.*, mémoire de magister, Université d'Alger, 2016.

Plusieurs études ont traité le thème de l'histoire sociale du Maghreb antique. Parmi les travaux réalisés, il convient de citer celui de l'évolution de la société latine à partir des sources législatives, étudiée par Ismā'īl Ḥamīsī[126]. Mahā 'Aysawīa a dressé un large tableau de la société libyque depuis la préhistoire[127], Aksīl Laḥlū[128] et Maryam Ṭayyab[129] ont travaillé sur les structures sociales au Maghreb, Bint al-Nabī Muqaddam sur la famille[130] et Kāhīna Qbāylī sur la problématique des esclaves[131]. Wahība Būnḏawīa a étudié la présence des juifs dans le Maghreb antique[132]. Enfin Muḥammad Qāsīm a étudié l'évolution sociale et démographique à l'Ouest de la Maurétanie Césarienne[133]. L'intérêt s'est porté même à l'étude du quotidien de l'armée romaine au Maghreb par Farīda Būḥalaf[134]. Le thème des jeux a été traité par Ğāliyya Naṣāḥ[135] et Riḍā Ban 'Allāl[136]. En revanche, les problématiques religieuses sont encore discrètes, nous pouvons citer le mémoire de Muḫtar Nāyar sur les religions païennes du Maghreb durant l'occupation romaine[137], celui de Mağīd Mhannī sur les aspects de la religion romaine au Maghreb[138], de Muḥammad Ban 'Abd al-Mu'-

126   Ismā'īl Ḥamīsī, *Taṭawwur al-muğtama'*.

127   Mahā 'Aysawī, *al-Muğtama' fī bilād al-Maġrib al-qadīm min 'uṣūr mā qabla al-tārīḫ ilā 'ašiyyat al-fatḥ al-islāmī*, thèse de doctorat, Université de Constantine, 2010.

128   Aksīl Laḥlū, *al-Tarkība al-iğtimāi'yya li-l-Maġrib al-qadīm : 146q.m 40m.*, mémoire de magister, Université d'Alger, 2016.

129   Maryam Ṭayyib, *al-Nuẓum al-iğtimā'iyya fī Nūmīdiyā : min maṭla' al-qarn al-awwal mīladī ilā nihāyat al-qarn al-ṯāliṯ mīladī*, mémoire de magister, Université d'Adrar, 2014.

130   Bint al-Nabī Muqaddam, *al-Usra fī bilād al-Maġrib al-qadīm ḫilāl al-'ahd al-rūmānī al-imbrāṭūrī al-a'alā 27 qabla al-mīlād -284 al-mīlādī*, thèse de doctorat, Université d'Alger, 2013.

131   Kāhīna Qbāylī, *al-'Abīd fī bilād al-Maġrib ḫilāl al-'ahd al-rūmānī 146 q m-430m*, mémoire de magister, Université d'Alger, 2006 ; Idem, *al-Ḥayāt al-iğtmā'iyya fī al-Maġrib al-qadīm ḫilāl al-qarn al-rābi' wa al-ḫāmis fī ẓill al iḥtilāl al-rūmānī : al-fi'āt wu al-ṭabaqāt al-iğtima'iyya*, thèse de doctorat, Université d'Alger, 2016.

132   Wahība Būnḏawī, *al-Yahūd fī bilad al-Maġrib fī al-'uṣūr al-qadīma 814 q.m-146q.m.*, mémoire de magister, Université d'Alger, 2012.

133   Muḥammad Qāsim, *al-Waḍ'iyya al-iğtmā'iyya wa-l-dīmūğrafiyya li-ğarb Mūrīṭaniyya al-Qayṣariyya min 42 ilā sanat 284m.*, mémoire de magister, Université d'Oran, 2015.

134   Farīda Būḥalaf, *al-Ğayš al-rūmānī wa ḥayātuhu fī al-Maġrib al-qadīm min sanat 146 q m-40 m.*, mémoire de magister, Université d'Alger, 2014.

135   Ğāliyya Naṣāḥ, *Maẓāhir al-tasliyya wa al-tarfīh fī muqāṭa'at Afrīqiyya al-rūmāniyya min muntaṣaf al-qarn 2 q. m. ilā al-qarn al-rābi' al-mīladī*, mémoire de magister, Université d'Alger, 2010.

136   Riḍā Ban 'Allāl, *al-'Arabāt fī al-ḥawḍ al-ġarbī li-l-baḥr al-abyaḍ al-mutawassaṭ fī al-'uṣūr al-qadīma*, mémoire de magister, Université d'Alger, 2001 ; Idem, *Al-al'āb fī al-Maġrib al-qadīm aṯnā āl-iḥtilāl al-rūmānī*, thèse de doctorat, Université d'Alger, 2012.

137   Muḫtar Nāyar, *al-Diyāna al-waṭaniyya fī bilād al-Maġrib al-qadīm aṯnā' al-iḥtilāl al-rūmānī al-'ahd al-imbrāṭūrī al-a'lā*, mémoire de magister, Université d'Oran, 2006.

138   Mağīd Mhannī, *Maẓāhir al-diyāna al-rūmāniyya fī bilād al-Maġrib al-qadīm*, mémoire de magister, Université d'Alger, 2013.

min sur les croyances post mortem[139], ainsi que celui de Saʿīd Būʿlam sur la présence des divinités orientales en Numidie[140].

La résistance maghrébine à la romanisation demeure encore d'actualité. On note le travail de Muḥammad al-ʿArbī ʿAqqūn sur la campagne de Jules César en Afrique[141], ainsi que celui de Ḥamādūš Būlaḥrāṣ[142], de Fatḥī Dardār[143] ou de ʿAmr Būṣbīʿ[144] sur le même sujet. Būzakrī Yāsīna a réalisé une analyse du processus d'occupation de la Maurétanie Césarienne[145]. Mais ce qui a suscité le plus d'intérêt sont les fortifications romaines, étudiées par ʿAbd al-Qādir Saḥrāwī[146] et de ʿAzzūz Aʿrab[147]. Souvent le choix s'est porté sur des contextes géographiques différents, à l'instar de Naṣīra Sāḥīr qui s'est intéressée à la Maurétanie Tingitane[148], de Bint al-Nabī Muqaddam à la politique romaine envers les tribus du Maghreb antique[149], de Ǧamāl Masarhī à la résistance numide dans les Aurès[150]. Nāṣar al-Dīn Tamām a traité le même sujet en Maurétanie Sétifienne[151]. ʿAbd al-Nāṣir Masʿūd a choisi de se concentrer sur

139 Muḥammad Ban ʿAbd al-Muʾmin, *Aqāʾid al-mawt ʿinda sukkān al-Maġrib al-qadīm*, thèse de doctorat, Université d'Oran, 2012.

140 Saʿīd Būʿlam, *al-Āliha al-šarqiyya fī muqaṭaʿat Nūmīdiya : Izys, Mythra, Kīrys anmūḏaǧan*, mémoire de magister, Université d'Alger, 2013.

141 Muḥammad al-ʿArbī ʿAqqūn, *Ḥamlat Yūlyūs Qayṣar ʿalā Ifrīqiyya 47-46 qabla al-mīlād*, *mémoire de magister*, Université de Constantine, 1996.

142 Ḥamādūš Būlaḥrāṣ, *Siyāsat Yūlyūs Qayṣar al-tawasuʿiyya wa-inʿikāsātuhā ʿalā Nūmīdiyā : 49 qabla al-mīlād-44 qabla al-mīlād*, mémoire de magister, Université d'Alger, 2014.

143 Fatḥī Dardār, *al-Ṯawra al-nūmīdiyya fī muwāǧahat al-tadaḫḫul al-rūmanī : 111-46 q. m.*, mémoire de magister, Université d'Alger, 2016.

144 ʿAmr Būṣbīʿ, *al-Ḥarb al-ahlīya bayna Būmbay wa Qayṣar wa inʿikāsatuhā ʿalā mamlakat Nūmīdiya : 44-49 q m.*, mémoire de magister, Université d'Alger, 2014.

145 Būzakrī Yāsīn, *Ḥarakāt al-istīṭān al-rūmānī fī Mūrīṭaniyyā al-Qayṣariyya ḫilāl al-ʿahd al-imbrāṭūrī al-awwal*, mémoire de magister, Université d'Alger, 2013.

146 ʿAbd al-Qādir Saḥrāwī, *al-Taḥṣīnāt al-ʿaskarīya al-rūmāniyya bi-Nūmīdiyā wa Mūrīṭāniyyā al-Qayṣariyya ḫilāl al-ʿahd al-imbrāṭūrī al-awwal*, mémoire de magister, Université d'Oran, 2002.

147 ʿAzzūz Aʿrab, *al-Taḥṣīnāt al-rūmāniyya ǧanūb Nūmīdiya wa Mūrīṭaniyya al-qayṣariyya q 1-3 m wā aṯāruhā*, mémoire de magister, Université d'Alger, 2010.

148 Naṣīra Sāḥīr, *Mūrīṭaniyyā al-Tanǧiyya, baḥṯ ḥawla al-līmas wa muqāwamat al-Mūr*, mémoire de magister, Université d'Alger, 2001.

149 Bint al-Nabī Muqaddam, *Siyāsat al-Rūmān tuǧāh qabāʾil bilād al-Maġrib al-qadīm ḫilāl al-ʿahd al-imbrāṭūrī al-awwal*, *mémoire de magister*, Université d'Oran, 2004.

150 Ǧamāl Masarhī, *al-Muqāwama al-nūmīdiyya li-al-iḥtilāl al-rūmānī fī al-ǧanūb al-šarqī al-Ǧazāʾirī : ṯawrāt al-Awrās wa al-tuḫūm al-ṣaḥrāwiyya namūḏaǧan*, mémoire de magister, Université de Constantine, 2009 ; Idem, *Awḍāʿ al-šarq al-Ǧazāʾirī al-qadīm min zawāl al-mamlaka al-Nūmīdiyya ḥattā al-ġazawāt al-wandāliyya 46 qabla al-mīlād -429 mīlādi : dirāsa taḥlīliyya ḥawla al-wāqiʿ al-siyāsī wa al-iqtiṣādī fī ẓill al-iḥtilāl al-rūmānī*, thèse de doctorat, Université de Batna, 2018.

151 Nāṣar al-Dīn Tamām, *Muqāwamat sukkān Mūrīṭāniyyā al-sṭāyfiyya li-l-iḥtilāl al-rūmānī bayna al-qarnayn al-ṯāliṯ wa al-rābiʿ mīlādi*, mémoire de magister, Université d'Alger, 2014.

la période antonine[152] et Mbārka Qūrārī a étudié la paix romaine dans les provinces africaines[153].

Le champ de recherche sur l'histoire économique a présenté un intérêt pour plusieurs auteurs qui ont orienté leurs préoccupations, suite à l'étude de Muḥammad al-Bašīr Šnītī[154], sur divers aspects de la vie économique. Nous pouvons citer le magister de Āsiyā Masʿūdī sur l'échange commercial avec l'Italie[155], du doctorat de Ḥadīǧa Manṣūrī sur l'évolution économique en Maurétanie Césarienne[156], de Šāfiya Šāran sur le commerce de la Numidie et de la Maurétanie Césarienne durant l'occupation romaine[157], de Šafīqa Āyt ʿAllāq sur le réseau routier de la meme province[158]. Saʿdiyya Sarqīn a étudié la richesse économique de la Numidie[159], Faṭīma Kablī les infrastructures économiques du Maghreb[160], Sihām Haddād les ports de l'Est algérien[161]. Dalīla Būrni[162] et al-Ǧūdī Ḥammūma[163] ont étudié le système des impôts. Nūra ʿAmrān a travaillé sur les financiers étrangers dans les provinces africaines[164]. Le travail de Muḥammad Tikyalīn appréhende le même sujet d'une manière

152 ʿAbd al-Nāṣir Masʿūd, *al-Tawassuʿ al-rūmānī fī-bilād al-Maġrib al-qadīm wa-rudūd fīʾl al-sukkān al-maḥaliyyīn ḫilāl ʿahd al-Usrat al-Anṭūniyya*, mémoire de magister, Université de Bechar, 2010.

153 Mbārka Qūrārī, *al-Silm al-rūmānī fī al-muqāṭaʿa al-Afrīqiyyā fī ʿahd al-abāṭira al-awāʾil li-l-usra al-antūniyya*, mémoire de magister, Université d'Alger, 2012.

154 Muḥammad al-Bašīr Šnītī , *al-Awḍāʿ al-iqtiṣādiyya*.

155 Āsiyā Masʿūdī, *al-Tabādul al-tiǧārī bayna al-Maġrib al-qadīm wa Īṭāliyā ḫilāla al-ʿahd al-imbrāṭūrī al-awwal qarn 1-3 lil-mīlād*, mémoire de magister, *Université d'Alger*, 1988.

156 Ḥadīǧa Manṣūrī, *al-Taṭawwurāt al-iqtṣādiyya*.

157 Šāfiya Šāran, *al-Našāṭ al-tiǧārī fī Nūmīdiyā wa Mūrīṭaniyā al-Qayṣariyya aṯnāʾ al-iḥtilāl al-rūmānī: al-ʿahd al-imbrāṭūrī al-awwal*, thèse de doctorat, Université d'Alger, 2001.

158 Šafīqa Āyt ʿAllāq, *Šabakat al-ṭuruqāt al-rūmāniyya fī al-ǧiha al-šarqiyya li-Mūrīṭaniyyā al-Qayṣariyya*, mémoire de magister, Université d'Alger, 2012.

159 Saʿdiyya Sarqīn, *Ahāmiyyat Nūmīdiyā al-iqtṣādiyya bi-l-nisba li-Rūmā min sanat 64 q.m li-nihāyat al-qarn al-ṯānī*, mémoire de magister, Université de Constantine. 1983.

160 Faṭīma Kablī, *al-Ḫalfiyya al-iqtiṣādiyya li-l-iḥtilāl al-rūmānī li-bilād al-Maġrib al-qadīm wa aṯarihā ʿalā al-mūǧtamaʿ*, mémoire de magister, Université d'Alger, 2012 ; Idem, *al-Istīṭān al rūmanī fī šamāl Ifrīqiyā, dirāsa muqārana bilād al Maġrib wa Miṣr-namūdaǧan*, thèse de doctorat, Université d'Alger, 2019.

161 Sihām Haddād, *Silsilat mawāniʾ al-šarq al-qadīma. Dirāsa tārīḫiyya waṣfiyya iʿtimādan alā al-maṣādir al-mādiyya al-maḥaliyya*, mémoire de magister, Université de Constantine, 2009.

162 Dalīla Būrni, *Taṭawwur al-niẓām al-ḍarībī al-rūmānī fī Šamāl Ifrīqiyā*, mémoire de magister, Université d'Alger, 2001.

163 al-Ǧūdī Ḥammūma, *al-Ḍarāʾib al-rūmāniyya fī bilād al-Maġrib al-qadīm Munḏu suqūṭ Qarṭāǧa 146 qabla al-mīlād ilā nihāyat al-iḥtilāl al-rūmānī 430 li-l-mīlād*, mémoire de magister, Université d'Alger, 2015.

164 Nūra ʿAmrān, *Riǧāl al-mal wa al-aʿmal al-aǧānib fī-l-muqāṭaʿa al-ifrīqiyyā al-rūmāniyya 146 q.m-285m.*, mémoire de magister, Université d'Alger, 2011.

générale[165]. D'autres chercheurs ont investi la thématique de l'agriculture, à l'image de Muḥammad al-Ḥabīb B'šārī[166], de Ṣalīḥa Hālīt[167], ainsi que Saʿīd Bāḥmad sur l'annone[168] et de Ḥasnāwī Ṣafiya sur la loi Manciana et Hadriana[169], de Nādiya ʿAwn sur l'arboriculture au Maghreb[170], de Naṣīra Sāḥir[171], de Rafīqa Būydġaġn[172], ʿAbd al-Fattāḥ Ḥanniš[173] et de Sitī Ṣandūq[174] sur l'activité agricole et artisanale. L'exploitation de l'eau a été étudiée par Karīma Sīnī[175] ainsi que ʿAlī Ḥadīdī[176].

Cependant, peu d'études sont consacrées à l'administration romaine depuis le mémoire de M. Bouchenaki sur les Magistrats de la Confédération Cirtéenne[177] ou celui de M.B. Cheniti sur la politique de la romanisation au Maghreb[178]. Nous n'avons recensé que deux thèses, celle de Tasaʿdīt Ramḍān sur les reformes sévériennes[179] et celle de Wafiya Nsīġawī sur la situation de

165 Muḥammad Tikyalīn, *al-Iḥtilāl al-rūmānī li-Lībiya wa dawruhu fī al-taṭawwur al-iqtṣādī li-l-minṭaqa: baynu ul-qarnayn 1q.m-4m. Sīrīnāyka wa Trībūlītaniya*, thèse de doctorat, Université d'Alger, 2015.

166 Muḥammad al-Ḥabīb B'šārī, *Dawr al-muqāṭʿāt al-ifrīqiyya fī iqtiṣād Rūmā bayna 146 qabla al-mīlād wa 285 li-l-mīlād*, thèse de doctorat d'État, Université d'Alger, 2007.

167 Ṣalīḥa Hālīt, *al-Zirāʿa fī al-ʿahdayni al-qarṭāǧī wa al-rūmānī fī al-Maġrib al-qadīm*, mémoire de magister, Université d'Alger, 2013.

168 Saʿīd Bāḥmad, *al-Anūna fī al-Maġrib al-rūmanī, al-ḍarāʾib al-ʿayniyya li-intāǧ al-qamḥ wa zayt al-zaytūn*, mémoire de magister, Université d'Alger 2009.

169 Ḥasnāwī Ṣafiya, *Dawr qanūnā mankyana wa hadryana fī al-zirāʿa al-maġārbiyya al-qarnayn al-awwal wa-l-tānī li-l-mīlād*, mémoire de magister, Université d'Alger, 2015.

170 Nādiya ʿAwn, *al-Zirāʿa al-šaġariyya fī bilād al-Maġrib atnāʾ al-iḥtilāl al-rūmanī 146 q.m ilā 430 m al-zaytūn wa al-kurūm*, mémoire de magister, Université d'Alger, 2012.

171 Naṣīra Sāḥir, *al-Našāṭ al-zirāʿī wa al-ṣināʿī fī muqaṭaʿatay Mūrīṭaniyya al-Ṭanǧiyya wa Bītīka wa al-ḥaraka al-tiǧāriyya baynahumā hilal al-ʿahd al-imbraṭūrī al-rūmānī al-aʿalā*, thèse de doctorat, Université d'Alger, 2012.

172 Rafīqa Būydġaġn, *al-Zirāʿa fī al-Maġrib al-qadīm atnāʾ al-iḥtlāl al-rūmanī: min bidāyat al-qarn al-tānī qabla al-mīlād ilā al-qarn al-tānī mīlādī*, mémoire de magister, Université d'Alger, 2012.

173 ʿAbd al-Fattāḥ Ḥanniš, *al-Tawassuʿ al-zirāʿī fī Ifrīqiyya al-qadīma hilāl al-fatra al-rūmāniyya*, *mémoire de magister*, Université de Constantine, 2013.

174 Sitī Ṣandūq, *al-Tarwa al-ḥayawāniyya wa al-ġiṭāʾ al-nabātī fī al-Ǧazāʾir hilāl al-ʿuṣūr al-qadīma*, thèse de doctorat, Université d'Oran, 2015.

175 Karīma Sīnī, *al-Mawārid al-māʾiyya wa ṭuruq istiġlāluhā fī bilād al-Maġrib hilāl al-iḥtilāl al-rūmānī 146q.m-429m.*, mémoire de magister, Université d'Alger, 2011.

176 ʿAlī Ḥadīdī, *al-Māʾ fī tārīḫ al-Maġrib al-qadīm*, mémoire de magister, Université de Constantine, 2014.

177 N. Benseddik, « L'archéologie antique en Algérie ».

178 Muḥammad al-Ṣaġīr Ġanim, *al-Tawassuʿ al-fīnīqī*.

179 Ismāʿīl Ḥamīsī, *Taṭawwur al-muǧtamaʿ al-lātīnī*.

la proconsulaire sous l'emprise de Rome[180]. La même situation se présente pour l'histoire culturelle qui se résume à seulement deux mémoires : Celui de Masīka Tafāt sur les Africains dans la littérature latine[181] et celui de Nūr al-Sādāt Būqūfa sur la politique culturelle de Rome[182].

De même la géographie historique n'a pas suscité beaucoup d'intérêt, un mémoire fut soutenu sur la géographie historique du Maghreb antique, celui de Mṣasdaq Rabbī[183], ainsi que quelques monographies consacrées à la Maurétanie Sétifienne par Muḥammad al-Ḥabīb B'šārī[184], à la confédération cirtéenne par Muḥammad al-ʿArbī ʿAqqūn[185], au site de Portus Magnus par Muḥammad Ban ʿAbd al-Mu'min[186] et à celui de la cité de Tiddis par Ġaniyya Būgarra[187], de Cirta par Maḍwī Ḫāldiyya[188], de Tebessa par Laḥḍar Fāḍal[189] ou de Guelma par Salwā Būšārab[190]. A une échelle plus large, Ḥakīma ʿAzzūz a étudié la Maurétanie Césarienne[191] et Saḥnūn Šrāyaf à la vallée de Chelif[192].

180 Wafiya Nsīgawī, *Awḍāʿ Afrīqiyya al-Brūqunṣuliyya fī ẓill bidāyat al-iḥtilāl al-askarī al-rūmānī 27 q m–117m*, mémoire de magister, Université de Constantine, 2004.

181 Masīka Tafāt, *Musāhamat al-Afāriqa fī taṭwīr al-adab al-lātīnī min nihāyat al-qarn al-awwal ilā al-qarn al-rābiʿ mīladī*, mémoire de magister, Université d'Alger, 2011.

182 Nūr al-Sādāt Būqūfa, *Siyāsat Rūmā al-ṯaqāfiyya fī bilād al-Maġrib al-qadīm wa mawqif al-sukkān minhā 146 qabla al-mīlād-430 mīlād*, mémoire de magister, Université d'Adrar, 2016.

183 Mṣasdaq Rabbī, *al-Ǧuġrāfiyya al-tārīḫiyya li-bilād al-Maġrib al-qadīm min ḫilāl al-nuṣūṣ al-adabiyya al-iġrīqiyya wa al-latīniyya : mudun al-mūrīṭanyatayn al-ṭanǧiyya wa al-qayṣariyya namūdaǧan*, mémoire de magister, Université d'Alger, 2010.

184 Muḥammad al-Ḥabīb B'šārī, *Dirāsa Tārīḫiyya li-Muqāṭaʿat Mūrīṭāniyyā al-Saṭāyfiyya, mémoire de magister, Université d'Alger*, 2000.

185 Muḥammad al-ʿArbī ʿAqqūn, *al-Ittiḥād al-sīrtī munḏu istīlā' Sītyūs ʿalā Sīrtā 46 qabla al-mīlād ilā aḥdāṯ al-qarn al-rābiʿ : dirāsa fī-l-tārīḫ wa-āṯār nuẓum Sīrtā al-ʿatīqa*, thèse de doctorat d'État, Université de Constantine, 2005.

186 Muḥammad Ban ʿAbd al-Mu'min, *Purtus Magnus Baṭṭīwa, dirāsa mūnūġrāfiyya*, mémoire de magister, Université d'Oran, 2006.

187 Ġaniyya Būgarra, *Madīnat Tīdīs bayna al-naš'a al-tārīḫiyya wa al-baqāyā al-aṯariyya bidāyat min fatra faǧr al-tārīḫ wa ḥattā al-qarn 3m.*, mémoire de magister, Université de Constantine, 2007 ; Idem, *Madīnat Tīdīs wa al-muḥīṭ al-Sīrtī ḫilāl al-fatra al-rūmāniyya, dirāsa iǧtimāʿiyya wa iqtiṣādiyya*, thèse de doctorat, Université de Constantine, 2018.

188 Maḍwī Ḫāldiyya, *al-Tawāṣul al-ḥaḍārī bi-madīnat Qasanṭīna fī al-ʿuṣūr al-qadīma*, thèse de doctorat, Université d'Oran, 2017.

189 Laḥḍar Fāḍal, *Tibāssa fī al-ʿuṣūr al-qadīma*, thèse de doctorat, Université d'Oran, 2018.

190 Salwā Būšārab, *Iqlīm Gālma wa mā ǧāwarahā : dirāsa mūnūġrāfiyya munḏu faǧr al-tārīḫ li-nihayat al-iḥtilāl al-rūmānī min ḫilāl al-maṣādir al-mādiyya wa-l-adabiyya*, thèse de doctorat, Université de Batna, 2018.

191 Ḥakīma ʿAzzūz, *Muqāṭaʿat Mūrīṭāniyā ʿabra al-tārīḫ al-ṭabāʿī li-Plīnyūs, dirāsa mūrfūlūǧiyya, ṭabīʿiyya, wa-ʿumrāniyya*, mémoire de magister, Université d'Alger, 2016.

192 Šrāyaf Saḥnūn, *Dirāsa mūnūġrāfiyya li-ḥawḍ al-Šalif fī al-ʿahd al-rūmānī 40-429m.*, mémoire de magister, Université d'Alger, 2011.

L'antiquité tardive n'a pas suscité beaucoup d'études ; signalons le magister de Yūsuf ʿAybaš sur les Maures et les Byzantins, suivi d'un doctorat sur les conditions économiques et sociales du Maghreb au VIe siècle[193]. Laḥdar Fāḍal[194] et Farīda Būdarabza[195] ont étudié successivement le thème de la résistance et les fortifications byzantines. ʿImād Ṭawīl a traité la politique de Justinien au Maghreb[196]. Muḥammad al-Ṣālaḥ al-ʿŪd a tenté d'effectuer une étude sur la période vandale au Maghreb[197].

Les travaux sur l'histoire du christianisme ont porté en premier lieu sur le donatisme étudié par Ḥadīǧa Manṣūrī, en lien avec les révoltes du quatrième siècle[198], puis par A. Amrane[199]. Ḥamīda Našnaš a étudié le clergé au Maghreb antique[200]. Al-Rabīʿ ʿŪlmī[201] et Saʿīda Ūyaḥyā[202] ont appréhendé l'histoire du christianisme maghrébin d'une manière globale.

3.1.2   L'histoire de l'antiquité orientale

La situation des études de l'antiquité orientale du point de vue quantitatif est plus importante que celle qui a caractérisé l'histoire du Maghreb. Les premières thèses ont été soutenues à partir de la fin des années quatre-vingts,

---

193   Yūsuf ʿAybaš, *al-Mūr wa al-bizanṭiyīn* ; *al-Awḍāʿ al-iǧtimāʿiyya*.

194   Laḥdar Fāḍal, *Muqāwamat sukkān šamāl Ifrīqiyya li-l-iḥtilāl al-bīzanṭī*, mémoire de magister, Université d'Oran, 2000.

195   Farīda Būdarabza, *al-Taḥsīnāt al-bīzanṭiyya fī bilād al-Maġrib al-qadīm*, mémoire de magister, Université Oran, 2002.

196   ʿImād Ṭawīl, *Siyāsat Ǧustīniyyan fī šamāl Afrīqiyyā 533m/565m.*, mémoire de magister, Université d'Alger, 2014.

197   Muḥammad al-Ṣālaḥ Al-ʿŪd, *al-Taḥawwulāt al-ḥaḍāriyya fī šamāl Ifrīqiya fī al-fatra al-wandāliyya 429-534 li-l-mīlād, mémoire de magister*, Université de Constantine 2010 ; Idem, *al-Taġayyurāt al-iqtiṣādiyya wa al-iǧtimāʿiyya wa al-dīniyya fī bilād al-Maġrib ḫilāl al-fatratayn al-wandāliyya wa al-bīzanṭiyya : dirāsa muqārina*, thèse de doctorat, Université d'Alger, 2018.

198   Ḥadīǧa Manṣūrī, *al-Dūnātiyya*.

199   ʿAbd al-Ḥamīd ʿAmrān, *al-Ḥaraka al-dunātiyya bayna al-inšiqāq al-dīnī wa al-taḥarrur 305-411 li-l-mīlād, mémoire de magister*, Université de Constantine, 2005 ; Idem, *al-Diyāna al-masīḥiyya fī-l-Maġrib al-qadīm– al-našʾa wa al-Taṭawwur 180-430 li-l-mīlād*, thèse de doctorat, Université de Constantine, 2011.

200   Ḥamīda Našnaš, *Riǧāl al-dīn fī buldān al-Maġrib al-qadīm min ẓuhūr al-masīḥiyya fī nihāyat al-qarn al-ṯānī ilā ġāyat al-salām al-masīḥī sanat 313 li-l-mīlād : min ḫilāl Tartūlyānūs wa al-qiddīs Kībryānūs namūḏaǧan*, mémoire de magister, Université d'Alger, 2010 ; Idem, *Riǧāl al-dīn al-maġāriba fī ẓill al-ṣirāʿ al-dīnī al-masīḥī 284-430 mīlādī*, thèse de doctorat, Université d'Alger, 2017.

201   al-Rabīʿ ʿŪlmī, *al-Masīḥiyya fī Bilād al-Maġrib al-qadīm wa dawruhā fī aḥdāṯ al-qarnayn al-rābiʿ wa al-ḫāmis al-mīlādiyayn*, thèse de doctorat, Université de Batna, 2016.

202   Saʿīda Ūyaḥyā, *al-Diyāna al-masīḥiyya fī bilād al-Maġrib al-qadīm min nihāyat al-qarn al-ṯānī mīlādī ilā bidāyat al-qarn al-ḫāmis al-mīladī 180-411m : Qarṭāǧ wa Nūmīdiya namūḏaǧan*, thèse de doctorat, Université d'Alger, 2017.

mais le lancement réel de cette discipline ne remonte qu'aux années 2003-2005 (Fig. 5.3).

L'histoire de la Mésopotamie et les pays voisins a été initié par les coopérants du Proche Orient en charge de l'enseignenent aux départements d'histoire des universités d'Alger, de Constantine et d'Oran. Il s'agit en premier lieu du magister de'Abd al-'Azīz Ban Laḥraš qui a étudié l'évolution du système politique au 3e millénaire[203], suivi de Ḥūriyya 'Abd Allāh sur l'expansion assyrienne en Proche Orient[204]. Le contexte politique de cette civilisation a été traité aussi, par Nādiya Abarkān qui a orienté son regard vers l'Iran[205] et par Fayza Bḥāyar qui s'est focalisée à son tour sur l'Assyrie[206] et par Nağwa Rāšī qui a traité le concept de la cité état en Iraq[207]. Al-Ṭayyib Zīn al-'Ābidīn a traité les processus de l'unification de la Mésopotamie[208]. Les aspects de la religion ont été traités par Zakiyya al-Ṭāhar Al-Ḥāǧǧ qui a étudié les Assyriens et les Chaldéens à travers l'Ancien Testament[209], 'Abd al-Wahhāb Kīdār a traité de l'exil babylonien[210], Samiyya Ma'ūšī du rôle de l'institution du temple[211]. Balḫīr Baqa a étudié l'impact de la religion sur la vie intellectuelle[212]. La vie culturelle

---

203 'Abd al-'Azīz Ban Laḥraš, *Niẓām al-ḥukm fī ǧanūb bilād al-Rāfidayn*.

204 Ḥūriyya 'Abd Allāh, *al-Tawassu' al-Āšūrī*.

205 Nādiya Abarkān, *Īrān fī 'ahd al-malik Qubāḏ al-awwal wa al-azma al-mazdakiyya min 488 ilā 531 mīlādī*, mémoire de magister, Université d'Alger, 2012.

206 Fayza Bḥāyar, *Āšūr fī ẓill al-taǧayyurāt al-ǧiyyūsiyāsiyya li-l-minṭaqa fī mā bayna al-qarnayn 12-7 qabla al-mīlad*, mémoire de magister, Université d'Oran, 2015.

207 Nağwa Rāšī, *Niẓām al-dawla al-madīna fī al-'Irāq al-qadīm : Sūmar kanamūḏaǧ – 3000-2470 qabla al-mīlad*, mémoire de magister, Université d'Alger, 2014 ; Idem, *Niẓām al-dawla al-madīna fī al-šarq al-Adnā al-qadīm : Sūmar, Fīnīqiyya, al-Iǧrīq 3000-335q-m.*, thèse de doctorat, Université d'Alger, 2019.

208 Ṭayyib Zīn al-'Ābidīn, *Bilād al-Rāfidayn min al-inqisām ilā al-waḥda : al-'aṣr al-bābilī al-qadīm anmūḏaǧan, 2004-1595 qabla al-mīlad*, mémoire de magister, Université d'Alger, 2015 ; Idem, *Ab'ād al-fikr al-waḥdawī wa ta'ṯīrātuhu fī wāqi' al-ḥayāt al-siyāsiyya wa al-iqtiṣādiyya wa al-iǧtimā'iyya fī bilād al-Rāfidayn 2500-539 qabla al-mīlad*, thèse de doctorat, Université d'Alger, 2019.

209 Zakiyya al-Ṭāhar Al-Ḥāǧǧ, *al-'Ahd al-qadīm wa madā 'alāqat maḍmūnihi bi-l-dawla al-ašūriyya wa al-kaldaniyya wa mamlakat yahūda*, mémoire de magister, Université d'Alger, 2004.

210 'Abd al-Wahhāb Kīdār, *al-Nafī al Bābilī wa-āṯāruhu*, mémoire de magister, Université d'Alger, 2009 ; Idem, *Ẓāhirat al-nubuwāt 'inda Banī Isrā'īl wa-aṯaruhā fī al-takwīn al-dīnī wa-al-siyāsī li-mamlakatay Yahūdā wa al-Sāmira : min al-qarn al-rābi' 'ašar ḥattā al-qarn al-ḫāmis qabla al-mīlad*, thèse de doctorat, Université d'Alger, 2017.

211 Samiyya Ma'ūšī, *Mū'assasat al-ma'bad wa dawruhā fī ḥaḍārat Wādī al-rāfidayn*, mémoire de magister, Université d'Alger, 2010.

212 Balḫīr Baqa, *Āṯār diyānat wādī al-Rāfidayn 'alā al-ḥayāt al-fikriyya, Sūmar wa-Bābil 3200-539 qabla al-mīlad*, mémoire de magister, Université d'Alger, 2009 ; Idem, *Āṯār diyānat wādī al-Rāfidayn 'alā al-'Ahd al-Qadīm*, thèse de doctorat, Université d'Alger, 2017.

a fait l'objet de quelques thèses, comme par exemple Aḥmad Damāna qui a consacré une mémoire de magister à la vie littéraire et scientifique à Babylone et Ninive et sa thèse de doctorat à la civilisation du royaume d'Ebla au nord-ouest de la Syrie[213], de Ṣufyān Būslīn qui a présenté une thèse sur la vie politique et culturelle de Sumer[214], de Ǧamīla Ḥālfī qui a étudié le monde du livre et des bibliothèques en Mésopotamie[215] ou d'Ammār Yamùūn sur la transcription[216]. ʿAṭiyya Saʿd Ǧihād a étudié les valeurs esthétiques et l'art de la sculpture[217]. L'intérêt aux études de l'héritage législatif s'est traduit par les études de Faziyya Farāḥ[218], de Muḥammad Al-ʿĪhār[219], et de Salīm Saʿīdī sur le statut personnel dans la législation en Iraq[220]. Muḥammad Tikyalīn a étudié l'évolution politique de l'état Hittite en Anatolie[221].

Depuis les années quatre-vingt-dix, l'histoire de l'Arabie ancienne est introduite dans les travaux universitaires. L'usage des sources arabes éditées et de l'abondante documentation orientale a limité sa pertinence. Nous pouvons citer les deux thèses de al-Ṭahar Drāʿ qui a traité des religions anciennes dans la société du Ḥiǧāz préislamique[222], celle de ʿAbd al-Ḥamīd Bʿayaṭiš sur le royaume des Nabatéens[223] ou de Malīka Manṣūriyya qui a étudié l'évolution du

---

213 Aḥmad Damāna, *al-Ḥayāt al-adabiyya wa al-ʿilmiyya bi-Bābil wa Nīnwā min 1792 qabla al-mīlād ilā 539 qabla al-mīlād*, mémoire de magister, Université d'Alger, 2009; Idem, *al-Dawr al-ḥaḍārī li-Mamlakat Iblā min muntaṣaf al-alf 3 qabla al-mīlād ilā muntaṣaf al-alf 2 qabla al-mīlād, Dirāsa Tārīḫiyya aṯariyya*, thèse de doctorat, Université d'Alger, 2018.

214 Ṣufyān Būslīn, *al-Ḥayāt al-siyāsiyya wa al-taqāfiyya fī bilād Sūmar ḫilal ʿahd sulālat Ūr al-tāliṯ 2112-2004 q m.*, mémoire de magister, Université d'Alger, 2010.

215 Ǧamīla Ḥālfī *al-Maktaba wa-l-maktabāt fī bilād al-Rāfidayn 3200 ilā 626 qabla al-mīlād: Maktabat Āšur Bānībāl namūḏaǧan*, mémoire de magister, Université d'Alger, 2010; Idem, *al-Taʿlīm wa al-madāris al-taʿlīmiyya fī bilād al-Rāfidayn*, thèse de doctorat, Université d'Alger, 2017.

216 ʿAmmār Yamùūn, *al-Tadwīn fī bilād al-rāfidayn al-qadīma: 400 q.m 626 q.m. maktabat Nīnwā anmūḏaǧan*, mémoire de magister, Université d'Alger, 2016.

217 ʿAṭiyya Saʿd Ǧihād, *al-Qiyam al-ǧamāliyya fī ʿimārat al-Rafidayn – al-sūmariyya al-akadiyya al-babiliyya al-ašūriyya*, mémoire de magister, Université d'Alger, 2009; Idem, *Fann al-naḥt wa al-naqš al-āšūrī min 1595-612 q.m.*, thèse de doctorat, Université d'Alger, 2015.

218 Farāḥ Faziyya, *al-Tašrīʿ fī bilād al-Rāfidayn min al-alf al-tāliṯ ilā muntaṣaf al-alf al-ṯānī qabla al-mīlad: taṭawwuruhu wa aṯaruhu*, mémoire de magister, Université d'Alger, 2010.

219 Muḥammad Al-ʿĪhār, *Irhāṣāt al-tašrīʿ fī al-ʿIrāq al-qadīm al-asbāb al-natāʾiǧ wa al-inʿikāsāt*, mémoire de magister, Université d'Oran, 2014.

220 Saʿīdī Salīm, *al-Qānūn wa al-aḥwāl al-šaḫṣiyya fī kull min al-ʿIrāq wa Miṣr 2050-332 q m.*, mémoire de magister, Université de Constantine, 2010.

221 Muḥammad Tikyalīn, *al-Taṭawwur al-siyāsī li-l-dawla al-Ḥīṯiyya bayna taʾṯīr al-ṣirāʿāt al-dāḫiliyya wa al-tawassuʿāt al-ḫāriǧiyya*, mémoire de magister, Université d'Alger, 2005.

222 al-Ṭahar Drāʿ, *al-Diyānāt al-qadīma fī al-Ḥiǧāz; al-Muǧtamaʿ al-ʿarabī al-qadīm*.

223 ʿAbd al-Ḥamīd Bʿayaṭiš, *Mamlakat al-Anbaṭ wa dawruhā al-ḥaḍārī fī šibh al-Ǧazīra al-ʿarabiyya wa Sīnāʾ 4 q. m-106 m.*, mémoire de magister, Université d'Alger, 2009.

système politique dans la péninsule arabique[224]. Plusieurs travaux ont traité de la Mecque dans son environnement, à l'instar de la thèse de Ḥasān M'amrī sur la Mecque et ses relations avec la péninsule arabique[225], de celle de al-Rabī' 'Ūlmī sur le rayonnement religieux et culturel de la Mecque préislamique[226]. Salwā Būšārab a traité le même sujet mais à une échelle plus large[227]. L'aspect religieux de la péninsule arabique a été encore traité par Aḥmad Raqqād qui a étudié le pluralisme religieux[228], de Samīr Al-'Aydānī autour de la vie religieuse[229] ou de 'Abd al-Qādir Al-Muḫtār sur les fondements du phéno-mène des offrandes religieuses[230]. En revanche la dimension culturelle n'a bénéficié que de deux thèses, celle de Hāǧar Barkān sur le rôle civilisation-nel du royaume ghassanide[231], ou celui de 'Umar Kīḥal sur la vie littéraire des Lakhmides, suite à un mémoire de magister sur le royaume d'Al-Hira et son rôle civilisationnel[232].

L'histoire et la civilisation yéménites ont fait l'objet de plusieurs études. Nous citons la thèse de Balqāsam Raḥmānī sur les relations du sud de la péninsule arabique avec l'Afrique de l'Est. Ce chercheur a poursuivi ses travaux avec une thèse de doctorat sur l'influence civilisationnelle du Yemen[233]. Le Royaume

224   Malīka Manṣūriyya, *al-Niẓām al-siyāsī fī al-Ǧazīra al-'Arabiyya min al-qabīla ilā al-dawla : 300 q.m 'alā al-fatḥ al-islāmī*, mémoire de magister, Université d'Alger, 2016.

225   Ḥasān M'amrī, *Makka wa-'alāqatuhā ma'a šamāl wa ǧanūb šibh al-ǧazīra al-'arabiyya ḫilāl al-qarnayn 5 wa 6 mīlādī*, mémoire de magister, Université d'Alger, 2009.

226   al-Rabī' 'Ūlmī, *Makka wa dawruhā al-ṯaqāfī wa al-dīnī fī šibh al-Ǧazīra al-'arabiyya qabla al-Islām ḫilāl al-qarnayn al-ḫāmis wa al-sādis li-l-mīlād*, mémoire de magister, Université de Constantine, 2008.

227   Salwā Būšāra, *Makka wa 'alāqatuhā bi-l-ḥawāḍir al-ḥiǧāziyya wa l duwal al-muǧāwiru*, mémoire de magister, Université de Constantine, 2008.

228   Aḥmad Raqqād, *al-Ta'addudiyya al-dīniyya fī šibhi al-Ǧazīra al-'Arabiyya bayna al-waṭaniyya wa al-tawḥīd : dirāsa taḥlīliyya wa muqārina*, mémoire de magister, Université d'Alger, 2011.

229   Samīr Al-'Aydānī, *al-Ḥayāt al-dīniyya fī šamāl šibh al-Ǧazīra al-'arabiyya 1200q.m-600m.*, mémoire de magister, Université d'Alger, 2011.

230   'Abd al-Qādir al-Kīlānī A'mār Al-Muḫtār, *Murtakazāt al-fikr al-dīnī wa burūz ẓāhirat al-qarābīn fī Šibh al-Ǧazīra al-'Arabiyya wa-al-Šām wa-bilād al-Rāfidayn : dirāsa tārīḫiyya taḥlīliyya muqārana*, thèse de doctorat, Université d'Alger, 2014.

231   Hāǧar Barkān, *Mamlakat al-Ġassāsina wa dawruhā al-ḥaḍārī fī šamāl šibh al-Ǧazīra al-'arabiyya*, mémoire de magister, Université d'Alger, 2012.

232   'Umar Kīḥal, *Mamlakat al-Ḥīra wa dawruhā al-ḥaḍārī: min al-qarn al-ṯālit al-mīlādī ilā sanat 632 mīladiyya*, mémoire de magister, Université d'Alger, 2008 ; Idem, *al-Ḥayāt al-adabiyya fī dawlat al-Manāḏira min al-qarn al-ṯālit al-mīlādī ilā sanat 632 mīladiyya*, thèse de doctorat, Université d'Alger, 2017.

233   Balqāsam Raḥmānī, *'Alāqāt ǧanūb šibh al-Ǧazīra al-'arabiyya ; al-Āṯār al-ḥaḍāriyya*.

sabéen a bénéficié de l'étude de Muḥammad Kākī[234] et bien après celui de Karīma Ḥaddūš sur le commerce[235]. La question de la religion du Yémen n'a bénéficié que d'une seule étude, en l'occurrence, celle de Naǧiyya Saḥnīn[236]. La problématique de l'émigration yéménite, qui est souvent proposée comme un élément central pour argumenter l'hypothèse de l'origine arabe du Maghreb antique n'a pas fait objet d'une réflexion nouvelle. Deux études ont traité cette question, mais dans des contextes géographiques différents. Il s'agit du travail de Būmadyan Ban Muwaffaq qui a tenté de suivre ses déplacements vers l'Afrique de l'Est[237], celui de Māliya Baṣal qui a étudié les colonies yéménites en péninsule arabique[238], ainsi que la comparaison effectuée par Nādiya Māǧī avec l'émigration sémite[239]. Signalons un autre travail sur les colonies et l'urbanisme d'Al-Baʿsī Fayṣal Ḥusayn Nāṣir dans la région de Kur[240].

Nous avons recensé plusieurs études autour du Proche Orient. Il s'agit de la thèse de Fāṭima al-Zahrā' ʿAzzūz, sur les liens intellectuels et religieux entre les Phéniciens et les Hébreux, suivie d'un doctorat sur le même sujet[241]. Les

---

234   Muḥammad Kākī, *al-Wāqiʿ al-tiǧārī wa aṯaruhu fī izdihār al-mamlaka al-sabaʾiyya*, mémoire de magister, Université d'Alger, 2003 ; Idem, *Maẓāhir al-ḥaḍāra al-sabaʾiyya fī al-ǧanūb al-ʿarabī bidāyatan min al-alf al-awwal qabla al-mīlad wa ḥattā maṭlaʿ al-qarn al-sādis mīladī*, thèse de doctorat, Université de Constantine, 2016.

235   Karīma Ḥaddūš, *Tiǧārat mamlakat Saba' ʿalā ḍaw' kutub al-raḥḥāla wa dawruhā al-ḥaḍārī : kitāb al-ṭawāf ḥawla al-baḥr al-arītrī anmūḏaǧan*, mémoire de magister, Université d'Alger, 2010.

236   Naǧiyya Saḥnīn, *Al-diyāna fī al-Yaman al-qadīm min 1300 q. m. ʿalā qubayl ẓuhūr al-islām al-qarn 14 q.m–al-qarn 6m.*, mémoire de magister, Université d'Alger, 2008.

237   Būmadyan Ban Muwaffaq, *al-Hiǧra al-yamaniyya naḥwa al-šarq al-ifrīqī wa-āṯāruhā al-ḥaḍāriyya : al-Ṣūmāl wa al-Ḥabašā wa-Miṣr namūḏaǧan*, mémoire de magister, Université d'Alger, 2009 ; Idem, *al-Dawr al-ḥaḍāarī al-miṣrī fī al-šarq al-ifrīqī : bilād al-Nūba namūḏaǧan*, thèse de doctorat, Université d'Alger, 2014.

238   Māliya Baṣal, *al-Mustawṭana al-yamaniyya wa dawruhā al-ḥaḍārī fī wasaṭ wa šamal al-ǧazīra al-ʿarabiyya munḏu ẓuhūr al-duwal al-yamaniyya al-qadīma ilā ġāyat maǧī' al-Islām*, mémoire de magister, Université d'Alger, 2011 ; Idem, *al-ʿAlāqāt al-ḥaḍāriyya bayna al-Yaman wa manṭiqat al-Hilāl al-Ḫaṣīb*, thèse de doctorat, Université d'Alger, 2017.

239   Nādiya Māǧī, *Ḥarakāt al-istīṭān al-sāmiyya : al-fīnīqiyya – al-yamaniyya : dirāsa muqārana*, mémoire de magister, Université d'Oran, 2014.

240   Al-Baʿsī Fayṣal Ḥusayn Nāṣir, *Mustawṭanāt awdiyyat Kūr al-ʿAwāliq, al-ǧumhūriyya al-yamaniyya muḥāfaẓat Šabwa : dirāsa tārīḫiyya aṯariyya*, mémoire de magister, Université d'Alger, 2009 ; Idem, *Munšaʾāt al-rayy al-qadīma fī manṭiqat awdiyyat Kūr al-ʿAwāliq fī-l-Yaman-muḥāfaẓat Šabwa*, thèse de doctorat, Université d'Alger, 2014.

241   Fāṭima al-Zahrā' ʿAzzūz, *al-Rawābiṭ al-fikriyya al-fīnīqiyya al-ʿibrāniyya al-muʿtaqadāt al-dīniyya – al-ādāb – al-funūn min al-qarn al-ʿāšir qabla al-mīlād ilā al-qarn al-awwal li-l-mīlād, mémoire de magister, Université d'Alger, 2006 ; Idem, Taṯīr al-muʿtaqadāt al-fīnīqiyya fī-l-diyānat al-ʿibrāniyya min ḫilāl muktašafāt Ra's Šamrā wa nuṣūṣ al-ʿahd al-qadīm : dirāsa muqārina q 10-06 q-m.*, thèse de doctorat, Université d'Alger, 2011.

conflits autour du littoral phénicien ont fait l'objet des études de Ṭāriq Marīqī[242] et de Nağiyya Saḥnīn[243]. Salīma Labḫūr a étudié le royaume hébreu au temps de Solomon[244], Lwīza Ğalmam a traité la question de l'exode[245], Ḥalīma Sāyaḥla la problématique de l'ancienneté de l'implantation en Palestine[246]. Le commerce phénicien a été traité par Nūr al-Dīn Raḥīm[247], le commerce avec l'Egypte par ʿAmr Ḫayr[248], ainsi qu'avec l'ouest de la Méditerranée par Muḫtār Nāyar[249]. Faṭṭūma Ašlafa a traité des industries artisanales phéniciennes[250]. Enfin Šarīf Qūʾīš a traité du rôle civilisationnel de la flotte phénicienne à l'est de la Méditerranée[251].

Même si l'intérêt accordé à l'histoire de l'Egypte ancienne est très récent, le nombre et la variété des travaux recensés confirment l'importance de cet axe de recherche dans la production universitaire. Nous abordons cet axe par les travaux déjà cités d'Umm al-Ḫayr Al-ʿAqqūn[252], et de Slīman Ban al-Saʿdī sur la question des liens et des échanges entre le Maghreb antique et l'Egypte ancienne[253], quoique l'utilisation des sources pharaoniques actuelles est loin d'avoir apporté un éclairage pertinent sur le Maghreb antique. Néanmoins, cette abondance de documentation égyptienne a beaucoup favorisé la multi- plication des champs de recherche. Dans ce sens l'histoire économique a fait l'objet d'une thèse présentée par al-Zahrāʾ Al-Zuʿbī sur le commerce entre le

---

242   Ṭāriq Marīqī, *al-Sāḥil al-fīnīqī wa ṣirāʿ qiwā al-ğiwār al-ğuğrāfī : al-alf al-ṯāniyya q.m ilā bidāyat al-qarn 12 q.m.*, mémoire de magister, Université d'Alger, 2009.

243   Nağiyya Saḥnīn, *Ṣiraʿ al-qiwā al-qadīma ʿala Filisṭīn wa aṯaruhu min 1000 sana qabla al-mīlad ilā qubayl ẓuhūr al-Islām 6 m.*, thèse de doctorat, Université d'Alger, 2017.

244   Salīma Labḫūr, *al-Mamlaka al-ʿibrāniyya fī ʿahd Dāwūd wa Sulaymān mā bayna 1004 q. m.- 922. q.m.*, mémoire de magister, Université de Constantine, 2010.

245   Lwīza Ğalmam, *Ḫurūğ Banī Isrāʾīl min Miṣr bayna al-maṣādir al-dīniyya wa al-dirāsa al-aṯariyya : al-qarn al-sābiʿ ḥattā 13 q.m.*, mémoire de magister, Université d'Alger, 2016.

246   Ḥalīma Sāyaḥ, *Filasṭīn bayna al-Yahūd wa al-qurā al-qadīma*, mémoire de magister, Université d'Alger, 2014.

247   Nūr al-Dīn Raḥīm, *al-Tiğāra ʿinda al-fīnīqiyyīn 1200 q m-814 q m.*, mémoire de magister, Université de Constantine, 2010.

248   ʿAmr Ḫayr, *al-ʿAlāqa al-tiğāriyya bayna Fīnīqiyā wa Miṣr fīma bayna 2780 q.m. wa-l-qarn al-sādis q.m.*, mémoire de magister, Université d'Alger, 2012.

249   Muḫtār Nāyar, *al-Tiğāra al-baḥriyya fī al-ḥawḍ al-ğarbī li-l-baḥr al-Abyaḍ al-mutawssiṭ fī al-ʿuṣūr al-qadīma min al-Fīnīqiyyīn ilā ʿahd al-iḥtilal al-rūmanī*, thèse de doctorat, Université d'Oran, 2019.

250   Faṭṭūma Ašlaf, *al-Ṣināʿa al-ḥirafiyya al-fīnīqiyya 1200 q.m-322 q.m.*, mémoire de magis- ter, Université d'Alger, 2009 ; Idem, *al-Iqtiṣād al-fīnīqī fī-l-baḥr al-mutawassaṭ : 1200q.m.- 332q.m.*, thèse de doctorat, Université d'Alger, 2018.

251   Šarīf Qūʾīš, *Dawr al-baḥriyya al-fīnīqiyya fī rabṭ al-ʿalaqāt al-mubakkira bayn ḥawḍ al-šarqī li-l-baḥr al-abyaḍ al-mutawssiṭ wa ğarbihi*, mémoire de magister, Université d'Oran, 2015.

252   Umm al-Ḫayr Al-ʿAqqūn, *al-ʿAlāqāt al-ḥaḍāriyya*.

253   Slīman Ban al-Saʿdī, *ʿalāqat Miṣr bi-l-Maġrib al-qadīm*.

quatrième et le premier millénaire[254]. Si l'aspect politique n'a fait l'objet que d'une étude, celle d'ʿĀʾiša Būṯrīd[255], le contexte social a bénéficié de deux études, celle de Muḥammad Brahmī sur les aspects de la vie égyptienne à travers l'art pariétal[256] et celle de Ġaniyya Ban Ḥafṣī sur le statut de la femme dans la société pharaonique[257]. Par ailleurs, les études autour de l'histoire culturelle et civilisationnelle s'avèrent beaucoup plus importantes. Nous pouvons citer le travail de ʿAbd al-Raḥmān Ban ʿAṭī Allāh sur le rôle d'Alexandrie dans l'évolution des lettres et des sciences[258], et quelques années plus tard de Hāǧar Katfī al-Šarīf sur le même sujet[259]. Abū Bakr Marīqī a effectué une étude sur le rôle civilisationnel de la dynastie des Ptoléméens[260], Bašīr Qaffāf, sur les liens civilisationnels entre l'Egypte et l'Arabie[261]. Farīda Būdīfa a étudié les sciences chez les pharaons[262], al-Saʿīd Šlālqa a traité le thème de l'écriture et les ouvrages en Egypte ancienne[263]. Enfin, Naṣīra Ḥalīfī a étudié la vie littéraire en Egypte pharaonique[264].

En ce qui concerne l'histoire religieuse, les sujets traités sont aussi variés. Masʿūd Šabbaḥīa a réalisé une comparaison entre l'Egypte et la Mésopotamie,

254   al-Zahrāʾ Al-Zuʿbī, *Tiǧārat Miṣr al-firʿawniyya min āḫir al-alf al-rābiʿa ilā al-alf al-ūlā qabla al-mīlād, mémoire de magister, Université d'Alger*, 2008.

255   ʿĀʾiša Būṯrīd, *Niẓām al-ḥukm wa al-idāra fī Miṣr al-qadīma ḥattā al-dawla al-ḥadīṯa*, Diplôme des Études Supérieures, Université de Constantine, 1977.

256   Muḥammad Brahmī, *Maẓāhir al-ḥayāt al-miṣriyya al-qadīma min ḫilal al-fann al-miṣrī al-qadīm, al-rasm wa-l-naḥt namūḏaǧan : min al-ʿuṣūr al-qadīma 5000 q.m ʿalā ʿahd al-dawla al-wusṭā ḥawālī 1780 q.m.*, mémoire de magister, Université d'Alger, 2012.

257   Ġaniyya Ban Ḥafṣī, *Makānat al-marʾa wa dawruhā fī al-muǧtamaʿ al-firʿawnī 3200 q.m-1080 q.m.*, mémoire de magister, Université d'Alger, 2011.

258   ʿAbd al-Raḥmān Ban ʿAṭī Allāh, *Dawr madīnat al-Iskandariyya fī taṭwīr al-ādāb wa al-ʿulūm munḏu taʾsīsihā ḥattā al-niṣf al-ṯānī min al-qarn al-awwal qabla al-mīlād (331 qabla al-mīlād /30 qabla al-mīlād)*, mémoire de magister, Université d'Alger, 2010.

259   Hāǧar Katfī al-Šarīf, *Madīnat al-Iskandariyya wa ḥaḍāratuhā fī ʿahd al-baṭālima : dirāsa fī al-ǧānib al-iǧtimāʿī anmūḏaǧan 331-30q.m.*, mémoire de magister, Université d'Alger, 2016.

260   Marīqī, Abū Bakr. *al-Dawr al-ḥaḍārī li-l-baṭālat fī Miṣr : al-baḥṯ al-iqtiṣādī wa-al-iǧtimāʿī wa-al-ṯaqāfī namūḏaǧan*, mémoire de magister, Université d'Alger, 2008.

261   Bašīr Qaffāf, *al-Ṣilāt al-ḥaḍāriyya bayna Miṣr wa-šibh al-ǧazīra al-ʿarabiyya munḏu qiyām al-dawla al-wusṭā al-firʿawniyya ilā ġāyat nihāyat al-dawla al-ḥadīṯa, mémoire de magister, Université d'Alger*, 2009.

262   Farīda Būdīf, *al-ʿUlūm ʿinda al-farāʾina min 3200 q.m ilā 525 q.m.*, mémoire de magister, Université d'Alger, 2009.

263   al-Saʿīd Šlālqa, *al-Kitāba wa dawr al-kutub bi-Miṣr al-qadīma mā bayna 2100-1050 qabla al-mīlād, mémoire de magister, Université d'Alger*, 2010.

264   Naṣīra Ḥalīfī, *al-Ḥayāt al-adabiyya fī Miṣr al-qadīma : al-dawla al-qadīma wa al-dawla al-wusṭā namūḏaǧan 3500 q m-1778 q m.*, mémoire de magister, Université d'Alger, 2012.

avant d'étudier le mouvement religieux d'Akhenaton[265]. Laylā Būmrīš a effectué aussi une étude sur les rites funéraires et ensuite effectué la même comparaison[266]. Il se trouve que cette approche a été largement reprise. Anwar Mūḥammad Ṣāliḥ Zammūšīa a étudié l'influence religieuse sur les peuples environnants[267], Samīr Al-ʿAydānī le même sujet par rapport aux peuples de la mer[268]. Ḥālid Maḥfūẓ s'est aventuré même à effectuer une comparaison de la vie religieuse de l'Egypte avec celle des Mayas[269]. L'urbanisme funéraire a été traité par Zahiyya ʿIwağ[270]. Par Ṣabīḥa Ūkīl[271] et Ṣaḥbī Sūmiyya[272], la dualité art-religion a été largement reprise. Enfin Samīša Faīz a étudié le rôle religieux et politique des prêtres en Egypte pharaonique[273]. Pour la période romaine deux travaux ont évoqué l'histoire économique egyptienne, celui de ʿAbd al-Nūr Al-ʿAmrī[274] et de al-Ṭayyib Qadīm[275].

265 Masʿūd Šabbaḥī, *Diyānat Miṣr wa bilād al-Rāfidayn al-qadīma, al-simāt al-ḥuṣūṣiyya wa al-muqārana imtidādan min fatrat ma qabla al-usra ilā awāḥir al-alf al-ṯāliṯa q.m.*, mémoire de magister, Université de Constantine, 2001 ; Idem, *Ḥarakat Aḥnawn al-dīniyya 1367-1350 q.m : dirāsa taḥlīliyya*, thèse de doctorat, Université de Constantine, 2009.

266 Laylā Būmrīš, *al-Ṭuqūs al-ğanāʾiziyya al-firʿawniyya*, mémoire de magister, Université d'Alger, 2005 ; Idem, *Taṭawwur al-fikr al-dīnī fī Miṣr wa bilād al-Rāfidayn : dirāsa fī asāṭīr al-takwīn*, thèse de doctorat, Université d'Alger, 2013.

267 Anwar Mūḥammad Ṣāliḥ Zammūšī, *Malāmiḥ al-taʾṯīrāt al-dīniyya al-miṣriyya ladā šuʿūb al-ğiwār al-ğuğrāfī : al-Lībiyīn wa-al-Fīnīqiyīn namūḏağan 3200 qabla al-mīlād -865 al-mīlādī, mémoire de magister, Université d'Alger*, 2008.

268 Samīr Al-ʿAydānī, *al-ʿAlaqāt al-ḥaḍāriyya bayna Miṣr wa šuʿūb bilād al-Rafidayn "al-ʿalāqāt al-dīniyya anmūḏağan" : min bidāyat ʿaṣr al-dawla al-ḥadīṯa ḥattā al-tawāğud al-yūnānī fī Miṣr 1580 q.m.-332 q.m.*, thèse de doctorat, Université d'Alger, 2017.

269 Ḥālid Maḥfūẓ, *al-Ḥayāt al-dīniyya ladā al-Farāʿina 2780 qabla al-mīlād-1085 qabla al-mīlād wa al-Māyyā 600 qabla al-mīlād-1500 al-mīlād : dirāsa muqārana*, mémoire de magister, Université d'Alger, 2010.

270 Zahiyya ʿIwağ, *Taṭawwur al-ʿimāra al-ğanāʾiziyya fī Miṣr al-qadīma 3500-1075q-m.*, mémoire de magister, Université d'Alger, 2008.

271 Ṣabīḥa Ūkīl *al-Dīn wa-l-fann fī Miṣr al-qadīma 3200-1085 q m.*, mémoire de magister, Université d'Alger, 2009.

272 Ṣaḥbī Sūmiyya, *Taʾṯīr al-diyāna ʿalā al-ḥayāt al-iğtimāʿiyya wa-al-fikriyya fī Miṣr al-firʿawniyya*, mémoire de magister, ENS, Alger, 2005.

273 Samīša Faīz, *Dawr al-kahana al-dīnī wa al-siyasī fī Miṣr al-firʿawniyya : al-dawla al-qadīma 2690-2180 q.m – wa al-dawla al-ḥadīṯa 1580-1085 q.m namūḏağan*, mémoire de magister, Université d'Alger, 2012.

274 ʿAbd al-Nūr Al-ʿAmrī, *Siyāsat Rūmā al-iqtiṣādiyya fī Miṣr mā bayna al-qarn al-awwal qabla al-mīlād wa bidāyat al-qarn al-rābiʿ mīlādi 27 qabla al-mīlād -306 mīlādī wa al-natāʾiğ al-mutarattiba ʿanhā, mémoire de magister, Université d'Alger*, 2010.

275 al-Ṭayyib Qadīm, *al-Tağayyurāt al-iqtiṣādiyya fī Miṣr al-rūmāniyya : min nihāyat al-qarn al-awwal li-l-mīlād ilā al-qarn al-rābiʿ mīlādī, mémoire de magister, Université d'Alger*, 2012 ; Idem, *al-Dawr al-ḥaḍārī al-rūmānī fī Sūriyyā siyāsiyyan wa-iqtiṣādiyyan wa ṯaqāfiyyan : min 64 qabla al-mīlād ilā 394 mīlādi*, thèse de doctorat, Université d'Alger, 2018.

Contrairement à l'Egypte, la Grèce antique n'a suscité que peu d'études. Le thème des conquêtes d'Alexandre le Macédonien a été étudié par Ibrāhīm al-ʿĪd Bašī[276], ainsi que Fāṭima al-Zahrāʾ Ǧāwšī[277]. Ḥadīǧa Ṭahārī a étudié aussi le système militaire de la même période[278]. ʿAbd al-Ḥaqq Masʿī s'est concentré sur l'établissement grec au sud de l'Italie[279]. Amḥammad Sālam Muḥammad a étudié la vie religieuse et intellectuelle à Cyrène[280], ʿAbbās Masrūr la femme grecque[281], Karīm Mnāṣar le thème du théâtre grec[282] et enfin Nawāl Ṭabīb a tenté de traiter l'historicité des épopées grecques[283].

Le monde romain est peu étudié. Il s'agit de quelques travaux, tels que celui de Ḫālid Šahra sur les législations romaines[284], de Nuwwāra Saʿfa sur le rôle des esclaves dans l'évolution de l'empire romain[285] ou de Brāhīm Laḥsan sur les captifs[286]. Les réformes impériales ont suscité intérêt traduit par l'étude de Nūra Mūwwās sur les réformes du IIème siècle[287], de ʿAyša Muṣbāḥ sur celles

---

276   Ibrāhīm al-ʿĪd Bašī, *al-Tawassuʿ al-ʿaskarī al-maqdūnī min ḫilāl ḥamlāt al-Iskandar al-Akbar 336-323 qabla al-mīlād*, mémoire de magister, Université d'Alger, 1992.

277   al-Zahrāʾ Ǧāwšī, *Ḥamlat al-Iskandar al-Maqdūnī ʿalā bilād mā bayna al-Nahrayn 331-30 qabla al-mīlād : al-fatra al-hilīnistiyya*, mémoire de magister, Université d'Alger, 2013.

278   Ḥadīǧa Ṭahārī, *al-Niẓām al-ʿaskarī wa-aṯaruhu ʿalā al-niẓām al-siyāsī min Qūraš al-ṯānī ilā al-Iskandar al-Maqdūnī*, mémoire de magister, Université d'Alger, 2016.

279   ʿAbd al-Ḥaqq Masʿī, *al-Istīṭān al-iġrīqī fī ǧanūb Īṭāliyya wa Ṣiqiliyya bayna al-qarnayn al-ṯāmin wa al-sādis qabla al-mīlad*, mémoire de magister, Université d'Alger, 2008 ; Idem., *al-Muʾaṯṯirāt al-ḥaḍāriyya al-iġrīqiyya fī al-Maġrib al-qadīm min al-qarn al-sābiʿ qabla al-mīlād ilā al-qarn al-awwal mīladī*, thèse de doctorat, Université d'Alger, 2018.

280   Amḥammad Sālam Muḥammad, *al-Ḥayāt al-dīniyya wa al-fikriyya fī Qūrīnā aṯnāʾ al-ʿaṣr al-iġrīqī*, thèse de doctorat d'État, Université d'Alger, 2006.

281   ʿAbbās Masrūr, *al-Marʾa wa dawruhā al-ḥaḍārī fī al-muǧtamaʿ al-iġrīqī fī al-fatra al-klasīkiyya : al-marʾa al-aṯīniyya wa-l-isbarṭiyya namūḏaǧan*, mémoire de magister, Université d'Alger, 2016.

282   Karīm Mnāṣar, *Dawr al-masraḥ fī bilād al-Iġrīq*, mémoire de magister, Université d'Alger, 2008 ; Idem, *Našʾat al-masāriḥ wa al-mudarraǧāt al-rūmāniyya fī al-muqāṭaʿa al-Afrīqiyya wa taʾṯīrihā fī al-ḥayāt al-siyāsiyya wa al-iqtiṣādiyya wa al-iǧtimaʿiyya : al-qarn al-awwal – al-ṯāliṯ al-mīladī*, thèse de doctorat, Université d'Alger, 2017.

283   Nawāl Ṭabīb, *Al-Ḥaqāʾiq al-tārīḫiyya min ḫilāl adab al-malāḥim ʿinda al-Iġrīq al-Ilyāda namūḏaǧan*, mémoire de magister, Université d'Alger, 2012.

284   Ḫālid Šahra, *al-Tašrīʿ al-rūmānī fī al-ʿaṣr al-ǧumhūrī 509-27 qabla al-mīlād*, mémoire de magister, Université d'Alger, 2015.

285   Nuwwāra Saʿfa, *Dawr al-ʿabīd wa al-maʿtūqīn fī šibh Ǧazīra al-Iṭāliyya min fatra 55-54 q.m ilā fatra 193-211m.*, mémoire de magister, Université d'Alger, 2011.

286   Brāhīm Laḥsan, *al-Asrā ʿinda al-Rūmān ḫilāl al-niṣf al-ṯānī min al-ʿahd al-ǧamhūrī 378 q-m ilā 27 qabla al-mīlād*, mémoire de magister, Université d'Alger, 2016.

287   Nūra Mūwwās, *al-Iṣlāḥāt fī al-imbrāṭūriyya al-rūmāniyya ḫilāl al-ʿaṣr al-imbrāṭūrī al-ṯānī : 284 m.-395m.*, thèse de doctorat, Université d'Alger, 2016.

de l'empereur Dioclétien[288] ou de Saḥālī Aḥmad concernant les réformes de l'empereur Constantin[289]. L'histoire de l'empire de Byzance a été traitée, dans le contexte du VIe siècle par Yūsuf Ḥayāṭ[290] et à travers ses relations avec la péninsule arabique, par Umm Hānī Ramḍānī[291]. Un autre sujet mérite d'etre cité par son exception, il s'agit du mémoire de Būrni Dalīla consacré à la civilisation des Mayas[292].

3.2   *L'archéologie classique*

3.2.1   Les recherches archéologiques sur le terrain

Il est intéressant de constater que la régression de l'action archéologique ne remonte qu'à la fin des années quatre-vingt. Le bilan dressé par M. Bouchenaki confirme qu'entre 1962 et 1980[293] les interventions sur les sites de Tébessa[294], Sétif[295], Lambèse[296], Tiddis[297], Tipasa[298], Nador[299], Cherchell[300], Frenda[301],

---

288   ʿAyša Muṣbāḥ, *al-Iṣlāḥāt al- idāriyya wa al-ʿaskariyya li-l-imbraṭūr Daqlidyanūs fī Afrīqiyya : 285-304*, mémoire de magister, Université d'Alger, 2013.

289   Saḥālī Aḥmad, *Iṣlāḥāt Qusṭanṭīn al-awwal al-dīniyya wa al-siyāsiyya fī Urūbbā 306– 337*, *mémoire de magister, Université d'Alger*, 2016.

290   Yūsuf Ḥayāṭ, *al-Dawla al-bīzanṭiyya min al-naša ḥattā ʿahd Ǧīstinyān 284-565m.*, mémoire de magister, Université d'Alger, 2011.

291   Umm Hānī Ramḍānī, *Bīzanṭa wa šibh al-Ǧazīra al-ʿArabiyya min al-qarn al-ṯaliṯ mīlādī ilā al-qarn al-sādis mīlādī*, mémoire de magister, Université d'Alger, 2006 ; Idem, *Šibh al-Ǧazīra al-ʿArabiyya wa al-qiwā al-qadīma min al-qarn al-rābiʿ qabla al-mīlād ilā al-qarn al-ṯāliṯ mīlādī*, thèse de doctorat, Université d'Alger, 2013.

292   Būrni Dalīla, *Ḥaḍārat al-Māya : al-naša wa-l-taṭawwur*, thèse de doctorat, Université d'Alger, 2015.

293   M. Bouchenaki, *Récentes recherches et étude de l'Antiquité en Algérie*, op. cit., 9-28.

294   R. Lequément, « Fouilles à l'amphithéâtre de Tébessa 1965-1968 », *Bulletin d'Archéologie algérienne*, vol. 2, 1966-67, 107-122 ; Idem, *Fouilles de l'amphithéâtre de Tébessa*, thèse de doctorat de 3e cycle soutenue à Alger en 1969, 2e Supplément au Bulletin d'Archéologie algérienne, Alger, 1979.

295   A. Mohamedi, A. Benmansour, A. Amamra, E. Fentress, *Fouilles de Sétif 1977-1984*, Agence Nationale d'Archéologie et de Protection des Sites et Monuments Historiques, Supplément 5, B.A.A., Alger, 1991.

296   M. Janon, N. Benseddik, S. Roskams, *Fouilles de l'Asclépiéium de Lambèse 1984-1992*, doctorat non publié encore.

297   A. Berthier, *Tiddis, antique Castellum Tidditanorum*, Alger, 1972 ; Idem, *Tiddis. Cité antique de Numidie*, Institut de France, Mémoires de l'Académie des Inscriptions et Belles-Lettres, vol. 20, Paris, Diffusion de Boccard, 2000.

298   M. Bouchenaki, *Fouilles de la nécropole occidentale de Tipasa Matarès 1968-1972*, Alger, SNED, 1975.

299   L. Anselmino, M. Bouchenaki, A. Carandini, *Il castellum del Nador. Storia di una fattoria tra Tipasa e Caesarea I-VI sec. d. C.*, Roma, Monografie di archeologia libica 23, 1989.

300   N. Benseddik, T.W. Potter, *Fouilles du forum de Cherchel*, op. cit.

301   F. Kadra, *Les Djeddars. Monuments funéraires de la région de Frenda*, Alger, SNED, 1983.

ou Siga[302] permettent de mesurer l'ampleur de l'implication de l'Algérie dans le débat historique[303]. Les problématiques de la transition de l'antiquité au Moyen Âge, établie à Tébessa et à Sétif, les pratiques d'inhumations à travers les exemples de Sétif et de Tiddis, l'aménagement militaire à partir de l'étude de la Fabrica de Lambèse, ou le funéraire des tombeaux de Siga et des Djeddars étaient des thématiques qui avaient positionné les archéologues algériens à coté de plusieurs personnalités scientifiques françaises, italiennes ou allemandes. Plusieurs d'entre eux ont préparé leurs thèses dans des universités étrangères[304].

Mais à partir des années quatre-vingt le nombre de chantiers archéologiques a considérablement diminué. L'action archéologique est réduite à de simples opérations de gestion patrimoniale, et le Bulletin d'Archéologie Algérienne a cessé de paraître[305]. Cette situation illustre bien les prémices du dysfonctionnement de l'action archéologique et de la dégradation des outils de la recherche[306]. Nonobstant cela, quelques projets ont été initiés au niveau du CNRS sans que cette institution ne dispose des compétences nécessaires. Le projet de « *La cartographie archéologique numérique et l'introduction de l'utilisation de nouvelles technologies en archéologie* » mené dans le cadre d'une coopération avec le laboratoire de recherche archéologique de l'Université de Trento 2003-2010 n'a pas abouti et n'a livré jusqu'à présent aucune publication scientifique. Un autre programme de coopération algéro-français en collaboration avec le CNRS a été initié et développé entre 2006 et 2011 autour du site archéologique de Lambèse-Tazoult ; il s'est élargi en 2014 à l'étude de l'ensemble du site avec des déclinaisons de formation et de gestion patrimoniale. En dépit de l'importance de ses approches et ses problématiques, ce projet peine toujours

---

302   M. Bouchenaki, *Récentes recherches et étude de l'Antiquité en Algérie*. Op. cit., 24.

303   Plusieurs travaux ont marqué l'état de la recherche, voir P.A. Février, A. Gaspary, R. Guéry, *Fouilles de Sétif 1959-1966. Quartier nord-ouest rempart et cirque*, Supplément 1, *Bulletin d'archéologie algérienne*, Alger, 1970 ; R. Guéry, *La nécropole orientale de Sitifis (Sétif, Algérie). Fouilles de 1966-1967*, Paris, 1985 ; Idem, « Les thermes d'Ad Sava Municipium Hammam Guergour », B.A.A., vol. 2, 1966-67, 1967, 95-106 ; Ph. Leveau, *Caesarea de Maurétanie. Une ville romaine et ses campagnes*, Rome, Collection EFR, 70, 1984 ; E. Fentress, A. Aït Kaci, N. Bounssair, « Prospections dans le Belezma : rapport préliminaire », dans *Actes du colloque international sur l'histoire de Sétif : Sétif 8, 9, et 10 décembre 1990*, Bulletin d'Archéologie Algérienne, supplément 7, Alger, 1991, 107-13.

304   F. Kadra, *Etude des Djeddars. Mausolées de tradition berbère dans la Wilaya de Tiaret*, thèse de doctorat de 3e cycle, Aix-en-Provence, 1974 ; S. Ferdi, *Inventaire des mosaïques de Cherchel*, thèse de doctorat de 3e cycle, Aix-Marseille, 1982 ; N. Benseddik, *Le culte d'Esculape en Afrique*, thèse de doctorat, Paris 4, 1995.

305   N. Bensedik, *L'archéologie antique en Algérie hier et aujourd'hui*, op. cit., 198 ; F.X. Fauvelle et alii, « Les savoirs archéologiques au Maghreb », *Perspective*, 2, 2017, 15-29.

306   N. Bensedik, *L'archéologie antique en Algérie hier et aujourd'hui*, op. cit., 197.

à concrétiser le concept de l'archéologie programmée et à maintenir une réelle continuité de son action archéologique[307]. En revanche le CNRA s'est vu attribuer les interventions dites d'urgence ou de diagnostic sur le terrain en usant d'un potentiel incapable d'actualiser l'état des découvertes ou même de développer une stratégie de recherche par rapport à l'expansion urbaine de plus en plus envahissante au détriment du paysage archéologique. Cette tendance vers « l'Archéologie Préventive » s'est concrétisée lors des travaux liés au métro d'Alger en 2009 ; la station de la place des Martyrs a bénéficié d'une intervention de l'INRAP France. Le recours à cette prestation de service archéologique explique parfaitement la nouvelle tendance des structures du Ministère de la culture de n'accorder que peu d'intérêt à la recherche.

En revanche l'université privée des moyens institutionnels a perdu son rapport aux réalités archéologiques et aux outils de renouvèlement de l'état des connaissances[308]. Les fouilles pédagogiques à l'exemple de *Tigzirt*[309], de *Madaure*[310], de *Quiza*[311], ou de *Thabudeos*[312] n'ont pu livrer que peu de publications innovantes. Cela révèle un réel dysfonctionnement entre la mission d'une archéologie au service des sciences historiques et celle d'une archéologie exclusivement patrimoniale.

3.2.2   La production scientifique universitaire

Plusieurs thèses ont été soutenues dans des universités étrangères, notamment à Aix-Marseille, sous la direction de P.A. Février, qui a encadré le travail

---

307   Programme initié depuis 2006 par A.A. Malek. Depuis 2014, j'assure la codirection de ce programme comme représentant du CNRA.

308   K. Mazari, « Archéologues au bord de la crise de nerf », dans *Pratiquer les sciences sociales au Maghreb*, ed. M. Al-Moubaker et F. Pouillon, Centre Jacques Berque, Casablanca, 2014, 381.

309   Travaux dirigés par M.M. Fillah. Cf. M. Dorbane, « Notes sur une inscription latine découverte à Tigzirt antique, Iomnium », *L'Africa romana XVI*, Rabat, 2004, Roma, 2006, 1707-1710.

310   Travaux dirigés par Ibrāhīm Būraḥlī.

311   B. Boussadia et alii, « Les établissements humains littoraux de la basse vallée du Chlef Algérie depuis le premier âge du Fer jusqu'à la période musulmane », dans *Implantations humaines en milieu littoral méditerranéen : facteurs d'installation et processus d'appropriation de l'espace Préhistoire Antiquité Moyen Âge : actes des rencontres 15-17 octobre 2013 : XXXIVe Rencontre Internationale d'archéologie et d'histoire d'Antibes*, Dir. L.M. Ricardo, G. Villaescusa, Fr. Bertoncello, Antibes, 2014.

312   Y. Hadji, « Les découvertes archéologiques de Badias », dans *Libyca : Actes du colloque international La Numidie, Massinissa et l'histoire, Constantine, les 14, 15 et 16 mai 2016*, 285-299.

de F. Kadra sur les Djeddars[313], de S. Ferdi sur la Mosaïque de Cherchell[314] de M.M. Fillah sur les agglomérations antiques en Numidie[315] et de M. Orfalli sur l'Iconographie funéraire en Maurétanie Césarienne[316]. À l'université de Paris 1 Sorbonne A. Bouizem a soutenu une thèse de 3eme cycle sur les forums en Afrique du Nord[317], S. Deloum sur la Numismatique[318]. Quelques années plus tard, A.A. Malek a consacré sa thèse au jardin et aux représentations de la nature dans le Maghreb antique[319], et N.A. Wahab[320] a réalisé un corpus des mosaïques d'Hippone. H. Taoutaou a réalisé une thèse sur les arcs de triomphe[321], et récemment K. Zinai[322], sur le décor des thermes en Algérie. À Strasbourg B. Boussadia a préparé une thèse de 3eme cycle sur la céramique antique[323] et à Toulouse A. Soltani sur la numismatique préromaine[324].

En parallèle, la part des universités algériennes s'est limitée à quelques monographies à l'exemple de celle de Yammūna Baġdādī, qui a effectué une monographie sur la Maurétanie préromaine[325], de Nāṣir Ban Masʿūd, qui réa-lisé un corpus des marchés de la Numidie[326] et de Ǧahīda Mhantal Maqrūs qui

---

313 F. Kadra, *Etude des Djeddars. Mausolées de tradition berbère*, op. cit.

314 Titulaire d'un doctorat de 3e cycle en sciences de l'antiquité classique Institut pontifical d'archéologie sacrée Rome 1979, elle a soutenu une thèse de doctorat intitulée : *Inventaire des mosaïques de Cherchel*, op. cit.

315 M.M. Fillah, *Recherches sur les agglomérations antiques : le réseau urbain et le paysage rural en Numidie occidentale Algérie*, thèse de doctorat, Aix-Marseille 1, 1986.

316 M. Orfalli, *Inventaire des sculptures funéraires et votives de la Mauritanie césarienne*, thèse de doctorat, Aix-Marseille 1, 1989.

317 A. Bouizem, *La vie du forum dans les villes de l'Afrique du Nord romaine*, doctorat 3e cycle, Paris 1, 1979.

318 S. Deloum, *Le trésor monétaire de M'sila et l'étude des découvertes monétaires des Vè et VIè siècles trouvés en Afrique du Nord*, doctorat 3e cycle, Paris-Sorbonne, 1987.

319 A.A. Malek, *Le sentiment de la nature dans les domus de l'Afrique romaine II-V Siècles*, thèse de doctorat, Paris EHESS, 1999.

320 N.A. Wahab, *Corpus des mosaïques d'Hippone Algérie sur base topographique*, thèse de doctorat, Paris 4, 2005.

321 H. Taoutaou, Les arcs monumentaux romains d'Algérie : essai d'étude pour la sauvegarde et la mise en valeur, thèse de doctorat, Paris 1, 2005.

322 K. Zinai, *Le décor des thermes dans l'Algérie antique*, thèse de doctorat, Paris 1, 2014.

323 B. Boussadia, *La céramique campanienne : les collections de Cherchel et de Tipasa*, thèse de doctorat, Université de Strasbourg, 1985.

324 A. Soltani, *Le monnayage préromain de l'Afrique du Nord dans la collection du Musée natio-nal des antiquités d'Alger*, thèse de doctorat, Toulouse 2, 2005.

325 Yammūna Baġdādī, *Dirāsa ḥawla Mūrīṭaniyya*.

326 Nāṣar Ban Masʿūd, *Aswāq muqāṭaʿat Numīdiyā : dirāsa miʿmāriyya muqārina li-aswāq Tīmgād wa Kwīkūl Ǧamīla*, mémoire de magister, Université d'Alger, 1992.

a tenté de réaliser une monographie sur la cité de Satafis[327]. C'est seulement à partir des années 90 que le nombre de thèses est devenu significatif.

L'émergence d'une nouvelle génération de chercheurs s'avère beaucoup plus compliquée. N'ayant plus les mêmes prérequis ni les moyens nécessaires de réaliser leurs projets, elle a diversifié les thèmes de recherches, sans pouvoir atteindre la pertinence et la visibilité demandée. Nous avons regroupé cette production sous forme de dossiers thématiques.

Les questions du Territoire et de la cartographie archéologique ont suscité beaucoup de d'intérêt, en dépit de l'emprise de *l'Atlas archéologique* de S. Gsell qui persiste encore comme un outil incontournable. Effectivement à défaut d'avoir un programme institutionnel, plusieurs chercheurs ont préféré investir le terrain. Nous pouvons évoquer l'exemple de Suʿād Slīmanī qui s'est concentrée sur la région du Hodna[328] ; de Muḥammad Fawzī M'allam qui a soutenu une thèse sur la carte d'Ain el Arbi et d'Ain Makhlouf, une région importante dans le territoire de Calama[329]. Trois autres thèses ont traité du même thème en Maurétanie Césarienne, notamment la wilaya de Bouira par Hūriyya Ban Zītūn[330], la région de Tissemsilt par al-Ḥāǧǧ Labīb[331], le territoire de Chlef par Muḥammad Fūqa[332], et la région d'Ain Temouchent par Āmāl Ban Mahdī[333]. L'étude des voies à l'Est de cette province a été entreprise par Ǧamīla Šāwšī[334]. En Numidie un projet de carte archéologique de la région de Milev a été réalisé

---

327 Ǧahīda Mhantal Maqrūs, *Minṭaqat ʿAyn al-Kabīra : dirāsa tārīḫiyya wa aṯariyya*, mémoire de magister, Université d'Alger, 1996.

328 Suʿād Slīmanī, *Mūnšaʾāt al-rayy al-qadīma fī minṭaqat al-Ḥūḍna*, mémoire de magister, Université d'Alger, 2005 ; Idem, *Dirasa tārīḫiyya wa aṯariyya li-l-maʿālim al-qadīma al-mawǧūda bi-bilād al-Ḥūḍna*, thèse de doctorat, Université d'Alger, 2014.

329 Muḥammad Fawzī M'allam, *al-Ḥarīṭa al-aṯariyya li-baladiyyat ʿAyn al-ʿArbī wa ʿAyn Maḫlūf ǧanūb Gālma*, mémoire de magister, Université d'Alger, 2008 ; Idem, *al-Munšaʾāt wa al-maʿālim al-aṯariyya al-rīfiyya li-silsilat ǧabal Māwna wa ḍawāḫīha : ǧanūb Gālma*, thèse de doctorat, Université d'Alger, 2015.

330 Hūriyya Ban Zītūn, *al-Aṭlas aṯarī li-wilāyat al-Bawīra*, mémoire de magister, Université d'Alger, 2009.

331 al-Ḥāǧǧ Labīb, *Ǧard al-mawāqiʿ al-aṯariyya bi-wilāyat Tīsmsīlat*, mémoire de magister, Université d'Alger, 2010.

332 Muḥammad Fūqa, *Ḥarīṭa aṯariyya li-wilāyat al-Šilaf*, mémoire de magister, Université d'Alger, 2009.

333 Āmāl Ban Mahdī, *al-Ḥarīṭa al-aṯariyya li-manṭiqat ʿAyn Tamūšant*, mémoire de magister, Université d'Alger, 2016.

334 Ǧamīla Šāwšī, *Dirāsa aṯariyya li-l-mawāqiʿ al-sāḥiliyya mā bayn madīnatay Tāmanfūst wa Dallas fī al-ʿahd al-rūmānī*, mémoire de magister, Université d'Alger, 2015.

par ʿAmmār Nuwwāra[335], et en partie par Muṣṭafā Zaʿbāṭ[336]. L'occupation du sol a suscité le même intérêt. Wāʿmar Aʿīšūšan a réalisé une étude monographique sur quelques sites de l'Aurès, avant qu'il s'engage dans l'étude de la dualité ville/campagne dans le même territoire[337]. Au sud de cette chaine al-Saʿīd Trīʿāt a étudié les installations hydrauliques[338] ; Laylā Būʿazza a dressé l'état des sites de la région de Guelma et de Tebessa[339], Muḥammad al-Šarīf Ḥusīn a étudié l'occupation humaine de la région d'Oum el Bouaghi durant l'antiquité[340], et al-Ḥāǧǧ Labīb les fortifications romaines au sud de l'Ouencheris[341]. Enfin Yāsmīn Aggūnī a réalisé un survol des monuments archéologiques au nord ouest de la Maurétanie Césarienne[342].

À défaut de fouilles archéologiques, l'urbanisme antique n'a suscité que peu d'investissement. Nous pouvons citer le mémoire de Muḥammad Ḫayr Ūrfalli sur l'urbanisme punique au Maghreb[343] et le mémoire de Laḥsan Rābaḥ sur les mausolées numides[344]. Farīda ʿAmrūs a travaillé sur l'urbanisme funéraire depuis la période punique[345]. L'urbanisme militaire a fait l'objet de l'étude

---

335   ʿAmmār Nuwwāra, *al-Ḫarīṭa al-aṯariyya li-manṭiqat Mīla wa ḍawāḥīhā*, mémoire de magister, Université de Constantine, 2012.

336   Muṣṭafā Zaʿbāṭ, *al-Ḫarīṭa al-aṯariyya li-baladiyyatay Wād al-Aṯmaniyya wa ʿAyn al-Mulūk, Mīla*, mémoire de magister, Université d'Alger, 2011.

337   Wāʿmar Aʿīšūšan, *Dirāsa maydāniyya wa naẓariyya li-āṯār al-fatrat al-qadīma al-mawǧūda fī ǧibāl al-Awrās*, mémoire de magister, Université d'Alger, 2005 ; Idem, *al-ʿAlāqa bayna al-rīf wa-l-madīna fī iqlīmay al-Awrās wa al-Qabāʾil fī al-fatra al-rūmāniyya*, thèse de doctorat, Université d'Alger, 2016.

338   al-Saʿīd Trīʿāt, *Munšaʾāt al-rayy al-qadīma bi-l-tuḫūm al-Awrāsiyya al-ǧanūbiyya*, mémoire de magister, Université d'Alger, 2009 ; Idem, *al-Zirāʿa wa al-rayy ǧanūb al-Awrās fī al-fatra al-qadīma min ḫilāl al-muḫallafāt al-aṯariyya*, thèse de doctorat, Université d'Alger, 2017.

339   Laylā Būʿazza, *al-Maʿālim al-aṯariyya al-turāṯiyya fī wilāyat Gālma tašḫīṣ al-wāqiʿ wa iqtirāḥ al-ḥulūl*, mémoire de magister, Université de Constantine, 2011 ; Idem, *Dirāsa tārīḫiyya wa aṯariyya li-taṭawwur madīnat Tīfāst*, thèse de doctorat, Université d'Alger, 2019.

340   Muḥammad al-Šarīf Ḥusīn, *al-Taʿmīr al-bašarī bi-minṭaqat Umm al-Bawāqī, dirāsa tārīḫiyya wa aṯariyya min fatrat faǧr al-tārīḫ ilā ġāyat al-fatra al-bīzanṭiyya*, thèse de doctorat, Université d'Alger, 2018.

341   al-Ḥāǧǧ Labīb, *al-Taḥṣīnāt al-ʿaskariyya al-rūmāniyya ǧanūb al-Wanšarīs q 2-3m*, thèse de doctorat, Université d'Alger, 2018.

342   Yāsmīn Aggūnī, *al-Maʿālim al-aṯariyya li-l-ǧihat al-šamāliyya al-šarqiyya li-Mūrīṭāniyyā al-Qayṣariyya*, thèse de doctorat, Université d'Alger, 2019.

343   Muḥammad Ḫayr Ūrfalli, *Ḫaṣāʾiṣ al-ʿimara al-fīnīqiyya fī-l-Maġrib al-qadīm*, DEA, Université d'Alger, 1977.

344   Laḥsan Rābaḥ, *Madāfin ḥukkām al-Mūr wa al-Nūmīdiyyīn*, mémoire de magister, Université d'Alger, 1999.

345   Farīda ʿAmrūs, *al-Mabānī wa al-ṭūqūs wa al-šaʿāʾir al-ǧanāʾiziyya li-l-fatra al-Lūbiyya al-būniyya*, mémoire de magister, Université d'Alger, 2000 ; Idem, *al-Aḍriḥa al-ǧanāʾiziyya al-rūmāniyya bi-l-Ǧazāʾir : Dirāsa miʿmāriyya wa fanniyya*, thèse de doctorat, Université d'Alger, 2010.

de Muṣṭafā Dūrbān sur le camp romain de Tigzirt[346] et d'Usāma Baggār sur le grand camp de la IIIe Légion Augusta[347] ; Ḥakīma Ṭwāhrīa a effectué un double travail sur les maisons en Numidie et Afrique du nord[348]. Zakariyya Ḥalīf a effectué une étude sur l'urbanisme à Tipaza[349]. Le site de Timgad a fait l'objet de plusieurs études, nous signalons le travail de ʿIzz al-Dīn Ṣaddīqī sur le forum[350] et celui de Šarīf Riyyāš sur le théatre[351]. Wīza Balʿarbī a étudié les préssoirs de Madaure[352]. Les thermes de Guelma ont fait l'objet d'une étude par Riyyāḍ Daḥmān[353]. Le système hydraulique a été mis en lumière par Ṣūniyya Āyt ʿAbd al-Qawwī sur l'irrigation à Timgad[354], Kāhina Ḥaǧǧāǧ à Cuicul[355] et Yasmīna Mūsaʿb à Tipaza[356]. Les matériaux et les techniques de construction ont été étudiés, à Cherchel, par Ǧamīla Dūalī[357] et à Timgad par ʿAbd al-Raḥmān Āyt Ǧāmaʿ[358].

Plusieurs études ont été consacrées aux monographies de sites, à l'exemple des monographies de Satafis et de Cirta effectuées par Ǧahīda Mhantal

346 Muṣṭafā Dūrbān, *al-Muʿaskar al-rūmānī li-madīnat Tīgzīrt dirāsa miʿmāriyya wa aṯariyya*, mémoire de magister, Université d'Alger, 2000.

347 Usāma Baggār, *Muʿaskar al-firqa al-uġusṭisiyya al-ṯāliṯa fī Lumbāz 81-238*, mémoire de magister, Université d'Alger, 2014.

348 Ḥakīma Ṭwāhrī, *Manāzil ḏāt al-fināʾayn bi-iqlīm Nūmīdiyā : dirāsa li-manāzil Tīmgād, Ǧamīla, ʿAnnūna wa Ḥamīsa*, mémoire de magister, Université d'Alger, 2011 ; Idem, *Manāzil šamāl Afrīqiyyā ḫilāl al-fatra al-rūmāniyya*, thèse de doctorat, Université d'Alger, 2015.

349 Zakariyya Ḥalīf, *al-ʿImāra al-sakaniyya bi-madinat Tībāza : dirāsa l-namūḏaǧ min al-ḥayy al-sakanī al-ǧadīd*, mémoire de magister, Université d'Alger, 2017.

350 ʿIzz al-Dīn Ṣaddīqī, *Dirāsa aṯariyya li-furūm Tīmgād wa marāfiqihi*, mémoire de magister, Université d'Alger, 2008.

351 Šarīf Riyyāš, *Masraḥ Tīmgād wa Ǧamīla : dirāsa waṣfiyya w taḥlīliyya*, mémoire de magister, Université d'Alger, 2009.

352 Wīza Balʿarbī, *Maʿāṣir Mādūr : dirāsa aṯariyya taḥlīliyya*, mémoire de magister, Université d'Alger, 2006.

353 Riyyāḍ Daḥmān, *al-Ḥammāmat al-šarqiyya li-madīnat Gālma fī maǧālihā al-ʿumrānī al-rūmanī al-qadīm*, mémoire de magister, Université d'Alger, 2014.

354 Ṣūniyya Āyt ʿAbd al-Qawwī, *al-Rayy fī madinat Tūmgād : tamwīn tawzīʿ wa-taṣrīf al-miyāh*, mémoire de magister, Université d'Alger, 2006.

355 Kāhina Ḥaǧǧāǧ, *Ṭuruq tamwīn madīnat Kwīkūl Ǧamīla bi-l-miyāh fī al-ʿaṣr al-rūmānī : dirāsa waṣfiyya wa-miʿmāriyya*, mémoire de magister, Université d'Alger, 2011.

356 Yasmīna Mūsaʿbā, *Ṭuruq tamwīn madīnat Tībāza bi-l-miyāh fī al-fatra al-rūmāniyya*, mémoire de magister, Université d'Alger, 2014.

357 Ǧamīla Dūalī, *Tīqaniyyat al-bināʾ al-rūmānī fī al-ḥammāmāt al-ġarbiyya wa-l-masraḥ bi-madīnat Qayṣariyya- Šaršāl*, mémoire de magister, Université d'Alger, 2015.

358 ʿAbd al-Raḥmān Āyt Ǧāmaʿ, *Mawādd wa tiqaniyyāt al-bināʾ al-rūmāniyya bi-mawqiʿ Tāmūgādī al-aṯarī : dirāsa tiqaniyya wa aṯariyya*, mémoire de magister, Université d'Alger, 2016.

Maqrūs[359] ; de Madaure par Ibrāhīm Būraḥlī[360], de Diana Veteranorum, effectuée par Farīd Ṭāṭa[361], de Mila par Sumiya Ṣamat[362], du site de Baala dans la
région de Mila, par Asmāʾ Būgarra[363], et celle de Thibilis réalisée par al-ʿAmrī
Ūṣmanī[364]. Le site de Tubursicum Numidarum a fait l'objet de plusieurs études,
celles de Farīda Manṣūrī[365], de Ḥakīm Īdīrān[366] ou de Yāsīn Būlmīs[367]. Hmāma
Saʿīdī[368] a étudié les monuments de Sétif, ʿAbd al-Ḥakīm Ūʿkwār de Tobna[369],
et al-Sādaq ʿArbāwī les monuments de Mopht[370]. Bien que ces travaux aient
tenté d'actualiser la documentation, l'absence d'une réelle recherche de terrain
à limité leurs portées.

Le décor a fait l'objet de plusieurs études, notons la thèse de Muḥammad
al-Šarīf Ḥamza sur la mosaïque de la Maurétanie Césarienne[371] ; ou celle de
Naġma Sarrāġ Rmīlī sur l'iconographie à travers les représentations des vignes
ou de Dionysius[372], de Fatīḥa ʿAmmār sur la présence de la feuille de lierre dans

---

359 Ǧahīda Mhantal Maqrūs, *Minṭaqat ʿAyn al-Kabīra* ; Idem, *al-Taṭawwur al-ḥaḍārī bi-madīnat Qusanṭīna Kirta fī al-fatra al-qadīma*, thèse de doctorat, Université d'Alger, 2010.

360 Ibrāhīm Būraḥlī, *Mustaʿmarat Mādūrūs wa iqlīmuhā al-turābī*, thèse de doctorat, Université d'Alger, 2010.

361 Farīd Ṭāṭa, *Madīnat Zana "Diana Veteranorum" Tārīḫuhā wa Maʿālimuhā*, mémoire de magister, Université d'Alger, 2012.

362 Sumiya Ṣamat, *al-Maʿālim al-ʿumrāniyya bi-madīnat Mīla fī al-ʿahd al-qadīm : dirāsa mūnūǧrafiyya*, mémoire de magister, Université de Constantine, 2014.

363 Asmāʾ Būgarra, *Mawqiʿ al-Baʿāla, Mīla : dirāsu mūnūǧrāfiyya*, mémoire de magister, Université de Constantine, 2014.

364 al-ʿAmrī Ūṣmanī, *Madīnat Tibīlīs "Sallāwa ʿAnnūna" : dirāsa tārīḫya wa aṯariyya*, thèse de doctorat, Université d'Alger, 2016.

365 Farīda Manṣūrī, *Dirāsa tārīḫiyya wa aṯariyya li-madīna Tūbūrsīkūm Nūmīdarūm Ḥamīssa ḥāliyyan*, thèse de doctorat, Université d'Alger, 2017.

366 Ḥakīm Īdīrān, *Mustaʿmarat Tūbūsūktū al-rūmāniyya : dirāsa aṯariyya wa miʿmāriyya*, mémoire de magister, Université d'Alger, 2012.

367 Yāsīn Būlmīs, *al-Ḥayy al-sukkanī al-ǧanūbī al-ġarbī bi-al-mawqiʿ al-rūmānī "Tūbūrsīkūm Nūmīdārūm" Ḥamīsa ḥāliyan*, mémoire de magister, Université d'Alger, 2014.

368 Hmāma Saʿīdī, *Dirāsa aṯariyya li-maʿālim madīnat Siṭīf*, mémoire de magister, Université d'Alger, 2012.

369 ʿAbd al-Ḥakīm Ūʿkwār, *al-iqlīm al-idārī wa al-aṯarī li-baladiyya rūmāniyya : dirāsa ǧuġrā-fiyya wa aṯariyya li-madīnat Ṭubna*, mémoire de magister, Université d'Alger, 2010.

370 al-Sādiq ʿArbāwī *Madīnat Mūbt Mopht : dirāsa aṯariyya wa miʿmāriyya*, mémoire de magis-ter, Université d'Alger, 2015.

371 Muḥammad al-Šarīf Ḥamza, *Fusayfisāʾ Mūrīṭaniyya al-Qayṣariyya : al-tablīṭat al-ǧanāʾi-ziyya*, thèse de doctorat, Université d'Alger, 2012.

372 Naġma Sarrāġ Rmīlī, *al-Kurūm wa-l-ḥamr fī al-Ǧazāʾir al-qadīma muʿṭayyāt aṯariyya wa ikūnuġrāfiyya ḥawla zirāʿat al-kurūm wa taṣnīʿihā wa ʿibādat ilāh al-ʿinab wa-l-ḥamr fī al-marḥala al-qadīma*, mémoire de magister, Université d'Alger, 2009 ; Idem, *Fusayfisāʾ al-tayāzūs al-Diyūnīzī bi-Šamāl Afrīqiyyā al-rūmāniyya : dirāsa iknūǧrafia taḥlīliyya*, thèse de doctorat, Université d'Alger, 2018.

la mosaïque en Algérie[373] ; de Malīka Ḥasīsī- Daḥmanī sur la mosaïque dans la province de la Numidie[374]. Ilyās ʿArīfī a consacré son étude de mosaïque à la cité de Tebessa[375]. Kātiyā Ǧāmāʿ a effectué une étude sur le décor chrétien sur les monuments antiques[376].

Plusieurs autres mémoires de magister ont traité la thématique du décor, souvent réinvestis en doctorat, à l'exemple de Suhīla Kardīn sur les chapiteaux de Madaure[377] ; de Mīlūd Ūnīs sur la décoration architecturale à Cuicul et à Timgad[378] ; de Rašīd Ǧawād sur les sculptures de Lambèse et de Timgad[379] ; de Naṣīra Ban ʿAllāl sur l'iconographie des sarcophages[380] ; ou de Wardiyya ʿAlīlāš sur les stèles de Timgad[381]. Ḥasīna ʿAynūš a dressé un inventaire des statues exposées au Musée de Guelma, avant d'éffectuer une étude sur la sculpture mythologique en Algérie[382]. al-Ṭayyib Būsāḥa a étudié les stèles de Guelma, avant de s'occuper de l'analyse iconographique des habits dans les stèles antiques[383]. Zakiyya Zarwāl a réalisé une thèse sur le symbolisme païen en

---

373   Fatīḥa ʿAmmār, *Waraqāt al-lablab min ḫilāl al-lawḥat al-fusayfisāʾ al-rūmāniyya fī al-Ǧazāʾir*, mémoire de magister, Université d'Alger, 2012.

374   Malīka Ḥasīsī- Daḥmanī, *Fusayfisāʾ Nūmīdiya : Ǧamīla, Lambāz, Tīmgād, Tibassa, Qusanṭīna*, thèse de doctorat, Université d'Alger, 2010.

375   ʿArīfī, Ilyās, *Maǧmuʿat fusayfisāʾ minṭaqat Tibassa : dirāsa aṯariyya wa ǧard*, mémoire de magister, Université d'Alger, 2009 ; Idem, *Fusayfisāʾ Tibassa, Sūq Ahrās wa Ǧālma*, thèse de doctorat, Université d'Alger, 2019.

376   Kātiyā Ǧāmāʿ, *al-Zaḫrafa al-masīḥiyya ʿalā al-maʿālim al-aṯariyya fī muqāṭaʿat Nūmīdiyā : Dirāsa zuḫrufiyya wa iknūġrāfiyya*, thèse de doctorat, Université d'Alger, 2018.

377   Suhīla Kardīn, *Dirāsa fanniyya zuḫrufiyya li-l-ʿanāṣir al-miʿmāriyya al-muzayyina li-maʿālim al-mawqiʿ al-aṯarī Madūrūs fī al-fatra al-qadīma*, thèse de doctorat, Université d'Alger, 2018 ; Idem, *Tīǧān madīnat Madūrūs : ǧard wa dirāsa ḥawla al-zaḫrafa al-miʿmāriyya*, mémoire de magister, Université d'Alger, 2010.

378   Mīlūd Ūnīs, *Tīǧān madīnat Ǧamīla Kwīkūl : Dirāsa ḥawla al-zaḫrafat al-miʿmāriyya*, mémoire de magister, Université d'Alger, 2004 ; Idem, *al-Zaḫrafa al-miʿmāriyya fī madīnat Tīmgād Tāmūqādī : Dirāsa waṣfiyya taḥlīliyya li-l-Tīǧān*, thèse de doctorat, Université d'Alger, 2014.

379   Rašīd Ǧawād, *al-Naḥt al-timṯālī li-madīnatay Lumbāz wa Tīmgād*, mémoire de magister, Université d'Alger, 2012.

380   Naṣīra Ban ʿAllāl, *Tawābīt Nūmīdiyā wa-Mūrīṭānyā al-Qayṣariyya : Dirāsa ikūnūġrāfiyya wa taḥlīliyya*, mémoire de magister, Université d'Alger, 2009.

381   Wardiyya ʿAlīlāš, *Anṣāb madīnat Tīmgād*, mémoire de magister, Université d'Alger, 2009 ; Idem, *al-Naḥt al-naḏrī wa al-ǧanāʾizī li-muqāṭaʿat Nūmīdiyya fī al-fatra al-rūmāniyya*, thèse de doctorat, Université d'Alger, 2018.

382   Ḥasīna ʿAynūš, *Dirāsa tamāṯīl matḥaf Ǧālma : ǧard wa taḥlīl*, mémoire de magister, Université d'Alger, 2009 ; Idem, *al-Naḥt al-timṯalī al-mīṯūlūǧī bi-l-Ǧazāʾir ḫilāl al-fatra al-rūmāniyya, al-numīdiyya*, thèse de doctorat, Université d'Alger, 2017.

383   al-Ṭayyib Būsāḥa, *Dirāsa waṣfiyya taḥlīliyya li-anṣāb manṭiqat Ǧālma al-maḥfūẓa fī al-masraḥ al-rūmānī bi-Ǧālma*, mémoire de magister, Université d'Alger, 2010 ; Idem,

Numidie[384] ; Widād Barāknī pour sa part a étudié les sculptures de Juba II au musée de Cherchel[385].

Bien que les études céramologiques ont débuté en Algérie, cette discipline se résume à un mémoire et trois thèses autour des lampes dans le contexte muséal. Nous citons un mémoire de DEA de al-Mašrafī Fīlālī sur les lampes et les amphores[386], qui malheureusement n'a pas donné lieu à une suite. Sitī Ṣandūq a étudié la collection des lampes au musée de Zabāna (Oran)[387] ; Muṣṭafā Dūrbana réalisé une thèse sur la typologie de la céramique[388] ; al-Ḥanāfī Šurfa a réalisé un catalogue des objets céramiques au Musée de Sétif[389]. Fūziyya Wālī a effectué une étude typologique des lampes exposées au Musée de Timgad[390]. Le même travail a été effectué au Musée de Tebessa par Balqāsim ʿAmaǧ[391]. Deux études iconographiques ont été effectuées sur les lampes exposées au Musée des antiquités d'Alger par Yāsmīn Aggūnī[392] et Kātiyā Ǧāmāʿ qui s'est

Dirāsat al-libās al-rūmānī fī šamāl Ifrīqiyā min ḫilāl šawāhid al-tamāṯīl wa al-anṣāb, thèse de doctorat, Université d'Alger, 2019.

384 Zakiyya Zarwāl, *al-Ramziyya al-waṭaniyya fī iqlīm Nūmīdiyā fī al-fatra al-qadīma*, thèse de doctorat, Université d'Alger, 2017.

385 Widād Barāknī, *Dirāsa tiqaniyya wa fanniyya li-maǧmūʿāt al-ṣuwar al-naḥtiyya li-l-ʿāʾila al-malakiyya li-Yūbā al-ṯānī wa al-maḥfūẓa bi-matḥaf madīnat Šaršāl, mémoire de magister, Université d'Alger*, 2016.

386 al-Mašrafī Fīlālī, *al-Maṣābīḥ wa al-ǧirār al-rūmāniyya fī ʿaṣr Fīlībūs*, DEA, *Université d'Alger*, 1974.

387 Sitī Ṣandūq, *Dirāsa tanmīṭiyya li-l-maṣabīḥ al-maḥfūẓa bi al-matḥaf al-waṭanī Aḥmad Zabāna li-madīnat Wahrān*, mémoire de magister, Université d'Oran, 2007.

388 Muṣṭafā Dūrbān, *Anmāṭ al-faḫḫar al-qadīm fī al-Ǧazāʾir al-qadīma mā bayn al-qarn al-awwal qabla al-mīlad wa-l-qarn al-ṯāliṯ mīladī: dirāsa waṣfiyya wa tanmīṭiyya wa taḥlīliyya*, thèse de doctorat, Université d'Alger, 2010.

389 Šurfa al-Ḥanāfī, *Katālūǧ maǧmūʿāt al-faḫāriyya al-maʿrūḍa bi-l-Matḥaf al-ʿumūmī al-waṭanī Siṭīf: Dirāsa tanmīṭiyya wa waṣfiyya*, mémoire de magister, Université d'Alger, 2014.

390 Fūziyya Wālī, *Dirāsa tanmīṭiyya li-l-maṣābīḥ al-waṭaniyya al-maḥfūẓa bi-matḥaf Tīmgād*, mémoire de magister, Université d'Alger, 2009.

391 Balqāsim ʿAmaǧ, *Ǧard maǧmūʿat al-maṣābīḥ al-maḥfūẓa fī maʿbad Mīnaraf bi-Tibāssa: Dirāsa waṣfiyya wa tanmīṭiyya wa zuḫrufiyya*, mémoire de magister, Université d'Alger, 2012.

392 Yāsmīn Aggūnī, *al-Maṣābīḥ al-zaytiyya al-maḥfūẓa fī-l-Matḥaf al-waṭanī li-l-āṯār al-qadīma: dirāsa waṣfiyya tanmīṭiyya wa taḥlīliyya*, mémoire de magister, *Université d'Alger*, 2010.

concentré sur les lampes chrétiennes[393]. Nous signalons aussi, le mémoire d'Ayman Muḥammad Ṣālaḥ Ḥassūna sur la céramique découverte à Gaza[394].

Enfin, Nūriyya Aklī a étudié le mobilier en verre[395]. Tandis que Ḫūḫa ʿAyyatīsʾ s'est orientée vers l'étude de l'activité sidérurgique à travers les collections des musées de Cirta (Constantine) et de Bardo (Alger)[396]. Ǧūdī Balǧūdī a travaillé sur les activités minières[397]. Sufyān Būḏrāʿ[398] et Kāhina Būsaʿīd[399] ont étudié les outils de mesures.

L'épigraphie, à son tour, a fait l'objet de plusieurs études, nous citons l'exemple du magister de Salīm Drīsī, autour de la société de Sitifis[400], de Saʿīd Dallūm sur le trésor monétaire de Msila[401], et de Tawfīq Ḥammūm sur les élites de la confédertion cirtéenne[402]. Ḫadīǧa Ban ʿAyya a travaillé sur les stèles à Saturne de Lambèse[403], et al-Saʿīd Ḫāša sur la société à Auzia et en thèse de

---

393 Kātiyā Ǧāmāʿ, *Dirāsa tanmīṭiyya wa-iknūǧrāfiyya li-maǧmuʿat maṣābīḥ zaytiyya faḫḫāriyya maḥfūẓa fī al-Matḥaf al-waṭanī li-l-āṯār al-qadīma*, mémoire de magister, Université d'Alger, 2009.

394 Ayman Muḥammad Ṣālaḥ Ḥassūna, *al-Faḫḫār al-qadīm al-muktašaf fī Ġazza : dirāsa tiqaniyya wa-taḥlīliyya*, mémoire de magister, Université d'Alger, 2010.

395 Nūriyya Aklī, *al-Awānī al-zuǧāǧiyya al-musawwāt ʿalā qāʿida fī šamāl Ifrīqiyya*, mémoire de magister, Université d'Alger, 2001 ; Idem, *al-Ḥiraf wa al-ḥirafiyyūn fī Nūmīdiyā qabla al-ʿahd al-rūmānī*, thèse de doctorat, Université d'Alger, 2010.

396 Ḫūḫa ʿAyyatī, *al-Taʿdīn al-qadīm fī šamāl al-Ǧazāʾir : dirāsat al-adawāt al-maʿdaniyya al-mahfūẓa fī matḥaf Sīrta wa Bārdū*, mémoire de magister, Université d'Alger, 2002 ; Idem, *Ṭuruq taʿdīn al-nuḥās wa sabkihi min ḫilāl dirāsat ʿayyināt matḥafay Bārdū al-Ǧazāʾir al-ʿāṣima wa Sīrta*, thèse de doctorat, Université d'Alger, 2016.

397 Ǧūdī Balǧūdī, *al-Manāǧim al-qadīma fī al-Ǧazāʾir*, mémoire de magister, Université d'Alger, 2000.

398 Sufyān Būḏrāʿ, *Wasāʾil wa asalīb al-qiyāsāt wa al-awzān fī al-ʿahd al-qudīm : ul-muwāzīn wa al-maʿāyīr*, thèse de doctorat, Université d'Alger, 2016.

399 Kāhina Būsaʿīd, *Niẓām qiyās al-wazn wa al-siʿa al-rūmāniyya fī al-Ǧazāʾir : dirāsa tiqaniyya wa-taḥlīliyya*, mémoire de magister, Université d'Alger, 2005.

400 Salīm Drīsī, *Dirāsat mukawwināt muǧtamaʿ Sītīfīs min ḫilāl al-nuqūš al-latīniyya bayn al-qarnayn al-ṯānī wa-l-ṯāliṯ al-mīlādiyayn*, mémoire de magister, Université d'Alger, 1993.

401 Saʿīd Dallūm, *Kanz al-Mʾsīla al-naqdī nihāyat al-qarn al-ḫāmis wa bidāyat al-qarn al-sādis al-mīladiyayn : dirāsa tārīḫiyya wa naqdiyya*, thèse de doctorat d'État, 2007.

402 Tawfīq Ḥammūm, *Kahana wa kahanūt al-ʿahd al-imbrāṭūrī al-rūmānī al-awwal fī šamāl Ifrīqiyya min ḫilāl al-kitābāt al-lātīniyya*, mémoire de magister, Université d'Alger, 2000 ; Idem, *al-Nuḫab al-idāriyya wa-al-iǧtimāʿiyya li-l-kunfidirāliyya al-sirtiyya wa al-mudun al-kubrā bi-Nūmīdiyā aṯnāʾ al-iḥtilāl al-rūmānī : munḏu sanat 46 qabla al-mīlād ilā nihāyat al-qarn al-rābiʿ al-mīlādī*, thèse de doctorat, Université d'Alger, 2009.

403 Ḫadīǧa Ban ʿAyya, *al-Anṣāb al-naḏriya al-muhdāt li-l-ilāh Satūrn bi madīnat Lambīz*, mémoire de magister, Université d'Alger, 2012.

doctorat sur Cuicul[404]. Ḥayra ʿAšīṭ Hānī a effectué une étude onomastique de la cité de Madaure[405]. ʿUmar Kabbūr a présenté une thèse sur la société d'el Kantara dans la wilaya de Biskra[406]. Muḥannad Āklī Īḫarbān a étudié l'occupation humaine dans la région de Guelma à travers les inscriptions latines[407]. Ḥayāt Būslīmānī a étudié la société de Teveste, ainsi que celle des cités de la Maurétanie césarienne[408]. Ṣuriyya Madīwan a étudié la société de Tūbūrsīkūm Nūmīdarūm[409]. Enfin, Zuhīr Baḫḫūš, qui a entamé son magister sur la société de Timgad, a réalisé un doctorat sur l'onomastique entre la ville et la campagne dans les Aurès[410]. Il est à signaler que la majorité de ces travaux s'est limitée à une simple traduction de la documentation textuelle déjà publiée.

Le dossier de la Numismatique a fait l'objet de plusieurs études, notamment, les collections muséales. Nous citons les thèses de Tūfīq ʿAmrūnī[411], de Yāsmīna Amzyān qui a effectué une étude sur deux trésors de Cherchell et de Tigzirt[412], et de Dalīla Ḥawqlāwn qui a traité le sujet de la propagande impériale à travers

---

404   al-Saʿīd Ḫāša, *Dirāsa muǧtamaʿ Ūziyyā min ḫilāl al-kitābāt al-lātīniyya*, mémoire de magister, Université d'Alger, 2007 ; Idem, *Kwīkūl, dirāsa iǧtimāʿiyya wa aṯariyya*, thèse de doctorat, Université d'Alger, 2017.

405   Ḥayra ʿAšīṭ Hānī, *Dirāsat al-asmā wa al-diyāna bi-madīnat Madūr : dirāsa al-muǧtamaʿ al-Mādūrī*, mémoire de magister, Université d'Alger, 2012.

406   ʿUmar Kabbūr, *al-Muǧtamaʿ al-qadīm bi-minṭaqat al-Qanṭara min ḫilāl al-kitāba wa al-muḫallafāt al-aṯariyya ḫilāl al-fatra al-mumtadda mā bayna al-qarn al-awwal wa al-ṯāliṯ al-mīladiyayn*, thèse de doctorat, Université d'Alger, 2016.

407   Muḥannad Āklī Īḫarbān, *Dirāsa aṯariyya li-iqlīm Gālma al-qadīma min ḫilāl al-taǧammuʿāt al-sukkāniyya wa šabakāt al-ṭuruqāt wa al-nūqūšāt al-lātīniyya wa muḫtalaf al-lūqā al-aṯariyya*, thèse de doctorat, Université d'Alger, 2016.

408   Ḥayāt Būslīmānī, *Dirāsat mukawwināt muǧtamaʿ madīnat Tīfāstīs wa ḍawāḥīhā min ḫilāl al-kitābāt al-lātīniyya fī al-fatra al-mumtadda bayna al-qarnayn al-awwal wa al-ṯāliṯ li-l-mīlād*, mémoire de magister, Université d'Alger, 2009 ; Idem, *Dirāsat mukawwināt muǧtamaʿāt mudun Mūrīṭāniyyā al-Qayṣariyya min ḫilāl al-kitābāt al-lātīniyya fī al-fatra al-mumtadda bayna al-qarnayn al-awwal wa al-ṯāliṯ li-al-mīlād*, thèse de doctorat, Université d'Alger, 2017.

409   Ṣuriyya Madīwan, *Dirāsa muǧtamaʿ Tūbūrsīkūm Nūmīdarūm min ḫilal al-naqīšat al-lātīniyya*, mémoire de magister, Université d'Alger, 2013.

410   Zuhīr Baḫḫūš, *Dirāsa taḥlīliyya li-asmāʾ afrād muǧtamaʿ mustaʿmarat Tāmūgādī ḫilāl al-fatra al-mumtadda mā bayna al-qarnayn al-ṯānī wal-rābiʿ mīlādiyayn*, mémoire de magister, Université d'Alger, 2007 ; Idem, *al-tarkība al-bašariyya li-muǧtamaʿ al-rīf al-Awrāsī aṯnāʾ al-iḥtilāl al-rūmānī : dirāsa taḥlīliyya wa-muqāranatiyya maʿa asmāʾ afrād muǧtamaʿāt al-marākiz al-ḥaḍariyya al-rūmāniyya bi-l-Awrās*, thèse de doctorat, Université d'Alger, 2018.

411   Tūfīq ʿAmrūnī, *Dirāsat al-ḥaraka al-naqdiyya* ; *Dirāsat al-ʿumla al-mūrīṭaniyya*.

412   Yāsmīna Amzyān, *Dirāsat iqtiṣād al-imbrāṭūriyya al-rūmāniyya min ḫilāl dirāsat muqārana li-kanzayni naqdiyyayni li-Mūrīṭāniyyā al-Qayṣariyya : ḥālat Šaršāl wa Tigzīrt*, thèse de doctorat, Université d'Alger, 2010.

la collection de Lamasba, déposée au musée d'Alger, suivi d'un doctorat sur les trésors monétaires découverts en Afrique du Nord[413]. Zakiyya Zarwāl a réalisé un catalogue monétaire d'un trésor découvert à Arris[414], Hūsīn Ǧarmūn autour du trésor de Ghassira[415], et Īmān Būlaʿrās sur le trésor conservé au musée de Guelma[416]. Nūriyya Mūqrānī a écrit une thèse sur le trésor de Lambèse[417]. Anīsa Ġarbī a étudié le trésor du musée d'Annaba[418] et Ṣabrīna Baʿīš a réalisé un catalogue des monnaies exposées au Musée de Cirta à Constantine[419]. ʿAbd al-NāṣirŠ īkar a tenté d'analyser les signes de pouvoir de l'empereur Philipe[420] et Nūr al-Dīn Marzūqī a élargi son champ d'étude en proposant une analyse de la politique monétaire jusqu'à la période de Dioclétien[421]. Enfin Kalṯūm Aklī a effectué une lecture iconographique de la monnaie numide[422].

Plusieurs projets de thèses ont vu le jour, autour des collections de musées. Tūfīq ʿAmrūnī a étudié la collection numismatique préromaine du musée de

413   Dalīla Ḥawqlāwn, *al-Diʿāya ʿinda al-Rūmān fī al-imbrāṭūriyya al-suflā min ḫilāl kanz Lāmāsbā Marwāna maḥfūẓ bi-l-Matḥaf al-waṭanī li-l-āṯār al-qadīma al-Ǧazāʾir*, mémoire de magister, Université d'Alger, 2009 ; Idem, *Dirāsa aṯariyya wa naqdiyya li-l-ʿumlāt wa al-kunūz al-rūmāniyya al-muktašafa fī šamāl Afrīqiyā : al-muʾarraḫa li-l-qarnayn al-rābiʿ wa-al-ḫāmis al-mīlādiyayn*, thèse de doctorat, Université d'Alger, 2017.

414   Zakiyya Zarwāl, *Katalūǧ kanz naqdī li-madīnat Arīs maḥfūẓ bi-l-matḥaf al-waṭanī li-l-āṯār al-qadīma : Dirāsa naẓariyya wa ikūnūǧrāfiyya*, mémoire de magister, Université d'Alger, 2011.

415   Hūsīn Ǧarmūn, *al-Kanz al-naqdī li- Ġāsira : Dirāsa tiqaniyya wa īkūnūǧrāfiyya*, mémoire de magister, Université d'Alger, 2009.

416   Īmān Būlaʿrās, *al-Kanz al-naqdī li-manṭiqat Ḥammām Awlād ʿAlī al-maḥfūẓ bi-matḥaf Masraḥ Gālma : dirāsa tanmīṭiyya wa taḥlīliyya*, mémoire de magister, Université d'Alger, 2012.

417   Nūriyya Mūqrān, *al-Maǧmūʿat al-naqdiyya al-maḥfūẓa bi-matḥaf Lambazis : dirāsa tārīḫiyya wa naqdiyya*, mémoire de magister, Université d'Alger, 2012.

418   Anīsa Ġarbī, *Dirāsa taḥlīliyya tārīḫiyya aṯariyya li-kanz ʿAnnāba al-maḥfūẓ bi al-matḥaf al-waṭanī li-l-āṯar Sīrta Qusanṭīna*, mémoire de magister, Université d'Alger, 2009.

419   Ṣabrīna Baʿīš, *Katālūǧ maǧmūʿāt naqdiyya maḥfūẓa bi-matḥaf Sīrtā al-waṭanī : dirāsa tārīḫiyya wa naqdiyya*, mémoire de magister, Université d'Alger, 2011.

420   ʿAbd al-Nāṣir Šīkar, *Maẓāhir ḥukm al-imbrāṭūr Mārkūs Yūlyūs Fīlībūs al-mullāqab bi-l-ʿArabī : min ḫilāl iṣdārātihi al-naqdiyya 244-249*, mémoire de magister, Université d'Alger, 2012.

421   Nūr al-Dīn Marzūqī, *al-Siyāsa al-naqdiyya li-l-abāṭira al-rūmān wa aṯaruhā ʿalā al-ḥayāt al-iqtiṣādiyya wa al-iǧtmāʿiyya : min bidāyat al-ʿahd al-imbrāṭūrī ḥatta nihāyat ḥukm Daqlidyānūs 27 qabla al-mīlād 305 lil-mīlād*, mémoire de magister, Université d'Alger, 2014.

422   Kalṯūm Aklī, *Dirāsat ikunūǧrāfiyya li-l-muʾašširāt al-dīniyya min ḫilāl al-ʿumlat al-nūmīdiyya wa al-mūrīṭāniyya min al-qarn al-ṯāliṯ qabla al-mīlād ilā al-niṣf al-awwal baʿda al-mīlād*, thèse de doctorat, Université d'Alger, 2018.

Cirta, ainsi que celle de Juba II et Ptolémée[423] ; Anīsa Ġarbī celle du trésor d'Annaba déposé aussi à Cirta[424]. Sufyān Būḏrāʿ a dréssé un inventaire des objets exposés au Musée de Cirta[425]. H'mīda Fūralī a réalisé un inventaire des lampes chrétiennes déposées aux musées de Cirta et de Cuicul[426]. Salīḥa Dūnyā Maryam Qattāl[427] a réalisé un inventaire des stèles de Cuicul, Muḥammad Āklī Īḫarbān l'inventaire des objets exposés au même musée[428] ; al-ʿAmrī Ūṣmanī les stèles funéraires du musée de Sétif[429] ; Asmāʾ Bannūr a dressé un inventaire des outils de médecine déposés au musée des antiquités à Alger et au musée de Cuicul[430]. Malīka Ḥasīsī a éffectué une étude sur le Musée de Lambèse[431]. Enfin Farīda Manṣūrī a traité la collection monétaire de Guelma déposée au musée des antiquités d'Alger[432].

Pour la période byzantine, nous citons la thèse des fortifications byzantines de Salīm Drīsī[433] et de ʿIzz al-Dīn Maǧǧanī sur le mur byzantin de Milev[434].

423   Tūfīq ʿAmrūnī. *Dirāsat al-ḥaraka al-naqdiyya fī Šamāl Ifrīqiyyā 49 q.m-69m min al-niṣf al-awwal li-l-qarn qabla al-mīlad ilā al-niṣf al-ṯānī li-l-qarn 1 m.*, mémoire de magister, Université d'Alger, 2008 ; Idem, *Dirāsat al-ʿumla al-mūrīṭaniyya fī ʿahday Yūba al-ṯānī wa Baṭlīmūs 25 q m-40 m : muqāraba ǧadīda min ḫilal al-kūnūz al-muktašafa wa al-maǧmūʿa al-naqdiyya al-matḥafiya wa-l-ḥaṣṣa al-iqtiṣād al-naqdī wa al-tadāwul*, thèse de doctorat, Université d'Alger, 2015.

424   Anīsa Ġarbī, *Dirāsa taḥlīliyya tārīḫiyya aṯariyya li-kanz ʿAnnāba al-maḥfūẓ bi al-matḥaf al-waṭanī li-l-āṯar Sīrta Qusanṭīna*, mémoire de magister, Université d'Alger, 2009.

425   Sufyān Būḏrāʿ, *Ǧard wa dirāsa maʿrūḍāt ḥadīqat al-Matḥaf al-waṭanī Sīrtā – Qusanṭīna*, mémoire de magister, Université d'Alger, 2009.

426   H'mīda Fūralī, *Ǧard al-maṣābīḥ al-masīḥiyya al-maʿrūḍa fī kull min al-matḥaf al-waṭanī li- Sīrta wa matḥaf mawqiʿ Ǧamīla al-aṯarī*, mémoire de magister, Université d'Alger, 2012.

427   Salīḥa Dūnyā Maryam Qattāl, *Anṣāb madīnat Kwīkūl : ǧard wa dirāsa taḥlīliyya*, mémoire de magister, Université d'Alger, 2010.

428   Muhannad Āklī Īḫarbān, *Ǧard al-tuḥaf al-aṯariyya al-maʿrūḍāt bi-matḥaf Ǧamīla Kuwīkūl al-qadīma*, mémoire de magister, Université d'Alger, 2008.

429   al-ʿAmrī Ūṣmanī, *Dirāsa tanmīṭiyya wa ikūnūġrafiyya li-maǧmūʿat al-anṣāb al-maḥfūẓa fī matḥaf Siṭīf*, mémoire de magister, Université d'Alger, 2010.

430   Asmāʾ Bannūr, *Ǧard wa-dirāsat adawāt al-ṭibb al-rūmāniyya min ḫilāl maǧmūʿatay matḥaf mawqiʿ Ǧamīla wa-al-Matḥaf al-waṭanī li-al-āṯār al-qadīma : dirāst taḥlīliyya*, mémoire de magister, Université d'Alger, 2012.

431   Malīka Ḥasīsī, *Matḥaf Lāmbīz, dirāsat al-maǧmūʿāt al-aṯariyya*, mémoire de magister, Université d'Alger, 1999.

432   Farīda Manṣūrī, *Taṭawwur al-fann al-naqdī min ḫilāl maǧmūʿa naqdiyya min madīnat Gālma maḥfūẓa bi-l-matḥaf al-waṭanī li-l-āṯar al-qadīma*, mémoire de magister, Université d'Alger, 2013.

433   Salīm Drīsī, *al-Bīzanṭiyyūn fī Šamāl Ifrīqiyya aṯnāʾ al-iḥtilāl wa-l-ʿimāra al-difaʿiyya*, thèse de doctorat, *Université d'Alger*, 2008.

434   ʿIzz al-Dīn Maǧǧanī, *al-Sūr al-bīzanṭī li-madīnat Mīlaf*, mémoire de magister, Université d'Alger, 2010.

En revanche l'archéologie chrétienne n'est étudiée que par Rābaḥ Ḥāǧǧī Yāsīn autour des basiliques chrétiennes en Numidie[435], Faziya Mūkāḥ a travaillé sur l'urbanisme chrétien à Timgad[436] et ʿAbd al-Ḥaqq ʿĪd sur le quartier chrétien de Cuicul[437]. H'mīda Fūralī a réalisé un inventaire des lampes chrétiennes exposées aux Musées de Cirta et de Cuicul, ainsi qu'une étude sur les baptistères chrétiens[438]. Ḥasīna Faṣūlī a effectué une étude sur la mosaïque chrétienne[439].

3.2.3   La recherche en préhistoire

Les premières initiatives de la recherche préhistorique ont été conduites par le CRAPE à travers le recrutement de plusieurs étudiants de formation géomorphologique. Cette démarche, soutenue par les facilités de bourses de formation à l'étranger, a permis d'inscrire et de soutenir plusieurs thèses de 3eme cycle. Nous citons à titre d'exemples N. Ferhat[440], N. Saoudi[441], A. Amara[442], S. Hachi[443], qui ont réussi à transformer la plupart de leurs travaux en projets de recherche sur le terrain. Par ailleurs, un certain nombre de chercheurs issus de l'université d'Alger, qui ont réalisé leurs thèses aux universités françaises ont renforcé le corps des chercheurs enseignants de cette institution.

---

435 Rābaḥ Ḥāǧǧī Yāsīn, *al-bāzīlīkāt al-masīḥiyya fī muqāṭaʿat Nūmīdiyā: dirāsa aṯariyya wa-tanmīṭiyya*, thèse de doctorat, Université d'Alger, 2009.

436 Faziya Mūkāḥ, *al-ʿImāra al-dīniyya al-masīḥiyya fī madīnat Tīmgād al-aṯariyya al-muǧammaʿ al-masīḥī al-musammā al-kātūlīkī wa al-muǧammaʿ al-masīḥī al-musammā al-dūnātī: dirāsa aṯariyya*, mémoire de magister, Université d'Alger, 2013.

437 ʿAbd al-Ḥaqq ʿĪd, *al-Maǧmaʿ al-masīḥī al-ḥayy al-masīḥī bi Kwīkūl – Ǧamīla – Dirāsa miʿmāriyya wa fanniyya*, mémoire de magister, Université d'Alger, 2015.

438 H'mīda Fūralī, *Ǧard al-maṣābīḥ al-masīḥiyya al-maʿrūḍa fī kull min al-mathaf al-waṭanī li- Sīrta wa mathaf mawqiʿ Ǧamīla al-aṯarī*, mémoire de magister, Université d'Alger, 2012; Idem, *Buyūt al-taʿmīd fī muqāṭaʿat Nūmīdiya al-masīḥiyya, dirāsa aṯariyya wa tanmīṭiyya*, thèse de doctorat, Université d'Alger, 2018.

439 Ḥasīna Faṣūlī, *Fūsayfisāʾ faǧr al-masīḥiyya: dirāsa taḥlīliyya īknūǧrafiyya wa ramziyya wa tiqaniyya namūḏaǧ min al-Ǧazāʾir al-qadīma wa Tūnis wa Rūmā*, mémoire de magister, Université d'Alger, 2011.

440 N. Ferhat, *Les industries préhistoriques de la paléo vallée de Timimoun dans leur contexte stratigraphique. Sahara-Algérien*, thèse de doctorat de 3ème cycle, Université de Bordeaux 1, 1985.

441 N. Saoudi, *Pliocène et Pléistocène inférieur et moyen du Sahel occidental d'Alger*, thèse 3e cycle, Aix-Marseille 2, 1982.

442 A. Amara, *Contribution à l'étude des formations quaternaires et de la Préhistoire dans le Hodna oriental Algérie du Nord-Est*, thèse de 3e cycle, Université de Bordeaux 1, Bordeaux, 1981.

443 S. Hachi, *Les industries d'Afalou Bou Rhummel (Algérie) dans leurs relations avec l'Ibéromaurusien*, thèse de doctorat, Aix-Marseille 1, 1987.

Nous citons M. Sahnouni[444], A. Guelmaoui[445], A. Derradji[446], D.J. Hadjouis[447], M. Hachid[448], Ch. Y. Saoudi[449], N. Ait Sbaa[450], I. Amara[451], S. Merzoug[452] et S. Iddir[453]. Ayant une maitrise des outils méthodologiques, ils ont rédigé leur production scientifique en langue étrangère, selon les modèles de publications internationales. Cela leur à permis d'actualiser les données scientifiques des sites étudiés et des collections archéologiques, déjà étudiés depuis la période coloniale, et de produire par la même occasion, un discours scientifique soutenu.

3.2.4 Les fouilles préhistoriques

Bien que la préhistoire soit considérée comme une science récente, elle n'a pas échappé aux aléas du discours idéologique colonial. Plusieurs concepts

444 M. Sahnouni, *L'industrie sur galets du gisement villafranchien supérieur d'Ain Hanech (Sétif, Algérie Orientale) : approche morpho-technologique*, doctorat de 3e cycle, Université Pierre et Marie Curie, Paris, 1985 ; Idem, *Archaeological investigations at the Lower Palaeolithic site of Ain Hanech Algeria and their behavioral implications*, Ph.D. thesis, Indiana University, Bloomington, 1996.

445 A. Guelmaoui, *Essai d'analyse morpho technologique d'industries lithiques atériennes d'Algérie*, thèse de doctorat, Paris 10, 1986.

446 A. Derradji, *Contribution à l'étude sédimentologique des terrains quaternaires de la région de Nice. Origine et mise en place des couvertures limoneuses et sableuses des terrasses*, Museum National d'histoire naturelle, thèse de doctorat, Université Pierre et Marie Curie Paris VI, 1987.

447 D.J. Hadjouis, *Les bovidés du gisement atérien des Phacochères, Alger, Algérie. Contribution à l'étude des bovidés du Pléistocène moyen et supérieur du Maghreb*, thèse de doctorat de 3e cycle en Paléontologie des Vertébrés, Muséum National d'Histoire Naturelle et Paris VI, 1985 ; Idem, *Hominidés et grands mammifères dans leur contexte paléo-environnemental au cours du Quaternaire maghrébin*, HDR, Université de Perpignan, 2003.

448 M. Hachid, *Recherches méthodiques sur l'art rupestre de l'Atlas saharien. Étude de deux stations de la région de Djelfa Sud-Algérois*, doctorat de 3e cycle, Aix-en-Provence, 1982.

449 Ch. Y. Saoudi, *Les mammifères holocènes des gisements préhistoriques de Gueldaman-Akbou (Bejaia), Columnata (Tiaret) et Ti-n Hanakaten (Djanet) en Algérie*, doctorat de 3e cycle, Lyon 1, 1987. Cf. son ouvrage : *Le Pliocène et Pléistocène inférieur et moyen du Sahel occidental d'Alger : description matérielle*, Alger, 1989.

450 N. Ait Sbaa, *Les gravures du djebel serkout : contribution a la préhistoire de l'Ahaggar*, thèse de doctorat, Paris 1, 2001.

451 I. Amara, *L'art rupestre dans le sud-ouest de l'Atlas saharien Algérie : étude analytique et typologique des figurations de la période récente*, thèse de doctorat, Panthéon Sorbonne Paris-1, 2001.

452 Merzoug, S., *Comportements de subsistance des Ibéromaurusien d'après l'analyse archéo-zoologique des mammifères des sites de Tamar Hat Taza 1 et Columnata (Algérie)*, thèse de doctorat, Museum National d'Histoire Naturelle, Paris, 2005.

453 S. Iddir, *Peuplement holocène du bas Mertoutek zone centrale de la chaine Téfedest, massif de l'Ahaggar (Algérie)*, thèse de 3e cycle, Université Toulouse le Mirail – Toulouse 2, 2013.

liés à l'occupation humaine ont été développés, à l'exemple de la théorie de l'immigration Nord-Sud. La plupart de ces thèses ne cherchaient qu'à justifier un synchronisme des découvertes archéologiques maghrébines aux acquis européens[454]. La question du peuplement du Maghreb et du Sahara représente parfaitement cet état d'esprit[455]. En revanche l'évolution des pratiques de recherche liée à l'introduction de nouvelles préoccupations d'ordres technologiques et géoarchéologiques à permis de renouveler, voire même d'initier de nouveaux concepts. (Fig. 5.1)

Il parait évident qu'au vu du nombre de sites préhistoriques connus les opérations de fouilles restent très insuffisantes. Néanmoins l'implication des préhistoriens algériens s'est accrue dans le débat concernant l'humanité ancienne, l'émergence des industries lithiques[456] ou la richesse de l'art rupestre multiforme. Plusieurs chantiers ont fourni un matériel archéologique souvent étudié et analysé dans un contexte universitaire. Il s'agit de la fouille du site néolithique du Tin Hinakaten, qui remonte aux années 1976 sous la direction de G. Aumassip[457] ; de la fouille du site de Mechta- Afalou Bou-Rummel, conduite par S. Hachi, au cours des années quatre-vingt[458]. Le chantier de fouille mené par M. Sahnouni depuis 1992 a permis de mettre au jour de nombreux gisements archéologiques et paléontologiques à Ain Hanech et Ain Boucherit[459] qui remontent au Paléolithique inférieur, 24 millions d'années.

Cette découverte a donné lieu à repositionner l'Algérie dans les schémas de diffusion de la technologie lithique oldowayenne à travers l'Afrique et l'Europe. Dirigé par le même chercheur le chantier de Tighennif poursuit aussi les traces découvertes d'une version d'Homo Erectus producteur des industries acheuléennes. S. Merzoug dirige depuis quelques années des fouilles sur le site

454   N. Coye, « Préhistoire et protohistoire en Algérie au XIXe siècle : les significations du document archéologique », *Cahiers d'Études Africaines*, vol. 33, n. 129, 1993, 99-137.

455   G. Camps, *Les civilisations préhistoriques et du Sahara*, Paris, 1974.

456   Plusieurs études de cas ont permis de réviser la chrono-stratigraphie des industries lithiques.

457   G. Aumassip, *Algérie des premiers hommes*, Paris, Éditions de la Maison des Sciences de l'Homme, Éditions Ibis-Presse, 2001.

458   S. Hachi, *Les cultures de l'Homme de Mechta-Afalou. Le gisement d'Afalou Bou Rhummel massif des Babors Algérie. Les niveaux supérieurs 13000-11000 BP*, Mémoires du CNRPAH nouvelle série 2, Alger, 2003 ; Idem, *Aux origines des arts premiers en Afrique du Nord. Les figurines et les objets modelés en terre cuite de l'abri-sous-roche préhistorique d'Afalou Babors Algérie 18000-11000 BP*, Mémoires du CNRPAH nouvelle série n. 6, Alger, 2003.

459   M. Sahnouni et al., « 1.9-million- and 2.4-million-year-old artifacts and stone tool–cut marked bones from Ain Boucherit, Algeria », Science, vol. 362, n. 6420, 2018, 1297-1301, https://science.sciencemag.org/content/362/6420/1297 ; Idem, M. Sahnouni dir., Trad. R. Pigeaud, *Le Paléolithique en Afrique. L'histoire la plus longue*, Paris, Éditions Artcom' Errance, 2005.

Capsien de Medjez II dans la région de Sétif[460]. Ainsi que F. Kherbouche qui dirige la fouille des grottes de Gueldeman dans la région de Bejaia[461].

La richesse archéologique du Sahara lui a conféré un intérêt majeur, qui s'est traduit par la multiplication des études sur les installations mégalithiques et les stations de l'art rupestre. Les missions sur le terrain se sont renforcées après la création du Parc national du Tassili. Nous pouvons citer à titre d'exemple, les recherches menées sur les peintures et les gravures rupestres du Tassili des Ajjer, de l'Ahaggar et de l'Atlas saharien[462]. Plusieurs autres chantiers de fouilles ou de prospections dirigées par des chercheurs attachés au CNRPAH ont abouti à des soutenances de thèses ou des publications[463]. Au niveau de l'Université d'Alger, plusieurs projets méritent aussi d'être cités, nous signalons les fouilles dirigées par A. Derradji dans le site Errayeh Mostaganem qui ont livré un abondant matériel lithique remontant au paléolithique inférieur[464], ou les prospections de T. Sahed dans la région des Aurès[465].

3.2.5 La production universitaire en préhistoire

Au-delà de ces dimensions chronologiques et spatiales, un bon nombre de ces thèses est le fruit d'un travail de terrain et d'une meilleure ouverture sur les disciplines scientifiques. Néanmoins, cette production est loin de couvrir tout le potentiel archéologique de l'Algérie. Parmi les thèmes les plus abordés, il convient de citer les études des industries lithiques, la préhistoire du Sahara et la protohistoire. Plusieurs travaux sont liés aux nouvelles collections, issues des fouilles ou des prospections récentes. Il convient de citer, pour le paléolithique,

---

460 Merzoug, S. « A level prior to the Upper Capsian at Medjez II Algeria: Archaeozoological and taphonomical evidence combined with archaeological data », *Quaternary International*, vol. 320, 2014, 125-130.

461 F. Kherbouche, *Le néolithique tellien de la grotte de Gueldaman GLD1 Babors d'Akbou Algérie VIII-V millénaire BP*, thèse de doctorat, Toulouse 2, 2015 ; F. Kherbouche, et alii, « Middle Holocene hunting and herding at Gueldaman Cave Algeria: An integrated study of the vertebrate fauna and pottery lipid residues », *Quaternary International*, vol. 410, 2016, 50-60.

462 M. Hachid, *Le Tassili des Ajer aux sources de l'Afrique 50 siècles avant les pyramides*, Alger / Paris, 2000 ; Idem, *Les Premiers Berbères. Entre Méditerranée Tassili et Nil*, Alger / Aix-En-Provence, 2000.

463 'Abd al-Qādir Ḥaddūš, *al-Ahaggār al-markazī wa al-ǧanūbī fī faǧr al-tārīḫ*, thèse de doctorat, Université d'Alger, 2010.

464 A. Derradji, « Le site acheuléen d'Errayah Mostaganem Algérie dans son contexte géologique » *dans* Comptes Rendus, *Palevol* 51-2, 229-235, Feb. 2006 ; Id et alii, « Errayah un site Acheuléen récent dans la partie littorale nord-occidentale de l'Algérie Sidi- Ali Mostaganem », *L'Anthropologie*, vol. 121, n. 1-2, Mai 2017, 179-188.

465 T. Sahed, « Contribution à l'étude de la nécropole protohistorique de Sefiane région de N'gaous », *Anthropo*, vol. 21, 2010, 61-77.

les travaux effectués sur le littoral de Mostaghanem, à l'exemple de l'étude de
Salwā Šībān qui a consacré une étude morpho-stratigraphique du quaternaire
au littoral de Mostaganem[466], de Riḍā Ban Šarnīn qui a étudié le site acheuléen Errayeh[467] et de Fāraḥ Samrīk sur une collection lithique du même site[468].
Laṭīfa Maʿrūfa a orienté son étude vers la taphonomie[469] tandis que Samīra
Ṭarraḥ a étudié le gisement de sidi Moussa[470]. Les autres sites n'ont pas pu
fédérer la même dynamique. L'industrie lithique du site d'Ain Hennech a fait
l'objet d'une étude de la part de Marwān Rābḥī[471]. Yūsuf Būʿasal a traité la typologie des éclats de l'industrie dans la région de Tabelballa[472]. Ḥusīn Saḥnūn a
aussi effectué une étude morphotechnologique de l'industrie acheuliéne du
site Al-Māʾ al-Abyaḍ, à Tebessa[473].

Plusieurs approches taphonomiques ont été effectuées, notamment sur les
collections d'ossements de mammifères du pléistocène inférieur de la grotte de
Kīfān Balġūmarī au Maroc par Fatīḥa Šannān[474], la collection d'el Kherba d'Ain
el Hennech, Sétif, par Nādiya Qandī[475], et celle du site de St. Ruch, déposée

---

466   Salwā Šībān, *Dirāsa ǧiyūmūrfūlūǧiyya, mūrfūṭabāqiyyawa ṭabāqiyya li-takwīnāt al-zaman
       al-ǧiyūlūǧī al-rābiʿ bi-l-minṭaqa al-mumtadda ʿalā al-šarīṭ al-sāḥilī bi-wilāyat Mustaġānim :
       Šamāl al-Ǧazāʾir al-ġarbiyya*, mémoire de magister, Université d'Alger, 2013.

467   Riḍā Ban Šarnīn, *al-Mawqiʿ al-Ašūlī li-l-Rābiḥ Mustaġānim-al-Maġrib al-Ǧazāʾir : dirāsa
       iqtināʾ al-mādda al-awwaliyya wa tiknūlūǧiyyat al-ṣināʿa al-ḥaǧariyya*, mémoire de magis-
       ter, Université d'Alger, 2012.

468   Fāraḥ Samrīk, *Dirāsa mūrfū-tiknūlūǧiyya wa qiyāsiyya li-maǧmūʿa ḥaǧariyya ṣināʿiyya
       li-mawqiʿ al-Rayḥ bi-wilāyat Mustaġānim ġarb al-Ǧazāʾir*, mémoire de magister, Université
       d'Alger, 2008.

469   Laṭīfa Maʿrūf, *Dirāsa tafūnūmiyya li-l-mustawā al-aṯarī al-suflī li-l-mawqiʿ al-Ašūlī, al-Rayḥ,
       Sīdī ʿAlī, Mustaġānim al-Ǧazāʾir*, mémoire de magister, Université d'Alger, 2012.

470   Samīra Ṭarraḥ, *Dirāsat al-maǧmūʿa al-ḥaǧariyya li-l-ʿaṣr al-ḥaǧarī al-qadīm al-mawǧūda fī
       al-tarassūbat al-ḥamrāʾ li-mawqiʿ Wādī Sīdī Mūsā, Muḥammad Sīdī Šrīf Wīlīs wa al-Ḥamrā
       bi-Mustaġānim*, mémoire de magister, Université d'Alger, 2013.

471   Marwān Rābḥī, *al-Ṣināʿa al-ḥaǧariyya al-aldawāniyya li-mawqiʿ ʿAyn al-Ḥanaš*, mémoire
       de magister, Université d'Alger, 2006.

472   Yūsuf Būʿasal, *Dirāsa tanmīṭiyya wa-tiknūlūǧiyya li-ṣināʿa ḥaǧariyya ʿalā šaẓāyā
       bi-Tabalbālat manṭiqat al-Sāwra : maǧmūʿat matḥaf al-ǧiyūlūǧiyā bi-ǧāmiʿat al-Ǧazāʾiri*,
       mémoire de magister, Université d'Alger, 2015.

473   Ḥusīn Saḥnūn, *Dirāsa tiknū-mūrfūlūǧiyya li-l-ṣināʿat al-ḥaǧariyya al-Ašūliyya li-mawqiʿ
       al-Māʾ al-Abyaḍ bi minṭaqat Tibāssa*, mémoire de magister, Université d'Alger, 2009.

474   Fatīḥa Šannān, *Dirāsa mūrfūtriyya li-ḥamiyyāt ḍibāʿ wa snūriyyāt maġārat Kīfān
       Balġūmarī al Maġrib al-Aqṣā – al-blaystūsīn al-aʿlā wa muḥāwalat tašḥīṣ ʿalāqātihā bi-bāqī
       al-maǧmūʿāt al-ʿaẓmiyya*, mémoire de magister, Université d'Alger, 2012.

475   Nādiya Qandī, *al-Baqāyā al-ʿiẓmiyya al-ḥayawāniyya li-fatrat al-blūstūsīn al-asfal li-mawqiʿ
       al-ḥarba Galta al-Zarqa-Siṭīf al-Mustawa A, dirāsa ṭafūnūmiyya wa arkyū-zūlūǧiyya*,
       mémoire de magister, Université d'Alger, 2012.

au Musée A. Zabana à Oran, par ʿAbd al-Ḥafīẓ Qarrūǧ[476]. Šahrazād Massūsī a engagé plutôt une démarche paléobotanique pour l'étude du littoral de l'ouest algérien[477]. Tandis que Wahība Ḥarfūš[478] a traité la période du paléolithique inférieur à travers les perspectives de recherches en Algérie.

Quelques sites du type atérien ont été mis à jour. Nous signalons l'étude de l'industrie du site d'Ain Mharim à El Kala par Karīm Abarkān[479], l'étude de la collection lithique du site d'Aymi à Zemmouri el Bahri dans la wilaya de Boumerdès par Laṭīfa Ṣarī[480], ainsi que les collections des sites de Chaabya dans la wilaya de Mostaganem, par Ǧamāl Yaṭǧan[481] et celui de Chabat el Yhoudi à l'ouest algérien, par Sāmiyya ʿAwīmar[482].

Un nombre important de thèses a été consacré aux stations préhistoriques du Sahara, même si leur cartographie et inventaire sont loin d'être à jour. Plusieurs études ont été consacrées aux monographies de ces sites, notament au Tassili-Nager. Nous signalons le travail d'Ismāʿīl Īdīr qui a étudié le site de Tihoudine[483], celui de Badr al-DīnŠ ītwāḥ sur la station Aqnar Agherghar au grand Sahara[484] et de Ṣālaḥ Amuqrān qui a étudié le site du plateau d'Ambrum[485], de Nādiya Baḥra sur les stations rupestres de la région

---

476 ʿAbd al-Ḥafīẓ Qarrūǧ, *Dirāsa mūrfū-mitriyya li-l-ʿiẓām mawqiʿ San Rūš sābiqan ʿUyūn al-Turk- al-blaystūsan al-aʿlā al-maḥfūẓa fī al-matḥaf Aḥmad Zabāna bi-Wahrān*, mémoire de magister, Université d'Alger, 2012.

477 Šahrazād Massūsī, *al-Ǧiṭāʾ al-nabatī li-sāḥil ǧarb al-Ǧazāʾir fī al-blaystūsīn al-aʿlā*, mémoire de magister, Université d'Alger, 2001.

478 Wahība Ḥarfūš, *Dirāsa naqdiyya li-l-waḍʿiyya al-bāliyūlītī al-asfal fī al-Ǧazāʾir wa-al-āfāq al-mustaqbaliyya li-l-baḥṯ*, mémoire de magister, Université d'Alger, 2003.

479 Karīm Abarkān, *Tiknūlūǧiyyat al-ṣināʿāt al-ḥaǧariyya al-aṭariyya li-maḥaṭṭat ʿAyn maḥāram bi-l-Qāla, wilāyat al-Ṭāraf šarq al-Ǧazāʾir, mémoire de magister, Université d'Alger*, 2007.

480 Laṭīfa Ṣarī, *Dirāsa taḥlīliyya murfutiknūlūǧiyya wa tanmīṭiyya li-maǧmūʿat ṣināʿa ḥaǧariyya min al-waǧh al-taqāfī al-ībīrī al-Maǧribī bi-Zammūrī al-Baḥrī al-sāḥil al-šarqī li-l-Ǧazāʾir*, mémoire de magister, Université d'Alger, 2002.

481 Ǧamāl Yaṭǧan, *Dirāsa tiknūmūrfūlūǧiyya li-maǧmūʿa ṣināʿiyya ḥaǧariyya li-l-waǧh al-ṯaqāfī al-ʿAtīrī, li-l-mawqiʿ al-šaʿaybiyya al-Kaḥla bi-wilāyat Mustaǧānim al-sāḥil al-ǧarbi al-Ǧazāʾir*, mémoire de magister, Université d'Alger, 2012.

482 Sāmiyya ʿAwīmar, *Dirāsa mūrfūlūǧiyya wa tiknūlūǧiyya li-maǧmūʿāt ṣināʿiyya ḥaǧariyyaʿātiriyya li-mawqiʿ šuʿbat lihūdī bi-al-Sāḥil al-ǧarbī al-ǧazāʾirī, mémoire de magister, Université d'Alger*, 2009.

483 Ismāʿīl Īdīr, *al-Adawāt al-ḥaǧariyya li-mawqiʿ ʿIrq Tīhūdāyīn: dirāsa manhaǧiyya wa tanmīṭiyya, mémoire de magister, Université d'Alger*, 2003.

484 Badr al-Dīn Šītwāḥ, *Taṭbīq qawāʿid al-arkiyūzūlūǧiyya ʿalā al-īkūnūǧrāfiyya al-ḥayawāniyya li-maḥaṭṭatay Aqnār wa Aǧrǧār: al-Ṣaḥrāʾ al-kubrā al-Ǧazāʾir, mémoire de magister, Université d'Alger*, 2016.

485 Ṣālaḥ Amuqrān, *Dirāsat āṯār fatrat mā qabla al-tārīḫ li-haḍabat Ambrūm -Tasīlī Nāhagār, al-Ṣaḥrāʾ al-wusṭā al-Ǧazāʾir, mémoire de magister, Université d'Alger*, 2012.

d'Admr[486], de ʿIzz al-Dīn Farqī, sur les gravures de Oued Djerrat[487], ainsi que Ǧawhar Ūbrāham qui a réalisé une monographie des stations de l'art rupeste de la région de Tamanraset[488], de Samīr Naʿīmī sur les sites de d'Affifug et de Tourset à Djanet[489] et celui de ʿIzz al-Dīn Farqī sur les gravures de la station de Oued Garra, au Tassili[490].

Plusieurs études ont tenté d'étudier le contexte socio-économique de ce patrimoine rupestre. Hasība Safrwān a traité l'image feminine dans la région de Saffar[491], Dāwiya Šrīfī les représentations humaines dans l'art rupestre de l'Atlas saharien[492], Sīdī Muḥammad Ībāh, les aspects culturels et modes de vie dans la région de Tafdast au Hogar[493], ainsi que Karīm Abarkān qui a effectué une réflexion sur l'occupation humaine dans l'Atlas saharien[494]. D'autres sites ont suscité l'intérêt des chercheurs tels que le travail de Kamāl Būlġrāyf sur le site de Theniet el Had à Tissemsilt[495], de Ḥusīn Ballaḥraš sur la région d'El Bayed[496] et au nord celui de Wahība ʿAbd al-Wahhāb sur la faune de la

<hr>

486   Nādiya Baḥra, *Muḥāwalat dirāsa taḥlīliyya li-l-fann al-ṣaḥrī bi-manṭiqat Ādmr al-Tāsīlī Āzǧar- al-Ṣaḥrāʾ al-Wusṭā – al-Ǧazāʾir*, mémoire de magister, Université d'Alger, 2006.

487   Farqī, ʿIzz al-Dīn, *Dirāsa taḥlīliyya li-nuqūš wa wāǧihat maḥaṭṭat wadī Ǧarra -Tāsīlī-Nāǧar – al-Ṣaḥrāʾ al-Wusṭā, al-Ǧazāʾir*, mémoire de magister, Université d'Alger, 2009.

488   Ǧawhar Ūbrāham, *Dirāsat baʿḍ maḥaṭṭāt al-fann al-ṣaḥrī bi-nawāḥī Wilāyat Tamanrāst, manṭiqat al-Ahaggār, al-Ṣaḥrāʾ al-wusṭā, al-Ǧazāʾir*, mémoire de magister, Université d'Alger, 2007.

489   Samīr Naʿīmī, *Dirāsa tīqaniyya wa fanniyya li-mawqiʿay al-fann al-ṣaḥrī Afīf Ūǧ wa Tūrst bi Ǧanat Tasīlī-Nāǧar*, mémoire de magister, Université d'Alger, 2014.

490   ʿIzz al-Dīn Farqī, *Dirāsa taḥlīliyya li-nuqūš wa wāǧihat maḥaṭṭat wadī Ǧarra -Tāsīlī-Nāǧar – al-Ṣaḥrāʾ al-Wusṭā, al-Ǧazāʾir*, mémoire de magister, Université d'Alger, 2009.

491   Hasība Safrwān, *Wāqiʿiyyat ṣūrat al-unṭa fī al-rasm al-ṣaḥrī li-minṭaqat Ṣaffār wa ḍawāḥīhā al-Tasīlī-Naǧar, al-Ṣaḥrāʾ al-Wusṭā- al-Ǧazāʾir*, mémoire de magister, Université d'Alger, 2008.

492   Dāwiya Šrīfī, *Dirāsat al-ašḫāṣ al-mumāṯala fī al-nuqūš al-ṣaḥriyya bi-l-Aṭlas al-Ṣaḥrāwī*, mémoire de magister, Université d'Alger, 2012.

493   Sīdī Muḥammad Ībāh, *al-Maẓāhir al-ṯaqāfiyya wa-l-anmāṭ al-maʿīšiyya min ḫilal al-rusūmāt al-ṣaḥriyya bi-Tafdast al-Hūgār*, mémoire de magister, Université d'Alger, 2013.

494   Karīm Abarkān, *al-Taʿmīr al-bašarī ḫilāl al-hūlūsīn fī-l-Aṭlas al-ṣaḥrāwī al-šarqī: al-iṭār al-ṭabīʿī wa tiknūlūǧiyyat al-ṣināʿāt al-ḥaǧariyya li-mawqiʿ Maǧārat ʿAmūra, al-Ǧalfa*, thèse de doctorat, Université d'Alger, 2016.

495   Kamāl Būlġrāyf, *Dirāsa waṣfiyya wa-taḥlīliyya li-maḥaṭṭāt al-fann al-ṣaḥrī li-manṭiqat Ṯniyyat al-Ḥadd Wilāyat Tīsmsīlat al-Ǧazāʾir*, mémoire de magister, Université d'Alger, 2008.

496   Ḥusīn Ballaḥraš, *Dirāsa taḥlīliyya li-l-nuqūš al-ṣaḥriyya li-manṭiqat al-Bayyiḍ*, mémoire de magister, Université d'Alger, 2010 ; Idem, *Taṭbīq niẓām al-maʿlūmāt al-ǧuġrāfiyya ʿalā mawāqiʿ al-fann al-ṣaḥrī li-l-Aṭlas al-ṣaḥrāwī- manṭiqatay al-Bayyiḍ wa al-Ǧalfa namūḏaǧan*, thèse de doctorat, Université d'Alger, 2019.

grotte des Ours à Constantine[497], ou celui de Farīda Ūzānī sur l'alimentation au Maghreb préhistorique[498].

L'intérêt des études sur le Néolithique se revèlent importantes, quoiquelles se limitent à l'étude des collections. Nous signalons la thèse de Muḥammad ʿAllīš sur les aspects du néolithique dans la région de Tin Izran, au Tassili[499], de Fatīḥa Azbūǧan Ūtšarnān, sur les matériaux de l'industrie lithique à Timimoun[500], celle de Ramḍān Bakdā qui a étudié une collection des ossements conservée au musée de Zabana à Oran[501], et de Fūziyya Būšʿīyb sur les sites préhistoriques de l'Holocène à Mostaganem[502]. Le site de Tin Hanakaten a beneficié de plusieurs études. Nous signalons celle de Muḥammad Ḥammūdī qui a effectué une analyse d'une coupe du néolithique au site[503] ainsi que celle de Saʿīda Ban Ṣaddūq qui a travaillé sur la poterie néololithique[504]. L'analyse sédimenthologique éffectuée par Samīra Hāmil[505], ainsi que l'étude paléontologique de l'Holocène de Samīra ʿAmranī[506] ont permis de developper de nouvelles perspectives de recherches.

Les études consacrées à la protohistoire restent minimes. Nous citons le travail de Tāriq ʿAzīz Sāḥad qui a étudié les monuments funéraires de la région des

---

497   Wahība ʿAbd al-Wahhāb, *Dirāsa bālyuntūlūǧiyya wa ikūlūǧiyya li-mufradāt wa muzdawaǧāt al- ṣabiʿ li-mawqiʿ Kahf al-Diba, Hūlūsīn, Ǧabal al-Rakīna, Bātna*, mémoire de magister, Université d'Alger, 2012.

498   Farīda Ūzānī, *al-Taġdiyya ʿinda insān al-ʿaṣr al-ḥaǧarī al-qadīm al-mutaʾaḫḫir wa al-ʿaṣr al-ḥaǧarī al-ḥadīṯ fī al-Maġrib, al-Ǧazāʾir, Tūnis : dirāsa fāḥiṣat al-asnān wa al-amrāḍ al-siniyya*, mémoire de magister, Université d'Alger, 2008.

499   Muḥammad ʿAllīš, *Maẓhar min al-niyūlītī al-ṣaḥrāwī al-raʿawī al-aʿlā li-minṭaqat Tīn-Izran al-Tasīlī-Naǧar al-Ǧazāʾir*, mémoire de magister, Université d'Alger, 1999.

500   Fatīḥa Azbūǧan Ūtšarnān, *Dirāsa namaṭ istiġlāl al-māda al-awwaliyya fī mawqiʿ Ādǧī bi-Tīmīmūn wilāyat Adrār, al-ǧanūb al-ġarbī al-ǧazāʾirī*, mémoire de magister, Université d'Alger, 2009.

501   Ramḍān Bakdā, *Dirāsat al-baqāyā al-ʿaẓmiyya li-Mawqiʿ al-Razīqat al-Niyūlītī : al-Rāḥil Ḥāsī al-Ġalat bi-ʿAyn Tīmūšant al-maḥfūẓa bi-l-matḥaf al-waṭanī Aḥmad Zabāna bi-Wahrān*, mémoire de magister, Université d'Alger, 2012.

502   Fūziyya Būšʿīyb, *Dirāsat al-mawāqiʿ al-aṯariyya al-sāḥiliyya li-fatrat al-Hūlūsān li-manṭiqat al-Šamra Sīdī Laḥḍar : dirāsa mūrfū-tiknūlūǧiyya li-maǧmūʿāt ṣināʿiyya ḥaǧariyya*, mémoire de magister, Université d'Alger, 2015.

503   Muḥammad Ḥammūdī, *Dirāsa waǧh min al-niyūlītī al-ṣaḥrāwī : al-baqrī al-asfal ḥasba al-maqṭaʿ al-rābiʿ li-mawqiʿ Tīn Hnāktn-al-Ṭāsīlī Naǧar- al-Ǧazāʾir*, mémoire de magister, Université d'Alger, 2002.

504   Saʿīda Ban Ṣaddūq, *Dirāsat faḫḫār li-mustawayāt muḫtalifa li-mawqiʿ al-niyyūlūtī Tīn Hna Katān "Ṭāsīlī Naǧar" al-Ṣaḥrāʾ al-wusṭā*, mémoire de magister, Université d'Alger, 2011.

505   Samīra Hāmil, *Dirāsa rusūbiyya li-ʿayyināt min al-mawqiʿ al-aṯarī Tin-Hnaktn al-Tāsīlī Naǧar*, mémoire de magister, Université d'Alger, 2010.

506   Samīra ʿAmranī, *Dirāsa arkiyū-balnyūlūǧiyya li-Asāṭ al-hulusān bi-minṭiqat Tīn-Hunāktan al-Ṭasīlī-Naǧar, al-Ṣaḥrāʾ al-wusṭā*, mémoire de magister, Unéversité d'Alger, 2002.

Aurès, suivi d'un doctorat sur la question de l'occupation du sol protohistorique dans le Maghreb à partir de l'exemple des Aurès[507]. Dans la même perpsective, la thématique du peuplement a été reprise par Ḥafīẓa La'yāḍī sur le peuplement du Tassili[508], et par Marwān Rābḥī concernant l'Atlas saharien[509]. Laylā Mūqrānī a orienté son travail vers le littoral d'Alger au cours de l'Holocène[510]. L'archéologie funéraire a bénéficié aussi de quelques études, à commencer par celle de Ǧaʿfar Āyt Sī Aʿmur qui a étudié les couloirs couverts du site de Rahunat en Kabylie[511], celle de Muṣṭafā Rmīlī sur les monuments funéraires dans les hauteurs du Titteri[512] et celle de Mūrad Zrārqa[513], ainsi que celle de Wāfiya ʿĀdil, sur la même problématique dans la région de Guelma[514].

Plusieurs approches géographiques ont appréhendé cette période, sous fome de monographies régionales. Nous citons le travail de Mūsā Ḥalīl sur la répartition géographique des nécropoles mégalitiques de Sigus[515], de Mūḥammad al-Ṭāhir Al-Hāšmī qui a consacré une étude des monuments mégalitiques de

507   Tāriq ʿAzīz Sāḥad, *al-Maʿālim al-ǧanāʾiziyyya li-minṭaqat N'qāwus : maqbarat Sufyān-al-Ḥuḍna al-šarqiyya*, mémoire de magister, Université d'Alger, 1998 ; Idem, *al-Taʿmīr al-bašarī bi-bilād al-Maġrib fī fatrat faǧr al-tārīḫ – namūḏaǧ al-maʿālim al-ǧanāʾiziyya bi-manaṭiqat al-Awrās : dirāsa aṯariyya miʿmāriyya*, thèse de doctorat, Université d'Alger, 2009.

508   Ḥafīẓa La'yāḍī, *al-Tarkība al-bašariyya li-l-Ṭāsīlī-Nāǧar munḏu mā qabl al-tārīḫ ilā bidāyat al-ʿuṣūr al-tārīḫiyya*, mémoire de magister, Université d'Alger, 2011.

509   Marwān Rābḥī, *al-Taʿmīr al-bašarī li-faǧr al-tārīḫ bi-l-Aṭlas al-Ṣaḥrāwī : minṭaqa al-Idrīsiyya namūḏaǧan*, thèse de doctorat, Université d'Alger, 2012.

510   Laylā Mūqrānī, *al-Taʿmīr al-bašarī wa al-ḥaywānī li- bidāyat al-hūlūsīn al- sāḥil al- Ǧazā'ir al-ʿāṣima al-ġarbī min ḫilāl dirāsat aṯār maġārat al-Ṣahrā' al-kabīra*, mémoire de magister, *Université d'Alger*, 2016.

511   Ǧaʿfar Āyt Sī Aʿmur, *al-Mamarrāt al-muġaṭṭāt li-mawqiʿay Āṯ Rahunat wa Ibārīsn bi-manṭiqat al-Qabā'il : dirāsa aṯariyya wa miʿmāriyya*, mémoire de magister, *Université d'Alger*, 2012.

512   Muṣṭafā Rmīlī, *al-Maʿālim al-ǧanāʾiziyya li-faǧr al-tārīḫ bi-minṭaqat Ašīr- Ǧabal al-Tīṭrī*, mémoire de magister, Université d'Alger, 2002 ; Idem, *Dirāsa aṯariyya li-l- maʿālim wa-l-ṭuqūs al-ǧanāʾiziyya li- faǧr al-tārīḫ bi-minṭaqat al-Ḥuḍna*, thèse de doctorat, Université d'Alger, 2016.

513   Mūrad Zrārqa, *al-Maʿālim al-ǧanāʾiziyya al-mīǧālītiyya wa šibh al-mīǧalītiyya li-minṭaqat al-Burma wa Ǧabal al-Farṭas ǧanūb Qusanṭīna*, mémoire de magister, Université d'Alger, 2006 ; Idem, *al-Maʿālim al-ǧanāʾiziyya wa-l-ḥayāt al-sakaniyya li-ḥawḍ Būmrzūg fī bidāyat al-ʿuṣūr al-tārīḫiyya*, thèse de doctorat, Université d'Alger, 2013.

514   Wāfiya ʿĀdil, *Maqābir faǧr al-tārīḫ bi-manṭiqat Gālma- dirāsa waṣfiyya tanmīṭiyya*, thèse de doctorat, Université d'Alger, 2018.

515   Mūsā Ḥalīl, *al-Tawzī' al-ǧuġrāfī fī al-waṣf al-miʿmārī li-maʿālim al-maqbara al-mīǧalītiyya "al-Ṣfiyya" bi-minṭaqat Sīqūs – wilāyat Umm al-Buwāqī*, mémoire de magister, Université d'Alger, 2008.

quelques sites de la région d'El Djelfa[516], de Salma 'Amrānī qui a traité l'application des SIG à l'étude de quelques sites de la Kabylie[517].

Par ailleurs, la langue Libyque n'a fait l'objet que de peu d'études. Il s'agit du travail de Balqāsam Ša'lāl sur les stèles libyques[518], celui de 'Abd al-Ǧabbār 'Abbāsī, qui a étudié les inscriptions libyques dans les stations rupestres du Tassili[519], et enfin Yāsīn Sīdī Ṣalaḥ qui a effectué une étude iconographique sur inscriptions épigraphique dans les gravures rupestres dans la région de Tizi Ouzou[520].

L'analyse de cette production permet de constater que cette discipline a maintenu, durant ces trente dernières années, une augmentation constante en nombre de thèses soutenues. Mais si un nombre considérable de ces sujets s'est inscrit dans des projets de fouilles, le nombre de sites et des problématiques préhistoriques reste plus important. Ne citons que l'exemple de l'émergence de la civilisation capsienne et sa cartographie, qui est totalement absente de cette production universitaire.

4   Conclusion

Au terme de cette présentation synthétique de l'historiographie antique en Algérie, plusieurs points méritent d'être soulevés. D'abord, l'analyse de l'historique des soutenances permet de constater une discrétion de la production historiographique au cours des premières décenies après l'indépendance. Son émergence à partir des années quatre-vingt correspond aux grandes mutations de l'université, suite à l'arabisation et à la multiplication du nombre d'universités et d'étudiants. La géneralisation de la formation d'histoire au niveau de ces nouveaux centres explique parfaitement le phénomène d'accélération

---

516   Muḥammad al-Ṭāhar Al-Hāšmī, *Dirāsa ǧuġrāfiyya wa tanmīṭiyya li-l-ma'ālim al-ǧanā'iziyya li-fatrat faǧr al-tārīḫ li-mawāqi' 'Ayn al-Wakārīf wa Kāf al-Dašra wa mawqi' Adsām bi-al-Šāraf*, mémoire de magister, Université d'Alger, 2010.

517   Salma 'Amrānī, *Tawṯīq ba'ḍ al-maḥaṭṭāt al-aṯariyya li-l-Qabā'il al-Kubrā mā qabla al-tārīḫ wa faǧr al-tārīḫ bi-istiḥdām taṭbīqat niẓām al-ma'lūma al-ǧuġrāfiyya*, mémoire de magister, Université d'Alger, 2011.

518   Balqāsam Ša'lāl, *al-Anṣāb al-lībiyya ḏāt al-mašahid al-ikūnūǧrafiyya fī al-Ǧazā'ir ǧard wa taḥlīl*, mémoire de magister, Université d'Alger, 2009.

519   'Abd al-Ǧabbār 'Abbāsī, *al-Kitāba al-lībiyya al-barbariyya fī iṭār al-fann al-ǧidārī al-ṣaḥrawī: dirāsa aṯariyya li-maǧmū'a min al-kitāba al-ṣaḥriyya fī muḥīṭayhā al-ṭabī'ī wa al-aṯarī bi--l-Tāsīlī-Nāǧar*, mémoire de magister, Université d'Alger, 2005.

520   Yāsīn Sīdī Ṣalaḥ, *al-Tamṯīlāt al-ṣaḥriyya wa al-kitābāt al-muštaraka: dirāsa ikūnū ibīǧrafiyya li-ba'ḍ mawāqi' al-fann al-ṣaḥrī li-wilāyat Tīzī Wazzū. al-Ǧazā'ir*, mémoire de magister, Université d'Alger, 2012.

des soutenances, mais elle revèle un dysfonctionnement capital en matière d'orientation et d'encadrement. Car, au-delà de la grande diversité des intitulés, l'analyse du taux de fidélité des chercheurs aux thématiques engagées, laisse entrevoir un réel nomadisme entre les spécialités et les sujets de recherche. Le choix de ces thèmes étant généralement individuel, s'illustre en premier lieu par le taux de redondances des intitulés et notamment, par l'absence de prérequis lors de l'attribution des sujets.

Ainsi, l'absence de standards méthodologiques limite la visibilité et l'impact de cette production dans le domaine de la recherche. Les tendances observées en matière d'histoire orientale, d'histoire socio-économique ou d'histoire religieuse, n'échappent pas à cet état des lieux. En effet, mis à part les quelques travaux de terrain, notamment en préhistoire, les problématiques soulevés reposent souvent sur une documentation textuelle et n'arrivent pas à se détacher de l'héritage colonial.

Devant l'absence de grands travaux de synthèse, les projets d'inventaire et de cartographie restent inachevés et manquent d'une coordination dans le temps et dans l'espace. Les études des corpus, des cités, des vestiges, des objets ou de la Société peinent à s'adapter aux nouvelles attentes académiques et sociétales. Les débats sur les questions de l'identité, de l'occupation humaine ou même de l'histoire locale sont loin d'être résolus. L'Antiquité reste algérienne, en raison de l'handicap de la maitrise des langues anciennes et étrangères, en raison de la timidité de ces approches concernant le patrimoine, et par la frustration qu'elle engendre en matière de renouvellement des sources et surtout par son manque d'ambition de réconcilier le Maghreb avec sa profondeur territoriale et internationale.

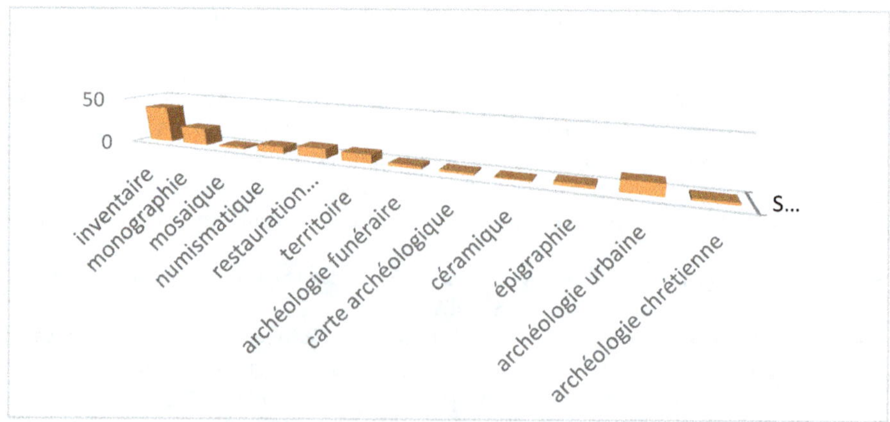

FIGURE 5.1   Répartition thématique des thèses en archéologie

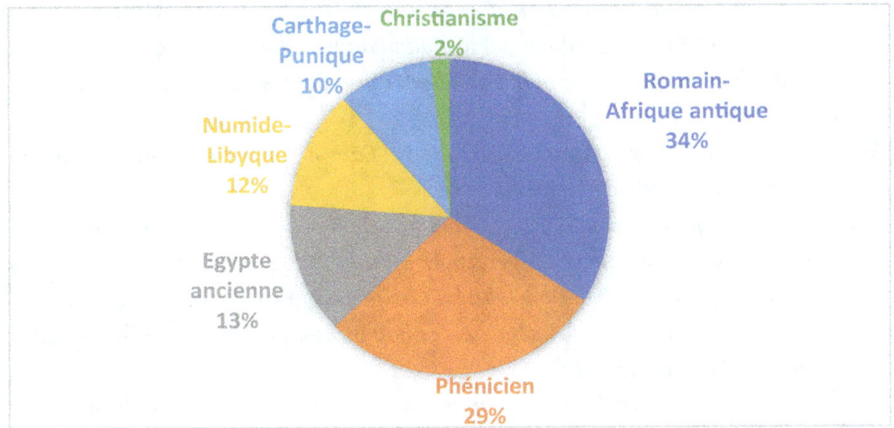

FIGURE 5.2 Répartition thématique des thèses d'histoire antique

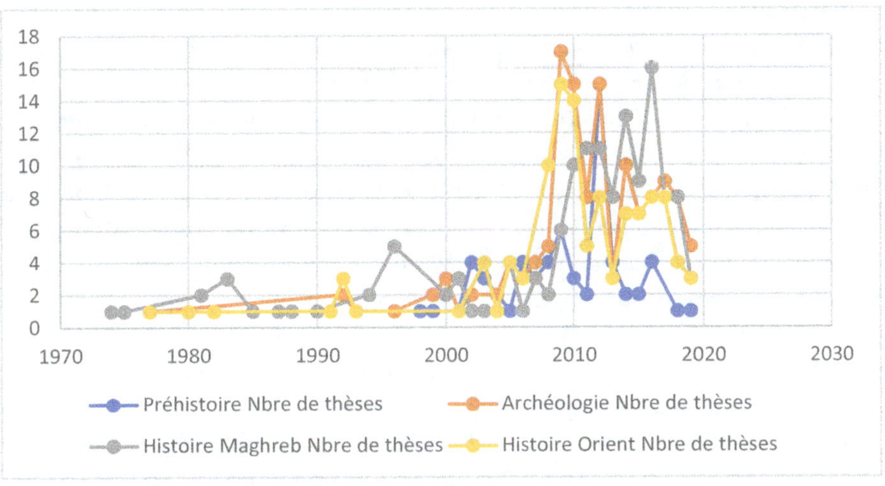

FIGURE 5.3 Évolution des soutenances

Bibliographie

'Abbāsī, 'Abd al-Ğabbār. *al-Kitāba al-lībiyya al-barbariyya fī iṭār al-fan al-ğidārī al-ṣaḥrawī: dirāsa aṯariyya li-maǧmūʿa min al-kitāba al-ṣaḥriyya fī muḥīṭayhā al-ṭabīʿī wa al-aṯarī bi-l-Tāsīlī-Nāǧar*, mémoire de magister, Université d'Alger, 2005.

'Abd al-Wahhāb, Wahība. *Dirāsa bālyuntūlūǧiyya wa ikūlūǧiyya li-mufradāt wa muzdawaǧāt al-ṣābiʿ li-mawqiʿ Kahf al-Diba, Hūlūsīn, Ğabal al-Rakīna, Bātna*, mémoire de magister, Université d'Alger, 2012.

ʿAbd Allāh, Ḥūriyya. *al-Ḥayāt al-ṯaqāfiyya wa-al-fikriyya fī bilād al-Rāfidayn: dirāsa taḥlīliyya, al-usṭūrāt wa al-malḥamāt namūḏağan, nihāyat al-qarn 25 qabla al-mīlād – nihāyat al-qarn 17 qabla al-mīlād*, thèse de doctorat, Université d'Alger, 2015.

ʿAbd Allāh, Ḥūriyya. *al-Tawassuʿ al-Āšūrī fī bilād al-Šām 911-612 qabla al-mīlād*, mémoire de magister, Université d'Alger, 1992.

ʿĀdil, Wāfiya. *Maqābir faǧr al-tārīḫ bi-manṭiqat Gālma- dirāsa waṣfiyya tanmīṭiyya*, thèse de doctorat, Université d'Alger, 2018.

ʿAdwānī, Muḥammad al-Ṭāhar. *Dirāsa li-l-ḥaḍāra fī ʿuṣūr mā qabla al-tārīḫ bi-al-Ṣaḥrāʾ al-Ǧazāʾiriyya wa ḫāṣṣatan aṯnāʾ al-ʿaṣr al-ḥaǧarī al-ḥadīṯ*, mémoire de magister, Université d'Alexandrie, 1983.

ʿAla, Ṣabāḥ. *al-Muʿtaqadāt al-dīniyya al-qarṭāǧiyya 814 q m-264 q m*. mémoire de magister, Université d'Alger, 2011.

ʿAla, Ṣabāḥ. *Muʿtaqdāt bilād al-Maġrib wa ʿalāqatuhā bi-muʿtaqadāt al-Šarq al-Adnāal-qadīm. al-Maġrib wa Miṣr namūḏağan*, thèse de doctorat, Université d'Alger, 2017.

ʿAlīlāš, Wardiyya. *al-Naḥt al-naḏrī wa al-ğanāʾizī li-muqāṭaʿat Nūmīdiyya fī al-fatra al-rūmāniyya*, thèse de doctorat, Université d'Alger, 2018.

ʿAlīlāš, Wardiyya. *Anṣāb madīnat Tīmgād*, mémoire de magister, Université d'Alger, 2009.

ʿAllīš, Muḥammad. *Maẓhar min al-niyūlītī al-ṣahrāwī al-raʿawī al-aʿlā li-minṭaqat Tīn-Izran al-Tasīlī-Naǧar al-Ǧazāʾir*, mémoire de magister, Université d'Alger, 1999.

ʿAmaǧ, Balqāsim. *Ǧard maǧmūʿat al-maṣābīḥ al-maḥfūẓa fī maʿbad Mīnaraf bi-Tibāssa: Dirāsa waṣfiyya wa tanmīṭiyya wa zuḫrufiyya*, mémoire de magister, Université d'Alger, 2012.

ʿAmmār, Fatīḥa. *Waraqāt al-lablab min ḫilāl al-lawḥat al-fusayfisāʾ al-rūmāniyya fī al-Ǧazāʾir*, mémoire de magister, Université d'Alger, 2012.

ʿAmrān, Nūra. *Riǧal al-māl wa al-aʿmāl al-ağānib fī-l-muqāṭaʿa al-ifrīqiyyā al-rumāniyya 146 q.m-285m.*, mémoire de magister, Université d'Alger, 2011.

ʿAmrān, ʿAbd al-Ḥamīd. *al-Diyāna al-masīḥiyya fī-l-Maġrib al-qadīm- al-našʾa wa al-Taṭawwur 180-430 li-l-mīlād*, thèse de doctorat, Université de Constantine, 2011.

ʿAmrān, ʿAbd al-Ḥamīd. *al-Ḥaraka al-dunātiyya bayna al-inšiqāq al-dīnī wa al-taḥarrur 305-411 li-l-mīlād*, mémoire de magister, Université de Constantine, 2005.

ʿAmrānī, Salma. *Tawṯīq baʿḍ al-maḥaṭṭāt al-aṯariyya li-l-Qabāʾil al-Kubrā mā qabla al-tārīḫ wa faǧr al-tārīḫ bi-istiḫdām taṭbīqat niẓām al-maʿlūma al-ǧuġrāfiyya*, mémoire de magister, Université d'Alger, 2011.

ʿAmranī, Samīra. *Dirāsa arkiyū-baliyūlūǧiyya li-Asāṭ al-hulusān bi-minṭiqat Tīn-Hunāktan al-Tasīlī-Naǧar, al-Ṣaḥrāʾ al-wusṭā*, mémoire de magister, Université d'Alger, 2002.

'Amrūnī, Tūfīq. *Dirāsat al-'umla al-mūrīṭaniyya fī 'ahdi Yūba al-ṯānī wa Baṭlīmūs 25 q m-40 m : muqāraba ǧadīda min ḫilal al-kūnūz al-muktašafa wa al-maǧmū'a al-naqdiyya al-matḥafiyyaa wa-l-ḥaṣṣa al-iqtiṣād al-naqdī wa al-tadāwul,* thèse de doctorat, Université d'Alger, 2015.

'Amrūnī, Tūfīq. *Dirāsa al-ḥaraka al-naqdiyya fī Šamāl Ifrīqiyyā 49 q.m-69m min al-niṣf al-awwal li-l-qarn qabla al-mīlad ilā al-niṣf al-ṯānī li-l-qarn 1 m.,* mémoire de magister, Université d'Alger, 2008.

'Amrūs, Farīda. *al-Aḍriḥa al-ǧanā'iziyya al-rūmāniyya bi-l-Ǧazā'ir : Dirāsa mi'māriyya wa fanniyya,* thèse de doctorat, Université d'Alger, 2010.

'Amrūs, Farīda. *al-Mabānī wa al-ṭūqūs wa al-ša'ā'ir al-ǧanā'iziyya li-l-fatra al-Lūbiyya al-Būniyya,* mémoire de magister, Université d'Alger, 2000.

'Aqqūn, Muḥammad al-'Arbī. *al-Ittiḥād al-sīrtī munḏu istīlā' Sītyūs 'alā Sīrtā 46 qabla al-mīlād ilā aḥdāṯ al-qarn al-rābi' : dirāsa fī-l-tārīḫ wa-āṯār nuẓum Sīrtā al-'atīqa,* thèse de doctorat d'État, Université de Constantine, 2005.

'Aqqūn, Muḥammad al-'Arbī. *Ḥamlat Yūlyūs Qayṣar 'alā Ifrīqiyya 47-46 qabla al-mīlād,* mémoire de magister, Université de Constantine, 1996.

'Arbāwī, al-Sādaq. *Madīnat Mūbt Mopht : dirāsa aṯariyya wa mi'māriyya,* mémoire de magister, Université d'Alger, 2015.

'Arīfī, Ilyās. *Fusayfisā' Tibassa, Sūq Ahrās wa Gālma,* thèse de doctorat, Université d'Alger, 2019.

'Arīfī, Ilyās. *Maǧmu'at fusayfisā' minṭaqat Tibassa : dirāsa aṯariyya wa ǧard,* mémoire de magister, Université d'Alger, 2009.

'Ašīṭ Hānī, Ḥayra. *Dirāsat al-asmā' wa al-diyāna bi-madīnat Madūr : dirāsat al-muǧtama' al-Mādūrī,* mémoire de magister, Université d'Alger, 2012.

'Aṭiyya, Sa'd Ǧīhad. *Fann al-naḥt wa al-naqš al-āšūrī min 1595-612 q.m.,* thèse de doctorat, Université d'Alger, 2015.

'Aṭiyya, Sa'd Ǧīhad. *al-Qiyam al-ǧamāliyya fī 'imārat al-Rafidayn – al-sūmariyya al-akadiyya al-babiliyya al-ašūriyya,* mémoire de magister, Université d'Alger, 2009.

'Awīmar, Sāmiyya. *Dirāsa mūrfūlūǧiyya wa tiknūlūǧiyya li-maǧmū'āt ṣinā'iyya ḥaǧariyya 'ātiriyya li-mawqi' šu'bat lihūdī bi-al-Sāḥil al-ǧarbī al-ǧazā'irī,* mémoire de magister, Université d'Alger, 2009.

'Awn, Nādiya. *al-Zirā'a al-šaǧariyya fī bilād al-Maǧrib aṯnā' al-iḥtilāl al-rūmanī 146 q.m ilā 430 m. al-zaytūn wa al-kurūm,* mémoire de magister, Université d'Alger, 2012.

'Aybaš, Yūsuf. *al-Awḍā' al-iǧtimā'iyya wa al-iqtiṣādiyya fī bilad al-Maǧrib aṯnā' al-iḥtilāl al-bizanṭī,* thèse de doctorat, Université de Constantine, 2007.

'Aybaš, Yūsuf. *al-Mūr wa al-bizanṭiyīn ḫilāl al-qarn 6 mīlādī,* mémoire de magister, Université de Constantine, 1996.

'Aynūš, Ḥasīna. *al-Naḥt al-timṯālī al-mīṯūlūǧī bi-l-Ǧazā'ir ḫilāl al-fatra al-rūmāniyya, al-numīdiyya,* thèse de doctorat, Université d'Alger, 2017.

ʿAynūš, Ḥasīna. *Dirāsat tamāṯīl matḥaf Gālma : ǧard wa taḥlīl*, mémoire de magister, Université d'Alger, 2009.

ʿAysawī, Mahā. *al-Muǧtamaʿ fī bilād al-Maġrib al-qadīm min ʿuṣūr mā qabla al-tārīḫ ilā ʿašiyyat al-fatḥ al-islāmī*, thèse de doctorat, Université de Constantine, 2010.

ʿAysawī, Mahā. *al-Nuqūš al-lūbiyya fī Šamāl Ifrīqiyya : dirāsa tārīḫiyya – luġawiyya*, mémoire de magister, Université de Constantine, 2002.

ʿAyyatī, Ḥūḫa. *al-Taʿdīn al-qadīm fī šamal al-Ġazāʾir : dirāsa al-adawāt al-maʿdaniyya al-maḥfūẓa fī matḥaf Sīrta wa Bārdū*, mémoire de magister, Université d'Alger, 2002.

ʿAyyatī, Ḥūḫa. *Ṭuruq taʿdīn al-nuḥās wa sabkihi min ḫilāl dirāsat ʿayyināt matḥafay Bārdū al-Ġazāʾir al-ʿāṣima wa Sīrta*, thèse de doctorat, Université d'Alger, 2016.

ʿAzzūz, Fāṭima al-Zahrāʾ. *al-Rawābiṭ al-fikriyya al-fīnīqiyya al-ʿibrāniyya al-muʿtaqadāt al-dīniyya – al-ādāb – al-funnūn min al-qarn al-ʿāšir qabla al-mīlād ilā al-qarn al-awwal li-l-mīlād*, mémoire de magister, Université d'Alger, 2006.

ʿAzzūz, Fāṭima al-Zahrāʾ. *Taʾṯīr al-muʿtaqadāt al-fīnīqiyya fī-l-diyānat al-ʿibrāniyya min ḫilāl muktašafāt Raʾs Šamrā wa nuṣūṣ al-ʿahd al-qadīm : dirāsa muqārina q 10-06 q-m.*, thèse de doctorat, Université d'Alger, 2011.

ʿAzzūz, Ḥakīma. *Muqāṭaʿat Mūrīṭāniyā ʿabra al-tārīḫ al-ṭabāʾiʿī li-Balīnyūs, dirāsa mūr-fūlūǧiyya, ṭabīʿiyya, wa-ʿumrāniyya*, mémoire de magister, Université d'Alger, 2016.

Abarkān, Karīm. *al-Taʿmīr al-bašarī ḫilāl al-hūlūsīn fī-l-Aṭlas al-ṣaḥrāwī al-šarqī : al-iṭār al-ṭabīʿī wa tiknūlūǧiyyat al-ṣināʿāt al-ḥaǧariyya li-mawqiʿ Maġārat ʿAmūra, al-Ǧalfa*, thèse de doctorat, Université d'Alger, 2016.

Abarkān, Karīm. *Tiknūlūǧiyya al-ṣināʿāt al-ḥaǧariyya al-aṯariyya li-mahaṭṭat ʿAyn Mahāram bi-l-Qāla, wilāyat al-Ṭāraf šarq al-Ġazāʾir*, mémoire de magister, Université d'Alger, 2007.

Abarkān, Nādiya. *Īrān fī ʿahd al-malik Qubāḏ al-awwal wa al-azma al-mazdakiyya min 488 ilā 531 mīlādī*, mémoire de magister, Université d'Alger, 2012.

Aggūnī, Yāsmīn. *al-Maṣābīḥ al-zaytiyya al-maḥfūẓa fī-l-Matḥaf al-waṭanī li-l-āṯār al-qadīma : dirāsa waṣfiyya tanmīṭiyya wa taḥlīliyya*, mémoire de magister, Université d'Alger, 2010.

Aggūnī, Yāsmīn. *al-Maʿālim al-aṯariyya li-l-ǧihat al-šamāliyya al-šarqiyya li-Mūrīṭāniyyā al-qayṣariyya*, thèse de doctorat, Université d'Alger, 2019.

Ait Amara O. *Recherche sur les Numides et les maures face à la guerre depuis les guerres puniques jusqu'à l'époque de Juba 1er*, Université Jean Moulin Lyon 3, 2007.

Ait Sbaa, N. *Les gravures du djebel Serkout : contribution a la préhistoire de l'Ahaggar*, Paris 1, 2001.

Aklī, Kaltūm. *Dirāsat ikunūġrāfiyya li-l-muʾašširāt al-dīniyya min ḫilāl al-ʿumlat al-nūmīdiyya wa al-mūrīṭāniyya min al-qarn al-ṯāliṯ qabla al-mīlād ilā al-niṣf al-awwal baʿda al-mīlād*, thèse de doctorat, Université d'Alger, 2018.

Aklī, Nūriyya. *al-Awānī al-zuǧāǧiyya al-musawwāt ʿalā qāʿida fī šamāl Ifrīqiyya*, mémoire de magister, Université d'Alger, 2001.

Aklī, Nūriyya. *al-Ḥiraf wa al-ḥirafiyyūn fī Nūmīdiyā qabla al-ʿahd al-rūmānī*, thèse de doctorat, Université d'Alger, 2010.

Aksīl, Laḥlū. *al-Tarkība al-iǧtimāʿiyya li-l-Maġrib al-qadīm : 146q.m 40m.*, mémoire de magister, Université d'Alger, 2016.

Al-Baʿsī, Fayṣal Ḥusayn Nāṣir. *Munšaʾāt al-rayy al-qadīma fī manṭiqat awdiyyat Kūr al-ʿAwāliq fī-l-Yaman-muḥāfaẓat Šabwa*, thèse de doctorat, Université d'Alger, 2014.

Al-Baʿsī, Fayṣal Ḥusayn Nāṣir. *Mustawṭanāt awdiyyat Kūr al-ʿAwāliq, al-ǧumhūriyya al-yamaniyya muḥāfaẓat Šabwa : dirāsa tārīḫiyya aṯariyya*, mémoire de magister, Université d'Alger, 2009.

Al-Ǧilālī, ʿAbd al-Raḥmān. *Tārīḫ al-Ǧazāir al-ʿāmm*, 1954, rééd. Beyrouth, Dār al-Ṯaqāfa, 1983.

Al-Ḥāǧǧ al-Ṭāhar, Zakiyya. *al-ʿAhd al-qadīm wa madā ʿalāqat maḍmūnihi bi-l-dawla al-āšūriyya wa al-kaldaniyya wa mamlakat yahūda*, mémoire de magister, Université d'Alger, 2004.

Al-Hāšmī, Mūḥammad al-Ṭāhar. *Dirāsa ǧuġrāfiyya wa tanmīṭiyya li-l-maʿālim al-ǧanāʾiziyya li-fatrat faǧr al-tārīḫ li-mawāqiʿ ʿAyn al-Wakārīf wa Kāf al-Dašra wa mawqiʿ Adsām bi-al-Šāraf*, mémoire de magister, Université d'Alger, 2010.

Al-Madanī, Aḥmad Tawfīq. *Tārīḫ al-Ǧazāir*, Ghardaïa, al-Maṭbaʿa al-ʿarabiyya, 1931.

Al-Mīllī, Mubārak. *Tārīḫ al-Ǧazāir fī-l-qadīm wa-l-ḥadīth*, al-Maṭbaʿa al-islāmiyya al-Ǧazāiriyya, 1928-1932, 2 vol.

Al-Muḫtār, al-Kīlānī Aʿmār ʿAbd al-Qādir. *Murtakazāt al-fikr al-dīnī wa burūz ẓāhirat al-qarābīn fī Šibh al-Ǧazīra al-ʿArabiyya wa-al-Šām wa-bilād al-Rāfidayn : dirāsa tārīḫiyya taḥlīliyya muqārana*, thèse de doctorat, Université d'Alger, 2014.

Al-Ṭayyib, Zīn al-ʿĀbidīn. *Abʿād al-fikr al-waḥdawī wa taʾṯīrātuh fī wāqiʿ al-ḥayāt al-siyāsiyya wa al-iqtiṣādiyya wa al-iǧtimāʿiyya fī bilād al-Rāfidayn 2500-539 qabla al-mīlād*, thèse de doctorat, Université d'Alger, 2019.

Al-Ṭayyib, Zīn al-ʿĀbidīn. *Bilād al-Rāfidayn min al-inqisām ilā al-waḥda : al-ʿaṣr al-bābilī al-qadīm anmūḏaǧan 2004-1595 qabla al-mīlād*, mémoire de magister, Université d'Alger, 2015.

Al-Zuʿbī, al-Zahrāʾ. *Tiǧārat Miṣr al-firʿawniyya min āḫir al-alf al-rābiʿa ilā al-alf al-ūlā qabla al-mīlād*, mémoire de magister, Université d'Alger, 2008.

Al-ʿAqqūn, Umm al-Ḫayr. *al-ʿAlāqāt al-ḥaḍāriyya wa al-siyāsiyya bayna Miṣr wa šamāl ǧarb Ifrīqiya mundu aqdam al-ʿuṣūr ḥattā nihāyat al-alf al-ṯāniya qabla al-mīlād*, mémoire de magister, Université d'Alexandrie, 1988.

Al-ʿAqqūn, Umm al-Ḫayr. *Al-Lībiyyūn wa taʾsīsuhum li-l-dawla fī Miṣr al-firʿawniyya*, thèse de doctorat d'État, Université Oran, 1996.

Al-ʿAmrī, ʿAbd al-Nūr. *Siyāsat Rūmā al-iqtiṣādiyya fī Miṣr mā bayna al-qarn al-awwal qabla al-mīlād wa bidāyat al-qarn al-rābiʿ mīlādi 27 qabla al-mīlād -306 mīlādī wa al-natāʾiǧ al-mutarattiba ʿanhā*, mémoire de magister, Université d'Alger, 2010.

Al-ʿAydānī, Samīr. *al-Ḥayāt al-dīniyya fī šamāl šibh al-Ǧazīra al-ʿarabiyya 1200q.m-600m.* mémoire de magister, Université d'Alger, 2011.

Al-ʿAydānī, Samīr. *al-ʿAlāqāt al-ḥaḍāriyya bayna Miṣr wa šuʿūb bilād al-Rafidayn "al-ʿalāqāt al-dīniyya anmūḏaǧan" : min bidāyat ʿaṣr al-dawla al-ḥadīṯa ḥattā al-tawāǧud al-yūnānī fī Miṣr 1580q.m-332 q.m.*, thèse de doctorat, Université d'Alger, 2017.

Al-ʿĪhār, Muḥammad. *Irhāṣāt al-tašrīʿ fī al-ʿIrāq al-qadīm al-asbāb al-natāʾiǧ wa al-inʿikāsāt*, mémoire de magister, Université d'Oran, 2014.

Al-ʿŪd, Muḥammad al-Ṣālaḥ. *al-Taġayyurāt al-iqtiṣādiyya wa al-iǧtimāʿiyya wa al-dīniyya fī bilād al-Maġrib ḥilāl al-fatratayn al-wandāliyya wa al-bīzanṭiyya : dirāsa muqārina*, thèse de doctorat, Université d'Alger, 2018.

Al-ʿŪd, Muḥammad al-Ṣālaḥ. *al-Taḥawwulāt al-ḥaḍāriyya fī šamāl Ifrīqiya fī al-fatra al-wandāliyya 429-534 li-l-mīlād*, mémoire de magister, Université de Constantine, 2010.

Albertini, E. *L'Afrique romaine*, Alger, 1922.

Amara, A. *Contribution à l'étude des formations quaternaires et de la Préhistoire dans le Hodna oriental Algérie du Nord-Est*, thèse de 3e cycle, Université de Bordeaux 1, 1981.

Amara, I. *L'art rupestre dans le sud-ouest de l'Atlas saharien Algérie : étude analytique et typologique des figurations de la période récente*, thèse de doctorat, Panthéon Sorbonne Paris-1, 2001.

Amuqrān, Ṣālaḥ. *Dirāsat āṯār fatrat mā qabla al-tārīḫ li-haḍabat Ambrūm -Tasīlī Nāhagār, al-Ṣaḥrāʾ al-wusṭā al-Ǧazāʾir*, mémoire de magister, Université d'Alger, 2012.

Amzyān, Yāsmīna. *Dirāsat iqtiṣād al-imbrāṭūriyya al-rūmāniyya min ḥilāl dirāsat muqārana li-kanzayni naqdiyyayni li-Mūrīṭāniyyā al-Qayṣariyya : ḥālat Šaršāl wa Tigzīrt*, thèse de doctorat, Université d'Alger, 2010.

Ašlaf, Faṭṭūma. *al-Iqtiṣād al-fīnīqī fī-l-baḥr al-mutawaṣṣaṭ : 1200q.m.-332q.m.*, thèse de doctorat, Université d'Alger, 2018.

Ašlaf, Faṭṭūma. *al-Ṣināʿa al-ḥirafiyya al-fīnīqiyya 1200q.m-322 q.m.*, mémoire de magister, Université d'Alger, 2009.

Aumassip, G. *Algérie des premiers hommes*. Éditions de la Maison des Sciences de l'Homme, Éditions Ibis-Presse, 2001.

Āyt Aʿmāra, Wīza. *Dawr al-safīna fī-l-tiǧara wa al-tawassuʿ al-istiṭānī fī al-baḥr al-mutawassiṭ al-qadīm*, mémoire de magister, Université d'Alger, 1996.

Āyt Ǧamaʿ, ʿAbd al-Raḥmān. *Mawādd wa tiqaniyyāt al-bināʾ al-rūmāniyya bi-mawqiʿ Tāmūgādī al-aṯarī : dirāsa tiqaniyya wa aṯariyya*, mémoire de magister, Université d'Alger, 2016.

Āyt Sī Aʿmur, Ǧaʿfar. *al-Mamarrāt al-muġaṭṭāt li-mawqiʿay Āṯ Rahūnat wa Ibārīsn bi-manṭiqat al-Qabāʾil : dirāsa aṯariyya wa miʿmāriyya*, mémoire de magister, Université d'Alger, 2012.

Āyt ʿAbd al-Qawwī, Ṣūniyya. *al-Rayy fī madīnat Tīmgād : tamwīn tawzīʿ wa-taṣrīf al-miyāh*, mémoire de magister, Université d'Alger, 2006.

Āyt ʿAllāq, Šafīqa. *Šabakat al-ṭuruqāt al-rūmāniyya fī-l-ǧihat al-šarqiyya li-Mūrīṭāniyyā al-Qayṣariyya*, mémoire de magister, Université d'Alger, 2012.

Azbūǧan Mūlda Ūtšarnān, Fatīḥa. *Dirāsa namaṭ istiǧlāl al-māda al-awwaliyya fī mawqiʿ Ādǧī bi-Tīmīmūn wilāyat Adrār, al-ǧanūb al-ǧarbī al-ǧazāʾirī*, mémoire de magister, Université d'Alger, 2009.

Aʿīšūšan, Wāʿmar. *al-ʿAlāqa bayna al-rīf wa-l-madīna fī iqlīmay al-Awrās wa al-Qabāʾil fī al-fatra al-rūmāniyya*, thèse de doctorat, Université d'Alger, 2016.

Aʿīšūšan, Wāʿmar. *Dirāsa maydāniyya wa naẓariyya li-āṯār al-fatrat al-qadīma al-mawǧūda fī ǧibāl al-Awrās*, mémoire de magister, Université d'Alger, 2005.

Aʿrab, ʿAzzūz. *al-Taḥṣīnāt al-rūmāniyya ǧanūb Nūmīdiya wa Mūrīṭaniyya al-qayṣariyya q 1-3 m wā aṯāruhā*, mémoire de magister, Université d'Alger, 2010.

Bʾšārī, Muḥammad al-Ḥabīb. *Dirāsa Tārīḫiyya li-Muqāṭaʿat Mūrīṭāniyyā al-Saṭāyfiyya*, mémoire de magister, Université d'Alger, 2000.

Bʾšārī, Muḥammad al-Ḥabīb. *Dawr al-muqāṭaʿāt al-ifrīqiyya fī iqtiṣād Rūmā bayna 146 qabla al-mīlād wa 285 li-l-mīlād*, thèse de doctorat d'État, Université d'Alger, 2007.

Bagdādī, Yammūna. *Dirāsa ḥawla Mūrīṭaniyya qabla al-iḥtilāl al-rūmānī*, mémoire de magister, Université d'Alger, 1994.

Baggār, Usāma. *Muʿaskar al-firqa al-uǧusṭisiyya al-ṯālita fī Lumbāz 81-238*, mémoire de magister, Université d'Alger, 2014.

Baghli, S.-A., Bouchenaki, M. « Recherches et travaux en 1975-1976 », *Bulletin d'Archéologie Algérienne*, vol. VI, 1975-1976, 7-14.

Baghli, S.-A., Bouchenaki, M., Février, P.-A. « Recherches et travaux, 1962-1965 », *Bulletin d'Archéologie Algérienne*, vol. I, 1962-1965 3-6 ; « Recherches et travaux 1966-1967 », *Bulletin d'Archéologie Algérienne*, vol. II, 1966-1967, 1-10 ; « Recherches et travaux 1967 », *Bulletin d'Archéologie Algérienne*, vol. III, 1968, 1-34 ; « Recherches et travaux, 1968-1969 », *Bulletin d'Archéologie Algérienne*, vol. IV, 1970, 9-40 ; « Recherches et travaux, 1970-1971 », *Bulletin d'Archéologie Algérienne*, vol. V, 1971-1974, 9-24.

Baghli, S.-A., Bouchenaki, M., Février, P.-A. « Bilan des activités archéologiques dans la wilaya de Constantine », *Recueil de la société archéologique de Constantine*, vol. 71, 1969-1971, 13-17.

Baḥḥūš, Zuhīr. *al-tarkība al-bašariyya li-muǧtamaʿ al-rīf al-Awrāsī aṯnāʾ al-iḥtilāl al-rūmānī : dirāsa taḥlīliyya wa-muqāranatiyya maʿa asmāʾ afrād muǧtamaʿāt al-marākiz al-ḥaḍariyya al-rūmāniyya bi-l-Awrās*, thèse de doctorat, Université d'Alger, 2018.

Baḥḥūš, Zuhīr. *Dirāsa taḥlīliyya li-asmāʾ afrād muǧtamʿa mustaʿmarat Tāmūgādī ḫilāl al-fatra al-mumtada mā bayna al-qarnayn al-ṯānī wal-rābiʿ mīlādiyayn*, mémoire de magister, Université d'Alger, 2007.

Bāḥmad, Saʿīd. *al-Anūna fī al-Maġrib al-rūmanī, al-ḍarāʾib al-ʿayniyya li-intāǧ al-qamḥ wa zayt al-zaytūn*, mémoire de magister, Université d'Alger, 2009.

Bāḥmad, Saʿīd. *al-Anūna fī al-Mašriq al-qadīm aṯnāʾ al-iḥtilāl al-rūmānī 31 q.m.-395m.*, thèse de doctorat, Université d'Alger, 2019.

Bāḥmān, Ḥasība. *Sukkān bilād al-Maġrib al-qadīm fī al-ʿahd al-qarṭāǧī 814 qabla al-mīlād-146 qabla al-mīlād*, mémoire de magister, Université d'Adrar, 2015.

Baḥra, Nādiya. *Muḥāwalat dirāsa taḥlīliyya li-l-fann al-ṣaḥrī bi-manṭiqat Ādmr al-Tāsīlī Āzǧar- al-Ṣaḥrāʾ al-Wusṭā – al-Ǧazāʾir*, mémoire de magister, Université d'Alger, 2006.

Bakdā, Ramḍān. *Dirāsat al-baqāyā al-ʿaẓmiyya li-Mawqiʿ al-Razīqat al-Niyūlītī : al-Rāḥil Ḥāsī al-Ġalat bi-ʿAyn Tīmūšant al-maḥfūẓa bi-l-matḥaf al-waṭanī Aḥmad Zābāna bi-Wahrān*, mémoire de magister, Université d'Alger, 2012.

Balǧūdī, Ǧūdī. *al-Manāǧim al-qadīma fī al-Ǧazāʾir*, mémoire de magister, Université d'Alger, 2000.

Ballaḥraš, Ḥusīn. *Dirāsa taḥlīliyya li-l-nuqūš al-ṣaḥriyya li-manṭiqat al-Bayyiḍ*, mémoire de magister, Université d'Alger, 2010.

Ballaḥraš, Ḥusīn. *Taṭbīq niẓām al-maʿlūmāt al-ǧuġrāfiyya ʿalā mawāqiʿ al-fann al-ṣaḥrī li-l-Aṭlas al-ṣaḥrāwī- manṭiqatay al-Bayyiḍ wa al-Ǧalfa namūḏaǧan*, thèse de doctorat, Université d'Alger, 2019.

Balʿābad, Zīnab. *al-Malāmiḥ al-ǧanāʾiziyya wa al-naḏriyya li-l-būniyyīn wa-l-nūmīdiyyīn fī al-mamlaka al-Nūmīdiyya : dirāsa taḥlīliyya min ḫilāl al-maʿālim al-aṯariyya*, thèse de doctorat, Université de Constantine, 2016.

Balʿābad, Zīnab. *al-Muqaddas wa-l-ramz min ḫilāl nuṣub maʿbad al-Ḥufra bi-Qusanṭīna al-qarnayn al-ṯāliṯ wa-l-ṯānī q.m.*, mémoire de magister, Université de Constantine, 2005.

Balʿarbī, Wīza. *Maʾāṣir Mādūr : dirāsa aṯariyya taḥlīliyya*, mémoire de magister, Université d'Alger, 2006.

Balʿīd, Ḥasān. *Ḥanabaʿl wa al-ḥarb al-būniyya al-ṯāniyya 218-202 qabla al-mīlād*, mémoire de magister, Université d'Alger, 2014.

Bāmbārk, Rūqiyya. *al-Lūġa al-lūbiyya al-qadīma min ḫilāl al-maṣādir al-mādiyya wa-l-kitābiyya*, mémoire de magister, Université d'Adrar, 2016.

Ban ʿAbd al-Muʾmin, Muḥammad. *Purtus Magnus Baṭṭīwa, dirāsa mūnūǧrāfiyya*, mémoire de magister, Université d'Oran, 2006.

Ban ʿAbd al-Muʾmin, Muḥammad. *ʿAqāʾid al-mawt ʿinda sukkān al-Maġrib al-qadīm*, thèse de doctorat, Université d'Oran, 2012.

Ban ʿAllāl, Naṣīra. *Tawābīt Nūmīdiyā wa-Mūrīṭānyā al-Qayṣariyya : Dirāsa ikūnūǧrāfiyya wa-taḥlīliyya*, mémoire de magister, Université d'Alger, 2009.

Ban ʿAllāl, Riḍā. *Al-alʿāb fī al-Maġrib al-qadīm aṯnāʾ āl-iḥtilāl al-rūmānī*, thèse de doctorat, Université d'Alger, 2012.

Ban ʿAllāl, Riḍā. *al-ʿArabāt fī al-ḥawḍ al-ġarbī li-l-baḥr al-abyaḍ al-mūtawassaṭ fī al-ʿuṣūr al-qadīma*, mémoire de magister, Université d'Alger, 2001.

Ban ʿAṭī Allāh, ʿAbd al-Raḥmān. *Dawr madīnat al-Iskandariyya fī taṭwīr al-ādāb wa al-ʿulūm munḏu taʾsīsihā ḥattā al-niṣf al-ṯānī min al-qarn al-awwal qabla al-mīlād (331 qabla al-mīlād /30 qabla al-mīlād)*, mémoire de magister, Université d'Alger, 2010.

Ban ʿAyya, Ḥadīǧa. *al-Anṣāb al-naḏrīya al-muhdāt li-l-ilāh Satūrn bi madīnat Lambīz*, mémoire de magister, Université d'Alger, 2012.

Ban al-Saʿdī, Slīman. *Šuʿūb al-baḥr wa ʿalāqatuhum bi-Miṣr 1300-1150 q.m : dirāsa tārīḫiyya*, mémoire de magister, Université d'Alexandrie, 1992.

Ban al-Saʿdī, Slīman. *ʿalāqat Miṣr bi-l-Maġrib al-qadīm munḏu faǧr al-tārīḫ ḥattā al-qarn 7q m.*, thèse de doctorat d'État, Université de Constantine, 2009.

Ban Būzīd, Laḥḍar. *al-Aṯar al-dīnī fī mašāhid al-rusūm al-ṣaḥriyya li-minṭaqat al-Ṭāsīlī-Nāǧar ḫilal marḥalat al-ruʾūs al-mustadīra : 8000 q m-2500 q m.*, mémoire de magister, Université d'Alger, 2010.

Ban Būzīd, Laḥḍar. *Ḥaḍārat al-ruʿāt fī al-niyūlītī bi-l-Ṭāsīlī-Nāǧar wa al-Hūgar min ḫilāl al-fann al-ṣaḥrī : 6000 q.m. 1000 q.m.*, thèse de doctorat, Université d'Alger, 2016.

Ban Drīs, ʿAmr. *al-Ṣirāʿ al-qarṭāǧī al-iġrīqī fī ġarb al-mūtawassiṭ : mā bayna al-qarnayn al-sādis wa al-rābiʿ q.m.*, DEA, Université d'Alger, 1982.

Ban Ḥafṣī, Ġaniyya. *Makānat al-marʾa wa dawruhā fī al-muǧtamaʿ al-firʿawnī 3200 q.m-1080 q.m.*, mémoire de magister, Université d'Alger, 2011.

Ban Laḥraš, ʿAbd al-ʿAzīz. *Bašariyyāt mā qabla al-insān*, thèse de doctorat d'État, Université de Constantine, 2003.

Ban Laḥraš, ʿAbd al-ʿAzīz. *Niẓām al-ḥukm fī ǧanūb bilād al-Rāfidayn al-qadīm min 3500 qabla al-mīlād ilā 2350 mīlādī*, mémoire de magister, Université de Constantine, 1987.

Ban Mahdī, Āmāl. *al-Ḫarīṭa al-aṯariyya li-manṭiqat ʿAyn Tamūšant*, mémoire de magister, Université d'Alger, 2016.

Ban Maqallātī, ʿĪsā. *Mamlakat Murīṭāniyyā bayna al-tabaʿiyya li-Rūma wa al-istiqlāliyya : min 25 qabla al-mīlād ilā 40 li-l-mīlād*, mémoire de magister, Université d'Alger, 2015.

Ban Masʿūd, Nāṣar. *al-ʿImāra al-ʿumūmiyya bi al-muqāṭaʿa al-nūmīdiyya al-rūmāniyya dirāsa aṯariyya taḥlīliyya li-ʿimārat al-munšaʾāt al-ʿumūmiyya bi-mudun al-muqāṭaʿa al-nūmīdiyya al-rūmāniyya*, thèse de doctorat, Université d'Alger, 2018.

Ban Masʿūd, Nāṣar. *Aswāq muqāṭaʿat Nūmīdiyā : dirāsa miʿmāriyya muqārina li-aswāq Tīmgād wa Kwīkūl Ǧamīla*, mémoire de magister, Université d'Alger, 1992.

Ban Muwaffaq, Būmadyan. *al-Dawr al-ḥaḍārī al-miṣrī fī al-šarq al-ifrīqī : bilād al-Nūba namūḏaǧan*, thèse de doctorat, Université d'Alger, 2014.

Ban Muwaffaq, Būmadyan. *al-Hiǧra al-yamaniyya naḥwa al-šarq al-ifrīqī wa-āṯāruhā al-ḥaḍāriyya : al-Ṣūmāl wa al-Ḥabaša wa-Miṣr namūḏaǧan*, mémoire de magister, Université d'Alger, 2009.

Ban Ṣaddūq, Saʿīda. *Dirāsat faḫḫār li-mustawayāt muḫtalifa li-mawqiʿ al-niyyūlūtī Tīn Hna Katān "Ṭāsīlī Nāǧar" al-Ṣaḥrāʾ al-wusṭā*, mémoire de magister, Université d'Alger, 2011.

Ban Šarnīn, Riḍā. *al-Mawqiʿ al-Ašūlī li-l-Rābiḥ Mustaǧānim-al-Maġrib al-Ǧazāʾir : dirāsa iqtināʾ al-mādda al-awwaliyya wa tiknūlūǧiyyat al-ṣināʿa al-ḥaǧariyya*, mémoire de magister, Université d'Alger, 2012.

Ban Zītūn, Ḥūriyya. *al-Aṭlas aṯarī li-wilāyat al-Bawīra*, mémoire de magister, Université d'Alger, 2009.

Bannūr, Asmāʾ. *Ǧard wa-dirāsat adawāt al-ṭibb al-rūmāniyya min ḫilāl maǧmūʿatay matḥaf mawqiʿ Ǧamīla wa-al-Matḥaf al-waṭanī li-al-āṯār al-qadīma : dirāsa taḥlīliyya*, mémoire de magister, Université d'Alger, 2012.

Baqa, Balḫīr. *Āṯār diyānat wādī al-Rāfidayn ʿalā al-ḥayāt al-fikriyya, Sūmar wa-Bābil 3200-539 qabla al-mīlād*, mémoire de magister, Université d'Alger, 2009.

Baqa, Balḫīr. *Āṯār diyānat wādī al-Rāfidayn ʿalā al-ʿAhd al-Qadīm*, thèse de doctorat, Université d'Alger, 2017.

Barāknī, Widād. *Dirāsa tiqaniyya wa fanniyya li-maǧmūʿāt al-ṣuwar al-naḥtiyya li-l-ʿāʾila al-malakiyya li-Yūbā al-ṯānī wa al-maḥfūẓa bi-matḥaf madīnat Šaršāl*, mémoire de magister, Université d'Alger, 2016.

Barkān, Hāǧar. *Mamlakat al-Ġassāsina wa dawruhā al-ḥaḍārī fī šamāl šibh al-Ǧazīra al-ʿarabiyya*, mémoire de magister, Université d'Alger, 2012.

Baṣal, Māliya. *al-Mustawṭana al-yamaniyya wa dawruhā al-ḥaḍārī fī wasaṭ wa šamal al-ǧazīra al-ʿarabiyya munḏu ẓuhūr al-duwal al-yamaniyya al-qadīma ilā ġāyat maǧīʾ al-Islām*, mémoire de magister, Université d'Alger, 2011.

Baṣal, Māliya. *al-ʿAlaqāt al-ḥaḍāriyya bayna al-Yaman wa manṭiqat al-Hilāl al-Ḫaṣīb*, thèse de doctorat, Université d'Alger, 2017.

Bašī, Ibrāhīm al-ʿĪd. *al-Būnya al-ǧuġrāfiyya wa al-ḥaḍāriyya fī al-ǧanūb al-šarqī al-ǧazāʾirī Tāsīlī – Nāǧar namūḏaǧan, dirāsa waṣfiyya li-l-minṭaqa fī al-marḥala al-qadīma*, thèse de doctorat d'État, Université d'Alger, 2005.

Bašī, Ibrāhīm al-ʿĪd. *al-Tawassuʿ al-ʿaskarī al-maqdūnī min ḫilāl ḥamlāt al-Iskandar al-Akbar 336-323 qabla al-mīlād*, mémoire de magister, Université d'Alger, 1992.

Baʿīš, Ṣabrīna. *Katālūǧ maǧmūʿāt naqdiyya maḥfūẓa bi-matḥaf Sīrtā al-waṭanī : dirāsa tārīḫiyya wa-naqdiyya*, mémoire de magister, Université d'Alger, 2011.

Benseddik, N., Leveau, Ph., Romane, F. *Les nouvelles inscriptions de Cherchel 1971-1974, Bulletin d'Archéologie Algérienne*, vol. V, 1976, 195-206.

Benseddik, N., Leveau, Ph., Romane, F. *Nouvelles inscriptions de Sétif*, BAA, T. VII, 1, 1977-1979, 33-52.

Benseddik, N. *Les troupes auxiliaires de l'armée romaine en Maurétanie Césarienne sous le Haut-Empire*, SNED, Alger, 1982.

Benseddik, N. *Fouilles du forum de Cherchel 1977-1981*, Alger, ANAPMSH, 1993.

Benseddik, N. *Le culte d'Esculape en Afrique*, Paris 4, 1995.

Benseddik, N. *Thagaste Souk-Ahras patrie de saint Augustin*, Alger, INAS, 2005.

Benseddik, N. « L'archéologie antique en Algérie hier et aujourd'hui », dans N. Benghabrit et M. Heddab Dir., *L'Algérie 50 ans après. Etat des savoirs en sciences sociales et humaines 1954-2004*, Oran, CRASC, 2008, 193-203.

Benseddik, N. *Esculape et Hygie en Afrique. Recherches sur les cultes guérisseurs*, Mémoires de l'AIBL, vol. 44., I et II, Paris, 2010.

Benseddik, N. *Cirta-Constantina et son territoire*, Errance-Actes Sud Arles, 2012.

Berthier, A. *Tiddis. Cité antique de Numidie*, Institut de France, Mémoires de l'Académie des Inscriptions et Belles-Lettres, vol. 20, Paris, Diffusion de Boccard, 2000.

Berthier, A. *Tiddis antique castellimi Tidditanorum*, Alger, 1972.

Bḥāyar, Fayza. *Āšūr fī ẓill al-taġayyurāt al-ǧiyyūsiyāsiyya li-l-minṭaqa fīmā bayna al-qarnayn 12-07 qabla al-mīlad*, mémoire de magister, Université d'Oran, 2015.

Bouchenaki, M. *Cités Antiques d'Algérie*, Alger, Ministère de la Culture, 1975.

Bouchenaki, M. *Fouilles de la nécropole occidentale de Tipasa*, Alger, Bibliothèque Nationale, 1975.

Bouchenaki, M. *Fouilles de la nécropole occidentale de Tipasa Matarès 1968-1972*, Alger, 1975.

Bouchenaki, M., L. Anselmino, A. Carandini. *Il castellum del Nador. Storia di una fattoria tra Tipasa e Caesarea 1-VI sec. d. C.*, Roma, Monografie di archeologia libica 23, 1989.

Bouchenaki, M. *Le Mausolée Royal de Maurétanie*, Alger, SNED. 1970.

Bouchenaki, M. « Contribution à la connaissance de la Numidie avant la conquête romaine », dans *Atti del I Congresso internazionale di studi fenici e punici Roma 5-10 novembre 1979*, Roma, 1983, 527-541.

Bouchenaki, M. « La recherche archéologique en Algérie », *Die Numider*, Rheinisches Landes Museum, Bonn, 1979, 2-3.

Bouchenaki, M. *Les Magistrats de La Confédération Cirtéenne*, DEA, Université d'Alger, 1967.

Bouchenaki, M. « Récentes recherches et études de l'antiquité en Algérie », *Antiquités africaines*, vol. 15, 1980, 9-28.

Bouchenaki, M. *Tipasa site du patrimoine mondial*, Alger, ENAG, 1989.

Bouizem, A. *La vie du forum dans les villes de l'Afrique du Nord romaine*, doctorat 3e cycle, Paris 1, 1979.

Boukechour, M.S. « L'écriture de l'histoire de l'Algérie, période coloniale 1830-1962 : sources et perspectives », *Revue des études humaines et sociales*, Université Chlef, vol. 16, 2016, 3-8.

Boussadia, B. et alii. « Les établissements humains littoraux de la basse vallée du Chlef Algérie depuis le premier âge du Fer jusqu'à la période musulmane », dans *Implantations humaines en milieu littoral méditerranéen : facteurs d'installation et processus d'appropriation de l'espace Préhistoire Antiquité Moyen Âge : actes des rencontres 15-17 octobre 2013 : XXXIVᵉ Rencontre Internationale d'archéologie et d'histoire d'Antibes*, Dir. L.M. Ricardo G. Villaescusa, Fr. Bertoncello, Antibes, 2014.

Boussadia, B. *La Céramique campanienne : les collections de Cherchel et de Tipasa*, doctorat 3e cycle, Strasbourg, 1985.

Brāhīmī al-Mīlī, Mubārak. *Tārīḫ al-Ǧazāir fī-l-qadīm wa-l-ḥadīt*, Constantine, al-Maṭbaʿa al- islāmiya al-Ǧazāiriya, 1928-1932.

Brahmī, Muḥammad. *Maẓāhir al-ḥayāt al-miṣriyya al-qadīma min ḫilal al-fann al-miṣrī al-qadīm, al-rasm wa-l-naḥt namūḏaǧan : min al-ʿuṣūr al-qadīma 5000 q.m ʿalā ʿahd al-dawla al-wusṭā ḥawālī 1780 q.m.*, mémoire de magister, Université d'Alger, 2012.

Būdarabza, Farīda. *al-Taḥṣīnāt al-bīzanṭiyya fī bilād al-Maġrib al-qadīm*, mémoire de magister, Université Oran 1, 2002.

Būdīf, Farīda. *al-ʿUlūm ʿinda al-farāʿina min 3200 q.m ilā 525 q.m.*, mémoire de magister, Université d'Alger, 2009.

Būḏrāʿ, Sufyān. *Ǧard wa dirāsa maʿrūḏāt ḥadīqat al-Matḥaf al-waṭanī Sīrtā – Qusanṭīna*, mémoire de magister, Université d'Alger, 2009.

Būḏrāʿ, Sufyān. *Wasāʾil wa asālīb al-qiyāsāt wa al-awzān fī al-ʿahd al-qadīm : al-mawāzīn wa al-maʿāyīr*, thèse de doctorat, Université d'Alger, 2016.

Būǧamʿa, Farīda. *al-Kitāba al-Lībiyya*, mémoire de magister, Université d'Alger, 2012.

Būgarra, Asmāʾ. *Mawqiʿ al-Baʿāla, Mīla : dirāsa mūnūǧrāfiyya*, mémoire de magister, Université de Constantine, 2014.

Būgarra, Ġaniyya. *Madīnat Tīdīs bayna al-našʾa al-tārīḫiyya wa al-baqāyā al-aṯariyya bidāyat min fatrat faǧr al-tārīḫ wa ḥattā al-qarn 3m.*, mémoire de magister, Université de Constantine, 2007.

Būgarra, Ġaniyya. *Madīnat Tīdīs wa al-muḥīṭ al-Sīrtī ḫilāl al-fatra al-rūmāniyya, dirāsa iǧtimāʿiyya wa iqtiṣādiyya*, thèse dedoctorat, Université de Constantine, 2018.

Būġrāra, Wafāʾ. *al-Ḥayāt al-taqāfiyya fī al-Maġrib al-qadīm bayna al-aṣāla wa taʾṯīr al-ṯaqāfa al-wāfida*, mémoire de magister, Université d'Adrar, 2014.

Būġrāra, Wafāʾ. *al-ʿAlāqa al-iǧtīmāʿiyya wa al-taqāfiyya bayna al-Maġrib al-qadīm wa šuʿūb al-baḥr al-abyaḍ al-mutawassaṭ*, thèse de doctorat, Université d'Adrar, 2018.

Būḫalaf, Farīda. *al-Ǧayš al-rūmānī wa ḥayātuhu fī al-Maġrib al-qadīm min sanat 146 q m- 40 m.*, mémoire de magister, Université d'Alger, 2014.

Būlaḫlūḫ, Muḥammad. *al-Tanẓīm al-ʿaskarī li-mamlakat Nūmīdiyā min sanat 220 ilā 46 q.m.*, mémoire de magister, Université d'Alger, 2016.

Būlaḫrāṣ, Ḥamādūš. *Siyāsat Yūlyūs Qayṣar al-tawasuʿiyya wa-inʿikāsātuhā ʿalā Nūmīdiyā : 49 qabla al-mīlād-44 qabla al-mīlād*, mémoire de magister, Université d'Alger, 2014.

Būlaʿrās, Īmān. *al-Kanz al-naqdī li-manṭiqat Ḥammām Awlād ʿAlī al-maḥfūẓ bi-matḥaf Masraḥ Gālma : dirāsa tanmīṭiyya wa taḥlīliyya*, mémoire de magister, Université d'Alger, 2012.

Būlġrāyf, Kamāl. *Dirāsa waṣfiyya wa-taḥlīliyya li-maḥaṭṭāt al-fann al-ṣaḫrī li-manṭiqat Ṯniyyat al-Ḥadd Wilāyat Tīsmsīlat al-Ǧazāʾir*, mémoire de magister, Université d'Alger, 2008.

Būlmīs, Yāsīn. *al-Ḥayy al-sukkanī al-ǧanūbī al-ġarbī bi-al-mawqiʿ al-rūmānī "Tūbūrsīkūm Nūmīdārūm" Ḫamīsa ḥāliyan*, mémoire de magister, Université d'Alger, 2014.

Būmaʿqal Mūlāy al-Ḥāǧǧ, Aḥmad, *Maẓāhir min al-taʾṯīr al-qarṭāǧī fī Nūmīdiyā : al-zirāʿa, al-diyāna wa al-luġa, min al-Qarn al-ṯāliṯ ilā 146 qabla al-mīlād*, mémoire de magister, Université d'Alger, 2009.

Būmaʿqal Mūlāy al-Ḥāǧǧ, Aḥmad. *al-Aǧānib fī madīnat Qarṭāǧa, min al-qarn al-rābiʿ ilā 146 qabla al-mīlād ; al-miṣriyyūn wa al-Iġrīqiyyūn namūḏaǧan*, thèse de doctorat, Université d'Alger, 2015.

Būmrīš, Laylā. *al-Ṭuqūs al-ǧanāʾiziyya al-firʿawniyya*, mémoire de magister, Université d'Alger, 2005.

Būmrīš, Laylā. *Taṭawwur al-fikr al-dīnī fī Miṣr wa bilād al-Rāfidayn : dirāsa fī asāṭīr al-takwīn*, thèse de doctorat, Université d'Alger, 2013.

Būnḍawī, Wahība. *al-Yahūd fī bilad al-Maġrib fī al-ʿuṣūr al-qadīma 814 q.m-146q.m.*, mémoire de magister, Université d'Alger, 2012.

Būqūfa, Nūr al-Sādāt. *Siyāsat Rūmā al-ṯaqāfiyya fī bilād al-Maġrib al-qadīm wa mawqif al-sukkān minhā 146 qabla al-mīlād-430 mīlād*, mémoire de magister, Université d'Adrar, 2016.

Būraḥlī, Ibrāhīm. *Mustaʿmarat Mādūrūs wa iqlīmihā al-turābī*, thèse de doctorat, Université d'Alger, 2010.

Būrni, Dalīla. *Ḥaḍārat al-Māya : al-našʾa wa-l-taṭawwur*, thèse de doctorat, Université d'Alger, 2015.

Būrni, Dalīla. *Taṭawwur al-niẓām al-ḍarībī al-rūmānī fī Šamāl Ifrīqiyā*, mémoire de magister, Université d'Alger, 2001.

Būsāḥa, al-Ṭayyib. *Dirāsa waṣfiyya taḥlīliyya li-anṣāb manṭiqat Ǧālma al-maḥfūẓa fī al-masraḥ al-rūmānī bi-Ǧālma*, mémoire de magister, Université d'Alger, 2010.

Būsāḥa, al-Ṭayyib. *Dirāsat al-libās al-rūmānī fī šamāl Ifrīqiyā min ḫilāl šawāhid al-tamāṯīl wa al-anṣāb*, thèse de doctorat, Université d'Alger, 2019.

Būšārab, Salwā. *Iqlīm Ǧālma wa mā ǧāwarahā : dirāsa mūnūǧrāfiyya mundu faǧr al-tārīḫ li-nihayat al-iḥtilāl al-rūmānī min ḫilāl al-maṣādir al-mādiyya wa-l-adabiyya*, thèse de doctorat, Université de Batna, 2018.

Būšārab, Salwā. *Makka wa ʿalāqatuhā bi-l-ḥawāḍir al-ḥiǧāziyya wa-l-duwal al-muǧāwira*, mémoire de magister, Université de Constantine, 2008.

Būsaʿīd, Kāhina. *Niẓām qiyyās al-wazn wa al-saʿa al-rūmāniyya fī al-Ǧazāʾir : dirāsa tiqaniyya wa-taḥlīliyya*, mémoire de magister, Université d'Alger, 2005.

Būṣbīʿ ʿAmr. *al-Ḥarb al-ahlīya bayna Būmbay wa Qayṣar wa inʿikāsatuhā ʿalā mamlakat Nūmīdiya : 44-49 q m.*, mémoire de magister, Université d'Alger, 2014.

Būslīmānī, Ḥayāt. *Dirāsat mukawwināt muǧtamaʿ madīnat Tīfāstīs wa ḍawāḥīhā min ḫilāl al-kitābāt al-lātīniyya fī al-fatra al-mumtadda bayna al-qarnayn al-awwal wa al-ṯāliṯ li-l-mīlād*, mémoire de magister, Université d'Alger, 2009.

Būslīmānī, Ḥayāt. *Dirāsat mukawwināt muǧtamaʿāt mudun Mūrīṭāniyyā al-Qayṣariyya min ḫilāl al-kitābāt al-lātīniyya fī al-fatra al-mumtadda bayna al-qarnayn al-awwal wa al-ṯāliṯ li-al-mīlād*, thèse de doctorat, Université d'Alger, 2017.

Būslīn, Ṣufyān. *al-Ḥayāt al-siyāsiyya wa al-taqāfiyya fī bilād Sūmar ḫilal ʿahd sulālat Ūr al-tāliṯ 2112-2004 q. m.*, mémoire de magister, Université d'Alger, 2010.

Būšʿīyb, Fūziyya. *Dirāsa al-mawāqiʿ al-aṯariyya al-sāḥiliyya li-fatrat al-Hūlūsān li-manṭiqat al-Šmra Sīdī Laḥḍar : dirāsa mūrfū-tiknūlūǧiyya li-maǧmūʿāt ṣināʿiyya ḥaǧariyya*, mémoire de magister, Université d'Alger, 2015.

Būṯrīd, ʿĀʾiša. *Niẓām al-ḥukm wa al-idāra fī Miṣr al-qadīma ḥattā al-dawla al-ḥadīṯa*, Diplôme des Études Supérieures, Université de Constantine, 1977.

Būydġaġn, Rafīqa. *al-Zirāʿa fī al-Maġrib al-qadīm aṯnāʾ al-iḥtlāl al-rūmanī : min bidāyat al-qarn al-ṯānī qabla al-mīlād ilā al-qarn al-ṯānī mīlādī*, mémoire de magister, Université d'Alger, 2012.

Būzakrī, Yāsīn. *Ḥarakāt al-istīṭān al-rūmānī fī Mūrīṭaniyyā al-Qayṣariyya ḫilāl al-ʿahd al-imbrāṭūrī al-awwal*, mémoire de magister, Université d'Alger, 2013.

Būʿasal, Yūsuf. *Dirāsa tanmīṭiyya wa-tiknūlūǧiyya li-ṣināʿa ḥaǧariyyaʿalā šaẓāyā bi-Tabalbālat manṭiqat al-Sāwra : maǧmūʿat matḥaf al-ǧiyūlūǧiyā bi-ǧāmiʿat al-Ǧazāʾir 1*, mémoire de magister, Université d'Alger, 2015.

Būʿazza, Laylā. *al-Maʿālim al-aṯariyya al-turāṯiyya fī wilāyat Gālma tašḫīṣ al-wāqiʿ wa iqtirāḥ al-ḥulūl*, mémoire de magister, Université de Constantine, 2011.

Būʿazza, Laylā. *Dirāsa tārīḫiyya wa aṯariyya li-taṭawwur madīnat Tīfāst*, thèse de doctorat, Université d'Alger, 2019.

Būʿlam, Saʿīd. *al-Āliha al-šarqiyya fī muqāṭaʿat Nūmīdiya : Izys, Mythra, Kīrys anmūdaǧan*, mémoire de magister, Université d'Alger, 2013.

Bʿayaṯīš, ʿAbd al-Ḥamīd. *Mamlakat al-Anbaṭ wa dawruhā al-ḥaḍārī fī šibh al-Ǧazīra al-ʿarabiyya wa Sīnāʾ min al-qarn al-rābiʿ q. m. ḥattā 106 m.*, mémoire de magister, Université d'Alger, 2009.

Camps, G. *Aux origines de la Berbérie : Massinissa ou les débuts de l'Histoire*, Alger, Imprimerie officielle, 1961.

Camps, G. *Les civilisations préhistoriques et du Sahara*, Paris, Doin, 1974.

Cantier, J. *L'Algérie au regard de l'histoire : un exemple d'évolution de l'historiographie coloniale*. Les cahiers d'Histoire Immédiate, Groupe de recherche en histoire immédiate, 1994, 29-55.

Carcopino, J. « La fin du Maroc romain », Ext. des *Mélanges d'archéologie et d'histoire de l'E.F. Rome*, 1940, 349-448.

Chachoua, K. « 2ᵉ Festival culturel panafricain d'Alger 1-4 juillet 2009. Colloque international sur l'anthropologie africaine, Pour une Anthropologie Sud/Sud », *Journal des anthropologues*, n. 118-119, 2009, 375-380.

Courtois, C. *Les Vandales et l'Afrique*, Paris-Alger, 1955.

Coye, N. « Préhistoire et protohistoire en Algérie au XIXe siècle : les significations du document archéologique », *Cahiers d'Études Africaines*, vol. 33, n. 129, 1993, 99-137.

Daḥmān, Riyyāḍ. *al-Ḥammāmat al-šarqiyya li-madīnat Gālma fī maǧālihā al-ʿumrānī al-rūmanī al-qadīm*, mémoire de magister, Université d'Alger, 2014.

Dahmani, S. *Hippo Regius Hippone à travers les siècles*, Ministère de l'Information et de la Culture de la R.A.D.P., Alger, 1973.

Dallūm, Saʿīd. *Kanz al-Mʾsīla al-naqdī nihāyat al-qarn al-ḫāmis wa bidāyat al-qarn al-sādis al-mīladiyayn : dirāsa tārīḫiyya wa naqdiyya*, thèse de doctorat d'État, 2007.

Damāna, Aḥmad. *al-Dawr al-ḥaḍārī li mamlakat Iblā min muntaṣaf al-alf 3 qabla al-mīlād ilā muntaṣaf al-alf 2 qabla al-mīlād, Dirāsa Tārīḫiyya aṯariyya*, thèse de doctorat, Université d'Alger, 2018.

Damāna, Aḥmad. *al-Ḥayāt al-adabiyya wa al-ʿilmiyya bi-Bābil wa Nīnwā min 1792 qabla al-mīlād ilā 5391792 qabla al-mīlād*, mémoire de magister, Université d'Alger, 2009.

Dardār, Fatḥī. *al-Ṯawra al-nūmīdiyya fī muwāǧahat al-tadaḫḫul al-rūmanī : 111-46 q. m.*, mémoire de magister, Université d'Alger, 2016.

Deloum, S. *Le trésor monétaire de M'sila et l'étude des découvertes monétaires des Ve et VIe siècles trouvés en Afrique du Nord*, doctorat 3e cycle, Paris-Sorbonne, 1987.

Derradji, A. *Contribution à l'étude sédimentologique des Terrains quaternaires de la région de Nice. Origine et mise en place des couvertures limoneuses et sableuses des terrasses*, Museum National d'histoire naturelle, doctorat 3e cycle, Université Pierre et Marie Curie Paris VI, 1987.

Derradji, A. et alii, « Errayah un site Acheuléen récent dans la partie littorale nord-occidentale de l'Algérie Sidi- Ali Mostaganem », *L'Anthropologie*, vol. 121, n. 1-2, 2017, 179-188.

Derradji, A. « Le site acheuléen d'Errayah Mostaganem Algérie dans son contexte géologique », *Comptes Rendus Palevol*, vol. 5, n. 1-2, 2006, 229-235.

Diehl, Ch. *L'Afrique byzantine. Histoire de la domination byzantine en Afrique 533-709*, Paris, 1896.

Djender, M. *Introduction à l'histoire de l'Algérie Systèmes historiques conception générale de l'histoire nationale*, Alger, SNED, 1968.

Dondin-Payre, M. « *L'exercitus Africae inspiratrice de l'armée française d'Afrique : Ense et aratro* », *Antiquités africaines*, vol. 27, 1991, 141-49.

Dondin-Payre, M. *Un siècle d'épigraphie classique Aspects de l'œuvre des savants français dans les pays du bassin méditerranéen*, Paris, 1988.

Dorbane, M. « Notes sur une inscription latine découverte à Tigzirt antique, Iomnium », *L'Africa romana XVI*, Rabat, 2004, Roma, 2006, 1707-1710.

Drāʿ, al-Ṭāhar. *al-Diyānāt al-qadīma fī al-Ḥiǧāz qabla al-Islām min ḫilāl al-maṣādir al-ʿarabiyya wa al-kutub al-samāwiyya*, mémoire de magister, Université de Constantine, 1991.

Drāʿ, al-Ṭāhar. *al-Muǧtamaʿ al-ʿarabī al-qadīm min ḫilāl kitābāt aṣḥāb al-siyar wa-al-kuttāb al-qudamāʾ*, thèse de doctorat d'État, Université de Constantine, 2003.

Drīsī, Salīm. *al-Bīzanṭiyyūn fī Šamāl Ifrīqiyya aṯnāʾ al-iḥtilāl wa-l-ʿimāra al-difāʿiyya*, thèse de doctorat, Université d'Alger, 2008.

Drīsī, Salīm. *Dirāsa mukawwināt muǧtamaʿ Sītīfīs min ḫilāl al-nuqūš al-latīniyya bayn al-qarnayn al-ṯānī wa-l-ṯāliṯ al-mīlādiyayn*, mémoire de magister, Université d'Alger, 1993.

Dūalī, Ǧamīla. *Tīqaniyyat al-bināʾ al-rūmānī fī al-ḥammāmāt al-ġarbiyya wa-l-masraḥ bi-madīnat Qayṣariyya- Šaršāl*, mémoire de magister, Université d'Alger, 2015.

Dūrbān, Muṣṭafā. *al-Muʿaskar al-rūmānī li-madīnat Tīgzīrt dirāsa miʿmāriyya wa aṯariyya*, mémoire de magister, Université d'Alger, 2000.

Dūrbān, Muṣṭafā. *Anmāṭ al-faḫḫar al-qadīm fī al-Ǧazāʾir al-qadīma mā bayna al-qarn al-awwal qabla al-mīlad wa-l-qarn al-ṯāliṯ mīladī : dirāsa waṣfiyya wa tanmīṭiyya wa taḥlīliyya*, thèse de doctorat, Université d'Alger, 2010.

Fāḍal, Laḫḍar. *Muqāwamat sukkān šamāl Ifrīqiyya li-l-iḥtilāl al-bīzanṭī*, mémoire de magister, Université d'Oran, 2000.

Fāḍal, Laḫḍar. *Tibāssa fī al-ʿuṣūr al-qadīma*, thèse de doctorat, Université d'Oran, 2018.

Faīz, Samīša. *Dawr al-kahana al-dīnī wa al-siyasī fī Miṣr al-firʿawniyya : al-dawla al-qadīma 2690-2180 q.m – wa al-dawla al-ḥadīṯa 1580-1085 q.m namūḏaǧan*, mémoire de magister, Université d'Alger, 2012.

Farāḥ, Faziyya. *al-Tašrīʿ fī bilād al-Rāfidayn min al-alf al-ṯaliṯ ilā muntaṣaf al-alf al-ṯānī qabla al-mīlad : taṭawwuruhu wa aṯaruhu*, mémoire de magister, Université d'Alger, 2010.

Farḥātī, Fatīḥa. *Nūmīdiyā min ḥukm Ġāyā ilā bidāyat al-iḥtilāl al-rūmānī, al-ḥayāt al-siyāsiyya wa al-ḥaḍāriyya 213-46.m.*, Université du Caire, 2003.

Farqī, ʿIzz al-Dīn. *Dirāsa taḥlīliyya li-nuqūš wa wāǧihat maḥaṭṭat wadī Ǧarra-Tāsīlī-Nāǧar – al-Ṣaḥrāʾ al-Wusṭā, al-Ǧazāʾir*, mémoire de magister, Université d'Alger, 2009.

Faṣūlī, Ḥasīna. *Fūsayfisāʾ faǧr al-masīḥiyya : dirāsa taḥlīliyya īknūǧrafiyya wa ramziyya wa tiqaniyya namawdaǧ min al-Ǧazāʾir al-qadīma wa Tūnis wa Rūmā*, mémoire de magister, Université d'Alger, 2011.

Fauvelle, F.X. et alii. « Les savoirs archéologiques au Maghreb », *Perspective*, 2, 2017, 15-29.

Fentress, E. et alii. « Prospections dans le Belezma : rapport préliminaire », dans *Actes du colloque international sur l'histoire de Sétif : Sétif 8, 9, et 10 décembre 1990*, *Bulletin d'Archéologie Algérienne*, supplément 7, Alger, 1991, 107-13.

Ferhat, N. *Les industries préhistoriques de la paléo vallée de Timimoun dans leur contexte stratigraphique. Sahara-algérien*, thèse de doctorat de 3ème cycle, Université de Bordeaux 1, 1985.

Février, P.A. *Approches du Maghreb romain*, vol. 1, Aix-en Provence, 1989.

Février, P.A. *Djemila*, Alger, 1968.

Février, P.A. « Le monde rural du Maghreb antique approche de l'historiographie du XIXᵉ siècle », *Histoire et archéologie de l'Afrique du Nord*, 3e Colloque International Montpellier, 111e Congrès national des Sociétés savants, Paris, 1986, 87-106.

Février, P.A., Gaspary, A., Guéry, R. « Fouilles de Sétif 1959-1966. Quartier nord-ouest rempart et cirque », *Bulletin d'Archéologie Algérienne*, supplément 1, Alger, 1970.

Fīlālī, al-Mašrafī. *al-Maṣābīḥ wa al-ǧirār al-rūmāniyya fī ʿaṣr Fīlībūs*, DEA, Université d'Alger, 1974.

Fillah, M.M. *Recherches sur les agglomérations antiques : le réseau urbain et le paysage rural en Numidie occidentale Algérie*, thèse de doctorat, Aix-Marseille 1, Dir. P.A. Février, 1986.

Fūqa, Muḥammad. *Ḫarīṭa aṯariyya li-wilāyat al-Šilaf*, mémoire de magister, Université d'Alger, 2009.

Fūralī, H'mīda. *Buyūt al-taʿmīd fī muqāṭaʿat Nūmīdiya al-masīḥiyya, dirāsa aṯariyya wa tanmīṭiyya*, thèse de doctorat, Université d'Alger, 2018.

Fūralī, H'mīda. *Ǧard al-maṣābīḥ al-masīḥiyya al-maʿrūda fī kull min al-mathaf al-waṭanī li- Sīrta wa mathaf mawqiʿ Ǧamīla al-aṯarī*, mémoire de magister, Université d'Alger, 2012.

Ǧalmam, Lwīza. *Ḫurūǧ Banī Isrāʾīl min Miṣr bayna al-maṣādir al-dīniyya wa al-dirāsa al-aṯariyya : al-qarn al-sābiʿ ḥattā 13 q.m.*, mémoire de magister, Université d'Alger, 2016.

Ǧāmāʿ, Kātiyā. *al-Zaḫrafa al-masīḥiyya ʿalā al-maʿālim al-aṯariyya fī muqāṭaʿat Nūmīdiyā : Dirāsa zuḫrufiyya wa ikūnūǧrāfiyya*, thèse de doctorat, Université d'Alger, 2018.

Ǧāmāʿ, Kātiyā. *Dirāsa tanmīṭiyya wa-ikūnūǧrāfiyya li-maǧmuʿat maṣābīḥ zaytiyya faḫḫāriyya maḥfūẓa fī al-Mathaf al-waṭanī li-l-āṯār al-qadīma*, mémoire de magister, Université d'Alger, 2009.

Ǧānim, Muḥammad al-Ṣaġīr. *al-Musāhama al-ḥaḍāriyya al-būniyya fī al-mamlaka al-nūmīdiyya*, thèse de doctorat d'État, Université de Constantine, 1996.

Ǧānim, Muḥammad al-Ṣaġīr. *al-Tawāǧud al-finīqī- al-būnī fī al-Ǧazāʾir*, doctorat troisième cycle, Université d'Alger, 1981.

Ǧānim, Muḥammad al-Ṣaġīr. *al-Tawassuʿ al-finīqī fī ġarb al-baḥr al-mutawassiṭ*, Diplôme d'Étude Superieur, Université d'Alger, 1974.

Ǧarbī, Anīsa. *Dirāsa taḥlīliyya tārīḫiyya aṯariyya li-kanz ʿAnnāba al-maḥfūẓ bi al-mathaf al-waṭanī li-l-āṯār Sīrta Qusanṭīna*, mémoire de magister, Université d'Alger, 2009.

Ǧarmūn, Ḥūsīn. *al-Kanz al-naqdī li- Ġāsīra : Dirāsa tiqaniyya wa ikūnūǧrāfiyya*, mémoire de magister, Université d'Alger, 2009.

Ǧawād, Rašīd. *al-Naḥt al-timṯālī li-madīnatay Lumbāz wa Tīmgād*, mémoire de magister, Université d'Alger, 2012.

Ǧāwšī, Fāṭima al-Zahrāʾ. *Ḥamlat al-Iskandar al-Maqdūnī ʿalā bilād mā bayna al-Nahrayn 331-30 qabla al-mīlād: al-fatra al-hilīnistiyya*, mémoire de magister, Université d'Alger, 2013.

Ǧrāya, Mūḥammad Rušdī. *al-Ṣaḥrāʾ al-Ǧazāʾiriyya ḫilāl al-ʿaṣr al-ḥaǧarī al-ḥadīṯ 6100 qabla al-mīlād-1000 qabla al-mīlād*, mémoire de magister, Université de Constantine, 2007.

Ǧrāya, Mūḥammad Rušdī. *Malāmiḥ al-ʿaṣr al-ḥaǧarī al-qadīm fī bilād al-Maġrib: dirāsa ḥaḍāriyya aṯariyya*, thèse de doctorat, Université d'Alger, 2012.

Guelmaoui, A. *Essai d'analyse morpho technologique d'industries lithiques atériennes d'Algérie*, doctorat, Paris 10, 1986.

Guéry, R. *Caesarea de Maurétanie. Une ville romaine et ses campagnes*, Collection de E.F.R. 70, Rome, 1984.

Guéry, R. *La nécropole orientale de Sitifis Sétif Algérie. Fouilles de 1966-1967*, Paris, 1985.

Guéry, R. « Les thermes d'Ad Sava Municipium, Hammam Guergour », *Bulletin d'archéologie Algérienne*, vol. 2, 1966-67, 95-106.

Hachi, S. « Aux origines des arts premiers en Afrique du Nord. Les figurines et les objets modelés en terre cuite de l'abri-sous-roche préhistorique d'Afalou, Babors, Algérie 18000-11000 BP », Mémoires du CNRPAH, nouvelle série, n. 6, Alger, 2003.

Hachi, S. « Les cultures de l'Homme de Mechta-Afalou. Le gisement d'Afalou Bou Rhummel massif des Babors Algérie. Les niveaux supérieurs 13000-11000 BP », Mémoires du CNRPAH, nouvelle série, n. 2, Alger, 2003.

Hachi, S. *Les Industries d'Afalou Bou Rhummel Algérie dans leurs relations avec l'Ibéromaurusien*, doctorat de 3e cycle, Dir. G. Camps, Aix-Marseille 1, 1987.

Hachid, M. *Recherches méthodiques sur l'Art rupestre de l'Atlas saharien. Étude de deux stations de la région de Djelfa Sud-Algérois*, thèse de 3e cycle, Aix-en-Provence, 1982.

Hachid, M. *Le Tassili des Ajer aux sources de l'Afrique. 50 siècles avant les pyramides*, Alger-Paris, 2000.

Hachid, M. *Les Premiers Berbères. Entre Méditerranée Tassili et Nil*, Alger, Aix-En-Provence, 2001.

Ḥadadū, Yuġūrṭa. *Ahamm mašāhid al-ḥayawānāt al-ṭabīʿiyya al-kabīra fī maḥaṭṭat al-nuqūš al-ṣaḥriyya li-l-Aṭlas al-ṣaḥrāwī wa ʿalāqatuhā bi-l-insān min al-nāhiya al-iǧtimāʿiyya wa al-ʿaqāʾidiyya*, mémoire de magister, Université d'Alger, 2006.

Haddād, Sihām. *Silsilat mawāniʾ al-šarq al-qadīma. dirāsa tārīḫiyya waṣfiyya iʿtimādan alā al-maṣādir al-mādiyya al-maḥalliyya*, mémoire de magister, Université de Constantine, 2009.

Ḥaddūš, Karīma. *Tiǧārat mamlakat Sabaʾ ʿalā ḍawʾ kutub al-raḥḥāla wa dawruhā al-ḥaḍārī: kitāb al-ṭawāf ḥawla al-baḥr al-arītrī anmūḏaǧan*, mémoire de magister, Université d'Alger, 2010.

Ḥaddūš, ʿAbd al-Qādir. *al-Ahaggār al-markazī wa al-ǧanūbī fī faǧr al-tārīḫ*, thèse de doctorat, Université d'Alger, 2010.

Ḥadīdī, ʿAlī. *al-Māʾ fī tārīḫ al-Maġrib al-qadīm*, mémoire de magister, Université de Constantine, 2014.

Hadji, Y. « Les découvertes archéologiques de Badias », dans *Libyca : Actes du colloque international La Numidie, Massinissa et l'histoire, Constantine, les 14, 15 et 16 mai 2016*, 285-299.

Hadjouis, D.J. *Hominidés et Grands mammifères dans leur contexte paléo-environnemental au cours du Quaternaire maghrébin*, thèse d'habilitation à diriger des recherches, Université de Perpignan, 2003.

Hadjouis, D.J. *Les Bovidés du gisement atérien des Phacochères Alger Algérie. Contribution à l'étude des Bovidés du Pléistocène moyen et supérieur du Maghreb*, thèse de 3ème cycle en paléontologie des vertébrés, Paris VI, Muséum National d'Histoire Naturelle, 1985.

Ḥaǧǧāǧ, Kāhina. *Ṭuruq tamwīn madīnat Kwīkūl Ǧamīla bi-l-miyāh fī al-ʿaṣr al-rūmānī : dirāsa waṣfiyya wa-miʿmāriyya*, mémoire de magister, Université d'Alger, 2011.

Ḥaǧǧī Yāsīn, Rābaḥ. *al-bāzīlīkāt al-masīḥiyya fī muqāṭaʿat Nūmīdiyā : dirāsa aṯariyya wa-tanmīṯiyya*, thèse de doctorat, Université d'Alger, 2009.

Ḥāldiyya, Maḍwī. *al-Tawāṣul al-ḥaḍārī bi-madīnat Qusanṭīna fī al-ʿuṣūr al-qadīma*, thèse de doctorat, Université d'Oran, 2017.

Ḥāldiyya, Maḍwī. *Mulūk bilād al-Maġrib al-qadīm qabla al-iḥtilāl al-rūmānī*, mémoire de magister, Université d'Oran, 2009.

Ḥalfa, ʿAbd al-Raḥmān. *al-Diyānāt al-waṭaniyya al-maġrībiyya al-qadīma mundu al-našʾa ilā suqūṭ Qarṭāǧa, 146 qabla al-mīlād*, mémoire de magister, Université de Constantine, 2008.

Ḥālfī, Ǧamīla. *al-Maktaba wa-l-maktabāt fī bilād al-Rāfidayn 3200 ilā 626 qabla al-mīlād : Maktabat Āšūr Bānībāl namūḏaǧan*, mémoire de magister, Université d'Alger, 2010.

Ḥālfī, Ǧamīla. *al-Taʿlīm wa al-madāris al-taʿlīmiyya fī bilād al-Rāfidayn*, thèse de doctorat, Université d'Alger, 2017.

Ḥālid, Šahra. *al-Tašrīʿ al-rūmānī fī al-ʿaṣr al-ǧumhūrī 509-27 qabla al-mīlād*, mémoire de magister, Université d'Alger, 2015.

Ḥalīf, Zakariyya. *al-ʿImāra al-sakaniyya bi-madinat Tībāza : dirāsa l-namūḏaǧ min al-ḥayy al-sakanī al-ǧadīd*, mémoire de magister, Université d'Alger, 2017.

Ḥalīfī, Naṣīra. *al-Ḥayāt al-adabiyya fī Miṣr al-qadīma : al-dawla al-qadīma wa al-dawla al-wusṭā namūḏaǧan 3500 q m-1778 q m.*, mémoire de magister, Université d'Alger, 2012.

Ḥalīl, Mūsā. *al-Tawzīʿ al-ǧuġrāfī fī al-waṣf al-miʿmārī li-maʿālim al-maqbara al-mīǧalītiyya "al-Ṣfiyya" bi minṭaqat Sīqūs – wilāyat Umm al-Buwāqī*, mémoire de magister, Université d'Alger, 2008.

Ḥālīt, Ṣalīḥa. *al-Zirāʿa fī al-ʿahdayni al-qarṭāǧī wa al-rūmānī fī al-Maġrib al-qdīm*, mémoire de magister, Université d'Alger, 2013.

Hamādī, Samīr. *Maẓāhir al-taʾṯīr al-ḥaḍārī al-fīnīqī fī al-ḍiffa al-šamāliyya al-ġarbiyya li-ḥawḍ al-baḥr al-abyaḍ al-mutawissaṭ: ǧuzur Ṣīqiliyya, Sardīniyya wa al-Balyar namūḏaǧan 1200-550 q.m.*, mémoire de magister, Université d'Alger, 2012.

Ḥamdāš, Fahīma. *al-Ḥayāt al-iqtiṣādiyya fī Ifrīqiyya al-Brūqunṣuliyya: min iṣlāḥāt aūǧusṭus ilā iṣlāḥāt Daqlidiyyānūs*, thèse de doctorat, Université d'Alger, 2018.

Ḥamdāš, Fahīma. *al-Ṣināʿāt al-ḥirafiyya fī Qarṭāǧa al-būnīqiyya*, mémoire de magister, Université d'Alger, 2009.

Hāmil, Samīra. *Dirāsa rusūbiyya li-ʿayyināt min al-mawqiʿ al-aṯarī Tin-Hnaktn al-Tāsīlī Nāǧar*, mémoire de magister, Université d'Alger, 2010.

Ḥamīsī, Ismāʿīl. *Taṭawwur al-muǧtamaʿ al-lātīnī min ḫilāl al-tašrīʿāt*, Université d'Alger, 1996.

Ḥammūdī, Muḥammad. *Dirāsa waǧh min al-niyūlītī al-ṣaḥrawī: al-baqrī al-asfal ḥasba al-maqṭaʿ al-rābiʿ li-mawqiʿ Tīn Hnāktn-al-Ṭāsīlī Nāǧar- al-Ǧazāʾir*, mémoire de magister, Université d'Alger, 2002.

Ḥammūm, Tawfīq. *al-Nuḫab al-idāriyya wa-al-iǧtimāʿiyya li-l-kunfidirāliyya al-sartūniyya wa al-mudun al-kubrā bi-Numīdiyā aṯnāʾ al-iḥtilāl al-rūmānī: munḏu sanat 46 qabla al-mīlād ilā nihāyat al-qarn al-rābiʿ al-mīlādī*, thèse de doctorat, Université d'Alger, 2009.

Ḥammūm, Tawfīq *Kahana wa kahanūt al-ʿahd al-imbrāṭūrī al-rūmānī al-awwal fī šamāl Ifrīqiyya min ḫilāl al-kitābāt al-lātīniyya*, mémoire de magister, Université d'Alger, 2000.

Ḥammūma, al-Ǧūdī. *al-Ḍarāʾib al-rūmāniyya fī bilād al-Maġrib al-qadīm munḏu suqūṭ Qarṭāǧa 146 qabla al-mīlād ilā nihāyat al-iḥtilāl al-rūmānī 430 li-l-mīlād*, mémoire de magister, Université d'Alger, 2015.

Ḥamza, Muḥammad al-Šarīf. *Fusayfisāʾ Mūrīṭaniyya al-Qayṣariyya: al-tablīṭat al-ǧanāʾiziyya*, thèse de doctorat, Université d'Alger, 2012.

Ḥanniš, ʿAbd al-Fattāḥ. *al-Tawassuʿ al-zirāʿī fī Ifrīqiyya al-qadīma ḫilāl al-fatra al-rūmāniyya*, mémoire de magister, Université de Constantine, 2013.

Ḥarfūš, Wahība. *Dirāsa naqdiyya li-l-waḍʿiyya al-bāliyūlītī al-asfal fī al-Ǧazāʾir wa-al-āfāq al-mustaqbaliyya li-l-baḥṯ*, mémoire de magister, Université d'Alger, 2003.

Ḥāriš, Muḥammad al-Hādī. *al-Taṭawwur al-siyāsī wa al-iqtiṣādī fī Numīdiyā munḏu iʿtilāʾ Māsīnīsā al-ʿarš ilā wafāt Yūbā al-awwal 203-46 qabla al-mīlād*, mémoire de magister, Université d'Alger, 1985.

Ḥāša, al-Saʿīd. *Dirāsat muǧtamaʿ Ūziyyā min ḫilāl al-kitābāt al-lātīniyya*, mémoire de magister, Université d'Alger, 2007.

Ḥāša, al-Saʿīd. *Kwīkūl, dirāsa iǧtimāʿiyya wa aṯariyya*, thèse de doctorat, Université d'Alger, 2017.

Ḥasīsī-Daḥmanī, Malīka. *Fusayfisāʾ Numīdiya: Ǧamīla, Lambāz, Tīmgād, Tibassa, Qusanṭīna*, thèse de doctorat, Université d'Alger, 2010.

Ḥasīsī, Malīka. *Matḥaf Lāmbīz, dirāsat al-maǧmūʿāt al-aṯariyya*, mémoire de magister, Université d'Alger, 1999.

Ḥasnāwī, Ṣafiya. *Dawr qanūnā mankyana wa hadryana fī al-zirāʿa al-maǧāribiyya al-qarnayn al-awwal wa-l-tānī li-l-mīlād*, mémoire de magister, Université d'Alger, 2015.

Ḥassūna, Ayman Muḥammad Ṣālaḥ. *al-Faḫḫār al-qadīm al-muktašaf fī Ġazza : dirāsa tiqaniyya wa-taḥlīliyya*, mémoire de magister, Université d'Alger, 2010.

Ḥawqlāwn, Dalīla. *al-Diʿāya ʿinda al-Rūmān fī al-imbrāṭūriyya al-suflā min ḫilāl kanz Lāmāsbā Marwāna maḥfūẓ bi-l-Matḥaf al-waṭanī li-l-āṯār al-qadīma al-Ǧazāʾir*, mémoire de magister, Université d'Alger, 2009.

Ḥawqlāwn, Dalīla. *Dirāsa aṯariyya wa naqdiyya li-l-ʿumlāt wa al-kunūz al-rūmāniyya al-muktašafa fī šamāl Afrīqiyā : al-muʾarraḫa li-l-qarnayn al-rābiʿ wa-al-ḫāmis al-mīlādiyayn*, thèse de doctorat, Université d'Alger, 2017.

Ḥayāṭ, Yūsuf. *al-Dawla al-bīzanṭiyya min al-našʾa ḥattā ʿahd Ǧīstinyān 284-565m.*, mémoire de magister, Université d'Alger, 2011.

Ḥayr, ʿAmr. *al-ʿAlāqa al-tiǧāriyya bayna fīnīqiyā wa Miṣr fima bayna 2780 q.m wa-l-qarn al-sādis q.m.*, mémoire de magister, Université d'Alger, 2012.

Heddouche, A. *Protohistoire de l'Ahaggar central et méridional*, doctorat, Université d'Alger, 2010.

Ḥusīn, Muḥammad al-Šarīf. *al-Taʿmīr al-bašarī bi-minṭaqat Umm al-Bawāqī, dirāsa tārīḫiyya wa aṯariyya min fatrat faǧr al-tārīḫ ilā ǧāyat al-fatra al-bīzanṭiyya*, thèse de doctorat, Université d'Alger, 2018.

ʿĪd, ʿAbd al-Ḥaqq. *al-Maǧmaʿ al-masīḥī al-ḥayy al-masīḥī bi kwīkūl – Ǧamīla – Dirāsa miʿmāriyya wa fanniyya*, mémoire de magister, Université d'Alger, 2015.

Iddir, S. *Peuplement holocène du bas Mertoutek zone centrale de la chaine Téfedest Massif de l'Ahaggar, Algérie. Archéologie et Préhistoire*, thèse de 3e cycle, Université Toulouse le Mirail – Toulouse 2, 2013.

Īdīr, Ismāʿīl. *al-Adawāt al-ḥaǧariyya li-mawqiʿ ʿIrq Tīhūdāyīn : dirāsa manhaǧiyya wa tanmīṭiyya*, mémoire de magister, Université d'Alger, 2003.

Īdīrān, Ḥakīm. *Mustaʿmarat Tūbūsūktū al-rūmāniyya : dirāsa aṯariyya wa miʿmāriyya*, mémoire de magister, Université d'Alger, 2012.

Īḫarbān, Muḥannad Āklī. *Dirāsa aṯariyya li-iqlīm Gālma al-qadīma min ḫilāl al-taǧammuʿāt al-sukkāniyya wa šabakāt al-ṭuruqāt wa al-nūqūšāt al-lātīniyya wa mūḫtalaf al-lūqā al-aṯariyya*, thèse de doctorat, Université d'Alger, 2016.

Īḫarbān, Muḥannad Āklī. *Ǧard al-tuḥaf al-aṯariyya al-maʿrūḍāt bi-matḥaf Ǧamīla Kuwīkūl al-qadīma*, mémoire de magister, Université d'Alger, 2008.

ʿIwaǧ, Zahiyya. *Taṭawwur al-ʿimāra al-ǧanāʾiziyya fī Miṣr al-qadīma 3500-1075q.m.*, mémoire de magister, Université d'Alger, 2008.

Jansen, J.C. *Une « Statuomanie » à l'algérienne Histoire de l'Algérie à la période coloniale. 1880-1914*, Paris, La Découverte, 2014.

Kabbūr, ʿUmar. *al-Mūǧtamaʿ al-qadīm bi-minṭaqat al-Qanṭara min ḥilāl al-kitāba wa al-muḥallafāt al-aṯariyya ḥilāl al-fatra al-mumtadda mā bayna al-qarn al-awwal wa al-ṯāliṯ al-mīladiyayn*, thèse de doctorat, Université d'Alger, 2016.

Kablī, Faṭīma. *al-Ḥalfiyya al-iqtiṣādiyya li-l-iḥtilāl al-rūmānī li-bilād al-Maġrib al-qadīm wa aṯarihā ʿalā al-mūǧtamaʿ*, mémoire de magister, Université d'Alger, 2012.

Kablī, Faṭīma. *al-Istīṭān al rūmanī fī šamāl Ifrīqiyā, dirāsa muqārana bilād al Maġrib wa Miṣr -namūḏaǧan*, thèse de doctorat, Université d'Alger, 2019.

Kadra, F. et Lequement, R. *Découverte d'une nécropole de basse époque à El Hadjar,* BAA III, 259-270, 1968.

Kadra, F. *Étude des Djeddars. Mausolées de tradition berbère dans la Wilaya de Tiaret*, thèse de doctorat de 3e cycle, Aix-en-Provence, 1974.

Kadra, F. *Les Djedars monuments funéraires berbères de la région de Frenda Wilaya de Tiaret*, Alger, 1983.

Kadra, F. « Note complémentaire sur les Djedars de la région de Frenda », *Bulletin d'archéologie Algérienne,* vol. VII, n. 1, 1985, 227-232.

Kadra, F. « Recherches et travaux 1977-1979 », *Bulletin d'archéologie Algérienne* vol. VII, n. 1, 1985, 9-28.

Kākī, Muḥammad. *al-Wāqiʿ al-tiǧārī wa aṯaruhu fī izdihār al-mamlaka al-Sabaʾiyya*, mémoire de magister, Université d'Alger, 2003.

Kākī, Muḥammad. *Maẓāhir al-ḥaḍāra al-sabaʾiyya fī al-ǧanūb al-ʿarabī bidāya min al-alf al-awwal qabla al-mīlad wa ḥattā maṭlaʿ al-qarn al-sādis mīladī*, thèse de doctorat, Université de Constantine, 2016.

Kardīn, Suhīla. *Dirāsa fanniyya zuḥrufiyya li-l-ʿanāṣir al-miʿmāriyya al-muzayyina li-maʿālim al-mawqiʿ al-aṯarī Madūrūs fī al-fatra al-qadīma*, thèse de doctorat, Université d'Alger, 2018.

Kardīn, Suhīla. *Tīǧān madīnat Madūrūs : ǧard wa dirāsa ḥawla al-zaḥrafa al-miʿmāriyya*, mémoire de magister, Université d'Alger, 2010.

Katfī al-Šarīf, Hāǧar. *Madīnat al-Iskāndariyya wa ḥaḍāratuhā fī ʿahd al-Baṭālima : dirāsa fī al-ǧānib al-iǧtimāʿī anmūḏaǧan 331-30q.m.*, mémoire de magister, Université d'Alger, 2016.

Kherbouche, F. et alii. « Middle Holocene hunting and herding at Gueldaman Cave Algeria : An integrated study of the vertebrate fauna and pottery lipid residues », *Quaternary International*, vol. 410, 2016, 50-60.

Kherbouche, F. *Le néolithique tellien de la grotte de Gueldaman GLD1 Babors d'Akbou Algérie VIII-V millénaire BP*, thèse de doctorat, Toulouse 2, 2015.

Kīdār, ʿAbd al-Wahhāb. *al-Nafī al-bābilī wa-āṯāruhu*, mémoire de magister, Université d'Alger, 2009.

Kīdār, ʿAbd al-Wahhāb. *Ẓāhirat al-nubuwāt ʿinda Banī Isrāʾīl wa-aṯaruhā fī al-takwīn al-dīnī wa-al-siyāsī li-mamlakatay Yahūdā wa al-Sāmira : min al-qarn al-rābiʿ ʿašar ḥatta al-qarn al-ḥāmis qabla al-mīlād*, thèse de doctorat, Université d'Alger, 2017.

Kīḥal, al-Bašīr. *al-Ḥuḍūr al-dīnī al-būnī fī Nūmīdiyā -814 qabla al-mīlād -146 qabla al-mīlād*, mémoire de magister, Université d'Alger, 2012.

Kīḥal, ʿUmar. *Mamlakat al-Ḥīra wa dawruhā al-ḥaḍārī : min al-qarn al-ṯāliṯ al-mīlādī ilā sanat 632 mīlādiyya*, mémoire de magister, Université d'Alger, 2008.

Kīḥal, ʿUmar. *al-Ḥayāt al-adabiyya fī dawlat al-Manāḏira min al-qarn al-ṯāliṯ al-mīlādī ilā sanat 632 mīlādiyya*, thèse de doctorat, Université d'Alger, 2017.

Labḥūr, Salīma. *al-Mamlaka al-ʿibrāniyya fī ʿahd Dāwūd wa Sulaymān mā bayna 1004 q. m.-922*, mémoire de magister, Université de Constantine, 2010.

Labīb, al-Ḥāǧǧ. *al-Taḥṣīnāt al-ʿaskariyya al-rūmāniyya ǧanūb al-Wanšarīs q 2-3m.*, thèse de doctorat, Université d'Alger, 2018.

Labīb, al-Ḥāǧǧ. *Ǧard al-mawāqiʿ al-āṯariyya bi-wilāya Tīsmsīlat*, mémoire de magister, Université d'Alger, 2010.

Lacheraf, M. *L'Algérie : nation et société*, Paris, Éditions François Maspero, 1965.

Laḥsan, Brāhīm. *al-Asrā ʿinda al-Rūmān ḫilāl al-niṣf al-ṯānī min al-ʿahd al-ǧamhūrī 378 q-m ilā 27 qabla al-mīlād*, mémoire de magister, Université d'Alger, 2016.

Larābī, Ḥalīma. *al-ʿAlāqā bayna Qarṭāǧa wa Rūmā min ḫilāl al-muʿāhadāt – 509-146 qabla al-mīlād*, mémoire de magister, Université d'Alger, 2016.

Lassus, J. *Visite à Timgad*, Alger Ministère de l'Éducation Nationale, Direction des affaires culturelles, 1969.

Laʿyāḏī, Ḥafīẓa. *al-Tarkība al-bašariyya li-l-Ṭāsīlī-Nāǧar mundu mā qabl al-tārīḫ ilā bidāyat al-ʿuṣūr al-tārīḫiyya*, mémoire de magister, Université d'Alger, 2011.

Leimdorfer, J.F. *Discours académique et colonisation. Thèmes de recherche sur l'Algérie pendant la période coloniale*, Paris, Publisud, 1992.

Lequément R. « Fouilles à l'Amphithéâtre de Tébessa 1965-1968 », *Bulletin d'Archéologie algérienne*, vol. 2, 1966-67, 107-122.

Lequément R. *Fouilles de l'Amphithéâtre de Tébessa*, thèse de doctorat de 3e cycle soutenue à Alger en 1969, 2ᵉ Supplément du *Bulletin d'Archéologie algérienne*, Alger, 1979.

Leveau, Ph. *Caesarea de Maurétanie. Une ville romaine et ses campagnes*, Collection EFR, 70, 1984.

Lucas, Ph. *L'Algérie des anthropologues*, Paris, Maspéro, 1992.

Maddād, Kamāl. *al-Ḍayʿāt al-rīfiyya al-rūmāniyya fī al-Šarq al-Ǧazāʾirī, dirāsa aṯariyya, taḥlīlyya wa tanmīṭiyya*, thèse de doctorat, Université d'Alger, 2019.

Madīwan, Ṣūriyya. *Dirāsa muǧtamaʿ Tūbūrsīkūm Nūmīdarūm min ḫilal al-naqīšat al-latīniyya*, mémoire de magister, Université d'Alger, 2013.

Maġārī, Nawāl. *Qarṭāǧa wa al-lībyyūn : Dirāsa fī al-ʿalāqa al-ḥaḍariyya 480-146 q.m.*, mémoire de magister, Université d'Alger, 2014.

Maġǧanī, ʿIzz al-Dīn. *al-Sūr al-bīzanṭī li-madīnat Mīlaf*, mémoire de magister, Université d'Alger, 2010.

Māǧī, Nadiyya. *Ḥarakāt al-istīṭān al-sāmiyya : al-fīnīqiyya – al-yamaniyya : dirāsa muqārana*, mémoire de magister, Université d'Oran, 2014.

Maḥbūs, Ǧamāl. *al-Ḥayāt al-dīniyya fī Qarṭāǧanna*, Université d'Oran, 2011.

Maḥfūẓ, Ḥālid. *al-Ḥayāt al-dīniyya ladā al-Farā'ina 2780 qabla al-mīlād-1085 qabla al-mīlād wa al-Māyyā 600 qabla al-mīlād-1500 al-mīlād : dirāsa muqārana*, mémoire de magister, Université d'Alger, 2010.

Malarkey, J. *The Colonial Encounter in French Algeria : a Study of the Development of Power Asymmetry and Symbolic Violence in the City of Constantine 1830-1970*, thèse d'anthropologie, Austin, Texas, 1980.

Malek, A.A. *Le sentiment de la nature dans les domus de l'Afrique romaine II-V Siècles*, thèse de doctorat, EHESS, Paris, 1999.

Malīzī, Rīma. *Qarṭāǧa wa al-baḥr 814-146 q m.* mémoire de magister, Université d'Alger, 2011.

Manṣūrī, Farīda. *Dirāsa tārīḫiyya wa aṯariyya li-madīna Tūbūrsīkūm Nūmīdarūm Ḥamīssa ḫāliyyan*, thèse de doctorat, Université d'Alger, 2017.

Manṣūrī, Farīda. *Taṭawwur al-fann al-naqdī min ḫilāl maǧmū'a naqdiyya min madīnat Ǧālma -maḥfūẓa bi-l-matḥaf al-waṭanī li-l-āṯar al-qadīma*, mémoire de magister, Université d'Alger, 2013.

Manṣūrī, Ḥadīǧa. *al-Dūnātiyya wa ṯawrat al-qarn al-rābiʿ fī šamal Ifrīqiyya*, mémoire de magister, Université d'Oran. 1987.

Manṣūrī, Ḥadīǧa. *al-Taṭawwurāt al-iqtṣādiyya li-Mūrīṭāniyya al-Qayṣariyya aṯnā' al-iḥtilāl al-rūmānī*, thèse de doctorat, Université d'Oran, 1996.

Manṣūriyya, Malīka. *al-Niẓām al-siyāsī fī al-Ǧazīra al-'Arabiyya min al-qabīla ilā al-dawla : 300q.m 'alā al-fatḥ al-islāmī*, mémoire de magister, Université d'Alger, 2016.

Marīqī, Abū Bakr. *al-Dawr al-ḥaḍārī li-l-baṭālat fī Miṣr : al-baḥṯ al-iqtiṣādī wa-al-iǧtimā'ī wa-al-ṯaqāfī namūḏaǧan*, mémoire de magister, Université d'Alger, 2008.

Marīqī, Ṭāraq. *al-Sāḥil al-fīnīqī wa ṣirā' qiwā al-ǧiwwār al-ǧuġrāfī : al-alf al-ṯāniyya q.m ilā bidāyat al-qarn 12 q.m.*, mémoire de magister, Université d'Alger, 2009.

Marzūqī, Nūr al-Dīn. *al-Siyāsa al-naqdiyya li-l-abāṭira al-rūmān wa aṯaruhā 'alā al-ḥayāt al-iqtiṣādiyya wa al-iǧtmā'iyya : min bidāyat al-'ahd al-imbrāṭūrī ḥatta nihāyat ḥukm Daqlidyānūs 27 qabla al-mīlād 305 lil-mīlād*, mémoire de magister, Université d'Alger, 2014.

Masarhī, Ǧamāl. *al-Muqāwama al-nūmīdiyya li-al-iḥtilāl al-rūmānī fī al-ǧanūb al-šarqī al-Ǧazā'irī : ṯawarāt al-Awrās wa al-tuḫūm al-ṣaḥrāwiyya namūḏaǧan*, mémoire de magister, Université de Constantine, 2009.

Masarhī, Ǧamāl. *Awḍā' al-šarq al-Ǧazā'irī al-qadīm min zawāl al-mamlaka al-Nūmīdiyya ḥattā al-ġazawāt al-wandāliyya 46 qabla al-mīlād -429 mīlādi : dirāsa taḥlīliyya ḥawla al-wāqi' al-siyāsī wa al-iqtiṣādī fī ẓill al-iḥtilāl al-rūmānī*, thèse de doctorat, Université de Batna, 2018.

Masrūr, 'Abbās. *al-Mar'a wa dawruhā al-ḥaḍārī fī al-muǧtama' al-iġrīqī fī al-fatra al-klasīkiyya : al-mar'a al-aṯīniyya wa-l-isbarṭiyya namūḏaǧan*, mémoire de magister, Université d'Alger, 2016.

Massūsī, Šahrazād. *al-Ġiṭāʾ al-nabatī li-saḥil ġarb al-Ǧazāʾir fī al-blaystūsīn al-aʿlā*, mémoire de magister, Université d'Alger, 2001.

Masʿī, Abd al-Ḥaqq. *al-Istīṭān al-iġrīqī fī ǧanūb Īṭāliyya wa Ṣiqiliyya bayna al-qarnayn al-ṯāmin wa al-sādis qabla al-mīlad*, mémoire de magister, Université d'Alger, 2008.

Masʿī, Abd al-Ḥaqq. *al-Muʾaṯṯirāt al-ḥaḍāriyya al-iġrīqiyya fī al-Maġrib al-qadīm min al-qarn al-sābiʿ qabla al-mīlād ilā al-qarn al-awwal mīladī*, thèse de doctorat, Université d'Alger, 2018.

Masʿūd ʿAbd al-Nāṣir, *al-Tawassuʿ al-rūmānī fī-bilād al-Maġrib al-qadīm wa-rudūd fī'l al-sukkān al-maḥaliyyīn ḫilāl ʿahd al-Usrat al-Anṭūniyya*, mémoire de magister, Université de Bechar, 2010.

Masʿūdī, Āsiyā. *al-Tabādul al-tiǧārī bayna al-Maġrib al-qadīm wa Īṭāliyā ḫilāla al-ʿahd al-imbrāṭūrī al-awwal qarn 1-3 lil-mīlād*, mémoire de magister, Université d'Alger, 1988.

Mattingly, D. *Imperialism, Power, and Identity. Experiencing the Roman Empire*, Princeton, Princeton University Press, 2013.

Mazari, K. « Archéologues au bord de la crise de nerf », dans *Pratiquer les sciences sociales au Maghreb*, ed. M. Al-Moubaker et F. Pouillon, Centre Jacques Berque, Casablanca, 2014.

Maʿrūf, Laṭīfa. *Dirāsa tafūnūmiyya li-l-mustawā al-aṯarī al-suflī li-l-mawqiʿ al-āšūlī, al-Rayh, Sīdī ʿAlī, Mustaġānim al-Ǧazāʾir*, mémoire de magister, Université d'Alger, 2012.

Maʿūšī, Samiyya. *Mūʾassassat al-maʿbad wa dawruhā fī ḥaḍārat Wādī al-Rāfidayn*, mémoire de magister, Université d'Alger, 2010.

Mercier, E. « La population indigène de l'Afrique sous la domination romaine vandale et byzantine », *Recueil de la société archéologique de Constantine*, vol. 30, 1896.

Merzoug, S. « A level prior to the Upper Capsian at Medjez II Algeria : Archaeozoological and taphonomical evidence combined with archaeological data », *Quaternary International*, vol. 320, 2014, 125-130.

Merzoug, S. *Comportements de subsistance des Ibéromaurusien d'après l'analyse archéo zoologique des mammifères des sites de Tamar Hat Taza 1, Algérie*, thèse de doctorat, Museum national d'histoire naturelle, Paris, 2005.

Mhannī, Maǧīd. *Maẓāhir al-diyāna al-rūmāniyya fī bilād al-Maġrib al-qadīm*, mémoire de magister, Université d'Alger, 2013.

Mhantal, Maqrūs Ǧahīda. *al-Taṭawwur al-ḥaḍārī bi-madīnat Qusanṭīna Kirta fī al-fatra al-qadīma*, thèse de doctorat, Université d'Alger, 2010.

Mhantal, Maqrūs Ǧahīda. *Minṭaqat ʿAyn al-Kabīra: dirāsa tārīḫiyya wa aṯariyya*, mémoire de magister, Université d'Alger, 1996.

Mnāṣar, Karīm. *Dawr al-masraḥ fī bilād al-Iġrīq*, mémoire de magister, Université d'Alger, 2008.

Mnāṣar, Karīm. *Naš'at al-masāriḥ wa al-mudarraǧāt al-rūmāniyya fī al-muqāṭa'a al-Afrīqiyya wa ta'ṯīrihā fī al-ḥayāt al-siyāsiyya wa al-iqtiṣādiyya wa al-iǧtima'iyya : al-qarn al-awwal –– al-ṯāliṯ al-mīladī*, thèse de doctorat, Université d'Alger, 2017.

Modéran, Y. « Mythe et histoire aux derniers temps de l'Afrique antique : à propos d'un texte d'Ibn Khaldûn », *Revue historique*, n. 618, 2001, 315-341.

Mohamedi, A., Benmansour, A., Amamra, A., Fentress, E. *Fouilles de Sétif 1977-1984*, Supplément 5, *Bulletin d'Archéologie Algérienne*, Alger, Agence Nationale d'Archéologie et de Protection des sites et Monuments Historiques, 1991.

Mokrenta, B. *L'Algérie antique Maurétanies Césarienne Sitifienne et Numidie à travers les sources arabes du Moyen-Age*, thèse de doctorat, Université Aix-en-Provence, 2005.

Muqaddam, Bint al-Nabī. *al-Usra fī bilād al-Maǧrib al-qadīm ḫilāl al-'ahd al-rūmānī al-imbrāṭūrī al-a'lā 27 qabla al-mīlād -284 al-mīlādī*, thèse de doctorat, Université d'Alger, 2013.

Muqaddam, Bint al-Nabī. *Siyāsat al-Rūmān tuǧāh qabā'il bilād al-Maǧrib al-qadīm ḫilāl al-'ahd al-imbrāṭūrī al-awwal*, mémoire de magister, Université d'Oran, 2004.

Mūkāḥ, Faziya. *al-'Imāra al-dīniyya al-masīḥiyya fī madīnat Tīmgād al-aṯariyya al-muǧamma' al-masīḥī al-musammā al-kātūlīkī wa al-muǧamma' al-masīḥī al-musammā al-dūnātī : dirāsa aṯariyya*, mémoire de magister, Université d'Alger, 2013.

Mūqrānī, Laylā. *al-Ta'mīr al-bašarī wa al-ḥayawānī li- bidāyat al-hūlūsīn al- sāḥil al- Ǧazā'ir al-'āṣima al-ǧarbī min ḫilāl dirāsat aṯār maǧārat al-Ṣaḥrā' al-kabīra*, mémoire de magister, Université d'Alger, 2016.

Mūqrānī, Nūriyya. *al-Maǧmū'at al-naqdiyya al-maḥfūẓa bi-mathaf Lambazis : dirāsa tārīḫiyya wa naqdiyya*, mémoire de magister, Université d'Alger, 2012.

Mūṣa'b, Yasmīna. *Ṭuruq tamwīn madīnat Tībāza bi-l-miyyāh fī al-fatra al-rūmāniyya*, mémoire de magister, Université d'Alger, 2014.

Muṣbāḥ, 'Ayša. *al-Iṣlāḥāt al- idāriyya wa al-'askariyya li-l-imbraṭūr Daqlidyanūs fī Afrīqiyya : 285-304*, mémoire de magister, Université d'Alger, 2013.

Mūwwās, Nūra. *al-Iṣlāḥāt fī al-imbrāṭūriyya al-rūmāniyya ḫilāl al-'aṣr al-imbrāṭuri al-ṯāanī : 284 m - 395m.*, thèse de doctorat, Université d'Alger, 2016.

M'allam, Muḥammad Fawzī. *al-Ḫarīṭa al-aṯariyya li-baladiyyat 'Ayn al-'Arbī wa'Ayn Maḫlūf ǧanūb Gālma*, mémoire de magister, Université d'Alger, 2008.

M'allam, Muḥammad Fawzī. *al-Munša'āt wa al-ma'ālim al-aṯariyya al-rīfiyya li-silsilat ǧabal Māwna wa ḍawāḥīha : ǧanūb Gālma*, thèse de doctorat, Université d'Alger, 2015.

M'amrī, Ḥasān. *Makka wa-'alāqatuhā ma'a šamāl wa ǧanūb šibh al-ǧazīra al-'arabiyya ḫilāl al-qarnayn 5 wa 6 mīlādī*, mémoire de magister, Université d'Alger, 2009.

Naṣāḥ, Ǧāliyya. *Maẓāhir al-tasliyya wa al-tarfīh fī muqaṭ'at Afrīqiyya al-rūmāniyya min muntaṣaf al-qarn 2 q m ilā al-qarn al-rābi' al-mīladī*, mémoire de magister, Université d'Alger, 2010.

Našnaš, Ḥamīda. *Riǧāl al-dīn al-maǧāriba fī ẓill al-ṣirā' al-dīnī al-masīḥī 284-430 mīlādī*, thèse de doctorat, Université d'Alger, 2017.

Našnaš, Ḥamīda. *Riǧāl al-dīn fī buldān al-Maġrib al-qadīm min ẓuhūr al-masīḥiyya fī nihāyat al-qarn al-ṯānī ilā ġāyat al-salām al-masīḥī sanat 313 li-l-mīlād : min ḫilāl Tartūlyānūs wa al-qiddīs Kībryānūs namūḏaǧan*, mémoire de magister, Université d'Alger, 2010.

Nāyar, Muḫtar. *al-Diyāna al-waṯaniyya fī bilād al-Maġrib al-qadīm aṯnā' al-iḥtilāl al-rūmānī al-ʿahd al-imbrāṭūrī al-aʿlā*, mémoire de magister, Université d'Oran, 2006.

Nāyar, Muḫtar. *al-Tiǧāra al-baḥriyya fī al-ḥawḍ al-ġarbī li-l-baḥr al-Abyaḍ al-mutawssiṭ fī al-ʿuṣūr al-qadīma min al-Fīnīqiyyīn ilā ʿahd al-iḥtilal al-rūmanī*, thèse de doctorat, Université d'Oran, 2019.

Naʿīmī, Samīr. *Dirāsa tīqaniyya wa faniyya li-mawqiʿay al-fann al-ṣaḫrī Afīf Ūǧ wa Tūrst bi Ǧanat : Tasīlī-Nāǧar*, mémoire de magister, Université d'Alger, 2014.

Nsīġawī, Wafiya. *Awḍāʿ Afrīqiyya al-Brūqunṣuliyya fī ẓill bidāyat al-iḥtilāl al-ʿaskarī al-rūmānī 27 q m-117m.*, mémoire de magister, Université de Constantine, 2004.

Nūr al-Dīn, Karīma. *Siyāsat Āl Barqa fī al-Ḥawḍ al-ġarbī li-l-mutawssiṭ : munḏu nihāyat al-ḥarb al-Būnīqiyya al-ūlā ilā wafāt Ḥannibaʿl 241-138 q.m.*, mémoire de magister, Université d'Alger, 2011.

Nuwwara, ʿAmmār. *al-Ḥarīṭa al-aṯariyya li-manṭiqat Mīla wa ḍawāḥīhā*, mémoire de magister, Université de Constantine, 2012.

Orfalli, M. *Inventaire des sculptures funéraires et votives de la Mauritanie césarienne*, thèse de doctorat, Aix-Marseille 1, 1989.

Oulebsir, N. *Les Usages du patrimoine. Monuments, musées et politique coloniale en Algérie 1830-1930*, Paris, Éditions de la Maison des sciences de l'homme, 2004.

Qadīm, al-Ṭayyib. *al-Dawr al-ḥaḍārī al-rūmānī fī Sūriyyā siyāsiyyan wa-iqtiṣādiyyan wa ṯaqāfiyyan : min 64 qabla al-mīlād ilā 394 mīlādi*, thèse de doctorat, Université d'Alger, 2018.

Qadīm, al-Ṭayyib. *al-Taġayyurāt al-iqtiṣādiyya fī Miṣr al-rūmāniyya : min nihāyat al-qarn al-awwal li-l-mīlād ilā al-qarn al-rābiʿ mīlādī*, mémoire de magister, Université d'Alger, 2012.

Qaffāf, Bašīr. *al-Ṣilāt al-ḥaḍāriyya bayna Miṣr wa-šibh al-ǧazīra al-ʿarabiyya munḏu qiyām al-dawla al-wusṭā al-firʿawniyya ilā ġāyat nihāyat al-dawla al-ḥadīṯa*, mémoire de magister, Université d'Alger, 2009.

Qandī, Nādiya. *al-Baqāyā al-ʿiẓmiya al-ḥayawāniyya li-fatrat al-blūstūsīn al-asfal li-mawqiʿ al-ḥarba Galta al-Zarqa-Siṭīf al-Mustawa A, dirāsa ṭafūnūmiyya wa arkyū-zūlūǧiyya*, mémoire de magister, Université d'Alger, 2012.

Qarrūǧ, ʿAbd al-Ḥafīẓ. *Dirāsa mūrfū-mitriyya li-l-ʿiẓām mawqiʿ San Rūš sābiqan ʿUyūn al-Turk- al-blaystūsan al-aʿlā al-maḥfūẓa fī al-matḥaf Aḥmad Zabāna bi-Wahrān*, mémoire de magister, Université d'Alger, 2012.

Qāsīm, Muḥammad. *al-Waḍʿiyya al-iǧtimāʿiyya wa-l-dīmūǧrafiyya li-ġarb Mūrīṭaniyya al-Qaysariyya min 42 ilā sanat 284m.*, mémoire de magister, Université d'Oran, 2015.

Qattāl, Salīḥa, Dūnyā Maryam. *Anṣāb madīnat Kwīkūl : ǧard wa dirāsa taḥlīliyya*, mémoire de magister, Université d'Alger, 2010.

Qaʿr al-Maṯrad, al-Saʿīd. *al-Zirāʿa fī bilād al-Maǧrib al-qadīm : malāmiḥ al-našʾa wa-al-taṯawwur ḥattā tadmīr Qarṯāǧa -146 qabla al-mīlād*, mémoire de magister, Université de Constantine, 2008.

Qbāylī, Kāhīna. *al- Ḥayāt al-iǧtimāʿiyya fī al-Maǧrib al-qadīm ḫilāl al-qarn al-rābiʿ wa al-ḫāmis fī ẓill al-iḥtilāl al-rūmānī : al-fiʾāt wa al-ṭabaqāt al-iǧtimāʿiyya*, thèse de doctorat, Université d'Alger, 2016.

Qbāylī, Kāhīna. *al-ʿAbīd fī bilād al-Maǧrib ḫilāl al-ʿahd al-rūmānī 146 q m-430m.*, mémoire de magister, Université d'Alger, 2006.

Qūrārī, Mbārka. *al-Silm al-rūmānī fī al-muqāṭ'a al-Afrīqiyyā fī ʿahd al-abāṭira al-awāʾil li-l-usra al-antūniyya*, mémoire de magister, Université d'Alger, 2012.

Qūʿīš, Šarīf. *Dawr al-baḥriyya al-fīnīqiyya fī rabṭ al-ʿalāqāt al-mubakkira bayn ḥawḍ al-šarqī li-l-baḥr al-abyaḍ al-mutawassiṭ wa ǧarbihi*, mémoire de magister, Université d'Oran, 2015.

Rābaḥ Laḥsan. *Madāfin ḥukkām al-Mūr wa al-Nūmīdiyyīn*, mémoire de magister, Université d'Alger, 1999.

Rabbī, Mṣasdaq. *al-Ǧuǧrāfiyya al-tārīḫiyya li-bilād al-Maǧrib al-qadīm min ḫilāl al-nuṣūṣ al-adabiyya al-iǧrīqiyya wa al-latīniyya : mudun al-mūrīṭanyatayn al-ṭanǧiyya wa al-qayṣariyya namūdaǧan*, mémoire de magister, Université d'Alger, 2010.

Rābḥī, Marwān. *al-Ṣināʿa al-ḥaǧariyya al-aldawāniyya li-mawqiʿ ʿAyn al-Ḥanaš*, mémoire de magister, Université d'Alger, 2006.

Rābḥī, Marwān. *al-Taʿmīr al-bašarī li-faǧr al-tārīḫ bi-l-Aṭlas al-Ṣaḥrāwī : minṭaqa al-Idrīsiyya namūdaǧan*, thèse de doctorat, Université d'Alger, 2012.

Raḥīm, Nūr al-Dīn. *al-Tiǧāra ʿinda al-fīnīqiyyīn 1200 q. m.-814 q. m.*, mémoire de magister, Université de Constantine, 2010.

Raḥmānī, Balqāsam. *al-Āṯār al-ḥaḍāriyya li-ʿalāqat al-Yaman bi-šamāl al-Ǧazīrat al-ʿArabiyya wa -Ifrīqiyyā qabla al-islām*, thèse de doctorat d'État, Université d'Alger, 2003.

Raḥmānī, Balqāsam. *ʿAlāqāt ǧanūb šibh al-Ǧazīra al-ʿarabiyya bi-šarq Ifrīqiyyā munḏu qiyām al-duwaylāt al-ʿarabiyya al-ǧanūbiyya ḥattā al-fatḥ al-islāmī*, mémoire de magister, Université d'Alger, 1993.

Ramḍān, Tasaʿdīt. *al-Iṣlāḥāt al-Sīfīriyya fī bilād al-Maǧrib al-qadīm 193-235 mīlādī*, mémoire de magister, Université d'Alger, 1990.

Ramḍānī, Umm Hānī. *Bīzanṭa wa šibh al-Ǧazīra al-ʿArabiyya min al-qarn al-ṯaliṯ mīlādī ilā al-qarn al-sādis mīlādī*, mémoire de magister, Université d'Alger, 2006.

Ramḍānī, Umm Hānī. *Šibh al-Ǧazīra al-ʿArabiyya wa al-qiwā al-qadīma min al-qarn al-rābiʿ qabla al-mīlād ilā al-qarn al-ṯāliṯ mīlādī*, thèse de doctorat, Université d'Alger, 2013.

Raqqād, Aḥmad. *al-Ta'addudiyya al-dīniyya fī šibhi al-Ǧazīra al-'Arabiyya bayna al-waṭaniyya wa al-tawḥīd : dirāsa taḥlīliyya wa muqārina*, mémoire de magister, Université d'Alger, 2011.

Rāšī, Naǧwa. *Niẓām al-dawla al-madīna fī al-šarq al-Adnā al-qadīm : Sūmar, Fīnīqiyya, al-Iǧrīq 3000-335q-m.*, thèse de doctorat, Université d'Alger, 2019.

Rāšī, Naǧwa. *Niẓām al-dawla al-madīna fī al-'Irāq al-qadīm : Sūmar kanamūdaǧ – 3000-2470 qabla al-mīlad*, mémoire de magister, Université d'Alger, 2014.

Remaoun, H. « L'intervention institutionnelle et son impact sur la pratique historiographique en Algérie : La politique d'Ecriture et de Réécriture de l'histoire, tendances et contre-tendances », *Insaniyat* 19-20, 2003, 7-40.

Rīǧī, Murād. *al-Tārīḫ al-'askarī li-Qarṭāǧa bi-Ṣiqiliyya bayna al-qarnayn al-sādis wa al-ṯāliṯ q. m.*, thèse de doctorat, Université d'Alger, 2017.

Rīǧī, Murād. *Ḥurūb Ṣiqiliyya bayna al-Qarṭāǧiyyīn wa al-Iǧrīq fī al-fatra bayn 580-265 q.m.*, mémoire de magister, Université d'Alger, 2011.

Riyyāš, Šarīf. *Masraḥ Tīmgād wa Ǧamīla : dirāsa waṣfiyya w taḥlīliyya*, mémoire de magister, Université d'Alger, 2009.

Rmīlī, Muṣṭafā. *al-Ma'ālim al-ǧanā'iziyya li-faǧr al-tārīḫ bi-minṭaqat Ašīr- Ǧabal al-Tīṭrī*, mémoire de magister, Université d'Alger, 2002.

Rmīlī, Muṣṭafā. *Dirāsa aṯariyya li-l- ma'ālim wa-l-ṭuqūs al-ǧanā'iziyya li- faǧr al-tārīḫ bi-minṭaqat al-Ḥudna*, thèse de doctorat, Université d'Alger, 2016.

Šabbaḥī, Mas'ūd. *Diyānat Miṣr wa bilād al-Rāfidayn al-qadīma, al-simāt al-ḫuṣṣūṣiyya wa al-muqārana imtidādan min fatra ma qābla al-usra ilā awāḫir al-alf al-ṯāliṯa q.m.*, mémoire de magister, Université de Constantin, 2001.

Šabbaḥī, Mas'ūd. *Ḥarakat Aḫnawn al-dīniyya 1367-1350 q.m : dirāsa taḥlīliyya*, doctorat, Université de Constantine, 2009.

Ṣaddīqī, 'Izz al-Dīn. *Dirāsa aṯariyya li- furūm Tīmgād wa marāfiqihi*, mémoire de magister, Université d'Alger, 2008.

Safrwan, Ḥasība. *Wāqi'iyat ṣūrat al-unṯa fī al-rasm al-ṣaḥrī li-minṭaqat Ṣaffār wa ḍawāḥīhā al-Tasīlī-Naǧar, al Ṣaḥrā' al-Wusṭā- al-Ǧazā'ir*, mémoire de magister, Université d'Alger, 2008.

Sāḥad, Ṭāriq 'Azīz. *al-Ma'ālim al-ǧanā'iziyya li-minṭaqat N'qāwus : maqbarat Sufyān- al-Ḥudna al-šarqiyya*, mémoire de magister, Université d'Alger, 1998.

Sāḥad, Ṭāriq 'Azīz. *al-Ta'mīr al-bašarī bi-bilād al-Maǧrib fī fatrat faǧr al-tārīḫ – namūḏaǧ al-ma'ālim al-ǧanā'iziyya bi-manaṭiqat al-Awrās : dirāsa aṯariyya mi'māriyya*, thèse de doctorat, Université d'Alger, 2009.

Saḥālī, Aḥmad. *Iṣlāḥāt Qusṭanṭīn al-awwal al-dīniyya wa al-siyāsiyya fī Urūbbā 306–337*, mémoire de magister, Université d'Alger, 2016.

Ṣaḥbī, Sūmiyya. *Ta'ṯīr al-diyāna 'alā al-ḥayāt al-iǧtimā'iyya wa-al-fikriyya fī Miṣr al-fir'awniyya*, mémoire de magister, ENS-Alger, 2005.

Sahed, T. « Contribution à l'étude de la nécropole protohistorique de Sefiane région de N'gaous », revue *Anthropo*, n. 21, 2010, 61-77.

Sāḥīr, Naṣīra. *al-Našāṭ al-zirāʿī wa al-ṣināʿī fī muqaṭaʿatay Mūrīṭaniyya al-Ṭanǧiyya wa Bītīka wa al-ḥaraka al-tiǧāriyya baynahumā ḥilal al-ʿahd al-imbraṭūrī al-rūmānī al-aʿlā*, thèse de doctorat, Université d'Alger, 2012.

Sāḥīr, Naṣīra. *Mūrīṭaniyya al-Tanǧiyya, baḥṯ ḥawla al-līmas wa muqāwamat al-Mūr*, mémoire de magister, Université d'Alger, 2001.

Sahli, M. Ch. *Décoloniser l'histoire. L'Algérie accuse le complot contre les peuples africains*, Édition ENAP, Alger, 1965.

Saḥnīn, Naǧiyya. *Al-diyāna fī al-Yaman al-qadīm min 1300 q. m. ʿalā qubayl ẓuhūr al-islām al-qarn 14 q.m–al-qarn 6m.*, mémoire de magister, Université d'Alger, 2008.

Saḥnīn, Naǧiyya. *Ṣirāʿ al-qiwā al-qadīma ʿala Filisṭīn wa aṯaruhu min 1000 sana qabla al-mīlad ilā qubayl ẓuhūr al-Islām 6 m.*, thèse de doctorat, Université d'Alger, 2017.

Sahnouni, M. *L'industrie sur galets du gisement villafranchien supérieur d'Ain Hanech, Sétif Algérie Orientale. Approche morpho-technologique*, doctorat de 3e cycle, Université Pierre et Marie Curie, Paris, 1985.

Sahnouni, M. *Archaeological investigations at the Lower Palaeolithic site of Ain Hanech Algeria and their behavioral implications*, Ph.D. thesis, University of Indiana, 1996.

Sahnouni, M., Ed. R. Pigeaud, trans., *Le Paléolithique en Afrique. L'histoire la plus longue*, Paris, Éditions Artcom' Errance, 2005.

Sahnouni, M. et al. « 1.9-million- and 2.4-million-year-old artifacts and stone tool–cut marked bones from Ain Boucherit, Algeria », *Science*, vol. 362, n. 6420, 2018, 1297-1301, https://science.sciencemag.org/content/362/6420/1297.

Saḥnūn, Ḥusīn. *Dirāsa tiknū-mūrfūlūǧiyya li-l-ṣināʿat al-ḥaǧariyya al-Ašūliyya li-mawqiʿ al-Māʾ al-Abyaḍ bi-minṭaqat Tibāssa*, mémoire de magister, Université d'Alger, 2009.

Saḥrāwī ʿAbd al-Qādir. *al-Taḥṣīnāt al-ʿaskaryīa al-rūmāniyya bi-Nūmīdiyā wa Mūrīṭāniyyā al-Qayṣariyya ḥilāl al-ʿahd al-imbrāṭūrī al-awwal*, mémoire de magister, Université d'Oran, 2002.

Sālam Muḥammad, Amḥammad. *al-Ḥayāt al-dīniyya wa al-fikriyya fī Qūrīnā aṯnāʾ al-ʿaṣr al-iġrīqī*, thèse de doctorat d'État, Université d'Alger, 2006.

Salama, P. « Vues nouvelles sur l'insurrection Maurétanienne dite 'de 253' : le dossier numismatique », dans *L'armée et des affaires militaires*, 113e Congrès national des Sociétés savants, Paris, 1991, 455-70.

Ṣamat, Samiya. *al-Maʿālim al-ʿumranī bi-madīnat Mīla fī al-ʿahd al-qadīm : dirāsa mūnūǧrafiyya*, mémoire de magister, Université de Constantine, 2014.

Samrīk, Fāraḥ. *Dirāsa mūrfū-tiknūlūǧiyya wa qiyāsiyya li-maǧmūʿa ḥaǧariyya ṣināʿiyya li-mawqiʿ al-Rayḥ bi-wilāyat Mustaġānam ġarb al-Ǧazāʾir*, mémoire de magister, Université d'Alger, 2008.

Ṣandūq, Sitī. *al-Ṯarwa al-ḥayawāniyya wa al-ġiṭāʾ al-nabātī fī al-Ǧazāʾir ḥilāl al-ʿuṣūr al-qadīma*, thèse de doctorat, Université d'Oran, 2015.

Ṣandūq, Sitī. *Dirāsa tanmīṭiyya li-l-maṣabīḥ al-maḥfūẓa bi al-matḥaf al-waṭanī Aḥmad Zabāna li-madīnat Wahrān*, mémoire de magister, Université d'Oran, 2007.

Šannān, Fatīḥa. *Dirāsa mūrfūtriyya li-ḥamiyyāt ḍibāʿ wa snūriyyāt maġārat Kīfān Balġūmarī al-Maġrib al-Aqṣā – al-blaystūsīn al-aʿlā wa muḥāwlat tašḫīṣ ʿalāqatuhā bi-bāqī al-maǧmūʿāt al-ʿaẓmiyya*, mémoire de magister, Université d'Alger, 2012.

Saoudi, Ch. Y. *Le Pliocène et Pléistocène inférieur et moyen du Sahel occidental d'Alger : Description matérielle*, Alger, 1989.

Saoudi, Ch. Y. *Les mammifères holocènes des gisements préhistoriques de Gueldaman-Akbou Bejaia Columnata Tiaret et Tin Hanakaten Djanet en Algérie*, thèse de doctorat, Dir. Cl. Guérin, Lyon 1, 1987.

Saoudi, N. *Pliocène et Pléistocène inférieur et moyen du Sahel occidental d'Alger*, thèse 3e cycle, Aix-Marseille 2, 1982.

Saqwān, Naǧla. *al-Taqāfa al-qarṭaǧiyya fī bilād al-Maġrib al-qadīm 814 q m-146 q m.*, mémoire de magister, Université d'Adrar, 2015.

Šāran, Šāfiya. *al-Našāṭ al-tiǧārī fī Nūmīdiyā wa Mūrīṭaniyā al-Qayṣariyya atnāʾ al-iḥtilāl al-rūmānī : al-ʿahd al-imbrāṭūrī al-awwal*, thèse de doctorat, Université d'Alger, 2001.

Šāran, Šāfiya. *Awḍāʿ al-Nūmīdiyyīn fī ẓill al-ḥukm al-rūmānī wa mawqifuhum minhu*, mémoire de magister, Université du Caire, 1983.

Sarḥān, Naǧat. *Baʿḍ min malāmiḥ al-ḥayāt al-yawmiyya fī al-muǧtamaʿ al-lībī al-qadīm*, mémoire de magister, Université de Constantine, 2005.

Ṣarī, Laṭīfa. *Dirāsa taḥlīliyya murfutiknūlūǧiyya wa tanmīṭiyya li-maǧmūʿat ṣināʿa ḥaǧariyya min al-waǧh al-taqāfī al-ībīrī al-Maġribī bi-Zammūrī al-Baḥrī al-sāḥil al-šarqī li-l-Ǧazāʾir*, mémoire de magister, Université d'Alger, 2002.

Sarqīn, Saʿdiyya. *Ahamiyyat Nūmīdiyā al-iqtṣādiyya bi-l-nisba li-Rūmā min sanat 64 q.m li-nihāyat al-qarn al-tānī*, mémoire de magister, Université de Constantine, 1983.

Sarrāǧ Rmīlī, Naǧma. *al-Kurūm wa-l-ḥamr fī al-Ǧazāʾir al-qadīma muʿṭayāt atariyya wa ikūnuġrāfiyya ḥawla zirāʿat al-kurūm wa taṣnīʿihā wa ʿibādat ilāh al-ʿinab wa-l-ḥamr fī al-marḥala al-qadīma*, mémoire de magister, Université d'Alger, 2009.

Sarrāǧ Rmīlī, Naǧma. *Fusayfisāʾ al-tayāzūs al-Diyūnīzī bi-Šamāl Afrīqiyyā al-rūmāniyya : dirāsa iknūǧrafia taḥlīliyya*, thèse de doctorat, Université d'Alger, 2018.

Ṣawšat, al-Madanī ʿAlī. *al-ʿAlāqāt al-lībiyya al-miṣriyya fī ẓill al-ṣirāʿ al-fārisī al-iġrīqī*, mémoire de magister, Université d'Oran, 2017.

Šāwšī, Ǧamīla. *Dirāsa atariyya li-l-mawāqiʿ al-sāḥiliyya mā bayn madīnatay Tāmanfūst wa Dallas fī al-ʿahd al-rūmānī*, mémoire de magister, Université d'Alger, 2015.

Sāyaḥ, Ḥalīma. *Filasṭīn bayna al-Yahūd wa al-qurā al-qadīma*, mémoire de magister, Université d'Alger, 2014.

Šaʿbān ʿAlī, Aḥmad. *al-Siyāsa al-ḫāriǧiyya li-mamlakatay Nūmīdiyā wa Murīṭāniyā fī ʿahd al-mamālik : min al-qarn al-tālit qabla al-mīlād ilā 40 li-l-mīlād*, mémoire de magister, Université d'Alger, 2010.

Saʿfa, Nuwwāra. *Dawr al-ʿabīd wa al-maʿtūqīn fī šibh Ǧazīra al-Iṭāliyya min fatra 55-54 q.m ilā fatra 193-211m.*, mémoire de magister, Université d'Alger, 2011.

Saʿīdī, Hmāma. *Dirāsa aṯariyya li-maʿālim madīnat Siṭīf*, mémoire de magister, Université d'Alger, 2012.

Saʿīdī, Salīm. *al-Qānūn wa al-aḥwāl al-šaḫṣiyya fī kull min al-ʿIrāq wa Miṣr 2050-332 q m.*, mémoire de magister, Université de Constantine, 2010.

Šaʿlāl, Balqāsim. *al-Anṣāb al-lībiyya ḏāt al-mašāhid al-ikūnūǧrafiyya fī al-Ǧazāʾir ǧard wa taḥlīl*, mémoire de magister, Université d'Alger, 2009.

Sī al-Hādī, Dahbiyya. *al-Mamālīk al-nūmīdiyya bayna Qarṭāǧa wa Rūmā min nihāyat al-qarn al-ṯālit q.m li-l-qarn al-awwal q.m : dirāsa siyāsiyya waʿaskariyya*, mémoire de magister, Université d'Alger, 2014.

Šībān, Salwa. *Dirāsa ǧiyūmūrfūlūǧiyya, mūrfūṭabāqiyyawa ṭabāqiyya li-takwīnāt al-zaman al-ǧyūlūǧī al-rābiʿ bi-l-minṭaqa al-mumtadda ʿalā al-šarīṭ al-sāḥilī bi-wilāyat Mustaǧānim : Šamāl al-Ǧazāʾir al-ǧarbiyya*, mémoire de magister, Université d'Alger, 2013.

Sīdī Muḥammad, Ībāh. *al-Maẓāhir al-ṯaqāfiyya wa-l-anmāṭ al-maʿīšiyya min ḫilal al-rusūmāt al-ṣaḫriyya bi-Tafdast al-Hūgār*, mémoire de magister, Université d'Alger, 2013.

Sīdī Ṣalaḥ, Yāsīn. *al-Tamṯīlāt al-ṣaḫriyya wa al-kitābāt al-muštaraka : dirāsa ikūnū-ibīǧrafiyya li-baʿḍ mawāqiʿ al-fann al-ṣaḫrī li-wilāyat Tīzī Wazzū. al-Ǧazāʾir*, mémoire de magister, Université d'Alger, 2012.

Šīkar, ʿAbd al-Nāṣir. *Maẓāhir ḥukm al-imbrāṭūr Mārkūs Yūlyūs Fīlībūs al-mullāqab bi-l-ʿArabī : min ḫilāl iṣdārātihi al-naqdiyya 244-249*, mémoire de magister, Université d'Alger, 2012.

Sīnī, Karīma. *al-Mawārid al-māʾiyya wa ṭuruq istiǧlāluhā fī bilād al-Maǧrib ḫilāl al-iḥtilāl al-rūmānī 146q.m-429m.*, mémoire de magister, Université d'Alger, 2011.

Šītwāḥ, Badr al-Dīn. *Taṭbīq qawāʿid al-arkyūzūlūǧiyya ʿalā al-īkūnūǧrāfiyya al-ḥayawāniyya li-mahaṭṭatay Aqnār wa Aǧrǧār : al-Ṣaḥrāʾ al-kubrā al-Ǧazāʾr*, mémoire de magister, Université d'Alger, 2016.

Slāḫǧa, Badr al-Dīn. *al-Maʿālim al-ǧanāʾiziyya li-fatrat faǧr al-tārīḫ bi manṭiqat Biskra "Ǧabal al-Zāb" : dirāsa aṯariyya wa miʿmāriyya*, mémoire de magister, Université d'Alger, 2012.

Šlālqa, al-Saʿīd. *al-Ḥayāt al-iqtiṣādiyya fī šibh al-Ǧazīra al-ʿArabiyya min al-qarn al-rābiʿ qabla al-mīlād ilā al-qarn al-sādis li-l-mīlād : al-zirāʿa wa al-tiǧāra anmūḏaǧan*, thèse de doctorat, Université d'Alger, 2015.

Šlālqa, al-Saʿīd. *al-Kitāba wa dawr al-kutub bi-Miṣr al-qadīma mā bayna 2100-1050 qabla al-mīlād*, mémoire de magister, Université d'Alger, 2010.

Slāṭniyya, ʿAbd al-Mālik. *Al-Mustawṭanāt al-finīqiyya – al-būniyya fī al-Ḥawḍ al-Ǧarbī li-l-baḥr al-mutawassiṭ*, thèse de doctorat, Université de Constantine, 2010.

Slīmānī, Aḥmad. *al-Ṣilāt al-qarṭāǧiyya al-lūbiyya min al-nawāḥī al-siyāsiyya wa al-iǧtimāʿiyya wa al-ḥaḍāriyya wa dalālāti al-nuqūš al-maktūba ; al-qarn 5 wabla al-mīlād 146 qabla al-mīlād*, Université d'Alger, 2011.

Slīmanī, Suʿād. *Dirāsa tārīḫiyya wa aṯariyya li-l-maʿālim al-qadīma al-mawǧūda bi-bilād al-Ḥuḍna*, thèse de doctorat, Université d'Alger, 2014.

Slīmanī, Suʿād. *Mūnšaʾāt al-ray al-qadīma fī minṭaqat al-Ḥuḍna*, mémoire de magister, Université d'Alger, 2005.

Šnītī, Muḥammad al-Bašīr. *Aḍwāʾ ʿalā tārīḫ al-Maġrib al-qadīm, buḥūṯ wa dirāsāt*, Dār al-Haqq, al-Ǧazāʾir, 2003.

Šnītī, Muḥammad al-Bašīr. *al-Awḍāʿ al-iqtiṣādiyya wa al-iǧtimāʿiyya fī al-Maġrib al-rūmānī wa dawruhā fī aḥdāṯ al-qarn al-rābiʿ al-mīlādī*, thèse de doctorat, Université d'Alger, 1981.

Šnītī, Muḥammad al-Bašīr. *Murīṭāniyyā al-Qayṣariyya : Dirāsa ḥawla al-līmas wa muqāwamat al-Mūr*, thèse de doctorat, Université d'Alger, 1992.

Šnītī, Muḥammad al-Bašīr. *Siyāsat al-rawmana fī bilād al-Maġrib min suqūṭ al-dawla al-Qarṭāǧiyya li-suqūṭ Mūrīṭaniyya 140q.m-40m.*, DEA, Université d'Alger, 1975.

Soltani, A. *Le monnayage préromain de l'Afrique du Nord dans la collection du Musée national des antiquités d'Alger*, thèse de doctorat, Toulouse 2, 2005.

Soufi, F. « En Algérie : l'histoire et sa pratique », dans *Savoirs historiques au Maghreb*, CRASC, Oran, 2006, 123-145.

Soufi, F. « Histoire et mémoire : l'historiographie coloniale », dans *Insaniyat*, n. 3, CRASC, Oran, 1997, 53-97.

Šrāyaf Saḥnūn. *Dirāsa mūnūgrāfiyya li-ḥawḍ al-Šalif fī al-ʿahd al-rūmānī 40-429m.*, mémoire de magister, Université d'Alger, 2011.

Šrīfī, Dāwiya. *Dirāsat al-ašḫāṣ al-mumāṯala fī al-nuqūš al-ṣaḥriyya bi-l-Aṭlas al-Ṣaḥrāwī*, mémoire de magister, Université d'Alger, 2012.

Šurfa, al-Ḥanāfī. *Katālūǧ maǧmūʿāt al-faḫāriyya al-maʿrāḍa bi-l-Matḥaf al-ʿumūmī al-waṭanī Siṭīf : Dirāsa tanmīṭiyya wa waṣfiyya*, mémoire de magister, Université d'Alger, 2014.

Ṭabīb, Nawāl. *Al-Ḥaqāʾiq al-tārīḫiyya min ḫilāl adab al-malāḥim ʿinda al-Iġrīq al-Ilyāda namūḏaǧan*, mémoire de magister, Université d'Alger, 2012.

Tafāt, Masīka. *Musāhamat al-Afāriqa fī taṭwīr al-adab al-lātīnī min nihāyat al-qarn al-awwal ilā al-qarn al-rābiʿ mīladī*, mémoire de magister, Université d'Alger, 2011.

Ṭahārī, Ḥadīǧa. *al-Niẓām al-ʿaskarī wa-aṯaruhu ʿalā al-niẓām al-siyāsī min Qūraš al-ṯānī ilā al-Iskandar al-Maqdūnī*, mémoire de magister, Université d'Alger, 2016.

Tamām, Nāṣir al-Dīn. *Muqāwamat sukkān Murīṭāniyyā al-sṭāyfiyya li-l-iḥtilāl al-rūmānī bayna al-qarnayn al-ṯālit wa al-rābiʿ mīlādi*, mémoire de magister, Université d'Alger, 2014.

Taoutaou, H. *Les arcs monumentaux romains d'Algérie : essai d'étude pour la sauvegarde et la mise en valeur*, thèse de doctorat, Paris 1, 2005.

Ṭarraḥ, Samīra. *Dirāsat al-maǧmūʿa al-ḥaǧariyya li-l-ʿaṣr al-ḥaǧarī al-qadīm al-mawǧūda fī al-tarassūbat al-ḥamrāʾ li-mawqiʿ Wādī Sīdī Mūsā, Muḥammad Sīdī Šrīf Wīlīs wa al-Ḥamrā bi-Mustaǧānim*, mémoire de magister, Université d'Alger, 2013.

Ṭāṭa, Farīd. *Madīnat Zana "Diana Veteranorum" Tārīḫuhā wa maʿālimuhā*, mémoire de magister, Université d'Alger, 2012.

Tauxier, H. « Études sur les migrations des tribus berbères avant l'islamisme », dans *Raf*. t. 6. 1862, 353-363.

Tāwrīrt, Muṣṭafā. *Al-ʿAlāqāt al-nūmīdiyya al-rūmāniyya bayna al-siyāda wa al-tabaʿiyya, 203 q, m-46 q, m.*, mémoire de magister, Université d'Alger, 2016.

Ṭayyib, Maryam. *al-Nuẓum al-iǧtimaʿiyya fī Nūmīdiyā : min maṭlaʿ al-qarn al-awwal mīladī ilā nihāyat al-qarn al-ṯāliṯ mīladī*, mémoire de magister, Université d'Adrar, 2014.

Tikyalīn, Muḥammad. *al-Iḥtilāl al-rūmānī li-Lībiya wa dawruhu fī al-taṭawwur al-iqtṣādī li-l-minṭaqa : bayna al-qarnayn 1q.m-4m. Sīrīnāyka wa Trībūlītaniya*, thèse de doctorat, Université d'Alger, 2015.

Tikyalīn, Muḥammad. *al-Taṭawwur al-siyāsī li-l-dawla al-Ḥīṭiyya bayna taʾṯīr al-ṣirāʿāt al-dāḫiliyya wa al-tawassuʿāt al-ḫāriǧiyya*, mémoire de magister, Université d'Alger, 2005.

Trīʿāt, al-Saʿīd. *al-Zirāʿa wa al-rayy ǧanūb al-Awrās fī al-fatra al-qadīma min ḫilāl al-muḫallafāt al-aṯariyya*, thèse de doctorat, Université d'Alger, 2017.

Trīʿāt, al-Saʿīd. *Munšaʾāt al-rayy al-qadīma bi-l-tuḫūm al-Awrāsiyya al-ǧanūbiyya*, mémoire de magister, Université d'Alger, 2009.

Ṭwāhrī, Ḥakīma. *Manāzil ḏāt al-fināʾayn bi-iqlīm Nūmīdiyā : dirāsa li-manāzil Tīmgād, Ǧamīla, ʿAnnūna wa Ḥamīsa*, mémoire de magister, Université d'Alger, 2011.

Ṭwāhrī, Ḥakīma. *Manāzil šamal Afrīqiyyā ḫilāl al-fatra al-rūmāniyya*, thèse de doctorat, Université d'Alger, 2015.

Ṭawīl, ʿImād. *Siyāsat Ǧūstīniyyan fī šamāl Afrīqiyyā 533m/565m.*, mémoire de magister, Université d'Alger, 2014.

Ūbrāham, Ǧawhar. *Dirāsat baʿḍ maḥaṭṭāt al-fann al-ṣaḫrī bi-nawāḥī Wilāyat Tamanrāst, manṭiqat al-Ahaggār, al-Ṣaḥrāʾ al-wusṭā, al-Ǧazāʾir*, mémoire de magister, Université d'Alger, 2007.

Ūkīl, Ṣabīḥa. *al-Dīn wa-l-fann fī Miṣr al-qadīma 3200-1085 q. m.*, mémoire de magister, Université d'Alger, 2009.

Ūkīl, Ṣabīḥa. *Ẓāhirat al-tawḥīd fī ḥaḍarat Wādī al-Rāfidayn bayn al-nuṣūṣ al-qadīma wa al-diyāna al-samāwiyya : daʿwat Nūḥ ʿalayhi al-salām anmūḏaǧan*, thèse de doctorat, Université d'Alger, 2017.

ʿUlmī, al-Rabīʿ. *al-Masīḥiyya fī Bilād al-Maǧrib al-qadīm wa dawruhā fī aḥdāṯ al-qarnayn al-rābiʿ wa al-ḫāmis al-mīlādiyayn*, thèse de doctorat, Université de Batna, 2016.

ʿŪlmī, al-Rabīʿ. *Makka wa dawruhā al-ṯaqāfī wa al-dīnī fī šibh al-Ǧazīra al-ʿarabiyya qabla al-Islām ḥilāl al-qarnayn al-ḥāmis wa al-sādis li-l-mīlād*, mémoire de magister, Université de Constantine, 2008.

Ūnīs, Mīlūd. *al-Zaḥrafa al-miʿmāriyya fī madīnat Tīmgād Tāmūqādī : Dirāsa waṣfiyya taḥlīliyya li-l-Tīǧān*, thèse de doctorat, Université d'Alger, 2014.

Ūnīs, Mīlūd. *Tīǧān madīnat Ǧamīla Kwīkūl : Dirāsa ḥawla al-zaḥrafat al-miʿmāriyya*, mémoire de magister, Université d'Alger, 2004.

Ūrfalli, Muḥammad Ḥayr. *Ḥaṣāʾiṣ al-ʿimāra al-fīnīqiyya fī-l-Maǧrib al-qadīm*, DEA, Université d'Alger, 1977.

Ūṣmanī, al-ʿAmrī. *Dirāsa tanmīṭiyya wa ikūnūǧrafiyya li-maǧmūwʿat al-anṣab al-maḥfūẓa fī matḥaf Siṭīf*, mémoire de magister, Université d'Alger, 2010.

Ūṣmanī, al-ʿAmrī. *Madīna Tibīlīs "Sallāwa ʿAnnūna" : dirāsa tārīḥiyya wa aṯariyya*, thèse de doctorat, Université d'Alger, 2016.

ʿUṯmān, Līnda. *al-ʿĀdāt al-dīniyya wa al-ṭuqūṣ wa al-šaʿāʾir al-ǧanāʾiziyya fī bilād al-Maǧrib al-qadīm fī-l-fatra al-lībiyya al-būniyya*, mémoire de magister, Université d'Alger 2, 2014.

Ūyaḥyā, Saʿīda. *al-Diyāna al-masīḥiyya fī bilād al-Maǧrib al-qadīm min nihāyat al-qarn al-ṯānī mīladī ilā bidāyat al-qarn al-ḥāmis al-mīladī 180-411m : Qarṭāǧ wa Nūmīdiya namūdaǧan*, thèse de doctorat, Université d'Alger, 2017.

Ūyaḥyā, Saʿīda. *Ṣilāt al-lībiyyīn bi-Miṣr mundu fatrāt mā qabla al-ūsrāt li-nihāyat al-ḥukm al-lībī fī Miṣr*, mémoire de magister, Université d'Alger, 2003.

Ūzānī, Farīda. *al-Taǧdiyya ʿinda insān al-ʿaṣr al-ḥaǧarī al-qadīm al-mutaʾaḥḥir wa al-ʿaṣr al-ḥaǧarī al-ḥadīṯ fī al-Maǧrib, al-Ǧazāʾir, Tūnis : dirāsa fāḥiṣat al-asnān wa al-amrāḍ al-siniyya*, mémoire de magister, Université d'Alger, 2008.

Ūʿkwār, ʿAbd al-Ḥakīm. *al-iqlīm al-idārī wa al-aṯarī li-baladiyya rūmāniyya : dirāsa ǧūǧrāfiyya wa aṯariyya li-madīnat Ṭubna*, mémoire de magister, Université d'Alger, 2010.

Vatin, J.C. *L'Algérie politique. Histoire et société*, Paris, Presse de la Fondation Nationale des Sciences Politiques, 1974.

Vatin, J.C. « Science historique et conscience historiographique de l'Algérie coloniale, I. 1840-1962 », *Annuaire de l'Afrique du Nord*, 1979, vol. 18, 1.

Wāʾil, Amḥammad. *Inʿikās marḥalat al-munāḥ al-amṯal ʿalā ṯaqāfat al-muǧtamʿāt fī al-Ṣaḥrāʾ al-wusṭā 7000 qabla al-mīlād ilā ǧāyat 2500 qabla al-mīlād*, mémoire de magister, Université d'Oran 1, 2014.

Wahab, N.A. *Corpus des mosaïques d'Hippone Algérie sur base topographique*, thèse de doctorat, Paris 4, 2005.

Wālī, Fūziyya. *Dirāsa tanmīṭiyya li-l-maṣābīḥ al-waṭaniyya al-maḥfūẓa bi-matḥaf Tīmgād*, mémoire de magister, Université d'Alger, 2009.

Yafṣaḥ, Nādiya. *Ālihat al-ḥiṣb al-būniyya al-nūmīdiyya fī Šamāl Afrīqiyyā*, mémoire de magister, Université d'Alger, 2004.

Yamùūn, 'Ammār. *al-Tadwīn fī bilād al-rāfidayn al-qadīma : 400 q.m. 626 q.m. maktabat Nīnwā anmūḏağan*, mémoire de magister, Université d'Alger, 2016.

Yatġan, Ğamāl. *Dirāsa tiknūmūrfūlūğiyya li-mağmūʿa ṣināʿiyya ḥağariyya li-l-wağh al-ṯaqāfī al-ʿAtīrī, li-l-mawqiʿ al-šaʿaybiyya al-Kaḥla bi-wilāyat Mustaġānam al-sāḥil al-ġarbi al-Ğazāʾir*, mémoire de magister, Université d'Alger, 2012.

Zaġbīb, Ḥasīna. *al-Ḥurūb al-ahliyya fī Rūmā wa aṯaruhā ʿalā bilād al-Maġrib : 88-31qabla al-mīlād*, mémoire de magister, Université d'Alger, 2012.

Zammūšī, Anwar Mūḥammad Ṣāliḥ. *Malāmiḥ al-taʾṯīrāt al-dīniyya al-miṣriyya ladā šuʿūb al-ğiwār al-ğuġrāfī: al-Lībiyīn wa-al-Fīnīqiyn namūḏağan 3200 qabla al-mīlād -865 al-mīlādī*, mémoire de magister, Université d'Alger, 2008.

Zarwāl, Zakiyya. *al-Ramziyya al-waṭaniyya fī iqlīm Nūmīdiyā fī al-fatra al-qadīma*, thèse de doctorat, Université d'Alger, 2017.

Zarwāl, Zakiyya. *Katalūğ kanz naqdī li-madīnat Arīs maḥfūẓ bi-l-matḥaf al-waṭanī li-l-āṯār al-qadīma : Dirāsa naẓariyya wa ikūnūğrafiyya*, mémoire de magister, Université d'Alger, 2011.

Zaʿbāṭ, Muṣṭafā. *al-Ḥarīṭa al-aṯariyya li-baladiyyatay Wād al-Aṯmaniyya wa ʿAyn al-Mlūk, Mīla*, mémoire de magister, Université d'Alger, 2011.

Zidane, M. *Djemila et Sétif: l'urbanisme compare de deux villes romaines d'Afrique du nord*, thèse de doctorat, Paris-Sorbonne, 2002.

Zinai, K. *Le décor des thermes dans l'Algérie antique*, thèse de doctorat, Paris I, 2014.

Zrārqa, Mūrad. *al-Maʿālim al-ğanāʾiziyya al-mīğālītiyya wa šibh al-mīğalītiyya li-minṭaqat al-Burma wa Ğabal al-Farṭas ğanūb Qasanṭīna*, mémoire de magister, Université d'Alger, 2006.

Zrārqa, Mūrad. *al-Maʿālim al-ğanāʾiziyya wa-l-ḥayāt al-sakaniyya li-ḥawḍ Būmrzūğ fī bidāyat al-ʿuṣūr al-tārīḥiyya*, thèse de doctorat, Université d'Alger, 2013.

6

Receptions of Classical Antiquity in Egypt and the Arab World: Parallel Narratives, Invisible Corpora and a Troubled Archive

Usama Gad

1　Introduction

In recent decades the origin of the historical entanglements between Greek, Latin and Arabic has enjoyed considerable scholarly attention. It is in this context that the study of the classical heritage in Islam and the translation movements from Medieval Greek into Arabic and again from Arabic into Medieval Latin has gained a good deal of interest in Western academia, and in the Arab world.[1] Nonetheless an "obsession with origins" and foundations, visible on both sides of the globe, is still regrettably present and has been rightly criticised by a growing number of scholars.[2] That is why modern narratives, receptions and trajectories of both classical traditions and classical antiquity, especially in connection with colonialism and empire, have become a focus of study in the fields of Classics and Middle Eastern studies.[3] In Classical Studies, scholars are now attempting to go beyond the traditional chronological confines of the field by treating, for example, the Latin language, literature and tradition in its entirety from its origin until its demise around 1800 CE.[4] Nevertheless, within

---

1　See most recently Dimitri Gutas, *Greek Thought* with bibliography. A short overview with bibliography is Uwe Vagelpohl, *Translation Literature*.

2　See Garth Fowden, *Before and After Muhammad* 4, and bibliography. Garth Fowden is one of the scholars who has most recently criticized the selectivity of the historians of both camps. The critique appears in the first pages of his recently published so-called programmatic book *Before and After Muhammad* (BAM). BAM is the name used by Garth Fowden himself when he talks to the author of this contribution about the ongoing Arabic translation of this book. A Turkish translation is already published. The intellectual, geographical and chronological range, visible from the subtitle "The First Millennium Refocused", of this book is telling *per se*, let alone the idea(s) behind the book and its content.

3　See e.g. Lorna Hardwick and Christopher Stray, *A Companion to Classical Receptions* and Lorna Hardwick, and Stephen Harrison, *Classics in the Modern World*.

4　See Koenig, *Latin and Arabic* as well as De Gussem et al., Editorial Note, iv–v. The note appeared in the recently published (June 2019) first volume of *The Journal of Latin Cosmopolitanism and European Literatures* (JOLCEL). Their justification of the journal's wide

these frames of both Classics and Middle Eastern Studies, modern *academic* and *official* narratives, corpora, and archives of classical antiquity in twentieth century Egypt and the wider Arab world remain largely unknown or, at best, marginalized.[5]

I do not intend here to write a comprehensive study of this under-researched and complex topic. Rather, I am presenting an introduction to the history of classical studies in the Arab world based in part on my experiences and observations as a scholar of Classics and papyrology in Egypt. Franz Rosenthal's statement in the first paragraph of the English preface to his original German anthology of the classical (Greco-Roman) heritage in Islam is – *mutatis mutandis* – true about this history and the vignettes which I present here: "The heritage of classical antiquity affected Islam to its core by virtue of the influence it had on religious disciplines, theology, mysticism and law. It did not leave Arabic philology, grammar, literary studies and the art of poesy altogether untouched. The following pages scarcely refer to any of these intellectual and literary activities. They are confined to the direct and obvious links between the two cultures, which mostly concern other branches of learning. Nevertheless, despite this limitation, the material that merits consideration remains very extensive. Hence, the choice of texts offered here is, in a way, arbitrary. I do not wish to claim – as many compilers of anthologies tend to do – that the texts chosen contain all that is best and most important on the

---

scope and comprehensive coverage of Latin is extremely intriguing "according to one conservative estimate by Jürgen Leonhardt (University of Tübingen), classical Latin texts, including all inscriptions, barely make up for 0.001% of all of extant Latinity – with 80% of that 0.001% consisting of late antique texts. However, instead of focusing on one particular historical period, JOLCEL will tackle the entire Latin tradition from antiquity to the early 1800s, when Latin's status as a truly living language of literary creation and education was nearing the end of its swan song.".

5   But see most recently Jennifer Baird and Zena Kamash, Remembering Roman Syria, and Sarah C. Humphreys and Rudolf G. Wagner, *Modernity's Classics*. It is to be noted that Ahmad Etman [Aḥmad ʿUthmān (1945–2013)], was the most active scholar in highlighting many aspects of the classical receptions in modern Arabic literature. He contributed to Lorna Hardwick and Christopher Stray, *A Companion to Classical Receptions*, see the bibliography of this chapter for more details about his contribution. Yet his premature death deprived us of his insights regarding "The impact of Classics in Egypt", a theme he presented in the 2010 conference held in London at the Open University, see Lorna Hardwick, and Stephen Harrison, *Classics in the Modern World* xxix–xxvii. According to Hardwick, Etman "… had extensive interests in the comparative histories of classical texts, both within antiquity and subsequently. He was an international authority on the history of classical scholarship in Egypt and on the role of the transmission of Greek texts through Latin and Arabic translations. In recent years, he contributed extensively on those topics to conferences in the UK and other western European countries", see Lorna Hardwick, In Memoriam 175.

subject. By using other passages, it would be quite feasible to provide a selection equal in scope and similar in context. However, I hope I have selected what is relevant and typical. If not superior to other, possible anthologies, this one should at any rate be of equal merit."[6]

2   Previous Overviews of the Topic

An Arabic introduction to the academic field of classical studies in the form of a narrative of the philological-historical scholarship of classical antiquity in which the concept, purpose, scope and history of classical scholarship are explored and presented, either in minute details or briefly, is entirely lacking.[7] Nevertheless, one could consider Ṭāhā Ḥusayn's monumental book *Mustaqbal al-Thaqāfa fī Miṣr* [The Future of Culture in Egypt], published in Cairo in 1937, as *the* Arabic introduction to Classical studies.[8] Despite the book's title, which only mentions culture, it is in fact a complete manifesto of Ḥusayn's opinions about a wide array of topics that are still of great importance to Egyptians and Arabs. Among many interconnected topics, he talked about modernity, heritage, culture, civilization and education. The Western Classical tradition was one of these topics. The most relevant parts about classical studies in Egypt are pages 18–51 and 161–175.[9] The former section (pp. 18–51) deals with the relationship, relevance and importance of the classical languages (Latin and Greek), cultures and civilization to Egypt. Ḥusayn dedicated the latter section (pp. 161–175) to the question of how Greek and Latin should fit into language courses and/or curricula of schools and the issue of education in Egypt after its nominal independence from the United Kingdom in accordance

---

6 Rosenthal, *The Classical Heritage* xv. Cf. the German original Rosenthal, *Das Fortleben der Antike* 5. The Arabic translation, done by the late Abdallah Hassan el-Mosallamy ['Abdallāh Ḥasan Al-Musallamī] and published in Cairo in 1993, is out of print and known to me only by title; Rosenthal, *Al-Turāth al-Qadīm*.

7 Eurocentric narratives of Western scholarship, ranging from the scholars of the Ptolemaic library of Alexandria to the present-day, are facing increasing critique and are slowly falling out of fashion in serious academic circles of Classics. Nevertheless such diachronical explorations and geographical expeditions are still available in printed books and in the wider academic and public cultures, cf. e.g. the first words about the concept and history of classical philology in Gerhard Jäger, *Einführung* 11–12 and 16–17, Nigel Wilson, *Griechische Philogie im Altertum* and John Edwin Sandys, *Short History*.

8 Ḥusayn, *Mustaqbal*. The book used here is the Arabic original, but see also the English translation by S. Glazer of 1954.

9 Page references are for the Arabic edition of 1996.

with the articles of the Anglo-Egyptian Treaty of 1936.[10] The topic of education in general was, and still is to a large degree, hotly debated among Egyptians. In the preface of his seminal book, Husayn makes it clear that he wrote or dictated the book verbatim in response to two interrelated incidents. The first was a national incident and the second a professional one. The national incident caused many discussions among Egyptian university students who directed their questions to Ṭāhā Ḥusayn, the first Egyptian lecturer of Classics in an environment of predominantly Western scholars and professors. The questions were mainly about Egypt's future after its independence following the above-mentioned Anglo-Egyptian Treaty of 1936. The professional stimulus was Ḥusayn's participation in two consecutive international conferences in Paris about culture and higher education. In the first conference, he represented the Ministry of Education and, in the second, he represented the Egyptian University. Instead of reporting to the ministry and/or the university, and in order to clarify his ideas and elaborate more about his answers to enthusiastic Egyptian students, he decided to write or dictate his thoughts in what became an epoch-marking book. It was published just one year after the conclusion of the Anglo-Egyptian Treaty of 1936. This book had a great influence on almost all Egyptian academic departments concerned with the study of Egyptian antiquity and the Arabic-Islamic Middle Ages.[11]

The importance of this work for our study stems not only from the fact that Ḥusayn himself was appointed in the first place as a lecturer of Greco-Roman History and then of Arabic language and literature, but also from the importance of the historical moment *per se*. Britain and the other European powers were competing with one another for domination of Egyptian educational, archaeological and cultural policies both in the nascent academia and beyond. It is therefore extremely hard to understand what Ḥusayn talks about in this book without knowing the historical context and milieu surrounding the related incidents. Appreciating Ḥusayn's introduction to classical studies requires some knowledge of modern Egyptian history under the British occupation. Donald Malcom Reid's article on "Cromer and the Classics" and his history of Cairo University are important in this regard.[12] Reid has also written two important studies on Egyptian identity in relation to archaeology, in which Greek and Roman heritage is also included.[13]

---

10   The treaty gave Egypt only nominal independence; hence it was unpopular.
11   See Ḥusayn, *Mustaqbal* 11–13.
12   Reid, Cromer and the Classics; Idem, *Cairo University*.
13   Reid, *Whose Pharaoh's?* and *Contesting Antiquity*, especially 229–259.

Other publications have dealt with the more contemporary history of Classical and Ancient Studies in Egypt and the wider Arab world. Ra'ūf 'Abbās' autobiography gives a good insight into the careers of historians and the development of academic departments (including Greco-Roman Studies) after the British left Egypt.[14] For an internal history of classical studies in Egypt one should consult the synoptic and panoramic overview of classical scholarship and classicists in Egypt over the hundred years from 1908 to 2008, written by the two most senior and insightful of Egyptian classicists: Aḥmad 'Uthmān [Ahmad Etman] and Muḥammad Ḥamdī Ibrāhīm.[15] In a consecutive series of studies, Peter Pormann has described and analysed many of the entanglements of Classics, the nineteenth century Arabic cultural awakening (*Al-Nahḍa*), Islam, Extremism, and Modernity.[16] In German, there is Michael Kreutz's book about Arabic Humanism.[17] The most important quantitative study of Arabic scholarly output in the field of classical studies is the unpublished MA thesis of Sāmiya Al-Kāfurī from 2004.[18] Al-Kāfurī's study was submitted to Cairo University's Department of Libraries, Information and Documents. Aḥmad 'Uthmān (1945–2013) was the external supervisor of this impressive and unique study of modern Egyptian knowledge production in Classics to the end of the last millennium. In addition to the fact that the thesis is a quantitative study done by an outsider, hence without analysis of the corpus, its main shortcoming is its focus on Egyptian productions, excluding any contributions to the field from other Arab countries. Nevertheless, it is an extremely informative work. Al-Kāfurī has been able to gather more than 1100 titles produced by 208 Egyptian classicists between 1925 and 2000. She made a list of all these titles arranged according to authors' first names, which is typical in Arabic, in the very beginning of her study (pp. 1–101).[19]

---

14   'Abbās, *Mashaynāhā*.

15   Etman ['Uthmān], Translation in the Intersections of Traditions and Ibrāhim, Mi'at 'Ām [One Hundred Years].

16   Peter Pormann, Cultural Awakening (Nahḍa), Classics and Islam, The Continuing Tradition and Classical Scholarship and Arab Modernity.

17   Kreutz, *Arabischer Humanismus*.

18   Al-Kāfurī, *Al-Intāj*.

19   Al-Kāfurī's list should be the starting-point in building a state-of-the-art relational database of Arab knowledge production in Classics. A first step would be updating whatever is missing (especially from Arab countries other than Egypt) from 1925 to 2000, adding the titles that appeared between 1918 and 1925 and those new titles that have been recently published between 2000 and 2018. It is a daunting and time-consuming activity, but a necessary one.

3   **The Chronological and Theoretical Frameworks of the Current
        Study and the Structure of the Explored Narratives, Corpora
        and the Troubled Archive**

I have decided to approach this topic using two different chronological and theoretical frameworks. We will begin with the chronological framework of this study. Arab scholars and intellectuals, mostly but not exclusively Egyptians, produced during the last one hundred years (1918–2018) an impressive body of knowledge about Greek and Roman classical antiquity. The corpora under survey here, the archives explored, and the narratives analyzed are mainly printed.[20] The language they used to produce these materials was neither the classical Arabic of the seventh century CE nor one of the medieval or modern Arabic vernaculars, but rather a standardized modern version called Modern Standard Arabic (MSA).[21] A bibliometric study, conducted fifteen years ago, has been able to record a solely Egyptian academic corpus of more than one thousand works on Greco-Roman Civilization printed from 1925 to 2000.[22] Adding another twenty-five years to this corpus to accommodate all the Arabic printed materials published in the long twentieth century from 1918 to 2018 and expanding the survey to include not just Egypt but rather the entire Arab world could double, if not triple, this corpus. The supplementary audio, visual, archival and other related materials, which have hardly been included in this first bibliographic survey, could bring the total number of records to several thousand. Nevertheless, the bulk of this body of knowledge, which is mostly

---

20   The archive is supplemented by audio, visual and archival material as appropriate. But, due to the nature of this material, it cannot be incorporated here. It is available on my website "Classics in Arabic".

21   Since 1973, Modern Standard Arabic has been an official language of the UN and its organs. The visibility of Arabic in commerce and modern politics outweighs its visibility in the academic and cultural spheres save for specialists. It is the official language of 27 states across the Middle East and North Africa with more than 420 million inhabitants. Standard Arabic is the language learned in school while local colloquial Arabic dialects are spoken at home and in daily life. Arabic speakers usually mix varying amounts of standard and colloquial Arabic in their speech depending on context. The Egyptian dialect of Arabic is well-understood across the Arab world due to the ground-breaking enterprise of the Egyptian visual media, especially comedy and satire. The written register of Arabic not only reflects all these modern realities, but also the complexities of Egypt's history and past, including the written culture. The fussy labels "Egyptian-Arabic" or simply "Arabic" obscure these facts, relevant to my study. For more details about these phenomena entangling linguistics, history and politics of Arabic see Kamusella, The Arabic Language, and for Egypt see David Wilmsen and Manfred Woidich, Egypt.

22   Al-Kāfurī, *Al-Intāj*.

academic in nature, remains unknown and hence invisible for outsiders and paradoxically enough for many insiders too.

It is true that an insider's resistance to the Western views of the region, expressed in academic publications, does actually exist. Yet this academic resistance is of course not uniform and had, and still has, many varying degrees of intensity. These degrees depend on the historical circumstance as well as the personal experience of every individual scholar in the Arab academic world. In an age in which western publications dominate the print culture in the field, one would expect that even insiders would submit to the grand European narrative of history to the degree that the Arab scholars and students of antiquity themselves would neglect an Arabic publication in favor of a European one. This is a complex scientific phenomenon that needs to be revisited again, but for the moment, one would not be surprised to see that such marginalization of the Arabic publications on the ancient world extends to Arab scholarship itself. In her bibliometric study about Egyptian scholarship in Classics, Al-Kāfurī has done a citation analysis on the titles she assembled. The results show an imbalance or bias against Arabic publications in favor of Western publications that can be observed even in scientific publications produced in Arabic. Such internal attitudes towards Arabic scholarship in classical studies are of course historical. They are connected to and no doubt feed upon external attitudes to the language and culture.[23] This attitude will likely persist as long as no comprehensive list of publications in Arabic in this field exists. The chart below illustrates this bias/imbalance and submission to European publishing power.[24]

In order to remedy this problem, I am trying to compile, revise and update on a regular basis a comprehensive catalogue of Arabic scholarly publications on all aspects of Greco-Roman studies. Yet this catalogue remains, unfortunately, far from complete. The task of compiling a bibliography of dissertations, monographs and journal articles written in Arabic and published in Arabic-speaking countries in the field of Classical studies, with transliterated titles and short abstracts for each recorded publication, is a daunting and time-consuming activity. The advent of digital culture and online catalogues of libraries, academic and cultural institutions has brought much more material to light and doubled the challenge. The process of assembling this corpus has proved to be an activity that goes beyond the limited time and financial resources of an academic who is overwhelmed with teaching and administrative activities

---

23   See Alastair Hamilton, Arabic Studies 166.

24   Or subjection to the "print-capitalism" as Benedict Anderson describes it, see Anderson, *Imagined Communities* 70.

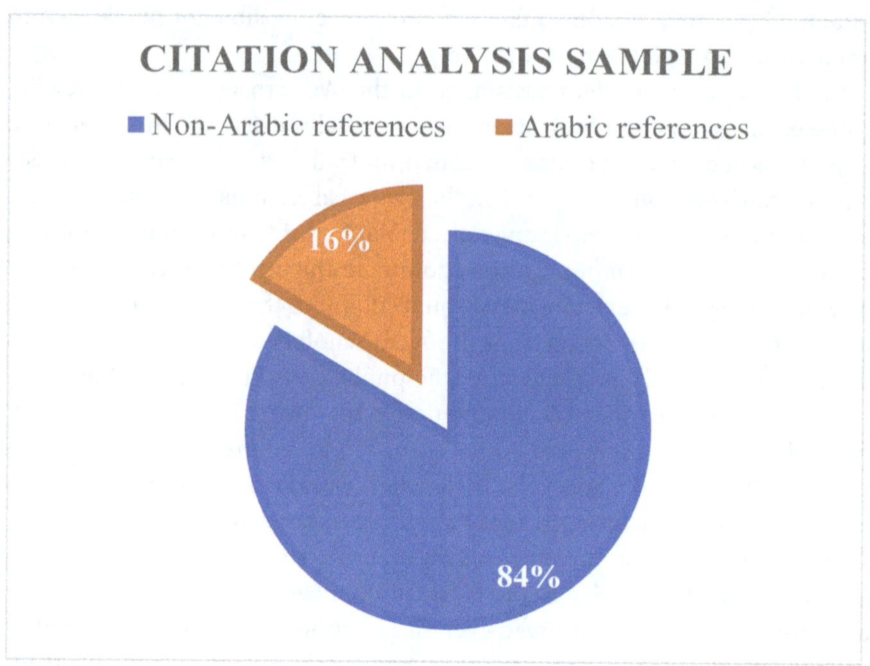

FIGURE 6.1   Citation analysis

in a post-colonial country striving to (re)build its academic, archaeological and cultural capacity, thus it remains a work in progress.

Nonetheless, such a mental exercise has been over the past years a rewarding activity to me, my students, and the readers of my academic website "Classics in Arabic".[25] The most important conclusion I learned was that Egyptian and Arab contributions to classical studies, along with the narratives and corpora they produced, remain largely an invisible and a troubled archive. The need to make them accessible to a specialist and general readership has never been more urgent and compelling than today in a global age in which digital culture is challenging the traditional and centuries-old concepts of print culture.[26]

25   Usama Gad, Classics in Arabic (2019). Classicsinarabic.blogspot.com. Retrieved 20 August 2019, from http://classicsinarabic.blogspot.com/.

26   The most important period of the print culture coincides with the high days of nationalism in Europe. For a detailed account see Anderson, *Imagined Communities* 67–82.

4   What Is the Aim of This Chapter and Who Is the Intended Audience?

The main aim of this chapter, as stated in the beginning, is not to provide a complete history of Egyptian and Arab scholarship in the field of classical studies in the period from 1908 to 2018. It is rather an insider's account, consisting mainly of vignettes, and not a complete narrative. Instead of narrating, the author presents to the reader a small range of the recurring topics and questions that have arisen in the classroom and in academic discussions during his career as a student, teacher, and researcher in the fields of Classics and papyrology in Egypt. Not infrequently, at the end of these events, the author has found himself in complete perplexity. The standard answers provided by the author, to himself, to his students and to the public were in many cases too Eurocentric, anachronistic, and too traditional to provide any real change on the ground. The difficult questions that started at the level of transferring European knowledge about the Classics into Arabic has never ended at the mere act of translating labels, concepts, definitions and aims to an audience with a collective cultural, linguistic, ethnic and religious memory and identity that is neither European nor Western. It is equally important to state here as well that the views and selected bibliography provided are not comprehensive. Additions, corrections or suggestions to this study are encouraged and extremely welcome.

The main audience of this paper is the European or Western reader to whom Greek and Latin are Classics. I hope that this presentation is provocative enough to stimulate further research and analysis of these parallel narratives and invisible corpora of Arabic classical scholarship.

5   Theoretical Frameworks of the Study

5.1   *Classical Studies between Europe, Egypt and the Middle East*

As long as the study of the Greek and Roman literature, culture and civilization is seen as a Western cultural enterprise – rather than an academic one – there will be no place for non-Western voices or perspectives in this field of study. It is true that many of the sources, archives, materials and modern intellectual capitals of Classical studies lie north of the Mediterranean Sea. Some of the countries that claim to be the legitimate heirs to the culture and civilization of the Greeks and Romans, such as Britain and Germany, were historically located at the margins of the Classical World, while others, like the

United States, obviously had no Greco-Roman presence at all. Even the core regions of Greco-Roman civilization, such as modern Italy and Greece, have undergone many profound cultural, linguistic and historical transformations that place the modern inhabitants of those countries at a great remove from the world of Classical Antiquity. Rome, Athens, Constantinople, Antioch and Alexandria, if we limit ourselves to the most important capitals and religious and cultural centers of the Roman Empire, are today located in modern nation-states whose inhabitants' psychological and intellectual attachments to and views of the Greeks and Romans are, in the best cases, highly tenuous.

Modern day popular religious and cultural orientations, even in Italy and Greece, are far removed from the popular and private manners and customs of the Greeks and Romans in the classical period. Nevertheless, the traditional official narratives of the European states mentioned above ascribe great cultural and national values to the languages and civilization of the Greeks and Romans. The canonized literature, culture and history of the Greeks and Romans, distant and foreign as they are, remain an integral part of the Western canon of Classics. This *per se* is not a problem, but the idea of appropriating this canon as mainly or exclusively Western and/or European is problematic. Many countries in the Middle East and North Africa have at least an equally valid claim to this canon. In Egypt, for example, the physical presence of the Greeks and Romans spanned more than a millennium. This is in addition to the profound influence of the Greco-Roman intellectual heritage in medieval Arabic-Islamic culture and on Egyptian modernity, for Egypt has a tradition of academic classical studies that is over one hundred years old.

This paper seeks to explore the history of the academic enterprise of Classics in modern Egypt, during what will be referred to as the long twentieth century of Egypt from 1918 until 2018. The exploration starts when the First World War ended and Ṭāhā Ḥusayn was appointed in the Egyptian University as the first Egyptian lecturer of Greek and Roman history and civilization. The year 2018 is used as the vantage point for a whole century of Egyptian classical scholarship for academic as well as cultural and political reasons that define the relationships between Egypt, Europe and Middle East.

5.2   *European Classics in Arabic Attire, or: What's in a Name?*
Classical studies is a modern academic discipline.[27] In its current make-up it is a culturally-motivated field of study whose origins, conventions and

---

27   Most relevant here is Sarah C. Humphreys, Classics and Colonialism 207–208; "Two features of ... history are particularly relevant for a discussion of the situation of western 'classical studies' today. First that the particular conjuncture of the disciplining process

configurations have developed in eighteenth- and nineteenth-century colonial Europe.[28] The image of noble perfection which it was once believed to have possessed has faded now both in Europe and North America.[29] This is part of a larger crisis that is affecting not only classical studies but all the fields in the humanities (*al-ādāb* in Arabic).[30] There is much to say here about the noble perfection of the name and content of classical studies, especially its connection with colonialism and the Middle East, but let us first define what is meant by classical studies in this paper. Then we will proceed to look at the various names given to the field at the international level before we go into the details of the modern Arabic labels of this field.

For the purpose of this study, the academic field of Classical studies is treated as broadly as possible to accommodate most of the Antiquity-related fields like classical philology, literature, history, drama, philosophy, archaeology, and Classical reception studies. In writing this introduction and in compiling the bibliography, a narrower disciplinary definition of Classics or of Classical studies that focuses exclusively on one sub-field of Classics while neglecting the others has been avoided.[31] Classical studies is here understood to be the academic field of study that focuses on both the material and intellectual culture of the Greek and Roman world. Whereas it is easy to translate the Arabic *al-ʿālam al-yūnānī wa al-rūmānī* to its English equivalent the "Greek and Roman world", it is hard to accept that the phrase "the tangible and

---

with the development of the modern university, and with intensified colonialism in Asia, positioned Graeco-Roman studies as a model for the disciplinization of other fields in the humanities and for the identification and study of classical texts in other civilizations. Second, that the period of disciplinary formation – essentially the nineteenth century – was one in which major transformations took place over a wide range of conception and institutions concerned with the self and its cultivation...." [emphasis is mine]. See also the opening words of Glenn W. Most about disciplinization, institutionalization and professionalization in Most, *Disciplining Classics* vii–xi.

28   Relevant to the topic discussed here is Reid, Cromer and the Classics. See also Barbara Goff, *Classics and Colonialism*; Mark Bradley, *Classics and Imperialism in the British Empire*; Phiroze Vasunia, *The Classics and Colonial India*; and Barbara Goff, *Your Secret Language*.

29   The most recent criticism I am aware of is Dan-el Padilla Peralta's paper about racial equity and knowledge production in the field which he presented in Future of Classics Panel of the annual joint conference of the American Institute of Archaeology and American Society of Classical Studies, "SCS-AIA annual meeting in San Diego 2019, Racial Equity and the Production of Knowledge," Future of Classics Panel (January 5, 2019).

30   See Culham, Edmunds et al., *Classics: A Discipline and Profession in Crisis?* Most, *Disciplining Classics* Hanson and Heath, *Who Killed Homer?* and Hanson, Heath and Thornton, *Bonfire of the Humanities*. For Egypt see Khaled Fahmy, The Crisis of the Humanities in Egypt.

31   Cf. the definition of classical studies in McGuire, *Introduction* 2 and 5.

intellectual heritage or remains" covers all the concepts and connotations of the Arabic phrase *al-āthār al-māddiyya wa al-fikriyya*. The word *al-āthār* has a broad spectrum of meanings in Arabic.[32] It could mean tracks, signs, marks, influences, traditions, works of art and literature, monuments, and antiquities. By modifying *al-āthār* with the adjective *al-māddiyya*, the author's approach is mostly identical to UNESCO's definition of tangible cultural heritage. By *al-āthār al-fikriyya* one could speak of the other side of the coin, i.e., all the intellectual heritage of the Greek and Roman world, whether this is an institution like democracy, an art like theatrical performance, or the memory of these people like reception studies.

The International Federation of Associations of Classical Studies (FIEC) lists 59 member associations worldwide.[33] The list is representative of how the field is labeled and where it is studied on the international level. The densest concentration of classical associations is in Greece, which is home to five associations, followed by Spain, France and Switzerland, which each have three, and finally Germany, Italy, the USA and Serbia, which each have two associations. Every other country represented in the FIEC has only one classical association. From the members' list, it seems that Classics is a European field of study par excellence. Nevertheless, not all these European countries define the field in the same way. Each has its own understanding of, and therefore its own label for, what is generally dubbed Classical Studies in English. The world of the Greeks and Romans is approached as a history, a philology, a culture, or a civilization. It is described as the Ancient, the Classical or simply the Greco-Roman world. A degree of differentiation between Greek and Hellenic and between Roman and Latin exists as well.

This is not at odds with the situation in the Arab world. Classical studies are known in Arabic under many names, which in most cases reflect the different theoretical approaches, concepts, methodologies and frameworks applied in practice. In the philological departments where the literature of the Greeks and Romans is the focus of study and research, the field is known as classical studies (*al-dirāsāt al-klāsikiyya*), Greek and Latin Studies (*al-dirāsāt al-Ighrīqiyya/al-Yūnāniyya wa al-Lātīniyya*) or Ancient European civilization (*al-ḥaḍāra al-ūrubiya al-qadīma*). Such philological departments existed traditionally only in Cairo (1925), 'Ayn Shams (1950) and Alexandria (1938) and

---

32   Cf. McGuire's note about the different meanings of the terms applied to the field in French, Italian, English and German. To him "German klassische Altertumswissenschaft, or simply Altertumswissenschaft is, more satisfactory than French and German philology or English Classical Philology, or Classical Scholarship, but there is no exact English equivalent.", McGuire, *Introduction* 6.

33   Founded in 1948.

more recently in Mansoura, Sohag and Damanhur universities (2007). In all these universities, classical philology departments are part of what are called faculties of letters (*kulliyāt al-ādāb*). All of the above-mentioned universities have established programs (BA, MA and PhD) in almost all the subspecialties of classical studies. No other Arab country boasts such expertise in the language and literature of the Greeks and Romans as Egypt. Greek and Latin philology departments are a purely Egyptian phenomenon in the modern history of the Arab world. The reason for this situation is the influence of Ṭāhā Ḥusayn, who himself was the first Egyptian classicist and is also commonly known as the dean of Arabic literature.[34]

When it comes, however, to such specialized fields as archaeology, philosophy and the history of the Greeks and Romans, Egypt is competing with almost every other Arab country. Greco-Roman history is studied throughout the Arab world in history departments as a subspecialty of history. In almost every Arab university there is a section (*shuʻba*) and/or specialism (*takhaṣṣuṣ*) in Greco-Roman history (*al-Tārīkh al-Yūnānī wa al-Rūmānī*). A plethora of titles for this specialism exists in the Arabic academic world reflecting again the diversity of concepts and approaches to the field. In addition to Greco-Roman history other labels are used for this field such as ancient history (*al-tārīkh al-qadīm*), history of the Greeks and Romans (*tārīkh al-Yūnān wa al-Rūmān*), "History of the Greek World" (*tārīkh bilād al-Ighrīq*), and "History of the Romans" (*tārīkh al-rūmān*). Greco-Roman philosophy is studied as a general rule in the Arab world in the department of philosophy (*qism al-falsafa*), which is also part of the Faculty of Arts and Letters. In most cases, it is not a subspecialty in these departments. Most of these departments also teach courses like "History and Philosophy of the Sciences" (*tārīkh al-ʻulūm wa falsafatuhā*), which would definitely contain a unit on the history of sciences in the Greco-Roman world. At ʻAyn Shams University in Cairo, Classical Archaeology is studied as a subspecialty in the archaeology department in the section of Greek and Roman archeology (*shuʻbat al-āthār al-yūnāniyya wa al-rūmāniyya*). This department at ʻAyn Shams University has been turned recently, i.e. 2020, into a Faculty of Archaeology emulating Cairo University, where Classical art and architecture is studied in a department of Greek and Roman archaeology (*qism al-āthār al-yūnāniyya wa al-rūmāniyya*).

---

34   See footnote 27 above about the influence of *"Graeco-Roman studies as a model for the disciplinization of other fields in the humanities and for the identification and study of classical texts in other civilizations"*.

5.3   *Historical Invisibility and Manufactured Marginalization*

Even though one or more of the sub-fields of Classical Studies is represented in almost every Arab country, no Arab country is present in the FIEC or any of its fourteen international Western-based, professional learned societies of Antiquity-related fields.[35] Egypt has its own very active society of classicists with an annual conference, proceedings, and publications, which is known as the *Egyptian Society of Greek and Roman Studies*. Despite the recent effort of the FIEC to declare Greek and Latin as common human heritage, there is still much that must be done in order to decolonize this field and achieve more visibility of its members regardless of their global location.

The Western-based FIEC and its supposedly international professional learned societies of Antiquity-related fields not only ignore and/or marginalize senior Arab professors in their internet presence, but also in their scientific committees. Even in matters related to the improvement of the working conditions of classicists in the Middle East and North Africa, the FIEC member associations do not usually consult local scholars. A good example of this can be seen in the recommendations of the working party of the International Association of Papyrologists.[36] The list of the names of the members of the working party who produced these recommendations (recorded in the footnote of the first page) includes no Arabic names. The main task of this group was "to study the complex legal, ethical and scholarly questions connected with the commerce in papyri and to make recommendations ... on measures that may appropriately serve the purposes of scholarship, support the development of papyrological studies in Egypt and further the preservation of the documentary heritage of Egypt and other countries". Yet from reading the document and the list of scholars involved one might assume that there are no papyrologists or classicists in Egypt! This problem is not limited to Egypt or papyrology alone, but rather can be observed in other Antiquity-related disciplines as well.[37]

Arabic scholarship in Classics is also largely invisible in the West. The standard international reference bibliography of classical scholarship, *L'Année Philologique*, contains to date only 100 records of Arabic publications.[38] The

---

35   For the names of the member organizations see the FIEC website, https://www.fiecnet .org/our-story. Accessed 17/02/ 2020.

36   The recommendation is published online in the website of the Belgium-based international association, https://www2.ulb.ac.be/assoc/aip/workingparty.pdf. Accessed 23/11/18.

37   See Blouin, The Committee Test.

38   Unlike the International Medieval Bibliography (http://cpps.brepolis.net/bmb/search. cfm) which is an open access database, the online database of *L'Année philologique* is

Bibliographie Papyrologique has, in its two versions, no mention of Arabic publications at all.[39] Arabic scholarship of classical antiquity has almost no place in these two major digital bibliographic projects nor in any of the printed handbooks, introductory books, biographies, or encyclopedias produced in the West.[40] Building authority over space and time is hard work and deconstructing it is even harder. Visibility is a key purpose and factor in this process. In the four volumes that have been published so far celebrating the story of papyrology from 1745 to 2012, only one Egyptian is portrayed – though there are many Egyptian classicists, ancient historians, Egyptologists and other practitioners of papyrology in Egypt who could have been featured in this encyclopedia. Even when Arab scholars are featured, they are given short shrift: the biography of Abdallah Hassan el-Mosallamy ['Abdallāh Ḥasan Al-Musallamī] (1934–98) of 'Ayn Shams University in Cairo, Egypt, in two pages (357–58) of the first volume of *Who's Who in Papyrology* is dwarfed by the biographies of seventy six hermae of Western papyrology.[41] This neglect seems to be innocent, but the historical roots of exclusion and expulsion are the other side of the coin which reveal its true nature.[42] Conscious or unconscious exclusion of indigenous scholars, cultures and languages in Classical studies is visible to everyone and cannot escape the eye.[43] In the Middle East and North Africa, scholars live in the shadow of the West and this exclusion resonates locally.

---

available only through institutional or individual subscriptions at https://about.brepolis .net/lannee-philologique-aph/. Accessed 21/08/19.

39   The papyrological database *Bibliographie Papyrologique* is, however, an open access database, whose most up-to-date version is available here http://www.aere-egke.be/BP/. Accessed 21/08/19. The bibliography could also be consulted through the search interface of papyri.info here http://www.papyri.info/bibliosearch. Accessed 21/08/19.

40   The same is also true about the first edition of *Who Was Who in Egyptology*, see Reid, *Contesting* 355.

41   See Capasso, *Hermae* i, 357–358. Note that this author produced as much work in Arabic as he did in English in the field of papyrology.

42   Exclusion and expulsion are done within the national boundaries, which shift over time and space. Their main drive is nationalism. The examples here are numerous and need a separate study. The prefaces of published bibliographies reveal a great deal of awareness among national scholars and societies of the importance of scholarly and research visibility beyond linguistic and cultural barriers, see for example the prefaces of Janson et al., *Swedish Archaeological Bibliography* and Callmer and Holmquist, *Swedish Archaeological Bibliography*. Interesting as well is the transnational, or more precisely transatlantic bibliographic coverage of Thompson who started at first with only American scholarship but later covered British scholarship as well, see Thompson, *A Bibliography of American doctoral dissertations* and Thompson, *A Bibliography of Dissertations in Classical Studies*.

43   The dynamic process is not always one-way, but it could also be reversed i.e. to fight for inclusion and to exercise critique. Thus, Classical knowledge is used by two African Americans "to advocate liberation and emancipation", see Malmud, Classics as a Weapon,

Even at the Pan-Arab level, bibliographies of Arabic scholarship in Classics are a rare phenomenon. Neither Egypt nor any other Arab country possesses a print or online catalogue of this modern corpus. This phenomenon is observed in almost all humanities disciplines in the modern Arab world. The phenomenon is complex and historically connected with colonialism – especially its language and education policies – and the postcolonial legacy in the region. Wholesale and oversimplifying statements about Arab universities' inability to start or feed a real, epistemological, cultural and social change are contradicted by, in the author's opinion, the "Arab Spring" as well as other uprisings in modern history. Al-Amīn's recent observation that "subordinate socialization triumphs over the function of social change in government universities" is true. To justify this by the predominance of politics in the governance of Arab universities is problematic and neither sufficient nor attainable.[44] Compared with the well-served Western printed corpus of Classical scholarship, the corpus of Arabic Classical scholarship is decentralized, scattered and uncatalogued. Many records whose titles are known to us are missing and/or out of print. Copies of known titles are dispersed among many publishing houses, libraries and institutions not only in Egypt but also across the entire Arab world. Rare books are a hard currency. To sum up, both outside and inside the Arab world, the archive of Arabic Classical scholarship is largely invisible.

5.4   *Classical Power Contestations over Space, Time and Materials*

The reasons behind the invisibility of scholars and marginalization of research from the Arab world are geographical and historical, intertwined and complex. It is true that the regional and international limitations of the print culture played a great role in this regard.[45] However, it should be borne in mind that these are often the result of deliberate policies and decisions. It is not surprising, then, that in the Arab countries there are still deliberate restrictions on access to books, libraries and knowledge. The Arab national libraries and public university libraries are late-comers in hard circumstances and contain the bare minimum of research material while the libraries of foreign institutions and research centers in the Arab world, representing the former colonizers of

---

89–103. Note how the author is sceptical about the idea of the democratic turn stating at the end of his contribution "the colour line in the United States persists", see ibid, 103. Greek tragedy could promote empire and at the same it could be deployed in an anti-war agenda, see in the relevant case of Iraq and Afghanistan, Rabinowitz, The Expansion of Tragedy as Critique, 120–130.

44   See Al-Amīn, Al-Jāmiʿāt Al-ʿArabiyya.

45   For an account of the introduction of the printing press in modern Egypt, see al-Ṭahṭāwī, *Takhlīṣ* 19–25 with bibliography.

the land and their allies, are crammed with books and monographs. Egyptian and Arab specialists and their students, not to mention the general public, are granted only limited access to these foreign research centers which hold the reins of knowledge, power and authority in disciplines related to the material and intellectual culture of the region.

It is a parallel narrative to the Western main narrative of Classical studies with its own subplots and historical and geographical trajectories. Classical studies in Egypt and the wider Arab world where Arabic is the dominant language and Islam is the majority religion, cannot be compared with Classics in West or South Africa, where the indigenous communities did not have contacts with the Greeks and Romans during the course of their history, but rather the Greco-Roman tradition was introduced to them by European colonizers.[46] The Classical heritage in the Arab world is tangibly and intangibly visible in every corner. Colonial armies invading the region came with their own different versions and memories of Greek and Roman textual and material culture. The languages they used and the cultures they represented came to compete unequally with Arabic and still do.

Consequently, the print and digital invisibility of Arabic Classical scholarship makes the Arab researchers themselves invisible not only in the West but, as stated earlier, everywhere else where Western scholarship is authoritative. It is not surprising, then, that biographical dictionaries of Classical and papyrological scholars do not record any information whatsoever about Arabic classicists or papyrologists, dead or alive, except for one case. Despite his fame and popularity in the West, Ṭāhā Ḥusayn's classical training and career have been largely ignored. The prominent Egyptian papyrologist ʿAbdallāh Ḥasan Al-Musallamī was only mentioned in a Western publication thanks to the pen of his colleague ʿAliyya Ḥanafi [Alia Hanafi].[47] Famous and senior Egyptian and Arab classicists are consigned to oblivion in Western circles.

Another notable case both for internal and external reasons is Muṣṭafā Al-ʿAbbādī (1928–2017). Al-ʿAbbādī was a well-known Greco-Roman historian

---

46   This is not to say that classics has evolved in the Arab world out of internal factors and/or to exclude the importance of drawing comparisons between classical education in both regions. The relationship between Classics in Egypt and the Egyptian political influences on African independence movements may however prove to be fruitful, for the role and the rhetoric of colonial commissions in this part of Africa, see Goff, Classics in West African Education, 157–169 with bibliography. South Africa is an interesting case where drama and politics are used by both sides of the struggle, for an introduction see Van Zyl Smit, Multicultural reception, 373–385. In the same vein see Etman, Translation in the Intersections of Traditions, 141–152.

47   See Capasso, *Hermae* 357–358.

of Alexandria University. He was known in Western academia, not only because of his scholarship, but also, and most importantly, because of his endeavors to revive the library of Alexandria. It took him many years to persuade the government of Egypt to support the project. The Egyptian government and UNESCO agreed to support the library in 1986. In 2002, the library was opened as the Bibliotheca Alexandrina, causing more controversy than was satisfactory even to Al-ʿAbbādī himself. One day after its official inauguration, Al-ʿAbbādī, who was not invited to the ceremony, expressed his worry that his dream of a "world-class research centre" was turning into a "cultural centre".[48]

The self-imposed or forced absence and marginalization of Arab Classical scholars in Western and international congresses and associations is closely tied to this scholarly invisibility in addition to linguistic, economic and geo-political factors. Gregory Crane, the American digital classicist behind the famous Perseus Digital Library, the largest open access digital library in Classics and its editor-in-chief, has succinctly summarized the power of the print culture when he wrote; "Few Classicists, for example, realize that the University of Cairo supports one of the most active programs in Greek and Latin in the world because they publish largely in Arabic and because print culture, with its massive libraries, favored a handful of universities in the first world.".[49]

Therefore, the socio-cultural politics surrounding the production of the Arabic corpus of Classical scholarship is an integral part of the corpus. The geopolitical and historical context is also important in any analysis of it. Knowledge and power are two ingredients that are hardly missed in the dramatically shifting, and in many cases volatile, political milieu of the Middle East and North Africa. A good example is the case of ʿAbd al-Raḥmān Badawī, the classical philosopher who fled from Jamāl ʿAbd al-Nāṣir's Egypt, in September 1967, to Libya, where he witnessed Muʿammar al-Qadhdhāfī's *coup d'état* in September 1969 and his subsequent declaration on 15 April, 1973, of "a cultural revolution" during a public speech in Zuwwāra near Tunisia. Badawī describes the cultural revolution he witnessed as an attempt to get rid of all the imported theories that contradicted the September 1st Revolution along with abolishing all laws and liberating the people while militarizing them at the same time.[50] Despite his imprisonment and subsequent departure from the country, Badawī managed during his six-year residence in Libya to produce

---

48   The whole story is told by Wakin, Successor, and for more details around the politics surrounding this project, see Ali, Power.

49   See Crane, Rethinking the Humanities, and about Perseus Digital Library itself see Lang, Review.

50   Badawī, *Sirat* ii, 174–278 and for the full story of his stay in Libya see Ibid, 105–162.

two important volumes about Carneades and Synesius of Cyrene and what he called the history of Libyan philosophy in the Greek and Roman Period.[51]

5.5   *What Is a Troubled Archive?*

For our purposes the archive consists of all the media, print or digital, that have been used by modern Egyptians and Arabs to construct their Greco-Roman past or to accommodate the Greeks and Romans into their national past. Recent incidents in the Middle East, especially after 2011, have put the ancient heritage of the region at risk and have thus increased the significance of this archive both to insiders and outsiders. The advent of digital culture has enlarged the number of records in this troubled archive and subsequently the will to investigate its "power/knowledge" or (*pouvoir/savoir*) syndrome.[52] Regarding the extent of the academic archive, it can be safely claimed that the corpus of Arabic academic scholarship on the Classics is very extensive and covers nearly all aspects of Greco-Roman antiquity. Any student in Egypt or in any other Arab country is able to consult introductory books as well as specialized dissertations in Classical Philology, Literature, History, Religion and Mythology, Archaeology, Numismatics, Philosophy and Ancient Science, Papyrology, and Epigraphy. With a reading ability in a modern European language, a student whose first language is Arabic has more than enough resources in order to obtain a good and balanced introduction to the fundamental narratives, theories, concepts, opinions and practices of this large field of study.

The history of Arabic cultural interactions with Greek and Latin makes the perspective gained from examining the archive of the Arabic tradition of Classical studies unique compared it with the English, French, German or Italian traditions of Classical scholarship, or those of other modern European languages and cultures. The legacy of European colonialism and its history of hegemony and interventionism in the Arab world provide a transnational socio-political context to this troubled archive. The digital culture, particularly social media, the Arab Spring, and the recent global challenges complicate things further. The geopolitical and strategic importance of the Arab world, with its material and intellectual Greco-Roman heritage, the trajectory of the recent global challenges, the crisis of the humanities with its cultural, economic, and socio-political dimensions, all add volumes to the complexities already arising from these texts. This large corpus, the knowledge it translates, embodies and contests, and its context can constitute a major source for the study of

---

51   See Badawī, *Tārīkh al-falsafa.*

52   The reference here is to a central theme in Foucault's works, see Ellen Feder, Power/ knowledge 55–68.

the entangled processes of knowledge production and power consumption. The complex questions about knowledge and the power that arise from the corpus *per se*, or if we use Foucault's expression its *"system of thoughts"*,[53] do not easily lend themselves to simple answers and need a detailed analysis that goes beyond the current limitation of space and time. Without a comprehensive catalogue of the archive of Arabic Classical studies production described above, any account of Arab scholarship in Classical Antiquity-related fields is incomplete. Nonetheless, a starting point will be made here.

5.6 *Indigenous Cultures, Public Discourses and Academic Systematization of Knowledge Production in the Arab World*

The starting point for our narrative is the year 1918. In this year Ṭāhā Ḥusayn was appointed as lecturer of Greek and Roman history and civilization at the Egyptian University. The university sent him in May of 1914 to the University of Montpellier to study for a second degree in history after he had already obtained the *al-ʿĀlamiyya* degree from the newly inaugurated Egyptian University.[54] In 1918/19, he returned to Egypt with a second PhD from the Sorbonne in ancient history and he was assigned to teach the history of the Ancient Orient.[55] In 1922/23, he gave four lectures a week on the general history of Greece from 432 BCE to the rise of Macedon, the Macedonian kingdom and the role of Alexander the Great in the expansion of Greek civilization in the East and in Egypt, Greco-Roman Relations [to start in the second term], and readings in the historical texts of the Greeks, Romans and Egyptians.[56] In 1923/24, he continued teaching these lectures. The suggestion of teaching "ancient languages" was approved in this year too and a new department under the name *madrasat al-lughāt al-qadīma* (Department of Ancient Languages) was opened. This year also witnessed the transition of the Egyptian University (predecessor of Cairo University) from a private into a state university. In 1924/25, he taught the same course Ancient History of the East but handled only three topics: Egypt under the Macedonians (viz Ptolemaic), Foundations of the Roman Republic, and Rome and Greece.[57]

This does not mean that the modern Arab interest in the Greek and Roman civilization and/or the ancient world before 1918 was irrelevant. On

---

53   This is the title that Michel Foucault chose for his chair at *Collège de France* where he taught from 1971–1984, see François Ewald and Alessandro Fontana, Forward ix.

54   See Budayr, *al-Amīr Aḥmad Fuʾād* 200. *Al-ʿĀlamiyya* was the Arabic term used at the time for PhD degrees from the Egyptian University.

55   Ibid 158 and 205.

56   Ibid 178.

57   Ibid 185.

FIGURE 6.2   Ṭāhā Ḥusayn, the third from left in the second row, among the students of
the Archaeology class of 1908/09
SOURCE BUDAYR, *AL-AMĪR AḤMAD FU'ĀD*, UNNUMBERED IMAGES

the contrary, the Egyptian national discourses about the past, tradition and heritage were important factors that led to the systematization of academic study and knowledge production in this domain. These national and pan-Arab discourses were the driving forces behind the establishment of departments such as the department of Islamic Civilization and Archaeology at the Egyptian University. Ḥusayn was not only among the first students to attend the classes offered in both subjects in December 1908, but he also excelled in both.

The role of antiquities in these discourses is a central one.[58] The idea of establishing an Egyptian Arabic university appeared in the course of these debates.[59] The Egyptian national university was originally a private (*ahlī*) initiative not only by Egyptian intellectuals and politicians but also by writers and activists from other Arab countries like Jurjī Zaydān. In 1908 the first Egyptian and Arab University was established as a private university. Then it

---

58   The role of antiquities in the modern Egyptian discourse about heritage and past is a central one. See Reid, Whose Pharaohs 2002 and Contesting Antiquity 2015.

59   Reid, *Cairo University* 1990 gives the full account of the nascent Egyptian academia, in which not only Egyptians took part, but also Europeans and non-Egyptian Arabs.

became a state university, known from 1925 to 1938 as the Egyptian University. From 1938–53 it was known as Fu'ād I University, and from 1953 until now as Cairo University.[60] Most of the subsequent Egyptian and Arab universities that developed from this date on followed the model and the path of the first modern Egyptian university.

6   Egypt's Classics: Re-readings in Arabic

6.1   *Ṭāhā Ḥusayn Bey: The First Egyptian Classicist*
The most important figure of this cultural and academic debate both within Egypt and between Egypt and Europe or the West is of course Ṭāhā Ḥusayn. As a professor of Arabic language and literature, he was known as the dean of Arabic literature, but his pioneering role in Greek and Roman studies as an academic discipline is known, both nationally and internationally, by only a few. After a whole century of Egyptian scholarship in Classics, the legacy of his first appointment, at the Egyptian University as a lecturer of Greek and Roman history and civilization in the department of archaeology, and his teaching, research, and viewpoints, are still visible both at the academic and public levels.

The scholarly and public debate he started in 1922 with the publication of his seminal book *The Future of Culture in Egypt*, about Egypt's academic and cultural future, still rages in the academic, cultural and political circles of the Egyptian intelligentsia. The name he coined for the scientific study of the material and intellectual heritage of the Greeks and Romans in Egypt is not only still in use among academics, but it also still determines the context in which this highly specialized field is offered. The disputes and sometimes imaginary cultural wars continue to be lost and won in exactly the same cultural, ideological and political plane that he defined one hundred years ago, that of the European civilization vis-à-vis the trinity of Egyptian, Arabic and Islamic civilization. His inspiration, or, according to his critics, bedazzlement, by the European Enlightenment, must be critically analyzed in the context of his academic career and his endeavors to promote the right of Egyptians to consider themselves equal to the Europeans in terms of their share in Greco-Roman cultural heritage.

---

60   For the complete story see Reid, *Cairo University*.

FIGURE 6.3   Ṭāhā Ḥusayn, the second from left in the second row from the back. He is
standing among the students of the Islamic Civilization class of 1908/09
SOURCE, BUDAYR, *AL-AMĪR AḤMAD FU'ĀD*, UNNUMBERED IMAGES

6.2   *Classics in Arabic: Translating the Untranslatable*

Translation of complete works of foreign authors into Arabic seems to be a
beloved tradition of medieval as well as modern Arabic translators. Ḥunayn
b. Isḥāq (192/808–260/873) was the chief translator of Galen and the so-called
Corpus Hippocratium into Arabic.[61] Ḥunayn and his son Isḥāq, followed by Abū
Bishr Mattā (d. 328/940) and Yaḥyā b. ʿAdī (d. 363/974), translated Aristotle into
Arabic.[62] The translation movement under the Abbasids focused on the practical sciences, philosophy and medicine. Another modern translation movement from European languages occurred in the nineteenth century which, like
the earlier Abbasid translation movement, concentrated for the most part on
the translation of works in what were perceived to be practical disciplines.[63]
By the turn of the twentieth century, a shift towards the translation of high

---

61   About Ḥunayn see Strohmaier, Ḥunayn b. Isḥāq al-ʿIbādī, in *EI²*, ii, 578–81, for Galen
in Arabic, see R. Walzer, Djālīnūs, in *EI²*, ii, 402–403 and for Hippocrates in Arabic, see
A. Dietrich, Buqrāṭ in *EI²*, supplement, 154.

62   About Isḥāq see Strohmaier, Isḥāq b. Ḥunayn, in *EI²*, iv, 110; on Yaḥyā see Endress, Yaḥya b.
ʿAdī, in *EI²*, xi, 245–6 and for Aristotle in Arabic see Walzer, Arisṭūṭālīs, in *EI²*, i, 631.

63   The history of translation in Egypt is intertwined with education and culture. See
Newman's overview of al-Ṭahṭāwī, *Takhlīṣ* 47–71; and Sadgrove, Tardjama in *EI²*, x,
232–233.

literature (*al-ādāb*) was noticeable.[64] The duality of practicality and impracticality in the Egyptian educational system may have its roots in this period and in this shift of focus in translation. Sciences, seen as practical, were now regarded as untranslatable while the humanities and social sciences, regarded as unpractical (theoretical), were considered translatable. The modern Arabic culture received anew Greek thought. It was literature's turn this time. The significant lesson to be learned from both translation movements remains *mutatis mutandi* the same, i.e. "the translation movement made Islamic civilization the successor to Hellenistic civilization. As such, not only did it ensure the survival of Hellenism at a time when the Latin West was ignorant of it and the Byzantine East busy suppressing it, but it also proved that it can be expressed in languages and adopted in cultures other than Greek, and that it is international in scope and the common property of all mankind."[65]

6.3 *The Homeric Quest in Arabic*

The Homeric quest in modern Arabic Classical scholarship is in all probability a transfer of the Homeric complex from the Western sphere. Sūlaymān al-Bustānī's verse translation of Homer's *Iliad* published by *al-Hilāl* printing press in 1904 predated not only Ḥusayn's interest in Classics but also the Egyptian University itself.[66] The translation was highly appreciated by Egyptian and other Arab intellectuals and writers of the time because it was the first complete translation of the epic into Arabic. The translation's significance is due also to its detailed documentation of the translator's strategies and to its erudite and extensive comparative introduction to the poem. The title of the translation in Arabic is extremely long and reads as follows: *Homer's Iliad: translated in Arabic verse, annotated with historical and literary commentaries, an introduction about Homer's life and poetry, [a comparative study about] Greek and Arabic literature, a general glossary and an index.* The introduction and comparative study occupy 200 pages of this first class annotated translation. The translation proper runs from page 201 to page 1149. Every *nashīd* (book) of the Arabic translation of the Iliad is introduced with a synopsis of the events. The glossary and indices occupy the rest of the book, from pages 1150 to 1260. Though al-Bustānī relied heavily on modern European translations of the Iliad, he seems also to have consulted an original Greek version. Exactly one hundred years after this first translation, a second Arabic translation of

---

64   See Christoff, Tardjama in *EI²*, supplement, 788–790.
65   For a summary and bibliographic survey see the authoritative article by Gutas, Tardjama, in *EI²*, x, 224–231 and *cf.* 232.
66   al-Bustānī, *'Iliāzat Hūmīrus.*

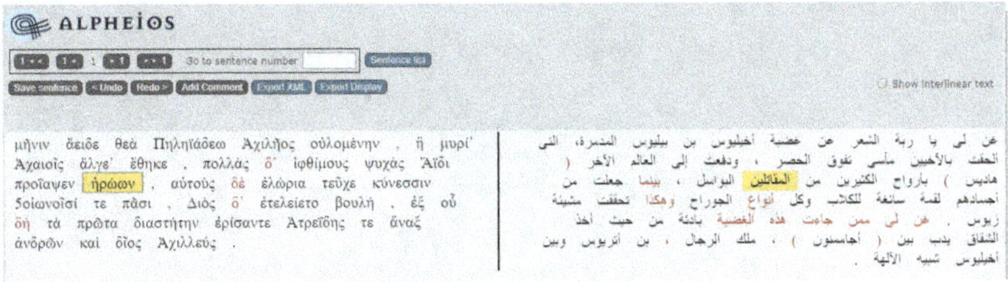

FIGURE 6.4   Translation alignment 1

Homer's Iliad appeared again in Cairo, but this time in prose. The uniqueness
of this new translation stems not only from the fact that it is the first direct
translation of this epic from Ancient Greek into Arabic, but also from the team
work behind it and the leader or the maestro who coordinated the whole sym-
phony. The editor of this *opus magnus* was the late Aḥmad ʿUthmān, who was
assisted by four other Egyptian classicists: Luṭfī ʿAbd al-Wahhāb Yaḥyā (books
1–3), Munīra Karawān (books 7–12), Al-Saʿīd ʿAbd al-Salām al-Barāwī (books
14–18) and ʿĀdil al-Naḥḥās (books 21–24). The editor introduced this edition
with an extensive study of the Iliad. He first discussed earlier translations of
the Iliad, especially that of al-Bustānī, then he introduced the Arabic reader
to the Wolfian Homeric question, the Homeric style, Greek hexameter, similes
in the Homeric poem, a synopsis of the whole narrative and the individual
events in each book, an overview of Homeric studies from ancient times until
now, the reception of the Iliad and Homer throughout the ages and a bibliography of all these topics (pp. 7–113). Throughout his introduction runs the
theme and question "who is the other in the Iliad?". The Arabic translation of
the twenty-four books follows from pages 117–800 and an index of mythical
characters and biographies of the translators concludes the translation. The
book was published by the Egyptian National Centre of Translation in two
large hardcover editions in 2004 and 2008.

6.4   *The Corpus of Twentieth-Century Egypt's Greek-into-Arabic Translation Movement*

After experimental indirect translations, which included adaptations of European classics, mainly French baroque plays, aimed at performance in the rising
Egyptian theatre, a literary translation movement of Greek and Latin texts was
launched in the Arab world; especially in Egypt. From 1925 to 2000 a total of
205 books on Classics were translated into Arabic, of which 36% were monographs. The chart below illustrates the percentage of translation activity compared to production of original studies.

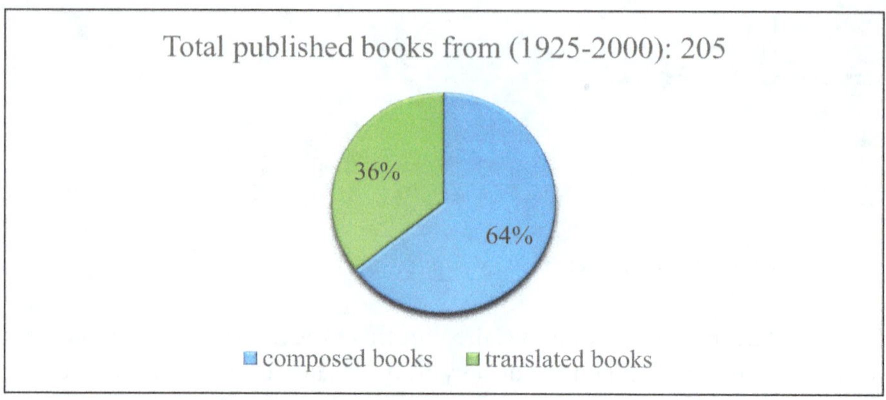

FIGURE 6.5 Translated books

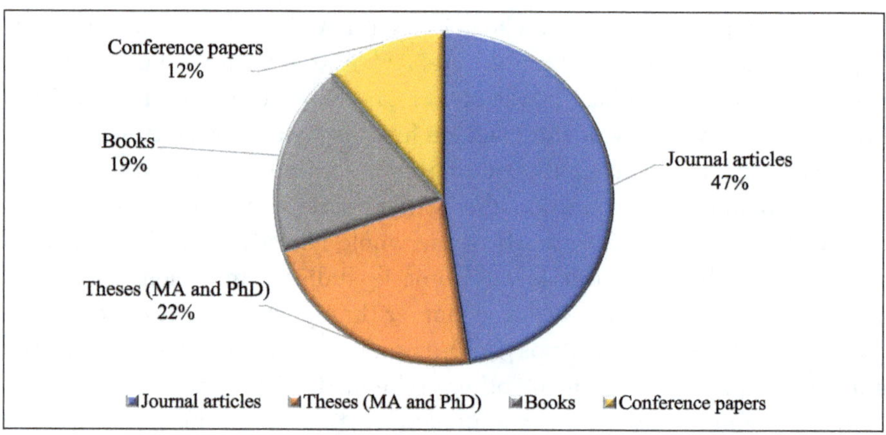

FIGURE 6.6 Snapshot 1: Produced knowledge by topic

6.5   *Quantitative Snapshots of the Egyptian School of Classical Studies*
Publications in the field of Greek and Latin literature comprise more than a
third (37 %) of the total number of Arabic publications in the discipline of
Classical Studies. A quarter (25 %) of the publications concern Greek and
Roman history and 18 % are in the field of papyrology. The chart below shows
the chronological distribution of modern Arabic scholarship on the Classical
World from 1925 to 2000. One can see that publications in this field are growing
steadily. Almost all these publications have appeared in Arabic and in Egypt.

There are however some books that have been published outside of Egypt,
mainly in Greece, Italy and Kuwait, but also the UK, Lebanon and Saudi
Arabia, in addition to other countries. The publications in Greece, Italy, and
the UK are dissertations since many Egyptian classicists completed their MA
or PhD degrees in these countries. The publications in Kuwait are mainly

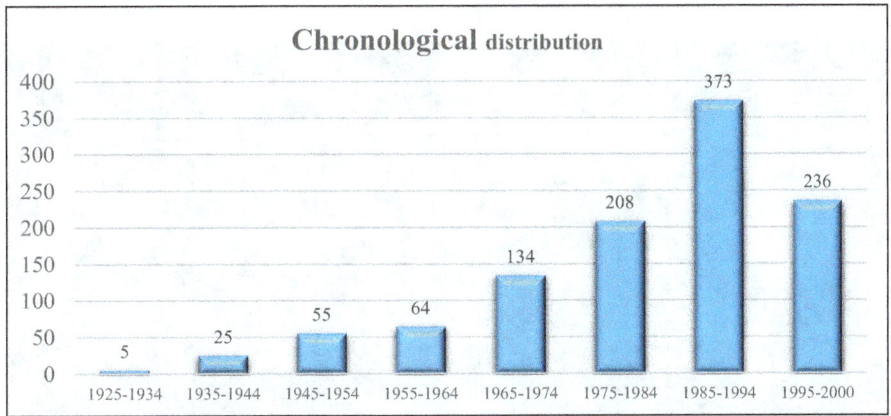

FIGURE 6.7   Snapshot 2: Chronological distribution

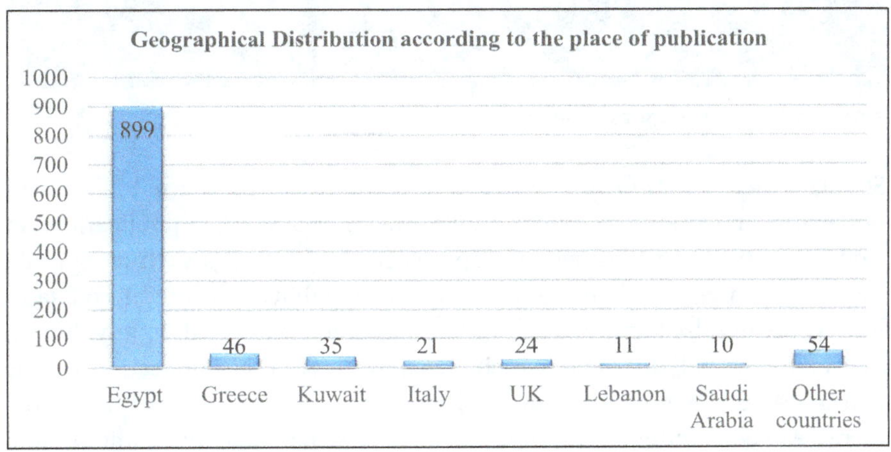

FIGURE 6.8   Snapshot 3: Geographical distribution

translations of Greek and Latin drama done by Egyptian scholars who taught in the Kuwaiti Higher Institute for Theatrical Arts. These positions were virtually a monopoly of Egyptian classicists. The translations were published by the Kuwaiti Ministry of Media and Culture in a series entitled *Works from the International Theater* (*Min al-Maṣraḥ al-ʿĀlamī*). Saudi Arabian publications of classical monographs are mostly ad hoc projects that serve certain particular purposes such as the recently published series *The Arabian Peninsula in the Classical Sources* (*Al-Jazīra al-ʿArabiyya fī al-Maṣādir al-Klāsikiyya*). The chart above illustrates these trends.

Most of the Arabic scholarship in Classical studies is published in specialized journals, as al-Kāfūrī has shown in her study. The graph below illustrates this trend. One of the main periodicals is the ʿAyn Shams Journal of Papyrological

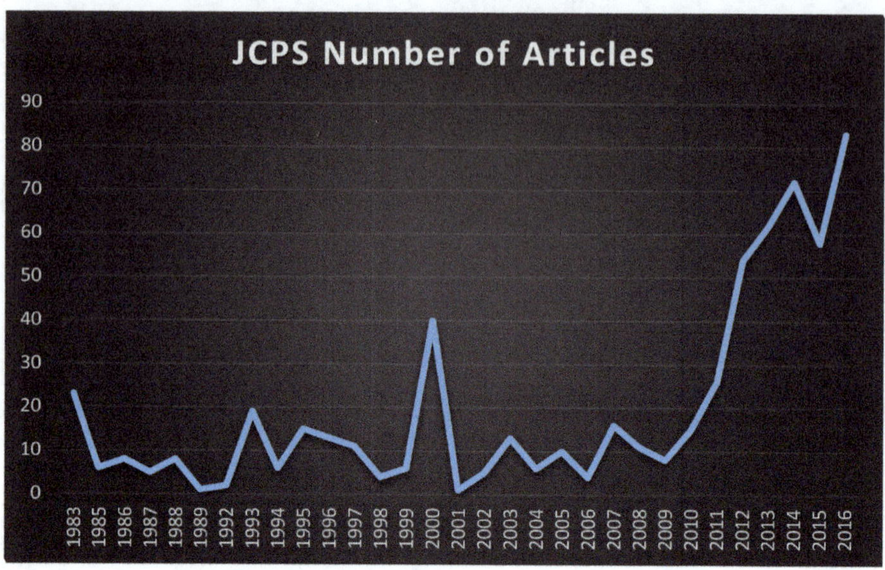

FIGURE 6.9 Snapshot 4: JCPS number of articles

Studies (*Majallat Markaz al-Dirāsāt al-Bardiyya*). This journal has been published almost every year since 1983. The journal accepts publications in Arabic or any other language of papyrological scholarship such as English, French, German or Italian, though most of its publications are of course in Arabic. Six hundred and eleven articles have been published, in 31 volumes, between 1983 and 2016, and the chart below shows that publication in this journal is steadily growing. Starting from 2010 there has been a remarkable increase in publications in this journal. It is also remarkable that in the volume for 2000 the number of articles reached 40 papers. Perhaps this is related to the fact this particular volume contains the papers presented to the center in its thematic conference *Palestine in the Light of Papyri and Inscriptions*.

Another important journal is *Classical Papers* (*Majallat Awrāq Klāsikiyya*). This journal is published by the department of Greek and Latin studies of Cairo University. It is a peer-reviewed journal of papers in the field of classical studies, as its name indicates. The first volume appeared in 1991 and the most recent one, volume 13, appeared in 2017. Between 1996 and 2003 there were no issues of this journal. Most of the published papers are written in Arabic, but there are also contributions in English and French written by Egyptian classicists as well as international scholars. Many of these papers are of an interdisciplinary nature focusing on the receptions of Classical works not only in modern Arabic literature, but also in English, French, and German litera-ture. This is consistent with the fact that the philological department of Cairo

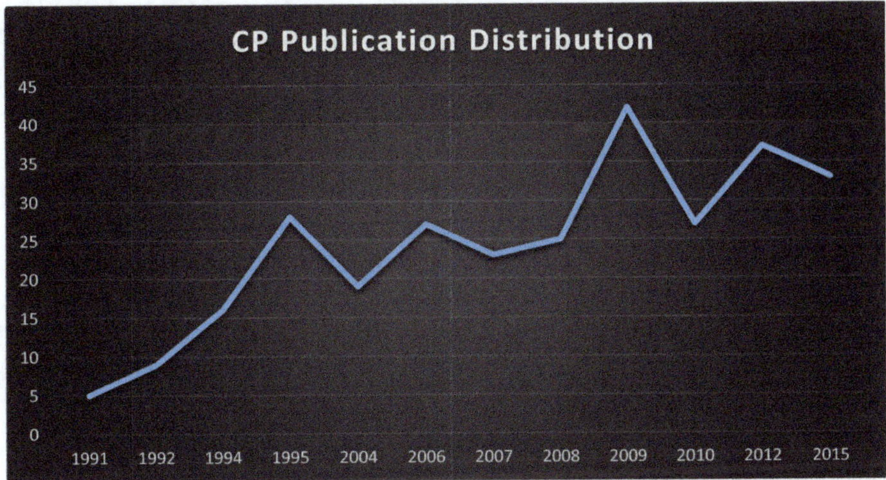

FIGURE 6.10   Snapshot 5: CP publication distribution

University has an internationally renowned research profile in comparative literature and reception studies. This research trend goes back to its founding father, Ṭāhā Ḥusayn, and it has been kept alive and even extended to a wider level by Aḥmad ʿUthmān, the founder of *Classical Papers*. It has been customary since ʿUthmān's time that the head of the department is also the editor-in-chief of this journal. Two hundred and ninety-one papers were published in the first 12 volumes, up until 2015. The chart above shows a fluctuation in publication. The drop in publications in the journal seen after 2010 is closely connected to the boom in publication in the journal of the *Center of Papyrological Studies* of ʿAyn Shams University. It is not clear if there is a connection between these two trends. It is important to note that the two periodicals serve as the main publication outlets for the majority of Egyptian classicists.

6.6   *Translation of the Classics by Egyptian Scholars: A Translation of the European Translation(s) or a New Reading of the Classics?*

Ṭāhā Ḥusayn's publication in 1921 of his Arabic translation of the *Athenian Constitution* (Greek: Ἀθηναίων πολιτεία) was a pioneering event in the history of Greek and Roman Studies in Egypt, as well as for other Egyptian Antiquity-related fields. Ḥusayn was the founding father of Egyptian classical studies and the main person behind the idea of opening up the gates of knowledge for Egyptians to study the Classical heritage of Egypt on their own terms through the establishment of academic departments specializing in the study of the world of the Greeks and Romans in the nascent Egyptian academic system. After earning a doctorate from the Sorbonne with a thesis on Ibn Khaldun in 1918, Ḥusayn returned to Egypt to be appointed as a lecturer of Greek and Roman history in the new Egyptian University. There, as he himself recounts in the preface to his translation, he began to teach ancient Greek history in Arabic to a class of students unfamiliar with Greek and Latin. This is the experience that led him to translate Aristotle's *Constitution of the Athenians*. In 1921 he finished the translation of the Greek text and published it. The text of Aristotle's lost work was found in a papyrus sheet from Egypt proudly smuggled by Sir E.A. Wallis Budge in 1889 and published in 1891 by Frederic G. Kenyon.[67] Ḥusayn was introduced to the text during his doctoral studies at the Sorbonne and was familiar with both the text and its translations for more than thirty years. In addition to the wide international scholarly and public attention that this discovery has drawn, there are three facts that might have drawn the attention of Ḥusayn the student and the professor to this text. First of all, the text was ascribed to Aristotle with his long history in Arabic-Islamic culture as the "first master". Secondly, it was lost and rediscovered on a papyrus roll from Egypt. Thirdly, it dealt with a constitution or a system of governance, i.e. *Nizām* as he rendered it in Arabic. These three foundational ideas would be inherited by the Egyptian school of Classical Studies and would be ever-present in Egyptian debates about antiquity and modernity. Ḥusayn's book consists of a dedication to Qāsim Amīn, an introduction to the text with a biography of Aristotle's life and list of his main works (pp. 7–42), the translation proper (43–180), a table of contents (181–192) and a few footnotes dealing mainly with explanations of some technical and historical terms along with explanatory information about the figures that appear throughout the text. Ḥusayn's translation has continued to serve as the archetype of almost all academic Greek and Latin translation into Arabic up to the present day. His translation, or more accurately Arabic reading of the Greek, is not a mechanical rendering of a text into a hollow culture, but in itself an interesting journey of cultural transfers and bidirectional diachronic and synchronic discourse with Greece, Europe, Abbasid Baghdad, and the modern Egyptians who were involved in long-standing debates and disputes about land ownership, systems of government, the rights of citizens and many more questions that are still relevant at the present moment. There is no place to elaborate on the strategic decision taken by Ḥusayn in rendering this text into Arabic, but an excerpt from the second page gives us a glimpse of how all this works in a Greek source

---

67   Papyrus 131 now in the British library. The story of its smuggling is told by Budge himself in *By Nile and Tigris*, ii, 147–48.

text (ST) transferred eloquently into a multi-layered Arabic target text (TT) so that one can barely recognize that it is not an original text.[68]

"The *Nizām* [i.e. system] of governance at that time was an absolute system of minority rule. The relation of the poor to the rich was exactly like that of a lowly servant [to a master]. This submissiveness was not confined to men only but shared by their children and wives as well. They were called *mawālī* (*pelatai*) and *musaddasīn* (*ektimorai*) i.e. they farmed the land of the rich in exchange for only one sixth of its fruits (*thamarātihi*). The whole land was in the hands of a small sect (*ṭā'ifa*) of people. If the farmers failed to produce what had been asked of them, they and their families, including their children, were liable to be sold. In such cases the debtor was subjected to physical execution. This remained the case up to the time of Solon, the first leader of the democratic faction. The people were suffering first and foremost because of this *Niẓām* and they were furious about not having their share of the land. But there were many other reasons for their indignation. In reality they had nothing."

Besides the text's clear tone of modernity, which could be another reason why Ḥusayn chose it in the first place to read with his students, the target text has been Egyptianized to the degree that it became an idealized meta-text tied not only to Ṭāhā Ḥusayn as a historical figure, but also to the Egyptian and Arab context, or more precisely, the modern quest for modernity, independence and democracy. A key word here is the book's title, *System* (*niẓām*). It may suffice just to mention that the main demand of the Egyptians in Tahrir square from the first days of the 25th of January revolution in 2011 was "The People want the Fall of the System". Echoes of this revolutionary slogan and demand were heard not only in Egypt but across the Arab world from the Gulf to the Atlantic Ocean in 2011. Ḥusayn's text and context, not only the present one but also almost all his texts and contexts, were read and re-read until they became consciously and unconsciously rooted in modern Egyptian and Arab culture. He did not, in the present example, merely translate Aristotle's Greek words and historical understanding of Solon (c. 630 BCE–560 BCE), who was known in Antiquity as the lawmaker and the first leader of the people (τοῦ δήμου), but instead he modernized Solon's position by unilaterally and undemocratically electing him as the first leader of the "democratic faction" in the Arabic target text. In the Arabic translation Solon is no longer a Greek lawmaker and a statesman but rather a partisan leader. The poor people of Athens are no longer enslaved (ἐδούλευον) client (πελάται) tenants paying a sixth of their produce as rent to the rich oligarchy that owned almost all arable lands in the city-state,

---

68   The Arabic translation can be seen below in the translation alignment and cf. the translation of the same text by the Syrian père Austin Barbara, *Dustūr Al-Āthiniyyin.*

FIGURE 6.11 Translation Alignment 2: Alignment of the Greek original with the
English and Arabic translations of the above-mentioned paragraph
from Aristotle's Constitution of the Athenians by the software
aligner Ugarit. An interactive text and Epidoc XML-compliant file of
this alignment is available at http://www.ugarit.ialigner.com/align3
.php?function=update&id=26905

rather they are likened in Ḥusayn's historically multi-layered translation to the
peasants of Greco-Roman Egypt, to modern Egyptian servants in the palaces of
their European colonizers, and even to clients (*mawālī*) of the Umayyad period
toiling on the land in an imagined golden age of Islam. There is a great deal
of addition, omission, substitution, and re-ordering on the linguistic, cultural
and historical meta-level in this Egyptianized translation, though it should
be noted that this practice was not without parallel in the French, German,
Italian, and English translations of this text that were available to Ḥusayn at
that time. Ḥusayn has done an excellent job in domesticating the Greek text
of Aristotle's *Constitution of the Athenians* to an eloquent Modern Standard
Arabic that is hardly a translation.

Ḥusayn's new readings of the Classics during his pioneering academic and
professional career at the Egyptian University were not confined to Greek
Aristotelian philosophy or papyrology. In 1939 he directed his literary, scholarly and educational attention to the rising Egyptian theatre, which according
to his views needed the original classics of the Greek drama. In this year he
published the first collection of direct Modern Standard Arabic translations of

Greek literary texts. In this book, to which he gave the title [*A selection*] *From Greek Drama*, he translated, single-handedly, four of Sophocles' seven extant plays: *Electra, Ajax, Antigone,* and *Oedipus Tyrannus*.[69] This was the first direct translation of Ancient Greek literature to Modern Standard Arabic after experimental indirect translations, which included adaptations of European classics, mainly French baroque plays, aimed at performance in the rising Egyptian theatre. In 1944, after unsuccessful attempts from the 1930s, Ṭāhā Ḥusayn was able to establish the Egyptian National Institute of Dramatic Arts, which is now known as The Higher Institute of Dramatic Arts.[70]

6.7   *Ḥusayn, the Patriarch of Egyptian Classics and Its Linguistic and Cultural Heresies*

Ḥusayn's second relevant book for our study, *The Future of Culture in Egypt,* contains a detailed account of all his endeavors to introduce the study of Greek and Latin language and literature to Egyptian high schools and the nascent national university. Passionate, eloquent, influential and charismatic as he was, he not only coined the name of this branch of study in use to the present day in Egypt (Ancient European Civilization), he also initiated most of its controversies. It was, and still is, extremely hard to see from his elaborate introduction where his ideas about the Classics, European civilization and culture begin and where his Egyptian and Arab identity start. The idea of the Classics was entangled with his strong belief about the supremacy of modern European civilization to a significant degree. The public and the academic were also mixed in a perplexing approach. In this book he explicitly expressed such a view in statements like "the supreme idol of the Egyptian in his material and spiritual life is/should be the European", "There is/should be no difference in mentality between the Egyptian and the European" and "We [i.e. the Egyptians] should bluntly and defiantly adopt the standards of the modern European civilization in every aspect of our life".[71] The book with its bold statements and ideas unleashed a controversy in Egypt and the wider Arab world that has not ended until this day. This debate has overshadowed all of his endeavors to introduce Greek and Latin to Egypt and the Arab world in general.

---

69   Ḥusayn, *Min al-Adab al-Tamthīlī.*

70   See Hammouda, et al., Egypt, in WECT, iv, 97. On the early stage of translations of classical drama, which is closely connected with the rise of the Egyptian theatre, see Hammouda, et al., Egypt, in WECT, iv, 72–77 and 82–84.

71   Ḥusayn, *Mustaqbal,* 11–51.

The historical moment itself might justify this unreasonable entanglement, but his own personal life and professional career as a university teacher, or more precisely the first Egyptian academic in a milieu of European professors, was also normative. Unfortunately, most of Ṭāhā Ḥusayn's short lived dreams about universalizing education in the Classical languages, culture and civilization in Egypt went unfulfilled. In 1970, three years before the death of Ṭāhā Ḥusayn himself, ʿAbd al-Muʿṭī Shaʿrāwī gave a disappointed account of the fate of Greek and Latin education in the departments of the Egyptian universities, where he complains about the ever-diminishing study hours given to these two languages in departments like philosophy, history and English literature. In the last part of his short article, he illustrates the severe consequences of neglecting the original Greek texts in some Arabic translations of Classical literature with examples of an unsatisfactory translation of Plato's *Phaedrus* into Arabic by a philosophy professor who does not know Greek.[72]

This case is unfortunately not unique. This phenomenon has persisted in Egyptian academia from the moment of its official start in 1925 to the time of writing (2017). One of the early accounts of this phenomenon, or structural characteristic, is to be found in an anecdote by Ṭāhā Ḥusayn from 1937. Ḥusayn, who was then a professor of Arabic literature at Fuʾād I University, describes in his book how the university's council, consisting of all of the university's professors (both Egyptians and non-Egyptians), insisted on refusing to introduce the study of Greek and Latin languages to the relevant faculties and departments of the university. Greek and Latin studies ended up being introduced in the university with a crippling restriction; to be taught *only* in the newly inaugurated Greek and Latin Studies department. The terrible consequence was and still is that "... a professor of legal history and/or Roman (civil) law in the Egyptian university does not know Latin and cannot read a simple source text written in it (Hussein 1938. 172)."

The question of the status of Greek and Latin in education is of course not unique to the Arab countries. Moreover, the whole question of the status of these languages is an organic growth from the socio-cultural history of the modern Arab world, where the question of the Arabic language itself has been a major theme of controversy and debate. In a personal interview from 2017, Sayyid ʿUmar [Sayed Omar] of ʿAyn Shams University (one of the most prominent figures in the fields of Classics, Ancient History and Papyrology in Egypt), said in response to a question about the importance of Greek-Arabic or Latin-Arabic lexica for modern Arabic scholarship on ancient history "we do not need them. The English, German and other modern European lexica

---

72   See Shaʿrāwī, Mustaqbal 107–109.

[e.g. LSJ or Preisigke Wörterbuch] are more than enough [for us]". For a person like him, educated in Germany,[73] this makes perfect sense, but for many other scholars of ancient history in Egypt who do not know Greek, Latin or any modern European language other than English, this is problematic.

6.8   *Ṭāhā Ḥusayn, the Pioneering Egyptian Latinist*

Certainly Arabic-speaking students and scholars of the ancient world, and particularly the Roman one, do not lack the necessary tools to understand ancient languages and cultures. On the contrary, the Arab students of classical Latin are served with many books that illustrate to them the grammar and syntax of this ancient language. The first of these books is called *The Latin Language* [*Al-lugha al-Lātīniyya*], and it was most probably the first of its kind, as stated also by the authors in the preface of the first edition in 1946.[74] The second edition of this book appeared two years later in 1948 in Cairo. It was written by three authors: Muḥammad Maḥmūd al-Salāmunī, Jack Joseph Cohen and ʿAbd al-Laṭīf Aḥmad ʿAlī. All of them were mentioned as working in the Faculty of Arts at Fuʾād I University in the preface to the book. Ṭāhā Ḥusayn is said to be the person who commissioned the composition of this grammar when he was dean of the faculty.[75] He and Muḥammad Salīm Sālim, the then head of the Association for Reviving Ancient Studies (*Jamāʿat Iḥyāʾ al-Dirāsāt al-Qadīma*) later revised the grammar. The authors also acknowledged the help of a lecturer by the name of G. Holland, who was said to be working in the same university. The book has seven extensive lessons of Latin grammar, explained using classical Arabic grammatical terminology, in addition to four glossaries (a Latin-Arabic glossary of nouns, another for verbs, an Arabic-Latin glossary for words other than verbs and an Arabic-Latin glossary of Verbs) and an index of grammar rules. It seems that the second volume of this grammar has never appeared.[76] The second Latin textbook that appeared was Amīn Salāma's translation of Frank Prescott Moulton's *Introductory Latin* under the title *Qawāʿid al-Lātīniyya al-Mubassaṭa* [*Simplified Latin Grammar*] in 1947.[77] Another Latin grammar from this period is *Al-Madkhal ilā al-Lughat al-Lātīniyya* [*Introduction to the Latin Language*] by Muḥammad Salīm Sālim

---

73   He obtained his PhD in 1978 from the Institut für Altertumskunde der Universität zu Köln (Arbeitsstelle für Papyrologie, Epigraphik und Numismatik).

74   Al-Salāmunī et al., *Al-Lātīniyya* v.

75   Al-Salāmunī et al., *Al-Lātīniyya* iv.

76   The same is also true about *Al-Badāʾiʿ* the first book series sponsored by the association. Al-Salāmūnī, Cohen, and ʿAlī, *Al-Lughat al-Lātīniyya*.

77   Moulton, *Introduction*; Salāma, *Qawāʿid*.

and Aḥmad ʿAbd al-Raḥīm Abū Zayd published in Cairo in 1949.[78] Muḥammad Salīm Sālim was an assistant professor of ancient studies (*al-dirāsāt al-qadīma*) while Abū Zayd seems to have been a junior lecturer of Latin in the Egyptian University. In 1963 a second edition of this book appeared, followed by a third edition in 1964. It seems that the book enjoyed great popularity until 1990, the year of its last edition. The book consists of an introduction, twenty-seven lessons, a model exam for the students of the first year in several university departments (Arabic, History, Geography and Philosophy), a Latin-Arabic glossary, an Arabic-Latin glossary, paradigms for Latin nouns, adjectives and verbs, and an index of grammar rules. More recently there is *Al-Lugha al-Lātīniyya* [*The Latin Language*] by Aḥmad al-Sammān and Muḥammad Sāmī al-Bājūrī, published in Cairo in 2002.[79] This book, in addition to a general introduction including a short history of Latin and a synopsis of the most salient features of its classical pronunciation, is divided in twenty-six lessons, with ample translation exercises from Latin into Arabic and from Arabic into Latin. At the end of the book students can find paradigms of all the Latin verbs as well as two glossaries: Latin-Arabic and Arabic-Latin.

6.9   *Ṭāhā Ḥusayn's Jamāʿat al-Badāʾiʿ* (*Association of Classics*)

The first Egyptian learned society for Greek and Latin Studies was *The Society for the Revival of Ancient Studies* (*Jamāʿat Iḥyāʾ al-Dirāsāt al-Qadīma*) which was founded in 1945.[80] It is very interesting that the members called themselves a *jamāʿa*, a term that in most cases refers to a first community of believers and their concept of *ijmāʿ* (doctrinal agreement).[81] These believers were: Ṭāhā Ḥusayn, Muḥammad Salīm Sālim, ʿAbd al-Laṭīf Aḥmad ʿAlī, Jack Joseph Cohen, Muḥammad Maḥmūd al-Salāmūnī and Muḥammad Ṣaqr Khafāja. It seems that this jamāʿa had its first headquarters in the Faculty of Arts of Fuʾād I University and that all of these scholars were working in the Department of Ancient Studies, one of the early names given to the department of Greek and Latin studies and the name that is seen in most of their publications and professional titles. During the ten years between 1945 and 1955 the society issued a number of publications, the first of which, entitled *al-Badāʾiʿ* i.e. *The Finest Masterpieces*, appeared in 1945 by protégé of Ṭāhā Ḥusayn and head of the society, Muḥammad Salīm Sālim.[82]

------

78   Abū Zayd and Sālim, *Al-Madkhal.*
79   Al-Bājūrī and Al-Sammān, *Lugha.*
80   Khafāja, Baʿth 160 and cf. also Al-Salāmūnī et al., *Al-Lātīniyya*, iii.
81   About this philosophical and religious meaning see Gardet, Jamāʿa, in *EI*[2], ii, 411.
82   Sālim, *Al-Badāʾiʿ.*

Al-Badāʾiʿ was initially conceived by the head of the society and its first author as a series of translations of the finest master pieces of Greek and Latin authors. Its first volume contained Sālim's translation of Euripides' *Andromache* (not the finest drama, according to some critics), ʿAlī's translation of Lysias' speech *On the killing of Eratosthenes*, and Khafāja's translation of Demosthenes' first *Olynthiac*. Each translation was preceded by an introduction to the author's life, treatises and artistic merits. A second volume of this series has never appeared, yet direct translations of Greek and Latin authors into Arabic by these classicists and their students continued to be published, both under the auspices of the society and elsewhere. The translation of the second book of Herodotus' *Histories* (concerning Egypt) appeared in 1945 by Wahīb Kāmil under the sponsorship of this society.[83] In addition to the translation the book contained an introduction to Herodotus' life, his writing-style, the second book of his *Histories*, and his assumed visit to Egypt. The first edition of Ibrāhīm Nushī's *magnum opus* entitled *History of Egypt in the Ptolemaic Period* (*Tārīkh Miṣr fī ʿAṣr al-Baṭālima*), appeared in Cairo in this same very productive year.[84] Then in 1954 there appeared under the auspices of the society a translation of H. Idris Bell's *Egypt from Alexander the Great to the Arab Conquest: A Study of the Diffusion and Decay of Hellenism*.[85] Two editions of this translation, with additional comments and bibliography in the footnotes by the translators, appeared in 1968, in Cairo, and 1973, in Beirut.[86] Last but not least, Khafāja has translated Legrand's book about Alexandrine Poetry (*La Poésie Alexandrine*).[87] Legrand published his book in Paris in 1924 and Khafāja's translation appeared in Cairo in 1955.[88]

7   Classics in Arabic: Not a Conclusion

Views about Arabic scholarship in Classical Studies are varied, as stated at the start of this overview. Yet none of these views are based on a comprehensive

---

83   Kāmil, *Hīrūdut*.

84   Nushī, *Tārīkh*.

85   Bell, *Egypt*.

86   It is worth noting here that the third edition that appeared in Beirut in 1973 was revised by ʿAbd al-Laṭīf Aḥmad ʿAlī when he was teaching at Beirut Arab University, see ʿAlī, *Miṣr min al-Iskandar*, iv.

87   Legrand, *La Poésie*. On all these publications, see the review presented by Khafāja, Baʿth 159–164.

88   It is noteworthy here to state that Legrand was Khafāja's doctoral supervisor, see Ibrāhīm, Miʾat ʿĀm 8.

survey of the Arabic publications of the field. This is of course due to the lack of a bibliographical database of the field and its subspecialties that covers the publications in Egypt as well as in other Arab countries. The reasons behind the lack of such a bibliography are manifold, but the most important factor behind this shortcoming is the fact that Arabic publications are widely dispersed, without regards to discipline, chronology and place of publication, in libraries throughout the Arab world. Another crucial factor is the fact that, even with the help of online databases and other digital media, such a project is a time-consuming activity that requires a lot of financial and human resources. It is extremely difficult to hunt down every publication in the field, to read it, review it, and to write a balanced review and/or a summary of its content. Nevertheless, it is a rewarding activity.

Arabic-language scholarship in Classical Studies now covers almost every branch of the field. It is more than adequate for enabling any student whose first language is Arabic to obtain a balanced introduction to the fundamental theories, concepts, and opinions of this large field of study. Every student in Egypt is now able to consult introductory books as well as specialized dissertations and theses on Greco-Roman history, religion, mythology, archeology, numismatics, philosophy, science, papyrology and epigraphy, as well as numerous grammars of Greek and Latin, all written in Arabic.

Of course, to rely only on research in one language, especially in advanced stages of study like doctoral and post-doctoral research, is extremely problematic. This is true whether that one language is Arabic or a European language such as German, French, Italian or English. Living in a monolingual bubble of scholarship, no matter how successful the particular tradition of scholarship is, while ignoring scholarship in other languages, is a grave mistake. Just as Arab classicists must continue to follow and utilize European-language scholarship in their field, there is no excuse for the Western community of classicists completely ignoring Arabic Classical scholarship. Modern Arabic scholarship in the Classics is extremely important not only because it sometimes has presented itself as a mode of resistance to the grand European narrative of history, but because it has been, not infrequently, a shadow of it. Arabic Classical scholarship presents a distinct view of the history and heritage of the Greek and Roman world. This feature, in addition to the historical roots of its language and culture, the geographical location occupied by the main audience of this scholarship, and the long history of relations and intellectual exchanges between the Arab countries and Europe, provides Arabic Classical scholarship with a great deal of importance in and of itself as well as for any Western scholar interested in the history and heritage of the Greeks and Romans.

Acknowledgments

This chapter has been written mostly at the Library of the Institute of Classical Studies, University of London, as part of my Visiting Fellowship's Project "Digital Classics in Arabic", generously funded by the British Academy.

Bibliography

'Abbās, Ra'ūf, *Mashaynāhā Khuṭan* [*Inescapable Destinies; An Autobiography*], Cairo, 2004.

'Abd al-Ḥayy, Salāh, *Adab al-riḥalāt 'inda al-Yūnān wa al-Rūmān min khilāl al-Ūdisiyya wa al-Argūnawtīka wa al-Ilyāda* [Greek and Roman Travel Literature through the Odyssey, the Argonautica and the Iliad], PhD. diss., 'Ayn Shams University, Cairo, 2004.

'Abd al-Ḥayy, Salāh, al-Juz' al-Limnī bi-Malḥamat al-Argūnautīka Ṣūra 'Ākisa li al-mujtama' al Hillīnistī, in *Majallat Markaz al-Dirāsāt al-Bardiyya* [*Journal of the Center of Papyrological Studies*] J C P S 31 (2014), 131–150.

Abū Zayd, Aḥmad 'Abd al-Raḥīm, and Sālim, Muḥammad Salīm, *Madkhal ilā al-Lughat al-Lātīniyya* [*Introduction to the Latin Language*], Cairo, 1949.

Ali, Amro, "Power, Rebirth, and Scandal: A Decade of the Bibliotheca Alexandrina," in *Jadaliyya*, October 17, 2012, https://www.jadaliyya.com/Details/27221. Accessed January 02, 2019.

Anderson, Benedict, *Imagined Communities: Reflections on the Origin, and Spread of Nationalism*, London, 1983.

Awrāq Klāssikiyya [*Classical Papers*], Cairo University, 1991, https://acl.journals.ekb.eg/. Accessed November 10, 2020.

Badawī, 'Abd al-Raḥmān, *Tārīkh al-falsafa fī Lībiya: Karniyādis al-Qūrīnāī wa Sūnasiyūn al-Qūrīnāī* [*History of Libyan philosophy: Carneades and Synesius of Cyrene*], 2 vols., Beirut, Dār Ṣādir, 1971.

Badawī, 'Abd al-Raḥmān, *Sīrat Ḥayātī* [*My Autobiography*], 2 vols., Beirut, 2000.

Baird, Jennifer and Kamash, Zena, Remembering Roman Syria: valuing Tadmor-Palmyra, from 'discovery' to destruction in *Bulletin of the Institute of Classical Studies (BICS)* 62.1 (2019), 1–29.

Al-Bājūrī, Muḥammad Sāmī Zakī, and Al-Sammān, Aḥmad Fu'ād, *Al-Lughat Al-Lātīniyya* [*The Latin Language*], Cairo, 2002–2003.

Barbara, Augustin, *Dustūr Al-Āthiniyyin: ta'līf Ārisṭu* [*Constitution of the Athenians: A Treatise by Aristotle*], Damascus, 2013.

Bell, Harold Idris, *Egypt from Alexander the Great to the Arab Conquest: A Study of the Diffusion and Decay of Hellenism*, Oxford, 1948.

Bell, Harold Idris, Arabic translation of the above by Aḥmad, ʿAbd al-Laṭīf, *Miṣr min al-Iskandar al-Akbar ḥattā al-Fatḥ al-ʿArabī: Dirāsa fī Intishār al-Ḥaḍāra al-Hillīniyya wa Iḍmiḥlālihā*, Cairo, 1954, Cairo, 1964 (rev. ed.).

"Bibliographie Papyrologique (BP)," http://www.aere-egke.be/BP/. Accessed August 21, 2019.

Blouin, Katherine, "The Committee Test: Wonder how male & Eurocentric your Antiquity-related field is? Try the Committee Test!" In *Everyday Orientalism*, https://everydayorientalism.wordpress.com/2018/02/13/wonder-how-male-euro centric-your-antiquity-related-field-is-try-the-committee-test/. Accessed 23/11/18.

Bradley, Mark (ed.), *Classics and Imperialism in the British Empire*, Oxford, 2010.

Budayr, Aḥmad ʿAbd al-Fattāḥ, *al-Amīr Aḥmad Fuʾād wa-nashʾat al-Jāmiʿa al-Miṣrīya* [Prince Aḥmad Fuʾād and the Foundation of the Egyptian University], Cairo, 1950.

Budge, Ernest A. Wallis, *By Nile and Tigris: A narrative of journeys in Egypt and Mesopotamia on behalf of the British Museum between the years 1886 and 1913*, London, 1920.

Bulletin of the Center of Papyrological Studies (BCPS), ʿAyn Shams University, Cairo, 1985–, https://bcps.journals.ekb.eg/. Accessed November 10, 2020.

al-Bustānī, S., ʾIliāzat Hūmīrus muʿarraba naẓman wa ʿalayha sharḥ tārīkhī wa hiya muṣaddara bi muqaddima fī Hūmīrus wa shiʿrihi wa ādāb al-yūnān wa al-ʿarab wa mudhayyala bi muʿjam ʿām wa fahāris [*Homer's Iliad: translated in Arabic verse, annotated with historical and literary commentaries, an introduction about Homer's life and poetry, [a comparative study about] the Greek and the Arabic literature, a general glossary and an index*], Cairo, 1904.

Butler, Beverley, *Return to Alexandria: An Ethnography of Cultural Heritage, Revivalism, and Museum History*, Walnut Creek (California, USA), 2007.

Callmer, Christian and Holmqvist, Wilhelm (eds.), *Swedish archaeological bibliography: 1949–1953*, Stockholm, 1956.

Capasso, Mario, *Hermae: scholars and scholarship in papyrology*, 4 vols., Pisa, 2007–2015.

Christoff, M., Tardjama, in *Encyclopaedia of Islam*, 2nd edition, Leiden, 1960–2005, Supplement, 788–790.

Classical Receptions Journal (CRJ), Oxford, 2009-.

Crane, Gregory Ralph, Rethinking the Humanities and advancing civilization in a violent world, in *The Stoa: A Blog for Digital Classics* (2010). Retrieved 28 August 2019, from https://blog.stoa.org/archives/1299.

Culham, Phyllis, Lowell Edmunds, and R. Alden Smith (eds.), *Classics: A Discipline and Profession in Crisis?* Lanham, 1989.

De Gussem, Jeroen et al., Editorial Note in *Journal of Latin Cosmopolitanism and European Literatures* 1 (2019), iv–v.

Dietrich, A. Buqrāṭ, in *Encyclopaedia of Islam*, 2nd edition, Leiden, 1960–2005, Supplement, 154.

Elamine, Adnan [Al-Amīn, ʿAdnān], Al-Jāmiʿāt Al-ʿArabiyya wa taḥaddiyāt al-taghyīr al-ijtimāʿī [Arab Universities and the Challenges of Social Change] in *Omran* [ʿUmrān] 26 (2018), 61–84.

Endress, G., Yaḥyā b. ʿAdī, in *Encyclopaedia of Islam*, 2nd edition, Leiden, 1960–2005, xi, 245–246.

Etman, Ahmed [ʿUthmān, Aḥmad], Translation at the Intersection of Traditions: The Arab Reception of the Classics in Lorna Hardwick and Christopher Stray (eds.) *A Companion to Classical Receptions*, Oxford, 2008, 141–152.

Ewald, François and Fontana, Alessandro, Foreword in Daniel Defert (ed.) *Michel Foucault: Lectures on the Will to Know*, London, 2013, ix.

Fahmy, Khaled [Fahmī, Khālid], The Crisis of the Humanities in Egypt in *Comparative Studies of South Asia, Africa and the Middle East*, 37.1 (2017), 142–148.

Feder, Ellen K., Power/Knowledge, in Dianna Taylor (ed), *Michel Foucault: Key Concepts*, Durham, 2011, 55–68.

Fowden, Garth, *Before and After Muḥammad: The First Millennium Refocused*, Princeton, 2014.

Gad, Usama, "Classics in Arabic,", http://classicsinarabic.blogspot.com/. Accessed 10/11/2020.

Gad, Usama, Aligned Greek, Arabic and English translation of Constitution of the Athenians, "Ugarit, Translation Alignment Editor", http://www.ugarit.ialigner.com/align3.php?function=update&id=26905. Accessed August 12, 2019.

Gardet, L., *Jamāʿa*, in *Encyclopaedia of Islam*, 2nd edition, Leiden, 1960–2005, x, 224–231.

Goff, Barbara (ed.), *Classics and Colonialism*, London, 2005.

Goff, Barbara, Classics in West African Education in Hardwick, Lorna and Stephen Harrison (eds.) *Classics in the Modern World*, Oxford 2013, 157–169.

Goff, Barbara, (ed.), *Your Secret Language: Classics in the British Colonies of West Africa*, London, 2013.

Gutas, Dimitri, *Greek Thought, Arabic Culture: The Graeco-Arabic Translation Movement in Baghdad and Early ʿAbbāsid Society (2nd–4th/8th–10th Centuries)*, London, 1998.

Gutas, Dimitri, Arabic translation of the above by Niqūlā Ziyāda, *Al-Fikr al-Yūnānī wa al-Thaqāfa al-ʿArabiyya: Ḥarakat al-Tarjama al-Yūnāniyya – al-ʿArabiyya fī Baghdād wa al-Mujtamaʿ al-ʿAbbāsī al-Mubakkir (al-Qarn al-Thānī – al-Qarn al-Rābiʿ h./al-Qarn al-Thāmin – al-Qarn al-ʿĀshir m.)*, Beirut, 2003.

Gutas, Dimitri, Tardjama, in *Encyclopaedia of Islam*, 2nd edition, Leiden, 1960–2005, x, 224–231.

Hamilton, Alastair, Arabic Studies in Europe in *Encyclopaedia of Arabic Language and Linguistics* ii, 166–172.

Hanson, Victor Davis and Heath, John, *Who Killed Homer? The Demise of Classical Education and the Recovery of Greek Wisdom*. New York, 1998.

Hanson, Victor Davis, Heath, John and Thornton, Bruce S., *Bonfire of the Humanities: Rescuing Classics in an Impoverished Age*, Wilmington, 2001.

Hardwick, Lorna and Stray, Christopher (eds.), *A Companion to Classical Receptions*, Oxford, 2007.

Hardwick, Lorna and Harrison, Stephen (eds.), *Classics in the Modern World*, Oxford, 2013.

Hardwick, Lorna, In Memoriam: Professor Ahmed Etman (1945–2013) in *Classical Receptions Journal* 6.1 (January 2014), 175.

Humphreys, Sarah C. and Wagner, Rudolf G. (ed.), *Modernity's Classics*, Heidelberg, 2013.

Humphreys, Sarah C., Classics and Colonialism in Most, Glenn W. (ed.) *Disciplining Classics-Altertumswissenschaft als Beruf*, Göttingen, 2002, 207–251.

Ḥusayn, Ṭāhā, *Min al-Adab al-Tamthīlī al-Yūnānī* [*Selections from Greek Drama*], Cairo, 1939.

Ḥusayn, Ṭāhā, *Mustaqbal al-Thaqāfa fī Miṣr* [*The Future of Culture in Egypt*], Cairo, 1937, repr. Cairo, 1996.

Ḥusayn, Ṭāhā, English translation of the above by Glazer, Sidney, *The Future of Culture in Egypt*, Washington, 1954.

Ḥusayn, Ṭāhā, *Niẓām al-Athīniyyin* [*The Constitution of the Athenians*], Cairo, 1921.

Ibrāhim, Muḥammad Ḥamdī, Mi'at ʿām min al-Dirāsāt al-Klāsīkiyya fī Jāmiʿat al-Qāhira [One Hundred Years of Classical Studies in Cairo University] in *Awrāq Klāsīkiya* [*Classical papers*], 8 (2008), 7–16.

"International Federation of the Societies of Classical Studies (FIEC)", https://www.fiecnet.org/our-story. Accessed February 17, 2020.

International Journal of the Classical Tradition (IJCT), published by Springer, 1994–.

Jäger, Gerhard, *Einführung in die Klassische Philologie*, München, 1990.

Janson, Sverker, Olof Vessberg, and Bengt J.N. Thordeman, *Swedish Archaeological Bibliography*: 1. Uppsala, 1951.

Journal of Nationalism, Memory and Language Politics (JNMLP), published by De Gruyter on behalf of Charles University, 2017–.

Al-Kāfurī, Sāmiya, *Al-Intāj al-Fikrī al-Misrī fī Majāl al-Dirāsāt al-Yūnāniya wa al-Latīniya: Dirāsa Bibliomitriya* [*The Intellectual Egyptian Production in the field of the Greek and Latin studies: A Bibliometric Study* (MA unpublished diss. Cairo University)], Cairo, 2004.

Kāmil, Wahīb, *Hīrūdut fī Miṣr* [*Herodotus in Egypt*], Cairo, 1945.

Kamusella, Tomasz, The Arabic Language: A Latin of Modernity? in *Journal of Nationalism, Memory & Language Politics* 11.2 (2017), 117–145.

Khafāja, Muḥammad Ṣaqr, Baʿth al-dirāsāt al-Yūnāniyya wa al-Latīniyya fi Miṣr al-Ḥadītha [The Renaissance of Greek and Latin Studies in Modern Egypt], in *Majallat maʿhad al-dirasāt al-islāmiyya fī Madrīd* 3 (1955), 160–164.

Koenig, Daniel G., ed. *Latin and Arabic: Entangled Histories*, Heidelberg, 2019.

Kreutz, Michael, *Arabischer Humanismus in der Neuzeit*, Berlin, 2007.

Lang, Sarah, Review of 'Perseus Digital Library' Gregory Crane (ed.), 1985–2017 in *RIDE: A Review Journal for Digital Editions and Resources* 8 (2018). doi: 10.18716/ride.a.8.3. Accessed 03.12.2019.

Legrand, Ph. E., *La Poésie Alexandrine*, Paris, 1924.

Legrand, Ph. E., Arabic translation of the above by Khafāja, Muḥammad Ṣaqr, *Shiʿr al-Ruʾāt: Al-Adab al-Yūnānī fī ʿAṣr al-Iskandariyya*, Cairo, 1955.

Malamud, Margret, Classics as a Weapon: African Americans and the Fight for Inclusion in American Democracy, in Hardwick, Lorna and Stephen Harrison (eds.) *Classics in the Modern World: A Democratic Turn?* Oxford, 2013, 89–103.

McGuire, Martin R.P., *Introduction to classical scholarship, a syllabus and bibliographical guide*, Washington, 1961.

Most, Glenn W. (ed.), *Disciplining Classics—Altertumswissenschaft Als Beruf*, Göttingen, 2002.

Moulton, Frank Prescott, *Introductory Latin*, Boston, 1909.

Moulton, Frank Prescott, Arabic translation of the above by Salāma, Amīn, *Qawāʿid al-Lātīniyya al-Mubassaṭa* [*Simplified Latin Grammar*], Cairo, 1947.

Nuṣḥī, Ibrāhīm, *Tārīkh Miṣr fī ʿAṣr al-Baṭālima* [*History of Egypt in the Ptolemaic Period*], 2 vols, Cairo, 1946, 4 vols (rev. ed.), Cairo, 1980/1981.

"Papyri.info, Bibliography", http://www.papyri.info/bibliosearch. Accessed August 21, 2019.

"Perseus Digital Library", http://www.perseus.tufts.edu. Accessed November 6, 2020.

Pormann, Peter, The Arab Cultural Awakening (Nahḍa), 1870–1950, and the Classical Tradition in *International Journal of the Classical Tradition* 13.1 (2006), 3–20.

Pormann, Peter, Classics and Islam: From Homer to Al-Qāʾida in *International Journal of the Classical Tradition* 16.2 (2009), 197–233.

Pormann, Peter, The Continuing Tradition of Arab Humanism in *International Journal of the Classical Tradition* 17.1 (2010), 95–106.

Pormann, Peter, Classical Scholarship and Arab Modernity in Humphreys, Sarah C. and Wagner, Rudolf G. *Modernity's Classics* (eds.) Heidelberg, 2013, 123–141.

Rabinowitz, Nancy Sorkin, The Expansion of Tragedy as a Critique in Hardwick, Lorna and Stephen Harrison (eds.) *Classics in the Modern World: A Democratic Turn?*, Oxford, 2013, 119–130.

Reid, Donald Malcolm, *Cairo University and the Making of Modern Egypt*, Cambridge, 1990.

Reid, Donald Malcolm, Cromer and the Classics: Imperialism, Nationalism and the Greco-Roman Past in Modern Egypt in *Middle Eastern Studies* 32.1 (1996), 1–29.

Reid, Donald Malcolm, *Whose Pharaohs? Archaeology, Museums, and Egyptian National Identity from Napoleon to World War I*, Berkeley, 2002.

Reid, Donald Malcolm, *Contesting Antiquity in Egypt: Archaeologies, Museums, and the Struggle for Identities from World War I to Nasser*, Cairo, 2015.

Rosenthal, Franz, *Das Fortleben der Antike im Islam*, Stuttgart, 1965.

Rosenthal, Franz, *The Classical Heritage in Islam*, London, 1975.

Rosenthal, Franz, Arabic translation of the above by Al-Musallamī, ʿAbdallāh Ḥasan, *Al-Turāth al-Qadīm fī al-Ḥaḍāra al-Islāmiyya*, Cairo, 1993.

Sadgrove, P.C., Tardjama, in *Encyclopaedia of Islam*, 2nd edition, Leiden, 1960–2005, x, 232–233.

Al-Salāmūnī, Muḥammad Maḥmūd, Cohen, Jack Joseph, and ʿAlī, ʿAbd al-Laṭīf Aḥmad, Supervised by Ṭāhā Ḥusayn and Muḥammad Salīm Sālim, *Al-Lughat al-Lātīniyya: Al-Juzʾ al-Awwal* [*The Latin Language: Part One*], Cairo, 1948.

Sālim, Muḥammad Salīm, *Al-Badāʾiʿ* [*The Finest Masterpieces*], Cairo, 1945.

Sandys, John Edwin, *A Short History of Classical Scholarship from the Sixth Century B.C. to the Present Day*, Cambridge, 1915.

Shaʿrāwī, ʿAbd al-Muʿṭī, Mustaqbal al-dirāsāt al-klāsīkiīya fī Misr [Future of Classical studies in Egypt] in *Al-Majalla* 159 (March 1970), 103–109.

al-Shayyāl, Jamāl al-Dīn, *Tārīkh al-tarjama fī Miṣr fī ʿahd al-ḥamla al-Faransiyya* [History of Translation in Egypt during the French expedition], Cairo, 1949.

al-Shayyāl, Jamāl al-Dīn, *Tārīkh al-tarjama wa-al-ḥaraka al-thaqāfiya fī ʿaṣr Muḥammad ʿAlī* [History of Translation and the Cultural Movement during the era of Muhammad Ali], Cairo, 1951.

Strohmaier, G., Isḥāq b. Ḥunayn al-ʿIbādī, in *Encyclopaedia of Islam*, 2nd edition, Leiden, 1960–2005, ii, 578–581.

Strohmaier, G., Isḥāq b. Ḥunayn, in *Encyclopaedia of Islam*, 2nd edition, Leiden, 1960–2005, iv, 110.

al-Ṭahṭāwī, Rafāʿa Rāfiʿ, *Takhlīṣ Al-Ibrīz fī talkhīṣ Bārīz aw al-Dīwān al-Nafīs bi-Iwān Bārīs* [*An Imam in Paris: Account of a Stay in France by an Egyptian Cleric (1826–1831)*], trans. Newman, Daniel L., London, 2011.

Thompson, Lawrence, *A Bibliography of American Doctoral Dissertations in Classical Studies and Related Fields*, Hamden, CT, 1968.

Thompson, Lawrence, *A Bibliography of Dissertations in Classical Studies: American, 1946–1972; British, 1950–1972; with a Cumulative Index, 1861–1972.* Hamden, CT, 1976.

Vagelpohl, Uwe, Translation Literature in *Encyclopaedia of Arabic Language and Linguistics*, iv, 542–548.

Van Zyl Smit, Betine, Multicultural Reception: Greek Drama in South Africa in the Late Twentieth and Early Twenty-first Centuries in Hardwick, Lorna and Christopher Stray (eds.) *A Companion to Classical Receptions*, Oxford, 2008, 373–397.

Vasunia, Phiroze, *The Classics and Colonial India*, Oxford, 2013.

Wakin, Daniel J., Successor to Ancient Alexandria Library Dedicated in New York Times, October 17/2002, Section A, 14.

Walzer, R. Arisṭūṭālīs, in *Encyclopaedia of Islam*, 2nd edition, Leiden, 1960–2005, i, 631.

Walzer, R. Djālīnūs, in *Encyclopaedia of Islam*, 2nd edition, Leiden, 1960–2005, ii, 402–403.

Wehr, Hans, *A Dictionary of Modern Written Arabic*, Urbana, 1979.

Wilmsen, David, and Woidich, Manfred, Egypt in *Encyclopedia of Arabic Language and Linguistics* ii, 1–12.

Wilson, Nigel, Griechische Philologie im Altertum in *Einleitung in die griechische Philologie*, Nesselrath, Heinz-Günthner (ed.), Leipzig, 1977.

Abbreviations of Periodicals, Encyclopedias and Dictionaries

BCPS   *Bulletin of the Center of Papyrological Studies* ('Ayn Shams University, Cairo, 1985–)

IJCT   *International Journal of the Classical Tradition* (Published by Springer, 1994–)

JNMLP   *Journal of Nationalism, Memory and Language Politics* (Published by De Gruyter on behalf of Charles University, 2017–)

JOLCEL   *Journal of Latin Cosmopolitanism and European Literatures* (Ghent University, Ghent, 2019–)

WECT   *The World Encyclopaedia of Contemporary Theatre* (London, 1994–2000)

EI²   *The Encyclopaedia of Islam*, second edition (Leiden, 1960–2005)

Interviews

Fahmy, Khalid [Fahmī, Khālid], personal interview (13/11/2017): His Majesty Sultan Qaboos Bin Sa'id, Professor of Modern Arabic Studies at Cambridge University.

Sayyid, 'Umar [Sayed Omar], personal interview (29/10/2017): Prof. *emeritus* of papyrology, Greek and Latin Studies at 'Ayn Shams University.

PART 2

The Study of the Middle Ages

∵

7

The Study of Byzantine History in Egypt (1945–2017)

Abdelaziz Ramadan

The study of Byzantine history emerged in Egypt after World War II as a branch of Islamic and Medieval history. After the war for almost two decades a sort of such study can be traced but without real Byzantinists.

1 The Pre-Revolutionary Situation

Although the first Egyptian university had been founded by – and named after – King Fu'ād in 1925, the chair of medieval history in the Faculty of Arts was only established in 1937 by Muḥammad Muṣṭafā Ziyāda (1900–68) who, seven years earlier, had completed his PhD in Liverpool, with a dissertation entitled *Foreign Relations of Egypt in the Fifteenth Century*, supervised by the famous medievalist G.W. Copland. Meanwhile, another medievalist, ʿAzīz Sūryāl ʿAṭṭiyya (1898–1988), returned to King Fu'ād University in 1939 after many years of studying in the universities of Liverpool and London. He moved to Alexandria as soon as King Fārūq University was established, in 1942, and held the foundation chair in medieval history in the Faculty of Arts till 1954.[1] Muṣṭafā Ziyāda's preoccupation with writing about Islamic history and editing Arabic sources,[2] and Sūryāl ʿAṭṭiyya's concentration on the Crusades and Coptic history, did not give them any room for interest in Byzantine history. Their postgraduate students followed the same pattern and devoted themselves mainly to Islamic and Crusade studies.[3] This pattern was only broken,

---

1   On Sūryāl ʿAṭṭiyya's brilliant career abroad from 1955 until his death in 1988, see ʿAbd al-Ẓāhir, *Suryāl ʿAṭṭiyya* 7–10.

2   On Muṣṭafā Ziyāda's contributions to the editing of Arabic manuscripts, see the pamphlet of Rabīʿ, *Manhaj Taḥqīq at-Turāth* 1–10.

3   Muṣṭafā Ziyāda supervised about 35 master's and doctoral dissertations. Their titles reveal that the history of the Ayyubids and Mamluks received the greatest share of his interest (11 dissertations in Mamluk history and 8 in Ayyubid history). The other dissertations were divided between the history of the Crusades (4), Islamic civilization (4), Abbasids (4), and one dissertation each on the history of early Islam, the Umayyads, Fatimids, the Maghrib,

relatively speaking, when some of these students had the opportunity to study for a doctorate abroad. All of them were occupied with studying topics related to Islamic-Byzantine relations. In 1946, a student specializing in Islamic history from the Faculty of Arts at King Fārūq University, Muḥammad ʿAbd al-Hādī Shuʿayra (d. 1977), completed his doctoral dissertation entitled *La lutte entre Arabes et Byzantins: la conquête et l'organisation des frontières aux VIIe et VIIIe siècles* at the University of Paris.[4] At about the same time, another graduate of King Fārūq University, Muḥammad ʿAlī Fahmy,[5] earned his PhD degree from the University of London with a dissertation entitled *Muslim Sea-Power in the Eastern Mediterranean from the Seventh to the Tenth Century.*[6] In 1949, the future medievalist Ibrāhīm Aḥmad al-ʿAdawī (d. 2004) returned from Liverpool to the Faculty of Dār al-ʿUlūm[7] at King Fuʾād University carrying his doctoral dissertation *Egyptian Maritime Power in the Early Middle Ages: from the Arab Conquest of Egypt to the Fall of the Fatimids (640–1171)*. A quick look at these dissertations' bibliographies may explain why these researchers were directed to study such subjects, since it reveals an obvious lack of knowledge of Greek and complete dependence on modern Western studies, Arabic sources and the very few Greek texts then available in modern Western translations.[8]

This beginning seems to have largely determined the shape and nature of what can be described as the pre-revolutionary study of Byzantine history. It seems that most of the generation of pioneers who graduated from Liverpool and London were greatly influenced by the historiographical school of

---

and Muslims in Norman Sicily. He also supervised a dissertation [of Ḥakīm Amīn, 1955] entitled *Al-Jamāʿāt al-Rahbāniya fī Wādī al-Naṭrūn fī al-Qarn al-Rabiʿ al-Mīlādī* [Monastic Communities in Fourth Century Wādī al-Naṭrūn]. See Kutabī, *Muṣṭafā Ziyāda* 35–7. See also: Dissertations awarded 400–403.

4   It was published under the same titles by *Société de publications Égyptiennes*, Alexandria 1947.

5   Fahmy was not a member of the university faculty. As recorded in the list of contributors in *Islamic Review* (March 1952), he was working at that time as an inspector of social studies for secondary schools in the Alexandria zone.

6   This dissertation was completed under the guidance of the famous Bernard Lewis. It was published under the same title in London 1950 and re-published in Cairo in 1966 in two volumes, the first carrying the same title, while the second was entitled *Muslim Naval Organisation from the Seventh to Tenth Century*.

7   The English translation is 'Faculty of Religious Sciences', a college specializing in Arabic and religious sciences.

8   In his review of Fahmy's book, the eminent Byzantinist Romilly Jenkins found that "it is disappointing that Dr. Fahmy attempts to sketch the organization of Muslim sea-power without a knowledge of Greek, and hence without reference to an enormous number of Greek terms and Greek documents which would have helped and illuminated his study". Jenkins, Review 180–81.

"Political History". Even ʿAbd al-Hādī Shuʿayra, who completed his doctorate in the milieu of the *Annales* school in France, appeared more influenced by traditional political and dynastic history when he chose to translate into Arabic Alexander Vasiliev's monumental study *Byzance et les Arabes*, the first western work about Byzantine history to be translated into Arabic, in 1949.[9] This also explains why the contribution to the study of Byzantine history during the 1950s and 1960s was confined to the translation and publication of studies relating to Islamic–Byzantine relations.

Ibrāhīm al-ʿAdawī was the most active and engaged scholar in Byzantine history during this period. Besides his first book *Byzantium and Islam* (Cairo, 1951), he published three articles, one of which dealt with the Muslim–Byzantine competition over Crete in the ninth century[10] and another with political representation between the Abbasids and the Byzantines.[11] The title of the third article, "Studies in Byzantine History",[12] is problematic, since it only focuses on the early Arab–Byzantine frontiers, in particular on the system of *themata*. It seems that Ibrāhīm al-ʿAdawī did not intend any kind of misinformation, and this was no more than an expression of a trend among the medievalists of this time that considered Islamic-Byzantine relations as the most important part of Byzantine history. This trend was implicitly criticized by none other than leading medievalist Muṣṭafā Ziyāda. In his introduction to Ibrāhīm al-ʿAdawī's *Byzantium and Islam*, he acknowledged the difficulty of separating the study or the teaching of Byzantine history from Islamic history, but on the other hand he claimed that this should not prevent medievalists from producing works in "pure" Byzantine studies.[13]

2   Impact of the July Revolution: the 1950s and the 1960s

This initial status for the study of Byzantine history remained essentially unchanged after the July Revolution in 1952. It maintained its basic line of adhering to the school of political history and studying Islamic–Byzantine relations exclusively. However, a remarkable change in its form and content

---

9   Affiliation to the school of political history may be also reflected by the first Arabic translation of a western survey of Byzantine history, Norman Baynes's *The Byzantine Empire*, which was done in 1950 by Ḥusayn Muʾnis (1911–96), Professor of Islamic History at King Fuʾād University.

10   Al-ʿAdawī, Iqrīṭish 53–68.

11   Al-ʿAdawī, Al-Tamthīl 113–122.

12   Al-ʿAdawī, Dirāsāt 75–93.

13   Al-ʿAdawī, *Bīzanṭa wa al-Islām* iii–iv.

can be observed as a result of the increasing relationship between historical writing and political ideology in the post-revolutionary period. The spread of the new revolutionary spirit and ideas not only changed the names of the three existing universities but also prompted medievalists to adjust their interests and attitudes. In his study *Historians, State, and Politics in Twentieth Century Egypt*, Gorman has analyzed the impact of the new climate created by the July Revolution on the study and teaching of modern history, referring in detail to historians who warmly embraced the new political demands of nationalism, Arabism, and socialism.[14]

Medievalists were not isolated from this climate, in fact many of them soon adapted to it and competed to echo the revolutionary rhetoric and nationalist tone of the 1950s and 1960s,[15] and this largely determined the themes, contents, and even the formula of their studies' titles.[16] Ibrāhīm al-ʿAdawī's post-revolutionary writings are a clear indicator of this adjustment. The terms *ʿArab* and *ʿArabī* began to appear in their titles with the same frequency as *Muslims* and *Islamic*.[17] The contents and titles of these studies became more rhetorical and a reminder of the early Muslims' past glories. In the preface of his monograph *The Umayyads and Byzantines: The Mediterranean an Islamic Lake*, he stressed the concept of "political and social vigilance", the role of religion's "social system" in the unity of the Islamic world, and the importance of the Mediterranean to achieve "global leadership".[18] Another medievalist from

---

14 Groman, *Historians* 29.

15 It was not strange during the 1950s and 1960s to find a prominent medievalist such as Saʿīd ʿĀshūr writing a considerable book entitled *Revolution of the People: a Presentation of the National Movement in Egypt in the Nineteenth and Twentieth Centuries with a Detailed Study of the Revolution of July 23, 1952*. Also, Ibrāhīm al-ʿAdawī published in the 1950s and 1960s books entitled *Gamāl ʿAbd al-Nāṣir*; *The Vigilance of Sudan*; *The Leaders of Arab Liberation in Modern Era*; *Infiltration Movements against Arab Nationalism*; *ʿUmar Makram: Hero of the Popular Resistance*; *The Arab Society: Its Components and Universal Mission*; *The Conflict between Arab Nationalism and the New Colonialism*. It seems that the last three books, which were published between 1967 and 1969, were influenced by the atmosphere of the defeat of the 1967 War.

16 As Gorman also has pointed out "There were opportunities to make considerable profit for those willing to write on subjects from a politically acceptable viewpoint". Groman, *Historians* 60.

17 Also, it seems that Ibrāhīm al-ʿAdawī found the title of his monograph *Byzantium and Islam* became unsuitable for the requirements of the period, so he republished it in 1958 under the new title *The Islamic State and the Empire of the Rūm*. Using the term the Islamic state and using a term that has an ethnic connotation seem to be meaningful.

18 Ibrāhīm al-ʿAdawī appeared to be addressing the political power when wrote: "Today, Islamic countries are passing through an important stage of political and social vigilance and working to achieve a decent place among the nations of the world. This stage requires careful study of the fundamentals of the Islamic countries, and an understanding of the

the University of Alexandria (formerly King Fārūq University), ʿUmar Kamāl Tawfīq, published two books in 1959 and 1966 dealing with the eastern politics of Emperors Nikephoros II Phocas (963–969) and John Tzimisces (969–976). In both books, he evidently sought to link his approach to the contemporary political discourse that was hostile to colonialism and imperialism. He portrayed tenth-century Byzantium as a crusader and imperialist power, and presented the two Emperors' policies as a "religious war",[19] a "prelude to the Crusades", and a part of the persistent European ambitions in the Arab-Islamic Near East.[20]

From the same origins as this growing relationship between historical writing and political ideology, another phenomenon was also born during the 1950s and 1960s and left a profound impact on the study of medieval history that has continued until now. It is the emergence of what can be described as the "encyclopedic" medievalist, whose writing could, and should, cover many periods and fields of medieval and Islamic history. This phenomenon seemed more pronounced among the medievalists of Cairo University (formerly King Fuʾād University), who have pursued the line of Muṣṭafā Ziyāda that gathers the history of the Crusades, Ayyubids, Mamluks, Byzantines, and medieval Europe in one branch known as *Tārīkh al-ʿUṣūr al-Wūsṭā* (history of the Middle Ages). Given that Byzantine history was the least of the areas of these medievalists' interests, and that the new political demands had prompted some of them to expand their scope of writing even beyond the "history of the Middle Ages", we can imagine the status of the post-revolutionary study of Byzantine history at Cairo University in both quantity and quality.

Ibrāhīm al-ʿAdawī is a shining example of this new phenomenon. He almost abandoned his previous interest in Islamic-Byzantine relations in favor of

---

developments that they have passed, through a scientific study, so that leaders of the Islamic world can follow the guidance of these studies to direct their countries towards what achieves its pride and glory". Al-ʿAdawī, *Al-Umawiyyūn* iii–vi. A similar rhetoric can be easily extracted from his monograph *Arab Fleets in the Mediterranean*, Al-ʿAdawī, *Al-Asāṭīl* vi. However, this tone is absent from his study *Muslim Embassies to Europe in Middle Ages*, which includes a considerable part relating to embassies to Byzantium.

19   This is evident in the title of his first book: *Emperor Nikephore Phokas and the Recovery of the Holy Lands.*

20   ʿUmar Tawfīq's keenness to address the political authorities may be evident in the preface of his second book: "Perhaps this study will be a lesson and useful for the Arab Islamic nation, which is facing today the recent attempts by the foreign colonizer to occupy its homeland ... The Arab nation today is in dire need of unity under wise leadership so that it can vigorously and successfully confront the dangers surrounding it". Tawfīq, *Yūḥanā Tzimisces* v–vi. It should be noted that ʿUmar Tawfīq wrote this book between the two wars of 1956 and 1967, and this may have affected his preface.

many other fields. With the exception of his monograph *The Umayyads and Byzantines*, which may have been written before the revolution, Ibrāhīm al-ʿAdawī's post-revolutionary publications dealt with various topics in Islamic, medieval, modern, and even ancient history.[21] His only article on Byzantine history written after the revolution appeared in Kuwait in 1973 and deals with the laws of agrarian reform in Byzantium.[22] Based on the information available on the website of the Egyptian Universities Libraries Consortium (*EULC*), he supervised about forty-five master's and doctoral dissertations from 1967 to his death in 2004.[23] Only two of them dealt with subjects related to Islamic-Byzantine relations.[24]

The study of Byzantine history was also outside the area of interest of the two prominent pupils of Muṣṭafā Ziyāda, Ḥasan Ḥabashī (1915–2005)[25] and Saʿīd ʿAbd al-Fattāḥ ʿĀshūr (1922–2009).[26] Despite their relatively long

---

21   In the fields of Islamic and medieval history, he published books entitled: *Ibn Baṭṭūṭa*; *The Arab Navies in the Mediterranean*; *Muslims and Germans: Islam in the Western Mediterranean*; *The Arab society and anti-Populism*; *Arabs and Tartars*; *Ibn ʿAbd al-Ḥakam: Pioneer of the Arab Historians*; *Mūsā Ibn Nuṣayr: The Founder of Arab Maghrib*. In Ancient history: *History of the Ancient World*. In modern history: *Islamic East in the Modern Era*.

22   Tawfīq, Qawānīn al-Iṣlāḥ 149–72. This is the only study written by Ibrāhīm al-ʿAdawī that deals with a subject in pure Byzantine history.

23   As the *EULC* website records, Ibrāhīm al-ʿAdawī supervised nine dissertations in Fatimid and Ayyubid history, seven in the history of the Maghrib and Andalus, five in Ottoman history, five in the history of the Umayyads and Abbasids, three about early Islamic history, two in Mamluk history, three on Islamic civilization, three on the Islamic history of the Gulf region, and one on Mongol history. Strangely enough, he also supervised three dissertations in modern history entitled *The history of Palestinian resistance (1917–35)*; *The Iranian Threat to the Arab Gulf in the First Half of the Twentieth Century*; *Ẓāhir al-ʿUmar in Palestine and ʿAlī Beg al-Kabīr in Egypt: a Comparative Historical Study*.

24   These dissertations as follows: Ramaḍān, A.A., *Al-ʿAlāqāt*; Al-Qirsh, *Al-ʿAlāqāt*. He also supervised a master's dissertation at Kuwait University: Al-Ḥamd, *Al-Imbrāṭūriyya*.

25   Ḥasan Ḥabashī completed his master's dissertation *Nūr a-Dīn Maḥmūd and the Crusades* in 1938 under the supervision of Muṣṭafā Ziyāda (published in Cairo in 1948), then moved to Ibrāhīm Pāshā University (later ʿAyn Shams University) in 1950 as a lecturer in Islamic History. In 1955, he completed his doctoral dissertation *Historical Studies on the Inbāʾ al-Ghumar of Ibn Ḥajar* at the University of London under the direction of the eminent scholar Bernard Lewis. Although he devoted most of his studies to the history of the Crusades and Mamluks, his interest extended to writing about the history of early Islam and modern Algeria. He also made great efforts in editing some Arabic sources and translating, from English and French, a large number of sources on the Crusades and a few western studies on Muslim Spain, non-Muslims in Islam, and even modern Zanzibar.

26   There is no doubt that Saʿīd ʿĀshūr in his post-doctoral studies was following Ziyāda's footsteps. Under the supervision of the latter, he completed in 1944 a master's dissertation entitled *Cyprus and the Crusades* (published in Cairo, 1957) and the doctoral dissertation *Social Life in Mamluk Egypt* (published in Cairo in 1963 under the title *The Egyptian*

academic lives and the abundance and diversity of their studies, neither of them published a single article relating to Byzantine history.[27] According to the *EULC* website, of the thirty-four dissertations supervised by Ḥasan Ḥabashī in the Faculty of Arts at ʿAyn Shams University from 1964 to 1975,[28] only one deals with a topic related to early Byzantine history.[29] Similarly, Saʿīd ʿĀshūr supervised some twenty-eight dissertations between 1967 and 2005,[30] two of which concerned Byzantine history.[31]

On the other hand, the lack of strict and precise boundaries in academic historical writing at Cairo University necessarily led to the emergence of inadequate studies written by non-specialists during the 1950s and the 1960s. The references of these studies reveal a full reliance on citations from the few Western surveys of Byzantine history that were available at that time, and an apparent ignorance of the source language, or perhaps a lack of knowledge of the sources themselves. Fortunately, however, the number of these studies can be counted on the fingers of one hand. In 1956, a thirty-four-page monograph entitled *Iconoclasm in the Byzantine State* was published by Ibrāhīm ʿAlī Ṭarkhān (d. 1985), whose studies were mainly focused on the history of the Muslim kingdoms of West Africa and the feudal system in medieval Egypt.[32]

    Society in the Era of the Mamluk Sultans). However, his contribution, which is close to seventy studies, is not only confined to the history of the Crusades and the Mamluks, but also covers the history of the Fatimids, Ayyubids, Ottomans, and medieval Europe, besides writing on Islamic civilization and editing some Arabic sources.

27   Even when Ḥasan Ḥabashī translated into Arabic the two narratives of Geoffrey de Villehardouin and Robert de Clari about the fourth crusade in 1964 and 1982, respectively, or the *Alexiad* of Ana Komnena in 2004, this was simply an extension of his project of translating the sources of the Crusades. His translation of Donald Nicol's *A Biographical Dictionary of the Byzantine Empire* (published in 2003) is his only work directly related to Byzantine history.

28   These dissertations are as follows: nine on Abbasid history, seven on editions of Arabic manuscripts, five in Mamluk history, three in the Crusades, three in the history of the Maghreb and Andalus, one on the historian Ibn al-Athīr, and one each on the Buwayhids, Umayyads, Mongols and the Ḥijāz.

29   It is the MA dissertation of Raʾfat ʿAbd al-Ḥamīd, the future medievalist at ʿAyn Shams University from the mid-1970s until his death in 2001, which is entitled *Constantine I's Policy Toward the Christian Sects*.

30   According to the *EULC* website, there are twelve on Mamluk history, eight on the Crusades, two in Islamic history of Oman, and one each on the history of the Maghreb, Mongols, Umayyads, and Islamic Africa.

31   See, Ṣāliḥ, *Siyāsat*; Zayyān, A.H., al-*Imbrāṭūr Aliksīyūs*.

32   Under the supervision of Muṣṭafā Ziyāda, Ibrāhīm Ṭarkhān obtained his MA degree in 1949 and his PhD in 1955; the title of his MA dissertation was *Islamic Feudal System in the Middle Ages until the End of the Ayyubid Era*, while his PhD dissertation was entitled *Feudal Systems in the First and Second Mamluk States*. He moved to Cairo University

It was the only study written by Ibrāhīm Ṭarkhān about Byzantine history. Although it is the first Arabic study that dealt with a purely Byzantine subject, it is entirely based on a few classic Western surveys of Byzantine history,[33] and just as it did not rely on any Byzantine source, it also overlooked Western studies available at that time on the same subject.[34]

Al-Sayyid al-Bāz al-ʿArīnī (d. 1969) was also a true embodiment of the status of Byzantine studies at Cairo University during this period. He was awarded MA and PhD degrees in the history of medieval Egypt under the supervision of Muṣṭafā Ziyāda in 1944 and 1955, respectively.[35] As a member of this "encyclopedic" generation, his studies covered all the fields that were regarded as components of discipline known as the "History of the Middle Ages".[36] Among the few dissertations he supervised, there is only one master's dissertation on Islamic-Byzantine relations, entitled *The Islamic East and the Byzantine State in the time of the Ayyubids*, which was completed in 1968 by the future medievalist Zubayda Muḥammad ʿAṭāʾ. Compared with other contemporary medievalists at Cairo University, al-ʿArīnī was the most active contributor to the study of Byzantine history. His MA dissertation included as an appendix a translation of the tenth-century text *Eparchion Biblion*. This translation does not need to be evaluated here, as it has already been implicitly criticized.[37] In 1956, he published a small eighteen-page pamphlet about the Byzantine *themata*,[38] largely

---

(Khartoum Branch) and was a professor of medieval history when he published the two dissertations in one volume entitled *Feudal Systems in the Medieval Middle East*, which was published in Cairo in 1968. He published many articles about Islam and the Arabs in Africa and three books about West African Islamic States of Ghana, Mali and Bornu. He also published in the 1950s and 1960s books entitled *The Visigoths*; *Egypt in the Era of the Circassian Mamluk State*; and *Muslims in Medieval Europe*.

33 Specifically those written by Norman Baynes, Henry Moss, John Bury, Charles Diehl, George Finlay, Edward Gibbon, Charles Oman, and Alexander Vasiliev.

34 Such as: Martin, *Iconoclastic Controversy*; Ostrogorsky, Les débuts 235–55; Lander, Iconoclastic controversy 127–49.

35 Al-Bāz al-ʿArīnī's MA dissertation entitled *ʿAbd al-Raḥmān ibn Naṣr al-Shayzarī's Kitāb Nihāyat al-Rutbah fī Ṭalab al-Ḥisba, with a Historical Introduction on the Office of Muḥtasib in Egypt till 254/868*, and the title of his PhD dissertation is *Equestrian in Egypt under the Mamluk Sultans*.

36 In the 1960s, al-Bāz al-ʿArīnī published books entitled *Middle East and the Crusades*; *Historians of the Crusades*; *Byzantine Egypt*; *The European Civilization in the Middle Ages*; *The Ayyubids*; *The Mongols*; *The Arab Society*; *History of Europe in Middle Ages*.

37 In his monograph *State and Trade in the Middle Byzantine Period*, Wisām Faraj pointed out that al-Bāz al-ʿArīnī relied on the English translation of this text and was unable to obtain the Greek text, nor did he see the Latin or French translation, which is the best translation of the text. Faraj, Al-Dawla 59.

38 Al-ʿArīnī, *Ajnād*.

based on the articles of E.W. Brooks and Charles Diehl.[39] What really deserves attention is his 931-page monumental survey *The Byzantine State*.[40] The uniqueness of this work and its high level compared with other works of this period will certainly shock readers, especially chapter one, entitled "The evolution of the study of Byzantine history". However, this surprise will dissipate quickly upon comparing this chapter with the first chapter of Vasiliev's *History of the Byzantine Empire (324–1453)*, entitled "The study of Byzantine history", from which it appears to be a direct translation.

Unlike at Cairo University, the post-revolutionary study of Byzantine history was moving, albeit slowly, in a somewhat different direction at the University of Alexandria. From the beginning, Sūryāl ʿAṭṭiyya sought to develop a more specific definition of "the history of the Middle Ages". He excluded from its framework the history of the Mamluks and the Ayyubids, with a major focus on the history of the Crusades. His immediate disciple and successor, Joseph Yūsuf (1925–93), followed him. Joseph Yūsuf earned his master's degree in 1950 and his doctorate in 1954 under the supervision of Sūryāl ʿAṭṭiyya with two dissertations dealing with the Seventh Crusade against Egypt[41] and King Louis IX in the Levant.[42] His long academic career, which made him one of the most productive medievalists of his time, was almost entirely devoted to the history of the Crusades[43] and medieval European history. Joseph Yūsuf's writing on Byzantine history was limited and confined to subjects related to his primary

---

39   Brooks, Byzantine Themes 67–7; Diehl, régime des themes 276–92. In addition to using few Arabic sources, al-ʿArīnī did not forget to quote from the traditional surveys of Baynes, Bury, Runciman and Vasiliev.

40   Al-ʿArīnī, Al-*Dawla*.

41   Published in 1960 under the title *The Defeat of Louis IX on the Nile Riverbanks,* and republished in 1969 under the title *The Crusader Aggression on Egypt: The Defeat of Louis IX in Mansoura and Fāraskūr*.

42   Joseph Yūsuf published his PhD dissertation in 1956 under the title *Louis IX in the Middle East (1250–54): The Palestinian Issue in the Period of the Crusades*, and he republished it in 1971 under the new title *The Crusader aggression on the Levant: The Defeat of Louis IX in the Holy Lands*.

43   Joseph Yūsuf published books entitled *Union and the Movements of Arab Vigilance during the Crusader Aggression; Studies in the Relations between East and West in Middle Ages; In the History of the Crusader Movement*. He also published articles entitled: The Personal Motive in the Crusader Movement; Western Colonial Aggression against the Arab World: Ancient and Modern Common Divisors; Zionism in Palestine as a Natural Extension of Crusader Colonialism. It is worth mentioning that the titles of Joseph Yūsuf's works during the 1950s and 1960s evidently reflect the revolutionary national tone. This can be easily noted in using words as "aggression", "union", and "Arab vigilance". Also, there is a clear connection between the titles and contents of his articles and the growing anger toward Israel and the West during the 1960s.

area of interest. With the exception of his textbook *History of the Byzantine Empire (284–1453)*,[44] which seems to have served an educational purpose, he approached Byzantine history only when he addressed the Byzantine role in the first Crusade in his book *Arabs, Byzantines and Latins in the First Crusade*,[45] or as an introductory chapter to his book *Islam and Christianity: The Conflict of their Powers in the Middle Ages*.[46]

In the same period, the University of Alexandria also witnessed the emergence of another prominent medievalist, 'Umar Kamāl Tawfīq (d. 1986), who returned in 1952 from the University of Pennsylvania with a doctoral dissertation entitled *Nūr al-Dīn and the Revival of Muslim Power (1146–1174)*, supervised by John Lamonte. Compared with Joseph Yūsuf, his few studies reflect a balanced interest in both Byzantine history and the history of the Crusades.[47] 'Umar Tawfīq also seemed more interested in promoting the study of Byzantine history among postgraduate students. In his book *History of the Byzantine State*, he criticized scholars who "do not tend to study Byzantine history and regard it as a bleak and boring story". According to him, "there is no way to get a complete picture of the history of Arabs and Muslims in the Middle Ages without studying Byzantine history", and "if the ancient Arabs have learned a lot about the Byzantines because of their close connections with them, the modern Arab students of history should be interested in Byzantine history. For us, its importance in many respects exceeds the importance of the history of Europe in the Middle Ages."[48]

Although 'Umar Tawfīq seems to have been more interested than Joseph Yūsuf in directing most of his postgraduate students to study topics from

---

44   Yūsuf, *Tārīkh*.

45   Yūsuf, *Al-'Arab*.

46   This chapter deals with Muslim-Byzantine relations in Syria and its frontiers in early Islam (626–37), originally an article presented at the fourth international conference of Bilād al-Shām, Amman 1985. This book contains three other chapters. The second chapter deals with the history of Arab civilization. The third represents the first publication of his future small monograph *In the History of the Crusader Movement*, while the fourth is a re-publication of his monograph *Union and the Movements of Arab Vigilance during the Crusader Aggression*.

47   In addition to the two books mentioned earlier, which deal with the eastern policies of the Emperors Nickephoros II Phocas and John Tzimisces, 'Umar Tawfīq published two books entitled *The Crusader Kingdom of Jerusalem; Islamic Diplomacy and the Peaceful Relations with the Crusaders*. It is important to note the titles of the studies contain the words "diplomatic" and "peace", as they were written around the time of the 1979 Egyptian-Israeli peace treaty. Prof. Albrecht Fuess, Marburg University, drew my attention to this observation during the discussions of the Conference *Modern Arabic Historical Scholarship on the Ancient and Medieval Periods*, held at the University of Trier, 23–4 November 2017.

48   Tawfīq, *Tārīkh* 5, 12.

Byzantine history for their MA and PhD dissertations, the two were similar in maintaining the traditional adherence to the school of political history, and in not going beyond the familiar trend of studying the political relations between Muslims and Byzantines. ʿUmar Tawfīq supervised only seven dissertations, five of which dealt with topics related to Islamic-Byzantine relations,[49] while Joseph Yūsuf, according to the *EULC* website, supervised about twenty-two dissertations, most of which were concerned with the history of the Crusades and of which only five dealt with Byzantine-Islamic relations.[50]

3　　　Cairo University: the 1970s and Beyond

There is no doubt that the foundation established by the medievalists of the 1950s and 1960s at the universities of Cairo and Alexandria clearly defined the course of studying medieval history in general and Byzantine history in particular at the two universities from the 1970s onwards.

At Cairo University, three new researchers joined Saʿīd ʿĀshūr in the early 1970s as faculty members specializing in medieval history. All of them were directed to study the history of the Ayyubids, Mamluks and Crusades. The first one, Hassanein Rabie (Ḥasanayn Rabīʿ, b. 1938), was trained by al-Bāz al-ʿArīnī and wrote under his guidance a master's thesis entitled *The Financial System of Egypt in the Ayyubid Era* (completed and published in Cairo 1964). In the late 1960s, he obtained his doctorate from the University of London with a dissertation entitled the *Financial System of Egypt (1169–1341)*, supervised by Bernard Lewis.[51] Saʿīd ʿĀshūr was the supervisor of the two other prominent historians, Muḥammad Amīn (1938–2015) and Ḥāmid Zayyān (b. 1946). Muḥammad Amīn completed his master's dissertation *Sulṭān al-Ṣāliḥ Najm al-Dīn Ayyūb (1240–49)* in 1968 and his doctoral dissertation *History of the Waqfs in Egypt under the Mamluk Sultans (1250–1517)* in 1972. Ḥāmid Zayyān received his master's and PhD degrees in 1970 and 1973, respectively, with dissertations entitled *Aleppo in the Zengid Period (1095–1183)* and *Relations between Sicily, Egypt and Syria during the Crusades (1069–1261)*.

As products of the Cairo University School founded by Muṣṭafā Ziyāda and his students Saʿīd ʿĀshūr and al-Bāz al-ʿArīnī, the three new medievalists were

---

49　　Ghunaym, *Al-ʿAlāqāt* and *Al-dawla*; Faraj, *Al-ʿAlāqāt*; Ṣidqī, *Al-ʿAlāqāt*; Al-ʿAbd al-Ghanī, *Thawrat*.

50　　Al-ʿAbd al-Ghanī, *Thawrat*, and *Armīniya*; Nawār, *Al-ʿAlāqāt*; ʿAbdallāh, *Thīyūfīlūs*, and *Al-ʿAlāqāt*.

51　　Published by Oxford University Press, London 1972.

not very concerned with Byzantine history. Apart from writing a textbook entitled *Studies in the History of the Byzantine State*,[52] Hassanein Rabie devoted himself mainly to the history of Mamluk and Ayyubid Egypt.[53] Muḥammad Amīn was preoccupied with writing about Islamic history and editing Arabic sources.[54] Ḥāmid Zayyān's studies concentrated on the history of Islam, medieval Egypt and the Crusades.[55] However, he wrote a small study entitled *Muslim Prisoners of War in the Byzantine Territories*,[56] which was criticized by a recent study for presenting inconsistent views and not taking note of many Arabic and Byzantine texts essential for the topic.[57]

Laylā ʿAbd al-Jawād Ismāʿīl (1952–2009) was the first researcher at Cairo University to deal with topics from Byzantine history in both her master's and doctoral dissertations. In 1980, under the supervision of Hassanein Rabie, she completed a master's dissertation entitled *Foreign Policy of the Latin Kingdom of Constantinople (1204–61)*.[58] In 1984, she received her doctorate under the supervision of Muḥammad Amīn with a dissertation entitled *The Byzantine State under Heraclius and its Relations with Muslims*.[59] Her postdoctoral research was influenced by the traditional trend of the Cairo University School, which did not favor limiting interest to one field. However, she showed a balanced interest in both Byzantine history and the history of medieval Egypt.[60] With

---

52   Rabie, *Dirāsāt*.

53   Rabie was the only medievalist at Cairo University, after Muṣṭafā Ziyāda, who was keen to publish, in English, studies focused on the history of Ayyubids and Mamluks. He published articles dealing with the size and value of the Iqṭāʿ, financial aspects of the Waqf, Mamluk cavalry, relations between the Safavids of Persia and the Mamluks of Egypt and Syria, Agriculture in Medieval Egypt, and Mamluk Campaigns against Rhodes.

54   Amīn's preoccupation with editing Arabic sources made him produce very few studies. He published books entitled *History of Islamic Yemen in the First Three Centuries of the Hijra*; *Financial and Economic System of Islam*; *Arabs and Islam from the Prophetic Period to the End of the Umayyad Caliphate*.

55   In addition to some textbooks, Zayyān published studies entitled *Emperor Fredrick Barbarossa and the Third Crusade*; *History of Islamic Civilization in Sicily and its Impact on Europe*; *The Abbasid Caliphate under the Mamluk State: The Abbasid Caliph al-Mustaʾīn billah*; *The Scholars between War and politics in the Ayyubid Era: The Family of Shaykh al-Shuyūkh*; *Life in the Arabian Gulf in the Light of the Travels of Ibn Baṭṭūṭa*; *Islamic Conquest of Egypt*.

56   Zayyān, *Al-Asrā*.

57   Ramaḍān, Treatment 156 n.9.

58   Ismāʿīl, *Al-Siyāsa*.

59   Published under the same title in Cairo 1985. See, Ismāʿīl, *Al-Dawla*.

60   Besides some textbooks on the history of medieval Egypt, Ismāʿīl was mainly concerned with the Mamluks. She published a book entitled *Būlāq in the Era of the Circassian Mamluks 1382–1517*, and articles entitled: Deputy of the Sultanate (*Nāʾib al-Salṭana*) in Cairo during the Era of the Bahri Mamluk State and Cannabis (*Hashīsh*) Abuse and

the exception of a monograph entitled *History of the Rus in the Arabic sources*[61] and an article about Byzantine relations with the Magyars[62] as well as another about their relations with the Bulgars,[63] most of her studies about Byzantine history were committed to the traditional line of studying Islamic-Byzantine relations based mainly on Arabic texts and the available modern Western studies. She published a monograph dealing with Byzantine relations with Tulunid and Ikhshidid Egypt,[64] and an article discussing Byzantine relations with the Bahri Mamluk State (1261–1382).[65] In addition she published two articles about Constantinople as presented in al-ʿUmarī's *Masālik al-Abṣār wa Mamālik al-Amṣār*,[66] and the other writings of Muslim geographers and travelers.[67] She also wrote another article about the Bulgars' role in resisting the campaign of Maslama b. ʿAbd al-Malik against Constantinople (717–18).[68]

The interest of Laylā Ismāʿīl in studying topics related to Islamic-Byzantine relations is probably due to her limited knowledge of Greek and Latin, even if the collection of Byzantine primary sources *Corpus Scriptorum Historiae Byzantinae* (CSHB) began to appear in the references of some of her studies. The same can be said of another researcher at Cairo University in the late 1980s and early 1990s, Muḥammad Zakī al-Wisīmī. He studied his MA under the supervision of Hassanein Rabie and finished it in 1988 with a dissertation dealing with the Byzantine relations with the Seljuk Sultanate of Rum under the Komnenoi (1081–1185).[69] In 1994 he completed his doctoral dissertation *The Seljuk Sultanate of Rum (1185–1243)*.[70] His move from Cairo University to work at King Saud University for almost two decades seems a significant reason for the small number of studies. According to his curriculum vitae available on the website of King Saud University, he published only two articles, one of which is related to the history of Mamluks,[71] while the other deals with the Mosque of Constantinople and its political role.[72]

Control in Mamluk Egypt. Also, she jointly published with Rabie a book entitled *History of the Kingdom of Hormuz from its Rise to Fall in 1622*.

61   Ismāʿīl, *Tārīkh*.
62   Ismāʿīl, Ḥamalāt 71–102.
63   Ismāʿīl, Aḍwāʾ Jadīda 309–358.
64   Ismāʿīl, *Al-Ṭūlūniyyīn*.
65   Ismāʿīl, ʿAlāqa 57–125.
66   Ismāʿīl, Mamlakat 281–321.
67   Ismāʿīl, Al-Qusṭanṭīniyya 151–201; 109–145.
68   Ismāʿīl, Dawr al-Bulghār 83–113.
69   Al-Wisīmī, ʿAlāqa.
70   Al-Wisīmī, *Salṭanat*.
71   Its title is: Political Relations between the Karaman Emirate and the Circassian Mamluk State.
72   Al-Wisīmī, Jāmiʿ 39–73.

The direct result of the Cairo School's lack of interest in the study of Byzantine history, and its loose conception of the branch of "History of the Middle Ages", can be seen in the current generation of faculty members. This generation includes four young researchers, three of whom completely excluded Byzantine history from their research interests, both in their dissertations and in postdoctoral studies.[73] The only researcher who has shown an interest in the study of Byzantine history is Amāl Ḥāmid Zayyān (b. 1979). In 2005, she completed a master's thesis entitled *Emperor Alexios I Komenenos and the First Crusade in the Light of the Alexiad*, which was supervised by Hassanein Rabie and Laylā Ismāʿīl.[74] She moved to the Girls College at ʿAyn Shams University to complete her doctorate under the supervision of ʿAliyya ʿAbd al-Samīʿ al-Janzūrī, and received it in 2009 with a thesis entitled *The Political Role of the Historian Michael Psellos in the Byzantine State (1041–1078)*.[75] However, despite her comparative advantage over her colleagues at Cairo University, Amāl Zayyān's post-doctoral research showed a marginal interest in the study of Byzantine history. She published about eight articles, most of which were devoted to the history of the Crusades and the Mamluks,[76] and only two are related to Byzantine History. The first deals with the embassy of

---

73   The first one is Mūḥammad ʿAbd al-Naʿīm (b. 1966), who completed in 1993 his master's thesis entitled *The Eastern Desert of Egypt in the Ayyubid and Mamluk Periods*, under the supervision of Saʿīd ʿĀshūr. He received his doctorate in 2000 with a thesis entitled *The Tutush Family in Syria and its Foreign Policy (1078–1117)*, under the supervision of Ḥāmid Zayyān. He published seven articles devoted entirely to the history of the Crusades, the Ayyubids and Mamluks. The second is Mūḥammad al-Zāmil (b. 1969) who, under Hassanein Rabie's supervision, received his master's degree in 2000 with a thesis entitled *The Role of European Powers in the Economic Siege of the Mamluk Sultanate (1291–1517)*, and his PhD in 2007 with a thesis entitled *The Economic Conditions in Egypt under the Mamluk Sultans (1453–1517)*. These two theses were published in 2008 and 2009 under the titles *Economic Siege of Egypt in the Late Middle Ages* and *Economic Transformation in Late Medieval Egypt*. The third researcher is Mūḥammad Ramaḍān al-Baṭrān (b. 1967) who, under Hassanein Rabie's supervision, received a master's degree and a doctorate in 1999 and 2007, respectively, with theses entitled *Banū Artaq and their Foreign Policy during the Crusades*, and *The French Role in the Crusades against Syria (1145–1240)*. Al-Zāmil and al-Baṭrān are not known to have published a single article since they received their doctorates.

74   Published under the same title in Cairo 2010. See, Zayyān, A.H., *Al-Imbrāṭūr*.

75   Published under the same title in Cairo 2012. See, Zayyān, A.H., *Al-Muʾarrikh*.

76   These articles deal with Gaza in light of al-ʿUmarī's *Masālik al-Abṣār fī Mamālik al-Amṣār*, the role of the al-Qalqashandī family in the scientific communication between Egypt and Jerusalem, the role of the amīr ʿAlam al-Dīn Sunjur al-Shujāʿī in the struggle over the Mamluk sultanate, the political role of the Sheikh Taqī al-dīn b. Taymiyya, and the image of the Franks in the writings of Muslims during the Crusades.

Emperor Anastasius II to the Umayyad Caliph al-Walīd b. ʿAbd al-Malik in 714,[77] while the other discusses the campaign of Emperor John II against Shayzar in 1138.[78]

4 Alexandria University: the 1970s and Beyond

Most likely, the relatively late interest shown by Cairo University medievalists in the study of Byzantine history during the 1980s[79] was largely influenced by changes that had been in force for more than a decade before at both Alexandria University and ʿAyn Shams University. The trend supported by ʿUmar Tawfīq and, to some extent, Joseph Yūsuf, at the University of Alexandria had its clear impact on Ismat Ghunaym (d. 1999) in the late 1960s. She was the first Alexandrian researcher who devoted most of her studies to Byzantine political history, primarily Byzantine-Islamic relations. Under the supervision of ʿUmar Tawfīq, she began her career in 1968 with a master's dissertation dealing with Byzantine political relations with the Fatimids.[80] In 1973, she obtained her PhD with a dissertation entitled *The Political Relations between the Byzantine State and Islamic Crete (827–961)*.[81] During the post-doctoral stage, she published an article about the battle of Manzikert according to Psellos's *Chronography*,[82] monographs entitled *The Empire of Justinian*,[83] *German-Byzantine Relations during the Second Crusade in the Light of Kinnamos*,[84] and a book entitled *Studies in the History of the Byzantine Empire of Nicaea*.[85]

---

77 Zayyān, A.H., Sifārat, 93–115.

78 Zayyān, A.H., Ḥamlat, 21–50. She also wrote an article dealing with the earthquake of 1063 according to the Byzantine historian *Michael Attaleiates*, which will be published in *AFAAShU.*

79 There was not much interest in the study of Byzantine history at Cairo University during the 1970s and 1980s. With the exception of the dissertations of ʿAbd al-Jawād and al-Wasīmī, Cairo University professors did not supervise any dissertations in the field. In contrast, according to *EULC* website, Rabie, for instance, supervised four dissertations on the history of the Crusades and one about Ayyubid history.

80 Ghunaym, *Al-ʿAlāqāt.*

81 Published in Alexandria 1983 under the title *The Byzantine State and Islamic Crete.* See, Ghunaym, *Al-Dawla.*

82 Ghunaym, Maʿrakat Manzikert 205–48.

83 Ghunaym, *Imbrāṭūriyyat Jūstīniān.*

84 Ghunaym, *Kīnnāmūs.*

85 Ghunaym, *Dirāsāt.* It includes articles dealing with the Fourth Crusade and the responsibility of its deviation against Constantinople, Theodore Lascaris and revival of the Byzantine Empire in Nicaea, and the Battle of Pelagonia.

The titles of Ismat Ghunaym's studies imply that the study of Byzantine history at the University of Alexandria began to take a different path since the early 1970s. It was the first time an Alexandrian researcher had dealt with topics that lie at the heart of pure Byzantine history. She herself wrote in the introduction to her book *Studies in the History of the Byzantine Empire of Nicaea,* that "these studies are new and diverse". The Latin texts, which were quoted and translated into Arabic in some of her studies, hint at her knowledge of Latin. But this picture may be overly optimistic. In her study about the Fourth Crusade and the responsibility of its deviation against Constantinople, for instance, although she quoted the CSHB Latin text of the Byzantine historian Nicetas Choniates's famous cry, "O City of Byzantium",[86] she relied in its Arabic translation on the literal quotation from Isḥāq ʿUbayd's (Ebeid's) book *Rome and Byzantium from the Photian Schism to the Latin Invasion of Constantinople 869–1204,*[87] which had been well-known among medievalists for more than a decade.[88] The absence of a reference to Isḥāq ʿUbayd either in the footnotes or the bibliography of this study, despite the direct quotation from him, may cast doubt on its originality.

As a graduate of the Alexandria University School, Ismat Ghunaym had to expand the scope of her studies to harmonize with the Alexandrian definition of the so-called branch of "History of the Middle Ages". She wrote studies about the Avars, medieval European women and relations between the Ayyubids and Crusaders.[89] It can be said, however, that Ismat Ghunaym's interest in studying Byzantine history, regardless of her studies' content, was unique and never repeated again by her contemporaries or later medievalists at the University of Alexandria. Her colleague, Maḥmūd Saʿīd ʿUmrān (1933–2015), was more inclined to study the history of the Crusades. His postgraduate studies may reflect the slight difference between the concerns of Joseph Yūsuf and ʿUmar Tawfiq. Under the supervision of Joseph Yūsuf, he was directed to study the Fifth Crusade in his master's thesis (awarded in 1973),[90] while in 1975 he finished under the supervision of ʿUmar Tawfiq a PhD dissertation about the eastern policy of the Byzantine Emperor Manuel I Komnenos (1143–80).[91]

---

86   Ghunaym, *Dirāsāt* 114.
87   ʿUbayd, *Rūmā* 324.
88   ʿUbayd's book had been published in 1970.
89   She published monographs entitled *Women in Western Europe in the Middle Ages; The Avars; The Ayyubids and the Crusaders.*
90   Published in Alexandria 1978 under the title *The Fifth Crusade: The Campaign of Jean de Brienne against Egypt.*
91   Published in 1985 with the title *The Eastern Policy of the Byzantine Empire in the Reign of Emperor Manuel.* See, ʿUmrān, *Al-Siyāsa.*

During his long academic career, Saʿīd ʿUmrān was one of the most active and productive medievalists at Alexandria University. According to his website, he participated in a large number of local and international conferences and wrote about sixty-nine articles. However, the number of his published articles is only about twenty-five, mostly relating to the history of the Crusades,[92] and some of which deal with foreign travelers to the Middle East[93] and medieval historical writing and coins.[94] Also, in addition to publishing his doctoral and master's dissertations, he published nearly twenty books, more than half of them textbooks and the rest dealing with subjects ranging from the history of the Crusades to Medieval Europe and its relationship with the Mongols.[95]

The study of Byzantine history has not received much attention from Saʿīd ʿUmrān, and except for three studies closer to the Crusades than to Byzantine history,[96] only about four of his studies are concerned with topics related to Byzantine history. In two of these studies, which depended mainly on the letters of Patriarch Nicholas I Mystikos[97] and the *Chronography* of Michael Psellos,[98] he appeared to be more a translator than a researcher. Indeed, Saʿīd ʿUmrān himself did not try to pretend otherwise. In his study dealing with Psellos' narrative on the reign of Emperor Romanos IV Diogenes (1068–71), he explained that "the researcher's plan in this study is limited to translating what

---

92   Saʿīd ʿUmrān published some eight articles about the Crusades entitled: The Role of the Crusader Movement in the Composition of the Kingdom of Portugal; William Adams and Restoration of the Holy Lands; The Siege of the Crusaders and the Fatimid Forces of Saladin; The Ideas of Pierre Dubois to Restore the Holy Lands; the Seljuk Diplomacy (1192–1246); Legend of John the Presbyter and its Role in the Crusaders' Alliance with Mongols against Muslims (1146–1291). He also published in English articles entitled: King Amalric and the Siege of Alexandria 1167; Truces between Moslems and Crusaders (1174–1217).

93   He published articles entitled: Arculf and his Journey to the East; Writings of the Traveler Arculf as a Source for Syria in the Era of the Rightly-Guided Caliphate; Egypt in the Writings of Foreign Travelers during the Byzantine Era; The Journey of Antonius the Martyr to Syria and Egypt (560–70); Egypt and Syria in the Writings of Foreign Travelers during the Byzantine Era; Jerusalem and the al-Aqṣa Mosque in the Writings of Foreign Travelers (670–80); Missionaries to the East: The Journey of Jordan of Catalonia; Egypt and Syria in the Writings of the Traveler John Mandeville (1346–47); The Journey of the Russian Afanasy Nikitin.

94   ʿUmrān, Al-Nuqūd 36–54.

95   He published books entitled: *The Vandal Kingdom of North Africa*; *Crusader Leaders Captured in the Hands of Muslims*; *Europe and Mongols*; *Mongols, Europeans, Crusaders and the Jerusalem Issue*; *Studies in the Relations between East and West*; *Studies in Medieval Sources*; *Money in Medieval Europe*.

96   These studies are: Maʿrakat 89–99; Shārl 169–96; John Kinnamos 45–55.

97   ʿUmrān, *Nīqūlā Mistīqūs*.

98   ʿUmrān, Al-Imbrāṭūr 55–96.

Psellos recorded in his famous chronicle, based on the English translation, and then comment on the historical material in footnotes when clarification must be provided to the reader".[99] These two studies, and indeed many other studies of Saʿīd ʿUmrān, reflect a typical trend in modern Arab historical research, particularly in the field of medieval history, namely the design of research based on a historical source once this source becomes available in one of the modern Western translations.[100]

In the other two studies, Saʿīd ʿUmrān seemed to follow the traditional line of studying Islamic-Byzantine relations. One of these studies is in English and deals with the cultural influences and peaceful relations between Muslims and Byzantines,[101] while most of the second study which is entitled "Fortifications of the City of Constantinople in the Face of Foreign Invasion",[102] focuses on the Muslims' attempts to conquer Constantinople. This study was the subject of a master's dissertation completed under his supervision in 2000 and entitled *Immunity of Constantinople in the Face of Internal Revolutions and External Invasions in the Middle Ages*.[103] This seems to reflect a unique approach that may distinguish Saʿīd ʿUmrān from others, which is to guide graduate students to broaden and deepen topics he himself has already dealt with in whole or in part. It is therefore not strange to find a clear match between the subjects and fields of research interest of Saʿīd ʿUmrān and his students. Among the nearly forty dissertations supervised by him, nine relate to Byzantine history and deal with topics about early Byzantine historical sources, coins, travelers and Islamic-Byzantine relations. The remaining dissertations supervised by him were distributed in the fields of the history of the Crusades and medieval Europe.

With the exception of Ismat Ghunaym, and to a certain degree Saʿīd ʿUmrān, the course of medieval studies at the University of Alexandria seems to have been moving since the 1980s onwards in favor of the trend set by Suryāl ʿAṭṭiyya and his student Joseph Yūsuf. The early death of ʿUmar Tawfīq, as well as his work during the last years of his life at Kuwait University, was one of the factors

---

99   Ibid. 56.
100   This may explain the great number of Saʿīd ʿUmrān's studies dealing with medieval chronicles based on their English translations. He published articles entitled: King Clovis in the Light of Gregory of Tours' History of the Franks; The Chronicle of the Fall of Lisbon in 1147; Arabs in the Chronicle of the Syriac Historian Zacharias of Mytilene; New Light on the Chronicle of the Fall of Silves in 1189. The same applies to his many works dealing with topics in the light of travelers' writings.
101   ʿUmrān, Religious Policy 330–47.
102   ʿUmrān, Taḥsīnāt 308–39.
103   ʿAbd al-Rashīd, *Ḥasānat al-Qusṭanṭīniyya*.

influencing this process. A new generation of Alexandrian medievalists, who were trained by Joseph Yūsuf and Saʿīd ʿUmrān, was interested mainly in the history of the Crusades, and to a lesser extent medieval European history. The contribution of this generation to the study of Byzantine history can be counted on the fingers of one hand.

This generation includes four researchers. The first is Ibrahīm Khamīs, who received his master's degree in 1980 with a dissertation about the Knights Templar and their political relations with Muslims in the Near East until the end of Saladin's rule (1118–93) and his PhD in 1983 with a dissertation about political relations between the Knights Templar and the Muslims in Egypt and Syria (1193–1291).[104] According to the EULC website, his contribution to the study of Byzantine history was limited to an article dealing with the peace treaties between Muslims and Byzantines in the second half of the seventh century.[105] The second researcher, Ḥasan ʿAbd al-Wahāb, received his MA and PhD in 1982 and 1987, respectively, with two dissertations about Caesarea under Latin rule and its political relations with the Muslims of the Near East (1101–1265)[106] and the Teutonic Knights and their political relations with the Muslims of Egypt and Syria (1190–1291).[107] Based on the EULC and King Saud University websites, where he has been working for many years, all his studies are devoted to the economic and social history of the Crusades.[108]

The early death of the third researcher, Suhayr Niʿnaʿ (d. 2007), was the reason for the small number of studies which she produced. With the exception of her master's and doctoral dissertations on the history of the Crusades, in 1988 and 1995 respectively,[109] she published two articles dealing with women in Byzantine Egypt and medieval Alexandria as described by the foreign travelers. The last researcher of this generation, Ibrāhīm Saʿīd Fahīm, completed his MA dissertation in 1991 about Jaffa's role in the Crusader-Islamic conflict 1099–1291, and his doctoral dissertation in 1997 about European pilgrimage to

---

104 In Alexandria in 2002, the two dissertations were published in one volume entitled *Studies in the History of Crusades: The Knights Templar.*

105 Khamīs, Muʿāhadāt al-Salām 265–97.

106 Published in Alexandria in 1990 under the title *Caesarea of Syria during the Islamic Era.*

107 Published in Alexandria in 1989 under the title *History of the Teutonic Knights in the Holy Lands.*

108 He published articles entitled: Missionary Attempts in the Levant during the Crusades; The Speech of Pope Urban II at the Council of Clermont, as well as a book entitled *Studies in the Economic History of the Crusades.*

109 The title of her MA dissertation is *The Crusade of Peter Lusignan against Alexandria,* and her PhD entitled *Jabla and its Role in the Islamic-Crusader Conflict (1099–1291).*

holy places in the Islamic Near East (1291–1517).[110] Like his colleagues, the study of Byzantine history did not feature in his research interests.[111]

5   ʿAyn Shams University: a Paradigm Shift

While this was the status of the study of Byzantine history since the 1970s in the two oldest universities in Egypt, the third university – in terms of date of establishment – ʿAyn Shams University, witnessed in the same period what can be described as a paradigm shift in the study of Byzantium.

The branch of the "History of the Middle Ages" at ʿAyn Shams University appeared relatively late and in a more specific concept than the other two universities. Since its emergence in the late 1960s, the history of the Ayyubids, the Mamluks and the Crusades has been excluded from its framework which has been limited to the study of medieval European and Byzantine History. This difference may seem unjustified in light of the presence of graduates from the universities of Alexandria and Cairo as faculty members in the Department of History since its inception in the early 1950s, namely ʿAbd al-Hādī Shuʿayra and Ḥasan Ḥabashī. However, the presence of these two scholars, as well as their areas of research interest, may be the only reasonable explanation of this difference.

ʿAbd al-Hādī Shuʿayra's interest in studying Islamic-Byzantine relations in a few of his studies stemmed mainly from his being a specialist in Islamic history. With the exception of his doctoral dissertation *La lutte entre Arabes et Byzantins* and his translation of Vasiliev's *Byzance et les Arabes*,[112] he published only one article about the Byzantine-Islamic frontier,[113] while most of his other studies focus on the history of the medieval Maghrib,[114] the Umayyads and the Abbasids.[115] On the other hand, the appointment of Ḥasan Ḥabashī as a lecturer of Islamic history in 1950, and the focus of his research on the history of

---

110   The two dissertations were published under the same titles in Alexandria, 2007.

111   Based on the EULC website, he published books entitled: *Studies in the History of the Middle Ages and its Civilization; Studies in the History of East-West Relations in the Middle Ages; Books and Writings from the Library of the Carolingian State*. He also published an article entitled *Rhodes at the Crossroads of Two Eras: The Diary of the Turkish Siege of the Island (1480) in European Sources*.

112   See notes 4 and 9.

113   Shuʿayra, Al-Murābiṭūn 147–68.

114   He published a book entitled *The Political History of the Almoravids*, and an article about Libyan Islamic coastal anchors.

115   He published articles entitled: The Allied Kingdoms: Transoxiana and the Islamic State until the Days of Al-Muʿtasim; Le statut des pays de ʿAhd aux VIIᵉ et VIIIᵉ siècles [in

the Crusades and the Mamluks, may explain why these two fields are excluded from the branch of 'History of the Middle Ages' at 'Ayn Shams University. This may also explain why no master's or doctoral dissertation related to the history of the Byzantine Empire or medieval Europe was defended until 1970.

The real beginning of medieval studies at 'Ayn Shams University was in 1968, when the chair of medieval history was filled by a graduate of the University of Alexandria, Isḥāq Tāwḍrūs 'Ubayd (also spelled Ishaq Tawdros Ebeid, b. 1933), who returned that year from the University of Nottingham with a PhD dissertation entitled *The Attitude of Western Churchmen towards the Byzantine Empire in the Period (1054–1204)*, which was supervised by Bernard Hamilton.[116] It is the first doctoral dissertation, and perhaps the only one written by an Egyptian Byzantinist studying abroad, that does not focus on Byzantine-Muslim relations. The abundance of Greek and Latin extracts through its 600 pages may explain why he was commissioned to study such a topic. In fact, many of Isḥāq 'Ubayd's subsequent studies reflect a good knowledge of the source language, especially Latin, which enabled him to extract his material from the original sources directly. This is abundantly illustrated in the rich footnotes and appendices that are replete with Latin extracts from the chronicles and literary, philosophical and theological writings.[117]

In his postdoctoral studies, Isḥāq 'Ubayd showed a balanced interest in both medieval European and Byzantine history. In addition to his studies that focus on the history of the Western Church and the feudal system,[118] he produced three studies related to Byzantine history directly. In 1969, he published two articles, the first in English which assesses the extent of Pope Innocent III's responsibility for the deviation of the Fourth Crusade to Constantinople

---

French]; Regional Divisions in the First Abbasid Period and The Emergence of the Islamic Near East.

116   This dissertation was developed and published in Arabic (Cairo, 1970) under the title *Rome and Byzantium from the Photian Schism to the Latin Invasion of Constantinople (869–1204)*. See, 'Ubayd, *Rūmā*.

117   This is explained by 'Ubayd in the introductions of some of his studies. For example, in the introduction to his book *European Middle Ages: The Era of Darkness*, he pointed out that "this book is primarily documentary, intended to provide the reader with a clear picture of the conditions of Europe when entering the Dark Ages. In the preparation of this book, I have tried to reflect the spirit of the time by relying on the primary and literary sources, whether prose, poetry, or narrations, so the footnotes are full of a great number of Latin texts". 'Ubayd, *Al-'Uṣūr* i–ii.

118   His studies focused on the history of the western church and the feudal system. He published articles entitled: Abelard the free theologian; Aurelius Prudentius Clemens and his '*Contra Symmachum*'; Joan of Arc: a vision through the sources. He also published books entitled: *Knights and Serfs in the Feudal Society*; *Inquisition: Origin and Activities*.

in 1204,[119] and the second about the story of St. Helena's finding of the True Cross between mythology and historical reality.[120] In 1975, Benghazi University published his important book about the last centuries of Byzantium, which is entitled *The Byzantine State in the Paleologian Era*.[121] Also, he marginally approached early Byzantine history in other studies that deal with the period of Germanic invasions in the western part of the Roman Empire, which he preferred to refer to as the "Dark Age". This was the topic of two of his major works, published in Cairo 1972 and 1977, entitled *The Roman Empire between Religion and Barbarism*;[122] and *From Alaric to Justinian: A Study in the Annals of the Dark Ages*.[123]

Some of 'Ubayd's studies also reflect an interest in editing unpublished Arabic manuscripts related to early Byzantine history. For example, the appendices of his book *The Roman Empire between Religion and Barbarism* include two Arabic manuscripts entitled *Yūliyānūs al-ʿAṣī* (Julian the Apostate)[124] and *Qawānīn al-Majmaʿ al-Maskūnī al-awwal al-Multaʾim fī Nīqīyah* (the Canons of the First Ecumenical Council, held in Nicaea).[125] Other manuscripts were edited and published in English in independent articles, such as a manuscript dealing with the events of the Alexandria Church following the Ecumenical Council of Chalcedon,[126] and a manuscript on the Emperor Julian.[127]

In the early 1970s, two new researchers joined Isḥāq 'Ubayd as faculty members specializing in medieval history. The first is 'Alī al-Ghamrāwī (1926–93) who graduated from the Department of Greek and Latin Studies at the Faculty of Arts, 'Ayn Shams University in 1946. He completed his MA dissertation in Latin literature in 1958 under the direction of Salīm Sālim.[128] In 1967, he received his doctorate from the University of Munich with a dissertation entitled *Lexikographische Studien über die lateinischen Pflanzennamen bei Dioskurides und Pseudo-Apuleius*. As a specialist in Latin philology, al-Ghamrāwī returned

---

119   'Ubayd, Was Pope Innocent III, 3–19.

120   'Ubayd, Qiṣṣat 5–21.

121   'Ubayd, *Al-Dawla*.

122   'Ubayd, *Al-Imbrāṭūriyya*.

123   'Ubayd, *Min Alārīk*. Later, 'Ubayd relied heavily on these two works to publish in 1990 and 1995 his two books *European Middle Ages: The Era of Darkness* and *Europe in the Sea of Darkness*.

124   Preserved in the Egyptian National Library (*Dār al-Kutub al-Miṣriyya*), no. 1649.

125   Preserved in the Library of the Coptic Studies Institute in Cairo (*Maktabat Maʿhad al-Dirāsāt al-Qibṭiyya bil-Qāhira*).

126   'Ubayd, Concerning the happenings of 207–242.

127   'Ubayd, Julian the Apostate 121–2.

128   This dissertation is in English and entitled *Cicero's Oration pro Q. Roscio Comoedo: Edition and Commentary*.

to the Department of Greek and Latin studies for a few years, then moved to the Department of History in the early 1970s. This classical background may explain why he devoted most of his post-doctoral studies to medieval and modern European historiography,[129] and why the study of Byzantine history was completely absent from his research interests.

Unlike al-Ghamrāwī, the second medievalist, Ra'fat 'Abd al-Ḥamīd, was more inclined to study Byzantine history, especially its early period. In 1970, under the supervision of Ḥasan Ḥabashī, he completed a master's dissertation about Constantine I's policy toward the Christian Sects. In 1974, he received his doctorate under the supervision of 'Abd al-Mun'im Mājid (1921–99)[130] with a dissertation entitled *Athanasius: his thought and relationship with the Byzantine State.* This beginning seems to have shaped Ra'fat 'Abd al-Ḥamīd's subsequent research interests in studying issues related to the transition period which extended from the Roman to the Byzantine periods, a period that he alternatively called the late Roman or the early Byzantine era.[131]

After receiving his doctorate, Ra'fat 'Abd al-Ḥamīd spent nearly three years translating Joan Hussey's *The Byzantine World*. He then began his ambitious project to study relations between the state and the church in the fourth century. He published his doctoral and master's dissertations as the second and third volumes of his book *The State and the Church*. He then added a fourth volume covering the reigns of Emperors Valens and Theodosius I.[132] It seems that he died before completing the first volume. According to the introduction

---

129   Al-Ghamrāwī published books entitled: *Topics in Medieval European Culture*; *The Germanic Epic*; *Modern Research in the History of the Middle Ages: Sixteenth-Seventeenth Centuries*; *Modern Collections of Medieval European Sources: Sixteenth-Twentieth Centuries*. He also published articles entitled: Pre-Carolingian Hagiographical Sources; Historiographical Views in Medieval European History before the Tenth Century; Religious Writings in the Literature of Latin Theologians from the Sixth Century to the Eighth Century; A Bibliographical Report on the Eighteenth-Century French Research on Medieval European History.

130   Mājid was then a professor of Islamic history specializing in the history of medieval Egypt. He published an article about Crete between the Ikhshids, the Fatimids and the Byzantines. The presence of two supervisors specializing in Islamic history can be explained by the absence of a professor specializing in medieval history at 'Ayn Shams University at the time.

131   See the study added by him as an introduction to his translation of Joan Hussey: *Al-'Ālam al-Bīzanṭī* 42.

132   'Abd al-Ḥamīd, *Al-Dawla*. Volumes 2 and 3 were published in 1980 and 1982 respectively with the subtitles "*Constantine*" and "*Athanasius*", then they were republished in 2000 with new sub-titles: *Qayṣar wa al-Masīḥ* [Caesar and Christ], and *al-Wathaniyya wa al-Masīḥiyya* [Paganism and Christianity]. The fourth volume was published in 2001 with the subtitle *al-Masīḥiyya al-Jadīda* [New Christianity].

to the fourth volume, he pointed out that the first volume was still in progress and would be devoted to the analysis of historical and ecclesiastical sources. In this book, as reflected in the bibliography, he has used a number of sources from the collections of *Patrologia Graeca* and *Patrologia Latina*, and he was keen to record the Latin titles of many other sources, although he relied on their English translations in the collections of *Nicene* and *Ante Nicene Fathers*.

Ra'fat 'Abd al-Ḥamīd's interest in the religious conditions of the fourth century was also reflected in a number of his other studies. He published an article comparing the causes of Roman persecution of Christians before and after the recognition of Christianity by Constantine the Great,[133] and another discussing the position of the Church of Jerusalem towards the Episcopal conflict on spiritual leadership.[134] He also published an article dealing with the Palestinian church historian Sozomenos,[135] and two articles analyzing the reasons and circumstances behind the assassinations of Arius[136] and Julian.[137]

However, as a product of the 'Ayn Shams school, as well as the concept of specialization prevalent in other universities, Ra'fat 'Abd al-Ḥamīd had to diversify the scope of his studies and not limit them to one framework. In addition to other articles dealing with issues from the early Byzantine period, such as the reasons for the Nika insurrection of 532,[138] and the Byzantine-Persian conflict on the Arabian Peninsula in the sixth century,[139] he wrote articles about the principles of Byzantine diplomacy,[140] the eleventh-century chronicler Michael Psellos,[141] and the Byzantine position on the Crusades.[142] He also published articles on medieval Papal thought,[143] the German monarchy[144] and the role of Muslim leaders during the Crusades.[145]

---

133 'Abd al-Ḥamīd, Al-Ittiḥād al-Rūmānī 8–38.

134 'Abd al-Ḥamīd, Kanīsat al-Quds 65–126.

135 'Abd al-Ḥamīd, Sūzūmenūs 85–128.

136 'Abd al-Ḥamīd, Ightiyāl Ariyūs 49–91.

137 'Abd al-Ḥamīd, Maṣra' Jūliān 481–533.

138 'Abd al-Ḥamīd, Al-Thawra 25–88.

139 'Abd al-Ḥamīd, Al-Ṣirā' 263–326.

140 'Abd al-Ḥamīd, Qawā'id 29–82.

141 'Abd al-Ḥamīd, Psellūs 151–224. It is worth mentioning that 'Abd al-Ḥamīd gathered his studies about Byzantine history in one book entitled *Byzantium between thought, religion and politics*, published in Cairo 1997. See, 'Abd al-Ḥamīd, *Bīzanṭah bayn al-fikr*.

142 'Abd al-Ḥamīd, Bīzanṭa 67–121.

143 Their titles are: The Papal Supremacy between Theory and Practice; The Papal Crusader Thought in the Face of Temporal Power.

144 Their titles are: German Monarchy between Inheritance and Election; The Italian Issue in German Politics.

145 Their titles are: Emir Fakhruddīn ibn Sheikh in the Court of History; Al-Malik al-Kāmil between Excess and Negligence in the Face of the Crusaders.

There is no doubt that both Isḥāq ʿUbayd and Raʾfat ʿAbd al-Ḥamīd, especially the latter, gave a strong impetus to the study of Byzantine history at ʿAyn Shams University. Isḥāq ʿUbayd supervised a considerable number of master's and doctoral dissertations in the field,[146] and although the number of dissertations supervised by Raʾfat ʿAbd al-Ḥamīd was very few, they were all related to the field.[147] In addition, the two scholars were keen to prepare a new generation specialized in Byzantine studies and proficient in the source languages, by directing their students to obtain a Bachelor of Greek and Latin studies. This generation, represented by two researchers, Ṭāriq Muḥammad (b. 1965) and ʿAbd al-ʿAzīz Ramaḍān (b. 1973), emerged during the 1990s and continues to play a key role in the study of Byzantine history in Egypt to this day.

Ṭāriq Muḥammad (Tarek Muhammad), who graduated from Manṣūra University in 1987, received his master's degree from Banhā University in 1993 with a dissertation entitled *The Army in the Byzantine Empire from the Beginning of the Seventh Century to the End of the Ninth Century*, under the supervision of Usāma Zakī Zayd.[148] Then he moved that year to work at ʿAyn Shams University as an assistant lecturer. In 1999, he completed a doctoral dissertation entitled *The Rus and the International Community (945–1045)*,[149] supervised by Raʾfat ʿAbd al-Ḥamīd. His postdoctoral studies show remarkable activity. He distinguished himself from his generation with his obvious interest in establishing contact with Western scholars, participating in international conferences and publishing in international journals.

Of course, the most appropriate and affordable way to do so for Muḥammad, and indeed for other Arabic-speaking scholars, is to deal with issues related to Muslim-Byzantine relations based largely on Arabic sources and, to a lesser extent, on Greek texts. In his English articles, he devoted much of his attention to the study of the military aspects of these relations. This may be an extension of the interest in military history which he showed in his MA dissertation. He published two articles discussing the late Mamluk writer Ibn Manglī as evidence for the knowledge and use of Greek fire by Muslims since the beginning of the ninth century until the end of the Mamluk period,[150] as well as two other articles dealing with Arab military skills and tactics during the early conquests

---

146   Dissertations such as: Puṭrus, *Al-Arman*; Al-Sayyid, *Al-Imbrāṭūr*; Maqāmī, *Al-ʿAlāqāt*; Fahmī, *Al-Sanawāt*; Zīdān, *Al-Dawla*.

147   These dissertations as follow: Al-Birī, *Al-ʿAlāqāt*; Muḥammad, T., *Al-Rūs*; Ramaḍān, A.M., *Bīzanṭa*.

148   Professor of medieval history at Ṭanṭā University, whose research interests focus on the history of the Crusades and medieval England.

149   Published under the same title in Cairo, 2001.

150   Muḥammad, T., Ibn Manglī and Naval Warfare 55–80; Ibn Manglī 25–43.

of Syria,[151] and the papyrological evidence for the role of Copts in the Islamic navies during the seventh and eighth centuries.[152] In addition to these topics of a military nature, he published a large article that presents a list of about sixty Byzantine civil functions and titles mentioned in Arabic historical sources and analyzes the extent to which the Arabs could understand their meanings as explained in the Greek texts.[153]

However, Muḥammad published other articles that go beyond this traditional line of studying Muslim-Byzantine relations based mainly on the Arabic sources. Most of these articles deal with the Islamic rituals as perceived in Byzantine literature, especially theological writings. In two of these articles, he examines the understanding by the Byzantine theologians of the Muslim ritual of *al-Takbīr* or saying *Allahu Akbar*.[154] In a third article, he seeks to explain how Byzantine theologians dealt with the marriage of the Prophet Muḥammad to Zaynab b. Jaḥsh, and their discussion of whether it was a marriage or adultery.[155] He also devoted articles to addressing the conversion from Islam to Christianity as presented by the Byzantine author of *Digenes Akrites*,[156] and the Greek text *Parastaseis Syntomi Chronikai* as a real guide to the sculptures of eighth-century Constantinople by comparing it with other Greek and Arabic sources.[157]

In his studies in Arabic, Muḥammad showed a similar interest in Muslim-Byzantine relations. Nearly three of these articles are in line with the themes of some of his research in English. These articles deal with the Byzantine titles and functions between the Arab concept and the Byzantine reality,[158] Greek Fire in the light of Arabic and Greek sources,[159] and the image of Islam in *Digenes Akrites*.[160] In two other articles, he deals with Greek and Arabic sources as

---

151   Muḥammad, T., Had the Arabs 83–96.
152   Muḥammad, T., The Role 1–32.
153   Muḥammad, T., The Civil 356–82.
154   Muḥammad, T., The Concept of al-Takbīr 77–97; Alla Wa Koubar 296–315.
155   Muḥammad, T., The Byzantine Theologians, 139–60.
156   Muḥammad, T., The Conversion 121–39.
157   Muḥammad, T., Parastaseis 77–98. Muḥammad's English articles, whether published in local or international journals, are not confined to Byzantine history but extended to cover other topics closer to Islamic history. He published articles entitled: Clysma in the Literary and Documentary Arab Sources; Al-Fākihī and the Religious Life at Pre-Islamic Makka; Al-Ghazālī and the Sources of his MS. *Al-Tibr al-Masbūk fī Naṣīḥat al-Mulūk*: The Greek and Persian Sources; Greek Intellectual Influence on Islamic Political Thought: The Case of al-Ghazālī; Aspects of Greek Wisdom in the Thought of Al-Ghazālī; Is the Poetry of the Time of Saladin a Reliable Source of his Deeds?.
158   Muḥammad, T., Al-Waẓāʾif 7–82.
159   Muḥammad, T., Al-Nār 115–59.
160   Muḥammad, T., Malḥamat 3–72.

evidence of relations between the two sides. One of these articles discusses the account of the Arab prisoner Hārūn b. Yaḥyā, preserved in Ibn Rustah's *al-Aʿlāq al-Nafīsa*,[161] the other deals with the chronicle of Theophanes the Confessor as evidence for the Islamic conquests of the Levant.[162] Finally, he devoted two articles to the cultural relations between the two sides, namely language and translation issues. One of these articles analyzes the extent to which Muslim Arabs knew Greek during the middle Byzantine period,[163] and the other deals with the translation of the Holy Qurʾān into Greek in the ninth century.[164]

Outside of the framework of Muslim-Byzantine relations, Muḥammad published other articles in Arabic dealing with various topics of Byzantine history, some of which seem to be an extension of the subjects of his master's and doctoral dissertations. One of these articles discusses whether the 907 and 911 treaties between the Rus and Byzantines should be seen as one or two treaties.[165] Two other articles deal with the Byzantine military strategy according to the *Taktika* of Emperor Leo VI,[166] and the Byzantine Imperial guard.[167] He also published two articles dealing with the ceremonies of imperial banquets during the reign of Leo VI,[168] and Constantinople in the Crusader writings (1097–1204).[169] In addition, he published in Egyptian journals two articles in English dealing with the Byzantine expedition of Nicetas on Egypt (609–10), and the *De Administrando Imperio* of Emperor Constantine VII as evidence for Turkic settlement in the Caucasus and Steppes. Finally, Muḥammad published three books containing some of his previously published articles as well as other new articles. The titles of these books are *Blossoms of Byzantine Thought*,[170] *Byzantium: City of Civilization and Institutions*,[171] and *Muslims in*

---

161   Muḥammad, T., Hārūn 44–52.

162   Muḥammad, T., Futūḥ 13–70.

163   Muḥammad, T., Ilmām 215–36.

164   Muḥammad, T., Al-Bīzanṭiyyūn 83–130.

165   Muḥammad, T., Muʿāhadatā 11–43.

166   Muḥammad, T., Fann al-Qitāl 147–84.

167   Muḥammad, T., Al-Ḥaras 181–230.

168   Muḥammad, T., Al-Maʾādib 57–118.

169   Muḥammad, T., Al-Qusṭanṭīniyya 261–325.

170   Muḥammad, T., Quṭūf. In this book, Muḥammad adds three new chapters about Byzantine literature, the life of the Egyptian saint Mary, and Emperor Constantine VII's *De Thematibus*. A chapter dealing with Digenes Akrites seems to be taken from one of his published articles on this topic.

171   Muḥammad, T., Bīzanṭa. It includes the articles al-Qusṭanṭīniyya, al-Waẓāʾif, al-Nār, Muʿāhadatā, as well as two articles published for the first time in this book, al-Maʾādib and al-Ḥaras.

Christian Thought.[172] He also published a textbook entitled *Byzantines and the Islamic World.*[173]

There is no doubt that the abundance and diversity of Muḥammad's studies, whether published locally or internationally, reflect an important step in the path of the qualitative shift in the study of Byzantine history drawn by Isḥāq ʿUbayd and Raʾfat ʿAbd al-Ḥamīd at ʿAyn Shams University since the early 1970s. This path and shift seem to have been visible to Muḥammad since his early beginnings. In the introduction to his very short bibliographical list of the Byzantine studies in Egypt published in 1998, he assumes that there are three generations of Egyptian Byzantinists who embody the past, the present and the future. He probably made a wrong judgment about the past when he placed Al-Bāz al-ʿArīnī and Saʿīd ʿĀshūr as the sole representatives of the first generation, and when he considered Isḥāq ʿAbīd and Raʾfat ʿAbd al-Ḥamīd and Wesam Farag (Wisām Faraj)[174] as a second generation. I think that these latter three scholars are in fact the real founders of Byzantine studies in Egypt. However, Muḥammad clearly expressed an optimistic view of the development of Byzantine studies at the time and for the future.[175]

The second researcher in this generation, ʿAbd al-ʿAzīz Ramaḍān, took a slightly different course in his studies. He graduated from ʿAyn Shams University in 1994 and received a master's degree in 2000 with a thesis entitled *Byzantine-Latin Relations under the Reign of Emperor Manuel I Komnenos (1143–1180)*, under the supervision of Raʾfat ʿAbd al-Ḥamīd.[176] In late 2003, he received his doctorate under the supervision of Isḥāq ʿUbayd with a thesis entitled *Byzantine Women from the Ninth to Twelfth Centuries.*[177] In the post-doctoral period of his studies, Ramaḍān, in comparison to Muḥammad, proved to be less productive and interested in publishing in English. However, the titles of his studies show that he was the least affected by the areas of his dissertations for his master's and doctorate, and that he focused almost exclusively on Byzantine studies,[178] with only one article published outside the framework

---

172   Muḥammad, T., *Al-Muslimūn*. It includes his two articles Futūḥ and Malḥamat.

173   Muḥammad, T., *Al-Bīzanṭiyyūn wa al-ʿĀlam*.

174   Professor of medieval history at Manṣūra University, whose contribution will be discussed later.

175   Muḥammad, T., Byzantine Studies 79–92.

176   Published in Cairo 2007 under the title *Byzantium and Western Europe 1143–1180*.

177   Published in Cairo 2005 under the title *Women and Society in the Byzantine Empire, Ninth-Twelfth Centuries*.

178   Ramaḍān played a role in determining the specialization of new faculty members at the Faculty of Arts, ʿAyn Shams University. He jointly supervised with Isḥāq ʿUbayd the theses of three young researchers. Two of them were directed to specialize in the history of Western Europe in the Middle Ages, and the third in the history of Byzantine Egypt.

of the study of Byzantine history. In addition, these titles indicate that he was most influenced by the trend of ʿAbd al-Ḥamīd and ʿUbayd in his interest in the early Byzantine era and in subjects related to popular religious thought, law and diplomacy.

In his book *Road to Byzantium: Studies on thought, religion and politics in the eastern late Roman Empire*,[179] Ramaḍān republished six articles originally published in a number of local journals. The first article analyzes the available evidence of the Byzantines' concept of identity and whether they considered themselves Greeks or Romans.[180] The second article discusses the position of the imperial authority towards the public entertainments, *Ludi Publici*, and how it was able to deal with the contradiction between this inherited Roman obsession and the rigid ideology of the Church.[181] In the third and fourth articles, Ramaḍān deals with the right of Church asylum between legal theory and practice,[182] and the conflict between science and popular religious belief, taking medicine as a model.[183] The last two articles discuss misogyny as revealed in the monastic writings of the fourth and fifth centuries,[184] and the imperial authority's selection criteria for its ambassadors and envoys to the outside world.[185]

Following the usual practice of those Egyptian Byzantinists who publish in English, especially internationally, Ramaḍān has devoted three studies in English to dealing with aspects of Islamic-Byzantine relations. He wrote a long article discussing the considerations that shaped the policy of the Byzantines towards Arab prisoners of war during the ninth and tenth centuries and the mechanisms they used to integrate them into society.[186] In another article, he

---

Under their supervision, Sāmir Qandīl completed his master's thesis in 2009, entitled *Gerbert (Pope Sylvester II) and his Role in Political and Cultural Life in Western Europe (945–1003)*. In 2016, Qandīl received his PhD degree with a dissertation entitled *European Perceptions of Islam and Muslims from the Ninth Century until the End of the Eleventh Century*. Ramaḍān and ʿUbayd also supervised the master's and doctoral dissertations of ʿUmar Imām, which were completed in 2009 and 2015, respectively. Their titles are *Vikings and the Carolingian Empire (814–911)*; *The Image of Islam and Muslims in Italian Writings (Fourteenth and Fifteenth Centuries)*. Under their supervision also, the third researcher, Usāma Istiqlāl completed in 2016 his MA thesis entitled *Medicine and Methods of Cure in Egypt during the Byzantine Era*.

179   Ramaḍān, *Al-Ṭarīq*.
180   Ramaḍān, Al-Hūwiyyatayn 39–74.
181   Ramaḍān, Siyāsat Abāṭirat 9–85.
182   Ramaḍān, Ḥaqq al-Lujūʾ 131–58.
183   Ramaḍān, Al-Bīzanṭiyyūn 33–98.
184   Ramaḍān, Ṣūrat al-Marʾa 31–52.
185   Ramaḍān, Maʿāyīr 11–119.
186   Ramaḍān, Treatment 155–94.

discusses the popular Islamic and Byzantine concept of the intervention of
supernatural powers, especially religious ones, in the course of the wars of both
sides.[187] The last article deals with the Islamic conquests of Syria as portrayed
in the eastern Christian sources.[188] Islamic-Byzantine relations also captured
Ramaḍān's interest in two articles in Arabic, one of which dealt with the image
of Islam as presented in the apocalypse of Pseudo Methodius.[189] The other discussed the motives for apostasy from Islam and Byzantine policy mechanisms
to promote conversion to Christianity and assimilation of apostates in society.[190]
He also published two articles dealing with English migration to Byzantium in
1066 and the evidence of the English element's presence within it until 1204,[191]
and the political and religious connotations of the tradition of Bride Shows in
the Byzantine court,[192] as well as a bibliographic article which lists the websites of Byzantine studies available until 2002.[193]

Ramaḍān has also made efforts for the promotion of Byzantine studies at
ʿAyn Shams University. This may be reflected in the comparison of the number
of master's and doctoral dissertations which were completed during the period
from the establishment of the branch of History of the Middle Ages at ʿAyn
Shams until 2003, the year in which Ramaḍān received his doctorate, and the
number of theses that were completed from 2003 until now. While only three
dissertations were supervised by Raʾfat ʿAbd al-Ḥamīd, and six by Isḥāq ʿUbayd,
Ramaḍān supervised jointly with ʿUbayd about six theses from 2003 to 2013,[194]
the ten years in which Ṭāriq Muḥammad was absent from ʿAyn Shams because
of his work at Taif University in Saudi Arabia.

---

187   Ramaḍān, Supernatural 1–34.
188   Ramaḍān, Islamic 7–22.
189   Ramaḍān, Ṣūrat al-Islām 9–32.
190   Ramaḍān, Siyāsat Bīzanṭa 103–57. This article has been fully developed and published in
      English. See Ramaḍān, Arab Apostates 273–314.
191   Ramaḍān, Al-Murtazaqa 161–95.
192   Ramaḍān, ʿUrūḍ 75–88.
193   Ramaḍān, Madkhal 75–103.
194   These dissertations are: ʿAbdallāh, *Al-ʿAlāqāt*; Al-Rāghī, *Manāṭiq*; Aḥmad, *Al-Bīzanṭiyyūn*;
      ʿAbd al-Rāzīq, *Jūrj Jimīstūs*; Sulaymān, M., *Al-Jadal*; al-Tājūrī, *Al-Ḥayāt*. Ramaḍān also
      contributed to the promotion of the study of Byzantine history in some other universi-
      ties. He supervised the master's and doctoral theses of Mutṣafā al-Shaʿīnī at South Valley
      University, and the doctoral theses of Hiba al-ʿAwāydī of The Girls' College at ʿAyn Shams
      University and Imān Siqiyyū at al-Azhar University. See Al-Shaʿīnī, *Niswat*; *Al-Muʿtaqadāt*;
      Al-ʿAwāydī, *Al-Ajānib*; Siqiyyū, *Al-Ḥayāt*.

6   The Impact of the Cairo School on New Universities

The expansion of public universities in Egypt since the early 1970s has increased the number of history departments. This, in turn, created demand for new faculty members to meet the needs of the different history branches. It was clear at the time that ʿAyn Shams University, whose branch of "History of the Middle Ages" was newly founded, would not benefit from the new situation, and that the competition for filling the new posts would be restricted to the graduates of the universities of Cairo and Alexandria, the only graduates available at the time. There is no doubt that the results of this competition have had a clear impact on the concept of the medieval history branch in new universities. Although the lines of any imaginable mental map are complicated and intertwined, one can trace the impact of the Cairo School on the universities of Upper Egypt, and of the Alexandria School on the universities of the Delta with the exception of Zaqāzīq.

The impact of Cairo University, both in terms of the phenomenon of the encyclopedic historian and in terms of its conception of the components of the medieval history branch, can be seen clearly in the case of Zubayda Muḥammad ʿAṭāʾ (b. 1944). She graduated from Cairo University in 1964 and received her master's degree in 1968 under the supervision of al-Bāz al-ʿArīnī, with a thesis entitled *The Islamic East and the Byzantine State in the Time of the Ayyubids*.[195] She completed her PhD in 1972 under the supervision of Saʿīd ʿĀshūr with an edition of the ninth volume of the Mamluk historical manuscript of Baybars al-Dawādār's *Zubdat al-Fikra fī Tārīkh al-Hijra*.[196] She began her career at al-Minyā University, after its founding in 1970, and then moved to Ḥilwān University after the establishment of the Faculty of Arts there in 1995. Most of her research interests focused on the history of the Copts[197] and Jews, especially in Medieval and Modern Egypt, and extended to cover the Arab-Israeli conflict.[198] Some articles have also been published by her on

---

195   Published under the same title in Cairo 1996. See ʿAṭāʾ, Al-*Sharq*.

196   Published under the same title in Cairo 2001.

197   ʿAṭāʾ published two great books on Copts in Christian and Islamic Egypt, as well as other books entitled: *The Egyptian Peasant between the Coptic and Islamic Eras*; *The Minyā Region in the Byzantine Era*; *The Economic Life in Byzantine Egypt*. She also published articles dealing with the internal markets in Byzantine Egypt, and the Coptic character and its position on the church and state in the Byzantine era.

198   She published books entitled: *The Jews of Egypt: Political History*; *The Jews of Egypt: Social and Economic History*; *Israel in the Nile*; *Jews and their Trade in Islamic Egypt*; *Israeli Ambitions in Africa and the Nile*; *Arabism of Jerusalem According to Waqf documents*; *Jews of the Arab World: Claims of Persecution*.

the history of the Crusades, the Ayyubids, and the Mamluks.[199] However, the study of Byzantine history was not entirely absent from 'Aṭā''s research interests. In addition to a book dealing with Byzantine history from Constantine to Anastasius,[200] she published another book about Byzantine relations with the Rum Seljuks and Ottomans,[201] and articles dealing with the Byzantine soldier,[202] and the image of the feudal knight in the Byzantine and Carolingian popular epics, *Digenes Akrites* and *La Chanson de Roland*.[203]

Other examples of the Cairo school's impact on Upper Egyptian universities can be seen clearly in the research interests of faculty members such as Muḥammad Maḥmūd al-Ḥūwayrī (1936–2003)[204] and Ḥasan 'Abd al-Jalīl al-Baṭṭāwī[205] at Asyūṭ University, and 'Ādil 'Abd al-Ḥāfiz Ḥamza (b. 1958)[206] at al-Minyā University. All of them devoted their studies to the history of the Crusades, the Ayyubids and the Mamluks, without any interest in the study of Byzantine history. The same applies to those who have dealt with topics related to Byzantine history, whether in a master's or doctoral thesis, such as Aḥmad 'Abd al-Karīm Sulaymān (1939–2015)[207] at Fayyūm Univesity, 'Izz

---

199   She published two articles dealing with the Crusade of Louis IX against Tunisia and the school libraries in the Ayyubid and Mamluk periods.

200   'Aṭā', *Al-Dawla*.

201   'Aṭā', *Al-Turk*.

202   'Aṭā', Al-Muqātil 83–140.

203   'Aṭā', Ṣūrat 67–115.

204   Under Sa'īd 'Āshūr's supervision, al-Ḥūwayrī completed his MA and PhD in 1972 and 1978, respectively. Their titles are *Aswān in the Middle Ages*, and *The Cultural Conditions in the Levant in the Twelfth and Thirteenth Centuries*. They were published under the same titles in Cairo in 1979 and 1980. He also published books and monographs entitled: *A Vision on the Fall of the Roman Empire*; *The Lombards in History and Civilization*; *Egypt in the Middle Ages: Political and Cultural Conditions*; *Egypt in the Middle Ages from the Christian Era until the Islamic Conquest*; *Al-'Ādil al-Ayyūbī*; *The History of the Ottoman Empire in the Middle Ages*; *The Coast of East Africa from the Dawn of Islam until the Portuguese Invasion*.

205   Al-Baṭṭāwī completed his MA and PhD in 1995 and 2000, respectively, under the supervision of Sa'īd 'Āshūr. His master's thesis is entitled *The Owners of the Turban (al-Mu'ammamūn) in the Mamluk Sultans' Era*. It was published in Cairo 2007. His PhD thesis is entitled *Social Contrast and Doctrinal Differences in the Crusader Society of Syria (1097–1187)*. He devoted all his postdoctoral studies to the history of the Crusades, the Ayyubids and the Mamluks.

206   Ḥamza received his MA and PhD from al-Minyā University under the supervision of Sa'īd 'Āshūr and Zubayda 'Aṭā' in 1986 and 1990. His MA thesis is entitled *Political Relations between the Holy Roman Empire and the Islamic East*. The title of his PhD is *Aleppo in the Era of the Mamluk Sultans (1250–1517)*. They were published under the same titles in Cairo 1989 and 2000. He published articles about ports and customs in Mamluk Egypt, Aleppo in the Ayyubid era, and Saladin's letter to Baldwin IV of Jerusalem in 1174.

207   Aḥmad Sulaymān received his MA and PhD from Cairo University under the supervision of Muḥammad Amīn in 1972 and 1980. His MA thesis is entitled *Agricultural Life in*

al-ʿArab Sulaymān (1956–2013) at Asyūṭ University,[208] and Najlāʾ Muṣṭafā Shīḥa (b. 1970) at Banī Suwayf University.[209] The only students of the Cairo school who showed an interest in the study of Byzantine history in the Universities of Upper Egypt are Muḥammad ʿAbd al-Shāfī al-Maghribī (b. 1964) at the University of South Valley,[210] and Sihām ʿAbd al-ʿAẓīm (b. 1969) at Ḥilwān University.[211] The emergence of other faculty members interested in the study of Byzantine history in the universities of Upper Egypt began only recently as a result of direct contact with ʿAyn Shams University.[212]

Mamluk Egypt, while the title of his PhD is *Relations between the Byzantine Empire and the Islamic Powers in the Eastern Mediterranean in the Tenth and Eleventh Centuries*. With the exception of a small monograph dealing with the battle of Adrianople in 378, most of his studies focused on the history of the Mamluks and the Mongols. See, *Maʿrakat*.

208　Under the supervision of al-Ḥūwayrī, ʿIzz al-ʿArab Sulaymān received his MA in 1993 and PhD in 1997 with theses entitled: *The Policy of the Fatimid State towards the Crusader Movement*, and *The Foreign Policy of the Byzantine State in the Era of the Angeloi (1185–1204)*. See, Sulaymān, al-*Siyāsa*. His postdoctoral research is devoted to the history of the crusades and the Mamluks.

209　Shīḥa received her MA from Cairo University in 1999 under the supervision of Hassanein Rabie and Laylā Ismāʿīl, with a thesis entitled *Constantinople in the Tenth Century*. See, Shīḥa, *Al-Qusṭanṭīniyya*. She received her doctorate from Banī Suwayf University in 2007 with a thesis entitled *European Communities in Mamluk Egypt (1250–1517)*, under the supervision of Hassanein Rabie. She devoted all her post-doctoral studies to the history of the Crusades and the Mamluks.

210　Under the supervision of al-Ḥūwayrī he received his MA in 1991 and PhD in 2000 with theses entitled *The Kingdom of the Jewish Khazars and its Relationship with the Byzantines and Muslims in the Seventh and Eighth Centuries*, and *The Political and Cultural Situation in Asia Minor in the Twelfth Century*. He published three articles dealing with the blind, caring for the elderly in Byzantium and the position of the Byzantine monasteries of the opposite sex. See, Al-Maghrabī, *Mamlakat*; Al-ʿUmyān; Riʿāyat 192–231; Mawqif 27–88.

211　ʿAbd al-ʿAẓīm received her master's and doctorate in 1997 and 2001 under the supervision of Zubayda ʿAṭāʾ at al-Minyā University, with theses entitled *Islamic-Byzantine Relations under the Ducas Dynasty (1059–81)*, and *The Internal Revolutions and Strife in the Byzantine Empire and their Impact on Byzantine-Islamic Relations in the Eleventh Century*. See, ʿAbd al-ʿAẓīm, al-*ʿAlāqāt*; al-*Thawarāt*. She published papers dealing with relations between Muslims and Byzantines (1059–1081), Byzantine military strategy and tactics in the Justinianic era, the presence of foreign children in the Byzantine court, Persian Christians and their role in Byzantine-Persian relations between the fourth and seventh centuries, the policy of displacement in the Byzantine territories, and Byzantine prisoners in Persia from the early fourth century to the early seventh century. ʿAbd al-ʿAẓīm, Al-ʿAlāqāt 257–64; al-Taktīk 57–116; Ẓāhirat 119–71; Masīhiyyū 3–39; Siyāsat 245–76; al-Asrā 153–80.

212　In 2006 a faculty member at Fayyūm University, Muḥammad Zāyid ʿAbdallāh (b. 1976), completed a master's thesis entitled *Byzantine-German relations 962–1059* under the supervision of Isḥāq ʿUbayd and ʿAbd al-ʿAzīz Ramaḍān. He continued his doctorate at Fayyūm University and received it in 2010 under the supervision of Aḥmad ʿAbd al-Karīm Sulaymān, with a thesis entitled *The Common Class during the Middle Byzantine Period*.

The impact of the Cairo school was not limited to the universities of Upper Egypt but also spread to a spot of the Delta when one of its graduates, Qāsim ʿAbduh Qāsim (b. 1942), established the branch of medieval history at Zaqāzīq University. As a direct disciple of Saʿīd ʿĀshūr, Qāsim remained committed to the traditional line of his teacher by dedicating all his studies to the history of the Crusades, the Ayyubids and the Mamluks, without producing a single paper in Byzantine history. However, unlike ʿĀshūr, Qāsim tried to draw the attention of some of his disciples to the importance of the study of Byzantine history and not ignoring it completely. He encouraged some graduate students to dedicate one of their theses to Byzantine History, and the other to the History of the Crusades or the Mamluks. This was the case of Ḥātim al-Ṭaḥāwī (b. 1962) who completed his master's thesis on the crusader economy in 1993 and a doctoral thesis in 1997 entitled *Economic Relations between the Byzantine Empire and the Italian Commercial Cities (1081–1204).*[213] Another student, Zaynab ʿAbd al-Majīd ʿAbd al-Qawī (b. 1958), completed in 1985 a master's thesis entitled *Political and Religious Relations between the Byzantines and Western Europe (1071–1101),*[214] and a PhD in 1993 dealing with the English role in the crusades.[215] Two of Qāsim's other students following the same pattern in their choice of

----

See, ʿAbdallāh, *Al-ʿAlāqāt*; *Ṭabaqāt*. ʿAbdallāh's postdoctoral studies showed a particular interest in Byzantine and medieval Western history. He published articles entitled: Byzantine *Typika* as a Source for Studying Medicine and Public Health in the Byzantine State; The Romans and the Persecution of the Christians in the Writings of Eusebius of Caesarea; The Arab *Skenites* 'Tents Dwellers' in Palaestina *Tertia*; *The Constructions of Constantine I in Jerusalem (306–37) and their Religious and Political Connotations*. See, ʿAbdallāh, al-Tīpīkā 223–58; al-Rūmān 160–75, al-ʿArab 129–68; Munshaʾāt 331–53. Another young faculty member at the university of South Valley, Muṣṭafā al-Shaʿīnī, received his MA and PhD in 2012 and 2017 under the supervision of ʿAbd al-ʿAzīz Ramaḍān. His theses are entitled *Imperial Byzantine Women in the Komnenian Era (1081–1185)*, and *Popular Beliefs in the Byzantine Empire, Ninth-Twelfth Centuries*. See, Al-Shaʿīnī, Niswat; *Al-Muʿtaqadāt*.

213   Published in Cairo 1998 under the title *Byzantium and Italian Cities: Trade Relations (1081–1204)*. See, Al-Ṭaḥāwī, *Bīzanṭa*. Al-Ṭaḥāwī's postdoctoral research focused on the translation of the Byzantine and Latin sources of the Ottoman Conquest of Constantinople in 1453, the Ottoman Empire in the fourteenth and fifteenth centuries, Baghdad and Mecca in Chinese sources, and Tamerlane's relations with the Near East. He published an article about the Red Sea in the Byzantine Sources of the sixth century. See, Al-Ṭaḥāwī, Al-Baḥr.

214   ʿAbd al-Qawī, *Al-ʿAlāqāt*.

215   The postdoctoral research of ʿAbd al-Qawī focused on medieval English history. She published monographs dealing with Eleanor of Aquitaine and the Jews of England (1066–1290), as well as two articles on the English Parliament in the thirteenth century and the University of Oxford.

thesis topics, became the first specialists in medieval history at the University of Manūfiyya.[216]

The legacy of the Cairo School in the other universities cannot be left without shedding light on its impact on the founders of the medieval history branch at Al-Azhar University and the Girls College at 'Ayn Shams University, 'Afāf Sayyid Ṣabra (b. 1943) and 'Aliyya 'Abd al-Samī' al-Janzūrī (1941–2010). Ṣabra obtained her master's and doctorate from Cairo University in 1970 and 1977, respectively, under the supervision of Sa'īd 'Āshūr and Hassanein Rabie, with theses dealing with the *Dīwān al-Inshā'* under the Ayyubids and Mamluks,[217] and the relationship of Venice with Egypt and Syria from the twelfth to the fourteenth centuries.[218] Her postdoctoral research focused on the history of the Mamluks, the Crusades, and Islamic civilization.[219] Her interest in the study of Byzantine history is limited to a book dealing with the relations between the Byzantine and Carolingian empires during Charlemagne's time, and an Arabic translation of Procopius's *Gothic Wars*.[220] Unlike Ṣabra, al-Janzūrī was a unique case of mixing the two different concepts of the medieval history branch at Cairo and 'Ayn Shams Universities, which eventually produced a model similar to that found at Alexandria University. She received her master's and her doctorate from the Girls College at 'Ayn Shams University in 1969 and 1972, respectively, under the supervision of Ḥasan Ḥabashī and Sa'īd 'Āshūr. Her theses concentrated on the history of the Crusades and dealt with the impact of the advent of the Crusades on political life in Syria and the Crusader County of Edessa. However, her postdoctoral research showed a considerable interest in Byzantine and European medieval history. In addition to three studies that follow the traditional path of studying Islamic-Byzantine relations,[221] she paid

---

216   The first is Muḥammad Fatḥī al-Shā'ir who completed his master's thesis in 1976 about al-Sharqiyya region in the eras of the Ayyubids and the Mamluks, and a doctorate in 1984 entitled *The Eastern Policy of the Byzantine Empire in the Era of Justinian*. See, Al-Shā'ir, *Al-Siyāsa*. His contribution to the study of Byzantine history was limited to a small study entitled *The Cultural Links between Byzantium and the Levant in the Eighth and Ninth Centuries*. See, Al-Shā'ir, *Al-Ṣilāt*. The second is Ṣabrī Salīm Abū al-Khayr whose master's thesis was completed in 1987 about the Fourth Crusade, while his PhD dealt with the Mongols. See, Abū al-Khayr, al-Ḥamla.

217   Published in Cairo 1990.

218   Published in Cairo 1983.

219   She published books entitled: *The Political History of the Khwarizmī State*; *Studies in the History of the Crusades*; *Orientalists and the Problems of Civilization*; *The History of Independent States in the Islamic Near East*; *The History of Islamic Civilization*; *The History of the Rightly-Guided Caliphs*.

220   Ṣabra, *Al-Imbrāṭūriyyatān*.

221   These studies deal with the Islamic *thughūr* (frontier regions) on Byzantine borders, the Byzantine naval attacks on the shores of Islamic Egypt, the truce of Ṣafar in 970, and

particular attention to the study of Byzantine imperial women in two studies entitled *Empress Irene*, and *Women in Byzantine Civilization*.[222] She also published a book dealing with Russian-Byzantine relations under the Macedonian dynasty (867–1056).[223]

7 The Impact of the Alexandria School on New Universities

While the influence of the Cairo School was particularly pronounced in the Upper Egyptian universities, the impact of the Alexandria School was somewhat apparent in Delta universities. The Alexandrian graduates competed to fill the vacant positions in the history departments of the Delta, bringing with them the Alexandria school's conception of what should be included in the medieval history branch. This may explain the absence of Byzantinists until the turn of the millennium in a university like Ṭanṭā, which separated from the University of Alexandria in 1972.

Usāma Zakī Zayd (b. 1943) and Ḥusayn Muḥammad ʿAṭṭiyya (b. 1945) are the founders of the medieval history branch in Ṭanṭā. Both completed their master's and PhD degrees in the history of the Crusades under the supervision of Joseph Yūsuf. Their postdoctoral studies followed the traditional path of their supervisor, that is to study the history of the Crusades or medieval European history, without producing a single paper in Byzantine history. This situation has only changed at the beginning of the third millennium with the appearance of al-Amīn ʿAbd al-Ḥamīd Abū Siʿda (Abouseada, b. 1963), the founder of the study of Byzantine history in Ṭanṭā. He began his career in 1992 with a master's thesis entitled *Relations between the Byzantine Empire and the Islamic Powers in the Levant during the Reign of Michael VIII Palœologus (1259–82)*, under the supervision of Ḥusayn ʿAṭṭiyya.[224] He moved to the University of Birmingham and received his doctorate in 2000, under the supervision of John Haldon, with a thesis entitled *Byzantium and Islam (Ninth–Tenth Centuries): A Historical Evaluation of the Role of Religion in Byzantine-Muslim Relations*. Although these titles suggested that Abū Siʿda would exclusively follow the traditional pattern of studying Islamic-Byzantine relations, his post-doctoral studies proved otherwise. Alongside one article dealing with the image of Byzantium in the

---

Byzantine Islamic relations from 1028 to 1056. See, Al-Janzūrī, *Al-Thughūr*; *Hajamāt*; *Al-ʿAlāqāt al-Islāmiyya* 81–101.

222　Al-Janzūrī, *Al-Imbrāṭūra; Al-Marʾa*.
223　Al-Janzūrī, *Al-ʿAlāqāt al-Bīzanṭiyya*.
224　Abū Siʿda, *Al-ʿAlāqāt*.

Arabic epic *Dhāt al-Himma*,[225] he devoted articles to Byzantine compulsory monasticism,[226] the Italian adventurer Neri Acciaiuoli in Greece,[227] the Polish policy toward Byzantium (965–1453),[228] and the death penalty in Byzantium.[229]

On the other hand, the Alexandrian concept of the medieval history branch was not followed by some graduates of Alexandria University themselves in universities such as Manṣūra and Banhā. Wisām ʿAbd al-ʿAzīz Faraj (also spelled Wesam Farag, b. 1946) is the most prominent example. He began his career at the University of Alexandria as an assistant lecturer in 1968. He completed in 1973 a master's thesis dealing with Byzantine-Umayyad relations in the reign of Emperor Leo III (717–40) under the supervision of Joseph Yūsuf and ʿUmar Tawfīq.[230] In 1975, Manṣūra University, established in 1972, granted him the opportunity to continue his doctoral studies at the University of Birmingham. In 1979 he completed there a PhD thesis entitled *Byzantium and its Muslim Neighbors during the Reign of Basil II (976–1025)*, under the supervision of the noted Byzantinist and numismatist Michael Hendy. The observations that can be gleaned from the writings of his professors and western colleagues suggest that he was not just a doctoral student who went for a degree, but a researcher who interacted with the surrounding environment so positively that he still lived in their memory, even though years had passed.[231] Faraj's success in Birmingham was unique for an Arab and never repeated, although four Egyptian researchers followed him there.[232]

---

225   Abū Siʿda, Bīzanṭa 275–317.

226   Abū Siʿda, Al-Dīriyya 232–92.

227   Abū Siʿda, Nīrī 25–71.

228   Abū Siʿda, Al-Siyāsa 217–63.

229   Abū Siʿda, ʿUqubat 11–124.

230   Faraj, *Al-ʿAlāqāt*.

231   See Herrin, J., Polla ta ete (repeat three times) to Bryer, In L. Brubaker & K. Linardou (eds.), Food and Wine in Byzantium: In Honour of Professor A.A.M. Bryer; Idem, Authority across the Byzantine Empire: Margins and Metropolis, Princeton & Oxford 2013, 58; M. Hendy, Studies in the Byzantine Economy 300–1450, Cambridge 1985, 269; Haldon, J.F., Kudāma ibn Djaʿfar and the Garrison of Constantinople, *Byz* 48/1 (1975), 78–90.

232   Two Egyptian researchers, ʿAbd al-Raḥman Sālim from the Faculty of Religious Sciences at Cairo University and Samīra Yūnis ʿAbd al-Qādir (b. 1951) from al-Azhar University, completed their doctorates at the University of Birmingham in 1983 and 1984, under the supervision of Antony Bryer and John Haldon. Sālim's PhD thesis was entitled *War and Peace in Caliphate and Empire: Political Relations between the Abbasids and Byzantium (794–847)* and ʿAbd al-Qādir's thesis was entitled *Byzantium and its Arab Neighbours under the Successors of Basil II (1025–1071)*. Two other researchers, Abū Siʿda from Ṭanṭā University and Muḥammad Abū Ḥadīd (b. 1967) from Banhā University, followed them. Abū Ḥadīd received his doctorate in 2002 under the supervision of John Haldon, with a thesis entitled *Byzantine-Abbasid Warfare: Structure, Strategy and Organisation of the Abbasid Army (750–1258)*. The post-doctoral contributions of the three scholars are

Faraj presented his first paper "the truce of Safar" at the eleventh spring symposium held at the center for Byzantine Studies at the University of Birmingham in 1977.[233] He continued his early interest in Islamic-Byzantine relations in two articles published in the prominent journals *Byzantinische Zeitschrift* and *Byzantine and Modern Greek Studies*. The first article deals with Leo of Tripoli's Attack on Thessaloniki in 904,[234] while the second discusses Byzantine-Fatimid conflicts of interest in Northern Syria in the later tenth century.[235] He also participated in international conferences of Byzantine studies. At the 15th annual conference of Byzantine studies in 1989, held at the department of Classics, University of Massachusetts at Amherst, he participated with a paper entitled "The After-Effects of the Byzantine Offensive against Dar al-Islam: The Demographic Dimensions".[236] He also published an article entitled "Papst Benedikt XVI. und das byzantinische Zitat. Versuch eines Brückenschlags".[237]

While Faraj's international articles were devoted to issues related to Islamic-Byzantine relations, his articles in Egyptian journals tended to deal with purely Byzantine topics. In these articles, he paid particular attention to the society, economy and administration in the Middle Byzantine era. He published studies dealing with the State and trade,[238] the economic policy of the successors of Justinian (565–82),[239] agricultural property laws in the tenth century,[240] the phenomenon of personal dependence between masters and clients,[241] the society of Constantinople,[242] the religious dimensions and political significance of emperor Leo VI's fourth marriage,[243] and the continuity and discontinuity in

---

limited. Sālim published a monograph entitled *The Muslims and Byzantines in the Era of the Prophet: A Study in the Roots of the Conflict and its Development between Muslims and Byzantines until the Death of the Prophet*. He also published two articles dealing with the cultural communication between the Abbasids and Byzantines in the reign of Caliph al-Ma'mūn (812–833), and Muslim-Byzantine relations under Caliph Abū Bakr (632–634). Sālim, *Al-Muslimūn*; al-Ittiṣāl 163–190; al-ʿAlāqāt 55–109. ʿAbd al-Qādir published only one monograph entitled *The Normans and the Byzantine Empire in the Eleventh century*. See, ʿAbd al-Qādir, *al-Nūrmān*.

233   Faraj, *Truce of Safar* 1–12.
234   Faraj, Some Remarks 133–9.
235   Faraj, Aleppo Question 44–59.
236   Faraj, The After-Effects 1–18.
237   Faraj, Papst Benedikt 63–77.
238   Faraj, *Al-Dawla*.
239   Faraj, Al-Siyāsa 13–65.
240   Faraj, Qwānīn 299–342.
241   Faraj, Al-Atbāʿ 89–136.
242   Faraj, Aḍwāʾ 65–135.
243   Faraj, *Al-Zawāj*.

government titles and positions.[244] Other articles sought to understand the Byzantine political ideology,[245] the factors which determined the policies of Emperor Basil II,[246] the Slavic presence in the Balkans 591–1018,[247] and the nature of Greek fire and its impact on the maritime activity of the Muslims.[248]

There is no doubt that Faraj represents a milestone in the development of the study of Byzantine history in Egypt, and in the shift away from the trends of the Alexandria School and its concept of the branch of medieval history. His influence was not limited to his immediate students, but extended to many researchers of the new generation in various Egyptian universities, such as Muḥammad and Ramaḍān in ʿAyn Shams, Abū Siʿda in Ṭanṭā, Hānī al-Bashīr in Ḥilwān,[249] Muḥammad ʿUthmān ʿAbd al-Jalīl in Port Said,[250] and al-Mutawallī Tamīm in Damanhūr.[251] However, it seems that Faraj's immediate students among faculty members at Manṣūra University, unfortunately, were not keen to develop his model or even try to replicate it. Although his student, and at the same time his colleague, ʿAbd al-Ghanī ʿAbd al-ʿĀṭī (b. 1944) completed under his supervision in 1981 a PhD entitled *The Eastern Policy of the Byzantine Empire*

244   Faraj, Al-Alqāb 295–339.

245   Faraj, Al-Dawlah al-Bīzanṭiyya 147–74.

246   Faraj, Basil II 97–130.

247   Faraj, Al-Slāv 141–201.

248   Faraj, Al-Nār 287–305.

249   Al-Bashīr (b. 1965) received his doctorate from Ṭanṭā University in 1999 with a thesis entitled *Relations between the Byzantine Empire and the First Bulgarian State 681–1018*, under the supervision of Faraj and Usāma Zayd. See, Al-Bashīr, *Bīzanṭa*. He published papers dealing with the *Breviarium* of *Patriarch Nicephorus*, the development of the Byzantine navy and its military activity during the eighth and tenth centuries, the role of the Armenians in the army and the political life of the Byzantine state from the beginning of the seventh century until the end of the tenth century, and Byzantine civilization in the light of the Islamic sources of the tenth and eleventh centuries. Al-Bashīr, Niqfūrūs 39–75; Taṭawūr 145–202; Dawr 71–102; al-Ḥaḍāra 394–451.

250   ʿAbd al-Jalīl (b. 1960) received his master's and doctorate under the supervision of Usāma Zayd at Ṭanṭā University in 1992 and 1997, with theses dealing with the revolt of Thomas the Slav 821–823, and the foreign policy of Epirus 1205–1340. He published papers dealing with the Samaritans in Palestine and their relationship with Byzantium (305–361), The Byzantine Duchy of Morea under the Paleologoi (1383–1460), the embassy of Pope John I to Constantinople in 526, and the sect of silent asceticism and its political and religious role in Byzantium in the fourteenth century. ʿAbd al-Jalīl, *Thawrat*; *Epīrūs*; al-Sāmiriyyūn 75–106; Dūqiyyat 327–60; Sifārat 229–253; Jamāʿat 239–52.

251   Tamīm (b. 1965) received his master's and doctorate in 1996 and 2004, under the supervision of Faraj, with theses entitled *The Pechenegs and Byzantines: Study in the Northern Policy of Byzantium (580–1122)*, and *The Kingdom of Hungary and its Relations with the Byzantine Empire (1000–1453)*. Tamīm, *Al-Bushnāq*; *Mamlakat*.

under the Emperor Alexius I Komnenos (1081–1118),[252] his postdoctoral research focused on the history of Islamic Yemen, the Crusades, the Ayyubids and the Mamluks, with only one article on Byzantine history entitled "The Bogomil Movement in the Byzantine State in the Eleventh and Twelfth centuries".[253] Another student, Aḥmed Kāmil ʿAbd al-Maqṣūd (b. 1961), produced only his MA and PhD, which were completed in 1996 and 2004 under the titles *Catalan Groups in the Byzantine Empire* and *The Second Bulgarian State (1185–1396).*[254]

Two other researchers at Banhā University succeeded in overcoming the Alexandrian concept of the medieval history branch. The first is Fāʾiz Najīb Iskandar (b. 1944) who completed his doctoral and master's theses in 1976 and 1980, under the supervision of Joseph Yūsuf. His master's thesis was entitled *The Art of War and Fighting among the Crusaders and Muslims in the Near East during the First Half of the Thirteenth Century*, while the title of his doctoral thesis is *The Lesser Armenian Kingdom between the Crusaders and the First Mamluk State*. Although some of Iskandar's post-doctoral studies dealt with topics from the history of the Mamluks, the Crusades, and the Vandals in North Africa, his main concern was the history of Armenia and Georgia (Bilād al-Kurj). In this context, he wrote a number of studies dealing with the Islamic-Byzantine conflict over these regions. He published two studies about the Islamic conquests of Armenia (632–661) and Georgia in the late twelfth century. He also published studies entitled *Armenia between the Byzantines and the Rightly-Guided Caliphs in the Light of the Writings of the Armenian Historian Gevond,*[255] *Armenia between the Byzantines and the Seljuk Turks (1000–71) According to Aristakis of Lastivert,*[256] *The Byzantine Invasion of Armenia in 1045,*[257] *Georgia between the Muslims and Byzantines,*[258] and *Muslims, Byzantines and Armenians in the Light of the Writings of the Armenian Historian Sebeos (632–61).*[259] Iskandar also paid attention to Seljuk-Byzantine relations in two studies dealing with the battle of Manzikert 1071,[260] as well as an article about the eleventh-century family of Bryennios,[261] and an article on Niketas Choniates.[262]

---

252   See, ʿAbd al-ʿĀṭī, *Al-Siyāsa al-Sharqiyya.*

253   ʿAbd al-ʿĀṭī, Ḥarakat 68–118.

254   See, ʿAbd al-Maqṣūd, *Al-Jamāʿāt; Al-Dawla.*

255   Iskandar, *Gīvūnd.*

256   Iskandar, *Arīsītākīs.*

257   Iskandar, *Ghazw.*

258   Iskandar, *Bilād al-Kurj.*

259   Iskandar, *Al-Muslimūn.*

260   Iskandar, *Al-Bīzanṭiyyūn; Mawqiʿat.*

261   Iskandar, Usrat 83–118.

262   Iskandar, Nīkītās 363–85.

The second scholar at Banhā University is Wadīʿ Fatḥī ʿAbdallāh (b. 1949) who differs from Iskandar in that he devoted all his attention from the beginning to the study of Byzantine history. He received his MA and PhD in 1982 and 1987 under the supervision of Joseph Yūsuf, with theses devoted to Islamic-Byzantine relations. His master's thesis dealt with the political relations between the Byzantine Empire and the Abbasid Caliphs during the reign of Emperor Theophilus (829–42),[263] while his doctoral thesis dealt with political relations between the Byzantine Empire and the Islamic Near East (741–820).[264] In his post-doctoral studies, he continued his interest in Islamic-Byzantine relations. He published a monograph entitled *Byzantium and the Muslims of Southern Italy and Sicily under the Reign of Basil I (867–66)*,[265] and an article entitled "The Byzantine Attack on Damietta in 853: A New Vision of the Byzantine-Islamic Maritime Conflict in the Ninth Century".[266] He also devoted three studies to Byzantine historiography. He published a monograph about *Theophylact Simocatta*,[267] and an article about *Joseph Genesius*.[268] He was also interested in dealing with the Byzantine rebellions and devoted monographs to the Norman rebel Roussel de Bailleul (1073–76),[269] and the revolt of Nikephoros Botaneiates in (1077–78).[270] Finally, two other articles were devoted to the reign of Emperor Nikephoros I, one dealing with his tax and financial reform,[271] while the other discussed his relationship with the Church.[272]

8   Conclusion

The study of Byzantine history in Egypt was strongly influenced by the circumstances that accompanied the establishment of the branch of medieval history in the three oldest universities.

In Cairo University, the medievalists remained committed to the concept formulated by the founder of the medieval history section, Muṣṭafā Ziyāda,

---

263   ʿAbdallāh, W.F., Thīyūfīlūs.
264   ʿAbdallāh, W.F., *Al-ʿAlaqāt*.
265   ʿAbdallāh, W.F., *Bīzanṭa*.
266   ʿAbdallāh, W.F., *Al-Hujūm* 627–96.
267   ʿAbdallāh, W.F., *Thīyūfīlākt*.
268   ʿAbdallāh, W.F., Jūsīf 273–345.
269   ʿAbdallāh, W.F., *Rūsīl*.
270   ʿAbdallāh, W.F., *Thawrat*.
271   ʿAbdallāh, W.F., Al-Iṣlāḥ 189–259.
272   ʿAbdallāh, W.F., Al-ʿAlāqa 107–60.

about the components of the branch since the late 1930s. It was a loose concept that prevented the existence of clear boundaries between the fields of medieval and Islamic history and produced the phenomenon of the encyclopedic medievalist who can write not only on the history of medieval Egypt, Europe, Byzantium and the Crusades, but also on the other various fields of history. This has adversely affected the study of Byzantine history in terms of quantity and quality until the 1980s. Despite the emergence of faculty members who turned part of their attention to the study of Byzantine history, such as Laylā Ismāʿīl, this did not lead to what can be described as a revolution in this study, especially with continued adherence to the need to expand the scope of research interest to include the history of the Ayyubids, Mamluks and the Crusades.

This was not the case at the University of Alexandria, whose specialists adhere to the conception formulated by the founder of the medieval history section there, Sūryāl ʿAṭṭiyya. The trend towards limiting the branch of medieval history to more specific content, compared with Cairo University, allowed the study of Byzantine history to appear on the map of the Alexandrian medievalists' concerns from an early date. Although this was initially associated, as in the case of Joseph Yūsuf and ʿUmar Tawfīq, with a basic interest in the history of the Crusades, it soon produced a specialist, Ismat Ghunaym, who devoted most of her research interest to Byzantine history. However, while the first and second generations of Sūryāl ʿAṭṭiyya's students achieved a relative balance in their studies among the three components of the medieval branch in Alexandria: Byzantine history, Western Europe, and the Crusades, as evidenced in Saʿīd ʿUmrān's studies, the third generation brought the situation back to Sūryāl ʿAṭṭiyya's time with its exclusive interest in the history of the Crusades.

The different concepts of Cairo and Alexandria about the branch of medieval history produced a difference in newly established universities since the 1970s. The impact of the Cairo School of medieval history in universities such as Zaqāzīq, Ḥilwān and the Upper Egyptian universities, has produced a situation almost identical to that of Cairo University in these smaller universities. The influence of the Alexandria School has appeared in universities such as Ṭanṭā, Banhā and Manṣūra. Its students in Ṭanṭā continued to adhere to the approach of Sūryāl ʿAṭṭiyya, which is exclusively concerned with studying the history of the Crusades, and this delayed the emergence of a specialist in Byzantine history at Ṭanṭā University until the beginning of this century. The students of the Alexandria School in Manṣūra and Banhā succeeded in freeing themselves from the Alexandrian concept of the branch of medieval history. Therefore, from the birthplace of the Alexandria School, Wisām Faraj at Manṣūra University emerged as one of the three pioneers of the study of Byzantine history in Egypt during the 1970s. The other two pioneers, Isḥāq ʿUbayd and Raʾfat ʿAbd al-Ḥamīd, succeeded in establishing a branch of medieval history at ʿAyn Shams University starting in the 1970s in accordance with a more specific conception of the field than those held by the medievalists of the universities of Cairo and Alexandria. They focused on studying the history of Byzantium and medieval Europe as key components of the branch, as well as preparing a new generation of researchers with a good degree of knowledge in the source languages.

Despite the fact that there are about ten researchers in Byzantine studies who received PhD degrees from abroad, of whom five studied at the Center for Byzantine Studies in Birmingham, the impact of Western universities, especially British ones, did not appear clearly except in the cases of Isḥāq ʿUbayd and Wisām Faraj. All the doctoral dissertations prepared abroad dealt with topics related to Islamic-Byzantine relations, with the exception of Isḥāq ʿUbayd's thesis, which dealt with Latin-Byzantine relations. On the one hand, this suggests that Western supervisors wanted to take advantage of these researchers' Arabic language skills, and on the other hand it might suggest an attempt to avoid the difficulties of Latin or Greek for some of them. In fact, even at home, Islamic-Byzantine relations, from the beginning of Byzantine studies in Egypt until now, has been the preferred field for many researchers, especially for those who aspire to publish in international journals.

In conclusion, the study of Byzantine history has been developing since the 1970s in the universities of ʿAyn Shams and Manṣūra. However, the current scene is not entirely satisfactory, as the number of researchers interested in the field can be counted on the fingers of one hand. It seems that there are still major obstacles to progress in the study of Byzantine history, such as the loose concepts of the branch of medieval history in many Egyptian universities, the lack of interest in the source languages or modern research languages, and most importantly living conditions that do not allow full-time research and force many to leave to work in the universities of the Gulf oil countries, which ends the research lives of some of them. However, the hope for this progress is still in the hands of a number of aspiring young researchers, such as Ṭāriq Muḥammad, ʿAbd al-ʿAzīz Ramaḍān, al-Amīn Abū Siʿda and a few others.

Bibliography

ACPSI *Annals of the Center of Papyrological Studies and Inscriptions*, ʿAyn Shams University

ACRHS	*Annals of Center for Research and Historical Studies*, Faculty of Arts, Cairo University
AEH	*Annals of the Egyptian Historian*, Faculty of Arts, Cairo University
AESGRS	*Annals of the Egyptian Society of Greek and Roman Studies*, Faculty of Arts, Cairo University
AH (Cai.)	*The Arab Historian* (Cairo)
AH (Bag.)	*The Arab Historian* (Baghdad)
AFAAShU	*Annals of the Faculty of Arts, ʿAyn Shams University*
AnIsl	*Annales islamologiques*
ASIMH	*Annals of the Seminar of Islamic and Medieval History*, Egyptian Society for Historical Studies
BFAAU	*Bulletin of the Faculty of Arts, Alexandria University*
BFABU	*Bulletin of the Faculty of Arts, Banha University*
BFACU	*Bulletin of the Faculty of Arts, Cairo University*
BFAHU	*Bulletin of the Faculty of Arts, Hilwan University*
BFAKU	*Bulletin of the Faculty of Arts, Kuwait University*
BFAMU	*Bulletin of Faculty of Arts, Mansoura University*
BFASCU	*Bulletin of Faculty of Arts, Suez Canal University*
BFASU	*Bulletin of the Faculty of Arts, Sanaʿa University*
BFASVU	*Bulletin of the Faculty of Archaeology, South Valley University*
BFATU	*Bulletin of the Faculty of Arts, Ṭanṭā University*
BFAZU	*Bulletin of the Faculty of Arts, Zagazig University*
BFAUAEU	*Bulletin of the Faculty of Arts, United Arab Emirates University*
BFDUCU	*Bulletin of the Faculty of Dār al-ʿUlūm, Cairo University*
BFEṬ	*Bulletin of the Faculty of Education in Ṭāʾif*
BMGS	*Byzantine and Modern Greek Studies*
BSl	*Byzantinoslavica*
BSOAS	*Bulletin of the School of the Oriental and African Studies*
BZ	*Byzantinische Zeitschrift*
EH	*The Egyptian Historian*, Faculty of Arts, Cairo University
EHR	*Egyptian Historical Review*, Egyptian Society for Historical Studies
CChO	*Collectanea Christiana Orientalia*
HE	*Historical Events*, Faculty of Arts, Cairo University
HFAD	*Humanities, Faculty of Arts in Damanhūr*
HF	*History and Future*, Faculty of Arts, Minia University
IJMH	*International Journal of Maritime History*
JCS	*Journal of Coptic Studies*
JHS	*Journal of Hellenic Studies*

| *JMIH* | *Journal of Medieval and Islamic History*, Faculty of Arts, ʿAyn Shams University |

JMIH *Journal of Medieval and Islamic History*, Faculty of Arts, ʿAyn Shams University

MS *Mediaeval Studies*

NTIW *Nadwat al-Tārīkh al-Islāmī wa al-Wasīṭ*, Faculty of Arts, ʿAyn Shams University

NTI *Nadwat al-Tārīkh al-Islāmī*, Faculty of Dār al-ʿUlūm, Cairo University

PI *Pax Islamica*

RJFAMU *Research Journal of Faculty of Arts, Menoufia University*

ʿAbd al-Ḥamīd, R., Kanīsat al-Quds fī al-ʿAsr al-Bīzanṭī [The Church of Jerusalem in the Byzantine Era], in *EHR* 25 (1978), 65–126.

ʿAbd al-Ḥamīd, R., Mīkhāʾīl Psellūs min khilāl Kitābihi al-Tārīkh al-Zamanī [Michael Psellos through his Chronographia], *BFASU* 2 (Mar. 1979), 151–224.

ʿAbd al-Ḥamīd, R., *Al-Dawla wa al-Kanīsa* [*The State and the Church*], 3 vols., Cairo, 1980–2000.

ʿAbd al-Ḥamīd, R., Al-Thawra al-Shaʿbiyya fī al-Qusṭanṭīniyya sanat 532 [The popular revolution of Constantinople in 532], in *EHR* 32 (1985), 25–88.

ʿAbd al-Ḥamīd, R., Qawāʿid al-Diblūmāsiyya al-Bīzanṭiyya [The principles of Byzantine diplomacy], in *EHR* 33 (1986), 29–82.

ʿAbd al-Ḥamīd, R., Al-Idṭihād al-Rūmānī li al-Masīḥyyīn bayn al-Iʿtiqād al-Kanasī wa al-Fikr al-Siyāsī [Roman persecution of Christians between ecclesiastical belief and political thought], in *BFAUAEU* 3 (1987), 8–38.

ʿAbd al-Ḥamīd, R., Al-Ṣirāʿ al-Dūwalī ḥawla Shibh al-Jazīra al-ʿArabiyya fī al-Qarn al-Sādis [International conflict on the Arabian Peninsula in the sixth century], in *AH* (Cai.) ½ (1994), 263–326.

ʿAbd al-Ḥamīd, R., Sūzūmenūs al-Muʾarrikh al-Ghazāwī fī al-Qarn al-Khāmis [Sozomenos, A Gazan historian in fifth century], in H. Zayān (ed.), *Aʿmāl Nadwat Filisṭīn ʿabra al-ʿUṣūr*, Cairo University, 1996, 85–128.

ʿAbd al-Ḥamīd, R., Ightiyāl Ariyūs [The assassination of Arius], in *BFAMU* 19 (Aug. 1996), 49–91.

ʿAbd al-Ḥamīd, R., *Bīzanṭa bayn al-fikr wa al-Dīn wa al-Siyāsa* [*Byzantium between thought, religion and politics*], Cairo, 1997.

ʿAbd al-Ḥamīd, R., Maṣraʿ Jūliān al-Imbrāṭūr al-Faylasūf [The death of Julian, the Philosopher-Emperor], in A. al-Rubāʿī (ed.), *Quṭūf Dāniyya Muhdāh ilā Nāṣir al-Dīn al-Asad*, Amman, 1997, 481–533.

ʿAbd al-Ḥamīd, R., Bīzanṭa wa Khiyānat al-Qāḍiyyat al-Ṣalībiyya [Byzantium and betrayal of the Crusader cause], in Idem, *Qaḍāyā min Tārīkh al-Ḥurūb al-Ṣalībiyya*, Cairo, 1998, 67–121.

'Abd al-'Āṭī, A.M., *Al-Siyāsa al-Sharqiyya li al-Imbrāṭūriyya al-Bīzanṭiyya fī 'Ahd al-Imbrāṭūr Aliksīyūs al-Awwal Komnīn 1081–1118* [*The Eastern Policy of the Byzantine Empire under the Emperor Alexius I Komnenos 1081–1118*], Cairo, 1983.

'Abd al-'Āṭī, A.M., Ḥarakat al-Būjūmīl fī al-Dawla al-Bīzanṭiyya fī al-Qarnayn al-Ḥādī 'Ashr wa al-Thānī 'Ashr li al-Mīlād [The Bogomil Movement in the Byzantine State in the Eleventh and Twelfth centuries], in *BFAMU* 12 (May, 1992), 68–118.

'Abd al-'Aẓīm, S.M., *Al-'Alāqāt al-Islāmiyya al-Bīzanṭiyya fī 'Aṣr Usrat Dūqās (1059–1081)* [Byzantine-Islamic Relations in the era of the Dukas Dynasty 1059–1081 AD], MA dissertation, Faculty of Arts, Al-Minyā University, 1997.

'Abd al-'Aẓīm, S.M., Al-'Alāqāt bayn al-Muslimīn wa al-Bīzanṭiyyin min 1059–1018 (451–474) [Relations between Muslims and the Byzantines from 1059–1018 AD (451–474 A.H.)], in *HF* 1/1 (Jan., 1997), 257–64.

'Abd al-'Aẓīm, S.M., *Al-Thawrāt wa al-Fitan al-Dākhiliyya fī al-Imbrāṭūriyya al-Bīzanṭiyya wa atharuha 'alā al-'Alāqāt al-Bīzanṭiyya al-Islāmiyya fī al-Qarn al-Ḥādī 'Ashar al-Mīlādī* [Revolutions and internal strife in the Byzantine Empire and their impact on Byzantine-Islamic relations in the eleventh century AD], PhD dissertation, Faculty of Arts, Al-Minyā University, 2001.

'Abd al-'Aẓīm, S.M., Al-Istrātījiyya wa al-*Taktīk* al-'Askarī fī 'Ahd Justīnyān [Byzantine Strategy and Military Tactics during the Reign of Justinian], in *EH* 33 (2008), 57–116.

'Abd al-'Aẓīm, S.M., Ẓāhirat Wujūd al-Abnā' al-Ajānib fī al-Balāṭ al-Bīzanṭī [The phenomenon of the presence of foreign sons in the Byzantine court], in *HF* 1 (2008), 119–171.

'Abd al-'Aẓīm, S.M., Masīḥiyyu Fāris wa Dawruhum fī al-'Alāqāt al-Fārisiyya fī mā bayn al-Qarn al-Rābi' wa al-Sābi' al-Mīlādiyayn [The Christians of Persia and their role in the Persian-Byzantine relations between the fourth and seventh centuries AD], in *AFAAShU* 8 (2013–2014), 3–39.

'Abd al-'Aẓīm, S.M., Siyāsat al-Tahjīr fī al-Arāḍī al-Bīzanṭiyya [The politics of displacement in the Byzantine lands], in *BFAAU* 73 (2014), 245–276.

'Abd al-'Aẓīm, S.M., Al-Asrā al-Bīzanṭiyyūn ladā al-Furs min Bidāyat al-Qarn al-Rabi' ilā Bidāyat al-Qarn al-Sabi' al-Mīlādiyayn [Byzantine prisoners of war with the Persians from the beginning of the fourth century to the beginning of the seventh century AD], in *AFAAShU* 9 (2014–2015), 153–180.

'Abd al-Jalīl, M.U., *Thawrat Tūmās al-Saqalabī fī al-Imbrāṭūriyya al-Bīzanṭiyya (205–207/821–823)* [Thomas the Slav's revolt in the Byzantine Empire 205–207 AH/ 821–823 AD], MA dissertation, Faculty of Arts, Ṭanṭā University, 1992.

'Abd al-Jalīl, M.U., *Epīrūs wa Siyāsatuhā al-Khārijiyya 1205–1340* [Epirus and its foreign policy 1205–1340 AD], PhD dissertation, Faculty of Arts, Ṭanṭā University, 1997.

'Abd al-Jalīl, M.U., Al-Sāmiriyyūn fī Falasṭīn wa 'Alāqatuhum bi al-Imbrāṭūriyya al-Bīzanṭiyya (305–361) [The Samaritans in Palestine and their Relationship with the Byzantine Empire 305–361 AD], in *EH* 28 (Jan., 2005), 75–106.

'Abd al-Jalīl, M.U., Dūqiyyat al-Mūra al-Bīzanṭiyya fī 'Ahd Āl Pālīyūlūghūs 1383–1460 [The Duchy of Byzantine Morea during the reign of the Palaeologus family from 1383–1460 AD], in *EH* 29 (Jan., 2006), 327–360.

'Abd al-Jalīl, M.U., Sifārat al-Pāpā Yūḥanā al-Awwal ilā al-Qusṭanṭīniyya 'Am 526 [Embassy of Pope John I to Constantinople in 526 AD], in *Al-Insāniyyāt* 35 (Oct., 2010), 229–253.

'Abd al-Jalīl, M.U., Jamā'at al-Zuhd al-Ṣāmit wa Dawruhā al-Siyāsī wa al-Dīnī fī Bīzanṭa fī al-Qarn al-Rābi' 'Ashar [The Sect of Silent Asceticism and its political and religious role in Byzantium in the fourteenth century], in *JMIH* 8 (2013–2014), 239–252.

'Abd al-Maqṣūd, A.K., *Al-Jamā'āt al-Qaṭālūniyya fī al-Imbrāṭūriyya al-Bīzanṭiyya* [Catalan Groups in the Byzantine Empire], MA dissertation, Faculty of Arts, Manṣūra University, 1996.

'Abd al-Maqṣūd, A.K., *Al-Dawla al-Bulghāriyya al-Thāniyya 1185–1396* [The Second Bulgarian State 1185–1396 AD], PhD dissertation, Faculty of Arts, Manṣūra University, 2004.

'Abd al-Qādir, S.Y., *Al-Nūrmān wa al-Dawla al-Bīzanṭiyya fī al-Qarn al-Ḥādī 'Ashar al-Mīlādī [The Normans and the Byzantine State in the Eleventh Century AD]*, Cairo, 1995.

'Abd al-Qawī, Z.A., *Al-'Alāqāt al-Siyāsiyya wa al-Dīniyya bayn al-Dawla al-Bīzanṭiyya wa Gharb Urupā fī al-Fatra min 1071–1101* [Political and religious relations between the Byzantine state and Western Europe 1071–1101 AD], MA dissertation, Faculty of Arts, Zagazig University, 1985.

'Abd al-Rashīd, R.A., *Ḥaṣānat al-Qusṭanṭīniyya fī Mūwājahat al-Thawra al-Dākhiliyya wa al-Ghazawāt al-Khārijiyya fī al-'Uṣūr al-Wusṭā* [The immunity of Constantinople in the face of internal revolt and external invasions of the Middle Ages], MA dissertation, Faculty of Arts, Alexandria University, 2000.

'Abd al-Rāzīq, A.A.D., Rū'yat Jūrj Jimīstūs Plīthūn li Iḥyā' al-Dawla al-Bīzanṭiyya 1360–1453 [George Gemistus Plethons' View to revive the Byzantine State 1360–1453], MA dissertation, Faculty of Arts, 'Ayn Shams University, 2016.

'Abd al-Ẓāhir, Ḥ., *Al-Mū'arrikh al-Miṣrī 'Azīz Suryāl 'Aṭṭiyya [The Egyptian Historian 'Azīz Suryāl 'Aṭṭiyya]*, Cairo, 2004.

'Abdallāh, M.Z., Al-'Alāqāt al-Bīzanṭiyya al-Almāniyya 962–1059 [Byzantine-German relations 962–1059], MA dissertation, Faculty of Arts, 'Ayn Shams University, 2006.

'Abdallāh, M.Z., Ṭabaqat al-'Āmma fī al-Imbrāṭūriyya al-Bīzanṭiyya khilāl al-'Aṣr al-Bīzanṭī al-Awsaṭ [The Common Class during the Middle Byzantine period], PhD thesis, Faculty of Arts, Fayoum University, 2009.

'Abdallāh, M.Z., Al-Tīpīkā al-Bīzanṭiyya Maṣdar li al-Ṭibb wa al-Ṣiḥḥat al-'Āmma fī al-Dawlat al-Bīzanṭiyya [Byzantine typika as a source for studying medicine and public health in Byzantine state], in *ASIMH* 1 (2011), 223–58.

'Abdallāh, M.Z., Al-Rūmān wa Idṭihād al-Masīḥiyyīn fī Kitābāt Yūsībīus al-Qayṣārī [The Romans and the persecution of the Christians in the writings of Eusebius of Caesarea], in A.M. Ramaḍān et al. (eds.), *Quṭūf min al-Tārīkh al-Islāmī wa al-Wasīṭ* [Selections from Islamic and Medieval History], Cairo, 2012, 160–75.

'Abdallāh, M.Z., Al-ʿArab al-Iskīnāʾī Sākinū al-Khiyām fī Wilāyat Filasṭīn al-Thālitha khilāl al-ʿAṣr al-Bīzanṭī [The Arab Skenites "tents dwellers" in Palaestina Tertia], in *BFASCU* 7 (2013), 129–68.

'Abdallāh, M.Z., Munshaʾāt Qusṭanṭīn al-Awwal (306–337) fī Madinat al-Quds wa Dalālātuhā al-Dīniyya wa al-Siyāsiyya [The Constructions of Constantine I in Jerusalem (306–337) and their Religion and Political Connotations], in *AH* (*Cai.*) 23 (2015), 331–53.

'Abdallāh, W.F., *Al-ʿAlāqāt al-Siyāsiyya bayn al-Imbrāṭūriyya al-Bīzanṭiyya wa al-Khilāfa al-ʿAbbāsiyya fī ʿAhd al-Imbrāṭūr Thiyūfīlūs (214–228/ 829–842)* [Political Relations between the Byzantine Empire and the Abbasid Caliphate during the reign of Emperor Theophilos 214–228 AH/ 829–842], MA dissertation, Faculty of Arts, Alexandria University, 1982.

'Abdallāh, W.F., *Al-ʿAlāqāt al-Siyāsiyya bayn Bīzanṭa wa al-Sharq al-Adnā al-Islāmī (124–205/742–820)* [*Political Relations between Byzantium and the Islamic Near East 124–205 AH/ 742–820 AD*], Alexandria, 1990.

'Abdallāh, W.F., *Bīzanṭa wa Mulslimū Janūb Iṭāliyā wa Ṣiqiliyya fī ʿAhd Bāsīl al-Awwal al-Maqdūnī 867–886* [*Byzantium and the Muslims of southern Italy and Sicily during the reign of Basil I of Macedon 867–886 AD*], Alexandria, 1992.

'Abdallāh, W.F., *Rūsīl Bāylūl al-Nūrmānī al-Thāʾir fī Asia al-Ṣughrā (1073–1076)* [*Roussel de Bailleul, a Norman rebel in Asia Minor 1073–1076 AD*], Cairo, 1995.

'Abdallāh, W.F., *Al-Mūʾarrikh al-Bīzanṭī Thīyūfīlākt Symūkātā min Khilāl Muʾallafihi 'al-Tārīkh'* [*The Byzantine Historian Theophylact Simocatta through his "History"*], Cairo, 1995.

'Abdallāh, W.F., Al-Iṣlāḥ al-Ḍarībī wa al-Mālī fī al-Imbrāṭūriyya al-Bīzanṭiyya zaman Niqfūr al-Awwal (802–811) [Tax and Financial Reform in the Byzantine Empire at the time of Nikephoros I, 802–811 AD], in *HF* (Jan., 2000), 189–259.

'Abdallāh, W.F., Al-Hujūm al-Bīzanṭī ʿalā Dumyāṭ sanat 853 [Byzantine attack on Damietta in 853 AD], in *BFABU* 11/2 (July, 2004), 627–696.

'Abdallāh, W.F., Al-ʿAlaqa bayn al-Dawla wa al-Kanīsa fī ʿAṣr Niqfūr al-Awal (802–811) [The Relationship between the State and the Church in the era of Nikephoros I 802–811 AD], in *EH* 28 (Jan., 2005), 107–160.

'Abdallāh, W.F., Thawrat Niqfūr Būtanyātīs wa Ṣadāha fī al-Imbrāṭūriyya al-Bīzanṭiyya 1077–1078 [The revolt of Nikephoros Botaneiates and its Impact in the Byzantine Empire 1077–1078], in: *Majallat Markaz al-Khidma lil-Istishārāt al-Baḥthiyya*, Faculty of Arts, al-Munūfiya University, 2006.

'Abdallāh, W.F., Jūsīf Ginisius Mū'arrikh li Ḥukm al-Imbrāṭūr Mīkhā'īl al-Thānī al-'Amūrī 820–829 [Joseph Genesius, a historian of the reign of Emperor Michael II the Amorian, 820–829 AD], in *JMIH* 5 (2006–2007), 273–345.

Abū al-Khayr, S., *Al-Ḥamla al-Ṣalībiyya al-Rābi'a wa Suqūṭ al-Qusṭanṭīniyya* [Fourth Crusade and the fall of Constantinople], MA dissertation, Faculty of Arts, Zaqāzīq University, 1987.

Abū Si'da, A.A., *Al-'Alāqāt bayn al-Imbrāṭūriyya al-Bīzanṭiyya wa al-Qiwā al-Islāmiyya fī al-Mashriq fī 'Ahd Mīkhā'īl al-Thāmin Pālīyūlūg (657–681/1259–1282)* [Relations between the Byzantine Empire and the Islamic powers in the East during the reign of Michael VIII Palaeologus (657–681 AH / 1259–1282 AD)], MA dissertation, Faculty of Arts, Ṭanṭā University, 1992.

Abū Si'da, A.A., Bīzanṭa fī al-Malāḥim al-'Arabiyya; Qirā'a fī Sīrat Dhāt al-Himma [Byzantium in the Arab Epics: A Reading in the Biography of the Princess Dhat al-Himma], in *BFAHU* 9–10 (2001), 275–317.

Abū Si'da, A.A., Nīrī Akyāūlī: al-Ḥayyā al-Siyāsiyya li Mughāmir Iṭālī fī Bilād al-Yūnān fī al-Qarn al-Rābi' al-Mīlādī [Neri Acciaiuoli: The Political Life of an Italian Adventurer in Greece in the Fourteenth Century AD], in *RJFAMU* 55 (Oct., 2003), 25–71.

Abū Si'da, A.A., Al-Dayriyya al-Ijbāriyya fī al-Dawla al-Bīzanṭiyya [Mandatory monasticism in the Byzantine state], in *BFAMU* 43/1 (Aug., 2008), 232–92.

Abū Si'da, A.A., 'Uqubat al-I'dām fī al-Dawla al-Bīzanṭiyya bayn al-Wāqi' wa al-Qānūn [The death penalty in the Byzantine state between reality and the law], in *ACRHS* (2016).

Al-'Abd al-Ghanī, A.M., *Thawrat Bardās Sklīrūs fī al-Dawla al-Bīzanṭiyya wa Mawqif al-Duwal al-Islāmiyya minhā (366–379/976–989)* [Bardas Skleros' Revolt in the Byzantine Empire and the Position of the Neighboring Islamic States Towards It, 366–379 AH / 976–989 AD], MA dissertation, Faculty of Arts, Alexandria University, 1980.

Al-'Abd al-Ghanī, A.M., *Armīniyā wa 'Alāqatuhā al-Siyāsiyya bikulli min al-Bīzanṭiyyin wa al-Muslimīn (33–457/653–1064)* [*Armenia and its political relations with the Byzantines and Muslims 33–457 AH / 653–1064 AD*], Kuwait, 1989.

Al-'Adawī, I., Dirāsāt fī al-Tārīkh al-Bīzanṭī [Studies in Byzantine History], in *EHR* 2/2 (1949), 75–93.

Al-'Adawī, I., Iqrīṭish bayna al-Muslimīn wa al-Bīzanṭiyyin fī al-Qarn al-Tāsi' [Crete between Muslims and Byzantines in the ninth century], in *EHR* 3/2 (1950), 53–68.

Al-'Adawī, I., *Bīzanṭa wa al-Islām* [*Byzantium and Islam*], Cairo, 1951.

Al-'Adawī, I., Al-Tamthīl al-Siyāsī bayn al-Khilāfa al-'Abbāsiyya wa al-Dawla al-Bīzanṭiyya [Political representation between the Abbasid caliphate and the Byzantine state], in *EHR* 4/2 (1952), 113–22.

Al-'Adawī, I., *Al-Umawiyyūn wa al-Bīzanṭiyyūn: al-Baḥr al-Mutawassiṭ Buḥayra Islāmiyya* [*Umayyads and Byzantines: the Mediterranean an Islamic Lake*], Cairo, 1953.

Al-ʿAdawī, I., *Al-Asāṭīl al-ʿArabiyya fī al-Baḥr al-Mutawassiṭ* [*Arab Navies in the Mediterranean*], Cairo, 1957.

Al-ʿAdawī, I., *Al-Sifārāt al-Islāmiyya ilā Ūrūpā fī al-ʿUṣūr al-Wūsṭā* [*Muslim Embassies to Medieval Europe*], Cairo, 1957.

Al-ʿAdawī, I., Qawānīn al-Iṣlāḥ al-Zirāʿī fī al-Dawlat al-Bīzanṭiyya [Laws of Agrarian Reform in the Byzantine State], in *BFAKU* 3–4 (1973), 149–72.

Al-ʿArīnī, A.A., *Ajnād al-Rūm* [*The Byzantine Themes*], Cairo, 1956.

Al-ʿArīnī, A.A., *Al-Dawla al-Bīzanṭiyya 323–1081* [*The Byzantine state 323–1081*], Cairo, 1965.

Aḥmad, M.M.H., Al-Bīzanṭiyyūn wa al-Lātīn 1096–1204: Rūʾyat al-Akhar [The Byzantines and the Latins 1096–1204: the image of the other], MA dissertation, Faculty of Arts, ʿAyn Shams University, 2016.

ʿAṭāʾ, Z.M., *Bilād al-Turk fī al-ʿUṣūr al-Wūsṭā: Bīzanṭa wa Salājiqat al-Rūm wa al-ʿUthmāniyyūn* [*The Land of the Turks in the Middle Ages: Byzantium, the Rūm Seljuks and the Ottomans*], Cairo, n.d.

ʿAṭāʾ, Z.M., *Al-Dawla al-Bīzanṭiyya min Qusṭanṭīn ilā Anastasīyūs* [*The Byzantine state from Constantine to Anastasius*], Cairo, 1970.

ʿAṭāʾ, Z.M., Al-Muqātil al-Bīzanṭī [The Byzantine Fighter], in *HF* 1/1 (1991), 83–140.

ʿAṭāʾ, Z.M., Ṣūrat al-Fāris al-Iqṭāʿī wa al-Ṣirāʿ al-Islāmī al-Masīḥī kamā waradat fī Malāḥim al-Qarn al-Ḥādīʿashar al-Mīlādī al-Bīzanṭiyya wa al-Lātīniyya [The image of the feudal knight and Islamic-Christian conflict as mentioned in Byzantine and Latin epics of the eleventh century], in *HF* 5/3 (1991), 67–115.

ʿAṭāʾ, Z.M., *Al-Sharq al-Islāmī wa al-Dawlat al-Bīzanṭiyya zaman al-Ayyūbiyyīn* [*The Islamic East and the Byzantine State during the Time of the Ayyubids*], Cairo, 1996.

Al-ʿAwāydī, H.R.M., Al-Ajānib fī Bīzanṭa min al-Qarn al-ʿāshir ilā al-Qarn al-thānī ʿashar [Foreigners in Byzantium, 10th–12th Centuries], PhD dissertation, Girls College, ʿAyn Shams University, 2016.

Al-Bashīr, H.A., *Bīzanṭa wa Bulghāria 681–1018* [*Byzantium and Bulgaria 681–1018 AD*], Cairo, 2001.

Al-Bashīr, H.A., *Al-Dawla al-Bīzanṭiyya 641–711* [*Byzantine State 641–711 AD*], Cairo, 2002.

Al-Bashīr, H.A., Al-Ḥaḍāra al-Bīzanṭiyya fī ḍawʾ al-Maṣādir al-Islāmiyya li al-Qarnayn al-ʿĀshir wa al-Ḥādī ʿashar al-Mīlādiyayn [Byzantine Civilization in the Light of Islamic Sources of the Tenth and Eleventh Centuries AD], in *BFATU* 26/1 (Jan., 2003), 394–451.

Al-Bashīr, H.A., Niqfūrūs Paṭriark al-Qusṭanṭīniyya (806–815) wa Mūʾallafuhu al-Tārīkh al-Mukhtaṣar [Nicephorus, Patriarch of Constantinople (806–815 AD), and his *Short History*], in *EH* 26 (Jan. 2003), 39–75.

Al-Bashīr, H.A., Taṭawwūr al-Baḥriyya al-Bīzanṭiyya wa Nashāṭuhā al-ʿAskarī Khilāl al-Qarnayn al-Thāmin wa al-ʿĀshir li al-Mīlād [The development of the Byzantine

Navy and its military activity during the eighth and tenth centuries AD], in *HF* 1/1 (Jul., 2003), 145–202.

Al-Bashīr, H.A., Dawr al-Arman fī al-Jaysh wa al-Ḥayāt al-Siyāsiyya li al-Dawla al-Bīzanṭiyya min Bidāyat al-Qarn al-Sābiʿ ḥattā Nihāyat al-Qarn al-ʿĀshir al-Mīlādī [The role of the Armenians in the army and the political life of the Byzantine state from the beginning of the seventh century until the end of the tenth century AD], in *AH* (Cai.) 14 (March, 2006), 71–102.

Al-Birī, M.M.A., Al-ʿAlāqāt bayn al-Imbrāṭūriyya al-Bīzanṭiyya wa al-Muslimīn fī Ṣiqiliyya wa Janūb Iṭāliyā zaman al-Usrat al-Maqdūniyya [Relations between the Byzantine Empire and Muslims in Sicily and Southern Italy in the time of the Macedonian Dynasty], MA dissertation, Faculty of Arts, ʿAyn Shams University, 1996.

Brooks, E.W., Arabic Lists of the Byzantine Themes, in *JHS* 21 (1901), 67–77.

Diehl, Ch., L'origine du régime des thèmes dans l'empire byzantin, in Idem, Études byzantines, Paris, 1905, 276–92.

Fahmī, G.A., *Al-Sanawāt al-Akhīra li al-Usrat al-Maqdūniyya 1025–1056* [The last years of Macedonian Dynasty 1025–1056], MA dissertation, Faculty of Arts, ʿAyn Shams University, 2002.

Faraj, W.A. [Farag], The Truce of Safar A.H. 359 / December–January 969–970 A.D., in *Proceedings of the Eleventh Spring Symposium of Byzantine Studies*, University of Birmingham, 1977, 1–12.

Faraj, W.A. [Farag], *Byzantium and its Muslim Neighbours During the Reign of Basil II (976–1025)*, PhD thesis, University of Birmingham, 1979.

Faraj, W.A. [Farag], *Al-ʿAlāqāt bayn al-Imbrāṭūriyya al-Bīzanṭiyya wa al-Dawla al-Umawiyya ḥattā Muntaṣaf al-Qarn al-Thāmin al-Mīlādī* [*Relations between the Byzantine Empire and the Umayyad State until the mid-eighth century AD*], Alexandria, 1982.

Faraj, W.A. [Farag], Al-Imbrāṭūr Bāsīl al-Thānī Saffāḥ al-Bulghār (976–1025): al-ʿAwāmil allatī Atharat ʿalā al-Siyāsa fī ʿAṣrihi [Emperor Basil II, the Bulgar Slayer (976–1025 AD): Factors that influenced politics in his time], in *NTIW* 1 (1982), 168–202.

Faraj, W.A. [Farag], Basil II "The Bulgar Slayer" 976–1025 A.D.: The Factors which determined the Policies of his Reign, in *BFAMU* 3–4 (1982), 97–130.

Faraj, W.A. [Farag], Qawānīn al-Milkiyya al-Zirāʿiyya fī al-Imbrāṭūriyya al-Bīzanṭiyya fī al-Qarn al-ʿĀshir al-Mīlādī [Laws of agricultural property in the Byzantine Empire in the tenth century AD], in *NTIW* 2 (1983), 299–342.

Faraj, W.A. [Farag], Al-Slāv fī shibh Jazīrat al-Balqān wa Juhūd al-Imbrāṭūriyya al-Bīzanṭiyya li Istirdād Siyādatihā (951–1018) [Slavs in the Balkan Peninsula and the efforts of the Byzantine Empire to recover its sovereignty 951–1018 AD], in *EHR* 30–31 (1983–1984), 141–201.

Faraj, W.A. [Farag], Aḍwāʾ ʿalā Mujtamaʿ al-Qusṭanṭīniyya: Dirāsa fī al-Tārīkh al-Ijtmāʿī li Madinat Qusṭanṭīn ḥattā Nihāyat al-Qarn al-Ḥādī ʿashar al-Mīlādī [Spotlight on

348   RAMADAN

Constantinople Society: A study in the social history of the city of Constantine until the end of the eleventh century AD], in *BFAMU* 5 (1984), 65–135.

Faraj, W.A. [Farag], Al-Atbāʿ wa al-Sāda: Dirāsa fī Zāhirat al-Tabaʿiyya al-Shakhṣiyya fī al-ʿAṣr al-Bīzanṭī al-Awsaṭ [Clients and Masters: A study in the phenomenon of personal dependency in the middle Byzantine era], in *HER* 32 (1985), 89–135.

Faraj, W.A. [Farag], Al-Dawla wa al-Tijāra fī al-ʿAṣr al-Bīzanṭī al-Awsaṭ [State and Trade in the Middle Byzantine Period], *BFAKU* 53 (1987–1988).

Faraj, W.A. [Farag], Some Remarks on Leo of Tripoli's Attack on Thessaloniki in 904 A.D., in *BZ* 82 (1989), 133–9.

Faraj, W.A. [Farag], The After-Effects of the Byzantine Offensive against Dar al-Islam: The Demographic Dimensions, in *BFAMU* 10 (1990), 1–18.

Faraj, W.A. [Farag], The Aleppo Question: A Byzantine-Fatimid Conflict of Interests in Northern Syria Towards the End of the 10th Century A.D., in *BMGS* 14 (1990), 44–59.

Faraj, W.A. [Farag], Al-Siyāsa al-Māliyya li al-Dawla al-Bīzanṭiyya fī Awākhir al-Qarn al-Sādis al-Mīlādī (565–582) [The financial policy of the Byzantine state in the late 6th century AD (565–582 AD], in *Historical research papers dedicated by faculty members in the Department of History to Kuwait University on the occasion of the 25th anniversary of its foundation*, Kuwait, 1990, 13–65.

Faraj, W.A. [Farag], *Al-Zawāj al-Rābiʿ li al-Imbrāṭūr Liū al-Sādis: al-Abʿād al-Dīniyya wa al-Dalāla al-Siyāsiyya* [*The Fourth Marriage of Emperor Leo VI: Religious Dimensions and Political Significance*], Alexandria, 1991.

Faraj, W.A. [Farag], Al-Nār al-Ighrīqiyya: Ṭabīʿat Tarkībihā wa Atharuha fī Nashāṭ al-Muslimīn al-Baḥrī [Greek Fire: The Nature of Its Structure and Its Impact on Muslim Maritime Activity], in *Nadwat al-Ḥaḍārat al-Islāmiyya wa ʿĀlam al-Biḥār*, Union of Arab Historians, Cairo, 1994, 287–305.

Faraj, W.A. [Farag], Al-Alqāb wa al-Manāṣib fī Bīzanṭa bayn al-Istimrāriyya wa al-Inqiṭāʿ [Titles and government positions in Byzantium between continuity and discontinuity], in *Yearbook of the Egyptian Society for Greek and Roman Studies*, Cairo, 1998, 295–339.

Faraj, W.A. [Farag], Al-Dawla al-Bīzanṭiyya bayn Awhām al-Naẓariyya wa Ḥaqīqat al-Huwiyya [The Byzantine state between illusions of theory and fact of identity], in *Journal of Archaeological Society of Alexandria* 46 (2001), 147–174.

Faraj, W.A. [Farag], Papst Benedikt XVI. und das byzantinische Zitat. Versuch eines Brückenschlags, in G.K. Hasselhoff & M. Meyer–Blanck (eds.), Religion und Rationalit? [Studien des Bonner Zentrums für Religion und Gesellschaft, Band 4], Würzburg, 2008, 63–77.

Ghunaym, Ismat, *Al-ʿAlāqāt al-Siyāsiyya bayn al-Dawlatayn al-Bīzanṭiyya wa al-Fāṭimiyya 969–1094* [*Political relations between the Byzantine and Fatimid states 969–1094*], MA, Faculty of Arts, Alexandria University, 1968.

Ghunaym, Ismat, *Imbrāṭūriyyat Jūstīnian* [*The Empire of Justinian*], Jeddah, 1977.

Ghunaym, Ismat, Ma'rakat Manzikert fī Ḍaw' Wathā'iq Psellūs [The Battle of Manzikert in the light of Psellos], in *BFAAU* 28 (1980), 205–48.

Ghunaym, Ismat, *Al-Dawla al-Bīzanṭiyya wa Krīt al-Islāmiyya* [*The Byzantine State and Islamic Crete*], Alexandria, 1983.

Ghunaym, Ismat, *Al-'Alāqāt al-Bīzanṭiyya al-Almāniyya athnā' al-Ḥamlat al-Ṣalībiyyat al-Thāniyya fī ḍaw' Wathā'iq Kīnnāmūs* [*Byzantine-German Relations during the Second Crusade in the Light of Kinnamos*], Alexandria, 1988.

Ghunaym, Ismat, *Dirāsāt fī Tārīkh Imbrāṭūriyyat Nīqiyya al-Bīzanṭiyya* [*Studies in the History of the Byzantine Empire of Nicea*], Alexandria, 1991.

Al-Ḥamd, A.A., *Al-Imbrāṭūriyya al-Bīzanṭiyya wa al-Umarā' al-Ṣalībiyyūn 1098–1118* [*The Byzantine Empire and the Crusader Princes 1098–1118*], MA dissertation, Faculty of Arts and Education, University of Kuwait, 1976.

Iskandar, F.N., *Armīniyā bayn al-Bīzanṭiyyīn wa al-Khulafā' al-Rāshidīn fī Ḍaw' Kitābāt al-Mü'arrikh al-Armanī Gīvūnd* [*Armenia between the Byzantines and the Righty-Guided Caliphs in the Light of the Writings of the Armenian Historin Gevond*], Alexandria, 1982.

Iskandar, F.N., *Armīniyā bayn al-Bīzanṭiyyīn wa al-Atrāk al-Salājika (392–453/1000–1071) fī Muṣannaf Arīsītākīs* [*Armenia between the Byzantines and the Seljuk Turks (1000–1071) According to Aristakis of Lastivert*], Alexandria, 1983.

Iskandar, F.N., *Al-Bīzanṭiyyīn al-Atrāk al-Salājiqa fī Ma'rakat Malāzkird (463/1071) fī Muṣannaf Niqfūr Brīnyūs* [*The Byzantines and the Seljuk Turks in the Battle of Manzikert (463 AH/1071 AD) in the Work of Nikephoros Bryennios*], Alexandria, 1984.

Iskandar, F.N., Usrat Brīnyūs wa Dawruha fī Tārīkh al-Imbrāṭūriyya al-Bīzanṭiyya [*The Bryennios Family and Its Role in the History of the Byzantine Empire*], in *EHR* 33 (1986), 83–118.

Iskandar, F.N., *Bilād al-Kurj bayn al-Muslimīn wa al-Bīzanṭiyyīn* [*Georgia between the Muslims and Byzantines*], Alexandria, 1988.

Iskandar, F.N., *Ghazw al-Imbrāṭūriyya al-Bīzanṭiyya li Armīniyā Sanat 437/1045* [*The Byzantine Invasion of Armenia in 437 AH/1045 AD*], Alexandria, 1988.

Iskandar, F.N., *Mawqi'at Malāzkird wa Ṣadāha fī al-Qusṭanṭīniyya (26 Ughusṭus 1071–4 Ughusṭus 1072)* [*The Battle of Manzikert and its Impact in Constantinople (26 August 1071 AD–4 August 1072 AD)*], Alexandria, 1988.

Iskandar, F.N., *Al-Muslimūn wa al-Bīzanṭiyyūn wa al-Arman fī Ḍaw' Kitābāt al-Mü'arrikh al-Armanī Sībyūs 11–40/632–661* [*Muslims, Byzantines and Armenians in the Light of the Writings of the Armenian Historian Sebeos 11–40 AH/632–61*], Sanaa, 1993.

Iskandar, F.N., Nīkītās Khūnyātis wa I'tirāfuhu bi Tasāmuḥ al-Muslimīn wa Barbariyyat al-Ṣalībiyyīn: Qirā'a Naqdiyya li Tajāwuzāt al-Ḥamla al-Ṣalībiyya al-Rābi'a (600–1204) [Niketas Choniates and his recognition of the tolerance of Muslims and the barbarism of the Crusaders: a critical reading of the excesses of the Fourth Crusade 600 AH/1204 AD], in *BFABU* 7 (Jan., 2002), 363–385.

Ismāʿīl, L.A., *Al-Siyāsa al-Khārijiyya li al-Mamlakat al-Latīniyya fī al-Qusṭanṭīniyya* [*The Foreign Policy of the Latin Kingdom of Constantinople*], MA, Faculty of Arts, Cairo University, 1980.

Ismāʿīl, L.A., *Al-Dawla al-Bīzanṭiyya fī ʿAṣr Hiraql wa ʿAlāqatuhā bi al-Muslimīn* [Byzantine state in the era of Heraclius and its relationship with Muslims], Cairo, 1985.

Ismāʿīl, L.A., ʿAlāqat al-Dawla al-Bīzanṭiyya bi-Salṭanat al-Mamālīk al-Baḥriyya (1261–1382) [The relationship of the Byzantine state with the Kingdom of the Bahri Mamluks 1261–1382], in *BFACU* 46–47 (1986), 57–125.

Ismāʿīl, L.A., ʿAlāqat Dawlat al-Rūm bi-Miṣr ʿAṣray al-Ṭūlūnyyīn wa al-Ikhshīdiyyīn [The relationship of the Byzantine state with Egypt in the time of the Tulunids and Ikshids], Cairo, 1988.

Ismāʿīl, L.A., Al-Qusṭanṭīniyya fī Ḍawʾ Kitābāt al-Jughrāfiyyīn wa al-Raḥḥāla al-Muslimīn [Constantinople in light of the writings of Muslim Geographers and Travelers], in *EH* 3 (Jan., 1989), 151–201 and 4 (Jul., 1989), 109–45.

Ismāʿīl, L.A., Ḥamalāt Mānuel Komnīnūs ʿalā al-Majar (1151–1167) fī Ḍawʾ Kitābāt Ḥanā Kīnnāmūs [The Campaigns of Manuel Komnenos against Hungary (1151–1167) in the light of John Kinnamos], in *EHR* 37 (1990), 71–102.

Ismāʿīl, L.A., *Tārīkh al-Rūs min khilāl al-Maṣādir al-ʿArabiyya* [*History of the Rus through Arabic sources*], Cairo, 1990.

Ismāʿīl, L.A., Dawr al-Bulghār fī Mūwājahat Ḥamlat Maslamah b. ʿAbd al-Malik ʿalā Al-Qusṭanṭīniyya [The role of the Bulgarians in Confronting the Campaign of Maslamah b. ʿAbd al-Malik against Constantinople], in *EH* 6 (Jan., 1991), 83–113.

Ismāʿīl, L.A., Aḍwāʾ Jadīdah ʿalā Tārīkh Bulghāria taḥt al-Ḥukm al-Bīzanṭī (1018–1097) [New Light on the History of Bulgaria under Byzantine Rule 1018–1097], in *EH* 14 (Jan., 1995), 309–58.

Ismāʿīl, L.A., Mamlakat al-Qusṭanṭīniyya fī *Masālik al-Abṣār wa Mamālik al-Amṣār* li al-ʿUmarī [The Kingdom of Constantiople in al-ʿUmarī's *Masālik al-Abṣār wa Mamālik al-Amṣār*], in *AH* (Cai.) 15 (Mar., 2007), 281–321.

Al-Janzūrī, *Al-Thughūr al-Bariyya al-Islāmiyya ʿalā Ḥudūd al-Dawla al-Bīzanṭiyya* [*Islamic Thughūr on the borders of the Byzantine state*], Cairo, 1979.

Al-Janzūrī, *Al-Imbrāṭūra Irīn* [*Empress Irene*], Cairo, 1981.

Al-Janzūrī, *Al-Marʾa fī al-Ḥaḍāra al-Bīzanṭiyya* [*Women in the Byzantine Civilization*], Cairo, 1982.

Al-Janzūrī, *Hajamāt al-Rūm al-Baḥriyya ʿalā Shawāṭiʾ Miṣr al-Islāmiyya* [*Byzantine Naval attacks on the shores of Islamic Egypt*], Cairo, 1985.

Al-Janzūrī, Al-ʿAlāqāt al-Islāmiyya al-Bīzanṭiyya fī al-Niṣf al-Akhīr mi al-Qarn al-Rābiʿ al-Hijrī/ al-ʿĀshir al-Mīlādī fī Ḍawʾ al-Ittifāqiyya al-Ḥalabiyya al-Bīzanṭiyya 539/970 [Byzantine Islamic relations in the last half of the fourth century AH / tenth century AD in light of the Byzantine-Aleppine Agreement 539 AH / 970 AD], in *Majallat Dirāsāt ʿArabiyya wa Islāmiyya*, Center for Languages and Translation at Cairo University 7 (1988), 81–101.

Al-Janzūrī, *Al-ʿAlāqāt al-Bīzanṭiyya al-Rūsiyya fī ʿAhd al-Usra al-Maqdūniyya (867–1056)* [*Byzantine-Russian Relations during the Macedonian Dynasty 867–1056 AD*], Cairo, 1989.

Jenkins, R., Review of Fahmy's Muslim Sea-Power in the Eastern Mediterranean from the Seventh to the Tenth Century A.D., in *BSOAS* 14/1 (1952), 180–1.

Khamīs, I., Muʿāhadāt al-Salām bayn al-Muslimīn wa al-Bīzanṭiyyin fī al-Niṣf al-Thānī min al-Qarn al-Sābiʿ [Peace treaties between Muslims and Byzantines in the second half of the seventh century], in *BFAAU* 41 (1993), 265–297.

Kutabī, M.S.M., *Al-Muʾarrikh Muḥammad Muṣṭafā Ziyāda* [*The Historian Muḥammad Muṣṭafā Ziyāda*], Cairo, 2011.

Lander, G.B., Origin and Significance of the Byzantine Iconoclastic controversy, in *MS* 2/1 (1940), 127–49.

Al-Maghribī, M.A., *Mamlakat al-Khazar wa ʿAlāqatuha bi al-Bīzanṭiyyīn wa al-Muslimīn fī al-Qarnayn al-Sābiʿ wa al-Thāmin* [The Kingdom of the Jewish Khazars and its relationship with the Byzantines and Muslims in the 7th and 8th centuries], Alexandria, 2002.

Al-Maghribī, M.A., Riʿāyat al-Musinnīn fī al-Dawlat al-Bīzanṭiyya [Care of the elderly in the Byzantine state], in *BFASVU* 6 (2011), 192–231.

Al-Maghribī, M.A., Al-ʿUmyān fī al-Dawla al-Bīzanṭiyya [The Blind in the Byzantine state], in *EHR* 48 (2012–13).

Al-Maghribī, M.A., Mawqif al-Adyira al-Bīzanṭiyya min al-Jins al-Akhar [The position of the Byzantine monasteries towards the opposite sex], in *HFAD* 40 (2013), 27–88.

Martin, E.J., *A History of the Iconoclastic Controversy*, London, 1930.

MA and PhD Dissertations awarded at the Egyptian Universities from their foundation to 1967, in *EHR* 13 (1967), 400–403.

Maqāmī, N.I., *Al-ʿAlāqāt bayn al-Dawla al-Bīzanṭiyya wa al-Nūrmān fī Janūb Itāliā wa Siqilliyya (1025–1197)* [Relations between the Byzantine State and the Normans in Southern Italy and Sicily 1025–1197 AD], PhD dissertation, Faculty of Arts, ʿAyn Shams University, 1989.

Muḥammad, T.M., *Al-Jaysh fī al-Imbrāṭūriyya al-Bīzanṭiyya mundhu bidāyat al-qarn al-sābiʿ ilā nihāyat al-qarn al-tāsiʿ* [The army in the Byzantine Empire from the beginning of the seventh century to the end of the ninth century], MA dissertation, Faculty of Arts, Benha University, 1993.

Muḥammad, T.M., The Byzantine Studies in Egypt: A Brilliant Future. Bibliographical Study, in *AESGRS* 3 (1998), 79–92.

Muḥammad, T.M., *Al-Rūs wa al-Mujtama' al-Duwalī 945–1054* [The Rus and the International Community 945–1045], Cairo, 2001.

Muḥammad, T.M., Mu'āhadatān 907 wa 911 bayna al-Bīzanṭiyyīn wal-Rūs: Ithnatān am Waḥida? [The Treaties of 907 and 911 between the Byzantines and the Russians: two or one?], in *EH* 24 (2001), 11–43.

Muḥammad, T.M., *Quṭūf al-Fikr al-Bīzanṭī* [Blossoms of Byzantine Thought], Cairo, 2002.

Muḥammad, T.M., *Al-Bīzanṭiyyūn wa al-'Ālam al-Islāmī* [Byzantines and the Islamic World], Cairo, 2003.

Muḥammad, T.M., Fann al-Qitāl 'ind al-Bīzanṭiyyīn: Dirasa fī al-Istrātījiyya al-'Askariyya fī Ḍaw' *Taktīkā* Līyū al-Ḥakīm [The Byzantines Art of Warfare: A Study on Military Strategy in the Light of Leo the Wise's *Taktika*], in H. al-Ṭaḥāwī (ed.), *Dirāsāt fī Tārīkh al-'Uṣūr al-Wūsṭā*: Majmū'at Abḥāth Muhdāh ilā Qāsim 'Abduh Qāsim, Cairo, 2003, 147–84.

Muḥammad, T.M., Ibn Manglī between the Arab and Byzantine Worlds, New Evidence, in *JMIH* 3 (2003), 25–43.

Muḥammad, T.M., Malḥamat Dijīnīs Akrītīs wa Rū'yat al-Akhar: Dirāsa fī Bāṭin al-Naṣṣ wa Īdiyūlūjiyyat al-Mu'allif [The epic of Digenes Akrites and the Image of the Other: a Study in the Text and the Ideology of the author], in *BFAZU*, Special Issue (2004), 3–72.

Muḥammad, T.M., Hārūn b. Yaḥyā (300/9120): Maṣdar min Maṣādir al-Tārīkh al-Bīzanṭī [Hārūn b. Yaḥyā (300/912) as a Source for Byzantine History], in *BFEGT* 6 (2004–5), 44–52.

Muḥammad, T.M., Al-Nār al-Ighrīqiyya fī ḍaw' al-Kitābāt Islāmiyya wal-Bīzanṭiyya [Greek Fire in the light of Islamic and Byzantine Writings], in *JMIH* 4 (2004–5), 115–59.

Muḥammad, T.M., Can Parastaseis Syntomi Chronikai be considered a real guide to the Sculptures of Constantinople during the Isaurian Period?, in *BSl* 64 (2006), 77–98.

Muḥammad, T.M., Futūḥ al-Shām wa Filasṭīn fī Ḍaw' Ḥawliyyat Thīyūfānīs: Dirāsa Idiyūlūjiyyat al-Mu'allif tijāh al-Islām [The conquests of Syria and Palestine in the light of the chronicle of Theophanes the Confessor: A Study of the Author's Ideology towards Islam], in *AH* (Cai.) 14 (2006), 13–70.

Muḥammad, T.M., Al-Qusṭanṭīniyya fī al-Kitābāt al-Ṣalībiyya 1096–1204: Dirāsa Taḥlīliyya li al-Rū'ā al-Ṣalībiyya li Madīnat Qusṭanṭīn [Constantinople in the Crusader Writings 1096–1204 AD: An Analytical Study of the Crusader Views about the City of Constantine], in *EH* 29 (2006), 261–325.

Muḥammad, T.M., *Al-Muslimūn fī al-Fikr al-Masīḥī* [Muslims in Christian Thought], Cairo, 2008.

Muḥammad, T.M., The Role of the Copts in the Islamic Navigation in the 7th–8th Centuries: the Papyrological Evidence, in *JCS* 10 (2008), 1–32.

Muḥammad, T.M., Had the Arabs Military Skills or Tactics during their Early Conquests of *Bilād al-Shām?*, in J.P. Monferrer-Sala, V. Christides, and Th. Papadopoullos (eds.), *East and West: Essays on the Byzantine and the Arab Worlds in the Middle Ages*, Supplement G of *Graeco-Arabica*, New Jersey, 2009, 83–96.

Muḥammad, T.M., The Byzantine Theologians on Muḥammad and Zaynab b. Jaḥsh: Marriage or Adultery?, in *BSl* 67 (2009), 139–160.

Muḥammad, T.M., Ibn Manglī and Naval Warfare: The Question of Greek Fire between the Muslims and Byzantines, in *IJMH* 21/1 (June 2009), 55–80.

Muḥammad, T.M., The Conversion from Islam to Christianity as viewed by the Author of Digenes Akrites, in *CChO* 7 (2010), 121–49.

Muḥammad, T.M., Al-Waẓā'if wa al-Alqāb al-Bīzanṭiyya bayn al-Mafhūm al-'Arabī wa al-Wāqi' al-Bīzanṭī [Byzantine Functions and Titles between the Arab Concept and the Byzantine reality], in *JMIH*, Special Edition 2 (2011), 7–82.

Muḥammad, T.M., Ilmām al-'Arab al-Muslimīn bil-Rūmiyya fī al-'Aṣr al-Bīzanṭī al-Awsaṭ [Familiarity of Arab Muslims with Greek in the Middle Byzantine era], in *BCPSAShU* 28/1 (2011), 215–36.

Muḥammad, T.M., *Alla Wa Koubar* in the Byzantine Conception, in *Selected Papers of the Second International Conference "The World of Islam: History, Society, Culture"*, *Moscow, October, 28–30, 2010*, = *PI* 8 (2012), 296–315.

Muḥammad, T.M., The Civil Byzantine Functions and Titles as known by the Arabs in the Middle Byzantine Period, in *International Symposium of the Byzantine Studies 'Byzantium and the Arabs', University of Thessaloniki 15–18 December 2011*, Thessaloniki, 2013, 356–82.

Muḥammad, T.M., Al-Bīzanṭiyyūn wa Tarjamat al-Qur'ān ilā al-Yūnāniyya fī al-Qarn al-Tāsi' al-Mīlādī: al-Juz' al-Thalāthūn Anmūdhajan [Byzantines and the translation of the Qur'ān into Greek in the ninth century: Part XXX as a Case-Study], in *JMIH* 8 (2013–14), 83–130.

Muḥammad, T.M., The Concept of al-Takbīr in the Byzantine Theological Writings, in *BSl* 72/1–2 (2014), 77–97.

Muḥammad, T.M., *Bīzanṭa: Madīnat al-Nuẓum wa al-Ḥaḍāra* [Byzantium: City of Civilization and Institutions], Cairo, 2015.

Muḥammad, T.M., Al-Ma'ādib al-Imbrāṭūriyya fī 'Ahd al-Imbrāṭūr Līyū al-Sādis al-Ḥakīm (886–912) [Imperial banquets under the Emperor Leo VI], in Idem, *Bīzanṭa*, 57–118.

Muḥammad, T.M., Al-Ḥaras al-Imbrāṭūrī al-Bīzanṭī min al-Qarn al-Sābi' ilā al-Qarn al-Tāsi' [Byzantine Imperial Guard from the 7th to the 9th century], in Idem, *Bīzanṭa*, 181–230.

Nawār, N.M.A., *Al-'Alāqāt al-Siyāsiyya bayn al-Imbrāṭūriyya al-Bīzanṭiyya wa al-Khilāfa al-'Abbāsiyya fī 'Ahd al-Imbrāṭūr Mīkhā'īl al-Thānī al-'Amūrī* [Political Relations between the Byzantine Empire and the Abbasid Caliphate during the reign of

Emperor Michael II the Amorian], PhD dissertation, Faculty of Arts, Alexandria University, 1987.

Ostrogorsky, G., Les débuts de la querelle des images, in *Mélanges Charles Diehl I*, Paris, 1930, 235–255.

Puṭrus, A.M., *Al-Arman wa ʿAlāqatuhum bi al-Muslimīn wa al-Bīzanṭiyyīn 1701–1171* [Armenians and their relations with the Byzantines and Muslims 1071–1171], MA dissertation, Faculty of Arts, ʿAyn Shams University, 1986.

Al-Qirsh, A.H., *Al-ʿAlāqāt al-Ḥaḍāriyya bayn al-Bīzanṭiyyīn wa al-Muslimīn fī al-Shām wa Misr fī al-ʿaṣr al-Umawī* [*The Cultural Relations between Byzantines and Muslims in Syria and Egypt during the Umayyad Era*], PhD dissertation, Faculty of Dār al-ʿUlūm, Cairo University, 2003.

Rabie, H.M., *Dirāsāt fī Tārīkh al-Dawlat al-Bīzanṭiyya* [*Studies in the History of the Byzantine State*], Cairo, 1952.

Rabie, H.M., *Manhaj Taḥqīq al-Turāth al-Tārīkhī ʿinda Muḥammad Muṣṭafā Ziyāda* [Muḥammad Muṣṭafā Ziyāda: His Method of Editing Historical Manuscripts], Cairo, 2004.

Al-Rāghī, Z.A., *Manāṭiq al-Ḥudūd al-Islāmiyya al-Bīzanṭiyya fī al-Qarn al-ʿĀshir al-Mīlādī* [Byzantine-Islamic Border Areas in the 10th century A.D.], PhD dissertation, Faculty of Arts, ʿAyn Shams University, 2015.

Ramaḍān, A.A., *Al-ʿAlāqāt bayn al-Usra al-Maqdūniyya wa al-Khilāfa al-Fāṭimiyya* [*The Relations between the Macedonian Dynasty and the Fatimid Caliphate*], MA dissertation, Faculty of Arts, Cairo University (Khartoum branch), 1980.

Ramaḍān, A.M. [Abdelaziz Ramadan], ʿUrūḍ Zawāj al-ʿArāʾis fī al-Balāṭ al-Bīzanṭī 788–882: Al-Dalālāt al-Siyāsiyya wa al-Dīniyya [Bride-Shows in the Byzantine court 788–882: Political and religious connotations], in *JMIH* 2 (2002), 75–88.

Ramaḍān, A.M. [Abdelaziz Ramadan], Madkhal ilā Mawāqiʿ al-Dirāsāt al-Bīzanṭiyya ʿalā Shabakat al-Internet [An Introduction to the Websites of Byzantine studies], in *JMIH* 3 (2003), 75–103.

Ramaḍān, A.M. [Abdelaziz Ramadan], Al-Murtazaqa al-Injilīz fī al-Imbrāṭūriyya al-Bīzanṭiyya 1066–1204 [English mercenaries in the Byzantine Empire 1066–1204], in *JMIH* 4 (2004–5), 161–195.

Ramaḍān, A.M. [Abdelaziz Ramadan], Al-Bīzanṭiyyūn bayn al-Huwiyyatayn al-Yūnāniyya wa al-Rūmāniyya [Byzantines between the Greek and Roman identities], in *EH* 28 (2005), 39–74.

Ramaḍān, A.M. [Abdelaziz Ramadan], *Al-Marʾa wa al-Mujtamaʿ fī al-Imbrāṭūriyyat al-Bīzanṭiyya min al-Qarn al-Tāsiʿ ilā al-Qarn al-Thānī ʿashar* [Women and Society in the Byzantine Empire, 9th–12th Centuries], Cairo, 2005.

Ramaḍān, A.M. [Abdelaziz Ramadan], Al-Bīzanṭiyyūn bayn ʿIlāj al-Aṭibāʾ wa Muʿjizāt al-Qiddīsīn: Dirāsa fī Hajūgrāfiyā al-ʿAṣr al-Bākir [The Byzantines between the

treatment of doctors and the miracles of the saints: a study in early hagiography],
in *JMIH* 5 (2006), 33–98.

Ramaḍān, A.M. [Abdelaziz Ramadan], Ṣūrat al-Islām fī Nubūʾat Mīthūdīyūs al-Majhūl
[image of Islam in the apocalypse of Pseudo Methodius], in *EHR* 44 (2006), 9–32.

Ramaḍān, A.M. [Abdelaziz Ramadan], *Bīzanṭa wa al-Gharb al-Urūbbī 1143–1180*
[Byzantium and the European West 1143–1180], Cairo, 2007.

Ramaḍān, A.M. [Abdelaziz Ramadan], Siyāsat Bīzanṭa al-Tanṣīriyya tijāh al-ʿAnāṣir
al-ʿArabiyya al-Muslima: al-Qurūn min al-Sābiʿ ilā al-Ḥādī ʿashar [Byzantine policy
of Converting to Christianity towards the Arab-Muslim elements: 7th–11th centu-
ries], in *HE* 7 (2007), 103–157.

Ramaḍān, A.M. [Abdelaziz Ramadan], The Treatment of Arab Prisoners of War in
Byzantium, 9th–10th Centuries, in *AnIsl* 43 (2009), 155–94.

Ramaḍān, A.M. [Abdelaziz Ramadan], Islamic Conquests of Bilād al-Shām as Portrayed in the Eastern Christian Sources, in A.M. Ramaḍān et al. (eds.), *Quṭūf min
al-Tārīkh al-Islāmī wal-Wasīṭ* [Blossoms of the Islamic and Medieval History], Cairo,
2012, 7–22.

Ramaḍān, A.M. [Abdelaziz Ramadan], Ḥaqq al-Lujūʾ ilā al-Kanīsa fī al-ʿAṣr al-Bīzanṭī
al-Bākir: al-Naẓariyya al-Qānūniyya wa al-Taṭbīq al-ʿAmalī [The right of Church
Asylum in the early Byzantine period: legal theory and practice], in *JMIH* 8 (2013–
14), 131–58.

Ramaḍān, A.M. [Abdelaziz Ramadan], Ṣūrat al-Marʾa fī al-Adab al-Rahbānī fī al-
Qarnyn al-Rābiʿ wa al-Khāmis al-Mīlādīayn [The image of women in monastic literature during the fourth and fifth centuries], in *ACPSI* 31 (2014), 31–52.

Ramaḍān, A.M. [Abdelaziz Ramadan], Supernatural Powers in Arab-Byzantine
Warfare, 7th–11th Centuries, as reflected by Popular Imagination, in *JMIH* 9 (2014–
15), 1–34.

Ramaḍān, A.M. [Abdelaziz Ramadan], Maʿāyīr Ikhtiyār al-Mabʿūthīn al-Diblūmāsiyyīn
fī al-ʿAṣr al-Bīzanṭī al-Bākir [Selection Criteria of Diplomatic Envoys in the Early
Byzantine Era], in *ACRHS* Special Issue (2016), 11–119.

Ramaḍān, A.M. [Abdelaziz Ramadan], Siyāsat Abāṭirat Usratay Qusṭanṭīn wa
Thīyūdūsīyus tijāh al-ʿUrūḍ al-ʿĀma bayn al-Mawrūth al-Rūmānī wa al-Idiyūlūjiyya
al-Kanasiyya [The policy of the Constantinian and Theodosian emperors towards
the *publici ludi* between the Roman heritage and the church ideology], in *AEH*
Special Issue (2016), 9–85.

Ramaḍān, A.M. [Abdelaziz Ramadan], *Al-Ṭarīq ilā Bīzanṭa: Dirāsāt ḥawl al-Fikr wa
al-Dīn wa al-Siyāsa fī Sharq al-Imbrāṭūriyya al-Rūmāniyya al-Mutaʾakhkhira* [Road
to Byzantium: Studies on thought, religion and politics in the eastern late Roman
Empire], Amman, 2017.

Ramaḍān, A.M. [Abdelaziz Ramadan], Arab Apostates in Byzantium: Evidence from
Arabic Sources, in *Byzantina Symmeikta* 29 (2019), 273–314.

Ṣabra, A.S., *Al-Imbrāṭūriyyatān al-Bīzanṭiyya wa al-Rūmāniyya al-Gharbiyya zaman Shārlamān* [*The Byzantine and Western Roman Empires in the Time of Charlemagne*], Cairo, 1982.

Ṣaliḥ, N.U., *Siyāsat al-Dawlat al-Bīzanṭiyya fī Ḥawḍ al-Baḥr al-Mutawassiṭ fī ʿAhd al-Usrat al-Aysūriyya (717–802)* [The politics of the Byzantine state in the Mediterranean basin during the Isaurian Dynasty 717–802], MA dissertation, Faculty of Arts, Cairo University, 1991.

Sālim, A., Al-Ittiṣāl al-Thaqāfī bayn al-Khilāfa al-ʿAbbāsiyya wa al-Imbrāṭūriyya al-Bīzanṭiyya fī ʿAṣr al-Maʾmūn (198–218 /813–833) [Cultural contact between the Abbasid Caliphate and the Byzantine Empire in the Al-Maʾmun era 198–218 AH/ 813–833 AD], in *BFDUCU* 18 (1995), 163–90.

Sālim, A., *Al-Muslimūn wa al-Rūm fī ʿAṣr al-Nubūwah: Dirāsa fī Judhūr al-Ṣirāʿ wa Taṭawwūruhu bayn al-Muslimīn wa al-Bīzanṭiyyin ḥatta wafāt al-Rasūl* [*The Muslims and Byzantines in the Era of the Prophecy: A Study in the Roots of the Conflict and its Development between Muslims and Byzantines until the Death of the Prophet*], Cairo, 1997.

Sālim, A., Al-ʿAlāqāt bayn al-Muslimīn wa al-Rūm fī ʿAṣr Abī Bakr (11–13 /632–634) [Relations between Muslims and Byzantines in the era of Abu Bakr (11–13 AH / 632–634 AD], in *NTI* 2 (2006), 55–109.

Al-Sayyid, W.A.M., Al-Imbrāṭūr Mūrīs 582–602: Aḥwāl al-Imbrāṭūriyya al-Bīzanṭiyya fī ʿAhdihi [Emperor Maurice (582–602): The conditions of the Byzantine Empire in his reign], MA dissertation, Faculty of Arts, ʿAyn Shams University, 1988.

Al-Shaʿīnī, M.M., Niswat al-ʿArsh al-Bīzanṭī fī ʿAṣr Usrat Kūmnīnūs 1081–1185 [Imperial Byzantine Women in the Komnenian era 1081–1185], MA dissertation, Faculty of Arts in Qena, South Valley University, 2012.

Al-Shaʿīnī, M.M., Al-Muʿtaqadāt al-Shaʿbiyya fī al-Imbrāṭūriyya al-Bīzanṭiyya min al-Qarn al-Tāsiʿ ilā al-Qarn al-Thānī ʿashar [Popular beliefs in the Byzantine Empire, 9th–12th centuries], PhD dissertation, Faculty of Arts in Qena, South Valley University, 2017.

Al-Shāʿir, *Al-Siyāsa al-Sharqiyya li al-Imbrāṭūriyya al-Bīzanṭiyya fī al-Qarn al-Sādis (ʿAṣr Justīnyān)* [*Eastern Policy of the Byzantine Empire in the 6th Century: The Age of Justinian*], Cairo, 1989.

Al-Shāʿir, *Al-Ṣilāt al-Ḥaḍāriyya bayna Bīzanṭa wa al-Mashriq al-Islāmī fī al-Qarnayn al-Thāmin wa al-Tāsiʿ li al-mīlād* [*The Cultural links between Byzantium and the Islamic East in the eighth and ninth centuries AD*], Cairo, 1991.

Shīḥa, N.M., Madīnat al-Qusṭanṭīniyya fī al-Qarn al-ʿĀshir [Constantinople in the 10th Century], MA dissertation, Faculty of Arts, Cairo University, 1999.

Shuʿayra, A., Al-Murābiṭūn fī al-Thughūr al-Barriyya al-Rūmiyya ʿinda Jibāl Ṭūrūs fī Ṣadr al-Dawlat al-ʿAbbāsiyya [Volunteer Fighters in the Byzantine Themes in the Area of the Taurus Mountain during the early Abbasid Period], in A. Badawī (ed.), *Ilā Ṭāhā Ḥusayn fī ʿĪd Mīlādihi al-Sabʿīn*, Cairo, 1962, 147–168.

Ṣidqī, M.Ḥ., *Al-ʿAlāqāt al-Bīzanṭiyya al-Turkiyya fī Ḍawʾ Kitāb al-Alixiād* [Byzantine-Turkish Relations in Light of the Book of Alexiad], MA dissertation, Faculty of Arts, Alexandria University, 1979.

Siqiyyū, I.M., *Al-Ḥayāt al-Thaqāfiyya wa al-ʿIlmiyya fī al-Dawlat al-Bīzanṭiyya 867–1056* [Cultural and Scientific Life in the Byzantine State, 867–1056], Cairo, 2013.

Sulaymān, A.A., *Maʿrakat Adrīyānūpil bayn al-Qūṭ wa al-Rūmān* [The Battle of Adrianople between the Goths and Romans in 378], Cairo, 1990.

Sulaymān, I.A., Al-Siyāsa al-Khārijiyya li al-Imbrāṭūriyya al-Bīzanṭiyya fī ʿAhd Usrat Anjīlūs (1185–1259) [Foreign Policy of the Byzantine Empire during the Angelus Dynasty 1185–1259 AD], PhD dissertation, Faculty of Arts in Sohag, South Valley University, 1997.

Sulaymān, M., Al-Jadal al-Nisṭūrī wa Aṣdāʾuhu fī al-Imbrāṭūriyya al-Bīzanṭiyya 428–491 [The Nestorian controversy and its echoes in the Byzantine Empire 428–491], PhD dissertation, Faculty of Arts, ʿAyn Shams University, 2016.

Al-Ṭaḥāwī, H.A., *Bīzanṭa wa al-Mudun al-Iṭāliyya 1081–1204: al-ʿAlāqāt al-Tijāriyya* [*Byzantium and the Italian Cities 1081–1204 AD: Trade Relations*], Cairo, 1998.

Al-Ṭaḥāwī, H.A., Al-Baḥr al-Aḥmar fī al-Maṣādir al-Bīzanṭiyya (6th Century) [The Red Sea in Byzantine Sources (6th century AD)], in *BFAZU* 55 (2016), 73–108.

Al-Tājūrī, M.U., *Al-Ḥayāt al-Dīniyya fī Shamāl Afrīqiyyā min al-Iḥtilāl al-Bīzanṭī ḥattā al-Fatḥ al-ʿArabī 533–698* [Religious life in North Africa from the Byzantine occupation until the Arab Conquest 533–698], PhD dissertation, Faculty of Arts, ʿAyn Shams University, 2017.

Tamīm, A.A., *Al-Bushnāq wa al-Bīzanṭiyyūn: Dirāsa fī Siyāsat Bīzanṭa al-Shimāliyya 580–1122* [The Pechenegs and Byzantines: Study in the Northern Policy of Byzantium 580–1122 AD], MA dissertation, Faculty of Arts, Manṣūra University, 1996.

Tamīm, A.A., *Mamlakat al-Majar wa ʿAlāqātuhā bi al-Imbrāṭūriyya al-Bīzanṭiyya 1000–1453* [The Kingdom of Hungary and its Relations with the Byzantine Empire 1000–1453 AD], PhD dissertation, Faculty of Arts, Manṣūra University, 2004.

Ṭarkhān, I.A., *Al-Ḥaraka al-lā-Iqūniyya fī al-Dawla al-Bīzanṭiyya* [*Iconoclasm in the Byzantine State*], Cairo, 1956.

Tawfīq, O.K., *Al-Imbrāṭūr Niqfūr Phūqās wa Istirjāʿ al-Arāḍī al-Muqaddasa* [*Nikephore Phokas and the Recovery of the Holy Lands*], Alexandria, 1959.

Tawfīq, O.K., *Al-Imbrāṭūr Yūhanā Tzimisces wa Siyāsatuhu al-Sharqiyya 969–979* [*Emperor John Tzimisces and his Eastern Politics 969–979*], Alexandria, 1966.

Tawfīq, O.K., *Tārīkh al-Dawlat al-Bīzanṭiyya*, Alexandria, 1977.

ʿUbayd, Isḥāq, [Ebeid, Ishaq], Was Pope Innocent III an accomplice in the diversion of the Fourth Crusade? in *EHR* 16 (1969), 3–19.

ʿUbayd, Isḥāq, [Ebeid, Ishaq], Qiṣṣat ʿUthūr al-Qiddīsa Hīlāna ʿalā Kashabat al-Ṣalīb: Usṭūra am Ḥaqīqa? [The story of the finding of the True Cross by St. Helena: Myth or Reality? in *EHR* 17 (1970), 5–21.

'Ubayd, Isḥāq, [Ebeid, Ishaq], *Rūmā wa Bīzanṭa min Qaṭīʿat Phūtius wa ḥattā al-Ghazw al-Lāṭīnī li-Madīnat Qusṭanṭīn 869–1204* [*Rome and Byzantium from the Photian Schism till the Latin invasion of Constantinople 869–1204*], Cairo, 1970.

'Ubayd, Isḥāq, [Ebeid, Ishaq], *Al-Imbrāṭūriyya al-Rūmāniyya bayn al-Dīn wa al-Barbariyya* [*Roman Empire between Religion and Barbarism*], Cairo, 1972.

'Ubayd, Isḥāq, [Ebeid, Ishaq], Concerning the happenings which befell the Alexandrian Church after the Ecumenical Council of Chalcedon (Arabic Manuscript), in *AFAAShU* 13 (1973), 207–42.

'Ubayd, Isḥāq, [Ebeid, Ishaq], *Al-Dawla al-Bīzanṭiyya fī ʿAsr Pālīyūlūghūs* [*The Byzantine state in the Palaeologian Era*], Benghazi, 1975.

'Ubayd, Isḥāq, [Ebeid, Ishaq], *Min Alārīk ilā Justinian: Qirāʾa fī Ḥawliyyāt al-ʿUṣūr al-Muẓlima* [*From Alaric to Justinian: A Reading in the Annals of the Dark Ages*], Cairo, 1977.

'Ubayd, Isḥāq, [Ebeid, Ishaq], Julian the Apostate as portrayed in an Arabic Manuscript, in *Seminario Internazionale: Roma e Lʾ Egitto Nellʾ Antichità Classica*, Cairo, 1989, 121–2.

'Umrān, M.S., Maʿrakat Ḥārim: al-Taḥāluf al-Bīzanṭī al-Ṣalībī al-Armīnī ḍidd Nūr ad-Dīn Zinkī (1164) [The Battle of Harim: A Byzantine Crusader Armenian alliance against Nūr ad-Dīn Zinkī in 1164], in *AH* (Bag.) 8 (1977), 89–99.

'Umrān, M.S., *Nīqūlā Mistīqūs wa ʿAlāqat al-Imbrāṭūriyya al-Bīzanṭiyya bil-Qiwā al-Islāmiyya min Khilāl Murāsalātihi* [*Nicholas Mysticus and the relationship of the Byzantine Empire with Muslim Powers through his correspondence*], Beirut, 1980.

'Umrān, M.S., Al-Imbrāṭūr al-Bīzanṭī Rūmānūs al-Rābiʿ (1068–1071) fī Dawʾ Ḥawliyyat Mīkhāʾīl Psellūs [The Byzantine Emperor Romanos IV (1068–1071) in the light of the Chronography of Michael Psellos], in *BFAAU* 31 (1982–3), 55–96.

'Umrān, M.S., *Al-Siyāsa al-Sharqiyya li al-Imbrāṭūriyya al-Bīzanṭiyya fī ʿAhd Manuel al-Awwal 1143–1180* [*The Eastern Policy of the Byzantine Empire under Manuel I Komnenos 1143–1180*], Alexandria, 1985.

'Umrān, M.S., Taḥṣīnāt Madīnat al-Qusṭanṭīniyya fī Mūwājahat al-Ghazawāt al-Khārijiyya [Fortification of Constantinople in the face of foreign invasions], in *Nadwat al-Ḥaḍāra al-Islāmiyya wa ʿilm al-Biḥār, Union of Arab Historians*, Cairo, 1994, 308–39.

'Umrān, M.S., John Kinnamos as a Historian of the Second Crusade, in *Uluslararasi Hacli Seferleri Sempozyumu, Turkish Historical Society*, Istanbul, 1997, 45–55.

'Umrān, M.S., Shārl Kūnt Anjū bayn al-Qusṭanṭīniyya wa Tūnis wa al-Quds (1266–1285) [Charles Count of Anjou between Constantinople and Tunis and Jerusalem 1266–1285], in *AH* (Cai.) 6 (1998), 169–196.

'Umrān, M.S., Al-Nuqūd al-Bīzanṭiyya [Byzantine Coins], *Abjadiyyāt, Bibliotheca Alexandrina* 5 (2010), 36–54.

'Umrān, M.S., Religious Policy or Policy of War between Constantinople, Damascus and Bagdad, in *Selected Papers of the Second International Conference "The World of Islam: History, Society, Culture", Moscow, October, 28–30, 2010,* = *PI* 8 (2012), 330–47.

Al-Wisīmī, M.Z., 'Alāqat Salṭanat Salājiqat al-Rūm bi al-Dawlat al-Bīzanṭiyya fī 'Aṣr Usrat Kūmnīn 1081–1185 [The Relations of the Seljuk Sultanate of Rum with the Byzantine State under the Komnenoi 1081–1185], MA, Faculty of Arts, Cairo University, 1988.

Al-Wisīmī, M.Z., Salṭanat Salājiqat al-Rūm 1185–1243 [The Seljuk Sultanate of Rum 1185–1243], PhD dissertation, Faculty of Arts, Cairo University, 1994.

Al-Wisīmī, M.Z., Jāmi' al-Qusṭanṭīniyya al-Awwal wa Dawruhu al-Siyāsī [The First Mosque of Constantinople and its Political Role], in *BFACU* 6/2 (Apr., 2000), 39–73.

Yūsuf, J.N., *Al-'Arab wa al-Rūm wa al-Latīn fī al-Ḥarb al-Ṣalībiyya al-Ūlā* [*The Arabs, Byzantines and Latins in the First Crusade*], Alexandria, 1963.

Yūsuf, J.N., *Tārīkh al-Imbrāṭūriyya al-Bīzanṭiyya 284–1453* [*History of the Byzantine Empire 284–1453*], Alexandria, 1984.

Yūsuf, J.N., *Al-Islām wa al-Masīḥiyya wa Ṣirā' al-Qiwā baynahuma fī al-'Uṣūr al-Wūsṭā* [*Islam and Christianity: The Conflict of their Powers in the Middle Ages*], Alexandria, 1986.

Zayyān, A.H., Sifārat al-Imbrāṭūr Anāstāsīyūs al-Thānī ilā al-Khalīfa al-Umawī al-Walīd ibn 'Abd al-Malik 'Ām 714 [The embassy of Emperor Anastasius II to the Umayyad Caliph al-Walīd b. 'Abd al-Malik in 714], in *Symposium of the Arab Historians Union in Cairo 2009. History of the Arab World through the Ages: Delegations and embassies,* Cairo, 2009, 93–115.

Zayyān, A.H., *Al-Imbrāṭūr Aliksīyūs al-Awwal Kumnīn wa al-Ḥamla al-Ṣalībiyya al-Ūlā fī Ḍaw' Kitāb al-Aliksīyād* [Emperor Alexios I Komenenos and the First Crusade in the light of the *Alexiad*], Cairo, 2010.

Zayyān, A.H., *Al-Dawr al-Siyāsī li al-Mū'arrikh Mīkhā'īl Psīllūs 1041–1078* [The Political Role of the Historian Michael Psellos in the Byzantine State 1041–1078], Cairo, 2012.

Zayyān, A.H., Ḥamlat al-Imbrāṭūr Ḥanā al-Thānī Kumnīn 'alā Madīnat Shayzar 'Ām 1138 [the campaign of Emperor John II against Shayzar in 1138], in *JMIH* 9 (2014–15), 2150.

Zayyān, Ḥ., *Al-Asrā al-Muslimūn fī Bilād al-Rūm* [Muslim Prisoners of War in the Byzantine Territories], Cairo, 1982.

Zīdān, N.A., Al-Dawla al-Bīzanṭiyya fī 'Ahd al-Imbraṭūrayn Justīn al-Thānī wa Tībirīus 565–582 [The Byzantine State under the Emperors Justin II and Tiberius 565–582], MA dissertation, Faculty of Arts, 'Ayn Shams University, 2004.

8

Hichem Djaït, maître d'une école historique pour l'étude de l'Islam

Khaled Kchir

1 Introduction : Hichem Djaït, historien de l'islam des origines

En guise d'introduction, nous essayerons de restituer l'itinéraire d'un savant et intellectuel tunisien qui s'est consacré à l'étude des origines de l'islam[1]. Les points de vue et les enseignements de Hichem Djaït (Hišām Ğaʿayṭ) ont essaimé et marqué au moins deux générations d'historiens de la Tunisie indépendante. Dans le cadre de ce bilan historiographique, je ne peux que saluer les efforts téméraires, mais discrets du maître, d'ouvrir le champ de la recherche historique à tous les mouvements et courants. Ce texte est un hommage et une reconnaissance à Hichem Djaït.

Agrégé d'histoire, H. Djaït a soutenu une thèse d'État en Sorbonne, sur la ville de Kūfa qu'il a publiée sous le titre de *al-Kūfa. Naissance de la ville islamique*, en 1986 chez Maisonneuve & Larose à Paris. Il est à rappeler que lorsqu'il partit en France poursuivre ses études supérieures, il n'y avait pas d'historiens tunisiens travaillant sur l'Orient. Historien médiéviste, certes, mais il est aussi un intellectuel habité par la situation des peuples musulmans au lendemain des indépendances. Son engagement dans son époque le mène à écrire deux essais mondialement connus et traduits dans plusieurs langues. L'auteur y a exprimé sa pensée vivante, oscillante entre le passé et le présent ainsi qu'une conscience aigüe des différences entre l'Orient et l'Occident, marquée par le poids de l'histoire et l'impact de la modernité. Il s'agit de *La personnalité et le*

---

[1] Le 1ᵉʳ juin 2021 à l'aube, Hichem Djaït a cessé de penser, à l'âge de 86 ans. Je suis profondément affecté de faire part de ce triste départ. Lorsque je lui ai parlé de cet article, il m'a humblement répondu, qu'il le lira une fois publié. Ce texte lui est dédié, en reconnaissance à son œuvre grandiose et en hommage à sa mémoire. Le grand maître nous a quittés en faisant ses adieux à la vie, mais restera présent parmi nous, à travers son œuvre. Le maître a vécu heureux, il a bien savouré les plaisirs de la vie ; la recherche et les découvertes en faisaient partie. Il a été aimé, apprécié et respecté. Sa vie durant, il a défendu sa liberté qu'il érigea en vertu absolue. La connaissance était pour lui la voie initiatique pour approcher le vrai. En guise d'adieu, le maître publia son testament intellectuel où il a démontré sa manière de *Penser l'histoire, penser la Religion*, Tunis, Cérès, 2021. Qu'il repose en paix.

devenir arabo-islamiques et *L'Europe et l'Islam*, parus à Paris chez Seuil, respectivement en 1974 et 1978.

En 1989 Hichem Djaït publie *La Grande Discorde, Religion et politique dans l'Islam des origines*, ouvrage nourri de ses travaux et de son dialogue avec ses étudiants[2]. Insatisfait de son décryptage de la situation après la mort du prophète, H. Djaït remonte le temps vers les origines. Il déconstruit tout ce qui a été écrit à propos de la vie du Prophète. Une trilogie naît chez Fayard[3]. H. Djaït y tente une énième biographie du prophète (en arabe)[4], en partant de la plausibilité du nom de Muḥammad ! Dans cette recherche novatrice, l'auteur croise les dimensions politique, religieuse, sociologique, historique, anthropologique et psychologique.

L'intérêt pour la naissance de l'islam en Arabie et en Irak n'a pas empêché H. Djaït d'écrire l'histoire de l'islamisation du Maghreb et de l'Ifriqiyya (la Tunisie actuelle). Cette histoire a fait l'objet de plusieurs articles qu'il publia chez Amal Editions, en 2004 sous le titre *La fondation du Maghreb islamique*.

Par ailleurs, le médiéviste n'hésite pas à s'exprimer en tant qu'intellectuel pour déplorer la situation des sociétés arabo-islamiques contemporaines. Il aborde la question à travers la culture, à laquelle il consacre des études en langue arabe, dont il publia une sélection sous le titre *Azmat al-Ṯaqāfa al-islāmiyya* paru à Beyrouth chez Dar al-Talīʿa en 2000. Ce livre a été publié en français, chez Fayard en 2007, sous le titre *La crise de la culture islamique*. Tous ces ouvrages ont été traduits et/ou réédités.

Il a été professeur invité dans plusieurs universités, dont l'Université McGill à Montréal, l'Université Berkeley en Californie, l'École des Hautes Etudes à Paris, le Collège de France ...

Presque vingt ans après un départ forcé à la retraite, H. Djaït est nommé Président de l'Académie tunisienne Bayt al-Hikma. Bien que tardive, cette reconnaissance lui a permis d'instituer un nouveau conseil scientifique ouvert à des personnalités scientifiques, en Tunisie et à l'étranger

À partir des thèses soutenues sous sa direction, nous essayerons de démontrer que Hichem Djaït représente une école historienne qui a pu dépasser l'approche *sacrée* de l'islam des origines. Qu'ils soient compagnons ou proches parents du prophète, tous les personnages de l'époque sont abordés en tant

---

2   Voir compte rendu de l'ouvrage publié par K. Kchir, *in Correspondances*, 18, 1990. En retour, naîtra *La seconde discorde* de B. Bin Ḥusayn, une de ses étudiantes.

3   La trilogie a été traduite en français et en anglais, *La vie de Muḥammad.* t. 1 *Révélation et prophétie*, 2001 ; t. 2, *La prédication prophétique à La Mecque*, 2008 ; t. 3, *Le parcours du Prophète à Médine et le triomphe de l'Islam*, 2012.

4   K. Kchir, « Hichem Djaït, *Fī l-Sīra al-Nabawiyya: I. al-Wahy wa l-Qurʾān wa l-Nubuwwa*, Note de lecture », *IBLA*, (2005), 132-136.

qu'*acteurs*, dans une historicité désacralisée. Pour réaliser ce travail, nous avons procédé à une sélection des travaux réalisés sous la direction du maître qui reflètent clairement la conception d'un grand programme, réalisé par étapes, chacune étant confiée à un doctorant. Pour bien cerner la naissance de l'islam, le milieu dans lequel il a baigné et son évolution durant les quatre premiers siècles de l'hégire, H. Djaït chargea Salwā Bilḥāj Ṣāliḥ d'une thèse sur le christianisme arabe. Le rôle des compagnons dans l'édification de l'Islam est confié à Ḥayāt ʿAmāmū; Riḍāʾ Būqirra s'est occupé de l'opposition politique et de la naissance du šīʿisme; quant au ḫāriǧisme, il fera l'objet de la recherche de Laṭīfa al-Bakkāy. Le dépassement du califat primitif et de l'opposition naissante, prendra forme dans le cadre de l'État omeyyade, qui a fait l'objet de la thèse de B. Bin Ḥusayn.

2 Le maître : nouvelle approche des origines de l'islam et nouvelles pistes

Toute la difficulté réside pour nous, dans la reconstruction de l'itinéraire d'un savant qui a fait école. Hichem Djaït fait partie de la première génération d'historiens tunisiens qui optent pour l'histoire du Moyen Orient sous les directives du Šayḫ Claude Cahen, qui essaye de mettre en application un vaste programme de recherche qui va couvrir l'histoire du Moyen Orient durant tout le Moyen Âge. « Une répartition des tâches » est arrêtée entre J. Chebbi H. Djaït, R. Daghfous, M. Chapoutot, O. Saïdi, Y. Raghib, etc. … avait pour objectif la production d'un savoir académique bien assis, obéissant aux règles heuristiques, sur la période allant du Ier siècle h/VIIème, jusqu'à l'orée des temps modernes.

Cette approche sera relayée par le futur maître dans le sens des questions pointues. En effet, de retour à Tunis, agrégé, docteur d'État, H. Djaït se lance à son tour dans l'aventure de la transmission du savoir, en assumant sur rôle de promoteur-développeur de la recherche.

En parallèle, son enseignement porte sur les temps fondateurs de l'islam : l'Arabie des VI–VII siècles, comme cadre socio-culturel et anthropologique qui permettra à l'Appel de l'Envoyé de Dieu d'éclore. L'originalité de son approche du milieu qurayšite et de ses acteurs retiendra l'attention et l'intérêt de ses étudiants tant à l'Ecole Normale Supérieure qu'à la Faculté des Lettres et Sciences Humaines. Sollicité pour encadrer les mémoires et thèses, H. Djaït n'hésite pas à engager les jeunes dans la voie de la recherche sur les fondements de l'islam, se réservant la personnalité de Muḥammad qui va couronner son enseignement, ses recherches et sa carrière. Ainsi, dès le départ, le choix programmatique de H. Djaït était clair. Il s'attelait à déconstruire les lieux communs et à procéder à une archéologie des écrits sur l'islam et ses fondateurs. Selon ses instructions, rien n'est épargné, car tout devait passer au crible de la critique historique.

Il tenait à distinguer entre patrimoine, mémoire et histoire ; car selon lui le patrimoine est ce qu'hérite une communauté, un peuple ou même l'humanité entière, des prédécesseurs dans tous les domaines. Cependant l'histoire signifie le questionnement du passé proche ou lointain pour essayer de le comprendre. Pour ce faire, il est nécessaire de le déchiffrer sur la base de sources en tant que moyens d'extraction de données, conformément à une méthode appropriée. Suite à quoi, commence l'épreuve de l'histoire, c'est à dire l'élucidation et l'approche de la vérité ou l'extraction d'une logique aux événements et aux structures, avec comme objectif ultime, la contribution à l'enrichissement de la connaissance et à faire comprendre l'histoire. Ce « rappel à l'ordre » méthodologique évident s'impose car, selon H. Djaït, les Arabes vivent actuellement un blocage face au patrimoine sacralisé. En effet, la conscience arabe est engloutie dans le présent avec les problèmes de l'identité et du rapport à l'autre, qui entravent la marche de l'histoire académique. Quand il arrive à cette conscience de s'intéresser à l'histoire, c'est bien pour l'instrumentaliser et la soumettre à ses soucis immédiats. Sinon, elle ne s'intéresse guère à l'histoire et la laisse aux orientalistes qu'elle condamne et vénère en même temps !

Ainsi l'écriture de l'histoire sérieuse, objective et forcément *en empathie* avec son sujet est un moyen important pour rehausser le niveau de la connaissance et de la culture. C'est d'autant plus vrai que l'historien authentique est celui qui dispose d'un *background* solide en matière de culture générale, englobant la sociologie, l'économie, l'anthropologie et même la philosophie, pour pouvoir forger une réflexion diffuse dans son discours, sans concession en matière de rigueur scientifique. Hichem Djaït insiste par ailleurs sur le sens de l'évolution historique et sur la *sensibilité* qui doit appuyer l'explication logique des faits et la soutenir. En cas d'impossibilité d'atteindre la vérité, le principe conducteur chez H. Djaït, est de poser les problématiques[5].

Il conclut sur une interprétation différente des causes de la discorde – *sport favori* de H. Djaït – et annonce la couleur, en fait un projet de cours, véritable laboratoire, où H. Djaït affine ses expériences. *La seconde discorde*, sera confiée

---

5 لابد لكل دراسة أن يكون لها "....طابع الشمولية و الدقة ......مع تشكيل الإشكالية، كلما استحال الخروج بحقيقة دامغة ... ومن خصال كل مبحث أن يستفز الاعتراض أو النقد، و أنا بدوري لا أتماشى مع آخر ماجاء في الخاتمة.... من أن موت النبي أعطى الانطلاقة لتفجير وحدة المسلمين" تقديم لكتاب حياة عمامو ص 9.

à Buṭayna Bin Ḥusayn qui la publiera en arabe, juste après la soutenance de sa thèse sur l'État omeyyade.

3   Une leçon de méthode sans cesse rappelée et renouvelée

Hichem Djaït est obnubilé par les sources et leur critique. Il ne cesse d'y revenir, comme le prouve la fin de sa trilogie où il évoque le livre perdu de Musʿab Ibn ʿUqba, dont le nom est une énigme en soi, en rappelant qu'il est incidemment connu par les critiques d'Ibn Saʿd. Aussi avance-t-il l'hypothèse que le livre a été expurgé, puis rejeté, avant de tomber en désuétude, depuis le VIIIème siècle !

Pour H. Djaït, les sources de l'époque abbasside ne donnent pas d'explications ni de raisons franches et claires quant aux relations entre Muḥammad et ses vis-à-vis (groupes ou individus). Bien plus, leurs auteurs laissent libre cours à leur imagination et à l'imaginaire de la société.

4   De la pratique d'une psycho-histoire

Cette voie a été ouverte par le maître à ses élèves puisqu'il a sans cesse insisté sur l'affect et le sentimental toujours à découvrir pour comprendre l'attraction de l'islam sur les contemporains du prophète. Pour H. Djaït, l'introduction de cette dimension s'impose, pour comprendre les faits politiquement.

Sur ce plan, les sources sont d'un grand apport en matière première et en données brutes, à critiquer et à évaluer à l'aune de la critique historique.

5   Du renouvellement des lectures

H. Djaït innove aussi en remettant en question la *Hiǧra* secrète de Muḥammad suite à *un complot*. Il écrit que « La *Hiǧra* imaginaire. Il est absolument impossible d'y croire »[6].

A l'origine de l'exil (*Hiǧra*), H. Djaït met en valeur le premier contact du prophète avec les six Yaṯribites au cours du *haǧǧ*, car ils étaient en contact direct avec les juifs, leurs protégés, parmi lesquels l'idée de monothéisme est assez connue et répandue. Cet environnement socio-culturel accueillera le prophète mecquois, poussé à l'exil par sa propre communauté. Ils acceptent la foi et la prophétie. Ibn Isḥāq (acquis) s'efforce même de démontrer rationnellement,

---

6   *La vie de Muḥammad*, t. 3, 26.

sous forme d'explication logique leur adhésion à l'Islam. Selon lui, les juifs les menaçaient de la venue d'un prophète chez eux pour les exterminer. Aussi, ils s'empressèrent de prendre les devants, en attirant Muḥammad pour le gagner de leur côté. Leur objectif était de faire appel à lui, pour arbitrer le conflit qui déchirait Aws et Ḥazraǧ. Il s'agit donc de mobiles politiques que la sagesse imposait.

Ibn Isḥāq plante un décor harmonieux pour illustrer un contexte déterminé par une acception matérialiste de l'histoire. Il mettait côte à côte la crainte des juifs arabisés et bien adaptés, mais qui se sentaient menacés et la division des habitants de Yaṯrib.

Ainsi, H. Djaït rappelle et appelle au retour aux sources. Selon lui les discours sont non seulement tardifs et contextualisés, mais théologiques, politiques ou idéologiques ; d'où la nécessité de les dépasser, sans les laisser de côté, pour ne pas brouiller la lecture des données brutes. Une relecture introspective des textes classiques transformerait la *Hijra* en une affaire de revanche ḫazraǧite et de rééquilibrage par rapport aux Aws et aux juifs. D'ailleurs, lors de la *Bay'a* de 'Aqaba, sur les douze *muḥāyi'*, deux seulement sont Awsites et ne représentent que leurs personnes ! Au cours de cette phase ('Aqaba I) H. Djaït relève les confusions chronologiques chez Ibn Isḥāq (peut être chez Ibn Hišām) au sujet de la prière du vendredi (non encore décrétée) et au sujet de la *Qibla*.

Contrairement à Ibn Isḥāq, H. Djaït considère que le pacte de 'Aqaba II est un traité politique, qui induit la reconnaissance de Muḥammad en tant que prophète-messager d'une part, et la conversion à l'islam, de l'autre.

Sur les traces de Wellhausen[7], H. Djaït démontre que le prophète est certes un messager, mais il a été surtout un arbitre et un chef militaire. Ce sont ses combats, ses faits d'armes et ses victoires qui ont façonné son statut de guide commandeur. Toutefois, son objectif ultime demeure la diffusion de l'appel à Dieu d'où l'équation difficile du pouvoir au service de la religion.

Toujours dans le même volume de la *Sīra*, d'autres interprétations novatrices défrayent les chroniques, comme les messages du prophète aux délégations tribales, où la signification de *al-Nās kāffa* « كافة الناس » (« *Tout le monde* ») est à relativiser, puisqu'elle concernait « tous les Arabes ».

Après cette notice bio-bibliographique succincte, revenons à la carrière d'enseignant chercheur. Dès son retour en Tunisie, à la fin des années 1970, en précurseur, il ouvre la voie à ses étudiants pour continuer sur ses pas. Il les oriente vers l'époque originelle, selon une approche nouvelle, où tous les

---

7　Ḫālid Kšīr [Khaled Kchir], « Waqʻu Kitāb « Julius Wellhausen » wa Istiʻmālātuhu fī-l-ʻĀlam al-ʻArabī. al-Tārīḫ al-Islāmī bayn al-Ḏākira wal-Istišrāq », *Maǧallat Maʻhad al-Ādāb al-ʻArabiyya*, IBLA, 206/ 2010-2, p. 83-100.

fondateurs de l'Islam autour du prophète, baignent dans une historicité désacralisée (c'est l'objet d'une partie du tome 1 de la trilogie consacrée à la vie du prophète).

6 Quelques exemples pour mieux fixer notre bilan : sur les pas du maître

Sur les pas du maître Claude Cahen, Hichem Djaït charge chaque étudiant d'élucider un dossier. On remarquera que tous les travaux ont été réalisés en langue arabe[8]. Dans le feu de l'action, il encadrait avec l'humilité propre aux savants.

Les étudiants de H. Djaït ont compris que la condition *sine qua non* pour travailler sous sa direction était de se départir et de se dégager de toute appartenance ou influence doctrinale ou religieuse. L'impératif à respecter était de désacraliser les temps fondateurs et leur reflet dans les sources, enjolivés et idéalisés par des littératures rivales, défendant chacune une doctrine. Méthodologiquement, H. Djaït imposait la démarcation et bannissait de son discours les vérités et les développements fondés sur « *un tel a dit ou écrit* ».

Année	Auteur	Intitulé de la thèse
1981	R. Būqirra	*Les mouvements šīʿītes et ʿalaouites au Hedjaz et en Iraq durant la première moitié du II h/VIII J. C. analyse politico-doctrinale*
1996	Ḥ. Qṭāṭ	*Approche d'anthropologie historique des Arabes au VIème siècle*
1996	Ḥ. ʿAmāmū	*Les compagnons et leur rôle dans la fondation de l'islam*
1996 (1997)	S. Bilḥāj Ṣāliḥ	*Le christianisme arabe et son évolution*
1996 (2001)	L. Bakkāy	*Le mouvement des ḫāriǧītes- leur origine et leur développement jusqu'à la fin de l'ère omeyyade*
1997 (2008)	B. Bin Ḥusayn	*L'État omeyyade*

---

8 On relèvera que la fin des années 1970 a été marquée par une vague d'arabisation des programmes sans précédent, aussi bien dans les lycées que dans les facultés.

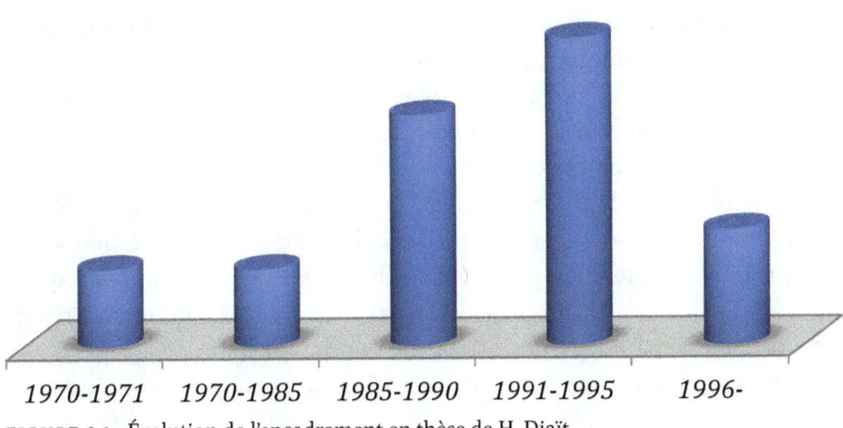

FIGURE 8.1 Évolution de l'encadrement en thèse de H. Djaït

Les travaux choisis, reflètent l'emprunte du maître, décelable à travers les problématiques suggérées et les questionnements traités ; ainsi garde-t-il sa vue d'ensemble du haut de sa chaire dans les sens propre et figuré. H. Djaït considère qu'il est de son devoir d'épuiser les interrogations historiques-clés, bien adossées aux problématiques *historiographiques* sans cesse remises en cause. C'est bien là son sceau. Le tableau ci-après présente sommairement les thèses de doctorat dirigées par le Professeur H. Djaït (nous proposons une traduction en français des intitulés des thèses) :

6.1 S. Bilḥāj Ṣāliḥ, *al-Masīḥiyya al-ʿArabiyya wa taṭawwurātuhā*

Pour saisir l'intérêt de la thèse de S. Bilḥāj Ṣāliḥ dans le cadre du vaste programme de recherche de H. Djaït, il y a lieu de rappeler ce qu'a écrit l'auteure dans son introduction. Elle y insiste sur les usages relativement récents des méthodes des sciences humaines et sociales par les historiens arabes, qui commencent à donner des fruits. Elle relève aussi la nécessité de dépasser la perception classique d'une Arabie païenne en contradiction avec la nouvelle croyance qu'est l'islam. Il est grand temps selon S. Bilḥāj Ṣāliḥ d'aborder les autres croyances des Arabes dont le monothéisme chrétien. Le renouvellement de ce champ de recherche s'impose en parallèle avec celui de l'islam, car l'étude du christianisme arabe a été dominée par des prêtres. De la plupart de leurs études, se dégage un faux lieu commun, présentant les Arabes chrétiens comme "ennemis de l'islam".

L'auteure construit un plan tripartite où elle entrecroise l'approche chronologique et thématique. Elle aborde ainsi les différentes églises et archevêchés dont dépendaient les communautés arabes chrétiennes jacobite, melkite et nestorienne. Avec le temps, une législation stricte a vu le jour pour régir les relations entre chrétiens en général et Arabes et musulmans, pour ce qui a trait entre autres à la liberté. S. Bilḥāj Ṣāliḥ passe en revue la répartition des diocèses et archevêchés des différentes communautés arabes chrétiennes qui dépendaient des grandes églises orientales syriaque, melkite, jacobite, nestorienne et celles du Yaman et de Naǧrān.

L'exemple bien développé est celui de la grande tribu nomade des Taġlib qui nomadisait sur les confins syro-irakiens du nord et qui a défendu sa foi chrétienne dans le cadre de son archevêché tribal qui a perduré jusqu'au Xème siècle[9]. Quant aux Naǧrānites éxilés par ʿUmar, ils s'installèrent près de Kūfa où ils se convertirent au nestorianisme et non à l'islam !

Cette église a même dépêché une délégation de prosélytes en Chine pour convertir les Chinois au Xème siècle. À cela s'ajoutent les archevêchés de Ḥira et Anbār, dont relevaient des dizaines de monastères, véritables creusets d'acculturation et fiefs d'intégration entre chrétiens et musulmans. L'auteure insiste sur l'ancrage et l'ancienneté du christianisme en Arabie et au Yaman, sans compter l'Irak et la Syrie, lors de l'avènement de l'islam et notamment chez les Arabes nomades. Les Taġlib n'ont pas quitté leurs villages.

Parmi les résultats auxquels aboutit cette thèse, la persistance du christianisme arabe avec ses deux colorations et son attachement référentiel au courant syriaque, sauf que le clergé non arabe expliquerait ses limites modestes et la désaffection des Arabes. La marginalisation progressive des Arabes sous les Abbassides expliquerait leur islamisation, sous l'effet des relations de parenté. Les chrétiens arabes n'ont pas vécu comme une minorité opprimée ni fermée. Ils étaient complètement intégrés dans la société. En tant que foi, le christianisme n'a pas réussi à créer ou souder une coalition de résistance avant et après l'avènement de l'islam. Culturellement, les Arabes chrétiens n'étaient pas différents de ceux convertis à l'islam, aussi ont-ils prêté aux musulmans main forte lors des conquêtes de l'empire Sassanide.

Fidèles au nouvel État, ils vont relancer les circuits commerciaux grâce à leurs expériences, et leurs fortunes et développer à l'intérieur de *Dār al Islām* le commerce, les finances et l'artisanat. Cependant, l'auteure relève que les bédouins appartenaient plutôt à l'église jacobite, c'est ainsi qu'ils ont gardé leurs traditions, dont la poésie arabe sous toutes ses formes, face à une culture naissante fondée sur le Coran.

En face, les Arabes nestoriens citadins ont joué un rôle fondamental dans le développement des différents domaines du savoir, à commencer par l'arabisation et la transmission des savoirs antiques et tous les legs scientifiques

---

9 S. Bilḥāj Ṣāliḥ a consacré son mémoire à l'étude de cette tribu. *Taġlib bayna al-Masīḥiyya wal-islam*, 1988.

hellénistique, persan et syriaque. Ils ont aussi brillé par leurs travaux originaux en matière de mathématiques, de philosophie et de médecine. Ils sont aussi à l'origine du *'Ilm al-kalām* (théologie). Selon S. Bilḥāj Ṣāliḥ, l'hostilité envers les chrétiens a commencé avec les fuqahā' du XIème siècle, dont Šāfiʿī.

S. Bilḥāj Ṣāliḥ finit sa thèse en relevant un paradoxe. En effet, dans un État où la liberté de conscience est respectée, le christianisme a fini par disparaître ! D'un autre côté, elle relève que l'affrontement entre islam et christianisme s'est fait dans un cadre *arabo-arabe*, d'où sa particularité. Il n'a donc rien à voir avec le conflit ouvert à partir du XIème siècle dans le cadre des Croisades.

Parallèlement à cette recherche qui encadre la naissance de l'islam et son développement, H. Djaït a chargé Ḥayāt Qṭāṭ d'instruire le dossier du contexte anthropologique de la naissance de l'islam.

6.2 Ḥayāt Qṭāṭ, *Muqāraba fī-'l Anthrūbūlūğiya tārīḫiyya lil-ʿArab fī al-Qarn al-sādis mīlādī*

Ḥayāt Qṭāṭ définit d'abord le milieu naturel hostile de la naissance de l'islam qui explique pour une large part, la prédominance du nomadisme comme mode de vie adapté. Dans ce pays hostile, la vie urbaine est réduite à quelques noyaux au Ḥiğāz et sur la côte orientale de l'Arabie. La seconde partie est consacrée à l'étude des structures sociales dans une dialectique famille-clan-tribu ; régie par les formes d'organisation et les rites religieux.

Dans la troisième partie, Ḥayāt Qṭāṭ analyse le livre d'Ibn al-Kalbī pour étudier les liens de parenté, les types de mariages, les liens de sang et leurs répercussions sur les différentes formes de pouvoir en Arabie pré-islamique.

Pour mieux fixer notre bilan, voici quelques jalons du renouvellement de l'appréhension de l'islam des origines.

6.3 ʿAbd al-Salām Bisbās, *Ibn Šihāb al-Zuhrī. Mu'assis Madrasat al Maġāzī bil-Madīna*

Soucieux d'aborder les cadres initiaux qui vont fossiliser les récits retraçant la *Sīra* (biographie) du prophète et ses *Maġāzī* (faits d'armes ou conquêtes), transformés en socle sur lequel sera fondée la légitimité abbasside, H. Djaït dirige un mémoire sur la source des sources, à savoir Zuhrī qui allait inaugurer le corpus qui va compléter le Coran. Il a été le transmetteur hybride dans une phase transitionnelle, entre le *rāwī* et le ʿālim au service de l'État, en l'occurrence omeyyade.

Dans cette recherche oriente les questions et affûte la critique historique pour dégager le maillon initial fort qui précède celui du prophète. C'est al-Zuhrī qui invente la chaîne de transmission (*sanad/isnād*) des actes et paroles du prophète et fonde le proto-*hadīth*. Il structure la *Sīra*, qui sera relayée et restructurée par Ibn Ishaq puis relue et réécrite par Ibn Hišām, qui en scelle le plan. Une des conclusions de ce mémoire est que la succession chronologique est née dans le *laboratoire* des *Maġāzī*, où les événements ont subi une refonte et un remodelage, conformes à l'idéale *vitae* de Muḥammad.

Le monde tribal dont l'agglomération a constitué l'ossature de la *Umma* naissante est étudié dans le cadre d'une *micro-storia* qui ne dit pas son nom a été tentée à trois reprises : une monographie consacrée à la tribu de Taġlib, une autre aux notables de Bāhila. Un troisième mémoire est consacré aux femmes en 1996.

6.4 Laṭīfa al-Bakkāy, *Ḥarakat al-Ḥawāriǧ. Naš'atuhā wa Taṭawwuruhā ilā Nihāyat al-'Ahd al-Umawī (37-132h)*

Ce livre[10] est à l'origine une thèse soutenue en 1996. H. Djaït a confié cette recherche à Laṭīfa al-Bakkāy en vue de compléter le panorama des balbutiements de la vie politique, à travers les premiers opposants, en l'occurrence les Ḥāriǧites. Dans cette recherche l'auteure s'est bien gardée de prendre position. H. Djaït tenait à orienter ses étudiants vers des pistes apparemment connues. Il écrit dans sa préface que beaucoup de chercheurs pensent que le mouvement Ḥāriǧite a fait l'objet d'intérêt de plusieurs chercheurs depuis des années, et qu'en reprenant ce sujet, L. Bakkāy s'est fixé le défi de renouveler la question. Au bout du compte, elle a démontré que ce mouvement méritait d'être réétudié.

6.5 Ḥayāt 'Amāmū, *Aṣḥāb Muḥammad wa-Dawruhum fī Naš'at al-Islām*

La préface du livre de Ḥayāt 'Amāmū est une leçon de méthode aux futurs chercheurs. H. Djaït y distingue entre mémoire, histoire et patrimoine et insiste sur le fait que les Arabes soient obsédés par le passé sacralisé, ou au contraire méprisé. Aussi sont-ils incapables d'aborder un sujet aussi brûlant qui traite de la naissance d'une grande religion, rarement étudiée par les Arabes contemporains. D'un autre côté, l'angle d'attaque précis de cette naissance a été rarement pris au sérieux par les chercheurs musulmans ou orientalistes. Leur intérêt a souvent été focalisé sur la personnalité centrale du prophète, aux dépens de son entourage proche qui l'a soutenu et construit avec lui et sous sa direction et sa protection l'islam, à la fois religion, communauté et État.

Dans sa thèse, 'Amāmū commence par définir le concept de la « *suhba* » et le rôle de ceux qui en furent désignés et qualifiés dans l'édification de l'islam autour du prophète, en insistant sur le changement de l'acception et l'évolution

---

10   Laṭīfa al-Bakkāy *Ḥarakat al-Ḥawāriǧ : Naš'atuhā wa Taṭawwuruhā ilā Nihāyat al-'Ahd al-Umawī (37-132h)*, Beyrouth, Dār al-Ṭalī'a, 2001.

de son sens entre les sources originales et les sources tardives. Elle n'oublie pas de rappeler sa signification dans le patrimoine islamique.

Cette approche relativise le rôle de l'individu (en l'occurrence le prophète communiquant avec l'au-delà) et fouille dans les profondeurs de la société qurayšite, mosaïque multicolore. Quant aux biographies des compagnons, elles ont été systématiquement analysées (âges, origines, situations, …), afin « … de déterminer la nature politique, religieuse et sociale de l'islam dans sa phase prophétique »[11].

Pour Ḥayāt ʿAmāmū, cette recherche fouille dans le rôle assumé par les compagnons pour asseoir l'islam, en tant que religion, foi et institution politico-religieuse. C'est le point de départ d'un examen minutieux des rapports entre les compagnons et leurs contemporains. Le dénominateur commun qui traverse ces problématiques est l'emprunte du maître bien marquée à savoir les luttes politico-doctrinales tardives qui ont plus ou moins dénaturé, déformé et entaché les données des sources[12].

Par ailleurs, Djaït démontre et rappelle dans la préface que « le déterminisme strict dans le cours de l'histoire n'existe pas. Il y aurait plutôt un semblant de logique interne et une série de causes à long et court termes, selon la volonté des hommes, leurs objectifs et leurs ambitions »[13]. L'esprit d'émulation l'intéressait à plus d'un titre surtout s'il fait progresser la science historique, ayant pour objet les origines de l'islam.

6.6 Buṯayna Bin Ḥusayn, *al-Dawla al-Umawiyya wa muqawwimātuhā al-īdyūlūǧiyya wal-iǧtimāʿiyya*

Soutenue en 1997, cette thèse a été publiée en 2008. Sa thématique s'insère dans le programme heuristique de Hichem Djaït, puisque Buṯayna Bin Ḥusayn s'est intéressée à la période fondatrice en aval. Son mémoire et sa thèse ont porté sur la concrétisation définitive d'un État islamique, au bout d'un demi-siècle de luttes et de de balbutiements. Elle a procédé par étapes : le mémoire est consacré à l'édification de l'État omeyyade entre 661 et 715 ap. J.C., focalisé sur les rôles des califes fondateurs Muʿāwiya et ʿAbd al-Malik b. Marwān.

Pour le besoin de la recherche, elle a décomposé les différentes institutions d'un État bien établi : califat, chancelleries, *dīwān*, police, justice, monnaie.

Elle démontre que cet État arabe est une synthèse des traditions culturelles arabe, byzantine et persane. C'est ce qu'on appellera l'État islamique. Entre

---

11   Ḥayāt ʿAmāmū, *Aṣḥāb Muḥammad wa-Dawruhum fī Našʾat al-Islām*, Tūnis, Dār al-Janūb li-al-Našr, 1996, (= Préface, p.12).

12   Ibid.

13   Idem, 9.

deux tendances profane et religieuse, cet État naissant a réorganisé ses rapports avec les forces sociales en présence (Qurayšites, *Anṣār, Ašrāf,* Syriens, Irakiens, *Mawlās, ḏimmīs* …). Il apparait ainsi que la thèse est venue continuer et compléter le travail préliminaire du mémoire.

À partir d'une approche macro-historique situant l'État Omeyyade dans le temps et dans l'espace, le lecteur découvre l'aboutissement d'un long cheminement, sur un empire aux dimensions jamais atteintes, par les Romains ni les Chinois, avec une centralisation du pouvoir évidente. La thèse est une démonstration de la fragilité de cette équation : immensité géographique depuis les confins de la Chine jusqu'en Espagne et l'adaptation ou création d'institutions appropriées, à toutes les échelles de la gestion d'un empire conquis par la force des armes.

L'étude des institutions à l'échelle centrale et régionale a fait l'objet de la première partie. La seconde met en valeur les fondements matériels et symboliques du pouvoir depuis les fortunes personnelles au protocole, en passant par la couronne, le trône, le sceptre, la monnaie et les édifices prestigieux, imposant respect et soumission. Buṯayna Bin Ḥusayn a ensuite étudié les fondements idéologiques de cet État, démontrant que, contrairement aux accusations de leurs opposants, les Omeyyades ont fondé leur pouvoir sur l'islam. Les assises sociales sont analysées à part, où on relève l'importance des princes de la famille, dans le cadre d'une monarchie naissante, au sein d'un État de moins de trente ans d'âge. Autour d'eux, les réseaux d'influence s'articulaient sous forme de cercles concentriques : *Ašrāf,* chefs de tribus ou parents du prophète, *fuqahā'*, personnel au service de l'État, agents des différents *dīwān*, etc … Face à ce pouvoir, se dressaient les opposants *se structurant progressivement au sein de mouvements bien distincts.*

Deux ans plus tard, Butayna Bin Ḥusayn publie *al-Fitna al-Ṯāniya.* Cette *seconde discorde* se déclencha lors d'une crise de succession au sein de la famille élargie[14].

Dans la préface de ce livre, Hichem Djaït s'exprime clairement sur l'originalité de l'école tunisienne dans le domaine de l'histoire « … qui a accédé à un niveau appréciable, grâce au recours aux méthodes modernes »[15].

Par ailleurs, d'autres aspects de l'histoire sociale des Arabes entre les VIe et VIIe siècles ont fait l'objet d'autres travaux sous la direction du maître. Nous

---

14   Au lendemain de l'écrasement du califat rival à Makka, ʿAbd al-Malik eut à affronter la première tentative de *putsh* à Damas. Elle a fait l'objet d'une longue étude par Buṯayna Bin Ḥusayn et Khaled Kchir, « La révolte de ʿAmr Ibn Saʿīd al-Ašdaq. Une nouvelle lecture », dans *Les mouvements sociaux dans le monde arabo-islamique*, Tunis, 2011, 17-105.

15   Voir l'extrait dans notre conclusion.

nous sommes contentés ici d'en présenter quelques exemples. Pour mieux illustrer notre propos et étayer notre hypothèse, nous nous étendrons sur un travail réalisé en deux étapes, celle du mémoire et celle de la thèse. Il s'agit du travail de Riḍā' Būqirra sur les mouvements pro-alides.

6.7 Étude du *šīʿisme*. Riḍā' Būqirra, *al-Ḥarakāt al-šīʿiyya al-ʿalawiyya fīl-Ḥiǧāz wal-ʿIrāq fīl-niṣf al-Awwal min al-Qarn al-ṯānī h. Taḥlīl siyāsī ʿaqāʾidī*

Mémoire d'aptitude à la recherche soutenu à l'École Normale Supérieure qui fait partie d'un vaste projet programmatique de Hichem Djaït de cerner l'histoire de l'islam, durant les deux premiers siècles en Arabie et dans les provinces orientales.

Le sujet traite des mouvements šīʿites et ʿalaouites au Ḥiǧāz et en Iraq durant la première moitié du IIᵉh/VIIIᵉ J.C. Analyse politico-doctrinale. Comme l'indique le sous-titre du mémoire, Riḍā' Būqirra s'est attelé à analyser l'élaboration des choix politiques et doctrinaux des mouvements nés d'une opposition aristocratique exclue de pouvoir. Grâce à une propagande efficiente, ils vont se transformer en mouvements radicaux.

Dans une approche dynamique et synchronique, le jeune chercheur aborde la renaissance de šīʿisme au deuxième siècle pour démontrer qu'entre le premier et le deuxième siècle, il y a eu un changement et une rupture qui vont déterminer les destinées d'un islam pertinent avec ses différents rites, dont le šīʿisme.

Le premier chapitre insiste sur la nature d'un mouvement autour du prince Zayd face à un État omeyyade. Ce mouvement marque la transformation de l'échiquier socio-politique. Au-delà des trois cercles, tribu-clan-famille, nous sommes face à un prince, en l'occurrence Zayd, face à un État dont l'armée a tué froidement son grand-père al-Ḥusayn. Mais à la légitimité par l'ascendance, Zayd ajoutait les fondements d'une idéologie politico-religieuse naissante et qui se perfectionnera au cours des siècles.

La problématique même du mémoire démontre l'enchevêtrement des actions menées, des influences et retours entre idées politiques et opérations militaires. Il en résultera des doctrines nées de cette alchimie qui mêleront « volonté divine » et revendications alaouites. Dans un va-et-vient entre l'événementiel et le doctrinal -en cours d'élaboration- le chercheur démontre que le tournant fatidique a été celui de la prise du pouvoir par les Abbassides, une autre branche des Hāšimites (*Āl al-Bayt*), au sens large (membres de la maison). C'est ainsi qu'il arrive à démêler les orientations des différentes branches de la famille alaouite. Les descendants de Ḥasan, exclus de la vie politique et scientifique, compenseront par la charge de recueillir l'aumône du prophète et son cousin ʿAlī. La branche ḥusaynite, guidée par Zayd b. ʿAlī b. al-Ḥusayn compensera en optant pour le savoir. Les descendants d'al-Ḥusayn deviendront des savants et des guides qui attirent les musulmans de tous les coins de la terre.

Cette branche inventera puis entretiendra la culture du martyr et de la repentance qui perdure jusqu'à nos jours, et dont dérivera le proto-soufisme avec les pleureurs pénitenciers. Toujours selon l'approche anthropologique, Riḍāʾ Būqirra situe la troisième branche ʿalīde « marginale » représentée par un autre petit-fils de ʿAlī, né d'un autre mariage avec al-Ḥanafiyya. Avec cette branche nait le testament d'allégeance. Ce prince excentré qui ne descend pas de Fāṭima « trahira » la cause et prêtera serment posthume aux cousins des ʿalīdes, les Abbassides. Un autre tournant et pris par l'État islamique.

Ce mémoire démontre en définitive que la clé de voûte du courant ʿalīde de *Āl al-Bayt* est forgée au cours de cette période et pas avant. Elle est le fruit d'une pensée en quête de légitimité face à la logique de la raison d'État développée par les Omeyyades puis par leurs « cousins » Abbassides, avec à chaque fois une exclusion du sommet de l'État ; « … leurs droits ont longuement été bafoués », dixit ʿUmar b. ʿAbd al-ʿAzīz, le calife omeyyade reconnu « juste » dans la mémoire ʿalīde et abbasside, qui ne reconnaissait que les descendants de Fāṭima. Historiquement, il semblerait qu'il aurait été l'inventeur du « *Fatimisme* », construit par l'ascendance (le sang) et par la fixation des critères de *l'imāmat*. Cette approche anthropologique suggérée par Hichem Djaït, aboutit à une nouvelle lecture, une mise à plat du šīʿisme (sans parti pris ni animosité). Le courant des Kaysaniyya émerge par sa fidélité aveugle aux *Šīʿa* hāšimites, seuls restés fidèles à Ibn al-Ḥanafiyya, après l'allégeance accordée par Abū Hāšim ʿAbd Allāh b. Muḥammad b. ʿAlī b. al-Ḥanafiyya[16].

Ce mémoire met à plat toutes les dissensions originelles qui ont donné naissance aux différentes « sectes » et ramifications ʿalaouites (par procuration, c'est Fāṭima qui a été déterminante dans les délimitations du nouvel échiquier).

L'auteur dégage deux courants auxquels vont s'agglutiner tous les mouvements *šīʿites* du IIᵉ siècle h/VIIIᵉ ap. J.C. Le courant théo-doctrinal avec une

---

16 Selon nous, cette opposition vite écartée, pourrait être abordée d'un autre point de vue, car elle «a opposé » Fāṭima à al-Ḥanafiyya, par-delà ʿAlī. Nous serions face à des séquelles d'un matriarcat évanescent, dont la persistance demeurera symbolique, au sein d'une doctrine politico-religieuse. Les précurseurs auraient défendu une sorte de « féminisme », où le souvenir des femmes et leur mémoire sont déterminantes. Nos sources parlent des femmes « *barza* » qui côtoyaient les hommes dans les conseils politiques, dont Umm Hāšim, veuve de Yazīd b. Muʿāwiya, qui a épousé Marwān b. al-Ḥakam, en secondes noces. En s'offrant à lui, et lui offrit le califat. Elle sauva ainsi la dynastie omeyyade. Il est à rappeler l'épisode du Ǧamal qui cache ʿĀʾiša, sans descendance. C'est dire le rôle des femmes dans une tradition arabe pré-islamique qui perdurait encore.

coloration politique négative et qui donnera naissance aux deux grands rites :
imāmite (duodécimain) et *ismā'īlite*.

L'étude s'est développée à propos de ces deux courants autour de trois questions socio-historiques : la théorie révolutionnaire, l'éveil ḥasanite face au pouvoir abbasside et la perdurance du mouvement ḥusaynite sous les Omeyyades
puis les Abbasides jusqu'en 148 h.

À travers une analyse fine, Būqirra démontre la récupération de la tradition
de résistance 'alaouite par les Abbassides pour prendre le pouvoir. Très vite, ils
vont réprimer cette même opposition qui les porta au pouvoir.

La notion de *Āl al-Bayt* est définitivement scindée en deux : les descendants
de 'Alī d'un côté et les descendants de 'Abbās de l'autre. Les *Šī'a* évolueront
selon deux mouvances : militante versée dans l'action politico-militaire, l'autre
plutôt intellectuelle, se consacrait au développement des idées qui consti-
tueront les fondements d'une idéologie et d'une doctrine originales, bien
avant la doctrine sunnite. Ce n'est donc pas par hasard, que les Omeyyades
aient demandé à Zuhrī de constituer le premier noyau du corpus de *Ḥadīṯ*. Au
cours de la même période les tendances extrémistes ont vu le jour. La scène
politico-religieuse était définitivement meublée, chaque force prit place dans
un équilibre plus ou moins stable, autour du pouvoir politique comme système
de régulation.

Dans ce mémoire, la pensée *šī'īte* est épurée par le dégagement des idées
anachroniques (*imāmat, 'iṣma, 'ilm ilāhī*) projetées à partir de temps postérieurs, et ce conformément à une méthode de démantèlement de socles idéologiques immuables dans leurs apparences. De cette manière les tendances
sont réduites à leurs propres dimensions, sur la base d'une mise en perspective
des sources « *sunnītes et šī'ītes, disponibles en Tunisie* ». Ce mémoire met en
valeur les rivalités entre 'Alaouites et Abbassides, qui cachent à leur tour des
rivalités entres Fatimides et Ḥanifites.

Par petites touches, Riḍā' Būqirra est arrivé à dépeindre un tableau multicolore qui rend bien la diversité des tendances au sein des premiers mouvements
šī'ītes, nés dans les interstices de contact d'une communauté naissante entre
un ordre ancien et un ordre en éclosion. Dans un jeu d'échelles, Buqirra situe
l'émergence d'un nouveau *leadership* entre famille et communauté religieuse.
Il a démontré que les actions menées par les *Šī'ītes* n'avaient pas pour objectif
de semer le chaos et l'anarchie, bien au contraire ces actions ressortent sous
un autre jour.

Ce sont des tentatives de réformes sur les plans : politique, religieux et
militaire dans une lutte contre le pouvoir absolu des califes et pour « rapa-
trier » le califat à Médine. Pour preuve, le mouvement de Zayd a eu des sym-
pathisants parmi les savants sunnītes. Riḍā' Būqirra en conclut que la doctrine

zaydite était proche de celle de *Ahl al-Sunna*. Al-Mahdī (Muḥammad al-Nafs al-Zakiyya) apparait dans cette recherche, comme le candidat le plus apte que n'importe quel prince abbasside.

Quant à l'aspect armé improvisé, il serait la preuve que les *šīʿītes* ne remettaient pas en cause l'ordre social et que le IIe siècle h, aurait été *le siècle ʿalaouite*, à travers le monde musulman, y compris dans le palais califal. Ce travail est repris et élargi dans une thèse de troisième cycle consacrée aux mouvements *šīʿītes*.

7   En guise de conclusion

Dans cette enquête nous avons essayé de démontrer qu'à partir de questionnements, doutes, hypothèses et problématiques Hichem Djaït a réalisé un vaste programme de recherche sur les différents cadres de la naissance de l'islam (social, culturel, sans oublier le fond psychologique).

Son va-et-vient entre les temps fondateurs et actuels, a permis à Hichem Djaït de définir ses *outils* et d'établir ses *distances* qui ont été à l'origine de deux essais clés qui préfigurent l'identité de l'historien. L'archéologie des savoirs à laquelle il s'est adonné, lui a ouvert des voies multiples de remise en question d'idées reçues et d'une vulgate fossilisée. Ce caractère novateur attira plusieurs jeunes chercheurs tunisiens qui l'ont choisi comme encadrant. Sous son influence, leurs travaux ont essayé de développer les hypothèses et les problématiques qu'il a posées.

Telles des pièces d'un puzzle, ces mémoires et thèses constituent aujourd'hui un large tableau historique de la naissance et du développement de l'Islam. Dans ce tableau, les différentes dimensions s'entrelacent, se superposent et se complètent.

À la lumière des résultats glanés dans les différents travaux retenus dans cette enquête, notre hypothèse se dégage clairement et se confirme. En effet, il nous est permis de considérer que Djaït est le maître d'une école historienne digne de ce nom, qui propose une lecture académique, pluridisciplinaire et iconoclaste à partir d'une approche « profane » de l'islam des origines.

Au bout de cinquante ans de carrière, Hichem Djaït a rendu possible une historiographie critique et un discours historique objectif outrepassant les parti pris doctrinaux et les polémiques idéologiques qui renvoient à des luttes et dissensions politiques.

Annexe : Extraits d'une préface de Hichem Djaït

Pour finir, voici des extraits qui résument le statut de Hichem Djaït et qui étayent notre hypothèse de départ, selon laquelle il est le maître d'une école d'histoire de l'islam. Ce sont des extraits de sa préface au livre de Buṯayna Bin Ḥusayn, *La seconde discorde*[17] :

> *Ce livre fait partie d'une vague d'ouvrages qui ont vu le jour depuis une cinquantaine d'années et prouvent que les musulmans ont accédé à la science moderne, dans l'interprétation de l'histoire de l'islam. Depuis trente ans, l'école tunisienne a prouvé ses performances dans ce domaine, suite au travail réalisé par les historiens irakiens entre les années 1950 et les années 1980*
>
> *... Ce qui a été réalisé par l'école tunisienne dans le champ de la recherche historique honore la nation arabe et le monde islamique en général. Or cet effort n'est pas assez connu ...*
>
> *Sur cette modeste terre qui a enfanté Ibn Ḫaldūn, l'histoire a brillé d'un éclat moderne, après l'indépendance, dans plusieurs domaines et en particulier celui de l'histoire académique de l'islam ... Le monde arabe est certes submergé par ses problèmes auxquels il accorde toute son importance, il est encore loin de la recherche scientifique avec ses différents affluents et demeure atteint d'un complexe d'infériorité envers l'occident et sa production. Mais tôt ou tard, viendra le jour où on reconnaîtra les apports des XXᵉ et XXIᵉ siècles, ainsi que les changements radicaux qu'ils ont réalisés dans le décryptage du passé et dans le questionnement de la grande civilisation qui est la nôtre. C'est une des plus grandes cultures humaines comparable à celles de la Chine, de l'Inde et de l'Europe. 7-8.*

Bibliographie

ʿAmāmū, Ḥayāt. *Aṣḥāb Muḥammad wa-Dawruhum fī Naš'at al-Islām*, Tūnis, Dār al-Janūb li-al-Našr, 1996.

Al-Bakkāy, Laṭīfa. *Ḥarakat al-Ḫawāriǧ. Naš'atuhā wa Taṭawwuruhā ilā Nihāyat al-ʿAhd al-Umawī (37-132h)*, Bayrūt, Dar al-Talīʿa, 2001.

Bilḥāj Ṣāliḥ, Salwā. *Al-Masīḥiyya al-ʿArabiyya wa taṭawwurātuhā*, Bayrūt, Dār al-Talīʿa, 1997.

Bin Ḥusayn, Buṯayna. *Al-Dawla al-Umawiyya wa muqawwimātuhā al-īdyūlūǧiyya wal-iǧtimāʿiyya*, 1997.

Bin Ḥusayn, Buṯayna et Khaled Kchir. « La révolte de Amr b. Saʿīd al-Ašdaq. Une nouvelle lecture », dans *Les mouvements sociaux dans le monde arabo-islamique : Actes du Vème colloque international organisé par le Laboratoire du monde arabo-islamique médiéval*, Tūnis, 2006, 17-105.

Bisbās, ʿAbd al-Salām. *Ibn Šihāb al-Zuhrī. Muʾassis Madrasat al-Maǧāzī bil-Madīna*, C.A.R. (= mastère), 1986.

Būqirra, Riḍāʾ. *al-Ḥarakāt al-šīʿiyya al-ʿalawiyya fil-Ḥiǧāz wal-ʿIrāq fil-niṣf al-awwal min al-qarn al-Ṯānī h. Taḥlīl siyāsī ʿaqāʾidī*, C.A.R. (= mastère), 1981.

Djaït, Hichem. [Ǧaʿayṭ, Hišām]. *La personnalité et le devenir arabo-islamiques*, Paris, Seuil, 1974.

Djaït, Hichem. [Ǧaʿayṭ, Hišām]. *L'Europe et l'Islam*, Paris, Seuil, 1978.

Djaït, Hichem. [Ǧaʿayṭ, Hišām]. *La Grande Discorde, Religion et politique dans l'Islam des origines*, Paris, Gallimard, Bibliothèque des Histoires, 1989.

Djaït, Hichem. [Ǧaʿayṭ, Hišām]. *Fī l-Sīra al-Nabawiyya: I. al-Waḥy wa l-Qurʾān wa l-Nubuwwa*, Bayrūt, Dar al-Talīʿa, 1999 ; *II. Tarīḫiyyat al-Daʿwa al-Muhammadiyya fī Makka*, 2007 ; *III. Masīrat Muhammad fil-Madīna wa Intisār al-Islām*, 2015.

Djaït, Hichem. [Ǧaʿayṭ, Hišām]. *La vie de Muḥammad : Révélation et prophétie*, Paris, Fayard, 2007.

Djaït, Hichem. [Ǧaʿayṭ, Hišām]. *La vie de Muḥammad : La prédication prophétique à La Mecque*, Paris, Fayard, 2008.

Djaït, Hichem. [Ǧaʿayṭ, Hišām]. *La vie de Muḥammad : Le parcours du Prophète à Médine et le triomphe de l'Islam*, Paris, Fayard, 2012.

Djaït, Hichem. [Ǧaʿayṭ, Hišām]. *Penser l'histoire, penser la religion*, Tunis, Cérès, 2021.

Djaït, Hichem. [Ǧaʿayṭ, Hišām]. *The Life of Muḥammad*, 3 vol., Carthage, Bayt al-Hikma, Academy of Sciences, Letters and Arts, (History Collection), 2014.

Kchir, Khaled [Kšīr, Ḥālid]. « *La grande discorde* de Hichem Djaït », Compte rendu dans *Correspondances* 18 (1990), 3-4.

Kchir, Khaled [Kšīr, Ḥālid]. « H. Djaït, *Fī l-Sīra al-Nabawiyya: I. al-Waḥy wa l-Qurʾān wa l-Nubuwwa*, Note de lecture », *IBLA* (2005), 132-136.

Kchir, Khaled [Kšīr, Ḥālid]. « Waqʿu Kitāb « Julius Wellhausen » wa Istiʿmālātuhu fil-ʿĀlam al-ʿArabī. al-Tārīḫ al-Islāmī bayn al-Ḏākira wal-Istišrāq », *Maǧallat Maʿhad al-Ādāb al-ʿArabiyya*, *IBLA* 206 (2010-2012), 83-100.

Qṭāṭ, Ḥayāt. *Muqāraba fī-Anṯrūbūlūǧya tārīḫiyya li-l-ʿArab fil-Qarn al-sādis mīladī*, 1996.

9

The Umayyads in Contemporary Arabic Historical Writing

Abdulhadi Alajmi

1 The Umayyads as the Benchmark of the History of Islam

This chapter does not attempt to include all of the modern Arabic studies on the Umayyad period. The selected material aims to show the most significant characteristics and tendencies of this scholarship. The Umayyads and their state are the ideal paradigm against which the transformations and developments of Arabic historiography can be gauged, with all their objectivity, traditionalism, conflict, sectarianism, bias and politics in both classical and modern times.[1]

2 An Overview of the Historiography of the Umayyad Period

It is evident that the study of the history of the Umayyad state holds a special appeal, as it is deemed interesting for both the general reader in the Arab World and academic specialists. Such interest is associated with the significance, nature and circumstances of the era, especially the conflicts and the events that occurred during that period. Writing about the Umayyads and their state is characterized by dependence upon a massive traditional heritage of Arab-Islamic primary sources (i.e. *ummahāt al-kutub*),[2] as well as modern and contemporary sources,[3] according to the nature and intellectual approaches of each school. Those models likely represented "original" historical efforts, which constituted, along with others, a historical continuum not only for the Umayyad state, but also in respect to Islamic history in general. Theoretically, there is no agreed-upon historical periodization of the scholarly literature on

---

1   The current chapter does not aim to cover all Arabic studies on the Umayyads, rather it will highlight particular trends and give examples of representative works.
2   Such as al-Ṭabarī, al-Balādhurī, al-Wāqidī, al-Baghdādī, Ibn Hishām, al-Qāsim, Ibn Sallām, etc.
3   Many studies which examined, analyzed and studied it.

© KONINKLIJKE BRILL NV, LEIDEN, 2021 | DOI:10.1163/9789004460089_010

the Umayyads, yet an overview of such literature depends, in its holistic view, upon two principal tendencies:

1) The first tendency, which is influenced by popular and established accounts which are part of a context of extensive writings represented in the early Islamic historical sources, especially those accounts dating from the establishment of Abbasid rule (132–158 AH/750–775 CE),[4] with all their intense crises and ambivalences (the Shīʿī reading in particular), which still maintain the antagonistic Abbasid view of the Umayyads.

2) Another tendency represented by those studies that are marked by a sense of unburdening of the prejudiced historical heritage (consistent with the collective imaginary), with a degree of caution being exercised by those writings towards the texts and which condemn the Umayyads and their iconic figures. Added to this, it seems that there were attempts to revisit some conventional historical views, not only those related to the Umayyads in particular, but also those related to Islamic history (in general). Both tendencies[5] endorsed a large variety of Arab and Western literature, the majority of which was centered upon two opposing (attack/defense)[6] paradigms.

3   "History" and the Umayyads

Upon observing the history of scholarship on the Umayyads, one finds that it went through various stages, which moved slowly from the conventional and cognitive stage (driven by factors of narrative and description), to the ideological and the populist (which teems with the sensitivities of the present such as the sectarian, and Arabist/nationalist trends) to reach the comprehensiveness and wide range it enjoys now.

---

4   The rise of the Abbasid state and the onset of its political history (132–158 AH/750–775 CE), which was officially established in the aftermath of the murder of the caliph Marwān b. Muḥammad (127–132 AH/745–750 CE), who was the last Umayyad caliph.

5   Out of this problematic, the current research proceeds towards a simple conception to show how the historical writing about the Umayyads was divided, whether negatively or positively, and through which I attempt to showcase my vision regarding the risk involved in being limited by this framework, formed due to the recognition by narrators, historians and jurists that the function of texts and narratives can fall short of being neutral; they might select whatever meets and serves their standpoints or the authorities' standpoints, which eventually led to the creation of a different image. As a consequence, any critique, questioning of, or attempt to comprehend some of those writings made one open to skepticism and censure.

6   In a future project I plan to compile a comprehensive, annotated bibliography of modern Western and Arabic scholarship on the Umayyads with classification of the studies.

It is undeniable that the Umayyad state, founded in 41 AH/661 CE by Muʿāwiya b. Abī Sufyān (41–60 AH/661–680 CE), continued for the entirety of its sovereignty, which lasted approximately 90 years, to face challenges and conflicts, and failed to stand up to them until it eventually fell with the death of Marwān b. Muḥammad, the last of the Umayyad caliphs, in 132 AH/750 CE. It should be noted that not much historiographical literature can be dated to the Umayyad period, especially in comparison with the later Abbasid era.

Since the earliest moments of the clash or the underlying conflict between the power-holders in Iraq and Bilād al-Shām (the Levant), ʿAlī and Muʿāwiya, the slander campaigns by their respective opponents on the one hand and the refutations of the attacks by their advocates on the other have been a lingering feature in Islamic historical writing.[7] Going beyond the primary sources, it will be noted that contemporary historical writings are also partially polarized to a great extent, in terms of their own fixation, reading, and controlled historical discourse, and by the pressure of a "for-or-against" paradigm, often driven by sectarian or political considerations.

Before considering recent scholarship that falls within the "for or against" paradigm, we will look with interest at some of the works of what I refer to as the "systematic" or "interpretative"[8] type. The systematic/interpretative studies include the earliest pioneering modern Arabic studies on the Umayyad period. There is necessarily some overlap between these works and those of the "for-or-against" paradigm, however, the general context of the systematic/ interpretative paradigm remains consistent in its pursuit of a more modern and comprehensive understanding of Umayyad history, even though some of this literature retains features of conflict or bias.[9]

Out of this early historiographical literature, some authors stand out, like Muḥammad al-Khudarī, a lecturer in Islamic History at the Egyptian University,[10] with his two-volume book *Lectures on the History of the Islamic Nations* [*Muḥāḍarāt fī tārīkh al-Umam al-Islāmiyya*], which was published in 1916. The significance of al-Khudarī's writings lies in the fact they belong

---

7   From the first half of the first century AH to the present day.

8   Meaning that these authors did not merely compile the narratives from the medieval sources but also attempted to interpret them.

9   In general, these writings cannot be separated or categorized under a particular category or pattern. Many of them intersect with the studies of the "for or against" paradigm, being supportive in certain incidents and events and opposed in others. This makes it difficult to classify them in a single pattern.

10   He also was an inspector in the Egyptian ministry of education. In his *Muḥāḍarāt fī Tārīkh al-Umam al-Islāmīya*, which appeared in two volumes in lecture form, he broadly examined the Umayyad state, the basis for its inception, the conquests it undertook, and its caliphs.

to an early type of scholarly literature that may be categorized as being flexible enough to enable various readings of texts and accounts, whereby minor details were composed with an orientation that neither promotes clashes and conflict (with an opponent), nor enunciates contradiction or rupture. Instead, al-Khudarī's lectures were, for his successors, an example of how to keep in check the trends aiming at deepening the schism and divergence in the controversial issues of Islamic history.

Zakariyyā al-Nuṣūlī's *The Umayyad State in Syria* [*Al-Dawla al-Umawiyya fī al-Shām*], published in 1926, also presents extensive information on the history of the Umayyad state, including its onset, conquests, civilization, its society, and finally its fall. Rafīq al-Mahāynī's work on medieval Islamic history, published in 1947, is likewise noteworthy.[11] Even though what is included in this book is a trifling and simplified overview of the Umayyad state, it is important to note that it was one of the earliest studies that made extensive use of the primary sources. Such an attitude is also represented in the writings of Ismāʿīl al-Rāwī, who published his *Iraq during the Umayyad Period* [*Al-ʿIrāq fī al-ʿAṣr al-Umawī*] in 1959. Al-Rāwī differed from the others in that he provided an acceptable historical background despite his attempts to diverge in favor of the analytical and interpretive approach. In addition, though his work was specifically linked to Iraq, al-Rāwī maintained the historical paradigm as a referential point of departure relating to his arguments. Sayyida Ismāʿīl Kāshif, a famous professor of medieval and Islamic history at ʿAyn Shams University in Cairo, wrote important studies on the caliph Al-Walīd b. ʿAbd al-Malik (86/705–96/715) and the Umayyad governor of Egypt ʿAbd al-Azīz b. Marwān (d. 86/705) in the 1960s. Likewise, Diyāʾ al-Dīn al-Rayyis wrote a monograph about the caliph ʿAbd al-Malik (65/685–86/705) that was published in 1969 [*ʿAbd al-Malik b. Marwān wa al-Dawla al-Umawiyya*]. This book provides an in-depth view of the Umayyad state in ʿAbd al-Malik's time, though it is influenced by the author's pronounced nationalist bias.

Later, other publications appeared, like Nabīh ʿĀqil's *The Umayyad Caliphate* [*Khilāfat Banī Umayya*] in 1972, Yūsuf al-ʿIsh's *The Umayyad State and the Factors that Preceded and Paved the Way for It* [*Al-Dawla al-Umawiyya wa al-Aḥdāth allatī Sabaqathā wa Mahhadat lahā*], as well as *The Umayyad Empire in the East* [*Al-Dawla al-Umawiyya fī al-Sharq*] by Muhammad al-Tayyib al-Najjār, who is considered to be one of the pioneering figures in modern scholarship on Islamic history. Both Al-ʿIsh and Al-Najjār developed a sophisticated understanding of what had been previously achieved in terms of an acceptable reading in referentiality and historical vision vis-à-vis the Umayyads and their state

---

11   Al-Mahāynī, *Tārīkh*.

(although Al-ʿIsh adopted the Arabist factor as a paradigm for the Umayyad state and its historiography).

There are other studies that deserve mention here, such as ʿAbbās Maḥmūd al-ʿAqqād's *Muʿāwiya b. Abī Sufyān*, published in 1966.[12] This book applies the approach of analytical foundationalism to the figure of Muʿāwiya, especially in terms of social empirical standards and individual experience. This approach has thrived in subsequent Arabic historiographical writing. Although al-ʿAqqād was willing to reference the viewpoints of contemporary advocates and opponents, he has been criticized for not including a comprehensive bibliography of the primary sources that he used. We should also mention here ʿUmar Abu al-Naṣr's study on the fall of the Umayyad state [*Al-Ayyām al-Akhīra li al-Dawla al-Umawiyya*] in 1962,[13] and the important taxonomical studies of Husayn ʿAṭwān, such as his book on the Umayyads and the concept of the caliphate [*Al-Umawiyyūn wa al-Khilāfa*],[14] in which he focuses on examining the cognitive and intellectual factors of what the caliphate represented as an institution during the Umayyad period.

Other studies followed the same trend, such as ʿAbd al-Halīm ʿUways' *The Umayyads between External Attacks and Internal Decline* [*Banū Umayya bayna al-Ḍarabāt al-Khārijiyya wa al-Inhiyār al-Dākhilī*], Ibrāhīm Aḥmad Al-ʿAdawī's *The Resistance to the Umayyad State and its Message* [*Al-Dawla al-Umawiyya: Muqāwamatuhā wa Risālatuhā*], Ḥusayn al-Ḥajj Ḥasan's *The Civilization of the Arabs in the Umayyad Period* [*Haḍārat al-ʿArab fī al-ʿAṣr al-Umawī*], Aḥmad Shalabī's section on the Umayyads in his encyclopedia of Islamic history [*Mawsūʿat al-Tārīkh al-Islāmī wa al-Ḥaḍāra al-Islāmiyya: Al-Dawla al-Umawiyya*], published in 1970 and others.[15] The studies of Suhayl Zakkār along with Ibrāhīm Bayḍūn's *Political History of the Arabs from the Birth of Islam until the Fall of Baghdad* [*Tārīkh al-ʿArab al-Siyāsī min Fajr al-Islām ḥattā Suqūṭ Baghdād*], Muḥammad Suhayl Ṭaqqūsh's *History of the Umayyad State* [*Tārīkh al-Dawla al-Umawiyya*], and Ḥusayn Muʾnis' edition of al-Maqrīzī's *The Conflict and Enmity between the Umayyads and the Hashimites* [*Al-Nizāʿ wa al-Takhāṣum fī mā bayna Banī Umayya wa Banī Hāshim*], also fall into the interpretive survey literature category that has attempted to broadly assimilate the history of the Umayyad period and its multifarious factors.[16]

---

12   Al-ʿAqqād, *Muʿāwiya*.

13   Abū al-Naṣr, *Al-Ayyām*. See also his book *ʿAbd al-Malik b. Marwān*.

14   ʿAṭwān, *Al-Umawiyyūn*. See also his book *Al-Walīd b. Yazīd*.

15   ʿUways, *Banū Umayya*; Al-ʿAdawī, *Al-Dawla*; Ḥasan, *Ḥaḍāra*; Shalabī, *Mawsūʿa*.

16   Bayḍūn, *Tārīkh*; Ṭaqqūsh, *Tārīkh*; Al-Maqrīzī, *Al-Nizāʿ*. Ṭaqqush's books show the influence of Arab nationalist thought.

We may add to the above works Muḥammad Māhir Hammāda's *Political Documents from the Umayyad Period* [*Al-Wathāʾiq al-Siyāsiyya al-ʿĀʾida li al-ʿAṣr al-Umawī*] published in 1985, Maḥmūd Shākir's volume on the Umayyad period within his general history of Islam [*Al-Tārīkh al-Islāmī: Al-ʿAhd al-Umawī*], and ʿAbd al-Shāfiʿ Muḥammad ʿAbd al-Laṭīf's *The Islamic World in the Umayyad Period* [*Al-ʿĀlam al-Islāmī fī al-ʿAṣr al-Umawī*].[17] Although some of these works, such as those of Maḥmūd Shākir, were written from a conservative point of view, in general, these writings are distinguished by being reciprocally supportive as well as being well-constructed and precise.

In his *Sword and Politics in Islam: the Conflict between Prophetic Islam and Umayyad Islam* [*Al-Sayf wa al-Siyāsa fī al-Islām: Al-Ṣirāʿ bayna al-Islām al-Nabawī wa al-Islām al-Umawī*], Ṣāliḥ al-Wardānī likewise provides a significant systematic and interpretive paradigm, which seeks to mix the political and the historical, yet without sacrificing the text's objectivity and vitality.[18] Such an approach is also attempted by ʿAbd al-ʿAzīz al-Thaʿālibī in his *The Fall of the Umayyad Empire and Rise of the Abbasid Empire* [*Suqūṭ al-Dawla al-Umawiyya wa Qiyām al-Dawla al-ʿAbbāsiyya*], in which he attempts to center stage the classical or traditional heritage vis-à-vis the Umayyad-Abbasid conflict, meanwhile using it in new contexts.[19]

We may look with special interest at Rafīq al-ʿAẓm's (d. 1925) viewpoints in his *Famous Personalities of Islam in War and Politics* [*Ashhar Mashāhīr al-Islām fī al-Ḥurūb wa al-Siyāsa*].[20] This book, published in 1909, is one of the earliest modern Arabic historical studies. In it al-ʿAzm portrayed in painstaking detail the reign of Muʿāwiya, the iconic founder of the Umayyad state. Most of the above-mentioned studies on the Umayyads showcase a systematic and interpretative tendency with high observational dynamics, broadened or narrowed in line with the breadth or narrowness of the events. Some of these studies included bibliographical sections, which were a new and modern feature that appeared at this time not only in literature on the Umayyads, but also in studies on Arab and Islamic culture as a whole.

Also of great interest is the earliest historical-fictional literature on the Umayyads, that is the works written by Jurjī Zaydān[21] as a series of historical novels, all of which deal with the stages of Islamic history from its inception until the modern era. This series included *Ghādat Karbalāʾ*, which appeared in

---

17   Ḥammāda, *Al-Wathāʾiq*; Shākir, *Al-Tārīkh*; ʿAbd al-Laṭīf, *Al-ʿĀlam*.

18   Al-Wardānī, *Al-Sayf*.

19   Al-Thaʿālibī, *Suqūṭ*.

20   Al-ʿAẓm, *Ashshar*.

21   Born in Beirut in 1861, and died in 1914.

1901, *al-Ḥajjāj b. Yūsuf,* published in 1902, *Fatḥ al-Andalus,* published in 1904, and finally *Abū Muslim al-Khurāsānī,* published in 1905. This latter novel is particularly significant, despite the fact that it portrays an Abbasid figure. Its importance lies not only in the events related to this character, but also in its showcasing of the events that contributed to the fall of the Umayyad state out of the ruins of which the Abbasid state arose, albeit under the guise of a fictional textual background that is intertwined with the historical.

These works, and others that followed the same pattern, stood for the essence of the ideas that foregrounded their own understandings of the nature of the Umayyad state, with its allegiances, influences, and reciprocal variables, in an (often acceptable) objectivity, even though they still follow traditional patterns of historical writing in many respects. This literature is noteworthy for not depending upon the influence of the Western schools, especially upon those trends in orientalist scholarship which were quite explicit regarding their non-neutrality in their discussion of the history of the Islamic state in general, and the Umayyad state in particular.

4 The Western School and Its Impact on the Trends in Arabic Umayyad Studies

Proximity to the Western school has been subject of heated debate. At one stage, such proximity, as a factor in dealing with the Western school and the literature produced by it, especially what was written about the Umayyads in their general approaches, played a role in framing the modernist patterns in Arabic historiographical scholarship and casting them in their current shape. Here my primary focus is not the Western historical scholarship on the Umayyads and its related tendencies. Rather, what is important is to focus on the influence of Western scholarship on modern Arab scholarship on Islamic history in general and on the Umayyads in particular. Those Arab readings of Western orientalist scholarship have centered on two focal points, regardless of the various details.

The first focal point is represented by doubt and its related tools of uncertainty and suspicion. This category is shaped by the nature of its own writings, with all its outlines and sub-details, represented by a group of researchers and scholars with a specific referentiality,[22] in particular the writing model of the sectarian Sunnī trend and those currents adopting its method.[23] The second

---

22 Mostly Sunnī, Salafist or fundamentalist.
23 Literature published in Saudi Arabia largely tends to follow this approach.

focal point is characterized by openness and positivity. The proponents of this trend regard proximity to the ideas of Western Scholarship as one necessary stage in the development of Arabic Islamic scholarship in general. One of the first modern Arabic works on early Islamic history which engaged Western scholarship and ideas was the Egyptian thinker Ṭāhā Husayn's (d. 1973) famous study on the first Islamic Civil War entitled *The Great Civil War* [*Al-Fitna al-Kubrā*]. This book embodies a significant stage in the development of Islamic historical writing in general. In his work Ḥusayn investigated the most momentous conflict in Islamic history and raised a number of issues and problematics and liberated himself from the authority of many traditional texts in favor of a critical historiographical approach.

Literature on the Umayyads follows this general framework. It proceeded from research projects that worked on introducing the Umayyads in a wider historical context, connected with the context of the map of the continuum of interactions and relations and the human factor within this continuum.[24] In the context of this framework or trend, the works of some prominent modern Arab historians such as Hichem Djaït [Hishām Ja'ayṭ], Maḥmūd Ismā'īl 'Abd al-Rāziq, Riḍwān al-Sayyid, 'Abdallāh al-'Arawī, and more recently 'Abd al-'Azīz al-Hallābī,[25] as well as other famous intellectuals who were not strictly-speaking historians, such as the Iraqi sociologist 'Alī al-Wardī (d. 1995), and the North African philosophers Muḥammad 'Ābid al-Jābirī (d. 2010) and Muḥammad Arkūn (d. 2010) are characterized by the tendency to employ a critical methodology and by their attempts to fill in the established gaps in a mystified history (one in which the concepts of myth, sanctity and the forbidden play a role). These scholars have exhibited an ability to access the unsaid in the texts, where, according to them, many of the accounts and narratives have lost their traditional function, and were subjected to verifiable, open debate and discussion.

In his *The Arab Political Mind* [*Al-'Aql al-Siyāsī al-'Arabī*], for example, al-Jābirī argues that social forces formed an alliance and upheaval that led to the fall of the Umayyads.[26] Arkūn argues in his *Critique of the Islamic Mind*

---

24   Although the majority of these writings are not exclusively dedicated to discussing the Umayyads and their state, they reflect a general framework and a modernist model for writing about them.

25   Although in a number of his writings al-Hallābī was influenced by the same prevalent tendency in Saudi Arabia, that is, the Salafist tendency, especially with regard to the Shī'ī movement writings and the attempt to critique any of its historical fallacies or errors, he should be given credit for coming up with new interpretations and deeply discussing the unsaid in other issues.

26   Al-Jābirī addressed what he labelled the consecration of the state of preordination and renunciation, and termed this bond "the historical block;" see Al-Jābirī, *Al-'Aql*.

[*Naqd al-'Aql al-Islāmī*] that religion was subjected to politics through the experience of the Umayyads, while al-Hallābī refuses to accept the accounts attributed to the controversial narrator of early Islamic traditions 'Abdallāh b. Saba'.[27]

In these writings, an "abrupt" attitude is noted, in one way or another, in retreating away from the power (or authority) of the text, to retreat away from the power of the symbolic, the sacred, and the ideal, by means of showing contradiction, confusion, detecting bias, and distancing oneself from justification and apology. Such a modernist tendency of writing about the Umayyads can be viewed as a radical shift from the dominance of the ideological over the cognitive. Nonetheless, an in-depth look at the modernist works shows that they continued, with a few exceptions, to reproduce and rehabilitate the conflict between the advocates and the opponents, albeit to a less acute degree. Therefore, in such studies Umayyad history continued to be an offshoot of the ideological struggle latent in the history of the Islamic state.

After reviewing some of the most outstanding tendencies that contributed to and influenced the growth of modern Arabic historical scholarship on the early Islamic period, we will now focus on examining the dominant contemporary patterns in modern Arabic scholarship on the Umayyads. These represent a significant shift in the treatment of Umayyad history in general, particularly in light of the aforementioned trends.

5 The Umayyads and the Formation of Their Image in Arabist or Arab Nationalist Literature

The Umayyads have been an attractive subject to the scholars that adopted the Arab nationalist tendency and who largely oriented history's compass towards them. According to this group of historians and writers, the Umayyad represented the most effective form of the Arabist state. Indeed, many Arab nationalist writers celebrated what they regarded as Umayyad *realpolitik* and secularism.

Riḍwān al-Sayyid has argued that in the past six decades there had been a strong call to rewrite Arab history,[28] which specifically highlighted the need to use modern methodology and to be independent from Orientalist writings. Yet this could not be fulfilled, as historical writing in Bilād al-Shām, Iraq and Egypt developed trends and factors that were consistent with the societal

---

27 A similar approach was taken by Murtaḍā al-'Askarī in his book *'Abd Allāh b. Saba' wa Asāṭīr Ukhrā*, which was published in 1972.

28 Al-Sayyid, *Kitābat*.

discourse in those countries, subsequent to Arab nationalism becoming the first mobilizing political force of the masses.

With the dominance of the Arabist tendency, whose ideological basis was framed by a number of its early founders like the Syrian intellectuals ʿAbd al-Raḥmān al-Kawākibī (d. 1902), Sāṭiʿ al-Ḥuṣrī (d. 1968), Michel ʿAflaq (d. 1989), Qusṭanṭīn Zurayq (d. 2000) and others, Arab historians of the medieval Islamic period also began to direct the field of historical studies towards the same Arabist approach, given that it became necessary to look for historical roots to support and institutionalize this approach. Indeed, this enterprise or trend was embraced by a myriad of historians and writers, with Umayyad history becoming a rich ground for the application of this approach. The Iraqi historiographical school in particular, which has acted as the gateway between Shīʿī Iran and the Sunnī Arab countries, is one of the significant examples of this historiographical trend. Iraq, an Islamic country that was at times a hub of the Islamic conquests, a center of opposition to the Umayyads and later a haven for the Abbasid state, a land of great sectarian and cultural diversity, became a widely used example of the meaning of historical writing geared towards consecrating the concepts of nationalism and Arabism, and the transformation of these concepts into an ideological doctrine which colored the image of the Umayyads in the works of nationalist historians. It is interesting that an in-depth look at the origins of this trend, which treated the Umayyads as an example of an "Arab state", uncovers a great disparity in the inability to find a unified memory underlying the studies produced by this school, as well as the absence of agreement on the broad outlines of Umayyad history. This can be seen[29] in a wide array of studies produced by scholars of the Arabist tendency[30] which we will look at later. It should be noted that changes in these writings reflected changes in contemporary political and social conditions (as in pre-Saddam and post-Saddam Iraq, for example).

The dynamics of these writings also indicate that the Umayyad state has been considered an integral part of historical heritage, burdened with the nature of sectarian and societal conflict as signified by its main protagonists (i.e. Arab and non-Arab). Subsequently, this conflict led some historians to

---

29   Naturally there are exceptions to this approach, but generally, the field has been dominated by ideological, sectarian, and partisan tendencies.

30   Until the fall of the Baathist regime. A glance at the literature on the Umayyads from the 1920s until the end of the twentieth century reveals that the Shīʿī vision, for example, was not allowed to be extensively articulated. Later, with the fall of the Baathist regime at the beginning of the current century, the situation changed. New ideas, trends and visions have come into play, commensurate with the societal, economic and political developments that are taking place in Iraq.

consolidate the Arabist tendency for the benefit of the nationalist perspective. This tendency was invoked by historians as a counterpoint to the Persian/Shīʿī tide.[31]

A look at one of the most significant historians of the Arabist trend, namely, ʿAbd al-ʿAzīz al-Dūrī (d. 2010), whose works represent a qualitative shift in the contemporary Arab historical consciousness and its attitudes, confirms that the Umayyads, out of all of the Islamic dynasties, were the most popular model for followers of this trend. With his proficiency in turning the wheel of historical scholarship towards defending faith, jihad, Arabism, nationalism, etc., al-Dūrī signified a key cornerstone in the nature of this thought. We can see this clearly in al-Dūrī's most famous studies. Crammed with significant data and details, this substantial body of historical scholarship has largely been restricted to and geared towards expressing the nationalist trend. For example, in his *Introduction to the Formative Period of Islam* [*Muqaddima fī Tārīkh Ṣadr al-Islām*], considered to be a principal reference on the formative period of Islamic history which presents an in-depth portrait of early Islamic history while taking into account broad trends and attitudes,[32] we notice how al-Dūrī[33] hastens to disclose his own perceptions regarding the Umayyads when he argues: "The Arabs were portrayed in the Umayyad age as Bedouins [*Aʿrāb*], whereas the foundations of Arab civilization and culture were set up in that period … there was an attempt to belittle their conquests in the East, albeit they represent the second major wave of Arab expansion … It is evident that the majority of scholars in the Umayyad age were Arabs."[34] Here he asserts that the Umayyads laid the foundations of Arab sovereignty and statehood as the general circumstances for such rule were favorable. He also maintains that the Umayyad state was a natural phenomenon in the general development of history. Therefore, and according to this recurrent pattern in al-Dūrī's writings, (which generally depart from a search for the historical roots of Arab nationalism), history was the ideal theory as a point of departure; any national thought cannot thrive away from history and its augmentations. Al-Dūrī's attempt to

---

31 Upon which its intellectual mechanisms and its sectarian referentiality are based. In the face of this, this trend envisioned the Umayyads in particular, as an ideal historical model. However, the problem was that the Arabist, nationalist ideology whereby some of those writings were produced, led to a chauvinistic attitude towards certain perceptions and mobilization of the historical memory towards those perceptions. Moreover, such an ideological literature, which believes only in the ideology that produced it, regarded many of the other historical texts as hostile and even as worthless.

32 Al-Dūrī, *Muqaddima*.

33 Al-Dūrī, *Muqaddima*, 22.

34 Al-Dūrī, *Muqaddima*, 70.

re-introduce the experience of the victorious, prevailing, and conquering Arab element, represented in the Umayyad state's dominion and its expansive conquests, was marked by restricting this aspect within the nature of the relationship between Arabism and Islam. Consequently, other historians were likewise driven to work in keeping with this trend or approach. Umayyad history, it may be argued, could have absorbed the very idiosyncrasy of its own incidents in many events, yet according to the rationale of the Arabists themselves, al-Dūrī among them, Umayyad history fell short of reducing the history of Islam in its entirety within it.

We may ask whether Umayyad history, written with an "Arabist" tendency, was the same history that al-Dūrī referred to when he exclaimed: "Do we want a history that drags [us] back and cripples [our] mobility, or do we want one as a springboard to reach a better future?" And we may also ask whether this contradicts al-Dūrī's own interest in historical phenomena within the history of Islam, such as populism, to which he devoted much of his effort, and nationalism, to which he was dedicated.

In this same vein, Ṣāliḥ Aḥmad al-ʿAlī (d. 2003),[35] another prominent Iraqi historian of the medieval period who was engrossed in the idea of history and the reading of its roots, characteristics and connotations, also tried to highlight the contribution of the Arabs to the general cultural and intellectual accomplishments of human civilization. Al-ʿAlī pursued the same road taken by al-Dūrī in writing about the Umayyads. His book *ʿUmar b. ʿAbd al-ʿAzīz: Khāmis al-Khulafāʾ al-Rāshidīn* (on the fifth Umayyad caliph ʿUmar b. ʿAbd al-ʿAzīz) presents a view connected with the contemporary process of sanctification of the history of some of the iconic figures of early Islamic history.[36] Though he provided an effective historical portrayal of the character of the caliph, he could not get away from the grips of the Arabist and nationalist historical outlook in his discussion and general view of Umayyad history. In his work Umayyad history is neither a history of Muslim societies, a history of Islamic states, nor a corrective vision of a human reality teeming with factors, possibilities and contradictions, inasmuch as it is a history of Islam itself, perceived through the mirror of the heroic and iconic religious figures who lived during the Umayyad age.

Under the same impact of the ideologies of nationalism and Arabism and their ramifications lies *The Umayyad State and the Events which Preceded it and Paved the Way for it beginning from the Murder of ʿUthmān* [*Al-Dawla al-Umawiyya wa al-Aḥdāth allatī Sabaqathā wa Mahhadat lahā Ibtidāʾan min*

---

35   For more information on him see Maṭbaʿī, *Al-Muʾarrikh*.
36   Al-ʿAlī, *ʿUmar b. ʿAbd al-ʿAzīz*.

Fitnat ʿUthman] by the Syrian-Lebanese historian Yūsuf al-ʿIsh (d. 1967), who was one of the prominent historians of the Levantine school.[37] This book is by and large illustrative of the type of historical studies which emanated from the Arabist perspective in its view of the Umayyad period. Similar is *The Political Factions from the Emergence of Islam until the Fall of the Umayyad State* [*Al-Hizbiyya al-Siyāsiyya mundhu Qiyām al-Islām ḥattā Suqūṭ al-Dawla al-Umawiyya*] by Riyāḍ ʿĪsā, a work on the history of the political factions in Islam from its beginning until the end of the Umayyad period.[38] This book, despite its equanimity, is in the end not dissimilar to those studies whose point of departure was the promotion of the issues and problematics of Arab nationalism through the history of the Umayyad state. A similar approach was taken by Ḍiyāʾ al-Dīn al-Rayyis in his book *ʿAbd al-Malik b. Marwān Muwaḥḥid al-Dawla al-ʿArabiyya: Ḥayātuhu wa ʿAṣruhu*,[39] considered one of the earliest modern works dealing with the Umayyad caliph ʿAbd al-Malik b. Marwān. We can discern from the book's first pages the author's intention of portraying this iconic figure, not only as one of the most celebrated Umayyad caliphs, but as the unifier of the Arab state. This can be seen through his practice of ascribing meanings to texts and narratives far beyond what could reasonably be ascribed to them, in order to support his ideological tendency.

Finally, we should mention Suhayl Taqqūsh's history of the Umayyad state [*Tārīkh al-Dawla al-Umawiyya*].[40] Despite Taqqūsh's assertion that his book discusses the state's political aspect and that it was written with objectivity and impartiality, it is in fact strongly influenced by the Arabist, nationalist tendency. The author argues that the Umayyad state "maintained, despite its negative aspects, a gleaming image in the mind of the Arabs and a bright and pride-filled chapter in their history. Yet, anti-Umayyad ideas circulated and found those detractors who would disseminate them."[41]

6 Umayyad Studies and Sectarianism (the Doctrinal Conflict)

The cognitive and cultural production of any region, nation or people is not cut off from society and its prevailing circumstances. To a large extent, historians are governed by their environment and by the prevailing views of their time,

---

37 Al-ʿIsh, *Al-Dawla al-Umawiyya*.

38 ʿĪsā, *Al-Ḥizbiyya*.

39 Al-Rayyis, *ʿAbd al-Malik*.

40 Ṭaqqūsh, *Tārīkh*.

41 Ṭaqqūsh, *Tārīkh*, 8.

especially the political, social and sectarian views. It is fair to say that contemporary tendencies in scholarship on the Umayyad period have been subject to, and polarized by, sectarian conflict. As successive defeats saw the ebb of the Arabist tide and the decline of the ideas supporting it, a new trend of historical writing, i.e. the doctrinal and sectarian tendency, emerged. It is this trend that adopted and favored doctrinally and ideologically oriented writings over other trends or approaches. It can be seen as a sort of counterattack against the nationalist idea, whereby historical scholarship on the Umayyads seems to take a new route, namely, the route of religious reverence and glorification.

By examining some contemporary studies on the Umayyad state, we can see how this sectarian tendency, and the Sunnī–Shīʿī conflict, in particular, became the arena in which doubt and skepticism grew and were nourished by the two parties in question.[42] This is evident also in the wide and extensive circulation of studies on the Umayyad period. Some works[43] were discreet in their treatment of the Sunnī–Shīʿī conflict that took place during the Umayyad age and thus discuss it in a restrained, critical fashion. Harsh accusations, even those which have placed blame on specific events, did not infiltrate such studies and books. Instead, they demonstrated scientific rigor and did not slip over the slope of objectivity. This may indicate how intellectual and sectarian conflicts can be correlated with the nature of current politics. Of course any discussion of the historical repercussions and contexts of the Umayyad period comes subtly into contact with the sectarian conflict through the context of the historical narratives pertaining to the Umayyad state and its iconic figures. Some of the opposing scholarship also used the same contexts of the historical narratives of the Umayyad state and utilized its iconic figures from whom a core foundation was formed, which colored many of those writings within the context of the sectarian perceptions of the disagreed-with other. Consequently, the production of such scholarship has become a part of the context of the reciprocal historical perceptions pertaining to each party of the conflict.[44]

---

42   To be fair, the conflict between Islamic denominations and sects was not only exclusive to Sunnīs and Shīʿīs; the dispute is not therefore one created by the religious text and/or its interpretations. There are auxiliary factors like the writings themselves, which invoke those disagreements and which create a site of oppression and conflict. These writings are fundamentally influenced by a problematic factor rather than a historical one, and perceive of the contexts associated with religion and its interpretations as their ultimate goal. The authors' intellectual dispositions, social roots and political stations are not excluded here.

43   For example, in Iraq from the time of the monarchy through the revolutionary governments to the Saddam Hussein period.

44   This reality changed completely in the post-Saddam Hussein era and with the fall of the Baath Party when sectarian tendencies were expressed much more openly and directly.

7 The Shīʿī Tendency

We can see this trend by looking at a number of academic journals and periodicals in some of the Iraqi universities such as *Dirāsāt Islāmiyya Muʿāṣira* (Contemporary Islamic Studies) published by the University of Karbala. Here we find a literature unburdened of the conditions of the "politicized" past on the one hand, and on the other hand we find an increase in the accusatory and selective tendencies as well as the intensified and widespread sense of historical oppression (*maẓlūmiyya*) related to the history of *Ahl al-Bayt* (The Family of the Prophet). To better understand this trend, it is necessary to examine some of the issues of this journal and the articles published within them.[45] A study on the revenge inflicted by some of the Umayyad rulers against their foes and opponents,[46] for example, seeks to demonstrate that the Umayyad state applied the famous principle "the end justifies the means", that the Umayyads committed the most abhorrent forms of oppression and crimes prohibited by the Islamic faith and against all principles and well-established moral values, that the Umayyads established an hereditary regime confined to the Umayyad household only, and that they showed fierce and unremitting hostility toward the *Ahl al-Bayt*.

It appears here that sectarian viewpoints which had previously been restricted in historical scholarship for political reasons during the years of Baathist rule suddenly became widespread with its fall. Thus we find a great increase in sectarian and doctrinal historical debates and clashes along with anti-rational readings of the historical sources which go as far as to deny some incidents, negate others, or question the historically established perceptions vis-à-vis some events.

In recent years treatments of Umayyad history from sectarian religious perspectives like the above-mentioned example have proliferated in the journals, periodicals and publishing houses for no acceptable reason save for the regime or the authorities' acceptance of the ideologization and sectarianization of the nature of historical writing. Not only have the iconic religious, military, and political figures of the Umayyad period been used in the new sectarian historiography, even the literary figures of the period have been dragged

---

45 *Dirasat Islamiya Muʾasira* is a peer-reviewed academic journal issued by the Faculty of Islamic Sciences at Karbala University, which publishes academic articles in the fields of Qurʾānic studies and Arabic language and literature in view of scientific promotion. It commissions acclaimed experts in Iraq to review research submitted for publication. Research is published by the Karbala University Press. The first volume was published in 2010.

46 Al-Ḥilfī, Khalaf, and ʿUmrān, Thaʾr.

into the doctrinal debates. A study on the Umayyad poet Al-Kumayt al-Asadī ["Mu'ashshirāt al-ḥukm al-Umawī wa al-ʿAlawī fī *Hāshimīyāt* Kumayt al-Asadī,"] published in post-Saddam Iraq, uses its treatment of the poet to show that Umayyad rule was based on vagaries, violence, injustice, and oppression of the people, and that al-Asadī rejected this.[47] It also argues that the Umayyads used religion merely as an instrument to advance their tyrannical goals. In contrast, ʿAlī b. Abī Ṭālib is presented as a sensible, courageous man, who cared for the people's welfare, defended the Islamic community and ran the Islamic system based on the Prophetic tradition and the law.

In the same vein is an article entitled "The effect of the Revolution of Ḥusayn on the Pillars of the Umayyad State" ["Athar Thawrat al-Imam al-Ḥusayn fī Arkān al-Dawla al-Umawiyya: Al-Khalīfa al-Umawī al-Thālith Muʿāwiyah b. Yazīd b. Muʿāwiya ka Namūdhaj"].[48] It argues that Ḥusayn's revolution was like a torch that lit the dark corners of the earth, to eradicate from society the underlying injustice instilled by tyrants and oppressors. This approach can be seen in other articles from the journal in question such as "The military and political dimensions of Ḥusayn's Revolt and the Reasons for the Choice of Kufa as its Launching-Point" ["Al-Thawra al-Ḥusayniyya: Dirāsa fī Abʿādihā al-Siyāsiyya wa al-ʿAskariyya wa Asbāb Ikhtiyār al-Kūfa Munṭalaqan li al-Taḥarruk wa Dalālāt al-Rasāʾil al-Kūfiyya li al-Imām al-Ḥusayn"], "The Social Dimensions of Ḥusayn's Uprising" ["Al-Buʿd al-Ijtimāʿī li Nahḍat al-Imām al-Ḥusayn"], and "Manifestations of Sympathy for the Imams of the Ahl al-Bayt" ["Maẓāhir al-ʿĀṭifa ʿan Aʾimmat Ahl al-Bayt ʿalayhim al-Salām ʿalā Istishhād al-Imām al-Ḥusayn ʿalayhi al-Salām: Dirāsa Tārīkhiyya."]49

Such articles characterize the Umayyad age as one of injustice, tyranny and impiety. At the same time, they represent Shīʿī symbols (especially ʿAlī and Ḥusayn) as figures embodying future victory, which is interpreted as the triumph of Islam and the rise of the Islamic status quo from deviation to integrity and from tyranny to justice.

In very serious terms infused with ideas of oppression, some studies in the same journal have attributed the Islamic world's deteriorating conditions to the hegemony of the tyrannical Umayyad regime. It is asserted that self-indulgence, subornment, suppression of uprisings, oppression of non-Arab Muslims, persecution and displacement of those with different political doctrines, emasculation of the humanitarian sense, and the eradication of any

---

47   Āʾīnawand and Naṣīḥat, Muʾashshirāt.
48   Al-Suwaytī, Athar.
49   Dakhīl, Al-Thawra; Shahid, Al-Buʿd; ʿAbd al-Razzāq, ʿAbbūd, and ʿAṭiyya Maẓāhir.

nuance for freedom through false religious anesthesia were the causes of the fall of the Umayyads and their state.

Such, then, are the accusations, critique, denunciation, denigration and skepticism directed towards the Umayyads and their image in this quite alarming historiographical tendency. Even more alarming is the fact that such biased and partisan studies appear in peer-reviewed academic journals that are supposed to show impartiality, reasoning and objectivity.

8 The Sunnī Trend

The scholars who generally adopt anti-Shīʿī sectarian positions, often empathize with certain iconic historical figures from the early Islamic period,[50] or are reluctant to investigate or even allude to the deeper causes of the historical incidents related to them. In order to illustrate the Sunnī trend in sectarian historiographical discourse I will focus on Saudi Umayyad scholarship for a number of reasons, the most important of which is the conservative standpoint that colors such writings, especially concerning the conflicts that occurred among the Prophet's Companions (Ṣaḥāba) after the murder of the third caliph ʿUthmān in 35/656. In the works of the Saudi historians the major conflicts between the Prophetic Companions,[51] are often approached with caution and disconcert and expressed in an idiom that suggests impartiality.

Scholarship on the Umayyads from Saudi Arabia or from the Sunnī standpoint in general refrains from discussing the conflicts between the Prophetic Companions under the pretext of fairness and objectivity, but such studies often appear to be at odds with historical facts. Sometimes these works go even further by negating entire events, such as the denying the existence of some historically celebrated characters or certain well-verified incidents,[52] in addition to showing reticence regarding discussion of many of Muʿāwiya's policies.

A peculiar feature of Saudi scholarship on the Umayyads is that there is little discernible clash between the historical and the text, except when it comes to the iconic figures and the Prophetic Companions. It is in the latter cases where this discrepancy stands out, crystallized in the authors' positions vis-à-vis those events in which they clearly articulate the Sunnī standpoint. The "who-is-right-and-who-is-wrong" viewpoint, for example, remains significantly dominant

---

50   Affiliated to the Salafī or Sunnī trend in general.

51   For example the battles of al-Jamal, Ṣiffīn, and Karbala, as well as Ḥasan's concession to Muʿāwiya/Yazīd and al-Walīd and what was raised in that regard.

52   See Al-Hallābī, ʿAbd Allāh b. Saba'; Al-Ghāmiḍī, Suqūṭ.

throughout much of the Salafī and Sunnī-influenced historical scholarship, especially when it comes to discussing the murder of Ḥusayn, though these studies differ, in varying degrees, in deciding to what extent that blame should be placed in the events which ultimately led to the tragedy of his death at the Battle of Karbala (61/680). Curiously enough, this trend can be perceived as a kind of "pro-Umayyad" tendency, with many studies vehemently defending the Umayyads, especially with regards to Umayyad treatment of the opposition to their rule. Two examples of this trend are *The Caliphate of Muʿāwiya b. Abī Sufyān* [*Khilāfat Muʿāwiya b. Abī Sufyān*] by ʿUmar Sulaymān al-ʿUqaylī,[53] and ʿAbīr al-ʿAbbād's thesis entitled "An Objective, Neutral Study of the Umayyads" ["Dirāsa Taʾṣīliyyah Mawḍūʿiyya Muḥāyida li Inṣāf Banī Umayya"].[54] Such tendencies in modern scholarship have relied to a great degree upon primary source texts and narratives known to be biased against the Shīʿī point of view, a practice detrimental to objective, rational historical research.

To be fair, some in the new generation of Sunnī historians have applied a critical, modernist approach. Al-Hallābī, in particular, has been at the forefront of this trend in Saudi Arabia. Al-Hallābī and those who follow his approach represent a new attempt to reconcile historical reality, on the one hand, with mystification and sanctity, on the other, and to address the dialectic relationship between ideology and utopia in expression of the collective imaginary's sociology of Islamic history. For example, in al-Hallābī's "Shedding light on the Supposed Role of the Qurʾān Reciters in the Battle of Ṣiffīn" ["Ilqāʾ al-Ḍawʾ ʿalā al-Dawr al-Mazʿūm li al-Qurrāʾ fī Maʿrakat Ṣiffīn,"] he rejects the claim that the faction of the Qurʾān Reciters was responsible for the cessation of combat, the agreement to arbitrate the claims of both factions, and the decision to appoint Abū Mūsā al-Ashʿarī as ʿAlī's representative at the arbitration following the battle.[55] He also argues that these claims were nothing but "historical libels", invented and recorded in later historical sources for religious and political purposes.

An examination of the issues of the journal *Al-Adab wa al-ʿUlūm al-Insāniyya* (published by King ʿAbd al-ʿAzīz University) reveals more examples of the Sunnī approach to Umayyad history. An article on "The Political Conditions in Oman during the Umayyad Period" ["Al-Awḍāʾ al-Siyāsiyya li Bilād ʿUmān fī al-ʿAṣr al-Umawī (41–132 AH/661–750 CE)"][56] attempts to show that, despite

---

53   Al-ʿUqaylī, *Khilāfat Muʿāwiya*. The author addressed the controversial issues between ʿAlī and Muʿāwiya after Caliph ʿUthmān's demise, based on the political dispute, with some of the other aspects being discarded.

54   Al-ʿAbbād, Dirāsa.

55   Al-Hallābī, Ilqāʾ al-Ḍawʾ.

56   Al-Jumayḥ, Al-Awḍāʾ.

the violent attempts by the Umayyads to subjugate the region of Oman, the Umayyads were enlightened administrators. For example, the author states that "the resolute policy of 'Abd al-Malik and his son al-Walīd and their effective administrative command were also important."[57] A study on the reforms of the Umayyad governor Ziyād b. (Abīhi) 'Ubayd in Iraq (in the period between 45–53 AH/665–673 CE)[58] discusses the nature of Ziyād's efforts and reforms in Iraq with an account of their development and significance. In his *The Islamic World during the Umayyad Period: a Political Study* [*Al-'Ālam al-Islāmī fī al-'Aṣr al-Umawī (41–132 AH/661–750 CE): Dirāsah Siyāsiyya*],[59] 'Abd al-Laṭīf argues that the memory of the Umayyads was distorted by their opponents. He lists the factors that cause historians to discredit the Umayyads, whose rule, in his opinion, was the most exemplary and remarkable in the history of the Islamic dynasties. He also suggests that literature on the Umayyad age has showcased a hostile attitude based on the accounts of their detractors. As a result the history of the Umayyads and their caliphs became twisted, tainted by falsehoods, distortion, and deviation from historical facts.

It is evident that the sectarian Sunnī tendency in Umayyad studies presents an idealized image of the dynasty. It is based on certain ideological assumptions such as that the Umayyad state and its iconic figures must be safeguarded due to the aura of sacredness accorded them in the Islamic historical texts, especially those texts associated with the symbolic and the mystified aspects of these figures. This highly restrictive historical reading will certainly continue to embolden more identification between the historical and the ideological.

Within the same framework of scholarship of this tendency and approach in Saudi Arabia comes Ḥamdī Shāhīn's *The Maligned Umayyad State: A Study on the Accusations and the Responses to them for a Corrective Vision of Islamic History* [*Al-Dawla al-Umawiyya al-Muftarā 'alayhā: Dirāsat al-Shubuhāt wa al-Radd 'alayhā: Ru'ya Taṣḥīḥiyya li al-Tārīkh al-Islāmī (al-'aṣr al-Umawī)*].[60] In this work Shāhīn attempts to give the impression that the history of the Umayyad State was subject to much distortion, falsification, and slander. He claims that his study has rectified many of the misconceptions about the Umayyads, refuted the slanders made about them, and discussed the reasons for the distortion of Umayyad history. The same attitude is taken by Al-Sallābī in his *The Umayyad State: its Bloom and its Decline* [*Al-Dawla al-Umawiyya:*

---

57 Significant not only to Oman, but also to all regions of the Islamic state, p. 155.

58 Al-Mulhim, Iṣlāḥāt.

59 'Abd al-Laṭīf, *Al-'Ālam al-Islāmī*.

60 Shāhīn, *Al-Dawla*.

'Awāmil al-Izdihār wa Tadā'iyāt al-Inhiyār].[61] Al-Sallābī's point of departure is
the defense of the Umayyads and their iconic figures and the refutation of any
falsehoods related to them. This standpoint is also evident in a dissertation entitled "The Influence of Shī'ism on the Historical Narratives of the First Century
A.H." ["Athar al-Tashayyu' 'alā al-Riwāyāt al-Tārīkhiyya fī al-Qarn al-Awwal
al-Hijrī"].[62] The author of this dissertation likens some of the pro-Shī'ī narrators to priests who take their information from demons who eavesdrop on the
heavens and, not content with this, still mix their own lies into the accounts!
In his *Political History of the Arab Empire: the Age of the Umayyad Caliphates*
[*Al-Tārīkh al-Siyāsī li al-Dawla al-'Arabiyya: 'Aṣr al-Khulafā' al-Umawiyyīn*],[63]
Mājid 'Abd al-Mun'im argues that the Arab-Islamic conquests reached their
utmost range during the Umayyad period. Furthermore, this was the era in
which the empire attained its ultimate character through Arabization. The
Saudi historian 'Abīr al-'Abbād's doctoral thesis, entitled "An Objective, Neutral
Study of the Umayyads" [Dirāsa Ta'ṣīliyya Mawḍū'iyya Muḥāyada li Inṣāf Banī
Umayya], maintains that the Umayyad state has been defamed in history and
that this must be redressed.[64] The Egyptian historian Muhammad 'Amāra's
works also express the sectarian Sunnī tendency.[65] We can see, then, that
there exists a discourse amply devoted to this clash between the historical and
the religious, producing utopian and ideological perceptions – in the historical sense.

Influenced by the so-called "contemporary Sunnī standpoint" in its scope,
reading, and historical discourse, this literature cannot in fact be more than a
partisan pro-Umayyad point of view.[66] The presence of such apologetics in academic journals and periodicals raises the question of to what extent the

---

61   Al-Ṣallābī, *Al-Dawla*.

62   Walī, Athar.

63   'Abd al-Mun'im, *Al-Tārīkh al-Siyāsī*.

64   Al-'Abbād, Dirāsa.

65   An Egyptian historian who has published many books such as *'Umar b. 'Abd al-'Azīz: The
     Conscience of the Islamic Community and the Fifth Rightly-Guided Caliph* [*'Umar b. 'Abd
     al-'Azīz: Damīr al-Umma wa Khāmis al-Rāshidīn*] in 1985.

66   When it comes to the discussion of some events that represent a breakpoint base like
     the battles of al-Ḥarra (63/683), Ṣiffīn (37/651), and the murder of al-Ḥusayn (61/680),
     personalities like Mu'āwiya and Yazīd, and themes like the oppression of the Shī'a, this
     trend is manifestly palpable. When the standpoint regarding the martyrdom of al-Ḥusayn
     is discussed, we discern a negative view of al-Ḥusayn's rebellion against the caliph Yazīd
     coloring the Salafist historical reading or what stems out of this context. This Salafist
     reading often relies heavily on the interpretations of the Andalusī Mālikī jurist Abū Bakr
     b. al-'Arabī (d. 543/1148) whose work is characterized by a clear pro-Umayyad bias, espe-
     cially visible in his book *Al-'Awāṣim min al-Qawāṣim*.

contexts of the doctrinal and historical dimensions intersect in this scholarship. One cannot deal with any of these writings as if they represent the historical truth, upon which one may build without verification or in-depth investigation, even though some of these works quote extensively from extracts, texts and accounts in the primary sources. Use of these writings should be undertaken with caution; historical writings based on these sectarian tendencies will remain precarious and will not contribute to the discipline of history unless the distorting effect of their sectarian viewpoint is taken into account. Finally, there are undeniably more circumspect and methodical readings that follow the same course of the Sunnī/Shīʿī apologetic schools, but what is of interest here are the popular ones which influence the current historical discourse vis-à-vis their tendencies and their perceptions of the Umayyad period.

9   The Umayyads and the Methodological Tendency/Attempts to (Humanize) Islamic Historical Writing in General (The North African School)

This tendency is associated with a critical question: to what extent are the viewpoints of the medieval Muslim historians still reproduced and to what destination will this lead us? Identifying an historical school's features and characteristics, especially if it is a contemporary and not a deeply rooted, established and ancient school, is closely connected with the effort of examining the intellectual and cognitive productions contained in its memory.

Through an examination of the works of some of the leading figures of the North African school and its academic and intellectual contributions related to the history of the Islamic world and the Umayyad period in particular, we find a complex interlacing web between reason and the imaginary, where the religious is intensely present within the old, textual register. This school institutionalizes and follows a critical, iconoclastic methodology which deconstructs and re-configures history in a way that is not restricted to narrative and description, but which also pays attention to various aspects and details, especially economic and cultural ones, in a kind of interweaving of history and sociology, although it eventually reaches conclusions that are also largely ideological in nature.

The Tunisian historian Hishām Jaʿayṭ [Hichem Djaït] is an excellent example of this school. His works are concerned with reading the roots and meanings of historical events and their implications for political, social and cultural reality, a reading that appears to back away from the sanctifying and justifying style, and which is keen to adhere to the methodology of academic critique.

This is particularly evident in his book *The Civil War: The Dialectic of Religion and Politics in Early Islam* [*Al-Fitna: Jadaliyyat al-Dīn wa-al-Siyāsa fī al-Islām al-Mubakkir*].[67] This book is a very important example of modern historical scholarship on the medieval Islamic period. It presents a reading of a history replete with events, accounts and characters using critical analysis and interrogation of what is beyond the texts, especially political conflicts and factionalism. This is also the case in Ja'ayṭ's other works such as *Kufa: The Birth of the Arab-Islamic City* [*Al-Kūfa: Nash'at al-Madīna al-'Arabiyya al-Islāmiyya*]; *Revelation, Quran, and Prophecy* [*Al-Waḥy wa al-Qur'ān wa al-Nubuwwa*]; and *The Prophet's Life in Medina and the Triumph of Islam* [*Masīrat Muḥammad fī al-Madīna wa Intiṣār al-Islām*],[68] in which he adopted the same analytical approach he used in writing his first book, *The Civil War*, but to a lesser degree.

Ja'ayṭ makes use of the methodologies and conceptions provided by modern historical schools. His work may be seen as an attempt to move away from blindly following the lead of orientalist scholarship to critiquing it whilst using its tools. Ja'ayṭ is also careful to present the human dimension of Islamic culture as reflected in the early struggles and rivalries between Prophetic Companions, as well as the rise of religious factions and parties.

Ja'ayṭ's approach summons the reports and narratives of the early Islamic factional and sectarian conflicts, which are latent within some of the early historical texts, with the aim of analyzing them in a free atmosphere. However, this approach, dominated by ideas of conflict, clash, revenge and interests, remains an exclusionary one that overrides "shadow" texts, narratives and accounts.

Another representative historian of the North African school is Ḥayāt 'Amāmū. She wrote a book entitled *Struggle for Power and Doubts of Legitimacy* [*Al-Ṣirā' 'alā al-Sulṭa wa Hājis al-Shar'iyya*]. In this book, 'Amāmū tackled specifically the development of the system of rule in Islam. This, in turn, led her to discuss the Umayyad dynasty and its legitimacy and seizure of power. She analyzes the *bay'a* (oath of allegiance) to the Muslim ruler. She focuses in particular on Mu'āwiya b. Abī Sufyān (41–60 AH/661–680) and the transformation of the caliphate from a system of selection by council (*shūrā*) to one of hereditary rule by the Umayyad family. The publications of 'Amāmū are characterized by the same methodology as Ja'ayṭ's works in terms of collecting historical narrations and texts and comparing them and delving deeply into the momentous events of Islamic history. 'Amāmū's book contains perceptive analysis of the justifications given for the seizure of power by the Umayyads. She devotes a

---

67   Ja'ayṭ, *Al-Fitna*.
68   Ja'ayṭ's focus in these publications centers on criticizing ideologies, finding facts, tying and interpreting them within a coherent broad vision.

large part of her book to the question of Umayyad legitimacy while addressing other issues like the Caliphate, the idea of the rule of the Community and the understanding of the foundations of the Umayyad dynasty. ʿAmāmū also tackled the controversial question of the acceptance of the concept of dynastic family rule by the wider society. This is considered to be an important criterion for public approval of the Umayyad dynasty and the newly devised form of succession and rule that emerged.

In her article "Muʿāwiya b. Abī Sufyān: the Arabs and the Mediterranean Sea" ["Muʿāwiya b. abī Sufyān al-ʿArab wa al-Baḥr al-Mutawassaṭ"], Ḥayāt ʿAmāmū presents another good example of how to deconstruct and analyze classical Arabic historical narratives.[69] She implicitly criticizes some earlier studies on the establishment of Islamic naval power, which tried to ascribe this event to the period before Muʿāwiya. She argues that though there were half-hearted earlier attempts to establish a fleet, these were unsuccessful in having any impact on the balance of power between the Caliphate and Byzantium. According to the evidence compiled by ʿAmāmū, Muʿāwiya was the most determined proponent of the idea of an Islamic navy. She cites the correspondence between the second caliph, ʿUmar b. al-Khaṭṭāb, and Muʿāwiya, then governor of Syria, in which the latter asks for the former's permission to start seafaring expeditions. In this article, ʿUmāmū shows her effective methods of tackling the texts related to the events of the early Islamic period, subjecting them to a critical research methodology which is distant from the realm of the sacred and the unseen worlds.

Another book, written by Buthayna Bin Ḥusayn from the same North African school, addresses the second great civil war in the time of the Umayyad caliph Yazīd b. Muʿāwiya (60–64/680–683) and is entitled *The Second Civil War in the Time of Yazīd b. Muʿāwiya* [*Al-Fitna al-Thāniya fī ʿAhd al-Khalīfa Yazīd b. Muʿāwiya*]. In this two-part, 700-page book, Bin Ḥusayn compiles several narrations in the classical Arabic sources and follows closely the same methodology and approach used by Jaʿayṭ in his book about the First Civil War. Jaʿayṭ acknowledges the place of Buthayna Bin Ḥusayn and her book in the North African school of historiography saying "... what the Tunisian school achieved in the domain of historical studies is considered a source of pride. Let us remember many names from several generations such as Muḥammmad al-Ṭālibī, Muḥammad Ḥasan, Ḥayāt Qṭāṭ, Ḥayāt ʿAmāmū, Buthayna Bin Ḥusayn and others. I had the honor of supervising some of them or contributing to their academic training."[70]

---

69   ʿAmāmū, "Muʿāwiya b. Abū Sufyān," in *Aʿmāl Muhdāt li ʿAbd al-Majīd Sharafī* 195–240.

70   Buthayna Bin Ḥusayn, *Al-Fitna*, p. 8.

10   Epigraphy as a New Gateway into Umayyad History

The last few decades have witnessed significant developments in the study of Arabic epigraphy and inscriptions related to the early period of Islam. Important inscriptions have been discovered that date back to the early centuries of the Hijra. Of course, for our purposes, we will focus on inscriptions from the Umayyad period. Arabic Epigraphy is divided into three major subfields: petroglyphs, graffiti, and tombstones. It should be pointed out that typically the Arabic inscriptions are arranged and studied according to the collection to which they belong (from a single site or region) rather than by chronological period.

The known corpus of Umayyad petroglyphs is not very large. Some discoveries were made in Syria, Jordan, Lebanon and Palestine and published by foreign researchers. It is widely known that Mu'āwiya's Dam Graffiti in Ṭā'if was published by Miles in the 1950s.[71] At the beginning of this century, Sa'd al-Rashīd conducted a field survey in the Medina area. He examined Al Khanq Dam, also known as the Dam of Medina, and published its petroglyphs including a foundation inscription which dates back to Mu'āwiya's caliphate.[72] Al-Rāshid wrote a book entitled *Early Islamic Inscriptions from Mecca: A Study* [*Kitābāt Islāmiyya Mubbakira min Makka al-Mūkarrama: Dirāsa wa Taḥqīq*] in which he published an inscription that asks Allah's mercy for the Umayyad caliph 'Abd al-Malik b. Marwān (65–85/685–705) in addition to other inscriptions that date to the Umayyad era.[73] Al-Rāshid has published other important works including a book on inscriptions mentioning individuals that lived in the Umayyad and Abbasid periods; a study entitled "A Rock Inscription from the Umayyad era from an unspecified location in the Southern Hijaz" ["Naqsh Mū'arrakh min al-'Aṣr al-Umawī Majhūl al-Mawqi' min Minṭaqat Janūb al-Hijāz"]; and *Newly Discovered Islamic Inscriptions from Medina* [*Nuqūsh Islāmiyya Jadīda min Minṭaqat al-Madīna al-Munawwara*] which includes inscriptions from the Umayyad period.[74]

There are many inscriptions belonging to persons known to have lived during the Umayyad period. In her doctoral dissertation, Maysā' al-Ghubbān published three inscriptions for a client (*mawlā*) or a son of a client of the

---

71   Miles, Early Islamic Tombstones.

72   Al-Rāshid, *Dirāsāt fī al-Āthār al-Islāmiyya al-Mubakkira fī al-Madina al-Munawwara*, 46.

73   Al-Rāshid, *Kitābāt Islāmiyya min Makka*, 151–152.

74   Al-Rāshid, *Kitābāt Islāmiyya ghayr Manshūra*; Ibid., Naqsh Mu'arrakh, in *Dirāsāt fī al-Āthār* i, 265–270; Ibid., Nuqūsh Islāmiyya Jadīda min Minṭaqat al-Madīna al-Munawwara, in *Mudāwilāt al-Liqā' al-'Ilmī*, 117–153.

caliph Muʿāwiya b. Abī Sufyān.[75] In addition, her thesis includes an inscription for a client of the famous jurist ʿUrwa b. al-Zubayr (d. 94/712–713) with a date of 80 AH, along with other inscriptions containing dates from the Umayyad period.[76]

It is also worth mentioning the work of the Syrian historian, al-ʿIsh.[77] He has written a paper entitled "Unpublished Arabic Inscriptions in Asīs Mountain in Syria" ["Kitābāt ʿArabiyya ghayr Manshūra Wujidat fī Jabal Asīs fī Sūriyya"] in which he published an inscription that carries the name of Khālid b. Amīr al-Muʾminīn (Khālid son of the Commander of the Faithful), which causes al-ʿIsh to suspect that it refers to Khālid, the son of the caliph al-Walīd b. ʿAbd al-Malik (86–96/705–715). The inscription also contains the names Muḥammad and Ibrāhīm, both sons of the caliph al-Walīd. In addition, there are other inscriptions in the collection from the Umayyad period.

A group of researchers led by ʿAbdallāh al-Saʿīd known as the "Desert Team" [Farīq al-Ṣaḥrāʾ] has been active in discovering and publishing early Arabic inscriptions and they maintain a website.[78] They have written a book on the inscriptions found in the desert region of Ḥismā in northern Saudi Arabia.[79] A memorial inscription was published in this book which dates from the reign of the Umayyad caliph ʿAbd al-Malik b. Marwān along with other Umayyad inscriptions. A tombstone belonging to the Umayyad prince Muḥammad b. Khālid b. ʿAbd al-Malik b. al-Ḥārith b. al-Ḥakam has been discovered in Jordan, though it has a date from the Abbasid era.[80]

There are very few inscriptions from the Umayyad period that deal with actual events. An exception is an inscription that records the construction of the Great Mosque of Mecca by the caliph ʿAbd al-Malik b. Marwān.[81] Another inscription found in Ḥismā and published by ʿAbdallāh b. Saʿīd is dated "Year of the Conquest of the Sea." Al-Saʿīd believes that this inscription dates back to the governorship of Muʿāwiya b. Abī Sufyān over Syria during the rule of the third caliph ʿUthmān b. ʿAffān (23–35/644–656).

---

75   Al-Ghubbān, Al-Kitābāt al-Islāmiyya, 101–120.

76   Al-Ghubbān, Al-Kitābāt al-Islāmiyya, 207.

77   Muḥammad Abū al-Faraj al-ʿIsh, Kitābāt ʿArabiyya.

78   Their twitter account is called "Farīq al-Ṣaḥrāʾ" accessed December 5, 2019, https://twitter .com/AlsahraTeam. They also have a website called "Farīq al-Ṣaḥrāʾ," accessed December 5, 2019, alsahra.org. Many Arabic inscriptions from the early Islamic period are published on both sites.

79   ʿAbdallāh Al-Saʿīd, Muḥammad Shafīq al-Bayṭar, Saʿd Sulaymān Saʿīd, and Aḥmad Muḥammad al-Dāmigh, Nuqūsh Ḥismāʾ.

80   Karīm, Shāhid Qabr.

81   Al-Ḥārithī, Naqsh Kitābī Nādir.

There are a number of studies concerning both dated and undated inscriptions from the Umayyad period. These inscriptions are divided into two types: graffiti mentioning well-known figures from the Umayyad age and graffiti containing dates from the Umayyad period. An example of the former type of graffiti is cited in Aḥmad Saʿīd b. Qashāsh's study entitled "The Graffiti of the Prophetic Companion Khālid b. al-ʿĀṣ (d. 13 AH) and his sons in the Bāḥa Region" ["Nuqūsh al-Ṣaḥābī al-Jalīl Khālid b. al-ʿĀṣ (13 AH) Huwa wa Abnāʾuhu fī Minṭaqat al-Bāḥa"].[82] The importance of this inscription lies in the fact that it is the only graffiti that goes back to a contemporary of the Prophet. Moreover, both Khālid b. al-ʿĀṣ and his son, Al-Ḥārith, were appointed at different times as governors of Mecca, the father in the time of Muʿāwiya and the son in the time of Yazīd b. Muʿāwiya. Al-Ḥārith has his own graffiti on the same rock.

There are also dated inscriptions from the Umayyad period which have been published by many scholars. The Jordanian historian Jumʿa Maḥmūd Karīm has published an article on "Islamic Inscriptions dating back to the Umayyad and Abbasid ages from the south of Jordan. A Comparative, Analytical and Epigraphical Study" ["Nuqūsh Islāmiyya Taʿūdu li al-ʿAṣrayn al-Umawī wa al-ʿAbbāsī min Janūb al-Urdun: Qirāʾa wa Taḥlīl wa Muqārana"] along with another study entitled "A Kūfic Inscription dating back to the Umayyad period from southeast Al-Ghura in al-Jafar district" ["Naqsh Kūfī Yaʿūdu li al ʿAṣr al-Umawī min Janūb Sharq al-Ghura, Qaḍāʾ al-Jafar"].[83] Al-Jabbūr wrote his MA thesis on the Wadī Salmā inscriptions while in Jordan, Sulaymān al-Farḥāṭ and Sāmī al-Nawāfila have published Kufic inscriptions from the region of Al-Dīsah Waram.[84]

There are also inscriptions that have been discovered along the Pilgrimage (Ḥajj) routes, such as the Syrian route. These inscriptions were examined by Ḥayāt b. ʿAbdallāh al-Kilābī in her book entitled *The Islamic Inscriptions along the Pilgrimage Route from the Levant* [*Al-Nuqūsh al-Islāmiyya ʿalā al-Ṭarīq al-Ḥajj al-Shāmī*].[85] A recently published paper on inscriptions dating back to the Umayyad and ʿAbbasid periods by Aḥmad al-ʿAbbūdī and others entitled, "Dated Islamic Graffiti from Al Aqraʿ mountain north of Al-ʿAllā in the Governorate of Medina" ["Nuqūsh Islāmiyya Mūʾarrakha min Jabal al-Aqrʿa Shimāl Muḥāfaẓat al-ʿAllā bi-Minṭaqat al-Madīna al-Munawwwara"] presents

---

82 Qashāsh, Nuqūsh.

83 Karīm, Nuqūsh Islāmiyya; Naqsh Kūfī.

84 Al-Jabbūr, Al-Athār al-Islāmiyya fī Wādī Salmā, 27; Sulaymān al-Farḥāt and Sāmī al-Nawāfila, Kitābāt Kūfiyya.

85 Al-Kilābī, Al-Nuqūsh al-Islāmiyya ʿalā Ṭarīq al-Ḥajj al-Shāmī, 64–72.

some inscriptions by pilgrims dating back to the Umayyad period.[86] In 2015, Muḥammad b. ʿAbd al-Raḥmān al-Thaniyān republished all the inscriptions found in the Kingdom of Saudi Arabia from the first century AH.[87]

The study of tombstones and their inscriptions is another important sub-field of Arabic epigraphy. In the 1950s a tombstone from Iraq that dates back to 64/684 was published in an article entitled "The Stone of Ḥuffnat al-Bayḍ."[88] A comprehensive study of the tombstones in Mecca is ʿAbd al-Raḥmān al-Zahrānī's book entitled *Islamic Inscriptions from Mecca from the First to Seventh Centuries A.H.* [*Kitābāt Islāmiyya min Makka al-Mukarrama*].[89] It is true that the book does not contain inscriptions that have been definitively assigned to the Umayyad period but more research and analysis should be done on this matter. Finally, it is important to point out that internet web-sites and social media networks are playing a big role in making early Arabic inscriptions available to the general public and scholars alike.[90]

11 Conclusion

After examining the various trends in Arabic academic writing tendencies on the Umayyad Period we reach the following conclusions:

First of all, it appears that the modern studies on the Umayyads can be divided into two major types. On the one hand there are those studies influenced by the popular and established accounts, which were part of a broader context consistent with the earlier Islamic historical sources. On the other hand, there are those studies that are unhampered by the prejudiced historical heritage and the current popular imagination. A great deal of modern Arabic and Western scholarship falls within these two trends, having been polarized by these two opposing approaches.

Secondly, these two trends were parallel with another category of scholarship, that of historical or methodological survey literature. The survey works attempted to stand at an equal distance, and sought a revitalized understanding

---

86   Aḥmad b. Muḥammad al-ʿAbbūdī, Fuʾād b. Ḥasan al-ʿĀmir, and Kāmil b. ʿAlī al-Ghānim, *Nuqūsh Islāmiyya*, 30–35.

87   Al-Thāniyān, *Nuqūsh al-Qarn al-Hijrī al-Awwal*, 52–102.

88   Al-Rassām, *Ḥajar Ḥuffnat al-Abyaḍ*.

89   Al-Zahrānī, *Kitābāt Islāmiyya*.

90   For example, Muḥammad al-Maghdawī has made great efforts to collect all of the inscriptions from Medina and the surrounding area and post them on his twitter account: "Nawādir al-Āthār wa al-Nuqūsh," accessed December 5, 2019, https://twitter.com/mohammed93athar.

of the Umayyad history within the general framework of Islamic history or what can be labelled the human effort impact framework.

Thirdly, with the rise of a new generation and the advent of new schools of historical writing, especially those influenced by Western approaches, a modernist approach towards the writing of Umayyad history has emerged, exemplified by the "critical or deconstructive methodology."

The question remains: what is the value of these studies as academic/cognitive/cultural phenomena if they are unable to collectively advance a theoretical paradigm that is bold enough to revisit and rethink their viewpoints, correct their mistakes and develop new projects for the modernization of the field? What is the significance of these writing tendencies if they can be used to generate a state of ideological vigilance or invoke the history of hatred and bigotry "with or against" the other?

Bibliography

Al-ʿAbbād, ʿAbīr bint Ḥamd b. ʿAlī, Dirāsa Taʾṣiliyya Mawḍūʿiyya Muḥāyada li Inṣāf Banī Umayya, PhD dissertation, Qasīm University, 2010.

Al-ʿAbbūdī, Aḥmad b. Muḥammad, Fuʾād b. Ḥasan al-ʿĀmir, Kāmil b. ʿAlī al-Ghānim, Nuqūsh Islāmiyya Muʾarrakha min Jabal al-Aqraʿ Shimāl Muḥāfaẓat al-ʿAllā bi Minṭaqat al-Madīna al-Munawwara, *Majallat Kulliyat al-Siyāḥa wa al-Āthār* 29, no. 1 (2017), 30–35.

ʿAbd al-Laṭīf, ʿAbd al-Shāfī Muḥammad, *Al-ʿĀlam al-Islāmī fī al-ʿAṣr al-Umawī*, Cairo [?], 1984.

ʿAbd al-Munʿim, Mājid, *Al-Tārīkh al-Siyāsī li al-Dawlat al-ʿArabiyya: ʿAṣr al-Khulafāʾ al-Umawiyyin*, vol. 3, Cairo, 1996.

ʿAbd al-Razzāq, Aḥmad Bahāʾ and Wasīm ʿAbbūd ʿAṭṭiyya, Maẓāhir al-ʿĀṭifa ʿan Aʾimmat Ahl al-Bayt ʿalayhim al-Salām ʿalā Istishhād al-Imām al-Ḥusayn ʿalayhi al-Salām: Dirāsa Tārīkhiyya, *Majallat Kulliyat al-Islāmiyya al-Jāmiʿiyya – Najaf* 43, no. 1 (2017), 695–716.

Abū Dayya, ʿAdnān Aḥmad Qāsim, Nuqūd Āl al-Bayt fī ʿAhd al-Khalīfa Marwān b. Muḥammad, *Majallat al-Jāmiʿa al-Islāmiyya li al-Buḥūth al-Insāniyya*, 17, no. 2 (2009), 169–213.

Abū al-Naṣr, ʿUmar, *Al-Ayyām al-Akhīra li al-Dawla al-Umawiyya*, Beirut, 1962.

Abū al-Naṣr, ʿUmar, ʿAbd al-Malik b. Marwān, Beirut, 1962.

Al-ʿAdawī, Ibrāhīm Aḥmad, *Al-Dawla al-Umawiyya: Muqawwimātuhu wa Risālatuhu*, Cairo, 1996.

Āʾinawand, Ṣādiq, and Nāhīd Naṣīḥat, Muʾashshirāt al-Ḥukm al-Umawī wa al-ʿAlawī fī *Hāshimiyāt* Al-Kumayt al-Asadī, *Kulliyyat al-Islāmiya – Jāmiʿat Najaf* 33 (2015), 13–42.

Al-ʿAjamī, ʿAbd al-Hādī, Al-Tārīkh kamā Yaktubuhu al-Munhazimūn: Mawqaʿat al-Ḥarra (63 h./683m.) Namūdhajan, *Majallat Kulliyat al-Ādāb – Jāmiʿat Iskandariyya* 73 (2014), 279–331.

Al-ʿAlī, Ṣāliḥ Aḥmad, ʿUmar b. ʿAbd al-ʿAzīz: Khāmis al-Khulafāʾ al-Rāshidīn, Beirut, 2000.

ʿAmāmū, Ḥayāt, Muʿāwiya b. Abī Sufyān: Al-ʿArab wa al-Baḥr al-Mutawassaṭ, in *Aʿmāl Muhdāt li ʿAbd al-Majīd Sharafī*, Tunis, 2010, 195–240.

ʿAmāmū, Ḥayāt, *Al-Ṣirāʿ ʿalā al-Sulṭa wa Hājis al-Sharʿiyya*, Jubayl, 2010.

ʿAmāmū, Ḥayāt, *Aslamat Bilād al-Maghrib: Islām al-Taʾsīs min al-Futūḥāt ilā Ẓuhūr al-Niḥal*, Tunis, 2004.

ʿAmāmū, Ḥayāt, Min al-Khilāfa al-Rāshida fī al-Madīna ilā Taʾsīs al-Dawla al-Umawiyya bi Dimashq, paper presented at the conference *Al-Qabīla wa al-Madīna wa al-Majāl*, Tunis, 2003.

ʿAmāmū, Ḥayāt, *Taṣnīf al-Qudāmā fī al-Sīra al-Nabawiyya*, Tunis, 1997.

ʿAmāmū, Ḥayāt, *Aṣḥāb Muḥammad wa Dawruhum fī Nashr al-Islām*, Tunis, 1996.

ʿAmāra, Muḥammad, ʿUmar b. ʿAbd al-ʿAzīz: Ḍamīr al-Umma wa Khāmis al-Rāshidīn, Beirut, 1985.

Al-ʿĀqil, Nabīh, *Khilāfat Banī Umayya*, Beirut, 1972.

Al-ʿAqqād, ʿAbbās Maḥmūd, *Muʿāwiya b. Abī Sufyān*, Cairo, 1949.

ʿArafa, Thurayāʾ Ḥāfiẓ, Al-Ḥayāt al-Iqtiṣādiyya fī Bilād al-Shām fī al-ʿAṣr al-Umawī, PhD dissertation, Umm al-Qurā University, 1989.

Arkūn, Muḥammad, *Min al-Ijtihād ilā Naqd al-ʿAql al-Islāmī*, Beirut, 1991.

Al-ʿAskarī, Murtaḍā, *Abdallāh b. Sabaʾ wa Asāṭīr Ukhrā*, Beirut, 1972.

ʿAṭwān, Ḥusayn, *Al-Umawiyyūn wa al-Khilāfa*, Beirut, 1986.

ʿAṭwān, Ḥusayn, *Al-Walīd b. Yazīd*, Beirut, 1981.

Al-ʿAẓm, Rafīq, *Ashhar Mashāhīr al-Islām fī al-Ḥurūb wa al-Siyāsa*, 4 vols., Cairo, 1909.

Bin Ḥusayn, Buthayna, *Al-Fitna al-Thāniya fī ʿAhd al-Khalīfa Yazīd b. Muʿāwiya*, Beirut, 2013.

Dakhīl, Muḥammad Ḥasan, Al-Thawra al-Ḥusayniyya: Dirāsa fī Abʿādihā al-Siyāsiya wa al-ʿAskariyya wa Asbāb Ikhtiyār al-Kūfa Munṭalaqan li al-Taḥarruk wa Dalālāt al-Rasāʾil al-Kūfiyya li al-Imām al-Ḥusayn, *Majallat Markaz Dirāsāt al-Kūfa* 28, no. 1 (2013), 157–177.

Al-Dūrī, ʿAbd al-ʿAzīz, *Muqaddima fī Tārīkh Ṣadr al-Islām*, Beirut, 2007.

Al-Farhāt, Sulaymān, and Sāmī al-Nawāfila, Kitābāt Kūfiyya min Minṭaqat Al-Dīsah Waram, *Ḥawliyyat Dāʾirat al-Āthār al-ʿĀmma* 49 (2005), 29–38.

"Farīq al-Ṣaḥrāʾ", https://twitter.com/AlsahraTeam. Accessed December 5, 2019.

"Farīq al-Ṣaḥrāʾ", alsahra.org. Accessed December 5, 2019.

Al-Ghāmidī, Saʿd b. Hudhayfa, *Suqūṭ al-Dawlat al-ʿAbbāsiyya wa Dawr al-Shīʿa bayn al-Ḥaqīqa wa al-Ittihām*, Riyadh [?], 1981.

Al-Ghubbān, Maysā' bint 'Alī b. Ibrāhīm, Al-Kitābāt al-Islāmiyya al-Mubakkira fī Haḍbat Hismā fī Minṭaqat Tabūk: Dirāsa Taḥlīliyya Āthāriyya wa Lughawiyya, PhD dissertation, Malik Saʿūd University, 2017.

Hādī, Raʿd Ṣāliḥ, Aswāq al-ʿIrāq al-Islāmiyya fī al-ʿAṣr al-Umawī, *Majallat Dirāsāt Tarbawiyya* 24 (2013), 153–178.

Al-Hallābī, ʿAbd al-ʿAzīz, ʿAbdallāh b. Saba': Dirāsa li al-Riwāyāt al-Tārīkhīyya ʿan Dawrihi fī al-Fitna, *Ḥawliyyat Ādāb al-Kuwayt* 8, (1986–87).

Ḥammāda, Muḥammad Māhir, *Al-Wathā'iq al-Siyāsiyya al-ʿĀ'ida li al-ʿAṣr al-Umawī*, 4 vols., Beirut, 1985.

Al-Ḥārithī, Nāṣir b. ʿAlī, Naqsh Kitābī Nādir Yu'arrikh ʿImārat al-Khalīfa al-Umawī ʿAbd al-Malik b. Marwān li al-Masjid al-Ḥarām 78 h., ʿĀlam al-Makhṭuṭāt wa al-Nawādir 12, no. 2 (2007), 533–543.

Ḥasan, Ḥusayn al-Ḥājj, *Ḥaḍarat al-ʿArab fī al-ʿAṣr al-Umawī*, Beirut, 1994.

Al-Ḥilfī, Ṣabbīḥ Nūrī Khalaf and Buthayna ʿĀdil ʿUmrān, Tha'r baʿḍ Rijālāt al-Ḥukm al-Umawī min al-Munāwi'īn wa al-Muʿāriḍīn lahum, *Majallat Dirāsāt Tārīkhiyya – Jāmiʿat Baṣra* 15 (December, 2013), 97–142.

Ḥusayn, Ṭāhā, *Al-Fitna al-Kubrā*, 2 vols., Cairo, 1953.

ʿĪsā, Riyāḍ, *Al-Hizbiyya al-Siyāsīya mundhu Qiyām al-Islām ḥattā Suqūṭ al-Dawla al-Umawiyya*, n.p., 1992.

Al-ʿIsh, Yūsuf, *Al-Dawla al-Umawiyya wa al-Aḥdāth allatī Sabaqathā wa Mahhadat lahā Ibtidā'an min Fitnat ʿUthmān*, Damascus, 1982.

Al-ʿIsh, Muḥammad Abū al-Faraj, Kitābāt ʿArabiyya ghayr Manshūra Wujidat fī Jabal Asīs, *Majallat al-Ḥawliyyāt al-Athariyya al-Suriyya* 13 (1963), 281–293.

Jaʿayṭ, Hishām [Djaït, Hichem], *Masīrat Muḥammad fī al-Madīna wa Intiṣār al-Islām*, Beirut, 2015.

Jaʿayṭ, Hishām [Djaït, Hichem], *Al-Fitna: Jadaliyyat al-Dīn wa al-Siyāsa fī al-Islām al-Mubakkir*, Beirut, 2008.

Jaʿayṭ, Hishām [Djaït, Hichem], *Fī al-Sīra al-Nabawiyya: Al-Waḥy wa al-Qur'ān*, Beirut, 1999.

Jaʿayṭ, Hishām [Djaït, Hichem], *Al-Kūfa: Nash'at al-Madīna al-ʿArabiyya al-Islāmiyya*, Beirut, 1986.

Al-Jabbūr, Khālid Sulaymān, Al-Āthār al-Islāmiyya fī Wādī Salmā: Masājid, Nuqūsh, Fakhkhār, MA dissertation, Yarmuk University, 1999.

Al-Jumayḥ, Ibrāhīm ʿAbd al-ʿAzīz, Al-Awḍāʿ al-Siyāsiyya li Bilād ʿUmān fī al-ʿAṣr al-Umawī (41–132 h./661–750 m.), *Majallat Jāmiʿat al-Malik ʿAbd al-ʿAzīz* 9, no. 1 (1996), 129–194.

Al-Jumayḥ, Ibrāhīm ʿAbd al-ʿAzīz, Maẓāhir al-Nashāṭ al-Iqtiṣādī fī Mawāsim al-Ḥajj fī al-ʿAṣr al-Umawī (41–132 h./661–750m.), *Majallat Jāmiʿat al-Malik ʿAbd al-ʿAzīz* 7 (1994), 147–190.

Karīm, Jumʿa Maḥmūd, Shāhid Qabr al-Amīr al-Marwānī Muḥammad b. Khālid b. ʿAbd al-Malik b. al-Ḥārith b. Ḥakam min Janūb al-Urdunn, *Dirāsāt – al-Jāmiʿa al-Urdunniyya* 28, no. 1 (2001), 132–158.

Karīm, Jumʿa Maḥmūd, Naqsh Kūfī Yaʿūdu li al-ʿAṣr al-Umawī min Janūb Sharq al-Ghura-Qaḍāʾ al-Jafar, *Dirāsāt – al-Jāmiʿa al-Urdunniyya* 28, no. 2 (2001), 391–413.

Karīm, Jumʿa Maḥmūd, Nuqūsh Islāmiyya Taʿūdu li al-ʿAṣrayn al-Umawī wa al-ʿAbbāsī min Janūb al-Urdunn: Qirāʾa, Taḥlīl, wa Muqārana, *Majallat Jāmiʿat Dimashq* 18, no. 2 (2002), 295–299.

Kāshif, Al-Sayyida Ismāʿīl, ʿAbd al-ʿAzīz b. Marwān, Cairo, 1967.

Kāshif, Al-Sayyida Ismāʿīl, *Al-Walīd b. ʿAbd al-Malik*, Cairo, 1962.

Khaṭīb, Shahīd, Al-Buʿd al-Ijtimāʿī li Nahḍat al-Imām al-Ḥusayn, *Dirāsāt Islāmiyya Muʿāṣira* 8 (2013), 311–326.

Al-Khuḍarī, Muḥammad Bak, *Muḥāḍarāt fī Tārīkh al-Umam al-Islāmiyya*, 2 vols., Cairo, 1916.

Al-Khuḍarī, Muḥammad Bak, *Al-Dawla al-Umawiyya*, Beirut, n.d.

Al-Kilābī, Ḥayāt bint ʿAbdallāh, Al-Nuqūsh al-Islāmiyya ʿalā Ṭarīq al-Ḥajj al-Shāmī, Riyadh, 2009.

Al-Mahāynī, Rafīq, *Tārīkh al-Khilāfa al-Umawiyya wa al-ʿAbbāsiyya wa al-Duwal al-Islāmiyya wa al-ʿUṣūr al-Wusṭā fī Urubbā*, Damascus, 1947.

Al-Maqrīzī, Taqī al-Dīn, *Al-Nizāʿ wa al-Takhāṣum fī mā bayna Banī Umayya wa Banī Hāshim*, ed. Ḥ. Muʾnis, Cairo, 1988.

Maṭbaʿī, Ḥamīd, *Al-Muʾurrikh Ṣāliḥ Aḥmad al-ʿAlī*, Baghdad, 2001.

Miles, George C., Early Islamic Tombstones from Egypt in the Museum of Fine Arts, Boston, *Ars Orientalis* 2 (1957), 215–226.

Al-Mulḥim, Muḥammad b. Nāṣir b. Aḥmad, Iṣlāḥāt Ziyād b. (Abīhi) ʿAbīd fī al-ʿIrāq fī al-Fatra mā bayn 45–53 h./665–673 m., *Majallat Jāmiʿat Al-Malik ʿAbd al-ʿAzīz* 11, no. 1 (2001), 105-.

Al-Najjār, Muḥammad Ṭayyib, *Tārīkh al-ʿĀlam al-Islāmī: Al-Dawla al-Umawiyya*, Riyadh, 1985.

Al-Najjār, Muḥammad Ṭayyib, *Al-Dawla al-Umawiyya fī al-Sharq: bayn ʿAwāmil al-Bināʾ wa Maʿāwil al-Fanāʾ*, Cairo, 1977.

"Nawādir al-Āthār wa al-Nuqūsh", https://twitter.com/mohammed93athar. Accessed December 5, 2019.

Al-Nuṣūlī, Anīs Zakariyyāʾ, *Al-Dawla al-Umawiyya fī al-Shām*, Baghdad, 1926.

Qashāsh, Aḥmad b. Saʿīd, *Nuqūsh al-Ṣaḥābī al-Jalīl Khālid b. al-ʿĀṣ wa Abnāʾihi fī Minṭaqat al-Bāḥa*, Beirut, 2015.

Al-Rāshid, Saʿd b. ʿAbd al-ʿAzīz, Naqsh Muʾarrakh min al-ʿAṣr al-Umawī Majhūl al-Mawqiʿ min Minṭaqat Janūb al-Ḥijāz, in *Dirāsāt fī al-Āthār*, vol. 1, Riyadh, 1992.

Al-Rāshid, Saʿd b. ʿAbd al-ʿAzīz, *Kitābāt Islāmiyya ghayr Manshūra min (Ruwāwa) al-Madīna al-Munawwara: Dirāsa wa Taḥqīq*, Riyadh, 1993.

Al-Rāshid, Saʿd b. ʿAbd al-ʿAzīz, *Kitābāt Islāmiyya min Makka al-Mukarrama (Dirāsa wa Taḥqīq)*, Riyadh, 1995.

Al-Rāshid, Saʿd b. ʿAbd al-ʿAzīz, *Dirāsāt fī al-Āthār al-Islāmiyya al-Mubakkira fī al-Madīna al-Munawwara*, Riyadh, 2000.

Al-Rāshid, Saʿd b. ʿAbd al-ʿAzīz, Nuqūsh Islāmiyya Jadīda min Minṭaqat al-Madīna al-Munawwara, in *Mudāwalāt al-Liqāʾ al-ʿIlmī al-Sanawī al-Rābiʿ li Jamʿiyyat al-Tārīkh wa al-Āthār fī Duwal Majlis al-Taʿāwun li Duwal al-Khalīj al-ʿArabiyya*, Sharjah, 2002, 117–153.

Al-Rassām, ʿIzz al-Dīn al-Ṣandūq, Ḥajar Ḥafnat al-Abyaḍ, *Sumer* 11, no. 2 (1955), 213–218.

Al-Rāwī, Ismāʿīl, *Al-ʿIrāq fī al-ʿAṣr al-Umawī*, Baghdad, 1959.

Al-Rayyis, Ḍiyāʾ al-Dīn, ʿAbd al-Malik b. Marwān wa al-Dawla al-Umawiyya, Cairo, 1969.

Al-Rayyis, Ḍiyāʾ al-Dīn, ʿAbd al-Malik b. Marwān Muwaḥḥid al-Dawla al-ʿArabiyya: Ḥayātuhu wa ʿAṣruhu, Cairo, 1962.

Al-Saʿīd, ʿAbdallāh, Muḥammad Shafīq al-Bayṭār, Saʿd Sulaymān Saʿīd, and Aḥmad Muḥammad al-Dāmigh, *Nuqūsh Ḥismā: Kitābāt min Ṣadr al-Islām Shimāl Gharb al-Mamlaka*, Riyadh, 2018.

Al-Ṣallābī, *Al-Dawla al-Umawiyya: ʿAwāmil al-Izdihār wa Tadāʿiyyāt al-Inhiyār*, Beirut, 2008.

Al-Sayyid, Riḍwān, Kitābat al-Tārīkh al-ʿArabī, ʿArab 48 (October 31, 2010).

Shāhīn, Ḥamdī, *Al-Dawla al-Umawiyya al-Muftarā ʿalayhā: Dirāsat al-Shubuhāt wa al-Radd ʿalayhā: Ruʾyah Taṣḥīḥiyya li al-Tārīkh al-Islāmī (al-ʿAṣr al-Umawī)*, Cairo, 2001.

Shākir, Maḥmūd, *Al-Tārīkh al-Islāmī: al-ʿAhd al-Umawī*, 7 vols., Beirut, 2000.

Shalabī, Aḥmad, *Mawsūʿat al-Tārikh al-Islāmī wa al-Ḥaḍārat al-Islāmiyya: Al-Dawla al-Umawiyya*, Cairo, 1970.

Suhayl, Muḥammad, *Tārīkh al-Dawla al-Umawiyya*, Beirut, 1988.

Al-Suwaytī, Muḥammad Ḥusayn ʿAlī, Athar Thawrat al-Imām Ḥusayn fī Arkān al-Dawlat al-Umawiyya (Al-Khalīfa al-Umawī al-Thālith Muʿāwiya b. Yazīd b. Muʿāwiya Anmūdhajan), *Majallat Kulliyat al-Tarbiyya – Wāsiṭ* 12, no. 1 (2012), 179–209.

Ṭaqqūsh, Muḥammad Suhayl, *Tārīkh al-Dawla al-Umawiyya*, Beirut, 1998.

Al-Thaʿālibī, ʿAbd al-ʿAzīz, *Suqūṭ al-Dawlat al-Umawiyya wa Qiyām al-Dawlat al-ʿAbbāsiyya*, Beirut, 1995.

Al-Thāniyān, Muḥammad b. ʿAbd al-Raḥmān, *Nuqūsh al-Qarn al-Hijrī al-Awwal al-Muʾarrakha fī al-Mamlaka al-ʿArabiyya al-Saʿūdiyya: Dirāsa Taḥlīliyya Jadīda*, Riyadh, 2015.

Al-ʿUqaylī, ʿUmar Sulaymān, *Khilāfat Muʿāwiya b. Abī Sufyān*, Riyadh, 1984.

ʿUways, ʿAbd al-Ḥalīm, *Banū Umayya bayn al-Ḍarabāt Khārijiyya wa al-Inhiyār al-Dākhilī*, Cairo, 1987.

Walī, ʿAbd al-ʿAzīz Muḥammad Nūr, Athar al-Tashayyuʿ ʿalā al-Riwāyāt al-Tārīkhiyya fī al-Qarn al-Awwal al-Hijrī, PhD dissertation, [Saudi Arabia?], 1994.

Al-Wardānī, Ṣāliḥ, Al-Sayf wa al-Siyāsa fī al-Islām: Al-Ṣirāʿ bayn al-Islām al-Nabawī wa al-Islām al-Umawī, Cairo, 1999.

Al-Zahrānī, ʿAbd al-Raḥmān, Kitābāt Islāmiyya min Makka al-Mukarrama (q. 1–7 h./7–13 m.), Riyadh, 2013.

Zīdān, Jurjī, Abū Muslim al-Khurasānī, n.p., 1905.

Zīdān, Jurjī, Fatḥ al-Andalus, n.p., 1904.

Zīdān, Jurjī, Al-Ḥajjāj b. Yūsuf, n.p., 1902.

Zīdān, Jurjī, Ghādat Karbalāʾ, n.p., 1901.

10

Historical Writing in Modern Iraq: Personalities and Trends

Nasir al-Kaabi

1   Introduction

Historical writing in Iraq took a fixed path prior to the establishment of history departments and the emergence of the first generation of Western-influenced academic historians in the country. The roots of the beginnings modern Iraqi historiographical school can perhaps be traced to the late Ottoman period, between the mid-nineteenth and the early twentieth century. In general, the historical scholarship of this period represented the local traditional style of history-writing before its intermixing with and influence by Western methodologies.

Various factors contributed to stimulating historical writing in Iraq. Some of these factors were connected to contemporary technological and institutional developments. For example, telegraph lines deepened the connections between Iraq and its surrounding Ottoman environment and the period saw the spread of printing presses and modern schools. History was introduced as a regular subject in middle schools for the first time in 1870, and in elementary schools in 1873.[1]

These factors resulted in the appearance of a group of authors in Iraq at the end of the Ottoman period who wrote on historical topics. An outstanding example was Sulaymān Fāʿiq b. Ṭālib Kahiyya (d. 1896) who has been described as "the most prominent historian of the late Ottoman period".[2] Statistics reveal that there were 271 authors of historical works in late Ottoman Iraq, who wrote 755 books in various languages. Eighty percent of these works were written in Arabic.[3] It should be noted that these are not all "pure" historical works, some of them are mixed with other genres such as literature, *fiqh*, Qurʾānic exegesis, and other traditional Islamic disciplines.

---

1   Raʾūf, *Al-Tārīkh*.
2   Ibid., 75.
3   Ibid.

In the middle of the twentieth century the characteristics of academic historical writing clearly emerged, especially after the establishment of Baghdad University and its history department. An elite of Iraqi historians who had studied in Western universities and who wrote works influenced by modern Western methodologies appeared. A document issued by the Iraqi Ministry of Education for the Foreign Ministry in 1953 contains some useful information. Entitled "Historians," it specifies eight of the most famous historians working in Iraq and asks the Foreign Ministry to make them known to the outside world through the Iraqi embassies abroad and facilitate their involvement in international conferences. The names of the historians are as follows: Majīd Khaddūrī (Washington, USA), Zakī Ṣāliḥ (Professor in the Teachers' College in Baghdad), Ṣāliḥ Aḥmad al-ʿAlī (Professor in the Faculty of Letters in Baghdad), Fāḍil Ḥusayn (Professor in the Teachers' College, Baghdad), ʿAbd al-ʿAzīz al-Dūrī (Dean of the Faculty of Letters, Baghdad), Muḥammad al-Hāshimī (Professor in the Teachers' College, Baghdad), Jawād ʿAlī (Secretary of the Iraqi Scientific Academy, Baghdad), Muṣṭafā Jawād (Professor in the Teachers' College, Baghdad).[4]

The preceding list does not include all of the major Iraqi historians but it is comprehensive in terms of the major trends in Iraqi historical scholarship at that time. A number of factors influenced the determination of each trend and the overall diversity of the trends. These factors include political events, the various political factions, and changes of government which usually entailed changes in the historical vision along with the emergence of projects for the rewriting of history according to the ideology of the new government. The sending of Iraqi students to Western universities to study history and the influence of Western methodologies and styles of history writing also played a role. Finally, the influence of regional, Arab ideological currents cannot be ignored as these were part of the Iraqi historians' milieu. In the following section a general classification of the nature of the trends in Iraqi historical writing from the establishment of the Iraqi state in 1921 until the American invasion of 2003 will be presented.

2   History Writing Outside of the University

We will focus on two major scholars in this category who showed the characteristics of historians in their works and their style of writing. The first of these is ʿAbbās al-ʿAzzāwī (1890–1971). As was typical in late Ottoman Iraq he had a

---

4   *Milaff Jawād ʿAlī.*

traditional religious education rather than formal academic training in history. His early education was in the Ottoman primary schools [*madāris rushdiyya*] where the curriculum was heavily influenced by the traditional religious education system. Later he studied under and received a certificate [*ijāza*] from Muḥammad Shukrī al-Alūsī (1856–1924), one of the most famous Sunnī religious scholars in Iraq during this period.

A dominant theme in al-ʿAzzāwī's work is that the nation [*umma*] has a constant need to evoke historical experiences in order to remind people about the recent and distant past, with the goal of making history a tool for the revival of the nation. Al-ʿAzzāwī's concept of the nation is limited to Iraqi society with its various sects and does not extend to the other Arab countries, despite the strong influence of Arab nationalist ideas on the historical vision of his time. The titles of most of al-ʿAzzāwī's works confirm that Iraq was the center of his attention and research. His famous eight volume work *Iraq between Two Occupations* [*Al-ʿIraq bayna Iḥtilālayn*], published between 1935 and 1956, is a history of Iraq from the Mongol conquest in 1258 until the British conquest in 1917.[5] He also wrote an encyclopedic work on the clans of Iraq [*ʿAshāʾir al-ʿIraq*] as well as studies on particular sects, such as a history of the Yazīdī sect [*Tārīkh al-Yāzīdiyya*] and another on the Yārsānī or Kākāʾī sect [*Al-Kakāʾiyya*].[6] Other works of his concerning Iraqi history and culture include a study on music in Iraq during the Mongol and Turkman periods [*Al-Mūsīqā al-ʿIrāqiyya fī ʿAhd al-Mughūl wa al-Turkmān*], a study on Astronomy in Iraq [*Tārīkh ʿIlm al-Falak fī al-ʿIrāq wa ʿAlāqatihi bi al-Aqṭār al-ʿArabiyya wa al-Islāmiyya*], a history of taxes in Iraq [*Tārīkh al-Ḍarāʾib al-ʿIrāqiyya*], a history of coinage in Iraq [*Tārīkh al-Nuqūd al-ʿIrāqiyya*], a history of Arabic literature in Iraq [*Tārīkh al-Adab al-ʿArabī fī al-ʿIrāq*] and even a study on the date-palm in Iraq [*Al-Nakhīl fī al-ʿIrāq*].[7]

The other non-academic historian who enjoyed great success was ʿAbd al-Razzāq al-Ḥasanī (1903–1997). He received a traditional education before pursuing higher studies at the Teachers' College [*Dār al-Muʿallimīn al-ʿĀliya*]. His early interest was journalism and he founded two newspapers, *Al-Mufīd* in 1922 and *Al-Fayḥāʾ* in 1927. He was also involved in politics. He took part in the 1941 movement of Rashīd ʿAlī for which he was imprisoned in the Al-Faw prison. His employment in the bureau of the Royal Council of Ministers [*Majlis al-Wuzarāʾ*], where he organized official documents, had a great impact on his

---

5 Al-ʿAzzāwī, *Al-ʿIrāq*.

6 Al-ʿAzzāwī, *Al-ʿAshāʾir*; Idem, *Tārīkh al-Yāzīdiyya*; Idem, *Al-Kakāʾiyya*.

7 Al-ʿAzzāwī, *Al-Mūsīqā*; Idem, *Tārīkh ʿIlm al-Falak*; Idem, *Tārīkh al-Ḍarāʾib*; Idem, *Tārīkh al-Nuqūd*; Idem, *Tārīkh al-Adab*; Idem, *Tārīkh al-Nakhīl*.

historical works which are based on and contain examples of official Iraqi documents from the period of the monarchy (1921–58). His works are especially valuable because many of the documents from this period were burned or destroyed following the overthrow of the monarchy in 1958.

His most famous books include *A History of the Iraqi Ministries* [*Tārīkh al-Wizārāt al-ʿIrāqiyya*] in ten volumes, *A Political History of Iraq* [*Tārīkh al-ʿIrāq al-Siyāsī*], *The Great Iraqi Revolution* [*Al-Thawra al-ʿIrāqiyya al-Kubrā*], *A History of the Iraqi Political Parties* [*Tārīkh al-Aḥzāb al-Siyāsiyya fī al-ʿIrāq*], and *Iraq in the Occupation and Mandate Periods* [*Al-ʿIrāq fī Dawray al-Iḥtilāl wa al-Intidāb 1935–1938*].[8] Most of these books rely on official documents to narrate modern Iraqi history along with personal interviews with prominent individuals who contributed to the political and social history of Iraq during this period.

Al-Ḥasanī's books did not achieve widespread circulation among the public, a fact about which he frequently complained. In addition, some of his books were resented by members of various sects and religions in Iraq because of their many errors in describing the beliefs and practices of these religious communities. Examples are his books on the Bahá'í religion [*Al-Bābiyyūn wa al-Bahā'iyyūn fī Ḥāḍirihim wa Māḍīhim*], the Yazīdīs [*ʿAbadat al-Shayṭān fī al-ʿIrāq: Majmūʿat Muʿāhadāt wa Tatabbuʿāt Shakhṣiyya fī al-Madhhab al-Yazīdī*] and the Mandaeans or Sabians [*Al-Ṣāʾiba fī Ḥāḍirihim wa Māḍīhim*].[9] The last book in particular caused considerable controversy and provoked a response from the head of the Sabian sect due to the major errors that it contained. Another feature of al-Ḥasanī's books was that they were repetitive and he often recycled entire chapters from earlier books in his later works.

A comparison of the works produced by al-ʿAzzāwī and al-Ḥasanī reveals some similarities. Both authors relied heavily on archival material. They also both chose to focus on local Iraqi history without paying much attention to Arab or World history. On the other hand, there are also some important differences between the two. Al-ʿAzzāwī's works were concerned with cultural and social history for the most part and he showed little interest in political history, while al-Ḥasanī's works were overwhelmingly focused on political history.[10]

---

8   Al-Ḥasanī, *Tārīkh al-Wizārāt*; Idem, *Tārīkh al-ʿIrāq al-Siyāsī*; Idem, *Al-Thawra*; Idem, *Tārīkh al-Aḥzāb*; Idem, *Al-ʿIrāq fī Dawray*.

9   Al-Ḥasanī, *Al-Bābiyyūn*; Idem, *ʿAbadat*; Idem, Al-Ṣāʾiba.

10   Fāliḥ Ḥasan ʿAlī, *ʿAbd al-Razzāq al-Ḥasanī*.

3   The Writing of National (Local) History

The studies produced by the followers of this trend in historical writing are not restricted to Iraq, most of them treat a large number of cities, garrison towns [*amṣār*], and regions throughout the Arab world. The historians of this tendency believed that local and regional histories were more important for understanding historical events than broad, nationalist histories based on the idea of the empire-state with a single, unique center opposed to various peripheral regions. An outstanding example of historians who pursued this style of scholarship is Ṣāliḥ Aḥmad al-ʿAlī (1918–2003). He produced a series of studies focusing on the histories of early Islamic cities as self-sufficient entities with their own demographic, intellectual, and political characteristics. The titles of his works embody this vision. His doctoral thesis at Oxford concerned the social and administrative organization of early Islamic Basra.[11] In Arabic he wrote works on the western quarters of medieval Baghdad [*Baghdād, Madīnat al-Salām: Al-Jānib al-Gharbī*], the administration of Medina in the early Islamic period [*Dawlat al-Rasūl fī al-Madīna: Dirāsa fī Takwīnihā wa Tanẓīmihā*], early Islamic Kufa [*Al-Kūfa wa Ahluhā fī Ṣadr al-Islām: Dirāsa fī Aḥwālihā al-ʿUmrāniyya wa Sukkānihā wa Tanẓīmihim*], the short-lived Abbasid capital at Sāmarāʾ [*Sāmarāʾ: Dirāsa fī al-Nashʾa wa al-Bunya al-Sukkāniyya*], the tribal composition of early Islamic Fusṭāṭ [*Ahl al-Fusṭāṭ: Dirāsa fī Tarkībihim al-Qabalī*], administration and urbanism in the early Islamic Hijaz [*Al-Ḥijāz fī Ṣadr al-Islām: Dirāsa fī Aḥwālihi al-ʿUmrāniyya wa al-Idāriyya*], and the province of Aḥwāz (Khuzistan) under the early Islamic empire [*Al-Aḥwāz fī al-ʿUhūd al-Islāmiyya al-Ūlā*].[12] He also translated the important works of Jacob Lassner and George Makdisi on Abbasid Baghdad from English into Arabic.[13]

In these studies, al-ʿAlī gave an exhaustive treatment of the most important Arab cities or *amṣār* from the early Islamic period. He emphasized that each of these cities represented a semi-independent unit on the demographic, political, administrative, intellectual and spiritual levels and that they somewhat resembled city-states. For example, in his discussion of the Abbasid capital at Sāmarrāʾ he states that "in creating Sāmarrāʾ the caliph al-Muʿtaṣim aimed to establish a complete city that would be a seat for him, his army, court, and the administrative institutions of the empire as well as a civilizational center that would stimulate economic life and culture, which had advanced greatly during

---

11   Al-ʿAlī, Early History of Basrah.
12   Al-ʿAlī, *Baghdād, Madīnat al-Salām*; Idem, *Dawlat al-Rasūl*; Idem, *Al-Kūfa*; Idem, *Samarrāʾ*; Idem, *Ahl al-Fusṭāṭ*; Idem, *Al-Ḥijāz*.
13   Lassner, *Khiṭaṭ Baghdād*; Makdisi, *Khiṭaṭ Baghdād fī al-Qurūn al-Wusṭā*.

this period. He also intended that the new city would reduce the population of Baghdad without completely extinguishing it."[14] In his study on Medina he presents each of the factions composing the Islamic state in Medina as well as its administrative organization, politics, internal opposition, external challenges, institutions, and military. This pattern was reflected in his studies on other Islamic cities and *amṣār*.

It appears that al-ʿAlī's characterization of the early Islamic settlements as semi-independent political and administrative units, and his belief in the importance of this phenomenon for understanding the nature of the Arab-Islamic state, were due to the influence of his academic milieu in Oxford where he was exposed to scholarship on the city-state in European history, and also to the general post second world war climate which saw the collapse of the British Empire in the Middle East and the emergence of the independent Arab nation-states as important political actors in the region.

4 Marxist Historical Scholarship

From the mid-1940s onwards the historical materialist approach spread among some of the Arab researchers who had completed their higher education in the Soviet Union. Their historical vision and much of their work was informed by the concept of class struggle in history. They chose subjects which were in keeping with their materialist conception of history such as feudalism, land ownership, and social movements in Islamic history which they examined as part of larger processes in World History. The most famous pioneer of this approach was Ḥusayn Qāsim al-ʿAzīz (1922–95) who forcefully expressed and championed these ideas in his works. In a number of works he applied the historical materialist methodology in an attempt to comprehend Islamic history, especially the social protest movements in Islamic history. Al-ʿAzīz's book on the anti-Abbasid revolutionary movement led by Bābak (d. 223/838) [*Al-Bābakiyya: Al-Intifāḍa ḍidd al-Khilāfat al-ʿAbbāsiyya*] is a foundational study not only in terms of the subject but also the methodology employed. It is based on his PhD thesis, which was defended at Moscow University in 1966. In his preface he critiques the primary and secondary sources concerning this event and he ventures to describe some of the previous researchers who dealt with Bābak's revolt and similar movements as "scholars of the bourgeoisie who were filled with hatred of mass-revolutionary movements."[15] He casts doubt

---

14   Al-ʿAlī, *Samarrāʾ*, 5.

15   Al-ʿAzīz, *Al-Bābakiyya*, 6.

on their conclusions and their interpretations of these events and defends the historical-materialist approach against its critics. He denounces "slanderous accusations of licentiousness, wife-sharing, and drunken orgies" that were made against communist movements by hostile sources.[16] In the course of his criticism of "bourgeois scholars" he praises the role of orientalism in preserving and publishing the classical Arabic-Islamic corpus, however, he notes that orientalist scholarship has also been affected by the penetration of bourgeois ideas and opinions that are hostile to popular movements.[17] Al-ʿAzīz also criticizes Arab historians, particularly the Iraqis among them, who have been influenced by Western studies.

Al-ʿAzīz's historical writings on various subjects are frequently transformed into critiques of capitalist thought. He criticized the famous Iraqi historian ʿAbd al-ʿAzīz al-Dūrī (much of whose work focused on the economic history of the Islamic period) whom he claimed had "fallen into serious errors despite his pretense of an objective, scientific style."[18] Al-Dūrī claimed that Bābak's revolt against the Abbasids was due to hatred of Arab-Islamic rule by the local population in the province of Adharbayjān whereas al-ʿAzīz maintained that the revolt's causes were socioeconomic and that it was a popular movement opposed to the interests of the feudal aristocratic ruling class.[19]

In Al-ʿAzīz's vision of early Islamic history the dynamic factor was the relationship between a ruling Arab feudal aristocracy and the masses inhabiting the empire (he uses the term *ariqqāʾ*, or slaves, for the latter). He does not regard religion as a significant factor in this. In his view the relationship between the Arab ruling aristocracy and the non-Arabs was motivated primarily by class. Their attitude towards the non-Arab common class was one of scorn and disdain, while they treated old Persian aristocracy (*ashrāf al-ʿajam*) with respect and honor due to their common socioeconomic interests.

In his book on Bābak's revolt he equates the concept of slaves [Arabic *ʿabīd* or *ariqqāʾ*], which is present in Marxist theory, with the classical Arabic term *mawālī* [non-Arab converts to Islam in the early post-conquest period, often translated as "clients"]. According to al-ʿAzīz, despite the difference in name, in practice the *ariqqāʾ* and *mawālī* were equivalent because neither category of persons was permitted to hold high level positions in the army or administration.

---

16   Ibid., 7.
17   Ibid., 7.
18   Ibid., 35.
19   Ibid., 36.

Al-ʿAzīz uses Marxist terminology throughout his studies to understand Islamic history. He tries to analyze the decline and fall of the Umayyad caliphate, the Abbasid revolution, and the establishment of the Abbasid state within a borrowed Marxist intellectual framework. He employs many examples and details from the Arabic-Islamic sources to create a model of Islamic history which corresponds to the general principles of the Marxist theory of history. He denies religion a primary or even a secondary role as a moving force in history, particularly as a motivating factor for the masses. For al-ʿAzīz the opposition movements during the Abbasid period "arose as a result of the cooperation of diverse peoples against the authority of the ruling class and not due to racial or religious differences as many researchers claim in their interpretations and as the Abbasids themselves claimed in their propaganda against these movements in order to incite the Muslims against the rebels and to depict their efforts to suppress these peasant rebellions as a holy war." From this statement we can see that religion was not an influential factor in causing popular revolts and opposition movements but rather it was employed by the ruling class as a means of confronting such movements.

5 Historical Writing from a Nationalist Conception to an Islamic Conception

The 1950s saw great changes in Iraq and the Arab world, such as the rise of nationalist ideas followed by the appearance of political Islam, which was seen as an instrument to combat the Marxist current which was dominant in the region at that time. The transition from the idea of Arab nationalism to the concept of the "Islamic Umma" also brought major changes in its wake. The aftermath of the Second World War witnessed new challenges for the Arab world, such as the establishment of the state of Israel in 1948, and the Arab nationalist trend grew in popularity, reaching its apogee in the 1950s. Many Iraqi thinkers and academics participated directly in the nationalist movements. In May 1941 Iraq was divided by a power struggle between two factions, one pro-British and the other completely opposed to the British presence in the country. The efforts of the latter faction resulted in a sort of limited independence for Iraq. One of the most prominent Iraqi historians, Jawād ʿAlī (1908–87), participated in the May 1941 movement for which he was subsequently jailed under the charge of supporting the Axis powers.[20]

---

20   Jawād ʿAlī, *Abḥāth*, 20–32.

It was in the context of these momentous international and regional developments that Jawād ʿAlī wrote his monumental ten-part history of the Arabs before Islam [*Al-Mufaṣṣal fī Tārīkh al-ʿArab qabla al-Islām*, henceforth referred to as *al-Mufaṣṣal*]. The aims of this work were closely connected to the nationalist ideological milieu. This is evident from Jawād ʿAlī's words upon the completion of his project "I thank God for giving me the strength to accomplish this idea which I have loved and this project whose foundations I laid long ago, the project of recording the history of the Arabs before Islam ... I feel great joy for having performed the work incumbent upon me and for participating in this national duty which is in my opinion of the greatest importance ..."[21] It should be noted that Jawād ʿAlī's project on the history of the pre-Islamic Arabs was carried out in two complementary stages. The first stage consisted of an eight-part book bearing the title *Tārīkh al-ʿArab qabla al-Islām*, which was written between 1950 and 1959, a turbulent time with many changes of government and important events on the regional level which left an impact on this work.[22] Later he released an expanded and updated version of this book with two additional parts entitled *Al-Mufaṣṣal fī Tārīkh al-ʿArab qabla al-Islām*. The *Mufaṣṣal* was conceived as an encyclopedic work in the philological tradition of the German school of oriental studies.

In the *Mufaṣṣal* a strong nationalist interpretation of history is evident. Jawād ʿAlī treats the Arabs even in Antiquity as a member of a shared homeland and language family and defines their boundaries in relation to other groups. He does not share the view held by some Arab nationalist writers that all of the ancient Semitic peoples were "Arabs."[23] He writes "In my opinion Arabism [*al-ʿurūba*] does not need to add these other peoples to the Arabs, in order to prove the early origins of the Arabs, for God has given these other peoples histories and then erased them, however, He has given the Arabs an ancient history that continues until the present day. The Arabs have no inferiority complex that would make them claim as their own peoples whose relation to them cannot be proved."[24]

Then we move from Jawād ʿAlī's work on the Arabs before Islam to his book on the history of the Arabs during the Islamic period [*Tārīkh al-ʿArab fī al-Islām*], which was intended as the introduction to a second multi-volume project on the Arabs after the coming of Islam. This work exhibits a change in the author's vision, goals and methodology which corresponded to rapidly

---

21   Jawād ʿAlī, *Tārīkh al-ʿArab qabla al-Islām* ii, 6.
22   *Milaff Jawād ʿAlī*, 669.
23   Jawād ʿAlī, *Al-Mufaṣṣal*, i, 7.
24   Jawād ʿAlī, Ibid., i, 8.

occurring changes in Iraqi society and politics. Though it is a small volume and intended only as an introduction to a much larger encyclopedic project on Islamic history that Jawād ʿAlī never completed, this work affords us a valuable glimpse into the life and times of its author and the conditions under which he wrote. He refers directly to this background with the phrase "The Hegemony of Public Opinion."[25] For Jawād ʿAlī the study of medieval Islamic history plays a role in treating the problems of the modern Islamic world. The largest part of the book is concerned with methodological issues, namely, the proper approach to writing a history of Islam. This concern is expressed in the title of the first chapter: "The Importance of Islamic History and How to Write it."[26]

The book's goals are the study of history and an examination of the causes of prosperity and decline. Among the lessons which Jawād ʿAlī attempts to convey to his readers is the connection between contemporary problems and the past. In his opinion there is a strong connection between the experiences of the nascent Islamic community in the seventh century AD and the problems of the modern Islamic world in which he lived. He diagnoses the problems of contemporary Islamic society as "intellectual stagnation, ignorance, and blind fanaticism reminiscent of the fanaticism of Quraysh in the time of the Prophet."[27] After this description of the problems confronting modern Islamic society, he concludes that the solution lies in "studying the distant causes and reasons for these ills, which entails a return to the past in order to benefit from its lessons in the treatment of contemporary problems and in order to understand why these problems have persisted until the present."[28]

The idea of reviving the Islamic *umma* in order to confront present decline and combat the dominant ideological currents of the time, especially the spread of communist thought, is one of the pressing duties of the historian of Islam, according to Jawād ʿAlī. The year in which he published his book on the history of the Arabs in the Islamic period, 1961, witnessed a flourishing of communist and leftist thought in Iraq. The monarchy and its aristocratic supporters had recently been overthrown and replaced by a republican government dominated by military officers led by ʿAbd al-Karīm Qāsim. There was an enormous degree of sympathy for communism and for the plight of the common and lower classes in society. At the same time Islamist factions made their appearance as a response to the leftist currents and they proposed their own solutions to society's problems.

---

25   Jawād ʿAlī, *Tārīkh al-ʿArab fī al-Islām*, 12.

26   Ibid., 6.

27   Ibid., 7.

28   Ibid., 78.

Jawād ʿAlī believes that the study of Islamic history has an important role to play in providing an Islamic response to the challenges facing the *umma* in the contemporary period. According to him, the historian must choose subjects that are relevant to the contemporary period. He says that the discipline of Islamic history is "responsible for finding answers to the difficult problems and issues that are related to the history of Islam, and it will assist the Islamic world in treating the ailments from which it suffers, ailments that are mostly ancient, inherited by the East from the periods preceding the emergence of Islam and which have no relation to Islam itself."[29]

It appears that the transformation of Jawād ʿAlī's outlook from a nationalist to an Islamic one had a great impact on his view of orientalism. Although in his earlier works on pre-Islamic history he praised the works of the orientalists, he later took a negative stance toward orientalist scholarship on the Islamic period.[30] He considered religion to be a major motivating and guiding factor of orientalist scholarship which determined its attitudes towards Islam. According to him the religion and sect of orientalists had a real influence on how they presented Islam in their work and caused some to have unobjective conclusions. He states that: "The Christian orientalists were clergymen or graduates of theology faculties and they treated sensitive subjects in Islam, trying with all of their effort to find a Christian origin, whereas the Jewish orientalists, especially after the establishment of Israel and the espousal of the Zionist ideology by most of them attempted to derive everything Arab and Islamic from a Jewish origin. Both groups allowed their sympathies and religious views to guide their conclusions."[31] Therefore, Jawād ʿAlī's criterion for reception of orientalist scholarship was determined by religious factors, historical context, and the nature of the subject.

6   Between Economic History and Nationalist History

There was another group of historians who were concerned with the economic history of Islam, however, they approached it from a non-Marxist perspective. Their methodological inspiration came from Western Europe. Some of them studied in Europe shortly before the Second World War and after it when Europe was suffering severe economic difficulties as a result of devastation from the war. There was an attempt to search for universal solutions, relying

---

29   Ibid., 7.
30   Jawād ʿAlī, *Tārīkh al-ʿArab qabla al-Islām* I, 123, 140–141.
31   Ibid., i, 6.

not only on experiences and examples from Western history, but also seeking to benefit from the historical experiences of other regions, including the Orient with its venerable empires such as the Abbasid caliphate which was seen as the apogee of the Islamic Empire. This trend interacted with the rise of nationalism in the Arab world. For this reason, the study of the economic history of the Islamic world was framed by Arab nationalist thought. 'Abd al-'Azīz al-Dūrī (1919–2010) was perhaps the most prominent of the historians who fall into this category. He wrote his PhD thesis on the economic history of early Abbasid Iraq, entitled "Studies on the economic life of Mesopotamia in the 10th century" [later published in Arabic as *Tārīkh al-'Irāq al-Iqtiṣādī fī al-Qarn al-Rābi' al-Hijrī*], at the School of Oriental and African Studies in London, followed by a book in Arabic entitled *An Introduction to Arab Economic History* [*Muqaddima fī al-Tārīkh al-Iqtiṣādī al-'Arabī*].[32]

Al-Dūrī was a contemporary of Jawād 'Alī and Ṣāliḥ Aḥmad al-'Alī. Their presence indicated a trend toward increasing specialization within the field of Islamic history in Iraq during the 1950s and 1960s. Jawād 'Alī had written his doctoral thesis in Hamburg on the *Mahdī* according to the Twelver Shī'īs, a subject concerning the history of religions, while Ṣāliḥ Aḥmad al-'Alī started his career with a thesis on the social and administrative organization of early Islamic Basra and continued to focus heavily on social history. Al-Dūrī focused on economic history and for him the concept of the Arab Nation [*Al-Ummat al-'Arabiyya*] was the key to understanding the progression of Arab-Islamic history.

Al-Dūrī consolidated his vision of Islamic history with a series of studies in the realm of ideological history. Between 1960 and 1965 he wrote his famous trilogy "The Historical Roots" ["Al-Judhūr al-Tārīkhiyya"] which consisted of three volumes: *The Historical Roots of Arab Nationalism* [*Al-Judhūr al-Tārīkhiyya li al-Qawmiyya al-'Arabiyya*], *The Historical Roots of Ethnic Chauvinism* [*Al-Judhūr al-Tārīkhiyya li al-Shu'ūbiyya*], *The Historical Roots of Arab Socialism* [*Al-Judhūr al-Tārīkhiyya li al-Ishtirākiyya al-'Arabiyya*].[33] The 1960s saw the struggle for the realization of the ideal of Arab unity, a concept that was very popular among the Arab intellectual classes. The question asked was how can the Arab intellectual contribute to the contest from his position? In the books mentioned above al-Dūrī sought to establish roots for the concepts of nationalism and the Arab Nation, concepts that were new to traditional Arab culture.[34] Al-Dūrī calls for

---

32   Al-Dūrī, Studies; Idem, *Tārīkh al-'Irāq al-Iqtiṣādī*; Idem, *Muqaddima*.

33   Al-Dūrī, *Al-Judhūr al-Tārīkhiyya li al-Qawmiyya*; Idem, *Al-Judhūr al-Tārīkhiyya li al-Shu'ūbiyya*; Idem, Al-Judhūr al-Tārīkhiyya li al-Ishtirākiyya.

34   Kawtharānī, *Tārīkh*, 285–287.

limiting the subjects of historical research and the means of interpreting them: "Historical studies must be based on the history of the Nation if we want to understand its trends and developments. When history is dragged behind tales of dynasties and exceptional individuals, it is diverted from the destiny of the Nation and distanced from the desired goal."[35] This attitude was not limited to the subjects of research but also included the interpretation of the central events in Islamic history. The Arab-Islamic conquests were described as having been motivated primarily by the spirit of Arab nationalism, despite the clear importance of economic and religious factors in this event. Furthermore, the term *umma* in the Qur'ān and the Hadiths was anachronistically given the meaning "Arab Nation."

From the 1980s onwards al-Dūrī lessened his heavy reliance on the concept of the "Arab Nation" in his analysis of Islamic history. In his book *The Historical Formation of the Arab Nation: A Study on Identity and Consciousness* [*Al-Takwīn al-Tārīkhī li al-Ummat al-ʿArabiyya: Dirāsa fī al-Huwiyya*] published in 1984, he reformulated his idea of the Arab Nation from a historical-developmental point of view. This approach was relatively different from the one that he had espoused in the earlier trilogy on "historical roots."[36] It seems that he had a falling out with the Baath party and its extreme nationalist ideology. Nonetheless, he continued to believe in the idea of the Arab Nation and he still accorded to the Arabs a greater role in Islamic Civilization than to other peoples such as the Persians and the Turks.

7　　The State and History Writing in Iraq

When the earliest history departments were established in Iraq they were supervised and funded by the government. This was the case in the University of Baghdad, where the first history department in Iraq was opened in 1949. At the same time a policy of sending Iraqi students to study abroad in Western universities was also pursued. Prior to 1958 there was no direct, overt government intervention in the writing of history, but this changed with the overthrow of the monarchy and the coming of the republic. During this period state intervention in the production of historical scholarship gradually increased and works were subject to censorship. Such government interference became even more pronounced following the Baathist coup of 1968 and the rise to prominence of Ṣaddām Ḥusayn, who was then vice-president of the republic. In 1979

35　　Al-Dūrī, *Al-Judhūr al-Tārīkhiyya li al-Qamwiyya*, 9.
36　　Kawtharānī, *Tārīkh*, 288.

Ṣaddām Ḥusayn held his first meeting with Iraq's leading historians, among the invitees were ʿAbd al-ʿAzīz al-Dūrī, Ṣāliḥ Aḥmad al-ʿAlī, and Jawād ʿAlī. The topic of the meeting was how to interpret history and its stages according to the ideology of the Baath movement and how to avoid historical interpretations that went against Baathist doctrine.

It seems that this meeting was decisive in reinforcing state intervention in Iraqi historical scholarship. This was accompanied by a policy of Baathification [*tabʿīth*] which entailed the entry of university professors, willingly or unwillingly, into the ranks of the Baath party. A generation of historians emerged who believed in and defended the ideas of the Baath movement. This milieu affected the writing of MA and PhD theses in history. Every thesis had to be approved by the censors from the Baath party.

A large team of Iraqi historians were commissioned to write a comprehensive, encyclopedic history of Iraq and its civilization through all periods in light of the ideology of the government and the Baath party. The result was the 13-volume *Civilization of Iraq* [*Ḥaḍārat al-ʿIrāq*] published in 1985. The guiding principle of this book was to rewrite the history of Iraq from prehistory until the assumption of power by the Baath party according to the Baathist interpretation of history. This work was preceded by large volume entitled *Iraq in History* [*Al-ʿIrāq fī al-Tārīkh*].

In order to support the use of the Baathist ideology in historical scholarship, research institutions were founded. One of these was the *Institute of Arab History* [*Maʿhad al-Tārīkh al-ʿArabī*], which was established in 1971. Though it formally belonged to the Arab League, the institute was funded and supervised by the Iraqi state. It was very productive, in a single year the institute oversaw dozens of university theses in history, all of which reflected Baathist ideological positions. Another institute, named *The Founding Leader's Institue* [*Maʿhad al-Qāʾid al-Muʾassis*], in honor of the founder of the Baath party Michel ʿAflaq, was established at Al-Mustanṣiriyya University in Baghdad and it also played an important role in the supervision of many theses in history which adhered to Baathist viewpoints. During the Iran-Iraq war (1980–88) the Iraqi government opened a *Center for Iranian Studies* [*Markaz al-Dirāsāt al-Īrāniyya*] at the University of Basra, the purpose of which was to supply Iraq's decision makers with historical and intelligence information on Iran.

The Iraqi state's ideological influence was also exerted on historical and archeological journals. The journal *Sumer* (established in 1945), was Iraq's most famous journal of history and archeology and it enjoyed international renown. Its articles were published both in Arabic and in English. After 1979, it too was subjected to the views of the Baath party. An introduction was written for every issue which attempted to demonstrate the connection between the national heritage and the Baathist vision. The English section of the journal suffered from neglect due to the Baath party's Arabization policies. Other publications such as the cultural journal *Al-Mawrid* and the historical journal *Al-Muʾarrikh al-ʿArabī* underwent a similar experience.

In 1999 the president of Iraq, Ṣaddām Ḥusayn, held his second meeting with Iraqi historians, 20 years after the first meeting in 1979. This time a new generation of Iraqi scholars attended. The lectures delivered during this meeting were published under the title *Conversations of President Ṣaddām Ḥusayn with Iraqi Historians* [*Aḥādīth al-Raʾīs Ṣaddām Ḥusayn bi al-Baḥithīn wa al-Muʾarrikhīn wa Asātidhat al-Tārīkh fī al-ʿIrāq*]. The themes discussed at this meeting differed from those of the first meeting. Arab nationalist discourse was largely absent from the 1999 meeting. Instead, the focus was on Islamic history as well as modern history, particularly the history of the United States. This change in emphasis appears to have been due to several factors, among them the strained relations that Iraq had with many of the Arab states after its defeat in the 1991 Gulf War and the economic blockade imposed on Iraq with the participation of the United States and some Arab countries.[37]

8   Sectarian Historical Writing

It seems that the trend in contemporary Iraqi historiography of writing about the histories of religious sects and groups in a defensive, apologetic manner was a result of violent political changes to which Iraq was subjected. With the fall of Ṣaddām Ḥusayn's regime in 2003 there was a desire on the part of many to write the history of religious communities and sects in a new way, free from ideological constraints imposed by the previous regime. This trend is plainly visible through an examination of the theses produced in history departments and research units after 2003. One sees an abundance of theses which treat the histories of sects and ethnic groups in a deferential and celebratory way. A good example of this trend is Dr. ʿAbd al-Jabbār Nājī, one of Iraq's most famous living historians. We can detect two main phases in his research and writing, before and after the American invasion of Iraq in 2003 with its subsequent effects. In the first phase of his career as a historian he focused on the medieval Islamic city. In this choice of subject he was influenced by his MA supervisor in Iraq Ṣāliḥ Aḥmad al-ʿAlī. He earned his PhD from the School of Oriental and African Studies in London with a thesis on Basra in the late medieval period under the supervision of the famous orientalist Bernard Lewis (1919–2018). In

---

37   See Ṣaddām Ḥusayn, *Al-Tārīkh Nabḍ Ḥayy*.

a way this thesis was a continuation of that of Ṣāliḥ Aḥmad al-ʿAlī who had written about early Islamic Basra. Upon his return to Iraq, ʿAbd al-Jabbār Nājī wrote a number of works on historical thought. His crowning achievement in this period, however, was a volume entitled *Studies in the History of the Arab Islamic City* [*Dirāsāt fī Tārīkh al-Madīna al-ʿArabiyya al-Islāmiyya*]. This is a comprehensive work on the cities of the medieval Islamic world and it brings up to date the work that Ṣāliḥ Aḥmad al-ʿAlī had done previously on some of these cities.[38]

From the beginning of the 1980s historical scholarship in Iraq was subject to the heavy hand of the censor while Baathist ideology was imposed on all types of academic production in the field of history such as theses, journals, and monographs. This influence extended to the very choice of subject for a history dissertation. The treatment of the histories of religious sects and communities was strongly discouraged and any such studies of this nature that were produced reflected the Sunnī point of view.

After the fall of the Baathist regime in 2003, the previously taboo or marginalized subject of sectarian history became popular with researchers. A multitude of dissertations were written on topics related to the history of Shīʿism. Unfortunately, these studies lacked objectivity due to their great bias. The main goal of such studies was reconsideration of Shīʿī history for the Shīʿī society itself. It was within this context that a major change occurred in the scholarly production of ʿAbd al-Jabbār Nājī. An example of this is the long preface which he wrote for his Arabic translation of Petersen's important monograph *ʿAlī and Muʿāwiyya in Early Arabic Tradition* [*ʿAlī wa Muʿāwiyya fī al-Riwāya al-ʿArabiyya al-Mubakkira*] which was the first work that he published following the invasion of 2003. In this preface he attempts to reconsider how the Islamic caliphate was stolen from the "legitimate caliph" ʿAlī b. Abī Ṭālib.[39] He focuses intensively on this issue again in another book which he published in 2006 entitled *Shīʿism and Orientalism* [*Al-Tashayyuʿ wa al-Istishrāq*]. In this book his goal is not only to critique the treatment of Shīʿism by the orientalists, but also to convey to the Shīʿī community the necessity of playing its role in the political arena and to highlight the great importance of Shīʿī studies in the various national "schools" of oriental studies, especially in the American and Israeli schools which have devoted a great deal of resources to the topic and have produced more research on Shīʿism than all of the other orientalist schools.

---

38   Nājī, *Al-Mudun*, 130–140.

39   Peterson, *ʿAlī*, Introduction.

9   Conclusion

Based on the preceding sketch of historical writing in modern Iraq we can make a few general observations. First of all, it is apparent that student missions to European and American universities had a great influence on the development of historical studies in Iraq. Most of the early Iraqi academic historians employed the ideas and methodologies of the western orientalist schools in their writings. The history department of the University of Baghdad was the first institution to accept the Western traditions of historiography and it in turn influenced the other history departments in Iraq which were subsequently established.

Iraqi historical writing was also influenced by the surrounding political and ideological context. The state and the party played an especially influential role during the years of Baathist rule (1968–2003). At that time the Baath party exerted strong control over the history curriculum at all levels and its ideology influenced university dissertations.

Within the Arab world the Iraqi historiographical school rivaled the Egyptian school. Although the Egyptian school was older, some of the works produced by Iraqi historians in the field of early Islamic history surpassed those of their Egyptian counterparts in terms of depth, treatment, and the new results of their research. This is particularly the case with the works of the three most famous Iraqi historians: Jawād ʿAlī, Ṣāliḥ Aḥmad al-ʿAlī, and ʿAbd al-ʿAzīz al-Dūrī.

Translated by Amar S. Baadj

Bibliography

ʿAlī, Fāliḥ Ḥasan, ʿAbd al-Razzāq al-Ḥasanī Muʾarrikhan, Baghdad, 2010.

ʿAlī, Jawād [Ali, Javad], Der Mahdi der Zwölfer-Schia und seine vier Safire, PhD dissertation, Hamburg University, 1939.

ʿAlī, Jawād [Ali, Javad], *Tārīkh al-ʿArab qabla al-Islām*, 8 vols., Baghdad, 1956–1960.

ʿAlī, Jawād [Ali, Javad], *Tārīkh al-ʿArab fī al-Islām*, Baghdad, 1961.

ʿAlī, Jawād [Ali, Javad], *Al-Mufaṣṣal fī Tārīkh al-ʿArab qabla al-Islām*, 10 vols., Beirut, 1968–1974.

ʿAlī, Jawād [Ali, Javad], *Abḥāth fī Tārīkh al-ʿArab qabla al-Islām*, ed. Naṣīr al-Kaʿbī [Nasir al-Kaabi], Beirut, 2011.

Al-ʿAlī, Ṣāliḥ Aḥmad, Early History of Basrah: A Study of the Organization of an Islamic Misr, PhD dissertation, Oxford, 1949.

Al-ʿAlī, Ṣāliḥ Aḥmad, *Al-Tanẓīmāt al-Ijtimāʿiyya wa al-Iqtiṣādiyya fī al-Baṣra fī al-Qarn al-Awwal al-Hijrī*, Baghdad, 1953.

Al-ʿAlī, Ṣāliḥ Aḥmad, *Al-Ḥijāz fī Ṣadr al-Islām: Dirāsa fī Aḥwālihi al-ʿUmrāniyya wa al-Idāriyya*, Beirut, 1990.

Al-ʿAlī, Ṣāliḥ Aḥmad, *Baghdād Madīnat al-Salām, Al-Jānib al-Gharbī: Inshāʾuhā wa Tanẓīm Sukkānihā fī al-ʿUhūd al-ʿAbbāsiyya al-Ūlā*, 2 vols., Baghdad, 1985.

Al-ʿAlī, Ṣāliḥ Aḥmad, *Ahl al-Fusṭāṭ: Dirāsa fī Tarkībihim al-Qabalī wa Marākiz Idāratihim*, Beirut, 2000.

Al-ʿAlī, Ṣāliḥ Aḥmad, *Sāmarrāʾ: Dirāsa fī al-Nashʾa wa al-Bunya al-Sukkāniyya*, Beirut, 2001.

Al-ʿAlī, Ṣāliḥ Aḥmad, *Dawlat al-Rasūl fī al-Madīna: Dirāsa fī Takwīnihā wa Tanẓīmihā*, Beirut, 2003.

Al-ʿAlī, Ṣāliḥ Aḥmad, *Al-Kūfa wa Ahluhā fī Ṣadr al-Islām*, Beirut, 2003.

Al-ʿAlī, Ṣāliḥ Aḥmad, *Al-Ahwāz fī al-ʿUhūd al-Islāmiyya al-Ūlā*, Baghdad, n.d.

Al-ʿAzīz, Ḥusayn Qāsim, *Al-Bābakiyya: Al-Intifāḍa ḍidd al-Khilāfat al-ʿAbbāsiyya*, Baghdad and Beirut, 1966, repr. Damascus, 2000.

Al-ʿAzzāwī, ʿAbbās, *Al-Nakhīl fī al-ʿIrāq*, Baghdad, 1926.

Al-ʿAzzāwī, ʿAbbās, *Al-ʿIrāq bayna Iḥtilālayn*, Baghdad, 1935.

Al-ʿAzzāwī, ʿAbbās, *Tārīkh al-Yāzīdiyya*, Baghdad, 1936.

Al-ʿAzzāwī, ʿAbbās, *ʿAshāʾir al-ʿIrāq*, Beirut, 1937.

Al-ʿAzzāwī, ʿAbbās, *Al-Kākāʾiyya*, Baghdad, 1949.

Al-ʿAzzāwī, ʿAbbās, *Al-Mūsīqā al-ʿIrāqiyya fī ʿAhd al-Mughūl*, Baghdad, 1951.

Al-ʿAzzāwī, ʿAbbās, *Tārīkh ʿIlm al-Falak fī al-ʿIrāq wa ʿAlāqātuhu bi al-Aqṭār al-ʿArabiyya al-Islāmiyya*, Baghdad, 1958.

Al-ʿAzzāwī, ʿAbbās, *Tārīkh al-Nuqūd al-ʿIrāqiyya*, Baghdad, 1958.

Al-ʿAzzāwī, ʿAbbās, *Tārīkh al-Adab al-ʿIrāqī*, Baghdad, 1958.

Al-ʿAzzāwī, ʿAbbās, *Tārīkh al-Ḍarāʾib al-ʿIrāqiyya*, Baghdad, 1959.

Al-Dūrī, ʿAbd al-ʿAzīz, Studies on the Economic Life of Mesopotamia in the 10th Century, PhD dissertation, SOAS, University of London, 1942.

Al-Dūrī, ʿAbd al-ʿAzīz, *Tārīkh al-ʿIrāq al-Iqtiṣādī fī al-Qarn al-Rābiʿ al-Hijrī*, Baghdad, 1948.

Al-Dūrī, ʿAbd al-ʿAzīz, *Al-Nuẓum al-Islāmiyya*, Baghdad, 1950, repr. Beirut, 2008.

Al-Dūrī, ʿAbd al-ʿAzīz, English translation of the above by Ali, Razia, *Early Islamic Institutions: Administration and Taxation from the Caliphate to the Umayyads and ʿAbbāsids*, London and New York, 2011.

Al-Dūrī, ʿAbd al-ʿAzīz, *Baḥth fī Nashʾat ʿIlm al-Taʾrīkh ʿinda al-ʿArab*, Beirut, 1960.

Al-Dūrī, ʿAbd al-ʿAzīz, English translation of the above by Conrad, Lawrence I., *The Rise of Historical Writing Among the Arabs*, Princeton, 1983.

Al-Dūrī, ʿAbd al-ʿAzīz, *Al-Judhūr al-Tārīkhiyya li al-Qawmiyya al-ʿArabiyya*, Baghdad, 1961.

Al-Dūrī, ʿAbd al-ʿAzīz, *Al-Judhūr al-Tārīkhiyya li al-Shuʿūbiyya*, Beirut, 1962.

Al-Dūrī, ʿAbd al-ʿAzīz, Al-Judhūr al-Tārīkhiyya li al-Ishtirākiyya al-ʿArabiyya, *Al-Aqlām* 8 (August 1965), 3–25.

Al-Dūrī, ʿAbd al-ʿAzīz, *Muqaddima fī al-Tārīkh al-Iqtiṣādī al-ʿArabī*, Beirut, 1969.

Al-Dūrī, ʿAbd al-ʿAzīz, German translation of the above by Jacobi, Juergen, *Arabische Wirtschaftsgeschichte*, Munich and Zurich, 1979.

Al-Dūrī, ʿAbd al-ʿAzīz, *Al-Takwīn al-Tārīkhī li al-Ummat al-ʿArabiyya*, Beirut, 1984.

Al-Dūrī, ʿAbd al-ʿAzīz, English translation of the above by Conrad, Lawrence I., *The Historical Formation of the Arab Nation: A Study in Identity and Consciousness*, New York, Sydney, and London, 1987.

Al-Ḥasanī, ʿAbd al-Razzāq, *Al-Bābiyyūn wa al-Bahāʾiyyūn fī Ḥāḍirihim wa Māḍihim*, Sidon, 1930.

Al-Ḥasanī, ʿAbd al-Razzāq, *Al-Yāzīdiyya am ʿabadat al-Shayṭān*, Sidon, 1931.

Al-Ḥasanī, ʿAbd al-Razzāq, *Al-Ṣāʾiba fī Ḥāḍirihim wa Māḍīhim*, Sidon, 1931.

Al-Ḥasanī, ʿAbd al-Razzāq, *Tārīkh al-Wizārāt al-ʿIrāqiyya*, Sidon, 1933.

Al-Ḥasanī, ʿAbd al-Razzāq, *Al-ʿIrāq fī Dawray al-Iḥtilāl wa al-Intidāb*, Sidon, 1948.

Al-Ḥasanī, ʿAbd al-Razzāq, *Tārīkh al-ʿIrāq al-Siyāsī*, Sidon, 1957.

Al-Ḥasanī, ʿAbd al-Razzāq, *Tārīkh al-Aḥzāb al-Siyāsiyya fī al-ʿIrāq*, Beirut, 1980.

Ḥusayn, Ṣaddām, *Al-Tārīkh Nabḍ Ḥayy wa Fiʾl Inṣānī: Aḥādīth al-Raʾīs al-Qāʾid khilāl Liqāʾāt Siyādatihi bi al-Bāḥithīn wa al-Muʾarrikhīn wa Asātidha al-Tārīkh fī al-ʿIrāq*, Baghdad, 1999.

Kawtharānī, Wajīh, *Tārīkh al-Taʾrīkh: Ittijāhāt, Madāris, Manāhij*, Beirut, 2012.

Lassner, Jacob, *Khiṭaṭ Baghdād fī al-ʿUṣūr al-ʿAbbāsiyya al-Ūlā*, trans., Ṣāliḥ Aḥmad al-ʿAlī, Baghdad, 1984.

Maqdisī, George, *Khiṭaṭ Baghdād fī al-Qurūn al-Wusṭā*, trans. Ṣāliḥ Aḥmad al-ʿAlī, Beirut, 2014.

Milaff Jawād ʿAlī, Al-Majmaʿ al-ʿIlmī al-ʿIrāqī, unnumbered, 1/10/1953.

Nājī, ʿAbd al-Jabbār, Baṣra: 295–447/907–1055, PhD dissertation, SOAS, University of London, 1970.

Nājī, ʿAbd al-Jabbār, *Dirāsāt fī Tārīkh al-Mudun al-ʿArabiyya al-Islāmiyya*, Beirut, 2001.

Nājī, ʿAbd al-Jabbār, *Al-Tashayyuʿ wa al-Istishrāq*, Beirut, 2011.

Peterson, E.L., ʿAlī wa Muʿāwiyya fī al-Riwāya al-ʿArabiyya al-Mubakkira, trans. ʿAbd al-Jabbār Nājī, Beirut, 2009.

Raʾūf, ʿImād ʿAbd al-Salām, *Al-Tārīkh wa al-Muʾarrikhūn al-ʿIrāqiyyūn fī al-ʿAhd al-ʿUthmānī*, Beirut, 2009.

11

L'histoire sociale et économique médiévale de Al-Maġrib et Al-Andalus chez les chercheurs arabes

Brahim El Kadiri Boutchich et Azeddine Guessous

L'importance accordée à l'histoire économique et sociale dans le monde arabe réside dans le nombre et la nature des publications. Des recherches ayant fait l'objet de thèses et abordant des sujets originaux et inédits, utilisant de nouvelles méthodes, de nouvelles approches et de nouveaux thèmes, ne sont pas encore publiées. Ainsi, pour atteindre un tel niveau, la recherche historique a subi les multiples vicissitudes de l'orientalisme dirigée par l'esprit colonial et post-colonial. L'orientalisme, son idéologie et ses écrits sur le monde arabe, ont orienté, non sans impact, les recherches scientifiques en général et la recherche historique en particulier. Dans un premier temps, et compte tenu des incompréhensions, les écrits historiques se sont fixés comme objectif de réfuter les maladresses et les interprétations erronées de l'orientalisme. Ensuite, faisant appel aux méthodes des écoles historiques occidentales ainsi qu'à l'héritage épistémologique de l'orientalisme, plusieurs recherches ouvertes sur d'autres horizons plus larges, et bénéficiant de sources nouvelles publiées ou manuscrites jusqu'alors inexploitées, ont vu le jour. En outre, les recherches en histoire économique et sociale sur l'occident musulman et l'histoire des mentalités font partie de cette catégorie.

Cependant, plusieurs thèmes abordés dans des thèses de troisième cycle et de doctorat d'Etat portaient sur la vie sociale, sur le commerce et sur son impact socio-économique, ainsi que sur l'histoire des mentalités et ses aspects réels et mythiques. C'est pourquoi certains chercheurs ont travaillé sur les mariages, l'éducation des enfants, ou le rôle des femmes dans la société. D'autres se sont penchés sur l'étude des classes sociales, des *faqihs*, des esclaves, des sufis, des marginaux, sur l'opinion publique et le rapport entre gouvernant et gouvernés, l'influence de l'homme sur son espace et son comportement vis-à-vis de son milieu et les ressources naturelles lors des famines et des épidémies, l'activité agricole et les problèmes d'irrigation, l'artisanat, les voies commerciales …

Ces études se sont basées sur un nombre considérable de sources, publiées ou manuscrites, ainsi que sur les études récentes rédigées en arabe, en anglais, en espagnol ou en français. Dès lors, ces travaux sont devenus des références incontournables en histoire économique et sociale, à la fois en ce qui concerne

© KONINKLIJKE BRILL NV, LEIDEN, 2021 | DOI:10.1163/9789004460089_012

l'occident musulman et sur l'histoire de l'islam à l'époque médiévale. Outre les outils utilisés, l'objectif de ce travail est de faire connaître ces recherches aux occidentaux dans l'esprit d'établir des liens étroits au profit des recherches historiques.

Ainsi, notre présentation reposera sur deux axes :

1. Présenter les plus importantes réalisations, publications et thèses consacrées à l'histoire économique et sociale d'Al-Maġrib et Al-Andalus dans le monde arabe et essentiellement au Maroc à travers trois générations :

   – La génération des années 1970, comprenant des pionniers comme Maḥmūd Ismāʿīl, qui a jeté les bases d'une école ayant influencé les écrits historiques en Orient et en Occident.

   – La génération de chercheurs des années 1990 dont certains ont fondé des unités de recherche et de formation sur l'histoire économique et sociale. Ils ont à la fois publié et dirigé des recherches pointues et ont élaboré de nouveaux instruments d'analyse.

   – La troisième génération, celle du troisième millénaire, qui a suivi l'itinéraire de ses prédécesseurs en réalisant des recherches sur l'histoire économique et sociale ainsi que sur l'histoire des mentalités.

2. Le deuxième axe permettra de mettre en relief les nouveaux outils de travail, les sources mobilisées, les méthodes adoptées, ainsi que les nouveaux objets envisagés dans le domaine de l'histoire économique et sociale tout comme l'histoire des mentalités.

1 Pionniers des années 1970

L'importance accordée à l'histoire économique et sociale devient apparente lors de la réactualisation des approches dans les écrits historiques dans le monde arabe suite au contact avec les méthodes des écoles historiques occidentales. Sur la base de la conviction qu'il faut procéder à une nouvelle lecture de l'histoire et de ses sources, ont émergé des écrits sur des aspects encore non élucidés, tels que le social et l'économique. C'est ainsi que des publications ont vu le jour dans le monde arabo-musulman, telle l'étude de Sāliḥ Aḥmad Al-ʿAlī[1], ou celle de Abd al-ʿAzīz al-Dūrī[2]. Ces deux ouvrages ont été suivis par la publication occidentale d'Eliyahu Ashtor[3]. Il est relativement évident que

---

1 Sāliḥ Aḥmad Al-ʿAlī, *Al-Tanẓīmāt al-iqtiṣādiyya wa al-iǧtimāʿiyya fī al-Baṣra fī al-qarn al awwal al-hijrī.*

2 ʿAbd al-ʿAzīz al-Dūrī, *Muqaddima fī al-tārīḫ al-iqtiṣādī-l-ʿarabī.*

3 Eliyahu Ashtor, *A Social and Economic History of the Near East in the Middle Ages.*

le choix des tendances et des visions plus avancées de ces publications avait des échos dans les milieux scientifiques concernés ainsi que dans la recherche historique en général.

Par ailleurs, la présence du maître Maḥmūd Ismāʿīl ʿAbd al-Rāziq, au Maroc avait marqué de manière cruciale la focalisation sur l'histoire économique et sociale de l'occident musulman. Illustre historien chercheur, pionnier, intervenant, il continue jusqu'à présent de faire des percées dans le sujet en question. Son ouvrage, consistant en une approche sociologique de la pensée musulmane[4], retrace sa vision socio-économique de l'ensemble de l'histoire de l'islam, et donnant ainsi les contours d'une histoire vue d'en bas. Y sont regroupés les visions à la fois historique et théorique avec une induction à laquelle il a consacré le dernier tome. Profondément conscient de la crise de la pensée musulmane qui réside selon lui en la méthode, il ne cesse d'insister dans ses écrits, et essentiellement dans ses préfaces, sur le problème en question. L'intérêt accordé à l'histoire socio-économique émane de ses premières publications, soulevant des questions sur l'histoire de l'islam[5], où il présente une lecture sociologique des révoltes de l'occident musulman au deuxième siècle de l'hégire. Il réside aussi dans ses essais sur la pensée et l'histoire[6], qui contiennent une interprétation sociologique du mouvement Almoravide. Ses dernières publications sur les marginaux illustrent bel et bien sa persévérance dans cette perspective: *al-Muhammašūn fī-l-tārīḫ al-islāmī*, un ensemble d'études sur les cultivateurs, les esclaves, les artisans et les classes démunies et marginalisées, traite de la nature des causes et des revendications de leurs mouvements populaires et de leurs révoltes (ex. les révoltes des Zinǧ en Iraq, des Ḥarāfiš en Egypte, des Ḥaddādūn en Al-Andalus.). Il en déduit que chaque fois que le problème socio-économique s'aggrave, la société est poussée à l'extrémisme.

L'influence de Maḥmūd Ismāʿīl sur la recherche historique ne se limite pas à ces écrits; il a eu un impact plus opérationnel et direct sur des chercheurs et a aussi supervisé des thèses originales, au Maroc, en Algérie, en Tunisie et en Egypte. Il a établi, pour ainsi dire, une école historique sur le thème en question avec des perspectives nouvelles non seulement sur les méthodes mais également sur la conception de l'histoire elle-même. Une école pour une histoire vue d'en bas. Il va de soi que Maḥmūd Ismāʿīl et ses étudiants, devenus par la suite des professeurs éminents influencés par l'école *Les Annales E.S.C.*, ont le

---

4 Maḥmūd Ismāʿīl ʿAbd al-Rāziq, *Susyulūǧiyā-l-fikr al-islāmī* en dix volumes.
5 Maḥmūd Ismāʿīl ʿAbd al-Rāziq, *Qaḍāyā fī-l-tārīḫ al-islāmī: minhaǧ wa taṭbīq*.
6 Maḥmūd Ismāʿīl ʿAbd al-Rāziq, *Maqālāt fī l-fikr wa-l-tārīḫ*.

mérite d'écrire une histoire économique et sociale de al-Maġrib et al-Andalus avec de nouveaux thèmes et de nouvelles approches.

En 1980, Al-Ḥabīb Al-Ǧanhānī a publié un recueil d'études portant sur l'économique et le social de l'histoire de Al-Maġrib[7]. L'ouvrage comprend deux études sur la fiscalité sous les Umayyades et sous les Fatimides, l'une consacrée à l'aspect économique et social dans le mouvement ḫariǧite et l'autre aux informations précieuses que présentent les sources des *ṭabaqāts* pour traiter de la vie quotidienne de la société. *Tabaqāt al-mašāyiḫ* de Abī-l-ʿAbbās Al-Darǧīnī a été pris comme exemple. Toutefois, dans son introduction l'auteur se montre optimiste au regard de l'intérêt que les jeunes chercheurs accordent à ce choix, mais ce travail n'a pas eu de suite et n'a eu aucun impact sur les études en l'histoire économique et sociale.

2　　　　Les érudits des années 1990

Les années 1990 ont vu se réaliser des recherches plus poussées sur les composantes de l'histoire économique et sociale, abordant aussi l'histoire des mentalités ou de la vie familiale. Elles se sont penchées sur des classes sociales précises, telles que la *ʿāmma*, les esclaves, ou les rapports entre les classes. D'autres ont étudié le lien entre le politique et le social. La quasi-totalité de ces travaux ont été dirigés par Maḥmūd Ismāʿīl. À l'origine ce sont des thèses d'État, excepté celle de l'*iqṭāʿ* en Al-Andalus qui a fait l'objet de thèse de troisième cycle.

En 1989 Aḥmad Al-Ṭāhirī a publié son étude sur la *ʿāmma* de Cordoue[8]. Elle cible la classe sociale de la *ʿāmma*, son rôle économique dans le domaine agricole, artisanal, industriel et commerciale. Elle aborde par ailleurs les différentes catégories de la *ʿāmma*, notamment la structure sociale dans sa formation ethnique et hiérarchique, ainsi que des aspects de la vie socio-culturelle, le statut de la *ʿāmma* vis-à-vis des autres classes, et leur mode vie sociale influencé par leur niveau économique. L'auteur a également abordé la culture de la *ʿāmma* et son rapport avec son niveau socio-économique durant la période califale en al-Andalus. Enfin, il a traité du rôle politique de la *ʿāmma* de Cordoue.

Brahim El Kadiri Boutchich (Ibrāhīm al-Qādirī Būtašīš) a publié en 1992 son travail sur le féodalisme en al-Andalus[9]. Il s'agit d'une étude sur les effets et les

---

7　Al-Ḥabīb Al-Ǧanhānī, *Dirasāt magribīya fī-l-tārīḫ al-iqtiṣādī wa-l-iǧtimāʿī li-l-Maġrib al-Islāmī.*
8　Aḥmad Al-Ṭāhirī, *ʿAmmat Qurṭuba fī ʿaṣr al-ḫilāfa.*
9　Brahim El Kadiri Boutchich [Ibrāhīm al-Qādirī Būtašīš], *Aṯar al-iqṭāʿ fī tārīḫ al-Andalus al-siyāsī min muntasaf al-qarn al-ṯāliṯ al-hiǧrī ḥattā ẓuhūr al-ḫilāfa (250 H/316 H).*

conséquences du féodalisme comme modèle économique sur le politique en al-Andalus. L'auteur a traité en premier lieu des manifestations structurelles du féodalisme dans le domaine économique concernant le statut de la terre, les activités économiques et la structure sociale. Il s'est ensuite penché sur l'influence du féodalisme sur le pouvoir central et sur les activités militaires en analysant la désintégration politique et militaire qu'a connu al-Andalus à cause de celui-ci. Enfin, l'auteur a terminé son étude en démontrant la façon dont le système féodal a été la cause de multiples révoltes aussi bien dans l'espace rural que dans les milieux urbains - d'où la chute du féodalisme en al-Andalus.

En 1993 Brahim El Kadiri Boutchich a publié un travail[10] d'une importance capitale sur la vie sociale, avec un accent particulier sur l'histoire des mentalités sous les Almoravides. Il a consacré le premier chapitre à la vie familiale et à la vie conjugale en particulier, le rôle de la femme et l'éducation des enfants. Le deuxième chapitre traite des coutumes et des superstitions populaires telles que la nourriture, l'habillement, les fêtes, les moyens de distraction, la santé, la mort et les funérailles, la sorcellerie et l'astrologie. Le troisième chapitre est consacré aux sufis, aux saints et aux marabouts, aux rapports entre l'état de crise et l'apparition du sufisme ainsi qu'aux opinions vis-à-vis du pouvoir et la société.

Dans le même sens, Brahim El Kadiri Boutchich a publié son deuxième ouvrage sur les Almoravides[11]. L'étude se penche sur la population, se base sur une classification ethnique et considère aussi sa croissance démographique. Elle traite ensuite du statut des *ḏimmīs*, leurs rapports avec le pouvoir et la société. L'auteur aborde ensuite la structure sociale et l'ordre des classes, leurs hiérarchies ainsi que leur niveau de vie, et termine avec un chapitre sur la structure tribale de l'espace rural de l'époque ainsi qu'une étude sur l'aspect socio-économique, l'organisation des tribus y compris leurs coutumes et leurs rapports avec le pouvoir.

'Abd al-Illah Binmalīḥ publie une autre approche originale sur l'esclavage en occident musulman[12]. Cette étude est intéressante en ce qu'elle informe sur les différentes sources d'approvisionnement en matière d'esclavage et les différentes origines ethniques des esclaves, y compris leur présence dans les secteurs économiques, sociaux, politiques, militaires et culturels. L'auteur a aussi présenté les multiples facettes de leurs situations de démunis et marginalisés

---

10   Brahim El Kadiri Boutchich, *Al-Maġrib wa Al-Andalus fī ʿaṣr Al-Murābiṭīn: al-muǧtamaʿ, al-ḏihniyāt, al-awliyāʾ*.

11   Brahim El Kadiri Boutchich, *Mabāḥiṯ fī-l-tārīḫ al iǧtimāʿī fī-l-Maġrib wa-l-Andalus ḫilāla ʿaṣr Al-Murābiṭīn*.

12   ʿAbd al-Illah Binmalīḥ, *Al-Riqq fī bilād Al-Maġrib wa-l-Andalus*.

dans la société. Il s'est penché sur leur statut légal et juridique, sur leurs activités dans les domaines économiques ainsi que sur leur statut social et leur activité culturelle. Un chapitre est consacré à leur culture et à leur créativité en littérature populaire, sujet qui relève de l'histoire des mentalités. En dernier lieu il étudie leur rôle dans le domaine politique.

Pouvoir et opinion publique sont un autre thème, nouveau, développé dans un ouvrage de Azeddine Guessous[13]. L'étude porte sur la relation entre gouvernants et gouvernés. L'auteur a démontré, d'abord, l'existence d'une opinion publique pendant cette période que les gouvernants prenaient en considération ; ils dirigeaient en grande partie leur politique en fonction de celle-ci. Il a défini les composants de la relation entre gouvernants et gouvernés pour évoquer, ensuite, l'opinion publique vis-à-vis l'unité politique et religieuse concernant la doctrine sunnite entreprise par les Almoravides, et ce du Sahara jusqu'en al-Andalus. Ensuite, il a traité de l'opinion publique des villes envers le pouvoir et sa politique générale. Il a aussi abordé l'opinion publique dans l'espace rural chez les grandes factions tribales en définissant les tribus alliées et celles qui se sont opposées par la suite. L'ouvrage se termine par un chapitre intéressant sur la liberté d'expression. Il y est exposée la façon dont le pouvoir s'est comporté envers les opposants, sa politique culturelle envers la philosophie, les *uṣūl al-fiqh* et la théologie, *'ilm al-kalām* et le sufisme. Pour terminer, il a présenté une nouvelle interprétation de l'autodafé de l'ouvrage de Al-Ġazālī, *Iḥyā' 'ulūm al-dīn*.

3   Une UFR pour l'histoire économique et sociale

À Meknès, en 1999, à la faculté des lettres et des sciences humaines, une unité de formation et de recherche spécialisée en histoire économique et sociale sous la responsabilité de Brahim El Kadiri Boutchich a été accréditée. Il est certain que le parcours scientifique est important dans ce choix thématique : tout s'ajoute à ses intérêts, le domaine de l'histoire des mentalités. La durée de formation se situait entre 1999 et 2003, allait jusqu'en 2013 de la phase de recherche basée essentiellement sur la question de méthode et celle des sources. C'est ainsi qu'apparaissent des études aussi originales que les précédentes, traitant de l'histoire économique et sociale ou celle des mentalités avec une génération qui s'est chargée de la continuité de la recherche. À cet effet,

---

13   Azeddine Guessous, *Mawqif al-ra'iyya min al-sulṭa al-siyāsīya fī Al-Magrib wa Al-Andalus 'alā 'ahd al-Murābitīn: dirāsa fī 'ilm al-iǧtimā' al siyāsī*.

nous allons recueillir quelques travaux. Signalons que ce choix ne remet pas en cause la qualité des autres recherches.

Saʿīd Binḥamāda a réalisé un travail sur l'eau et l'homme en al-Andalus[14]. Le travail étudie l'impact de l'eau sur l'espace géographique urbain et rural, sur l'individu et dans la société, et ce dans les connaissances de l'utilisation de l'eau ou dans le domaine représentatif et imaginaire. L'étude a pu montrer comment dans l'espace rural ou urbain, l'eau est un élément de conflit ou de solidarité au sein de la société ; il a aussi étudié l'aspect culturel lié à l'eau dans la société et dans la pensée andalouse. Il ne manque pas d'élucider son importance chez les sufis et dans leurs miracles.

La Société et la Guerre de Ḥamīd Tītāw, comme son titre l'indique[15], s'intéresse à la sociologie de la guerre, la polémologie, et à ses retombées sur la société. Le chercheur a réussi à élucider comment la guerre a constitué le comportement de l'individu, du pouvoir et de l'ensemble de la société. La guerre a détruit aussi bien les familles que l'individu. C'est ce que l'on peut observer sur les hommes en tant que guerriers, leurs femmes et leurs enfants. D'où l'émergence de nouveaux comportements et valeurs sociales. C'est ce qui justifie son effet sur le domaine culturel. Pour le pouvoir mérinide, la guerre était l'un des fondements principaux de son existence, chose que l'on peut percevoir à travers le domaine fiscal et politique. L'étude a abordé la destruction que subissent les activités économiques dans le domaine agricole, industriel et commercial. À cela, il faut ajouter l'enrôlement de ces travailleurs dans l'armée. L'étude s'est aussi intéressée aux retombées de la croissance démographique sur le paysage de désolation qu'a connu l'espace mérinide.

Le travail de ʿAbd-al-Hadī-l-Bayyāḍ aborde les répercussions des catastrophes naturelles sur le comportement et sur les mentalités[16], la façon dont elles étaient considérées, les tentatives pour affronter la sécheresse, les épidémies, les criquets et les séismes. Il a montré comment ces catastrophes étaient à la fois la cause de tumultes spasmodiques dans la société et une raison pour établir une solidarité populaire dans de pareilles conditions. Le pouvoir s'est mobilisé pour venir en aide aux populations sinistrées et pour apaiser les conséquences des catastrophes ayant nourri l'idée d'épargne individuelle et collective dans la société et le pouvoir.

---

14   Saʿīd Binḥamāda, *Al-Mā' wa-l-insān bi al-Andalus ḫilāla-l-qarnayn 7 H-8 H/ 13 A.D.-14 A.D.: Ishām fī dirāsat al-maǧāl wa-l-muǧtamaʿ wa-l-dhihniyāt.*

15   Ḥamīd Tītāw, *Al-Muǧtamaʿ wa-l-ḥarb fī-l-Maǧrib al-aqṣā ḫilāla-l-ʿaṣr al-marīnī 869 A.H./1456 A.D.: musāhama fī dirāsat in'ikāsāt al-ḥarb ʿalā-l-binyāt al-iqtisādiya wa-l-iǧtimāʿīya wa-l-dhihniya.*

16   ʿAbd-al-Hādī-l-Bayyāḍ, *Al-Kawāriṯ al-ṭabīʿiyya wa āṯaruhā fī sulūk wa ḏihniyat al-insān fī-l-Maǧrib wa-l-Andalus.*

Ḥamīd Ǧmīlī propose une recherche originale sur l'histoire démographique et la question des données statistiques[17]. L'étude a présenté les facteurs sociaux et religieux qui ont contribué au peuplement de la région et au métissage entre les habitants et les différentes immigrations qu'a connu l'espace d'Al-Maġrib. Ensuite il a abordé le rôle de l'économie dans le domaine agricole, industriel, artisanal, commercial et fiscal, se concentrant sur la procuration des données statistiques. Puis il a abordé le phénomène de l'urbanisation et son rapport avec la croissance démographique dans les différentes villes et services publics. Le travail s'est aussi penché sur les conséquences que la guerre a provoqué sur la démographie, surtout lors de la chute d'un pouvoir et l'avènement d'un autre, ainsi que sur les répercussions des catastrophes naturelles, comme les famines et les épidémies.

4 Documentation et méthodes

Les travaux recueillis sur l'histoire sociale et économique, nous l'avons déjà dit, ont touché de nouveaux objets avec de nouvelles approches. C'est ainsi qu'ils ont franchi des horizons jusqu'alors inexplorés dans la recherche historique du monde musulman médiéval, pour examiner des documents vierges, spécialement de l'occident musulman. Ils se sont ouverts à d'autres disciplines et d'autres méthodes en utilisant différents types de sources.

4.1 *Documentation*

En matière de documentation, les recherches mentionnées ont fait usage d'une quantité considérable de sources, manuscrites ou imprimées. Ce qui est une évidence dans ces travaux, mais aussi un point commun. La liste des références manuscrites montre l'effort déployé pour les atteindre. Les manuscrits sont consultables sur place dans les bibliothèques mais cela nécessite des déplacements à Rabat ou à Fès, à l'Escurial, à Paris, en Algérie et au Caire, sans parler du problème du déchiffrement de l'écriture des manuscrits. De plus, ces références, comme les sources imprimées utilisées, touchent des disciplines différentes : histoire, jurisprudence, fiqh, médecine, géographie, hagiographie, hérésiographie, biographie, voyage, poésie, proverbe populaire, littérature, ouvrages scientifiques et techniques, etc., et tout document pouvant fournir des informations sur le thème et l'époque en question. Une pléthore de

---

17 Ḥamīd Ǧmīlī, *Ǧawānib mina-l-tārīḫ al-dimuġrāfi bi-l-Maġrib al-Aqṣā ḫilāla-l-ʿasr al waṣīṭ 6-8 A.H.*

documents appartenant à des catégories scientifiques et littéraires différentes, nécessite une connaissance de la langue utilisée, son style et sa manière d'aborder les choses pour pouvoir la comprendre. Afin d'être en mesure de répondre aux questions et objets nouveaux, les chercheurs ont ainsi dépassé, dans leurs méthodes de travail, la conception classique des documents. Cette spécificité les a conduits à travailler sur des informations inédites. Elles ont également permis de prouver, de réfuter ou combler des vides, de dissiper des équivoques, et prévenir et concevoir des maladresses méthodologiques et terminologiques.

Une même vision vaste et profonde des sources s'applique aux études récentes, y compris les études en langue arabe. La liste de ces références inclut des travaux en anglais, en espagnol, en français et même parfois en italien ou en allemand. Toute recherche est susceptible de fournir une idée, une interprétation ou une vision capable de servir à la méthode ou à l'analyse. C'est pourquoi on trouve des ouvrages de méthode, de théories ou d'autres champs disciplinaires en sociologie, en anthropologie, ethnologie, sociologie politique, sondage, etc.

Selon Fernand Braudel, une documentation exhaustive nécessite, notamment pour l'historien, un effort particulier pour traiter des sujets, affronter des problématiques et des phénomènes sur une longue durée.

4.2 *Méthodes et approches*

Une telle documentation avait pour objectif d'aborder des thèmes allant au-delà de l'histoire classique évènementielle tournant autour du pouvoir et ses exploits. Ces recherches se sont tournées vers la société, les mentalités et vers les classes marginalisées afin de compenser la platitude de l'histoire narrative et évènementielle et se pencher sur l'histoire problématique. Nous sommes convaincus que l'histoire chronologique ne représente qu'un aspect superficiel de l'histoire. L'objectif de ce parcours est de pénétrer les zones à questions pointues dans la perspective de démanteler les mécanismes complexes des mentalités, du social économique et de l'anthropologique, dépasser l'individu pour atteindre le groupe, comprendre les structures sociales, investir les phénomènes naturels comme le climat, les catastrophes, les épidémies, la sécheresse et les classes sociales, s'introduire dans les demeures pour découvrir les décors, le comportement, les sentiments, les tabous, appréhender les rapports qui les relient, se pencher sur la magie, la sorcellerie et les interdits. Somme toute, dresser une histoire vue d'en bas, autrement dit, une histoire subalterne. Cela a permis d'écrire une histoire qui commence par une ou plusieurs questions et qui s'achève par d'autres questions. Il faut signaler que la vision de ces recherches a considérablement été influencée par l'école *Les Annales E.S.C.* et sa vision interdisciplinaire de l'histoire.

L'ensemble des travaux, y compris ceux qui figurent sur la liste ci-dessous, ont utilisé plusieurs méthodes dans leurs approches pour étudier des thèmes nouveaux et audacieux. Ils ont opté pour l'histoire problématique exigeant une relecture de la documentation classique et un effort considérable pour affranchir et surmonter la diversité des autres sources référentielles. Ils ont adopté, par conséquent et sans exception, la démarche des approches anthropologiques, sociologiques, ethnologiques, sémiologiques pour étudier le pouvoir symbolique ou les mythes conçus dans l'avènement d'un pouvoir. N'oublions pas, toutefois, l'histoire de la démographie, afin de tirer le maximum de ce que recèle la structure des informations des textes, ainsi que les informations en elles-mêmes. Cela a permis de comprendre le comportement, la mentalité et l'impact psychologique de l'homme sur son environnement. C'est ce que l'on peut observer dans les études qui ont abordé la famille, le père, la mère, l'éducation des enfants, l'habillement, les loisirs, la femme, les sufis, la magie, les classes sociales, les _dhimmīs_, les marginaux, mendiants, esclaves, prostitués ou malfaiteurs. Le changement que les catastrophes naturelles ont provoqué dans les mentalités, les rapports sociaux, ou les rapports de l'homme à la gestion de ses ressources naturelles. D'autres études se sont penchées sur la sociologie politique et sur les éléments qui régissent les relations entre gouvernants et gouvernés, notamment la sécurité, les impôts et la politique fiscale.

En outre, une autre qualité de taille dans l'esprit de ces recherches est qu'elles abordent à la fois l'aspect théorique et historique des thèmes choisis. Qualité constituante des méthodes utilisées dans la structure, la vision et l'analyse de ses travaux. Elles mettent aussi en évidence la discussion des idées, des interprétations et de la vision des autres recherches, et d'une manière intermittente, des autres disciplines qu'elles ont investies.

5   Pour conclure ...

L'ensemble des travaux ont fait l'objet d'une thèse d'État ou nationale. Il s'agit de recherches réalisées sous la supervision d'un directeur de recherche, acceptées pour être soutenues devant un jury pour être évaluées et défendues : des travaux inédits de premier choix en histoire économique et sociale et en histoire des mentalités. Certains chercheurs, après avoir obtenu leurs diplômes, ont continué dans la même optique tout en abordant d'autres champs de recherche, en publiant des articles dans des revues spécialisées comme _Hesperis Tamuda, La recherche historique Dirasāt tārīḫīya, Al-ʿUṣur al-ǧadīda_ ..., ou en participant à des colloques et des conférences. Cependant, cet effort individuel n'a pas été sous-tendu par un effort de groupe ; bien que le travail individuel soit fructueux, il reste lacunaire en l'absence de groupe de recherche institutionnalisé. Celui-ci constitue, à coup sûr, une force propulsive au niveau de la recherche et de la qualité innovante de la production scientifique.

Le constat est aussi déconcertant que saugrenu, vu les ressources humaines qualifiées, les méthodes adoptées, les outils de travail dont on dispose, ou l'expérience accumulée. Certes, ces projets exigent plus de moyens financiers mais cela n'empêche pas de continuer le travail dans cette voie.

Par ailleurs, nous pensons, tout en espérant que ce ne soit pas mal interprété, qu'il existe une certaine négligence en occident à l'égard de la production scientifique dans le monde arabo-musulman dans ce domaine. Il est certain que la lecture de la littérature que nous venons de citer épargne un grand effort, aussi bien sur le plan bibliographique ou méthodologique que sur le choix des champs de recherche abordés. Nous sommes convaincus que cet exposé se prête à discussions chez les islamisants, les historiens, les anthropologues et les sociologues, et aussi chez les historiens, anthropologues et sociologues d'autres centres d'intérêt cognitifs. Si nous avons évoqué ces derniers, c'est parce qu'en occident, toutes les disciplines (ou presque) concernant le monde islamique sont regroupées, pour une raison quelconque, incompréhensible, dans un seul département ou institut. Cela nous rappelle les propos significatifs de Maxime Rodinson que nous citons sur ce fait : « Il n'y a pas d'orientalisme, de sinologie, d'iranologie, etc. Il y a des disciplines scientifiques définies par leur objet et leur problématique spécifique, comme la sociologie, la démographie, l'économie politique, la linguistique, l'anthropologie ou l'ethnologie, les diverses branches de l'histoire généralisante, etc. Elles peuvent être appliquées à divers peuples ou régions à une époque ou à une autre, en tenant compte des particularités de ces peuples ou régions de ces époques. »[18].

Notre exposé qui ne prétend aucunement à l'exhaustivité, touche à sa fin avec l'espoir qu'il contribuera d'une manière ou d'une autre au décloisonnement espéré afin de promouvoir la recherche, qui, longtemps, est restée enfermée dans une espèce d'égocentrisme intellectuel. D'autant qu'il serait inconvenant et inconvenable de se fier à une seule littérature provenant d'un seul pays pour faire des recherches[19]. Nous espérons que cette présentation fournira des informations que nous souhaitons positives pour différents domaines de recherches.

---

18   Maxime Rodinson, *La fascination de l'islam*, 142.

19   Voir dans ce sens les propos Maxime Rodinson, Ibid., 143 et aussi ceux de Claude Cahen, *Introduction à l'histoire du monde musulman médiéval*, VIIe-XVe siècle, 12-15.

Liste à titre indicatif

La liste ci-dessous est présentée à titre indicatif seulement sur les recherches
en histoire économique et sociale et l'histoire des mentalités. Elle comprend
des travaux publiés ainsi que d'autres en cours de publication. Ceux-ci ont fait
l'objet de thèse de doctorat, que nous classons suivant un ordre chronologique
selon la date des soutenances.

Publications

Brāhīm El Kadiri Boutchich, *Iḍā'āt ḥawla turāṯ al-ġarb al-islāmī wa tārīḫihi –l-iqtiṣādī
wa-l-iǧtimā'ī*, Beyrouth, Dar al-Ṭalī'a, 2002.

Maḥmūd Ismā'īl 'Abd al-Rāziq, *Al-Muhammašūn fī -l-tārīḫ al-islāmī*, Le Caire, Ru'ya,
2004.

Brāhīm El Kadiri Boutchich, *Bayna Aḫlāqiyāt al-'Arab wa dihniyyāt al-ġarb : dirāsa
fī -l-untrūbūlūǧiyya al-iǧtimā'iyya wa-al-ṯaqāfiyya*, Le Caire, Ru'ya, 2005.

Maḥmūd Ismā'īl 'Abd al-Rāziq, *Al-Istūġrāfiyā wa -l-mīṯūlūǧiyyā*, Le Caire, Ru'ya, 2009.

Brāhīm El Kadiri Boutchich, *Al-Muhammašūn fī-l-tārīḫ al-ġarb al-islāmī*, Le Caire,
Ru'ya, 2014.

Brāhīm El Kadiri Boutchich, *Al-Aqalliyya -l-islāmiyya fī Sīsīliyya bayna al-indimāǧ wa
ṣirā' al-huwiyya*, Meknes, Université Mulay Ismā'īl, Faculté des lettres, 2016.

Thèses en cours de publication

Muḥammad Yāsir Al-Hilālī, *Muǧtma' al-maġrib al-aqsā ḫilāla -l-qarnayn 8-9 A. H./14-15
A. D. Musāhama fī ba'ḍ muṣṭalaḥāt al-taratub al-iǧtimā'ī : « Al-'āmma », « al-ḫāṣṣa »,
« al-ṭabaqa », « al-martaba »*, 2000.

Mūlūd 'Aššaq, *Imārat Barġawāṭa, musāhama fī dirāsat al-binyat al -iqtiṣādiyya
wa -l-iǧtimā'iyya wa -l-ḏihniyya*, 2006.

Ḥasan Laġrāyb, *Al-Aqalliyya al-masīḥiyya bi -l-maġrib al-aqṣā ḫilāla -l-'aṣr al-wasīṭ :
musāhama fī dirāsat al-ta'āyuš bayna mukawwināt al-muǧtama' al-maġribī
mina -l-qarn 5 A.H. ḥattā -l-qarn 8 A.H.*, 2008.

Abd al-Maǧīd 'Āmir Muḥammad, *Al-waqf wa Aṯaruhu fī -l-ḥayāt al-iqtiṣādiyya
wa -l-iǧtimā'iya bi -l-maġrib al-Aqṣā ḫilāla -l-qarnayn 7 wa 8 A.H.*, 2009.

Muḥamamad Laṭif, *Al-ḥayāt al-usariyya bi -l-maġrib al-aqṣā ḫilāla al-'aṣr -l-marīnī*,
2009.

Rašīd al-yamlūlī, *Al-Ḍarā'ib fī -l-ġarb al-islāmī ḫilāla -l-'aṣr al-wasīṭ wa aṯaruhā fī -l-tārīḫ
al-siyasī*, 2011.

Mūlay al-Ḥasan 'Amġār, *Al-Ḥiraf wa -l-ḥirafiyyūn bi -l-Maġrib al-Aqṣā ḫilāla -l-'aṣr
al-marīnī*, 2011.

Aḥmad Ṣādīqī, *Al-Kitāb fī -l-Maġrib wa -l-Andalus: Ishām fī dirāsat in'ikās ṯaqāfat
al-kitāb 'alā al-muǧtama'*, 2012.

Muṣṭafā Al-Dūblālī, *Al-Maḥḍūrāt fī muǧtamaʿ al-maġrib al-aqṣā ḫilāla –l-ʿaṣr al-wasīṭ*, 2013.

En 18-19-20 avril 2018 s'est tenu à Tétouan un colloque international sous le thème *Histoire sociale et économique et histoire des mentalités : Qaḍāyā wa iškāliyāt*, en hommage au Pr. Dr. Brahim El Kadiri Boutchich. Toutes les interventions sont nouvelles, nous allons en recueillir quelques-unes à titre d'information :

Ǧaʿfar b. Al-Ḥāǧ al-Sulamī, *Usṭūrat al-kīmiyāʾ fī -l-ġarb al-islāmī.*
Azeddine Guessous, *Al-Sulṭa al-muwaḥḥidiyya: al-usṭūra wa -l-mutaḫayyal.*
Nādiya al-ʿAšīrī, *La beauté féminine en Al-Andalus.*
Saʿīd Binḥamāda, *Taqālīd al-naẓāfa wa -l-taǧmīl bi muǧtamaʿ Al-Maġrib wa Al-Andalus : dirāsa fī -l-qiyam wa -l-sulūk.*
ʿAbd-Al-Salam al-Ǧaʿmāṭī, *Ẓāhirat tazwīr al-ʿumlāt fī tārīḫ al-Maġrib wa -l-Andalus.*
Twātiya Būdaliya, *Qaḍāyā -l-ḥaml fī nawāzil al-ġarb al-islāmī.*
Nawāl Bilmadanī, *Fiʾāt al-šuyūḫ bi muǧtamaʿ -l-ġarb al-islāmī.*
Muṣṭafā Našāṭ, *muqaddimāt al-taʿāṭī lil qinnab al-hindī (Al-Ḥašīša) bi -l-Maġrib al-wasīṭ.*

Bibliographie

ʿAbd al-Rāziq, Maḥmūd Ismāʿīl. *Qaḍāyā fī -l-tārīḫ al-islāmī : minhaǧ wa taṭbīq*, Beyrouth, Dar al-ʿŪda, 1974.

ʿAbd al-Rāziq, Maḥmūd Ismāʿīl. *Maqālāt fī l-fikr wa -l-tārīḫ*, Casablanca, Dar al-rašād al-ḥadīṯa, 1979.

ʿAbd al-Rāziq, Maḥmūd Ismāʿīl. *Susyulūgiyā -l-fikr al-islāmī*, Casablanca, Dār al-ṯaqāfa, 1980.

ʿAbd al-Rāziq, Maḥmūd Ismāʿīl. *Al-Muhammašūn fī-l-tārīḫ al-islāmī*, Le Caire, Ruʾya, 2004.

Al-ʿAlī, Sāliḥ Aḥmad. *Al-Tanẓīmāt al-iqtiṣādiyya wa al-iǧtimāʿiyya fī Al-Baṣra fī al-qarn al awwal al hijrī*, Bagdad, 1953.

Ashtor, Eliyahu. *A Social and Economic History of the Near East in the Middle Ages*, Berkeley, 1976.

Al-Bayyāḍ, ʿAbd al-Hādī. *Al-Kawāriṯ al-ṭabīʿiyya wa āṯaruhā fī sulūk wa ḏihniyat al-insān fī -l-Maġrib wa -l –Andalus*, Beyrouth, Dār al-Ṭalīʿa, 2008.

Binḥamāda, Saʿīd. *Al-māʾ wa -l-insān bi Al-Andalus ḫilāla -l-qarnayn 7 H-8 H/ 13 A.D.- 14 A.D.: Ishām fī dirāsat al-maǧāl wa -l -muǧtamaʿ wa -l-dhihniyāt*, Beyrouth, Dar al-Ṭalīʿa, 2007.

Binmalīḥ, ʿAbd-al-Illah. *Al-Riqq fī bilād Al-Maġrib wa -l-Andalus*, Beyrouth, Dar al-Intišār al-ʿarabī, 2004.

Boutchich, Brahim El Kadiri [Būtašīš, Ibrāhīm al-Qādirī]. *Aṯar al-iqṭāʿ fī tārīḫ Al-Andalus al-siyāsī min muntasaf al-qarn al-ṯāliṯ al-hiǧrī ḥatā ẓuhūr al-ḫilāfa (250 H./316H.)*, Rabat, ʿUkāẓ, 1992.

Boutchich, Brahim El Kadiri [Būtašīš, Ibrāhīm al-Qādirī]. *Al-Maġrib wa Al-Andalus fī ʿaṣr Al-Murābitīn : al-muǧtamaʿ, al-ḏihniyāt, al-awliyāʾ*, Beyrouth, Dar al-Ṭalīʿa, 1993.

Boutchich, Brahim El Kadiri [Būtašīš, Ibrāhīm al-Qādirī]. *Mabāḥit fī -l-tārīḫ al iǧtimāʿī fī -l- Maġrib wa -l- Andalus ḫilāla ʿaṣr Al-Murābitīn*, Beyrouth, Dar al-Ṭalīʿa, 1998.

Cahen, Claude. *Introduction à l'histoire du monde musulman médiéval, VII-XV siècle*, Paris, Librairie d'Amérique et d'Orient, 1982.

Al-Dūrī, ʿAbd al-ʿAzīz. *Muqaddima fī al-tarīḫ al-iqtiṣādī -l-ʿarabī*, Beyrouth, 1969.

Al-Ǧanhānī, Al-Ḥabīb. *Dirasāt magribiyya fī -l-tarik al -iqtiṣādi wa-l-iǧtimāʿī li -l-maġrib al islāmī*, Beyrouth, Dar al-Talīʿa, 1980.

Ǧmīlī, Ḥamīd. *Ǧawānib min al-tārīḫ al-dimuġrāfi bi-l-Maġrib al-Aqṣa ḫilāla -l-ʿasr al wasīṭ 6-8 H.*, Fès, Markaz Tāfilālt, 2016.

Guessous, Azeddine., *Mawqif al-raʾiyya min al-ṣulta al-siyāsiyya fī Al-Maġrib wa Al-Andalus ʿalā ʿahd Al-Murābitīn: dirāsa fī ʿilm al-iǧtimāʿ al-siyāsī*, Casablanca, Ifrīqiyā al-sharq, 2014.

Rodinson, Maxime. *La fascination de l'islam*, Paris, François Maspero, 1982.

Al-Ṭāhirī, Aḥmad. *ʿĀmmat Qurṭuba fī ʿaṣr al-ḫilāfa*, Rabat, ʿUkāẓ, 1980.

Tītāw, Ḥamīd. *Al-Muǧtamaʿ wa -l-ḥarb fī-l-Maġrib al-aqṣā ḫilāla -l-aṣr al-marīnī 869 H./1456 J.-C.: musāhama fī dirāsat inʿikāsāt al-ḥarb ʿalā -l-binyāt al-iqtisādiyya wa -l-iǧtimāʿiyya wa -l-dhihniyya*, Casablanca, Fondation du roi Abdul-Aziz, 2009.

12

Les travaux d'histoire médiévale dans les universités algériennes: bilan et tendances actuelles

Allaoua Amara

La période coloniale en Algérie (1830-1962) est marquée par la constitution de savoirs historiques et l'élaboration de nouvelles approches sur le passé médiéval du Maghreb[1]. Les ouvrages édités permettent de mettre en exergue ce que les auteurs de la période coloniale pensent de l'histoire d'un ancien territoire romain reconquis par la France après douze siècles de domination islamique. Les travaux de Henri Fournel[2], Ernest Mercier[3], Gabriel–Isidore Faure–Biguet[4], de Beylié[5], Georges Marçais[6], Émile-Félix Gauthier[7], Robert Brunschvig[8], Lucien Golvin[9], Hady Roger Idris[10] et Charles-André Julien[11] symbolisent cette historiographie coloniale. Leurs visions sont très diversifiées : des siècles obscurs à la catastrophe hilālienne, la plupart de ces auteurs dressent des portraits classiques stéréoptypés du déclin du Moyen Âge maghrébin. De l'autre côté, des Algériens, amateurs d'histoire et surtout militants réformistes et indépendantistes, répondent aux thèses colonialistes par des écrits défendant l'ancrage arabo-islamique de l'Algérie. Aḥmad Tawfīq al-Madanī[12], Mubārak

---

1   Je tiens à remercier Virginie Prévost pour sa relecture et ses suggestions.

2   Henri Fournel, *Les Berbers*.

3   Ernest Mercier, *Histoire de l'établissement des Arabes dans l'Afrique septentrionale selon les documents fournis par les auteurs arabes et notamment par l'Histoire des Berbères d'Ibn Khaldoun* ; *Histoire de l'Afrique septentrionale (Berbérie) depuis les temps les plus reculés jusqu'à la conquête*.

4   Gabriel–Isidore Faure–Biguet, *Histoire de l'Afrique septentrionale sous la domination musulmane*.

5   De Beylié, *La Kalaa des Beni-Hammad*.

6   Georges Marçais, *La Berbérie musulmane et l'Orient au Moyen Âge* ; *L'Algérie médiévale, monuments et paysages historiques*.

7   Émile-Félix Gauthier, *L'islamisation de l'Afrique du Nord*.

8   Robert Brunschvig, *La Berbérie orientale sous les Ḥafṣīdes*.

9   Lucien Golvin, *Le Maghreb central à l'époque des Zirides*.

10   Hady Roger Idris, *La Berbérie orientale sous les Zirīdes X-XIIᵉ*.

11   Charles-André Julien, *Histoire de l'Afrique du Nord*.

12   Aḥmad Tawfīq al-Madanī, *Tārīḫ al-Ǧazā'ir* (Histoire de l'Algérie).

Brāhīmī al-Mīlī[13] et ʿAbd al-Raḥmān al-Ǧilālī[14] sont les grandes figures de cette écriture de l'histoire médiévale de l'Algérie et du Maghreb. À partir de la fin des années quarante, Mohamed Cherif Sahli[15], théoricien du nationalisme algérien, appelle à décoloniser l'histoire. C'est à la suite de ces écritures que se développent les premiers travaux d'histoire médiévale dans les universités algériennes au lendemain de l'indépendance nationale[16].

1   Petite chronologie des travaux d'histoire médiévale

Au lendemain de l'indépendance de l'Algérie en 1962, les recherches sur l'histoire médiévale sont centrées sur l'unique université d'Alger, fondée en 1909. Cette période marque une transition se prolongeant jusqu'à la fin des années soixante, durant laquelle l'enseignement de l'histoire est arabisé, provoquant le départ des médiévistes français. Spécialiste des relations catalano-maghrébines à la fin du Moyen Âge, Charles-Emmanuel Dufourcq est le principal spécialiste de cette période, sur laquelle il dirige une dizaine de mémoires et de thèses de doctorat. Tous les travaux portent généralement sur les relations entre la péninsule Ibérique et le Maghreb d'une part[17], et l'émigration des musulmans d'Andalousie vers les pays du Maghreb d'autre part[18].

L'arabisation et la politique nationaliste provoquent un changement d'orientation des recherches sur l'histoire médiévale du Maghreb, dont le but est de mettre en lumière les origines arabo-islamiques de l'Algérie. Muḥammad

---

13   Mubārak Brāhīmī al-Mīlī, *Tārīḫ al-Ǧazāʾir fī-l-qadīm wa-l-ḥadīṯ* (Histoire ancienne et moderne de l'Algérie).

14   ʿAbd al-Raḥmān al-Ǧilālī, *Tārīḫ al-Ǧazāʾir al-ʿāmm* (Histoire générale de l'Algérie).

15   Mohamed Cherif Sahli, *Décoloniser l'histoire, introduction à l'histoire du Maghreb*.

16   Ce texte fait suite aux inventaires et articles que j'ai publiés entre 2010 et 2014, comme *L'histoire de l'Algérie dans la recherche universitaire en France (1968-2008)*, Constantine, Publications de la Faculté des lettres et sciences humaines, 2010 ; « Ḫamsūn sana min al-baḥt fī al-tārīḫ al-wasīṭ bi-l-ǧāmiʿa al-ǧazāʾiriya (1962-2012) », *Al-Mawaqif, Revue des études et des recherches sur la société et l'histoire*, 7 (2012), p. 109-141 ; *Niṣf Qarn min al-baḥt al-tārīḫī bi-l-ǧāmiʿa al-ǧazāʾiriyya (1962-2012)*, Constantine, Publications de la faculté des lettres et civilisation islamique, 2013 (en collaboration avec Mouloud Aouimeur).

17   À titre d'exemple, Henri Dravet, *Rapports entre la Couronne d'Aragon et le sultanat mérinide au temps d'Abou El Hassan 1334-1334*, diplôme d'études supérieures, 1966 ; Georgette Géorgopolous, *Castille et le Maroc de 1333 à 1339 d'après les chroniques castillanes*, diplôme d'études supérieures, 1968.

18   Nadjem Eddine Gais, *Aperçu sur la population musulmane de Majorque au XIVᵉ siècle*, diplôme d'études supérieures, 1970 ; Xavier Lecour Bessad Grandmaison, *L'émigration des musulmans de Majorque vers le Maghreb au XVIᵉ siècle entre 1334 et 1381*, diplôme d'études supérieures, 1966.

al-Hādī Šaʿīra, un médiéviste égyptien de l'université d'Alger, dirige des mémoires en langue arabe sur le Maghreb médiéval. Parmi les acteurs algériens de cette tendance figure notamment Mūsā Laqbāl (m. 2009), auteur d'un mémoire rédigé en arabe sur la situation politique et administrative du Maghreb sous les Omeyyades[19] et qui soutiendra une thèse de doctorat d'État à l'université du Caire en 1975 sur le rôle des Kutāma dans l'histoire du califat fatimide[20]. Sa thèse, publiée quatre ans plus tard, exercera une influence capitale sur la vision de l'histoire du Maghreb médiéval et servira de modèle à plusieurs travaux postérieurs.

Cette génération compte quatre autres médiévistes. Le premier est Brahim Fekhar (m. 2017), spécialiste de l'ibaḍisme maghrébin dont la thèse soutenue à l'université de Paris-Sorbonne en 1971 porte sur *Les communautés ibadites en Afrique du Nord (Lybie-Tunisie et Algérie) depuis les Fatimides*[21]. Il deviendra le chef de file des médiévistes à l'université d'Oran. Le second est Rachid Bourouiba (m. 2007), à la fois archéologue et historien, s'intéressant à l'archéologie islamique[22] et à l'histoire des villes médiévales d'Algérie. Il dirige notamment plusieurs campagnes de fouilles à la Qalʿa des Banī Ḥammād (1971-1974) et publie plusieurs études sur les Ḥammadides[23] et l'histoire des villes de l'Algérie[24]. Attallah Dhina (m. 1987) est un autre médiéviste consacrant ses études au bas Moyen Âge et plus particulièrement aux ʿAbdalwadides de Tlemcen. Sa thèse de troisième cycle (Université de Paris Sorbonne) a pour titre *Essai sur les structures politiques, sociales et économiques de l'État tlemcenien à l'époque d'Abū Ḥammū Mūsā I et d'Abū Tāšufīn I*[25] tandis que sa thèse de doctorat d'État porte sur *Les États de l'Occident musulman aux XIIIᵉ, XIVᵉ et XVᵉ siècles, institutions gouvernementales et administratives*[26]. Le dernier médiéviste de la génération postindépendance « fondatrice » des études médiévales à l'université d'Alger est Abdelhamid Hadjiat, dont les travaux sont focalisés

---

19   Mūsā Laqbāl, *Al-waḍʿiyya al-siyyāsiya wa-l-idāriyya li-l-Maġrib al-islāmī (45-122H)*, mémoire de diplôme d'études approfondies, 1967.

20   Mūsā Laqbāl, *Dawr Kutāma fī tārīḫ al-ḫilāfa al-fāṭimiyya*.

21   Brahim Fekhar, *Les communautés ibadites en Afrique du Nord (Lybie-Tunisie et Algérie) depuis les Fatimides*, thèse de doctorat d'État, Université Paris-Sorbonne, 1971 (inédite).

22   Rachid Bourouiba, *Apports de l'Algérie à l'architecture religieuse arabo-islamique*, Alger ; id., *Les inscriptions commémoratives des mosquées d'Algérie*.

23   Rachid Bourouiba, *Les H'ammadides*.

24   Rachid Bourouiba, *Cités disparues : Tahert, Sedrata, Achîr, Kalaa des Béni-Hammad*.

25   Attallah Dhina, *Essai sur les structures politiques, sociales et économiques de l'État tlemcenien à l'époque d'Abū Ḥammū Mūsā I et d'Abū Tāšufīn I*, thèse de doctorat de 3ᵉᵐᵉ cycle, Université de Paris Sorbonne, 1971. Éd. Alger, Office des publications universitaires, 1985.

26   Attallah Dhina, *Les États de l'Occident musulman aux XIIIᵉ, XIVᵉ et XVᵉ siècles, institutions gouvernementales et administratives*, éd. Alger, ENAL, 1984.

sur le Maghreb central sous le règne de l'émir ʿabdalwadide Abū Ḥammū Mūsā
II. Ces deux derniers médiévistes originaires de Tlemcen veulent montrer la
splendeur d'un État médiéval en Algérie, dont le centre de gravité se trouve
à Tlemcen.

Cette génération est donc à l'origine des premiers travaux sur l'histoire
médiévale en Algérie indépendante, même si elle est déjà en retard par rapport aux nouvelles approches appliquées dans les études historiques à cette
époque. Formés sur place et soutenant leurs thèses à l'étranger, ces médiévistes
ne mettent pas à profit les sources juridiques et hagiographiques, dont l'utilisation en Occident remonte au début du XXᵉ siècle. Leur vision de l'histoire
demeure classique et prisonnière du récit historique, d'autant que le recours à
la critique textuelle est presque inexistant. C'est à partir de cette vision que se
développent les travaux que je vais présenter dans ce texte.

Avec la création de deux départements d'histoire à l'université d'Oran et à
l'université de Constantine au début des années soixante-dix, les travaux sur
l'histoire médiévale connaissent une évolution lente, mais permettant de dis-
puter, dans une certaine mesure, le monopole exercé par l'université d'Alger.
Au sein de cette dernière une deuxième génération de médiévistes est formée,
composée essentiellement de Muḥammad Banʿamīra, Muḥammad al-Ṣālaḥ
Marmūl, Muḫtār Ḥasānī et ʿAlī Ǧawdat. Les sujets traités par ces derniers dans
leurs thèses de doctorat de troisième cycle ou de mémoires d'études approfondies portent généralement sur le Maghreb central médiéval, en particulier sur les Rustumides pour ʿAlī Ǧawdat[27] ou les Fatimides pour Muḥammad
al-Ṣālaḥ Marmūl[28], les Zanāta pour Muḥammad Banʿamīra[29] et le conflit
fatimido-omeyyade pour Muḫtār Ḥasānī[30]. Une remarque s'impose pour l'ensemble de ces travaux : ils sont d'emblée en décalage par rapport aux approches
développées dans les pays voisins ou occidentaux. Les livres publiés confirment
déjà l'arabisation des recherches sur l'histoire médiévale en Algérie. Depuis, les
recherches dans ce domaine s'expriment uniquement en langue arabe, à l'exception des ouvrages publiés plus tard par Rachid Bourouiba et moi-même.

Au département de Constantine, ʿAbd al-ʿAzīz Fīlālī est une figure mar-
quante des premiers médiévistes. Formé localement au début des années 1970,
il poursuit ses études supérieures à l'université d'Alexandrie où il soutient

---

27   Alī Ǧawdat, *Al-ʿAlāqāt al-ḫāriǧiyya li-l-dawla al-rustumiyya*.

28   Muḥammad al-Ṣālaḥ Marmūl, *al-siyāsa al-dāḫiliyya li-dawla al-fāṭimiyya*, thèse de docto-
      rat de 3ᵉ cycle, 1976. Éd. Alger, Office des publications universitaires, 1983.

29   Muḥammad Banʿamīra, *Dawr Zanāta fī al-ḥaraka al-maḏhabiyya fī al-Maġrib al-islāmī*,
      thèse de doctorat de 3ᵉ cycle, université d'Alger, 1978. Éd. Alger, ENAL, 1984.

30   Muḫtār Ḥasānī, *al-Ṣirāʿ bayna al-fāṭimiyyīn wa-l-umawiyyīn ʿalā al-siyāda fī al-Maġrib
      al-islāmī*.

une thèse de magister sous la direction d'Aḥmad Muḫtār al-ʿAbbādī sur les relations politiques entre l'État omeyyade en al-Andalus et les dynasties du Maghreb[31]. Au département d'histoire de l'université d'Oran, Brahim Fekhar dirige la plupart des thèses, avant d'être secondé, à partir des années 1990, par Mahdī Ġāzī Ġāšim al-Šammarī, un historien irakien naturalisé algérien un peu plus tard, assurant la direction de l'immense majorité des thèses de magister et de doctorat.

La politique mise en place par le ministère de l'Enseignement supérieur et de la Recherche Scientifique à l'époque vise la formation des historiens algériens dans les universités proche-orientales après des études de premier cycle aux universités d'Alger, Oran et Constantine. Parmi les médiévistes formés d'abord localement (aux Universités d'Oran et de Constantine en particulier) dans les universités égyptiennes figure d'abord Būba Maġġānī, auteure d'une thèse de magister sur le rôle des Arabes yéménites dans l'histoire du Maghreb au cours des trois premiers siècles de l'hégire[32]. Ayant soutenu un mémoire de diplôme d'études approfondies à l'université d'Oran sur les Midrānides de Siğilmāsa[33], Nūr al-Hudā Būḫalfa (m. 2017) poursuit ses études en Jordanie où elle fait une thèse de magister sous la direction de ʿAbd al-ʿAzīz al-Dūrī sur l'islam et l'arabisation du Maghreb au cours des trois premiers siècles de l'hégire[34].

En 1980, l'université de Bagdad est aussi la destination de plusieurs étudiants ; deux d'entre eux se spécialisent dans l'histoire médiévale. Ibrāhīm Baḥḥāz, qui réalise une thèse de magister sur la vie économique et culturelle de l'État rustumide[35], et ʿAbd al-Ḥamīd Ḥāldī, auteur d'une thèse sur la vie culturelle au Maghreb central sous les Ḥammadides[36]. Dès le début des années 1980, la formation doctorale des étudiants en Égypte reprend. Trois universités sont concernées Le Caire, Aïn-Chems et Alexandrie. Au total, sept

---

31   ʿAbd al-ʿAzīz Fīlālī, *al-ʿAlāqāt al-siyāsiyya bayna al-dawla al-umawiyya fī al-Andalus wa duwal al-Maġrib*.

32   Būba Maġġānī, *Aṯar al-ʿArab al-yamaniyya fī tārīḫ bilād al-Maġrib fī al-qurūn al-ṯalāṯa al-ūlā li-l-hiğra*.

33   Nūr al-Hudā Būḫalfa, *Dawlat Banī Wāsūl fī Siğilmāsa, ʿalāqātuhā wa dawruhā al-ḥaḍārī fī al-Maġrib al-wasīṭ*, Université d'Oran, 1976.

34   Nūr al-Hudā Būḫalfa, *al-islām wa-l-taʿrīb fī al-Šamāl al-Ifrīqī fī al-qurūn al-ṯalāṯa li-l-hiğra*, Amman, l'Université jordanienne, 1984.

35   Ibrāhīm Baḥḥāz, *al-Dawla al-rustumiyya (160-298/777-909), dirāsa fī-l-awḍāʿ al-iqtiṣādiyya wa-l-ḥayāt al-fikriyya* (l'État rustumide (160-298/777-909), étude sur la situation économique et la vie intellectuelle), thèse de magister, Université de Bagdad, 1984, éd. Alger, Lafoumik, 1985.

36   ʿAbd al-Ḥamīd Ḥāldī, *al-Ḥaraka al-fikriyya fī-l-Maġrib al-Awṣaṭ (al-dawla al-ḥammādiyya 408-547/1016-1152)* (le mouvement intellectuel au Maghreb central : l'État ḥammadide 408-547/1016-1152), thèse de magister, Université de Bagdad, 1983.

médiévistes y sont formés : Fāṭima Balhawwārī[37], ʿAbd al-Nāṣir Ǧabbār[38], Rašīd Bāqa[39], Masʿūd Mazhūdī[40], ʿĪsā Bandīb[41], Kamāl Banmārs[42] et ʿĀšūr Būšāma[43]. Ils sont par la suite recrutés dans les quatre départements d'histoire à l'époque, où ils soutiendront leurs thèses de doctorat d'État une dizaine d'années plus tard. Une lecture rapide des travaux réalisés par ces médiévistes à l'étranger et poursuivis en Algérie permet de cerner les principales tendances de l'époque : une domination de l'histoire du Maghreb et peu d'intérêt accordé à l'Occident chrétien voire à l'Orient musulman médiéval. Kamāl Banmārs est le seul à focaliser ses recherches sur l'Orient musulman, plus précisément sur les croisades, tandis que ʿAbd al-Nāṣir Ǧabbār et Rašīd Bāqa consacrent leurs thèses de magister aux relations entre le Maghreb et l'Europe méditerranéenne, sans parvenir à travailler sur les archives latines. Tous les autres s'intéressent au Maghreb médiéval.

Après les missions égypto-irakiennes, la politique menée par le ministère de l'Enseignement supérieur et de la Recherche Scientifique opte pour la formation locale des historiens médiévistes à quelques exceptions près[44], comme le cas de Allaoua Amara en France ou Naṣīra ʿAzrūdī en Égypte. Le premier fait ses études à l'université de Poitiers puis à l'université de Paris I Panthéon-Sorbonne

---

37 Fāṭima Balhawwārī, *al-Fāṭimiyūn wa ḥarakāt al-muʿāraḍa fī al-Maġrib al-islāmī* (les Fatimides et les mouvements d'opposition au Maghreb islamique), Université d'Aïn-Chems, 1991. Éd. Oran, Dār al-misk li-l-ṭibāʿa wa-l-našr, 2011.

38 ʿAbd al-Nāṣir Ǧabbār, *Banū Ḥafṣ wa-l-qiwā al-ṣalībiyya fī Ġarb al-Baḥr al-mutawassaṭ* (les Ḥafṣides et les Croisés en Méditerranée occidentale), thèse de magister, Université du Caire, 1991.

39 Rašīd Bāqa, *al-ʿalāqāt al-tiǧāriyya bayna Flūrasnā wa salatant al-mamālīk fī-l-qarn al-ḫāmis ʿašar al-mīlādī* (les relations commerciales entre Florence et le sultanat mamlūke au XVᵉ siècle), thèse de magister, Université du Caire, 1989.

40 Masʿūd Mazhūdī, *Al-Ibāḍiyya fī-l-Maġrib al-awsaṭ min suqūṭ al-dawla al-rustumiyya ilā hiǧrat Banī Hilāl ilā bilād al-Maġrib (296-442/909-1058)* (L'ibaḍisme au Maghreb central, de la chute de l'État rustumide à la migration des Hilāliens au Maghreb), thèse de magister, Université du Caire, 1988.

41 ʿĪsā Bandīb, *al-Tiǧāra fī ʿaṣr dawlat al-murābiṭīn (480-540)* (Le commerce à l'époque de l'État almoravide), thèse de magister, Université du Caire, 1990.

42 Kamāl Banmārs, *Al-ʿalāqa bayna al-Mawṣil wa Ḥalab wa dawruhā fī-l-ḥurūb al-ṣalībiyya (1071-1187)* (la relation entre Mossoul et Alep et son rôle dans les croisades), thèse de magister, Université d'Aïn-Chems, 1991.

43 ʿĀšūr Būšāma, *ʿAlāqāt al-dawla al-ḥafṣiyya maʿa duwal al-Maġrib wa-l-Andalus* (les relations de l'État ḥafṣide avec les États du Maghreb et d'al-Andalus), thèse de magister, Université du Caire, 1991.

44 Il faudra aussi citer, bien que leur influence soit inexistante au sein des universités algériennes : Said Dahmani, *La conquête de l'Ifrīqiya et ses artisans*, thèse de doctorat de 3ᵉ cycle, Université de Paris 1, 1973 ; Djamel Eddin Souidi, *Généalogie et pouvoir au Maghreb du IIᵉ au VIIᵉ siècle/VIIIᵉ-XIIIᵉ siècle*, doctorat nouveau régime, Université Paris 1, 1996.

où il soutient une thèse de doctorat sur les Ḥammadides[45] et la seconde fait une thèse sur les migrations andalouses au Maghreb central[46].

2   Une présence notable de l'histoire médiévale

La multiplication des études médiévales dans les universités algériennes s'explique aussi par la création de nombreux départements d'histoire à partir des années 1990, et notamment au début des années 2000. Cette période coïncide avec la promulgation du décret 98/254 relatif à la formation doctorale. En suppriment la thèse de magister et en procédant à la réorganisation des études supérieures, la durée de préparation des mémoires de magister est fixée à une année tandis que celle des thèses de doctorat est fixée à cinq années, ce qui entraîne une augmentation considérable du nombre de sujets traités dans le cadre de la formation-recherche. De 1962 à la fin de l'année 2017,

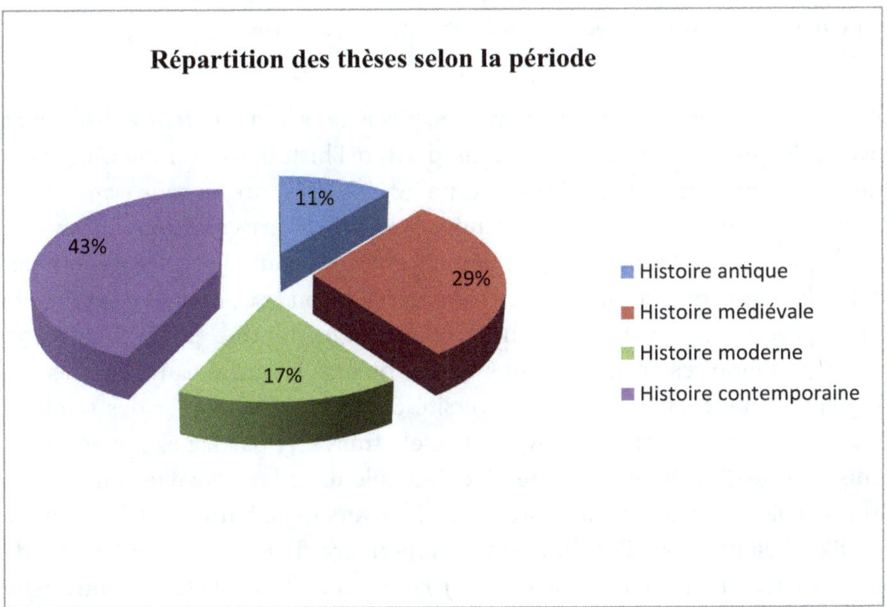

FIGURE 12.1   Répartition des thèses selon la période

---

45   Allaoua Amara, *Pouvoir, économie et société dans le Maghreb hammadide (395/1004-547/1152)*, thèse de doctorat nouveau régime, Université Paris 1 Panthéon-Sorbonne, 2002.

46   Naṣīra ʿAzrūdī, *Haǧarāt al-Andalusiyīn ilā al-Maġrib al-awsaṭ munḏu awāʾil al-qarn al-ṯānī al-hiǧrī (al-ṯāmin al-mīlādī) ḥattā awāḫir al-qarn al-ṯāmin al-hiǧrī (al-rābiʿ ʿašar al-mīlādī)*, thèse de magister, Université d'Alexandrie, 2007.

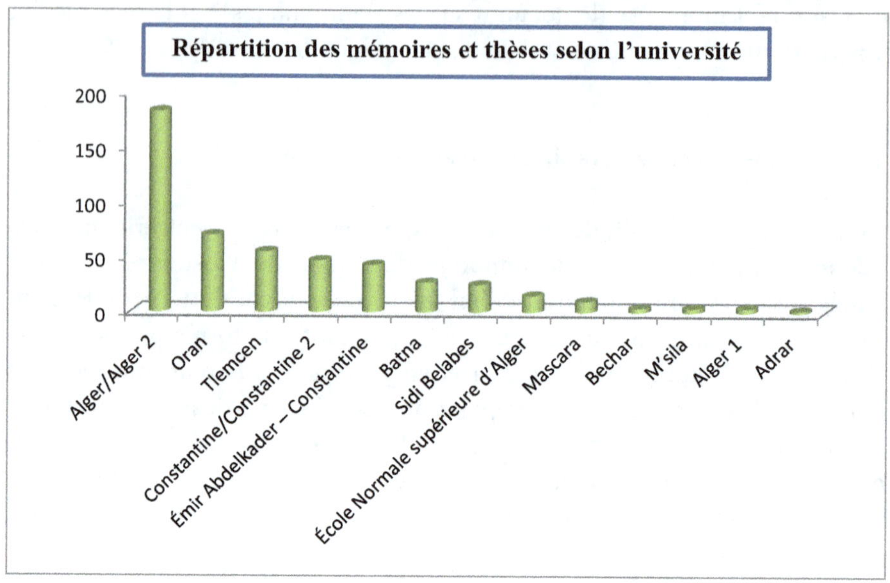

FIGURE 12.2   Répartition des mémoires et thèses selon l'université

l'histoire médiévale occupe la deuxième place dans les recherches historiques avec 488 mémoires et thèses soutenus, derrière l'histoire contemporaine (712), devançant largement l'histoire moderne (278) et l'histoire antique (179).

Le département d'histoire de l'université d'Alger arrive largement en tête sur le plan quantitatif avec 183 mémoires et thèses soutenus, suivi de loin par celui de l'université d'Oran (70) et celui de Tlemcen (55). Malgré l'ancienneté du département d'histoire de l'université de Constantine (fondée en 1969), seuls 47 mémoires et thèses soutenus ont pu être recensés, suivi de près par le département d'histoire de l'université de l'Émir Abdelkader des sciences islamiques (fondée en 1984) avec 43 sujets traités. À partir des années 2010, l'histoire médiévale occupe une place notable dans les nouvelles universités et les écoles normales supérieures, soit : l'université de Batna (27), l'université de Sidi Belabès (25), l'École normale supérieure d'Alger (15), l'université de Mascara (10), l'université de Bechar (4), l'université de M'sila (4) et l'université d'Adrar (2).

Les chiffres obtenus démontrent une centralité algéroise car l'université d'Alger continue de jouer un rôle essentiel dans la recherche-formation en histoire médiévale, mais une tendance s'affirme à l'ouest du pays avec notamment les universités d'Oran (70) et de Tlemcen (55). À l'est du pays, Constantine est le principal centre en histoire médiévale avec ses deux universités, Constantine 2

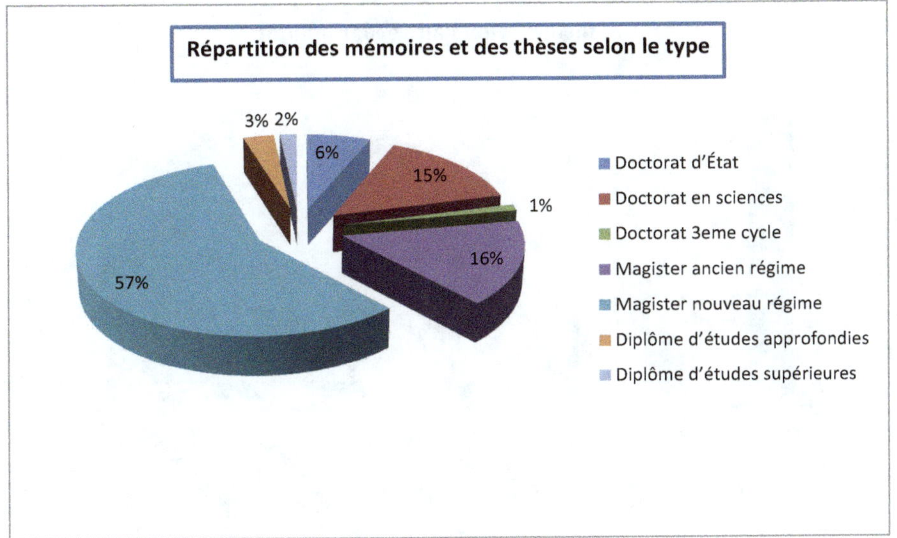

FIGURE 12.3   Répartition des mémoires et des thèse selon le type

(47) et Émir Abdelkader (43). D'autres universités sont à signaler, notamment celles de Batna 1 (27), Sidi Belabes (25) et Mascara (10).

Les données chiffrées sont à relativiser. En effet, seulement 27 thèses de doctorat d'État et 63 thèses de doctorat en sciences figurent parmi les 488 mémoires et thèses soutenus, représentant une faible part de l'ensemble des travaux. Ces chiffres renvoient donc à des mémoires dont les recherches sont très peu approfondies.

3   Un Moyen Âge essentiellement musulman

À l'exception de 19 mémoires et thèses, tous les sujets traités portent sur l'histoire de l'Islam médiéval. En outre, la présence des aires non islamiques dans les recherches universitaires est liée à l'étude des relations des territoires musulmans avec la Chrétienté latine, soit en Orient au temps des Croisades, soit en Occident (l'Europe méditerranéenne). Les relations économiques sont l'un des facteurs de cette présence, liée également à la diffusion de l'averroïsme en Occident médiéval. Mais cet intérêt rencontre un obstacle majeur : une connaissance médiocre du latin, expliquant le fait que la plupart de ces études soient uniquement fondées sur des sources arabes ou sur des travaux rédigés dans des langues européennes modernes.

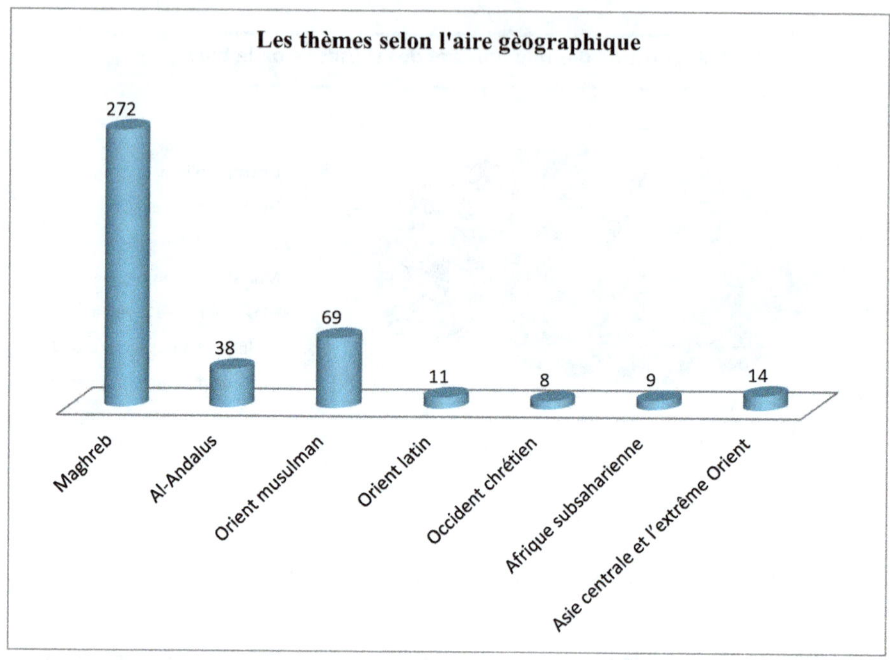

FIGURE 12.4   Les thèmes selon l'aire géographique

L'Orient médiéval est essentiellement musulman (59) même si nous trouvons 8 mémoires et thèses en rapport avec les principautés latines du Proche-Orient et les croisades. De même, l'Asie centrale et l'Extrême-Orient sont peu présentés avec seulement 14 mémoires et thèses. La plupart des travaux sont fondés sur des sources arabes et des études modernes en raison d'une méconnaissance des langues des peuples orientaux, et du latin dans le cas des principautés latines.

4   Le Maghreb central au cœur des recherches

Parmi les 310 sujets étudiés relatifs à l'Occident musulman, le Maghreb totalise 272 mémoires et thèses, devançant largement al-Andalus (38). Si un nombre important de thèmes concerne l'ensemble du Maghreb musulman (92), le Maghreb central constitue le territoire le mieux représenté avec 153 sujets, devant le Maghreb extrême (14) et l'Ifrīqiya (13). Considéré comme le territoire médiéval de l'Algérie, le Maghreb central est donc au centre des recherches universitaires en Algérie depuis l'indépendance du pays. Cette orientation s'explique par la politique de recherche visant à mener des travaux sur le passé médiéval de l'Algérie. L'objectif est donc de mettre en exergue ce passé sur lequel est fondée l'idéologie de l'État-nation.

Cependant, la première période musulmane est peu présente dans ces travaux en raison de la rareté des témoignages textuels et archéologiques. On retient notamment un seul mémoire sur l'époque omeyyade au Maghreb, et un autre sur la diffusion de l'islam. La dynastie rustumide est la mieux cernée par ces études, dont les auteurs sont originaires en grande partie des territoires à majorité ibaḍite. La majorité écrasante de ces travaux concerne donc la deuxième période musulmane allant de la deuxième moitié du XIe siècle au début du XVIe siècle.

Après l'orientation andalouse des premiers travaux, dont l'initiateur est Charles-Emmanuel Dufourcq, le Maghreb central trouve une place notable à partir des années 1970. Ainsi, les travaux universitaires suivants dirigés par l'égyptien Muḥammad al-Hādī Ša'īra commencent à aborder l'histoire du Maghreb, notamment du Maghreb central, comme mentionné plus haut. Les années 1980 marquent la confirmation de cette tendance, comme c'est le cas dans la thèse de magister de Laṭīfa Bašarī[47] sur le commerce extérieur de Tlemcen sous l'émirat ziyyānide, celle de 'Abd al-Ḥafīḏ Manṣūr[48] sur la situation sociale et économique sous l'imamat rustumide, ou encore celle de Muḫtār Ḥasānī[49] sur la situation sociale et économique de l'État ziyyānide. Cependant, cette place importante du Maghreb central ne signifie pas pour autant l'abandon total des recherches sur le reste du Maghreb islamique et de l'Orient. Ainsi, Muḥammad Lamīn Balġīṭ[50] réalise une thèse de magister sur le rôle du *ribāṭ* dans l'Occident musulman sous les Almoravides et les Almohades, tandis que Būziyyānī Darrāġī[51] s'intéresse à l'étude des conséquences de l'esprit de clivage sur l'émergence du pouvoir au Maghreb islamique. D'autres thèses sont consacrées à al-Andalus et même à l'Orient musulman, comme celle de Muḥammad Arazqī Farrād[52] sur les puissances maghrébines en al-Andalus

---

47   Laṭīfa Bašarī, *al-Tiǧāra al-ḫāriǧiyya li-Tilimsān fī 'ahd al-imāra al-rustumiyya*, thèse de magister, Université d'Alger, 1987.

48   'Abd al-Ḥafīḏ Manṣūr, *al-awḍā' al-iǧtimā'iyya wa-l-iqtiṣādiyya fī 'ahd al-imāra al-rustumiyya 144-296H/760-909*, thèse de magister, Université de Constantine, 1984.

49   Muḫtār Ḥasānī, *al-awḍā' al-iǧtimā'iyya wa-l-iqtiṣādiyya li-l-dawla al-ziyyāniyya 633-962/1235-1554*, thèse de magister, Université d'Alger, 1987.

50   Muḥammad Lamīn Balġīṭ, *al-rubuṭ bi-l-Maġrib al-islāmī wa dawruhum fī 'aṣr al-Murābiṭīn wa-l-Muwaḥidīn*, thèse de magister, Université d'Alger, 1987. Éd. Alger, Dār ǧusūr, 2014.

51   Būziyyānī Darrāġī, *al-'aṣabiyya al-qabaliyya wa aṯaruhā 'alā al-nuẓum wa-l-'alāqāt fī al-Maġrib al-islāmī*, thèse de magister, Université d'Alger, 1988.

52   Muḥammad Arazqī Farrād, *al-Qiwā al-maġrībiyya fī al-Andalus fī 'ahd mulūk al-ṭawā'if*, thèse de magister, Université d'Alger, 1988.

sous les Taïfas, celle de Baššār Qwīdar[53] sur le rôle des Barāmika dans le califat abbasside, ou encore celle de Rašīd Tūmī[54] sur les relations extérieures des Hauteville de Sicile.

Ces tendances se poursuivent dans les années 1990. Le Maghreb en général et le Maghreb central en particulier conservent une majorité écrasante parmi les sujets traités. Mais ce qu'il y a de nouveau par rapport aux décennies précédentes, ce sont les soutenances de thèses de doctorat d'État. C'est le cas par exemple de celle de ʿAbd al-ʿAzīz Fīlālī[55] sur la cité de Tlemcen sous les Ziyyānides : étude sociale, politique, urbaine et culturelle, celle de Būba Maǧǧānī sur l'organisation administrative du Maghreb sous les Fatimides[56], celle d'Ibrāhīm Baḥḥāz[57] sur la justice au Maghreb islamique, de la conquête à l'avènement des Fatimides, ainsi que celle de Masʿūd Mazhūdī[58] sur le djebel Nafūsa, de la conquête islamique à la présence hilālienne.

Le département d'histoire de l'université Émir Abdelkader des sciences islamiques se distingue par la formation de plusieurs spécialistes de l'Orient médiéval. Fondés essentiellement sur des textes narratifs, leurs travaux sont marqués par une ignorance presque totale des recherches récentes notamment en langues européennes.

Deux thèses de doctorat d'État soutenues respectivement à l'université d'Alger et à l'université d'Oran ouvrent la voie à l'émergence de plusieurs travaux sur al-Andalus islamique, réalisés par ʿAbd al-Qādir Būbāya[59] sur les

---

53   Baššār Qwīdar, *Dawr usrat al-barāmika fī tārīḫ al-ḫilāfa al-ʿabbāssiyya*, thèse de magister, Université d'Alger, 1986.

54   Rašīd Tūmī, *al-ʿalāqāt al-ḫāriǧiyya li-dawlat al-Nūrmān fī ǧanūb Īṭāliyya wa Ṣiqiliyya*, thèse de magister, Université d'Alger, 1988.

55   ʿAbd al-ʿAzīz Fīlālī, *Tilimsān fī al-ʿahd al-zayyānī, dirāsa iǧtimāʿiyya wa siyyāsiyya wa ʿumrāniyya wa ṯaqāfiyya*, thèse de doctorat d'État, Université d'Alger, 1996. Éd. Alger, ENAG, 2011, 2 vol.

56   Būba Maǧǧānī, *al-Nuẓum al-idāriyya fī bilād al-Maǧrib fī al-ʿahd al-fāṭimī*, Thèse de doctorat d'État, université de Constantine, 1996. Éd. partielle, Constantine, Dār Bahāʾ al-Dīn, 2009.

57   Ibrāhīm Baḥḥāz *Al-Qaḍāʾ fī-l-Maǧrib al-islāmī min tamāmi al-fatḥ ḥattā qiyām al-ḫilāfa al-fāṭimiyya (96–296/715–909)*, thèse de doctorat d'État, Université de Constantine, 1997. Éd. Ghardaïa, Association Turāṯ, 2006, 2 vol.

58   Masʿūd Mazhūdī, *Ǧabal Nafūsa min al-fatḥ al-islāmī ilā hiǧrat Banī Hilāl ilā al-Maǧrib*, thèse de doctorat d'État, Université de Constantine, 1997. Éd. Fondation Thawalt, 2003.

59   ʿAbd al-Qādir Būbāya, *al-Barbar fī al-Andalus wa mawqifihim min fitnat al-qarn al-ḫāmis al-hiǧrī*, thèse de doctorat d'État, Université d'Oran, 2002. Éd. Beyrouth, Dār al-kutub al-ʿilmiyya, 2011.

Berbères en al-Andalus et Muḥammad Lamīn Balġīt[60] sur la vie intellectuelle en al-Andalus sous les Almoravides.

5   La domination de l'histoire évènementielle

La tendance visant à étudier l'histoire évènementielle des mondes médiévaux demeure majoritaire pendant la première décennie du XXIᵉ siècle. Outre les évènements politiques et militaires, sont étudiées les organisations politiques, administratives et judiciaires. On peut citer à titre d'exemple le mémoire de Ġāziyya Harbāš[61] sur la révolte des Banī Ġāniyya, Muṣṭafā Ban Wāz[62] sur l'organisation judiciaire des Ḥafṣīdes, ʿAbd al-Ḥafīẓ Ḥīmī[63] sur les fonctions auxiliaires du système judiciaire en al-Andalus et Ḥamīd Zīdūr[64] dont le thème porte sur les positions politique et militaire des Berbères en al-Andalus. C'est dans cette thématique que s'inscrit la thèse de doctorat de ʿUmar Būḫārī[65], se concentrant sur les royaumes des Taïfas. Sont également abordées les relations politiques ou militaires entre les pouvoirs musulmans et les chrétiens d'Occident, ce que fait par exemple Fūḍīl Būṣṣūf[66], auteur d'un mémoire sur les relations entre l'Andalus islamique et l'Espagne chrétienne sous les Taïfas. C'est aussi le cas de la thèse de Muṣṭafā Ban Ḥusayn[67] sur les Mongols et leurs relations avec les puissances musulmanes et chrétiennes. Dans ce genre de thèmes, les études sont principalement fondées sur les sources arabes et ne font pas cas des travaux récents rédigés dans des langues européennes ou asiatiques.

---

60   Muḥammad Lamīn Balġīt, *al-Ḥayāt al-fikriyya fī al-Andalus fī ʿahd al-murābiṭīn*, thèse de doctorat d'État, Université d'Alger, 2003. Alger, Dār ġusūr, 2014.

61   Ġāziyya Harbāš, *Ṯawrat Banī Ġāniyya 580-633*, thèse de magister, Université d'Oran, 2002.

62   Muṣṭafā Ban Wāz, *Niẓām al-qaḍāʾ ʿinda al-ḥafṣiyīn 625-981H/1281-1573*, mémoire de magister, Université de Bechar, 2007.

63   ʿAbd al-Ḥafīẓ Ḥīmī, *al-Waẓāʾif al-musāʿida li-l-qaḍāʾ fī-l-Andalus ḫilāl al-qarnayn 3 wa 4 hiǧriyayn/9 wa 10 milādiyayn*, mémoire de magister, Université d'Oran, 2007.

64   Ḥamīd Zīdūr, *al-Barbar bayn al-muʿāraḍa wa-l-muwālāt fī ʿahd al-imāra al-umawiyya bi-l-Andalus (138-316/756-928)*, mémoire de magister, Université d'Oran, 2009.

65   ʿUmar Būḫārī, *al-Barbar fī al-Andalus fī ʿahd al-ṭawāʾif fī al-qarn al-ḫāmis al-hiǧrī*, thèse de doctorat, Université de Tlemcen, 2015.

66   Fūḍīl Būṣṣūf, *al-ʿAlāqāt al-siyāsiyya bayna al-Andalus al-islāmiyya wa Isbāniyya al-naṣrāniyya fī ʿaṣr mulūk al-ṭawāʾif*, mémoire de magister, Université de Constantine, 2011.

67   Muṣṭafā Ban Ḥusayn, *al-Maġūl wa ʿalāqatihim bi-l-qiwā al-masīḥiyya wa-l-islāmiyya fī Urūba wa-l-Mašriq 612-659/1215-1260*, thèse de magister, Université d'Alger, 2010.

6   Histoire de la vie culturelle et des mentalités

L'histoire culturelle occupe une place non négligeable dans les recherches universitaires en Algérie, notamment depuis l'édition de nouveaux catalogues de savants (*fahāris, barāmiǧ*) et de dictionnaires biographiques. Cet intérêt ne remonte en fait qu'aux années 1990 avec la réalisation de plusieurs travaux de valeur inégale. Plusieurs thèses de doctorat d'État soulignent cette tendance, comme celles de Muḥammad Lamīn Balǧīṭ[68] sur la vie intellectuelle en al-Andalus sous les Almoravides, de Naǧīb Ban Ḥayra[69] sur la vie scientifique à Ḫurasān, de Našīda Rāfʿī[70] sur la vie intellectuelle au Maghreb sous les Fatimides, ou encore la thèse de Būʿlām Sāḥī[71] sur la vie culturelle en Ifrīqiya sous les Aġlabides. Plus récemment, citons la thèse de Zaynab Razīwī[72] sur les savoirs au Maghreb central à la fin du Moyen Âge.

Pour les thèses de magister, nous pouvons citer à titre d'exemple celles de Muḥammad al-Šarīf Sīdī Mūsā[73] sur la vie culturelle à Bougie du VIIᵉ au Xᵉ siècle de l'hégire, et de Saʿdī Šaḥḥūm[74] sur la vie culturelle à Cordoue d'après le *Muqtabis* d'Ibn Ḥayyān. Les mémoires de magister de Ṭayyib Būsaʿd[75] sur la vie culturelle de l'émirat aġlabide, de Ḥāǧ ʿAbd al-Qādir Yaḥlaf[76] sur l'apport culturel des Berbères en al-Andalus, de Saʿīd ʿUqba[77] sur la vie intellectuelle à Bougie au XIIIᵉ siècle d'après le *ʿUnwān al-dirāya* d'al-Ġubrīnī, de ʿAbbās Qwīdar[78] sur la vie culturelle au Maghreb central au Xᵉ siècle et de ʿAllāl Ban

---

68   Muḥammad Lamīn Balǧīṭ, *al-Ḥayāt al-fikriyya bi-Andalus fī ʿaṣr al-Murābiṭīn*, op. cit.

69   Naǧīb Ban Ḥayra, *al-Ḥayāt al-ʿilmiyya fī-l-duwaylāt al-islāmiyya bi-l-Mašriq (Ḫurasān wa bilād mā warā' al-nahrayn*, thèse de doctorat d'État, Université Émir Abdelkader-Constantine, 2004.

70   Našīda Rāfʿī, *Al-Ḥayāt al-fikriyya wa-l-ṯaqāfiyya fī-l-Maġrib fī-l-ʿaṣr al-fāṭimī (296-362H)*, thèse de doctorat d'État, Université d'Alger, 2005.

71   Būʿlām Sāḥī, *Al-Ḥayāt al-ʿilmiyya fī Ifrīqiya fī ʿaṣr al-dawla al-Aġlabiyya (184-226H/800-909)*, thèse de doctorat d'État, Université d'Alger, 2009.

72   Zaynab Razīwī, *al-ʿUlūm wa-l-Maʿārif al-ṯaqāfiyya fī al-Maġrib al-awsaṭ mā bayna al-qarnayn 7-9 hiǧrī/13-15 mīlādī*, thèse de doctorat, Université de Belabes, 2016.

73   Muḥammad al-Šarīf Sīdī Mūsā, *al-Ḥayāt al-fikriyya bi-Biǧāya min al-qarn al-sābiʿ ilā al-qarn al-ʿāšir*, thèse de magister, Université d'Alger, 2002.

74   Saʿdī Šaḥḥūm, *al-Ḥayāt al-ʿilmiyya fī Qurṭuba min ḫilāl al-muqtabis d'Ibn Ḥayyān*, thèse de magister, Université d'Alger, 2002.

75   Ṭayyib Būsaʿd, *al-Ḥayāt al-ṯaqāfiyya wa-l-ʿilmiyya fī-l-imāra al-aġlabiyya wa ʿalāqatihā bi-l-ḫilāfa al-ʿabbasiyya*, mémoire de magister, Université d'Alger, 2003.

76   Ḥāǧ ʿAbd al-Qādir Yaḥlaf, *al-Ishām al-fikrī li-l-barbar bi-l-Andalus min al-ʿahd al-ʿāmirī ilā nihāyat al-wuǧūd al-murābiṭī (371-539/981-1148)*, mémoire de magister, Université d'Oran, 2009.

77   Saʿīd ʿUqba, *al-Ḥayāt al-ʿilmiyya wa-l-fikriyya bi-Biǧāya ḫilāl al-qarn 7H/13 min ḫilāl kitāb ʿunwān al-dirāya*, mémoire de magister, Université Émir Abdelkader-Constantine, 2009.

78   ʿAbbās Qwīdir, *al-Ḥayāt al-ṯaqāfiyya fī-l-Maġrib al-Awsaṭ ḫilāl al-qarn al-rābiʿ al-hiǧrī/ al-ʿāšir al-mīlādī*, mémoire de magister, Université de Sidi Belabes, 2010.

'Amar[79] sur le mouvement intellectuel et les familles savantes de Constantine à la fin du Moyen Âge s'inscrivent également dans cette perspective. Les familles savantes d'origine andalouse installées dans le Maghreb central sont soigneusement étudiées par Rafīq Ḥalīfī[80]. Les familles savantes en Afrique subsaharienne font également l'objet de recherches par Raḍwān Huwārī[81], d'après le corpus biographique d'Aḥmad Bābā al-Tinbuktī.

Plusieurs thèses et mémoires sur les méthodes d'enseignement au Maghreb médiéval s'ajoutent à cet axe de recherches. C'est le cas de ceux de Sāmiya Magrī[82] sur l'enseignement chez les ibaḍites au Maghreb, de la chute de la dynastie rustumide à la fondation des cercles savants, de Balqāsam Fīlālī[83] sur l'enseignement et la prédication almohades et de 'Abd al-Ḥalīl Garyān sur la politique d'enseignement de l'État ziyyānide[84].

Les thèmes traités en histoire culturelle se répètent peu. Les nouvelles approches méthodologiques, notamment le recours à l'histoire quantitative et aux approches épistémologique et onomastique, sont rarement appliquées avant 2006. Parmi les travaux méritant une attention particulière, notons celui de Mas'ūd Brīka[85] sur les élites de Bougie et le pouvoir ḥafṣide, marqué par le recours à l'histoire quantitative et aux approches sociologiques.

7   Les branches de l'islam et les minorités religieuses

Les différentes branches de l'islam au Maghreb ont fait l'objet de plusieurs travaux depuis la thèse de doctorat de Brahim Fekhar sur les ibaḍites, soutenue à l'université de Paris en 1971. Parmi ces travaux, on peut citer la thèse de doctorat

79   'Allāl Ban 'Amar, *al-Ḥaraka al-'ilmiyya wa buyūtāt al-'ulamā' fī madīnat Qasanṭīna*, mémoire de magister, Université Émir Abdelkader-Constantine, 2012.

80   Rafīq Ḥalīfī, *Al-Buyūtāt al-andalusiyya fī al-Magrib al-awsaṭ min nihāyat al-qarn 3 ilā nihāyat al-qarn 9 hiğrī*, mémoire de magister, Université Émir Abdelkader-Constantine, 2008.

81   Raḍwān Huwārī, *Buyūtāt al-'ulamā' fī al-Sūdān al-Ġarbī min ḫilāl kitāb nayl al-ibtihāğ bi-taṭrīz al-dībāğ li-Aḥmad Bābā al-Tinbuktī*, mémoire de magister, Université de Tlemcen, 2013.

82   Sāmiya Magrī, *al-Ta'līm 'inda al-ibāḍiyya fī bilād al-Magrib min suqūṭ al-dawla ilā ta'sīs niẓām al-'azzāba (296-409/909-1018)*, mémoire de magister, Université de Constantine, 2006.

83   Balqāsam Fīlālī, *al-Ta'līm wa-l-da'wa al-muwaḥidiyya 510-524/1116-1129*, mémoire de magister, Université de Constantine, 2004.

84   'Abd al-Ḥalīl Garyān, *al-Siyāsa al-ta'līmiyya li-dawla al-ziyyāniyya 633-962/1236-1554*, mémoire de magister, Université de Constantine, 2004.

85   Mas'ūd Brīka, *al-Nuḫba wa-l-sulṭa fī Biğāya al-ḥafṣiyya (7-9H/13-15M)*, mémoire de magister, Université Émir Abdelkader-Constantine, 2009. Éd. Alger, Mim Edition, 2014.

d'État de Mas'ūd Mazhūdī[86] sur les ibaḍites du djebel Nafūsa, le mémoire de magister de Faṭīma Maṭahrī[87] sur la ville de Tāhart sous les Rustumides, ou encore la thèse de doctorat de 'Umar Sulaymān Bū'asbāna[88] sur le recueil de biographies ibaḍite attribué à al-Wisyānī. Bien que les études ibaḍites soient peu développées avant les années 2000, on assiste depuis une dizaine d'années à des travaux plus importants portant sur le peuplement ibaḍite, son organisation communautaire et sa production intellectuelle.

L'ismaélisme et le califat fatimide au Maghreb font également l'objet de nombreuses recherches depuis la thèse de doctorat d'État de Mūsā Laqbāl sur les Kutāma et les Fatimides. Quatre thèses de doctorat d'État et une thèse de magister y sont consacrées. La première est l'œuvre de Būba Maġġānī[89], portant sur l'organisation administrative du Maghreb fatimide. La seconde est celle de Našīda Rāf'ī[90] sur la vie culturelle du Maghreb sous les Fatimides. Quant à la troisième, ayant pour auteur Ismā'īl Sāmi'ī[91], elle est consacrée au grand juriste et cadi fatimide al-Qāḍī al-Nu'mān (m. 363/979). Ce dernier fait l'objet d'une thèse de magister soutenue à la même période par Muḥammad Gwīsam[92]. Enfin, Faṭma Balhuwārī est l'auteure d'une thèse sur les activités économiques au Maghreb fatimide[93]. Les études ismaéliennes connaissent un développement notable au début des années 2000 avec la réalisation de plusieurs travaux, comme celui de Yūsuf Bardūdī[94] sur la doctrine ismaélite et l'urbanisme au Maghreb central.

La phase malikite du Maghreb fait l'objet de nombreuses recherches centrées essentiellement sur le Maghreb central, parmi lesquelles les thèses de

---

86 Mas'ūd Mazhūdī, *Ǧabal Nafūsa min al-fatḥ al-islāmī ilā hiǧrat Banī Hilāl ilā al-Maġrib (21-442/642-4053)*, thèse de doctorat d'État, Université de Constantine, 1997.

87 Faṭīma Maṭahrī, *Madīnat Tīhart al-rustumiyya, dirāsa tārīḫiyya ḥaḍāriyya*, mémoire de magister, Université de Tlemcen, 2010.

88 'Umar Sulaymān Bū'asbāna, *Maǧmū'at siyar al-Wisyānī, dirāsa wa taḥqīq*, thèse de doctorat, Université Émir Abdelkader-Constantine, 2006. Éd. Mascate, Ministère des affaires religieuses, 2009, 3 vol.

89 Būba Maġġānī, *al-Nuẓum al-idāriyya*, op. cit.

90 Našīda Rāf'ī, *al-Ḥayāt al-fikriyya wa-l-taqāfiyya*, op. cit.

91 Ismā'īl Sāmi'ī, *al-Qāḍī al-Nu'mān, ḥayātuh wa ǧuhūduh fī našr al-da'wa al-ismā'īliyya wa taṭawwurihā fī-l-dawr al-maġribī*, thèse de doctorat d'État, Université Émir Abdelkader-Constantine, 2003. Éd. *al-Dawla al-fāṭimiyya wa ǧuhūd al-Qāḍī al-Nu'mān fī irsā' da'ā'im al-ḫilāfa al-fāṭimiyya*, Amman, Markaz al-našr al-ǧāmi'ī, 2010.

92 Muḥammad Gwīsam, *Taṭawwur al-fikr al-siyāsī al-ismā'īlī min ḫilāl fikr al-Qāḍī al-Nu'mān b. Muḥammad (313-363/929-979)*, thèse de magister, Université de Constantine, 2003.

93 Faṭma Balhuwārī, *al-Našāṭ al-iqtiṣādī fī bilād al-Maġrib al-islāmī ḫilāl al-qarn al-rābi' al-hiǧrī*, 10 mīlādī, thèse de doctorat d'État, Université d'Oran, 2006.

94 Yūsuf Bardūdī, *al-Maḏhab al-ismā'īlī wa-l-'umrān fī-l-Maġrib al-awsaṭ 280/893-362/973*, mémoire de magister, Université Émir Abdelkader-Constantine, 2012.

magister de Ṣabra Ḥaṭīf[95] sur les juristes malikites et le pouvoir ziyyānide, de Laḥḍar Būlṭīf[96] sur les juristes malikites et les Almohades, ou encore l'étude de Šuʿayb Ḥannūf[97] sur les doctrines en Occident musulman sous les Almoravides, et celle de Qāda Sbaʿ[98] sur le malikisme au Maghreb central jusqu'au milieu du Xᵉ siècle. D'autres travaux s'inscrivent dans cette tendance, comme celui de Nasīm Nawwār[99], Saʿīda Lūzrī[100], Hafīẓ Kaʿwān[101], Fūzī Ramḍānī[102], Mūsā Hīšām[103] et de ʿAbd al-Qādir Būʿaqqāda[104]. Ces études sont généralement fondées sur une documentation textuelle, majoritairement narrative et juridique, et l'exploitation de textes inédits. Cependant, elles partent d'un point commun : la primauté du sunnisme au Maghreb bien avant la malikisation du pays.

Les autres courants islamiques au Maghreb et en Orient font cependant l'objet d'un nombre réduit de travaux, parmi lesquels les mémoires de magister de ʿAbd al-Qādir Būʿaqqāda[105] sur l'influence des doctrines islamiques disparues sur la jurisprudence, de ʿAbd al-Ḥamīd al-ʿĀbad[106] sur les rapports entrete-

95   Ṣabra Ḥaṭīf, *Fuqahāʾ Tilimsān wa-l-ṣulṭa fī al-Maġrib al-awsaṭ ḥilāl al-ʿahd al-ziyyānī (633-791/1235-1388), al-ǧihāz al-dīnī wa-l-taʿlīmī*, thèse de magister, Université Émir Abdelkader-Constantine, 2004. Éd. Alger, Ǧusūr édition, 2011.

96   Laḥḍar Būlṭīf, *Fuqahāʾ al-mālikiyya wa-l-taġruba al-siyāsiyya al-muwaḥidiyya fī-l-Ġarb al-islāmī*, thèse de magister, université Émir Abdelkader-Constantine, 2002. Éd. Herdon, The International Institute of Islamic Thought, 2009.

97   Šuʿayb Ḥannūf, *al-Awḍāʿ al-maḏhabiyya fī bilād Ġarb al-islāmī ḥilāl al-ʿaṣr al-murābiṭī (451-541/1055-1146)*, mémoire de magister, Université d'Alger 2, 2010.

98   Qāda Sbaʿ, *al-Maḏhab al-mālikī fī-l-Ġarb al-islāmī ilā muntaṣaf al-qarn al-ḥāmis al-hiǧrī*, mémoire de magister, Université d'Oran, 2010.

99   Nasīm Nawwār, *al-Ṣīrāʿ al-sunnī al-šīʿī bi-bilād al-Maġrib wa aṯaruhu fī taǧdīd al-fiqh al-mālikī*, mémoire de magister, Université d'Alger 2, 2011.

100   Saʿīda Lūzrī, *Al-Maḏhab al-mālikī fī al-Maġrib al-awsaṭ duḥūlah wa intišārih*, mémoire de magister, Université d'Alger 2, 2010.

101   Hafīẓ Kaʿwān, *Aṯar fuqahāʾ al-mālikiyya al-iǧtimāʿī wa-l-ṯaqāfī bi-Ifrīqiyya*, mémoire de magister, Université de Batna, 2010.

102   Fūzī Ramḍānī, *Dawr al-mālikiyya fī-l-ḥayāt al-fikriyya fī Miṣr ḥilāl al-ʿaṣr al-ayyūbī (567-648/1171-1250)*, mémoire de magister, École Normale Supérieure d'Alger, 2010.

103   Mūsā Hīšām, *al-Maḏhab al-sunnī fī al-Maġribayn al-adnā wa-l-awsaṭ 296-547 H*, thèse de doctorat, Université d'Alger 2, 2011.

104   ʿAbd al-Qādir Būʿaqqāda, *Al-Ḥaraka al-fiqhiyya bi-l-Maġrib al-awsaṭ bayn al-qarnayn 7-9 H/13-15M*, thèse de doctorat, Université d'Alger 2, 2015.

105   ʿAbd al-Qādir Būʿaqqāda, *Al-Maḏāhib al-fiqhiyya al-mundaṯira wa aṯaruhā fī al-tašrīʿ al-islāmī fī al-qarnaynī al-ṯānī wa-l-ṯāliṯ li-l-hiǧra*, mémoire de magister, Université d'Alger, 2004. Éd. *Waqāʾiʿ al-ḥaraka al-maḏhabiyya bi-l-Maġrib al-islāmī*, Alger, Dār al-Ḥaldūniyya, 2018.

106   ʿAbd al-Ḥamīd al-ʿĀbad, *ʿAlāqat fuqahāʾ al-sunna bi-l-dawla al-ʿabbāsiyya fī ʿaṣrihā al-awwal*, mémoire de magister, Université de Batna, 2009.

nus par les juristes sunnites avec le califat abbasside, de Badrīna Ziyyān[107] sur le maître des ḥanbalites Ibn ʿAqīl de Ḫālid ʿAllāl Kabīr[108] sur le mouvement ḥanbalite en Orient aux XIIe et XIIIe siècles. S'y rapportent également les sujets de recherches d'Umm al-Ḫayr ʿUṯmānī, ayant pour thème le muʿtazilisme d'après le *Kitāb al-bayān wa-l-tabyīn* d'al-Ǧāḥiẓ, de Muḥammad Naṣīr sur la diffusion de l'ašʿarisme au Maghreb au cours des Xe et XIe siècles et de Muṣṭafā Maġzāwī[109] sur le même sujet.

En revanche les minorités non musulmanes sont peu étudiées, à l'exception d'un certain nombre de mémoires de magister comme celui de Samīr Ṭabbī[110] sur le rôle des *ḏimmī*-s dans le califat abbasside, de ʿĀšūr Manṣūriyya[111] sur la tolérance religieuse en al-Andalus sous les Omeyyades, de Ṣafiyy al-Dīn Muḥyaddīn[112] sur le rôle des Mozarabes dans l'histoire d'al-Andalus, de la thèse de doctorat de Fāṭima Būʿmāma[113] sur les juifs au Maghreb islamique, et de la thèse de magister de Masʿūd Kuwātī[114] sur le même sujet. Par ailleurs, Muḥammad al-Amīn Wald al-Nān[115] consacre une thèse de doctorat aux juifs et aux chrétiens d'al-Andalus, de la chute du califat omeyyade à la fin des Almoravides. Il est à noter que l'immense majorité de ces travaux se fonde sur une documentation textuelle arabo-islamique. Cependant, les écrits produits par ces minorités ne sont pas exploités de manière directe.

---

107   Badrīna Ziyyan, *Šayḫ al-ḥanābila Abū-l-Wafāʾ b. ʿAqīl, ḥayātuh wa aʿmāluh al-siyāsiyya wa-l-iǧtimāʿiyya wa-l-ʿilmiyya 431-513/1040-1119*, mémoire de magister, Université d'Alger 2, 2010.

108   Ḫālid ʿAllāl Kabīr, *al-Ḥaraka al-ʿilmiyya al-ḥanbaliyya wa aṯaruhā fī al-Mašriq al-islāmī ḫilāl al-qarnayn 6-7H*, thèse de doctorat d'État, Université d'Alger, 2005.

109   Muṣṭafā Maġzāwī, *Dawr al-ʿāmil al-siyāsī fī intišār al-maḏhab al-ašʿarī fī al-Mašriq al-islāmī wa maġribih mundu muntaṣaf al-qarn 5 hiǧrī ilā bidāyat al-qarn 8 hiǧrī*, mémoire de magister, Université d'Alger 2, 2008.

110   Samīr Ṭabbī, *Dawr ahl al-ḏimma fī al-dawla al-islāmiyya fī al-ʿaṣr al-ʿabbāsī (132-447H)*, mémoire de magister, Université de Batna, 2007.

111   ʿĀšūr Manṣūriyya, *al-Tasāmuḥ al-dīnī fī ẓill al-dawla al-umawiyya bi-l-Andalus (138-422H)*, mémoire de magister, Université de Batna, 2007.

112   Ṣafiyy al-Dīn Muḥyaddīn, *al-Mustaʿrabūn wa dawruhum fī tārīḫ al-Andalus (138-483/755-1090)*, mémoire de magister, Université d'Oran, 2005.

113   Fāṭima Būʿmāma, *al-Yahūd fī al-Maġrib al-islāmī*, thèse de doctorat, Université d'Alger 2, 2010.

114   Masʿūd Kuwātī, *Al-Yahūd fī al-Maġrib al-islāmī min al-fatḥ al-islāmī ilā suqūṭ al-dawla al-muwaḥidiyya*, thèse de magister, Université d'Alger, 1992. Éd. Alger, Dār Hūma, 2000.

115   Muḥammad al-Amīn Wald al-Nān, *Al-Yahūd wa-l-naṣārā fī al-Andalus min suqūṭ al-ḫilāfa al-umawiyya ilā nihāyat al-ḥukm al-murābiṭī (422-529/1030-1141)*, thèse de doctorat, Université d'Oran, 2013.

8   Les courants mystiques

Le soufisme et les courants mystiques constituent un autre champ de recherches universitaires en Algérie. Depuis une dizaine d'années, les travaux se multiplient, notamment depuis la découverte et l'édition de nouveaux textes hagiographiques. Le Maghreb central est au centre de ces premières monographies hagiographiques, comme le montrent les thèses de Ṭāhar Būnābī[116] et de ʿAbīd Būdāwud[117]. Les travaux du premier sont représentatifs de cette orientation, notamment parce qu'ils exploitent un nombre considérable de textes hagiographiques inédits dans l'étude de différents courants mystiques. Ils sont suivis notamment par le mémoire de magister sur le mouvement mystique au Maghreb central sous les Ziyyānides de Āmāl Ladraʿ[118], par les travaux de Sihām Daḥmānī[119] sur la sainteté féminine au Maghreb et par ceux de Zaynab Malyānī[120] sur le soufisme au Maghreb sous les Almoravides et les Almohades. Enfin, deux mémoires concernent deux autres aires géographiques : al-Andalus et l'Orient. Le premier est l'œuvre de Fātima al-Zahrāʾ Ġaddū[121] portant sur l'autorité politique et les saints en al-Andalus sous les Almoravides et les Almohades, tandis que le second, de Fatīḥa Mazyānī[122], est consacré au mouvement mystique en Orient.

L'édition critique et l'étude des textes hagiographiques complètent cette tendance, comme c'est le cas dans le travail de Ṭāhar Manzal sur le manuscrit

---

116   Ṭāhar Būnābī, *al-Ḥaraka al-ṣūfiyya fī al-Maġrib al-awsaṭ ḫilāl al-qarnayn 6-7H/12-13M*, thèse de magister, Université d'Alger, 2001. Éd. *al-Taṣawwuf fī al-Ġazāʾir ḫilāl al-qarnayn 6-7H musāhama fī al-tārīḫ al-dīnī wa-l-iǧtimāʿī li-l-ǧazāʾir ḫilāl al-ʿaṣr al-wasīṭ*, Aïn M'lila, Dār al-Hudā, 2004 ; id. *Al-ḥaraka al-ṣūfiyya fī al-Maġrib al-awsaṭ ḫilāl al-qarnayn 8-9H/14-15M*, thèse de doctorat, Université d'Alger 2, 2010. Éd. *ʿAṣr al-mutaṣawwifa bi-l-Maġrib, dirāsa fī al-ḥaraka al-ṣūfiyya ḫilāl al-ʿaṣr al-wasīṭ*, M'sila, Publications de la Faculté des sciences humaines et sociales, 2017, 4 vol.

117   ʿAbīd Būdāwud, *Ẓāhirat al-taṣawwuf fī al-Maġrib al-awsaṭ mā bayn al-qarnayn al-sābiʿ wa-l-tāsiʿ al-hiǧriyayn*, thèse de magister, Université d'Oran, 2000. Éd. Oran, Dār al-ġarb al-islāmī li-l-našr wa-l-tawzīʿ, 2003.

118   Āmāl Ladraʿ, *al-Ḥaraka al-ṣūfiyya fī bilād al-Maġrib al-awsaṭ ḫilāl al-ʿaṣr al-ziyyānī (633/1236-962/1555)*, mémoire de magister, Université de Constantine, 2006.

119   Sihām Daḥmānī, *al-Marʾa wa-l-taṣawwuf fī al-Maġrib al-islāmī al-qurūn 6-9H/12-15M*, mémoire de magister, Université de Constantine, 2006.

120   Zaynab Malyānī, *al-Taṣawwuf fī al-Maġrib al-islāmī fī ʿaṣray al-murābiṭīn wa-l-muwaḥiddīn*, mémoire de magister, Université d'Alger, 2006.

121   Fātima al-Zahrāʾ Ġaddū, *al-Sulṭa wa-l-mutaṣawwifa fī al-Andalus fī ʿahd al-murābiṭīn wa-l-muwaḥidīn 479-635/1086-1238)*, mémoire de magister, Université de Constantine, 2008.

122   Fatīḥa Mazyānī, *Al-Ḥaraka al-ṣūfiyya wa aṯaruhā fī al-Mašriq al-islāmī ḫilāl al-qarn 7H/13M*, mémoire de magister, Université d'Alger 2, 2010.

du dictionnaire bio-hagiographique d'Ibn Ṣaʿd al-Tilimsānī (m. 901/1496) intitulé *al-Naǧm al-ṭāqib fīmā li-awliyyāʾ Allāh min mafāḥir*[123].

9 Des études sociales fondées sur la documentation juridico-hagiographique

Les textes hagiographiques et juridiques, récemment mis au jour, sont à l'origine de plusieurs travaux sur les sociétés du Maghreb médiéval. Depuis une
dizaine d'années, on assiste au développement de ce type de thèmes, même
si les approches méthodologiques sont en décalage selon les principaux
départements d'histoire. Les sources documentaires de la plupart de ces travaux sont les textes hagiographiques produits par les auteurs du Maghreb
central, notamment Ibn Marzūq (m. 781/1380), Abū ʿImrān Mūsā al-Māzūnī
(m. vers 833/1429) et Ibn Ṣaʿd al-Tilimsānī (m. 901/1496). De même, les textes
juridiques malikites et ibaḍites sont mis à profit depuis notamment la thèse
de magister de Dalāl Luwātī[124] sur les masses populaires de Kairouan sous les
Aġlabides, dans laquelle un nombre considérable de textes juridiques et narratifs est exploité. Le corpus juridique le plus utilisé ces dernières années est
celui d'*al-Durar al-maknūna fī nawāzil Māzūna*, édité par Muḫtār Ḥasānī. Il
est à l'origine de plusieurs travaux comme celui de Nūr al-Dīn Ġardāwī[125] sur
les aspects économiques et culturels au Maghreb à la fin du Moyen Âge, de
ʿAlī Šaʿwa[126] sur la vie sociale au Maghreb, celui de Hanā Šaqṭamī[127] sur la vie
rurale au Maghreb central et enfin celui de Muḥammad Lamine Būḥallūfa[128]
sur les *ḏimmī-s* au Maghreb central.

Le corpus du *Miʿyār* d'al-Wanšarīsī (m. 914/1509) constitue également la
base documentaire de plusieurs études socio-économiques parmi lesquelles
nous pouvons citer celle de ʿUmar Balbašīr sur la vie culturelle, sociale et

---

123 Ṭāhar Manzal, *al-Naǧm al-ṭāqib fīmā li-awliyyāʾ Allāh min mafāḥir*, mémoire de magister,
Université de Constantine 2, 2013.

124 Dalāl Luwātī, *ʿĀmmat al-Qayrawān fī al-aṣr al-aġlabī*, thèse de magister, Université de
Constantine, 2002. Éd. Le Caire, Dār Ruʾā, 2015.

125 Nūr al-Dīn Ġardāwī, *Ǧawānib min al-ḥayāt al-iqtiṣādiyya wa-l-fikriyya fī al-Maġrib al-islāmī
ḫilāl al-qarnayn al-ṯāmin wa-l-tāsiʿ al-hiǧriyayn min ḫilāl nawāzil al-Māzūnī*, mémoire de
magister, Université d'Alger, 2006.

126 ʿAlī Šaʿwa, *al-Ḥayāt al-iǧtimāʿiyya min ḫilāl al-durar al-maknūna fī nawāzil Māzūna*,
mémoire de magister, Université d'Alger, 2008.

127 Hanā Šaqṭamī, *al-Ḫiṭāb al-fiqhī wa-l-rif fī al-Maġrib al-awsaṭ min ḫilāl al-durar al-maknūna
fī nawāzil Māzūna*, mémoire de magister, Université de Constantine 2, 2013.

128 Muḥammad Lamine Būḥallūfa, *Ahl al-ḏimma fī al-Maġrib al-awsaṭ min ḫilāl nawāzil
al-Wanšarīsī*, mémoire de magister, Université d'Oran, 2015.

économique au Maghreb central et extrême[129]. S'inscrivent également dans cette perspective les mémoires de magister de Mas'ūd Karbū' sur les mesures de poids et de capacité d'après le *Mi'yār*[130] et de 'Abd al-Raḥīm Būḥālfa[131] sur le régime foncier au Maghreb central et les modes d'exploitation agricole. Un nombre non négligeable de travaux relatifs aux aspects socio-économiques et urbains se fonde sur ces textes juridiques, comme c'est le cas dans les thèses et mémoires de Maryāma La'nānī[132] sur la famille andalouse sous les Almoravides et les Almohades, de Sumaya Mazdūr[133] sur les pestes et les famines, de 'Ābad Bandūmī[134] sur les catastrophes naturelles et les épidémies au Maghreb, de 'Abīd Būdawud[135] sur le *waqf* au Maghreb islamique, de 'Abd al-'Azīz Ḥağ Kūla[136] sur la vie sociale et économique en al-Andalus et de L'arbī Laḥḍar[137] sur les métiers dans la ville de Tlemcen sous les Ziyyānides. Le travail de Sanā 'Aṭṭābī[138] sur l'organisation urbaine du Maghreb central est basé sur une large documentation juridique appuyée par des données archéologiques et archivistiques. De même, Nasīm Ḥasblāwī[139] exploite une large documentation juridique

---

129   'Umar Balbašīr, *Ğawānib min al-ḥayāt al-fikriyya wa-l-iğitimā'iyya wa-l-iqtiṣādiyya fī al-Maġribayn al-awsaṭ wa-l-aqṣā min ḫilāl al-mi'yār li-l-Wanšarīsī*, thèse de doctorat, Université d'Oran, 2010.

130   Mas'ūd Karbū', *Nawāzil al-nuqūd wa-l-makāyīl wa-l-mawāzīn fī kitāb al-mi'yār li-l-Wanšarīsī*, mémoire de magister, Université de Batna, 2014.

131   'Abd al-Raḥīm Būḥālfa, *al-Arḍ wa istiġlālihā fī al-Maġrib al-awsaṭ min ḫilāl nawāzil al-Wanšarīsī*, mémoire de magister, Université de Constantine 2, 2014.

132   Maryāma La'nānī, *al-Usra al-andalusiyya fī 'aṣray al-murābiṭīn wa-l-muwaḥḥidīn*, mémoire de magister, Université de Constantine, 2009.

133   Sumaya Mazdūr, *al-Awbi'a wa-l-mağā'āt bi-l-Maġrib al-awsaṭ min nihāyat al-qarn al-sābi' ilā maṭla' al-qarn al-tāsi' al-hiğrī*, mémoire de magister, Université de Constantine, 2010.

134   'Ābad Bandūmī, *al-Kawāriṯ al-ṭabī'iyya wa-l-ğawā'iḥ wa-l-awbi'a fī al-Maġrib al-awsaṭ wa aṯaruhā fī al-muğtama' fī-l-qarnayn al-sābi' wa-l-tāsi' al-hiğriyayn*, mémoire de magister, Université de Mascara, 2011.

135   'Abīd Būdawud, *Intišār ẓāhirat al-awqāf fī al-Maġrib al-islāmī mā bayn al-qarnayn al-ṯāmin wa-l-tāsi' al-hiğriyayn (13-14M)*, thèse de doctorat, Université d'Oran, 2006. Éd. *al-Waqf fī al-Maġrib al-islāmī mā bayn al-qarnayn al-sābi' wa-l-tāsi ' al-hiğriyayn (13-15 mīlādī) wa dawruh fī al-ḥayāt al-iqtiṣādiyya wa-l-iğtimā'iyya*, Sidi Belabes, Maktabat al-Rašād, 2011.

136   'Abd al-'Azīz Ḥağ Kūla, *al-Ḥayāt al-iğtimā'iyya wa-l-iqtiṣādiyya bi-l-Andalus min ḫilāl al-nawāzil al-fiqhiyya*, mémoire de magister, Université d'Alger 2, 2011.

137   L'arbī Laḥḍar, *al-Ḥiraf fī madīnat Tilimsān 'alā al-'ahd al-ziyyānī (633-962/1335-1554)*, mémoire de magister, Université de Mascara, 2011.

138   Sanā 'Aṭṭābī, *al-Ḫiṭāb al-fiqhī wa-l-'umrān fī al-Maġrib al-awsaṭ*, mémoire de magister, Université Émir Abdelkader-Constantine, 2008. Sa thèse de doctorat, soutenue sous ma direction en mars 2018 a porté sur le droit musulman et l'organisation urbaine à travers la ville de Tlemcen.

139   Nasīm Ḥasblāwī, *al-Muğtama' al-andalusī min ḫilāl kutub al-nawāzil bayn al-qarnayn 4-7 hiğrī, 10-13 mīlādī*, thèse de doctorat, Université d'Alger 2, 2017.

dans son étude sur la société de l'Andalus d'après les consultations juridiques malikites.

La thèse de 'Abd al-Nāṣir Ǧabbār[140] propose une lecture des textes fondamentaux de l'islam et des traités de droit malikite afin de déterminer le statut des prisonniers de guerre en islam et le sort des captifs, dont le rachat est mis en lumière.

10   **Les monographies locales**

L'histoire locale occupe une place grandissante depuis la soutenance de thèse de 'Abd al-'Azīz Fīlālī sur la ville de Tlemcen sous les Ziyyānides en 1996. Plusieurs travaux sont réalisés, notamment à l'université Émir Abdelkader, sur les villes du Maghreb central : la ville de Māzūna et sa région au Moyen Âge par Ǧaniyya 'Abbāsī[141], Biskra et sa région par Du'ā' Idrīsī[142], Ouargla par 'Ammār Ǧarā'issa[143], M'sila et sa région par Salīḥa Raḥlī[144], Ṭubna par 'Abd al-Nūr Grārī[145], Bougie par Āmina Būdšīš[146], Tāhart par Faṭīma Maṭharī[147], Oran par Warda Šargī[148], et Constantine par Muḥammad Gwīsam[149]. D'autres cités du Maghreb central sont concernées par des recherches en cours, comme Alger[150],

---

140   'Abd al-Nāṣir Ǧabbār, *al-Asr wa-l-fidā' : dirāsa fī al-mafāhīm wa tabādul al-asrā bayna al-muslimīn wa a'dā'ihim min ma'rakat Badr sanat 2 hiǧrī ilā 331/942*, thèse de doctorat, Université de Constantine 2, 2015.

141   Ǧaniyya 'Abbāsī, *Māzūna wa nāḥiyatuhā fī al-'aṣr al-wasīṭ, dirāsa munuǧrāfiyya*, mémoire de magister, Université Émir Abdelkader-Constantine, 2012.

142   Du'ā' Idrīsī, *al-Madīna al-dawla fī al-Maǧrib al-awsaṭ al-islāmī : Biskra namūḏaǧan*, mémoire de magister, Université Émir Abdelkader-Constantine, 2012.

143   'Ammār Ǧarā'issa, *al-Madīna al-dawla fī al-Maǧrib al-awsaṭ: Wārǧlān namūḏaǧan*, mémoire de magister, Université Émir Abdelkader-Constantine, 2008.

144   Salīḥa Raḥlī, *Masīla wa ǧihātihā fī al-'aṣr al-wasīṭ*, mémoire de magister, Université de Batna, 2014.

145   'Abd al-Nūr Grārī, *Ṭubna wa dawruhā al-ḥaḍārī min al-fatḥ ḥattā nihāyat al-qarn al-ḥāmis al-hiǧrī*, mémoire de magister, Université d'Alger 2, 2009.

146   Āmina Būdšīš, *Biǧāya, dirāsa tārīḫiyya wa ḥaḍāriyya*, mémoire de magister, Université de Tlemcen, 2008 ; id., *Madīnat Biǧāya min al-'ahd al-ḥammādī ilā al-ǧazw al-isbānī*, thèse de doctorat, Université de Tlemcen, 2017.

147   Faṭīma Maṭharī, op. cit.

148   Warda Šargī, *Madīnat Wahrān ḫilāl al-'aṣr al-wasīṭ, dirāsa munūǧrāfiyya*, mémoire de magister, Université Émir Abdelkader-Constantine, 2014.

149   Muḥammad Gwīsam, *Madīnat Qasanṭīna mā bayna al-qarnayn 7-9 hiǧrī, dirāsa siyāsiya wa 'umrāniyya wa iǧtimā'iyya wa ṭaqāfiyya*, thèse de doctorat, Université d'Alger 2, 2015.

150   La ville d'Alger a été le sujet de Zaynab Mūsāwī sous ma direction, mais elle est malheureusement décédée avant la soutenance de son mémoire de magister. Ce sujet a été repris par 'Abd al-Qādir Qrīšān, doctorant à l'université Émir Abdelkader-Constantine.

Bône[151] et Ténès[152]. L'étude de Ġaniyya ʿAbbāsī sur la petite ville de Māzūna est la plus pertinente, car l'auteure a pu mettre en lumière l'émergence et le développement d'une ville à partir des matériaux archéologiques et des sources textuelles, en exploitant en grande partie les sources locales manuscrites.

L'histoire locale ne se limite pas à l'étude de la ville et son territoire rural : plusieurs travaux sont consacrés à l'histoire régionale. Ainsi, la thèse de magister de Mūsā Raḥmānī[153] a pour aire géographique le massif de l'Aurès. De même, Ṣūraya Madyāza[154] consacre son mémoire de magister à la région du Zāb depuis la conquête omeyyade au départ des Fatimides en Orient.

11   **La géographie historique et l'étude du peuplement**

Parmi les tendances les plus récentes en histoire médiévale en Algérie, figure celle de la géographie historique. Après plusieurs travaux sur la ville au Maghreb central, comme ceux de Nawāl Balmadānī[155] et de Ṭāhar Ṭawīl[156] ou sur des tribus, comme ceux de Muḥammad Banʿamīra[157] sur les Zanāta, de Riḍā Baniyya[158] sur les Ṣanhāǧa, de Maftāḥ Ḥalfāt[159] sur les Zawāwa, de ʿAbd al-Raḥmān Ballāǧ[160] sur les Miknāsa et de Ḥāǧ ʿAbd al-Qādir Yaḥlaf[161] sur les Ṣanhāǧa d'al-Andalus, des recherches sur la géographie historique des entités formant le Maghreb central sont en cours. Parmi elles, la région de l'Aurès

---

151   C'est le sujet de thèse de doctorat de Ḥafīẓ Kaʿwān, Université de Batna 1.

152   C'est le sujet de thèse de doctorat de Yūsuf Bardūdī, Université de Constantine 2.

153   Mūsā Raḥmānī, *al-Awrās fī al-ʿaṣr al-wasīṭ min al-fatḥ al-islāmī ilā intiqāl al-ḫilāfa al-fāṭimiyya ilā Miṣr (27-362/637-972)*, mémoire de magister, Université de Constantine, 2007.

154   Ṣūraya Madyāza, *Bilād al-Zāb min al-fatḥ al-islāmī ilā intiqāl al-ḫilāfa al-fāṭimiyya ilā Miṣr*, mémoire de magister, Université de Batna, 2010.

155   Nawāl Balmadānī, *al-Madīna bi-l-Maġrib al-awsaṭ min ḫilāl al-maṣādir al-tārīḫiyya wa-l-ǧuġrāfiyya*, mémoire de magister, Université d'Oran, 2006.

156   Ṭāhar Ṭawīl, *al-Taṭawwur al-tārīḫī li-l-madīna bi-l-Maġrib al-awsaṭ min al-niṣf al-ṯānī li-l-qarn al-ṯānī li-l-hiǧra ilā al-qarn al-ḫāmis al-hiǧrī*, mémoire de magister, Université Émir Abdelkader-Constantine, 2008. Éd. Alger, Maṭbaʿat Ḥasnāwī, 2011.

157   Muḥammad Banʿamīra, *Dawr Zanāta fī al-ḥaraka al-maḏhabiyya*, op. cit.

158   Riḍā Baniyya, *Ṣanhāǧa al-Maġrib al-awsaṭ min al-fatḥ al-islāmī ḥatta ʿawdat al-fāṭimiyīn ilā Miṣr (80-362/699-973)*, mémoire de magister, Université de Constantine, 2006.

159   Maftāḥ Ḥalfāt, *Qabīlat Zawāwa mā bayn al-qarnayn 7 wa 9H/12-15M*, thèse de doctorat, Université d'Alger, 2010. Éd. Alger, Dār al-amal, 2011.

160   ʿAbd al-Raḥmān Ballāǧ, *Qabīlat Miknāsa al-barbariyya wa dawruhā al-siyāsī wa-l-maḏhabī fī bilād al-Maġrib min al-qarn al-ṯānī ilā al-qarn al-rābiʿ al-hiǧrī*, mémoire de magister, Université de Bechar, 2007.

161   Ḥāǧ ʿAbd al-Qādir Yaḥlaf, *al-Dawr al-siyyāsī wa-l-ishām al-fikrī li-Ṣanhāǧa bi-l-Andalus*, thèse de doctorat, Université d'Oran.

est étudiée par Ṭāhar Ṭawīl, la région du Zāb par Sādiq Ziyyānī et la région de l'Ouersenis-Banū Ṭūǧīn par Maḥmūd 'Abbād[162]. L'étude du peuplement rural et de la toponymie reste un domaine peu développé en Algérie. Il n'y a que le département d'histoire de l'université Émir Abdelkader à Constantine qui commence à former les doctorants à la géographie historique, à la toponymie et à l'étude des transformations socioculturelles depuis la fin de l'Antiquité.

Les faits migratoires au Maghreb médiéval intéressent de plus en plus les universitaires algériens. La dernière étude sur le sujet est l'œuvre de Ṭāhar Baḥadda[163], intitulée « Les migrations au Maghreb et leurs conséquences du XIIᵉ au XIVᵉ siècle ».

12   Retour à la biographie

Le début des années 2000 est marqué par un intérêt particulier pour la biographie « savante », comme l'attestent les nombreuses études réalisées. Ainsi, Ismā'īl Sām'ī et Muḥammad Gwīsam ont tous les deux consacré leurs thèses à al-Qāḍī al-Nu'mān b. Muḥammad, grand cadi et juriste ismaélite du califat fatimide au Maghreb. De même, le juriste malikite Muḥammad b. 'Abd al-Karīm al-Maǧīlī fait l'objet d'un travail biographique par Munīra Būǧrāra[164], tout comme les Rāzī d'al-Andalus[165], les Ibn Marzūq de Tlemcen[166], Abū 'Uṯmān Sa'īd al-'Uqbānī de Tlemcen[167] et Ibn 'Aqīl de Bagdad[168].

162   Les trois doctorants sont inscrits sous ma direction à l'Université Émir Abdelkader-Constantine.

163   Ṭāhar Baḥadda, *al-Hiǧra fī al-Maǧrib al-awsaṭ wāqi'uhā wa āṯārihā min muntaṣaf al-qarn al-sādis ilā awāḫir al-qarn al-ṯāmin* (12-14 mīlādī), thèse de doctorat, Université d'Oran, 2017.

164   Munīra Būǧrāra, *Muḥammad b. 'Abd al-Karīm al-Maǧīlī wa musāhamatihi fī al-ṯaqāfa al-islāmiyya fī Ǧarb Ifrīqiyya* (823-909/1417-1503), thèse de magister, Université Émir Abdelkader-Constantine, 2003.

165   Muḥammad Būšrīṭ, *Āl al-Rāzī wa āṯārihim al-tārīḫiyya wa-l-ǧuǧrāfiyya* (250-379), thèse de magister, Université d'Oran, 2004.

166   Naṣr al-Dīn Bandāwud, *'Ulamā' usrāt al-Marāziqa wa dawruhā al-ṯaqāfī bi-Tilmsān min qarn 7 ilā 13H/10-16M*, thèse de magister, Université d'Oran, 2004. Éd. Tlemcen, Dār al-našr al-ǧami'ī al-ǧadīd, 2011.

167   Šahrazād Raffāf, *Abū 'Uṯman Sa'īd al-'Uqbānī ḥayātuh wa āṯāruh*, mémoire de magister, Université de Bechar, 2006.

168   Badrīna Zayyān, op. cit.

13   Historiographie médiévale et histoire des sciences

Outre les travaux réalisés dans les départements de physique et mathématique sur l'histoire des sciences, les départements d'histoire connaissent depuis une dizaine d'années des recherches s'inscrivant dans la même perspective. La majeure partie de ces travaux ne suit toutefois pas l'évolution des recherches sur l'histoire des sciences. Deux exemples illustrent cette tendance : la thèse de magister de Nūr al-Dīn Zarhūnī[169] sur la médecine arabe en al-Andalus au XIIe siècle et celle de Bakīr Bū'arwa[170] sur les astronomes d'al-Andalus de la fondation de l'émirat omeyyade à la fin des Taïfas. La thèse de Hādī Ğallūl[171] sur les sciences religieuses au Maghreb central suit également cette approche classique de l'étude de l'histoire des sciences. Plus récemment, Naṣīra 'Azrūdī[172] a consacré sa thèse de doctorat à l'histoire de l'astronomie au Maghreb central.

Il faut cependant mentionner des travaux sur l'historiographie arabe médiévale, comme ceux de Āsiya Sāḥlī[173] sur la production et la transmission du savoir historique au Maghreb central, ceux de 'Alī Ziyyān[174] sur le savoir historique en al-Andalus au XIe siècle, ou encore ceux de Baššār Qwīdar[175] dont le thème est relatif à l'écriture de l'histoire chez Ibn al-Aṯīr et de Qaddūr Wahrānī[176] sur al-Qalqašandī. Plus récemment, la thèse de 'Abd al-Karīm Ḥasāyan[177] portait sur l'écriture de l'histoire au Maghreb central sous les Ziyyānides.

---

169   Nūr al-Dīn Zarhūnī, *al-Ṭibb wa-l-ḫadamāt al-ṭibbiyya fī al-Andalus ḫilāl al-qarn al-sādis ḥiğrī*, thèse de magister, Université d'Oran, 2002.

170   Bakīr Bū'arwa, *'Ulamā' al-falak bi-l-Andalus min bidāyat al-dawla al-umawiyya ḥattā nihāyat mulūk al-ṭawā'if (138-484/775-1088)*, mémoire de magister, Université d'Alger, 2009.

171   Hādī Ğallūl, *al-'Ulūm al-dīniyya fī al-Maġrib al-awsaṭ min al-qarn 2 ilā al-qarn 8 ḥiğrī (8-14m)*, thèse de doctorat, Université de Sidi Belabes, 2017.

172   Naṣīra 'Azrūdī, *Taṭawwur 'ilm al-falak bi-l-Maġrib al-awsaṭ ḫilāl al-fatra al-wusṭā*, thèse de doctorat, Université de Sidi Belabès, 2017.

173   Āsiya Sāḥlī, *Intāğ wa intiqāl al-ma'ārif al-tārīḫiyya fī al-Maġrib al-awsaṭ*, mémoire de magister, Université Émir Abdelkader-Constantine, 2009. La soutenance de sa thèse sur la place de l'histoire dans les champs du savoir dans le Maghreb médiéval est prévue pour la fin de 2018.

174   'Alī Ziyyān, *al-Ma'rifa al-tārīḫiyya fī al-Andalus ḫilāl al-qarn al-ḫāmis al-hiğrī*, mémoire de magister, Université de Constantine, 2011.

175   Baššār Qwīdar, *Manhağiyyat Ibn al-Aṯīr fī al-ta'rīḫ li-l-qiwā al-mu'āriḍa li-l-ḫilāfa al-'abbāsiyya fī al-dāḫil wa-l-ḫāriğ*, thèse de doctorat d'État, Université d'Alger, 2007.

176   Qaddūr Wahrānī, *Manhağ al-kitāba al-tārīḫiyya 'inda al-Qalqašandī min ḫilāl kitāb ma'āṯir al-anāfa fī ma'ālim al-ḫilāfa*, thèse de doctorat, Université d'Oran, 2014.

177   'Abd al-Karīm Ḥasāyan, *Ḥarakat al-ta'līf al-tārīḫī bi-l-Maġrib al-awsaṭ ḫilāl al-'ahd al-ziyyānī (633-962/1235-1554)*, thèse de doctorat, Université de Sidi Belabes, 2017.

14 Des aspects sociaux et urbains

Nous avons noté que des recherches s'intéressent aux aspects de la vie quotidienne et urbaine, comme c'est le cas de la thèse de doctorat de Būdāliyya Tuwātiyya[178] sur l'environnement en al-Andalus, de celle de Ḥayra Siyāb[179] sur l'usage des eaux au Maghreb médiéval, ou de celle de Malīka Ḥamdī[180] sur le rôle des femmes andalouses depuis la conquête arabe à la chute de Grenade, ou encore du mémoire de Baḫta Ḥāǧ Ǧallūl[181] sur la place de la femme dans la société ziyyānide. Quelques aspects de la vie sociale, tels que la pauvreté au Maghreb islamique[182] et les cérémonies au Maghreb central sous les Ziyyānides, sont également étudiés[183].

15 Conclusion

Au terme de cette présentation, il convient de rappeler que l'histoire médiévale au sein des universités algériennes est avant tout islamique, car l'immense majorité des recherches ne concerne que les pays musulmans. En revanche, la présence des autres mondes médiévaux est insignifiante. Les quelques travaux recensés sont fondés sur une documentation de seconde main en raison d'une méconnaissance des langues anciennes. Par ailleurs, ce Moyen Âge est essentiellement maghrébin, l'Orient musulman est faiblement représenté, et surtout, la qualité des travaux reste médiocre.

Il y a certainement une lacune historiographique concernant les premiers siècles. Outre l'absence de travaux sérieux sur les processus d'islamisation et d'arabisation, ces premiers siècles n'attirent pas les chercheurs, faute de sources et réflexions sur le Maghreb central.

---

178 Būdāliyya Tuwātiyya, *al-Bayʿa fī bilād al-Andalus ʿaṣray al-ḫilāfa wa mulūk al-ṭawāʾif*, thèse de doctorat, Université d'Oran, 2014.

179 Ḥayra Siyāb, *al-Miyāh wa dawruhā al-ḥaḍārī fī bilād al-Maġrib al-islāmī*, thèse de doctorat, Université d'Oran, 2014.

180 Malīka Ḥamdī, *al-Ishāmāt al-ḥaḍāriyya li-l-marʾa al-andalusiyya min al-fatḥ al-islāmī ilā suqūṭ Ġarnāṭa (92-897/711-1492)*, thèse de doctorat, Université d'Alger 2, 2014.

181 Baḫta Ḥāǧ Ǧallūl, *al-Marʾa fī al-muǧtamaʿ al-ziyyānī (633-962/1235-1554)*, mémoire de magister, Université d'Oran, 2015.

182 Baḫta Ḥalīlī, *al-Faqr fī al-Maġrib al-islāmī mā bayna al-qarnayn al-sābiʿ wa-l-tāsiʿ al-hiǧriyayn, wāqiʿuh wa āṯāruh*, thèse de doctorat, Université de Mascara, 2016.

183 Suhayla Dahmaš, *al-ʿĀdāt al-iḥtifāliyya, musāhama fī al-tārīḫ al-dīnī wa-l-iǧtimāʿī fī al-Maġrib al-awsaṭ al-ziyyānī (633-962/1235-1555)*, mémoire de magister, Université de M'sila, 2016.

Il convient aussi de noter que la diversité des thèmes traités ne signifie pas pour autant que les recherches universitaires sur le Moyen Âge sont en bonne voie, car la plupart d'entre elles s'inspirent des visions classiques imposées par les médiévistes égyptiens dans les années 1970-1980. Cependant, nombreuses sont celles qui apportent des connaissances nouvelles et contribuent indiscutablement à enrichir les champs des recherches d'histoire médiévale.

Enfin, notons l'absence de la dimension internationale dans la plupart des travaux réalisés. L'édition de ces recherches sur le Moyen Âge ne se fait qu'en arabe, la connaissance des autres langues étant réduite au français, et la diffusion des ouvrages publiés étant restreinte. Rares sont ceux qui publient dans d'autres langues que l'arabe, et rares aussi sont ceux qui exploitent les recherches publiées en langues non arabes.

Références bibliographiques

Al-ʿĀbad, ʿAbd al-Ḥamīd. *ʿAlāqat fuqahāʾ al-sunna bi-l-dawla al-ʿabbāsiyya fī ʿaṣrihā al-awwal*, Université de Batna, 2009.

ʿAbbāsī, Ġaniyya. *Māzūna wa nāḥiyatuhā fī al-ʿaṣr al-wasīṭ, dirāsa munuġrāfiyya*, Université Émir Abdelkader-Constantine, 2012.

ʿAṭṭābī, Sanā. *al-Ḫiṭāb al-fiqhī wa-l-ʿumrān fī al-Maġrib al-awsaṭ*, Université Émir Abdelkader-Constantine, 2008.

ʿAzrūdī, Naṣīra. *Haǧarāt al-Andalusiyīn ilā al-Maġrib al-awsaṭ munḏu awāʾil al-qarn al-ṯānī al-hiǧrī (al-ṯāmin al-mīlādī) ḥattā awāḫir al-qarn al-ṯāmin al-hiǧrī (al-rābiʿ ʿašar al-mīlādī)*, Université d'Alexandrie, 2007.

ʿAzrūdī, Naṣīra. *Taṭawwur ʿilm al-falak bi-l-Maġrib al-awsaṭ ḫilāl al-fatra al-wusṭā*, Université de Sidi Belabès, 2017.

Amara, Allaoua. « Ḫamsūn sana min al-baḥṯ fī al-tārīḫ al-wasīṭ bi-l-ǧāmiʿa al-ǧazāʾiriya (1962-2012) », *Al-Mawaqif, Revue des études et des recherches sur la société et l'histoire* 7 (2012), 109-141.

Amara, Allaoua. *L'histoire de l'Algérie dans la recherche universitaire en France (1968-2008)*, Constantine, Publications de la Faculté des lettres et sciences humaines, 2010.

Amara, Allaoua. *Niṣf qarn min al-baḥṯ al-tārīḫī bi-l-ǧāmiʿa al-ǧazāʾiriyya (1962-2012)*, Constantine, Publications de la faculté des lettres et civilisation islamique, 2013 (en collaboration avec Mouloud Aouimeur).

Amara, Allaoua. *Pouvoir*, économie et société *dans le Maghreb hammadide (395/1004-547/1152)*, Université Paris 1 Panthéon-Sorbonne, 2002.

Arazqī Farrād, Muḥammad. *al-Qiwā al-maġrībiyya fī al-Andalus fī ʿahd mulūk al-ṭawāʾif*, Université d'Alger, 1988.

Baḥadda, Ṭāhar. *al-Hiǧra fī al-Maġrib al-awsaṭ wāqiʿuhā wa āṯāruhā min muntaṣaf al-qarn al-sādis ilā awāḫir al-qarn al-ṯāmin (12-14 mīlādī)*, Université d'Oran, 2017.

Baḥḥāz, Ibrāhīm. *al-Dawla al-rustumiyya (160-298/777-909), dirāsa fī-l-awḍāʿ al-iqtiṣādiyya wa-l-ḥayāt al-fikriyya*, Alger, Lafoumik, 1985.

Baḥḥāz, Ibrāhīm. *al-Qaḍāʾ fī-l-Maġrib al-islāmī min tamāmi al-fatḥ ḥattā qiyām al-ḫilāfa al-fāṭimiyya (96-296/715-909)*, Ghardaïa, Association Turāṯ, 2006.

Balbašīr, ʿUmar. *Ǧawānib min al-ḥayāt al-fikriyya wa-l-iǧitimāʿiyya wa-l-iqtiṣādiyya fī al-Maġribayn al-awsaṭ wa-l-aqṣā min ḫilāl al-miʿyār li-l-Wanšarīsī*, Université d'Oran, 2010.

Balġīt, Muḥammad Lamīn. *al-Ḥayāt al-fikriyya fī al-Andalus fī ʿahd al-murābiṭīn*, Alger, Dār ǧusūr, 2014.

Balġīt, Muḥammad Lamīn. *al-Rubuṭ bi-l-Maġrib al-islāmī wa dawruhum fī ʿaṣr al-Murābiṭīn wa-l-Muwaḥidīn*, Alger, Dār ǧusūr, 2014.

Balhuwārī, Fāṭima. *al-Fāṭimiyūn wa ḥarakāt al-muʿāraḍa fī al-Maġrib al-islāmī*, Oran, Dār al-misk li-l-ṭibāʿa wa-l-našr, 2011.

Balhuwārī, Fāṭima. *al-Našāṭ al-iqtiṣādī fī bilād al-Maġrib al-islāmī ḫilāl al-qarn al-rābiʿ al-hiǧrī*, 10 mīlādī, Université d'Oran, 2006.

Ballāġ, ʿAbd al-Raḥmān. *Qabīlat Miknāsa al-barbariyya wa dawruhā al-siyāsī wa-l-maḏhabī fī bilād al-Maġrib min al-qarn al-ṯānī ilā al-qarn al-rābiʿ al-hiǧrī*, Université de Bechar, 2007.

Balmadānī, Nawāl. *al-Madīna bi-l-Maġrib al-awsaṭ min ḫilāl al-maṣādir al-tārīḫiyya wa-l-ǧuǧrāfiyya*, Université d'Oran, 2006.

Ban ʿAmar, ʿAllāl. *al-Ḥaraka al-ʿilmiyya wa buyūtāt al-ʿulamāʾ fī madīnat Qasanṭīna*, Université Émir Abdelkader-Constantine, 2012.

Ban Ḫayra, Naǧīb. *al-Ḥayāt al-ʿilmiyya fī-l-duwaylāt al-islāmiyya bi-l-Mašriq – Ḫurasān wa bilād mā warāʾ al-nahr*, Université Émir Abdelkader-Constantine, 2004.

Ban Ḥusayn, Muṣṭafā. *al-Maǧūl wa ʿalāqatihim bi-l-qiwā al-masīḥiyya wa-l-islāmiyya fī Urūba wa-l-Mašriq 612-659/1215-1260*, Université d'Alger, 2010.

Ban Wāz, Muṣṭafā. *Niẓām al-qaḍāʾ ʿinda al-ḥafṣiyīn 625-981H/1281-1573*, Université de Bechar, 2007.

Banʿamīra, Muḥammad. *Dawr Zanāta fī al-ḥaraka al-maḏhabiyya fī al-Maġrib al-islāmī*, Alger, ENAL, 1984.

Bandāwud, Naṣr al-Dīn. *ʿUlamāʾ usrāt al-Marāziqa wa dawruhā al-ṯaqāfī bi-Tilmsān min qarn 7 ilā 13H/10-16M*, Tlemcen, Dār al-našr al-ǧāmiʿī al-ǧadīd, 2011.

Bandīb, ʿĪsā. *al-Tiǧāra fī ʿaṣr dawlat al-murābiṭīn (480-540)*, Université du Caire, 1990.

Bandūmī, ʿĀbad. *al-Kawāriṭ al-ṭabīʿiyya wa-l-ǧawāʾiḥ wa-l-awbiʾa fī al-Maġrib al-awsaṭ wa aṯaruhā fī al-muǧtamaʿ fī-l-qarnayn al-sābiʿ wa-l-tāsiʿ al-hiǧriyayn*, Université de Mascara, 2011.

Baniyya, Riḍā. *Ṣanhāǧa al-Maġrib al-awsaṭ min al-fatḥ al-islāmī ḥatta ʿawdat al-fāṭimiyīn ilā Miṣr (80-362/699-973)*, Université de Constantine, 2006.

Banmārs, Kamāl. *al-ʿAlāqa bayna al-Mawṣil wa Ḥalab wa dawruhā fī-l-ḥurūb al-ṣalībiyya (1071-1187)*, Université d'Aïn-Chems, 1991.

Bāqa, Rašīd. *al-ʿAlāqāt al-tiğāriyya bayna Flūransā wa salṭanat al-mamālīk fī-l-qarn al-ḫāmis ʿašar al-mīlādī*, Université du Caire, 1989.

Bardūdī, Yūsuf. *al-Maḏhab al-ismāʿīlī wa-l-ʿumrān fī-l-Maġrib al-awsaṭ 280/893-362/973*, Université Émir Abdelkader-Constantine, 2012.

Bašarī, Laṭīfa. *al-Tiğāra al-ḫāriğiyya li-Tilimsān fī ʿahd al-imāra al-rustumiyya*, Université d'Alger, 1987.

Bourouiba, Rachid. *Apports de l'Algérie à l'architecture religieuse arabo-islamique*, Alger, ENAL et Office des publications universitaires, 1986.

Bourouiba, Rachid. *Cités disparues : Tahert, Sedrata, Achîr, Kalaa des Béni-Hammad*, Alger, Ministère de l'information, 1982.

Bourouiba, Rachid. *Les H'ammadides*, Alger, ENAL, 1984.

Bourouiba, Rachid. *Les inscriptions commémoratives des mosquées d'Algérie*, Alger, Office des publications universitaires, 1984.

Brāhīmī al-Mīlī, Mubārak. *Tārīḫ al-Ğazāʾir fī-l-qadīm wa-l-ḥadīṯ*, Constantine, al-Maṭbaʿa al-islāmiya al-Ğazāʾiriya, 1928-1932.

Brīka, Masʿūd. *Al-Nuḫba wa-l-sulṭa fī Biğāya al-ḥafṣiyya (7-9H/13-15M)*, Alger, Mim Edition, 2014.

Brunschvig, Robert. *La Berbérie orientale sous les Ḥafsīdes, des origines à la fin du XVe siècle*, Paris, Librairie d'Amérique et d'Orient Adrien-Maisonneuve, 1940-1946.

Būʿaqqāda, ʿAbd al-Qādir. *al-Ḥaraka al-fiqhiyya bi-l-Maġrib al-awsaṭ bayn al-qarnayn 7-9 H/13-15M*, Université d'Alger 2, 2015.

Būʿaqqāda, ʿAbd al-Qādir. *al-Maḏāhib al-fiqhiyya al-mundaṯira wa aṯaruhā fī al-tašrīʿ al-islāmī fī al-qarnaynī al-ṯānī wa-l-ṯāliṯ li-l-hiğra*, Université d'Alger, 2004.

Būʿarwa, Bakīr. *ʿUlamāʾ al-falak bi-l-Andalus min bidāyat al-dawla al-umawiyya ḥattā nihāyat mulūk al-ṭawāʾif (138-484/775-1088)*, Université d'Alger, 2009.

Būʿasbāna, ʿUmar Sulaymān. *Mağmūʿat siyar al-Wisyānī, dirāsa wa taḥqīq*, Mascate, Ministère des affaires religieuses, 2009.

Būʿmāma, Fāṭima. *al-Yahūd fī al-Maġrib al-islāmī*, Université d'Alger 2, 2010.

Būbāya, ʿAbd al-Qādir. *al-Barbar fī al-Andalus wa mawqifihim min fitnat al-qarn al-ḫāmis al-hiğrī*, Beyrouth, Dār al-kutub al-ʿilmiyya, 2011.

Būdawud, ʿAbīd. *al-Waqf fī al-Maġrib al-islāmī mā bayn al-qarnayn al-sābiʿ wa-l-tāsiʿ al-hiğriyayn (13-15 mīlādī) wa dawruh fī al-ḥayāt al-iqtiṣādiyya wa-l-iğtimāʿiyya*, Sidi Belabes, Maktabat al-Rašād, 2011.

Būdawud, ʿAbīd. *Ẓāhirat al-taṣawwuf fī al-Maġrib al-awsaṭ mā bayn al-qarnayn al-sābiʿ wa-l-tāsiʿ al-hiğriyayn*, Oran, Dār al-ġarb al-islāmī li-l-našr wa-l-tawzīʿ, 2003.

Būdšīš, Āmina. *Biğāya, dirāsa tārīḫiyya wa ḥaḍāriyya*, Université de Tlemcen, 2008.

Būdšīš, Āmina. *Madīnat Biğāya min al-ʿahd al-ḥammādī ilā al-ġazw al-isbānī*, Université de Tlemcen, 2017.

Būġrāra, Munīra. *Muḥammad b. ʿAbd al-Karīm al-Maġīlī wa musāhamatuhu fī al-ṯaqāfa al-islāmiyya fī Ġarb Ifrīqiyya (823-909/1417-1503)*, Université Émir Abdelkader-Constantine, 2003.

Būḫālfa, ʿAbd al-Raḥīm. *al-Arḍ wa istiġlāluhā fī al-Maġrib al-awsaṭ min ḫilāl nawāzil al-Wanšarīsī*, Université de Constantine 2, 2014.

Būḫālfa, Nūr al-Hudā. *al-Islām wa-l-taʿrīb fī al-Šamāl al-Ifrīqī fī al-qurūn al-ṯalāṯa li-l-hiǧra*, Université d'Amman, 1984.

Būḫālfa, Nūr al-Hudā. *Dawlat Banī Wāsūl fī Siǧilmāsa, ʿalāqātuhā wa dawruhā al-ḥaḍārī fī al-Maġrib al-wasīṭ*, Université d'Oran, 1976.

Būḥallūfa, Muḥammad Lamine. *Ahl al-ḏimma fī al-Maġrib al-awsaṭ min ḫilāl nawāzil al-Wanšarīsī*, Université d'Oran, 2015.

Būḫārī, ʿUmar. *al-Barbar fī al-Andalus fī ʿahd al-ṭawāʾif fī al-qarn al-ḫāmis al-hiǧrī*, Université de Tlemcen, 2015.

Būlṭīf, Laḫḍar. *Fuqahāʾ al-mālikiyya wa-l-taġruba al-siyāsiyya al-muwaḥḥidiyya fī-l-Ġarb al-islāmī*, Herdon, The International Institute of Islamic Thought, 2009.

Būnābī, Ṭāhar. *ʿAṣr al-mutaṣawwifa bi-l-Maġrib, dirāsa fī al-ḥaraka al-ṣūfiyya ḫilāl al-ʿaṣr al-wasīṭ*, M'sila, Publications de la Faculté des sciences humaines et sociales, 2017.

Būnābī, Ṭāhar. *al-Taṣawwuf fī al-Ǧazāʾir ḫilāl al-qarnayn 6-7H musāhama fī al-tārīḫ al-dīnī wa-l-iǧtimāʿī li-l-ǧazāʾir ḫilāl al-ʿaṣr al-wasīṭ*, Aïn M'lila, Dār al-Hudā, 2004.

Būsaʿd, Ṭayyib. *al-Ḥayāt al-ṯaqāfiyya wa-l-ʿilmiyya fī-l-imāra al-aġlabiyya wa ʿalāqatihā bi-l-ḫilafa al-ʿabbāsiyya*, Université d'Alger, 2003.

Būšāma, ʿĀšūr. *ʿAlāqāt al-dawla al-ḥafṣiyya maʿa duwal al-Maġrib wa-l-Andalus*, Université du Caire, 1991.

Būšrīṭ, Muḥammad. *Āl al-Rāzī wa āṯāruhum al-tārīḫiyya wa-l-ǧuġrāfiyya (250-379)*, Université d'Oran, 2004.

Būṣṣūf, Fūḍīl. *al-ʿalāqāt al-siyāsiyya bayna al-Andalus al-islāmiyya wa Isbāniyya al-naṣrāniyya fī ʿaṣr mulūk al-ṭawāʾif*, Université de Constantine, 2011.

Būziyyānī, Darrāǧī. *al-ʿAṣabiyya al-qabaliyya wa aṯaruhā ʿalā al-nuẓum wa-l-ʿalāqāt fī al-Maġrib al-islāmī*, Université d'Alger, 1988.

Dahmani, Said. *La conquête de l'Ifrīqiya et ses artisans*, Université de Paris 1, 1973.

Daḥmānī, Sihām. *al-Marʾa wa-l-taṣawwuf fī al-Maġrib al-islāmī al-qurūn 6-9H/12-15M*, Université de Constantine, 2006.

Dahmaš Suhayla. *al-ʿĀdāt al-iḥtifāliyya, musāhama fī al-tārīḫ al-dīnī wa-l-iǧtimāʿī fī al-Maġrib al-awsaṭ al-ziyyānī (633-962/1235-1555)*, mémoire de magister, Université de M'sila, 2016.

De Beylié, Léon. *La Kalaa des Beni-Hammad, une capitale berbère de l'Afrique du Nord au XIᵉ siècle*, Paris, Ernest Leroux, 1909.

Dhina, Attallah. *Essai sur les structures politiques, sociales et économiques de l'État tlemcenien à l'époque d'Abū Ḥammū Mūsā I et d'Abū Tāšufīn I*, Alger, Office des publications universitaires, 1985.

Dhina, Attallah. *Les États de l'Occident musulman aux XIIIᵉ, XIVᵉ et XVᵉ siècles, institutions gouvernementales et administratives* Alger, ENAL, 1984.

Dravet, Henri. *Rapports entre la Couronne d'Aragon et le sultanat mérinide au temps d'Abou El Hassan 1334-1334*, Université d'Alger, 1966.

Faure-Biguet, Gabriel-Isidore. *Histoire de l'Afrique septentrionale sous la domination musulmane*, Paris, Henri Charles-Lavauzelle, 1905.

Fekhar, Brahim. *Les communautés ibadites en Afrique du Nord (Lybie-Tunisie et Algérie) depuis les Fatimides*, Université Paris-Sorbonne, 1971.

Fīlālī, ʿAbd al-ʿAzīz. *al-ʿAlāqāt al-siyāsiyya bayna al-dawla al-umawiyya fī al-Andalus wa duwal al-Maġrib*, Alger, SNED, 1982.

Fīlālī, ʿAbd al-ʿAzīz. *Tilimsān fī al-ʿahd al-zayyānī, dirāsa iġtimāʿiyya wa siyāsiyya wa ʿumrāniyya wa ṯaqāfiyya*, Alger, ENAG, 2011.

Fīlālī, Balqāsim. *al-Taʿlīm wa-l-daʿwa al-muwaḥḥidiyya 510-524/1116-1129*, Université de Constantine, 2004.

Fournel, Henri. *Les Berbers : étude sur la conquête de l'Afrique par les Arabes, d'après les textes arabes imprimés*, Paris, Imprimerie nationale, 1875-1881.

Ğabbār, ʿAbd al-Nāṣir. *al-Asr wa-l-fidāʾ : dirāsa fī al-mafāhīm wa tabādul al-asrā bayna al-muslimīn wa aʿdāʾihim min maʿrakat Badr sanat 2 hiğrī ilā 331/942*, Université de Constantine 2, 2015.

Ğabbār, ʿAbd al-Nāṣir. *Banū Ḥafṣ wa-l-qiwā al-ṣalībiyya fī Ġarb al-Baḥr al-mutawassaṭ*, Université du Caire, 1991.

Ğaddū, Fātima al-Zahrāʾ. *al-Sulṭa wa-l-mutaṣawifa fī al-Andalus fī ʿahd al-murābiṭīn wa-l-muwaḥidīn 479-635/1086-1238)*, Université de Constantine, 2008.

Gais, Nadjem Eddine. *Aperçu sur la population musulmane de Majorque au XIVᵉ siècle*, Université d'Alger, 1970.

Ğallūl, Hādī. *al-ʿUlūm al-dīniyya fī al-Maġrib al-awsaṭ min al-qarn 2 ilā al-qarn 8 hiğrī (8-14m)*, Université de Sidi Belabes, 2017.

Ġarāʾissa, ʿAmmār. *al-Madīna al-dawla fī al-Maġrib al-awsaṭ: Wārğilān namūḏağan*, Université Émir Abdelkader-Constantine, 2008.

Ġardāwī, Nūr al-Dīn. Ğawānib min al-ḥayāt al-iqtiṣādiyya wa-l-fikriyya fī al-Maġrib al-islāmī ḫilāl al-qarnayn al-ṯāmin wa-l-tāsiʿ al-hiğriyayn min ḫilāl nawāzil al-Māzūnī, Université d'Alger, 2006.

Garyān, ʿAbd al-Ḥalīl. *al-Siyāsa al-taʿlīmiyya li-dawla al-ziyyāniyya 633-962/1236-1554*, Université de Constantine, 2004.

Gauthier, Émile-Félix. *L'islamisation de l'Afrique du Nord : les siècles obscurs du Maghreb*, Paris, Payot, 1927.

Ğawdat, ʿAlī. *al-ʿAlāqāt al-ḫāriğiyya li-l-dawla al-rustumiyya*, Alger, SNED, 1984.

Géorgopolous, Georgette. *Castille et le Maroc de 1333 à 1339 d'après les chroniques castillanes*, Université d'Alger, 1968.

Al-Ǧilālī, ʿAbd al-Raḥmān. *Tārīḫ al-Ǧazāʾir al-ʿāmm*, 1954, rééd. Beyrouth, Dār al-Ṯaqāfa, 1983.

Golvin, Lucien. *Le Maghreb central à l'époque des Zirides, recherches d'archéologie et d'histoire*, Paris, Arts et métiers graphiques, 1957.

Grārī, ʿAbd al-Nūr. *Ṭubna wa dawruhā al-ḥaḍārī min al-fatḥ ḥattā nihāyat al-qarn al-ḫāmis al-hiǧrī*, Université d'Alger 2, 2009.

Gwīsam, Muḥammad. *Madīnat Qasanṭīna mā bayna al-qarnayn 7-9 hiǧrī, dirāsa siyāsiya wa ʿumrāniyya wa iǧtimāʿiyya wa ṯaqāfiyya*, Université d'Alger 2, 2015.

Gwīsam, Muḥammad. *Taṭawwur al-fikr al-siyāsī al-ismāʿīlī min ḫilāl fikr al-Qāḍī al-Nuʿmān b. Muḥammad (313-363/929-979)*, Université de Constantine, 2003.

Ḥāǧ Ǧallūl, Baḫta. *al-Marʾa fī al-muǧtamaʿ al-ziyyānī (633-962/1235-1554)*, Université d'Oran, 2015.

Ḥaǧ Kūla, ʿAbd al-ʿAzīz. *al-Ḥayāt al-iǧtimāʿiyya wa-l-iqtiṣādiyya bi-l-Andalus min ḫilāl al-nawāzil al-fiqhiyya*, Université d'Alger 2, 2011.

Ḥāldī, ʿAbd al-Ḥamīd. *al-Ḥaraka al-fikriyya fī-l-Maġrib al-Awsaṭ (al-dawla al-ḥammādiyya 408-547/1016-1152)*, Université de Bagdad, 1983.

Ḥalfāt, Maftāḥ. *Qabīlat Zawāwa mā bayn al-qarnayn 7 wa 9H/12-15M*, Alger, Dār al-amal, 2011.

Ḥalīfī, Rafīq. *al-Buyūtāt al-andalusiyya fī al-Maġrib al-awsaṭ min nihāyat al-qarn 3 ilā nihāyat al-qarn 9 hiǧrī*, Université Émir Abdelkader-Constantine, 2008.

Ḥalīlī, Baḫta. *al-Faqr fī al-Maġrib al-islāmī mā bayna al-qarnayn al-sābiʿ wa-l-tāsiʿ al-hiǧriyayn*, wāqiʿuh wa āṯāruh, Université de Mascara, 2016.

Ḥamdī, Malīka. *al-Ishāmāt al-ḥaḍāriyya li-l-marʾa al-andalusiyya min al-fatḥ al-islāmī ilā suqūṭ Ġarnāṭa (92-897/711-1492)*, Université d'Alger 2, 2014.

Ḥannūf, Šuʿayb. *al-Awḍāʿ al-maḏhabiyya fī bilād Ġarb al-islāmī ḫilāl al-ʿaṣr al-murābiṭī (451-541/1055-1146)*, Université d'Alger 2, 2010.

Harbāš, Ǧāziyya. *Ṯawrat Banī Ġāniyya 580-633*, Université d'Oran, 2002.

Ḥasānī, Muḫtār. *al-Awḍāʿ al-iǧtimāʿiyya wa-l-iqtiṣādiyya li-l-dawla al-ziyyāniyya 633-962/1235-1554*, Université d'Alger, 1987.

Ḥasānī, Muḫtār. *al-Ṣirāʿ bayna al-fāṭimiyyīn wa-l-umawiyyīn ʿalā al-siyāda fī al-Maġrib al-islāmī*, Université d'Alger, 1979.

Ḥasāyan, ʿAbd al-Karīm. *Ḥarakat al-taʾlīf al-tārīḫī bi-l-Maġrib al-awsaṭ min ḫilāl al-ʿahd al-ziyyānī (633-962/1235-1554)*, Université de Sidi Belabes, 2017.

Ḥasblāwī, Nasīm. *al-Muǧtamaʿ al-andalusī min ḫilāl kutub al-nawāzil bayn al-qarnayn 4-7 hiǧrī, 10-13 mīlādī*, Université d'Alger 2, 2017.

Ḥaṭīf, Ṣābra. *Fuqahāʾ Tilimsān wa-l-sulṭa fī al-Maġrib al-awsaṭ ḫilāl al-ʿahd al-ziyyānī (633-791/1235-1388), al-ǧihāz al-dīnī wa-l-taʿlīmī*, Alger, Ǧusūr édition, 2011.

Ḥīmī, ʿAbd al-Ḥafīẓ. *al-Waẓāʾif al-musāʿida li-l-qaḍāʾ fī-l-Andalus ḫilāl al-qarnayn 3 wa 4 hiǧriyayn/9 wa 10 mīlādiyayn*, Université d'Oran, 2007.

Hišām, Mūsā. *al-Maḏhab al-sunnī fī al-Maġribayn al-adnā wa-l-awsaṭ 296-547 H*, Université d'Alger 2, 2011.

Huwārī, Raḍwān. *Buyūtāt al-ʿulamāʾ fī al-Sūdān al-Ġarbī min ḫilāl kitāb nayl al-ibtihāǧ bi-taṭrīz al-dībāǧ li-Aḥmad Bābā al-Tinbuktī*, Université de Tlemcen, 2013.

Idris, Hady Roger. *La Berbérie orientale sous les Zirīdes X-XIIᵉ siècles*, Paris, Adrien-Maisonneuve, 1962.

Idrīsī, Duʿāʾ. *al-Madīna al-dawla fī al-Maġrib al-awsaṭ al-islāmī: Biskra namūḏaǧan*, Université Émir Abdelkader-Constantine, 2012.

Julien, Charles-André. *Histoire de l'Afrique du Nord: Tunisie–Algérie-Maroc depuis la conquête arabe à 1830*, Paris, Payot, 1931.

Kaʿwān, Hafīẓ. *Aṯar fuqahāʾ al-mālikiyya al-iǧtimāʿī wa-l-ṯaqāfī bi-Ifrīqiyya*, Université de Batna, 2010.

Kabīr, Ḫālid ʿAllāl. *al-Ḥaraka al-ʿilmiyya al-ḥanbaliyya wa aṯaruhā fī al-Mašriq al-islāmī ḫilāl al-qarnayn 6-7H*, Université d'Alger, 2005.

Karbūʿ, Masʿūd. *Nawāzil al-nuqūd wa-l-makāyīl wa-l-mawāzīn fī kitāb al-miʿyār li-l-Wanšarīsī*, Université de Batna, 2014.

Kuwātī, Masʿūd. *al-Yahūd fī al-Maġrib al-islāmī min al-fatḥ al-islāmī ilā suqūṭ al-dawla al-muwaḥḥidiyya*, Alger, Dār Hūma, 2000.

Laʿnānī, Maryāma. *al-Usra al-andalusiyya fī ʿaṣray al-murābiṭīn wa-l-muwaḥḥidīn*, Université de Constantine, 2009.

Ladraʿ, Āmāl. *al-Ḥaraka al-ṣūfiyya fī bilād al-Maġrib al-awsaṭ ḫilāl al-ʿaṣr al-ziyyānī (633/1236-962/1555)*, Université de Constantine, 2006.

Laḫḍar, Lʿarbī. *al-Ḥiraf fī madīnat Tilimsān ʿalā al-ʿahd al-ziyyānī (633-962/1335-1554)*, Université de Mascara, 2011.

Laqbāl Mūsā, *al-Maġrib al-islāmī min bināʾ muʿaskar al-Qaran ilā nihāyat ṯawrāt al-Ḫawāriǧ*, Alger, SNED, 1979.

Laqbāl Mūsā, *Al-waḍʿiyya al-siyāsiya wa-l-idāriyya li-l-Maġrib al-islāmī (45-122H)*, Université d'Alger, 1967.

Lawātī, Dalāl. *ʿĀmmat al-Qayrawān fī al-aṣr al-aġlabī*, Le Caire, Dār Ruʾā, 2015.

Lecour Bessad Grandmaison, Xavier. *L'émigration des musulmans de Majorque vers le Maghreb au XVIᵉ siècle entre 1334 et 1381*, Université d'Alger, 1966.

Lūzrī, Saʿīda. *al-Maḏhab al-mālikī fī al-Maġrib al-awsaṭ duḫūlah wa intišārih*, Université d'Alger 2, 2010.

al-Madanī, Aḥmad Tawfīq. *Tārīḫ al-Ǧazāʾir*, Ghardaïa, al-Maṭbaʿa al-ʿarabiya, 1931.

Madyāza, Ṣūraya. *Bilād al-Zāb min al-fatḥ al-islāmī ilā intiqāl al-ḫilāfa al-fāṭimiyya ilā Miṣr*, Université de Batna, 2010.

Maġġānī, Būba. *al-Nuẓum al-idāriyya fī bilād al-Maġrib fī al-ʿahd al-fāṭimī*, Université de Constantine, 1996.

Maġġānī, Būba. *Aṯar al-ʿArab al-yamaniyya fī tārīḫ bilād al-Maġrib fī al-qurūn al-ṯalāṯa al-ūlā li-l-hiǧra*, Constantine, Dār Bahāʾ al-Dīn, 2009.

Maǧǧānī, Būba. *Min qaḍāya al-tārīḫ al-fāṭimī fī dawrihī al-maġribī*, Constantine, Dār Bahā' al-Dīn, 2009.

Magrī, Sāmiya. *al-Ta'līm 'inda al-ibāḍiyya fī bilād al-Maġrib min suqūṭ al-dawla ilā ta'sīs niẓām al-'azzāba (296-409/909-1018)*, Université de Constantine, 2006.

Maġzāwī, Muṣṭafā. *Dawr al-'āmil al-siyāsī fī intišār al-maḏhab al-aš'arī fī al-Mašriq al-islāmī wa maġribih mundu muntaṣaf al-qarn 5 hiǧrī ilā bidāyat al-qarn 8 hiǧrī*, Université d'Alger 2, 2008.

Malyānī, Zaynab. *al-Taṣawwuf fī al-Maġrib al-islāmī fī 'aṣray al-murābiṭīn wa-l-muwaḥḥiddīn*, Université d'Alger, 2006.

Manṣūr, 'Abd al-Ḥafīḏ. *al-Awḍā' al-iǧtimā'iyya wa-l-iqtiṣādiyya fī 'ahd al-imāra al-rustumiyya 144-296H/760-909*, Université de Constantine, 1984.

Manṣūriyya, 'Āšūr. *al-Tasāmuḥ al-dīnī fī ẓill al-dawla al-umawiyya bi-l-Andalus (138-422H)*, Université de Batna, 2007.

Manzal, Ṭāhar. *al-Naǧm al-ṭāqib fī mā li-awliyyā' Allāh min mafāḫir*, Université de Constantine 2, 2013.

Marçais, Georges. *L'Algérie médiévale, monuments et paysages historiques*, Paris, Arts et métiers graphiques, 1957.

Marçais, Georges. *La Berbérie musulmane et l'Orient au Moyen Âge*, rééd. Casablanca, Éditions Afrique Orient, 1991.

Marmūl, Muḥammad Ṣālaḥ. *al-Siyāsa al-dāḫiliyya li-l-dawla al-fāṭimiyya*, Alger, Office des publications universitaires, 1983.

Maṭahrī, Faṭīma. *Madīnat Tīhart al-rustumiyya, dirāsa tārīḫiyya ḥaḍāriyya*, Université de Tlemcen, 2010.

Mazdūr, Sumaya. *al-Awbi'a wa-l-maǧā'āt bi-l-Maġrib al-awsaṭ min nihāyat al-qarn al-sābi' ilā maṭla' al-qarn al-tāsi' al-hiǧrī*, Université de Constantine, 2010.

Mazhūdī, Mas'ūd. *al-Ibāḍiyya fī-l-Maġrib al-awsaṭ min suqūṭ al-dawla al-rustumiyya ilā hiǧrat Banī Hilāl ilā bilād al-Maġrib (296-442/909-1058)*, Université du Caire, 1988.

Mazhūdī, Mas'ūd. *Ǧabal Nafūsa min al-fatḥ al-islāmī ilā hiǧrat Banī Hilāl ilā al-Maġrib*, Fondation Thawalt, 2003.

Mazyānī, Fatīḥa. *al-Ḥaraka al-ṣūfiyya wa aṯaruhā fī al-Mašriq al-islāmī ḫilāl al-qarn 7H/13M*, Université d'Alger 2, 2010.

Mercier, Ernest. *Histoire de l'Afrique septentrionale (Berbérie) depuis les temps les plus reculés jusqu'à la conquête française (1830)*, Paris, Ernest Leroux, 1888.

Mercier, Ernest. *Histoire de l'établissement des Arabes dans l'Afrique septentrionale selon les documents fournis par les auteurs arabes et notamment par l'Histoire des Berbères d'Ibn Khaldoun*, Constantine, L. Marle Librairie, 1875.

Muḥyaddīn, Ṣafiyy al-Dīn. *al-Musta'rabūn wa dawruhum fī tārīḫ al-Andalus (138-483/755-1090)*, Université d'Oran, 2005.

Nuwwār, Nasīm. *al-Ṣīrā' al-sunnī al-šī'ī bi-bilād al-Maġrib wa aṯaruhu fī taǧdīd al-fiqh al-mālikī*, Université d'Alger 2, 2011.

Qwīdar, ʿAbbās. *al-Ḥayāt al-ṯaqāfiyya fi-l-Maġrib al-Awsaṭ ḫilāl al-qarn al-rābiʿ al-hiǧrī/ al-ʿāšir al-mīlādī*, Université de Sidi Belabes, 2010.

Qwīdar, Baššār. *Dawr usrat al-Barāmika fī tārīḫ al-ḫilāfa al-ʿabbāsiyya*, Université d'Alger, 1986.

Qwīdar, Baššār. *Manhaǧiyyat Ibn al-Aṯīr fī al-taʾrīḫ li-l-qiwā al-muʿāriḍa li-l-ḫilāfa al-ʿab- bāsiyya fī al-dāḫil wa-l-ḫāriǧ*, Université d'Alger, 2007.

Rāfiʿī, Našīda. *al-Ḥayāt al-fikriyya wa-l-ṯaqāfiyya fī-l-Maġrib fī-l-ʿaṣr al-fāṭimī (296-362H)*, Université d'Alger, 2005.

Raffāf, Šahrazād. *Abū ʿUṯman Saʿīd al-ʿUqbānī ḥayātuh wa āṯāruh*, Université de Bechar, 2006.

Raḥlī, Salīḥa. *Masīla wa ǧihātihā fī al-ʿaṣr al-wasīṭ*, Université de Batna, 2014.

Raḥmānī, Mūsā. *al-Awrās fī al-ʿaṣr al-wasīṭ min al-fatḥ al-islāmī ilā intiqāl al-ḫilāfa al-fāṭimiyya ilā Miṣr (27-362/637-972)*, Université de Constantine, 2007.

Ramḍānī, Fūzī. *Dawr al-mālikiyya fī-l-ḥayāt al-fikriyya fī Miṣr ḫilāl al-ʿaṣr al-ayyūbī (567- 648/1171-1250)*, École normale supérieure d'Alger, 2010.

Razīwī, Zaynab. *al-ʿUlūm wa-l-Maʿārif al-ṯaqāfiyya fī al-Maġrib al-awsaṭ mā bayna al-qarnayn 7-9 hiǧrī/13-15 mīlādī*, Université de Belabes, 2016.

Šaʿwa, ʿAlī. *al-Ḥayāt al-iǧtimāʿiyya min ḫilāl al-durar al-maknūna fī nawāzil Māzūna*, Université d'Alger, 2008.

Šaḫḫūm, Saʿdī. *al-Ḥayāt al-ʿilmiyya fī Qurṭuba min ḫilāl al-muqtabis li Ibn Ḥayyān*, Université d'Alger, 2002.

Sāḫī, Būʿlām. *al-Ḥayāt al-ʿilmiyya fī Ifrīqiya fī ʿaṣr al-dawla al-Aġlabiyya (184-226H/800- 909)*, Université d'Alger, 2009.

Sāḫlī, Āsiya. *Intāǧ wa intiqāl al-maʿārif al-tārīḫiyya fī al-Maġrib al-awsaṭ*, Université Émir Abdelkader-Constantine, 2009.

Sahli, Mohamed Cherif. *Décoloniser l'histoire, introduction à l'histoire du Maghreb*, Paris, Maspero, 1965.

Sāmiʿī, Ismāʿīl. *al-Dawla al-fāṭimiyya wa ǧuhūd al-Qāḍī al-Nuʿmān fī irsāʾ daʿāʾim al-ḫilāfa al-fāṭimiyya*, Amman, Markaz al-našr al-ǧāmiʿī, 2010.

Šaqṭamī, Hanā. *al-Ḫiṭāb al-fiqhī wa-l-rīf fī al-Maġrib al-awsaṭ min ḫilāl al-durar al-maknūna fī nawāzil Māzūna*, Université de Constantine 2, 2013.

Šargī, Warda. *Madīnat Wahrān ḫilāl al-ʿaṣr al-wasīṭ, dirāsa munūǧrāfiyya*, Université Émir Abdelkader-Constantine, 2014.

Sbaʿ, Qāda. *al-Maḏhab al-mālikī fī-l-Ġarb al-islāmī ilā muntaṣaf al-qarn al-ḫāmis al-hiǧrī*, Université d'Oran, 2010.

Sīdī Mūsā, Muḥammad Šarīf. *al-Ḥayāt al-fikriyya bi-Biǧāya min al-qarn al-sābiʿ ilā al-qarn al-ʿāšir*, Université d'Alger, 2002.

Siyāb, Ḫayra. *al-Miyāh wa dawruhā al-ḥaḍārī fī bilād al-Maġrib al-islāmī*, Université d'Oran, 2014.

Souidi, Djamel Eddin. *Généalogie et pouvoir au Maghreb du IIe au VIIe siècle/VIIIe-XIIIe siècle*, Université Paris 1 Panthéon-Sorbonne, 1996.

Ṭabbī, Samīr. *Dawr ahl al-ḏimma fī al-dawla al-islāmiyya fī al-ʿaṣr al-ʿabbāsī (132-447H)*, Université de Batna, 2007.

Ṭawīl, Ṭāhar. *al-taṭawwur al-tārīḫī li-l-madīna bi-l-Maġrib al-awsaṭ min al-niṣf al-ṯānī li-l-qarn al-ṯānī li-l-hiǧra ilā al-qarn al-ḫāmis al-hiǧrī*, Alger, Maṭbaʿat Ḥasnāwī, 2011.

Tūmī, Rašīd. *al-ʿAlāqāt al-ḫāriǧiyya li-dawlat al-Nūrmān fī ǧanūb Īṭāliyya wa Ṣiqiliyya*, Université d'Alger, 1988.

Tuwātiyya, Būdāliyya. *al-Bayʿa fī bilād al-Andalus ʿaṣray al-ḫilāfa wa mulūk al-ṭawāʾif*, Université d'Oran, 2014.

ʿUqba, Saʿīd. *al-Ḥayāt al-ʿilmiyya wa-l-fikriyya bi-Biǧāya ḫilāl al-qarn 7H/13 min ḫilāl kitāb ʿunwān al-dirāya*, Université Émir Abdelkader-Constantine, 2009.

Wahrānī, Qaddūr. *Manhaǧ al-kitāba al-tārīḫiyya ʿinda al-Qalqašandī min ḫilāl kitāb maʾāṯir al-anāfa fī maʿālim al-ḫilāfa*, Université d'Oran, 2014.

Wald al-Nān, Muḥammad al-Amīn. *al-Yahūd wa-l-naṣārā fī al-Andalus min suqūṭ al-ḫilāfa al-umawiyya ilā nihāyat al-ḥukm al-murābiṭī (422-529/1030-1141)*, Université d'Oran, 2013.

Yaḫlaf, Ḥāǧ ʿAbd al-Qādir. *al-Dawr al-siyāsī wa-l-ishām al-fikrī li-Ṣanhāǧa bi-l-Andalus*, Université d'Oran.

Yaḫlaf, Ḥāǧ ʿAbd al-Qādir. *al-Ishām al-fikrī li-l-barbar bi-l-Andalus min al-ʿahd al-ʿāmirī ilā nihāyat al-wuǧūd al-murābiṭī (371-539/981-1148)*, Université d'Oran, 2009.

Zarhūnī, Nūr al-Dīn. *al-Ṭibb wa-l-ḫadamāt al-ṭibbiyya fī al-Andalus ḫilāl al-qarn al-sādis hiǧrī*, Université d'Oran, 2002.

Zīdūr, Ḥamīd. *al-Barbar bayn al-muʿāraḍa wa-l-muwālāt fī ʿahd al-imāra al-umawiyya bi-l-Andalus (138-316/756-928)*, Université d'Oran, 2009.

Ziyyān, ʿAlī. *Al-Maʿrifa al-tārīḫiyya fī al-Andalus ḫilāl al-qarn al-ḫāmis al-hiǧrī*, Université de Constantine, 2011.

Ziyyan, Badrīna. *Šayḫ al-ḥanābila Abū-l-Wafāʾ b. ʿAqīl, ḥayātuh wa aʿmāluh al-siyāsiyya wa-l-iǧtimāʿiyya wa-l-ʿilmiyya 431-513/1040-1119*, Université d'Alger 2, 2010.

13

Mamluk Studies in the Arab World

Emad Abou-Ghazi

1   Introduction

The aim of this chapter is to present a brief overview of the trends in modern Arabic scholarship on the history of the Mamluk period. It begins in the nineteenth century – when historical writing gradually became academic and relied on the methodologies of historical research – and continues for a period of a century and half, during which time history departments and professional historical societies appeared throughout the Arab world.

It is perhaps not surprising that Egypt produced the largest number of studies on the Mamluk period out of all of the Arabic-speaking countries, since it was the center of the Mamluk state. The universities in Bilād al-Shām and the Ḥijāz, regions which were also subject to Mamluk rule, occupy second place in terms of their interest in this period. They are followed by those countries whose universities employed Egyptian academics who specialized in Mamluk studies. The most notable of these is Kuwait, where two of the most prominent Egyptian historians of the Mamluks worked for a long time in the national university. Researchers from the Maghrib have mostly focused on the history of relations between their region and the Mamluk state. They have particularly distinguished themselves in the field of "Khaldunian" studies.

I will combine three different approaches in this study of Arabic historical scholarship on the Mamluk period: the first of these is a chronological survey of the field, the second is discussion of some of the prominent scholars who have shaped the field, and the third is a consideration of the problems and themes that have occupied the attention of researchers. In addition this paper will look at the contributions to the study of Mamluk history in related disciplines such as archeology and archival studies, as well as some philosophical, sociological, literary, and linguistic scholarship concerning the Mamluk period, and studies which were produced by independent scholars who operated outside of the academic system.

© KONINKLIJKE BRILL NV, LEIDEN, 2021 | DOI:10.1163/9789004460089_014

2   The Beginnings

Modern education began in Egypt during the first half of the nineteenth century under Muḥammad ʿAlī Bāshā as part of his state-building endeavor. However, the schools that he founded and the student missions that he sent to Europe were focused mainly on the practical, applied disciplines such as medicine, engineering, agriculture, translation, and administration. History was offered as a subject of study only in some of the new schools.[1] In 1872 *Dār al-ʿUlūm* was founded as the first school of higher studies devoted to the humanities.[2] Despite the early beginning of modern education in Egypt, historical writing remained influenced by the medieval style. We may consider Rifāʿa al-Ṭahṭāwī (1801–73) and ʿAlī Bāshā Mubārak (1824–93) to represent the beginning of the transition from traditional historical writing, which followed the style of the classical works, to modern academic historical writing.

Al-Ṭahṭāwī discussed the Mamluks in a number of his writings. In his book *Manāhij al-Albāb al-Miṣriyya fī Manāhij al-Ādāb al-ʿAṣriyya* which was published in 1869, he made negative references to the Mamluks and criticized their rule.[3] Perhaps he was influenced by the position of Muḥammad ʿAlī Bāshā against the Mamluks and by the views of the French expedition. Some pages in his book *Al-Murshid al-Amīn li al-Banāt wa al-Banīn* are devoted to a discussion of the reign of Shajar al-Durr and her establishment of the Mamluk state.[4] He wrote a study on the history of Birkat al-Azbakiyya (the Azbakiyya Lake) which was established by the Mamluks.[5] In the context of his discussions on various historical and legal matters he often makes references to affairs which date back to the Mamluk period.[6]

ʿAlī Mubārak devoted 67 pages in the first part of his famous book *Al-Khiṭaṭ al-Tawfīqiyya al-Jadīda li Miṣr al-Qāhira, wa Muduniha wa Bilādihā al-Qadīma wa al-Shahīra* to the history of the Baḥrī and Circassian Mamluks.[7] He was influenced by the style of the medieval historians in his division of the subject and he followed the reigns of the sultans of the two Mamluk dynasties. His main focus was on the influence which political changes exerted on the architectural development of the city of Cairo.[8] For the most part his writing fol-

---

1   For the history of education in Muḥammad Alī's Egypt see ʿAbd al-Karīm, *Taʿlīm* i.
2   On Dār al-ʿUlūm see *Taqwīm Dār al-ʿUlūm* i.
3   Al-Ṭahṭāwī, *Manāhij*, 313–314.
4   Al-Ṭahṭāwī, *Murshid*, 187–189.
5   Al-Ṭahṭāwī, *Aʿmāl* v, 389–401.
6   Al-Ṭahṭāwī, *Manāhij*, 356; Idem, *Aʿmāl* iv, 525, 554, *Aʿmāl* v, 21–39.
7   The first edition was published in 1888–89 at the Būlāq press by order of the Khedive Tawfīq.
8   ʿAlī Mubārak, *Khiṭaṭ* I, 79–145.

lowed the style and language of the medieval sources, however, he concluded the chapter with thirteen pages in which he presented the development of the administrative system during the Ayyubid and Mamluk periods.[9] In parts two through six of the book, in the course of his presentation of the buildings of Cairo and the surrounding quarters, he takes up the history of the Mamluks and the biographies of people who lived during the Mamluk period. The historical narrative in these parts appears in the context of his discussion of the architectural development of the city. He relies on medieval narrative sources and documents that date back to the Mamluk period.

Similar to 'Alī Bāshā Mubārak's treatment of Mamluk history within his history of the architectural development of Cairo is Amīn Sāmī Bāshā's (1857–1941) discussion of the Mamluks in his study on the Nile, *Taqwīm al-Nīl*. In the first three pages he discusses the Nile floods during the Ayyubid and Mamluk periods and he presents in greater detail the writings of the Mamluk historians on the measurements of the Nile and on its floods. Then in the first chapter he gives a rather detailed chronological history of the Mamluk period.[10]

This early period also witnessed the contribution of the Lebanese man of letters and historian Jurjī Zīdān (1861–1914). He mentioned the Mamluks briefly in various parts of his survey of Islamic history and civilization entitled *Tārīkh al-Tamaddun al-Islāmī*.[11] For example, he discusses the birth of their state in his discussion of the Islamic dynasties, their military system, the land tenure system under their rule and their naval wars.[12] In the third part of his book, concerning Islamic Civilization and the sciences, he discusses the role of Ibn Khaldūn in the development of historiography as well as the contributions of other historians from the Mamluk period. He also mentions the importance of the hospitals and schools founded by the Mamluks.[13] In the fourth part of this book he discusses the Mamluks again in the context of the Mongol invasion of the Near East and later their relations with Tamerlane when the latter occupied Bilād al-Shām. Then he discusses the condition of Egypt and Syria on

---

9   Ibid, 146–158.

10   Sāmī, *Taqwīm*.

11   The first edition of this work was published between 1902 and 1906. Zīdān began writing a series of articles on Islamic history for the journal *Hilāl* and later decided to combine them and publish them in a 6-volume book. It is considered one of the first scholarly, academic treatments of Islamic history in Arabic.

12   Zīdān, *Tārīkh al-Tamaddun* i, 99, 165–166, 174, 209.

13   Ibid iii, 100, 207, 223.

the eve of the Ottoman conquest.[14] In part five he discusses the architectural achievements of the Ayyubids and Mamluks in Egypt.[15]

'Alī Bak Bahjat (1858–1924), the pioneer of Islamic archeology in Egypt, was perhaps the first person to write about the history of the Mamluk period in an academic way.[16] He published his studies in French in the journal of the Egyptian Scientific Academy (*Majallat al-Majma' al-'Ilmī al-Miṣrī*) and he presented them in the form of lectures at the meetings of the Academy.[17] At the same time he published studies in Arabic in the journal *Majallat al-Mawsū'āt*, which began to appear towards the end of the nineteenth century. Sometimes he wrote his articles under the pen name "Atharī" (Archeologist). His works on the Mamluk period combine archeology, social history, architectural history, and studies on the primary sources. Among the most important of his publications is a study on the *Ṣubḥ al-A'shā* of al-Qalqashandī, an essential primary source which is relied upon by all students of medieval Islamic administration and medieval Arabic documents. He presented this paper in October 1899 at the Congress of Orientalists in Rome and published it in Arabic in the journal *Mawsū'āt* in December of the same year.[18] In addition, he wrote about the archeological and cultural aspects of the Bīmāristān al-Manṣūrī (Manṣūrī Hospital) and he published a study on the historical geography of Egypt during the Mamluk period.[19] His last article on the Mamluk period concerned the *kharāj* (land tax) in Egypt.[20] His letters to the Swiss orientalist Max van Berchem

---

14   Ibid iv, 504, 513–515.

15   Ibid v, 632–633.

16   'Alī Bahjat was born in 1858 in the village of Bahā' al-'Ajūz in the governorate of Banū Suwayf. He studied at al-Madrasa al-Nāṣiriyya, then at the Preparatory School, followed by two years at the Engineering School before transferring to the School of Languages where he completed his education. He worked as translator for the Preparatory School, then as inspector of primary schools for the Ministry of *Waqfs*, then as director of the translators in the Ministry of Education before turning his attention to the field of archeology on which he made a great impact. See Muṣṭafā 'Abd al-Rāziq, *Fī Rithā'* 103–104; Ḍiyā' and 'Imād Abū Ghāzī, *'Alī Bahjat.*

17   The Egyptian Scientific Academy is the oldest continuously operating scientific society in Egypt. It was founded in 1859 by decree of Sa'īd Pasha who ordered that it be modelled after the scientific society that Bonaparte established during the French invasion of Egypt (1798–1801). For this reason, it considers itself to be a continuation of the earlier society founded by the French. See Ibrāhīm al-Dasūqī, *Al-Tārīkh al-Thaqāfī* 40–52.

18   The journal appeared on the first and fifteenth day of each hijrī month. Bahjat, Aḥmad b. 'Alī al-Qalqashandī wa Kitābuhu Ṣubḥ al-A'shā 111–123.

19   Bahjat, Al-Bīmāristān, 329–39; Idem, Nubdha Jughrāfiyya Tārīkhiyya fī mā kānat 'alayha Miṣr fī 'Ahd Dawlat al-Mamālīk al-Baḥriyya wa al-Burjiyya, 198–210.

20   Bahjat, Al-Kharāj fī Miṣr, 433–44.

reveal that he was also working on a comprehensive study of Mamluk heraldry but it appears that this work was never published.[21]

3   The Egyptian University

The Egyptian University (later King Fuʾād University and now Cairo University) was founded in 1908. Islamic history was taught as a regular subject from 1911 onwards. The first professor who taught this subject was Muḥammad ʿAfīfī al-Khuḍarī, who published his lectures in two parts in 1916 under the title *History of the Islamic Nations* (*Muḥāḍarāt fī Tārīkh al-Umam al-Islāmiyya*). His account stops with the Mongol invasion of the Middle East and the fall of the Abbasid Caliphate in Baghdad, the very moment when the Mamluk state was born.[22] Al-Khuḍarī was not an historian by training, he graduated from Dār al-ʿUlūm al-ʿUlyā as a specialist in *sharʿiyya* and he worked in the religious courts. The Egyptian University appointed him, rather than Jurjī Zīdān, to teach the new course in Islamic history because of fear that the appointment of the latter, a Christian from the Levant, would provoke opposition from conservative elements in the society.

The university began granting doctoral degrees in 1914.[23] The first person to obtain a doctorate from the university was Ṭāhā Ḥusayn, who was awarded his degree in Arabic Literature in May 1914.[24] He would later become the first Egyptian student to obtain a doctorate on a subject related to the history of the Mamluk period. Following his graduation from the Egyptian University he was sent to Paris on scholarship where he completed a second doctoral thesis in January 1918 on the topic "A Critical Analytical Study of the Social Philosophy of Ibn Khaldūn."[25] Ṭāhā Ḥusayn's friend, the Egyptian historian Muḥammad ʿAbdallāh ʿInān, translated this thesis from French to Arabic and it was published in Cairo in 1925. It can be considered one of the first studies by any Arab author on an aspect of the intellectual history of the Mamluk period.[26]

Before its transformation into a government university, the Egyptian University accepted seven doctoral theses. Only one of these, that of Aḥmad Bīlī on Ṣalāḥ al-Dīn al-Ayyūbī, which was approved in April, 1920, dealt with the

---

21   Lūqā, *ʿAlī Bahjat*, 61.
22   Ayman Fuʾād al-Sayyid, Ruwwād, 291–303.
23   Al-Jamīʿī, *Al-Jāmiʿa al-Miṣriyya*, 48.
24   Al-Jāmiʿī, *Ṭāhā Ḥusayn*, 8–11.
25   Ibid, 17–19.
26   Ṭāhā Ḥusayn, *Falsafa*.

history of the medieval period.[27] In 1925 the old Egyptian University became
the Faculty of Letters in the now public Egyptian University and a new chapter began in the history of Arabic Mamluk studies. A generation of academics
arose who would establish the first Arab "school" of Mamluk studies and specialized studies on the Mamluk period continued to progress from that time
onwards. The first MA thesis on Mamluk history to be accepted by the history
department of the Faculty of Letters was that of Jamāl al-Dīn Surūr in 1937 on
"Al-Ẓāhir Baybars and the Civilization of Egypt during his Reign." In 1943 Surūr
defended his doctoral thesis on "Politics and Civilization and Egypt during the
Period of the Qalāwūnid Dynasty."[28] These theses were published in 1938 and
1947 respectively.[29] It should be pointed out that although Surūr wrote both
his MA and PhD theses on Mamluk history, he later focused his attention on
the history of the Fatimid period and he continued his academic career in the
discipline of Islamic history.[30]

'Alī Ibrāhīm Ḥasan also obtained the doctorate in 1943 with a thesis on
"Al-Nāṣir Muḥammad Qalāwūn – his Life and the Administrative System during his Reign." In 1945 Ḥāmid Muṣṭafā 'Ammār, who would later specialize in
child-pedagogy, defended an MA thesis on "Relations between the Mamluks
and the African states." In 1949 two MA theses concerning Mamluk history were
accepted: that of Aḥmad Mukhtār al-'Abbādī on "The Rise of the First Mamluk
State in Egypt," and the second by Sa'īd 'Abd al-Fattāḥ 'Ashūr on "Cyprus and
the Crusades," a subject with a very strong connection to the Mamluks.[31] There
was a long interval before the publication of 'Ashūr's thesis.[32]

Such was the beginning of academic Mamluk studies in Egypt. Thereafter,
MA and PhD theses treating various aspects of Mamluk history followed in
rapid succession throughout the second half of the twentieth century. New
history departments were established throughout Egypt during this period,
however, the most important contributions to Mamluk history in Egypt were
made in three universities: Cairo University, Alexandria University, and the
University of Zaqāzīq. I will now focus on three individuals who made significant contributions to the field of Mamluk studies both in Egypt and in other
Arab countries: Muḥammad Muṣṭafā Ziyāda, Sa'īd 'Abd al-Fattāḥ 'Ashūr, and

---

27   Al-Jamī'ī, *Al-Jāmi'a*, 50.
28   *Al-Kitāb al-Fiḍḍī*, 171–72.
29   Surūr, *Al-Ẓāhir Baybars*; Idem, *Dawlat Qalāwūn*.
30   At Cairo University Ayyubid and Mamluk history were taught in the section of the History
      of the Middle Ages while Islamic history covered the history of Islam until the fall of the
      Fatimid Caliphate. *Al-Kitāb al-Fiḍḍī*, 111.
31   *Al-Kitāb al-Fiḍḍī*, 171–74, 176, 186.
32   'Ashūr, *Qubrus*.

Qāsim ʿAbduh Qāsim. They represent three successive generations of Mamluk studies specialists.

4   Three Pioneers/Three Generations

Muḥammad Muṣṭafā Ziyāda is considered the pioneer of Mamluk studies and the founder of the school of Mamluk studies in the Egyptian universities and in several other Arab universities. He graduated from the royal teachers' college in 1921 and completed his studies at Liverpool University where he earned a BA in medieval and modern history in 1925, followed by a PhD in medieval history in 1930.[33] Upon his return to Egypt he was appointed professor of the history of the Middle Ages at the Egyptian University. He thereby introduced a new specialization to the Egyptian and Arab academic worlds for he combined the teaching of medieval Islamic and European history. His doctoral thesis was about "The Foreign Relations of Egypt during the 15th Century," and reflects his interest in Mamluk history.[34]

Ziyāda published his first Arabic study in the journal of the Faculty of Letters of the Egyptian University in 1938 with the title "Some New Observations on the History of the Mamluk State in Egypt."[35] In this article he considered some problems that had attracted his attention while editing Taqī al-Dīn al-Maqrīzī's famous chronicle *Al-Sulūk li Maʿrifat Duwal al-Mulūk* such as the origin of the term "Baḥrī" which is applied to the first Mamluk state, the role of Baybars in the establishment of this state, the revival of the Abbasid Caliphate in Mamluk Cairo, and the controversies surrounding the lineage of Abbasid caliphs of Cairo. He concluded his article with an explanation of some Mamluk administrative terms. In 1949 he published a book entitled "The Egyptian Historians of the 15th Century."[36] This is an important study on one of the most brilliant periods of Arabic historical writing. Ziyāda divides the historians of that period into three generations: the first generation consisting of al-Maqrīzī and his contemporaries, the second consisting of Ibn Taghrībardī and his contemporaries, and the last consisting of Ibn Iyās and the historians of his time. A few years later he published an article in the *Egyptian Historical Journal* on the famous Circassian Mamluk period chronicler Ibn Iyās.[37] In 1951 he pub-

---

33   *Al-Kitāb al-Fiḍḍī*, 54–5.
34   ʿĀshūr, Al-Duktur Muḥammad Muṣṭafā Ziyāda, 3–14; Ayman Fuʾād al-Sayyid, Ruwwād, 297.
35   Ziyāda, Baʿd al-Mulāḥaẓāt.
36   Ziyāda, *Muʾarrikhūn*.
37   Ziyāda, Muqtabisāt.

lished an article in the same journal about the end of the Mamluk period in Egypt in which he analyzed the causes of the Mamluk collapse and addressed aspects of Mamluk–Ottoman relations.[38] Another article of his concerned the building policies in the time of the sultan Al-Nāṣir based on al-Maqrīzī's chronicle *Al-Sulūk*.[39] At a symposium on archeology and history in 1962 he presented an important study on Mamluk socioeconomic history.[40] Prior to this he had directed his student, Saʿīd ʿAbd al-Fattāḥ ʿĀshūr, to study the society of the Mamluk period, thereby guiding research on the Mamluk period in a new direction far from the traditional topics of political and military history.

Ziyāda also published studies in English on Egypt and the Crusades (1942), relations between Egypt and Cyprus (1943), and Mamluk expeditions against Rhodes in the fifteenth century (1945), all of which were later translated into Arabic.[41] He made great contributions to the publication of Mamluk sources as well. He edited six volumes of al-Maqrīzī's chronicle *Al-Sulūk* with copious annotation. In 1940 he edited al-Maqrīzī's treatise on famines (*Ighāthat al-Umma bi Kashf al-Ghumma*), one of the most precious sources for Mamluk history, with the assistance of his colleague Jamāl al-Dīn Surūr. This edition includes an analytical introduction to the source in which the editors discuss al-Maqrīzī's methodology in the writing of social and economic history, and the various economic and critical theories which al-Maqrīzī advanced in his small but important treatise.[42]

Saʿīd ʿAbd al-Fattāḥ ʿĀshūr continued to advance the trail that had been blazed by his teacher, Ziyāda, in the field of Mamluk studies. From the 1950s until his death in 2009, ʿĀshūr was one of the most prominent specialists on Mamluk history in Egypt and in the Arab world. He is considered the second founder, after Ziyāda, of the Egyptian school of medieval history in general and in particular of the school of Mamluk studies. He obtained his PhD in 1955 with a thesis on the social history of Egypt during the Mamluk period. This work opened a new path of research in Mamluk studies, focusing on the study of classes, social forces, customs, traditions, aspects of daily life, and various religious trends and sects. ʿĀshūr later encouraged his students in Egypt, Kuwait, Lebanon, Saudi Arabia, and other Arab countries to pursue research on similar themes. He published a revised version of his doctoral thesis with the title *Egyptian Society in the Age of the Mamluk Sultans*. In this book he

---

38   Ziyāda, Nihāya.

39   Ziyāda, Ḥaraka.

40   Ziyāda, Sirāsāt fī'l Tārīkh al-Iqtiṣādī wa al-Ijtimāʿī.

41   ʿĀshūr, Al-Duktūr Muḥammad Muṣṭafā Ziyāda, 9.

42   ʿĀshūr, Al-Duktūr Muḥammad Muṣṭafā Ziyāda, 9–14; Ayman Fuʾād al-Sayyid, Ruwwād, 296–98.

first examined the structure of Egyptian society during the Mamluk period, then discussed the conditions of the different classes in Egyptian society, intellectual and religious life, holidays and celebrations, family names, followed by an analysis of what he considered to be "social diseases" during the Mamluk period.[43]

ʿĀshūr published 22 books, most of which deal with the Mamluk period. Among the most important of these are: *Egypt and Syria in the Age of the Ayyubids and Mamluks*, *The Ayyubids and Mamluks in Egypt and Syria*, and *The Mamluk Period in Egypt and Syria*.[44] The latter was for many years considered the essential reference work on Mamluk history for history students studying the Mamluk period in the Egyptian universities and other Arab universities. It covers the political, economic, and social history of the Mamluk period in Egypt and Syria from the founding of the Mamluk state until its fall. He also wrote a book on the Mamluks in Egypt during the Baḥrī Mamluk period as well as some general works on the history of the Middle Ages, which include sections devoted to the Mamluk period such as his *Studies in the History of the Middle Ages* which is a collection of some of his articles and *The History of Relations between the East and the West during the Middle Ages*.[45]

He wrote tens of articles and conference papers, the bulk of which deal with Mamluk history. These include two important articles on the socioeconomic aspects of the Mamluk period. The first is about the peasantry and feudalism (*al-iqṭāʿ*) during the Ayyubid and Mamluk periods.[46] In this article he begins with a discussion of the origin of the *iqṭāʿ* system in Islamic history, its institutionalization in Egypt under the Ayyubids, and its full maturity in the Mamluk period. He then discusses the differences between feudalism in Mamluk Egypt and the West and he tries to glean from the sources information about the effects of the *iqṭāʿ* system on the peasants. The second article looks at the problem of economic decline in late Mamluk Egypt as depicted in passages of Ibn Iyās' chronicle.[47] Another article that he wrote is called "Pictures of Medieval Cairene Society."[48] His contributions to the study of Mamluk foreign policy

---

43   ʿĀshūr, *Al-Mujtamaʿ al-Miṣrī*.

44   ʿĀshūr, *Miṣr wa al-Shām*; Idem, *Al-Ayyūbiyyin wa al- Mamālīk*; Idem, *Al-ʿAṣr al-Mamālīkī*.

45   ʿĀshūr, *Miṣr fī ʿAṣr Dawlat al-Mamālīk al-Baḥriyya*; Idem, *Buḥūth wa Dirāsāt*; Idem, *Tārīkh al-ʿAlāqāt bayn al-Sharq wa al-Gharb*.

46   ʿĀshūr, *Al-Fallāḥ wa al-Iqṭāʿ*.

47   ʿĀshūr, *Al-Tadahwur al-Iqtiṣādī*.

48   ʿĀshūr, *Ṣuwar*.

include articles on Mamluk relations with Ethiopia and with the Kingdom of Lesser Armenia.[49]

His second area of focus was the history of the Crusades. He contributed a survey book as well as a number of more specialized studies on this topic. He also devoted a great deal of effort to the edition of Mamluk primary sources. He completed the edition of al-Maqrīzī's chronicle *Al-Sulūk* that his teacher Ziyāda had begun, and he edited the chronicles of Ibn Aybak al-Dawādar (*Kanz al-Durar*) and Ibn Duqmāq (*al-Jawhar al-Thamīn*).

Qāsim ʿAbduh Qāsim is considered the third pioneer of Mamluk studies and the founder of the new school of Mamluk studies at Zaqāzīq University beginning in the 1970s. Within a short time, this school became the most important center of Mamluk studies in Egypt. Qāsim was one of the most distinguished students of ʿĀshūr. Like his teacher he focused on the social history of the Mamluk period. He also added a new perspective to Mamluk studies by combining history with the study of literary sources of various genres. He devoted particular attention to the study of popular literature from the Mamluk period and relied on it as a source for the history of the period. Since 1976 he has written 25 books and more than 80 shorter studies.[50] His most important works include his MA thesis on the Nile in the Mamluk period, later published as *The Nile and Society in Egypt during the Period of the Mamluk Sultans*, and his doctoral thesis on the non-Muslims (*ahl al-dhimma*) in medieval Egypt which was published and reprinted many times.[51] On the same theme he wrote a book on the history of the Jews in Egypt from the Arab conquest until the Ottoman conquest, and a study on the Christians in Egypt during the Mamluk period.[52]

Qāsim's research took several directions. In the beginning he focused on the socioeconomic history of the Mamluk period. His publications in this field, in addition to those mentioned above, include a volume of collected studies on the social history of Mamluk Egypt, studies on the markets of Cairo in the Mamluk period (1976), a study on famines and plagues in Mamluk Egypt (1983), another on the crafts and industries related to daily life during the Mamluk period (1988), and a study on the archives of St. Catherine's Monastery in Sinai as a source for social history.[53]

---

49 ʿAshūr, Baʿḍ Aḍwāʾ Jadīda ʿalā al-ʿAlāqāt bayna Miṣr wa al-Ḥabasha; Idem, *Ṣalṭanat al-Mamālīk wa Mamlakat Armīniyya al-Ṣughrā.*

50 ʿAmr ʿAbd al-ʿAzīz Munīr, *Qāsim ʿAbduh Qāsim,* 20–30.

51 Qāsim ʿAbduh Qāsim, *Al-Nīl wa al-Mujtamaʿ;* Idem, *Ahl al-Dhimma fī Miṣr al-ʿUṣūr al-Wusṭā.*

52 Qāsim ʿAbduh Qāsim, *Al-Yahūd fī Miṣr.*

53 Qāsim ʿAbduh Qāsim, *Dirāsāt fī Tārikh Miṣr al-Ijtimāʿī;* ʿAmr ʿAbd al-ʿAzīz Munīr, *Qāsm ʿAbduh Qāsim,* 20–27.

His second area of concentration, which he also pioneered for the field of Mamluk studies, was the use of literature and folklore as an entry to the study of history. His studies in this field include *Between Literature and History, Between History and Folklore, Popular Epics as a Source for the Study of Social History* (1986), *The Historical Personality in the Epic of Al-Ẓāhir Baybars* (1986), *Popular Literature as a Tool for the Study of Cultural History* (1988), *The Popular Heritage in Historical Studies – the Khiṭaṭ of al-Maqrīzī as an Applied Study* (1994), *Shajar al-Durr between the Popular Epic and History* (1999), *Literary Narratives and History: Rivalry or Integration?* (2005), *The Literary Narrative and History* (2009).[54]

He also wrote about Mamluk political history in such works as *The Ayyubids and the Mamluks* (with ʿAlī al-Sayyid), *The Age of the Mamluk Sultans: Political and Social History*, and *On the History of the Ayyubids and Mamluks*.[55] Other works that touch on political themes are his biography of the sultan Quṭuz, a study on Mamluk Jerusalem, a history of the struggle for Egypt during the Crusades, and a study on the understanding of authority during the Mamluk period.[56] He published two studies on Mamluk foreign relations, the first regarding the policy of the Circassian Mamluks in the Red Sea Basin, and the second on relations between the Mamluks and Ethiopia. The cultural history of the Mamluk period was treated in his study on historical thought in the works of the Mamluk scholar al-Sakhāwī and in a book on culture and the sciences in the Mamluk period.[57] He also translated a number of important western studies from English to Arabic about topics such as the history of the Crusades and historical methodology.

The three pioneers mentioned above not only succeeded in training three successive generations of historians specialized in Mamluk studies, but also in establishing new history departments and developing the field of historical studies in Arab universities outside of Egypt where they supervised dissertations and trained scholars.

---

54   Qāsim ʿAbduh Qāsim, *Bayn al-Adab wa al-Tārīkh*; Idem, *Bayn al-Tārīkh wa al-Fulklūr*; ʿAmr ʿAbd al-ʿAzīz Munīr, *Qāsim ʿAbduh Qāsim*, 20–27.

55   Qāsim ʿAbduh Qāsim and ʿAlī al-Sayyid ʿAlī, *Al-Ayyūbiyyin wa al-Mamālīk*; Qāsim, *Fī Tārīkh al-Ayyūbiyyin wa al-Mamālīk*.

56   Qāsim ʿAbduh Qāsim, *Al-Malik al-Muẓaffar Sayf al-Dīn Quṭuz* (He later revised this study and published it under the title *Al-Sulṭān al-Muẓaffar Sayf al-Dīn Quṭuz Baṭal Maʿrakat ʿAyn Jālūt*); ʿAmr ʿAbd al-ʿAzīz Munīr, *Qāsim ʿAbduh Qāsim*, 20–27.

57   Ibid.

5 The Egyptian Society of Historical Studies

The establishment of the Egyptian Society of Historical Studies in 1945 was an additional factor in the spread and growth of Mamluk studies.[58] The Society, along with Muḥammad Muḥammad Muṣṭafā, undertook the publication of one of the most important late Mamluk sources, Ibn Iyās' chronicle *Badāʾiʿ al-Ẓuhūr*. The Society's journal (*al-Majalla al-Miṣrīya li al-Dirāsāt al-Tārīkhiyya*) published tens of articles on Mamluk history.[59] The Society also organized many academic conferences which were related to the history and culture of the Mamluk period and attended by specialists such as: a symposium on the historian al-Maqrīzī on the occasion of the 600th anniversary of his birth (May 1966), a conference on the encyclopedist al-Qalqashandī (1968), a conference on the historian Ibn Taghrībardī (March 1972), a conference on the historian Ibn Iyās (December 1973), a conference on al-Suyūṭī and his times (1976), and a conference on the biographer al-Sakhāwī (1981).[60] All of the above-mentioned conferences were concerned with the lives of famous scholars who lived during the Mamluk period and the papers that were presented at these conferences dealt with various aspects of the political, social, cultural and intellectual life of the period.

The Society also hosted a number of conferences dealing with general issues in the history of Egypt and the region which included contributions on the Mamluk period. Examples of these are the conference on the development of land tenure in Egypt (1988) and a conference on the Egyptians and authority through the ages (2001) in which Qāsim ʿAbduh Qāsim presented a study on the concept of authority in the Mamluk period. The Society dedicated its regular meeting in 1970–71 to the question of "Land and Peasant in Egypt throughout the Ages" and Saʿīd ʿAbd al-Fattāḥ ʿĀshūr presented his study on the peasants and feudalism during the Ayyubid and Mamluk periods on this occasion. In recent years the Society has organized regular seminars devoted to the history of the Middle Ages, of which the Mamluk period forms an essential part.

---

58 A royal decree was issued on July 30, 1945 for the creation of the Society of Historical Studies. In 1952 it became the Egyptian Society of Historical Studies. See Al-Jamīʿī, *Al-Jamʿiyya al-Miṣriyya li al-Dirāsāt al-Tārīkhiyya*, 13.

59 Ibid, 47–79.

60 *Dirāsāt ʿan al-Maqrīzī; Al-Muʾarrikh Ibn Taghrībardī; Ibn Iyās Dirāsāt wa Buḥūth.*

6   Mamluk Studies in the Eastern Arab World

Historians in Bilād al-Shām gave attention to the Mamluk period in the context of their studies on the history of their region. We see this clearly in the
works of the first generation of modern Syrian, Lebanese, and Palestinian
historians. Philip Ḥittī devoted a portion of his history of Syria, Lebanon, and
Palestine to the history of the Mamluk period in Bilād al-Shām. This book was
first published in English in 1951 and translated into Arabic before the close of
the decade.[61] Niqūlā Ziyāda addressed Mamluk history in several of his works.
The most important of these is his book about Damascus during the Mamluk
period.[62] Muḥammad ʿAlī Makkī wrote a history of Lebanon from the Arab
Conquest until the Ottoman conquest.[63] When Yarmūk University in Jordan
established a commission to write a multi-volume history of Bilād al-Shām, the
veteran editor and historian Iḥsān ʿAbbās wrote a section devoted to the history
of Bilād al-Shām under the Mamluks.[64] More recent works which treat Mamluk history in the course of longer regional histories include Mufīd al-Zaydī's
section on the Mamluk period in the *Encyclopedia of Islamic History* (*Mawsūʿat
al-Tārīkh al-Islāmī*), Ṭāriq Aḥmad Qāsim's study on the history of Lebanon in
the Middle Ages, and Sūzī Ḥammūd's reference work on the history of Lebanon in the medieval period, which covers the period from the Rāshidūn to the
end of Mamluk rule.[65]

The late 1950s and early 1960s saw many studies on Mamluk history produced by academics in Syria and Lebanon. Perhaps this was connected to the
period of Egyptian-Syrian unification (1958–61). Notable studies include that
of Laylā Ṣabbāgh on the history of Damascus in the sixteenth century and
Muḥammad Aḥmad Dahmān's study on the conflict between the Mamluks
and the Turks.[66] Mamluk studies subsequently suffered a temporary decline
but it returned as a major subject of interest in the late 1970s. Among the studies that appeared at this time are Muḥammad ʿAdnān Bakhīt's work on Karak
in the Mamluk period, Yūsuf Darwīsh Ghawānmah's study on the political history of eastern Jordan during the Baḥrī Mamluk period, and a study by the

---

61   Philip Ḥittī, *Tārīkh Sūrīya*.

62   This was republished in the ninth volume of Ziyāda's complete works.

63   Makkī, *Lubnān 635–1516*.

64   ʿAbbās, *Tārīkh Bilād al-Shām fī ʿAṣr al-Mamālik*.

65   Al-Zaydī, *Mawsūʿat al-Tārīkh al-Islāmī*; Ṭāriq Aḥmad Qāsim, *Tārīkh Lubnān al-Wasīṭ*; Sūzī
      Ḥammūd, *Lubnān fī al-ʿAṣr al-Wasīṭ*.

66   Laylā al-Ṣabbāgh, *Ḥawla Tārīkh al-Shām*; Muḥammad Aḥmad Dahmān, *Al-ʿIrāk bayn
      al-Mamālīk wa al-Atrāk*.

Syrian historian Ibrāhīm Zaʿrūr on the social history of Bilād al-Shām during the Ayyubid and Mamluk periods.[67]

The Lebanese historian ʿUmar ʿAbd al-Salām al-Tadmurī has been one of the most prominent specialists in Mamluk studies from the eastern Arab world since the 1970s. He has published more than 80 studies and editions of texts, most of which concern the Mamluk period. Al-Tadmurī studied at the Azhar in Cairo where he wrote his MA and PhD on the history of the city of Tripoli (in Lebanon). After extensive revision he published his MA thesis under the title *The Cultural History of Tripoli during the Middle Ages*.[68] His PhD thesis on the political and civilizational history of Tripoli was published in two volumes, the second of which deals with the city's history under the Mamluks.[69] His other works include a study on the mosques and schools of Tripoli during the Mamluk period and a sixteen-volume encyclopedia of the Muslim scholars in Lebanese history, of which six volumes deal exclusively with scholars from the Mamluk period, as well as tens of articles.[70] He has edited many important manuscripts from the Mamluk period. The most important of these is the massive chronicle *Tārīkh al-Islām* by al-Dhahabī.[71]

The twenty-first century has seen wide interest in Mamluk studies in the Palestinian, Jordanian, Lebanese, and Syrian universities with a focus on various aspects of the history of these countries during the Mamluk period. Some examples are the study by ʿAwād ʿArār on the population of Palestine during the Mamluk period, that of Marwān ʿAbd al-Qādir Bakīr from Birzeit University about the Palestinian cities during the Mamluk period, Mubārak al-Ṭirāwanaʾs study on social life in Bilād al-Shām during the Circassian Mamluk period, ʿUmar Mūsā Mishʿalʾs study on Al-Ẓāhir Baybars in Jerusalem, Muḥammad Zāriʿ al-Asṭalʾs thesis on intellectual life in Mamluk Jerusalem, the volume by Ilyās Dāwūd al-Qaṭṭār on Lebanon during the Mamluk period (part of a series on Lebanese history), Hāla al-Rifāʿīʾs doctoral thesis on the chancellery letters from the Baḥrī Mamluk period, and Ṭāhā al-Zaʿārīrʾs study on the crafts and industries in southern Bilād al-Shām during the Ayyubid and Mamluk periods.[72]

---

67 Bakhīt, *Mamlakat Karak*; Ghawānma, *Al-Tārīkh al-Siyāsī*; Zaʿrūr, *Al-Ḥayāt al-Ijtimāʿiyya*.

68 Al-Tadmurī, *Al-Ḥayāt al-Thaqāfiyya fī Ṭarāblus*. The original title of his MA thesis which he obtained from the Azhar was Ṭarāblus al-Shām Madīnat al-Ṣumūd wa al-ʿIlm fī al-ʿUṣūr al-Wusṭā.

69 Al-Tadmurī, *Tārīkh Ṭarāblus al-Siyāsī wa al-Ḥaḍārī ʿabr al-ʿUṣūr*.

70 Al-Tadmurī, *Tārīkh wa Āthār Masājid wa Madāris Ṭarāblus*; Idem, *Mawsūʿat ʿUlamāʾ al-Muslimīn fī Tārīkh Lubnānī*; Idem, *Al-Mustadrak ʿalā Mawsūʿat ʿUlamāʾ al-Muslimīn fī Tārīkh Lubnān al-Islāmī*.

71 Al-Dhahabī, *Tārīkh al-Islām*.

72 ʿArār, Sukkān; Bakīr, Al-Madīna; Ṭirāwana, *Al-Ḥayāt al-Ijtimāʿiyya*; Mishʿal, Min Tārīkh al-Ḥaraka al-ʿUmrāniyya; Al-Asṭal, Al-Ḥayāt al-Fikriyya; Al-Qaṭṭār, Lubnān; Hāla al-Rifāʿī, Al-Rasāʾil al-Dīwāniyya; Al-Zaʿārīr, Al-Ṣināʿāt wa al-Ḥiraf.

Muḥammad Maḥmūd al-ʿAnāqira from the Jordanian University has written many important studies on the Mamluk period. These include a study on economic life in the Ḥijāz during the Mamluk period, a study on pilgrimage routes during the Mamluk period, a book on the schools in Mamluk Egypt, a study on schools in Mamluk Jerusalem, and a study co-written with Fāṭima al-Rabīdī about the Riwāq al-Maghāriba (dormitory for the students from the Maghrib) at the Azhar and its role in the intellectual life of the Mamluk period.[73] ʿAmmār Muḥammad al-Nahār from Damascus University has written a new theoretical study on the history of the Baḥrī Mamluks.[74]

The Saudi universities have produced a number of studies concerned with the history of the Ḥijāz during the Mamluk period. Examples are Āmina Jallāl's study on the pilgrimage routes during the Mamluk period and Ṣāliḥ al-Maʿtūq's study on the *hadith* sciences, which discusses the study of the hadith in Mecca during the Mamluk period.[75] Saudi studies concerning Mamluk history outside of the Arabian Peninsula include Hanādī Ibrāhīm Abū Khadīja's thesis on women in Bilād al-Shām during the Mamluk period and Shaykha al-Dawsirī's study on women's *waqfs* (charitable endowments) in Mamluk Damascus and their influence on the intellectual life of the period.[76]

The Kuwaiti and Iraqi universities have also made important contributions to Mamluk studies. Perhaps the reason for this is connected to the presence of the three Egyptian pioneers of Mamluk studies in these countries at various times between the 1940s and 1990s. The leading Kuwaiti scholar in Mamluk studies is Ḥayāt Nāṣir al-Ḥajjī who has been active in the field for four decades. Among her most important contributions are her study on the amīr Tankiz al-Ḥussāmī and her valuable book on the conditions of the common classes during the Mamluk period (1984) which treats the role of the common people in the political circumstances of the time, the economic conditions of the period, and the daily social life of the common classes.[77] She has also written a book on aspects of the civilization of the Mamluk period and a study on society and authority during the Baḥrī Mamluk period which relies on documents.[78]

---

73   Al-ʿAnāqira, *Al-Ḥayāt al-Iqtiṣādiyya fī al-Ḥijāz fī ʿAṣr Dawlat al-Mamālīk*; Idem, *Al-Ḥayāt al-Iqtiṣādiyya fī al-Ḥijāz wa ʿAlāqātuhā al-Tijāriyya bi al-Dawlat al-Mamlūkiyya*; Idem, *Ṭuruq al-Ḥajj*; Idem, *Madāris al-Quds*; Al-ʿAnāqira and Fāṭima al-Rabīdī; *Al-Dawr al-ʿIlmī*.

74   Al-Nahār, *Al-Dirāsāt al-Naẓariyya*.

75   Āmina Ḥusayn Muḥammad Jallāl, *Ṭuruq al-Ḥajj*; Ṣāliḥ Yūsuf al-Māʿtūq, *ʿIlm al-Ḥadīth*.

76   Abū Khādīja, *Al-Marʾa fī Bilād al-Shām*; Shaykha bint Muḥammad al-Dawsirī, *Awqāf al-Nisāʾ fī Bilād al-Shām*.

77   Ḥayāt Nāṣir al-Ḥajjī, *Al-Amīr Tankiz*.

78   Ḥayāt Nāṣir al-Ḥajjī, *Ṣuwar min al-Ḥaḍāra al-ʿArabiyya al-Islāmiyya fī Salṭnat al-Mamālīk*; Idem, *Al-Sulṭa wa al-Mujtamaʿ*.

There are a number of recent Iraqi studies on Mamluk history. From al-Mustanṣirīya University there is a study by Anwār Jāsim Ḥasan on relations between the Mamluk state and the dynasties of the Maghrib (2007), Maḥmūd Kāmil Ṣāliḥ's study on the Arabs and their role in the Mamluk state (2010), and Saḥar ʿAbdallāh's study on concubines during the Mamluk period.[79] At Wāsiṭ University Thāmir Muṣṭāf has written on the role of women in daily life during the Baḥrī Mamluk period.[80] ʿAbīr ʿUnāyyit Saʿīd from al-Anbar University has written about public services in Egypt during the same period.[81] Fatḥī al-Lahībī and Fāʾiz al-Ḥadīdī have presented a new interpretation of Mamluk history.[82] Yāsir al-Mashhadānī has written a study of Mamluk relations with India.[83]

7 Mamluk Studies in the Maghrib

In the nations of the Maghrib, studies on the Mamluk period have often been included within larger works on medieval Islamic history. Interest in Mamluk history in these countries has been relatively limited in comparison with the state of the field in Egypt and the countries of the Mashriq. This is to be expected since the Maghrib never formed part of the Mamluk Empire. One of the earliest studies from this region related to the Mamluks is the work by Muḥammad al-ʿArūsī al-Maṭwī, a professor at the Zaytūna University in Tunis, on the history of the Crusades (1954).[84] The role of the Mamluks in the Crusades is discussed at length in this book. One of the most prominent specialists on the Mamluk period from the Maghrib is Mūnīra Chapoutot al-Rammādī at the University of Tunis, most of whose publications are in French. She has succeeded in establishing a Tunisian school of Mamluk studies. Among the recent Tunisian studies on the Mamluk period are Rashīda Bilsurūr's study on Mamluk Alexandria, Luṭfī bin Mīlād's study on relations between Ifrīqīyā and the Mashriq between the 11th and 16th centuries, which is based on his doctoral thesis, the same author's study on diplomatic relations between the Hafsid sultanate and the Circassian Mamluks, and Bilqāsim Ṭabbābī's work on society

---

79   Anwār Jāsim Ḥasan al-ʿAnabkī, Al-ʿAlāqāt al-Khārijiyya; Maḥmūd Kāmil Ṣāliḥ, Al-ʿArab wa Makānatuhum; Saḥar ʿAbdallāh, Al-Jawārī.
80   Thāmir Nuʿmān Muṣṭāf, Dawr al-Marʾa.
81   ʿAbīr ʿUnayyit Saʿīd, Al-Khadamāt al-ʿĀmma.
82   Al-Lahībī and al-Ḥadīdī, *Jawānib*.
83   Yāsir al-Mashhadānī, *Al-ʿAlāqāt*.
84   Al-Maṭwī, *Al-Ḥurūb al-Ṣalībiyya*.

and authority during the medieval Islamic period, which takes Mamluk Egypt and Syria as a case study.[85]

A number of theses have been written on Mamluk history and related topics in the Algerian universities. At the University of Constantine, Yūsuf ʿĀbid has written on Hafsid–Mamluk relations (1994). Fatḥiyya Mazyānī from Algiers University defended a thesis on sufism in the Mashriq during the fourteenth century (2009). At the same university, Al-Ḥajj ʿAfīf defended a doctoral thesis on the Maghāriba and Andalusians in Egypt and Bilād al-Shām during the Mamluk period.[86] ʿAbd al-Raḥmān Bilaʿraj at Tlemcen University has written a study on political and cultural relations between the Mamluks and the states in the Maghrib.[87]

One of the leading historians of the medieval period in Morocco is Ibrāhīm al-Qādirī Būtashīsh. Among his works touching on the history of the Mamluk period is his study on the *iqṭāʿ*.[88] Scholars from the Maghrib have shown a great interest in the editing and study of manuscripts from the Mamluk period located in the manuscript collections of the region. The Tunisian scholar Muḥammad al-Ḥabīb al-Hayla wrote a study on the administrative system of the Circassian Mamluk state based on rare manuscript sources which he presented at an international conference in Cairo organized by the Egyptian Ministry of Culture in 1969, celebrating the one thousandth anniversary of the founding of Cairo.[89] The Moroccan researcher Aḥmad al-Saʿīdī wrote a study on a Mamluk manuscript entitled *Adab al-Dunyā wa al-Dīn*, which was discovered in an obscure library in southern Morocco and appears to have been copied in the fourteenth century.[90]

8 The Trajectories of Mamluk Studies

The first studies on the Mamluks focused above all on the general political history: the founding of the first and second Mamluk states, the histories and biographies of the sultans, and the great transformations that occurred during the some of their reigns. The studies of Jamāl al-Dīn Surūr mentioned above are good examples of this type of writing. Other works in this category include

---

85   Rashīda Bilsurūr, *Markaz Tijārī*; Luṭfī bin Mīlād, *Ifrīqiyyā wa al-Mashriq al-Muṭawassiṭī*; Bilqāsim Ṭabbābī, *Dirāsāt fī al-Sulṭa wa al-Mujtamaʿ*.

86   See ʿAllāwa ʿAmāra, Khamsūn Sana min al-Baḥth.

87   ʿAbd al-Raḥmān Bilaʿraj, ʿAlāqāt.

88   Būtashīsh, Hal ʿArafa al-Mujtamaʿ al-ʿArabī al-Iqṭāʿ?

89   Muḥammad al-Ḥabīb al-Hayla, Al-Nuẓum al-Idāriyya.

90   Aḥmad al-Saʿīdī, Makhṭuṭa Mamlūkiyya.

'Alī Ibrāhīm Ḥasan's history of the Baḥrī Mamluks and his book on Egypt in the Middle Ages, Aḥmad Mukhtār al-'Abbādī's work on the rise of the Baḥrī Mamluk state, the studies by Ḥakīm Amīn 'Abd al-Sayyid and Ibrāhīm Ṭarkhān on the Circassian Mamluk state, Naẓīr Ḥassān Sa'dāwī's article, and Fayṣal Shillī's study on Bilād al-Shām in the Circassian Mamluk period.[91]

Another group of studies concerns the history of the administration during the Mamluk period. One of the most important surveys of Mamluk administrative history is a two volume work by 'Abd al-Mun'im Mājid.[92] Ḥāmid Zayyān studied the position of the Abbasid caliphate in Mamluk Cairo, focusing on the caliph Al-Musta'īn Billāh al-'Abbāsī and his attempt to combine the authority of both caliph and sultan.[93] More recently, 'Uthmān 'Alī 'Aṭā' has worked on the institution of *majālis al-shūrā* (advisory councils) during the Mamluk period.[94] He has tried to change the common stereotype of the Mamluk state as a despotic, authoritarian entity by demonstrating the importance of the councils and the sultans' recourse to them in political, economic, and religious matters.

There are many works on Mamluk military history, such as an article by 'Alī Ibrāhīm Ḥasan on the army and navy during the Mamluk period, Nabīl 'Abd al-'Azīz's study on weapons storehouses and their contents during the Ayyubid and Mamluk periods, Nadīm Aḥmad Fahīm's work on military science and the Mamluk army during the Baḥrī period, and Aḥmad Ramaḍān Aḥmad's study on the science of naval combat in the medieval Mediterranean.[95]

One of the subjects that has attracted great attention from specialists in Mamluk history is the *iqṭā'*. Though the *iqṭā'* had already appeared in the Mashriq well before the Mamluks took power, it constituted an essential feature of the Mamluk period. Study of the *iqṭā'* began quite early but it remains an open field within Mamluk studies. Ibrāhīm Ṭarkhān's book on the *iqṭā'* systems in the medieval Middle East (1968) is the most comprehensive study on the *iqṭā'*.[96] Ṭarkhān wrote his MA thesis in 1957 on the *iqṭā'* system down to the end of the Ayyubid period and in 1957 he wrote an article entitled "The

---

91   'Alī Ibrāhīm Ḥasan, *Arā'*; Idem, *Tārīkh al-Mamālīk al-Baḥriyya*; Idem, *Miṣr fī al-'Uṣūr al-Wusṭā*; Aḥmad Mukhtār al-'Abbādī, *Qiyām Dawlat al-Mamālīk al-Ulā*; Ḥakīm Amīn 'Abd al-Sayyid, *Qiyām Dawlat al-Mamālīk al-Thāniya*; Ṭarkhān, *Miṣr fī 'Aṣr al-Mamālīk al-Jarākisa*; Naẓīr Ḥassān al-Sa'dāwī; *Dawlat al-Barrayn wa al-Baḥrayn*; Fayṣal Shillī; *Bilād al-Shām fī Ẓill al-Dawla al-Mamlūkiyya al-Thāniya*.

92   'Abd al-Mun'im Mājid, *Nuẓum*.

93   Ḥāmid Zayyān; *Ṣafḥa min Tārīkh al-Khilāfa al-'Abbāsiyya*.

94   'Uthmān 'Alī 'Aṭā'; *Majālis al-Shūrā*.

95   'Alī Ibrāhīm Ḥasan, *Al-Jaysh wa al-Baḥriyya*; Nabīl 'Abd al-'Azīz, *Khazā'in*; Nadīm Aḥmad Fahīm, *Al-Fann al-Ḥarbī*; Aḥmad Ramaḍān Aḥmad, *Tārīkh Fann al-Qitāl al-Baḥrī*.

96   Ṭarkhān, *Al-Nuẓum al-Iqṭā'iyya*.

Islamic Iqṭāʿ: its Origins and Development – a Comparative Study".[97] In the same year Al-Sayyid al-Bāz al-ʿArīnī wrote a book about the *iqṭāʿ* in the Middle East from the 7th to the 13th centuries.[98] Before this, in 1956, he had published an article about the Mamluk horsemen and a book about the military *iqṭāʿ* in the Mamluk period.[99] ʿAlī al-Zayn wrote a book about *iqṭāʿ* contracts which includes a chapter about the conditions and forms of such contracts during the Mamluk period.[100]

The study of the *iqṭāʿ* paved the way for further studies on the social and economic conditions of the Mamluk age. The first turning point came in the early 1950s when Muḥammad Muṣṭafā Ziyāda oriented his pupil, Saʿīd ʿĀshūr, towards the study of the social history of the Mamluk period. The latter, in turn, guided his pupils in the same direction. Since that time the field of Mamluk studies has expanded to embrace various topics in social and economic history.

The oldest study on Mamluk social history may be Ḥasan Ibrāhīm's article on famines in Egypt published in 1946.[101] It appears to be influenced by al-Maqrīzī's treatise on famines *Ighāthat al-Umma bi Kashf al-Ghumma*, which had been edited and published a few years earlier by Muḥammad Muṣṭafā Ziyāda and Jamāl al-Dīn Surūr. The study of the social history of the period moved in several directions. Some studies focused on social classes, sects, and factions. Examples of these are Qāsim ʿAbduh Qāsim's studies on the Christians and Jews of the Mamluk period and ʿUmar Jamāl's study of the lives of the craftsmen in Mamluk Cairo.[102] Other publications deal with the common classes. Examples are Ḥayāt al-Ḥajjī's work on the common people and Maḥāsin al-Waqqād's study on the popular classes in Mamluk Cairo.[103] The lives, customs, and behavior of the upper classes have been studied by Aḥmad ʿAbd al-Rāziq in his work on family relations in Mamluk terminology, by Nabīl ʿAbd al-ʿAzīz in his studies about equestrian sports and palace cuisine during the Mamluk period, and by Al-Sayyid Ṣalāḥ al-Dabīkī in his work on the *Awlād al-Nās* (descendants of Mamluks).[104]

Some studies have focused on various societal phenomena of the period. An important work of social history is Naẓīr Hassān al-Saʿdāwī's study on the

---

97   *Al-Kitāb al-Fiḍḍī*, 174; Ṭarkhān, Al-Iqṭāʿ al-Islāmī.

98   Al-Sayyid al-Bāz al-ʿArīnī, Al-Iqṭāʿ fī al-Sharq al-Awsaṭ.

99   Al-Sayyid al-Bāz al-ʿArīnī, Al-Fāris al-Mamlūkī; Ayman Fuʾād Sayyid, *Ruwwād*, 303.

100   ʿAlī al-Zayn, *Al-ʿĀdāt wa al-Taqālīd fī al-ʿUhūd al-Iqṭāʿiyya*.

101   Ḥasan Ibrāhīm; Akhṭar al-Majāʿāt.

102   ʿUmar Jamāl, Al-Ḥayāt al-Ḥirfiyya.

103   Maḥāsin al-Waqqād, *Al-Ṭabaqāt al-Shaʿbiyya*.

104   Aḥmad ʿAbd al-Rāziq, Al-ʿAlāqāt al-Usriyya; *Al-Khayl wa Riyāḍātuhu*; Idem, *Al-Maṭbakh al-Sulṭānī*; Al-Dubaykī, *Awlād al-Nās*.

maẓālim courts (special courts overseen by the sultan).[105] ʿAlī al-Sayyid ʿAlī has written numerous studies on social history, many of which are collected in his volume *Studies on the Social History of the Mamluk Period* (*Buḥūth fī al-Tārīkh al-Ijtimāʿī min al-ʿAṣr al-Mamlūkī*).[106] The notable studies in this collection include his comparison of the Black Death and *al-Fanāʾ al-Kabīr* (as the great plague of the fourteenth century was known in Arabic sources) and a study on Cairo in the eyes of European travelers of the 14th and 15th centuries.[107] ʿAmr ʿAbd al-ʿAzīz Munīr has written about itinerant physicians of the Mamluk period known as *al-ṭuruqiyya*; on tricksters in Egypt and Bilād al-Shām during the Ayyubid and Mamluk periods; and on the uses and production of, and attitudes towards "alternative foods" in Mamluk Egypt.[108] Majdī ʿAbd al-Rashīd Baḥr has studied the Egyptian village during the Mamluk period.[109]

A number of studies have been written about economic crises and their effects on society. Ḥasan Ḥabashī wrote about hoarding of foodstuffs during the Mamluk period and its impact on the health of the population.[110] Muḥammad al-Zāmil has written on economic transformations at the end of the Mamluk period.[111] The "meat crisis" during the Circassian Mamluk period and its effect on Egyptian society was the subject of a study by Muḥammad ʿAbd al-Naʿīm.[112] Muṣṭafā Wajīh Muṣṭafā has written about nutrition in Mamluk Egypt.[113] One of the most recent works to examine the crisis of the Mamluk system from its political, economic, and social aspects is Aḥmad ʿAbd al-Rāziq Muḥammad's study on the decline of the Mamluk state in Egypt.[114]

Numerous studies have been written on the economic and financial system of the Mamluk period. ʿĀmir Najīb Mūsā Nāṣir wrote about Egyptian economic life under the Mamluks, Al-Bayyūmī Ismāʿīl on the financial system of Egypt and Syria during the Mamluk period, and ʿUmar Jamāl on the political economy of the Mamluk province of Damascus.[115]

Some of the studies on Mamluk economic history have also focused on international trade and trade routes during that period. Naʿīm Zakī Fahmī

105 Naẓīr Ḥassān al-Saʿdāwī, *Ṣuwar wa Maẓālim.*
106 ʿAlī al-Sayyid ʿAlī, *Buḥūth fī al-Tārīkh al-Ijtimāʿī.*
107 ʿAlī al-Sayyid ʿAlī, *Al-Fanāʾ al-Kabīr*; Idem, *Al-Qāhira fī ʿUyūn al-Raḥḥāla al-Urubiyyin.*
108 ʿAmr Munīr, *Jamāʿāt dūn al-Iʿtirāf.*
109 Majdī ʿAbd al-Rashīd Baḥr, *Al-Qarya al-Miṣriyya.*
110 Ḥasan Habashī, *Al-Iḥtikār al-Mamlūkī.*
111 Muḥammad Fatḥī al-Zāmil, *Al-Taḥawwulāt.*
112 Muḥammad ʿAbd al-Naʿīm Muḥammad ʿAbduh, *Azmat al-Luḥūm.*
113 Muṣṭafā Wajīh Muṣṭafā, *Al-Ghadhāʾ.*
114 Aḥmad ʿAbd al-Rāziq Muḥammad, *ʿAwāmil Inhiyār.*
115 ʿĀmir Najīb Mūsā Nāṣir, *Al-Ḥayāt al-Iqtiṣādiyya*; Al-Bayyūmī Ismāʿīl, *Al-Nuẓum al-Māliyya*; ʿUmar Jamāl, *Al-Siyāsa al-Iqtiṣādiyya.*

wrote a study on the international trade routes between East and West at the end of the Middle Ages.[116] Fārūq 'Uthmān Abāẓa has written on the effects that the opening of the maritime trade route around the Cape of Good Hope had on the economy of the Mediterranean Basin in the sixteenth century.[117] Ṣubḥī Labīb studied the trade policies of the Ayyubids and Mamluks.[118] Joseph Nasīm Yūsuf has written on Mamluk trade relations with the Italian city-states while Rashīd Bāqa focused specifically on trade relations between Florence and the Mamluk state.[119] Muḥammad Fatḥī al-Zāmil has studied the economic blockades of Egypt in the late medieval period.[120]

Researchers have shown great interest in Mamluk foreign policy. 'Abd al-'Azīz al-Ahwānī, a specialist in the literature of al-Andalus, studied embassies from the sultans of Granada to the Mamluk state during the fifteenth century.[121] Sulaymān 'Aṭiyya's thesis deals with Mamluk policy in the Red Sea until the end of Barsbāy's reign.[122] Ḥasan Ḥabashī produced a study on the Cypriot assault on Alexandria in 1365 relying on the important account by al-Nuwayrī.[123] 'Ādil Zaytūn wrote a book on East–West relations in the Middle Ages.[124] Ḥayāt al-Ḥajjī has published a study on relations between the Mamluks and the Spanish kingdoms during the 14th and 15th centuries.[125] 'Afāf Sayyid Ṣabra wrote about Venetian relations with Egypt and Bilād al-Shām.[126] Byzantine relations with the Mamluks have been studied by Laylā 'Abd al-Jawād.[127] Ṣubḥī 'Abd al-Mun'im Muḥammad wrote a study on Ilkhanid policy towards the Mamluks during the reign of the Ilkhan Abū Sa'īd Khudābanda.[128] Muḥammad Najīb al-Wasīmī has studied the relations between the Turcoman principality of Qarāmān in Anatolia and the Circassian Mamluks.[129] Sūzī Ḥammūd wrote a book on power struggles in the Near East in the Zenkid, Ayyubid and Mamluk periods.[130] Relations between Egypt and the Maghrib during the Mamluk

116   Na'īm Zakī Fahmī, *Ṭuruq al-Tijāra*.
117   Fārūq 'Uthmān Abāẓa, *Athar Taḥawwul*.
118   Ṣubḥī Labīb, *Siyāsat Miṣr al-Tijāriyya*.
119   Joseph Nasīm Yūsuf, *'Alāqāt*; Rashīd Bāqa, *Al-'Alāqāt al-Tijāriyya*.
120   Muḥammad Fatḥī al-Zāmil, *Al-Ḥiṣār al-Iqtiṣādī*.
121   'Abd al'Azīz al-Ahwānī, *Sifāra Siyāsiyya*.
122   Sulaymān 'Aṭiyya, *Siyāsat al-Mamālīk fī al-Baḥr al-Aḥmar*.
123   Ḥasan Ḥabashī, *Hujūm al-Qabāriṣa*.
124   'Ādil Zaytūn, *Al-'Alāqāt bayn al-Sharq wa al-Gharb*.
125   Ḥayāt Nāṣir al-Ḥajjī, *Al-'Alāqāt bayn Salṭanat al-Mamālīk wa al-Mamālik al-Isbāniyya*.
126   'Afāf Sayyid Ṣabra, *'Alāqat al-Bunduqiyya*.
127   Laylā 'Abd al-Jawād, *'Alāqat al-Dawla al-Bīzanṭiyya*.
128   Ṣubḥī 'Abd al-Mun'im Muḥammad, *Siyāsat al-Mughūl*.
129   Muḥammad Najīb al-Wasīmī, *Al-'Alāqāt al-Siyāsiyya*.
130   Sūzī Ḥammūd, *Al-Fāṭimiyūn, wa al-Zankiyūn wa al-Ayyubiyūn wa al-Mamālik*.

period have been studied by Najlāʾ Muḥammad Raḥūma while ʿAbd al-Raḥmān al-Aʿraj has published an article on the political relations between the Hafsids and the Baḥrī Mamluk state.[131] The tenth volume in the series *International Relations in Islamic History (Al-ʿAlāqāt al-Duwaliyya fiʾl Tārīkh al-Islāmī)* is dedicated to the Mamluk period.[132]

A number of reference aids for the study of the Mamluk period, such as specialized dictionaries, atlases, and catalogues of sources, have also been published. Muḥammad Aḥmad Dahmān published a dictionary of terminology from the Mamluk period.[133] A dictionary of the names of Mamluk sultans and amirs was written by ʿAbdallāh ʿAbd al-Ḥāfiẓ.[134] Aḥmad Saʿīd Sulaymān's dictionary of ruling dynasties has a special section devoted to the Mamluks.[135] The *Atlas of Islamic History (Aṭlas Tārīkh al-Islām)* has a section on the Mamluk period while Sāmī al-Maghlūth has published an atlas of Mamluk history.[136] The most important catalogue of archival sources is Muḥammad Muḥammad Amīn's catalogue of the documents of Cairo from the Middle Ages.[137]

9   Cultural History

In the field of cultural history, a large number of studies have been written on the historians and scholars of the Mamluk period and their works. We have already mentioned Muḥammad Muṣṭafā Ziyāda's book about the historians of the fifteenth century. Muḥammad ʿAbdallāh ʿInān wrote a two-volume book on sources for the history of Egypt during the Islamic period.[138] Mamluk sources and historians take up the greatest space in this work. Jamāl al-Dīn al-Shayyāl wrote a study on al-Maqrīzī's minor works.[139] Ayman Fuʾād al-Sayyid has written numerous studies on al-Maqrīzī as well as a book on historical writing in fifteenth century Egypt.[140] This leads us to our next topic, which is a discussion

---

131   Najlāʾ Muḥammad Raḥūma Ḥammād, *Al-ʿAlāqāt bayn Miṣr wa al-Maghrib*; ʿAbd al-Raḥmān al-Aʿraj, *Al-ʿAlāqāt al-Siyāsiyya.*

132   Nādiya Maḥmūd Muṣṭafā (ed.), *Al-ʿAlāqāt al-Duwaliyya fī al-Tārīkh al-Islāmī.*

133   Muḥammad Aḥmad Dahmān, *Muʿjam.*

134   ʿAbdallāh ʿAṭiyya ʿAbd al-Ḥāfiẓ, *Muʿjam Asmāʾ.*

135   Aḥmad al-Saʿīd Sulaymān, *Tārīkh al-Duwal al-Islāmiyya wa Muʿjam al-Usar al-Ḥākima.*

136   Ḥusayn Muʾnis, *Aṭlas*; Sāmī b. ʿAbdallāh b. Aḥmad al-Maghlūth, *Aṭlas.*

137   Muḥammad Muḥammad Amīn, *Fihrist.*

138   Muḥammad ʿAbdallāh ʿInān, *Miṣr al-Islāmiyya.*

139   Jamāl al-Dīn al-Shayyāl, *Muʾallafāt al-Maqrīzī.*

140   Ayman Fuʾād al-Sayyid, *Al-Maqrīzī wa Kitābuhu al-Mawāʿiẓ wa al-Iʿtibār*; Idem, *Ṭarīqat al-Taʾlīf*; Idem, *Khuṭuṭ al-Maqrīzī*, Idem, *Al-Kitāba al-Tārīkhiyya fī Miṣr fī al-Qarn al-Khāmis ʿAshar al-Mīlādī.*

of Khaldūnian studies or the study of the life and works of the great intellectual ʿAbd al-Raḥmān b. Khaldūn, a field which unites many different disciplines.

10 Khaldūnian Studies

From the time that Ṭāhā Ḥusayn wrote his thesis at the Sorbonne on the social philosophy of Ibn Khaldūn, which was translated into Arabic in 1925, the study of Ibn Khaldūn has been a shared concern of departments of history, philosophy, sociology, psychology, and literature in the faculties of letters and it has even become a focus in the sphere of political science. It has also connected all of the abovementioned disciplines to the field of Mamluk studies.

The printing of numerous editions of Ibn Khaldūn's *Muqaddima* since the late nineteenth century and the publication of studies on Ibn Khaldūn by authors who had no formal ties to academia have helped to propel interest in Khaldūnian studies. In the 1930s the young Moroccan scholars Muḥammad ʿAllāl al-Fāsī and ʿAbd al-ʿAzīz b. Idrīs printed an edition of the Muqaddima with notes. This edition inspired the learned but non-academic author Shakīb Arslān to write his study on Ibn Khaldūn's *History* (of which the Muqaddima is only the introduction) which was published in Cairo and Fez in 1936.[141] In this work Arslān criticizes some of Ibn Khaldūn's opinions and conclusions.

We turn now to the academic studies on Ibn Khaldūn. In 1944 Muṣṭafā al-Khashshāb wrote his MA thesis on "Social Philosophy according to Ibn Khaldūn and Auguste Comte."[142] Al-Khashshāb later took a position in the sociology department of Cairo University. In the early 1960s the famous Iraqi sociologist and thinker ʿAlī al-Wardī delivered a series of lectures in Cairo at the Maʿhad al-Dirāsāt al-ʿArabiyya al-ʿĀliyya (now Maʿhad al-Buḥūth wa al-Dirāsāt al-ʿArabiyya) that were later collected and published under the title *The Logic of Ibn Khaldūn in Light of his Civilization and Personality*.[143] The renowned Egyptian philosopher ʿAbd al-Raḥmān al-Badawī and the Syrian thinker Taysīr Shaykh al-Arḍ both wrote studies on Ibn Khaldūn in the 1960s.[144] An important book was also published during this decade by the Arab nationalist thinker Sāṭiʿ al-Ḥuṣrī under the title *Studies on the Muqaddima of Ibn Khaldūn*.[145]

---

141 Shakīb Arslān, *Tārīkh Ibn Khaldūn*.

142 *Al-Kitāb al-Fiḍḍī*, 176.

143 Alī al-Wardī, *Manṭiq Ibn Khaldūn*.

144 ʿAbd al-Raḥmān Badawī, *Muʾallafāt Ibn Khaldūn*; Taysīr Shaykh al-Arḍ; *Ibn Khaldūn*.

145 Sāṭiʾ al-Ḥuṣrī, *Abū Khaldūn*.

In the 1970s 'Uthmān Mawāfī published a study entitled *Ibn Khaldūn: Critic of History and Literature*.[146] In 1978 the Tunisian scholars 'Abd al-Karīm Marrāq, 'Alī al-Shanūfī, and 'Alī Ṣaḥābī published a study that approached the Muqaddima from their diverse backgrounds in history and philosophy departments.[147] Jihād Nu'mān, a psychologist, wrote about Ibn Khaldūn's concept of instincts and their control.[148] In the 1980s the Lebanese linguist Mīshīl Zakariyyā wrote a study on the faculty of speech in the Muqaddima.[149]

In 1996 Maḥmūd Ismā'īl 'Abd al-Rāziq, professor of Islamic history at 'Ayn Shams University and author of a history of political movements in Islam and a sociology of Islamic thought, wrote a series of critical articles in which he doubted the originality of Ibn Khaldūn's ideas in the Muqaddima. His writings provoked a major controversy not only in academic circles but also in the media. He expanded his articles and published them in one book in 1999.[150] The reformist writer Aḥmad Ṣubḥī Manṣūr wrote another study on the Muqaddima.[151] The Moroccan academic and novelist Binsālim Ḥamīsh, who specializes in philosophy, wrote a book entitled *Khaldūnian Studies in Light of the Philosophy of History* (1998) and another entitled *On Reading Ibn Khaldūn* (1999). He also wrote an historical novel about Ibn Khaldūn (1997). Ṣalāḥ al-Dīn Basyūnī has written a study of political economy according to Ibn Khaldūn.[152]

The six hundredth anniversary of Ibn Khaldūn's death in 2006 was an occasion for numerous commemorative academic and cultural conferences in Morocco, Algeria, Tunisia and Egypt at which dozens of new studies were presented. It was also the occasion for the launch of a new critical edition of Ibn Khaldūn's works under the direction of Ibrāhīm Shabbūḥ in Tunis. Sāmiya al-Sā'ātī, professor of sociology at 'Ayn Shams University, wrote a book called *Ibn Khaldūn as Innovator: A New Reading of his Sociological Thought and Methodology*.[153] Qāsim 'Abduh Qāsim presented two studies on Ibn Khaldūn for the commemoration jointly sponsored by the Egyptian High Council for Culture and the Alexandria Library: *Ibn Khaldūn and how the Arab Historians have Read him* and *Crisis of the Intellectual in the Shadow of Authoritarianism:*

---

146   'Uthmān Mawāfī, *Ibn Khaldūn Nāqid al-Tārīkh wa al-Adab*.

147   'Abd al-Karīm al-Marrāq, 'Alī al-Shanūfī and 'Alī Ṣaḥḥābī, *Aḍwā' 'alā Muqaddimat Ibn Khaldūn*.

148   Jihād Nu'mān, *Ibn Khaldūn wa 'Ilm al-Nafs*.

149   Mīshāl Zakariyyā, *Al-Malak al-Lisāniyya*.

150   Maḥmūd Ismā'īl 'Abd al-Rāziq, *Nihāyat Usṭūra*.

151   Aḥmad Ṣubḥī Manṣūr, *Muqaddimat Ibn Khaldūn*.

152   Ṣalāḥ al-Dīn Basiyūnī Ruslān, *Al-Siyāsa wa al-Iqtiṣād*.

153   Sāmiya al-Sā'ātī, *Ibn Khaldūn Mubdi'an*.

Ibn Khaldūn as a Case-Study.[154] In Tunis ʿAbd al-Wahhāb Būhadība and Mūnīra Chapoutot published a book entitled *In the Footsteps of Ibn Khaldūn* (*ʿAlā Khuṭā Ibn Khaldūn*).[155] In 2007 *Dār al-Kutub al-Miṣriyya* published a joint volume by specialists from diverse disciplines under the title *Ibn Khaldūn in the Light of Contemporary Research*.[156] The veteran editor and historian Ayman Fuʾād al-Sayyid presented three studies on Ibn Khaldūn in 2008: "Ibn Khaldūn in Egypt and his influence on the Egyptian Historiographical School of the 9th Century AH (15th century AD)," "Manuscripts in the Age of Ibn Khaldūn," and a study on the treatment of non-Muslims by Ibn Khaldūn in his history.[157] Al-Sayyid also edited and published volume 5 of Ibn Khaldūn's History in 2010 for the new Tunisian edition.

11   Language, Literature and Popular Culture in the Mamluk Period

Among the intellectual disciplines that have interacted with Mamluk studies are the fields of linguistics, literature, and popular literature. In 1941 the department of Arabic language and literature at the Egyptian University granted a doctoral degree to Suhayr al-Qalamāwī for a thesis on "The Literary Aspect of the Thousand and One Nights."[158] With this thesis the Egyptian University set a precedent for the academic study of popular or folk literature. In the same year ʿAbd al-Wahhāb ʿAzzām, professor of Arabic literature, edited the *Majālis* of Sulṭān al-Ghūrī and published the text with a full study, thereby introducing the study of the literature, language, and popular culture of the Mamluk period.[159]

In 1946 ʿAbd al-Ḥamīd Yūnis defended an MA thesis on *Sīrat Baybars* (the Baybars Epic), one of the most important popular epics from the Mamluk period, which presents a fantastic vision of the establishment of the Mamluk dynasty in Egypt.[160] Yūnis later became the founder of a "school" of Egyptian academics who focused on the study of popular literature. In 1961 Mīkhāʾil Najm Khūrī defended a thesis on the Baybars Epic at the American University of Beirut.[161] General interest in Mamluk popular culture in Egypt began even earlier when Jūrj Yaʿqūb Laṭīf Khayyāl published his studies on the famous

---

154   ʿAmr ʿAbd al-ʿAzīz Munīr, *Qāsim ʿAbduh Qāsim*, 26.
155   ʿAbd al-Wahhāb Būhadība and Mūnīra Chapoutot, *ʿAlā Khuṭā Ibn Khaldūn*.
156   Muḥammad Ṣābir ʿArab (ed.), *Ibn Khaldūn fī Dirāsāt ʿAṣriyya*.
157   Ayman Fuʾād al-Sayyid, Makhṭūṭāt ʿAṣr Ibn Khaldūn; Idem, Maṣādir Ibn Khaldūn.
158   *Al-Kitāb al-Fiḍḍī*, 166.
159   ʿAbd al-Wahhāb ʿAzzām, *Majālis al-Sulṭān al-Ghūrī*.
160   *Al-Kitāb al-Fiḍḍī*, 168.
161   Mīkhāʾīl Najm Khūrī, Sīrat al-Malik al-Sulṭān Baybars.

Mamluk-period author of shadow-plays Ibn Dāniyāl al-Mawṣilī in 1910.[162] Ibn Dāniyāl and the Mamluk shadow-play attracted the attention of many later scholars as well. Fuʾād Ḥasanayn published articles on the topic in 1942 and 1943 and Ibrāhīm Ḥamāda edited the texts of Ibn Dāniyāl's plays and shadow-plays.[163] Muḥammad Qandīl al-Baqlī wrote about the musical scales in the colloquial poetry of Ibn Sūdūn.[164]

Muḥammad Rajab al-Najjār, who obtained his PhD from Cairo University in the field of popular literature and later became professor of folklore at the University of Kuwait, played a very important role in the study of Mamluk popular culture. He wrote a book on the medieval stories of vagabonds and scoundrels, edited the popular tale known as *Sīrat ʿAlī al-Zabīq*, and wrote many studies on popular satirical poetry which focus mainly on compositions from the Mamluk period.[165] He published these studies in various journals and collected some of them in a volume entitled *Popular Satirical Poetry in the Mamluk Period*.[166] One of the essential articles in this volume is a study on popular political satire along with a second on social satire.

Qāsim ʿAbduh Qāsim was the first to employ both formal and popular literature from the Mamluk period as sources for studying its history. His student, ʿUmar ʿAbd al-ʿAzīz Munīr, followed in his footsteps. Munīr's contributions to the study of Mamluk folk culture include an edition of *Ṭayf al-Khayyāl*, a book on *Egypt and the Nile between History and Folklore* and a study on Jerusalem in Arabic tales of the 12th and 13th centuries.[167]

A number of important literary and intellectual studies of the Mamluk period have appeared. ʿAbd al-Laṭīf Ḥamza has written on the intellectual movements in Ayyubid and early Mamluk Egypt and on literature in Egypt from the Ayyubids until the French expedition.[168] Muḥammad Kāmil Ḥusayn has published a study on Shīʿism in the Egyptian poetry of the Ayyubid and Mamluk periods.[169] Muḥammad Rizq Salīm wrote a study on intellectual and literary production in the Ayyubid and Mamluk periods.[170] Aḥmad Ṣādiq al-Jamāl wrote about the Egyptian colloquial literature of the Mamluk period.[171]

---

162 Jūrj Yaʿqūb, *Ṭayf al-Khayyāl li Ibn Daniyāl al-Mawṣilī*.

163 Fuʾād Ḥasanayn, *Muḥammad b. Dāniyāl*; Ibrāhīm Ḥammāda (ed.), *Khayyāl al-Ẓill wa Tamthīliyāt Ibn Dāniyāl*.

164 Muḥammad Qandīl al-Baqlī, *Al-Awzān*.

165 Muḥammad Rajab al-Najjār, *Ḥikāyāt*; Idem (ed.), *Sīrat ʿAlī al-Zabīq*.

166 Muḥammad Rajab al-Najjār, *Al-Shiʿr al-Shaʿbī al-Sākhir*.

167 ʿUmar ʿAbd al-ʿAzīz Munīr, *Miṣr wa al-Nīl*; Idem, *Al-Quds fī al-Asāṭīr*.

168 ʿAbd al-Laṭīf Ḥamza, *Al-Ḥaraka al-Fikriyya*; Idem, *Al-Adab al-Miṣrī*.

169 Muḥammad Kāmil Ḥusayn, *Al-Tashayyuʿ*.

170 Muḥammad Rizq Salīm, *ʿAṣr Salāṭīn al-Mamālīk*.

171 Aḥmad Ṣādiq al-Jamāl, *Al-Adab al-ʿĀmmī fī al-ʿAṣr al-Mamlūkī*.

Muḥammad Zaghlūl Salām and Muḥammad Kāmil Fiqī have written books on Arabic literature during the Mamluk period and Muḥammad Munʿim Khafājī wrote a book on literary life in Egypt during the Mamluk and Ottoman periods.[172]

Linguists have also contributed to our understanding of the Mamluk period. Al-Badrāwī Zahrān has written linguistic studies on the Arabic of the medieval period.[173] Muḥammad Qandīl Baqlī has written studies on the terms in al-Qalqashandī's *Ṣubḥ al-Aʿshā* and on the language used in the archival documents from Mamluk Egypt.[174]

It is worth mentioning that the Mamluk period has been a great source of inspiration for writers and artists in the twentieth century, some of whom have written works which take place during that period. The famous modern novels about the Mamluk epoch include Jurjī Zīdān's *Shajar al-Durr*, Saʿīd al-ʿAryān's *ʿAlā Bāb Zuwayla*, *Wā Islāmāh* by ʿAlī Aḥmad Bakthīr, Saʿīd Makkāwī's *Al-Sāʾirūn Niyāman*, *Al-Zaynī Barakāt* by Jamāl al-Ghīṭānī, and *Al-ʿAllāma* by Binsālim Ḥamūsh. The Mamluk period has also been a fertile source of inspiration for the theatre. Plays with Mamluk themes include Tawfīq al-Ḥakīm's *Al-Sulṭān al-Ḥāʾir*, *Idārat ʿUmūm al-Zīr* by Ḥusayn Muʾnis, *Al-Fīl yā Malik al-Zamān*, *Mughāmarat Raʾs al-Mamlūk Jābir*, and *Al-Malik Huwa al-Malik* by Saʿdallāh Wannūs. Three films which are set in the Mamluk period are *Lājīn*, *Wā Islāmāh*, and *Al-Mamālīk*.

12   Archeology and Art

The academic field of Mamluk studies owes its start to an archeologist, ʿAlī Bahjat, who was active at the end of the nineteenth century. Archeologists and historians of art and architecture have continued to make important contributions to our understanding of the Mamluk period.

Ayyubid and Mamluk heraldry, of which hundreds of examples have survived, attracted the attention of scholars since the nineteenth century. The publication of Mayer's work on oriental heraldry in the 1930s led to a revival of interest in the topic. In 1941 articles were published on heraldry by two professors of Islamic archeology, Jamāl Muḥriz and Muḥammad Muṣṭafā.[175] In his

---

172   Muḥammad Zaghlūl Salām, *Al-Adab fī al-ʿAṣr al-Mamlūkī*; Muḥammad Kāmil al-Fiqī, *Al-Adab al-ʿArabī fī al-ʿAṣr al-Mamlūkī*; Muḥammad ʿAbd al-Munʿim Khafājī, *Al-Ḥayāt Al-Adabiyya*.

173   Al-Badrāwī Zahrān, *Fī ʿIlm al-Lugha al-Tārīkhī*.

174   Muḥammad Qandīl al-Baqlī, *Al-Taʿrīf bi Muṣṭalaḥāt Ṣubḥ al-Aʿshā*; ʿImād Abū Ghāzī, *Mulāḥaẓāt ʿalā Taṭawwur al-Lugha fī ʿAṣr al-Mamālīk*.

175   Jamāl Muḥammad Muḥriz, *Al-Runūk*; Muḥammad Muṣṭafā, *Al-Runūk fī ʿAṣr al-Mamālīk*.

book on the royal emblems and symbols of the Nile Valley, 'Abd al-Rahmān Zakī has devoted a section to Ayyubid and Mamluk heraldry.[176] In the 1970s, Ahmad 'Abd al-Rāziq, a researcher at 'Ayn Shams University, published the first book in Arabic on Islamic heraldry.[177] The Lebanese historian al-Tadmurī has written an article about the emblems preserved in the Mamluk buildings of Tripoli.[178]

Mamluk numismatics has also received its share of attention. One of the prominent researchers in the field is Ra'fat al-Nabrāwī who has published extensively on Mamluk coinage.[179] Muhammad 'Abd al-Sattār 'Uthmān edited al-Maqrīzī's treatise on coinage and published it with a detailed study of the manuscript and of the Mamluk currency system.[180]

Muhammad Mustafā has studied illustrated manuscripts of training manuals for horsemanship and combat that were written toward the end of the Mamluk period.[181] His most important contribution, however, is his edition of Ibn Iyās' chronicle in six volumes with full indices, a project which lasted for fifty years! 'Abd al-Rahmān Zakī made use of his military background in preparing an important study on the use of firearms in the Mamluk period, which he presented in 1973 at a conference on Ibn Iyās.[182]

Corruption and bribery during the Mamluk period have been thoroughly studied by Ahmad 'Abd al-Rāziq Ahmad in his book *Al-Badhal wa al-Bartala fī Zaman al-Mamālīk*, which traces the practice of bribery in the sources for the Mamluk period.[183] Corruption extended into the high levels of the Mamluk administration. Administrative positions were purchased with bribes from the sultan and as a consequence the positions went to those who could pay the most and not those who were most qualified to carry out the work. Furthermore, the main concern of the appointees to government posts was to recover the money that they had spent in order to obtain their jobs. In order to achieve this, they saddled the inhabitants of the areas which they administered with heavy additional taxes and fees. This practice became commonplace at the very time that the condition of the majority of the population was going from bad to worse and they were unable to sustain additional new burdens. Ahmad

---

176   'Abd al-Rahmān Zakī, *Al-A'lām wa Shārāt al-Malik*.
177   Ahmad 'Abd al-Rāziq Ahmad, *Al-Runūk*.
178   'Umar 'Abd al-Salām Tadmurī, *Runūk al-Mamālīk wa Rusūmuhum*.
179   Ra'fat al-Nabrāwī, *Al-Nuqūd al-Islāmiyya fī Misr 'Asr Dawlat al-Mamālīk al-Jarākisa*; Idem, *Al-Nuqūd*.
180   Al-Maqrīzī, *Shudhūr al-'Uqūd fī Dhikr al-Nuqūd*, ed. Muhammad 'Abd al-Sattār 'Uthmān.
181   Muhammad Mustafā, *Makhtūt Musawwar*.
182   'Abd al-Rahmān Zakī, *Ibn Iyās wa Istikhdām al-Asliha al-Nāriyya*.
183   Ahmad 'Abd al-Rāziq Ahmad, *Al-Badhl wa al-Bartala*.

observes the negative effects that this administrative corruption had on the political, economic, and social conditions of the period. He shows how bribery led to the decline of the justice system and highlights its pernicious effects on the Mamluk military.

Hani Ḥamza, an Egyptian specialist on medieval Islamic architecture, has recently written a two-volume work, directed toward both a scholarly and general readership, entitled *Mamluk Egypt: A New Interpretation*.[184] The first volume is concerned with the period of the Baḥrī Mamluks and the second with the Circassian Mamluk period. It is a critical re-reading of Egypt's history from the founding of the Mamluk state until its fall. Ḥamza tries to correct some of the common misconceptions about the Mamluk period. He criticizes the use of contemporary standards to judge the history of past ages. In Volume Two he examines the various groups of sultans who ruled during the Circassian or second Mamluk period and the rise and fall of each group, the internal and external struggles of the Mamluk state, and he discusses the ability of the Mamluks to recover from crises time and time again. In the tenth chapter of this volume he discusses the transition from Mamluk to Ottoman rule, the suffering of the Egyptians during this period, and their resistance. Ḥamza's study can be considered one of the important recent works to present a different vision of the Mamluk age. It also runs counter to a new common trend in the Egyptian school of Ottoman studies which tries to portray the period of Ottoman rule over Egypt and much of the Arab world in a positive light. This trend has two sources: the first stems from the influence of the critiques of oriental studies and of Eurocentrism, the second is the influence exerted by the political Islamist factions that have been on the rise in the region in recent years. Ḥamza's background in the history of art and architecture history enables him to use the Mamluk architectural legacy as a window to observe the development of Egyptian society during this period. In his second volume he has applied a method which combines traditional narration with chronology according to the reigns of the sultans with pauses for analysis of various historical phenomena.

13 The School of Arabic Document Studies and Its Impact on Mamluk Studies

The emergence of archival studies in the Arab universities in the 1950s saw the appearance of a new generation of scholars who combined the study of

---

184 Hānī Ḥamza, *Miṣr al-Mamlūkiyya*.

history, archeology and documents. At their head was 'Abd al-Laṭīf Ibrāhīm, the founder of the school of Arabic document studies. Ibrāhīm wrote his ground-breaking doctoral dissertation in the middle of the 1950s on the Arabic documents from the reign of the Mamluk sultan Qanṣūh al-Ghūrī.[185] In his study he published documents from the *waqfs* (charitable endowments) of the sultan, discussed the development of the *waqf* system, and showed how documents of legal transactions were composed and authenticated and how the documentation system developed during the Mamluk period. This was followed by other studies, such as the publication of a document of the amir Akhūr Qarāqujā al-Ḥasanī and a pioneering study on documentation and authentication in private documents of the Circassian Mamluk period through the study of the certifications on the back of a document of the sultan al-Ghūrī.[186] The latter work was considered a supplement to his dissertation. Between 1956 and 1984 Ibrāhīm published more than 30 studies on Arabic documents of which 17 deal with the Mamluk period. In most of his studies he published documents of various legal transactions, presenting individual examples of each transaction, such as documents concerning *waqfs*, sale, exchange, lease, and donation. His studies are regarded as revolutionary in the analysis of private legal documents from the Mamluk period.[187] He also studied public Arabic documents and their style of composition through analysis of the decrees preserved in the library of St. Catherine's Monastery in Sinai, which shed light on relations between the state and the monks of the monastery during the Mamluk period.[188] He brought his previous training in history and archeology to his research on documents and his studies serve as a guide to archeologists on how to benefit from documents in their work.

Ibrāhīm presented two particularly important studies at the second (1957) and third (1959) conferences on Archeology in the Arab Countries, which were selected to be republished by the Arab Organization for Culture and the Sciences in a special volume on Islamic archeology.[189] In one of these studies he located, through the use of Mamluk documents, the ruins of the of the fortress erected by the Mamluk amir Yashbak b. Mahdī al-Dāwadār, who held the position of Great Dāwadār (an important position in the late Mamluk court meaning "bearer of the Sultan's inkwell") under the sultan Qāyitbāy, in the area of

---

185 'Abd al-Laṭīf Ibrāhīm, Dirāsāt Tārikhiyya wa Athariyya fī Wathāʾiq min 'Aṣr al-Ghūrī.

186 'Abd al-Laṭīf Ibrāhīm, Wathīqat al-Amīr Akhūr Qarāqujā al-Ḥasanī; Idem, Al-Tawthīqāt al-Sharʿiyya.

187 See 'Imād Abū Ghāzī, Ruwwād al-Dirāsāt Al-Akādīmiyya fī Majāl al-Wathāʾiq.

188 'Abd al-Laṭīf Ibrāhīm, Fī Maktabat Dayr Sānt Kātrīn.

189 'Abd al-Laṭīf Ibrāhīm, Al-Wathāʾiq fī Khidmat al-Āthār: Al-ʿAṣr al-Mamlūkī; Idem, Al-Wathāʾiq fī Khidmat al-Āthār: Wathīqat Waqf Qāyitbāy.

al-Silsila in Alexandria, commanding the entrance to the old port along with the famous citadel of Qāyitbāy. This discovery was published in an article entitled "From the Documents of Arab History."[190] He wrote a number of studies in which he gleaned information about the political, social, and cultural history of Egypt during the Mamluk and Ottoman periods from the Arabic documents. An example is his study of a *waqf* document for the school of the Mamluk amir Ṣarghatmish.[191] From this document Ibrāhīm made valuable observations about the education system of the Baḥrī Mamluk period. He also studied a document for the *waqf* of the famous historian Ibn Taghrībardī and produced studies on *waqf* documents for sacred places.[192] A main focuses of his research was the history of schools during the Mamluk and Ottoman periods as seen in the documents. One of his pioneering studies in this domain concerned the funds of the schools. He also studied the art of the book during the Mamluk period including binding, decoration, and calligraphy. His studies on schools and book production were combined and published in a two-volume book entitled *Studies on Islamic Books and Libraries*.[193] In fact, this was the only book that he published, as the rest of his studies consist of many separate articles.

Ibrāhīm must also be credited with founding a school of Arabic document studies. Beginning in the 1960s he trained a generation of specialists in document and archival studies whom he encouraged to study Arabic documents from different perspectives with the goal of attaining a comprehensive vision of medieval Arabic document production. Many of the studies by Ibrāhīm's students focus on the Arabic documents of the Mamluk period, which are divided among three major archival collections: the collection entitled "Documents of Amirs and Sultans" in the Egyptian National Archives, the historical archive collection in the Ministry of *Waqfs*, and the documents in the library of St. Catherine's Monastery. In addition, there is also a group of Mamluk period documents in al-Ḥaram al-Sharīf in Jerusalem which were discovered in the 1970s. The dissertations by Ibarāhīm's students concerning Mamluk period documents include: Zaynab Maḥfūẓ Hannā's MA and PhD theses, Jamāl al-Khūlī's MA thesis (later published as a book), the MA thesis of Ibrāhīm al-Sayyid, and the PhD thesis of ʿImād Abū Ghāzī.[194]

---

190   ʿAbd al-Laṭīf Ibrāhīm, Min Wathāʾiq al-Tārīkh al-ʿArabī.

191   Naṣṣān Jadīdan min Wathīqat al-Amīr Ṣarghatmish.

192   ʿAbd al-Laṭīf Ibrāhīm, Waqfiyyat Ibn Taghrī Bardī; Idem, Wathāʾiq al-Waqf ʿalā al-Amākin al-Muqaddasa.

193   ʿAbd al-Laṭīf Ibrāhīm, *Dirāsāt fī al-Kutub wa al-Maktabāt al-Islāmiyya*.

194   Zaynab Muḥammad Maḥfūẓ Hannāʾ, Al-Taṭawwur Al-Diblūmātī; Idem, Wathāʾiq al-Bayʿ; Jamāl Ibrāhīm Mursī al-Khūlī, Dirāsa Muqārana li Wathāʾiq al-Istibdāl; Idem, Ithbāt

Since the 1950s, document-based studies have progressed in Egypt and throughout the Arab world and they have resulted in a major transformation in our historical knowledge of the Mamluk period, shedding light on new aspects of the period and changing many of our conceptions. We will discuss here some of the scholars who came after Ibrāhīm and made valuable contributions to the history of the Mamluk period through their use of documents. Tawfīq Iskandar worked on an Arabic document found in the Venetian archives concerning an embassy from Sultan Qāyitbāy to the Venetian Republic in 1490 which signed a treaty relinquishing Mamluk control over Cyprus. Unfortunately, Iskandar did not complete publication of the document.[195] Instead, he published an important study on the system of exchange in medieval Egyptian external trade.[196] He also translated and published an important collection of the writing of the scholars of the Annales school of historiography.[197] Ḥasan ʿAlī al-Ḥilwa obtained a BA in philosophy before turning his attention to the study of Arabic documents. He earned a diploma in archival studies in Paris, and then a PhD from Cairo University. He published a *waqf* document of the sultan al-Manṣūr Qalāwūn for his hospital complex (the Bīmāristān).[198]

In the 1950s and 1960s Aḥmad Darrāj produced some of the most important research based on medieval Arabic documents. He completed his PhD in France on the reign of the sultan Barsbāy.[199] He published a *waqf* document of Barsbāy with an Arabic introduction, along with a number of articles in Arabic based on the archival sources from the Mamluk period.[200] Although Darrāj was a professor of Islamic History at Cairo University (in Cairo University Islamic history includes the period from the rise of Islam to the end of the Fatimid period while the Ayyubid and Mamluk periods are considered part of Medieval history), his most important studies concern the history of the Mamluk period. His article on "Jam Sultan and International Diplomacy" concerns the decision of the Mamluks to grant refuge to the prince and pretender to the Ottoman throne Jam and the ensuing international controversy that this caused.[201] He also studied the *hisba* and its effect on Mamluk economic

---

al-Milkiyya fī al-Wathāʾiq al-ʿArabiyya; Muḥammad Ibrāhīm al-Sayyid, Al-Brūtukūl al-Khitāmī; ʿImād Abū Ghāzī, Dirāsa Diblūmātiyya.

195   Tawfīq Iskandar, *Tārīkh Miṣr fī Maḥfūẓāt al-Bunduqiyya.*

196   Tawfīq Iskandar, Nuẓum al-Muqāyaḍa.

197   Tawfīq Iskandar, *Buḥūth fī al-Tārīkh al-Iqtiṣādī* (trans.), introduction.

198   Ḥasan ʿAlī al-Ḥilwa, *Kitābā Waqf.*

199   He completed his doctoral thesis in the 1950s, but it was not published until the beginning of the following decade. Ahmad Darrag [Aḥmad Darrāj], L'Égypte sous le règne de Barsbay, 825–841/1422–1438.

200   Aḥmad Darrāj, Ḥujjat Waqf.

201   Aḥmad Darrāj, Jam Ṣulṭān.

life, the changes in Red Sea trade at the end of the Mamluk period, a study on Mamluks and Franks in the fifteenth century, and another on the documents of Dayr Sahyūn in Jerusalem.[202]

Muḥammad Muḥammad Amīn earned his PhD in 1972 with a thesis on the *waqfs* in Egypt during the Mamluk period, which he later published as a book.[203] Although ʿAbd al-Laṭīf Ibrāhīm was the first person to undertake the study of Mamluk *waqf* documents with his doctoral thesis on the *waqfs* of the sultan al-Ghūrī, Amīn's study is considered to be the first comprehensive study of the entire Mamluk *waqf* system and its influence on the society and economy of the period, as he did not study the *waqf* documents from a single reign but rather for the entire Mamluk period. Most of Amīn's subsequent work focused on the editing and publication of Arabic documents from the Mamluk period, especially documents of legal transactions that had never before been published. Examples are a *tafwīḍ* (partnership) document from the reign of Ṭūmān Bāy, a document of *isjāl ʿadāla* (attestation of good character for a witness) from the Mamluk period, and a *manshūr iqṭāʿī* (document for an *iqṭāʿ* grant) from the reign of al-Ghūrī which is the only surviving document of this kind from the medieval period.[204] He also published an abridged catalogue of the medieval documents in Cairo followed by an appendix in which he published nine new documents.[205]

Qāsim ʿAbduh Qāsim relied heavily on documentary evidence in his PhD thesis – later published as a book – on the non-Muslims in Egypt during the Middle Ages.[206] He also published documents from St. Catherine's Monastery and contributed a study on the importance of the monastery's archives as a source for social history.[207] Muṣṭafā Abū Shaʿīshaʿ had training both in history and in document studies. His works include a study on the marks used by notaries in the fifteenth century and a study of examples of documents from the Mamluk period.[208] There are also archeologists who contributed to the study of documents. Among them are ʿAbd al-Sattār ʿUthmān, who published a

---

202   Aḥmad Darrāj, Al-Ḥisba, Idem, Īḍāḥāt Jadīda; Idem, *Al-Mamālīk wa al-Faranj*; Idem, *Wathāʾiq Dayr Dayr Ṣaḥyūn*.

203   Muḥammad Muḥammad Amīn, *Al-Awqāf wa al-Ḥayāt al-Ijtimāʿiyya*.

204   Muḥammad Muḥammad Amīn, Tafwīḍ; Idem, Al-Shāhid al-Adl; Idem, Manshūr bi Manḥ Iqṭāʿ.

205   Muḥammad Muḥammad Amīn, *Fihrist*.

206   Qāsm ʿAbduh Qāsim, *Ahl al-Dhimma fī Miṣr*.

207   Qāsim ʿAbduh Qāsim, Nashr wa Taḥqīq Wathīqa min Wathāʾiq Dayr Sānt Kātrīn; Idem, Wathāʾiq Dayr Sānt Kātrīn Masdarān li al-Tārīkh al-Ijtimāʿī.

208   Muṣṭafā Abū Shaʿīshaʿ, Aʿlām al-Muwaththiqīn; Idem, Min al-Wathāʾiq al-ʿArabiyya.

document of Jamāl al-Dīn the Ustādar, and Rāshid Saʿad al-Qaḥṭānī's study on
the *waqf* documents of the sultan al-Ashraf Shaʿban for Mecca and Medina.[209]

Another example of the new information that the documents can offer to
better our understanding of the Mamluk period can be seen in the study of
ʿImād Abū Ghazī on the sale of lands by the treasury during the Circassian
Mamluk period.[210] This study is based on documents from the Mamluk period
as well as the registers for military stipends (*dafātir al-rizq al-jayshiyya*) and
the registers for *waqf* stipends (*dafātir al-rizq al-iḥbāsiyya*) which date from the
Ottoman period. The data for the military stipend registers derives from the
financial administration registers (*dafātir al-idāra al-māliyya*) of the Circassian
Mamluk period which were last recorded in 891 AH/1486 CE during the reign
of Qāyitbāy. The data for the registers of stipends of *waqfs* comes from the
cadastral survey registers (*dafātir al-tarbīʿ*) of 931 AH/1525 CE These documents
and registers provide new information which has changed the prevailing consensus about the supposed absence of private ownership of agricultural land
and its near total domination in one form or another by the state. This assumption had been based on information repeated in traditional sources such as the
chronicles, books of *fiqh*, and tax and administrative manuals. However, the
Mamluk documents and Ottoman registers paint a different picture. They confirm that the Circassian Mamluk period witnessed an increase in sale of state
property by the treasury. During this period, private ownership of farmlands
increased greatly in Egypt, resulting in the appearance of a new class of private
agricultural landowners during this period whose backbone was formed by the
awlād al-nās (descendants of Mamluks). The Ottoman occupation prevented
the full development of this class.[211]

Aḥmad al-Miṣrī's studies of the Mamluk period rely heavily on the documentary evidence as well. He has written about the Hafsid position towards
the Mamluk–Ottoman struggle, Qāyitbāy's *waqf* of al-Dashīsha al-Kubrā, the
litigation system during the mamluk period, and he has published unique
documents from the period.[212] Other key studies on the documents from the
Mamluk period are: Muḥammad Māhir Ḥammāda's study on political and
administrative documents of the Mamluk period; Muḥammad ʿIsā Ṣāliḥiyya's
work on the Ḥaram al-Sharīf documents from Jerusalem; Ḥayāt Nāṣir al-Ḥajjī's
study on the *waqf* system in the reign of al-Nāṣir Muḥammad b. Qalāwūn; and

---

209   Muḥammad ʿAbd al-Sattār ʿUthmān, *Wathīqa*; Rāshid Saʿd Rāshid al-Qaḥṭānī, *Awqāf*.

210   ʿImād Abū Ghazī, *Dirāsa Diblūmātiyya fī Wathāʾiq al-Bayʿ*.

211   ʿImād Abū Ghazī, *Taṭawwur al-Ḥiyāza al-Zirāʿiyya fī Miṣr fī ʿAṣr al-Mamālīk al-Jarākisa*;
      Idem, *Fī Tārīkh Miṣr al-Ijtimāʿī*.

212   Muḥammad al-Miṣrī, *Mawqif Banī Ḥafṣ*; Idem, *Min Wathāʾiq al-Maktaba al-Waṭaniyya bi
      Bārīs*; Idem, *Niẓām al-Taqāḍī*; Idem, *Wathīqat Taghyīr Shurūṭ*; Idem, *Min Daʿāwā al-Naṣb*.

Muḥammad al-ʿAnāqira and Fāṭima al-Barīdī's study on two *ijāzas* (certificates granted by teachers to pupils) for the judge Kamāl al-Dīn al-Nabulsī.[213] ʿUmar Jamāl from Sūhāj University has written about a decree of the sultan al-Ashraf Shaʿbān for the Frankish pilgrims and merchants in Jerusalem. He has also published a *waqf* document of Khawājā Sharaf al-Dīn Yūnis b. ʿAlī al-Ṣābūnī al-Ḥalabī and he has written about the date and fruit tree orchards of Mt. Sinai during the Mamluk period. The abovementioned works are just some examples of the important studies by historians and archeologists that were landmarks in the production of new knowledge due to their reliance on primary documents, however, they constitute merely a representative selection and by no means exhaust the full Arab contribution to the field of Mamluk archival studies.

14 Studies from Outside of the Academic Community

There are numerous studies on the Mamluk period written by scholars who were not formally connected to the academic world. The earliest of these studies may be a book written by Anwar Zaqalma entitled *The Mamluks in Egypt*.[214] The year of publication written in the book is 1995, but upon reading the book it is clear that it must have been written prior to 1936. The author talks about the system of *imtiyāzāt* (capitulations) which was not abolished until 1937, he refers to the Egyptian University rather than the later names of that institution (Fuʾād I University and then Cairo University), and the book contains texts that the author had published in 1919 in the journal *Al-Hilāl*. The book deals mostly with the foreign affairs of the Mamluk state. Zaqalma makes extensive use of the primary sources and he analyzes the history of the period with a critical spirit.

One of the most famous non-academic works which discussed Mamluk history in depth is Ṣubḥī Waḥīda's *On the Egyptian Question*.[215] Waḥīda served as secretary general of the Union of Egyptian Industries (*Ittiḥād al-Ṣināʿāt al-Miṣriyya*) at the beginning of the 1950s, when his book was published, and he died shortly thereafter. By the Egyptian Question he meant the problem of

---

213 Muḥammad Māhir Ḥammāda, *Al-Wathāʾiq al-Siyāsiyya wa al-Idāriyya*; Muḥammad ʿĪsā al-Ṣāliḥiyya, *Min Wathāʾiq al-Ḥaram al-Qudsī al-Sharīf*; Ḥayāt Nāṣir al-Ḥajjī, *Al-Sulṭān al-Nāṣir Muḥammad b. Qalāwūn wa Niẓām al-Waqf*; Muḥammad al-ʿAnāqira wa Fāṭima al-Rabīdī, *ʿIjāzatān*; ʿUmar Jamāl, *Marsūm al-Sulṭān al-Ashraf*; Idem, *Wathīqa Waqf al-Khawājā*; Idem, *Basātīn al-Nakhīl*.
214 Anwar Zaqalma, *Al-Mamālīk fī Miṣr*.
215 Ṣubḥī Waḥīda, *Fī Uṣūl al-Masʾala al-Miṣriyya*.

the British occupation of Egypt since 1882, however, the author attempts to get to the roots of the issue which he traces deep into the past, well before Egypt's collision with the West. A fundamental chapter in this book, entitled "The Mongol Rule", is devoted to the study of Egypt's economic condition during the Mamluk period. He attempts to link the disruptions caused by Mamluk rule to the severe economic decline which Egypt was suffering from in his time. In his view, many of Egypt's problems can be traced back to the Mamluk period. He analyzes the Mamluk phenomenon, the government, administration, and the condition of the Egyptian people during the Mamluk period. The book had a wide impact in cultural and political circles when it was published. Its popularity was due to the change of regime in Egypt that occurred when the Free Officers took power in 1952, but it enjoyed another wave of popularity in the mid-1970s, a time which saw the beginning of changes in the Egyptian political system, and it was reprinted following the January 2011 revolution.

Mention should also be made of the work of Aḥmad Ṣādiq Saʿd. Saʿd was one of the leaders of the Egyptian communist movement from the late 1930s onwards. In the 1970s he devoted his attention to the study of Egyptian history from the Marxist perspective. He adopted the concept of the Asiatic Mode of Production which Karl Marx had proposed in some of his writings on India and the pre-capitalist Eastern societies. Saʿd began by publishing his ideas in articles in the monthly journal *Al-Ṭalīʿa*. Then he widened his research and published a series of books in which he attempted to apply the Asiatic Mode of Production to Egyptian history. One of these books is *Egyptian Socio-Economic History in the Light of the Asiatic Mode of Production*, in which he devotes the tenth and final chapter to Egypt during the Ayyubid and Mamluk periods.[216] In this work he presents a new vision of Egyptian history, different from that of the traditional historiographical schools, and also from classical Marxism. He argues that the dominant mode of production in Egyptian history differed fundamentally from the Slave and Feudal modes of production. This Egyptian mode of production had two basic characteristics: a production base of peasant village communes and a centralized state that had economic tasks and possessed the society's revenue. Saʿd's book is one of the pioneering Arabic works in this field.

15   Final Observations

Two factors in the second half of the twentieth century contributed to the development of Mamluk studies. The first is the great effort which was made

---

216   Aḥmad Ṣādiq Saʿd, *Fī Ḍawʾ al-Namaṭ al-Āsiyāwī*, 383–509.

to edit Mamluk primary sources, thereby enabling researchers to study different aspects of this period. Editing of Mamluk sources began in the nineteenth century, but it made a great leap in the twentieth century. *Dār al-Kutub al-Miṣriyya* played a major role in the publication of these sources along with some of the academic departments in the Egyptian universities. The great editors of sources from the Mamluk period include: Muḥammad Muṣṭafā Ziyāda, Ḥasan Ḥabashī, Saʿīd ʿĀshūr, Muḥammad Muṣṭafā, Muḥammad Amīn, ʿAzīz Suryāl ʿAṭiyya, Jamāl al-Dīn al-Shayyāl, Ṣalāḥ al-Dīn al-Munajjid, ʿUmar ʿAbd al-Salām al-Tadmurī, Ayman Fuʾād al-Sayyid, and ʿAmr ʿAbd al-ʿAzīz Munīr.

The second factor was the discovery and availability of the surviving documents from the period, which number a few thousand in total. These documents shed light on previously obscure aspects of Mamluk history. There is no doubt that the main credit in recognizing the importance of these documents and utilizing them goes to ʿAbd al-Laṭīf Ibrāhīm, who began in the 1950s to establish a scientific foundation for the study, analysis, and understanding of the Mamluk documents.

It is important to note that in Cairo University Mamluk studies branched off from the general study of Islamic history. At the Egyptian University (now Cairo University) a chair in Islamic history was created along with a chair in the history of the Middle Ages. The latter was responsible for the history of medieval Europe, the history of the Crusades, and the history of the Ayyubid and Mamluk periods. From this time onwards the Ayyubid and Mamluk periods were studied together and they were separated from general Islamic history which, in the case of Egypt and Bilād al-Shām, ended with the fall of the Fatimid Caliphate. This division of Islamic history did not occur for any clear methodological reason but rather due to the competition that existed between the chairs. The situation did not repeat itself in the other Egyptian and Arab universities. Nevertheless, even in Cairo University some of the specialists in Mamluk history treated the period as if it were part of general Islamic history, while others who had earned their doctorates in the field of Mamluk history completely avoided Mamluk history in their later careers, such as Jamāl al-Dīn Surūr. Some of the professors who held chairs in Islamic history also wrote studies on the Mamluk period, including scholars such as Aḥmad Darrāj; Ḥasan Maḥmūd, in his study of foreign embassies to the late Mamluk state; Ḥusayn Muʾnis, who entered Mamluk studies through his specific field of the history of al-Andalus with a study on a Spanish embassy to the Mamluks; and both ʿAbd al-Munʿim Mājid and Maḥmūd Ismāʿīl ʿAbd al-Rāziq, who held professorships in Islamic history at ʿAyn Shams University.[217]

---

217 Ḥasan Aḥmad Maḥmūd, Al-Baʿthāt al-Diblūmāsiyya; Ḥusayn Muʾnis, Sifāra.

At the same time, a general trend arose in Egypt of studying Ayyubid and Mamluk history together due to the many shared features of the two states and especially because the first Mamluk state had its origins in the Ayyubid sultanate. The study of the Crusades was also closely linked to this field because most of the Crusades occurred during the Ayyubid and Mamluk periods.

Some scholars have also combined the study of Mamluk history with the study of Ottoman Egypt. They even consider the Ottoman period to be the "Third Mamluk Period" (after the Baḥrī/Kipchak and Burjī/Circassian Mamluk periods) due to the continued dominance of Mamluk amirs in Egypt under the shadow of the Ottoman government. Some scholars consider the period from the middle of the thirteenth century until the end of the eighteenth century to be the "Mamluk–Ottoman Period." The most famous scholar to hold this view was Louis ʿAwaḍ, a professor of English literature who later turned to the study of Egyptian intellectual history with his book on the foreign influences in modern Egyptian literature.[218] In an earlier study, Anwar Zaqalma divided the Mamluk Age into four periods: the Baḥrī Mamluks, the Circassian Mamluks, the Mamluk Begs (or the Mamluks under Ottoman rule), and the Mamluks of Muḥammad ʿAlī (al-mamālīk al-ʿAlawiyya). Zaqalma argued that Muḥammad ʿAlī did not completely exterminate the Mamluks in the Massacre of the Citadel, but rather he continued to use them as the Ottomans had done before him. According to Zaqalma, the role of the Mamluks in Egyptian life continued until the revolution of Aḥmad ʿUrābī in 1882 which resulted in their final disappearance from the political scene.[219]

Some of the studies concerned with the history of the sixteenth century combine the history of the Circassian Mamluks with the beginning of the Ottoman period. An example is a study by Aḥmad Fuʾād al-Mutawallī, professor of Turkish at ʿAyn Shams University, on the Ottoman occupation of Syria and Egypt.[220] In this work he relies on a large number of Arabic and Turkish documents, some of which he has published for the first time. He confirms the existence of relations between Khayr-Bak, the Mamluk governor of Aleppo, and the Ottomans years before the Ottoman invasion. Another scholar who has treated Circassian Mamluk and early Egyptian Ottoman history together is Muḥammad Anīs, Professor of Modern History at Cairo University, in his studies of the historians who were alive at the time of the Ottoman invasion and occupation of Egypt and Bilād al-Shām.[221]

---

218   Louis ʿAwaḍ, Al-Muʾaththirāt.
219   Anwar Zaqalma, *Al-Mamālīk fī Miṣr*, 25–30.
220   Aḥmad Fuʾād Mutawallī, *Al-Fatḥ al-ʿUthmānī*.
221   Muḥammad Anīs, Madrasat al-Tārīkh al-Miṣrī fī al-ʿAṣr al-ʿUthmānī.

A last observation is that Mamluk studies are not limited to history departments. They have also appeared in departments of Arabic language and literature, sociology, and philosophy, and later in the departments of archival and document studies, as well as in the departments of Islamic archeology, and they have even extended into departments of political science.

Translated by Amar S. Baadj

Bibliography

Abāẓa, Fārūq ʿUthmān, *Athar Taḥawwul al-Tijāra al-ʿĀlamiyya ilā Ṭarīq Raʾs al-Rajāʾ al-Ṣāliḥ ʿalā Miṣr wa ʿĀlam al-Baḥr al-Mutawassiṭ athnāʾ al-Qarn al-Sādis ʿAshar*, Cairo, 1985.

Al-ʿAbbādī, Aḥmad Mukhtār, *Qiyām Dawlat al-Mamālīk al-Ūlā fī Miṣr wa Shām*, Beirut, 1969.

ʿAbbās, Iḥsān, *Tārīkh Bilād al-Shām fī ʿAṣr al-Mamālīk (648/1250–923/1517)*, Yarmuk, 1998.

ʿAbdallāh, Saḥar, Al-Jawārī fī ʿAṣr al-Mamālīk: Dirāsa Tārīkhiyya, *Majallat al-Ustādh* 208, no. 1 (2014).

ʿAbd al-ʿAzīz, Nabīl, Khazāʾin al-Silāḥ wa Muḥtawayātuhā ʿalā ʿAṣr al-Ayyūbiyyin wa al-Mamālīk, *Al-Majalla al-Tārikhiyya al-Miṣriyya* (1976), 107–154.

ʿAbd al-ʿAzīz, Nabīl, *Al-Khayl wa Riyāḍātuhā fī ʿAṣr Salāṭīn al-Mamālīk*, Cairo, 1986.

ʿAbd al-ʿAzīz, Nabīl, *Al-Maṭbakh al-Sulṭānī fī ʿAṣr al-Ayyūbiyyin wa al-Mamālīk*, Cairo, 1989.

ʿAbd al-Ḥāfiẓ, ʿAbdallāh ʿAṭiyya, *Muʿjam Asmāʾ Salāṭīn wa Umarāʾ al-Mamālīk fī Miṣr wa al-Shām min khilāl mā Warida ʿalā ʿAmāʾirihim wa fī al-Wathāʾiq wa al-Maṣādir al-Tārīkhiyya*, Cairo, n.d.

ʿAbd al-Jawād, Laylā, ʿAlāqat al-Dawlat al-Bīzanṭiyya bi Salṭanat al-Mamālīk al-Baḥriyya (659–874h./1361–1382m.), *Majallat Kulliyat al-Ādāb – Jāmiʿat al-Qāhira*, 46–47 (1986), 57–131.

ʿAbd al-Karīm, Aḥmad ʿIzzat, *Ḥawla Tārīkh al-Taʿlīm fī ʿAṣr Muḥammad ʿAlī* (Al-Taʿlīm fī Miṣr fī al-Qarn al-Tāsiʿ ʿAshar 1), Cairo, 2011.

ʿAbd al-Rāziq, Maḥmūd Ismāʿīl, *Nihāyat Usṭūra: Naẓariyāt Ibn Khaldūn Muqtabisa min Rasāʾil Ikhwān al-Ṣafāʾ*, Cairo, 1999.

ʿAbd al-Rāziq, Muṣṭafā, Fī Rithāʾ ʿAlī Bahjat, *Majallat al-Majmaʿ al-ʿIlmī al-Miṣrī* 6 (1923–24), 103–104.

ʿAbd al-Sayyid, Ḥakīm Amīn, *Qiyām Dawlat al-Mamālīk al-Thāniya*, Cairo, 1967.

ʿAbduh, Muḥammad ʿAbd al-Naʿīm Muḥammad, Azmat al-Luḥūm wa Atharuhā ʿalā al-Mujtamaʿ al-Miṣrī fī ʿAṣr Dawlat al-Mamālīk al-Jarākisa, *Ḥawliyyāt Markaz al-Buḥūth wa al-Dirāsāt al-Tārīkhiyya – Jāmiʿat al-Qāhira* (October, 2011).

Abū Ghāzī, Ḍiyāʾ, and ʿImād Abū Ghāzī [Emad Abou-Ghazi], *ʿAlī Bahjat 1858–1924*, Cairo, 1976.

Abū Ghāzī, ʿImād [Abou-Ghazi, Emad], Dirāsa Diblūmātiyya fī Wathāʾiq al-Bayʿ min Amlāk Bayt al-Māl fī ʿAṣr al-Mamālīk al-Jarākisa, PhD dissertation, Cairo University, 1975.

Abū Ghāzī, ʿImād [Abou-Ghazi, Emad], Taṭawwur al-Ḥiyāza al-Zirāʿiyya fī Miṣr fī ʿAṣr al-Mamālīk al-Jarākisa, *al-Majalla al-Tārīkhiyya al-Miṣriyya* 39 (1996).

Abū Ghāzī, ʿImād [Abou-Ghazi, Emad], *Fī Tārīkh Miṣr al-Ijtimāʿī – Taṭawwur al-Ḥiyāza al-Zirāʿiyya Zaman al-Mamālīk al-Jarākisa*, Cairo, 2000.

Abū Ghāzī, ʿImād [Abou-Ghazi, Emad], Mulāḥaẓāt ʿalā Taṭawwur al-Lugha fī ʿAṣr al-Mamālīk: Dirāsa fī Ḍawʾ al-Wathāʾiq al-Qānūniyya, in Qāsim ʿAbduh Qāsim (ed.), *Bayn al-Tārīkh wa al-Adab al-Shaʿbī*, Cairo, 2013.

Abū Ghāzī, ʿImād [Abou-Ghazi, Emad], Ruwwād al-Dirāsāt al-Akādīmiyya fī Majāl al-Wathāʾiq, *Majallat al-Dirāsāt al-Tārīkhiyya wa al-Ḥaḍariyya al-Miṣriyya* 1, no. 1 (2016), 337–361.

Abū Khadīja, Hanādī Ibrāhīm, Al-Marʾa fī Bilād al-Shām khilāl al-ʿAṣr al-Mamlūkī, PhD dissertation, King ʿAbd al-ʿAzīz University, 2009.

Abū Shaʿīshaʿ, Muṣṭafā, Min al-Wathāʾiq al-ʿArabiyya fī al-ʿUṣūr al-Wusṭā Tawkīl Sharʿī, *Majallat al-Maktabāt wa al-Maʿlūmāt al-ʿArabiyya* 1, no. 3 (1981), 108–127.

Abū Shaʿīshaʿ, Muṣṭafā, Aʿlām al-Muwaththiqīn fī al-Qarn al-Tāsiʿ al-Hijrī, *Majallat al-Maktabāt wa al-Maʿlūmāt al-ʿArabiyya* 3, no. 1 (1983), 55–128.

Aḥmad, Aḥmad ʿAbd al-Rāziq, Al-Runūk fī ʿAṣr Salāṭīn al-Mamālīk, *Al-Majalla al-Tārīkhiyya al-Miṣriyya* 21 (1974), 67–116.

Aḥmad, Aḥmad ʿAbd al-Rāziq, Al-ʿAlāqāt al-Usriyya fī al-Muṣṭalaḥ al-Mamlūkī, *Al-Majalla al-Tārīkhiyya al-Miṣriyya* 23 (1976), 155–181.

Aḥmad, Aḥmad ʿAbd al-Rāziq, *Al-Runūk al-Islāmiyya*, Cairo, 1978.

Aḥmad, Aḥmad ʿAbd al-Rāziq, *Al-Badhl wa al-Barṭala Zaman Salāṭīn al-Mamālīk: Dirāsa ʿan al-Rashwa*, Cairo, 1979.

Aḥmad, Aḥmad Ramaḍān, *Tārīkh Fann al-Qitāl al-Baḥrī fī al-Baḥr al-Mutawassiṭ: al-ʿAṣr al-Wasīṭ*, Cairo, n.d.

Al-Ahwānī, ʿAbd al-ʿAzīz, Sifāra Siyāsiyya min Gharnāṭa ilā al-Qāhira fī al-Qarn al-Tāsiʿ al-Hijrī (Sana 844h.), *Majallat Kulliyyat al-Ādāb – Jāmiʿat al-Qāhira* 16, no. 1 (May 1954), 95–121.

ʿAlī, ʿAlī al-Sayyid, Al-Fanāʾ al-Kabīr wa al-Mawt al-Aswad fī al-Qarn al-Rābiʿ ʿAshar Mīlādī – Dirāsa Muqārana bayn al-Sharq wa al-Gharb, *Al-Majalla al-Tārīkhiyya al-Miṣriyya* 33 (1986), 149–188.

ʿAlī, ʿAlī al-Sayyid, Al-Qāhira fī ʿUyūn al-Raḥḥāla al-Ūrūbiyyin fī al-Qarn al-Rābiʿ ʿAshar wa al-Qarn al-Khāmis ʿAshar, *Fikr* 13 (October 1988), 66–98.

ʿAlī, ʿAlī al-Sayyid, *Buḥūth fī al-Tārīkh al-Ijtimāʿī fī al-ʿAṣr al-Mamlūkī*, Cairo, 2014.

ʿAlī, ʿAlī al-Sayyid and Qāsim ʿAbduh Qāsim, *Al-Ayyūbiyyin wa al-Mamālīk*, Cairo, 1995.

Amīn, Muḥammad Muḥammad, *Al-Awqāf wa al-Ḥayāt al-Ijtimāʿiyya fī Miṣr 648–923 h./1250–1517m. Dirāsa Tārikhiyya Wathāʾiqiyya*, Cairo, 1980.

Amīn, Muḥammad Muḥammad, Tafwīḍ min ʿAṣr al-ʿĀdil Ṭūmān Bāy Ṣāniʿ al-Salāṭīn, *Al-Majalla al-Tārīkhiyya al-Miṣriyya* 27 (1981), 55–80.

Amīn, Muḥammad Muḥammad, *Fihrist Wathāʾiq al-Qāhira ḥattā Nihāyat ʿAṣr Salāṭīn al-Mamālīk*, Cairo, 1981.

Amīn, Muḥammad Muḥammad, Al-Shāhid al-ʿAdl fī al-Qaḍāʾ al-Islāmī mʿa Nashr wa Taḥqīq Isjāl ʿAdāla min ʿAṣr Salāṭīn al-Mamālīk, *Hawliyyāt Islāmiyya* 18 (1982), 1–14.

Amīn, Muḥammad Muḥammad, Manshūr bi Manḥ Iqṭāʿ min ʿAṣr al-Sulṭān al-Ghūrī, *Hawliyyāt Islāmiyya* 19 (1983), 1–18.

ʿAmmāra, ʿAllāwa [Amara, Allaoua], Khamsūn Sana min al-Baḥth fī al-Tārīkh al-Wasīṭ bi al-Jāmiʿa al-Jazāʾiriyya (1962–2012), *Mawāqif-Majallat al-Dirāsāt wa al-Buḥūth fī al-Mujtamaʿ wa al-Tārīkh* 7 (December 2012).

Al-ʿAnāqira, Muḥammad Maḥmūd, *Al-Ḥayāt al-Iqtiṣādiyya fī al-Ḥijāz fī ʿAṣr Dawlat al-Mamālīk (648–923h./1250–1517m.)*, Riyadh, 2006.

Al-ʿAnāqira, Muḥammad Maḥmūd, Madāris al-Quds fī al-ʿAṣr al-Mamlūkī (648–923 h./ 1250–1517m.), *Majallat Waqāʾiʿ Tārīkhiyya* (2006).

Al-ʿAnāqira, Muḥammad Maḥmūd, Ṭuruq al-Ḥajj wa Masālikuhā fī al-ʿAṣr al-Mamlūkī, in *Buḥūth wa Dirāsāt Muhdā ilā al-Ustādh al-Duktūr Ṣāliḥ Darādaka bi Munāsabat Bulūghihi Sinn al-Sabʿīn*, Amman, 2009.

Al-ʿAnāqira, Muḥammad Maḥmūd, *Al-Madāris fī Miṣr fī ʿAṣr Dawlat al-Mamālīk*, Cairo, 2016.

Al-ʿAnāqira, Muḥammad Maḥmūd, and Fāṭima al-Rabīdī, Ijāzatān ʿIlmiyyatān li al-Qāḍī Kamāl al-Dīn al-Nablusī fī al-ʿAhd al-Mamlūkī, *Majallat Waqāʾiʿ Tārīkhiya* 19 (2013).

Al-ʿAnāqira, Muḥammad Maḥmūd, Al-Dawr al-ʿIlmī li Riwāq al-Maghāriba fī Jāmiʿ al-Azhar fī al-ʿAṣr al-Mamlūkī, *Majallat al-Muʾarrikh al-Miṣrī* (2014).

Al-ʿAnbakī, Anwār Jāsim Ḥasan, Al-ʿAlāqāt al-Khārijiyya li Dawlat al-Mamālīk maʿa Bilād al-Maghrib (660/1262–923/1517), PhD dissertation, al-Mustanṣiriyya University, 2007.

Anīs, Muḥammad, Madrasat al-Tārīkh al-Miṣrī min al-ʿAṣr al-ʿUthmānī, in *Abḥāth al-Nadwa al-Duwaliyya li Tārīkh al-Qāhira: Mārs–Abrīl 1969*, iii, Cairo 1971, 1079–1156.

ʿArab, Muḥammad Ṣābir, ed., *Ibn Khaldūn fī Dirāsāt ʿAṣriyya*, Cairo, 2007.

Al-Aʿraj, ʿAbd al-Raḥmān, Al-ʿAlāqāt al-Siyāsiyya bayna al-Dawlat al-Ḥafṣiyya wa al-Mamālīk al-Baḥriyya bayn al-Qarnayn 7–8 h./13–14m., *Dawriyyat Kān al-Tārīkhiyya* 29 (September 2015), 61–67.

ʿArār, Shafīq ʿAwwād ʿAbd al-Karīm, Sukkān Filasṭīn fī al-ʿAhd al-Mamlūkī, MA dissertation, Birzeit University, 2004.

Al-'Arīnī, Al-Sayyid al-Bāz, Al-Fāris al-Mamlūkī, *Al-Majalla al-Tārīkhiyya al-Miṣriyya* 5 (1956), 47–71.

Al-'Arīnī, Al-Sayyid al-Bāz, Al-Fāris al-Mamlūkī, Al-Iqṭā' fī al-Sharq al-Awsaṭ mundhu al-Qarn al-Sābi' ilā al-Qarn al-Thānī 'Ashar al-Mīlādī, *Ḥawliyyāt Kulliyyat al-Ādāb – Jāmi'at 'Ayn Shams* 2 (1957), 113–148.

Arslān, Shakīb, *Tārīkh Ibn Khaldūn*, Cairo, 1936.

'Āshūr, Sa'id 'Abd al-Fattāḥ, Al-Duktūr Muḥammad Muṣṭafā Ziyāda, *Majallat Kulliyyat al-Ādāb* 4, (n.d.), 3–14.

'Āshūr, Sa'id 'Abd al-Fattāḥ, *Miṣr fī 'Aṣr Dawlat al-Mamālīk al-Baḥriyya*, n.p., 1959.

'Āshūr, Sa'id 'Abd al-Fattāḥ, *Al-Mujtamā' al-Miṣrī fī 'Āsr Salāṭīn al-Mamālīk*, Cairo, 1962.

'Āshūr, Sa'id 'Abd al-Fattāḥ, *Al-'Āṣr al-Mamālīkī fī Miṣr wa al-Shām*, Cairo, 1965.

'Āshūr, Sa'id 'Abd al-Fattāḥ, Ba'ḍ Aḍwā' Jadīda 'alā al-'Alāqāt bayn Miṣr wa al-Ḥabasha fī al-'Uṣūr al-Wusṭā, in *Al-Majalla al-Tārīkhiyya al-Miṣriyya* 14 (1968), 1–43.

'Āshūr, Sa'id 'Abd al-Fattāḥ, Ṣuwar min Mujtama' al-Qāhira fī al-'Uṣūr al-Wusṭā, *Al-Majalla al-Tārīkhiyya al-Miṣriyya* 18 (1971), 161–171.

'Āshūr, Sa'id 'Abd al-Fattāḥ, *Miṣr wa al-Shām fī 'Aṣr al-Ayyūbiyyin wa al-Mamālīk*, Cairo, 1972.

'Āshūr, Sa'id 'Abd al-Fattāḥ, Al-Fallāḥ wa al-Iqṭā' fī 'Aṣr al-Ayyūbiyyin wa al-Mamālīk, in *Al-Fallāḥ wa al-Arḍ 'alā Marr al-'Uṣūr*, Cairo, 1974, 211–224.

'Āshūr, Sa'id 'Abd al-Fattāḥ, *Al-Ayyūbiyyin wa al-Mamālīk fī Miṣr wa al-Shām*, Cairo, 1976.

'Āshūr, Sa'id 'Abd al-Fattāḥ, *Buḥūth wa Dirāsāt fī Tārīkh al-'Uṣūr al-Wusṭā*, Beirut, 1977.

'Āshūr, Sa'id 'Abd al-Fattāḥ, Al-Tadahwur al-Iqtiṣādī fī Dawlat Salāṭīn al-Mamālīk fī Ḍaw' Kitābāt Ibn Iyās, in *Ibn Iyās: Dirāsāt wa Buḥūth*, Cairo, 1977, 13–88.

'Āshūr, Sa'id 'Abd al-Fattāḥ, *Tārīkh al-'Alāqāt bayn al-Sharq wa al-Gharb fī al-'Uṣūr al-Wusṭā*, Cairo, 2003.

Al-Asṭal, Muḥammad Zāri', Al-Ḥayāṭ al-Fikriyya wa al-Thaqāfiyya fī Madīnat al-Quds fī al-'Ahd al-Mamlūkī (648/1250–922/1516), PhD dissertation, The Islamic University of Gaza, 2014.

'Aṭā', 'Uthmān 'Alī, *Majālis al-Shūrā fī 'Aṣr Salāṭīn al-Mamālīk*, Cairo, 2008.

'Aṭiyya, Sulaymān, Siyāsat al-Mamālīk fī al-Baḥr al-Aḥmar ḥattā Nihāyat 'Aṣr al-Sulṭān Barsbāy (1250–1428), PhD dissertation, Cairo University, 1959.

'Awaḍ, Luwīs, *Al-Mu'aththirāt al-Ajnabiyya fī al-Adab al-'Arabiyy al-Ḥadīth*, Cairo, 1963. This work was reprinted as *Tārīkh al-Fikr al-Miṣrī al-Ḥadīth min al-Ḥamla al-Fransiyya ilā 'Aṣr Ismā'īl*, Cairo, 1987.

Badawī, 'Abd al-Raḥmān, *Mu'allafāt Ibn Khaldūn*, Cairo, 1962.

Bahjat, 'Alī [Atharī], *Al-Bīmāristān al-Manṣūrī, Majallat al-Mawsū'āt* 1, no. 1 (April 11, 1899), 329–339.

Bahjat, 'Alī [Atharī], Aḥmad b. 'Alī al-Qalqashandī wa Kitābuhu Ṣubḥ al-A'shā, *Majallat al-Mawsū'āt* 4, no. 2 (December 1899), 111–123.

Bahjat, ʿAlī [Atharī], Nubdha Jughrāfiyya Tārīkhiyya fī mā Kānat ʿalayhi Miṣr fī ʿAhd Dawlat al-Mamālīk al-Barriyya wa al-Baḥriyya, *Majallat al-Mawsūʿāt* 7, no. 2 (February 1, 1900), 198–210.

Bahjat, ʿAlī [Atharī], Al-Kharāj fī Miṣr, *Majallat al-Mawsūʿāt* 14, no. 2 (May 16, 1900), 433–444.

Baḥr, Majdī ʿAbd al-Rashīd, *Al-Qarya al-Miṣriyya fī ʿAṣr Salāṭīn al-Mamālīk*, Cairo, 1999.

Bakhīt, Muḥammad ʿAdnān, *Mamlakat al-Karak fī al-ʿAhd al-Mamlūkī*, Amman, 1976.

Bakīr, Marwān ʿAbd al-Qādir, Al-Madīna al-Filasṭīniyya fī ʿAhd al-Mamālīk, MA dissertation, Birzeit University, 2005.

Bāqa, Rashīd, Al-ʿAlāqāt al-Tijāriyya bayna Flūrinsā wa Salṭanat al-Mamālīk fī al-Qarn al-Khāmis ʿAshar al-Mīlādī, MA dissertation, Cairo University, 1989.

Al-Baqlī, Muḥammad Qandīl, *Al-Awzān al-Mūsīqiyya fī Azjāl Ibn Sūdūn*, Cairo, 1972.

Al-Baqlī, Muḥammad Qandīl, *Al-Taʿrīf bi Muṣṭalaḥāt Ṣubḥ al-Aʿshā*, Cairo, 1983.

Al-Bayyūmī, Ismāʿīl, *Al-Nuẓum al-Māliyya fī Miṣr wa al-Shām Zaman Salāṭīn al-Mamālīk*, Cairo, 1998.

Bilaʿraj, ʿAbd al-Raḥmān, ʿAlāqāt Duwal al-Maghrib al-Islāmī bi Duwal al-Mamālīk Siyāsiyyan wa Thaqāfiyyan bayn al-Qarnayn al-Sābiʿ wa al-Tāsiʿ al-Hijrīyayn, PhD dissertation, Tlemcen, 2013.

Bilsurūr, Rashīda, *Markaz Tijārī fī Miṣr al-Suflā: Al-Iskandariyya khilāl al-ʿAhd al-Mamlūkī*, Tunis, 2007.

Binmīlād, Luṭfī [Ben Miled, Lotfi], *Ifrīqiyyā wa al-Mashriq al-Mutawassaṭī min Awāsiṭ al-Qarn 5h./11 m. ilā Maṭlaʿ al-Qarn 10 h./16m.: Waqāʾiʿ al-Infiṣāl wa Taḥaddiyāt al-Ittiṣāl*, Tunis, 2011.

Būḥadība, ʿAbd al-Wahhāb, Mūnīra Chapoutot, ʿAlā Khuṭā Ibn Khaldūn, Tunis, 2006.

Būtashīsh, Ibrāhīm al-Qādirī [Boutchich, Brahim El Kadiri], Hal ʿArafa al-Mujtamaʿ al-ʿArabī al-Iqṭāʿ?, *Al-Waḥda* 57 (June 1989), 98–109.

Al-Dabīkī, Al-Sayyid Ṣalāḥ, *Awlād al-Nās fī ʿAṣr Salāṭīn al-Mamālīk (648–923h./1250–1517m.)*, Cairo, 2016.

Dahmān, Muḥammad Aḥmad, Al-ʿIrāk bayn al-Mamālīk wa al-Atrāk, in *Al-Tārīkh wa al-Āthār: al-Ḥalqa al-Dirāsiyya al-Ūlā (al-Qāhira 4–9 Fabrāyir 1961)*, Cairo, 1961, 185–191.

Dahmān, Muḥammad Aḥmad, *Muʿjam al-Alfāẓ al-Tārikhiyya fī al-ʿAṣr al-Mamlūkī*, Beirut and Damascus, 1990.

Darrāj, Aḥmad [Darrag, Ahmad], Jam Ṣulṭān wa al-Diblūmāsiyya al-Duwaliyya, *Al-Majalla al-Tārikhiyya al-Miṣriyya* 8 (1959), 201–242.

Darrāj, Aḥmad [Darrag, Ahmad], *L'Egypte sous le Règne de Barsbay 825–841 / 1422–1438*, Damascus, 1961.

Darrāj, Aḥmad [Darrag, Ahmad], *Al-Mamālīk wa al-Faranj fī al-Qarn al-Tāsiʿ al-Hijrī al-Khāmis ʿAshar Mīlādī*, Cairo, 1961.

Darrāj, Aḥmad [Darrag, Ahmad], *Ḥujjat Waqf al-Ashraf Barsbāy*, Cairo, 1963.

Darrāj, Aḥmad [Darrag, Ahmad], Al-Ḥisba wa Atharuhā ʿalā al-Ḥayāt al-Iqtiṣādiyya fī Miṣr al-Mamlūkiyya, Al-Majalla al-Tārīkhiyya al-Miṣriyya 14 (1968), 109–142.

Darrāj, Aḥmad [Darrag, Ahmad], Īḍāḥāt Jadīda ʿan al-Taḥawwul fī Tijārat al-Baḥr al-Aḥmar mundhu Maṭlaʿ al-Qarn al-Tāsiʿ al-Hijrī, in Al-Muḥāḍarāt al-ʿĀmma li al-Jamʿiyya al-Miṣriyya li al-Dirāsāt al-Tārīkhiyya, Al-Mawsim al-Thānī 1967–1968, Cairo, 1968, 185–220.

Darrāj, Aḥmad [Darrag, Ahmad], Wathāʾiq Dayr Ṣahyūn bi al-Quds al-Sharīf, Cairo, 1968.

Al-Dasūqī, Wāʾil Ibrāhīm, Al-Tārīkh al-Thaqāfī li Miṣr al-Ḥadītha – al-Muʾassasāt al-ʿIlmiyya wa al-Thaqāfiyya fī al-Qarn al-Tāsiʿ ʿAshar, Cairo, 2012.

Dirāsāt ʿan al-Maqrīzī: Majmūʿat Abḥāth al-Ḥalqa al-Dirāsiyya ʿan al-Maqrīzī, Cairo, 1971.

Al-Dawsirī, Shaykha bint Muḥammad, Awqāf al-Nisāʾ fī Bilād al-Shām wa Atharuhā fī al-Ḥayāt al-ʿĀmma fī al-ʿAṣr al-Mamlūkī: Dirāsa Tārīkhiyya Miʿmāriyya, Riyadh, 2006.

Fahīm, Nadīm Aḥmad, Al-Fann al-Ḥarbī li al-Jaysh al-Miṣrī fī al-ʿAṣr al-Mamlūkī al-Baḥrī, Cairo, 1983.

Fahmī, Naʿīm Zakī, Ṭuruq al-Tijāra al-Duwaliyya wa Maḥaṭṭātuhā bayna al-Sharq wa al-Gharb Awākhir al-ʿUṣūr al-Wusṭā, Cairo, 1973.

Al-Fiqī, Muḥammad Kāmil, Al-Adab al-ʿArabī fī al-ʿAṣr al-Mamlūkī, Cairo, 1983.

Ghawānmah, Yūsuf Darwīsh, Al-Tārīkh al-Siyāsī li Sharq al-Urdunn fī al-ʿAṣr al-Mamlūkī al-Awwal: al-Mamālik al-Baḥriyya, Amman, 1982.

Ḥabashī, Ḥasan, Al-Iḥtikār al-Mamlūkī wa ʿAlāqatuhu bi al-Ḥālat al-Ṣiḥḥiyya, Ḥawliyyāt Kulliyyat al-Ādāb – Jāmiʿat ʿAyn Shams 9 (1964), 133–157.

Ḥabashī, Ḥasan, Hujūm al-Qabāriṣa ʿalā al-Iskandariyya 767/1365 min Nuṣūṣ Jadīda li al-Nuwayrī, Al-Majalla al-Tārīkhiyya al-Miṣriyya 15 (1965), 1–35.

Al-Ḥadīdī, Fāʿiz ʿAlī and Al-Lahībī, Fatḥī Sālim Ḥamīdī, Jawānib min al-Ḥayāt al-Siyāsiyya wa al-Iqtiṣādiyya wa al-Ijtimāʿiyya fī al-ʿAṣr al-Mamlūkī: Tafsīr Jadīd, Mosul, 2014.

Al-Ḥajjī, Ḥayāt Nāṣir, Al-ʿAlāqāt bayn Salṭanat al-Mamālīk wa al-Mamālik al-Isbāniyya fī al-Qarnayn al-Thāmin wa al-Tāsiʿ al-Hijrī/ al-Rābiʿ ʿAshar wa al-Khāmis ʿAshar al-Mīlādī: Dirāsa wa Wathāʾiq, Kuwait, 1980.

Al-Ḥajjī, Ḥayāt Nāṣir, Al-Amīr Tankīz al-Ḥusāmī Naʾib al-Shām fī Fatra min 712–741 h./ 1312–1340 m., Ḥawliyyāt Kulliyyat al-Ādāb – Jāmiʿat al-Kuwayt 1, no. 4 (1980).

Al-Ḥajjī, Ḥayāt Nāṣir, Aḥwāl al-ʿĀmma fī Ḥukm al-Mamālīk 678–741 h./ 1279–1382m. Dirāsa fī al-Jawānib al-Siyāsiyya wa al-Iqtiṣādiyya wa al-Ijtimāʿiyya, Kuwait, 1984.

Al-Ḥajjī, Ḥayāt Nāṣir, Ṣuwar min al-Ḥaḍāra al-ʿArabiyya al-Islāmiyya fī Salṭanat al-Mamālīk, Kuwait, 1992.

Al-Ḥajjī, Ḥayāt Nāṣir, Al-Sulṭa wa al-Mujtamaʿ fī Salṭanat al-Mamālīk Fatrat Ḥukm al-Mamālīk al-Baḥriyya min Sana 661/1262 ilā Sana 784/1382 Dirāsa Tārīkhiyya

Wathāʾiqiyya fī Waqāʾiʿ al-Mumārisāt al-Mukhtalifa al-Sulṭāniyya wa al-Amīriyya, Kuwait, 1997.

Al-Ḥajjī, Ḥayāt Nāṣir, *Al-Sulṭān al-Nāṣir Muḥammad b. Qalāwūn wa Niẓām al-Waqf fī ʿAhdihi maʿa Taḥqīq wa Dirāsat Waqf Siryāqūs*, Maktabat al-Fallāḥ, n.d.

Ḥammād, Najlāʾ Muḥammad Raḥūma, *Al-ʿAlāqāt bayna Miṣr wa al-Maghrib fī ʿAhd Salāṭīn al-Mamālīk*, Alexandria, 2011.

Ḥammāda, Ibrāhīm, ed., *Khayyāl al-Ẓill wa Tamthīliyyāt Ibn Dāniyāl*, Cairo, 1963.

Ḥammāda, Muḥammad Māhir, *Al-Wathāʾiq al-Siyāsiyya wa al-Idāriyya li al-ʿAṣr al-Mamlūkī (656–922/1258–1516) Dirāsa wa Nuṣūṣ*, Beirut, 1980.

Ḥammūd, Sūzī, *Lubnān fī al-ʿAṣr al-Wāsiṭ mundhu al-ʿAhd al-Rāshidī ilā Nihāyat ʿAhd al-Mamālīk (648/1250–923/1517)*, Beirut, 2009.

Ḥammūd, Sūzī, *Al-Fāṭimiyyūn wa al-Zankiyyūn wa al-Ayyūbiyyūn wa al-Mamālīk wa Ṣirāʿuhum ḥawl al-Ṣulṭa fī al-Mashriq al-ʿArabī (362/973–923/1517)*, Beirut, 2010.

Ḥamza, ʿAbd al-Laṭīf, *Al-Ḥarakat al-Fikriyya fī Miṣr fī al-ʿAṣrayn al-Ayyūbī wa al-Mamlūkī al-Awwal*, Cairo, 1947.

Ḥamza, ʿAbd al-Laṭīf, *Al-Adab al-Miṣrī min Qiyām al-Dawlat al-Ayyūbiyya ilā Majīʾ al-Ḥamlat al-Fransiyya*, Cairo, n.d.

Ḥamza, Hānī, *Miṣr al-Mamlūkiyya: Qirāʾa Jadīda*, 2 vols., Cairo, 2012–2014.

Ḥannā, Zaynab Muḥammad Maḥfūẓ, Al-Taṭawwur al-Diblūmātī li Marāsim Dīwān al-Inshāʾ bi Dayr Sānt Kātrīn min al-Qarn al-Khāmis ilā al-Qarn al-ʿĀshir al-Hijrī, MA dissertation, Cairo University, 1977.

Ḥasan, ʿAbd al-Ghanī, *Jurjī Zīdān*, Cairo, 1970.

Ḥasan, ʿAlī Ibrāhīm, Arāʾ fī Tārīkh Dawlat al-Mamālīk al-Baḥriyya, *Majallat Kulliyyat al-Ādāb – Jāmiʿat Fuʾād al-Awwal* 7, no. 2 (1944), 69–87.

Ḥasan, ʿAlī Ibrāhīm, Al-Jaysh wa al-Baḥriyya fī ʿAṣr al-Mamālīk, *Rasāʾil Idārat al-Shuʾūn al-ʿĀmma bi Wizārat al-Difāʿ al-Waṭanī* 53 (1944).

Ḥasan, ʿAlī Ibrāhīm, Akhṭar al-Majāʿāt fī Miṣr mundhu ʿAhd al-Farāʿina ilā Nihāyat ʿAṣr al-Mamālīk, *Majallat al-Kātib* (June, 1946).

Ḥasan, ʿAlī Ibrāhīm, *Miṣr fī al-ʿUṣūr al-Wusṭā*, Cairo, 1949.

Ḥasan, ʿAlī Ibrāhīm, *Tārīkh al-Mamālīk al-Baḥriyya*, Cairo, 1967.

Ḥasanayn, Fuʾād, Muḥammad b. Dāniyāl, *Majallat al-Thaqāfa* 208, 209, 210 (1942–1943).

Al-Hayla, Muḥammad al-Ḥabīb, Al-Nuẓum al-Idāriyya bi Miṣr fī al-Qarn al-Tāsiʿ al-Hijrī min khilāl Kitāb *Rawḍat al-Adīb wa Nuzhat al-Arīb* li Muḥammad b. Ibrāhīm b. Ẓuhayr al-Ḥanafī al-Ḥamawī, in *Abḥāth al-Nadwa al-Duwaliyya li Tārīkh al-Qāhira*, Cairo, 1971, vol. 3, 1043–1095.

Al-Ḥilwa, Ḥasan ʿAlī, *Kitābā Waqf al-Sulṭān al-Manṣūr Qalāwūn ʿalā al-Bīmāristān al-Manṣūrī*, Cairo, 1975.

Ḥittī, Philip, *Tārīkh Sūriyya wa Lubnān wa Filasṭīn*, 2 vols., Beirut, 1958.

Ḥusayn, Muḥammad Kāmil, Al-Tashayyuʿ fī al-Shiʿr al-Miṣrī fī ʿAṣr al-Ayyūbiyyīn wa al-Mamālīk, *Majallat Kulliyyat al-Ādāb* 15, no. 1 (1953).

Husayn, Ṭāhā, *Falsafat Ibn Khaldūn al-Ijtimāʿī: Taḥlīl wa Naqd*, trans. Muḥammad ʿAbdallāh ʿInān, Cairo, 1925.

Al-Ḥuṣrī, Sāṭiʿ, *Abū Khaldūn: Dirāsāt ʿan Muqaddimat Ibn Khaldūn*, Cairo, 1967.

Ibn Iyās: Dirāsāt wa Buḥūth, Cairo, 1977.

Ibrāhīm, ʿAbd al-Laṭīf, Dirāsa Tārikhiyya wa Athariyya fī Wathāʾiq min ʿAṣr al-Ghūrī, PhD dissertation, Cairo University, 1955.

Ibrāhīm, ʿAbd al-Laṭīf, Wathīqat al-Amīr Akhūr Qarāqujā al-Ḥasanī: Dirāsa wa Nashr wa Taḥqīq, *Majallat Kulliyyat al-Ādāb – Jāmiʿat al-Qāhira* 18, no. 2 (1956).

Ibrāhīm, ʿAbd al-Laṭīf, Al-Tawthīqāt al-Sharʿiyya wa al-Ishhādāt fī Ẓahr Wathīqat al-Ghūrī: Dirāsa wa Nashr wa Taḥqīq, *Majallat Kulliyyat al-Ādāb – Jāmiʿat al-Qāhira* 19, no. 1 (1957).

Ibrāhīm, ʿAbd al-Laṭīf, *Dirāsāt fī al-Kutub wa al-Maktabāt al-Islāmiyya*, Cairo, 1962.

Ibrāhīm, ʿAbd al-Laṭīf, Naṣṣān Jadīdān min Wathīqat al-Amīr Ṣarghatmish, *Majallat Kulliyyat al-Ādāb – Jāmiʿat al-Qāhira* 28 (1966).

Ibrāhīm, ʿAbd al-Laṭīf, Fī Maktabat Dayr Sānt Kātrīn: Dirāsa fī al-Wathāʾiq al-ʿĀmma fī al-ʿUṣūr al-Wusṭā, *Majallat Jāmiʿat Umm Durmān al-Islāmiyya* 1 (1968).

Ibrāhīm, ʿAbd al-Laṭīf, Min Wathāʾiq al-Tārīkh al-ʿArabī, *Majallat Jāmiʿat al-Qāhira – Farʿ al-Kharṭūm* 2 (1971).

Ibrāhīm, ʿAbd al-Laṭīf, Waqfiyyat Ibn Taghrībardī, in *Al-Muʾarrikh Ibn Taghrībardī Jamāl al-Dīn Abū al-Maḥāsin Yūsuf 813–874 A . H .* , Cairo, 1974.

Ibrāhīm, ʿAbd al-Laṭīf, Al-Wathāʾiq fī Khidmat al-Āthār: Al-ʿAṣr al-Mamlūkī; Al-Wathāʾiq fī Khidmat al-Āthār: Wathīqat Waqf Qāyitbāy, in *Dirāsāt fī al-Āthār al-Islāmiyya*, Cairo, 1979.

Ibrāhīm, ʿAbd al-Laṭīf, Wathāʾiq al-Waqf ʿalā al-Amākin al-Muqaddasa, in *Al-Muʾtamar al-Awwal li Dirāsat Tārīkh al-Jazīra al-ʿArabiyya*, Riyadh, 1979.

ʿInān, Muḥammad ʿAbdallāh, *Miṣr al-Islāmiyya wa Tārīkh al-Khiṭaṭ al-Miṣriyya*, Cairo, 1969.

ʿInān, Muḥammad ʿAbdallāh, *Muʾarrikhū Miṣr al-Islāmiyya wa Maṣādir al-Tārīkh al-Miṣrī*, Cairo, 1969.

Iskandar, Tawfīq, *Tārīkh Miṣr fī Maḥfūẓāt al-Bunduqiyya – Wathāʾiq ghayr Manshūr, Al-Silsila al-Ūlā: Al-Muʿāhidāt (1)1 Sifārat Bīrū Dīdū wa Muʿāhadat Tanāzul Miṣr ʿan Qubruṣ 1490*, Cairo, 1956.

Iskandar, Tawfīq, Nuẓum al-Muqāyaḍa fī Tijārat Miṣr al-Khārijiyya fī al-ʿAṣr al-Wasīṭ, *Al-Majallat al-Tārīkhiyya al-Miṣriyya* 6 (1957), 37–46.

Iskandar, Tawfīq, *Buḥūth fī al-Tārīkh al-Iqtiṣādī*, Cairo, 1961.

Jalāl, Amina Ḥusayn Muḥammad, *Ṭuruq al-Ḥajj wa Murāfaqa fī al-Ḥijāz fī al-ʿAṣr al-Mamlūkī*, Mecca, 2005.

Al-Jamāl, Aḥmad Ṣādiq, *Al-Adab al-ʿĀmmī fī al-ʿAṣr al-Mamlūkī*, Cairo, 1966.

Jamāl, ʿUmar, Al-Ḥayāt al-Ḥirafiyya fī al-Qāhira al-Mamlūkiyya, MA dissertation, Sūhāj University, 2010.

Jamāl, ʿUmar, Al-Siyāsa al-Iqtiṣādiyya fī Niyābat Dimashq wa Āthāruhā fī ʿAṣr Salāṭīn al-Mamālīk, PhD dissertation, Sūhāj University, 2013.

Jamāl, ʿUmar, Marsūm al-Sulṭān al-Ashraf Shaʿbān ilā al-Ḥujjāj wa al-Tujjār al-Firanj fī al-Quds al-Sharīf wa al-Ṣādir fī Shahr Rajab Sana 776 A . H . : Dirāsa Tārīkhiyya Ḥaḍāriyya, *Majallat Kulliyyat al-Ādāb – Jāmiʿat Manṣūra* 55 (2014).

Jamāl, ʿUmar, Wathīqat Waqf al-Khawājā Sharaf al-Dīn Yūnus b. ʿAlī al-Ṣābūnī al-Ḥalabī, *Majallat Kulliyyat al-Ādāb – Jāmiʿat Manṣūra* 57 (2015).

Jamāl, ʿUmar, Basātīn al-Nakhīl wa al-Fākiha fī Ṭūr Sīnāʾ fī al-ʿAṣr al-Mamlūkī (648/1250–923/1517): Dirāsa fī Ḍawʿ Wathāʾiq Dayr Sānt Kātrīn, *Majallat Kulliyyat al-Ādāb – Jāmiʿat Asyūṭ* 59 (2016).

Al-Jamīʿī, ʿAbd al-Munʿim, *Al-Jāmiʿa al-Miṣriyya wa al-Mujtamaʿ*, Cairo, 1983.

Al-Jamīʿī, ʿAbd al-Munʿim, *Al-Jamʿiyya al-Miṣriyya li al-Dirāsāt al-Tārīkhiyya: Dirāsa Tārikhiyya li Muʾassasa ʿIlmiyya: 1945–1985*, Cairo, 1985.

Al-Jamīʿī, ʿAbd al-Munʿim, *Ṭāhā Ḥusayn wa al-Jāmiʿa al-Miṣriyya*, Cairo, 2007.

Khāfājī, Muḥammad ʿAbd al-Munʿim, *Al-Ḥayāt al-Adabiyya fī Miṣr fī al-ʿAṣr al-Mamlūkī wa al-ʿUthmānī*, Cairo, 1984.

Al-Khūlī, Jamāl Ibrāhīm Mursī, Dirāsa Muqārana li Wathāʾiq al-Istibdāl fī Miṣr fī al-ʿAṣrayn al-Mamlūkī wa al-ʿUthmānī fī al-Qarn al-ʿĀshir al-Hijrī, MA dissertation, Cairo University, 1974.

Al-Khūlī, Jamāl Ibrāhīm Mursī, *Ithbāt al-Milkiyya fī al-Wathāʾiq al-ʿArabiyya*, Cairo, 1994.

Khūrī, Mīkhāʾil Najm, Sīrat al-Malik al-Sulṭān al-Ẓāhir Baybars, MA dissertation, American University in Beirut, 1961.

Al-Kitāb al-Fiḍḍī li Kulliyyat al-Ādāb: 1925–1950, Cairo, 1950.

Labīb, Ṣubḥī, Siyāsat Miṣr al-Tijāriyya fī ʿAṣray al-Ayyūbiyyin wa al-Mamālīk, *Al-Majalla al-Tārīkhiyya al-Miṣriyya* 28–29 (1981–82), 117–146.

Lūqā, Anwar, ʿAlī Bahjat: Awwal Atharī Miṣrī, Cairo, 2003.

Al-Maghlūth, Sāmī b. ʿAbdallāh b. Aḥmad, *Aṭlas Tārīkh al-ʿAṣr al-Mamlūkī*, Riyadh, 2013.

Maḥmūd, Ḥasan Aḥmad, Al-Baʿthāt al-Diblūmāsiyya li Dawlat Salāṭīn al-Mamālīk ka mā Waṣafahā Ibn Iyās, in *Ibn Iyās Dirāsāt wa Buḥūth – Muḥāḍarāt Ulqiyat fī Nadwat al-Jamʿiyya al-Miṣriyya li al-Dirāsāt al-Tārīkhiyya wa al-Majlis al-Aʿlā li Riʿāyat al-Funūn wa al-Ādāb wa al-ʿUlūm al-Ijtimāʿiyya 16–21 Dīsambir 1973*, Cairo, 1977, 37–46.

Mājid, ʿAbd al-Munʿim, *Nuẓum Dawlat Salāṭin al-Mamālīk wa Rusūmuhum: Dirāsa Shāmila fī al-Nuẓum al-Siyāsiyya*, 2 vols., Cairo, 1974.

Makkī, Muḥammad ʿAlī, *Lubnān 635–1516 min al-Fatḥ al-ʿArabī ilā al-Fatḥ al-ʿUthmānī*, Beirut, 1977.

Manṣūr, Aḥmad Ṣubḥī, *Muqaddimat Ibn Khaldūn: Dirāsa Uṣūliyya Tārīkhiyya*, Cairo, 1998.

Al-Maqrīzī, Taqī al-Dīn, *Shudhūr al-ʿUqūd fī Dhikr al-Nuqūd*, edition and study by Muḥammad ʿAbd al-Sattār ʿUthmān, Cairo, 1990.

Marrāq, ʿAbd al-Karīm, ʿAlī al-Ṣaḥābī, ʿAlī al-Shanūfī, *Aḍwāʾ ʿalā Muqaddimat Ibn Khaldūn: Dirāsa wa Nuṣūṣ Mustarsila*, Tunis, 1978.

Al-Mashhadānī, Yāsir, *Al-ʿAlāqāt al-Miṣriyya al-Hindiyya fī al-ʿAṣr al-Mamlūkī: Dirāsa fī al-Jawānib al-Siyāsiyya wa al-Ḥaḍāriyya*, Mosul, 2015.

Maʿtūq, Ṣāliḥ Yūsuf, ʿIlm al-Ḥadīth fī Makka al-Mukarrama khilāl al-ʿAṣr al-Mamlūkī, PhD dissertation, Umm al-Qurā University, 1407 AH.

Al-Maṭwī, Muḥammad al-ʿArūsī, *Al-Ḥurūb al-Ṣalībiyya fī al-Mashriq wa al-Maghrib*, Tunis, 1954.

Mawāfī, ʿUthmān, *Ibn Khaldūn: Nāqid al-Tārīkh wa al-Adab*, Cairo, 1975.

Mishʿal, ʿUmar Mūsā, Min Tārīkh al-Ḥarakat al-ʿUmrāniyya fī Filasṭīn fī al-ʿAhd al-Mamlūkī- ʿAmāʾir al-Ẓāhir Baybars: al-Khalfiyyāt wa al-Abʿād – Khān al-Ẓāhir bi al-Quds, *Ḥawliyyāt al-Quds* 12 (Winter 2011), 63–85.

Al-Miṣrī, Aḥmad, Mawqif Banī Ḥafṣ min al-Ṣirāʿ al-Mamlūkī al-ʿUthmānī fī Ḍawʾ Aḥad Khiṭābāt al-Sulṭān Bāyazīd al-Thānī, *Ḥawliyyāt Islāmiyya* 35 (2001), 1–15. Republished in *Majallat al-Maktabāt wa al-Maʿlūmāt al-ʿArabiyya* 21 (2001), 171–187.

Al-Miṣrī, Aḥmad, Wathīqat Taghyīr Shurūṭ al-Intifāʿ bi al-Waqf min al-ʿAṣr al-Mamlūkī li al-Sayfī Qilij b. ʿAbdallāh al-Sharīfī, *Majallat Kulliyat al-Ādāb – Jāmiʿat Banī Suwayf* 5 (2003) 60–89. Republished in *Hawliyyāt Islāmiyya* 38 (2004), 1–15.

Al-Miṣrī, Aḥmad, Min Wathāʾiq al-Makataba al-Waṭaniyya bi Bārīs: Wathīqat al-Dashīsha al-Kubrā li al-Sulṭān Qayitbāy, *Majallat Kulliyyat al-Ādāb – Jāmiʿat Banī Suwayf* 20 (2011), 103–134.

Al-Miṣrī, Aḥmad, Niẓām al-Taqāḍī fī Miṣr al-Mamlūkiyya maʿa al-Taṭbīq ʿalā daʿawā Ilghāʾ Istibdāl, *Majallat al-Rūznāma* 9 (2011), 35–92.

Mubārak, ʿAlī, *Al-Khiṭaṭ al-Tawfīqiyya al-Jadīda*, Cairo, 1969.

Muḥammad, Aḥmad ʿAbd al-Rāziq, ʿAwāmil Inhiyār Dawlat Salāṭīn al-Mamālīk fī Miṣr, Cairo, 2017.

Muḥammad, Ṣubḥī ʿAbd al-Munʿim, *Siyāsat al-Mughūl al-Īlkhāniyyin tujāhu Duwlul al-Mamālīk fī Miṣr wa al-Shām Zaman al-Īlkhān Abī Saʿīd b. Khudābandah (716–7136h.)*, Cairo, 1999.

Muḥriz, Jamāl Muḥammad, Al-Runūk, *Majallat al-Muqtaṭaf* 98, Part 5 (May 1941), 461–468.

Munīr, ʿAmr ʿAbd al-ʿAzīz, *Miṣr wa al-Nīl bayn al-Tārīkh wa al-Fūlklūr*, Cairo, 2009.

Munīr, ʿAmr ʿAbd al-ʿAzīz, *Al-Quds fī al-Asāṭīr al-ʿArabiyya*, Cairo, 2009.

Munīr, ʿAmr ʿAbd al-ʿAzīz, (ed.), *Qāsim ʿAbduh Qāsim bayn al-Tārīkh wa al-Adab al-Shaʿbī*, Cairo, 2013.

Munīr, ʿAmr ʿAbd al-ʿAzīz, Jamāʿāt dūna al-Iʿtirāf: Muqāraba ḥawla Ahl Ḥiyal fī Miṣr wa al-Shām fī ʿAṣray al-Ayyūbiyyin wa al-Mamālīk, *Majallat Kulliyyat al-Ādād bi Qināʾ – Jāmiʿat Janūb al-Wādī* (2014).

Munīr, ʿAmr ʿAbd al-ʿAzīz, Al-Aṭʿima al-Badīla fī Miṣr al-Mamlūkiyya: Mumārasāt wa Ṣināʿa wa Mawqif, forthcoming in *Majallat Jāmiʿat al-Shāriqa*.

Mu'nis, Ḥusayn, *Aṭlas Tārikh al-Islām*, Cairo, 1987.

Mu'nis, Ḥusayn, Sifārat Badrūmārtīr Dānjalāriyyā Safīr al-Malikayn al-Kāthūlīkiyyayn ilā al-Sulṭān al-Ghūrī Dīsambar 1501–Fabrāyir 1502, in *Abḥāth al-Nadwa al-Duwaliyya li Tārīkh al-Qāhira*, i, Cairo, 1970, 429–482.

Al-Mu'arrikh Ibn Taghrī Bardī Jamāl al-Dīn Abū al-Maḥāsin Yūsuf 813–874 h., Cairo, 1974.

Muṣṭāf, Thāmir Nu'mān, Dawr al-Mar'a fī al-Ḥayāt al-'Āmma fī 'Aṣr al-Mamālīk al-Baḥriyya 648/1250–784/1382, *Majallat Wāsiṭ li al-'Ulūm* 23 (n.d.), 267–302.

Muṣṭafā, Muḥammad, Al-Runūk fī 'Aṣr al-Mamālīk, *Majallat al-Risāla*, 400 (1941), 269–271.

Muṣṭafā, Muḥammad, Makhṭūṭ Muṣawwar fī Ta'līm Funūn al-Qitāl wa al-Furūsiyya min Awākhir 'Aṣr al-Mamālīk al-Jarākisa, *Majallat al-Majm' al-'Ilmī al-Miṣrī* 51 (1969/1970).

Muṣṭafā, Muṣṭafā Wajīh, *Al-Ghidhā' fī Miṣr 'Aṣr Salāṭīn al-Mamālīk: Dirāsa fī al-Tārīkh al-Ijtimā'ī*, Cairo, 2016.

Muṣṭafā, Nādiya Maḥmūd, ed., *Min Taṣfiyyat al-Wujūd al-Ṣalībī ilā Bidāyat al-Hajma al-Ūrūbiyya*, vol. 10 of *Al-'Alāqāt al-Duwaliyya fī al-Tārīkh al-Islāmī*, Cairo, 1996.

Mutawallī, Aḥmad Fu'ād, *Al-Fatḥ al-'Uthmānī li al-Shām wa Miṣr wa Muqddimātuhu min Wāqi' al-Wathā'iq wa al-Maṣādir al-Turkiyya wa al-'Arabiyya al-Mu'āṣira lahu*, Cairo, 1976.

Al-Nabrāwī, Ra'fat, *Al-Nuqūd al-Islāmiyya fī Miṣr: 'Aṣr Dawlat al-Mamālīk al-Jarākisa*, Cairo, 1996.

Al-Nabrāwī, Ra'fat, *Al-Nuqūd mundhu Bidāyat al-Qarn al-Sādis ḥattā Nihāyat al-Qarn al-Tāsi' al-Hijrī*, Cairo, 2000.

Al-Nahār, 'Ammār Muḥammad, Al-Dirāsāt al-Naẓariyya al-Jadīda fī 'Aṣr Dawlat al-Mamālīk al-Baḥriyya (684/1250–784/1382), *Dirāsāt Tārīkhiyya* 117/118 (Kānūn al-Thānī – Ḥazīrān, 2012), 243–294.

Al-Najjār, Muḥammad Rajab, *Ḥikāyāt al-Shaṭṭār wa al-'Ayyārūn fī al-Tūrāth al-'Arabī*, Kuwait, 1981.

Al-Najjār, Muḥammad Rajab, *Sīrat 'Alī al-Zabīq*, Cairo, 2005.

Al-Najjār, Muḥammad Rajab, *Al-Shi'r al-Sha'bī al-Sākhir fī 'Uṣūr al-Mamālīk*, Cairo, 2015.

Nāṣir, 'Āmir Najīb Mūsā, *Al-Ḥayāt al-Iqtiṣādiyya fī Miṣr fī al-'Aṣr al-Mamlūkī*, Cairo, 2003.

Al-Nu'mān, Jihād, *Ibn Khaldūn fī 'Ilm al-Nafs: Baḥth ḥawla Mafhūmihi li al-Gharā'iz wa Murāqabatihā*, Beirut, n.d.

Al-Qaḥṭānī, Rāshid Sa'd Rāshid, *Awqāf al-Sulṭān al-Ashraf Sha'bān 'alā al-Ḥaramayn*, Riyadh, 1994.

Qāsim, Qāsim 'Abduh, *Ahl al-Dhimma fī Miṣr al-'Uṣūr al-Wusṭā*, Cairo, 1977.

Qāsim, Qāsim 'Abduh, Nashr wa Taḥqīq Wathīqa min Wathā'iq Dayr Sānt Kātrīn al-Khāṣṣa, *Al-Majalla al-Tārīkhiyya al-Miṣriyya* 25 (1978), 257–275.

Qāsim, Qāsim ʿAbduh, *Al-Nīl wa al-Mujtamaʿ fī ʿAṣr Salāṭīn al-Mamālīk*, Cairo, 1978.

Qāsim, Qāsim ʿAbduh, *Dirāsāt fī Tārīkh Miṣr al-Ijtimāʿī – ʿAṣr Salāṭīn al-Mamālīk*, Cairo, 1979.

Qāsim, Qāsim ʿAbduh, *Bayn al-Adab wa al-Tārīkh*, Cairo, 1986.

Qāsim, Qāsim ʿAbduh, *Al-Yahūd fī Miṣr mundhu al-Fatḥ al-ʿArabī ḥattā al-Ghazw al-ʿUthmānī*, Cairo, 1987.

Qāsim, Qāsim ʿAbduh, *Bayn al-Tārīkh wa al-Fulklūr*, Cairo, 1993.

Qāsim, Qāsim ʿAbduh, *ʿAṣr Salāṭīn al-Mamālīk – al-Tārīkh al-Siyāsī wa al-Ijtimāʿī*, Cairo, 1998.

Qāsim, Qāsim ʿAbduh, *Al-Malik al-Muẓaffar Sayf al-Dīn Quṭuz*, Damascus, 1999.

Qāsim, Qāsim ʿAbduh, *Wathāʾiq Dayr Sānt Kātrīn Māṣdaran li al-Tārīkh al-Ijtimāʿī*, *Majallat Arabīkā* (2001), 245–269.

Qāsim, Qāsim ʿAbduh, *Fī Tārīkh al-Ayyūbiyyin wa al-Mamālīk*, Cairo, 2001.

Qāsim, Qāsim ʿAbduh, *Ahl al-Dhimma fī Miṣr min al-Fatḥ al-Islāmī ḥattā Nihāyat al-Mamālīk: Dirāsa Wathāʾiqiyya*, Cairo, 2003.

Qāsim, Ṭāriq Aḥmad, *Tārīkh Lubnān al-Wasīṭ*, Beirut (?), 2007.

Al-Qaṭṭār, Ilyās Dāwūd, *Lubnān al-Wasīṭ ʿAhd Salāṭīn al-Mamālīk*, Beirut, 2015.

Al-Rifāʿī, Hāla Nawwāf Yūsuf, Al-Rasāʾil al-Dīwāniyya fī ʿAṣr Dawlat al-Mamālīk al-Ūlā (648/1250–784/1382): Dirāsa Tārīkhiyya, Siyāsiyya, wa Idāriyya, PhD dissertation, The Jordanian University, 2015–2016.

Ruslān, Ṣalāḥ al-Dīn Basyūnī, *Al-Siyāsa wa al-Iqtiṣād ʿinda Ibn Khaldūn*, Cairo, 1999.

Al-Saʿātī, Sāmiya, *Ibn Khaldūn Mubdiʿan: Qirāʾa Jadīda li Fikrihi wa Minhajihi fī ʿIlm al-Ijtimāʿ*, Cairo, 2006.

Al-Ṣabbāgh, Laylā, Ḥawla Tārīkh al-Shām fī al-Qarn al-ʿĀshir al-Hijrī/ al-Sādis ʿAshar al-Mīlādī, in *Al-Tārīkh wa al-Āthār: Al-Ḥalqa al-Dirāsiyya al-Ūlāʾ (al-Qāhira 6–9 Fabrāyir 1961)*, Cairo, 1961, 193–203.

Ṣabra, ʿAfāf Sayyid, ʿAlāqat al-Bunduqiyya bi Miṣr wa al-Shām fī al-Fatra min 1100–1400, Cairo, 1983.

Saʿd, Aḥmad Ṣādiq, *Fī Ḍawʾ al-Namaṭ al-Āsiyawī li al-Intāj: Tārīkh Miṣr al-Ijtimāʿī-Iqtiṣādī*, Beirut, 1979.

Al-Saʿdāwī, Naẓīr Ḥassān, *Ṣuwar wa Maẓālim min ʿAṣr al-Mamālīk*, Cairo, 1966.

Al-Saʿdāwī, Naẓīr Ḥassān, Dawlat al-Barrayn wa al-Baḥrayn, *Al-Majalla al-Tārīkhiyya al-Miṣriyya* 13 (1967), 129–168.

Saʿīd, ʿAbīr ʿUnayyit, Al-Khadamāt al-ʿĀmma li Dawlat al-Mamālīk al-Baḥriyya fī Miṣr 648/1250–784/382, PhD dissertation, Anbar University, 2012.

Al-Saʿīdī, Aḥmad, Makhṭūṭa Mamlūkiyya fī Janūb al-Maghrib: Dirāsa Kūdīkūlūjiyya fī Adab al-Dunyā wa al-Dīn li al-Māwardī, *Journal of Islamic Manuscripts* 7, no. 2 (2016), 244–260.

Salām, Muḥammad Zaghlūl, *Al-Adab fī al-ʿAṣr al-Mamlūkī*, Cairo, 1971.

Al-Ṣāliḥ, Maḥmūd Kāmil, Al-ʿArab wa Makānatuhum fī Dawlat al-Mamālīk, PhD dissertation, al-Mustansiriyya University, 2010.

Ṣāliḥiyya, Muḥammad ʿĪsā, Min Wathāʾiq al-Ḥaram al-Qudsī al-Sharīf al-Mamlūkiyya, *Ḥawliyyāt Kulliyyat al-Ādāb – Jāmiʿat Kuwayt* 6, no. 26 (1985).

Salīm, Muḥammad Rizq, ʿAṣr Salāṭīn al-Mamālīk wa Nitājuhu al-ʿIlmī wa al-Adabī, Cairo, 1955.

Sāmī, Amīn Bāshā, *Taqwīm al-Nīl*, Cairo, 1915.

Sayyid, Ayman Fuʾād, Ruwwād al-Dirāsāt al-Tārīkhiyya fī al-ʿUṣūr al-Wusṭā wa al-Islāmiyya, *Al-Majalla al-Tārīkhiyya al-Miṣriyya* 39 (1996), 291–303.

Sayyid, Ayman Fuʾād, Ṭarīqat al-Taʾlīf ʿinda al-Qudamāʾ min khilāl Musawwadat al-Maqrīzī li Kitāb al-Khiṭaṭ, in *Dirāsat al-Makhṭūṭāt al-Islāmiyya bayna Iʿtibārāt al-Mādda wa al-Bashar*, London, 1997, 153–161.

Sayyid, Ayman Fuʾād, *Al-Kitāba al-Tārīkhiyya fī Miṣr fī al-Qarn al-Khāmis ʿAshar al-Mīlādī*, Cairo, 2007.

Sayyid, Ayman Fuʾād, Ibn Khaldūn fī Miṣr wa Atharuhu ʿalā Madrasat al-Tārīkh al-Miṣrī fī al-Qarn al-Tāsiʿ al-Hijrī/ al-Khāmis ʿAshar al-Mīlādī, in *Kitāb Ibn Khaldūn wa Manābiʿ al-Ḥadātha*, 2 vols., Carthage, 2008, vol. 2, 549–560.

Sayyid, Ayman Fuʾād, Khuṭūṭ al-Maqrīzī fī Kitāb al-Makhṭūṭāt al-Muwaqqaʿa, in *Aʿmāl al-Muʾtamar al-Duwalī al-Thānī li Markaz al-Makhṭūṭāt*, Alexandria, 2008, 123–140.

Sayyid, Ayman Fuʾād, Makhṭuṭāt ʿAṣr Ibn Khaldūn, in *Kitāb Ibn Khaldūn bayn al-Andalus wa Miṣr*, Madrid, 2008.

Sayyid, Ayman Fuʾād, Maṣādir Ibn Khaldūn ʿan Tārīkh ghayr al-Muslimīn fī Kitāb al-ʿIbar, in *Kitāb Dirāsāt Adabiyya wa Lughawiyya Muhdā ilā al-Ustādh al-Duktūr ʿĀdil Sulaymān Jamāl bi Munāsabat Bulūghihi al-Sabʿīn*, Cairo, 2012, 539–550.

Sayyid, Ayman Fuʾād, *Al-Maqrīzī wa Kitābuhu al-Mawāʿiẓ wa al-Iʿtibār bi Dhikr al-Khiṭaṭ wa al-Āthār*, London, 2013.

Al-Sayyid, Muḥammad Ibrāhīm, Al-Brutukūl al-Khitāmī li al-Wathāʾiq al-ʿArabiyya fī Miṣr fī al-Rubʿ al-Awwal min al-Qarn al-Sādis ʿAshar Mīlādī: Wathāʾiq al-Bayʿ wa al-Waqf wa al-Istibdāl, MA dissertation, Cairo University, 1975.

Shaykh al-Arḍ, Taysīr, *Ibn Khaldūn*, Beirut, 1966.

Al-Shayyāl, Jamāl al-Dīn, Muʾallafāt al-Maqrīzī al-Ṣaghīra, in *Majmūʿat Abḥāth al-Ḥalqa al-Dirāsiyya ʿan al-Maqrīzī*, Cairo, 1971.

Shillī, Fayṣal, *Bilād al-Shām fī Ẓill al-Dawlat al-Mamlūkiyya al-Thāniya (Dawlat al-Jarākisa al-Burjiyya: 1381–1517)*, Damascus, 2008.

Sulaymān, Aḥmad al-Saʿīd, *Tārīkh al-Duwal al-Islāmiyya wa Muʿjam al-Usar al-Ḥākima*, Cairo, 1969.

Surūr, Muḥammad Jamāl al-Dīn, *Al-Ẓāhir Baybars wa Ḥaḍārat Miṣr fī ʿAṣrihi*, Cairo, 1938.

Surūr, Muḥammad Jamāl al-Dīn, *Dawlat Banī Qalāwūn fī Miṣr*, Cairo, 1947.

Ṭabbābī, Bilqāsim, *Dirāsāt fī al-Sulṭa wa al-Mujtamaʿ fī al-ʿAṣr al-Islāmī al-Wasīṭ, Miṣr wa al-Shām fī al-ʿAhd al-Mamlūkī Anmūdhajān*, Tunis, 2013.

Al-Tadmurī, ʿUmar ʿAbd al-Salām, *Al-Ḥayāt al-Thaqāfiyya fī Ṭarāblus al-Shām khilāl al-ʿUṣūr al-Wusṭā min al-Fatḥ al-ʿArabī ḥattā Suqūṭ al-Imāra al-Ṣalībiyya*, Beirut, 1972.

Al-Tadmurī, ʿUmar ʿAbd al-Salām, *Tārīkh wa Āthār Masājid wa Madāris Ṭarāblus fī ʿAṣr al-Mamālīk min al-Fatḥ al-Manṣūrī ḥattā al-Ān*, Tripoli, 1974.

Al-Tadmurī, ʿUmar ʿAbd al-Salām, *Tārīkh Ṭarāblus al-Siyāsī wa al-Ḥaḍārī ʿabra al-ʿUṣūr*, 2 vols., Beirut, 1981.

Al-Tadmurī, ʿUmar ʿAbd al-Salām, *Mawsūʿat ʿUlamāʾ al-Muslimīn fī Tārīkh Lubnān al-Islāmī*, Beirut, 1990.

Al-Tadmurī, ʿUmar ʿAbd al-Salām, *Al-Mustadrak ʿalā Mawsūʿat ʿUlamāʾ al-Muslimīn fī Tārīkh Lubnān al-Islāmī*, Beirut, 1996.

Al-Tadmurī, ʿUmar ʿAbd al-Salām, Runūk al-Mamālīk wa Rusūmuhum ʿalā ʿImārat Ṭarāblus al-Qadīma, *Majallat Tārīkh al-ʿArab wa al-ʿĀlam*, n.d., 16–37.

Al-Ṭaḥṭāwī, Rifāʿa Rāfiʿ, *Al-Aʿmāl al-Kāmila*, ed. Muḥammad ʿAmmāra, 5 vols., Cairo, 2010.

Al-Ṭaḥṭāwī, Rifāʿa Rāfiʿ, *Manāhij al-Albāb al-Miṣriyya fī Manāhij al-Ādāb al-ʿAṣriyya*, Cairo, 2018.

Al-Ṭaḥṭāwī, Rifāʿa Rāfiʿ, *Al-Murshid al-Amīn li al-Banāt wa al-Banīn*, Cairo, 2018.

Taqwīm Dār al-ʿUlūm, Cairo, 2008.

Ṭarkhān, Ibrāhīm ʿAlī, Al-Iqṭāʿ al-Islāmī – Uṣūluhu wa Taṭawwuruhu – Dirāsa Muqārana, *Al-Majalla al-Tārīkhiyya al-Miṣriyya* 6 (1957), 47–76.

Ṭarkhān, Ibrāhīm ʿAlī, *Al-Nuẓum al-Iqṭāʿiyya fī al-Sharq al-Awsaṭ fī al-ʿUṣūr al-Wusṭā*, Cairo, 1968.

Ṭarkhān, Ibrāhīm ʿAlī, *Miṣr fī ʿAṣr Dawlat al-Mamālīk al-Jarākisa: 1382–1517*, Cairo, 1968.

Al-Ṭīrāwana, Mubārak, *Al-Ḥayāt al-Ijtimāʿiyya fī Bilād al-Shām fī ʿAṣr al-Mamālīk al-Jarākisa 784/1382–922/1516*, Amman, 2010.

ʿUthmān, Muḥammad ʿAbd al-Sattār, *Wathīqat Waqf Jamāl al-Dīn al-Ustādār*, Cairo, 1983.

Waḥida, Ṣubḥī, *Fī Usūl al-Masʾala al-Miṣriyya*, 2 vols., Cairo, 1974.

Al-Waqqād, Maḥāsin, *Al-Ṭabaqāt al-Shaʿbiyya fī al-Qāhira al-Mamlūkiyya*, Cairo, 1999.

Al-Wardī, ʿAlī, *Manṭiq Ibn Khaldūn fī Ḍawʾ Ḥaḍāratihi wa Shakhṣiyyatihi- Muḥāḍarāt*, Cairo, 1962.

Al-Wasīmī, Muḥammad Najīb, Al-ʿAlāqāt al-Siyāsiyya bayna Imārat Qarāmān wa Dawlat al-Mamālīk al-Jarākisa (659–874 h./1361–1382 m.), *Al-Majalla al-Tārīkhiyya al-Miṣriyya* 39 (1996), 9–40.

Yaʿqūb, Jūrj, *Ṭīf al-Khayyāl li Ibn Dāniyāl al-Mawṣilī*, vols. 1 and 2 published in Erlangen in 1910, volume 3 published in Berlin in 1912.

Yūsuf, Jūzīf Nasīm, ʿAlāqāt Miṣr bi al-Mamālik al-Tijāriyya al-Īṭāliyya fī Ḍawʾ Wathāʾiq Ṣubḥ al-Aʿshā, in *Dirāsāt fī Tārīkh al-ʿAlāqāt bayna al-Sharq wa al-Gharb fī al-ʿUṣūr al-Wusṭā*, Alexandria, 1988, 61–123.

Al-Zaʿārīr, Ṭāhā Ḥasan ʿUqāb, Al-Ṣināʿāt wa al-Ḥiraf fī Janūb Bilād al-Shām fī al-ʿAṣrayn al-Ayyūbī wa al-Mamlūkī, PhD dissertation, Yarmuk University, 2015–2016.

Zahrān, Al-Badrāwī, *Fī ʿIlm al-Lugha al-Tārīkhī: Dirāsa Taṭbīqiyya ʿalā ʿArabiyyat al-ʿUṣūr al-Wusṭā*, Cairo, 1979.

Zakariyyāʾ, Mīshīl, *Al-Malaka al-Lisāniyya fī Muqaddimat Ibn Khaldūn: Dirāsa Alsuniyya*, Beirut, 1986.

Zakī, ʿAbd al-Raḥmān, *Al-Aʿlām wa Shārāt al-Mulk fī Wādī al-Nīl*, Cairo, 1948.

Zakī, ʿAbd al-Raḥmān, Ibn Iyās wa Istikhdām al-Asliḥat al-Nāriyya fī Ḍawʾ mā Katabahu fī Kitāb Badāʾiʿ al-Zuhūr, in *Ibn Iyās: Dirāsāt wa Buḥūth*, Cairo, 1977, 97–136.

Al-Zāmil, Muḥammad Fatḥī, *Al-Taḥawwulāt al-Iqtiṣādiyya fī Miṣr Awākhir al-ʿUṣūr al-Wusṭā*, Cairo, 2008.

Al-Zāmil, Muḥammad Fatḥī, *Al-Ḥiṣār al-Iqtiṣādī ʿalā Miṣr Awākhir al-ʿUṣūr al-Wusṭā*, Cairo, 2009.

Zaqalma, Anwar, *Al-Mamālīk fī Miṣr*, Cairo, 1995.

Zaʿrūr, Ibrāhīm, Al-Ḥayāt al-Ijtimāʿiyya fī al-ʿAṣrayn al-Ayyūbī wa al-Mamlūkī, PhD dissertation, Damascus University, 1990.

Al-Zaydī, Mufīd, *Mawsūʿat al-Tārīkh al-Islāmī: Al-ʿAṣr al-Mamlūkī (648/1250–923/1517)*, Amman, 2003.

Al-Zayn, ʿAlī, *Al-ʿĀdāt wa al-Taqālīd fī al-ʿUhūd al-Iqṭāʿiyya*, Beirut and Cairo, 1977.

Zaytūn, ʿĀdil, *Al-ʿAlāqāt bayn al-Sharq wa al-Gharb fī al-ʿUṣūr al-Wusṭā*, Damascus, 1980.

Zayyān, Ḥāmid, *Ṣafḥa min Tārīkh al-Khilāfat al-ʿAbbāsiyya fī Ẓill Dawlat al-Mamālīk: Al-Khalīfa al-Mustaʿīn Billāh al-ʿAbbāsī Sulṭān al-Diyār al-Miṣriyya*, Cairo, 1978.

Zīdān, Jurjī, *Tārīkh al-Tamaddun al-Islāmī*, Beirut, 1902–1906.

Ziyāda, Muḥammad Muṣṭafā, Baʿḍ Mulāḥaẓāt Jadīda fī Tārīkh Dawlat al-Mamālīk bi Miṣr, *Majallat Kulliyyat al-Ādāb* 4 (1938), 71–88.

Ziyāda, Muḥammad Muṣṭafā, *Al-Muʾarrikhūn fī Miṣr fī al-Qarn al-Khāmis ʿAshar al-Mīlādī*, Cairo, 1949.

Ziyāda, Muḥammad Muṣṭafā, Nihāyat al-Salāṭīn al-Mamālīk fī Miṣr, *Al-Majalla al-Tārīkhiyya al-Miṣriyya* 4, no. 1 (1951), 203–230.

Ziyāda, Muḥammad Muṣṭafā, Dirāsāt fī al-Tārīkh al-Iqtiṣādī wa al-Ijtimāʿī in *Al-Tārīkh wa al-Āthār: al-Ḥalqa al-Dirāsiyya al-Ūlā*, Cairo, 1962, 241–250.

Ziyāda, Muḥammad Muṣṭafā, Ḥarakat al-Bināʾ wa al-Taʿmīr fī ʿAṣr al-Nāṣir min Kitāb al-Sulūk li Maʿrifat Duwal al-Mulūk li al-Maqrīzī, *Al-Majalla al-Tārīkhiyya al-Miṣriyya* 9–10 (1962), 241–250.

Ziyāda, Muḥammad Muṣṭafā, Muqtabasāt min Ibn Iyās, *Al-Majalla al-Tārīkhiyya al-Miṣriyya* 12, no. 1 (1965), 197–228.

14

Modern Egyptian Arabic Scholarship on Mamluk Arts and Architecture (1250–1517)

Hani Hamza

Western Middle Eastern studies, a term that has replaced the discredited "Orientalism" in the post-Edward Saʿīd world, has realized the need for native scholars with a deep understanding of their own civilization, speaking native languages such as Arabic, Persian, or Turkish. This has mostly been achieved by inviting scholars of Middle Eastern origins to Western institutions either permanently or as visitors. A wise practice, no doubt, but those scholars are the tip of the iceberg. The majority stay at home while research in the Western "host" institutions is conducted mainly, if not entirely, in European languages.

The massive scholarly production on Arab-Islamic history in Middle Eastern countries in their native Arabic is trapped in two prisons: the language barrier and extremely limited circulation. The need for propagating this mass of research work worldwide is apparent and pressing. This chapter will shed light on the research related to one particular field, period, and country; namely the Mamluk sultanates' (1250–1517) material culture. It will survey the history of writing on Mamluk arts and architecture by Egyptians in Arabic.

The aim is to survey the research institutions in Egypt for critical analysis of their scholarly production in Arabic, which is mainly unpublished, showing influences and trends. In a similar way the publishing venues in terms of periodicals, books, monographs, or proceedings of seminars will be surveyed and analyzed. As a result, a comprehensive and a selected bibliography are compiled based on the survey.

1 Note on Methodology

Unlike other disciplines – such as engineering, medicine, or sciences – writing or publishing history has no barrier to entry except in universities, peer-reviewed periodicals, and specialized publishing houses. Our study will therefore be limited to those venues starting from the 1970s with a historical background going back to the nineteenth century.

Egyptian scholars in the field of Mamluk material culture publish in many languages other than Arabic, such as English, French, or German, in Egypt and worldwide. A point of caveat is given here: this study will cover only the publications in Arabic and in Egypt.

The critical mass of scholarly production will be classified according to institutions and topics of research rather than on the production of individual scholars. For example, the production of universities, which are the major research institutions in Egypt, will be measured by theses or dissertations for obtaining a Master of Arts or Doctor of Philosophy degree, and by the specialized periodicals published by those universities. In a similar manner, other scientific and research centers and societies will be dealt with in terms of papers published in their peer-reviewed periodicals and/or specialized books. All will be classified by topics rather than authors; the latter will be mentioned in the bibliographical section of this study. The only exception, where the classification is based on authors, is the historical introduction, the beginnings.

2 The Beginnings

2.1 *The Comité de Conservation des Monuments de l'Art Arabe*

Interest in the Islamic arts and architecture ('Arabic arts,' as it was then called) was overshadowed for a while by the legacy of the ancient Egyptians. It emerged in the late eighteenth century by means of the drawings of the scientists and artists accompanying the expedition that took place during the French invasion of Egypt (1798–1801),[1] and those of other European travelers to Egypt in the following decades.[2] However, the first institutional attempt to study Islamic archaeology was the establishment of the *Comité de Conservation des Monuments de l'Art Arabe* (*Lajnat ḥifẓ al-athār al-ʿarabiyya*), known as the *Comité* for short, by a khedivial decree on 18 December 1881.[3] The *Comité*

---

1 After the failure of the invasion, the savants (between 150 and 160 scientists and artists) published in Paris, between the years 1809 and 1822, a multi-volume book with texts and illustrations compiling the results of their scientific labor in Egypt during the invasion. It is called *Description de l'Égypte – Waṣf Miṣr.*

2 Among the scores of European travelers to Egypt in the nineteenth century, three stand out for their contributions to drawing and publishing the Islamic art treasures in Egypt. Pascale Coste (1787–1879) was a French architect who came to Egypt in 1817 and spent 10 years in the service of Muḥammad ʿAlī. Emile Prisse d'Avennes (1807–79), a controversial French architect, archaeologist, and writer, came to Egypt in 1827 and spent 17 years at various assignments. He pretended to convert to Islam, donned native dress, and called himself Idrīs Effendī. Robert Hay (1799–1863), a Scottish traveler and archaeologist, spent the years from 1824 to 1834 in Egypt, living mostly at a tomb in Thebes (Luxor). He recorded many aspects of life in Cairo and its Islamic architecture in his book *Illustrations of Cairo* (London, 1840). See ʿUkāshā, *Miṣr fī ʿuyūn al-ghurābāʾ*, i: 203–47, 365–87.

3 Al-Ḥabashī and Warner, *Recording the Monuments*, 81.

belonged to the Ministry of Pious Endowments (*Wizārat al-awqāf*) until 1936, when it was transferred to the Ministry of Education (*Wizārat al-maʿārif al-ʿumūmiyya*).

The *Comité* was assigned four tasks according to its foundation decree.[4] The first was to survey and make an inventory of the Arabic (both Islamic and Coptic) monuments of Egypt. The second was to maintain, protect, and conserve the recorded monuments and to propose necessary repairs. The third was to study and approve the drawings and designs proposed for the repairs and maintenance of the monuments and to supervise their execution. The fourth was to store the drawings of the works undertaken at the library of the Ministry and inform them of the parts salvaged from the monuments that were to be moved to and stored at the *Antīqkhāna*.[5]

The *Comité* consisted of two commissions. The First Commission was assigned the task of identifying the monuments and creating an inventory, while the Second Commission was technical, assigned the task of assessing the condition of the monuments and proposing, designing, and supervising execution of the necessary repair works.[6] The *Comité* held 303 meetings and produced 909 reports which were published in a bulletin that started in 1882–83 with the last issue in 1961,[7] the year the *Comité* was abolished and replaced by the Supreme Council of Antiquities.[8]

In the absence of drawings or photos of many of the monuments that were ruined beyond recognition, it seems that the *Comité* took some liberties and improvised solutions that became the subject of criticism. The *Comité* policy of removing the shops, kiosks, and sometimes houses that had become attached to the monuments over the ages, and thus isolating the monuments from the surrounding buildings, has also been challenged on the grounds that this tears away the monuments from their natural human environment and from their communal life that developed over centuries.[9]

---

4   *Comité, Exercice* 1882–1883, 8–9.

5   Literally, 'House of Antiquities,' referring mainly to the Egyptian Museum. But actually, the parts that were salvaged from Islamic monuments that were ruined beyond repair were transferred to the arcades of the al-Ḥākim mosque and later moved to the Museum of Arab Arts (now the Museum of Islamic Art) after the latter was founded in 1903. See al-Ḥabashī and Warner, *Recording the Monuments*, 81–2.

6   Ibid., 81.

7   All issues of the *Comité* Bulletins are available online at the Islamic Art Network website: http://www.islamic-art.org/comitte/BArchMain.asp (last downloaded on 15 January 2018). Also available online in a digitalized format at the *Persee* site https://www.persee.fr/collection/ccmaa (last downloaded on 12 December 2020).

8   Al-Ḥabashī, Islamic Art Network, Comité Bulletins, Historical Background, http://www.islamic-art.org/Comitte/comite.asp (last downloaded on 15 January 2018).

9   Ormos, *Max Hertz Pasha* i, 64.

Another legacy of the *Comité* is that by and large it considered medieval Cairo to be primarily Mamluk, to the exclusion of other architectural styles, especially the Ottoman. According to the *Comité*, the Mamluk arts and architecture of Egypt were the quintessential representation of Arab and Egyptian art versus the Ottoman and Turkish.[10] This attitude, and the fascination with Mamluk architecture, gave birth to the neo-Mamluk style in the majority of religious and secular buildings of the nineteenth and early twentieth centuries in Egypt.[11] The study of Mamluk history in general, and of its material culture in particular, is a logical expression of this new trend.

2.2 *Founding Fathers: The Pioneer Historians*

Most of the early Egyptian archeologists/historians came from under the wings of the *Comité*, which was run by Europeans from the beginning until the Egyptians took over its administration by the 1930s. The following survey of a selection of early Egyptian scholars of Islamic arts and architecture will briefly cover their main fields of activities, topics of study, and major works. One should bear in mind that those early scholars covered all Islamic periods and styles; the Mamluk period was only one among them. Most of their work was informative and semi-educational, exposing merits and influences, rather than critical analysis.

2.2.1 ʿAlī Bahjat (1858–1924) علي بهجت

Linguist, archaeologist, and historian. He worked at the *Comité* and was the first Egyptian director of the Museum of Islamic Art in Cairo. He excavated Fusṭāṭ, edited *Ṣubḥ al-Aʿshā* by the Mamluk historian al-Qalqashandī (d. 821/1418), and published many articles on Islamic artifacts and Mamluk monuments, mainly in French, which were then translated into Arabic.[12]

2.2.2 Ḥasan ʿĀbd al-Wahhāb (1898–1967) حسن عبد الوهاب

Archeologist and historian. Worked at the *Comité* in restoration, conservation, and identification of Islamic monuments in Egypt. A prolific writer; author of many books and articles on Islamic monuments of Egypt in general and Mamluk architecture in particular.[13] His best-known monograph is on the mosques of Cairo.[14]

---

10   Sanders, *Creating Medieval Cairo*, 26, 41, 103.

11   Ibid., 56.

12   For a list of his works see Muḥammad, *ʿAlī Bahjat wa-muʾallafātuhu*, 17–31; for his biography see Lūqā, *ʿAlī Bahjat awwal atharī Miṣrī*, 10–87; Muḥammad, *ʿAlī Bahjat wa-muʾallafātuhu*, 15–17.

13   The most important articles are listed at the bibliographical section of this paper.

14   H. ʿĀbd al-Wahhāb. *Tārīkh al-masājid al-athariyya*, Cairo, 1994.

2.2.3   Farīd Shāfiʿī (1907–85)   فريد شافعي

Architect and academic, teaching at Faculty of Engineering at Cairo and King Saʿūd Universities. Designed many buildings in the Islamic style; the Aghā Khān mausoleum in Aswan and the mosque of the Egyptian Parliament are the best known. Author of many books and studies on Islamic arts. The most famous is his three-volume book on early Islamic architecture in Egypt. The first volume covers the period from the Islamic conquest of Egypt in 32/639 until the start of the Fatimid period in 358/968.[15] The second volume, on Fatimid military architecture, and the third, on Fatimid secular and religious architecture, have not yet been published.

2.2.4   Zakī Muḥammad Ḥasan (1908–1957)   زكي محمد حسن

Archaeologist and academician, he started as a curator at the Islamic Museum in Cairo from 1935 till 1939 He then moved to Cairo University, then Baghdad University, where he died at the young age of 49. A prolific writer of books and articles, mainly on Islamic minor arts. The most prominent is a monograph on Fatimid arts published by Dār al-athār al-ʿarabiyya (now the Museum of Islamic Art in Cairo).[16]

2.2.5   Aḥmad Fikrī (?–1975)   أحمد فكري

Historian and academician at Alexandria and Baghdad Universities, mainly working on the Islamic architecture of Morocco and Andalusia. Author of many books and articles. The most prominent is a four-volume work on Cairo mosques and madrasas: an introduction, a volume on the Fatimid era, a volume on the Ayyubid era, and a fourth volume, on the Mamluk era, which has not yet been published.[17]

2.2.6   ʿAbd al-ʿAzīz Marzūq (1904–76)   عبد العزيز مرزوق

Started at the Islamic Museum, then moved to teaching at Alexandria, Cairo, and Baghdad Universities. Author of many books and articles, mainly on minor arts, especially Mamluk textiles and Mamluk mosques.[18]

2.2.7   ʿAbd al-Raḥmān ʿAbd al-Tawwāb (1916–2016)   عبد الرحمن عبد التواب

Archaeologist and academic who founded the archaeology department at Sūhāj University. Best known for pioneering the use of manuscripts in the study of Islamic architecture, and his publication of the texts of tomb stelae or

---

15   F. Shāfiʿī. F. *al-ʿImāra al-ʿarabiyya fi Miṣr al-Islāmiyya: ʿaṣr al-wulāt 32–358 (639–969)*, Cairo, 1994.

16   Z. Ḥasan, *Kunūz al-Fāṭimiyyīn*, Cairo, n.d.

17   A. Fikrī, *Masājid al-Qāhira wa-madārisuhā*, 3 vols., Cairo, 1962, 1965, 1969.

18   For his biography and works see Zakī, *Kalimat rathāʾ*, 5–10.

gravestones of Aswan cemetery at *Le Bulletin de l'Institut Français d'Archéologie Orientale* (BIFAO).

2.2.8   Suʿād Māhir (1917–96)   سعاد ماهر

Academic and archeologist. She was a prolific writer on various topics in Islamic art, including the Mamluk period. Her best-known book is a five-volume study of the mosques of Egypt and the holy men buried in them.[19]

3   Universities

Universities are the locomotive of research work and the incubator for scholars in the humanities in Egypt. There are 25 state universities – at least one in almost every governorate (province) of Egypt. The oldest is Cairo University, founded in 1908, followed by Alexandria University, ʿAyn Shams University, and ʾAsyūṭ University, all founded in the 1940s and early 1950s.[20] The remaining provincial universities started as offshoots of the first four, then became independent.

Almost every university has a faculty of arts where the history and archaeology of Islamic arts and architecture are part of its curriculum. Cairo University, Fayyūm University, Sūhāj University, South Valley University in Qinā, and most recently Aswan (2014); all have a separate faculty for archaeology with departments for Pharaonic, Greco-Roman, Islamic, and restoration. There is no institute or center specializing in Mamluk studies in any Egyptian university.

In addition, there are 20 private universities in Egypt, teaching mainly medicine, technology, science, and engineering. Humanities are a low priority, if they exist at all, in most of the private universities. The private universities are relatively new; the first was opened in 1996. Since postgraduate study, particularly in the humanities, does not exist for all practical purposes at the private universities, it will not be covered in this study.

3.1   *Faculty of Archaeology, Cairo University*

I will treat this faculty in more detail since it is the pioneer and bastion of learning in the field of Islamic arts in general and Mamluk arts in particular.[21] It was founded in 1925 as a department within the Faculty of Arts and became

---

19   S. Māhir, *Masājid Miṣr wa-awlīyāʾuhā al-ṣāliḥūn*, 5 vols., Cairo, 2017.

20   University names apart from Cairo and Alexandria, which are mostly uncommon in English, will be transliterated as they are pronounced, not necessarily as they appear on the univesity logo or publications.

21   The department of Islamic Arts and Architecture of the American University in Cairo is another bastion of Mamluk studies and a pioneer in the field but it will not be treated here, as the language of research and teaching is English.

an independent faculty in 1970. The faculty offers extensive postgraduate programs in archaeology, history, and restoration. Its program has four general diplomas, ten specialized diplomas, and four vocational diplomas, based on a credit-hour system with no research dissertation requirement. The Master of Arts (MA) program includes 14 specializations, combining credit hours and research dissertation. The Doctor of Philosophy (PhD) is a pure research degree offered in 14 specializations covering a wide range of topics and different geopolitical zones. Both MA and PhD degrees require the successful defense of a dissertation. The programs are conducted in Arabic, except for a couple of specialized courses.[22]

The research output in terms of dissertations for the MA and PhD degrees will be classified on the basis of their subject topics. The following topics are identified.[23]

a. In the field of history of architecture:
   i. Monuments: a study covering a single building or part(s) of a single building.
   ii. Patronage: a study of the founder(s) and/or construction supervisors, or the type of owner(s).
   iii. Area: urban studies of a region, city, quarter, or street.
   iv. Theme: studies of a certain element of a building (*minbar, miḥrāb*, portal, flooring, etc.), typology/function (madrasa, *khānqā, ribāṭ*, etc.), or a given era (such as Turkish or Circassian).
b. In the field of minor arts covering objects in any of the following categories:
   v. Numismatics.
   vi. Textiles, carpets, or costumes.
   vii. Glass, ceramics, stone, or marble.
   viii. Illuminated manuscripts.
   ix. Ivory, woodwork, or metalwork.

The Faculty of Archaeology has awarded 64 PhD degrees in Mamluk arts and architecture (out of a total of 220 degrees) in the Islamic Department since 1970,[24] as shown in Table 14.1.[25]

---

22   fa-arch.cu.edu.eg/postgraduatePrograms.html (last downloaded on 15 January 2018).

23   The same classification will be used for all other universities as well.

24   A word of caution is necessary here. All the figures given throughout this chapter are those published or available up to the end of 2017. The lists are inherently incomplete, as they grow continuously, but the sample is large enough to reflect the true picture and trends of research work at present.

25   http://fa-arch.cu.edu.eg/AllPHDsIslamic.html (last downloaded on 6 January 2018).

TABLE 14.1   Number of PhD's in Mamluk arts and architecture in the Faculty of Archaeology, Cairo University

Period	No.
Prior to 1990	22
During the 1990s	12
During the 2000s	16
Since 2010	14

The classification of dissertations by topic is shown in Table 14.2.

TABLE 14.2   Classification by topic of PhD's in Mamluk arts and architecture in the Faculty of Archaeology, Cairo University

Topic	Totals
Number of PhD's in Islamic Dept.	220
Mamluk PhD's	64
Architecture	
Monument	1
Patron or reign of a sultan	9
Region, city, or street	15
Theme	22
Sub-total	47
Minor Arts	
Numismatics	5
Textiles, carpets, or costumes	2
Glass, ceramics, or marble	2
Manuscripts	2
Miscellaneous	6
Sub-total	17

The faculty awarded 116 MA degrees in the Mamluk arts out of 362 degrees in general Islamic arts. The breakdown by decade is shown in Table 14.3.[26]

---

26   http://fa-arch.cu.edu.eg/MSCsIslamicArchaeology.html (last downloaded on 6 January 2018). This website of the Faculty of Archaeology, Cairo University lists name of candidate, title of dissertation, and date. Classification and processing of the data is by the author.

TABLE 14.3   Number of MA's in Mamluk arts and architecture in the Faculty of Archaeology, Cairo University

Period	No.
Prior to 1980	31
During the 1980s	14
During the 1990s	28
During the 2000s	26
Since 2010	17

The classification of dissertations by topic is shown in Table 14.4.

TABLE 14.4   Classification by topic of MA's in Mamluk arts and architecture in the Faculty of Archaeology, Cairo University

Topic	Totals
Total number of MA's	362
Mamluk MA's	116
Architecture	
Monument	16
Patron or reign of a sultan	11
Region, city, or street	29
Theme	28
Sub-total	84
Minor Arts	
Numismatics	3
Textiles, carpets, or costumes	4
Glass, ceramics, or marble	6
Manuscripts	8
Ivory, woodwork, or metalwork	5
Miscellaneous	6
Sub-total	32

The number of degrees now under preparation will show us the study trends. Table 14.5 shows PhD's under preparation in 2017.[27]

TABLE 14.5　Number of PhD's under preparation in Mamluk arts and architecture in the Faculty of Archaeology, Cairo University in 2017

Topic	Totals
Total number of PhD's	52
Mamluk PhD's	7
Architecture	
Monument	
Patron or reign of a sultan	1
Region, city, or street	3
Theme	1
Sub-total	5
Minor Arts	
Numismatics	1
Textiles, carpets, or costumes	1
Glass, ceramics, or marble	0
Manuscripts	
Miscellaneous	
Sub-total	2

Table 14.6 shows MA's under preparation in 2017.[28]

TABLE 14.6　Number of MA's under preparation in Mamluk arts and architecture in the Faculty of Archaeology, Cairo University in 2017.

Topic	Totals
Total number of MA's	143
Mamluk MA's	4
Architecture	
Monument	0

27　Faculty of Archaeology, Cairo University website fa-arch.cu.edu.eg/PhdsIslamicCurrent. html (last downloaded on 7 January 2018).

28　Faculty of Archaeology, Cairo University website, fa-arch.cu.edu.eg/MscsIslamicCurrent. html (last downloaded 16 January 2018).

TABLE 14.6 (*cont.*)

Topic	Totals
Patron or reign of a sultan	0
Region, city, or street	1
Theme	1
Sub-total	2
Minor Arts	
Numismatics	0
Textiles, carpets, or costumes	0
Glass, ceramics, or marble	0
Manuscripts	1
Miscellaneous	1
Sub-total	2

Whereas the number of PhD's awarded in Mamluk-era studies up to 2017 is 64 out of total of 220, or 29%, it fell to 7 degrees out of 52 PhD's under preparation, representing only 13.46%. The MA degrees currently under preparation displays this trend even more dramatically: only 4 Mamluk dissertations out of a total of 143 currently under preparation in Islamic art in general (2.79%), compared with 116 MA degrees awarded up to 2017 out of 362 (29%). Obviously, current research is moving away from the Mamluk era, mainly to other geopolitical zones and mostly outside of Egypt.

3.2   *Other Universities*

The number of research degrees in other universities will be given in the same categories, but in less detail.

TABLE 14.7   Ṭanṭā University, Faculty of Arts, Islamic Department[a]

Total number of PhD's (7), MA's (35)	42
Architecture	
Monument	3
Patron or reign of a sultan	2

a   The Egyptian Universities Libraries Consortium (EULC), http://www.eulc.edu.eg/eulc_v5/libraries/start.aspx?fn=ExploreThesis&ScopeID=1.3.3.&ID_Scope=1.3.3.&Flag=L (last downloaded on 7 January 2018).

TABLE 14.7 Ṭanṭā University, Faculty of Arts, Islamic Department (*cont.*)

Region, city, or street	7
Theme	13
Sub-total	25
Minor Arts	
Numismatics	4
Textiles, carpets, or costumes	1
Glass, ceramics, or marble	1
Manuscripts	1
Ivory, woodwork, and metalwork	4
Miscellaneous	6
Sub-total	17

TABLE 14.8 ʿAyn Shams University Faculty of Arts and Faculty of Tourism & Hotels[a]

Total number Islamic arts dissertation/Mamluk dissertations	61/14
Architecture	
Monument	0
Patron or reign of a sultan	1
Region, city, or street	1
Theme	8
Sub-total	10
Minor Arts	
Numismatics	1
Textiles, carpets or costumes	0
Glass, ceramics or marble	0
Manuscripts	1
Ivory, woodwork and metalwork	2
Miscellaneous	0
Sub-total	4

a   Ain Shams, Faculty of Arts archives, courtesy of Ḥusām Ismāʿīl of the Islamic Department.

TABLE 14.9 Alexandria University, Faculty of Arts, Islamic Department[a]

PhD	9
MA	4
Architecture	
Monument	0
Patron or reign of a sultan	4
Region, city, or street	0
Theme	4
Sub-total	8
Minor Arts	
Numismatics	0
Textiles, carpets, or costumes	0
Glass, ceramics, or marble	0
Manuscripts	1
Ivory, woodwork, and metalwork	0
Miscellaneous	4
Sub-total	5

a EULC, http://www.eulc.edu.eg/eulc_v5/libraries/start.aspx?fn=ExploreThesis&ScopeID=1.7.8.&ID_Scope=1.7.8.&Flag=L (last downloaded on 14 January 2018).

TABLE 14.10 Alexandria University, Faculty of Tourism & Hotels[a]

PhD	8
MA	14
Architecture	
Monument	0
Patron or reign of a sultan	0
Region, city, or street	4
Theme	9
Sub-total	13
Minor Arts	
Numismatics	0
Textiles, carpets, or costumes	3
Glass, ceramics, or marble	0
Manuscripts	0
Ivory, woodwork, and metalwork	4
Miscellaneous	2
Sub-total	9

a Alexandria University Faculty of Tourism & Hotels archives, courtesy of Karīm Ḥamza of Damanhūr University.

TABLE 14.11 Sūhāj University Faculty of Archaeology[a]

PhD	11
MA	13
Architecture	
Monument	0
Patron or reign of a sultan	6
Region, city, or street	0
Theme	12
Sub-total	18
Minor Arts	
Numismatics	0
Textiles, carpets, or costumes	2
Glass, ceramics, stone, or marble	2
Manuscripts	2
Ivory, woodwork, and metalwork	0
Miscellaneous	0
Sub-total	6

a Sūhāj University Faculty of Archaeology archives, courtesy of ʿAbd al-Sattār ʿUthmān.

TABLE 14.12 South Valley University (Qinā),[a] Faculty of Archaeology[b]

No. of dissertations	10
Architecture	
Monument	0
Patron or reign of a sultan	0
Region, city, or street	3
Theme	5
Sub-total	8
Minor Arts	
Numismatics	0
Textiles, carpets, or costumes	0
Glass, ceramics, or marble	1
Manuscripts	0
Ivory, woodwork, and metalwork	
Miscellaneous	1
Sub-total	2

a Faculty of Archaeology, Qina University, http://www.svu.edu.eg/arabic/links/camps/qena/archeology/high%20graduate%20-2.html (last downloaded on 14 January 2018).

b   Previously within Faculty of Arts, Islamic Antiquities Department, until becoming a separate faculty in 2007. See http://www.svu.edu.eg/arabic/links/camps/qena/archeology/islam.html (last downloaded on 14 January 2018).

TABLE 14.13   Asyūṭ University, Faculty of Arts, Islamic Department[a]

Mamluk dissertations	10
Architecture	
Monument	0
Patron or reign of a sultan	1
Region, city, or street	2
Theme	4
Sub-total	7
Minor Arts	
Numismatics	0
Textiles, carpets, or costumes	1
Glass, ceramics, or marble	2
Manuscripts	
Ivory, woodwork, and metalwork	
Miscellaneous	
Sub-total	3

a   EULC, http://www.eulc.edu.eg/eulc_v5/libraries/start.aspx?fn=ExploreThesis&ScopeID=1.18.9.&ID_Scope=1.18.9.&Flag=L (last downloaded on 14 January 2018).

TABLE 14.14   Manṣūra University, Faculty of Arts and Faculty of Tourism[a]

Mamluk dissertations	7
Architecture	
Monument	1
Patron or reign of a sultan	1
Region, city, or street	2

a   EULC, http://www.eulc.edu.eg/eulc_v5/libraries/start.aspx?fn=ExploreThesis&ScopeID=1.1.9.&ID_Scope=1.1.9.&Flag=L (Faculty of Arts) (last downloaded on 14 January 2018) and http://www.eulc.edu.eg/eulc_v5/libraries/start.aspx?fn=ExploreThesis&ScopeID=1.1.14.&ID_Scope=1.1.14.&Flag=L (Faculty of Tourism and Hotels).

TABLE 14.14 Manṣūra University, Faculty of Arts and Faculty of Tourism (*cont.*)

Theme	1
Sub-total	5
Minor Arts	
Numismatics	1
Textiles, carpets, or costumes	0
Glass, ceramics, or marble	0
Manuscripts	0
Ivory, woodwork, and metalwork	0
Miscellaneous	1
Sub-total	2

TABLE 14.15 Minyā University, Faculty of Arts, Islamic Department[a]

Mamluk dissertations	9
Architecture	
Monument	0
Patron or reign of a sultan	0
Region, city, or street	6
Theme	3
Sub-total	9
Minor Arts	
Numismatics	0
Textiles, carpets, or costumes	0
Glass, ceramics, or marble	0
Manuscripts	0
Ivory, woodwork, and metalwork	0
Miscellaneous	0
Sub-total	0

a EULC, Faculty of Arts (last downloaded on 14 January 2018), http://www.eulc.edu.eg/eulc_v5/libraries/start.aspx?fn=ExploreThesis&ScopeID=1.2.4.&ID_Scope=1.2.4.&Flag=L and Faculty of Tourism and Hotels, http://www.eulc.edu.eg/eulc_v5/libraries/start.aspx?fn=ExploreThesis&ID_Scope=1.2.15.&orderType=&OrderKey=&frameName=&ScopeID=1.2.15.&PageNo=11 (last downloaded on 14 January 2018).

TABLE 14.16 Universities of Ḥilwān, Zaqāzīq, Kafr al-Shaykh, and Fayyūm[a]

Mamluk dissertations	8
Architecture	
Monument	0
Patron or reign of a sultan	0
Region, city, or street	1
Theme	6
Sub-total	7
Minor Arts	
Numismatics	0
Textiles, carpets, or costumes	0
Glass, ceramics, or marble	0
Manuscripts	1
Ivory, woodwork, and metalwork	
Miscellaneous	

a   EULC, Hilwān, Faculty of Arts, http://www.eulc.edu.eg/eulc_v5/libraries/start.aspx?fn=ExploreThesis&ScopeID=1.22.16.&ID_Scope=1.22.16.&Flag=L (last downloaded on 14 January 2018); Faculty of Tourism and Hotels, http://www.eulc.edu.eg/eulc_v5/libraries/start.aspx?fn=ExploreThesis&ID_Scope=1.22.12.&orderType=&OrderKey=&frameName=&ScopeID=1.22.12.&PageNo=8 (last downloaded on 14 January 2018); Kafr al-Shaykh Faculty of Arts, shttp://www.eulc.edu.eg/eulc_v5/libraries/start.aspx?fn=ExploreThesis&ScopeID=1.15.45.&ID_Scope=1.15.45.&Flag=L (last downloaded on 14 January 2018); Fayyūm Faculty of Archaeology, http://www.eulc.edu.eg/eulc_v5/libraries/start.aspx?fn=ExploreThesis&ScopeID=1.17.51.&ID_Scope=1.17.51.&Flag=L (last downloaded on 14 January 2018).

3.2.1   Statistical Analysis

The previous tables are combined in a single table, Table 14.17, where we can identify certain trends before we proceed to the critical evaluation phase.

Chart 14.1 shows the total number of dissertations in each Egyptian university that awarded at least one PhD or MA degree in the history of Mamluk arts and architecture from 1970 till now.

The Faculty of Archaeology of Cairo University has the lion's share, with more dissertations than all the other universities combined, as shown in Chart 14.2.

TABLE 14.17 Combined research topics in Mamluk Arts and Architecture for all Egyptian universities

	Cairo	Tanta	Alex	Sūhāj	'Ain Shams	Qinā	Assīūṭ	Manṣūra	Miniyyā	Others	Total	% Cairo U
Total Mamluk Dissertations	180	42	35	24	14	10	10	7	9	8	339	53%
Architecture												
Monument	17	3						1			21	
Patron or reign of a sultan	20	2	4	6	1		1	1			35	
Region, city, or street	44	7	4		1	3	2	2	6	1	70	
Theme	50	13	13	12	8	5	4	1	3	6	115	
Sub-total	131	25	21	18	10	8	7	5	9	7	241	54%
Minor Arts												
Numismatics	8	4			1			1			14	
Carpets/ textiles	6	1	3	2			1				13	
Glass/ceramic	8	1		2		1	2				14	
Manuscripts	10	1	1	2	1					1	16	
Ivory/ woodwork/ metalwork	5	4	4		2						15	
Miscellaneous	12	6	6			1		1			26	
Sub-total	49	17	14	6	4	2	3	2	0	1	98	50%

The share of Mamluk architecture vs. minor arts at Cairo University, the mother faculty, compared to all others, is shown in Chart 14.3.

As Chart 14.3 shows, the study of Mamluk architecture exceeds that of the minor arts with a ratio of 71% to 29%. Whereas architectural studies are dominated by two topics (area and theme), representing 72% of the dissertations, the minor arts studies are more evenly distributed over all the topics.

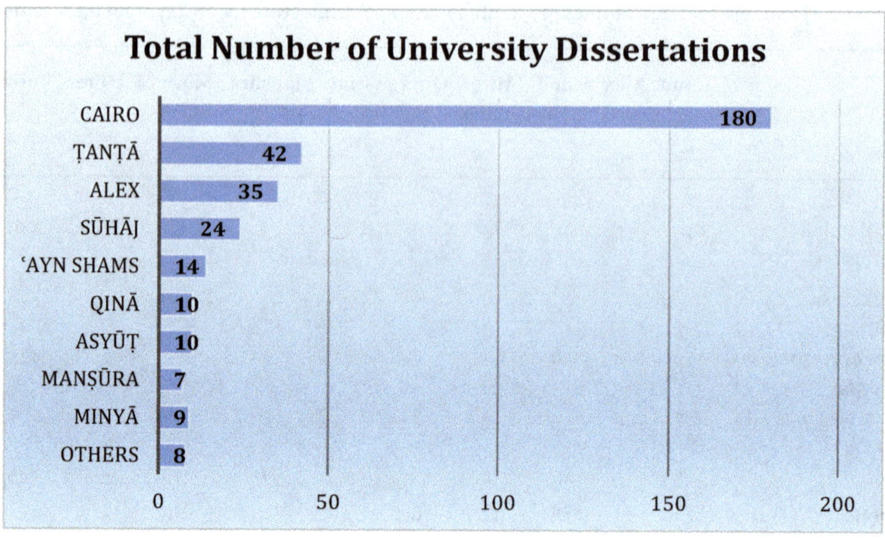

CHART 14.1 Total number of university dissertations

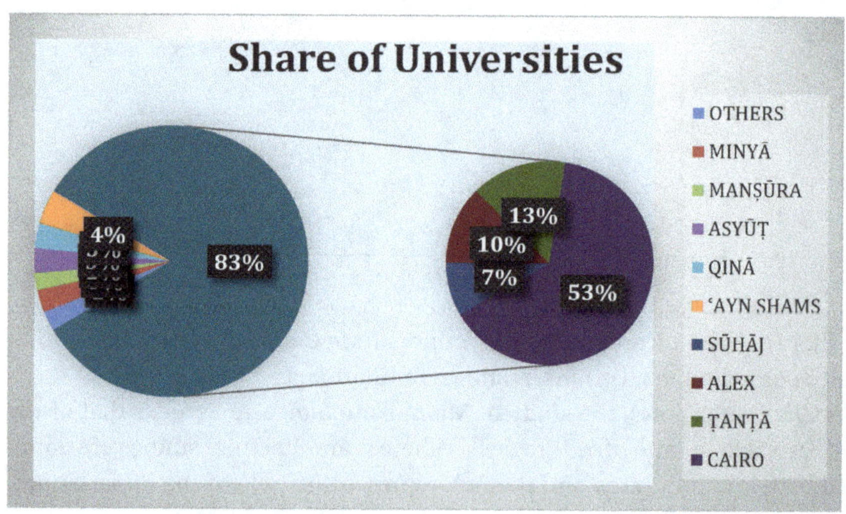

CHART 14.2 Share of universities

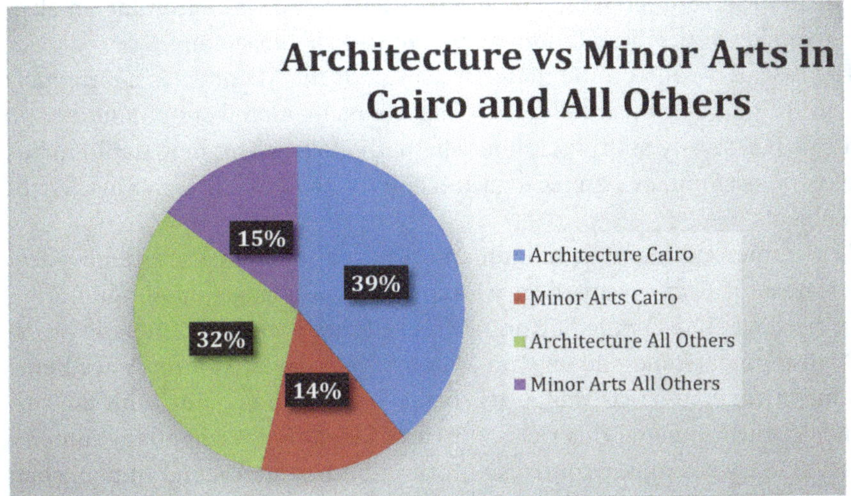

CHART 14.3 Architecture vs. minor arts in Cairo and all others

3.2.2   Preliminary Remarks on Research Content

Thorough evaluation of the corpus of scholarly production from Egyptian universities is neither possible nor intended here. Dissertations mostly follow a certain structure and methodology that is set out in research manuals.[29] After the introduction, a background study of the era and the research topic is given, covering the historical, political, geographical, and socioeconomic aspects. Normally an exhaustive description of the research object – a building, parts of a building, or an artifact(s) – is given in one or more chapters, detailing its elements and/or units. The description is followed by formal analysis of the elements of the object, emphasizing its origins, provenance, influence, development, and artistic and functional merits. A conclusion chapter ends the study by summarizing its contents and pointing to the new ideas and results presented. Following standard academic practice, all of the sources, figures, plates, annexes, etc., are listed.

A long title is normally used, defining the subject and period under study. In addition, many dissertations use subtitles to emphasize the methodology followed: a historical, architectural, artistic, documentary, or urban study. For example, many titles will be followed by words like *dirasa tārīkhiyya, miʾmāriyya, fanniyya, wathāʾiqiyya* or *ḥaḍāriyya*, as will be seen in the bibliographical part of this study. The absolute majority of dissertations are not published or posted

---

29   As an example, see Ismāʿīl, *Manhaj al-baḥth*, 127–50, and ʿAbd al-Wāḥid Taha, *Uṣūl al-baḥth al-tārīkhī*, Tripoli/Beirut, 2004.

on the internet, but left sitting on library shelves, though presenting an electronic version of the dissertation is a prerequisite for acceptance.

The research done on the material culture of the Mamluks is enormously rich in information on the different aspects of its architectural and artistic heritage. It is mostly multidisciplinary in methodology. This long tradition has resulted in accumulated knowledge and comprehensive scholarly coverage of the subjects.

The numerous Mamluk monuments that survived in Cairo and a few other areas in Egypt resulted in widespread consciousness and admiration of its heritage. The *Comité* beginnings turned into a massive scholarly investigation to understand and explain Mamluk heritage in its formal, aesthetic, and historical context, as well as its socioeconomic interaction with the surrounding environment. This rich landscape, aided by the abundant contemporary literary Mamluk narratives – both published books and unpublished manuscripts – propelled genuine research in academic institutions. Egyptian researchers extensively exploited the archival resources, such as endowment deeds (*waqf*), and monumental inscriptions to produce a truly multidisciplinary corpus of research.[30] The Museum of Islamic Art in Cairo, with its large collection of Mamluk artifacts, inspired another mass of scholarly literature on Mamluk minor arts.

Most of the research is devoted to the study of monuments, artifacts, urban areas, patronage structure, the comparative themes and influences of non-Mamluk heritage, or provenance of artifacts. Little research is done on theoretical subjects like iconography, symbolism, meaning, expressive intent, the praxis of abstract ideas like Sufism, or the relationship between the dead and the living expressed by the popular tradition of visiting cemeteries. The main exceptions are several studies devoted to urban jurisprudence (*fiqh al-ʿumrān*), investigating the rules governing the planning and construction of buildings within the urban areas.[31]

On the other hand, a few negative tendencies can be discerned within an otherwise erudite body of work. Exhaustive descriptions, unnecessary elaboration, long quotations from the sources, and digression to secondary topics

---

30   Access to archival materials at the Egyptian National Archives, Ministry of Pious Endowments, national or regional libraries or other repository of manuscripts and documents, is extremely difficult. A paranoia about security requires the researcher to go through long security checks to gain access to manuscripts and/or documents.

31   As an example, see Khālid ʿAzab, "Dawr al-fiqh al-Islāmı fı-l- ʿimārat al-madaniyya fı madīnatay al-Qāhira wa Rashīd fi-l-ʿaṣrayn al-mamlūkī wa-l-ʿUthmānī", unpublished MA thesis, Faculty of Archaeology, Cairo University, 1995.

are a few examples.[32] More serious is the redundancy of the topics. The same subjects appear again and again with slight modifications, adding little scholarly value. This is aggravated by the multiplicity of research institutions and apparent lack of coordination among them.[33]

There is an obvious need for more critical reading of the narratives and deeper analysis of the various points of view; the current practice of exhaustive formal analysis of origins, dating, and provenance is not sufficient. Also, we need to move more vertically toward deeper study of the subjects, including new lines of inquiry and study of the less popular and neglected monuments in Egypt, rather than moving in a horizontal direction towards studying remote geopolitical areas.

There needs to be more emphasis on changing the research strategies toward more interpretative research, free from the old diehard influence of the masters or current academic superiors. The field needs to open itself up to modern scholarship worldwide, especially from the west, and to avoid nationalistic discourse and uncalled-for patriotism. The secondary sources used by Egyptian scholars writing in Arabic are overwhelmingly local and in Arabic. The few foreign references cited are mainly old classical works that do not draw on the modern, up-to-date research published in specialized foreign periodicals or recent books and monographs. The Internet has made most of the modern research easily accessible. The language barrier is no excuse; fluency in a European language, preferably English, is necessary.

3.2.3   *Ad Ubi?* Where Are We Heading – Research Trends

As the statistics cited earlier show, the research trend in Egyptian universities is moving away from Mamluk studies, as the percentage of Mamluk dissertations relative to the total dissertations has dropped drastically.[34] The shift may be attributed to several reasons. One is the waning of interest in Mamluk architecture inspired by the *Comité* in the nineteenth and twentieth centuries

---

32   Some of the dissertations run into the thousands of pages and endless illustrations.

33   As indicated earlier, almost every Arts faculty of the 25 state universities (except Cairo University) has an Islamic arts department, in addition to the five archaeological faculties. Almost 7000 students graduate every year with a bachelor's degree in Islamic arts, according to a statement by Muḥammad Ḥamza al-Ḥadād, Dean of the Faculty of Archaeology of Cairo University, in *al-Yawm al-Sābiʿ*, 16 January 2018.

34   As mentioned earlier, PhD's awarded in the Mamluk era up to 2017 are 64 out of a total of 220, representing 29%. In more recent years the number is 7 degrees out of 52 PhD's under preparation, representing only 13.46%. Mamluk MA's have fallen even more dramatically; currently there are only 4 Mamluk dissertations out of a total of 143 in Islamic art in general, or 2.80%, compared with 116 MA degrees awarded out of 362, or 32%, prior to 2017.

and the increasing interest in other eras, such as the Fatimid and Ottoman periods. It may well be also that most of the important, glamorous Mamluk monuments, urban areas, patrons, or artifacts are already well studied, and the remaining, more modest ones are not attractive to researchers.

Researchers of Islamic arts and architecture at the Egyptian universities focus now on other geopolitical areas of the Islamic world: Morocco and Andalusia to the west; Muslim India, Transoxiana, Turkey, Persia, and even China to the north and east. This tendency is facilitated by the opening of the country, ease of travel, globalization, and above all, the Internet and modern communications.

4　　Research Papers Published in Peer-Reviewed Periodicals

4.1　　*Periodicals Published by Universities*

Periodicals are regularly issued by university faculties, representing the first venue for the publication of peer-reviewed research papers. Almost every faculty sponsors a periodical to publish the research in its field. However, there is no Egyptian periodical devoted to Mamluk studies. The following university periodicals have published, among other disciplines, research articles related to the history of Mamluk material culture.

Magazine of the Faculty of Archaeology of Cairo University

مجلة كلية الآثار جامعة القاهرة

The oldest of the specialized periodicals, published annually since 1975 with articles on Islamic, ancient Egyptian, and conservation topics. Twenty-one issues are available on the Internet, up to the 2010–11 issue.[35]

S H E D E T, Journal of the Faculty of Archeology of Fayyūm University

شدت – مجلة كلية الآثار جامعة الفيوم

Published annually since 2014.[36]

Annals of the Faculty of Arts of ʿAyn Shams University

حوليات كلية الآداب جامعة عين شمس

Published annually since 1951.[37]

35　Ibid.

36　Shedet is the ancient name of the city of Fayyūm. Issues are available online at the Fayyūm University website, http://www.fayoum.edu.eg/english/shedet/ISSUES.aspx (last downloaded on 14 January 2018).

37　EULC, http://www.eulc.edu.eg/eulc_v5/libraries/start.aspx?fn=BrowseAllSerialPapers&S copeID=1.7.8.&item_id=10718278 (last downloaded on 19 January 2018).

Bulletin of the Faculty of Arts of Alexandria University

مجلة كلية الآداب جامعة الإسكندرية

Published annually since 1943.[38]

Bulletin of the Faculty of Arts of Sūhāj University

مجلة كلية الآداب جامعة سوهاج

Published since 1978.[39]

Journal of the Faculty of Arts of University of the South Valley (Qinā)

مجلة كلية الآداب جامعة جنوب الوادي (قنا)

Published since 1990.[40]

The Periodical of the Faculty of Arts of Manṣūra University

دورية كلية الآداب جامعة المنصورة

Published annually since 1979.[41]

Journal of the Faculty of Arts of Ṭanṭā University

مجلة كلية الآداب جامعة طنطا

Published annually since 1982.[42]

Journal of the Faculty of Arts of Binhā University

مجلة كلية الآداب جامعة بنها

Published annually since 1991.[43]

Journal of the Faculty of Arts of Ḥilwān University

مجلة كلية الآداب جامعة حلوان

Published annually since 1995–96.[44]

---

38   EULC,   http://www.eulc.edu.eg/eulc_v5/libraries/start.aspx?fn=BrowseAllSerialPapers&
     ScopeID=1.7.8.&item_id=10718278 (last downloaded on 14 January 2018).

39   EULC,   http://www.eulc.edu.eg/eulc_v5/libraries/start.aspx?fn=BrowseAllSerialPapers&
     ScopeID=1.11.9.&item_id=10991012 (last downloaded on 14 January 2018).

40   Index of articles published at the journal is available online at the South Valley Uni-
     versity website: http://www.svu.edu.eg/arabic/links/camps/qena/art/makal.html (last
     downloaded on 14 January 2018).

41   EULC,   http://www.eulc.edu.eg/eulc_v5/libraries/start.aspx?fn=BrowseAllSerialPapers&
     ScopeID=1.1.9.&item_id=120135 (last downloaded on 14 January 2018).

42   EULC,   http://www.eulc.edu.eg/eulc_v5/libraries/start.aspx?fn=BrowseAllSerialPapers&
     ScopeID=1.3.3.&item_id=123574 (last downloaded on 14 January 2018).

43   EULC,   http://www.eulc.edu.eg/eulc_v5/libraries/start.aspx?fn=BrowseAllSerialPapers&
     ScopeID=1.19.5.&item_id=11384382 (last downloaded on 14 January 2018).

44   EULC,   http://www.eulc.edu.eg/eulc_v5/libraries/start.aspx?fn=BrowseAllSerialPapers&
     ScopeID=1.22.16.&item_id=11830141 (last downloaded on 14 January 2018).

Humanities, Faculty of Arts of Damanhūr University

إنسانيات كلية الآداب جامعة دمنهور

Published since 1998.[45]

History and Future Magazine of Minyā University

مجلة التاريخ والمستقبل جامعة المنيا

Published annually since 1998.[46]

The Egyptian Historian of the Faculty of Arts, Cairo University.

مجلة المؤرخ المصري كلية الآداب جامعة القاهرة

Published annually since 1988.[47]

All the above periodicals were surveyed for articles related to Mamluk art and architecture. Citations of the articles identified were classified by topic of research in a similar manner to the university dissertations. The results are shown in Table 14.18 and Chart 14.4.

TABLE 14.18 Research topics for all Egyptian Universities periodicals

University periodicals	Archaeology, Cairo	Fayūm, SHEDET	Annals, ʿAīn Shams	Bulletin, Sūhāj	Alex	Qinā	Manṣūra	Egyptian Historian	Hilwuan Tanta Banha Damn.	History & Future Minya	Total
Mamluk Papers	29	3	4	15	4	9	6	8	11	9	98
Architecture											
Monument	4	1	1	6	1	1	4	2	1	3	
Patron or reign of a sultan	2			1		1		2	2	1	9
Region, city, or street	2		2	2		1		1	2	1	
Theme	12			2	2	3	1	1	4	3	28
Sub-total	20	1	3	11	3	6	5	6	9	8	72

45 EULC, http://www.eulc.edu.eg/eulc_v5/libraries/start.aspx?fn=BrowseAllSerialPapers&ScopeID=1.111.2.&item_id=10710863 (last downloaded on 14 January 2018).

46 EULC, http://www.eulc.edu.eg/eulc_v5/libraries/start.aspx?fn=BrowseAllSerialPapers&ScopeID=1.2.4.&item_id=11383738 (last downloaded on 14 January 2018).

47 The first 23 issues are available online at Wadod: http://wadod.net/bookshelf/book/2813 (last downloaded on 14 January 2018).

TABLE 14.18 (*cont.*)

University periodicals	Archaeology, Cairo	Fayūm, SHEDET	Annals, ʿAīn Shams	Bulletin, Sūhāj	Alex	Qinā	Manṣūra	Egyptian Historian	Hilwuan Tanta Banha Damn.	History & Future Minya	Total
Minor Arts											
Numismatics	3			1		2					6
Carpets/textiles	1	1									2
Glass/ceramic/marble/stone	1	1		2	1				1		6
Manuscripts	1					1					2
Ivory/woodwork/metalwork								1			1
Miscellaneous	3		1	1			1	1	1	1	9
Sub-total	9	2	1	4	1	3	1	2	2	1	26

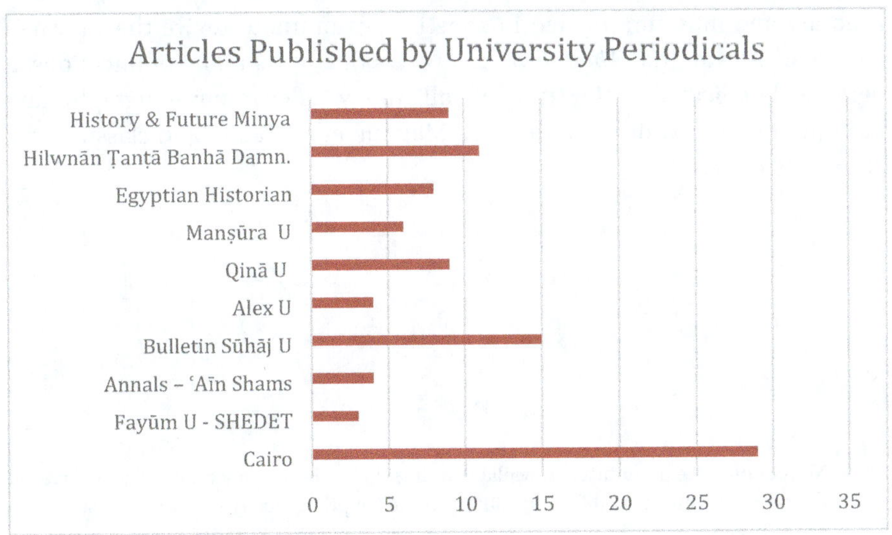

CHART 14.4 Articles published by university periodicals

4.2 Periodicals Issued by Cultural Centres and Societies

The Egyptian Society for Historical Studies

الجمعية المصرية للدراسات التاريخية

The society was founded in 1945. Beginning in 1948, it published a periodical called *The Egyptian Historical Review* (مجلة الجمعية التاريخية المصرية) as a venue
for research on the history of Egypt and related studies. Another periodical,
started in 2011, called *Annals of the Seminar on Islamic and Medieval History*
(حولية سمنار التاريخ الإسلامي والوسيط), is a venue for publication of the lectures and
studies given monthly at the society's premises.[48]

Institut Français d'Archéologie Orientale (French Institute for Oriental
Archaeology)
Founded in 1880 by the French government to study Egyptian culture from
prehistory to modern times. They publish two main periodicals. *Le Bulletin
de l'Institut Français d'Archéologie Orientale* (BIFAO),[49] published since 1901,
is almost entirely in French and English and is not covered here. The other
periodical, *Annales Islamologiques*[50] (حوليات إسلامية), published since 1954,
includes many articles in Arabic by Egyptian scholars.

Bibliotheca Alexandrina مكتبة الإسكندرية
A library and museum opened in 2002 in Alexandria to revive the vanished
Library of Alexandria. *Abgadiyat* (أبجديات) is one of its many publications, a
periodical dedicated to the study of calligraphy, paleography, epigraphy, and
inscriptions worldwide, including the Mamluk era.[51] Table 14.19 classifies the
articles by topic.

---

48 Neither of these periodicals is available online, to the best of my knowledge. I surveyed
the physical issues available at the library of the Egyptian Society for Historical Studies in
Nasr City, Cairo.

49 All the issues are available online at http://www.ifao.egnet.net/bifao/114/ (last downloaded on 14 January 2018).

50 All the issues are available online at http://www.ifao.egnet.net/anisl/ (last downloaded on
14 January 2018).

51 All the issues are available online at http://www.bibalex.com/calligraphycenter/abgadi-
yat/Issue/IssueList.aspx?page=Issues&lang=en (last downloaded on 14 January 2018).

TABLE 14.19 Research topics for all Egyptian Cultural Centers and Societies periodicals

	Egyptian Historical Review	Seminar of the Historical Society	*Abgadiyat*	*Annales Islamologiques*	Total
Mamluk papers	6	2	6	15	29
Architecture					
Monument	1		1	4	6
Patron or reign of a sultan	1			3	4
Region, city, or street			1	1	2
Theme	2	1	1	5	9
Sub-total	4	1	3	13	21
Minor Arts					
Numismatics			2		2
Carpets/textiles	1			1	2
Glass/ceramic/ marble/stone		1			1
Manuscripts					
Ivory/woodwork/ metalwork	1		1		2
Miscellaneous				1	1
Sub-total	2	1	3	2	8

4.3   *Periodicals Issued by the State Ministry for Antiquities*

The ministry issues several periodicals, two of them specializing in the study of Islamic arts. The first is *Islamic Archaeological Studies*, published since 1978, with five volumes surveyed till 1995. The second is the *Egyptian Journal for Islamic Archaeology* (*Mishkāh*), published since 2006, with five volumes surveyed till 2010–11. Neither is available online, so the figures in Table 14.20 are based on inspection of the physical volumes.

Thus, the total number of articles published by peer-reviewed periodicals reviewed by the author related to the study of Mamluk arts and architecture is 151 articles: 105 articles in architecture (70%) and 46 in minor arts (30%). The number of articles in each periodical is shown in Charts 14.5 and 14.6. We observe the same trend here as in dissertations: architectural studies dominate by a little more than 2 to 1; Cairo University still dominates, but to a lesser extent; and the topics are more or less evenly distributed.

TABLE 14.20 Research topics for The Ministry of Antiquities periodicals

Periodicals	*Islamic Archaeological Studies*	*Mishkāh, Egyptian Journal of Islamic Archaeology*	Total
Mamluk papers	17	7	24
Architecture			
Monument	5	1	6
Patron or reign of a sultan			
Region, city, or street		2	2
Theme	1	3	4
Sub-total	6	6	12
Minor Arts			
Numismatics	2		2
Carpets/textiles	1		1
Glass/ceramic/marble/stone	2		2
Manuscripts	1		1
Ivory/woodwork/metalwork	4		4
Miscellaneous	1	1	2
Sub-total	11	1	12

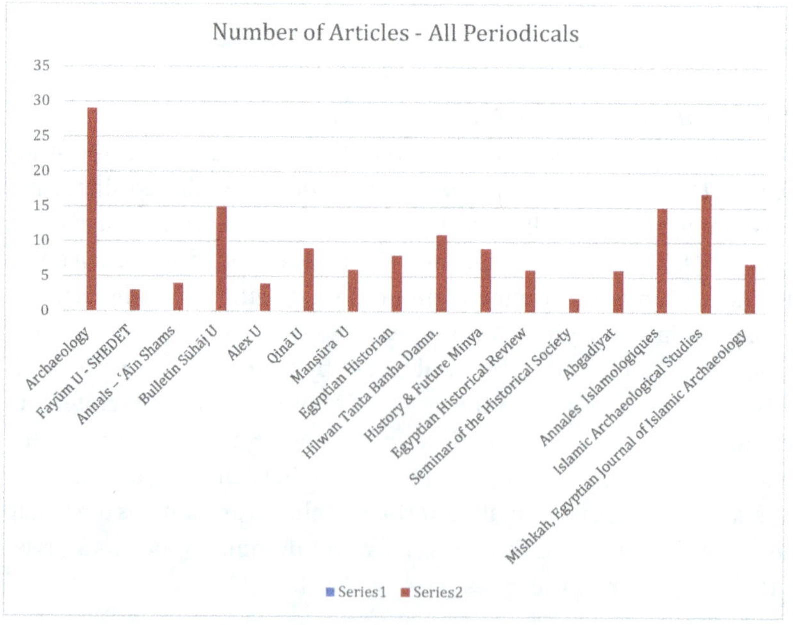

CHART 14.5 Number of articles – all periodicals

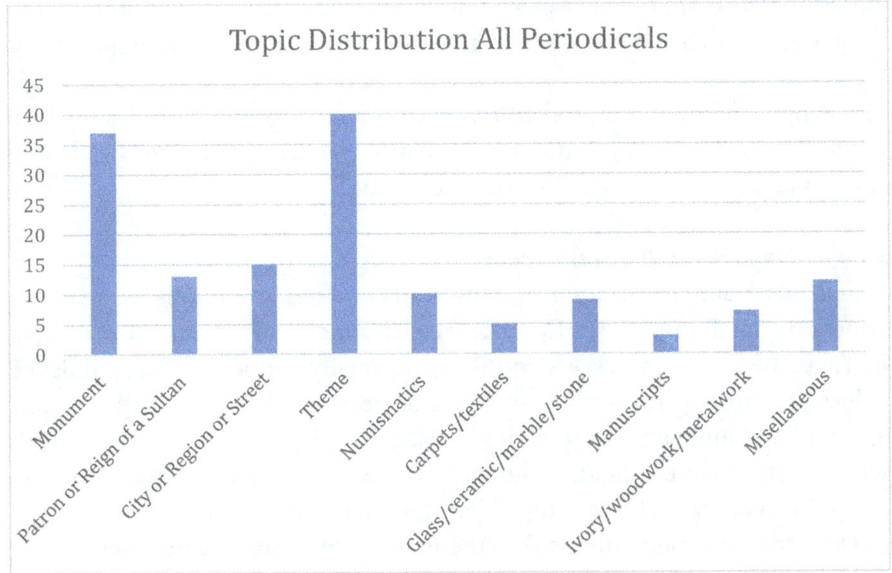

CHART 14.6 Topic distribution – all periodicals

4.4 *Monumental Inscriptions of Historic Cairo*

Though it is not a periodical yet, this project is a research tool of great importance. For almost 20 years, starting in 1997, its mission was to photograph, transcribe, and translate every inscription on an Islamic monument in Historic Cairo till 1800. It was carried out by a large team of specialists led by Bernard O'Kane of the American University in Cairo. The inscriptions are available online.[52]

4.5 *General Historical Periodicals Including History of Mamluk Material Culture (Articles Not Surveyed by the Author)*

The Arab Historian's Journal (*Majallat al-muʾarrikh al-ʿArabī*), an annual peer reviewed periodical issued by the Federation of Arab Historians established in 1992 in Cairo.[53] The journal has published twenty-seven issues since 1993.

The Journal of Architecture, Arts and Humanities, published The Arab Association of Civilization and Islamic Arts in Cairo.

---

52 http://islamicinscriptions.cultnat.org (last downloaded on 14 January 2018).

53 For more information about the federation, see: http://www.arabhistoryso.net (last downloaded on 12 December 2020).

Turāthiyāt, a semi-annual peer reviewed periodical published by the Manuscript Center of The Egyptian National Library and Archives in Cairo since 2003.

The Papyrus Studies and Inscriptions Institute belonging to ʿAyn Shams University, established in 1978, publishes a journal carrying its name with thirty-seven issues to date that can be accessed online.[54]

4.6   *Remarks on the Periodicals*

Unlike postgraduate research degrees in universities, the published research papers are not dominated by Cairo University, which makes them more diversified in content and form. We identified 13 university periodicals that published at least one article on Mamluk material culture, with a total of 98 articles. Government and independent societies have another 6 peer-reviewed periodicals with 53 articles in our field.[55] The history of Mamluk architecture still dominates the field (72%), but the topic distribution is more even.

One striking observation is that the number of postgraduate research dissertations, as shown earlier, is 335, more than double the 151 research papers published by periodicals. It is a huge difference when one considers that the effort, resources, and time necessary to produce a PhD or MA dissertation exceeds by far what is necessary to produce a research paper. Also, we note that most of the scholars publishing in the periodicals come from university faculties, and many contribute several papers. The observations on the evaluation of the content of research articles are very similar to the university production mentioned earlier and will not be repeated here.

Finally, we can conclude that the majority of postgraduate degree holders do not publish after they obtain the degree, and fewer scholars, mainly university faculty, keep on researching and publishing. One is tempted to believe that a great many researchers are motivated to obtain a higher degree to promote a professional non-academic career rather than because of a genuine interest in the research field.

---

54   https://bcps.journals.ekb.eg/issue_4483_4484_.html (last downloaded on 12 December 2020).

55   I covered only the periodicals specializing in historical studies and archaeology. Inevitably there must be some articles in our field published in other general periodicals that are not included here.

5 Book Series

There are not many specialized publishers for historical or archaeological studies, but specialized book series in the field are available. The first two listed are the most important.

History of the Egyptians series سلسلة تاريخ المصريين
A series of monographs published by the state-owned General Book Organization, it has published more than 300 titles since 1978. They focus on the history of Egypt from antiquity up to modern times, including the Mamluk period. Many dissertations on general Mamluk history have been published so far, including seven titles on Mamluk arts and architecture.[56]

Publications of the Ministry of Antiquities
The National Project for Registration and Documentation of the Islamic and Coptic Monuments (المشروع القومي لتسجيل وتوثيق الآثار الإسلامية والقبطية) is a series of booklets (20 so far) documenting individual monuments. Though not academic, it gives much data on the history and features of the monuments, many of which date to the Mamluk era.

The Historical Cairo Series, (مشروع القاهرة التاريخية), is another series of booklets documenting the renovation work done during restoration of a selected group of monuments. They are compiled by the work group of the Historic Cairo Project, which is practical rather than academic.

The Hundred Books series (مشروع المائة كتاب) is another publication on various historical and archaeological topics since 1985 with 33 monographs up to 2003 with only three on the Mamluks, mentioned in the bibliographical section of this paper.

6 Monographs

There are numerous monographs on Islamic arts and architecture by specialized academics, but they cover mostly broad subjects and different geopolitical eras, including the Mamluks. Citations of monographs that are related to Mamluk materials culture will be included in the general bibliography of this paper, but it is far from exhaustive.

---

56   Citations will be included in the general bibliography of this paper.

7   Conclusion

Egypt, as the base of the Mamluk Empire, is the repository of the most magnificent Mamluk monuments and artifacts. An old tradition of research to study, repair, preserve, and understand this rich repertoire has developed since the last quarter of the nineteenth century. The Mamluk arts and architectural style stood out as the quintessential expression of medieval Egyptian heritage; indeed, many have considered Mamluk architecture to be the national art of Egypt.[57]

A survey of the venues of research in this field gives a map of the academic institutions and throws light on their history and activities with a critical evaluation of the research characteristics of the field. In a similar way the publication venues for research papers, monographs, and books were surveyed and identified, creating the start of a comprehensive bibliographical database. The survey and classification were based on the topics rather than the scholars, with the exception of the historical introduction, for ease of research.

An obvious trend of Egyptian scholars moving away from research in the Mamluk era reflects modern globalization and awareness of the other geopolitical parts of wider Islamic heritage. In the same way, the interest of Western scholarly circles in Mamluk history and material culture has grown tremendously in recent years. The need to make the Egyptian Arabic scholarship available to Western scholars is now apparent and pressing. This study had two objectives: first, to show the research and publication venues in Egypt, and second, to present a reasonably comprehensive bibliographical database. A select and representative bibliography is shown in the annex here with full citations.[58]

Bibliography

Abgadīyat, http://www.bibalex.com/calligraphycenter/abgadiyat/Issue/IssueList.aspx? page=Issues&lang=en (2018).

Annales Islamologique, http://www.ifao.egnet.net/anisl/ (2018).

Comité, *Exercice 1882–1883*, Fascicule 1, Cairo, 1892.

Faculty of Archaeology, Cairo University website, http://fa-arch.cu.edu.eg (2018).

---

57   Paula Sanders, *Creating Medieval Cairo*, 142.
58   A comprehensive bibliography of Egyptian scholarship on Mamluk arts and architecture will hopefully be published on the Internet in the near future.

Faculty of Archaeology, South Valley University (Qinā), http://www.svu.edu.eg/arabic/index.html (2018).

Fayyūm University, http://www.fayoum.edu.eg/english/shedet/ISSUES.aspx (2018).

Al-Ḥabashī, A. and Warner, N., Recording the monuments of Cairo: An Introduction and overview, in *Annales Islamologique* 32 (1998), 81–990.

Islamic Art Network, Thesaurus Islamicus Foundation, http://www.islamic-art.org (2018).

Ismāʿīl, M.H. *Manhaj al-baḥth fī al-athār al-Islāmiyya*, Cairo, 2006.

Le Bulletin de l'Institut Français d'Archéologie Orientale (BIFAO), http://www.ifao.egnet.net/bifao/114/ (2018).

Lūqā, A. ʿAlī Bahjat awwal atharī Misrī, Kitab al-hilāl 639, December 2003.

Markaz Wadod li al-fahāris wa kutub al-taḥqīq (*Wadod*), http://wadod.net/bookshelf/book/2813 (2018).

Muhammad, ʿA.F. "ʿAlī Bahjat wa-muʾallafātuhu al-rāʾida fī al-āthār al-islāmiyya." *Majallat al-Kitāb al-ʿarabī*, Vol. 50 (July 1970), 15–31.

O'Kane, B. et al.. The Monumental Inscriptions of Historic Cairo, http://islamicinscriptions.cultnat.org (2018).

Ormos, I. *Max Hertz Pasha (1856–1919) His Life and Career*, 2 vols., Cairo, 2009.

Sanders, Paula. *Creating medieval Cairo: Empire, religion, and architectural preservation in nineteenth-century Egypt*, Cairo, 2008.

South Valley University, http://www.svu.edu.eg/arabic/links/camps/qena/art/makal.html (2018).

The Egyptian Universities Libraries Consortium (EULC), www.euclc.edu.eg (2018).

ʿUkāshā, Tharwat. *Miṣr fī ʿuyūn al-ghurābāʾ min al-raḥḥāla wa al-fannānīn wa al-udabāʾ (al-qarn al-tāsiʿ ʿashar)*, 2 vols., Cairo, 2003.

Selected Bibliography

Postgraduate Dissertations

ʿAbd al-Nūr, Ḥasan. "al-Sajjād al-Mamlūkī – dirāsah athariyya fanniyya fī ḍawʾ majmūʿat matḥaf al-fann wa-ṣināʿa bi-Vīyannā "wa-allatī yablughu ʿadaduhā 159 sajjāda", unpublished PhD dissertation, Faculty of Archaeology, Cairo University, 1992.

ʿAbd al-Wahhāb, Īmān. "Dawr nisāʾ al-balāṭ fī Miṣr fī al-ʿaṣr al-Mamlūkī (648–923/1250–1517)", unpublished PhD dissertation, Islamic Archaeology Department, Faculty of Arts, Ṭanṭā University, 2015.

al-Aḥlāwī, Muḥammd. "al-Nuqūsh al-kitābiyya ʿala al-nuqūd wa-l-ʿamāʾir al-Mamlūkiyya fī Sūriyyā (658–922/1260–151) dirāsah fanniyya muqārana", unpublished PhD dissertation, Islamic Archaeology Department, Faculty of Arts, Ṭanṭā University, 2013.

Aḥmad, Aḥmad. "al-Munsha'āt al-ṣinā'iyya fi al-'aṣr al-Mamlūkī min khilāl al-wathā'iq", unpublished MA dissertation, Faculty of Archaeology, Cairo University, 1988.

Aḥmad, Mamdūḥ. "Rusūm al-'amā'ir wa-l-tuḥaf al-taṭbīqiyya fī ṣuwar al-makhṭūṭāṭ fi-l-'aṣrayn al-'Ayyūbī wa-l-Mamlūkī", unpublished PhD dissertation, Faculty of Archaeology, Cairo University, 2006.

Aḥmad, Marwa. "Wāḥat a-Dākhila fī al-'aṣrayn al-Mamlūkī wa al-ḥadīth", unpublished MA dissertation, Islamic Department, Faculty of Tourism and Hotels, Alexandria University, 2005.

al-Ḥaddād, Muhammad. "Qarāfat al-Qāhira fī 'aṣr salāṭīn al-Mamālīk dirāsah athariyya ḥaḍāriyya", unpublished MA dissertation, Faculty of Archaeology, Cairo University, 1988.

al-Ḥusnī, Tāmir. "al-Asbila al-Mamlūkiyya al-baqiyya bi-madīnat al-Qāhira dirāsah athariyya fanniyya", unpublished MA dissertation, Faculty of Archaeology, Cairo University, 2012.

al-Labābda, 'Abd Allah. "al-Muqarnaṣāt fī al-'imāra al-Islāmiyya fī Miṣr fī al-'aṣr al-Mamlūkī", unpublished MA dissertation, Faculty of Archaeology, Cairo University, 2009.

al-Nabarāwī, Ra'fat. "Maskūkāt al-Mamālīk al-Jarākisa fī Mīṣr nuẓumuhā wa-qīmatuhā al-naqdiyya – dirāsah athariyya", unpublished PhD dissertation, Faculty of Archaeology, Cairo University, 1982.

al-Sa'īd, 'Amr. "'Amā'ir al-mar'a fī al-'aṣr al-Mamlūkī bi-l-Qāhira (648–923/1250–1517)", unpublished PhD dissertation, Islamic Archaeology Department, Faculty of Arts, Ṭanṭā University, 2016.

al-Shirārī, Muḥmmad. "Ba'ḍ maẓāhir al-ḥaḍāra fī al-Madīna al-munaūara fī al-'aṣr al-Mamlūkī (648–923/1250–1517)", unpublished PhD dissertation, Islamic Archaeology Department, Faculty of Arts, Alexandria University, 2015.

'Āmir, Samar. "al-Akhtām al-maṭbū'a 'ala al-makhṭūṭāṭ wa-l-wathā'iq al-Mamlūkiyya bi-Miṣr dirāsah athariyya fanniyya", unpublished MA dissertation, Faculty of Archaeology, Cairo University, 2016.

'Āzab, Khālid. "Daur al-fiqh al-Islāmī fī al-'imāra al-madaniyya fi madīnatāy al-Qāhira wa Rashīd al-'aṣrayn al-Mamlūki wa-l-'Uthmānī", unpublished MA dissertation, Faculty of Archaeology, Cairo University, 1995.

Bidir, Muna. "Madrasat Jamāl al-Dīn al-ustādār dirāsah mi'māriyya wathā'iqiyya", unpublished MA dissertation, Islamic Archaeology Department, Faculty of Arts, Ṭanṭā University, 2011.

Darwīsh, Maḥmūd. "al-Istaḥkamāt al-ḥarbiyya bi-madīnat Rashīd min al-'aṣr al-Mamlūkī ḥata 'aṣr Muḥammad 'Alī", unpublished PhD dissertation, Faculty of Archaeology, Cairo University, 1975.

Dāwūd, Māysā. "al-Mishkāwāt al-zujājīya fi-l-'aṣr al-Mamlūkī", unpublished MA dissertation, Faculty of Archaeology, Cairo University, n.d.

Faraj, Faraj. "al-Nuqūsh al-kitābiyya al-Mamlūkiyya ʿala al-ʿamāʾir fī Sūriyyā (658–922/1260–1516) dirāsah athāriyya fanniyya muqārana", unpublished PhD dissertation, Islamic Archaeology Department, Faculty of Arts, Sūhāj University, 2008.

Ghunim, Sāmī. "al-arbiṭa al-baqiyya bi-l-Qāhira khilāl al-ʿaṣr al-Mamlūkī "648–923 AH/1250–1517 AD", unpublished MA dissertation, Faculty of Archaeology, Cairo University, Cairo 1998.

Ḥamza, Hānī. "al-Turab al-Mamlūkiyya bi-madīnat al-Qāhira "648–923 AH/1250–1517 AD", unpublished PhD dissertation, Faculty of Archaeology, Cairo University, Cairo 2004.

Ḥasan, Muḥammad. "Taṣāwīr al-ʿuyūn fī al-makhṭūṭāṭ a-ṭibiyya al-Islāmiyya dirāsah athariyya fanniyya", unpublished MA dissertation, Faculty of Archaeology, Cairo University, 1995.

Ḥasan, Suʿād. "al-Ḥamāmāt fī Miṣr al-Islāmiyya", unpublished PhD dissertation, Faculty of Archaeology, Cairo University, 1984.

Ḥusnī, Madīḥa. "Qanāṭir al-mīyyāh fī Miṣr min al-ʿaṣr al-Ṭūlūnī ilā ʿaṣr Muḥammad ʿAlī Pāsha – dirāsah athariyya ḥadāriyya", unpublished MA dissertation, Faculty of Archaeology, Cairo University, 2004.

Ismāʾīl, Nuha. "al-Taʾthīrāt al-mutābādala bayn al-muṣawwirīn al-Muslīmīn wa al-ʾUrūbiyyīn mundhu al-qarn al-rābīʿ ʿashar al-milādī wa-ḥattā al-qarn al-sādis ʿashar al-milādī dirāsah athariyya fanniyya", unpublished MA dissertation, Faculty of Archaeology, Cairo University, 2014.

Mitwalī, ʿAlī. "Usus taṣmīm al-ʿamāʾir al-sakaniyya fī al-Qāhira fī al- ʿaṣrayn al-Mamlūkī wa-l-ʿUthmānī – dirāsah athariyya miʾmāriyya", unpublished PhD dissertation, Faculty of Archaeology, Cairo University, 2006.

Muḥammad, Amīna. "Qāʿāt sakaniyya wa quṣūr Mamlūkiyya taḥawwalat īlā munshʾāt dīniyya bi-madīnat al-Qāhira", unpublished MA dissertation, Faculty of Archaeology, Cairo University, 2005.

Muḥammad, Nuhā. "al-Ṭabaq al-najmī fī ʿamāʾir al-Qāhira fī ʿaṣr daulat al-Mamālīk al-Jarākisa dirāsah fanniyya taḥlīliyya muqārana (648–923/1250–1517)", unpublished MA dissertation, Islamic Archaeology Department, Faculty of Arts, Alexandria University, 2015.

Muḥammad, ʿAlāʾ. "Dirāsah athariyya fannīyya li-majmūʿa jadīda min al-zujāj al-Ayyūbī wa-l-Mamlūkī bi-matḥaf al-fann al-Islāmī bi al-Qāhira", unpublished PhD dissertation, Faculty of Archaeology, Cairo University, 2015.

Mūsa, Asmāʾ. "Athar al-takaddus al-ʿumrānī ʿala ʿimārat al-Qāhira fī al-ʿaṣrayn al-Ayyūbi wa-l-Mamlūki", unpublished MA dissertation, Faculty of Archaeology, Cairo University, 2001.

Mūsa, Jamāl. "al-Mansūjāt al- ḥarīriyya fī Miṣr al-Mamlūkiyya", unpublished MA dissertation, Faculty of Archaeology, Cairo University, 1976.

Muṣliḥ, ʿAbd Allah. "al-ʿAmāʾir al-dīniyya al-baqiyya fi al-ʾUrdun min al- ʿaṣrayn al-Mamlūki wa-l-ʿUthmānī – dirāsah athariyya miʾmāriyya", unpublished PhD dissertation, Faculty of Archaeology, Cairo University, 2012.

Nawijī, Ibrāhīm. "al-Masājid al-Islāmiyya fī al-madīnat al-qadīma bi-Ṭarāblus", unpublished MA dissertation, Faculty of Archaeology, Cairo University, 2010.

Nūwayṣar, Ḥusnī. "Munshaʾāt al-sultān Qaʾītbāy al-dīniyya bi-madīnat al-Qāhira – dirāsah miʾmāriyya athariyya", unpublished PhD dissertation, Faculty of Archaeology, Cairo University, 1975.

Qāsim, Yāsmīn. "Ẓāhirat al-ʿumrān al-raʾsī fī al-ʿamāʾir al-Mamlūkiyya bī-l-Qāhira", unpublished MA dissertation, Islamic Archaeology Department, Faculty of Arts, Sūhāj MA University, 2015.

Ṣāliḥ, Basma. "Iʿādat istikhdām al-ʿanāṣir al-miʿmāriyya fī al-ʿimāra al-Islāmiyya bi-madīnat al-Qāhira mundhu inshāʾihā ḥata nihāyat al-ʿaṣr al-Mamlūkī (358–923/969-1517)", unpublished PhD dissertation, Islamic Department, Faculty of Tourism and Hotels, Alexandria University, 2016.

Salīm, Sihām. "Fann tajlīd al-kitāb fi al-ʿaṣr al-Mamlūkī", unpublished dissertation, Faculty of Archaeology, Cairo University, 1975.

Saʿūdī, ʿAṭiyyāt. "al-Rukhām fī Miṣr fī ʿaṣr al-Mamālīk al-baḥriyya, dirāsah athariyya fannīyya", unpublished PhD dissertation, Faculty of Archaeology, Cairo University, 1994.

Sulaymān, Sawsān. "Munshaʾāt al-amīr Qajmas al-Isḥāqī, dirāsah athariyya miʿmāriyya", unpublished MA dissertation, Faculty of Archaeology, Cairo University, 1985.

ʿUthmān, Muḥammad. "Naẓariyyat al-waẓīfat ʿala al-ʿamāʾir al-dīniyya al-Mamlūkiyya al-bāqiya bi-madīnat al-Qāhira", unpublished PhD dissertation, Islamic Archaeology Department, Faculty of Arts in Asyūt, Asyūt University, 1979.

Yāghī, Ghazwān. "al-ʿAmāʾir al-sakaniyya al-baqīyya bi-madīnat al-Qāhira fī-l- ʿaṣr al-Mamlūkī – dirāsah athariyya ḥaḍāriyya", unpublished PhD dissertation, Faculty of Archaeology, Cairo University, 2005.

Periodicals

ʿAbd al-Malik, S.S. "al-Mawrūth al-tārīkhī fī khidmat al-iktishāfāt al-athāriyya, al-waqiʿ wa-l-maʾmūl: ṭarīq al-barīd wa-l-ḥajj al-miṣrī fī Sīnāʾ namūdhajan – thamāniya ʿashar ʿām min al-baḥth wa-l-tanqīb fī majāhil Sīnāʾ", *Mishkah* 5 (2010–1), 119–47.

ʿAbd al-Raḥīm, Khalaf. "Dirasa fī al-funūn al-Mamlūkiyya min khilāl munshāʾāt al-amīr Taqzdamur al-Ḥamawī", *Annales Islamologiques* 42 (2008), 49–78.

Abū Bakr, Niʿmat. "Minbar jāmiʿ al-Sitt Ṭāṭār al-Ḥijāziyya", *Dirāsāt athāriyya Islāmiyya* 1 (1978), 143–70.

ʿAlī, Bandar. "Izdihār ṣināʿat al-nasīj fi Miṣr fī al-ʿaṣr al-Mamlūkī", *Majallat al-jamʿiyya al-tārikhiyya al-Miṣriyya* 49 (2014–2015), 105–52.

ʿAwaḍ, Henry. "Dīnār Mamlūkī nādir." *Majallat kulliyat al-athār* [Cairo University] 2 (1977), 157–59.

ʿIlwān, Majdī. "Iḍāfa jadīda īla al-nuqūsh al-kitābiyya al-Islāmiyya al-muktashafa fī Miṣr", *Abgadiyat* [Bibliotheca Alexandrina] 7 (2012), 81–93.

al-Tuhamī, ʿĀʾisha. "al-Munshaʾāt al-miʿmāriyya lil sulṭāna Shajar al-Durr bi-madīnat al-Qāhira", *Majjalat al-muʾarrikh al-Miṣrī* 21 (1999), 27–77.

al-Wakīl, Fāyza. "Naqsh min ʿahd al-sulṭān Barqūq al-Mamlūkī al-Jarkasī muʾarrakh bi-shahr Dhī al-Ḥijja sanat 887AH bi-al-Ḥaram al-Makkī al-sharīf", *Majallat kulliyat al-athār* [Cairo University] 13 (2008), 103–14.

al-Waqqād, Maḥāsin. "al-Hidāyā wa al-tuḥuf zaman ṣalāṭīn al-Mamālīk al-baḥrīya (648–784/1250–1392)", *Ḥawliyyāt adāb ʿayn shams* 28 (2000), 186–240.

Najīb, Muṣṭafa. "Dirāsa li khizānāt al-zayt bi baʿḍ al-munshaʾāt al-dīniyya fī al-ʿaṣrayn al-Mamlūkī wa al-ʿUthmānī, dirāsah miʿmāriyya wathāʾiqiyya", *Majjalat kulliyat al-adāb* [South Valley University (Qinā)] 4 (1995), 419–98.

Ramaḍān, ʿĀṭif. "Rumūz al-arqām wa al-taqāwīm ʿala al-nuqūd fī al-ʿaṣr al-Islāmī", *al-Majalla al-ʿilmiyya li kulliyat adāb Sūhāj* 28 (2005), 5–231.

Sulaymān, Majāzī. "al-Thalj waʾl-thallājūn fī Miṣr wa al-Shām fī al-ʿaṣr al-Mamlūkī", *Ḥawliyyāt siminār al-tārīkh al-Islāmī wa al-wasīṭ* 1 (2010), 259–95.

ʿUthman, Muḥammad. "Wathīqat kashf qubbat Qalāwun al-muʾarrakha sanat 1167/1754 dirāsah athāriyya miʿmāriyya", *SHEDET* [Faculty of Archaeology, Fayyūm University] 3 (2016), 171–222.

Zakī, ʿAbd al-Raḥman. "al-Asbila al-athāriyya fī madīnat al-Qāhira", *Majallat kulliyat al-athār* [Cairo University] 2 (1978), 57–72.

Book Series and Monographs

ʿAbd al-Ḥamīd, ʿAlāʾ al-Dīn. *Shawāhid al-qubūr al-Ayyūbiyya wa al-Mamlūkiyya fī Miṣr*, Alexandria, 2013.

ʿAbd al-ʿAlīm, Fahmī. *Jāmiʿ al-Muʾayyad Shaykh, Silsilat al-thaqāfa al-athāriyya wa al-tārīkhiyya, Mashrūʿ al-miʾat kitāb* 22, Cairo, 1994.

ʿAbd al-ʿAlīm, Fahmī. *Al-ʿimāra al-Islāmiyya fī ʿaṣr al-mamālīk al-jarākisa (ʿaṣr al-Muwʾīad Shaykh), Silsilat al-thaqāfa al-athāriyya wa al-tārīkhiyya, Mashrūʿ al-miʾat kitāb* 33, Cairo, 2003.

Aḥmad, Nabīl. *Wathīqat al-sulṭān al-Muʾayyad Aḥmad b. al-Malik al-Ashraf abī al-Naṣr Īnāl al-ʿĀlāʾī (865–1460)*, Cairo, 1981.

Lamʿī, Ṣāliḥ. *al-Jāmiʿ al-abyaḍ bi-l-haush al-sulṭānī bi-qalʿat al-Qāhira*, Beirut, 1980.

Māḍī, Ibrāhīm. *Zayy ʾumarāʾ al-Mamālīk fī Miṣr wa al-Shām, Silsilat tārīkh al-Misriyyin* 581, Cairo, 2009.

Marzūq, ʿAbd al-ʿAzīz. *Tārīkh ṣināʿat al-nasīj fī al-Iskindariyya bain 331 BC wa 1517 AD*, Alexandria, 1955.

Rizq, ʿĀsim. *Dirāsāt fī al ʿimāra al-Islāmiyya (majmūʿat ibn Muzhir al-miʿmāriyya bi-al-Qāhira) 884/1479, dirāsa athāriyya miʿmāriyya, Silsilat al-thaqāfa al-athāriyya wa al-tārīkhiyya, Mashrūʿ al-miʾat kitāb* 25, Cairo, 1995.

Rizq, ʿĀsim. *Khānqāwāt al-ṣūfiyya fī Miṣr*, Cairo, 1997.

ʿUthmān, Muḥammad. *Wathīqat waqf Jamāl al-Dīn Yūsuf al-Ustādār dirāsah tārīkhiyya athāriyya wathāʾiqiyya*, Cairo, 1983.

15

Les études académiques arabes en histoire concernant « les relations Maghreb-Machreq » au Moyen Âge

Lotfi Ben Miled

1 Introduction

La question de la production scientifique en histoire dans le monde arabe pose plusieurs problèmes depuis plus de soixante-dix ans (1947-2017). En effet, elle est liée aux conditions dans lesquelles est né l'enseignement de l'histoire dans les universités arabes, conditions qui diffèrent d'un pays à l'autre, entre les universités elles-mêmes ainsi qu'entre des politiques éducatives divergentes.

Nul ne doute aujourd'hui que les politiques colonialistes ont eu leur effet au moment de la fondation des universités dans le monde arabe durant la première moitié du XXe siècle. Par là-même, les courants orientalistes occidentaux ont eu un impact sur les tendances adoptées au sein de ces universités, à divers modes et degrés.

En effet, si l'influence française a été sensible dans les universités de l'Afrique du Nord et du Levant, celle de la Grande-Bretagne a plutôt dominé dans les universités en Egypte et en Iraq, sans oublier l'influence de l'Orientalisme soviétique, plus tardif, certes, mais tout aussi imposant, en particulier au Yémen du Sud et en Syrie. Notons également l'influence grandissante, durant des décennies, de l'idéologie nationaliste arabe attisée par la question palestinienne.

Au Maghreb, plus particulièrement, la plupart des pères fondateurs des universités étaient d'anciens élèves issus d'universités françaises, ayant axé leurs premiers travaux sur les questions d'histoire politique et institutionnelle. Ils s'étaient tournés ensuite vers la grande nouveauté française du milieu du XXe siècle : l'Ecole des Annales.

Dans la région du Golfe arabo-persique, ce n'est qu'à la fin des années 1960 et au début des années 1970 qu'a commencé la recherche universitaire dans le domaine historique.

Nous abordons ici l'historiographie d'un thème important dans la recherche historique, celle des relations Maghreb-Machreq au cours du Moyen Âge, depuis la conquête arabo-musulmane jusqu'à l'invasion des Ottomans (de la deuxième moitié du Ier siècle de l'Hégire/VIIe siècle de l'ère chrétienne jusqu'à la première moitié du Xe siècle de l'Hégire/XVIe siècle de l'ère chrétienne).

Car, en effet, ce champ d'études a pris une importance accrue dans les travaux de recherche au Maghreb et en Égypte (puis dans le reste des pays du Machreq) à cause d'une nouvelle prise de conscience des liens historiques, humains et culturels avec le reste du monde arabe et plus précisément avec le monde arabo-islamique. Conscience d'autant plus attisée par les évènements majeurs qui ont secoué le Moyen-Orient depuis les années 1940, qui n'ont cessé d'interpeller le questionnement identitaire au niveau populaire et, par ricochet, au niveau de l'élite intellectuelle arabe.

2 Historiographie du thème des « relations Maghreb-Machreq » au Moyen Âge dans le monde arabe

2.1 *Questions de méthodologie : l'apport de l'École des Annales*

L'École des Annales est devenue, surtout depuis les années 1970, le cadre essentiel de la plupart des travaux de recherche dans les universités du Maghreb, notamment en Tunisie, avec une focalisation poussée sur le thème des conditions de vie matérielles et des structures mentales et socio-culturelles. Pour en saisir la portée et circonscrire les domaines de recherche il suffit de regarder du côté des travaux et activités du Centre d'Études et Recherches Économiques et Sociales (CERES) en Tunisie depuis la fin des années 1960 et le début des années 1970 jusqu'à aujourd'hui[1].

Ce qui est sûr c'est que les pères de l'École historique tunisienne actuelle (dans la spécialité du Moyen Âge musulman en particulier) étaient le produit de l'École française.

Les thèses classiques sur l'histoire de l'Ifriqiyya, comme celles de Pr. al-Ṭālibī (1921-2017) ou du Pr. Dašrāwī (1928-2007), étaient dirigées par Robert Brunschvig (1900-1990), père de l'historiographie maghrébine à l'Université française après Georges Marçais (1876-1962).

Avec le temps, cet élan méthodologique influencé par l'École des Annales s'est renforcé au Maghreb dans tous les départements d'Histoire ainsi que dans l'ensemble des universités. Malgré son essoufflement en France, il est resté

---

1 Voir le site du CERES : http://www.ceres.rnrt.tn.

extrêmement actif chez des historiens maghrébins comme, par exemple, le tunisien Hišām Ǧaʿayṭ (Hichem Djaït)[2] ou le marocain ʿAbdallāh Al-ʿArawī[3].

Dans la lignée de l'historiographie promue par l'École des Annales, des nouvelles problématiques ont été abordées à travers les conférences, articles, mémoires et thèses en Histoire concernant notamment les questions socio-économiques, la vie quotidienne ou les mentalités.

Ces nouvelles études ont abordé de nouveaux thèmes, questions et approches méthodologiques à partir de diverses sources comme, par exemple, les archives, les ouvrages de géographie, de voyages et de *ḥisba* (administration des marchés), la littérature, les *nawāzil* ou, la jurisprudence islamique.

La cartographie est devenue un outil de première importance, comme par exemple dans les travaux du tunisien Muḥammad Ḥasan[4]. De même, certaines données statistiques, mêmes si elles restent rares et fragmentaires, ont totalement renouvelé l'approche des questions démographiques et économiques.

Tous les travaux dont nous allons parler se sont engagés dans cette nouvelle voie consistant à écrire l'histoire des relations entre le Maghreb et le Machreq durant l'époque médiévale.

2.2 *Thèses et études académiques*

2.2.1 De la primauté égyptienne

Il était tout à fait naturel que la première étude académique se produise au sein de l'Université égyptienne puisqu'elle fut la première dans le monde arabe contemporain à avoir fondé un département d'études historiques depuis les années 1920. Néanmoins il a fallu attendre la fin de la Seconde Guerre Mondiale pour voir apparaître un net intérêt pour l'histoire du Maghreb.

En effet, le mémoire de magistère de Ḥusayn Muʾnis sur « La conquête arabe du Maghreb » en 1937 fut sans doute le premier d'une longue série de travaux de recherche des historiens égyptiens concernant l'histoire maghrébine[5]. Lorsque Muʾnis termine sa thèse de doctorat sur « L'aube de l'Andalousie musulmane ou l'époque des wullāt » (1943)[6], plusieurs historiens égyptiens diplômés des

---

2   Hišām Ǧaʿayṭ, *Taʾsīs al-Maǧrib al-islāmī*, Beyrouth, Dār al-ṭalīʿa, 2004. Même ouvrage en français : *La Fondation du Maghreb islamique*, Sfax, éditions Amal, 2004.

3   ʿAbdallāh Al-ʿArawī, *L'histoire du Maghreb : un essai de synthèse*, 2 volumes, éditions Maspero, Paris, 1970. Idem, *Ṯaqāfatunā fī ḍawʾ al-tārīḫ*, Beyrouth-Casablanca, Al-markaz al-ṯaqāfi al-ʿa-rabi, 1997 (4e édition).

4   Muḥammad Ḥasan, *Al-madīna wa-l-bādiya bi Ifrīqiyya fī-l-ʿahd al-ḥafṣī*, 2 tomes, Tunis, Publications de l'Université de Tunis I, 1999. Idem *Al-ǧuǧrāfya al-tārīḫiyya li Ifrīqiyya*, Benghazi (Libye) Dār al-kitāb al-ǧadīd, 2004.

5   Ḥusayn Muʾnis, *Fatḥ al-ʿArab li-l-Maǧrib*, Le Caire, 1947.

6   Idem, *Faǧr al-Andalus*, Le Caire, Dār al-Rašād, 2008 (1959).

universités égyptiennes, britanniques et françaises le suivent avec leurs thèses et travaux comme c'est le cas de Saʿd Zaġlūl ʿAbd al-Ḥamīd, Sālim ʿAbd al-ʿAzīz Sālim, Maḥmūd ʿAlī Makkī ou Aḥmad Muḫtār ʿAbbādī.

Viennent ensuite d'autres historiens égyptiens ayant travaillé sur l'histoire du Maghreb au Moyen Âge comme Ḥasan Maḥmūd, spécialiste des Almoravides (« Murābiṭūn »), Mahmūd Ismāʿīl ʿAbd al-Rāziq, Ibrāhīm Salāma, Saḥar ʿAbd al-ʿAzīz Sālim, ʿUbāda Kuhīla, ʿIssā Harīrī, etc …

À cet effort remarquable s'est ajouté un évènement majeur : la fondation de l'Institut égyptien des études islamiques à Madrid en 1950, et la création d'une revue spécialisée en son nom ayant publié quelques articles écrits par les historiens déjà cités, concernant les premières narrations de la conquête arabe du Maghreb et de l'Andalousie, ainsi que des travaux variés dus à d'autres historiens.

Néanmoins, ce n'est qu'à partir de 1967 que le Professeur Hasan Aḥmad Maḥmūd (spécialiste des Almoravides) commence à guider Maḥmūd Ismāʿīl ʿAbd al-Rāziq (Maḥmūd Ismāʿīl), le premier historien égyptien s'étant penché sur l'histoire des Aghlabides[7] et plus particulièrement sur leur politique étrangère. Il le fera dans un premier travail, avec des paragraphes concernant les Fatimides et les Abbassides, avant d'aborder dans sa thèse (1970) la question de l'avènement des Kharidjites au Maghreb[8].

D'ailleurs, la soutenance de la première thèse sur les relations entre l'Égypte et le Maghreb jusqu'à l'avènement des Fatimides date de 1974 mais nous ne savons pas si elle a été publiée[9]. Par ailleurs, la courte période fatimide en Ifrīqiyya (909-969) n'a pas été assez étudiée, en dehors de l'article publié dans la revue de l'Institut égyptien des études islamiques de Madrid durant les années cinquante[10].

On voit naître ensuite le travail d'Aḥmad Ḥasan Ḫuḍayrī sur les relations des Fatimides avec le Maghreb (969-1160)[11] ainsi que celui d'Aḥmad Tūḫī[12] et Saḥar ʿAbd al-ʿAzīz Sālim[13] sur les relations entre les Mamelouks et l'Andalousie.

---

7   Maḥmūd Ismāʿīl ʿAbd al-Rāziq, *Al-Aġāliba (184-296 H.), siyāsatuhum al-ḫāriǧiyya*, Le Caire, 2000 (3ᵉ édition).

8   Idem, *Al-Ḫawāriǧ fī bilād al-Maġrib, ḥattā muntaṣaf al-qarn al-rābiʿ al-hiǧrī*, Casablanca, Dar al-ṯaqāfa, 1985.

9   Hūriyya ʿAbdu, *ʿAlāqāt Miṣr bi-l-Maġrib al-ʿarabī min al-fatḥ ilā qiyām al-dawla al-fāṭimiyya*, Université du Caire, 1974.

10   Aḥmad Muḫtār Al-ʿAbbādī, « Siyāsat al-Fāṭimiyyīn naḥwa al-Maġrib wa-l-Andalus », *Maǧallat al-maʿhad al-miṣrī lil-dirāsāt al-islāmiyya*, Madrid, 5, 1957, 193-226.

11   Aḥmad Ḥasan Ḫuḍayrī, *Al-Fāṭimiyyūn wa bilād al-Maġrib (973-1171)*, Le Caire, Imprimerie Madbūli, 1996.

12   Aḥmad Ṭūḫi, *Al-Mamālīk wa-l-Andalus*, Université d'Alexandrie, 1983.

13   Saḥar ʿAbd al-ʿAzīz Sālim, « Ġarnāṭa wa ʿalāqātuhā bi-l Mamālik », in : *Buḥūṯ Mašriqiyya wa Maġribiyya*, Alexandrie, Sabab, 2001.

Pour sa part, Ibtisām Marʿī Ḥalfallah a étudié les relations entre le Califat almohade (avec aussi les Hafsides) et le Machreq musulman (et particulièrement l'Égypte jusqu'en 1509-1517) sans donner assez de détails sur la dernière période[14].

Nous remarquons que ces travaux ont mis l'accent sur le rôle de l'Égypte comme point de départ des conquêtes de l'Occident musulman et comme centre du Califat fatimide. D'ailleurs, l'Égypte est présentée dans un cadre de concurrence avec les puissances maghrébines, comme les Hafsides, y compris en ce qui concerne l'aide donnée d'une part ou de l'autre aux forces musulmanes qui luttaient contre les Croisés.

2.2.2   Du côté maghrébin

Les universités dans les pays du Maghreb sont nées postérieurement à celles du Machreq à l'heure des indépendances ; elles avaient des noyaux français déjà implantés à l'époque coloniale comme les Instituts des langues et d'archéologie en Tunisie et en Algérie dans lesquels s'était développé l'orientalisme colonialiste. Les pères de l'orientalisme français en Afrique du Nord dans le domaine des études médiévales étaient Georges Marçais en Tunisie, Robert Brunschvig en Algérie et Roger Le Tourneau au Maroc.

Durant la période de libération nationale (1945-1962), nous voyons apparaître le terme d'Occident musulman qui remplace petit à petit celui d'Afrique du Nord et celui, encore plus ancien, de Berbérie. Seulement, ce nouveau concept laisse entendre une relation d'opposition avec celui d'Orient musulman, voire même avec celui d'Occident chrétien.

Après la conquête des indépendances, et en réaction à la lecture colonialiste de l'Histoire du Maghreb, des travaux inédits ont vu le jour, en commençant par celui du tunisien Muḥammad al-Ṭālibī (Mohamed Talbi) sur l'émirat aghlabide (1966)[15] puis le travail de son compatriote Farḥāt Dašrāwī sur le Califat fatimide (1970)[16].

Ainsi, une nouvelle image de la Tunisie médiévale commence à se former : elle intègre désormais l'identité arabo-islamique à l'identité nationale en gestation après l'indépendance.

Ceci a coïncidé avec l'édition du premier ouvrage collectif écrit par des historiens et commissaires pédagogiques tunisiens, « Histoire générale de la Tunisie » paru en 1969 (2ème édition en 2008) et n'ayant pas été traduit en arabe. Hišām Ǧaʿayṭ en a rédigé le chapitre concernant l'Ifrīqiyya à l'époque

---

14   Ibtisām Marʿī Ḥalfallāh, *Al-ʿalāqāt bayna al-ḫilāfa al-muwaḥḥidiyya wal-mašriq al-islāmī*, Le Caire, Dār al-maʿārif, 1985.

15   Muḥammad al-Ṭālibī, *Al-dawla al-aġlabiyya*, op. cit.

16   Farḥāt Dašrāwī, *Al-ḫilāfa al-fāṭimiyya bi-l-Maġrib*, op. cit.

des gouverneurs (« *wullāt* ») de la province africaine sous le Califat, puis l'a réédité dans son ouvrage en arabe sur la Naissance du Maghreb musulman[17]. Deux autres chapitres concernant les époques Sanhajite et Hafside ont été aussi traduits en arabe (respectivement en 1992 et 1993), alors que Rāḍī Daġfūs a rassemblé ses études sur les Hilaliens et les a éditées en arabe dans le cadre d'un ouvrage à part[18].

Ces études ont abordé la question des relations Maghreb-Machreq de points de vue différents ; elles étaient pourtant unanimes sur la volonté de mettre en exergue l'importance de l'autonomie administrative de la province vis-à-vis du Califat au Machreq. Muḥammad al-Ṭālibī perçoit, dans le cadre de la seconde période de l'époque des gouverneurs (750-909) avec notamment la révolte des berbères, une période de véritable indépendance.

En Algérie indépendante (à partir de 1962), l'élite universitaire ne prit forme qu'à partir des années 1970 avec Rašīd Būrwība, ʿAtāllah Daḥīna, ʿAbd al-Ḥamīd Ḥāǧiyyāt qui ont fait leurs études en France. ʿAbd al-Raḥmān Ǧilālī[19] et Abū l-Qāsim Saʿdallāh[20] ont alors écrit deux ouvrages sur l'histoire générale de l'Algérie dans lesquels ils ont abordé les relations avec le Machreq, même si cela ne paraît pas suffisant. L'exception serait peut-être la thèse de Mūsā Laqbāl (mort en 2011) sur Kutāma et le califat fatimide en 1973[21], suivie bien plus tard par celle de l'algérienne Būba Maġānī sur les Yéménites au Maghreb musulman et qui fut éditée en 2009[22].

Enfin, au Maroc, après la publication de quelques articles sur les voyages au Machreq à l'époque mérinide par Muḥammad Mannūnī[23], il a fallu attendre les années 1990 pour voir la soutenance et l'édition de thèses sur ce thème des relations Maghreb-Machreq[24].

---

17   Hišām Ǧaʿayṭ, *Taʾsīs al- Maġrib al-Islāmī*, Beyrouth, éditions Al-Ṭalīʿa, 2004.

18   Rāḍī Daġfūs, *Buḥūṯ wa-dirāsāt fī l-tārīḫ al-ʿarabī al-islāmī*, Beyrouth, Dār al-Ġarb al-islāmī, 2005.

19   ʿAbd al-Raḥmān Ǧilālī, *Tārīḫ al-Ǧazāʾir al-ʿām*, Beyrouth-Alger, Dār Maktabat al-ḥayāt-Maktabat al-šārika al-Ǧazāʾiriyya , 2 tomes, 1965 (2ᵉ édition).

20   Abū l-Qāsim Saʿdallāh, *Tārīḫ al-Ǧazāʾir al-ṯaqāfī*, 10 volumes, Beyrouth, Dār al-Ġarb al-islāmī, Alger, Dar al-Basaʾir, 1998-2007.

21   Mūsā Laqbāl, *Dawr Kutāma fī tārīh al-ḫilāfa al- fāṭmiyya*, Alger, al-šārika al waṭaniyya lil-našr, 1979.

22   Būba Maġānī, *Aṯaru al-ʿArab al-yamāniyya fī tārīḫ bilād al-Maġrib fī l-qurūn al-ṯalāṯa al-ʿūlā li-l-hiǧrati*, Alger, Dār Bahāʾ al-Dīn, 2009.

23   Muḥammad Mannūnī, « Al-ǧazīra al-ʿarabiyya fī al- ǧuġrāfiya wa-l-rihalāt al-maġribiyya wa mā ilayhā », *Maǧallat al-Maǧmaʿ al-ʿilmī al-ʿirāqī* [Baghdad], 29 (1978), 150-187.

24   Ḥasan Malwānī, *Al-hiǧra bayna al-Mašriq wa-l-Maġrib munḏu al-fatḥ al-islāmī ḥattā awāsiṭ al-qarn 5 H./11*, thèse dirigée par : Hāšimī ʿAlawī Qāsimī, Faculté des Lettres de Fès [Maroc], 1996.

2.3 *Congrès et séminaires*

Nous constatons l'existence de deux séminaires, seulement, dans les années 1990, consacrés au thème des relations Maghreb-Machreq, alors que la plupart des congrès et séminaires concernent des régions ou capitales. Déjà en 1961, une communication dans le cadre du congrès s'étant déroulé à Damas sur Al-Ġazālī s'était intéressée à son impact intellectuel au Maghreb[25]. En 1969, quatre tunisiens ont participé au Congrès international qui s'est déroulé au Caire à l'occasion du Millénaire de la fondation de la capitale égyptienne[26] : Muḥammad Ḥabīb Belḫūǧa, par exemple, avec une conférence sur le Caire dans l'œuvre d'Ibn Rašīd de Ceuta (Sebta en arabe), et Ibrāhīm Šabbūḫ avec trois études.

Par la suite, au cours des années 1970 fut inaugurée à Amman (Jordanie) une série de colloques consacrés à l'histoire du Levant et nous y voyons participer deux marocains ('Abd al-Karīm Karīm[27] et 'Abd al-Hādi Tāzī[28]) ainsi qu'un tunisien (Habīb Ǧanḥānī[29]) ayant présenté des travaux sur les rapports entre le Califat en Orient et le Maghreb. Après neuf ans, Muḥammad Ḥabīb Hīla a présenté un travail sur Jérusalem du point de vue des voyageurs maghrébins[30].

Du côté maghrébin, le premier colloque fut organisé en Tunisie par le CERES (Centre des Études Économiques et Sociales de Tunis) sur le Maghreb musulman et sa civilisation, auquel ont participé des historiens du Machreq, et lors duquel Munīra Chapoutot a présenté le premier travail sur les rapports entre Ifrīqiyya et l'Égypte des Mamelouks[31].

Après deux ans, en 1975, eu lieu un autre colloque sur « Alexandrie à travers les âges » auquel ont participé deux spécialistes égyptiens de l'histoire du

---

25 Muhammad Muntasir Al-Kattani, « Al-Ġazālī wa-l-Maġrib », *Abū Ḥāmid Al-Ġazālī fī-l-ḏikrā al-mi'awiyya al-tāsi'a li mīlādihi (Mahraǧān Al-Ġazālī fī Dimašq, 1961)*, Le Caire, Al-maǧlis al-a'lā li ri'āyati al-adab wa-l-funūn, 1962, 699-715.

26 *Abḥāṯ al-nadwa al-duwaliyya li tārīḫ al-Qāhira* (Alfiyyat al-Qāhira, Le Caire, 1969), 3 volumes, Le Caire, Dār al-kitāb, 1970.

27 'Abd al-Karīm Karīm, « Bilād al-Šām wal-Magrib ḫilāl al-qarn 10h/16 », *Mu'tamar bilād al-Šām* Actes du 1ᵉ congrès d'histoire du Levant, Amman, Jordan University, 1974, vol. 1, 489-495.

28 'Abd al-Hādi Tāzī, « Bilād al-Šām fil-watā'iq al-diblumāsiyya al-magribiyya », *Mu'tamar bilād al-Šām* Actes du 1ᵉ congrès d'histoire du Levant, ibid., 431-488.

29 Habīb Ǧanḥānī, « Siyāsat al-ḫilāfa al-umawiyya tuǧāh al-Maġrib, lā siyyamā fi-l-maydān al-mālī », *Al-muǧtama' al-'arabī al-islāmī : al-ḥayāt al-'iqtiṣādiyya wal-'iǧtimā'iyya*, Kuwait, Coll. 'ālam al-ma'rifa, N° 319, 2005, 189-198.

30 Muḥammad Ḥabīb Hīla, « Al-Quds wa aṯaruhā al-ṯaqāfī bil-Maġrib wal-Andalus min ḫilāl kutub al-riḥalāt », *Mu'tamar bilād al-Šām*, Actes du 3ᵉ congrès d'histoire du Levant, Amman, 1980.

31 *Actes du 1ᵉʳ congrès de l'histoire et de la civilisation du Maghreb*, 1979.

Maghreb, Saʿd Zaġlūl ʿAbd al-Ḥamīd[32] et Aḥmad Muḫtār ʿAbbādī[33]. Dans deux autres colloques sur Ibn Ḫaldūn organisés à Rabat en 1979 puis à Tunis en 1980, nous ne trouvons point d'études sur la présence du grand savant maghrébin au Machreq ou plus particulièrement en Égypte, ni sur ses relations avec le pouvoir mamelouk, ni avec Tamerlan (en arabe et persan : Timūr Lang) ; ce sujet sera abordé lors du dernier colloque de Tunis en 2006[34].

D'autres colloques ont été organisés à la mémoire du fondateur de l'État omeyyade en Andalousie Abd al-Raḥmān 1er dit l'Exilé (en arabe : Al-Dāḫil)[35] ainsi que sur l'histoire de Tlemcen[36] et de Constantine[37], sur Al-Ġazālī à Rabat (1988)[38], à Kairouan (2009) et à Tunis (2011)[39].

Deux autres colloques ont été, cette fois-ci, consacrés aux relations Maghreb-Machreq : l'un a été organisé par l'Université de Banī Mallāl au Maroc (1994-1995)[40] et l'autre par l'Union des Historiens arabes au Caire (1997)[41]; leurs travaux ont été publiés.

Dans la région de la péninsule arabique, deux colloques se sont tenus à Riyad (1978) et à Abou Dhabi (1988)[42] dans lesquels des communications ont fait la lumière sur l'histoire de la présence des Maghrébins dans la région.

2.4   *Édition des manuscrits*

Nous devons d'abord reconnaître que l'initiative dans ce domaine revient aux Orientalistes européens. Il y a eu, ensuite, une vague de jeunes éditeurs de manuscrits à l'orée de la renaissance littéraire au Machreq dont nous pouvons citer quelques-uns des plus renommés : le syrien Ṣalāḥ al-Dīn al-Munaǧǧid

---

32   Saʿd Zaġlūl ʿAbd al-Ḥamīd, « Al-aṯar al-maġribī wa-l-andalusī fī l-muǧtamaʿ al-iskandarī », *Revue de la Faculté des Lettres d'Alexandrie*, 1975.

33   Aḥmad Muḫtār ʿAbbādī, « Dawr al-Maġāriba fi-l-ḥurūb al-ṣalībiyya », *Buḥuṯ fī tārīḫ al-ḥaḍāra al-islāmiyya, muhdāt ilā Aḥmad Fikrī* (Alexandrie, 1976), Alexandrie, Muʾassasat šabāb al-ǧāmiᶜa, 2000, 81-102.

34   Ayman Fuʾād Al-Sayyid, « Ibn Ḫaldūn wa makānatuhu fī Miṣr al-islāmiyya », *Ibn Ḫaldūn wa manābiʿ al-ḥadāṯa*, Tunis, Bayt al-ḥikma, 2006, t. 1.

35   Nous n'avons pas pu consulter les actes de ce colloque.

36   Tlemcen, 2013.

37   Constantine, 2015.

38   Rabat, 1988.

39   Neuvième centenaire du décès d'al-Gazali, Tunis, Bayt al-hikma, 2011.

40   « *Al-Maġrib-al-Mašriq : al-ʿalāqāt wa-l-ṣūra* », Actes des deux colloques de Mars 1994 et novembre 1997 à la Faculté des Lettres et sciences humaines (Beni Mellal), l'Université Qāḍī ʿIyāḍ (Marrakech) et le Groupe des Études et recherches sur les relations Maghreb-Machreq, 1999.

41   « *Al-Mašriq wa-ʿalāqātuhu bi-l-Maġrib* », Union des Historiens Arabes, Le Caire, 1997.

42   Colloque « Al-Ḫalīǧ al-ʿarabī wa makānatuhu fī-l-tārīḫ al-ʿarabī », Abou Dhabi, 1988.

qui a édité des textes de voyageurs maghrébins[43], le palestinien Iḥsān ʿAbbās et les égyptiens Abd al-Salām Hārūn, Šawqī Ḍayf, ʿAlī al-Muntaṣir al-Kittānī qui a édité les voyages d'Ibn Baṭṭūṭa[44] et Muḥammad Muṣṭafā Ziyāda ceux d'Ibn Ǧubayr[45].

Au Maghreb, nous trouvons d'abord les tunisiens Ḥasan Ḥusnī ʿAbd al-Wahhāb qui a édité une partie concernant Ifrīqiyya de l'ouvrage Masālik al-Abṣār d'al-ʿUmarī[46], Ibrāhīm Šabbūḥ qui a renouvelé en profondeur l'édition de la Muqaddima d'Ibn Ḥaldūn et même les volumes d'Al-ʿIbar[47], Ǧumʿa Šīḥa qui a édité avec le marocain Muḥammad bin Šarīfa le texte d'Ibn al-Ṣabbāḥ[48].

Ensuite, nous retrouvons l'algérien Ḥāǧ Ṣādiq[49] ainsi que les marocains Muḥammad Mannūnī[50], Muḥammad b. Tāwīt al-Ṭanǧī ayant édité l'autobiographie d'Ibn Ḥaldūn (son voyage au Maghreb et au Machreq)[51], Ḥasan Sāʾiḥ qui a édité Al-Balawī[52] et ʿAbd al-Hādī Tāzī[53].

Quant aux textes concernant directement les sujets du voyage et l'image géographique et culturelle dans le cadre des relations Maghreb-Machreq, nous devons citer l'édition par l'historien libanais ʿUmar ʿAbd al-Salām Tadmurī de l'ouvrage de ʿAbd al-Bāsiṭ b. Ḥalīl (m. 923/1514)[54] ainsi que le travail de

43   Ṣalāḥ Al-Dīn Al-Munaǧǧid, *Al-Mašriq fī naẓar al-Maǧāriba*, Beyrouth, 1963.

44   Abū ʿAbd Allāh Muḥammad Ibn Baṭṭūṭa, *Tuḥfat al-nuẓẓār fī ǧarāʾib al-amṣār wa- ʿaǧāʾib al-asfār*, dir. ʿAlī al-Muntaṣir al-Kittānī, Beyrouth, Muʾassasat al-Risāla, 1985.

45   Abū l-Ḥasan Muḥammad Ibn Ǧubayr, *Riḥla*, dir. Muḥammad Muṣṭafā Ziyāda, Le Caire, Imprimerie de la Commission de production, traduction et édition, 1939.

46   Ibn Faḍl Allāh Al-ʿUmarī, *Waṣf Ifrīqiyya wa-l-Andalus*, dir. Ḥasan Ḥusnī ʿAbd al-Wahhāb, Tunis, Imprimerie Al-Nahḍa (Renaissance), 1920.

47   Ibrāhīm Šabbūḥ vient de publier la première édition critique complète de l'ouvrage d'Ibn Haldūn, Dar Sadir, Bayrouth, 15 volumes, 2015.

48   ʿAbdallāh Ibn al-Ṣabbāḥ, *Nisbat al-aḥbār wa-taḏkirat al-aḥyār*, (*Riḥla ḥiǧāziyya*), dir. Ǧumʿa Šīḥa, Revue *Dirāsāt andalusiyya* (Tunis), Numéro double spécial 45-46 (2011).

49   Al-Zuhrī, *Kitāb al-ǧuǧrāfiya*, édition critique de Muḥammad Ḥāǧ Ṣādiq, Port Said (Egypte), Maktabat al-ṯaqāfa al-dīniyya, s.d.

50   Muḥammad Mannūnī, « Al-ǧazīra al-ʿarabiyya fī al- ǧuǧrāfiya wa-l-riḥalāt al-maǧribiyya wa mā ilayhā », *Maǧallat al-Maǧmaʿ al-ʿilmī al-ʿirāqī* [Baghdad], 29 (1978), 150-187.

51   ʿAbd al-Raḥmān Ibn Ḥaldūn, *Riḥlat ibn Ḥaldūn*, dir. Muḥammad ibn Tāwīt al-Ṭanǧī, Beyrouth, Dār al-Kutub al-ʿIlmiyya, 2004.

52   Ḥālid Ibn ʿĪsā al-Balawī, *Tāǧ al-mafriq fī taḥliyat ʿulamāʾ al-Mašriq*, dir. Al-Ḥasan Muḥammad Sāʾiḥ, Commission Mixte de l'édition du patrimoine (Maroc-Emirats Arabes Unis), 1970.

53   ʿAbd al-Hādī Tāzī, *Riḥlatu-l-riḥalāt: Makka fī miʾati riḥla maǧribiyya wa riḥla*, 2 tomes, London, Muʾassasatu-l-furqān li-l-turāṯ al-islāmī, 2005.

54   Zayn al-Dīn Ibn Ḥalīl, *Al-rawḍ al-bāsim fī ḥawādiṯ al-ʿumur wa-l-tarāǧim*, dir. ʿUmar ʿAbd Al-Salām Tadmurī, 4 tomes, Beyrouth, al-Maktaba al-ʿAṣriyya, 2014.

Muḥammad Ḥaqqī dans lequel il a édité une partie de l'ouvrage de Yāqūt al-Ḥamawī concernant la géographie du Maroc et de l'Andalousie[55].

De son côté, la palestinienne Zaynab Ṭāhir Sāqallāh a édité une partie de l'ouvrage d'Ibn Faḍlallāh al-ʿUmarī concernant la polémique entre les savants du Maghreb et du Machreq[56], alors que la marocaine Naǧāt Marīnī a rassemblé et édité les textes de Tāǧ al-Dīn b. Ḥammawayhī[57]. Ensuite, le mauritanien Ḥamallāh Wuld al-Sālim a rassemblé les textes de géographie et de voyages qui concernent le Sahara et les royaumes du Soudan[58], le marocain Muḥammad b. Šarīfa a rassemblé des biographies marocaines tirées des sources orientales[59] et enfin les deux tunisiens Muḥammad Ḥasan[60] et Aḥmad al-Bāhī[61] ont rassemblé les textes des voyageurs arabes du Moyen Âge concernant Kairouan et Sfax.

3   Domaines de recherche sur le thème des « relations Maghreb-Machreq »

3.1   *Histoire politique et diplomatique*

Nous pouvons résumer les questions abordées par les historiens arabes concernant les relations politiques entre le Maghreb et le Machreq comme suit :

D'abord, des études ayant mis l'accent sur la dépendance du Maghreb vis-à-vis du Machreq aux premiers siècles de l'Islam. Elles ont abordé particulièrement la question des conquêtes et des politiques menées par les représentants des califats omeyyade et abbasside et ont même insisté sur la dépendance de l'émirat aghlabide vis-à-vis du califat abbasside. Muḥammad al-Ṭālibī a étudié cette question dans sa thèse ainsi que dans article précédent[62]

---

55   Yāqūt Al-Ḥamawī, *Muʿǧam al-Andalus wa-l-Maġrib*, édition de Muḥammad Ḥaqqī, Benī Mellal (Maroc), 2011.

56   « *Fī l-inṣāf bayna al-Mašriq wa-l-Maġrib : Qiṭʿatun min masālik al-abṣār li-Ibn Faḍlallāh al-ʿUmarī* », étude et édition : Zaynab Ṭāhir Sāqallāh, Beyrouth, Dār al-madār al-islāmī, 2004.

57   Abū Muḥammad ʿAbd Allāh Ibn Ḥammawayhī, *Al-riḥla al-maġribiyya*, Textes rassemblées et éditées par Naǧāt al-Marīnī, Rabat, Centre Bābiṭīn de l'édition du patrimoine, 2011.

58   Ḥamallāh Wuld al-Sālim, *Ṣaḥrāʾ al-mulaṯṯamīn wa bilād al-Sūdān fī nuṣūṣ al-ǧuġrāfiyyīn wal-muʾarriḫīn al-ʿarab*, Beyrouth, Dār al-kutub al-ʿilmiyya, 2011.

59   Muḥammad Bin Šarīfa, *Tarāǧim maġribiyya min maṣādir mašriqiyya*, Casablanca, Imprimerie al-Naǧāḥ al-Ǧadīda, 1996.

60   Muḥammad Ḥasan, *Al-Qayrawān fī ʿuyūn al-raḥḥāla*, Carthage, Bayt al-Hikma, 2009.

61   Aḥmad Bāhī, *Sfāqs fī-l-maṣādir al-waṣīṭa*, Sfax, Imprimerie Gwīʿa, 2017.

62   Muḥammad al-Ṭālibī, « Ifrīqiyya wa-l-Mašriq ḫilāla al-qarn al-ṯāmin », *Al-dawla al-aġlabiyya*, op. cit., 21-81.

où il a abordé justement cette polémique que nous retrouvons de manière plus accentuée chez l'égyptien Maḥmūd Ismāʿīl[63].

Ensuite, nous retrouvons quelques travaux sur cette question et sur les relations politiques entre le Maghreb et le Machreq comme ceux de Farḥāt Dašrāwī[64] et de ʿAbd al-Ḥayy Šaʿbān[65] au colloque de Mahdiyya « Al-Qāḍī al-Nuʿmān » consacré aux études fatimides qui s'est déroulé en 1977 et 1981.

Les thèses égyptiennes déjà citées ont complété l'étude des relations politiques jusqu'au Vᵉ siècle de l'hégire (XIᵉ siècle de l'ère chrétienne). Pour ma part, j'ai essayé d'aborder cette question dans le cadre de ma thèse sur les relations entre l'Ifrīqiyya et l'Orient méditerranéen à l'époque des Ayyoubides et des Mamelouks en passant par les relations avec les Croisés et les Mongols jusqu'à celles avec les premiers Ottomans (1453)[66] puis avec les différents sultans ottomans durant un siècle (jusqu'en 1557).

Dans d'autres travaux, des sujets particuliers ont été également abordés, tels que les relations diplomatiques entre Saladin[67] et les Almohades ou avec Yūsuf b. Tāšfīn[68], etc ...

ʿAbd al-Hādī Tāzī a étudié de manière précise les documents diplomatiques concernant les relations entre le Maroc et les pays du Machreq[69] et a quelque peu exagéré l'apport diplomatique des textes d'Ibn Ḫaldūn[70] et d'Ibn Baṭṭūṭa[71].

Enfin, certains travaux, malgré la rareté des sources, ont pu aborder les relations entre le Maghreb central et les pays du Machreq[72] ainsi qu'avec le royaume mérinide[73].

---

63 Maḥmūd Ismāʿīl ʿAbd al-Rāziq, *Al-Aġāliba (184-296 H.), siyāsatuhum al-ḫāriǧiyya*, Le Caire, ʿAyn li-l-dirāsāt, 2000 (3ᵉ édition).

64 Farḥāt Dašrāwī, *Al-Ḫilāfa al-Fāṭimiyya bi-l-Maġrib*, op. cit.

65 Muḥammad ʿAbd al-Ḥayy Šaʿbān, « Limāḏa aqāma al-Fāṭimiyyun dawlatahum wa naqalūhā ilā miṣr ? », Colloque Al-Qāḍī al-Nuʿmān, Mahdia (Tunisie), 1981, 151-180.

66 Luṭfī Bin Mīlād [Lotfi Ben Miled], *Ifrīqiyya wa-l-Mašriq al-mutawassiṭī*, Tunis, Imprimerie al-Maġāribiyya, 2011.

67 ʿAbd al-Hādī Tāzī, « Sifārat Ṣalāḥ al-Dīn wa Yaʿqūb al-Manṣūr al-muwaḥḥidī », *Al-Akādimiyya*, Rabat, n°11, 1994, 105-131.

68 ʿAlī Qāsimī, « Bayna Yūsuf ibn Tāšfīn wa Ṣalāḥ al-Dīn al-ayyūbī », *Al-Tārīḫ al-ʿarabī*, n° 17, hiver 2001, 161-184.

69 ʿAbd al-Hādī Tāzī, *Tārīḫ al-Maġrib al-diblumāsī*.

70 Idem. « Ḥawla ifādat ibn Ḫaldūn ʿan al-ʿalāqāt al-duwaliyya li bilād al-maġrib », *Al-Ṯaqāfa*, Alger, N° 77, 1983, 27-35.

71 Idem. *Riḥlatu-l-riḥalāt*, op. cit.

72 Des travaux restés encore manuscrits, notamment le mémoire de Master de ʿAbd al-Raḥmān al-Aʿraǧ.

73 Par exemple : Rābiḥ Maġrāwī, « Al-ʿalāqāt al-Maġribiyya al-Mamlūkiyya fī al-ʿaṣr al-wasīṭ : qirāʾa fī nuṣūṣ Ibn al-Ḫaṭīb wa Ibn-Ḫaldūn », *Al-Maġrib wal-taḥawwulāt al-duwaliyya*,

3.2 *Mobilité des idées et des hommes*

Plusieurs travaux ont abordé les questions plus délicates des influences culturelles et de la mobilité des idées religieuses, en particulier entre le Maghreb et le Machreq. Parmi elles, notons l'étude de Maḥmūd ʿAlī Makkī sur le Chiisme en Andalousie à l'époque des Omeyyades[74] ainsi que l'un article de Muḥammad al-Ṭālibī sur la pénétration des idées chiites au Maghreb avant l'arrivée des missionnaires fatimides[75]. Ce dernier est, tout comme un des chapitres de la thèse de Farḥāt Dašrāwī, l'un des travaux les plus importants ayant abordé cette question, sans oublier ceux de l'égyptien Muḥammad Barakāt al-Bīlī sur le Chiisme au Maghreb[76] et de la libanaise Widād al-Qāḍī sur les Chiites de Baǧīla au Maroc[77].

En ce qui concerne les Kharidjites, nous avons d'abord la thèse de Maḥmūd Ismāʿīl ʿAbd al-Rāziq puis les travaux de la tunisienne Laṭīfa Bakkāy sur les origines du Khāridjisme et son expansion au Maghreb[78]. Les deux enseignants à l'université de la Zitūna, Aḥmad Maḥmūd Bakīr et ʿAbd al-Maǧīd bin Ḥamda, ont aussi écrit sur les écoles du Fiqh, du Kalām et surtout les Dhāhirites[79]. Naǧm al-Dīn Hintātī a étudié le Hanifisme, le Hanbalisme et l'Achʿarisme[80],

Actes du colloque en l'honneur du Pr. ʿUṯmān al-Manṣūrī, Faculté des Lettres et Sciences Humaines, Université Hassan II, Casablanca, 2010, 199-234.

74 Maḥmūd ʿAlī Makkī, « Al-tašayyuʿ fī-l-Andalus ilā nihāyat Mulūk al-Ṭawāʾif », *Maǧallat maʿhad al-dirāsāt al-islāmiyya* [Madrid], volume 2 (1954), 93-149.

75 Muḥammad al-Ṭālibī, « al-awḍāʿ allatī mahhadat li-qiyām al-dawla al-fāṭimiyya fī Ifrīqiyya », Colloque Qāḍī ʿIyāḍ des études fatimides, 2e session (Mahdiyya 4-7 août 1977), Tunis, Ministère des affaires culturelles, 1981, 29-36.

76 Muḥammad Barakāt Al-Bīlī, *Al-tašayyuʿ fī bilād al-Maǧrib al-islāmī ḥattā muntaṣaf al-qarn al-ḫāmis al-hiǧrī*, Le Caire, Dār al-nahḍa al-ʿarabiyya, 1993.

77 Widād Al-Qāḍī, « Al-šīʿa al-buǧaliyya fī-l-Maǧrib al-aqṣā », *Actes du 1er Congrès d'histoire et de civilisation du Maghreb*, Tunis, CERES, collection « Etudes économiques », tome 1, 1979, 165-194.

78 Laṭīfa Bakkāy, *Ḥarakāt al-Ḥawāriǧ*, Beyrouth, Dār al-ṭalīʿa, 2001.

79 ʿAbd al-Maǧīd Bin Ḥamda, *Al-madāris al-kalāmiyya bi Ifrīqiyya ilā ḍuhūr al-ašʿariyya*, Tunis, Dar al-ʿArab, 1986.

80 Naǧm al-Dīn Hintātī, « Taṭawwur mawqif ʿulamāʾ al-Mālikiyya bi-Ifrīqiyya min al-ḫawḍi fī l-masāʾil al-kalāmiyya ilā tabannīhim li-l-ʿaqīda al-ašʿariyya », *Revue de l'IBLA* [Tunis], 170 (1992), 297-322.

Idem : « Muḥāwala li-našr al-maḏhab al-ḥanbalī bi-Ifrīqiyya ḥawālay muntaṣaf al-qarn al-tāsiʿ milādi/al-ṯāliṯ hiǧrī », *Revue de l'IBLA* [Tunis], 173 (1994), 91-106.

Idem. : « Al-Maḏhab al-ḥanafī bi-l-Qayrawān fī l-qurūn al-wustā », *Al-Tārīḫ al-ʿarabī* [Maroc], 13 (2000), 227-258 .

Idem : *Al-Maḏhab al-Mālikī bi-l-Ġarb al-islāmī ilā muntaṣaf al-qarn 5 H./11 J.-C.*, Tunis, Tibr Azzamān, 2004.

alors que le marocain Yūsuf Aḥnāna[81] et le tunisien Mabrūk Manṣūri[82] ont écrit sur l'Achʿarisme.

D'ailleurs, en plus de l'article en espagnol de Maḥmūd ʿAli Makkī (en 1968) sur l'influence intellectuelle du Machreq en Andalousie[83], nous avons les travaux de Sālim Yāfūt sur Ibn Ḥazm et le Dhâhirisme[84] ainsi que d'autres travaux sur l'autodafé de l'ouvrage d'al-Ghazālī par les Almoravides[85].

ʿUmar b. Ḥammādī a révisé la question de l'influence orientale sur la pensée d'Ibn Tūmart[86]. Nelly ʿAmrī a également étudié l'influence du Machreq[87] au niveau du soufisme maghrébin et nous avons utilisé ses écrits à ce sujet dans notre étude des voyageurs irakiens au Maghreb[88]. Enfin, nous avons récemment publié un article à propos de l'influence orientale sur la pensée scientifique en Ifrīqīyya à l'époque hafside[89].

En ce qui concerne la mobilité des hommes et plus particulièrement leur implantation au Maghreb, nous avons un travail de l'algérienne Būba Maǧānī sur celle des Yéménites[90] ainsi que les écrits de Salwā Baḥriyya guidée par son professeur Rāḍī Daǧfūs sur les Yéménites au Maghreb et en Andalousie[91].

---

81 Yūsuf Aḥnāna, *Taṭawwur al-maḏhab al-ašʿarī fī l-Ġarb al-islāmī*, Rabat, Ministère des Habous et des Affaires Islamiques, 2007.

82 Mabrūk Mansūrī, « Al-Ašʿariyya fī bilād al-Maġrib ilā nihāyat al-qarn 6 H./ 12 wa mafhūm al-adwār al-ḥaḍāriyya », *Revue de l'IBLA* [Tunis] 192 (2003), 71-98.

83 Maḥmūd ʿAlī Makkī, *Ensayo sobre las aportaciones orientales en la España musulmana y su influencia en la formación de la cultura hispano-arabe*, Madrid, Instituto de estudios islámicos, 1968.

84 Sālim Yāfūt, *Ibn Ḥazm wa-l-fikr al-falsafī bi-l-Maġrib wa-l-Andalus*, Casablanca, Al-markaz al-ṯaqāfī al-ʿarabī, 1986.

85 Saʿd Ġrāb, « Ḥawla iḥrāq al-Murābiṭīn li-Iḥyāʾ al-Ġazālī », dans Idem, *Al-ʿāmil al-dīnī wal-huwiyya al-tūnisiyya*, Tunis, al-Dār al-Tūnisiyya li-l-Našr, 1990.

86 ʿUmar bin Ḥammādī, « Al-Ġazālī wa talāmiḏatuhu al-Maġāriba », *Neuvième centenaire de la mort de Ghazali*, Carthage, Bayt al-Hikma, 2011, 461-506.

87 Nelly ʿAmrī, *Al-taṣawwuf bi Ifrīqiyya fī-l-ʿaṣr al-wasīṭ*, Tunis, Ed. Contraste, 2009.

88 Luṭfī Bin Mīlād, [Lotfi Ben Miled, Lotfi], *Al-Huwiyyāt al-Mutašaẓẓiya wa Shatāt al-Nuḥab fī al-ʿĀlam al-Islāmī: Muḥāwala fī rasm Jawānib min Kharīṭat al-ʿAṣr al-Sunnī fī al-ʿAṣr al-Wasīṭ*, Tunis, Dār Miskilyānī, 2021 (sous presse).

89 Idem, « Al-Ḥarāk al-ṯaqāfī wa-l-fikrī bi-l-ʿalam al-islāmī wa-aṯaruhu fī ḥarakāt al-ʿulūm al-ʿaqliyya bi-Ifrīqiyya ilā nihāyat al-ʿaṣr al-wasīṭ », dans : Saʿīd Būsaklāwī, (dir.). *Al-ʿilm wa-l-taʿlīm fī bilād al-Maġrib min al-qarn al-tāsiʿ ilā al-qarn al-ṯāni ʿašar*, Wajda [Maroc], Centre d'études et de recherches humaines et sociales, 2016, 19-56.

90 Būba Maǧānī, *Aṯar al-ʿArab al-yamaniyya fī tārīḫ bilād al-Maġrib fī l-qurūn al-ṯalāṯa al-ūlā li-l-hiǧrati*, Alger, Dār Bahāʾ al-Dīn, 2009.

91 Salwā Baḥriyya, *Al-Yamaniyya fī-l-Maġrib wa-l-Andalus*, thèse de doctorat en histoire médiévale, Faculté des sciences humaines et sociales de Tunis, 1998-1999 (non publiée).

Maḥmūd Ismāʿīl ʿAbd al-Rāziq a publié un article sur la présence au Maghreb des soldats perses Khorassanides (1977)[92], alors que son élève marocain Ibrāhīm al-Qādirī Būtašīš (Brahim Kadiri Boutchich) a publié sa communication présentée en Iran dans la revue algérienne « ʿUṣūr » (époques) (2015)[93].

D'autre part, les articles de Muḥammad al-Ṭālibī sur les Orientaux (« Machāriqa ») dans *l'Encyclopédie tunisienne*[94] sont parmi les plus importants qui soient écrits sur la présence de cette catégorie sociale au Maghreb jusqu'au Vᵉ siècle de l'Hégire / XIᵉ siècle de l'ère chrétienne. Amīn Tawfīq Ṭībī, quant à il, a écrit sur les Aġzāz (1983)[95].

Enfin, nous avons étudié dans un article récent la manière avec laquelle ont été accueillis les nouveaux venus du Machreq au Maghreb et notamment les Iraqiens et les Perses à la fin de l'époque médiévale[96].

En ce qui concerne l'émigration contraire du Maghreb vers le Machreq, le premier travail l'ayant abordé a été celui du syrien ʿAlī Aḥmad sur les Andalous et les Maghrébins au Levant[97]. Ensuite, nous avons celui du tunisien Yūsif bin Sāsi sur les Maghrébins au Ḥiǧāz (1996)[98], puis celui de l'égyptien Aḥmad ʿAbd al-Laṭīf Ḥanafī sur les Maghrébins et Andalous en Égypte (2004)[99]. L'irakien ʿAbd al-Wāḥid Ṭāhā, dans un de ses ouvrages, a donné quelques indications sur les voyages entre le Maghreb et l'Iraq (2007)[100].

---

92 Maḥmūd Ismāʿīl ʿAbd al-Rāziq, « al-Furs fī bilād al-Maġrib », *Maġribiyyāt, dirāsāt ǧadīda*, Rabat, 1977.

93 Ibrāhīm al-Qādirī Būtašīš [Brahim El Kadiri Boutchich], « Al-adwār al-tārīḫiyya wa-l-ḥaḍāriyya li-l-Furs fī bilād al-Maġrib mundu intišār al-Islām ḥattā al-qarn al-ṯālit al-hiǧrī », *ʿUṣūr al-ǧadīda* [Université d'Oran-Algérie], n° double 14-15 (2014), 26-43.

94 Muḥammad al-Ṭālibī, « al-Mašāriqa », *L'Encyclopédie tunisienne*, fasc. n° 4, Carthage, Bayt al-Ḥikma, 1994, 200-204.

95 Amīn Tawfīq Ṭībī, « Al-Aġzāz wa-qudūmuhum ilā bilād al-Maġrib wa-l-Andalus », dans : Idem : *Dirāsāt wa-buḥūṯ fī tārīḫ al-Maġrib wa-l-Andalus*, Tunis-Tripoli (Lybie), Al-Dār al-ʿarabiyya li-l-Kitāb, 1983, 87-100.

96 Luṭfī Bin Mīlād, « Al-wāfidūn min al-Mašriq … », op. cit.

97 ʿAlī Aḥmad, *Al-Andalusiyyūn wa-l-Maġāriba fī bilād al-Šām ilā nihāyat al-qarn al-tāsiʿ H.*, Damas, Dār Ṭalas, 1985.

98 Yūsuf Bin Sāsi, *Al-Maġāriba bi-l-Ḥiǧāz min al-qarn 7 H. ilā l-qarn 9 H. (13-15 J.-C.)*, thèse dactylographiée, Faculté des Lettres de la Manouba [Tunisie].

99 Aḥmad Laṭīf Ḥanafī, *Al-Maġāriba wa-l-Andalusiyyūn fī Miṣr al-islāmiyya min ʿaṣr al-wullāt ḥattā nihāyat al-ʿaṣr al-fāṭimī*, 2 tomes, Coll : Histoire des Egyptiens (244), Le Caire, al-Hayʾa al-Miṣriyya al-ʿāmma li-l-Kitāb, 2005.

100 ʿAbd al-Wāḥid Ḏannūn Ṭāhā, *Al-riḥalāt al mutabādala bayna al-Ġarb al-islāmī wa-l-Mašriq*, Bayrouth, Dār al-madār, 2005.

En ce qui nous concerne, nous avons publié un article sur les voyages des Maghrébins en mer rouge, au Yémen et en Inde de 1098 à 1498 de l'ère chrétienne[101].

À ce jour, nous manquons encore d'informations sur la présence des Maghrébins en Asie centrale et orientale ; de plus, nous espérons voir bientôt un travail approfondi sur leur présence en Égypte à l'époque des Mamelouks.

3.3   Géographie et voyages

L'initiative dans ce domaine de recherche revient en vérité à l'arabisant russe Ignati Kratchkovski qui a écrit sur l'histoire de la littérature géographique arabe (1957)[102] ainsi qu'au français André Miquel qui a également consacré une œuvre monumentale à « la Géographie humaine du monde musulman jusqu'au milieu du XIe s. » (1973)[103].

En Tunisie, le Laboratoire de l'histoire du monde arabo-musulman a organisé un colloque sur les voyageurs et les voyages dans le monde arabo-musulman[104].

Plus particulièrement, la thèse de feu Muḥammad Sālaḥ Mġīrbī (m. 1993) soutenue à la Sorbonne sur « Les voyageurs de l'occident musulman du XIIe au XIVe siècles » reste le travail le plus important sur cette question[105].

À la même période, Ahmad Štīwī Buḫārī a étudié dans sa thèse quelques aspects de civilisation chez les voyageurs Maghrébins et Andalous (1988)[106].

D'ailleurs, le marocain ʿAbd al-Hādī Tāzī a beaucoup écrit sur les voyages d'Ibn Baṭṭūṭa et a aussi publié un article sur le voyage d'Ibn ʿAbīd al-Fāsī[107] ; de son côté, le tunisien Muḥammad al-Ṭālibī a écrit dans *l'Encyclopédie tunisienne* un article sur le voyage d'Ibn Ḫaldūn qui est, en fait, une traduction de son article dans *l'Encyclopédie de l'Islam*[108].

---

101   Luṭfī Bin Mīlād, « Al-Maġāriba wa tiǧārat al-Hind », *Annales islamologiques*, 51 (2017), 223-239.

102   Ignati Kratchkovski, *Tārīḫ al-adab al-ǧuġrāfī al-ʿarabī*, trad. arabe du russe, 2 tomes, Le Caire, Ligue des Etats arabes, 1961.

103   André Miquel, *La Géographie humaine du monde musulman jusqu'au milieu du XIe s.*, 4 tomes, Paris-EHESS, La Haye-Mouton, 1967-88.

104   Actes du colloque du Laboratoire d'histoire du monde arabe médiéval, (2006), *Revue Tunisienne des Sciences sociales*, Numéro spécial 139 (2010).

105   Ṣāliḥ Mġīrbī, *Adab al-riḥla fī al-Ġarb al-islāmī min al-qarn al-ṯānī ʿašar ilā l-qarn al-rābiʿ ʿašar*, trad en arabe par Mahmoud Tarchouna, Tunis, Centre National de Traduction, 2013.

106   Aḥmad Buhari Štīwī, *Ḥaḍārat al-ʿArab wa ṯaqāfatuhum fī riḥalāt al-Maġāriba bayna al-qarnayn al-sādis wa-l-ṯānī ʿašar H.*, Tunis, Centre de Publication Universitaire, 2018.

107   ʿAbd al-Hādī Tāzī, *Riḥlatu-l-riḥalāt : Makka fī miʾati riḥla maġribiyya wa riḥla*, 2 tomes, London, Muʾassasatu-l-furqān li-l-turāṯ al-islāmī, 2005.

108   Muḥammad al-Ṭālibī, « al-Mašāriqa », op. cit.

Plus tard, d'autres travaux sont venus approfondir quelques aspects particuliers de son voyage en Orient. La Saoudienne ʿAwāṭif Nawwāb a aussi écrit sur les voyages des Maghrébins et des Andalous comme source de l'Histoire de la péninsule arabique[109].

Du côté des voyageurs orientaux au Maghreb, viennent d'abord des articles sur le regard des Orientaux du Machreq envers les Maghrébins dont un article de Ṣalāḥ al-Dīn al-Munaǧǧid concernant la Tunisie à travers le regard d'Al-Qalqašandī (1980)[110] et d'autres travaux sur la géographie du Maghreb à travers Ibn Ḥawqal[111].

Ensuite, le syrien Aḥmad Badr a publié un article sur l'émigration orientale au Maghreb[112] et son compatriote ʿAlī Aḥmad a aussi écrit sur les voyageurs du Machreq au Maghreb[113]. Pour ma part, j'ai étudié la présence d'Ibn Ḫalīl au Maghreb[114].

4 Conclusion

Il est évident que les études sur les relations « Maghreb-Machreq » sont actuellement arrivées à un stade assez avancé, surtout du côté des chercheurs du Machreq qui ont beaucoup publié sur ce thème jusqu'au début du nouveau millénaire. Ces travaux ont notamment mis l'accent sur le thème des relations politiques et la présence humaine.

D'ailleurs, nous remarquons que la plupart de ces travaux proviennent des égyptiens et ce pour différentes raisons objectives dont, notamment, l'ancienneté et l'intensité des relations entre l'Égypte et le Maghreb, la dépendance à certaines périodes de l'histoire du Maghreb vis-à-vis de l'Égypte, l'échange du rôle de centre entre les deux pôles à travers l'histoire, etc. Ceci dit, ces travaux ont généralement tendance à appuyer l'idée de la pérennité du rôle central joué par l'Égypte.

---

109 ʿAwātif Muḥammad Yūsuf Nawwāb, *Al-Riḥalāt al-maġribiyya wa-l-andalusiyya, maṣdar min maṣādir tārīḫ al-Ḥiǧāz fī l-qarnayn al-sābiʿ wa-l-ṯāmin al-hiǧriyyayn : dirāsa taḥlīliyya muqārina*, Ryadh, Maktabat al-Malik Fahd al-waṭaniyya, 1996.

110 Ṣalāḥ al-Dīn Munaǧǧid, « Tūnis ʿinda-l-ǧuġrāfiyyīn al-mašāriqa min Ibn Hurdādba ilā al-Qalqašandī », *Al-Ḥayāt al-ṯaqāfiyya*, N° 7, janvier-février 1980, 24-29.

111 Par ex. : Yūsuf bin Aḥmad Ḥawāla, *Ibn Ḥawqal wa riḥalātuhu al-ǧuġrāfiyya li-l-ǧanāḥ al-ġarbī min al-dawla al-islāmiyya*, Koweït, Association géographique koweïtienne, 1992.

112 Aḥmad Badr, « Al-Andalusiyyūn wa-l-Maġāriba fī-l-Quds », *Awrāq* [Damas] 4 (1981), 123-139.

113 ʿAlī Aḥmad, *Al-Andalusiyyūn wa-l-Maġāriba fī bilād al-Šām*, op. cit.

114 Luṭfī Bin Mīlād, « Ṣūrat al-ġurabāʾ fī riḥlat Ibn Ḫalīl », *Revue Tunisienne des Sciences sociales* 164 (2013), 117-134.

Mis à part cette particularité, ces travaux ont montré la place importante qu'occupe le genre de récits de voyages au sein de l'historiographie arabo-musulmane.

Néanmoins, certaines questions fondamentales demandent à être approfondies, comme celle du commerce ou des relations économiques en général entre le Maghreb et le Machreq.

L'archéologie, ainsi que l'ensemble des archives et manuscrits éparpillés à travers le monde, devraient nous donner plus de détails sur les relations entre ces deux régions.

D'autre part, la coopération dans ces domaines de recherche entre les différentes universités arabes et entre les corps de chercheurs spécialisés reste très faible, à l'exception de quelques tentatives occasionnelles, en particulier au Maroc et en Tunisie.

Les nouvelles méthodes de recherche en histoire comparée sont, elles aussi, peu répandues.

Reste enfin la grande question, qui est de savoir si les chercheurs arabes ont su profiter des nouvelles méthodes de recherche afin de couvrir plus ou moins exhaustivement l'ensemble de ces domaines de recherche, notamment en ce qui concerne l'analyse des sources écrites en d'autres langues que l'arabe, dans le but de compléter les innombrables lacunes d'information historiographique sur les différentes questions qui fondent le thème des rapports « Maghreb-Machreq » au Moyen Âge.

Bibliographie thématique (sélective)

Éditions de sources
Récits de voyages

Al-ʿAbdarī, Muḥammad. *Al-Riḥla al-maġribiyya*, dir. Aḥmad bin Ǧiddū, sans date.

Al-Balawī, Ḫālid ibn ʿĪsā. *Tāǧ al-mafriq fī taḥliyat ʿulamāʾ al-Mašriq*, dir. Al-Ḥasan Muḥammad Al-Sāʾiḥ, Commission Mixte de l'édition du patrimoine (Maroc-Emirats Arabes Unis), 1970.

Ibn Baṭṭūṭa, Abū ʿAbdallāh Muḥammad. *Tuḥfat al-nuẓẓār fī ġarāʾib al-amṣār wa- ʿaǧāʾib al-asfār*, dir. ʿAlī al-Muntaṣir al-Kittānī, Beyrouth, Muʾassasat al-Risāla, 1985.

Al-Ġarnāṭī, Abū Ḥāmid ʿAbd al-Raḥīm. *Tuḥfat al-albāb wa-nuḫbat al-iʿǧāb*, dir. Ismāʿīl al-ʿArabī, Beyrouth, Dār al-Ǧīl, 1993.

Ibn Ǧubayr, Abū l-Ḥasan Muḥammad. *Riḥla*, dir. Muḥammad Muṣṭafā Ziyāda, Le Caire, Imprimerie de la Commission de production, traduction et édition, 1939.

Ibn Ḫaldūn, ʿAbd al-Raḥmān. *Riḥlat ibn Ḫaldūn*, dir. Muḥammad ibn Tāwīt al-Ṭanǧī, Beyrouth, Dār al-Kutub al-ʿilmiyya, 2004.

Ibn Ḫalīl, Zayn al-Dīn. *Al-rawḍ al-bāsim fī ḥawādiṯ al-ʿumur wa-l-tarāǧim*, dir. ʿUmar ʿAbd Al-Salām Tadmurī, 4 tomes, Beyrouth, al-Maktaba al-ʿAṣriyya, 2014.

Ibn Ḥammawayhī, Abū Muḥammad ʿAbd Allāh. *Al-riḥla al-maġribiyya*, Bribes rassemblées et éditées par Naǧāt al-Marīnī, Rabat, Centre Bābiṭayn de l'édition du patrimoine, 2011.

Ibn Rašīd, Abū ʿAbd Allāh Muḥammad. *Milʾu al-ʿayba bi-mā ǧumiʿa bi-ṭūli al-ġayba*, dir. Muḥammad al-Ḥabīb Bilḫūǧa, Tunis, Al-dār al-tūnisiyya li-l-našr, 1982.

Ibn al-Ṣabbāḥ, ʿAbd Allāh. *Nisbat al-aḫbār wa-taḏkirat al-aḫyār, (Riḥla ḥiǧāziyya)*, dir. Ǧumʿa Šīḥa, Revue *Dirāsāt andalusiyya* (Tunis), Numéro double spécial 45-46 (2011).

Al-ʿUmari, Ibn Faḍl Allāh. *Waṣf Ifrīqiyya wa-l-Andalus*, dir. Ḥasan Ḥusnī ʿAbd al-Wahhāb, Tunis, Imprimerie Al-Nahḍa (Renaissance) ; 1920.

Géographie et biographies

Bāhi, Aḥmad. *Sfāqs fī-l-maṣādir al-waṣīṭa*, Sfax, Imprimerie Gwīʿa, 2017.

Bin Šrīfa, Muḥammad. *Tarāǧim maġribiyya min maṣādir mašriqiyya*, Casablanca, Imprimerie al-Naǧāḥ al-Ǧadīda, 1996.

Ḥasan, Muḥammad. *Al-Qayrawān fī ʿuyūn al-raḥḥāla*, Carthage, Bayt al-Hikma, 2009.

Al-Munaǧǧid, Ṣalāḥ Al-Dīn. *Al-Mašriq fī naẓar al-Maġāriba*, Beyrouth, 1963.

Controverse

« *Fī l-inṣāf bayna al-Mašriq wa-l-Maġrib : Qiṭʿatun min masālik al-abṣār li-Ibn Faḍlallāh al-ʿUmarī* », étude et édition : Zaynab Ṭāhir Sāqallāh, Beyrouth, Dār al-madār al-islāmī, 2004.

Colloques spécialisés

Colloque sur les relations historiques et scientifiques entre les pays du Golfe arabe et les pays du Maghreb, Ryadh, 2008.

« *Al-Maġrib-al-Mašriq : al-ʿalāqāt wa-l-ṣūra* », Actes des deux colloques de Mars 1994 et novembre 1997 à la Faculté des Lettres et sciences humaines (Beni Mellal), l'Université Qāḍī ʿIyāḍ (Marrakech) et le Groupe des Études et recherches sur les relations Maghreb-Machreq, 1999.

« *Al-Mašriq wa-ʿalāqātuhu bi-l-Maġrib* », Union des Historiens Arabes, Le Caire, 1997.

Thèses

ʿAbdu, Hūriyya. *ʿAlāqāt Miṣr bi-l-Maġrib al-ʿarabī min al-fatḥ ilā qiyām al-dawla al-fāṭimiyya*, Université du Caire, 1974.

Bin Mīlād, Luṭfī [Ben Miled, Lotfi]. *Ifrīqiyya wa-l-Mašriq al-mutawassiṭī*, Tunis, Imprimerie al-Maġāribiyya, 2011.

Ḫalfallāh, Ibtisām Marʿī. *Al-ʿAlāqāt bayna al-ḫilāfa al-muwaḥḥidiyya wa-l-Mašriq al-ʿarabī ḥattā 1569*, Le Caire, Dār al-Maʿārif, 1985.

Ḥuḍayrī, Aḥmad Ḥasan. *Al-Fāṭimiyyūn wa bilād al-Maġrib (973-1171)*, Le Caire, Imprimerie Madbūli, 1996.

Mu'nis, Ḥusayn. *Faǧr al-Andalus*, Le Caire, Dār al-Rašād, 2008 (1959).

Ṭūḫī, Aḥmad. *Al-Mamālīk wa-l-Andalus*, Université d'Alexandrie, 1983.

Études
Voyages et voyageurs

Bin Mīlād, Luṭfī [Ben Miled, Lotfi]. « Ṣūrat al-ġurabā' fī riḥlat Ibn Ḫalīl », *Revue Tunisienne des Sciences sociales* 164 (2013), 117-134.

Daġfūs, Rāḍī (dir.). « Al-riḥla wa-l-raḥḥāla fī l-ʿālam al-ʿarabī al-islāmī », Actes du colloque du Laboratoire d'histoire du monde arabe médiéval (2006), *Revue Tunisienne des Sciences sociales*, Numéro spécial 139 (2010).

Ǧaḥma, Nawwāf ʿAbd al-ʿAzīz. *Raḥḥālat al-Ġarb al-Islāmī wa-ṣūrat al-Mašriq al-ʿarabī min al-qarn al-sādis ilā l-qarn al-ṯāmin H.*, Abou Dhabi, Dar al-Suwaidi, 2008.

Ḥamām, Muḥammad (dir.). *Al-riḥla bayna al-Šarq wa-l-Ġarb : Ittiṣāl am infiṣāl ?*, Actes d'un colloque de la Faculté des Lettres de Rabat, Casablanca, Imprimerie al-Naǧāḥ al-Ǧadīda, 2003.

Mġīrbī, Ṣāliḥ. *Adab al-riḥla fī al-Ġarb al-islāmi min al-qarn al-ṯani ʿašar ilā l-qarn al-rābiʿ ʿašar*, trad. en arabe par Mahmoud Tarchouna, Tunis, Centre National de Traduction, 2013.

Štīwī, Aḥmad. *Ḥaḍārat al-ʿArab wa ṯaqāfatuhum fī riḥalāt al-Maġāriba bayna al-qarnayn al-sādis wa-l-ṯāni ʿašar H.*, Tunis, Centre de Publication Universitaire, 2018.

Al-Ṭabbābī, Bilqāsim. « Ṣūrat Miṣr wa-l Miṣriyyin fī al-ʿahdayn al-Ayyūbī wa-l Mamlūkī min ḫilāl ar-raḥḥāla al-Maġāriba 586/1186 – 923/1517 », *Revue Tunisienne des Sciences sociales*, Numéro 139 (2010), 227-255.

Présence humaine

ʿAbd al-Ḥamīd, Saʿd Zaġlūl. « Al-aṯar al-maġribī wa-l-andalusī fī l-muǧtamaʿ al-iskandarī », *Revue de la Faculté des Lettres d'Alexandrie*, 1975.

Aḥmad, ʿAlī. *Al-Andalusiyyūn wa-l-Maġāriba fī bilād al-Šām ilā nihāyat al-qarn al-tāsiʿ H.*, Damas, Dār Ṭalas, 1985.

Badr, Aḥmad. « Al-Andalusiyyūn wa-l-Maġāriba fī-l-Quds », *Awrāq* [Damas] 4 (1981), 123-139.

Daġfūs, Rāḍī. « Al-Yamāniyyūn fī Ifrīqiyya », *Al-taḥarrukāt al-bašariyya wa-l-hiǧrāt al-yamāniyya ilā l-Šām wa šarq wa šamāl Ifrīqiyya qabla Ẓuhūr al-Islām wa-baʿdahu*, Colloque de Benghazi, 2001.

Daġfūs, Rāḍī. « Al-Ḥuḍūr al-yamāni fī Ifrīqiyya wa-l-Qayrawān fī l-qurūn al-ūlā li-l-hiǧra », *Išʿaʿ al-Qayrawān ʿabra al-ʿuṣūr* (Rayonnement de Kairouan à travers les âges), colloque de Kairouan (2009), 2010.

Daġfūs, Rāḍī. « Al-ʿawāmil al-iqtiṣādiyya li-hiǧrat banī Hilāl min Miṣr ilā Ifrīqiyya », *Awrāq* [Damas] 4 (1981), 3-18.

Daġfūs, Rāḍī. *Buḥūṯ wa-Dirāsāt fī l-tārīḫ al-ʿarabī al-islāmī*, Beyrouth, Dār al-Ġarb al-islāmī, 2005, 29-54.

Daġfūs, Rāḍī. « Al-hiǧra al-hilāliyya wa-inʿikāsātuhā fī Tūnis ʿabra al-tārīḫ », Centre d'Études et de Recherches Économiques et Sociales, 2005.

Daġfūs, Rāḍī. *Buḥūṯ fī tārīḫ Ifrīqiyya (Tūnis) wa-al-Yaman fī l-ʿahd al-islamī al-wasīṭ*, Amman, Dār Ǧalīs Al-Zamān, 2011, 83-131.

Daġfūs, Rāḍī. *Dirāsāt ʿan banī Hilāl wa-l-hiǧra al-hilāliyya*, Tunis, Centre de Publication Universitaire, 2015.

Ǧadla, Ibrāhīm. « Qabāʾil Riyāḥ min al-Nīl ilā al-Aṭlasī », *Revue Tunisienne des Sciences sociales* 127 (2004), 103-114.

Ḥanafī, Aḥmad Laṭīf. *Al-Maǧāriba wa-l-Andalusiyyūn fī Miṣr al-islāmiyya min ʿaṣr al-wullāt ḥattā nihāyat al-ʿaṣr al-fāṭimī*, 2 tomes, Coll : Histoire des Égyptiens 244, Le Caire, al-Hayʾa al-Miṣriyya al-ʿāmma li-l-Kitāb, 2005.

Maǧānī, Būba. *Aṯar al-ʿArab al-yamāniyya fī tārīḫ bilād al-Maġrib fī l-qurūn al-ṯalāṯa al-ūlā li-l-hiǧrati*, Alger, Dār Bahāʾ al-Dīn, 2009.

Malwānī, Ḥasan. *Al-hiǧra bayna al-Mašriq wa-l-Maġrib munḏu al-fatḥ al-islāmī ḥattā awāsiṭ al-qarn 5 H./11*, thèse dirigée par : Hāšimī ʿAlawī Qāsimī, Faculté des Lettres de Fès [Maroc], 1996.

Razzāz, Muḥammad. « Al-Hilāliyyūn fī l-Maġrib al-islāmī bayna iškāliyyat al-ġazwi wa l-hiǧra », *Al-Tārīḫ al-ʿarabī* [Maroc] 53 (2010), 213-228.

Al-Ṭālibī, Muḥammad [Talbi, Mohamed]. « al-Mašāriqa », *L'Encyclopédie tunisienne*, fasc. n° 4, Carthage, Bayt al-Ḥikma, 1994, 200-204.

Ṭībī, Amīn Tawfīq. « Al-Aġzāz wa-qudūmuhum ilā bilād al-Maġrib wa-l-Andalus », dans Idem. *Dirāsāt wa-buḥūṯ fī tārīḫ al-Maġrib wa-l-Andalus*, Tunis-Tripoli (Lybie), Al-Dār al-ʿarabiyya li-l-Kitāb, 1983, 87-100.

Relations avec la péninsule arabique

ʿAbd Wālī, Ǧamāl. « Makka min ḫilāl riḥlat al-Tuǧībī al-musammā ʿMustafād al-riḥla wa-l-iġtirābʾ », *Al-Riḥla wa-l-raḥḥāla fī l-ʿālam al-ʿarabī al-islāmī*, op. cit., 287-331.

Abū Diyyāk, Sālaḥ Muḥammad. « Al-tabādul al-fikrī bayna al-Maġrib wa-l-Andalus wa Šibh al-Ǧazīra al-ʿarabiyya », *Al-Dāra* [Riyadh] 4 (1988), 98-135.

Bābakr, Al-Ḥasan Ḥalīfa. « Al-ṣilāt al-fiqhiyya bayna al-Qayrawān wa-l-Madīna al-munawwra », Actes du colloque *Al-Qayrawān, markaz ʿilmī bayna al-Mašriq wa-l-Maġrib*, Tunis, 1995, 99-131.

Bin Sāsī, Yūsuf. *Al-Maǧāriba bī-l-Ḥiǧāz min al-qarn 7 H. ilā-l-qarn 9 H. (13-15 J.-C.)*, thèse dactylographiée, Faculté des Lettres de la Manouba [Tunisie].

Būlaġfān, Muḥammad. « Riḥalāt al-Andalus ilā l-Ḥaramayn », *Al-Andalus : Qurūn min al-taqallubāt wa-l-ʿaṭāʾ*, Riyadh, Bibliothèque Publique Abdelaziz, 1996.

Būtašīš, Ibrāhīm al-Qādirī [Boutchich, Brahim El Kadiri]. « Malāmiḥ min ḥaḍārat baʿḍ mudun al-Ǧazīra al-ʿarabiyya fi-l-ʿaṣr al-wasīṭ min ḫilāl adab al-ǧuġrāfiya wa-l-riḥalāt », *Al-Tārīḫ al-ʿarabī* [Maroc] 45 (2008), 309-330.

Kabānī, Saʿīd Ḥamad. *Al-Ṣilāt al-ʿaskariyya wa-l-iǧtimaʿiyya bayna al-Ġarb al-islāmī wa-bilād al-Hiǧāz ḫilāl al-ʿaṣr al-wasīṭ wa buldān al-Ḫalīǧ al-ʿarabī min al-qarn 1 H./7 ilā-l-qarn 6 H./12 : ishām fī dirāsat al-ṣilāt al-ḥaḍāriyya al-ḫalīǧiyya*, thèse de doctorat en histoire islamique dirigée par : Ibrāhīm al-Qādirī Būtašīš, Université de Meknès [Maroc].

Mannūnī, Muḥammad. « Al-ǧazīra al-ʿarabiyya fī al-ǧuġrāfiya wa-l-riḥalāt al-maġribiyya wa mā ilayhā », *Maǧallat al-Maǧmaʿ al-ʿilmī al-ʿirāqī* [Baghdad] 29 (1978), 150-187.

Marīnī, Sayf Šāhīn. *Al-ṣilāt al-tiǧāriyya bayna al-Andalus wa buldān al-Ḫalīǧ min al-qarn al-ṯāliṯ ilā l-qarn al-ḫāmis H.*, Doha, Faculté des Humanités, 2001.

Nawwāb, ʿAwāṭif Muḥammad Yūsuf. *Al-Riḥalāt al-maġribiyya wa-l-andalusiyya, maṣdar min maṣādir tārīḫ al-Ḥiǧāz fī l-qarnayn al-sābiʿ wa-l-ṯāmin al-hiǧriyyayn : dirāsa taḥlīliyya muqārina*, Riyadh, Maktabat al-Malik Fahd al-waṭaniyya, 1996.

Salāma, Ibrāhīm ʿAbd al-Munʿim. ʿUmān maʿbaran li tujjār al-Andalus ilā *Bilād Fāris wa Šarq Afrīqiyā (q. 3/9 - 5/11)*, Beyrouth, Muʾassasat al-Intišār al-ʿArabī, 2015.

Al-Siyābī, Aḥmad b. Saʿūd. *Al-Tawāṣul al-Ibāḍī bayna ʿUmān wa-l Bilād al-Maġāribiyya*, Oman, Maktabat al-Ḍāmirī li-l Našr wa-l Tawzīʿ, 2014.

Al-Tāzī, ʿAbd al-Hādī. « Riḥla Maġribī ilā Ḥaḍramawt ʿām 865/1460 », *Al-Mawrid*, 21/1 (1992), 19-40.

Al-Tāzī, ʿAbd al-Hādī. *Riḥlatu-l-riḥalāt : Makka fī miʾati riḥla maġribiyya wa riḥla*, 2 tomes, London, Muʾassasatu-l-furqān li-l-turāṯ al-islāmī, 2005.

Relations avec l'Iran

ʿAbd al-Rāziq, Maḥmūd Ismāʿīl. « al-Furs fī bilād al-Maġrib », *Maġribiyyāt, dirāsāt ǧadīda*, Rabat, 1977.

ʿArʿār, Murād. « Mulāḥaẓāt ḥawla al-Furs wa-l-Ḫurasāniyyin wa-ḥuḍūrihim bi-Ifrīqiyya », *Išʿāʿ al-Qayrawān*, op. cit., 165-194.

Būtašīš, Ibrāhīm al-Qādirī [Boutchich, Brahim El Kadiri]. « Al-adwār al-tārīḫiyya wa-l-ḥaḍāriyya li-l-Furs fī bilād al-Maġrib munḏu intišār al-Islām ḥattā al-qarn al-ṯāliṯ hiǧrī », *ʿUṣūr al-ǧadīda* [Université d'Oran-Algérie], n° double 14-15 (2014), 26-43.

Kaʿāk, ʿUthmān. *Al-ʿalāqāt bayna Tūnis wa-Īrān ʿabra al-Tārīḫ*, Tunis, S.T.D., 1972.

Kšīr, Ḫālid [Kchir, Khaled]. « Ibn Ḫaldūn wa-l-Furs », *al-Fikr al-ǧadīd* [Tunis] 2 (2016), 39-48.

Šabbūḥ, Ibrāhīm. « Baʿḍ muʾaṯṯirāt Īrān al-qadīma fī fann al-ʿimāra bi-Ifrīqiyya », *Al-Fikr* [Tunis], numéro spécial « Études iraniennes », 47ᵉ/1 (1971), 3-11.

Relations culturelles et idéologiques

Aḥnāna, Yūsuf. Taṭawwur al-maḏhab al-ašʿarī fī l-Ġarb al-islāmī, Rabat, Ministère des Habous et des Affaires Islamiques, 2007.

Bin Ḥammādī, ʿUmar. « Al-Ġazālī wa talāmiḏatuhu al-Maġāriba », *Neuvième centenaire de la mort de Ghazali*, Carthage, Bayt al-Hikma, 2011, 461-506.

Bin Mīlād, Luṭfī [Ben Miled, Lotfi]. « Al-Ḥarāk al-ṯaqāfī wa-l-fikrī bi-l-ʿālam al-islāmī wa-aṯaruhu fī ḥarakāt al-ʿulūm al-ʿaqliyya bi-Ifrīqiyya ilā nihāyat al-ʿaṣr al-wasīṭ », dans : Būsaklāwī, Saʿīd (dir.). *Al-ʿilm wa-l-taʿlīm fī bilād al-Maġrib min al-qarn al-tāsiʿ ilā al-qarn al-ṯāni ʿašar*, Wajda [Maroc], Centre d'études et de recherches humaines et sociales, 2016, 19-59.

Bin Mīlād, Luṭfī [Ben Miled, Lotfi]. *Al-Huwiyyāt al-Mutašaẓẓiya wa Shatāt al-Nuḥab fī al-ʿĀlam al-Islāmī: Muḥāwala fī rasm Jawānib min Kharīṭat al-ʿĀṣr al-Sunnī fī al-ʿĀṣr al-Wasīṭ*, Tunis, Dār Miskilyānī, 2021 (sous presse).

Bin Rumḍān, Rumḍān. « Madrasat al-iʿtizāl fi l-Qayrawān mā bayna al-qarn 2 H./8 ilā al-qarn 3 H./9, min al-ḏuhūr ilā al-ʿufūl », *Al-Ḥayāt al-ṯaqāfiyya* [Tunis] 201 (2009), 96-102.

Ġrāb, Saʿd. « Ḥawla iḥrāq al-Murābiṭīn li-Iḥyāʾ al-Ġazālī », dans Idem. *Al-ʿĀmil al-dīnī wal-huwiyya al-tūnisiyya*, Tunis, al-Dār al-Tūnisiyya li-l-Našr, 1990.

Hintātī, Naǧm al-Dīn. « Taṭawwur mawqif ʿulamāʾ al-Mālikiyya bi-Ifrīqiyya min al-ḫawḍi fi l-masāʾil al-kalāmiyya ilā tabannīhim li-l-ʿaqīda al-ašʿariyya », *Revue de l'IBLA* [Tunis] 170 (1992), 297-322.

Hintātī, Naǧm al-Dīn. « Muḥāwala li-našr al-maḏhab al-ḥanbalī bi-Ifrīqiyya ḥawālay muntaṣaf al-qarn al-tāsiʿ milādi/al-ṯāliṯ hiǧrī », *Revue de l'IBLA* [Tunis] 173 (1994), 91-106.

Hintātī, Naǧm al-Dīn. « Al-Maḏhab al-ḥanafī bi-l-Qayrawān fī l-qurūn al-wustā », *Al-Tārīḫ al-ʿarabī* [Maroc] 13 (2000), 227-258.

Hintātī, Naǧm al-Dīn. *Al-Maḏhab al-Mālikī bi-l-Ġarb al-islāmī ilā muntaṣaf al-qarn 5 H./11 J.-C.*, Tunis, Tibr Al- Zamān, 2004.

Makkī, Maḥmūd ʿAlī. « Al-tašayyuʿ fi-l-Andalus ilā nihāyat Mulūk al-Ṭawāʾif », *Maǧallat maʿhad al-dirāsāt al-islāmiyya* [Madrid], volume 2 (1954), 93-149.

Maʿmūrī, Muḥammad Ṭāhir. *Al-Ġazālī wa- ʿUlamāʾ al-Maġrib*, Tunis, Al-Dār al-Tūnisiyya li-l-Našr, Alger, al-Muʾassasa al-Waṭaniyya li-l-Kitāb, 1990.

Mansūrī, Mabrūk. « Al-Ašʿariyya fi bilād al-Maġrib ilā nihāyat al-qarn 6 H./ 12 wa mafhūm al-adwār al-ḥaḍāriyya », *Revue de l'IBLA* [Tunis] 192 (2003), 71-98.

Qablī, Muḥammad. « Ramz al-Iḥyāʾ wa-qaḍiyyat al-ḥukm fi l-Maġrib al-wasīṭ », dans Idem. *Murāǧaʿāt ḥawla al-muǧtamaʿ wa l-ṯaqāfa bi-l-Maġrib al-wasīṭ*, Casablanca, Dār Ṭubqāl, 1987.

Sī ʿAbd al-Qādir, ʿUmar. *Al-Tawāṣul al-ṯaqāfī bayn dawlat Banī Naṣr wa-l Mašriq fī ʿahd al-Mamālīk: 636/1238 – 898/1492*, Alger, Markaz al-Našr al-Jāmiʿī, 2014.

16

Modern Arabic Historical Scholarship on Medieval Europe: A Bibliographical Study

Al-Amin Abouseada

Early Arabic historiography on Medieval Europe has recently received some attention from western scholars. While some studies tend to discuss the perception of Europe in early Islamic literature,[1] almost all of these studies agree on the lack of interest shown in Medieval Arabic literature towards Europe, especially the western sphere. While this hypothesis seems to be plausible, a possible explanation can be largely attributed to religious, geographical, and linguistic barriers. Furthermore, there could have been other factors, which lie beyond the scope of this chapter.[2]

In pre- and early Islamic times, there were no records whatsoever of Arab travelers or merchants heading to Europe, as the main destinations for Arab trade were traditionally Yemen and Syria, with some vague references to Egypt. Al-Maqdisī, the Arab geographer and writer (d. 380 AH/990 CE), stated his lack of interest in writing about kingdoms of unbelievers (*kuffār*) as he never visited them and saw no benefit in speaking about them.[3]

When the Islamic conquests reached Iberia, the Arabs came into close contact with Western Europe. Thereafter, early Muslim writers and historians showed a relatively expanded knowledge of Medieval Europe. Arabic geographical works paid more attention to Europe in their presentation of the world's regions.

The turning point in Arabic knowledge on Europe was an Arabic translation of Orosius' (d. c. 417 CE) universal history, *Historiae adversus paganos*, which offers valuable information on Roman and early medieval Europe. The

---

1 For example works of Bernard Lewis, Daniel König and ʿAzīz al-ʿAẓma. See Bibliography.

2 Travel and presence of Muslims in the lands of non-Muslims (Dār al-Ḥarb) raised legal disputes. Some legal schools considered it impermissible for Muslims to live under non-Muslim rule, at least theoretically. See Lewis, *Islam and the West*, 50; Idem. *The Muslim discovery of Europe*, 61, 67.

3 Al-Maqdisī, *Aḥsan al-Taqāsīm*, Leiden, 9: "We mentioned only the kingdom of Islam, we did not pay attention to kingdoms of unbelievers as we neither visited them, nor do we see any advantage of speaking about them".

© KONINKLIJKE BRILL NV, LEIDEN, 2021 | DOI:10.1163/9789004460089_017

translation was recently reproduced with an introduction and notes.[4] This book was primarily translated into Arabic in al-Andalus during the reign of al-Ḥakam al-Mustanṣir Billah II (961–976 CE), presumably by some of the Latin clerics in Cordoba.[5] Some Arab historians referred to Orosius and his book as a source of their knowledge on Europe, this includes Ibn Juljul (d. after 377 AH/987 CE), al-Bakrī (d. 487 AH/1094 CE), and al-Maqrīzī.[6] It was, as Lewis noted, the only book which was translated from Latin during the medieval Arabic translation movement.[7]

Andalusia was always an active point of interaction between the Muslim world and Europe as armies, pilgrims, embassies, refugees, students, and merchants crossed borders between the two cultural zones. These interactions enriched Arab knowledge about Europe's history as well as its geography.[8]

The Crusader and Mamluk periods witnessed more close contacts between Muslims and Europe. This was reflected in the Arabic geographical works concerning Europe. As Koenig notes, Ibn Faḍlallāh al-ʿUmarī (d. 1349 CE) showed considerable knowledge of several European countries in his own time.[9] Nonetheless there were no individual historical or geographical works in Arabic from this period that were dedicated exclusively to Europe.

Under Ottoman rule the Arab world experienced a long period of isolation and intellectual idleness and there was less interest in Europe. There were a handful of missions and contacts between Europe and Muslim world, with a few Muslim persons travelling to Europe; they were mainly Ottoman officials and Moroccan merchants.[10]

In the beginning of the nineteenth century the Egyptian ruler Muḥammad ʿAlī (1805–1848 CE) dispatched the first Egyptian – perhaps the first Arab – students to study abroad in Paris. He sent with them the imām Rifāʿa Rāfiʿ al-Ṭahṭāwī (d. 1873 CE) to be their spiritual guide in Europe. Al-Ṭahṭāwī was an active person, a notable wit and a brilliant man. He mastered the French language and studied translation, eventually becoming one of the pioneer translators and intellectuals in the modern Arab world. His book on his trip to Paris offers valuable details on his experiences in Europe.[11]

---

4   Orosius, History of the World, an ancient Arabic translation, revised and edited by ʿAbd al-Raḥmān Badawī, Beirut, 1982.

5   Ibn Khaldūn, (d. 1406) mentioned the book and said it was translated into Arabic by a Christian judge, Tārīkh, 101.

6   Ūrūsiyūs, Tārīkh al-ʿĀlam, 21–33.

7   Lewis, The Muslim Discovery of Europe, 76.

8   See König, Arabic-Islamic perceptions of Western Europe in the Middle Ages.

9   König, Arabic-Islamic perceptions of Western Europe, 26–27.

10   Lewis, The Muslim Discovery of Europe, 117–119.

11   See D. Newman, An Imam in Paris: Al-Tahtawi's Visit to France (1826–31).

During the early twentieth century, the first modern universities were established in Egypt and the humanities were the first subjects to be studied in these universities. Though the University of Algiers, today called Benyoucef Benkhedda, was established in the nineteenth century by the French, it was in this early period under the tight supervision of the French colonial authorities and French was the primary language of instruction. Only in the second half of the twentieth century was it turned into a national university. It is worth noting that the well-known French orientalist and Byzantinist Marius Canard (d. 1982 CE) taught for several decades in the department of Oriental Studies at this university.

The establishment of national universities in the Arab world did not result in a sudden quick growth of Medieval studies. Although the humanities became a genuine discipline in all new universities, there were no independent departments of medieval history; rather, it became a branch of specialization taught within general history departments. Within this tiny branch there are usually three main areas of study: Medieval Europe, the Crusades, and Byzantine history. Some Egyptian universities, such as Cairo University, consider Ayyubid and Mamluk history as a course within the medieval branch, while other universities, in Egypt only, add a course on Byzantine Egypt. On the other hand, in Saudi Universities there is no separate Medieval history branch. The three abovementioned subjects are taught within the branch of Islamic history. Consequently, some young postgraduate students of medieval history are inclined to study topics related to Ayyubid and Mamluk history or relations between the Islamic world and medieval Europe. Occasionally some medievalists choose to be more specialized in the Crusades or Byzantine history rather than medieval Europe, with a few of them sticking to Byzantine Egypt.[12]

The following individuals can be considered the pioneers of medieval studies in the Arab world: ʿAzīz Suryāl ʿAtiyyāʾ (1898–1988), Joseph Nasīm Yūsuf (d. 1993), Alī Al-Ghamrāwī (d. 1993)[13], and Ḥasan Ḥabashī (d. 2005).[14] The most

---

12   Prof. Wisām Fāraj, Prof. Ḥusayn ʿAtiyya, Prof. Ṭariq Manṣūr, Prof. ʿAbd al-ʿAzīz Ramaḍān, Prof. Ḥātim al-Ṭahāwī (all Egyptians). In Saudi Arabia: Prof. ʿAlī Ūda al-Ghāmidi, Dr. ʿUmar Yamānī; Prof. ʿĀʾisha Abū al-Jadāyil (King Saud University) among others.

13   Originally he studied classics (Greek and Latin languages), obtaining his PhD in Germany. He is noted for contributing to editions of medieval sources, particularly the *Monumenta Germaniae Historica*, and showed an early interest in bibliographical studies. See Muḥammad Muʾnis ʿAwaḍ, al-Muʾarrikh al-Miṣrī ʿAlī Al-Ghamrāwī 1926–1993: Ḥayātuhu wa Muʾallafātuhu fī tārīkh Urūba fī al-ʿUṣūr al-Wusṭa.

14   Late professor of Medieval History, ʿAyn Shams University, Egypt. He translated several medieval sources, mostly from modern English translations including Anonymous Historian of the First crusades; William of Tyre; Robert Calri; Vilhardouin; The Continuation of William of Tyre; Joinville; *Alexiad* of Anna Comnena, Third Crusade Chronicles.

famous Arab medievalist is the late Saʿīd ʿAbd Al-Fattāḥ ʿĀshūr (d. 2009), whose works were, and are still, considered to be cornerstones of Arabic studies on medieval Europe. The most prolific Arabic medievalist was Isḥaq Tāwḍrūs ʿUbayd (also known as Ishaq Tawdros Ebeid).[15] Professor ʿUbayd composed several works on medieval Europe rather than following the general trend of Arab medievalists, who focused on European relations with the Islamic world or the Crusades. Another pioneering Arab medievalist was the late former Saudi Minister of Education and professor ʿAbd al-ʿAzīz al-Khuwayṭir (d. 2014) who obtained his PhD from the University of London, though it should be noted that most of his works tended to deal more with Islamic history.

After this first generation of Arab medievalists, the number of historians focusing on the Middle Ages increased considerably over a span of a half century. Most of them obtained their degrees at home in their national universities. Later, during the final decades of the last century, some Arab postgraduate students in medieval history acquired a unique chance to study in Europe and the United States. They became acquainted with more original medieval European sources, recent western studies, and modern library facilities. At the same time, they had to study Latin and Greek in preparation of their theses, according to the different criteria and standards applied by European universities. They returned home with more knowledge and languages, as well as copies of primary sources and modern reference works, all of which stirred the stagnant waters of medieval studies in their native countries. This paved a new path for medieval studies in the Arab world.

The accumulation of references, sources, knowledge, bibliographies and ideas related to the field of medieval studies increased sharply. Several other channels and factors contributed to this growth. In recent years many of the universities in Saudi Arabia and Egypt have established academic websites on which they put records of academic theses registered or completed in different colleges. Furthermore, the Supreme Council of Egyptian Universities has published online databases of MA and PhD theses, papers, and books written in different Egyptian universities.[16] The site is unique and helpful; it supports English, French, and Italian languages. Some Arab historians, especially in Egypt and North Africa, have personal academic pages on scientific sites such

---

15   Born in 1933 in Asyūṭ, Upper Egypt, graduate in history, Alexandria University 1955. His professional academic life started 1964 when he studied for his PhD in Nottingham University under the supervision of Bernard Hamilton. His thesis title was "The attitude of western churchmen toward the Byzantine empire from 1054 A.D. to 1204 A.D.". It was later published in Arabic under title "Ruma wa Bizanṭa" "Rome and Byzantium". See ʿAbd al-ʿAzīz Ramaḍān, Isḥāq Tāwḍrūs ʿUbayd: Masīrat ʿĀlim.

16   http://srv2.eulc.edu.eg/eulc_v5/libraries/start.aspx.

as Academia.edu, Google Scholar and Research Gate, or personal web pages or blogs. Some historians have published their papers online in full or at least provided abstracts for them. Simultaneously, most contemporary western medievalists also have their own pages on the same websites, making them better-known to Arab scholars and placing their articles and works within reach of Arab researchers.

The internet made a decisive contribution to the development of medieval European studies in the Arab world. It opened a wide window on the global academic world for Arab postgraduate students to grasp and communicate with their colleagues elsewhere. Most internet sites respect copyright and refrain from publishing entire books and texts. However, it should be noted that a large number of works on medieval European history, especially old collections of primary sources, were printed a long time ago, therefore they are no longer protected by copyright laws, and so they have been published fully and legally on several websites around the world.

Published books and papers online, particularly the free ones, offer a unique opportunity for Arab researchers to become acquainted with modern works in European languages.[17] The world wide web now provides free copies of non-copyrighted main primary sources of medieval History (*Patrologia Latina*, *Patrologia Graeca*, CSHB, RHC). All of these were once barely available at a few libraries in the entire Arab world. It should be remembered that at one time obtaining a single page from a collection of medieval European primary sources such as the *Patrologia Latina* would have been extremely hard and expensive. Now the entire collection is available for free, and legally, on the internet. In all Egypt there were only two or three printed copies of the *Patrologia*, in the Franciscan and Dominican libraries in Cairo, with restricted access, and expensive charges for photocopying. This made life miserable for researchers as I can attest from personal experience.

At the same time, with the social media revolution, several Arab postgraduate students created academic groups to discuss issues of common interest, and to upload scanned copies of books and papers. Unfortunately, this brilliant step proved to be a double-edged sword, as some simply appeared with nicknames asking for help with their theses, while others filled these groups with religious and political posts. Sometimes people uploaded books and papers in these groups without respecting copyright laws, a practice that can affect the publishers.

---

17   Most universities in Saudi Arabia, Egypt, and some other Arab countries offer free access
      for their staff and postgraduate students to international academic databases such as:
      Jstor, ProQuest, and Science Direct.

Some Arab publishers followed the example of the international publishing companies and created Arabic databases for Arabic academic works. Gradually these databases have appeared on the internet, though many are still deficient, poorly organized, and offer full text for only a limited selection of works, usually academic theses. Fortunately, most of the Egyptian and Saudi universities purchased subscriptions to these sites and offer full access to them.[18]

Al-Maktaba al-Shāmila (the Comprehensive Library) is a popular Arabic website which offers a huge searchable library of classical Arabic sources of all genres as well as some modern Arabic reference works.[19] All the works on the site are searchable texts with page numbers corresponding to the printed editions. From personal experience this site has become very popular in the Gulf countries, and less so in Egypt; this may be due to the limited internet speed in Egypt compared with the Gulf countries. There are also some internet sites and groups which offer both old and newer Arabic works and do not always respect the copyright rules. Moreover, there is a technical problem with most of the Arabic texts that are published on the internet by individuals. These texts are mostly PDF images, which contain unsearchable texts with immense file size and generally poor quality.

As the accumulation of non-Arabic primary sources and modern studies soared sharply, however, a new problem appeared; namely that of dealing with the languages of these primary sources, mainly medieval Greek and Latin. First of all, there are no specific courses in any Arab university offering a BA degree in Medieval European history. Consequently, studying Latin was imposed only as a sole requirement subject in the pre-master year, and usually consists of merely a few lessons which did not suffice to give students of medieval history the ability to read and translate medieval historical texts. Usually there is no similar option for a Greek course in this pre-master year.

To solve this problem, some Arab scholars[20] conceived a lengthy, extraordinary solution; they forced their postgraduate students to complete a second BA degree in Classical Studies in order to acquire the necessary knowledge of Latin and Greek before commencing their MA studies in medieval history. Some history students took this route while others were dismayed with the amount of time required to study for another BA degree and dropped out of the program.

---

18   These databases are Dar al-Mandumah for articles and theses; Ask Zad; Arabic eBook Collection; EBSCO; Nature Publisher Group; Al Jamea; Human Index; Arab Base; and others.

19   www.shamela.ws.

20   For example: Prof. Wisām Faraj (Wesam Farag), Manṣūra University. He obtained his PhD from Birmingham University, Centre for Byzantine & Ottoman and Modern Greek Studies, however, almost all of his works concern Byzantine History exclusively.

Other students paid private translators to translate the Latin and Greek texts required for their research. Obviously, therein lies another problem, since paying translators does not help those researchers with their limited knowledge of Latin or Greek to recognize the specific paragraphs that they would like to translate. In an attempt to compensate for their lack of linguistic skill, they follow the references in modern European-language secondary works to locate passages in the original Latin and Greek texts. Some have even tried to use their limited knowledge of Latin and Greek combined with machine translation systems such as Google Translate, or other software. Those who have better knowledge of Greek and Latin can attain some benefits through this method. It is worth noting that the Syrian Franciscan monk Manṣūr Mistriḥ, who has lived in Egypt for half a century, has always offered generous and free assistance with translating Latin. He continues to provide accurate and immediate translation for free to all students of Medieval history. Undoubtedly, postgraduate students need to have some basic knowledge of the ancient languages in order to determine the exact paragraphs that they need.

However, those Arab students of medieval history who manage to deal with Latin and Greek texts relying only on partial translation still lack a comprehensive view of the entire text, which they may not be able to fully read or comprehend. There are only a few Arab medievalists who can make free use of medieval European primary sources in their original languages. Gradually, more modern European translations have appeared for most of the medieval sources. Hence this became the magic and total solution for dealing with medieval sources. Furthermore, a few of these sources have been translated in turn into Arabic, but they are relatively very few compared with the number of primary sources related to the Crusades that have been translated into the same language. Almost none of the medieval European sources that were translated into Arabic were directly translated from their original languages such as Latin, Old French, and Byzantine Greek. The exception is the medieval Arabic translation of Orosius.

Even dealing with the modern European languages still constitutes a considerable challenge for the Arab medievalists. While most of them have a fair knowledge of English, only a few can write fluently in it. In recent years obtaining a higher degree in any field of postgraduate study in most Arab countries requires some knowledge of English. However, very few of the young Arab medievalists can write in English.

The problem widens and becomes more complicated when dealing with modern European languages apart from English. Most of the medievalists know some degree of French, fewer are acquainted with German, and fewer still know any of the other modern European languages. Nonetheless, recently some Arab medievalists have held post-doctoral positions in Germany, Italy and France, and some have participated in international conferences in Europe. Unquestionably, all these activities are widening the scope of medieval studies in the Arab world.

There are only limited cases of Arab medievalists who can read and write fluently in modern European languages apart from English, French and German. Hishām Ḥasan[21] is the only Arab medievalist, to my knowledge, who can read and write in Modern Greek, but most of his works are dedicated to Byzantine history. There is also the case of a young medievalist in Mansura University, Dr. Karīm ʿAbd al-Ghanī ʿAbd al-ʿĀṭī, who completed his PhD[22] in Arabic in 2015 and who can speak and write Bulgarian fluently. He participated in several academic events in Bulgaria. The Jordanian historian Muḥammad ʿAbduh Ḥatālma studied in Spain and has published some papers in Spanish; however, most of his works are devoted to the Moriscos and the fall of Muslim Spain.

A number of Arab medievalists have obtained PhD degrees from universities in Italy, Germany, and Spain. They attain a certain degree of knowledge of the language of the country they studied in, albeit without publishing any works in these languages apart from their own theses. Nonetheless this experience definitely broadened their scope, giving them a glimpse of the state of European scholarship, and enabled them to enrich the experiences their own postgraduate students as well as the field of Arabic medieval studies.

In recent years, an increasing number of Arabic works on medieval Europe have explored new topics and more significantly, have utilized the original Latin and Greek sources rather than depending mainly on modern European reference works. In Egypt several important new works have appeared which treat aspects of medieval European civilization. Most of the older Arabic studies on medieval Europe focused on political and military history, or on topics which allowed the authors to rely on Arabic primary sources in addition to, or instead of, medieval European sources.

---

21   Dr. Hishām M. Ḥasan born in Egypt 1975, studied classics in Egypt and obtained his PhD in Byzantine Philology at the Faculty of Arts in the University of Athens. He wrote his dissertation in Greek on *The Image of the Arabs in Byzantine Literature of the 7th and 8th Centuries*. Now he is working as a researcher in the Centre of Byzantine Research, National Hellenic Research Foundation in Athens in the Framework of the European Research Program *Krypidha*. He has written several works in Greek concerning Byzantine history and its relations with Muslims.

22   For his PhD thesis on medieval Balkan history see Karīm ʿAbd al-Ghanī ʿAbd al-ʿĀṭī, Qusṭanṭīn wa Mīthūdiyūs.

The entire body of Arabic research on Medieval Europe can be simply divided into four main groups according to their format: books, articles, theses, and translations (of primary sources and of modern studies).

Books constitute the main category, with the largest number of works. Indeed, there is a strong tendency for most Arab medievalists, who are generally university professors, to write a textbook, usually entitled "History of Medieval Europe", or "History and Civilization of Medieval Europe". Most of these works are predominantly simple, comprehensive, and depend little on primary sources. Some common titles used by Arab medievalists are "Studies in the history of Medieval Europe", or "Studies in Medieval History", in which the authors gather their different articles, similar to the Variorum Series in the West. Furthermore, many books deal with the typical subject of "Relations between East and West in the Medieval Period", or "The Impact of Arab or Islamic Civilization on Europe". Beyond these common titles only a limited number of monographs and books appear to examine other particular aspects of medieval European history. It should be noted that most of these studies, particularly the older ones, draw heavily on modern European studies, rather than on original Latin sources.

After more than half a century, the most well-known and popular book on the history and civilization of Medieval Europe by the late Egyptian historian Saʿīd ʿAbd Al-Fattāḥ ʿĀshūr, entitled *Tārīkh Urūba fī al-ʿUṣūr al-Wusṭā* (History of Medieval Europe), still constitutes the benchmark of all Arabic studies on medieval Europe. It was published in the middle of the last century and reprinted several times in Egypt and other Arab countries. The book consists of two volumes, the first is about political history, and the second is dedicated to the civilization of medieval Europe. Several other books on medieval Europe followed, but ʿĀshūr's book is still the touchstone and the first step for any postgraduate student in the Arab world, even though its first edition appeared around 1959. This essential textbook is very well organized, simple, and comprehensive. However, it lacks deep analysis and direct acquaintance with original medieval sources, as it refers only to two original sources, Tacitus' *Germanica* and Einhard's *Life of Charlemagne*, and even then only in their English translations. It is worth noting that his massive volume on the history of the crusades is equally admired across the Arab world. ʿĀshūr was a very prolific writer, he also composed several works on Muslim history and European–Muslim relations in the Middle Ages.

More recently, several other books followed, dealing with all aspects of medieval European history. They fluctuated in their topics and quality but most of them were either published dissertations, or textbooks for use in university courses. Among these works is a unique book entitled *Rūmā wa*

Bīzanṭa min Qaṭī'at Phūtius ḥattā al-Ghazw al-Lāṭīnī li-Madīnat Qusṭanṭīn 869–1204 [Rome and Byzantium from the Photian Schism until the Latin invasion of Constantinople 869–1204], which was originally a PhD thesis by Prof. Isḥāq Tāwḍrūs 'Ubayd.[23] The Arabic version (or translation) was printed in Cairo 1970. Two years later he published another work, *Al-Imbrāṭūriyya al-Rūmāniyya bayn al-Dīn wa al-Barbariyya* [Roman Empire between religion and Barbarism]. Both works, especially the first one, set a new benchmark for Arabic medieval studies. This is the only work to my knowledge whose author had a strong knowledge of the Latin language and fully utilized original medieval European sources with no reference whatsoever to Arabic sources or reference works.

Several modern studies have appeared in Arabic translation, offering an extensive and unique opportunity for young Arab medievalists to be acquainted with Western studies on medieval Europe. One may choose only two of them, each represent a separate trend of historical studies. The first and oldest is: Fisher's *History of Europe*, (first published in three volumes in London in 1937), which was translated into Arabic in 1969 by M.M. Ziyāda and al-Sayyid A. al-'Arīnī. The medieval section is a thin volume with vivid style, which offers direct illustration of the outlines of medieval Europe. The other book, which provides a deeper and more composite view, is Norman Cantor's *The Civilization of the Middle Ages* which was translated in two volumes under the title *al-Tārīkh al-Wasīṭ* by Qāsim 'Abduh Qāsim, and reprinted several times in Cairo. It remains in print now.

In the last few decades, various modern studies on medieval Europe have been translated into Arabic in several different Arab countries, undoubtedly enriching the development of medieval European studies in the Arab world. Recently there was an ambitious project at the National Translation Center in Cairo to translate the entire *New Cambridge Medieval History* into Arabic, but unfortunately bureaucratic obstacles meant the scheme was aborted.

The second category of publications consists of peer reviewed papers. These often provide a broader and deeper scope for investigation in medieval European studies. The allure of European–Muslim relations appears clearly, as approximately 35% of the papers by Arab historians of medieval Europe concern all aspects of these relations. In all Arab countries, publication of a number of academic papers, usually four or five, is an essential requirement for higher degrees. Nowadays the academic standards for these papers have

---

23   The original title of the PhD thesis is "The attitude of western churchmen toward the Byzantine empire from 1054 A.D. to 1204 A.D.", Nottingham University 1964, under supervision of late prof. Bernard Hamilton.

increased considerably. Progressively, new tight criteria were set and fresh ideas were required. Accordingly, an increasing number of Arabic papers have explored previously neglected aspects of medieval Europe, frequently dealing with internal medieval European topics rather than Islamic–European relations

Dissertations make up the third category of publications in the field. Academic theses necessarily attempt to explore new topics in medieval studies.[24] The increasing number of postgraduate students appearing every year creates an urgent need for finding new previously unexploited subjects for their theses. A proliferation of newly available European primary sources, thanks partially to the internet, and the pressure and encouragement exerted by thesis supervisors, have contributed to encourage students to break into new areas of research. Recently, or more accurately in the last two decades, i.e. after the internet revolution in academic studies, several excellent and original academic theses have been produced in the field of medieval European history, which should serve as models for future works.

Two of these works will be mentioned here. The first is Sāmir Qandīl's MA thesis from 2009 at 'Ayn Shams University entitled "Gerbert: Pope Sylvester II and his role in social and cultural life in Western Europe (945–1003)". The second is Yāsir 'Abdallāh's PhD thesis defended at the Girls' College of 'Ayn Shams University in 2007 which is entitled "Peter Abelard and his position in European Medieval Culture".

Both are strong theses that fit the European criteria for good academic works. The researchers, especially the first one, know the Latin language very well and were thereby able to fully utilize their original Latin sources. Furthermore, they read almost all of the modern works related to their field, not only in English as usual, but in other modern European languages too, not to mention the Arabic studies. They offer worthy and plausible arguments, vivid discussions on their works, and rich, comprehensive bibliographies. Unfortunately, on the other hand, some superficial nonacademic theses have been written as well. I refrain from referring to these works which are easy to spot by any specialist in the field.

Finally, to summarize the development of medieval studies in Arab world, one may hypothesize three distinct stages thereof. Certainly, these periods are approximate; their time span is slightly undefined. Nevertheless, each of

---

24   Note that in non-credit hours postgraduate programs the MA thesis is considered a full thesis, and often reaches a length of more than 200 pages. Even in credit hours programs the MA thesis is usually considered to be a complete work.

them constitutes a turning point in the development of medieval studies in the Arab world.

The first, or formative, period extends from the beginning to the middle of the twentieth century. At this time interest in medieval European studies was sporadic, with few libraries, only a handful of universities, and very limited resources throughout the mostly still colonized Arab world. In the entire Arab world there were only two universities: the University of Algiers[25] and Cairo University (founded 1908) in Egypt. During this period the early pioneer Arab medievalists focused mainly on general medieval history, dealing with the decline of the Roman Empire, the Germanic invasions, and the making of the European countries. At the same time, they gave some attention to the civilization of medieval Europe, mainly feudal systems, the church, and medieval universities. During this stage they drew heavily on modern European studies rather than on the original Latin and Greek sources.

The second period extends from the middle of the twentieth century to its end. In this epoch most of the Arab countries obtained their independence. Emerging from the colonial era they started building a new academic life and founded new national universities. In these new academic institutions, the humanities led the other disciplines; faculties of Arts and Sciences were usually the first faculties in every university.

An important feature of this period was the phenomenon of Arab academic missions abroad. Some postgraduate students completed their higher degrees in Europe. Most returned with new books,[26] ideas, experiences, conceptions, and academic contacts, which all have deeply impacted the field of medieval studies in the Arab world.[27] In this phase, most of the academic works tended to deal with the political history of medieval Europe and its relations with the Islamic world, while other works continued to cover the general history of Medieval Europe. However, general works on medieval European history continued to appear during this phase. Arab medievalists also began to focus on the histories of the individual European nations and countries during the medieval period and their relations with the Arabs. Unsurprisingly, the Christian Spanish kingdoms and their relations with the Muslims were a favorite subject.

---

25   Founded as a colonial French school in the middle of the nineteenth century.

26   Egyptian and Saudi authorities gave special allowances to their postgraduate students studying abroad to purchase reference works and even ship them home after finishing their courses.

27   For example Prof. Isḥāq Tawḍrūs ʿUbayd from Egypt and the late Prof. ʿAbd al-ʿAzīz al-Khuwayṭir from Saudi Arabia.

In this period some foreign institutions offered genuine help and support for Arab scholars of medieval European studies. In Egypt, for example, both the Franciscan and Dominican monasteries offered very rich libraries with unique reference works in all medieval and modern languages. The American University in Cairo and the Goethe Institute both offered inter-library loan services by which they made available articles and chapters of books to post-graduate students for a reasonable price.

The third period coincided with the beginning of the current millennium after the internet revolution. The availability of primary sources soared sharply, whether in their original languages or in modern translations. Secondary works in the modern European languages became increasingly available as well. Most of the Arab medievalists forged new research paths treating previously ignored subjects. medieval European civilization finally became an open and fertile field for study by the Arab medievalists.

Although the utilization of primary sources for medieval European history has increased dramatically over recent decades among Arab researchers, it is still mainly based on translations of these sources into modern European languages. Now almost all Arabic academic studies on medieval Europe are compelled to use the original medieval sources, if not in their original languages then at least in modern translations.

Gradually, due to the widespread availability of sources either in the original languages or in English translations, and the emergence of a new generation of Arab professors of medieval history – some of whom had studied abroad in Europe, developed their foreign language skills, and participated in international conferences – new criteria appeared in the field of medieval studies. In order to be accepted for publication academic papers are required to make use of original sources and the latest modern European works and no medieval history thesis in any university in the Arab world can now avoid dealing with primary sources.

Recently a number of Egyptian professors became particularly active in training new generations of Arab medievalists and encouraging them to explore new themes. Prof. Isḥāq Tāwḍrūs ʿUbayd was one of the pioneering medievalists in the Arab world. He obtained his PhD in England in 1968. He acquired an excellent knowledge of Latin; wrote several works on medieval Europe and mastered the whole texts of relevant medieval sources in their original Latin. He was the most prolific Arabic writer on medieval Europe. Upon his return to Egypt he created his own circle of brilliant medievalists; he insisted on utilizing the original sources and encouraged all of his students to acquire a basic knowledge of Latin.

Similarly, Prof. Usāma Zakī Zayd (Tanta University, Egypt), obtained his PhD in the field of the history of the Crusades. He has also written some papers on the history of the Lombards and about Lombard women. Later, he directed several of his students to focus on the history and civilization of medieval England. They selected research topics ranging from Roman Britain to the Hundred Years War. The main trend of these works fluctuated between the political and cultural history of the English (or Anglo-Saxon) kingdoms. Nowadays, some of his students have turned to the study of the Frankish kingdoms. This is mostly due to the availability of primary sources, whether in Latin or in modern English translation.

Likewise, Prof. ʿAfāf Ṣabra (Al-Azhar University, Egypt) is a prolific medievalist whose publications cover Islamic, Byzantine, and Medieval European history. Although there is a general impression in Egypt that students of al-Azhar usually have weaker English skills than their counterparts in other universities, Ṣabra has encouraged her students (who are mostly girls) to undertake research on topics in medieval European history that require extensive reliance on original European primary and secondary sources. Her students have undertaken theses on subjects such as the Venerable Bede, the Hanseatic League, Isidore of Seville, and Thomas Becket. "The Hanseatic League", is a much broader topic for a PhD dissertation than one would expect in a European department of medieval history, due to the greater degree of specialization there, but in the world of Arab medieval studies it represents the bold step of opening up a new and challenging subject that has not yet been studied by Arab medievalists.

In fact, it was not the works of Zayd and Ṣabra that represented a turning point in medieval studies per se, but rather their genuine efforts to pave new paths of research for their students and their advocating of new challenging ideas. This caused a move away from the traditional topics of Muslim–European relations. The daring steps of both professors certainly constituted a challenge to other professors to lead their students to explore ambitious new topics and ideas in their theses. Eventually this resulted in the creation of higher criteria for academic theses in the field.

More rigorous criteria required more reading as well as translation of medieval European primary sources and modern studies into Arabic. Indeed, translation into Arabic has been continuous since the beginning of medieval studies in the Arab world. The earliest Arabic translation of a medieval European source occurred in the Middle Ages with the translation of Orosius' universal history, *Historiae adversus paganos*, mentioned above. In modern times the earliest translation of European sources occurred in the middle of the twentieth century. The first modern Arabic translation of a medieval European primary source was of Tacitus's *Germania*.[28] Remarkably, it was translated from English rather than from the original Latin. A few years later the late Prof. Ḥasan Ḥabashī started a series of Arabic translations in which he translated (from the modern English translations) several key medieval sources including the works of Villehardouin, Robert de Clari, Anna Comnena, William of Tyre, and the continuation of William of Tyre. In total about 15 primary sources for medieval European history have been translated into Arabic. Almost all of them have been translated into Arabic from English translations rather than from the original Latin or other medieval languages such as Byzantine Greek or Old French. Early Arabic translations usually only consisted of a plain text with few comments, while later translations such as those made by Prof. Ḥ. al-Ṭaḥāwī[29] included a comprehensive study and extensive scholarly comments on every aspect of the text and its context.

Recently the Syrian historian Suhayl Zakkār has published a huge encyclopedia of the sources for the Crusades (al-Mawsūʻa al-Shāmila li al-Ḥurūb al-Ṣalībiyya). This work consists of over 50 large volumes. It includes fragments of primary Crusades sources from Latin, Syriac and other languages translated into Arabic.[30] This valuable encyclopedia has become a standard reference work among Arab researchers. Nevertheless, one may note that it focuses on the Crusades rather than on medieval Europe in general. Secondly, it does not offer a full translation of the texts themselves, but often includes only excerpts relevant directly to the history of the Crusades.

The number of modern European secondary works on medieval Europe in Arabic translation is considerably higher than that of translated primary sources. Approximately 88 such works have been translated into Arabic. Initially, the translations were mainly due to individual initiatives and efforts. Over the past two or three decades there have also been some institutional translation projects in Saudi Arabia, Egypt and other Arab countries.[31]

---

28   Tacitus, *Germania*, trans. Ibrāhīm ʻAlī Ṭarkhān, Cairo, 1959.

29   He translated into Arabic several Latin accounts of the Ottoman conquest of Constantinople in 1453 such as J.R. Melville Jones, *The siege of Constantinople 1453: seven contemporary accounts*, Amsterdam, 1972; Niccolò Barbaro *Diary of the Siege of Constantinople*, translated by J.R. Jones, New York, 1970.

30   It includes fragments of sources such as Matthew of Paris, Roger of Wendover, the *Song of Roland* and some others.

31   The so-called "One Thousand Books Project" in the 1960s. This was followed by a second series entitled "the second thousand books". In the UAE there is the project "Kalima".

Furthermore, some Arab universities have translation centers which offer generous funding for translations.[32]

The discipline of medieval European studies in the Arab world has always been far from static, and is always in need of closer surveys on the basis of careful examination of the available bibliographical data concerning Arabic studies on medieval Europe. The following statistical tables illustrate the main features and trends of modern Arabic historiography on medieval Europe. By my estimation there are around 544 Arabic works concerning medieval Europe. Undoubtedly, this number is not conclusive or totally accurate. Unfortunately, there are no specific bibliographical studies dedicated to history or branches of history in most Arab countries apart from some partial attempts by Egyptian researchers, but these pioneering works are neither sufficient nor comprehensive.[33]

TABLE 16.1   Division according to types

Works	Number
Books	168
Papers	129
Thesis	136
Arabic Translation of references	89
Arabic Translation of sources	14
Bibliography	5
Dictionaries	None
Encyclopedia	None
Others	None

Note: In Arabic academic journals, book reviews are rare. As a result, they are of minor importance, and I have not included them in the works surveyed here. The same can be said of both dictionaries and encyclopedias of history. No such works covering medieval Europe exist in Arabic. They are rare even in the other disciplines of history such as ancient, Islamic, and modern history. I have found only three works concerning individual medievalists.

32   In Saudi Arabia at King Saʿūd University, King ʿAbd al-ʿAzīz University, King Faisal University and other institutions.

33   Muḥammad Muʾnis ʿAwaḍ composed several bibliographical studies on the Crusades in general. Shaʿbān Ḥamza, an Egyptian researcher, composed a bibliography of all history theses in Egypt. Unfortunately, none of these works were dedicated to medieval Europe specifically nor did they have indices of proper names, but rather they were organized either by topics or titles with no indices to facilitate the usage and search thereof.

TABLE 16.2   Division according to topics

Works	Book	Thesis	Paper	Trans. ref.	Sum
Relations with Islamic world	46	25	46	33	150
General history	50	43	16	19	128
General civilization	14	5	7	6	32
Politics and war	14	5	7	6	32
Economy	8	12	7	5	32
Society & Feudal system	4	4	1	4	13
Thought & literature & Universities	11	11	21	10	53
Church & Religion	7	19	13	4	43
Mongols and Europe	7	1	3	–	11
Jews	3	2	2	1	8
Women	4	4	3	–	11
Arts	3	–	–	–	3

Note: Most of the Arabic studies on medieval Europe concern its relations with the Islamic world. This is mostly due to the easy availability of the Arabic primary sources and because young researchers wish to avoid dealing intensively with non-Arabic source languages. The early works focused mostly on political history. The Crusades, Byzantine history, and Muslim–Christian relations in the Middle Ages were popular topics with researchers as well.

TABLE 16.3   Divisions according to European countries

Country	Islam and med. west	General hist.	Civilization	Politics and war	Econ.	Society & Feudalism	Thought & literature & Univ.	Church & Religion[a]	Sum
All Europe	78	46	18	3	11	7	35	34	232
Roman Empire	3	6	1	–	–	1	1	–	12
Frankish kingdoms	23	14	4	8	4	2	11	2	68
England & Scotland	5	18	10	17	–	2	3	2	57
France	–	7	1	12	1	2	2	2	27
Germany & Holy Roman Empire	7	13	3	4	–	1	2	–	30

TABLE 16.3 Divisions according to European countries (*cont.*)

Country	Islam and med. west	General hist.	Civili-zation	Politics and war	Econ.	Society & Feudalism	Thought & litera-ture & Univ.	Church & Religion[a]	Sum
Italy (Venice & Sicily)	18	5	2	2	3	–	2	–	32
Iberia (Spain & Portugal and others	22	4	–	5	–	1	1	–	33
Poland	–	–	–	2	–	–	–	–	2
Russia	1	3	–	–	–	–	–	–	4
Scandinavia	1	–	–	–	–	–	–	–	1
Balkan & East Eu.	8	4	–	–	–	–	–	2	14
Other	–	11	–	–	–	–	–	–	11

a   Considering the Papacy as related to the whole of Europe and not only Italy.
Note: Most of the Arabic studies on medieval Europe focus on European relations with the Arabs and Islam. This was due to the fact that many researchers preferred topics that allowed them to make use of the Arabic primary sources with which they were most familiar.

The lion's share of studies on individual countries in the Middle Ages concern England, while a smaller number of studies are dedicated to medieval France, Germany, and Italy. A handful of studies have also been written about medieval Iberia, the Balkans, Russia and Poland, all of which have received relatively little attention from Arab medievalists. On the other hand, some regions such as Scandinavia, the Baltic region, Finland, and Romania have received almost no attention whatsoever from Arab medievalists. One may presume that language barriers are the main reasons for this. Some attention was given to the early Germanic peoples such as the Goths, Franks and Vandals. The Vikings and the Teutonic knights in the north received less attention.

1   Translated Works according to Their Original Languages

Most of the studies translated into Arabic are English works. Only a few non-English works have been translated. Recently some German, French, and a few Spanish works on the Middle Ages have appeared in Arabic translation. Unfortunately, in some cases the Arab translators did not bother to mention the bibliographical details of the original European book, nor the original language that it was translated from. Similarly, some of the translators tend to change the original titles completely and create totally different ones. Below are two examples:

> E.L. Ranelagh, *The Past We Share: The Near Eastern Ancestry of Western Folk Literature*, Indiana University, 1979. The Arabic translation carried a different title and it gave no indication of the original book. It was called *The Shared Past between the Arabs and the West: The Origins of Western Folk Literature* [*Al-Māḍī al-Mushtarak bayn al-ʿArab wa al-Gharb: Uṣūl al-Adab al-Shaʿbiyya al-Gharbiyya*]. This work was translated by the late Nabīla Ibrāhim in Kuwait in 1999.
>
> Sigrid Hunke, *Kamele auf dem Kaisermantel. Deutsch-arabische Begegnungen seit Karl dem Großen*, Stuttgart, 1976. This work was translated into Arabic under the title *Jimāl Tuzayyin Miʿṭaf al-Qayṣar, Liqāʾāt ʿArabiyya – Almāniyya mundhu ʿahd al-Qayṣar Shārlamān* [Camels decorated the Caesar's Mantle: Arab-German Encounters since the Time of Charlemagne] by Khālid Ghādirī in Damascus in 2008. An earlier Arabic translation of this same work by Ḥusām al-Shīmī appeared in Riyadh in 2001 with a different title: *Al-Ibil ʿalā Balāṭ Qayṣar* [*Camels in the court of Caesar*]. Neither translation mentioned the original German bibliographical data of the same book.

2   Divisions of Arab Works Written in European Languages

Only a handful works have been written in modern European languages by Arab medievalists. English is the main language used by most of the Arab writers. Writing in French is exclusive to medievalists from the Maghrib countries, with the exception of the Egyptian historian Fāʾiz Najīb Iskandar, who can write fluently in French.

3   Arab Historians of Medieval Europe by Nationality

Prima facie, Egyptian medievalists constitute the majority of Arab specialists on medieval Europe. Perhaps the reason is that only in Egyptian universities does there exist a separate branch for medieval Europe within history departments. The required subjects studied by students in this branch include: The Political history of Medieval Europe, the Civilization of Medieval Europe, the Crusades, Byzantine history, and Coptic Egypt. On the other hand, in Saudi Arabia medieval European history is merely a part of the Islamic history branch and students study only three subjects within it (Medieval Europe, Byzantium, and the Crusades). Sometimes these are optional subjects. Arab medievalists in other countries of the Mashriq (Syria, Iraq, Jordan, Saudi Arabia, etc.) have devoted most of their works to the Crusades and Byzantine–Muslim relations. Medievalists in the Maghrib have focused on the Byzantine and Vandal periods in North Africa (for example Mājida bin Kharbīṭ and Muḥammad al-Lubār).

4 The Main Themes of Arab Works on Medieval Europe

In conclusion, the main themes of the whole body of Arabic works on medieval Europe can be summarized in the following points. Firstly, the early Arabic studies on Medieval Europe rarely directly utilized European primary sources whether in their original languages or in English translation. In the early stages of development more attention was given to general history rather than cultural and religious themes. Simultaneously, efforts were dedicated more to medieval England than any other European country, perhaps because English was the most common foreign language of the Arab medievalists and also due to the relatively high availably of sources concerning England.

Concerning translation, it should be noted that translated studies have been translated from English. Even most of the medieval European primary sources were translated into Arabic from English translations rather than directly from the original Latin. At the same time, there are almost no bibliographical studies in Arabic dedicated exclusively to Medieval Europe. Few efforts have been made to fill the gap. There are no Arabic encyclopedias, biographical dictionaries, or historical dictionaries concerning medieval Europe. Also, one finds no authoritative geographical atlases of medieval Europe published in Arabic, only some handmade or Arabized maps within certain monographs. Finally, the internet paved the way for a revolution in Arabic historical studies in all fields, especially medieval studies.

In sum, the quality and quantity of Arabic studies on medieval Europe has increased considerably in the last few decades. The academic criteria were tightened everywhere. Within this context, closer and convenient connection with western institutions and medievalists will definitely contribute to the further growth and enrichment of the field of medieval European studies in the Arab world.

Bibliography

'Abd al-'Āṭī, Karīm 'Abd al-Ghanī, Qusṭanṭīn wa Mīthūdiyūs wa Dawruhumā fī al-Juhūd al-Tabshīrīyya li al-Kanīsa al-Bīzanṭiyya fī al-Niṣf al-Thānī min al-Qarn al-Tāsi' al-Mīlādī [Constantine and Methodius and their Role in the Missionary Activities of the Byzantine Church in the Second Half of the Ninth Century A.D.], PhD dissertation, Manṣūra University, 2015.

'Abdallāh, Yāsir, Ābīlār wa Makānatuhu fī al-Thaqāfa al-Ūrubiyya al-Wasīṭa (1079–1142 A.D.), [Peter Abelard and his Position in Medieval European Culture (1079–1142 A.D.)], PhD dissertation, 'Ayn Shams University, 2007.

'Āshūr, Sa'īd 'Abd al-Fattāḥ, Tārīkh Ūrūbā fī al-'Uṣūr al-Wusṭā, 2 vols, Cairo, 1975.

'Awaḍ, Muhammad Mu'nis, Al-Mu'arrikh al-Miṣrī 'Alī Al-Ghamrāwī 1926–1993: Ḥayātuhu wa Mū'allafātuhu fi Tārīkh Urūba fī al-'Uṣūr al-Wusṭa, 'Ālam al-Kutub, Saudi Arabia, 16:4 (1995), 286–289.

Al-'Aẓma, 'Azīz, [Aziz el Azmeh], Al-'Arab wa al-Barābira: Al-Muslimūn wa al-Ḥaḍārāt al-Ukhrā, London, 1991.

Al-'Aẓma, 'Azīz, [Aziz el Azmeh], Barbarians in Arab Eyes, Past and Present 134 (1992), 3–18.

Al-'Aẓma, 'Azīz, [Aziz el Azmeh], Mortal enemies, Invisible Neighbours: Northerners in Andalusi Eyes, in S.K. Jayyusi and M. Marín (eds), The Legacy of Muslim Spain, 2 vols, Leiden, 1992, i, 259–72.

Hermes, N. The [European] Other in Medieval Arabic Literature and Culture, New York, 2012.

Hunke, Sigrid, Kamele auf dem Kaisermantel. Deutsch-arabische Begegnungen seit Karl dem Großen, Stuttgart, 1976.

Hunke, Sigrid, Arabic translation of the above work as Al-Ibil 'alā Balāṭ Qayṣar [Camels in the court of Caesar], trans. Husām al-Shīmī, Riyadh, 2001.

Hunke, Sigrid, Second Arabic translation as Jimāl Tuzayyin Mi'ṭaf al-Qayṣar, Liqā'āt 'Arabiyya – Almāniyya mundhu 'ahd al-Qayṣar Shārlamān [Camels decorated the Caesar's Mantle: Arab-German Encounters since the Time of Charlemagne], trans. Khālid Ghādrī, Damascus, 2008.

Ibn Khaldūn, 'Abd al-Raḥmān b. Muḥammad, Tārīkh Ibn Khaldūn, Beirut, 2000.

König, Daniel, G., Arabic-Islamic perceptions of Western Europe in the Middle Ages, in: Christian-Muslim Relations: A Bibliographical History, vol. 5 (1350–1500), ed. D. Thomas, 17–34.

Lewis, Bernard, The Muslim discovery of Europe, BSOAS 20 (1957), 409–416.

Lewis, Bernard, Islam and the West, Oxford University, 1993.

Lewis, Bernard, The Muslim Discovery of Europe, London, 2001.

Newman, D. An Imam in Paris: Al-Tahtawi's Visit to France (1826–31), London, 2004.

Qandīl, Sāmir, Al-Ruʾā al-Ūrubiyya ʿan al-Islām wa al-Muslimīn: min al-Qarn al-Tāsiʿ ḥattā Nihāyāt al-Qarn al-Ḥādī ʿAshar al-Mīlādī [European Views of Islam and Muslims from the Ninth Century to the End of the Eleventh Century], PhD dissertation, ʿAyn Shams University, 2016.

Qandīl, Sāmir, Jīrbīrt "al-Bābā Sīlfistir al-Thānī" wa dawruhu fī al-Ḥayāt al-Siyāsiyya wa al-Thaqāfiyya fī Gharb Urubbā (945–1003) [Gerbert, "Pope Sylvester II," and his Role in the Political and Cultural Life of Western Europe 945–1003], MA dissertation, ʿAyn Shams University, 2009.

Ramaḍān, ʿAbd al-ʿAzīz, Isḥāq Tāwḍrūs ʿUbayd: Masīrat ʿĀlim [Ishaq Tawdros Ebeid: The Life of a Scholar], Miṣr al-Ḥadītha 16 (2017), 449–462.

Ranelagh, E.L., *The Past We Share: The Near Eastern Ancestry of Western Folk Literature*, Indiana, 1979.

Ranelagh, E.L., Translated into Arabic without reference to the original as *Al-Māḍī al-Mushtarak bayn al-ʿArab wa al-Gharb: Uṣūl al-Adab al-Shaʿbiyya al-Gharbiyya* [*The Shared Past between the Arabs and the West: The Origins of Western Folk Literature*], trans. Nabīla Ibrāhīm, Kuwait, 1999.

Al-Shallaq, Aḥmad Zakariyyāʾ, *Nahdat al-Kitāba al-Tārīkhiyya fī Miṣr*, Cairo, 2011.

Tacitus, *Tākītūs wa Shuʿūb Jarmāniya*, trans. Ibrāhīm ʿAlī Ṭarkhān, Cairo, 1959.

Tadmurī, ʿUmar ʿAbd al-Salām, Ḥasan Ḥabashī, Muḥammad Maḥmūd: al-Muʾarrikh Alladhī Aghnā al-Maktaba al-ʿArabiyya bi Muʾallafātihi [Muḥammad Maḥmūd: the Historian who Enriched the Arabic Library with His Works], in *Tārīkh Lubnān wa al-ʿĀlam* 26:219 (2006), 79–82.

Ūrūsiyūs, *Tārīkh al-ʿĀlam*, ed. ʿAbd al-Raḥmān Badawī, Beirut, 1982.